Recent
American Foreign Policy
BASIC DOCUMENTS 1941-1951

Recent
American Foreign Policy
BASIC DOCUMENTS 1941-1951

FRANCIS O. WILCOX

Chief of Staff, Senate Committee on Foreign Relations

and

THORSTEN V. KALIJARVI

Staff Associate, Senate Committee on Foreign Relations

With appreciation to E. Taylor Parks, Historical Adviser
of the Division of Historical Policy Research of the
Department of State

GREENWOOD PRESS, PUBLISHERS
WESTPORT, CONNECTICUT

The Library of Congress has catalogued this publication as follows:

Library of Congress Cataloging in Publication Data

Wilcox, Francis Orlando, 1908   ed.
  Recent American foreign policy.

  Based on A decade of American foreign policy;
basic documents 1941-1949, prepared by the staff of the
Committee on Foreign Relations of the U. S. Senate.
    1. U. S.--Foreign relations--1933-1945. 2. U. S.
--Foreign relations--1945-1953. I. Kalijarvi, Thorsten
Waino Valentine, joint ed. II. U. S. Congress.
Senate. Committee on Foreign Relations. A decade of
American foreign policy. III. Title.
[JX1416.W5 1972]   327.73   77-141283
ISBN 0-8371-5880-X

Originally published in 1952
by Appleton-Century Crofts

Reprinted by special arrangement with
Appleton-Century-Crofts, Educational Division,
Meredith Corporation

Reprinted from an original copy in the collections
of the University of Illinois Library

First Greenwood Reprinting 1972

Library of Congress Catalogue Card Number 77-141283

ISBN 0-8371-5880-X

Printed in the United States of America

This volume is respectfully dedicated to the two chairmen of the United States Senate Committee on Foreign Relations who contributed to the development of many of the documents contained herein and under whom the two editors have served.

SENATOR TOM CONNALLY OF TEXAS

and

SENATOR ARTHUR H. VANDENBERG OF MICHIGAN

In Memoriam

Foreword

In 1948 the Committee on Foreign Relations of the United States Senate requested the staff of the Committee, in collaboration with the Department of State, to arrange in a single volume, the more important documents and official statements bearing upon the foreign policy of the United States in the period following our entrance into World War II. Early in 1950 the project was completed and issued by the Government Printing Office under the title of *A Decade of American Foreign Policy: Basic Documents 1941-1949*.

The volume was designed especially to help members of Congress in their consideration of the basic problems involved in the development of American foreign policy since the War. It was favorably received both in government and academic circles. As a consequence, Appleton-Century-Crofts, Inc., invited the editors to reduce the work in size so that it might be published for wider circulation.

The general format of the original volume has been retained. Some fifty or sixty important documents have been added to cover the period through 1950 and early 1951. Extensive editing and excerpting has resulted in the elimination of considerable material which seems of less importance now in the light of historical perspective. Finally, brief editorial notes have been added which are designed to place each document in its proper setting and to give some continuity to the development of American policy.

The editors have undertaken the assignment because they are convinced that a first-hand knowledge of the basic documents is essential for an understanding of American foreign policy. They are in complete agreement with the publisher that a suitable collection lay at hand in the parent volume upon which this work is based.

No effort has been made to bring about uniformity of style or consistency in spelling. Except for the extensive excerpting done by the editors, the documents are reproduced as they first appeared.

Acknowledgment should be accorded the many contributors who helped prepare the original collection, notably E. Taylor Parks, Robert Lambert, Velma H. Cassidy, Marion S. Terrell, Beatrice C. Wharton, and the late Harley Notter of the State Department; Richard Heindel and Morella Hansen of the Committee Staff; and the Legislative Reference Service of the Library of Congress. In connection with the preparation of the present volume the editors wish especially to thank Carl Marcy, Morella Hansen and Mary Proctor of the Foreign Relations Committee Staff for their valuable assistance.

Francis O. Wilcox

Thorsten V. Kalijarvi

Washington, 1952

Contents

Part IV. UNITED NATIONS: SPECIALIZED AGENCIES

Part V. THE INTER-AMERICAN REGIONAL SYSTEM

Part VI. DEFEATED AND OCCUPIED AREAS

ITALY

VENEZIA GIULIA

BULGARIA

RUMANIA

Part VII. OTHER AREAS OF SPECIAL INTEREST TO THE UNITED STATES

CANADA

CHINA

GREECE

INDIA, PAKISTAN

CONTENTS

Recent
American Foreign Policy
BASIC DOCUMENTS 1941-1951

PART I

Wartime Documents Looking Toward Peace

1. THE FOUR FREEDOMS

Annual Message of the President to the Congress, January 6, 1941 (Excerpt) [1]

[Franklin D. Roosevelt's idea of the four freedoms will undoubtedly go down in history as one of the most important statements ever made on human liberty. Although the concept was incorporated in his message on the state of the union delivered to Congress some eleven months before Pearl Harbor, it was often referred to as one of the war aims of the Allied Powers. Mr. Roosevelt's recognition of the principle that human freedoms must be world-wide in scope, struck a responsive chord in the hearts of millions of people in many lands.]

In the future days, which we seek to make secure, we look forward to a world founded upon four essential human freedoms.

The first is freedom of speech and expression—everywhere in the world.

The second is freedom of every person to worship God in his way—everywhere in the world.

The third is freedom from want—which, translated into world terms, means economic understandings which will secure to every nation a healthy peacetime life for its inhabitants—everywhere in the world.

The fourth is freedom from fear—which, translated into world terms, means a world-wide reduction of armaments to such a point and in such a thorough fashion that no nation will be in a position to commit an act of physical aggression against any neighbor—anywhere in the world.

2. ATLANTIC CHARTER

Declaration by the President of the United States and the Prime Minister of the United Kingdom, August 14, 1941 [2]

[Four months before Pearl Harbor, President Roosevelt and Prime Minister Churchill met on the high seas and drew up the Atlantic Charter. The Charter not only provided an important statement of war aims for World War II; it

[1] Development of United States Foreign Policy, S. Doc. 188, 77th Cong., 2d sess., pp. 86-87.
[2] Cooperative War Effort, Department of State publication 1732, Executive Agreement Series 236, p. 4.

1

also notified the world that increasing coöperation between the two great English-speaking countries might be expected in the face of a common danger. At the time, there was much comment about the exact meaning of the Charter and the binding nature of the commitments assumed by the two governments. It was not drawn up as a formal international agreement.]

Joint declaration of the President of the United States of America and the Prime Minister, Mr. Churchill, representing His Majesty's Government in the United Kingdom, being met together, deem it right to make known certain common principles in the national policies of their respective countries on which they base their hopes for a better future for the world.

First, their countries seek no aggrandizement, territorial or other;

Second, they desire to see no territorial changes that do not accord with the freely expressed wishes of the peoples concerned;

Third, they respect the right of all peoples to choose the form of government under which they will live; and they wish to see sovereign rights and self-government restored to those who have been forcibly deprived of them;

Fourth, they will endeavor, with due respect for their existing obligations, to further the enjoyment by all States, great or small, victor or vanquished, of access, on equal terms, to the trade and to the raw materials of the world which are needed for their economic prosperity;

Fifth, they desire to bring about the fullest collaboration between all nations in the economic field with the object of securing, for all, improved labor standards, economic advancement and social security;

Sixth, after the final destruction of the Nazi tyranny, they hope to see established a peace which will afford to all nations the means of dwelling in safety within their own boundaries, and which will afford assurance that all the men in all the lands may live out their lives in freedom from fear and want;

Seventh, such a peace should enable all men to traverse the high seas and oceans without hindrance;

Eighth, they believe that all of the nations of the world, for realistic as well as spiritual reasons must come to the abandonment of the use of force. Since no future peace can be maintained if land, sea or air armaments continue to be employed by nations which threaten, or may threaten, aggression outside of their frontiers, they believe, pending the establishment of a wider and permanent system of general security, that the disarmament of such nations is essential. They will likewise aid and encourage all other practicable measures which will lighten for peace-loving peoples the crushing burden of armaments.

◇◇◇◇◇

3. DECLARATION BY UNITED NATIONS, JANUARY 1, 1942

A Joint Declaration by the United States, the United Kingdom, the Union of Soviet Socialist Republics, China, Australia, Belgium, Canada, Costa Rica, Cuba, Czechoslovakia(Dominican Republic,)El Salvador, Greece, Guatemala, Haiti, Honduras, India, Luxembourg, Netherlands, New Zealand, Nicaragua, Norway, Panama, Poland, South Africa, Yugoslavia [1]

[1] Cooperative War Effort, Department of State publication 1732, Executive Agreement Series 236, p. 1.

[Three weeks after Pearl Harbor, the great wartime coalition against fascist aggression achieved its first real unity when twenty-six states signed the United Nations Declaration. The signatory powers accepted the purposes and principles of the Atlantic Charter as their war aims, and pledged themselves to fight on with their full resources to final victory. Eleven of the twenty-six original signatories were American states. Twenty-one other countries subsequently adhered to the Declaration, making a total of forty-seven.]

The Governments signatory hereto,

Having subscribed to a common program of purposes and principles embodied in the Joint Declaration of the President of the United States of America and the Prime Minister of the United Kingdom of Great Britain and Northern Ireland dated August 14, 1941, known as the Atlantic Charter.

Being convinced that complete victory over their enemies is essential to defend life, liberty, independence and religious freedom, and to preserve human rights and justice in their own lands as well as in other lands, and that they are now engaged in a common struggle against savage and brutal forces seeking to subjugate the world,

DECLARE:

(1) Each Government pledges itself to employ its full resources, military or economic, against those members of the Tripartite Pact and its adherents with which such government is at war.

(2) Each Government pledges itself to cooperate with the Governments signatory hereto and not to make a separate armistice or peace with the enemies.

The foregoing declaration may be adhered to by other nations which are, or which may be, rendering material assistance and contributions in the struggle for victory over Hitlerism.

Done at Washington
January First, 1942

[The signatories to the Declaration by United Nations are as listed above.

The adherents to the Declaration by United Nations, together with the date of communication of adherence, are as follows:

Mexico	June 5, 1942	Peru	Feb. 11, 1945
Philippines	June 10, 1942	Chile	Feb. 12, 1945
Ethiopia	July 28, 1942	Paraguay	Feb. 12, 1945
Iraq	Jan. 16, 1943	Venezuela	Feb. 16, 1945
Brazil	Feb. 8, 1943	Uruguay	Feb. 23, 1945
Bolivia	Apr. 27, 1943	Turkey	Feb. 24, 1945
Iran	Sept. 10, 1943	Egypt	Feb. 27, 1945
Colombia	Dec. 22, 1943	Saudi Arabia	Mar. 1, 1945
Liberia	Feb. 26, 1944	Lebanon	Mar. 1, 1945
France	Dec. 26, 1944	Syria	Mar. 1, 1945]
Ecuador	Feb. 7, 1945		

◇◇◇◇◇◇

4. THE CASABLANCA CONFERENCE, JANUARY 14-24, 1943

Communiqué, January 26, 1943 [1]

[The main purpose of this meeting between President Roosevelt and Prime Minister Churchill was to agree upon the war strategy for 1943 against Germany, Italy, and Japan. The principal military decision reached was not to attempt a landing in northern France until 1944. Instead, it was decided to invade Sicily and eliminate Italy from the war. At the end of the meeting President Roosevelt announced that he and Churchill had agreed to accept nothing less than unconditional surrender from Germany, Japan, and Italy. The communiqué, which was released in 1943, because of security considerations does not include reference to the secret military agreements reached at the conference.]

On January 26, 1943, at 10 P.M., EWT, the following communiqué, cabled from Casablanca, Morocco, was made public:

The President of the United States and the Prime Minister of Great Britain have been in conference near Casablanca since January 14.

*   *   *

For 10 days the combined staffs have been in constant session, meeting 2 or 3 times a day and recording progress at intervals to the President and the Prime Minister.

The entire field of the war was surveyed theater by theater throughout the world, and all resources were marshaled for a more intense prosecution of the war by sea, land, and air.

Nothing like this prolonged discussion between two allies has ever taken place before. Complete agreement was reached between the leaders of the two countries and their respective staffs upon war plans and enterprises to be undertaken during the campaigns of 1943 against Germany, Italy, and Japan with a view to drawing the utmost advantage from the markedly favorable turn of events at the close of 1942.

Premier Stalin was cordially invited to meet the President and the Prime Minister, in which case the meeting would have been held very much farther to the east. He was unable to leave Russia at this time on account of the great offensive which he himself, as Commander in Chief, is directing.

The President and the Prime Minister realized up to the full the enormous weight of the war which Russia is successfully bearing along her whole land front, and their prime object has been to draw as much weight as possible off the Russian armies by engaging the enemy as heavily as possible at the best selected points.

Premier Stalin has been fully informed of the military proposals.

The President and the Prime Minister have been in communication with Generalissimo Chiang Kai-shek. They have apprised him of the measures which they are undertaking to assist him in China's magnificent and unrelaxing struggle for the common cause.

[1] Department of State Bulletin, January 30, 1943, pp. 93-94.

The occasion of the meeting between the President and the Prime Minister made it opportune to invite General Giraud (General Henri Honoré Giraud, High Commissioner of French Africa) to confer with the Combined Chiefs of Staff and to arrange for a meeting between him and General de Gaulle (General Charles de Gaulle, Fighting French Commander). The two generals have been in close consultation.

The President and the Prime Minister and their combined staffs, having completed their plans for the offensive campaigns of 1943, have now separated in order to put them into active and concerted execution.

◇◇◇◇◇

5. THE QUEBEC CONFERENCE, AUGUST 17-24, 1943

Joint Statement by Prime Minister Churchill and President Roosevelt, August 24, 1943 [1]

[This meeting dealt primarily with military problems. In Italy, Mussolini had fallen, and the Italians were sending out peace feelers during the Conference. On the political side, the chief accomplishment of the Quebec Conference was Anglo-American agreement on a draft for a four-power declaration concerning the establishment of an international security organization (subsequently adopted at the Moscow Conference), and an agreement to extend recognition to the French Committee of National Liberation under General de Gaulle. The Casablanca schedule for the invasion of France was re-affirmed, and a further decision was reached to supplement the Normandy landings with an invasion of southern France. As in the case of the Casablanca Conference, the communiqué which follows does not refer to the secret agreements reached.]

The Anglo-American war conference, which opened at Quebec on August 11, under the hospitable auspices of the Canadian Government, has now concluded its work.

The whole field of world operations has been surveyed in the light of the many gratifying events which have taken place since the meeting of the President and the Prime Minister in Washington at the end of May, and the necessary decisions have been taken to provide for the forward action of the fleets, armies, and air forces of the two nations.

Considering that these forces are intermingled in continuous action against the enemy in several quarters of the globe, it is indispensable that entire unity of aim and method should be maintained at the summit of the war direction.

Further conferences will be needed, probably at shorter intervals than before, as the war effort of the United States and British Commonwealth and Empire against the enemy spreads and deepens.

It would not be helpful to the fighting troops to make any announcement of the decisions which have been reached. These can only emerge in action.

[1] Department of State Bulletin, August 28, 1943, p. 121.

It may, however, be stated that the military discussions of the chiefs of staff turned very largely upon the war against Japan and the bringing of effective aid to China. Dr. T. V. Soong, representing the Generalissimo Chiang Kai-shek, was a party to the discussions. In this field, as in the European, the President and the Prime Minister were able to receive and approve the unanimous recommendation of the Combined Chiefs of Staff. Agreements were also reached upon the political issues underlying or arising out of the military operations.

It was resolved to hold another conference before the end of the year between the British and American authorities, in addition to any tri-partite meeting which it may be possible to arrange with Soviet Russia. Full reports of the decisions so far as they affect the war against Germany and Italy will be furnished to the Soviet Government.

Consideration has been given during the Conference to the question of relations with the French Committee of Liberation, and it is understood that an announcement by a number of governments will be made in the latter part of the week.

◇◇◇◇◇◇

6. FULBRIGHT RESOLUTION

House Concurrent Resolution 25—Seventy-eighth Congress, September 21, 1943 [1]

[After World War I, the Senate refused to approve the Treaty of Versailles, and the United States failed to become a member of the League of Nations. The American people were determined not to let that happen again. After Pearl Harbor, public opinion with reference to our participation in an international security organization developed rapidly under Congressional leadership. The first significant step in that direction came on September 21, 1943, when the House approved the Fulbright resolution by a vote of 360 to 29. The resolution put the House on record as favoring participation by the United States in a postwar international organization strong enough to keep the peace.]

Resolved by the House of Representatives (*the Senate concurring*), That the Congress hereby expresses itself as favoring the creation of appropriate international machinery with power adequate to establish and to maintain a just and lasting peace, among the nations of the world, and as favoring participation by the United States therein through its constitutional processes.

Passed the House of Representatives September 21, 1943.

[*Note:* The Connally Resolution (see No. 8 below) was passed by the Senate on Nov. 5, 1943.]

◇◇◇◇◇◇

[1] Toward the Peace—Documents, Department of State publication 2298, p. 4.

7. THE MOSCOW CONFERENCE, OCTOBER 19-30, 1943 [1]

[The Moscow Conference was significant in that it was the first wartime conference held by the three great powers in order to define their common objectives and coördinate their common efforts. In addition to discussing the steps necessary to shorten the war against Germany, representatives of the three powers issued declarations on their future policy with respect to Italy, Austria, and Germany. Most important, however, was their Declaration on General Security—also signed by China—in which the signatories recognized the necessity of establishing a general international organization for the maintenance of international peace and security.]

(a) Anglo-Soviet-American Communiqué, November 1, 1943

The Conference of (Foreign Secretaries) of the United States of America, Mr. Cordell Hull, of the United Kingdom, Mr. Anthony Eden, and of the Soviet Union, Mr. V. M. Molotov, took place at Moscow from the 19th to the 30th of October 1943. There were twelve meetings

[A list of participants in addition to the Foreign Secretaries follows here in the original.]

The agenda included all the questions submitted for discussion by the three Governments. Some of the questions called for final decisions and these were taken. On other questions, after discussion, decisions of principle were taken: these questions were referred for detailed consideration to commissions specially set up for the purpose, or reserved for treatment through diplomatic channels. Other questions again were disposed of by an exchange of views.

The Governments of the United States, the United Kingdom and the Soviet Union have been in close cooperation in all matters concerning the common war effort. But this is the first time that the Foreign Secretaries of the three Governments have been able to meet together in conference.

In the first place there were frank and exhaustive discussions of measures to be taken to shorten the war against Germany and her satellites in Europe. Advantage was taken of the presence of military advisers, representing the respective Chiefs of Staff, in order to discuss definite military operations, with regard to which decisions had been taken and which are already being prepared, and in order to create a basis for the closest military cooperation in the future between the three countries.

Second only to the importance of hastening the end of the war was the unanimous recognition by the three Governments that it was essential in their own national interests and in the interest of all peace-loving nations to continue the present close collaboration and cooperation in the conduct of the war into the period following the end of hostilities, and that only in this way could peace be maintained and the political, economic and social welfare of their peoples fully promoted.

This conviction is expressed in a declaration in which the Chinese Government joined during the Conference and which was signed by the three Foreign

[1] Toward the Peace—Documents, Department of State publication 2298, pp. 4-8; Department of State Bulletin, November 6, 1943.

Secretaries and the Chinese Ambassador at Moscow on behalf of their governments. This declaration, published today, provides for even closer collaboration in the prosecution of the war and in all matters pertaining to the surrender and disarmament of the enemies with which the four countries are respectively at war. It sets forth the principles upon which the four Governments agree that a broad system of international cooperation and security should be based. Provision is made for the inclusion of all other peace-loving nations, great and small, in this system.

The Conference agreed to set up machinery for ensuring the closest cooperation between the three Governments in the examination of European questions arising as the war develops. For this purpose the Conference decided to establish in London a European Advisory Commission to study these questions and to make joint recommendations to the three Governments.

Provision was made for continuing, when necessary, tripartite consultations of representatives of the three Governments in the respective capitals through the existing diplomatic channels.

The Conference also agreed to establish an Advisory Council for matters relating to Italy, to be composed in the first instance of representatives of their three Governments and of the French Committee of National Liberation. Provision is made for the addition to this council of representatives of Greece and Yugoslavia in view of their special interests arising out of the aggressions of Fascist Italy upon their territory during the present war. This Council will deal with day-to-day questions, other than military operations, and will make recommendations designed to coordinate Allied policy with regard to Italy.

The three Foreign Secretaries considered it appropriate to reaffirm, by a declaration published today, the attitude of their Governments in favor of restoration of democracy in Italy.

The three Foreign Secretaries declared it to be the purpose of their Governments to restore the independence of Austria. At the same time they reminded Austria that in the final settlement account will be taken of efforts that Austria may make towards its own liberation. The declaration on Austria is published today.

The Foreign Secretaries issued at the Conference a declaration by President Roosevelt, Prime Minister Churchill and Premier Stalin containing a solemn warning that at the time of granting any armistice to any German Government those German officers and men and members of the Nazi party who have had any connection with atrocities and executions in countries overrun by German forces will be taken back to the countries in which their abominable crimes were committed to be charged and punished according to the laws of those countries.

In the atmosphere of mutual confidence and understanding which characterized all the work of the Conference, consideration was also given to other important questions. These included not only questions of a current nature, but also questions concerning the treatment of Hitlerite Germany and its satellites, economic cooperation and the assurance of general peace.

(b) Declaration on Austria, November 1, 1943

The Governments of the United Kingdom, the Soviet Union and the United States of America are agreed that Austria, the first free country to fall a victim to Hitlerite aggression, shall be liberated from German domination.

They regard the annexation imposed upon Austria by Germany on March 15th, 1938, as null and void. They consider themselves as in no way bound by any changes effected in Austria since that date. They declare that they wish to see reestablished a free and independent Austria, and thereby to open the way for the Austrian people themselves, as well as those neighboring states which will be faced with similar problems, to find that political and economic security which is the only basis for lasting peace.

Austria is reminded, however, that she has a responsibility which she cannot evade for participation in the war on the side of Hitlerite Germany, and that in the final settlement account will inevitably be taken of her own contribution to her liberation.

(c) Declaration of Four Nations on General Security, November 1, 1943

The Governments of the United States of America, the United Kingdom, the Soviet Union and China:

united in their determination, in accordance with the Declaration by the United Nations of January 1, 1942, and subsequent declarations, to continue hostilities against those Axis powers with which they respectively are at war until such powers have laid down their arms on the basis of unconditional surrender;

conscious of their responsibility to secure the liberation of themselves and the peoples allied with them from the menace of aggression;

recognizing the necessity of ensuring a rapid and orderly transition from war to peace and of establishing and maintaining international peace and security with the least diversion of the world's human and economic resources for armaments;

jointly declare:

1. That their united action, pledged for the prosecution of the war against their respective enemies, will be continued for the organization and maintenance of peace and security.

2. That those of them at war with a common enemy will act together in all matters relating to the surrender and disarmament of that enemy.

3. That they will take all measures deemed by them to be necessary to provide against any violation of the terms imposed upon the enemy.

4. That they recognise the necessity of establishing at the earliest practicable date a general international organization, based on the principle of the sovereign equality of all peace-loving states, and open to membership by all such states, large and small, for the maintenance of international peace and security.

5. That for the purpose of maintaining international peace and security pending the re-establishment of law and order and the inauguration of a system of general security, they will consult with one another and as occasion

requires with other members of the United Nations with a view to joint action on behalf of the community of nations.

6. That after the termination of hostilities they will not employ their military forces within the territories of other states except for the purposes envisaged in this declaration and after joint consultation.

7. That they will confer and co-operate with one another and with other members of the United Nations to bring about a practicable general agreement with respect to the regulation of armaments in the post-war period.

V. MOLOTOV
ANTHONY EDEN
CORDELL HULL
FOO PING-SHEUNG

MOSCOW, *30th October, 1943.*

(d) Declaration Regarding Italy, November 1, 1943

The Foreign Secretaries of the United States of America, the United Kingdom and the Soviet Union have established that their three Governments are in complete agreement that Allied policy towards Italy must be based upon the fundamental principle that Fascism and all its evil influences and emanations shall be utterly destroyed and that the Italian people shall be given every opportunity to establish governmental and other institutions based upon democratic principles.

The Foreign Secretaries of the United States of America and the United Kingdom declare that the action of their Governments from the inception of the invasion of Italian territory, in so far as paramount military requirements have permitted, has been based upon this policy.

In the furtherance of this policy in the future the Foreign Secretaries of the three Governments are agreed that the following measures are important and should be put into effect:

1. It is essential that the Italian Government should be made more democratic by the introduction of representatives of those sections of the Italian people who have always opposed Fascism.

2. Freedom of speech, of religious worship, of political belief, of the press and of public meeting shall be restored in full measure to the Italian people, who shall also be entitled to form anti-Fascist political groups.

3. All institutions and organizations created by the Fascist regime shall be suppressed.

4. All Fascist or pro-Fascist elements shall be removed from the administration and from the institutions and organizations of a public character.

5. All political prisoners of the Fascist regime shall be released and accorded a full amnesty.

6. Democratic organs of local government shall be created.

7. Fascist chiefs and other persons known or suspected to be war criminals shall be arrested and handed over to justice.

In making this declaration the three Foreign Secretaries recognize that so long as active military operations continue in Italy the time at which it is possible to give full effect to the principles set out above will be determined by the Commander-in-Chief on the basis of instructions received through the

Combined Chiefs of Staff. The three Governments parties to this declaration will at the request of any one of them consult on this matter.

It is further understood that nothing in this resolution is to operate against the right of the Italian people ultimately to choose their own form of government.

(e) Declaration on German Atrocities, November 1, 1943

The United Kingdom, the United States and the Soviet Union have received from many quarters evidence of atrocities, massacres and cold-blooded mass executions which are being perpetrated by the Hitlerite forces in the many countries they have overrun and from which they are now being steadily expelled. The brutalities of Hitlerite domination are no new thing and all the peoples or territories in their grip have suffered from the worst form of government by terror. What is new is that many of these territories are now being redeemed by the advancing armies of the liberating Powers and that in their desperation, the recoiling Hitlerite Huns are redoubling their ruthless cruelties. This is now evidenced with particular clearness by monstrous crimes of the Hitlerites on the territory of the Soviet Union which is being liberated from the Hitlerites, and on French and Italian territory.

Accordingly, the aforesaid three allied Powers, speaking in the interests of the thirty-two [thirty-three] United Nations, hereby solemnly declare and give full warning of their declaration as follows:

At the time of the granting of any armistice to any government which may be set up in Germany, those German officers and men and members of the Nazi party who have been responsible for, or have taken a consenting part in the above atrocities, massacres and executions, will be sent back to the countries in which their abominable deeds were done in order that they may be judged and punished according to the laws of these liberated countries and of the free governments which will be created therein. Lists will be compiled in all possible detail from all these countries having regard especially to the invaded parts of the Soviet Union, to Poland and Czechoslovakia, to Yugoslavia and Greece, including Crete and other islands, to Norway, Denmark, the Netherlands, Belgium, Luxemburg, France and Italy.

Thus, the Germans who take part in wholesale shootings of Italian officers or in the execution of French, Dutch, Belgian or Norwegian hostages or of Cretan peasants, or who have shared in the slaughters inflicted on the people of Poland or in territories of the Soviet Union which are now being swept clear of the enemy, will know that they will be brought back to the scene of their crimes and judged on the spot by the peoples whom they have outraged. Let those who have hitherto not imbrued their hands with innocent blood beware lest they join the ranks of the guilty, for most assuredly the three allied Powers will pursue them to the uttermost ends of the earth and will deliver them to their accusers in order that justice may be done.

The above declaration is without prejudice to the case of the major criminals, whose offences have no particular geographical localisation and who will be punished by the joint decision of the Goverments of the Allies.

ROOSEVELT
CHURCHILL
STALIN

8. CONNALLY RESOLUTION

Senate Resolution 192—Seventy-Eighth Congress, November 5, 1943 [1]

[Some six weeks after the Fulbright resolution had been passed by the House, the Senate adopted the Connally resolution by a vote of 85 to 5. These two resolutions in effect gave a green light to the executive branch to coöperate with other nations in the establishment of a postwar international organization with full assurances to our allies that Congress would support our participation in it. Unlike the Fulbright resolution, the Connally resolution emphasized that the international organization would have to be based upon the sovereign equality of states.]

Resolved, That the war against all our enemies be waged until complete victory is achieved.

That the United States cooperate with its comrades-in-arms in securing a just and honorable peace.

That the United States, acting through its constitutional processes, join with free and sovereign nations in the establishment and maintenance of international authority with power to prevent aggression and to preserve the peace of the world.

That the Senate recognizes the necessity of there being established at the earliest practicable date a general international organization, based on the principle of the sovereign equality of all peace-loving states, and open to membership by all such states, large and small, for the maintenance of international peace and security.

That, pursuant to the Constitution of the United States, any treaty made to effect the purposes of this resolution, on behalf of the Government of the United States with any other nation or any association of nations, shall be made only by and with the advice and consent of the Senate of the United States, provided two-thirds of the Senators present concur.

9. THE CAIRO CONFERENCE, NOVEMBER 22-26, 1943 [2]

Statement by President Roosevelt, Generalissimo Chiang Kai-shek, and Prime Minister Churchill, December 1, 1943

[At Cairo, Roosevelt, Churchill, and Chiang Kai-shek reached agreement on the general objectives of the three governments with respect to the war in the Far East. Korea, they declared, should become free and independent, and the territory Japan had "stolen" from the Republic of China—such as Manchuria, Formosa, and the Pescadores—should be returned to her. Since

[1] Toward the Peace—Document of State publication 2298, p. 8.
[2] Toward the Peace—Documents, Department of State publication 2298, p. 14; Department of State Bulletin, December 4, 1943.

the Soviet Union was not at war with Japan, she was not represented at the Cairo Conference, although her agreement to the official communiqué was later obtained.]

The several military missions have agreed upon future military operations against Japan. The Three Great Allies expressed their resolve to bring unrelenting pressure against their brutal enemies by sea, land, and air. This pressure is already rising.

The Three Great Allies are fighting this war to restrain and punish the aggression of Japan. They covet no gain for themselves and have no thought of territorial expansion. It is their purpose that Japan shall be stripped of all the islands in the Pacific which she has seized or occupied since the beginning of the first World War in 1914, and that all the territories Japan has stolen from the Chinese, such as Manchuria, Formosa, and the Pescadores, shall be restored to the Republic of China. Japan will also be expelled from all other territories which she has taken by violence and greed. The aforesaid three great powers, mindful of the enslavement of the people of Korea, are determined that in due course Korea shall become free and independent.

With these objects in view the three Allies, in harmony with those of the United Nations at war with Japan, will continue to persevere in the serious and prolonged operations necessary to procure the unconditional surrender of Japan.

◇◇◇◇◇◇

10. THE TEHRAN CONFERENCE, NOVEMBER 28-DECEMBER 1, 1943 [1]

[The Tehran Conference was the first of the wartime conferences attended by Roosevelt, Churchill, and Stalin. The friendly spirit of coöperation that prevailed among the three is reflected in the tone of the communiqué. In addition to the declaration expressing their determination to work together to win the war, and the declaration relating to the independence of Iran, the three chiefs of state entered into a secret understanding that Russia would launch an offensive on the Eastern front to coincide with the landings of the Western Allies in Normandy. The latter agreement was not released until March 24, 1947.]

(a) Declaration of the Three Powers, December 1, 1943

We—the President of the United States, the Prime Minister of Great Britain, and the Premier of the Soviet Union, have met these four days past, in this, the Capital of our Ally, Iran, and have shaped and confirmed our common policy.

We express our determination that our nations shall work together in war and in the peace that will follow.

As to war—our military staffs have joined in our round table discussions,

1 Toward the Peace—Documents, Department of State publication 2298, pp. 15-16; Department of State Bulletin of December 4, 1943.

and we have concerted our plans for the destruction of the German forces. We have reached complete agreement as to the scope and timing of the operations to be undertaken from the east, west and south.

The common understanding which we have here reached guarantees that victory will be ours.

And as to peace—we are sure that our concord will win an enduring Peace. We recognize fully the supreme responsibility resting upon us and all the United Nations to make a peace which will command the goodwill of the overwhelming mass of the peoples of the world and banish the scourge and terror of war for many generations.

With our Diplomatic advisors we have surveyed the problems of the future. We shall seek the cooperation and active participation of all nations, large and small, whose peoples in heart and mind are dedicated, as our own peoples, to the elimination of tyranny and slavery, oppresssion and intolerance. We will welcome them, as they may choose to come, into a world family of Democratic Nations.

No power on earth can prevent our destroying the German armies by land, their U Boats by sea, and their war plants from the air.

Our attack will be relentless and increasing.

Emerging from these cordial conferences we look with confidence to the day when all peoples of the world may live free lives, untouched by tyranny, and according to their varying desires and their own consciences.

We came here with hope and determination. We leave here, friends in fact, in spirit and in purpose.

ROOSEVELT, CHURCHILL and STALIN

Signed at Tehran, *December 1, 1943*

(b) Declaration of the Three Powers Regarding Iran, December 1, 1943

The President of the United States, the Premier of the U. S. S. R. and the Prime Minister of the United Kingdom, having consulted with each other and with the Prime Minister of Iran, desire to declare the mutual agreement of their three Governments regarding their relations with Iran.

The Governments of the United States, the U. S. S. R., and the United Kingdom recognize the assistance which Iran has given in the prosecution of the war against the common enemy, particularly by facilitating the transportation of supplies from overseas to the Soviet Union.

The Three Governments realize that the war has caused special economic difficulties for Iran, and they are agreed that they will continue to make available to the Government of Iran such economic assistance as may be possible, having regard to the heavy demands made upon them by their world-wide military operations, and to the world-wide shortage of transport, raw materials, and supplies for civilian consumption.

With respect to the post-war period, the Governments of the United States, the U. S. S. R., and the United Kingdom are in accord with the Government of Iran that any economic problems confronting Iran at the close of hostilities should receive full consideration, along with those of other members of the United Nations, by conferences or international agencies held or created to deal with international economic matters.

The Governments of the United States, the U. S. R., and the United Kingdom are at one with the Government of Iran in their desire for the maintenance of the independence, sovereignty and territorial integrity of Iran. They count upon the participation of Iran, together with all other peace-loving nations, in the establishment of international peace, security and prosperity after the war, in accordance with the principles of the Atlantic Charter, to which all four Governments have subscribed.

WINSTON S. CHURCHILL
J. STALIN
FRANKLIN D. ROOSEVELT

(c) Military Conclusions of the Tehran Conference [1]

The Conference:—

(1) Agreed that the Partisans in Yugoslavia should be supported by supplies and equipment to the greatest possible extent, and also by commando operations:

(2) Agreed that, from the military point of view, it was most desirable that Turkey should come into the war on the side of the Allies before the end of the year:

(3) Took note of Marshal Stalin's statement that if Turkey found herself at war with Germany, and as a result Bulgaria declared war on Turkey or attacked her, the Soviet would immediately be at war with Bulgaria. The Conference further took note that this fact could be explicitly stated in the forthcoming negotiations to bring Turkey into the war:

(4) Took note that Operation OVERLORD would be launched during May 1944, in conjunction with an operation against Southern France. The latter operation would be undertaken in as great a strength as availability of landing-craft permitted. The Conference further took note of Marshal Stalin's statement that the Soviet forces would launch an offensive at about the same time with the object of preventing the German forces from transferring from the Eastern to the Western Front:

(5) Agreed that the military staffs of the Three Powers should henceforth keep in close touch with each other in regard to the impending operations in Europe. In particular it was agreed that a cover plan to mystify and mislead the enemy as regards these operations should be concerted between the staffs concerned.

FRANKLIN D. ROOSEVELT
JOSEPH V. STALIN
WINSTON S. CHURCHILL

TEHRAN, *December 1, 1943.*

◇◇◇◇◇◇

[1] Department of State press release 240, March 24, 1947.

11. THE CRIMEAN (YALTA) CONFERENCE, FEBRUARY 4-11, 1945 [1]

[At Yalta, Roosevelt, Churchill, and Stalin laid far-reaching plans for ending the war in Europe and Asia, and for dealing with the enemy countries in the postwar period. Among other things, agreement was reached to convene the United Nations Conference on International Organization at San Francisco. The famous Yalta voting formula—later to become Article 27 of the United Nations Charter—was also drafted. Arrangements were made for Russia's entry into the war against Japan, and in return, important concessions were made to Russia in the Far East.

The Yalta Agreements were not released in their entirety until March 24, 1947. They have aroused considerable controversy in the United States: first, because some of them were secret; second, because Congress did not have an opportunity to approve them; and third, because important decisions were made concerning China's future although China did not participate in the conference.]

(a) Protocol of Proceedings

The Crimea Conference of the Heads of the Governments of the United States of America, the United Kingdom, and the Union of Soviet Socialist Republics which took place from February 4th to 11th came to the following conclusions:

I. WORLD ORGANISATION

It was decided:

(1) that a United Nations Conference on the proposed world organisation should be summoned for Wednesday, 25th April, 1945, and should be held in the United States of America.

(2) the Nations to be invited to this Conference should be:

(a) the United Nations as they existed on the 8th February, 1945; and

(b) such of the Associated Nations as have declared war on the common enemy by 1st March, 1945. (For this purpose by the term "Associated Nation" was meant the eight Associated Nations and Turkey). When the Conference on World Organization is held, the delegates of the United Kingdom and United States of America will support a proposal to admit to original membership two Soviet Socialist Republics, i.e., the Ukraine and White Russia.

(3) that the United States Government on behalf of the Three Powers should consult the Government of China and the French Provisional Government in regard to decisions taken at the present Conference concerning the proposed World Organisation.

---

[1] Department of State press release 239, March 24, 1947. See report of the Conference, Department of State Bulletin, February 18, 1945, p. 213; the agreement regarding Japan has been printed as Department of State publication 2505, Executive Agreement Series 498.

(4) that the text of the invitation to be issued to all the nations which would take part in the United Nations Conference should be as follows:

INVITATION

"The Government of the United States of America, on behalf of itself and of the Governments of the United Kingdom, the Union of Soviet Socialist Republics, and the Republic of China and of the Provisional Government of the French Republic, invite the Government of _____ to send representatives to a Conference of the United Nations to be held on 25th April, 1945, or soon thereafter, at San Francisco in the United States of America to prepare a Charter for a General International Organisation for the maintenance of international peace and security.

"The above named governments suggest that the Conference consider as affording a basis for such a Charter the Proposals for the Establishment of a General International Organisation, which were made public last October as a result of the Dumbarton Oaks Conference, and which have now been supplemented by the following provisions for Section C of Chapter VI:

" 'C. VOTING

" '1. Each member of the Security Council should have one vote.

" '2. Decisions of the Security Council on procedural matters should be made by an affirmative vote of seven members.

" '3. Decisions of the Security Council on all other matters should be made by an affirmative vote of seven members including the concurring votes of the permanent members; provided that, in decisions under Chapter VIII, Section A and under the second sentence of paragraph 1 of Chapter VIII, Section C, a party to a dispute should abstain from voting.'

"Further information as to arrangements will be transmitted subsequently.

"In the event that the Government of _____ desires in advance of the Conference to present views or comments concerning the proposals, the Government of the United States of America will be pleased to transmit such views and comments to the other participating Governments."

TERRITORIAL TRUSTEESHIP

It was agreed that the five Nations which will have permanent seats on the Security Council should consult each other prior to the United Nations Conference on the question of territorial trusteeship.

The acceptance of this recommendation is subject to its being made clear that territorial trusteeship will only apply to (a) existing mandates of the League of Nations; (b) territories detached from the enemy as a result of the present war; (c) any other territory which might voluntarily be placed under trusteeship; and (d) no discussion of actual territories is contemplated at the forthcoming United Nations Conference or in the preliminary consultations, and it will be a matter for subsequent agreement which territories within the above categories will be placed under trusteeship.

II. Declaration on Liberated Europe

The following declaration has been approved:

"The Premier of the Union of Soviet Socialist Republics, the Prime Minister of the United Kingdom and the President of the United States of America have consulted with each other in the common interests of the peoples of their countries and those of liberated Europe. They jointly declare their mutual agreement to concert during the temporary period of instability in liberated Europe the polices of their three governments in assisting the peoples liberated from the domination of Nazi Germany and the peoples of the former Axis satellite states of Europe to solve by democratic means their pressing political and economic problems.

"The establishment of order in Europe and the re-building of national economic life must be achieved by processes which will enable the liberated peoples to destroy the last vestiges of Nazism and Fascism and to create democratic institutions of their own choice. This is a principle of the Atlantic Charter—the right of all peoples to choose the form of government under which they will live—the restoration of sovereign rights and self-government to those peoples who have been forcibly deprived of them by the aggressor nations.

"To foster the conditions in which the liberated peoples may exercise these rights, the three governments will jointly assist the people in any European liberated state or former Axis satellite state in Europe where in their judgment conditions require (a) to establish conditions of internal peace; (b) to carry out emergency measures for the relief of distressed peoples; (c) to form interim governmental authorities broadly representative of all democratic elements in the population and pledged to the earliest possible establishment through free elections of governments responsive to the will of the people; and (d) to facilitate where necessary the holding of such elections.

"The three governments will consult the other United Nations and provisional authorities or other governments in Europe when matters of direct interest to them are under consideration.

"When, in the opinion of the three governments, conditions in any European liberated state or any former Axis satellite state in Europe make such action necessary, they will immediately consult together on the measures necessary to discharge the joint responsibilities set forth in this declaration.

"By this declaration we reaffirm our faith in the principles of the Atlantic Charter, our pledge in the Declaration by the United Nations, and our determination to build in cooperation with other peace-loving nations world order under law, dedicated to peace, security, freedom and general well-being of all mankind.

"In issuing this declaration, the Three Powers express the hope that the Provisional Government of the French Republic may be associated with them in the procedure suggested."

III. Dismemberment of Germany

It was agreed that Article 12 (a) of the Surrender Terms for Germany should be amended to read as follows:

"The United Kingdom, the United States of America and the Union of Soviet Socialist Republics shall possess supreme authority with respect to Germany. In the exercise of such authority they will take such steps, including the complete disarmament, demilitarisation and dismemberment of Germany as they deem requisite for future peace and security."

The study of the procedure for the dismemberment of Germany was referred to a Committee, consisting of Mr. Eden (Chairman), Mr. Winant and Mr. Gousev. This body would consider the desirability of associating with a French representative.

IV. Zone of Occupation for the French and Control Council for Germany

It was agreed that a zone in Germany, to be occupied by the French Forces, should be allocated to France. This zone would be formed out of the British and American zones and its extent would be settled by the British and Americans in consultation with the French Provisional Government.

It was also agreed that the French Provisional Government should be invited to become a member of the Allied Control Council for Germany.

V. Reparation

*　　*　　*

[Approved protocol, printed following XIV.

VI. Major War Criminals

The Conference agreed that the question of the major war criminals should be the subject of enquiry by the three Foreign Secretaries for report in due course after the close of the Conference.

VII. Poland

The following Declaration on Poland was agreed by the Conference:

"A new situation has been created in Poland as a result of her complete liberation by the Red Army. This calls for the establishment of a Polish Provisional Government which can be more broadly based than was possible before the recent liberation of Western part of Poland. The Provisional Government which is now functioning in Poland should therefore be reorganized on a broader democratic basis with the inclusion of democratic leaders from Poland itself and from Poles abroad. This new Government should then be called the Polish Provisional Government of National Unity.

"M. Molotov, Mr. Harriman and Sir A. Clark Kerr are authorised as a commission to consult in the first instance in Moscow with members of the present Provisional Government and with other Polish democratic leaders from within Poland and from abroad, with a view to the reorganisation of the present Government along the above lines. This Polish Provisional Government of National Unity shall be pledged to the holding of free and unfettered elections as soon as possible on the basis of universal suffrage and secret ballot. In these elections all democratic and anti-Nazi parties shall have the right to take part and to put forward candidates.

"When a Polish Provisional Government of National Unity has been properly formed in conformity with the above, the Government of the U. S. S. R., which now maintains diplomatic relations with the present Provisional Government of Poland, and the Government of the United Kingdom and the Government of the United States of America will establish diplomatic relations with the new Polish Provisional Government of National Unity, and will exchange Ambassadors by whose reports the respective Governments will be kept informed about the situation in Poland.

"The three Heads of Government consider that the Eastern frontier of Poland should follow the Curzon Line with digressions from it in some regions of five to eight kilometres in favour of Poland. They recognise that Poland must receive substantial accessions of territory in the North and West. They feel that the opinion of the new Polish Provisional Government of National Unity should be sought in due course on the extent of these accessions and that the final delimitation of the Western frontier of Poland should thereafter await the Peace Conference."

VIII. YUGOSLAVIA

It was agreed to recommend to Marshal Tito and to Dr. Subasic:

(a) that the Tito-Subasic Agreement should immediately be put into effect and a new Government formed on the basis of the Agreement.

(b) that as soon as the new Government has been formed it should declare:

(i) that the Anti-Fascist Assembly of National Liberation (AVNOJ) will be extended to include members of the last Yugoslav Skupstina who have not compromised themselves by collaboration with the enemy, thus forming a body to be known as a temporary Parliament and

(ii) that legislative acts passed by the Anti-Fascist Assembly of National Liberation (AVNOJ) will be subject to subsequent ratification by a Constituent Assembly; and that this statement should be published in the Communiqué of the Conference.

IX. ITALO-YUGOSLAV FRONTIER

ITALO-AUSTRIA FRONTIER

Notes on these subjects were put in by the British delegation and the American and Soviet delegations agreed to consider them and give their views later.

X. YUGOSLAV-BULGARIAN RELATIONS

There was an exchange of views between the Foreign Secretaries on the question of the desirability of a Yugoslav-Bulgarian pact of alliance. The question at issue was whether a state still under an armistice regime could be allowed to enter into a treaty with another state. Mr. Eden suggested that the Bulgarian and Yugoslav Governments should be informed that this could not be approved. Mr. Stettinius suggested that the British and American Ambassadors should discuss the matter further with M. Molotov in Moscow. M. Molotov agreed with the proposal of Mr. Stettinius.

XI. South Eastern Europe

The British Delegation put in notes for the consideration of their colleagues on the following subjects:

(a) the Control Commission in Bulgaria.

(b) Greek claims upon Bulgaria, more particularly with reference to reparations.

(c) Oil equipment in Rumania.

XII. Iran

Mr. Eden, Mr. Stettinius and M. Molotov exchanged views on the situation in Iran. It was agreed that this matter should be pursued through the diplomatic channel.

XIII. Meetings of the Three Foreign Secretaries

The Conference agreed that permanent machinery should be set up for consultation between the three Foreign Secretaries; they should meet as often as necessary, probably about every three or four months.

These meetings will be held in rotation in the three capitals, the first meeting being held in London.

XIV. The Montreux Convention and the Straits

It was agreed that at the next meeting of the three Foreign Secretaries to be held in London, they should consider proposals which it was understood the Soviet Government would put forward in relation to the Montreux Convention and report to their Governments. The Turkish Government should be informed at the appropriate moment.

The foregoing Protocol was approved and signed by the three Foreign Secretaries at the Crimean Conference, February 11, 1945.

E. R. Stettinius, Jr.

M. Molotov

Anthony Eden

(b) Protocol on German Reparations

The Heads of the three governments agreed as follows:

1. Germany must pay in kind for the losses caused by her to the Allied nations in the course of the war. Reparation are to be received in the first instance by those countries which have borne the main burden of the war, have suffered the heaviest losses and have organized victory over the enemy.

2. Reparation in kind are to be exacted from Germany in three following forms:

(a) Removals within 2 years from the surrender of Germany or the cessation of organised resistance from the national wealth of Germany located on the territory of Germany herself as well as outside her territory (equipment, machine-tools, ships, rolling stock, German investments abroad, shares of industrial, transport and other enterprises in Germany etc.), these removals to be carried out chiefly for purposes of destroying the war potential of Germany.

(b) Annual deliveries of goods from current production for a period to be fixed.

(c) Use of German labour.

3. For the working out on the above principles of a detailed plan for exaction of reparation from Germany an Allied Reparation Commission will be set up in Moscow. It will consist of three representatives—one from the Union of Soviet Socialist Republics, one from the United Kingdom and one from the United States of America.

4. With regard to the fixing of the total sum of the reparation as well as the distribution of it among the countries which suffered from the German aggression the Soviet and American delegations agreed as follows:

"The Moscow Reparation Commission should take in its initial studies as a basis for discussion the suggestion of the Soviet Government that the total sum of the reparation in accordance with the points (a) and (b) of the paragraph 2 should be 20 billion dollars and that 50% of it should go to the Union of Soviet Socialist Republics."

The British delegation was of the opinion that pending consideration of the reparation question by the Moscow Reparation Commission no figures of reparation should be mentioned.

The above Soviet-American proposal has been passed to the Moscow Reparation Commission as one of the proposals to be considered by the Commission.

WINSTON S. CHURCHILL
FRANKLIN D. ROOSEVELT
JOSEPH V. STALIN

FEBRUARY 11, 1945.

(c) *Agreement Regarding Japan*

The leaders of the three Great Powers—the Soviet Union, the United States of American and Great Britain—have agreed that in two or three months after Germany has surrendered and the war in Europe has terminated the Soviet Union shall enter into the war against Japan on the side of the Allies on condition that:

1. The status quo in Outer-Mongolia (The Mongolian People's Republic) shall be preserved;

2. The former rights of Russia violated by the treacherous attack of Japan in 1904 shall be restored, viz:

(a) the southern part of Sakhalin as well as all the islands adjacent to it shall be returned to the Soviet Union,

(b) the commercial port of Dairen shall be internationalized, the preeminent interests of the Soviet Union in this port being safeguarded and the lease of Port Arthur as a naval base of the U. S. S. R. restored,

(c) the Chinese-Eastern Railroad and the South-Manchurian Railroad which provides an outlet to Dairen shall be jointly operated by the establishment of a joint Soviet-Chinese Company it being understood that the preeminent interests of the Soviet Union shall be safeguarded and that China shall retain full sovereignty in Manchuria;

3. The Kuril islands shall be handed over to the Soviet Union.

It is understood, that the agreement concerning Outer-Mongolia and the ports and railroads referred to above will require concurrence of Generalissimo Chiang Kai-shek. The President will take measures in order to obtain this concurrence on advice from Marshal Stalin.

The Heads of the three Great Powers have agreed that these claims of the Soviet Union shall be unquestionably fulfilled after Japan has been defeated.

For its part the Soviet Union expresses its readiness to conclude with the National Government of China a pact of friendship and alliance between the U. S. S. R. and China in order to render assistance to China with its armed forces for the purpose of liberating China from the Japanese yoke.

JOSEPH V. STALIN
FRANKLIN D. ROOSEVELT
WINSTON S. CHURCHILL

FEBRUARY 11, 1945

◇◇◇◇◇◇

12. THE BERLIN (POTSDAM) CONFERENCE, JULY 17-AUGUST 2, 1945

[The first and only meeting of the Big Three following the end of the war in Europe took place in Potsdam. There the powers agreed upon the principles to be followed in the treatment of Germany pending the final peace settlement, and they took the first steps toward the conclusion of peace treaties with the Axis satellite states. They also issued an ultimatum to Japan to end the war in the Far East. While the area of agreement was large, the Big Three failed to agree on such problems as the future of the Italian colonies, the disposition of the Dardanelles, the withdrawal of Soviet troops from Iran, and the future of Austria. It was at Potsdam that President Truman met Marshal Stalin for the first time. The third principal participant was Prime Minister Attlee.]

(a) Protocol of the Proceedings, August 1, 1945 [1]

The Berlin Conference of the Three Heads of Government of the U. S. S. R., U. S. A., and U. K., which took place from July 17 to August 2, 1945, came to the following conclusions:

I. ESTABLISHMENT OF A COUNCIL OF FOREIGN MINISTERS.

A. The Conference reached the following agreement for the establishment of a Council of Foreign Ministers to do the necessary preparatory work for the peace settlements:

"(1) There shall be established a Council composed of the Foreign Ministers of the United Kingdom, the Union of Soviet Socialist Republics, China, France, and the United States.

[1] Department of State press release 238, Mar. 24, 1947. *See* report on the Tripartite Conference at Berlin, Department of State Bulletin of Aug. 5, 1945, p. 153.

"(2) (i) The Council shall normally meet in London which shall be the permanent seat of the joint Secretariat which the Council will form. Each of the Foreign Ministers will be accompanied by a high-ranking Deputy, duly authorized to carry on the work of the Council in the absence of his Foreign Ministers, and by a small staff of technical advisers.

"(ii) The first meeting of the Council shall be held in London not later than September 1st 1945. Meetings may be held by common agreement in other capitals as may be agreed from time to time.

"(3) (i) As its immediate important task, the Council shall be authorized to draw up, with a view to their submission to the United Nations, treaties of peace with Italy, Rumania, Bulgaria, Hungary and Finland, and to propose settlements of territorial questions outstanding on the termination of the war in Europe. The Council shall be utilized for the preparation of a peace settlement for Germany to be accepted by the Government of Germany when a government adequate for the purpose is established.

"(ii) For the discharge of each of these tasks the Council will be composed of the Members representing those States which were signatory to the terms of surrender imposed upon the enemy State concerned. For the purposes of the peace settlement for Italy, France shall be regarded as a signatory to the terms of surrender for Italy. Other Members will be invited to participate when matters directly concerning them are under discussion.

"(iii) Other matters may from time to time be referred to the Council by agreement between the Member Governments.

"(4) (i) Whenever the Council is considering a question of direct interest to a State not represented thereon, such State should be invited to send representatives to participate in the discussion and study of that question.

"(ii) The Council may adapt its procedure to the particular problems under consideration. In some cases it may hold its own preliminary discussions prior to the participation of other interested States. In other cases, the Council may convoke a formal conference of the State chiefly interested in seeking a solution of the particular problem."

B. It was agreed that the three Governments should each address an identical invitation to the Governments of China and France to adopt this text and to join in establishing the Council. The text of the approved invitation was as follows:

Council of Foreign Ministers Draft for identical invitation to be sent separately by each of the Three Governments to the Governments of China and France.

"The Governments of the United Kingdom, the United States and the U. S. S. R. consider it necessary to begin without delay the essential preparatory work upon the peace settlements in Europe. To this end they are agreed that there should be established a Council of the Foreign Ministers of the Five Great Powers to prepare treaties of peace with the European enemy States, for submission to the United Nations. The

Council would also be empowered to propose settlements of outstanding territorial questions in Europe and to consider such other matters as member Governments might agree to refer to it.

"The text adopted by the Three Governments is as follows:

"In agreement with the Governments of the *United States and U. S. S. R., His Majesty's Government in the United Kingdom and U. S. S. R., the United States Government, the United Kingdom and the Soviet Government* extend a cordial invitation to the Government of *China (France)* to adopt the text quoted above and to join in setting up the Council. *His Majesty's Government, The United States Government, The Soviet Government* attach much importance to the participation of the *Chinese Government (French Government)* in the proposed arrangements and they hope to receive an early and favorable reply to this invitation."

C. It was understood that the establishment of the Council of Foreign Ministers for the specific purposes named in the text would be without prejudice to the agreement of the Crimea Conference that there should be periodical consultation between the Foreign Secretaries of the United States, the Union of Soviet Socialist Republics and the United Kingdom.

D. The Conference also considered the position of the European Advisory Commission in the light of the Agreement to establish the Council of Foreign Ministers. It was noted with satisfaction that the Commission had ably discharged its principal tasks by the recommendations that it had furnished for the terms of surrender for Germany, for the zones of occupation in Germany and Austria and for the inter-Allied control machinery in those countries. It was felt that further work of a detailed character for the coordination of Allied policy for the control of Germany and Austria would in future fall within the competence of the Control Council at Berlin and the Allied Commission at Vienna. Accordingly it was agreed to recommend that the European Advisory Commission be dissolved.

II. The Principles to Govern the Treatment of Germany in the Initial Control Period.

A. POLITICAL PRINCIPLES.

1. In accordance with the Agreement on Control Machinery in Germany, supreme authority in Germany is exercised, on instructions from their respective Governments, by the Commanders-in-Chief of the armed forces of the United States of America, the United Kingdom, the Union of Soviet Socialist Republics, and the French Republic, each in his own zone of occupation, and also jointly, in matters affecting Germany as a whole, in their capacity as members of the Control Council.

2. So far as is practicable, there shall be uniformity of treatment of the German population throughout Germany.

3. The purposes of the occupation of Germany by which the Control Council shall be guided are:

(i) The complete disarmament and demilitarization of Germany and the elimination or control of all German industry that could be used for military production. To these ends:—

(a) All German land, naval and air forces, the S. S., S. A., S. D., and Gestapo, with all their organizations, staffs and institutions, including the General Staff, the Officers' Corps, Reserve Corps, military schools, war veterans' organizations and all other military and semi-military organizations, together with all clubs and associations which serve to keep alive the military tradition in Germany, shall be completely and finally abolished in such manner as permanently to prevent the revival or reorganization of German militarism and Nazism;

(b) All arms, ammunition and implements of war and all specialized facilities for their production shall be held at the disposal of the Allies or destroyed. The maintenance and production of all aircraft and all arms, ammunition and implements of war shall be prevented.

(ii) To convince the German people that they have suffered a total military defeat and that they cannot escape responsibility for what they have brought upon themselves, since their own ruthless warfare and the fanatical Nazi resistance have destroyed German economy and made chaos and suffering inevitable.

(iii) To destroy the National Socialist Party and its affiliated and supervised organizations, to dissolve all Nazi institutions, to ensure that they are not revived in any form, and to prevent all Nazi and militarist activity or propaganda.

(iv) To prepare for the eventual reconstruction of German political life on a democratic basis and for eventual peaceful cooperation in international life by Germany.

4. All Nazi laws which provided the basis of the Hitler regime or established discriminations on grounds of race, creed, or political opinion shall be abolished. No such discriminations, whether legal, administrative or otherwise, shall be tolerated.

5. War criminals and those who have participated in planning or carrying out Nazi enterprises involving or resulting in atrocities or war crimes shall be arrested and brought to judgment. Nazi leaders, influential Nazi supporters and high officials of Nazi organizations and institutions and any other persons dangerous to the occupation or its objectives shall be arrested and interned.

6. All members of the Nazi Party who have been more than nominal participants in its activities and all other persons hostile to Allied purposes shall be removed from public and semi-public office, and from positions of responsibility in important private undertakings. Such persons shall be replaced by persons who, by their political and moral qualities, are deemed capable of assisting in developing genuine democratic institutions in Germany.

7. German education shall be so controlled as completely to eliminate Nazi and militarist doctrines and to make possible the successful development of democratic ideas.

8. The judicial system will be reorganized in accordance with the principles of democracy, of justice under law, and of equal rights for all citizens without distinction of race, nationality or religion.

9. The administration in Germany should be directed towards the decentralization of the political structure and the development of local responsibility. To this end:—

(i) local self-government shall be restored throughout Germany on democratic principles and in particular through elective councils as rapidly as is consistent with military security and the purposes of military occupation;

(ii) all democratic political parties with rights of assembly and of public discussion shall be allowed and encouraged throughout Germany;

(iii) representative and elective principles shall be introduced into regional, provincial and state (Land) administration as rapidly as may be justified by the successful application of these principles in local self-government;

(iv) for the time being, no central German Government shall be established. Notwithstanding this, however, certain essential central German administrative departments, headed by State Secretaries, shall be established, particularly in the fields of finance, transport, communications, foreign trade and industry. Such departments will act under the direction of the Control Council.

10. Subject to the necessity for maintaining military security, freedom of speech, press and religion shall be permitted, and religious institutions shall be respected. Subject likewise to the maintenance of military security, the formation of free trade unions shall be permitted.

B. ECONOMIC PRINCIPLES.

11. In order to eliminate Germany's war potential, the production of arms, ammunition and implements of war as well as all types of aircraft and seagoing ships shall be prohibited and prevented. Production of metals, chemicals, machinery and other items that are directly necessary to a war economy shall be rigidly controlled and restricted to Germany's approved post-war peacetime needs to meet the objectives stated in Paragraph 15. Productive capacity not needed for permitted production shall be removed in accordance with the reparations plan recommended by the Allied Commission on Reparations and approved by the Governments concerned or if not removed shall be destroyed.

12. At the earliest practicable date, the German economy shall be decentralized for the purpose of eliminating the present excessive concentration of economic power as exemplified in particular by cartels, syndicates, trusts and other monopolistic arrangements.

13. In organizing the German economy, primary emphasis shall be given to the development of agriculture and peaceful domestic industries.

14. During the period of occupation Germany shall be treated as a single economic unit. To this end common policies shall be established in regard to:

(a) mining and industrial production and its allocation;
(b) agriculture, forestry and fishing;
(c) wages, prices and rationing;
(d) import and export programs for Germany as a whole;
(e) currency and banking, central taxation and customs;
(f) reparation and removal of industrial war potential;
(g) transportation and communications.

In applying these policies account shall be taken, where appropriate, of varying local conditions.

15. Allied controls shall be imposed upon the German economy but only to the extent necessary:

(a) to carry out programs of industrial disarmament, demilitarization, of reparations, and of approved exports and imports.

(b) to assure the production and maintenance of goods and services required to meet the needs of the occupying forces and displaced persons in Germany and essential to maintain in Germany average living standards not exceeding the average of the standards of living of European countries. (European countries means all European countries excluding the United Kingdom and the U. S. S. R.).

(c) to ensure in the manner determined by the Control Council the equitable distribution of essential commodities between the several zones so as to produce a balanced economy throughout Germany and reduce the need for imports.

(d) to control German industry and all economic and financial international transactions including exports and imports, with the aim of preventing Germany from developing a war potential and of achieving the other objectives named herein.

(e) to control all German public or private scientific bodies, research and experimental institutions, laboratories, et cetera, connected with economic activities.

16. In the imposition and maintenance of economic controls established by the Control Council, German administrative machinery shall be created and the German authorities shall be required to the fullest extent practicable to proclaim and assume administration of such controls. Thus it should be brought home to the German people that the responsibility for the administration of such controls and any break-down in these controls will rest with themselves. Any German controls which may run counter to the objectives of occupation will be prohibited.

17. Measures shall be promptly taken:

(a) to effect essential repair of transport;

(b) to enlarge coal production;

(c) to maximize agricultural output; and

(d) to effect emergency repair of housing and essential utilities.

18. Appropriate steps shall be taken by the Control Council to exercise control and the power of disposition over German-owned external assets not already under the control of United Nations which have taken part in the war against Germany.

19. Payment of Reparations should leave enough resources to enable the German people to subsist without external assistance. In working out the economic balance of Germany the necessary means must be provided to pay for imports approved by the Control Council in Germany. The proceeds of exports from current production and stocks shall be available in the first place for payment for such imports.

The above clause will not apply to the equipment and products referred to in paragraphs 4 (a) and 4 (b) of the Reparations Agreement.

III. Reparations From Germany.

1. Reparation claims of the U. S. S. R. shall be met by removals from the zone of Germany occupied by the U. S. S. R., and from appropriate German external assets.

2. The U. S. S. R. undertakes to settle the reparation claims of Poland from its own share of reparations.

3. The reparation claims of the United States, the United Kingdom and other countries entitled to reparations shall be met from the Western Zones and from appropriate German external assets.

4. In addition to the reparations to be taken by the U. S. S. R. from its own zone of occupation, the U. S. S. R. shall receive additionally from the Western Zones:

(a) 15 per cent of such usable and complete industrial capital equipment, in the first place from the metallurgical, chemical and machine manufacturing industries as is unnecessary for the German peace economy and should be removed from the Western Zones of Germany, in exchange for an equivalent value of food, coal, potash, zinc, timber, clay products, petroleum products, and such other commodities as may be agreed upon.

(b) 10 per cent of such industrial capital equipment as is unnecessary for the German peace economy and should be removed from the Western Zones, to be transferred to the Soviet Government on reparations account without payment or exchange of any kind in return.

Removals of equipment as provided in (a) and (b) above shall be made simultaneously.

5. The amount of equipment to be removed from the Western Zones on account of reparations must be determined within six months from now at the latest.

6. Removals of industrial capital equipment shall begin as soon as possible and shall be completed within two years from the determination specified in paragraph 5. The delivery of products covered by 4 (a) above shall begin as soon as possible and shall be made by the U. S. S. R. in agreed installments within five years of the date hereof. The determination of the amount and character of the industrial capital equipment unnecessary for the German peace economy and therefore available for reparation shall be made by the Control Council under policies fixed by the Allied Commission on Reparations, with the participation of France, subject to the final approval of the Zone Commander in the Zone from which the equipment is to be removed.

7. Prior to the fixing of the total amount of equipment subject to removal, advance deliveries shall be made in respect to such equipment as will be determined to be eligible for delivery in accordance with the procedure set forth in the last sentence of paragraph 6.

8. The Soviet Government renounces all claims in respect of reparations to shares of German enterprises which are located in the Western Zones of Germany as well as to German foreign assets in all countries except those specified in paragraph 9 below.

9. The Governments of the U. K. and U. S. A. renounce all claims in respect of reparations to shares of German enterprises which are located in the Eastern Zone of occupation in Germany, as well as to German foreign assets in Bulgaria, Finland, Hungary, Rumania and Eastern Austria.

10. The Soviet Government makes no claims to gold captured by the Allied troops in Germany.

IV. Disposal of the German Navy and Merchant Marine

A. The following principles for the distribution of the German Navy were agreed:

(1) The total strength of the German surface navy, excluding ships sunk and those taken over from Allied Nations, but including ships under construction or repair, shall be divided equally among the U. S. S. R., U. K., and U. S. A.

(2) Ships under construction or repair mean those ships whose construction or repair may be completed within three to six months, according to the type of ship. Whether such ships under construction or repair shall be completed or repaired shall be determined by the technical commission appointed by the Three Powers and referred to below, subject to the principle that their completion or repair must be achieved within the time limits above provided, without any increase of skilled employment in the German shipyards and without permitting the reopening of any German ship building or connected industries. Completion date means the date when a ship is able to go out on its first trip, or, under peacetime standards, would refer to the customary date of delivery by shipyard to the Government.

(3) The larger part of the German submarine fleet shall be sunk. Not more than thirty submarines shall be preserved and divided equally between the U. S. S. R., U. K., and U. S. A. for experimental and technical purposes.

(4) All stocks of armament, ammunition and supplies of the German Navy appertaining to the vessels transferred pursuant to paragraphs (1) and (3) hereof shall be handed over to the respective powers receiving such ships.

(5) The Three Governments agree to constitute a tripartite naval commission comprising two representatives for each government, accompanied by the requisite staff, to submit agreed recommendations to the Three Governments for the allocation of specific German warships and to handle other detailed matters arising out of the agreement between the Three Governments regarding the German fleet. The Commission will hold its first meeting not later than 15th August, 1945, in Berlin, which shall be its headquarters. Each Delegation on the Commission will have the right on the basis of reciprocity to inspect German warships wherever they may be located.

(6) The Three Governments agreed that transfers, including those of ships under construction and repair, shall be completed as soon as possible, but not later than 15th February, 1946. The Commission will submit fortnightly reports including proposals for the progressive allocation of the vessels when agreed by the Commission.

B. The following principles for the distribution of the German Merchant Marine were agreed:—

(1) The German Merchant Marine, surrendered to the Three Powers and wherever located, shall be divided equally among the U. S. S. R., the U. K., and the U. S. A. The actual transfers of the ships to the respective countries shall take place as soon as practicable after the end

of the war against Japan. The United Kingdom and the United States will provide out of their shares of the surrendered German merchant ships appropriate amounts for other Allied States whose merchant marines have suffered heavy losses in the common cause against Germany, except that the Soviet Union shall provide out of its share for Poland.

(2) The allocation, manning, and operation of these ships during the Japanese War period shall fall under the cognizance and authority of the Combined Shipping Adjustment Board and the United Maritime Authority.

(3) While actual transfer of the ships shall be delayed until after the end of the war with Japan, a Tripartite Shipping Commission shall inventory and value all available ships and recommend a specific distribution in accordance with paragraph (1).

(4) German inland and coastal ships determined to be necessary to the maintenance of the basic German peace economy by the Allied Control Council of Germany shall not be included in the shipping pool thus divided among the Three Powers.

(5) The Three Governments agree to constitute a tripartite merchant marine commission comprising two representatives for each Government, accompanied by the requisite staff, to submit agreed recommendations to the Three Governments for the allocation of specific German merchant ships and to handle other detailed matters arising out of the agreement between the Three Governments regarding the German merchant ships. The Commission will hold its first meeting not later than September 1st, 1945, in Berlin, which shall be its headquarters. Each delegation on the Commission will have the right on the basis of reciprocity to inspect the German merchant ships wherever they may be located.

V. City of Koenigsberg and the Adjacent Area.

The Conference examined a proposal by the Soviet Government to the effect that pending the final determination of territorial questions at the peace settlement, the section of the western frontier of the Union of Soviet Socialist Republics which is adjacent to the Baltic Sea should pass from a point on the eastern shore of the Bay of Danzig to the east, north of Braunsberg-Goldap, to the meeting point of the frontiers of Lithuania, the Polish Republic and East Prussia.

The Conference has agreed in principle to the proposal of the Soviet Government concerning the ultimate transfer to the Soviet Union of the City of Koenigsberg and the area adjacent to it as described above subject to expert examination of the actual frontier.

The President of the United States and the British Prime Minister have declared that they will support the proposal of the Conference at the forthcoming peace settlement.

VI. War Criminals.

The Three Governments have taken note of the discussions which have been proceeding in recent weeks in London between British, United States, Soviet and French representatives with a view to reaching agreement on the methods of trial of those major war criminals whose crimes under the Moscow Declaration of October, 1943 have no particular geographical localisation. The Three Governments reaffirm their intention to bring these criminals to swift and sure justice. They hope that the negotiations in London will result in speedy agreement being reached for this purpose, and they regard it as a matter of great importance that the trial of these major criminals should begin at the earliest possible date. The first list of defendants will be published before 1st September.

VII. AUSTRIA.

The Conference examined a proposal by the Soviet Government on the extension·of the authority of the Austrian Provisional Government to all of Austria.

The three governments agreed that they were prepared to examine this question after the entry of the British and American forces into the city of Vienna.

It was agreed that reparations should not be exacted from Austria.

VIII. POLAND.

A. DECLARATION.

We have taken note with pleasure of the agreement reached among representative Poles from Poland and abroad which has made possible the formation, in accordance with the decisions reached at the Crimea Conference, of a Polish Provisional Government of National Unity recognized by the Three Powers. The establishment by the British and United States Governments of diplomatic relations with the Polish Provisional Government of National Unity has resulted in the withdrawal of their recognition from the former Polish Government in London, which no longer exists.

The British and United States Governments have taken measures to protect the interest of the Polish Provisional Government of National Unity as the recognized government of the Polish State in the property belonging to the Polish State located in their territories and under their control, whatever the form of this property may be. They have further taken measures to prevent alienation to third parties of such property. All proper facilities will be given to the Polish Provisional Government of National Unity for the exercise of the ordinary legal remedies for the recovery of any property belonging to the Polish State which may have been wrongfully alienated.

The Three Powers are anxious to assist the Polish Provisional Government of National Unity in facilitating the return to Poland as soon as practicable of all Poles abroad who wish to go, including members of the Polish Armed Forces and the Merchant Marine. They expect that those Poles who return home shall be accorded personal and property rights on the same basis as all Polish citizens.

The Three Powers note that the Polish Provisional Government of National Unity, in accordance with the decisions of the Crimea Conference, has agreed to the holding of free and unfettered elections as soon as possible on the basis of universal suffrage and secret ballot in which all democratic and anti-Nazi parties shall have the right to take part and to put forward candidates, and that representatives of the Allied press shall enjoy full freedom to report to the world upon developments in Poland before and during the elections.

B. WESTERN FRONTIER OF POLAND.

In conformity with the agreement on Poland reached at the Crimea Conference the three Heads of Government have sought the opinion of the Polish Provisional Government of National Unity in regard to the accession of territory in the north and west which Poland should receive. The President of the National Council of Poland and members of the Polish Provisional Government of National Unity have been received at the Conference and have fully presented their views. The three Heads of Government reaffirm their opinion that the final delimitation of the western frontier of Poland should await the peace settlement.

The three Heads of Government agree that, pending the final determination of Poland's western frontier, the former German territories cast of a line running from the Baltic Sea immediately west of Swinamunde, and thence along the Oder River to the confluence of the western Neisse River and along the Western Neisse to the Czechoslovak frontier, including that portion of East Prussia not placed under the administration of the Union of Soviet Socialist Republics in accordance with the understanding reached at this conference and including the area of the former free city of Danzig, shall be under the administration of the Polish State and for such purposes should not be considered as part of the Soviet zone of occupation in Germany.

IX. CONCLUSION OF PEACE TREATIES AND ADMISSION TO THE UNITED NATIONS ORGANIZATION.

The three Governments consider it desirable that the present anomalous position of Italy, Bulgaria, Finland, Hungary and Rumania should be terminated by the conclusion of Peace Treaties. They trust that the other interested Allied Governments will share these views.

For their part the three Governments have included the preparation of a Peace Treaty for Italy as the first among the immediate important tasks to be undertaken by the new Council of Foreign Ministers. Italy was the first of the Axis Powers to break with Germany, to whose defeat she has made a material contribution, and has now joined with the Allies in the struggle against Japan. Italy has freed herself from the Fascist regime and is making good progress towards reestablishment of a democratic government and institutions. The conclusion of such a Peace Treaty with a recognized and democratic Italian Government will make it possible for the three Governments to fulfill their desire to support an application from Italy for membership of the United Nations.

The three Governments have also charged the Council of Foreign Ministers with the task of preparing Peace Treaties for Bulgaria, Finland, Hungary and Rumania. The conclusion of Peace Treaties with recognized democratic governments in these States will also enable the three Governments to support applications from them for membership of the United Nations. The three Governments agree to examine each separately in the near future, in the light of the conditions then prevailing, the establishment of diplomatic relations with Finland, Rumania, Bulgaria, and Hungary to the extent possible prior to the conclusion of peace treaties with those countries.

The three Governments have no doubt that in view of the changed conditions resulting from the termination of the war in Europe, representatives of the Allied press will enjoy full freedom to report to the world upon developments in Rumania, Bulgaria, Hungary and Finland.

As regards the admission of other States into the United Nations Organization, Article 4 of the Charter of the United Nations declares that:

    1. Membership in the United Nations is open to all other peace-loving States who accept the obligations contained in the present Charter and, in the judgment of the organization, are able and willing to carry out these obligations;

    2. The admission of any such State to membership in the United Nations will be effected by a decision of the General Assembly upon the recommendation of the Security Council.

The three Governments, so far as they are concerned, will support applications for membership from those States which have remained neutral during the war and which fulfill the qualifications set out above.

The three Governments feel bound however to make it clear that they for their part would not favour any application for membership put forward by the present Spanish Government, which, having been founded with the support of the Axis Powers, does not, in view of its origins, its nature, its record and its close association with the aggressor States, possess the qualifications necessary to justify such membership.

X. Territorial Trusteeship.

The Conference examined a proposal by the Soviet Government on the question of trusteeship territories as defined in the decision of the Crimea Conference and in the Charter of the United Nations Organization.

After an exchange of views on this question it was decided that the disposition of any former Italian colonial territories was one to be decided in connection with the preparation of a peace treaty for Italy and that the question of Italian colonial territory would be considered by the September Council of Ministers of Foreign Affairs.

XI. Revised Allied Control Commission Procedure in Rumania, Bulgaria, and Hungary.

The three Governments took note that the Soviet Representatives on the Allied Control Commissions in Rumania, Bulgaria, and Hungary, have communicated to their United Kingdom and United States colleagues proposals for improving the work of the Control Commissions, now that hostilities in Europe have ceased.

The three Governments agreed that the revision of the procedures of the Allied Control Commissions in these countries would now be undertaken, taking into account the interests and responsibilities of the three Governments which together presented the terms of armistice to the respective countries, and accepting as a basis, in respect of all three countries, the Soviet Government's proposals for Hungary as annexed hereto. (Annex I)

XII. Orderly Transfer of German Populations.

The Three Governments, having considered the question in all its aspects, recognize that the transfer to Germany of German populations, or elements thereof, remaining in Poland, Czechoslovakia and Hungary, will have to be undertaken. They agree that any transfers that take place should be effected in an orderly and humane manner.

Since the influx of a large number of Germans into Germany would increase the burden already resting on the occupying authorities, they consider that the Control Council in Germany should in the first instance examine the problem, with special regard to the question of the equitable distribution of these Germans among the several zones of occupation. They are accordingly instructing their respective representatives on the Control Council to report to their Governments as soon as possible the extent to which such persons have already entered Germany from Poland, Czechoslovakia and Hungary, to submit an estimate of the time and rate at which further transfers could be carried out having regard to the present situation in Germany.

The Czechoslovak Government, the Polish Provisional Government and the Control Council in Hungary are at the same time being informed of the above and are being requested meanwhile to suspend further expulsions pending an examination by the Governments concerned of the report from their representatives on the Control Council.

XIII. Oil Equipment in Rumania.

The Conference agreed to set up two bilateral commissions of experts, one to be composed of United Kingdom and Soviet Members, and one to be composed of United States and Soviet Members, to investigate the facts and examine the documents, as a basis for the settlement of questions arising from the removal of oil equipment in Rumania. It was further agreed that these experts shall begin their work within ten days, on the spot.

XIV. Iran.

It was agreed that Allied troops should be withdrawn immediately from Tehran, and that further stages of the withdrawal of troops from Iran should be considered at the meeting of the Council of Foreign Ministers to be held in London in September, 1945.

XV. The International Zone of Tangier.

A proposal by the Soviet Government was examined and the following decisions were reached:

Having examined the question of the Zone of Tangier, the three Governments have agreed that this Zone, which includes the City of Tangier and the area adjacent to it, in view of its special strategic importance, shall remain international.

The question of Tangier will be discussed in the near future at a meeting in Paris of representatives of the Governments of the Union of Soviet Socialist Republics, the United States of America, the United Kingdom and France.

XVI. The Black Sea Straits.

The Three Governments recognized that the Convention concluded at Montreux should be revised as failing to meet present-day conditions.

It was agreed that as the next step the matter should be the subject of direct conversations between each of the three Governments and the Turkish Government.

XVII. International Inland Waterways.

The Conference considered a proposal of the U. S. Delegation on this subject and agreed to refer it for consideration to the forthcoming meeting of the Council of Foreign Ministers in London.

XVIII. European Inland Transport Conference.

The British and U. S. Delegations to the Conference informed the Soviet Delegation of the desire of the British and U. S. Governments to reconvene the European Inland Transport Conference and stated that they would welcome assurance that the Soviet Government would participate in the work of the reconvened conference. The Soviet Government agreed that it would participate in this conference.

XIX. Directives to Military Commanders on Allied Control Council for Germany.

The Three Governments agreed that each would send a directive to its representative on the Control Council for Germany informing him of all decisions of the Conference affecting matters within the scope of his duties.

XX. Use of Allied Property for Satellite Reparations or "War Trophies".

The proposal (Annex II) presented by the United States Delegation was accepted in principle by the Conference, but the drafting of an agreement on the matter was left to be worked out through diplomatic channels.

XXI. Military Talks.

During the Conference there were meetings between the Chiefs of Staff of the Three Governments on military matters of common interest.

ANNEX I

Text of a Letter Transmitted on July 12 to the Representatives of the U. S. and U. K. Governments on the Allied Control Commission in Hungary.

In view of the changed situation in connection with the termination of the war against Germany, the Soviet Government finds it necessary to establish the following order of work for the Allied Control Commission in Hungary.

1. During the period up to the conclusion of peace with Hungary the President (or Vice-President) of the ACC will regularly call conferences with the British and American representatives for the purpose of discussing the most important questions relating to the work of the ACC. The conferences will be called once in 10 days, or more frequently in case of need.

Directives of the ACC on questions or principle will be issued to the Hungarian authorities by the President of the Allied Control Commission after agreement on these directives with the English and American representatives.

2. The British and American representatives in the ACC will take part in general conferences of heads of divisions and delegates of the ACC, convoked by the President of the ACC, which meetings will be regular in nature. The British and American representatives will also participate personally or

through their representatives in appropriate instances in mixed commissions created by the President of the ACC for questions connected with the execution by the ACC of its functions.

3. Free movement by the American and British representatives in the country will be permitted provided that the ACC is previously informed of the time and route of the journeys.

4. All questions connected with permission for the entrance and exit of members of the staff of the British and American representatives in Hungary will be decided on the spot by the President of the ACC within a time limit of not more than one week.

5. The bringing in and sending out by plane of mail, cargoes and diplomatic couriers will be carried out by the British and American representatives on the ACC, under arrangements and within time limits established by the ACC, or in special cases by previous coordination with the President of the ACC.

I consider it necessary to add to the above that in all other points the existing Statutes regarding the ACC in Hungary, which was confirmed on January 20, 1945, shall remain in force in the future.

ANNEX II

Use of Allied Property for Satellite Reparations or "War Trophies".

1. The burden of reparation and "war trophies" should not fall on Allied nationals.

2. *Capital Equipment*—We object to the removal of such Allied property as reparations, "war trophies," or under any other guise. Loss would accrue to Allied nationals as a result of destruction of plants and the consequent loss of markets and trading connections. Seizure of Allied property makes impossible the fulfillment by the satellite of its obligation under the armistice to restore intact the rights and interests of the Allied Nations and their nationals.

The United States looks to the other occupying powers for the return of any equipment already removed and the cessation of removals. Where such equipment will not or cannot be returned, the U. S. will demand of the satellite adequate, effective and prompt compensation to American nationals, and that such compensation have priority equal to that of the reparations payment.

These principles apply to all property wholly or substantially owned by Allied nationals. In the event of removals of property in which the American as well as the entire Allied interest is less than substantial, the U. S. expects adequate, effective, and prompt compensation.

3. *Current Production*—While the U. S. does not oppose reparation out of current production of Allied investments, the satellite must provide immediate and adequate compensation to the Allied nationals including sufficient foreign exchange or products so that they can recover reasonable foreign currency expenditures and transfer a reasonable return on their investment. Such compensation must also have equal priority with reparations.

We deem it essential that the satellites not conclude treaties, agreements or arrangements which deny to Allied nationals access, on equal terms, to their trade, raw materials and industry; and appropriately modify any existing arrangements which may have that effect.

(b) Proclamation Defining Terms for Japanese Surrender, July 26, 1945 [1]

(1) We—The President of the United States, the President of the National Government of the Republic of China, and the Prime Minister of Great Britain, representing the hundreds of millions of our countrymen, have conferred and agree that Japan shall be given an opportunity to end this war.

(2) The prodigious land, sea and air forces of the United States, the British Empire and of China, many times reinforced by their armies and air fleets from the west, are poised to strike the final blows upon Japan. This military power is sustained and inspired by the determination of all the Allied Nations to prosecute the war against Japan until she ceases to resist.

(3) The result of the futile and senseless German resistance to the might of the aroused free peoples of the world stands forth in awful clarity as an example to the people of Japan. The might that now converges on Japan is immeasurably greater than that which, when applied to the resisting Nazis, necessarily laid waste to the lands, the industry and the method of life of the whole German people. The full application of our military power, backed by our resolve, *will* mean the inevitable and complete destruction of the Japanese armed forces and just as inevitably the utter devastation of the Japanese homeland.

(4) The time has come for Japan to decide whether she will continue to be controlled by those self-willed militaristic advisers whose unintelligent calculations have brought the Empire of Japan to the threshold of annihilation, or whether she will follow the path of reason.

(5) Following are our terms. We will not deviate from them. There are no alternatives. We shall brook no delay.

(6) There must be eliminated for all time the authority and influence of those who have deceived and misled the people of Japan into embarking on world conquest, for we insist that a new order of peace, security and justice will be impossible until irresponsible militarism is driven from the world.

(7) Until such a new order is established *and* until there is convincing proof that Japan's war-making power is destroyed, points in Japanese territory to be designated by the Allies shall be occupied to secure the achievement of the basic objectives we are here setting forth.

(8) The terms of the Cairo Declaration shall be carried out and Japanese sovereignty shall be limited to the islands of Honshu, Hokkaido, Kyushu, Shikoku and such minor islands as we determine.

(9) The Japanese military forces, after being completely disarmed, shall be permitted to return to their homes with the opportunity to lead peaceful and productive lives.

(10) We do not intend that the Japanese shall be enslaved as a race or destroyed as a nation, but stern justice shall be meted out to all war criminals,

---

[1] The Axis in Defeat, Department of State publication 2423, pp. 27-28; Department of State Bulletin, July 29, 1945.

This proclamation issued on July 26, 1945, by the heads of governments of the United States, United Kingdom, and China was signed by the President of the United States and the Prime Minister of the United Kingdom at Potsdam and concurred in by the President of the National Government of China, who communicated with President Truman by despatch. It is to be noted that the Soviet Union did not participate in this proclamation.

including those who have visited cruelties upon our prisoners. The Japanese Government shall remove all obstacles to the revival and strengthening of democratic tendencies among the Japanese people. Freedom of speech, of religion, and of thought, as well as respect for the fundamental human rights shall be established.

(11) Japan shall be permitted to maintain such industries as will sustain her economy and permit the exaction of just reparations in kind, but not those [industries] which would enable her to re-arm for war. To this end, access to, as distinguished from control of, raw materials shall be permitted. Eventual Japanese participation in world trade relations shall be permitted.

(12) The occupying forces of the Allies shall be withdrawn from Japan as soon as these objectives have been accomplished and there has been established in accordance with the freely expressed will of the Japanese people a peacefully inclined and responsible government.

(13) We call upon the government of Japan to proclaim now the unconditional surrender of all Japanese armed forces, and to provide proper and adequate assurances of their good faith in such action. The alternative for Japan is prompt and utter destruction.

PART II

Conferences on the Peace Settlement

〰〰

13. FIRST MEETING OF COUNCIL OF FOREIGN MINISTERS, LONDON, SEPTEMBER 11, TO OCTOBER 2, 1945

Report by Secretary Byrnes, October 5, 1945 [1]

[At the Potsdam Conference in 1945, the U.S., U.S.S.R. and U.K. agreed to establish the Council of Foreign Ministers. The immediate task of the Council, which was to be made up of the three powers plus China and France, was to draw up treaties of peace with Italy, Rumania, Bulgaria, Hungary, and Finland with a view to their submission to the other United Nations, and to propose settlements of territorial questions relating to the termination of the war in Europe. It was also charged with the responsibility for the preparation of a peace settlement for Germany. The excerpts which follow indicate the nature of the problems encountered by the great powers in their attempts to work out a peace settlement, and reflect the growing tension between East and West.

The first meeting, at which it was intended to provide directives for the preparation of treaties with Italy and the ex-satellite states, ended in a stalemate. Council members were unable to agree upon procedures to be followed in drawing up the treaties. In particular, the rôle of China, France, and the other United Nations was at issue.]

The first session of the Council of Foreign Ministers closed in a stalemate. But that need not, and should not, deprive us of a second and better chance to get on with the peace.

*   *   *

The first session of the Council, so far as the personal participation of the Foreign Ministers was concerned, was intended to provide directives for the deputies in the preparation of treaties for Italy, Rumania, Bulgaria, Hungary, and Finland.

*   *   *

So far as the Italian treaty was concerned I think we made very good progress toward agreement on directives to govern the work of our deputies.

1 Department of State publication 2398, Conference Series 78; Department of State Bulletin, October 7, 1945.

There was ready acceptance of our proposal that Italy should undertake to maintain a bill of rights which will secure the freedoms of speech, religious worship, political belief and public meeting envisaged for Italy in the Moscow Declaration of November 1943 and which will confirm the human rights and fundamental freedoms set forth in the Charter of the United Nations.

There was some difference among the conferees at the start as to providing for the limitation of armaments. But it was our feeling that Italy should rely on the United Nations for protection against aggression and should not engage in competition in armaments when all her resources are badly needed to restore her civilian economy. And this view gained general acceptance.

While the very controversial boundary dispute between Yugoslavia and Italy was not settled, it was encouraging to find that it was possible to agree that the line should in the main be governed by ethnic considerations and that regardless of its sovereignty there should be a free port at Trieste under international control.

The Council was in general agreement that the Dodecanese Islands should go to Greece although the assent of one member was qualified pending the study of certain questions by his government.

There was general agreement that the Italian colonies should come under the trusteeship provisions of the United Nations Charter. Various views were expressed as to the preferred form of trusteeship for the colonies.

The American Delegation was particularly gratified that the directive to the deputies, while not restricting their studies, called for special consideration of the American proposal for a truly international administration directly responsible to the United Nations with a view to the attainment of the greatest degree of independence of the inhabitants of two of the colonies at the end of ten years and independence for the people of a third colony at as early a date as possible.

This proposal was presented by the American Delegation when the Italian treaty first was taken up and was consistently adhered to.

It is our view that the object of a trusteeship should be to promote the self-government of the people of a colony and not to enrich a trustee or increase its economic or military power.

It was also agreed that Italian sovereignty should be restored on the conclusion of the treaty so that foreign troops may be withdrawn and, except as specially provided in the treaty, foreign controls within Italy terminated.

There was no definite understanding on reparations. The United States took the position that Italy could not pay anything like $600,000,000. Apart from certain foreign assets, she should be required to pay as reparations only such factory and tool equipment designed for the manufacture of war implements which are not required for the limited military establishment permitted to her and which cannot be readily converted to peaceful purposes. If she is stripped of more, then her economy cannot be restored.

We have contributed several hundred million dollars for the relief of the Italian people. Their condition is deplorable. We must continue to help them. But we cannot contribute more millions, if those millions are to be used to enable Italy to pay reparations to other governments. We did that for Germany after the last war. We shall not do it again.

Substantial progress was also made on the directives for the preparatory work on the Finnish treaty and the treaties with Rumania and Bulgaria. The principles suggested by the American Delegation and accepted for the Italian treaty for the safeguarding of human rights and fundamental freedoms are also to be incorporated in these treaties.

The directives concerning the limitation of armament for Rumania and Bulgaria are expected to follow the same general line as those accepted for Italy.

Before work could be commenced upon the directives for the Hungarian treaty the Soviet Delegation announced they felt obliged to withdraw their assent to the procedure previously accepted by the Council for dealing with peace treaties.

*   *   *

Had it not been for the difficulties experienced by the Allied Governments in agreeing upon a common policy in regard to the recognition of the Governments of Rumania and Bulgaria a more conciliatory spirit might possibly have prevailed and might greatly have helped to overcome the procedural difficulties of the Council.

No one present at the Council on September 11 questioned the decision taken by the Council that day inviting all five members to be present at all meetings.

Directives for the Italian treaty were under discussion for several days with China, not a party to the surrender terms, present, participating in the discussion, but not voting. No one objected.

Directives for the Finnish treaty were then considered, with the United States, France, and China present but not voting. No one objected.

Directives for the Rumanian treaty and then for the Bulgarian treaty were considered, with France and China present but not voting. No one objected.

It was only on September 22 that the Soviet Delegation took the position that the decision of the Council on Sepember 11 violated the Berlin agreement.

It will be recalled that the Berlin agreement set up a Council of the Soviet Union, Great Britain, France, China and the United States to undertake the necessary preparatory work for the peace settlements. It provided that the Council should draw up with a view to their submission to the United Nations peace treaties with Italy, Rumania, Bulgaria, Hungary, and Finland.

It provided that in the discharge of these tasks the Council will be composed of members representing those states which were signatory to the terms of surrender imposed upon the enemy state concerned, and for the purpose of the Italian settlement, France should be regarded as signatory to the surrender terms.

The Berlin agreement further provided that other members of the Council will be invited to participate when matters directly concerning them are under discussion.

This distinction between members of the Council who were parties to the surrender terms and those who were not, was not part of the original American proposal and was reluctantly accepted by us. We were fully aware that a member would not have the right to vote if not a party to the surrender terms, but we understood from the exchange of views at the table that all members would be allowed to participate in all discussions in the Council.

*   *   *

The Soviet Delegation's position was not simply that they wished to withdraw the invitation to China and France to participate without right to vote. Their position was that it was beyond the authority of the states signatory to the surrender terms to extend the invitation.

Although this construction of the Berlin agreement did not accord with the understanding of the American Delegation or the British Delegation or the President of the United States or the Prime Minister of Great Britain, the Soviet Delegation insisted that they could no longer discuss treaty matters in the presence of members who were not parties to the surrender terms.

*   *   *

The Berlin agreement expressly provided in section 4 of the article establishing the Council that the Council may adapt its procedures to the particular problems under discussion; that in some cases it may hold its own discussions prior to the participation of other interested states; and in other cases it may convoke a formal conference of states interested in particular problems.

I therefore proposed, with considerable reluctance, that we ask our French and Chinese colleagues to accept the position of the Soviet Delegation that the preparatory and exploratory work of the Council for the peace settlements be confined to the signatories of the surrender terms in question, provided that at the same time it should be agreed that a truly representative peace conference should be convoked before the end of the year. To ensure the calling of such a conference we thought that France and China, in the interest of peace, might make even this sacrifice.

This conference would be convoked for the purpose of considering the peace treaties with Italy, Rumania, Bulgaria, Hungary, and Finland. To the conference would be invited—

    (1) The five members of the Council of Foreign Ministers which are also the five permanent members of the United Nations Security Council;

    (2) All European members of the United Nations;

    (3) All non-European members of the United Nations which supplied substantial military contingents in the war against the European members of the Axis.

*   *   *

The Soviet Delegation stated, however, that they could not agree to the American proposal for a peace conference until they had returned to Moscow and had personal consultations with their Government.

It therefore became obvious that there could be no agreement unless the other delegations were prepared to yield their views and convictions to those of the Soviet Delegation. This none of the other delegations was prepared to do.

The United States is willing to dictate terms of peace to an enemy but is not willing to dictate terms of peace to its Allies.

*   *   *

The Soviet Delegation also reiterated their position that they would not discuss the treaties in the presence of members they now believed to be ineligible. This would have excluded China from the consideration of all treaties and France from the consideration of all but one without any assurance of participation in a peace conference.

It became apparent that agreement was impossible and further meetings were useless. The Chinese Foreign Minister who was presiding when the Council adjourned and at whose instance the Council had remained in session from Sunday until Tuesday, stated that under the circumstances he could not ask the Council to continue in session longer.

As the record stands the Foreign Minister of the Soviet Union has not rejected our proposal for a peace conference. During the discussions he admitted it was correct in principle. My hope is that, after he has conferred with his government, his government will agree that the nations that fought the war—the World War—shall have a chance to make the world peace.

* * *

◇◇◇◇◇

14. INTERIM MEETING OF FOREIGN MINISTERS OF THE UNITED STATES, THE UNITED KINGDOM, AND THE UNION OF SOVIET SOCIALIST REPUBLICS, MOSCOW, DECEMBER 16-26, 1945

Soviet-Anglo-American Communiqué, December 27, 1945 [1]

[The Moscow meeting of the foreign ministers of the U.S., U.K. and U.S.S.R. was far more successful than the London meeting of the Council. Satisfactory procedures for the preparation of the peace treaties were agreed upon in line with the American principle that all nations that helped win the war should participate in the peace. Moreover, as Secretary Byrnes pointed out, the great powers "reached understanding on all important items placed on our agenda with the exception of Iran."]

* * *

At the meeting which took place in Moscow from December 16 to December 26, 1945 of the Ministers of Foreign Affairs of the Union of Soviet Socialist Republics, the United States of America and the United Kingdom, agreement was reached on the following questions:

I. PREPARATION OF PEACE TREATIES WITH ITALY, RUMANIA BULGARIA, HUNGARY AND FINLAND

As announced on the 24th of December, 1945, the Governments of the Soviet Union, the United Kingdom, and the United States have agreed and have requested the adherence of the Governments of France and China to the following procedure with respect to the preparation of peace treaties:

1. In the drawing up by the Council of Foreign Ministers of treaties of peace with Italy, Rumania, Bulgaria, Hungary, and Finland, only members of the Council who are, or under the terms of the Agreement establishing

[1] Department of State publication 2448, Conference Series 79; Department of State publication 2653, Treaties and Other International Acts Series 1555.

the Council of Foreign Ministers adopted at the Berlin Conference are deemed to be, signatory of the Surrender Terms, will participate, unless and until the Council takes further action under the Agreement to invite other members of the Council to participate on questions directly concerning them. That is to say:

A) the terms of the peace treaty with Italy will be drafted by the Foreign Ministers of the United Kingdom, the United States, the Soviet Union and France;

B) the terms of the peace treaties with Rumania, Bulgaria, and Hungary by the Foreign Ministers of the Soviet Union, the United States and the United Kingdom;

C) the terms of the peace treaty with Finland by the Foreign Ministers of the Soviet Union and the United Kingdom.

The Deputies of the Foreign Ministers will immediately resume their work in London on the basis of understandings reached on the questions discussed at the first plenary session of the Council of Foreign Ministers in London.

2. When the preparation of all these drafts has been completed, the Council of Foreign Ministers will convoke a conference for the purpose of considering treaties of peace with Italy, Rumania, Bulgaria, Hungary and Finland. The conference will consist of the five members of The Council of Foreign Ministers together with all members of the United Nations which actively waged war with substantial military force against European enemy states, namely: Union of Soviet Socialist Republics, United Kingdom, United States of America, China, France, Australia, Belgium, Belorussian Soviet Socialist Republic, Brazil, Canada, Czechoslovakia, Ethiopia, Greece, India, the Netherlands, New Zealand, Norway, Poland, Union of South Africa, Yugoslavia, Ukrainian Soviet Socialist Republic. The conference will be held not later than May 1, 1946.

3. After the conclusion of the deliberations of the conference and upon consideration of its recommendations the States signatory to the terms of armistice with Italy, Rumania, Bulgaria, Hungary and Finland—France being regarded as such for the purposes of the peace treaty with Italy—will draw up final texts of peace treaties.

4. The final texts of the respective peace treaties as so drawn up will be signed by representatives of the States represented at the conference which are at war with the enemy states in question. The texts of the respective peace treaties will then be submitted to the other United Nations which are at war with the enemy states in question.

5. The peace treaties will come into force immediately after they have been ratified by the Allied States signatory to the respective armistices, France being regarded as such in the case of the peace with Italy. These treaties are subject to ratification by the enemy states in question.

II. FAR EASTERN COMMISSION AND ALLIED COUNCIL FOR JAPAN

A. FAR EASTERN COMMISSION

Agreement was reached, with the concurrence of China, for the establishment of a Far Eastern Commission to take the place of the Far Eastern

Advisory Commission. The Terms of Reference for the Far Eastern Commission are as follows:

I. Establishment of the Commission

A Far Eastern Commission is hereby established composed of the representatives of the Union of Soviet Socialist Republics, United Kingdom, United States, China, France, the Netherlands, Canada, Australia, New Zealand, India, and the Philippine Commonwealth.

II. Functions

A. The functions of the Far Eastern Commission shall be:

1. To formulate the policies, principles, and standards in conformity with which the fulfillment by Japan of its obligations under the Terms of Surrender may be accomplished.

2. To review, on the request of any member, any directive issued by the Supreme Commander for the Allied Powers or any action taken by the Supreme Commander involving policy decisions within the jurisdiction of the Commission.

3. To consider such other matters as may be assigned to it by agreement among the participating Governments reached in accordance with the voting procedure provided for in Article V-2 hereunder.

B. The Commission shall not make recommendations with regard to the conduct of military operations nor with regard to territorial adjustments.

C. The Commission in its activities will proceed from the fact that there has been formed an Allied Council for Japan and will respect existing control machinery in Japan, including the chain of command from the United States Government to the Supreme Commander and the Supreme Commander's command of occupation forces.

III. Functions of the United States Government

1. The United States Government shall prepare directives in accordance with policy decisions of the Commission and shall transmit them to the Supreme Commander through the appropriate United States Government agency. The Supreme Commander shall be charged with the implementation of the directives which express the policy decisions of the Commission.

2. If the Commission decides that any directive or action reviewed in accordance with Article II-A-2 should be modified, its decision shall be regarded as a policy decision.

3. The United States Government may issue interim directives to the Supreme Commander pending action by the Commission whenever urgent matters arise not covered by policies already formulated by the Commission; provided that any directive dealing with fundamental changes in the Japanese constitutional structure or in the regime of control, or dealing with a change in the Japanese Government as a whole will be issued only following consultation and following the attainment of agreement in the Far Eastern Commission.

4. All directives issued shall be filed with the Commission.

IV. Other Methods of Consultation

The establishment of the Commission shall not preclude the use of other methods of consultation on Far Eastern issues by the participating Governments.

V. Composition

1. The Far Eastern Commission shall consist of one representative of each of the States party to this agreement. The membership of the Commission may be increased by agreement among the participating Powers as conditions warrant by the addition of representatives of other United Nations in the Far East or having territories therein. The Commission shall provide for full and adequate consultations, as occasion may require, with representatives of the United Nations not members of the Commission in regard to matters before the Commission which are of particular concern to such nations.

2. The Commission may take action by less than unanimous vote provided that action shall have the concurrence of at least a majority of all the representatives including the representatives of the four following Powers: United States, United Kingdom, Union of Soviet Socialist Republics and China.

VI. Location and Organization

1. The Far Eastern Commission shall have its headquarters in Washington. It may meet at other places as occasion requires, including Tokyo, if and when it deems it desirable to do so. It may make such arrangements through the Chairman as may be practicable for consultation with the Supreme Commander for the Allied Powers.

2. Each representative on the Commission may be accompanied by an appropriate staff comprising both civilian and military representation.

3. The Commission shall organize its secretariat, appoint such committees as may be deemed advisable, and otherwise perfect its organization and procedure.

VII. Termination

The Far Eastern Commission shall cease to function when a decision to that effect is taken by the concurrence of at least a majority of all the representatives including the representatives of the four following Powers: United States, United Kingdom, Union of Soviet Socialist Republics and China. Prior to the termination of its functions the Commission shall transfer to any interim or permanent security organization of which the participating governments are members those functions which may appropriately be transferred.

It was agreed that the Government of the United States on behalf of the four Powers should present the Terms of Reference to the other Governments specified in Article I and invite them to participate in the Commission on the revised basis.

B. ALLIED COUNCIL FOR JAPAN

The following agreement was also reached, with the concurrence of China, for the establishment of an Allied Council for Japan:

1. There shall be established an Allied Council with its seat in Tokyo under the chairmanship of the Supreme Commander for the Allied Powers (or his Deputy) for the purpose of consulting with and advising the Supreme Commander in regard to the implementation of the Terms of Surrender, the occupation and control of Japan, and of directives supplementary thereto; and for the purpose of exercising the control authority herein granted.

2. The membership of the Allied Council shall consist of the Supreme Commander (or his Deputy) who shall be Chairman and United States member; a Union of Soviet Socialist Republics member; a Chinese member; and a member representing jointly the United Kingdom, Australia, New Zealand, and India.

3. Each member shall be entitled to have an appropriate staff consisting of military and civilian advisers.

4. The Allied Council shall meet not less often than once every two weeks.

5. The Supreme Commander shall issue all orders for the implementation of the Terms of Surrender, the occupation and control of Japan, and directives supplementary thereto. In all cases action will be carried out under and through the Supreme Commander who is the sole executive authority for the Allied Powers in Japan. He will consult and advise with the Council in advance of the issuance of orders on matters of substance, the exigencies of the situation permitting. His decisions upon these matters shall be controlling.

6. If, regarding the implementation of policy decisions of the Far Eastern Commission on questions concerning a change in the regime of control, fundamental changes in the Japanese constitutional structure, and a change in the Japanese Government as a whole, a member of the Council disagrees with the Supreme Commander (or his Deputy), the Supreme Commander will withhold the issuance of orders on these questions pending agreement thereon in the Far Eastern Commission.

7. In cases of necessity the Supreme Commander may take decisions concerning the change of individual Ministers of the Japanese Government, or concerning the filling of vacancies created by the resignation of individual cabinet members, after appropriate preliminary consultation with the representative of the other Allied Powers on the Allied Council.

III. KOREA

1. With a view to the re-establishment of Korea as an independent state, the creation of conditions for developing the country on democratic principles and the earliest possible liquidation of the disastrous results of the protracted Japanese domination in Korea, there shall be set up a provisional Korean democratic government which shall take all the necessary steps for developing the industry, transport and agriculture of Korea and the national culture of the Korean people.

2. In order to assist the formation of a provisional Korean government and with a view to the preliminary elaboration of the appropriate measures, there shall be established a Joint Commission consisting of representatives of the United States command in southern Korea and the Soviet command in northern Korea. In preparing their proposals the Commission shall consult with the Korean democratic parties and social organizations. The recommendations worked out by the Commission shall be presented for the consideration of the Governments of the Union of Soviet Socialist Republics, China, the United Kingdom and the United States prior to final decision by the two Governments represented on the Joint Commission.

3. It shall be the task of the Joint Commission, with the participation of the provisional Korean democratic government and of the Korean democratic

organizations to work out measures also for helping and assisting (trusteeship) the political, economic and social progress of the Korean people, the development of democratic self-government and the establishment of the national independence of Korea.

The proposals of the Joint Commission shall be submitted, following consultation with the provisional Korean Government for the joint consideration of the Governments of the United States, Union of Soviet Socialist Republics, United Kingdom and China for the working out of an agreement concerning a four-power trusteeship of Korea for a period of up to five years.

4. For the consideration of urgent problems affecting both southern and northern Korea and for the elaboration of measures establishing permanent coordination in administrative-economic matters between the United States command in southern Korea and the Soviet command in northern Korea, a conference of the representatives of the United States and Soviet commands in Korea shall be convened within a period of two weeks.

IV. CHINA

The three Foreign Secretaries exchanged views with regard to the situation in China. They were in agreement as to the need for a unified and democratic China under the National Government, for broad participation by democratic elements in all branches of the National Government, and for a cessation of civil strife. They reaffirmed their adherence to the policy of non-interference in the internal affairs of China.

Mr. Molotov and Mr. Byrnes had several conversations concerning Soviet and American armed forces in China.

Mr. Molotov stated that the Soviet forces had disarmed and deported Japanese troops in Manchuria but that withdrawal of Soviet forces had been postponed until February 1st at the request of the Chinese Government.

Mr. Byrnes pointed out that American forces were in north China at the request of the Chinese Government, and referred also to the primary responsibility of the United States in the implementation of the Terms of Surrender with respect to the disarming and deportation of Japanese troops. He stated that American forces would be withdrawn just as soon as this responsibility was discharged or the Chinese Government was in a position to discharge the responsibility without the assistance of American forces.

The two Foreign Secretaries were in complete accord as to the desirability of withdrawal of Soviet and American forces from China at the earliest practicable moment consistent with the discharge of their obligations and responsibilities.

V. RUMANIA

The three Governments are prepared to give King Michael the advice for which he has asked in his letter of August 21, 1945, on the broadening of the Rumanian Government. The King should be advised that one member of the National Peasant Party and one member of the Liberal Party should be included in the Government. The Commission referred to below shall satisfy itself that

(a) they are truly representative members of the groups of the Parties not represented in the Government;

(b) they are suitable and will work loyally with the Government.

The three Governments take note that the Rumanian Government thus reorganized should declare that free and unfettered elections will be held as soon as possible on the basis of universal and secret ballot. All democratic and anti-fascist parties should have the right to take part in these elections and to put forward candidates. The reorganized Government should give assurances concerning the grant of freedom of the press, speech, religion and association.

A. Y. Vyshinski, Mr. Harriman, and Sir A. Clark Kerr are authorized as a Commission to proceed to Bucharest immediately to consult with King Michael and members of the present Government with a view to the execution of the above-mentioned tasks.

As soon as these tasks are accomplished and the required assurances have been received, the Government of Rumania, with which the Soviet Government maintains diplomatic relations, will be recognized by the Government of the United States of America and the Government of the United Kingdom.

VI. BULGARIA

It is understood by the three Governments that the Soviet Government takes upon itself the mission of giving friendly advice to the Bulgarian Government with regard to the desirability of the inclusion in the Bulgarian Government of the Fatherland Front, now being formed, of an additional two representatives of other democratic groups, who (a) are truly representative of the groups of the parties which are not participating in the Government, and (b) are really suitable and will work loyally with the Government.

As soon as the Governments of the United States of America and the United Kingdom are convinced that this friendly advice has been accepted by the Bulgarian Government and the said additional representatives have been included in its body, the Government of the United States and the Government of the United Kingdom will recognize the Bulgarian Government, with which the Government of the Soviet Union already has diplomatic relations.

VII. THE ESTABLISHMENT BY THE UNITED NATIONS OF A COMMISSION FOR THE CONTROL OF ATOMIC ENERGY

Discussion of the subject of atomic energy related to the question of the establishment of a commission by the General Assembly of the United Nations. The Ministers of Foreign Affairs of the Union of Soviet Socialist Republics, the United States of America, and the United Kingdom have agreed to recommend, for the consideration of the General Assembly of the United Nations, the establishment by the United Nations of a commission to consider problems arising from the discovery of atomic energy and related matters. They have agreed to invite the other permanent members of the Security Council, France and China, together with Canada, to join with them in assuming the initiative in sponsoring the following resolution at the the first session of the General Assembly of the United Nations in January 1946:—

Resolved by the General Assembly of the United Nations to establish a Commission, with the composition and competence set out hereunder, to deal with the problems raised by the discovery of atomic energy and other related matters.

I. Establishment of the Commission

A Commission is hereby established by the General Assembly with the terms of reference set out under Section V below.

II. Relations of the Commission with the Organs of the United Nations

(a) The Commission shall submit its reports and recommendations to the Security Council, and such reports and recommendations shall be made public unless the Security Council, in the interests of peace and security, otherwise directs. In the appropriate cases the Security Council should transmit these Reports to the General Assembly and the members of the United Nations, as well as to the Economic and Social Council and other Organs within the framework of the United Nations.

(b) In view of the Security Council's primary responsibility under the Charter of the United Nations for the maintenance of international peace and security, the Security Council shall issue directions to the Commission in matters affecting security. On these matters the Commission shall be accountable for its work to the Security Council.

III. Composition of the Commission

The Commission shall be composed of one representative from each of those states represented on the Security Council, and Canada when that state is not a member of the Security Council. Each representative on the Commission may have such assistants as he may desire.

IV. Rules of Procedure

The Commission shall have whatever staff it may deem necessary, and shall make recommendations for its rules of procedure to the Security Council, which shall approve them as a procedural matter.

V. Terms of Reference of the Commission

The Commission shall proceed with the utmost dispatch and inquire into all phases of the problem, and make such recommendations from time to time with respect to them as it finds possible. In particular the Commission shall make specific proposals:

(a) For extending between all nations the exchange of basic scientific information for peaceful ends;

(b) For control of atomic energy to the extent necessary to ensure its use only for peaceful purposes;

(c) For the elimination from national armaments of atomic weapons and of all other major weapons adaptable to mass destruction;

(d) For effective safeguards by way of inspection and other means to protect complying states against the hazards of violations and evasions.

The work of the Commission should proceed by separate stages, the successful completion of each of which will develop the necessary confidence of the world before the next stage is undertaken.

The Commission shall not infringe upon the responsibilities of any Organ of the United Nations, but should present recommendations for the consideration of those Organs in the performance of their tasks under the terms of the United Nations Charter.

JAMES F. BYRNES
ERNEST BEVIN
V. MOLOTOV
Dec. 27–/45

◇◇◇◇◇◇

15. SECOND MEETING OF THE COUNCIL OF FOREIGN MINISTERS, PARIS

(a) First Part, April 25 to May 16, 1946
Report by Secretary Byrnes, May 20, 1946 [1]

[Representatives of the United States attended the second meeting of the Council with the hope that the way could be paved for a peace conference and the final approval of the peace treaties. But the ministers were unable to adjust their outstanding differences—particularly with respect to the Italian treaty and Germany—and as a result, progress at Paris was disappointingly small. This failure led Secretary Byrnes to comment: "The Council of Foreign Ministers was formed to facilitate and not obstruct the making of peace."]

*   *   *

We found that there were three basic issues outstanding on the Italian treaty: reparations, the colonies and the Italian-Yugoslav boundary, particularly as it concerns the Italian city of Trieste.

In summarizing the significance of these basic issues, I shall deliberately seek to avoid intensifying the conflict in viewpoints.

Our position on reparations is simple. To enable the Italian nation to live we have already advanced directly or indirectly $900,000,000. We should prefer in the interest of peace to forget about reparations. But we are willing to agree to limited reparations, provided these do not deprive Italy of resources necessary to enable her to subsist without external assistance.

If Italy requires help from others she will look to us. And we made it clear we are not going to advance millions of dollars to enable Italy to produce goods to be paid as reparations to any of our Allies.

The Soviet Government has insisted on reparations for itself of $100,-000,000. We have pointed out certain sources from which reparations can be taken which would not seriously affect the Italian economy and which would yield substantially the amount which the Soviets claim. But the Soviet Government is unwilling to count what she will obtain from some of these sources as reparations.

For example, she insists that some of the naval ships surrendered by Italy to the navies of the United States and Britain be shared with her. She declares the ships are war booty. But war booty belongs to the nation capturing it.

[1] Report on the Paris Conference of the Foreign Ministers of France, the Union of Soviet Socialist Republics, the United Kingdom, and the United States, which took place between Apr. 25 and May 16, 1946. Department of State publication 2537, Conference Series 86; Department of State Bulletin, June 2, 1946.

The Soviet Union has never shared with Allied nations any war booty captured by her. We are willing to give to her in lieu of reparations some of the naval ships surrendered to us. She demands the ships but refuses to consider them as a substitute for reparations. She insists upon being paid out of current production. We would have to finance the production, and therefore I refused to agree with the proposal.

Differences regarding the colonies have been narrowed but not resolved. The Soviet Government receded from its claim for a trusteeship of Tripolitania, first in favor of a joint Soviet-Italian trusteeship and later in favor of an Italian trusteeship as originally proposed by the French.

Our position has always been that the colonies should be placed under United Nations trusteeship, having as its objective the welfare of the inhabitants and their independence at the earliest practicable date. The Trusteeship Council should appoint a neutral administrator responsible to it, thus avoiding all possible rivalry between the powers. Libya and Eritrea should be granted independence in ten years.

It is open to question whether Italy is in an economic position to assume the responsibility of trusteeship and whether the return of the colonies to Italy as trustee takes sufficiently into account the wishes of the inhabitants. For these reasons it was with considerable reluctance that I indicated my willingness to yield to the French suggestion of an Italian trusteeship if that would bring about an agreement in the Council, and if it were agreed that a definite date would be fixed for the independence of Libya and Eritrea. But the French Government was unwilling to agree to a fixed date for independence.

* * *

It was my impression that agreement on reparations and the colonies as well as on a host of other questions would not be long delayed if only a solution of the Trieste problem could be found. The Soviet Representative finally indicated that there would be no serious question on the cession of the Dodecanese Islands to Greece but he refused to approve it until the other territorial dispositions could be agreed upon.

The experts appointed to investigate the Italian-Yugoslav frontier did not differ as to the facts. But the Soviet Representative differs from the other members of the Council as to the conclusions to be drawn from the facts. It is his position that Venezia Giulia must be treated as an inseparable whole, and that so treated the claim of Yugoslavia to the area is superior to that of Italy. The other Representatives believe that wise statesmanship as well as the explicit decision taken by the Council at London requires a boundary line which will in the main be an ethnic line leaving a minimum of people under alien rule.

It was wrong to give Italy the whole of Venezia Giulia after World War I. It would be equally wrong to give Yugoslavia the whole of Venezia Giulia now. It would transfer from Italy to Yugoslavia approximately 500,000 Italians.

The British and French experts proposed ethnic lines more favorable to Yugoslavia than our own. In an effort to reach agreement we stated we were willing to accept the British or French line or any other ethnic line that could be justified upon the basis of the London decision.

The American Delegation suggested a plebiscite for the area between the line proposed by the United States and the line proposed by the Soviet Union —but the Soviet Delegation would not consider a plebiscite except for the whole Venezia Giulia area. All of us are agreed that Yugoslavia and the countries of Central Europe which have for years used the port of Trieste shall have free access to Trieste at which there shall be a free port under international control. But we will continue to appeal to the Soviet Government and the Yugoslav Government not to press for a boundary line which will needlessly violate ethnic principles and will breed trouble in the future.

Agreement on the Balkan treaties is blocked principally by the inability of the Council to agree upon the economic clauses. Agreement on these provisions may have been delayed as part of a bargaining process, although so far the Soviet Government has stood out against the inclusion in the treaties of any provision which would promise freedom of commerce on the Danube, the gateway to Central Europe.

* * *

At the London meeting of the Council of Foreign Ministers when the Soviet Foreign Secretary seemed greatly concerned about the Soviet security requirements in the Balkans, I suggested a twenty-five year four-power treaty, to keep Germany disarmed as a means of preventing any real threat to Soviet security. I explained that we contemplated a similar joint guaranty of the disarmament of Japan.

I again proposed such a treaty in a talk with Generalissimo Stalin on December 24 while I was in Moscow. The Generalissimo said that if the United States made such a proposal he would wholeheartedly support it.

Later I also spoke to Mr. Bevin who advised me that he personally was most sympathetic to the suggestion.

In February I sent a working draft of the proposed treaty for German disarmament to the Soviet, British and the French Governments and the proposed treaty for Japanese disarmament to the Soviet, British and Chinese Governments. I invited their suggestions as to the draft.

I was informed by Mr. Bevin and M. Bidault that they favored the proposal in principle but would have a few suggestions to make. I did not hear from Mr. Molotov. Just before the Paris meeting I advised the Ministers I would like to discuss the proposal at Paris. The Soviet Minister agreed to discuss it informally but stated without specification that there were serious objections to the draft.

* * *

Later the Soviet Representative stated that when Generalissmo Stalin agreed with me to support the treaty I did not have a draft of it. He said that as it could not become effective until after a German treaty was signed, consideration of it could be delayed.

It is our sincere hope that after the Soviet Union studies our proposal and comes to appreciate our earnest desire to see Germany disarmed and kept disarmed, the Soviet Union will support it wholeheartedly.

* * *

Important as the German questions are and eager as we are to press for their speedy solution, we must not and cannot delay the peace settlements with other countries. At Potsdam it was agreed that the start should be made with Italy, Bulgaria, Hungary, Rumania and Finland. While Germany must remain under occupation for some time, we cannot fail to do our part to rid the rest of Europe of the burden of the forces of occupation. There can be no recovery in Europe until we do.

It is particularly important that we press forward vigorously with the Austrian treaty. The Moscow Declaration on Austria contemplated that Austria should be regarded more as a liberated than as a satellite country. It was agreed at Potsdam that no reparations would be taken from her. She was one of the first countries in Central Europe to have free elections following the liberation. The continuance of foreign troops in Austria is an undue burden on her economy.

In February we asked that the Austrian treaty be prepared along with other treaties for satellite states. At Paris I insisted upon its preparation but the Soviet Representative declined to discuss the Austrian treaty or say when he would consider it.

The making of peace with Austria is essential to the restoration of anything like conditions of peace in Europe. As long as there is no peace with Austria and foreign troops remain on her soil, military communication lines will continue to be maintained in Rumania and Hungary and possibly Italy.

It was for that reason that the American Delegation proposed that the Council at its next meeting on June 15 should conclude as far as possible its work on the proposed drafts, but that the date for the peace conference should be definitely for July 1 or July 15 and invitations should be issued at once.

It was our view that the Council had taken sufficient time to try to narrow their differences and at this stage with the principal issues defined, we should not deny to our other war partners their right to participate. The making of peace is not the exclusive prerogative of any four governments.

The Soviet Delegation insisted that invitations for the conference could not be sent until we had reconvened and agreed on all fundamental questions. Unanimous agreement was necessary and we were forced, therefore, to recess without agreement for the actual calling of the peace conference.

*   *   *

It is American policy to press unremittingly for the conclusion of peace settlements to make possible the withdrawal of troops from countries where they do not belong and where they impose unjustified economic and social difficulties upon the people. And even without waiting for the conclusion of peace treaties it is American policy to press for the reduction of occupation troops in all countries.

Our policy of continuing to press for the return of conditions of peace, without regard to the making of formal peace treaties, finally yielded some constructive results in the case of Italy. For months we have been urging the revision of the Italian armistice so as to restore virtually complete sovereignty to Italy except in the colonies and in the controversial Venezia Giulia area. At Paris this revision was agreed to.

While the absence of a peace treaty still handicaps Italy in her effort to rebuild her broken economic and political life, the revised armistice gives the Italian Government the largest possible freedom that can be given to it without a formal peace treaty.

Our problems are serious, but I am not discouraged. Our offensive to secure peace has only begun. We are determined to work for political and economic peace in Europe, in the Near East and in the rest of the world. We shall work for it in the peace conferences and in the councils of the United Nations. The objective of our offensive is not territory or reparations for the United States. The objective is peace—not a peace founded upon vengeance or greed, but a just peace, the only peace that can endure.

◇◇◇◇◇◇

(b) Second Part, June 15 to July 12, 1946

Report by Secretary Byrnes, July 15, 1946 [1]

[The Council continued its deliberations in June and July, and compromise solutions were finally reached on such controversial issues as Trieste, the Italian colonies, and reparations. It was agreed to convene a peace conference at Paris on July 29, 1946, for the settlement of certain unresolved issues, and for the consideration of the draft treaties of peace prepared by the Council. Said Secretary Byrnes: "We are on the road back to peace."]

*   *   *

The greatest struggle was over the Italian treaty, and the greatest issue involved in that treaty was the fate of Trieste and adjacent territory along the western shore of the Istrian Peninsula. The American Delegation, supported by the French and British, urged that Trieste and adjacent territory which are predominantly Italian should remain with Italy, and the predominantly Slavic hinterland should go to Yugoslavia.

The Soviet Union argued strongly that Trieste and adjacent territory should not be cut off from its immediate hinterland. While it admitted that a few cities and towns along the coast were predominantly Italian, it urged that the Istrian Peninsula should be regarded as a whole and that so regarded it was predominantly Yugoslav. This view was also urged by Czechoslovakia.

*   *   *

In an effort to break this deadlock the French informally suggested that Trieste and adjacent territory be separated from Italy but not ceded to Yugoslavia, and that its security and integrity be internationally guaranteed.

At first no one liked this proposal. But the more it was studied the more it seemed to offer a reasonable basis for agreement. It was recalled that before Italy entered World War I she had proposed that the Trieste area should become an autonomous state.

[1] Made on the occasion of the return of the Secretary of State from the Paris conference of the Foreign Ministers of France, the U.S.S.R., U.K., and U.S., which took place between June 15 and July 12, 1946. Department of State Bulletin, July 28, 1946; Department of State publication 2572; Conference Series 87.

Our delegation insisted that the area should be protected by the United Nations and not by joint agreement between Italy and Yugoslavia as the Soviets proposed, and not by the four principal Allied powers as suggested by the French. Our proposals were accepted.

The proposal as finally agreed upon leaves Gorizia and Montefalcone with Italy in the north and includes within the Free Territory of Trieste the rest of the area west of the agreed ethnic line.

It is true that the Free Territory of Trieste is predominantly Italian in the city and predominantly Slav outside of the city. But neither the Italians nor the Slavs in this territory are placed under alien rule. They are given home rule. The people will elect their own Assembly and the Assembly will elect the officials to administer the laws. They will be subject to supervision only by the United Nations Security Council and by an impartial governor appointed by the Security Council.

The prosperity and welfare of Trieste are linked not only with Italy but with Yugoslavia and the countries of central Europe. It is the natural outlet of central Europe to the Mediterranean. The only railroads entering Trieste come through Yugoslavia and are controlled by Yugoslavia. Representatives of that Government asserted that if Trieste were given to Italy they would divert traffic to Fiume or some other port in Yugoslavia.

Because of the bad feeling between the two peoples in that area, the control by the United Nations may prove to be the best means of preventing armed conflict and relieving tension.

*   *   *

No final decision was reached on the disposition of the Italian colonies.

It will be recalled that originally the Soviets had requested the trusteeship of Tripolitania. They stated they wanted a base in the Mediterranean for their merchant ships. The French favored Italy as trustee for all the colonies, and at the April session the Soviets expressed their willingness to accept the French proposal. Except for certain reservations in respect of Cyrenaica, the British were willing to accept our proposal to have all the colonies placed under the trusteeship of the United Nations.

*   *   *

It was finally agreed that the ultimate disposition of the colonies should be made by the four principal Allied powers in light of the wishes and welfare of the inhabitants and world peace and security, taking into account the views of other interested governments.

If the four principal Allied powers do not agree upon the disposition to be made of the colonies within a year after the coming into force of the treaty, they have bound themselves to make such disposition of them as may be recommended by the General Assembly of the United Nations.

*   *   *

The Soviets finally withdrew their objection to the cession of the Dodecanese to Greece and to the permanent demilitarization of the Islands.

It was, however, extremely difficult for us to reach agreement on reparations. The Soviets insisted that they were entitled to at least $100,000,000 reparations for the devastation of their territory by the Italian armies.

*   *   *

We had previously agreed that reparations could be taken in war plants not needed for Italian peacetime economy and could be paid out of Italian assets in Hungary, Rumania, and Bulgaria. But the Soviets insisted that part of the reparations should come from current or future production of Italian factories and shipyards.

We reluctantly agreed that the Soviets could receive reparations up to $100,000,000. But we required them to agree that, in so far as reparations were taken from Italian production, the deliveries must be arranged so as to avoid interference with economic reconstruction.

We further required the Soviets to agree that such deliveries should not commence for two years. In order to avoid our having to finance Italy's purchase of raw materials to furnish manufactured products to the Soviets, we also required agreement that the imported materials needed by Italy to make these deliveries should be supplied by the Soviets.

*   *   *

While the Council made real progress toward peace with Italy and the ex-satellite states, it made no progress at all on the German and Austrian questions.

*   *   *

The Soviets started the German discussion with a prepared statement on the draft treaty we had proposed to guarantee the continued demilitarization and disarmament of Germany for at least a quarter of a century. The Soviet statement reveals how hard-pressed the Soviets were to find real objection to a treaty which gives them the assurance that Germany should never again become a threat to their security or to the security of Europe.

I do not believe that the Soviets realize the doubts and suspicions which they have raised in the minds of those in other countries who want to be their friends by the aloofness, coolness, and hostility with which they have received America's offer to guarantee jointly the continued disarmament of Germany.

*   *   *

The Soviets stated that our proposed treaty was inadequate; that it did not assure the de-Nazification and democratization of Germany; that it did not assure them reparations. But these are political matters which are already dealt with in the Potsdam Agreement.

*   *   *

I certainly made clear in our earlier meeting in Paris that the proposed guaranty of German demilitarization was only a part of the German settlement. I proposed then and I proposed again at our recent meeting that deputies be appointed to start work on the whole settlement which the Allies expect the Germans to accept. The British and French accepted the proposal. The Soviets rejected it.

*   *   *

It is no secret that the four-power control of Germany on a zonal basis is not working well from the point of view of any of the four powers. Under the Potsdam Agreement Germany was to be administered as an economic unit and central administrative departments were to be established for this purpose.

But in fact Germany is being administered in four closed compartments with the movement of people, trade, and ideas between the zones more narrowly restricted than between most independent countries.

*   *   *

I made clear that we were unwilling to share responsibility for the economic paralysis and suffering we felt certain would follow a continuance of present conditions in Germany.

I then announced that as a last resort we were prepared to administer our zone in conjunction with any one or more of the other zones as an economic unit. I indicated that recently we had secured cooperation with the Soviet zone in one matter and with the British in another. I explained that our offer was made not in an effort to divide Germany but to bring it together.

*   *   *

Our military representative in Germany will this week be instructed to cooperate with any one or all of the three governments in essential administrative matters like finance, transportation, communication, trade, and industry. We will either secure economic cooperation between the zones or place the responsibility for the violation of the Potsdam Agreement.

Finally we came to a discussion of the Austrian problem. On June 1, I had circulated a proposed draft treaty recognizing the independence of Austria and providing for the withdrawal of the occupying troops. The British also had submitted a draft for consideration. I asked that the Deputies be directed to prepare the treaty.

The Soviets submitted a counterproposal calling first for further action to insure the de-Nazification of Austria and the removal of a large number of displaced persons from Austria whom they regard as unfriendly to them.

The British and French were willing to join us in submitting to the Deputies the consideration of the treaty and in requesting the Control Council to investigate and report on the progress of de-Nazification and on the problem of the displaced persons. But the Soviets were unwilling to agree to the Deputies' taking up the Austrian treaty until more tangible action was taken on these other two problems.

We recognize the seriousness of these problems and have been grappling with them. The problem of displaced persons is particularly difficult to solve. Where they are willing, we help them to return to their homes. But many refuse to return to their own countries because they fear death or imprisonment for their political views. Our tradition of protecting political refugees is too precious for us to consent to the mass expulsion of these people from our zone. The United Nations has a committee studying the problem, and we shall continue to do our part to try to find a solution, but it cannot be a cruel solution that will reflect discredit upon the American people.

*   *   *

16. PARIS PEACE CONFERENCE, JULY 29 TO OCTOBER 15, 1946

Report by Secretary Byrnes, October 18, 1946 [1]

[At the Paris Peace Conference, after some fifteen months of preparatory work, the peace treaties with Italy, Bulgaria, Hungary, Finland, and Rumania were put in final draft form by the twenty-one participating countries. The Conference adopted 107 recommendations, 59 by a two-thirds majority and 48 by a simple majority vote. Throughout the deliberations Russia and her satellite states voted consistently as a bloc, as the cleavage between East and West became more apparent. "The thing which disturbs me," said Secretary Byrnes after the Conference, "is not the lettered provisions of the treaties under discussion, but the continued if not increasing tension between us and the Soviet Union."]

*   *   *

These treaties are not written as we would write them if we had a free hand. They are not written as other governments would write them if they had a free hand. But they are as good as we can hope to get by general agreement now or within any reasonable length of time.

Our views on reparations are different from the views of countries whose territories were laid waste by military operations and whose peoples were brought under the yoke of alien armies and alien gestapos.

The reparation payments are heavy—excessively heavy in some cases. But their burdens should not be unbearable if the peoples on which they are laid are freed from the burdens of sustaining occupying armies and are given a chance to rebuild their shattered economic lives.

For Europe with her mingled national economies there are no ideal boundary settlements.

The proposed settlement for the Trieste area was long and warmly debated. The Conference approved the proposal of the Council of Foreign Ministers that this area should become a free territory under the protection of the United Nations. The Conference also by a two-thirds vote made recommendations for an international statute defining the responsibilities of the United Nations in relation to the free territory. Such recommendations are an expression of world opinion and cannot be arbitrarily disregarded.

Those recommendations of the Conference provide that the governor appointed by the Security Council should have sufficient authority to maintain public order and security, to preserve the independence and integrity of the territory, and to protect the basic human rights and fundamental freedoms of all the inhabitants.

The minority proposal which was supported by the Soviet Union, Yugoslavia, and other Slav countries would have made a figurehead of the United Nations governor and would have given Yugoslavia virtual control of the customs, currency, and foreign affairs of the territory. Certainly we could not

[1] Department of State publication 2682: Conference Series 90; Department of State Bulletin, October 27, 1946. See also, Paris Peace Conference: Selected Documents, Department of State publication 2868, Conference Series 103.

agree to that. It would make the territory a protectorate of Yugoslavia and would leave the United Nations powerless to prevent it becoming a battle-ground between warring groups. There must be no seizure of power in Trieste after this war as there was in Fiume after the last war.

*   *   *

At Potsdam in the summer of 1945 President Truman stressed the importance of providing for free navigation of the great international rivers in Europe on terms of equality for the commerce of all states.

President Truman was not seeking any special advantage for the United States. He was seeking to promote peace. He was seeking to ensure that these great waterways should be used to unite and not divide the peoples of Europe.

The Delegations representing the Soviet Republic and the Slav countries have vigorously opposed the proposal.

The Paris Conference recommended by a two-thirds vote that the treaties should ensure freedom of commerce on the Danube on terms of equality to all states.

I hope that when the Foreign Ministers meet we can agree upon the adoption of this recommendation.

In recent weeks much has been said about acrimonious debates and the divisions in the Paris Conference. Back of those debates and divisions were real and deep differences in interest, in ideas, in experience, and even in prejudices.

*   *   *

Two states can quickly reach an understanding if one is willing to yield to all demands. The United States is unwilling to do that. It is equally unwilling to ask it of another state.

Every understanding requires the reconciliation of differences and not a yielding by one state to the arbitrary will of the other.

Until we are able to work out definite and agreed standards of conduct such as those which govern decisions within the competence of the International Court of Justice, and such as those which we hope may be agreed upon for the control of atomic energy, international problems between sovereign states must be worked out by agreement between sovereign states.

But if states are to reach such agreements they must act in good faith and in the spirit of conciliation. They must not launch false and misleading propaganda against one another.

They must not arbitrarily exercise their power of veto, preventing a return to conditions of peace and delaying economic reconstruction.

No state should assume that it has a monopoly of virtue or of wisdom. No state should ignore or veto the aggregate sentiments of mankind.

States must not unilaterally by threats, by pressures, or by force disturb the established rights of other nations. Nor can they arbitrarily resist or refuse to consider changes in the relationships between states and peoples which justice, fair play, and the enlightened sentiments of mankind demand.

We must cooperate to build a world order, not to sanctify the *status quo,* but to preserve peace and freedom based upon justice.

And we must be willing to cooperate with one another—veto or no veto—

to defend, with force if necessary, the principles and purposes of the Charter of the United Nations.

Those are the policies we have pursued. In following those policies we have been criticized at times for being too "soft" and at times for being too "tough". I dislike both words. Neither accurately describes our earnest efforts to be patient but firm.

We have been criticized for being too eager to find new approaches after successive rebukes in our efforts to effectuate our policies. And we have likewise been criticized for not seeking new approaches. We will not permit the criticism to disturb us nor to influence our action.

We will continue to seek friendship with the Soviet Union and all other states on the basis of justice and the right of others, as well as ourselves, to opinions and ways of life which we do not and cannot share.

But we must retain our perspective.

We must guard against the belief that deep-rooted suspicions can be dispelled and far-reaching differences can be reconciled by any single act of faith.

The temple of peace must be built solidly, stone upon stone. If the stones are loosely laid, they may topple down upon us.

We must equally guard against the belief that delays or set-backs in achieving our objective make armed conflict inevitable. It is entirely possible that the failure or inability of the Soviet leaders to rid themselves of that belief lies at the very root of our difficulties. We will never be able to rid the world of that belief if we ourselves become victims to it.

*   *   *

But if the temple of peace is to be built the idea of the inevitability of conflict must not be allowed to dominate the minds of men and tear asunder a world which God made one.

It is that idea of the inevitability of conflict that is throttling the economic recovery of Europe. It is that idea that is causing artificial tensions between states and within states.

*   *   *

We deplore the tendency upon the part of the Soviet Union to regard states which are friendly to us as unfriendly to the Soviet Union and to consider as unfriendly our efforts to maintain traditionally friendly relations with states bordering on the Soviet Union.

We deplore the talk of the encirclement of the Soviet Union. We have it from no less authority than Generalissimo Stalin himself that the Soviet Union is in no danger of encirclement.

During the war the Baltic states were taken over by the U.S.S.R. The Polish frontier and the Finnish frontier have been substantially modified in Russia's favor. Königsberg, Bessarabia, Bukovina, and Ruthenia are to be given to her. In the Pacific, the Kuriles, Port Arthur, and Sakhalin have been assigned to her. Certainly the Soviet Union is not a dispossessed nation.

*   *   *

I should be less than frank if I did not confess my bewilderment at the motives which the Soviet Delegation attributed to the United States at Paris.

Not once, but many times, they charged that the United States had enriched itself during the war, and, under the guise of freedom for commerce and equality of opportunity for the trade of all nations, was now seeking to enslave Europe economically.

Coming from any state these charges would be regrettable to us. They are particularly regrettable when they are made by the Soviet Government to whom we advanced more than 10 million dollars of lend-lease during the war and with whom we want to be friendly in time of peace.

The United States has never claimed the right to dictate to other countries how they should manage their own trade and commerce. We have simply urged in the interest of all peoples that no country should make trade discriminations in its relations with other countries.

*   *   *

We want to assist in European reconstruction because we believe that European prosperity will contribute to world prosperity and world peace. That is not dollar democracy. That is not imperialism. That is justice and fair play.

We in America have learned that prosperity like freedom must be shared, not on the basis of "hand-outs," but on the basis of the fair and honest exchange of the products of the labor of free men and free women.

America stands for social and economic democracy at home and abroad. The principles embodied in the social and economic reforms of recent years are now a part of the American heritage.

*   *   *

Whatever political differences there may be among us, we are firmly and irrevocably committed to the principle that it is our right and the right of every people to organize their economic and political destiny through the freest possible expression of their collective will. We oppose privilege at home and abroad. We defend freedom everywhere. And in our view human freedom and human progress are inseparable.

*   *   *

◇◇◇◇◇◇

17. THIRD MEETING OF THE COUNCIL OF FOREIGN MINISTERS, NEW YORK CITY, NOVEMBER 4 TO DECEMBER 12, 1946

Report by the Department of State [1]

[The purpose of the third meeting of the Council of Foreign Ministers was to consider the recommendations of the Paris Peace Conference and to put the texts of the treaties with Italy, Bulgaria, Hungary, Finland, and Rumania in final form. For the most part, the recommendations of the Paris Conference were agreed upon by the Council. The treaties were later presented (February

[1] Department of State publication 2747, Conference Series 93; also Department of State Bulletin, February 2, 1947.

10, 1947) for signature by those states which took part in the Paris Conference and which were at war with the enemy state in question. In addition to completing the treaty texts, the Council devoted several meetings to Germany and Austria.]

I. Completion of Texts of Treaties of Peace with Italy, Rumania, Bulgaria, Hungary, and Finland

*   *   *

The Paris Peace Conference, through long discussion both in the commissions and in plenary sessions, had given the fullest possible consideration to every aspect of the peace treaties and had adopted 59 recommendations by two-thirds majority and 48 recommendations by a simple majority. For the most part, these recommendations related to questions which the Council of Foreign Ministers, despite protracted negotiation and discussion, had left in disagreement or had not considered. Thus the third session of the Council of Foreign Ministers in considering those issues which had previously divided the Council and Conference had the advantage of formal recommendations on these and other issues by the 21 nations at the Paris Conference. These recommendations and especially those backed by two thirds of the members of the Conference were a new factor in the work of the Council of Foreign Ministers and played a large if not determinant part in settling the still unsolved issues in these treaties. In effect the final texts of these treaties reveal that on the majority of issues final agreement was based upon the recommendations returned to the Council of Foreign Ministers by the Paris Conference.

This agreement was particularly evident in regard to the draft statute of the Free Territory of Trieste. Although the Council of Foreign Ministers last July had reached an agreement on the internationalization under the United Nations of this territory and on its proposed boundaries, no agreement had been reached by the special Commission on Trieste appointed by the Council of Foreign Ministers on the principles which were to govern the temporary regime and on the permanent statute for the area. Secretary Byrnes had made it clear that the United States, having agreed—contrary to its original position —to the internationalization of this area, was determined that the proposed Free Territory should be genuinely international in character and not a hotbed of friction and dispute between Italy and Yugoslavia. In view of the tension existing in the area and the rivalry between these two countries, the United States believed it to be essential that the representatives of the Security Council and the United Nations who were to assume responsibility for the integrity and security of this area must have adequate powers to discharge these responsibilities. As a neutral figure—representative of the United Nations as a whole—the proposed Governor for the Free Territory of Trieste would have no interest except to safeguard the security of the area and to promote the well-being and preserve the rights and freedoms of the inhabitants. The representatives of Great Britain and France had held similar views. The Soviet representative, however, had supported the claims of Yugoslavia to a special and privileged position in this territory and had opposed the granting to the Governor and to the United Nations what the United States regarded as absolutely essential powers for the maintenance of the international character and stability of the area. By a two-thirds vote the Paris Conference recommended the adoption of a French compromise proposal setting forth the principles for the organization of the Free Territory of Trieste, which were in basic accord with the views of the British and American Governments.

At the New York session of the Council of Foreign Ministers the principles for the permanent statute and provisional regime of the Free Territory of Trieste as recommended by the Conference were incorporated in a final draft after protracted negotiation. The statute as finally agreed upon has been incorporated as an annex to the peace treaty for Italy. If backed by an honest intention on the part of the states directly concerned to implement this statute as written, it provides the framework for the creation and maintenance of a genuine international regime for this troublesome and disputed area.

After agreement on the statute for the Free Territory of Trieste had been reached, the only other questions of importance still in dispute related to reparations, other economic clauses, and the question of freedom of navigation on the Danube River.

The reparation problem proved to be one of the most difficult. Marked difference in attitude existed between countries which had been devastated by one or another of these ex-enemy states and which therefore felt entitled to the maximum amounts possible, and between countries like the United States which felt that the most important thing was to build for a future in which the ex-enemy states would have some prospect of economic recovery. In the cases of Rumania, Hungary, and Finland, the reparation terms as set forth in their armistices provided for $300,000,000 of commodities at 1938 prices. Although the United States argued at great length that these three countries were not identical in the degree of their aggression nor equal in their capacity to pay, this Government was unable to obtain any change in the established arrangements which had already been implemented by bilateral agreements. In the case of Bulgaria, where the reparation terms were not fixed in the armistice, the situation was reversed, the Soviet Union arguing for an extremely low reparation obligation. Actually, the figure of $70,000,000 which was agreed on is not far out of line when compared with the obligation of Rumania, but it does throw into sharp contrast the burden of reparations placed on Hungary and Finland.

The problem of reparation is much simpler in the case of those four countries which were all net exporters than in the case of Italy. In order to find a practical means for payment by Italy, the formula previously agreed upon for Italian reparation to the Union of Soviet Socialist Republics—namely, that the reparation-receiving country must supply the required raw material —was utilized in connection with the other recipients. There were two particularly difficult problems: that of the relative treatment of Greece and Yugoslavia and that of whether Albania should be included at all. The first problem was resolved by giving Greece and Yugoslavia each the same total amount of $150,000,000 from Bulgaria and Italy. The second problem was resolved by giving a smaller payment of $5,000,000 to Albania.

It is also important to note that the commercial-policy provisions which this Government has urged from the very start are now incorporated in the treaties. These provisions establish, for a period of 18 months, an obligation on the part of the ex-enemy state not to discriminate among nations in matters pertaining to commerce and industry. This requirement is limited to 18 months in order to permit the concluding of commercial treaties. Furthermore, that period of time should determine whether international trade throughout the world will follow the liberal principles outlined in the American proposals for the expansion of world trade or whether various countries themselves will revert to discriminatory and restrictive-trade regulation. A similar provision with respect to aviation rights, including the first two freedoms of the air, is included in each treaty.

The question of including a clause expressing acceptance of the principle of free navigation on that great European waterway in the peace treaties with the ex-enemy states bordering on the Danube had been the subject of long dispute and acrimonious debate at previous sessions of the Council of Foreign Ministers, particularly at the Paris Peace Conference. In this case again the Conference had voted by a two-thirds majority for the inclusion in the appropriate treaties of some statement of the important principle of free navigation. It is gratifying to report that at the New York meeting the Soviet objections on this score were overcome, and the three Balkan treaties include the following statement of principle: "Navigation on the Danube shall be free and open for the nationals, vessels of commerce and goods of all States on the footing of equality with regard to port and navigation charges and conditions for merchant shipping." In order to reduce this general principle to specific operation, the Council of Foreign Ministers has agreed to call a conference within six months in which the United States, Great Britain, the Soviet Union, and France would participate, as well as the countries in the Danubian basin, for the purpose of establishing an international regime with respect to the Danube. The United States has very little direct interest in the Danube as such. The great concern of the United States has been to do all that it could to remove artificial barriers and discriminatory practices from national trade regulations and specifically from this vital waterway in southeastern Europe.

Other economic articles which dealt with such problems as restitution, compensation for damages, ex-enemy property in the United Nations, and the reinstatement of debt obligations posed certain difficulties of one kind or another; however, it is believed that the interests of the United States have been safeguarded so far as possible under the circumstances.

* * *

II. Preliminary Plans for Peace Settlements With Germany and Austria

In addition to completing final texts of the five peace treaties the Council of Foreign Ministers, as had been agreed in Paris, devoted several meetings of its New York session to the German and Austrian questions. As early as May 1946 Secretary Byrnes had endeavored without success to obtain agreement for the setting up of special deputies to start the preliminary work for the eventual peace settlement with Germany and to prepare a draft settlement with Austria so that without undue delay the Council of Foreign Ministers could take up these two questions vital to the entire future of Europe. The Soviet Government in May and again in July had been unwilling to agree to these proposals and had maintained that further study was required before deputies could be appointed to begin actual work concerning either a future German settlement or an Austrian treaty. At the New York session, however, these objections were overcome, and the following are the main points in the agenda adopted for the next meeting of the Council of Foreign Ministers to be held in Moscow on March 10, 1947:

1. Consideration of the report from the Allied Control Council;

2. Consideration of the form and scope of the provisional political organization of Germany;

3. Preparation of a peace treaty with Germany, taking into account the report to be received from the deputies and also including consideration of boundary questions, questions of the Ruhr and Rhineland, and others;

4. United States draft disarmament and demilitarization treaty and other measures for political, economic, and military control of Germany;

5. Consideration of the report already submitted by the Committee of Coal Experts; and

6. Consideration of the report of the deputies on the Austrian treaty.

The deputies appointed for discussion of German questions, who are now meeting in London, were instructed to: (*a*) hear the views of governments of neighboring Allied states and of other Allied states who participated with their armed forces in the common struggle against Germany and who wish to present their views on the German problem; (*b*) consider questions of procedure with regard to the preparation of a peace treaty for Germany; and (*c*) submit a report on the above matters to the Council of Foreign Ministers by February 25, 1947.

The deputies appointed for Austria were instructed to: (*a*) proceed with the preparation of a treaty recognizing the independence of Austria, taking into consideration the proposals already submitted by the Governments of the United States and the United Kingdom, as well as any further proposals which may be submitted by any member of the Council of Foreign Ministers; (*b*) hear the views of the governments of neighboring Allied states and of other Allied states who participated with their armed forces in the common struggle against Germany and who wish to present their views on the Austrian problem; and (*c*) submit proposals on the above matters to the Council of Foreign Ministers by February 25, 1947.

*   *   *

◇◇◇◇◇◇

18. FOURTH MEETING OF THE COUNCIL OF FOREIGN MINISTERS, MOSCOW, MARCH 10 TO APRIL 24, 1947

Report by Secretary Marshall, April 28, 1947 [1]

[The fourth meeting of the Council was devoted exclusively to Germany and Austria. Little progress was made. Basic differences over the future of Germany, the nature of her government, reparations, boundaries, and economic

[1] Department of State publication 2822, Conference Series 98; also Department of State Bulletin, May 11, 1947.

position in Europe, came to the fore and remained unresolved. Secretary Marshall, urging greater progress toward a peace settlement, commented: "The patient is sinking while the doctors deliberate."]

Tonight I hope to make clearly understandable the fundamental nature of the issues discussed at the Moscow Conference of Foreign Ministers.

* * *

There was a reasonable possibility, we had hoped a probability, of completing in Moscow a peace treaty for Austria and a four-power pact to bind together our four governments to guarantee the demilitarization of Germany. As for the German peace treaty and related but more current German problems, we had hoped to reach agreement on a directive for the guidance of our deputies in their work preparatory to the next conference.

In a statement such as this, it is not practicable to discuss the numerous issues which continued in disagreement at the Conference. It will suffice, I think, to call attention to the fundamental problems whose solution would probably lead to the quick adjustment of many other differences.

* * *

The critical and fundamental German problems to which I shall confine myself are: (a) the limits to the powers of the central government; (b) the character of the economic system and its relation to all of Europe; (c) the character and extent of reparations; (d) the boundaries for the German state; and (e) the manner in which all Allied states at war with Germany are represented in the drafting and confirmation of the treaty.

* * *

CENTRAL GOVERNMENT

This issue of the degree of centralization of the future German state is of greatest importance. Excessive concentration of power is peculiarly dangerous in a country like Germany which has no strong traditions regarding the rights of the individual and the rights of the community to control the exercise of governmental power. The Soviet Union appears to favor a strong central government. The United States and United Kingdom are opposed to such a government, because they think it could be too readily converted to the domination of a regime similar to the Nazis. They favor a central government of carefully limited powers, all other powers being reserved to the states, or *Länder* as they are called in Germany. The French are willing to agree only to very limited responsibilities for the central government. They fear a repetition of the seizure of power over the whole of Germany carried out by the Hitler regime in 1933.

* * *

GERMAN ECONOMY

Regarding the character of the German economic system and its relation to all of Europe, the disagreements are even more serious and difficult of adjustment. German economy at the present time is crippled by the fact that there is no unity of action, and the rehabilitation of Germany to the point where she is self-supporting demands immediate decision.

There is a declared agreement in the desire for economic unity in Germany, but when it comes to the actual terms to regulate such unity there are wide and critical differences. One of the most serious difficulties encountered in the effort to secure economic unity has been the fact that the Soviet-occupied zone has operated practically without regard to the other zones and has made few if any reports of what has been occurring in that zone. There has been little or no disposition to proceed on a basis of reciprocity, and there has been a refusal to disclose the availability of foodstuffs and the degree or character of reparations taken out of this zone.

This unwillingness of the Soviet authorities to cooperate in establishing a balanced economy for Germany as agreed upon at Potsdam has been the most serious check on the development of a self-supporting Germany and a Germany capable of providing coal and other necessities for the neighboring states who have always been dependent on Germany for these items. After long and futile efforts to secure a working accord in this matter, the British and American zones were combined for the improvement of the economic situation, meaning the free movement of excess supplies or produce available in one zone to another where there is a shortage. Our continuing invitation to the French and Soviets to join in the arrangement still exists. This merger is bitterly attacked by the Soviet authorities as a breach of the Potsdam Agreement and as a first step toward the dismemberment of Germany, ignoring the plain fact that their refusal to carry out that agreement was the sole cause of the merger. It is difficult to regard their attacks as anything but propaganda designed to divert attention from the Soviet failure to implement the economic unity agreed at Potsdam. Certainly some progress towards economic unity in Germany is better than none.

The character of the control over the Ruhr industrial center, the greatest concentration of coal and of heavy industries in Europe, continues a matter of debate. It cannot be decided merely for the purpose of reaching an agreement. Vitally important considerations and future consequences are involved.

REPARATIONS

The question of reparations is of critical importance as it affects almost every other question under discussion. This issue naturally makes a tremendous appeal to the people of the Allied states who suffered the terrors of German military occupation and the destruction of their cities and villages.

*   *   *

We believe that no reparations from current production were contemplated by the Potsdam Agreement. The Soviets strongly oppose this view. They hold that the previous discussions and agreements at Yalta authorize the taking of billions of dollars in reparations out of current production. This would mean that a substantial portion of the daily production of German factories would be levied on for reparation payments, which in turn would mean that the recovery of Germany sufficiently to be self-supporting would be long delayed. It would also mean that the plan and the hope of our Government, that Germany's economic recovery by the end of three years would permit the termination of American appropriations for the support of the German inhabitants of our zone, could not be realized.

The issue is one of great complications, for which agreement must be found in order to administer Germany as an economic whole as the four powers claim they wish to do.

There is, however, general agreement among the Allies that the matter of the factories and equipment to be removed from Germany as reparations should be re-examined. They recognize the fact that a too drastic reduction in Germany's industrial set-up will not only make it difficult for Germany to become self-supporting but will retard the economic recovery of Europe. The United States has indicated that it would be willing to study the possibility of a limited amount of reparations from current production to compensate for plants, previously scheduled to be removed as reparations to various Allied countries, which it now appears should be left in Germany; it being understood that deliveries from current production are not to increase the financial burden of the occupying powers or to retard the repayment to them of the advances they have made to keep the German economy from collapsing. The Soviet Government has made no response to this suggestion.

BOUNDARIES

The issue regarding boundaries to be established for Germany presents a serious disagreement and another example of complete disagreement as to the meaning of the pronouncement on this subject by the heads of the three powers. In the rapid advance of the Soviet armies in the final phase of the war, millions of Germans in eastern Germany fled to the west of the Oder River. The Soviet armies, prior to Potsdam, had placed Poles in charge of this area largely evacuated by the German population. That was the situation that confronted President Truman at Potsdam. Under the existing circumstances, the President accepted the situation for the time being with the agreed three-power statement, "The three heads of government reaffirm their opinion that the final delimitation of the western frontier of Poland should await the peace settlement."

The Soviet Foreign Minister now states that a final agreement on the frontier between Germany and Poland was reached at Potsdam, and the expression I have just quoted merely referred to the formal confirmation of the already agreed upon frontier at the peace settlement, thus leaving only technical delimitation to be considered.

The United States Government recognized the commitment made at Yalta to give fair compensation to Poland in the west for the territory east of the Curzon Line incorporated into the Soviet Union. But the perpetuation of the present temporary line between Germany and Poland would deprive Germany of territory which before the war provided more than a fifth of the foodstuffs on which the German population depended. It is clear that in any event Germany will be obliged to support, within much restricted boundaries, not only her pre-war population but a considerable number of Germans from eastern Europe. To a certain extent this situation is unavoidable, but we must not agree to its aggravation. We do not want Poland to be left with less resources than she had before the war. She is entitled to *more,* but it will not help Poland to give her frontiers which will probably create difficulties for her in the future. Wherever the frontiers are drawn, they should not constitute barriers to trade and commerce upon which the well-being of Europe is dependent. We must look toward a future where a democratic Poland and a democratic Germany will be good neighbors.

PEACE TREATY PROCEDURE

There is disagreement regarding the manner in which the Allied powers at war with Germany are to participate in the drafting and confirmation of the German peace treaty. There are 51 states involved. Of these, in addition to the four principal Allied powers, 18 were directly engaged in the fighting, some of course to a much greater extent than others. It is the position of the United States that all Allied states at war with Germany should be given an opportunity to participate to some degree in the drafting and in the making of the peace treaty, but we recognize that there would be very practical difficulties if not impossibilities in attempting to draft a treaty with 51 nations participating equally at all stages. Therefore, the United States Government has endeavored to secure agreement on a method which involves two different procedures, depending on whether or not the state concerned actually participated in the fighting. But all would have an opportunity to present their views, and rebut other views, and all would sit in the peace conference to adopt a treaty.

*   *   *

FOUR POWER PACT

The proposal for the Four Power Pact was advanced by the United States Government a year ago. It was our hope that the prompt acceptance of this simple pact ensuring in advance of the detailed German peace settlement that the United States would actively cooperate to prevent the rearmament of Germany would eliminate fears as to the future and would facilitate the making of a peace suitable to Europe's present and future needs.

*   *   *

However, the Soviet Government met our proposition with a series of amendments which would have completely changed the character of the pact, making it in effect a complicated peace treaty, and including in the amendments most of the points regarding the German problem concerning which there was, as I have pointed out, serious disagreement. I was forced to the conclusion by this procedure that the Soviet Government either did not desire such a pact or was following a course calculated to delay any immediate prospect of its adoption. Whether or not an agreement can finally be reached remains to be seen, but the United States, I think, should adhere to its present position and insist that the pact be kept simple and confined to its one basic purpose—to keep Germany incapable of waging war.

AUSTRIAN TREATY

The negotiations regarding the Austrian treaty resulted in agreement on all but a few points, but these were basic and of fundamental importance. The Soviet Union favors and the other governments oppose the payment of reparations and the cession of Carinthia to Yugoslavia.

But the Soviet Government attached much more importance to its demand that the German assets in Austria which are to be hers by the terms of the Potsdam Agreement should include those assets which the other three powers consider to have been taken from Austria and the citizens of the United Nations by force or duress by Hitler and his Nazi government following the taking over of Austria by military force in March 1938. The Soviet Government refused to consider the word *duress,* which in the opinion of the other three powers would be the critical basis for determining what property, that is, business, factories, land, forests, et cetera, was truly German property and not the result of seizures by terroristic procedure, intimidation, fake business acquisition, and so forth. The Soviet Union also refused to consider any process of mediation to settle the disputes that are bound to arise in such circumstances, nor would they clearly agree to have such property as they receive as German assets subject to Austrian law in the same manner as other foreign investments are subject to Austrian law.

The acceptance of the Soviet position would mean that such a large portion of Austrian economy would be removed from her legal control that Austrian chances of surviving as an independent self-supporting state would be dubious. She would in effect be but a puppet state.

All efforts to find a compromise solution were unavailable. The United States, in my opinion, could not commit itself to a treaty which involved such manifest injustices and, what is equally important, would create an Austria so weak and helpless as to be the source of great danger in the future.

*   *   *

SUMMARY

*   *   *

Agreement was made impossible at Moscow because, in our view, the Soviet Union insisted upon proposals which would have established in Germany a centralized government, adapted to the seizure of absolute control of a country which would be doomed economically through inadequate area and excessive population, and would be mortgaged to turn over a large part of its production as reparations, principally to the Soviet Union. In another form the same mortgage upon Austria was claimed by the Soviet Delegation.

Such a plan, in the opinion of the United States Delegation, not only involved indefinite American subsidy, but could result only in a deteriorating economic life in Germany and Europe and the inevitable emergence of dictatorship and strife.

*   *   *

The critical differences were for the first time brought into the light and now stand clearly defined so that future negotiations can start with a knowledge of exactly what the issues are that must be settled. The Deputies now understand the precise views of each government on the various issues discussed. With that they can possibly resolve some differences and surely can further clarify the problems by a studied presentation of the state of agreement and disagreement. That is the best that can be hoped for in the next few months. It marks some progress, however painfully slow. These issues are matters of vast importance to the lives of the people in Europe and to the future course of world history. We must not compromise on great principles in order to achieve agreement for agreement's sake. Also, we must sincerely try to understand the point of view of those with whom we differ.

*   *   *

◇◇◇◇◇◇

19. FIFTH MEETING OF THE COUNCIL OF FOREIGN MINISTERS, LONDON, NOVEMBER 25 TO DECEMBER 16, 1947

Report by Secretary Marshall, December 19, 1947 [1]

[The United States delegation attended the London meeting of the Council with the hope of bringing an end to the division of Germany. Indeed the basic issue at the meeting was whether the Allies could agree to reunite Germany. After interminable discussions, it became perfectly apparent that the objective could not be achieved. Said Secretary Marshall about the meeting: "It was but a dreary repetition of what had been said and resaid at the Moscow conference."]

*   *   *

In order to get the Conference started, it was finally agreed to accept the Soviet request that the preparation of a German peace treaty should be item two on the agenda. As a result, with the exception of one day of discussion of Austria and the Austrian treaty, it was not until after 10 days of meetings that the Conference really reached the heart of the German question. These first 10 meetings were devoted to futile and somewhat unreal discussion of the mechanisms for the preparation of an eventual German peace treaty before the question of whether or not there was to be a united Germany had even been considered. There was one question, however, of real substance during this phase of the discussion which had a direct application not only to a German peace treaty but also to the immediate situation in Germany. This was the question of the present and future frontiers of the German state. No serious consideration of a peace treaty could be undertaken without first considering what was to be the area of the future German state. Three delegations had already expressed their agreement that the area of the Saar should be separated from Germany and integrated into French economy. Mr. Molotov refused to commit his Government on this point.

On this vital matter of frontiers, three delegations agreed to the establishment of a frontier commission or commissions to make an expert study of any proposed changes from the prewar frontiers. Mr. Molotov refused to agree. It was impossible for me to reconcile his urgent insistence upon the necessity of expediting the preparation for a German peace treaty with his categoric refusal to agree to the appointment of boundary commissions,

_____

[1] Department of State Bulletin, December 28, 1947.

which three delegations considered to be an absolutely essential first step in any serious preparation for a future German peace settlement.

Many other questions concerning the actual preparation of any peace treaty were discussed without agreement.

It was during this stage of the debate that Mr. Molotov insisted that the Four Powers should agree upon the immediate establishment of a German central government. Although the United States had been, I believe, the first of the four occupying countries to suggest at Moscow the desirability for the earliest possible establishment of a German provisional central government, it was obvious that until the division of Germany had been healed and conditions created for German political and economic unity, any central government would be a sham and not a reality. This view was shared by the other western delegations but to Mr. Molotov was completely unacceptable. This was the first clear evidence of his purpose to utilize the meeting as an opportunity for propaganda declarations which would be pleasant to German ears.

After several days of consideration by the deputies, the Austrian treaty was again brought to the conference table on December 4. The sole issue discussed was the determination of what were the true German assets in eastern Austria to which the Soviet Union was fully entitled by the Potsdam agreement. This had been the stumbling block in reaching final agreement on the treaty draft, and it was an issue which would determine whether or not Austria would be under such complete economic domination by the Soviet Union that it would be virtually a vassal state.

The French had endeavored to break the impasse by submitting a compromise proposal, but this was categorically refused by the Soviet Delegate. In the last hour of the final session of the Conference Mr. Molotov indicated an apparent willingness to accept a percentage reduction in the Soviet claims, without specifying the actual amount involved in his proposal. The matter was immediately referred to the deputies, and I was informed just prior to my departure from England that the Soviet Government would submit later a detailed proposition.

It was not until the tenth meeting that the Conference finally came to the heart of the problem—to a consideration of the harsh realities of the existing situation in Germany.

Several more days were to elapse, however, before the Council really came to grips with these realities. Discussions of procedure—of what document to discuss—again intervened to delay our work. However, on Monday, December eighth, the procedural issues were resolved, and the Council began the consideration of the fundamental issues which eventually led to the adjournment of the session without agreement.

*   *   *

The United States Delegation considered that there were certain fundamental decisions which the four occupying powers should take if German unity was to be achieved. These were:

1. The elimination of the artificial zonal barriers to permit free movement of persons, ideas, and goods throughout the whole territory of Germany.

2. The relinquishment by the occupying powers of ownership of

properties in Germany seized under the guise of reparations without Four Power agreement.

3. A currency reform involving the introduction of new and sound currency for all Germany.

4. A definite determination of the economic burdens which Germany would be called upon to bear in the future, that is the costs of occupation, repayment of sums advanced by the occupying powers, and reparations.

5. An over-all export-import plan for all of Germany.

When these basic measures have been put into effect by the occupying powers, then the establishment under proper safeguards of a provisional government for all Germany should be undertaken.

Reparations soon emerged as a key issue. For the benefit of those not fully familiar with past negotiations on this subject, I wish to explain that a definite agreement had been concluded two years ago at Potsdam that reparation payments would be made by the transfer of surplus capital assets, that is, factories, machinery, and assets abroad, and not by payments from time to time out of the daily output of German production. One reason for this decision was to avoid an issue that would continue through the years between Germany and the Allies and between the Allies themselves concerning her ability to pay and the actual value of payments which had been made in goods. Also, it was clearly evident that for many years Germany would be involved in a desperate struggle to build up sufficient foreign trade to pay for the food and other items on which she will be dependent from outside sources. The best example of this phase of the situation that I can give is the present necessity for a Great Britain and the United States to pay out some 700 millions a year to provide the food and other items to prevent starvation and rather complete disintegration of that portion of Germany occupied by our forces.

In other words, reparations from current production—that is, exports of day to day German production with no return—could be made only if the countries at present supplying Germany—notably the United States—foot the bill. We put in and the Russians take out. This economic truth, however, is only one aspect of Soviet reparation claims. In the eastern zone of Germany the Soviet Union has been taking reparations from current production and has also, under the guise of reparation, seized vast holdings and formed them into a gigantic trust embracing a substantial part of the industry of that zone. This has resulted in a type of monopolistic strangle hold over the economic and political life of eastern Germany which makes that region little more than a dependent province of the Soviet Union. A very strong reason, in my opinion, for our failure to agree at London, was the Soviet determination not to relax in any way its hold on eastern Germany. Acceptance of their claims for reparations from current production from the western zones would extend that strangle hold over the future economic life of all Germany.

*   *   *

It finally became clear that we could make no progress at this time—that there was no apparent will to reach a settlement but only an interest in making more and more speeches intended for another audience. So I suggested that we adjourn. No real ground was lost or gained at the meeting, except that the outlines of the problems and the obstacles are much clearer. We cannot look forward to a unified Germany at this time. We must to the best we can in the area where our influence can be felt.

All must recognize that the difficulties to be overcome are immense. The problems concerned with the treaty settlements for Italy and the satellite countries were simple by comparison, since none of those countries were divided into zones of occupation and all of them had an existing form of government. Germany by contrast is subdivided into four pieces—four zones. No trace of national government remains.

There is another and I think even more fundamental reason for the frustration we have encountered in our endeavor to reach a realistic agreement for a peace settlement. In the war struggle Europe was in a large measure shattered. As a result a political vacuum was created, and until this vacuum has been filled by the restoration of a healthy European community, it does not appear possible that paper agreements can assure a lasting peace. Agreements between sovereign states are generally the reflection and not the cause of genuine settlements.

It is for this very reason, I think, that we encountered such complete opposition to almost every proposal the western powers agreed upon. The Soviet Union has recognized the situation in its frank declaration of hostility and opposition to the European Recovery Program. The success of such a program would necessarily mean the establishment of a balance in which the 16 western nations, who have bound their hopes and efforts together, would be rehabilitated, strong in forms of government which guarantee true freedom, opportunity to the invididual, and protection against the terror of governmental tyranny.

The issue is really clear-cut, and I fear there can be no settlement until the coming months demonstrate whether or not the civilization of western Europe will prove vigorous enough to rise above the destructive effects of the war and restore a healthy society. Officials of the Soviet Union and leaders of the Communist Parties openly predict that this restoration will not take place. We on the other hand are confident in the rehabilitation of western European civilization with its freedom.

Now, until the result of this struggle becomes clearly apparent, there will continue to be a very real difficulty to resolve, even on paper, agreed terms for a treaty of peace. The situation must be stabilized. Western nations at the very least must be firmly established on a basis of government and freedoms that will preserve all that has been gained in the past centuries by these nations and all that their cooperation promises for the future.

◇◇◇◇◇◇

20. SIXTH MEETING OF THE COUNCIL OF FOREIGN MINISTERS, PARIS, MAY 23 TO JUNE 20, 1949 [1]

Communiqué of June 21, 1949

[At the sixth meeting of the Council, held some eighteen months after the fifth meeting, the basic issue was still the question of German unity. While no real progress was made on this score, it was agreed that the occupying powers should consult in order to ease the economic difficulties arising from the existing division of Germany. Considerable progress was also made toward the conclusion of the Austrian treaty.]

The sixth session of the Council of Foreign Ministers attended by the Ministers of Foreign Affairs of France, Robert Schuman; of the Union of Soviet Socialist Republics, A. Y. Vyshinsky; of the United Kingdom, Ernest Bevin; and of the United States of America, Dean Acheson, took place in Paris from May 23 to June 20, 1949. During this meeting the German question and the Austrian treaty were discussed. The Council of Foreign Ministers took the following decisions.

I. THE GERMAN QUESTION

Despite the inability at this session of the Council of Foreign Ministers to reach agreement on the restoration of the economic and political unity of Germany, the Foreign Ministers of France, the Union of Soviet Socialist Republics, the United Kingdom, and the United States will continue their efforts to achieve this result and in particular now agree as follows:

1. During the course of the fourth session of the General Assembly of the United Nations to be convened next September, the four governments, through representatives at the Assembly, will exchange views regarding the date and other arrangements for the next session of the Council of Foreign Ministers on the German question.

2. The occupation authorities, in the light of the intention of the Ministers to continue their efforts to achieve the restoration of the economic and political unity of Germany, shall consult together in Berlin on a quadripartite basis.

3. These consultations will have as their purpose, among others, to mitigate the effects of the present administrative division of Germany and of Berlin, notably in the matters listed below:

(A) Expansion of trade and development of the financial and economic relations between the Western zones and the Eastern zone and between Berlin and the zones.

(B) Facilitation of the movement of persons and goods and the exchange of information between the Western zones and the Eastern zone and between Berlin and the zones.

(C) Consideration of questions of common interest relating to the administration of the four sectors in Berlin with a view to normalizing as far as possible the life of the city.

[1] Department of State Bulletin, July 4, 1949, pp. 857-864.

4. In order to assist in the work envisaged in paragraph 3, the respective occupation authorities may call upon German experts and appropriate German organizations in their respective jurisdictions for assistance. The Germans so called upon should exchange pertinent data, prepare reports and, if agreed between them, submit proposals to the occupation authorities.

5. The Governments of France, the Union of Soviet Socialist Republics, the United Kingdom, and the United States agree that the New York agreement of May 4, 1949, shall be maintained.[1] Moreover, in order to promote further the aims set forth in the preceding paragraphs and in order to improve and supplement this and other arrangements and agreements as regards the movement of persons and goods and communications between the Eastern zone and the Western zones and between the zones and Berlin and also in regard to transit, the occupation authorities, each in his own zone, will have an obligation to take the measures necessary to insure the normal functioning and utilization of rail, water, and road transport for such movement of persons and goods and such communications by post, telephone, and telegraph.

6. The occupation authorities will recommend to the leading German economic bodies of the Eastern and Western zones to facilitate the establishment of closer economic ties between the zones and more effective implementation of trade and other economic agreements.

II. THE AUSTRIAN TREATY

The Foreign Ministers have agreed:

(A) That Austria's frontiers shall be those of January 1, 1938;

(B) That the treaty for Austria shall provide that Austria shall guarantee to protect the rights of the Slovene and Croatian minorities in Austria;

(C) That reparations shall not be exacted from Austria, but that Yugoslavia shall have the right to seize, retain, or liquidate Austrian property, rights and interests within Yugoslav territory;

(D) That the Soviet Union shall receive from Austria $150,000,000 in freely convertible currency to be paid in six years:

(E) That the definitive settlement shall include:

(1) The relinquishment to Austria of all property, rights or interests held or claimed as German assets and of war industrial enterprises, houses, and similar immovable property in Austria held or claimed as war booty, on the understanding that the deputies will be instructed to define more accurately other categories of war booty transferred to Austria (with the exception of those oil assets and DDSG—Danube Shipping Company—properties transferred to the Soviet Union under other paragraphs of article 35 of the treaty indicated in the U. S. S. R. proposals of January 24, 1948, as revised, and retained in general under Austrian jurisdiction). Accordingly the assets of the DDSG in Bulgaria, Hungary, and Rumania as well as 100 percent of the assets of the

---

[1] Department of State Bulletin, May 15, 1949, p. 631.

company in eastern Austria in accordance with a list to be agreed upon by the deputies will be transferred to the U. S. S. R.

(2) That the rights, properties, and interests transferred to the U. S. S. R. as well as the rights, properties, and interests which the U. S. S. R. cedes to Austria shall be transferred without any charges or claims on the part of the U. S. S. R. or on the part of Austria. At the same time it is understood that the words "charges or claims" mean not only creditor claims as arising out of the exercise of the Allied control of these rights, properties, and interests after May 8, 1945, but also all other claims including claims in respect of taxes. It is also understood that the reciprocal waivers by the U. S. S. R. and Austria of charges and claims apply to all such charges and claims as exist on the date when Austria formalizes the rights of the U. S. S. R. to the German assets transferred to it and on the date of the actual transfer to Austria of the assets ceded by the U. S. S. R.

(F) That all former German assets which have become the property of the U. S. S. R. shall not be subject to alienation without the consent of the U. S. S. R.

(G) That the deputies shall resume their work promptly for the purpose of reaching agreement not later than September 1, 1949, on the draft treaty as a whole.

PART III

United Nations: Basic Organization

21. CHARTER OF THE UNITED NATIONS, JUNE 26, 1945 [1]

[The United Nations Charter was drafted and signed at the United Nations Conference on International Organization held at San Francisco from April 25 to June 26, 1945. In 1943, in the Moscow Declaration, the U.S., U.K., U.S.S.R., and China recognized the need for establishing a general international organization to maintain peace and security. At Dumbarton Oaks, these same four powers worked out a plan in the fall of 1944—the Dumbarton Oaks Proposals—which formed the basis for the drafting of the Charter.

The states invited to San Francisco were those which had declared war on Germany or Japan, and which had signed the United Nations Declaration of January 1, 1942. In addition, four other participating governments were invited by the Conference itself. Thus, fifty-one states became the original members of the United Nations.

The Charter became effective on October 24, 1945, following its ratification by the five Great Powers and a majority of the other signatories. The United States Senate approved ratification by the overwhelming vote of 89 to 2. At the end of 1950, sixty states were members.]

We the peoples of the United Nations determined

 to save succeeding generations from the scourge of war, which twice in our lifetime has brought untold sorrow to mankind, and

 to reaffirm faith in fundamental human rights, in the dignity and worth of the human person, in the equal rights of men and women and of nations large and small, and

 to establish conditions under which justice and respect for the obligations arising from treaties and other sources of international law can be maintained, and

 to promote social progress and better standards of life in larger freedom,

and for these ends

---

[1] The United States and the United Nations: Report by the President to the Congress for the Year 1946, Department of State publication 2735, United States-United Nations Report Series 7, pp. 195-221; Department of State publication 2349 and 2353, Conference Series 71 and 74, respectively. See text of Dumbarton Oaks proposals for a general international organization, Department of State publication 2349, Conference Series 71.

to practice tolerance and live together in peace with one another as good neighbors, and

to unite our strength to maintain international peace and security, and

to ensure, by the acceptance of principles and the institution of methods, that armed force shall not be used, save in the common interest, and

to employ international machinery for the promotion of the economic and social advancement of all peoples,

have resolved to combine our efforts to accomplish these aims.

Accordingly, our respective Governments, through representatives assembled in the city of San Francisco, who have exhibited their full powers found to be in good and due form, have agreed to the present Charter of the United Nations and do hereby establish an international organization to be known as the United Nations.

CHAPTER I. PURPOSES AND PRINCIPLES

ARTICLE 1

The Purposes of the United Nations are:

1. To maintain international peace and security, and to that end: to take effective collective measures for the prevention and removal of threats to the peace, and for the suppression of acts of aggression or other breaches of the peace, and to bring about by peaceful means, and in conformity with the principles of justice and international law, adjustment or settlement of international disputes or situations which might lead to a breach of the peace;

2. To develop friendly relations among nations based on respect for the principle of equal rights and self-determination of peoples, and to take other appropriate measures to strengthen universal peace;

3. To achieve international cooperation in solving international problems of an economic, social, cultural, or humanitarian character, and in promoting and encouraging respect for human rights and for fundamental freedoms for all without distinction as to race, sex, language, or religion; and

4. To be a center for harmonizing the actions of nations in the attainment of these common ends.

ARTICLE 2

The Organization and its Members, in pursuit of the Purposes stated in Article 1, shall act in accordance with the following Principles.

1. The Organization is based on the principle of the sovereign equality of all its Members.

2. All Members, in order to ensure to all of them the rights and benefits resulting from membership, shall fulfil in good faith the obligations assumed by them in accordance with the present Charter.

3. All Members shall settle their international disputes by peaceful means in such a manner that international peace and security, and justice, are not endangered.

4. All Members shall refrain in their international relations from the threat or use of force against the territorial integrity or political independence of any state, or in any other manner inconsistent with the Purposes of the United Nations.

5. All Members shall give the United Nations every assistance in any action it takes in accordance with the present Charter, and shall refrain from giving assistance to any state against which the United Nations is taking preventive or enforcement action.

6. The Organization shall ensure that states which are not Members of the United Nations act in accordance with these Principles so far as may be necessary for the maintenance of international peace and security.

7. Nothing contained in the present Charter shall authorize the United Nations to intervene in matters which are essentially within the domestic jurisdiction of any state or shall require the Members to submit such matters to settlement under the present Charter; but this principle shall not prejudice the application of enforcement measures under Chapter VII.

CHAPTER II. MEMBERSHIP

ARTICLE 3

The original Members of the United Nations shall be the states which, having participated in the United Nations Conference on International Organization at San Francisco, or having previously signed the Declaration by United Nations of January 1, 1942, sign the present Charter and ratify it in accordance with Article 110.

ARTICLE 4

1. Membership in the United Nations is open to all other peace-loving states which accept the obligations contained in the present Charter and, in the judgment of the Organization, are able and willing to carry out these obligations.

2. The admission of any such state to membership in the United Nations will be effected by a decision of the General Assembly upon the recommendation of the Security Council.

ARTICLE 5

A Member of the United Nations against which preventive or enforcement action has been taken by the Security Council may be suspended from the exercise of the rights and privileges of membership by the General Assembly upon the recommendation of the Security Council. The exercise of these rights and privileges may be restored by the Security Council.

ARTICLE 6

A Member of the United Nations which has persistently violated the Principles contained in the present Charter may be expelled from the Organization by the General Assembly upon the recommendation of the Security Council.

CHAPTER III. ORGANS

ARTICLE 7

1. There are established as the principal organs of the United Nations: a General Assembly, a Security Council, an Economic and Social Council, a Trusteeship Council, an International Court of Justice, and a Secretariat.

2. Such subsidiary organs as may be found necessary may be established in accordance with the present Charter.

ARTICLE 8

The United Nations shall place no restrictions on the eligibility of men and women to participate in any capacity and under conditions of equality in its principal and subsidiary organs.

CHAPTER IV. THE GENERAL ASSEMBLY

COMPOSITION

ARTICLE 9

1. The General Assembly shall consist of all the Members of the United Nations.

2. Each Member shall have not more than five representatives in the General Assembly.

FUNCTIONS AND POWERS

ARTICLE 10

The General Assembly may discuss any questions or any matters within the scope of the present Charter or relating to the powers and functions of any organs provided for in the present Charter, and, except as provided in Article 12, may make recommendations to the Members of the United Nations or to the Security Council or to both on any such questions or matters.

ARTICLE 11

1. The General Assembly may consider the general principles of cooperation in the maintenance of international peace and security, including the principles governing disarmament and the regulation of armaments, and may make recommendations with regard to such principles to the Members or to the Security Council or to both.

2. The General Assembly may discuss any questions relating to the maintenance of international peace and security brought before it by any Member of the United Nations, or by the Security Council, or by a state which is not a Member of the United Nations in accordance with Article 35, paragraph 2, and, except as provided in Article 12, may make recommendations with regard to any such questions to the state or states concerned or to the Security Council or to both. Any such question on which action is necessary shall be referred to the Security Council by the General Assembly either before or after discussion.

3. The General Assembly may call the attention of the Security Council to situations which are likely to endanger international peace and security.

4. The powers of the General Assembly set forth in this Article shall not limit the general scope of Article 10.

ARTICLE 12

1. While the Security Council is exercising in respect of any dispute or situation the functions assigned to it in the present Charter, the General

Assembly shall not make any recommendation with regard to that dispute or situation unless the Security Council so requests.

2. The Secretary-General, with the consent of the Security Council, shall notify the General Assembly at each session of any matters relative to the maintenance of international peace and security which are being dealt with by the Security Council and shall similarly notify the General Assembly, or the Members of the United Nations if the General Assembly is not in session, immediately the Security Council ceases to deal with such matters.

ARTICLE 13

1. The General Assembly shall initiate studies and make recommendations for the purpose of:

a. promoting international cooperation in the political field and encouraging the progressive development of international law and its codification;

b. promoting international cooperation in the economic, social, cultural, educational, and health fields, and assisting in the realization of human rights and fundamental freedoms for all without distinction as to race, sex, language, or religion.

2. The further responsibilities, functions, and powers of the General Assembly with respect to matters mentioned in paragraph 1 (b) above are set forth in Chapters IX and X.

ARTICLE 14

Subject to the provisions of Article 12, the General Assembly may recommend measures for the peaceful adjustment of any situation, regardless of origin, which it deems likely to impair the general welfare or friendly relations among nations, including situations resulting from a violation of the provisions of the present Charter setting forth the Purposes and Principles of the United Nations.

ARTICLE 15

1. The General Assembly shall receive and consider annual and special reports from the Security Council; these reports shall include an account of the measures that the Security Council has decided upon or taken to maintain international peace and security.

2. The General Assembly shall receive and consider reports from the other organs of the United Nations.

ARTICLE 16

The General Assembly shall perform such functions with respect to the international trusteeship system as are assigned to it under Chapters XII and XIII, including the approval of the trusteeship agreements for areas not designated as strategic.

ARTICLE 17

1. The General Assembly shall consider and approve the budget of the Organization.

2. The expenses of the Organization shall be borne by the Members as apportioned by the General Assembly.

3. The General Assembly shall consider and approve any financial and budgetary arrangements with specialized agencies referred to in Article 57 and shall examine the administrative budgets of such specialized agencies with a view to making recommendations to the agencies concerned.

VOTING

ARTICLE 18

1. Each member of the General Assembly shall have one vote.

2. Decisions of the General Assembly on important questions shall be made by a two-thirds majority of the members present and voting. These questions shall include: recommendations with respect to the maintenance of international peace and security, the election of the non-permanent members of the Security Council, the election of the members of the Economic and Social Council, the election of members of the Trusteeship Council in accordance with paragraph 1 (c) of Article 86, the admission of new Members to the United Nations, the suspension of the rights and privileges of membership, the expulsion of Members, questions relating to the operation of the trusteeship system, and budgetary questions.

3. Decisions on other questions, including the determination of additional categories of questions to be decided by a two-thirds majority, shall be made by a majority of the members present and voting.

ARTICLE 19

A Member of the United Nations which is in arrears in the payment of its financial contributions to the Organization shall have no vote in the General Assembly if the amount of its arrears equals or exceeds the amount of the contributions due from it for the preceding two full years. The General Assembly may, nevertheless, permit such a Member to vote if it is satisfied that the failure to pay is due to conditions beyond the control of the Member.

PROCEDURE

ARTICLE 20

The General Assembly shall meet in regular annual sessions and in such special sessions as occasion may require. Special sessions shall be convoked by the Secretary-General at the request of the Security Council or of a majority of the Members of the United Nations.

ARTICLE 21

The General Assembly shall adopt its own rules of procedure. It shall elect its President for each session.

ARTICLE 22

The General Assembly may establish such subsidiary organs as it deems necessary for the performance of its functions.

Chapter V. The Security Council

COMPOSITION

article 23

1. The Security Council shall consist of eleven Members of the United Nations. The Republic of China, France, the Union of Soviet Socialist Republics, the United Kingdom of Great Britain and Northern Ireland, and the United States of America shall be permanent members of the Security Council. The General Assembly shall elect six other Members of the United Nations to be non-permanent members of the Security Council, due regard being specially paid, in the first instance to the contribution of Members of the United Nations to the maintenance of international peace and security and to the other purposes of the Organization, and also to equitable geographical distribution.

2. The non-permanent members of the Security Council shall be elected for a term of two years. In the first election of the non-permanent members, however, three shall be chosen for a term of one year. A retiring member shall not be eligible for immediate re-election.

3. Each member of the Security Council shall have one representative.

FUNCTIONS AND POWERS

article 24

1. In order to ensure prompt and effective action by the United Nations, its Members confer on the Security Council primary responsibility for the maintenance of international peace and security, and agree that in carrying out its duties under this responsibility the Security Council acts on their behalf.

2. In discharging these duties the Security Council shall act in accordance with the Purposes and Principles of the United Nations. The specific powers granted to the Security Council for the discharge of these duties are laid down in Chapters VI, VII, VIII, and XII.

3. The Security Council shall submit annual and, when necessary, special reports to the General Assembly for its consideration.

article 25

The Members of the United Nations agree to accept and carry out the decisions of the Security Council in accordance with the present Charter.

article 26

In order to promote the establishment and maintenance of international peace and security with the least diversion for armaments of the world's human and economic resources, the Security Council shall be responsible for formulating, with the assistance of the Military Staff Committee referred to in Article 47, plans to be submitted to the Members of the United Nations for the establishment of a system for the regulation of armaments.

VOTING

ARTICLE 27

1. Each member of the Security Council shall have one vote.
2. Decisions of the Security Council on procedural matters shall be made by an affirmative vote of seven members.
3. Decisions of the Security Council on all other matters shall be made by an affirmative vote of seven members including the concurring votes of the permanent members; provided that, in decisions under Chapter VI, and under paragraph 3 of Article 52, a party to a dispute shall abstain from voting.

PROCEDURE

ARTICLE 28

1. The Security Council shall be so organized as to be able to function continuously. Each member of the Security Council shall for this purpose be represented at all times at the seat of the Organization.
2. The Security Council shall hold periodic meetings at which each of its members may, if it so desires, be represented by a member of the government or by some other specially designated representative.
3. The Security Council may hold meetings at such places other than the seat of the Organization as in its judgment will best facilitate its work.

ARTICLE 29

The Security Council may establish such subsidiary organs as it deems necessary for the performance of its functions.

ARTICLE 30

The Security Council shall adopt its own rules of procedure, including the method of selecting its President.

ARTICLE 31

Any Member of the United Nations which is not a member of the Security Council may participate, without vote, in the discussion of any question brought before the Security Council whenever the latter considers that the interests of that Member are specially affected.

ARTICLE 32

Any Member of the United Nations which is not a member of the Security Council or any state which is not a Member of the United Nations, if it is a party to a dispute under consideration by the Security Council, shall be invited to participate, without vote, in the discussion relating to the dispute. The Security Council shall lay down such conditions as it deems just for the participation of a state which is not a Member of the United Nations.

Chapter VI. Pacific Settlement of Disputes

ARTICLE 33

1. The parties to any dispute, the continuance of which is likely to endanger the maintenance of international peace and security, shall, first of all,

seek a solution by negotiation, enquiry, mediation, conciliation, arbitration, judicial settlement, resort to regional agencies or arrangements, or other peaceful means of their own choice.

2. The Security Council shall, when it deems necessary, call upon the parties to settle their dispute by such means.

ARTICLE 34

The Security Council may investigate any dispute, or any situation which might lead to international friction or give rise to a dispute, in order to determine whether the continuance of the dispute or situation is likely to endanger the maintenance of international peace and security.

ARTICLE 35

1. Any Member of the United Nations may bring any dispute, or any situation of the nature referred to in Article 34, to the attention of the Security Council or of the General Assembly.

2. A state which is not a Member of the United Nations may bring to the attention of the Security Council or of the General Assembly any dispute to which it is a party if it accepts in advance, for the purposes of the dispute, the obligations of pacific settlement provided in the present Charter.

3. The proceedings of the General Assembly in respect of matters brought to its attention under this Article will be subject to the provisions of Articles 11 and 12.

ARTICLE 36

1. The Security Council may, at any stage of a dispute of the nature referred to in Article 33 or of a situation of like nature, recommend appropriate procedures or methods of adjustment.

2. The Security Council should take into consideration any procedures for the settlement of the dispute which have already been adopted by the parties.

3. In making recommendations under this Article the Security Council should also take into consideration that legal disputes should as a general rule be deferred by the parties to the International Court of Justice in accordance with the provisions of the Statute of the Court.

ARTICLE 37

1. Should the parties to a dispute of the nature referred to in Article 33 fail to settle it by the means indicated in that Article, they shall refer it to the Security Council.

2. If the Security Council deems that the continuance of the dispute is in fact likely to endanger the maintenance of international peace and security, it shall decide whether to take action under Article 36 or to recommend such terms of settlement as it may consider appropriate.

ARTICLE 38

Without prejudice to the provisions of Articles 33 to 37, the Security Council may, if all the parties to any dispute so request, make recommendations to the parties with a view to a pacific settlement of the dispute.

CHAPTER VII. ACTION WITH RESPECT TO THREATS TO THE PEACE,
BREACHES OF THE PEACE, AND ACTS OF AGGRESSION

ARTICLE 39

The Security Council shall determine the existence of any threat to the peace, breach of the peace, or act of aggression and shall make recommendations, or decide what measures shall be taken in accordance with Articles 41 and 42, to maintain or restore international peace and security.

ARTICLE 40

In order to prevent an aggravation of the situation, the Security Council may, before making the recommendations or deciding upon the measures provided for in Article 39, call upon the parties concerned to comply with such provisional measures as it deems necessary or desirable. Such provisional measures shall be without prejudice to the rights, claims, or position of the parties concerned. The Security Council shall duly take account of failure to comply with such provisional measures.

ARTICLE 41

The Security Council may decide what measures not involving the use of armed force are to be employed to give effect to its decisions, and it may call upon the Members of the United Nations to apply such measures. These may include complete or partial interruption of economic relations and of rail, sea, air, postal, telegraphic, radio, and other means of communication, and the severance of diplomatic relations.

ARTICLE 42

Should the Security Council consider that measures provided for in Article 41 would be inadequate or have proved to be inadequate, it may take such action by air, sea, or land forces as may be necessary to maintain or restore international peace and security. Such action may include demonstrations, blockade, and other operations by air, sea, or land forces of Members of the United Nations.

ARTICLE 43

1. All Members of the United Nations, in order to contribute to the maintenance of international peace and security, undertake to make available to the Security Council, on its call and in accordance with a special agreement or agreements, armed forces, assistance, and facilities, including rights of passage, necessary for the purpose of maintaining international peace and security.

2. Such agreement or agreements shall govern the numbers and types of forces, their degree of readiness and general location, and the nature of the facilities and assistance to be provided.

3. The agreement or agreements shall be negotiated as soon as possible on the initiative of the Security Council. They shall be concluded between the Security Council and Members or between the Security Council and groups of Members and shall be subject to ratification by the signatory states in accordance with their respective constitutional processes.

ARTICLE 44

When the Security Council has decided to use force it shall, before calling upon a Member not represented on it to provide armed forces in fulfilment of the obligations assumed under Article 43, invite that Member, if the Member so desires, to participate in the decisions of the Security Council concerning the employment of contingents of that Member's armed forces.

ARTICLE 45

In order to enable the United Nations to take urgent military measures, Members shall hold immediately available national airforce contingents for combined international enforcement action. The strength and degree of readiness of these contingents and plans for their combined action shall be determined, within the limits laid down in the special agreement or agreements referred to in Article 43, by the Security Council with the assistance of the Military Staff Committee.

ARTICLE 46

Plans for the application of armed force shall be made by the Security Council with the assistance of the Military Staff Committee.

ARTICLE 47

1. There shall be established a Military Staff Committee to advise and assist the Security Council on all questions relating to the Security Council's military requirements for the maintenance of international peace and security, the employment and command of forces placed at its disposal, the regulation of armaments, and possible disarmament.

2. The Military Staff Committee shall consist of the Chiefs of Staff of the permanent Members of the Security Council or their representatives. Any Member of the United Nations not permanently represented on the Committee shall be invited by the Committee to be associated with it when the efficient discharge of the Committee's responsibilities requires the participation of that Member in its work.

3. The Military Staff Committee shall be responsible under the Security Council for the strategic direction of any armed forces placed at the disposal of the Security Council. Questions relating to the command of such forces shall be worked out subsequently.

4. The Military Staff Committee, with the authorization of the Security Council and after consultation with appropriate regional agencies, may establish regional subcommittees.

ARTICLE 48

1. The action required to carry out the decisions of the Security Council for the maintenance of international peace and security shall be taken by all the Members of the United Nations or by some of them, as the Security Council may determine.

2. Such decisions shall be carried out by the Members of the United Nations directly and through their action in the appropriate international agencies of which they are members.

ARTICLE 49

The Members of the United Nations shall join in affording mutual assistance in carrying out the measures decided upon by the Security Council.

ARTICLE 50

If preventive or enforcement measures against any state are taken by the Security Council, any other state, whether a Member of the United Nations or not, which finds itself confronted with special economic problems arising from the carrying out of those measures shall have the right to consult the Security Council with regard to a solution of those problems.

ARTICLE 51

Nothing in the present Charter shall impair the inherent right of individual or collective self-defense if an armed attack occurs against a Member of the United Nations, until the Security Council has taken the measures necessary to maintain international peace and security. Measures taken by Members in the exercise of this right of self-defense shall be immediately reported to the Security Council and shall not in any way affect the authority and responsibility of the Security Council under the present Charter to take at any time such action as it deems necessary in order to maintain or restore international peace and security.

CHAPTER VIII. REGIONAL ARRANGEMENTS

ARTICLE 52

1. Nothing in the present Charter precludes the existence of regional arrangements or agencies for dealing with such matters relating to the maintenance of international peace and security as are appropriate for regional action, provided that such arrangements or agencies and their activities are consistent with the Purposes and Principles of the United Nations.

2. The Members of the United Nations entering into such arrangements or constituting such agencies shall make every effort to achieve pacific settlement of local disputes through such regional arrangements or by such regional agencies before referring them to the Security Council.

3. The Security Council shall encourage the development of pacific settlement of local disputes through such regional arrangements or by such regional agencies either on the initiative of the states concerned or by reference from the Security Council.

4. This Article in no way impairs the application of Articles 34 and 35.

ARTICLE 53

1. The Security Council shall, where appropriate, utilize such regional arrangements or agencies for enforcement action under its authority. But no enforcement action shall be taken under regional arrangements or by regional agencies without the authorization of the Security Council, with the exception of measures against any enemy state, as defined in paragraph 2 of this Article, provided for pursuant to Article 107 or in regional arrangements directed against renewal of aggressive policy on the part of any such state, until such

time as the Organization may, on request of the Governments concerned, be charged with the responsibility for preventing further aggression by such a state.

2. The term enemy state as used in paragraph 1 of this Article applies to any state which during the Second World War has been an enemy of any signatory of the present Charter.

ARTICLE 54

The Security Council shall at all times be kept fully informed of activities undertaken or in contemplation under regional arrangements or by regional agencies for the maintenance of international peace and security.

CHAPTER IX. INTERNATIONAL ECONOMIC AND SOCIAL COOPERATION

ARTICLE 55

With a view to the creation of conditions of stability and well-being which are necessary for peaceful and friendly relations among nations based on respect for the principle of equal rights and self-determination of peoples, the United Nations shall promote:

   a. higher standards of living, full employment, and conditions of economic and social progress and development;

   b. solutions of international economic, social, health, and related problems; and international cultural and educational cooperation; and

   c. universal respect for, and observance of, human rights and fundamental freedoms for all without distinction as to race, sex, language, or religion.

ARTICLE 56

All Members pledge themselves to take joint and separate action in cooperation with the Organization for the achievement of the purposes set forth in Article 55.

ARTICLE 57

1. The various specialized agencies, established by intergovernmental agreement and having wide international responsibilities, as defined in their basic instruments, in economic, social, cultural, educational, health, and related fields, shall be brought into relationship with the United Nations in accordance with the provisions of Article 63.

2. Such agencies thus brought into relationship with the United Nations are hereinafter referred to as specialized agencies.

ARTICLE 58

The Organization shall make recommendations for the coordination of the policies and activities of the specialized agencies.

ARTICLE 59

The Organization shall, where appropriate, initiate negotiations among the states concerned for the creation of any new specialized agencies required for the accomplishment of the purposes set forth in Article 55.

ARTICLE 60

Responsibility for the discharge of the functions of the Organization set forth in this Chapter shall be vested in the General Assembly and, under the authority of the General Assembly, in the Economic and Social Council, which shall have for this purpose the powers set forth in Chapter X.

CHAPTER X. THE ECONOMIC AND SOCIAL COUNCIL

COMPOSITION

ARTICLE 61

1. The Economic and Social Council shall consist of eighteen Members of the United Nations elected by the General Assembly.

2. Subject to the provisions of paragraph 3, six members of the Economic and Social Council shall be elected each year for a term of three years. A retiring member shall be eligible for immediate re-election.

3. At the first election, eighteen members of the Economic and Social Council shall be chosen. The term of office of six members so chosen shall expire at the end of one year, and of six other members at the end of two years, in accordance with arrangements made by the General Assembly.

4. Each member of the Economic and Social Council shall have one representative.

FUNCTIONS AND POWERS

ARTICLE 62

1. The Economic and Social Council may make or initiate studies and reports with respect to international economic, social, cultural, educational, health, and related matters and may make recommendations with respect to any such matters to the General Assembly, to the Members of the United Nations, and to the specialized agencies concerned.

2. It may make recommendations for the purpose of promoting respect for, and observance of, human rights and fundamental freedoms for all.

3. It may prepare draft conventions for submission to the General Assembly, with respect to matters falling within its competence.

4. It may call, in accordance with the rules prescribed by the United Nations, international conferences on matters falling within its competence.

ARTICLE 63

1. The Economic and Social Council may enter into agreements with any of the agencies referred to in Article 57, defining the terms on which the agency concerned shall be brought into relationship with the United Nations. Such agreements shall be subject to approval by the General Assembly.

2. It may coordinate the activities of the specialized agencies through consultation with and recommendations to such agencies and through recommendations to the General Assembly and to the Members of the United Nations.

ARTICLE 64

1. The Economic and Social Council may take appropriate steps to obtain regular reports from the specialized agencies. It may make arrangements with the Members of the United Nations and with the specialized agencies to obtain reports on the steps taken to give effect to its own recommendations and to recommendations on matters falling within its competence made by the General Assembly.

2. It may communicate its observations on these reports to the General Assembly.

ARTICLE 65

The Economic and Social Council may furnish information to the Security Council and shall assist the Security Council upon its request.

ARTICLE 66

1. The Economic and Social Council shall perform such functions as fall within its competence in connection with the carrying out of the recommendations of the General Assembly.

2. It may, with the approval of the General Assembly, perform services at the request of Members of the United Nations and at the request of specialized agencies.

3. It shall perform such other functions as are specified elsewhere in the present Charter or as may be assigned to it by the General Assembly.

VOTING

ARTICLE 67

1. Each member of the Economic and Social Council shall have one vote.

2. Decisions of the Economic and Social Council shall be made by a majority of the members present and voting.

PROCEDURE

ARTICLE 68

The Economic and Social Council shall set up commissions in economic and social fields and for the promotion of human rights, and such other commissions as may be required for the performance of its functions.

ARTICLE 69

The Economic and Social Council shall invite any Member of the United Nations to participate, without vote, in its deliberations on any matter of particular concern to that Member.

ARTICLE 70

The Economic and Social Council may make arrangements for representatives of the specialized agencies to participate, without vote, in its deliberations and in those of the commissions established by it, and for its representatives to participate in the deliberations of the specialized agencies.

ARTICLE 71

The Economic and Social Council may make suitable arrangements for consultation with non-governmental organizations which are concerned with matters within its competence. Such arrangements may be made with international organizations and, where appropriate, with national organizations after consultation with the Member of the United Nations concerned.

ARTICLE 72

1. The Economic and Social Council shall adopt its own rules of procedure, including the method of selecting its President.

2. The Economic and Social Council shall meet as required in accordance with its rules, which shall include provision for the convening of meetings on the request of a majority of its members.

CHAPTER XI. DECLARATION REGARDING NON-SELF-GOVERNING TERRITORIES

ARTICLE 73

Members of the United Nations which have or assume responsibilities for the administration of territories whose peoples have not yet attained a full measure of self-government recognize the principle that the interests of the inhabitants of these territories are paramount, and accept as a sacred trust the obligation to promote to the utmost, within the system of international peace and security established by the present Charter, the well-being of the inhabitants of these territories, and, to this end:

a. to ensure, with due respect for the culture of the peoples concerned, their political, economic, social, and educational advancement, their just treatment, and their protection against abuses;

b. to develop self-government, to take due account of the political aspirations of the peoples, and to assist them in the progressive development of their free political institutions, according to the particular circumstances of each territory and its peoples and their varying stages of advancement;

c. to further international peace and security;

d. to promote constructive measures of development, to encourage research, and to cooperate with one another and, when and where appropriate, with specialized international bodies with a view to the practical achievement of the social, economic, and scientific purposes set forth in this Article; and

e. to transmit regularly to the Secretary-General for information purposes, subject to such limitation as security and constitutional considerations may require, statistical and other information of a technical nature relating to economic, social, and educational conditions in the territories for which they are respectively responsible other than those territories to which Chapters XII and XIII apply.

ARTICLE 74

Members of the United Nations also agree that their policy in respect of the territories to which this Chapter applies, no less than in respect of their metropolitan areas, must be based on the general principal of good-neighborliness, due account being taken of the interests and well-being of the rest of the world, in social, economic, and commercial matters.

CHAPTER XII. INTERNATIONAL TRUSTEESHIP SYSTEM

ARTICLE 75

The United Nations shall establish under its authority an international trusteeship system for the administration and supervision of such territories as may be placed thereunder by subsequent individual agreements. These territories are hereinafter referred to as trust territories.

ARTICLE 76

The basic objectives of the trusteeship system, in accordance with the Purposes of the United Nations laid down in Article 1 of the present Charter, shall be:

a. to further international peace and security;

b. to promote the political, economic, social, and educational advancement of the inhabitants of the trust territories, and their progressive development towards self-government or independence as may be appropriate to the particular circumstances of each territory and its peoples and the freely expressed wishes of the peoples concerned, and as may be provided by the terms of each trusteeship agreement;

c. to encourage respect for human rights and for fundamental freedoms for all without distinction as to race, sex, language, or religion, and to encourage recognition of the interdependence of the peoples of the world; and

d. to ensure equal treatment in social, economic, and commercial matters for all Members of the United Nations and their nationals, and also equal treatment for the latter in the administration of justice, without prejudice to the attainment of the foregoing objectives and subject to the provisions of Article 80.

ARTICLE 77

1. The trusteeship system shall apply to such territories in the following categories as may be placed thereunder by means of trusteeship agreements:

a. territories now held under mandate;

b. territories which may be detached from enemy states as a result of the Second World War; and

c. territories voluntarily placed under the system by states responsible for their administration.

2. It will be a matter for subsequent agreement as to which territories in the foregoing categories will be brought under the trusteeship system and upon what terms.

ARTICLE 78

The trusteeship system shall not apply to territories which have become Members of the United Nations, relationship among which shall be based on respect for the principle of sovereign equality.

ARTICLE 79

The terms of trusteeship for each territory to be placed under the trustee-ship system, including any alteration or amendment, shall be agreed upon by the states directly concerned, including the mandatory power in the case of territories held under mandate by a Member of the United Nations, and shall be approved as provided for in Articles 83 and 85.

ARTICLE 80

1. Except as may be agreed upon in individual trusteeship agreements, made under Articles 77, 79, and 81, placing each territory under the trustee-ship system, and until such agreements have been concluded, nothing in this Chapter shall be construed in or of itself to alter in any manner the rights whatsoever of any states or any peoples or the terms of existing international instruments to which Members of the United Nations may respectively be parties.

2. Paragraph 1 of this Article shall not be interpreted as giving grounds for delay or postponement of the negotiation and conclusion of agreements for placing mandated and other territories under the trusteeship system as provided for in Article 77.

ARTICLE 81

The trusteeship agreement shall in each case include the terms under which the trust territory will be administered and designate the authority which will exercise the administration of the trust territory. Such authority, hereinafter called the administering authority, may be one or more states or the Organization itself.

ARTICLE 82

There may be designated, in any trusteeship agreement, a strategic area or areas which may include part or all of the trust territory to which the agreement applies, without prejudice to any special agreement or agreements made under Article 43.

ARTICLE 83

1. All functions of the United Nations relating to strategic areas, including the approval of the terms of the trusteeship agreements and of their alteration or amendment, shall be exercised by the Security Council.

2. The basic objectives set forth in Article 76 shall be applicable to the people of each strategic area.

3. The Security Council shall, subject to the provisions of the trusteeship agreements and without prejudice to security considerations, avail itself of the assistance of the Trusteeship Council to perform those functions of the United Nations under the trusteeship system relating to political, economic, social, and educational matters in the strategic areas.

ARTICLE 84

It shall be the duty of the administering authority to ensure that the trust territory shall play its part in the maintenance of international peace and security. To this end the administering authority may make use of volunteer forces, facilities, and assistance from the trust territory in carrying out the obligations towards the Security Council undertaken in this regard by the administering authority, as well as for local defense and the maintenance of law and order within the trust territory.

ARTICLE 85

1. The functions of the United Nations with regard to trusteeship agreements for all areas not designated as strategic, including the approval of the terms of the trusteeship agreements and of their alteration or amendment, shall be exercised by the General Assembly.

2. The Trusteeship Council, operating under the authority of the General Assembly shall assist the General Assembly in carrying out these functions.

CHAPTER XIII. THE TRUSTEESHIP COUNCIL

COMPOSITION

ARTICLE 86

1. The Trusteeship Council shall consist of the following Members of the United Nations:

    a. those Members administering trust territories;

    b. such of those Members mentioned by name in Article 23 as are not administering trust territories; and

    c. as many other Members elected for three-year terms by the General Assembly as may be necessary to ensure that the total number of members of the trusteeship Council is equally divided between those Members of the United Nations which administer trust territories and those which do not.

2. Each member of the Trusteeship Council shall designate one specially qualified person to represent it therein.

FUNCTIONS AND POWERS

ARTICLE 87

The General Assembly and, under its authority, the Trusteeship Council, in carrying out their functions, may:

    a. consider reports submitted by the administering authority;

    b. accept petitions and examine them in consultation with the administering authority;

    c. provide for periodic visits to the respective trust territories at times agreed upon with the administering authority; and

    d. take these and other actions in conformity with the terms of the trusteeship agreements.

ARTICLE 88

The Trusteeship Council shall formulate a questionnaire on the political, economic, social, and educational advancement of the inhabitants of each trust territory, and the administering authority for each trust territory within the competence of the General Assembly shall make an annual report to the General Assembly upon the basis of such questionnaire.

VOTING

ARTICLE 89

1. Each member of the Trusteeship Council shall have one vote.
2. Decisions of the Trusteeship Council shall be made by a majority of the members present and voting.

PROCEDURE

ARTICLE 90

1. The Trusteeship Council shall adopt its own rules of procedure, including the method of selecting its President.
2. The Trusteeship Council shall meet as required in accordance with its rules, which shall include provision for the convening of meetings on the request of a majority of its members.

ARTICLE 91

The Trusteeship Council shall, when appropriate, avail itself of the assistance of the Economic and Social Council and of the specialized agencies in regard to matters with which they are respectively concerned.

CHAPTER XIV. THE INTERNATIONAL COURT OF JUSTICE

ARTICLE 92

The International Court of Justice shall be the principal judicial organ of the United Nations. It shall function in accordance with the annexed Statute, which is based upon the Statute of the Permanent Court of International Justice and forms an integral part of the present Charter.

ARTICLE 93

1. All Members of the United Nations are *ipso facto* parties to the Statute of the International Court of Justice.
2. A state which is not a Member of the United Nations may become a party to the Statute of the International Court of Justice on conditions to be determined in each case by the General Assembly upon the recommendation of the Security Council.

ARTICLE 94

1. Each Member of the United Nations undertakes to comply with the decision of the International Court of Justice in any case to which it is a party.
2. If any party to a case fails to perform the obligations incumbent upon it under a judgment rendered by the Court, the other party may have recourse to the Security Council, which may, if it deems necessary, make recommendations or decide upon measures to be taken to give effect to the judgment.

ARTICLE 95

Nothing in the present Charter shall prevent Members of the United Nations from entrusting the solution of their differences to other tribunals by virtue of agreements already in existence or which may be concluded in the future.

ARTICLE 96

1. The General Assembly or the Security Council may request the International Court of Justice to give an advisory opinion on any legal question.

2. Other organs of the United Nations and specialized agencies, which may at any time be so authorized by the General Assembly, may also request advisory opinions of the Court on legal questions arising within the scope of their activities.

CHAPTER XV. THE SECRETARIAT

ARTICLE 97

The Secretariat shall comprise a Secretary-General and such staff as the Organization may require. The Secretary-General shall be appointed by the General Assembly upon the recommendation of the Security Council. He shall be the chief administrative officer of the Organization.

ARTICLE 98

The Secretary-General shall act in that capacity in all meetings of the General Assembly, of the Security Council, of the Economic and Social Council, and of the Trusteeship Council, and shall perform such other functions as are entrusted to him by these organs. The Secretary-General shall make an annual report to the General Assembly on the work of the Organization.

ARTICLE 99

The Secretary-General may bring to the attention of the Security Council any matter which in his opinion may threaten the maintenance of international peace and security.

ARTICLE 100

1. In the performance of their duties the Secretary-General and the staff shall not seek or receive instructions from any government or from any other authority external to the Organization. They shall refrain from any action which might reflect on their position as international officials responsible only to the Organization.

2. Each Member of the United Nations undertakes to respect the exclusively international character of the responsibilities of the Secretary-General and the staff and not to seek to influence them in the discharge of their responsibilities.

ARTICLE 101

1. The staff shall be appointed by the Secretary-General under regulations established by the General Assembly.

2. Appropriate staffs shall be permanently assigned to the Economic and Social Council, the Trusteeship Council, and, as required, to other organs of the United Nations. These staffs shall form a part of the Secretariat.

3. The paramount consideration in the employment of the staff and in the determination of the conditions of service shall be the necessity of securing the highest standards of efficiency, competence, and integrity. Due regard shall be paid to the importance of recruiting the staff on as wide a geographical basis as possible.

CHAPTER XVI. MISCELLANEOUS PROVISIONS

ARTICLE 102

1. Every treaty and every international agreement entered into by any Member of the United Nations after the present Charter comes into force shall as soon as possible be registered with the Secretariat and published by it.

2. No party to any such treaty or international agreement which has not been registered in accordance with the provisions of paragraph 1 of this Article may invoke that treaty or agreement before any organ of the United Nations.

ARTICLE 103

In the event of a conflict between the obligations of the Members of the United Nations under the present Charter and their obligations under any other international agreement, their obligations under the present Charter shall prevail.

ARTICLE 104

The Organization shall enjoy in the territory of each of its Members such legal capacity as may be necessary for the exercise of its functions and the fulfillment of its purposes.

ARTICLE 105

1. The Organization shall enjoy in the territory of each of its Members such privileges and immunities as are necessary for the fulfillment of its purposes.

2. Representatives of the Members of the United Nations and officials of the Organization shall similarly enjoy such privileges and immunities as are necessary for the independent exercise of their functions in connection with the Organization.

3. The General Assembly may make recommendations with a view to determining the details of the application of paragraphs 1 and 2 of this Article or may propose conventions to the Members of the United Nations for this purpose.

CHAPTER XVII. TRANSITIONAL SECURITY ARRANGEMENTS

ARTICLE 106

Pending the coming into force of such special agreements referred to in Article 43 as in the opinion of the Security Council enable it to begin the exercise of its responsibilities under Article 42, the parties to the Four-Nation Declaration, signed at Moscow, October 30, 1943, and France, shall, in accordance with the provisions of paragraph 5 of that Declaration, consult with one another and as occasion requires with other Members of the United Nations with a view to such joint action on behalf of the Organization as may be necessary for the purpose of maintaining international peace and security.

ARTICLE 107

Nothing in the present Charter shall invalidate or preclude action, in relation to any state which during the Second World War has been an enemy of any signatory to the present Charter, taken or authorized as a result of that war by the Governments having responsibility for such action.

CHAPTER XVIII. AMENDMENTS

ARTICLE 108

Amendments to the present Charter shall come into force for all Members of the United Nations when they have been adopted by a vote of two thirds of the members of the General Assembly and ratified in accordance with their respective constitutional processes by two thirds of the Members of the United Nations, including all the permanent members of the Security Council.

ARTICLE 109

1. A General Conference of the Members of the United Nations for the purpose of reviewing the present Charter may be held at a date and place to be fixed by a two-thirds vote of the members of the General Assembly and by a vote of any seven members of the Security Council. Each Member of the United Nations shall have one vote in the conference.

2. Any alteration of the present Charter recommended by a two-thirds vote of the conference shall take effect when ratified in accordance with their respective constitutional processes by two thirds of the Members of the United Nations including all the permanent members of the Security Council.

3. If such a conference has not been held before the tenth annual session of the General Assembly following the coming into force of the present Charter, the proposal to call such a conference shall be placed on the agenda of that session of the General Assembly, and the conference shall be held if so decided by a majority vote of the members of the General Assembly and by a vote of any seven members of the Security Council.

CHAPTER XIX. RATIFICATION AND SIGNATURE

ARTICLE 110

1. The present Charter shall be ratified by the signatory states in accordance with their respective constitutional processes.

2. The ratifications shall be deposited with the Government of the United States of America, which shall notify all the signatory states of each deposit as well as the Secretary-General of the Organization when he has been appointed.

3. The present Charter shall come into force upon the deposit of ratifications by the Republic of China, France, the Union of Soviet Socialist Republics, the United Kingdom of Great Britain and Northern Ireland, and

the United States of America, and by a majority of the other signatory states. A protocol of the ratifications deposited shall thereupon be drawn up by the Government of the United States of America which shall communicate copies thereof to all the signatory states.

4. The states signatory to the present Charter which ratify it after it has come into force will become original Members of the United Nations on the date of the deposit of their respective ratifications.

ARTICLE 111

The present Charter, of which the Chinese, French, Russian, English, and Spanish texts are equally authentic, shall remain deposited in the archives of the Government of the United States of America. Duly certified copies thereof shall be transmitted by that Government to the Governments of the other signatory states.

In faith whereof the representatives of the Governments of the United Nations have signed the present Charter.

Done at the city of San Francisco the twenty-sixth day of June, one thousand nine hundred and forty-five.

◇◇◇◇◇

22. STATUTE OF THE INTERNATIONAL COURT OF JUSTICE, JUNE 26, 1945 [1]

[In addition to the organs handling political and economic questions, the United Nations agreed that it was essential to create machinery for the settlement of legal disputes. This task was assigned to an International Committee of Jurists made up of representatives of forty-five countries. The Committee met in Washington in April 1945, and drafted a statute which was later considered and approved by the San Francisco Conference.

The statute provided for a new court, although it is in many ways identical to the Permanent Court of International Justice which it replaced. The Court, which is the principal judicial organ of the United Nations, is an integral part of the United Nations system. All members of the United Nations are *ipso facto* members of the Court. The seat of the Court is at The Hague.]

ARTICLE 1

The International Court of Justice established by the Charter of the United Nations as the principal judicial organ of the United Nations shall be constituted and shall function in accordance with the provisions of the present Statute.

[1] Report to the President on Results of San Francisco Conference, June 26, 1945, also, Charter of the United Nations together with Statute of the International Court of Justice, June 26, 1945, Department of State publications 2349 and 2353, Conference Series 71 and 74. The statute was ratified along with the UN Charter on July 28, 1945, and went into effect on October 24, 1945.

CHAPTER I. ORGANIZATION OF THE COURT

ARTICLE 2

The Court shall be composed of a body of independent judges, elected regardless of their nationality from among persons of high moral character, who possess the qualifications required in their respective countries for appointment to the highest judicial offices, or are juris-consults of recognized competence in international law.

ARTICLE 3

1. The Court shall consist of fifteen members, no two of whom may be nationals of the same state.

2. A person who for the purposes of membership in the Court could be regarded as a national of more than one state shall be deemed to be a national of the one in which he ordinarily exercises civil and political rights.

ARTICLE 4

1. The members of the Court shall be elected by the General Assembly and by the Security Council from a list of persons nominated by the national groups in the Permanent Court of Arbitration, in accordance with the following provisions.

2. In the case of Members of the United Nations not represented in the Permanent Court of Arbitration, candidates shall be nominated by national groups appointed for this purpose by their governments under the same conditions as those prescribed for members of the Permanent Court of Arbitration by Article 44 of the Convention of The Hague of 1907 for the pacific settlement of international disputes.

3. The conditions under which a state which is a party to the present Statute but is not a Member of the United Nations may participate in electing the members of the Court shall, in the absence of a special agreement, be laid down by the General Assembly upon recommendation of the Security Council.

ARTICLE 5

1. At least three months before the date of the election, the Secretary-General of the United Nations shall address a written request to the members of the Permanent Court of Arbitration belonging to the states which are parties to the present Statute, and to the members of the national groups appointed under Article 4, paragraph 2, inviting them to undertake, within a given time, by national groups, the nomination of persons in a position to accept the duties of a member of the Court.

2. No group may nominate more than four persons, not more than two of whom shall be of their own nationality. In no case may the number of candidates nominated by a group be more than double the number of seats to be filled.

ARTICLE 6

Before making these nominations, each national group is recommended to consult its highest court of justice, its legal faculties and schools of law, and its national academies and national sections of international academies devoted to the study of law.

ARTICLE 7

1. The Secretary-General shall prepare a list in alphabetical order of all the persons thus nominated. Save as provided in Article 12, paragraph 2, these shall be the only persons eligible.

2. The Secretary-General shall submit this list to the General Assembly and to the Security Council.

ARTICLE 8

The General Assembly and the Security Council shall proceed independently of one another to elect the members of the Court.

ARTICLE 9

At every election, the electors shall bear in mind not only that the persons to be elected should individually possess the qualifications required, but also that in the body as a whole the representation of the main forms of civilization and of the principal legal systems of the world should be assured.

ARTICLE 10

1. Those candidates who obtain an absolute majority of votes in the General Assembly and in the Security Council shall be considered as elected.

2. Any vote of the Security Council, whether for the election of judges or for the appointment of members of the conference envisaged in Article 12, shall be taken without any distinction between permanent and non-permanent members of the Security Council.

3. In the event of more than one national of the same state obtaining an absolute majority of the votes both of the General Assembly and of the Security Council, the eldest of these only shall be considered as elected.

ARTICLE 11

If, after the first meeting held for the purpose of the election, one or more seats remain to be filled, a second and, if necessary, a third meeting shall take place.

ARTICLE 12

1. If, after the third meeting, one or more seats still remain unfilled, a joint conference consisting of six members, three appointed by the General Assembly and three by the Security Council, may be formed at any time at the request of either the General Assembly or the Security Council, for the purpose of choosing by the vote of an absolute majority one name for each seat still vacant, to submit to the General Assembly and the Security Council for their respective acceptance.

2. If the joint conference is unanimously agreed upon any person who fulfils the required conditions, he may be included in its list, even though he was not included in the list of nominations referred to in Article 7.

3. If the joint conference is satisfied that it will not be successful in procuring an election, those members of the Court who have already been

elected shall, within a period to be fixed by the Security Council, proceed to fill the vacant seats by selection from among those candidates who have obtained votes either in the General Assembly or in the Security Council.

4. In the event of an equality of votes among the judges, the eldest judge shall have a casting vote.

ARTICLE 13

1. The members of the Court shall be elected for nine years and may be re-elected; provided, however, that of the judges elected at the first election, the terms of five judges shall expire at the end of three years and the terms of five more judges shall expire at the end of six years.

2. The judges whose terms are to expire at the end of the above-mentioned initial periods of three and six years shall be chosen by lot to be drawn by the Secretary-General immediately after the first election has been completed.

3. The members of the Court shall continue to discharge their duties until their places have been filled. Though replaced, they shall finish any cases which they may have begun.

4. In the case of the resignation of a member of the Court, the resignation shall be addressed to the President of the Court for transmission to the Secretary-General. This last notification makes the place vacant.

ARTICLE 14

Vacancies shall be filled by the same method as that laid down for the first election, subject to the following provision: the Secretary-General shall, within one month of the occurrence of the vacancy, proceed to issue the invitations provided for in Article 5, and the date of the election shall be fixed by the Security Council.

ARTICLE 15

A member of the Court elected to replace a member whose term of office has not expired shall hold office for the remainder of his predecessor's term.

ARTICLE 16

1. No member of the Court may exercise any political or administrative function, or engage in any other occupation of a professional nature.

2. Any doubt on this point shall be settled by the decision of the Court.

ARTICLE 17

1. No member of the Court may act as agent, counsel, or advocate in any case.

2. No member may participate in the decision of any case in which he has previously taken part as agent, counsel, or advocate for one of the parties, or as a member of a national or international court, or of a commission of enquiry, or in any other capacity.

3. Any doubt on this point shall be settled by the decision of the Court.

ARTICLE 18

1. No member of the Court can be dismissed unless, in the unanimous opinion of the other members, he has ceased to fulfil the required conditions.

2. Formal notification thereof shall be made to the Secretary-General by the Registrar.

3. This notification makes the place vacant.

ARTICLE 19

The members of the Court, when engaged on the business of the Court, shall enjoy diplomatic privileges and immunities.

ARTICLE 20

Every member of the Court shall, before taking up his duties, make a solemn declaration in open court that he will exercise his powers impartially and conscientiously.

ARTICLE 21

1. The Court shall elect its President and Vice-President for three years; they may be re-elected.

2. The Court shall appoint its Registrar and may provide for the appointment of such other officers as may be necessary.

ARTICLE 22

1. The seat of the Court shall be established at The Hague. This, however, shall not prevent the Court from sitting and exercising its functions elsewhere whenever the Court considers it desirable.

2. The President and the Registrar shall reside at the seat of the Court.

ARTICLE 23

1. The Court shall remain permanently in session, except during the judicial vacations, the dates and duration of which shall be fixed by the Court.

2. Members of the Court are entitled to periodic leave, the dates and duration of which shall be fixed by the Court, having in mind the distance between The Hague and the home of each judge.

3. Members of the Court shall be bound, unless they are on leave or prevented from attending by illness or other serious reasons duly explained to the President, to hold themselves permanently at the disposal of the Court.

ARTICLE 24

1. If, for some special reason, a member of the Court considers that he should not take part in the decision of a particular case, he shall so inform the President.

2. If the President considers that for some special reason one of the members of the Court should not sit in a particular case he shall give him notice accordingly.

3. If in any such case the member of the Court and the President disagree, the matter shall be settled by the decision of the Court.

ARTICLE 25

1. The full Court shall sit except when it is expressly provided otherwise in the present Statute.

2. Subject to the condition that the number of judges available to con-

stitute the Court is not thereby reduced below eleven, the Rules of the Court may provide for allowing one or more judges, according to circumstances and in rotation, to be dispensed from sitting.

3. A quorum of nine judges shall suffice to constitute the Court.

ARTICLE 26

1. The Court may from time to time form one or more chambers, composed of three or more judges as the Court may determine, for dealing with particular categories of cases; for example, labor cases and cases relating to transit and communications.

2. The Court may at any time form a chamber for dealing with a particular case. The number of judges to constitute such a chamber shall be determined by the Court with the approval of the parties.

3. Cases shall be heard and determined by the chambers provided for in this Article if the parties so request.

ARTICLE 27

A judgment given by any of the chambers provided for in Articles 26 and 29 shall be considered as rendered by the Court.

ARTICLE 28

The chambers provided for in Articles 26 and 29 may, with the consent of the parties, sit and exercise their functions elsewhere than at The Hague.

ARTICLE 29

With a view to the speedy despatch of business, the Court shall form annually a chamber composed of five judges which, at the request of the parties, may hear and determine cases by summary procedure. In addition, two judges shall be selected for the purpose of replacing judges who find it impossible to sit.

ARTICLE 30

1. The Court shall frame rules for carrying out its functions. In particular, it shall lay down rules of procedure.

2. The Rules of the Court may provide for assessors to sit with the Court or with any of its chambers, without the right to vote.

ARTICLE 31

1. Judges of the nationality of each of the parties shall retain their right to sit in the case before the Court.

2. If the Court includes upon the Bench a judge of the nationality of one of the parties, any other party may choose a person to sit as judge. Such person shall be chosen preferably from among those persons who have been nominated as candidates as provided in Articles 4 and 5.

3. If the Court includes upon the Bench no judge of the nationality of the parties, each of these parties may proceed to choose a judge as provided in paragraph 2 of this Article.

4. The provisions of this Article shall apply to the case of Articles 26 and 29. In such cases, the President shall request one or, if necessary, two of the

members of the Court forming the chamber to give place to the members of the Court of the nationality of the parties concerned, and, failing such, or if they are unable to be present, to the judges specially chosen by the parties.

5. Should there be several parties in the same interest, they shall, for the purpose of the preceding provisions, be reckoned as one party only. Any doubt upon this point shall be settled by the decision of the Court.

6. Judges chosen as laid down in paragraphs 2, 3, and 4 of this Article shall fulfil the conditions required by Articles 2, 17 (paragraph 2), 20, and 24 of the present Statute. They shall take part in the decision on terms of complete equality with their colleagues.

ARTICLE 32

1. Each member of the Court shall receive an annual salary.

2. The President shall receive a special annual allowance.

3. The Vice-President shall receive a special allowance for every day on which he acts as President.

4. The judges chosen under Article 31, other than members of the Court, shall receive compensation for each day on which they exercise their functions.

5. These salaries, allowances, and compensation shall be fixed by the General Assembly. They may not be decreased during the term of office.

6. The salary of the Registrar shall be fixed by the General Assembly on the proposal of the Court.

7. Regulations made by the General Assembly shall fix the conditions under which retirement pensions may be given to members of the Court and to the Registrar, and the conditions under which members of the Court and the Registrar shall have their traveling expenses refunded.

8. The above salaries, allowances, and compensation shall be free of all taxation.

ARTICLE 33

The expenses of the Court shall be borne by the United Nations in such a manner as shall be decided by the General Assembly.

CHAPTER II. COMPETENCE OF THE COURT

ARTICLE 34

1. Only states may be parties in cases before the Court.

2. The Court subject to and in conformity with its Rules, may request of public international organizations information relevant to cases before it, and shall receive such information presented by such organizations on their own initiative.

3. Whenever the construction of the constituent instrument of a public international organization or of an international convention adopted thereunder is in question in a case before the Court, the Registrar shall so notify the public international organization concerned and shall communicate to it copies of all the written proceedings.

ARTICLE 35

1. The Court shall be open to the states parties to the present Statute.

2. The conditions under which the Court shall be open to other states shall, subject to the special provisions contained in treaties in force, be laid down by the Security Council, but in no case shall such conditions place the parties in a position of inequality before the Court.

3. When a state which is not a Member of the United Nations is a party to a case, the Court shall fix the amount which that party is to contribute towards the expenses of the Court. This provision shall not apply if such state is bearing a share of the expenses of the Court.

ARTICLE 36

1. The jurisdiction of the Court comprises all cases which the parties refer to it and all matters specially provided for in the Charter of the United Nations or in treaties and conventions in force.

2. The states parties to the present Statute may at any time declare that they recognize as compulsory *ipso facto* and without special agreement, in relation to any other state accepting the same obligation, the jurisdiction of the Court in all legal disputes concerning:

    a. the interpretation of a treaty;

    b. any question of international law;

    c. the existence of any fact which, if established, would constitute a breach of an international obligation;

    d. the nature or extent of the reparation to be made for the breach of an international obligation.

3. The declarations referred to above may be made unconditionally or on condition of reciprocity on the part of several or certain states, or for a certain time.

4. Such declarations shall be deposited with the Secretary-General of the United Nations, who shall transmit copies thereof to the parties to the Statute and to the Registrar of the Court.

5. Declarations made under Article 36 of the Statute of the Permanent Court of International Justice and which are still in force shall be deemed, as between the parties to the present Statute, to be acceptances of the compulsory jurisdiction of the International Court of Justice for the period which they still have to run and in accordance with their terms.

6. In the event of a dispute as to whether the Court has jurisdiction, the matter shall be settled by the decision of the Court.

ARTICLE 37

Whenever a treaty or convention in force provides for reference of a matter to a tribunal to have been instituted by the League of Nations, or to the Permanent Court of International Justice, the matter shall, as between the parties to the present Statute, be referred to the International Court of Justice.

ARTICLE 38

1. The Court, whose function is to decide in accordance with international law such disputes as are submitted to it, shall apply:

a. international conventions, whether general or particular, establishing rules expressly recognized by the contesting states;

b. international custom, as evidence of a general practice accepted as law;

c. the general principles of law recognized by civilized nations;

d. subject to the provisions of Article 59, judicial decisions and the teachings of the most highly qualified publicists of the various nations, as subsidiary means for the determination of rules of law.

2. This provision shall not prejudice the power of the Court to decide a case *ex aequo et bono,* if the parties agree thereto.

CHAPTER III. PROCEDURE

ARTICLE 39

1. The official languages of the Court shall be French and English. If the parties agree that the case shall be conducted in French, the judgment shall be delivered in French. If the parties agree that the case shall be conducted in English, the judgment shall be delivered in English.

2. In the absence of an agreement as to which language shall be employed, each party may, in the pleadings, use the language which it prefers; the decision of the Court shall be given in French and English. In this case the Court shall at the same time determine which of the two texts shall be considered as authoritative.

3. The Court shall, at the request of any party, authorize a language other than French or English to be used by that party.

ARTICLE 40

1. Cases are brought before the Court, as the case may be, either by the notification of the special agreement or by a written application addressed to the Registrar. In either case the subject of the dispute and the parties shall be indicated.

2. The Registrar shall forthwith communicate the application to all concerned.

3. He shall also notify the Members of the United Nations through the Secretary-General, and also any other states entitled to appear before the Court.

ARTICLE 41

1. The Court shall have the power to indicate, if it considers that circumstances so require, any provisional measures which ought to be taken to preserve the respective rights of either party.

2. Pending the final decision, notice of the measures suggested shall forthwith be given to the parties and to the Security Council.

ARTICLE 42

1. The parties shall be represented by agents.

2. They may have the assistance of counsel or advocates before the Court.

3. The agents, counsel, and advocates of parties before the Court shall

enjoy the privileges and immunities necessary to the independent exercise of their duties.

ARTICLE 43

1. The procedure shall consist of two parts: written and oral.

2. The written proceedings shall consist of the communication to the Court and to the parties of memorials, counter-memorials and, if necessary, replies; also all papers and documents in support.

3. These communications shall be made through the Registrar, in the order and within the time fixed by the Court.

4. A certified copy of every document produced by one party shall be communicated to the other party.

5. The oral proceedings shall consist of the hearing by the Court of witnesses, experts, agents, counsel, and advocates.

ARTICLE 44

1. For the service of all notices upon persons other than the agents, counsel, and advocates, the Court shall apply direct to the government of the state upon whose territory the notice has to be served.

2. The same provision shall apply whenever steps are to be taken to procure evidence on the spot.

ARTICLE 45

The hearing shall be under the control of the President or, if he is unable to preside, of the Vice-President; if neither is able to preside, the senior judge present shall preside.

ARTICLE 46

The hearing in Court shall be public, unless the Court shall decide otherwise, or unless the parties demand that the public be not admitted.

ARTICLE 47

1. Minutes shall be made at each hearing and signed by the Registrar and the President.

2. These minutes alone shall be authentic.

ARTICLE 48

The Court shall make orders for the conduct of the case, shall decide the form and time in which each party must conclude its arguments, and make all arrangements connected with the taking of evidence.

ARTICLE 49

The Court may, even before the hearing begins, call upon the agents to produce any document or to supply any explanations. Formal note shall be taken of any refusal.

ARTICLE 50

The Court may, at any time, entrust any individual, body, bureau, commission, or other organization that it may select, with the task of carrying out an enquiry or giving an expert opinion.

ARTICLE 51

During the hearing any relevant questions are to be put to the witnesses and experts under the conditions laid down by the Court in the rules of procedure referred to in Article 30.

ARTICLE 52

After the Court has received the proofs and evidence within the time specified for the purpose, it may refuse to accept any further oral or written evidence that one party may desire to present unless the other side consents.

ARTICLE 53

1. Whenever one of the parties does not appear before the Court, or fails to defend its case, the other party may call upon the Court to decide in favor of its claim.

2. The Court must, before doing so, satisfy itself, not only that it has jurisdiction in accordance with Articles 36 and 37, but also that the claim is well founded in fact and law.

ARTICLE 54

1. When, subject to the control of the Court, the agents, counsel, and advocates have completed their presentation of the case, the President shall declare the hearing closed.

2. The Court shall withdraw to consider the judgment.

3. The deliberations of the Court shall take place in private and remain secret.

ARTICLE 55

1. All questions shall be decided by a majority of the judges present.

2. In the event of an equality of votes, the President or the judge who acts in his place shall have a casting vote.

ARTICLE 56

1. The judgment shall state the reasons on which it is based.

2. It shall contain the names of the judges who have taken part in the decision.

ARTICLE 57

If the judgment does not represent in whole or in part the unanimous opinion of the judges, any judge shall be entitled to deliver a separate opinion.

ARTICLE 58

The judgment shall be signed by the President and by the Registrar. It shall be read in open court, due notice having been given to the agents.

ARTICLE 59

The decision of the Court has no binding force except between the parties and in respect of that particular case.

ARTICLE 60

The judgment is final and without appeal. In the event of dispute as to the meaning or scope of the judgment, the Court shall construe it upon the request of any party.

ARTICLE 61

1. An application for revision of a judgment may be made only when it is based upon the discovery of some fact of such a nature as to be a decisive factor, which fact was, when the judgment was given, unknown to the Court and also to the party claiming revision, always provided that such ignorance was not due to negligence.

2. The proceedings for revision shall be opened by a judgment of the Court expressly recording the existence of the new fact, recognizing that it has such a character as to lay the case open to revision, and declaring the application admissible on this ground.

3. The Court may require previous compliance with the terms of the judgment before it admits proceedings in revision.

4. The application for revision must be made at latest within six months of the discovery of the new fact.

5. No application for revision may be made after the lapse of ten years from the date of the judgment.

ARTICLE 62

1. Should a state consider that it has an interest of a legal nature which may be affected by the decision in the case, it may submit a request to the Court to be permitted to intervene.

2. It shall be for the Court to decide upon this request.

ARTICLE 63

1. Whenever the construction of a convention to which states other than those concerned in the case are parties is in question, the Registrar shall notify all such states forthwith.

2. Every state so notified has the right to intervene in the proceedings; but if it uses this right, the construction given by the judgment will be equally binding upon it.

ARTICLE 64

Unless otherwise decided by the Court, each party shall bear its own costs.

CHAPTER IV. ADVISORY OPINIONS

ARTICLE 65

1. The Court may give an advisory opinion on any legal question at the request of whatever body may be authorized by or in accordance with the Charter of the United Nations to make such a request.

2. Questions upon which the advisory opinion of the Court is asked shall be laid before the Court by means of a written request containing an exact statement of the question upon which an opinion is required, and accompanied by all documents likely to throw light upon the question.

ARTICLE 66

1. The Registrar shall forthwith give notice of the request for an advisory opinion to all states entitled to appear before the Court.

2. The Registrar shall also, by means of a special and direct communication, notify any state entitled to appear before the Court or international organization considered by the Court, or, should it not be sitting, by the President, as likely to be able to furnish information on the question, that the Court will be prepared to receive, within a time limit to be fixed by the President, written statements, or to hear, at a public sitting to be held for the purpose, oral statements relating to the question.

3. Should any such state entitled to appear before the Court have failed to receive the special communication referred to in paragraph 2 of this Article, such state may express a desire to submit a written statement or to be heard; and the Court will decide.

4. States and organizations having presented written or oral statements or both shall be permitted to comment on the statements made by other states or organizations in the form, to the extent, and within the time limits which the Court, or, should it not be sitting, the President, shall decide in each particular case. Accordingly, the Registrar shall in due time communicate any such written statements to states and organizations having submitted similar statements.

ARTICLE 67

The Court shall deliver its advisory opinions in open court, notice having been given to the Secretary-General and to the representatives of Members of the United Nations, of other states and of international organizations immediately concerned.

ARTICLE 68

In the exercise of its advisory functions the Court shall further be guided by the provisions of the present Statute which apply in contentious cases to the extent to which it recognizes them to be applicable.

CHAPTER V. AMENDMENT

ARTICLE 69

Amendments to the present Statute shall be effected by the same procedure as is provided by the Charter of the United Nations for amendments to that Charter, subject however to any provisions which the General Assembly upon recommendation of the Security Council may adopt concerning the participation of states which are parties to the present Statute but are not Members of the United Nations.

ARTICLE 70

The Court shall have power to propose such amendments to the present Statute as it may deem necessary, through written communications to the Secretary-General, for consideration in conformity with the provisions of Article 69.

◇◇◇◇◇◇

23. ACCEPTANCE OF COMPULSORY JURISDICTION OF INTERNATIONAL COURT OF JUSTICE, AUGUST 2, 1946

Senate Resolution 196—Seventy-ninth Congress

[Article 36 of the Statute of the International Court of Justice provides that any party to the Statute may accept the compulsory jurisdiction of the Court with respect to legal disputes that may arise in the future. On August 2, 1946, the Senate advised the President to make such a declaration on behalf of the United States. While the Senate resolution has been criticized because it exempts disputes within the domestic jurisdiction of the United States as determined by the United States, it was an important step forward in establishing the rule of law in the world. It was, in fact, a dramatic departure from the position the United States took in the inter-war years with respect to the judicial settlement of disputes when we refused even to become a member of the Permanent Court of International Justice.]

Resolved (*two-thirds of the Senators present concurring therein*), That the Senate advise and consent to the deposit by the President of the United States with the Secretary-General of the United Nations, of a declaration under paragraph 2 of article 36 of the Statute of the International Court of Justice recognizing as compulsory ipso facto and without special agreement, in relation to any other state accepting the same obligation, the jurisdiction of the International Court of Justice in all legal disputes hereafter arising concerning—

    a. the interpretation of a treaty;

    b. any question of international law;

    c. the existence of any fact which, if established, would constitute a breach of an international obligation;

    d. the nature or extent of the reparation to be made for the breach of an international obligation.

Provided, That such declaration shall not apply to—

    a. disputes the solution of which the parties shall entrust to other tribunals by virtue of agreements already in existence or which may be concluded in the future;

    b. disputes with regard to matters which are essentially within the domestic jurisdiction of the United States as determined by the United States; or

    c. disputes arising under a multilateral treaty, unless (1) all parties to the treaty affected by the decision are also parties to the case before the Court, or (2) the United States specially agrees to jurisdiction.

Provided further, That such declaration shall remain in force for a period of five years and thereafter until the expiration of six months after notice may be given to terminate the declaration.

◇◇◇◇◇◇

24. UNITED NATIONS PARTICIPATION ACT AS AMENDED [1]

AN ACT To provide for the appointment of representatives of the United States in the organs and agencies of the United Nations, and to make other provision with respect to the participation of the United States in such organization

[This 1945 act grants to the President the authority necessary for the effective participation of the United States in the United Nations. It was amended in 1949 so as to increase the strength of our mission to the United Nations and to enable our Government to coöperate with United Nations agencies (such as the Korean and Palestine Commissions) working in the field for the peaceful settlement of disputes. It will be noted that Section 6 of the Act has never become operative because no agreements have been concluded with the Security Council relating to the use of our armed forces under Article 43 of the Charter.]

Be it enacted by the Senate and House of Representatives of the United States of America in Congress assembled, That this Act may be cited as the "United Nations Participation Act of 1945."

SEC. 2. (a) The President, by and with the advice and consent of the Senate, shall appoint a representative and a deputy representative of the United States to the United Nations, both of whom shall have the rank and status of envoy extraordinary and ambassador plenipotentiary and shall hold office at the pleasure of the President. Such representative and deputy representative shall represent the United States in the Security Council of the United Nations and may serve ex officio as United States representative on any organ, commission, or other body of the United Nations other than specialized agencies of the United Nations, and shall perform such other functions in connection with the participation of the United States in the United Nations as the President may from time to time direct.

(b) The President, by and with the advice and consent of the Senate, shall appoint an additional deputy representative of the United States to the Security Council who shall hold office at the pleasure of the President. Such deputy representative shall represent the United States in the Security Council of the United Nations in the event of the absence or disability of both the representative and the deputy representative of the United States to the United Nations.

(c) The President, by and with the advice and consent of the Senate, shall designate from time to time to attend a specified session or specified sessions of the General Assembly of the United Nations not to exceed five representatives of the United States and such number of alternates as he may determine consistent with the rules of procedure of the General Assembly. One of the representatives shall be designated as the senior representative.

(d) The President may also appoint from time to time such other persons as he may deem necessary to represent the United States in the organs and agencies of the United Nations, but the representative of the United

States in the Economic and Social Council and in the Trusteeship Council of the United Nations shall be appointed only by and with the advice and consent of the Senate, except that the President may, without the advice and consent of the Senate, designate any officer of the United States to act, without additional compensation, as the representative of the United States in either such Council (A) at any specified session thereof, where the position is vacant or in the absence or disability of the regular representative, or (B) in connection with a specified subject matter at any specified session of either such Council in lieu of the regular representative. The President may designate any officer of the Department of State, whose appointment is subject to confirmation by the Senate, to act, without additional compensation, for temporary periods as the representative of the United States in the Security Council of the United Nations in the absence or disability of the representative and deputy representatives appointed under section 2 (a) and (b) or in lieu of such representatives in connection with a specified subject matter. The advice and consent of the Senate shall be required for the appointment by the President of the representative of the United States in any commission that may be formed by the United Nations with respect to atomic energy or in any other commission of the United Nations to which the United States is entitled to appoint a representative.

(e) Nothing contained in this section shall preclude the President or the Secretary of State, at the direction of the President, from representing the United States at any meeting or session of any organ or agency of the United Nations.

(f) All persons appointed in pursuance of authority contained in this section shall receive compensation at rates determined by the President upon the basis of duties to be performed but not in excess of rates authorized by sections 411 and 412 of the Foreign Service Act of 1946 (Public Law 724, Seventy-ninth Congress) for chiefs of mission and Foreign Service officers occupying positions of equivalent importance, except that no Member of the Senate or House of Representatives or officer of the United States who is designated under subsections (c) and (d) of this section as a representative of the United States or as an alternate to attend any specified session or specified sessions of the General Assembly shall be entitled to receive such compensation.

SEC. 3. The representatives provided for in section 2 hereof, when representing the United States in the respective organs and agencies of the United Nations, shall, at all times, act in accordance with the instructions of the President transmitted by the Secretary of State unless other means of transmission is directed by the President, and such representatives shall, in accordance with such instructions, cast any and all votes under the Charter of the United Nations.

SEC. 4. The President shall, from time to time as occasion may require, but not less than once each year, make reports to the Congress of the activities of the United Nations and of the participation of the United States therein. He shall make special current reports on decisions of the Security Council to take enforcement measures under the provisions of the Charter of the United Nations, and on the participation therein under his instructions, of the representative of the United States.

SEC. 5. (a) Notwithstanding the provisions of any other law, whenever the United States is called upon by the Security Council to apply measures which said Council has decided, pursuant to article 41 of said Charter, are to be employed to give effect to its decisions under said Charter, the President may, to the extent necessary to apply such measures, through any agency which he may designate, and under such orders, rules, and regulations as may be prescribed by him, investigate, regulate, or prohibit, in whole or in part, economic relations or rail, sea, air, postal, telegraphic, radio, and other means of communication between any foreign country or any national thereof or any person therein and the United States or any person subject to the jurisdiction thereof, or involving any property subject to the jurisdiction of the United States.

(b) Any person who willfully violates or evades or attempts to violate or evade any order, rule, or regulation issued by the President pursuant to paragraph (a) of this section shall, upon conviction, be fined not more than $10,000 or, if a natural person, be imprisoned for not more than ten years, or both; and the officer, director, or agent of any corporation who knowingly participates in such violation or evasion shall be punished by a like fine, imprisonment, or both, and any property, funds, securities, papers, or other articles or documents, or any vessel, together with her tackle, apparel, furniture, and equipment, or vehicle or aircraft, concerned in such violation shall be forfeited to the United States.

SEC. 6. The President is authorized to negotiate a special agreement or agreements with the Security Council which shall be subject to the approval of the Congress by appropriate Act or joint resolution, providing for the numbers and types of armed forces, their degree of readiness and general location, and the nature of facilities and assistance, including rights of passage, to be made available to the Security Council on its call for the purpose of maintaining international peace and security in accordance with article 43 of said Charter. The President shall not be deemed to require the authorization of the Congress to make available to the Security Council on its call in order to take action under article 42 of said Charter and pursuant to such special agreement or agreements the armed forces, facilities, or assistance provided for therein: *Provided,* That, except as authorized in section 7 of this Act, nothing herein contained shall be construed as an authorization to the President by the Congress to make available to the Security Council for such purpose armed forces, facilities, or assistance in addition to the forces, facilities, and assistance provided for in such special agreement or agreements.

SEC. 7. (a) Notwithstanding the provisions of any other law, the President, upon the request by the United Nations for cooperative action, and to the extent that he finds that it is consistent with the national interest to comply with such request, may authorize, in support of such activities of the United Nations as are specifically directed to the peaceful settlement of disputes and not involving the employment of armed forces contemplated by chapter VII of the United Nations Charter—

(1) the detail to the United Nations, under such terms and conditions as the President shall determine, of personnel of the armed forces of the United States to serve as observers, guards, or in any

noncombatant capacity, but in no event shall more than a total of one thousand of such personnel be so detailed at any one time: *Provided,* That while so detailed, such personnel shall be considered for all purposes as acting in the line of duty, including the receipt of pay and allowances as personnel of the armed forces of the United States, credit for longevity and retirement, and all other perquisites appertaining to such duty: *Provided further,* That upon authorization or approval by the President, such personnel may accept directly from the United Nations (a) any or all of the allowances or perquisites to which they are entitled under the first proviso hereof, and (b) extraordinary expenses and perquisites incident to such detail;

(2) the furnishing of facilities, services, or other assistance and the loan of the agreed fair share of the United States of any supplies and equipment to the United Nations by the National Military Establishment, under such terms and conditions as the President shall determine;

(3) the obligation, insofar as necessary to carry out the purposes of clauses (1) and (2) of this subsection, of any funds appropriated to the National Military Establishment or any department therein, the procurement of such personnel, supplies, equipment, facilities, services, or other assistance as may be made available in accordance with the request of the United Nations, and the replacement of such items, when necessary, where they are furnished from stocks.

(b) Whenever personnel or assistance is made available pursuant to the authority contained in subsection (a) (1) and (2) of this section, the President shall require reimbursement from the United Nations for the expense thereby incurred by the United States: *Provided,* That in exceptional circumstances, or when the President finds it to be in the national interest, he may waive, in whole or in part, the requirement of such reimbursement: *Provided further,* That when any such reimbursement is made, it shall be credited, at the option of the appropriate department of the National Military Establishment, either to the appropriation, fund, or account utilized in incurring the obligation, or to an appropriate appropriation, fund, or account currently available for the purposes for which expenditures were made.

(c) In addition to the authorization of appropriations to the Department of State contained in section 8 of this Act, there is hereby authorized to be appropriated to the National Military Establishment, or any department therein, such sums as may be necessary to reimburse such Establishment or department in the event that reimbursement from the United Nations is waived in whole or in part pursuant to authority contained in subsection (b) of this section.

(d) Nothing in this Act shall authorize the disclosure of any information or knowledge in any case in which such disclosure is prohibited by any other law of the United States.

SEC. 8. There is hereby authorized to be appropriated annually to the Department of State, out of any money in the Treasury not otherwise appropriated, such sums as may be necessary for the payment by the United States of its share of the expenses of the United Nations as apportioned by the General Assembly in accordance with article 17 of the Charter, and for all necessary salaries and expenses of the representatives provided for in section 2 hereof, and of their appropriate staffs.

* * *

◇◇◇◇◇◇

25. INTERNATIONAL ORGANIZATIONS IMMUNITIES ACT [1]

[Following World War II, when the United Nations and certain other international organizations established their headquarters in the United States, it became necessary to extend to such organizations certain privileges and immunities—relating to taxation, immunity from suit, property rights, and so on—so they could perform their functions effectively. The International Organizations Immunities Act lays down the scope of these privileges and immunities, and the conditions under which they are to be granted or revoked.]

AN ACT To extend certain privileges, exemptions, and immunities to international organizations and to the officers and employees thereof, and for other purposes

Be it enacted by the Senate and House of Representatives of the United States of America in Congress assembled,

TITLE I

SECTION 1. For the purposes of this title, the term "international organization" means a public international organization in which the United States participates pursuant to any treaty or under the authority of any Act of Congress authorizing such participation or making an appropriation for such participation, and which shall have been designated by the President through appropriate Executive order as being entitled to enjoy the privileges, exemptions, and immunities herein provided. The President shall be authorized, in the light of the functions performed by any such international organization, by appropriate Executive order to withhold or withdraw from any such organization or its officers or employees any of the privileges, exemptions, and immunities provided for in this title (including the amendments made by this title) or to condition or limit the enjoyment by any such organization or its officers or employees of any such privilege, exemption, or immunity. The President shall be authorized, if in his judgment such action should be justified by reason of the abuse by an international organization or its officers and employees of the privileges, exemptions, and immunities herein provided or for any other reason, at any time to revoke the designation of any international organization under this section, whereupon the international organization in question shall cease to be classed as an international organization for the purposes of this title.

[1] Public Law 291, 79th Cong., 1st sess., H. R. 4489.

SEC. 2. International organizations shall enjoy the status, immunities, exemptions, and privileges set forth in this section, as follows:

(a) International organizations shall, to the extent consistent with the instrument creating them, possess the capacity—

(i) to contract;

(ii) to acquire and dispose of real and personal property;

(iii) to institute legal proceedings.

(b) International organizations, their property and their assets, wherever located, and by whomsoever held, shall enjoy the same immunity from suit and every form of judicial process as is enjoyed by foreign governments, except to the extent that such organizations may expressly waive their immunity for the purpose of any proceedings or by the terms of any contract.

(c) Property and assets of international organizations, wherever located and by whomsoever held, shall be immune from search, unless such immunity be expressly waived, and from confiscation. The archives of international organizations shall be inviolable.

(d) Insofar as concerns customs duties and internal-revenue taxes imposed upon or by reason of importation, and the procedures in connection therewith; the registration of foreign agents; and the treatment of official communications, the privileges, exemptions, and immunities to which international organizations shall be entitled shall be those accorded under similar circumstances to foreign governments.

SEC. 3. Pursuant to regulations prescribed by the Commissioner of Customs with the approval of the Secretary of the Treasury, the baggage and effects of alien officers and employees of international organizations, or of aliens designated by foreign governments to serve as their representatives in or to such organizations, or of the families, suites, and servants of such officers, employees, or representatives shall be admitted (when imported in connection with the arrival of the owner) free of customs duties and free of internal-revenue taxes imposed upon or by reason of importation.

(Section 4 provides for amendments of the Internal Revenue Code in order to extend exemptions from Federal taxation to international organizations and their officers and employees.)

(Section 5 amends the Social Security Act to remove from covered employment services performed in the employ of an international organization, paralleling the employment-tax exemptions accorded by section 4. Provisions are made for refunding taxes collected prior to the effective date, January 1, 1946, of the exemptions and for excepting services rendered prior to that date.)

SEC. 6. International organizations shall be exempt from all property taxes imposed by, or under the authority of, any Act of Congress, including such Acts as are applicable solely to the District of Columbia or the Territories.

(Section 7 provides that alien officers and employees of international organizations and representatives of foreign governments therein shall enjoy the same privileges as officials of foreign governments in respect of laws regulating entering into and departure from the United States, alien registration and fingerprinting, registration of foreign agents, and selective training and service. The immigration laws are amended accordingly and, under section 7 (d) and 8 (b), the same procedure for deportation is made applicable to alien officers and employees of international organizations as in the case of officials of foreign governments.

(Under section 7 (b), all officials of international organizations, including American citizens, and representatives of foreign governments therein, are granted immunity from suit and legal process for acts performed in their official capacity. It should be noted that under this provision and section 8 (c) there is not extended full diplomatic immunity from judicial process as in the case of diplomatic officers.)

SEC. 8. (a) No person shall be entitled to the benefits of this title unless he (1) shall have been duly notified to and accepted by the Secretary of State as a representative, officer, or employee; or (2) shall have been designated by the Secretary of State, prior to formal notification and acceptance, as a prospective representative, officer, or employee; or (3) is a member of the family or suite, or servant, of one of the foregoing accepted or designated representatives, officers, or employees.

(b) Should the Secretary of State determine that the continued presence in the United States of any person entitled to the benefits of this title is not desirable, he shall so inform the foreign government or international organization concerned, as the case may be, and after such person shall have had a reasonable length of time, to be determined by the Secretary of State, to depart from the United States, he shall cease to be entitled to such benefits.

(c) No person shall, by reason of the provisions of this title, be considered as receiving diplomatic status or as receiving any of the privileges incident thereto other than such as are specifically set forth herein.

SEC. 9. The privileges, exemptions, and immunities of international organizations and of their officers and employees, and members of their families, suites, and servants, provided for in this title, shall be granted notwithstanding the fact that the similar privileges, exemptions, and immunities granted to a foreign government, its officers, or employees, may be conditioned upon the existence of reciprocity by that foreign government: *Provided*, That nothing contained in this title shall be construed as precluding the Secretary of State from withdrawing the privileges, exemptions, and immunities herein provided from persons who are nationals of any foreign country on the ground that such country is failing to accord corresponding privileges, exemptions, and immunities to citizens of the United States.

SEC. 10. This title may be cited as the "International Organizations Immunities Act."

TITLE II

(Title II is omitted because it bears no direct relationship to the International Organizations Immunities Act.)

✧✧✧✧✧✧

26. HEADQUARTERS OF THE UNITED NATIONS

(a) *Agreement Between the United Nations and the United States Regarding the Headquarters of the United Nations, Signed June 26, 1947, and Approved by the General Assembly October 31, 1947* [1]

[The location of a great international agency like the United Nations in the United States obviously raises many questions involving relations between the Organization and federal, state, and local authorities. What law is to be applied in the headquarters district? Suppose the United Nations wishes to establish its own postal system or its own aerodrome? Arrangements with respect to these and related problems were carefully worked out and incorporated in the Headquarters Agreement concluded between the United States and the United Nations in 1947. Federal, state, and local officials took part in the negotiations.]

The General Assembly,

Whereas the Secretary-General pursuant to resolution 99 (I) of 14 December 1946 signed with the Secretary of State of the United States of America on 26 June 1947 an Agreement between the United Nations and the United States of America regarding the Headquarters of the United Nations; and

Whereas the Secretary-General in accordance with the said Resolution has submitted the said Agreement to the General Assembly;

Having studied the report prepared on this matter by the Sixth Committee;

Endorses the opinions expressed therein;

Approves the Agreement signed on 26 June 1947; and

Authorizes the Secretary-General to bring that Agreement into force in the manner provided in Section 28 thereof and to perform on behalf of the United Nations such acts or functions as may be required by that Agreement.

The United Nations and the United States of America:

Desiring to conclude an agreement for the purpose of carrying out the resolution adopted by the General Assembly on 14 December 1946 to establish the seat of the United Nations in the City of New York and to regulate questions arising as a result thereof;

Have appointed as their representatives for this purpose:

The United Nations:

Trygve LIE, Secretary-General, and

The United States of America:

George C. MARSHALL, Secretary of State,

Who have agreed as follows:

---

[1] The United States and the United Nations; Report by the President to the Congress for the Year 1947, Department of State publication 3024, International Organization and Conference Series III, 1, pp. 220-234

ARTICLE I. DEFINITIONS

SECTION 1

In this agreement:

(*a*) The expression "headquarters district" means:

(1) the area defined as such in Annex 1;

(2) any other lands or buildings which from time to time may be included therein by supplemental agreement with the appropriate American authorities;

(*b*) the expression "appropriate American authorities" means such federal, state, or local authorities in the United States as may be appropriate in the context and in accordance with the laws and customs of the United States, including the laws and customs of the State and local government involved;

(*c*) the expression "General Convention" means the Convention on the Privileges and Immunities of the United Nations approved by the General Assembly of the United Nations on 13 February 1946, as acceded to by the United States;

(*d*) the expression "United Nations" means the international organization established by the Charter of the United Nations, hereinafter referred to as the "Charter";

(*e*) the expression "Secretary-General" means the Secretary-General of the United Nations.

ARTICLE II. THE HEADQUARTERS DISTRICT

SECTION 2

The seat of the United Nations shall be the headquarters district.

SECTION 3

The appropriate American authorities shall take whatever action may be necessary to assure that the United Nations shall not be dispossessed of its property in the headquarters district, except as provided in Section 22 in the event that the United Nations ceases to use the same, provided that the United Nations shall reimburse the appropriate American authorities for any costs incurred, after consultation with the United Nations, in liquidating by eminent domain proceedings or otherwise any adverse claims.

SECTION 4

(*a*) The United Nations may establish and operate in the headquarters district:

(1) its own short-wave sending and receiving radio broadcasting facilities, including emergency link equipment, which may be used on the same frequencies (within the tolerances prescribed for the broadcasting service by applicable United States regulations) for radio-telegraph, radio-teletype, radio-telephone, radio-telephoto, and similar services;

(2) one point-to-point circuit between the headquarters district and

the office of the United Nations in Geneva (using single sideband equipment) to be used exclusively for the exchange of broadcasting programmes and inter-office communications;

(3) low power; micro wave, low or medium frequencies, facilities for communication within headquarters buildings only, or such other buildings as may temporarily be used by the United Nations;

(4) facilities for point-to-point communications to the same extent and subject to the same conditions as committed under applicable rules and regulations for amateur operation in the United States except that such rules and regulations shall not be applied in a manner inconsistent with the inviolability of the headquarters district provided by Section 9 (a);

(5) such other radio facilities as may be specified by supplemental agreement between the United Nations and the appropriate American authorities.

(b) The United Nations shall make arrangements for the operation of the services referred to in this section with the International Telegraph Communication Union, the appropriate agencies of the Government of the United States and the appropriate agencies of other affected Governments with regard to all frequencies and similar matters.

(c) The facilities provided for in this section may, to the extent necessary for efficient operation, be established and operated outside the headquarters district. The appropriate American authorities will, on request of the United Nations, make arrangements, on such terms and in such manner as may be agreed upon by supplemental agreement, for the acquisition or use by the United Nations of appropriate premises for such purposes and the inclusion of such premises in the headquarters district.

SECTION 5

In the event that the United Nations should find it necessary and desirable to establish and operate an aerodrome, the conditions for the location, use and operation of such an aerodrome and the conditions under which there shall be entry into and exit therefrom shall be the subject of a supplemental agreement.

SECTION 6

In the event that the United Nations should propose to organize its own postal service, the conditions under which such service shall be set up shall be the subject of a supplemental agreement.

ARTICLE III. LAW AND AUTHORITY IN THE HEADQUARTERS DISTRICT

SECTION 7

(a) The headquarters district shall be under the control and authority of the United Nations as provided in this agreement.

(b) Except as otherwise provided in this agreement or in the General Convention, the federal, state and local law of the United States shall apply within the headquarters district.

(c) Except as otherwise provided in this agreement or in the General

Convention, the federal, state and local courts of the United States shall have jurisdiction over acts done and transactions taking place in the headquarters district as provided in applicable federal, state and local laws.

(*d*) The federal, state and local courts of the United States, when dealing with cases arising out of or relating to acts done or transactions taking place in the headquarters district, shall take into account the regulations enacted by the United Nations under Section 8.

SECTION 8

The United Nations shall have the power to make regulations, operative within the headquarters district, for the purpose of establishing therein conditions in all respects necessary for the full execution of its functions. No federal, state or local law or regulation of the United States which is inconsistent with a regulation of the United Nations authorized by this section shall, to the extent of such inconsistency, be applicable within the headquarters district. Any dispute, between the United Nations and the United States, as to whether a regulation of the United Nations is authorized by this section or as to whether a federal, state or local law or regulation is inconsistent with any regulation of the United Nations authorized by this section, shall be promptly settled as provided in Section 21. Pending such settlement, the regulation of the United Nations shall apply, and the federal, state or local law or regulation shall be inapplicable in the headquarters district to the extent that the United Nations claims it to be inconsistent with the regulation of the United Nations. This section shall not prevent the reasonable application of fire protection regulations of the appropriate American authorities.

SECTION 9

(*a*) The headquarters district shall be inviolable. Federal, state or local officers or officials of the United States, whether administrative, judicial, military or police, shall not enter the headquarters district to perform any official duties therein except with the consent of and under conditions agreed to by the Secretary-General. The service of legal process, including the seizure of private property, may take place within the headquarters district only with the consent of and under conditions approved by the Secretary-General.

(*b*) Without prejudice to the provisions of the General Convention or Article IV of this agreement, the United Nations shall prevent the headquarters district from becoming a refuge either for persons who are avoiding arrest under the federal, state, or local law of the United States or are required by the Government of the United States for extradition to another country, or for persons who are endeavouring to avoid service of legal process.

SECTION 10

The United Nations may expel or exclude persons from the headquarters district for violation of its regulations adopted under Section 8 or for other cause. Persons who violate such regulations shall be subject to other penalties or to detention under arrest only in accordance with the provisions of such laws or regulations as may be adopted by the appropriate American authorities.

ARTICLE IV. COMMUNICATIONS AND TRANSIT

SECTION 11

The federal, state or local authorities of the United States shall not impose any impediments to transit to or from the headquarters district of (1) representatives of Members or officials of the United Nations, or of specialized agencies as defined in Article 57, paragraph 2, of the Charter, or the families of such representatives or officials; (2) experts performing missions for the United Nations or for such specialized agencies; (3) representatives of the press, or of radio, film or other information agencies, who have been accredited by the United Nations (or by such a specialized agency) in its discretion after consultation with the United States; (4) representatives of non-governmental organizations recognized by the United Nations for the purpose of consultation under Article 71 of the Charter; or (5) other persons invited to the headquarters district by the United Nations or by such specialized agency on official business. The appropriate American authorities shall afford any necessary protection to such persons while in transit to or from the headquarters district. This section does not apply to general interruptions of transportation which are to be dealt with as provided in Section 17, and does not impair the effectiveness of generally applicable laws and regulations as to the operation of means of transportation.

SECTION 12

The provisions of Section 11 shall be applicable irrespective of the relations existing between the Governments of the persons referred to in that section and the Government of the United States.

SECTION 13

(a) Laws and regulations in force in the United States regarding the entry of aliens shall not be applied in such manner as to interfere with the privileges referred to in Section 11. When visas are required for persons referred to in that Section, they shall be granted without charge and as promptly as possible.

(b) Laws and regulations in force in the United States regarding the residence of aliens shall not be applied in such manner as to interfere with the privileges referred to in Section 11 and, specifically, shall not be applied in such manner as to require any such person to leave the United States on account of any activities performed by him in his official capacity. In case of abuse of such privileges of residence by any such person in activities in the United States outside his official capacity, it is understood that the privileges referred to in Section 11 shall not be construed to grant him exemption from the laws and regulations of the United States regarding the continued residence of aliens, provided that:

(1) No proceedings shall be instituted under such laws or regulations to require any such person to leave the United States except with the prior approval of the Secretary of State of the United States. Such approval shall be given only after consultation with the appropriate Member in the case of a representative of a Member (or a member of his family) or with the Secretary-General or the principal executive officer of the appropriate specialized agency in the case of any other person referred to in Section 11;

(2) A representative of the Member concerned, the Secretary-General or the principal Executive Officer of the appropriate specialized agency, as the case may be, shall have the right to appear in any such proceedings on behalf of the person against whom they are instituted;

(3) Persons who are entitled to diplomatic privileges and immunities under Section 15 or under the General Convention shall not be required to leave the United States otherwise than in accordance with the customary procedure applicable to diplomatic envoys accredited to the United States.

(c) This section does not prevent the requirement of reasonable evidence to establish that persons claiming the rights granted by Section 11 come within the classes described in that section, or the reasonable application of quarantine and health regulations.

(d) Except as provided above in this section and in the General Convention, the United States retains full control and authority over the entry of persons or property into the territory of the United States and the conditions under which persons may remain or reside there.

(e) The Secretary-General shall, at the request of the appropriate American authorities, enter into discussions with such authorities, with a view to making arrangements for registering the arrival and departure of persons who have been granted visas valid only for transit to and from the headquarters district and sojourn therein and in its immediate vicinity.

(f) The United Nations shall, subject to the foregoing provisions of this section, have the exclusive right to authorize or prohibit entry of persons and property into the headquarters district and to prescribe the conditions under which persons may remain or reside there.

SECTION 14

The Secretary-General and the appropriate American authorities shall, at the request of either of them, consult as to methods of facilitating entrance into the United States, and the use of available means of transportation, by persons coming from abroad who wish to visit the headquarters district and do not enjoy the rights referred to in this Article.

ARTICLE V. RESIDENT REPRESENTATIVES TO THE UNITED NATIONS

SECTION 15

(1) Every person designated by a Member as the principal resident representative to the United Nations of such Member or as a resident representative with the rank of ambassador or minister plenipotentiary,

(2) Such resident members of their staffs as may be agreed upon between the Secretary-General, the Government of the United States and the Government of the Member concerned,

(3) Every person designated by a Member of a specialized agency, as defined in Article 57, paragraph 2, of the Charter, as its principal resident representative, with the rank of ambassador or minister plenipotentiary at the headquarters of such agency in the United States, and

(4) Such other principal resident representatives of members of a specialized agency and such resident members of the staffs of representatives of a specialized agency as may be agreed upon between the principal executive

officer of the specialized agency, the Government of the United States and the Government of the Member concerned, shall whether residing inside or outside the headquarters district, be entitled in the territory of the United States to the same privileges and immunities, subject to corresponding conditions and obligations, as it accords to diplomatic envoys accredited to it. In the case of Members whose governments are not recognized by the United States, such privileges and immunities need be extended to such representatives, or persons on the staffs of such representatives, only within the headquarters district, at their residences and offices outside the district, in transit between the district and such residences and offices, and in transit on official business to or from foreign countries.

ARTICLE VI. POLICE PROTECTION OF THE HEADQUARTERS DISTRICT

SECTION 16

(a) The appropriate American authorities shall exercise due diligence to to ensure that the tranquillity of the headquarters district is not disturbed by the unauthorized entry of groups of persons from outside or by disturbances in its immediate vicinity and shall cause to be provided on the boundaries of the headquarters district such police protection as is required for these purposes.

(b) If so requested by the Secretary-General, the appropriate American authorities shall provide a sufficient number of police for the preservation of law and order in the headquarters district, and for the removal therefrom of persons as requested under the authority of the United Nations. The United Nations shall, if requested, enter into arrangements with the appropriate American authorities to reimburse them for the reasonable cost of such services.

ARTICLE VII. PUBLIC SERVICES AND PROTECTION OF THE HEADQUARTERS DISTRICT

SECTION 17

(a) The appropriate American authorities will exercise to the extent requested by the Secretary-General the powers which they possess with respect to the supplying of public services to ensure that the headquarters district shall be supplied on equitable terms with the necessary public services, including electricity, water, gas, post, telephone, telegraph, transportation, drainage, collection of refuse, fire protection, snow removal, et cetera. In case of any interruption or threatened interruption of any such services, the appropriate American authorities will consider the needs of the United Nations as being of equal importance with the similar needs of essential agencies of the Government of the United States, and will take steps accordingly, to ensure that the work of the United Nations is not prejudiced.

(b) Special provisions with reference to maintenance of utilities and underground construction are contained in Annex 2.

SECTION 18

The appropriate American authorities shall take all reasonable steps to ensure that the amenities of the headquarters district are not prejudiced and the purposes for which the district is required are not obstructed by any use made of the land in the vicinity of the district. The United Nations shall on its part take all reasonable steps to ensure that the amenities of the land in the vicinity of the headquarters district are not prejudiced by any use made of the land in the headquarters district by the United Nations.

SECTION 19

It is agreed that no form of racial or religious discrimination shall be permitted within the headquarters district.

ARTICLE VIII. MATTERS RELATING TO THE OPERATION OF THIS AGREEMENT

SECTION 20

The Secretary-General and the appropriate American authorities shall settle by agreement the channels through which they will communicate regarding the application of the provisions of this agreement and other questions affecting the headquarters district, and may enter into such supplemental agreements as may be necessary to fulfill the purposes of this agreement. In making supplemental agreements with the Secretary-General, the United States shall consult with the appropriate state and local authorities. If the Secretary-General so requests, the Secretary of State of the United States shall appoint a special representative for the purpose of liaison with the Secretary-General.

SECTION 21

(a) Any dispute between the United Nations and the United States concerning the interpretation or application of this agreement or of any supplemental agreement, which is not settled by negotiation or other agreed mode of settlement, shall be referred for final decision to a tribunal of three arbitrators, one to be named by the Secretary-General, one to be named by the Secretary of State of the United States, and the third to be chosen by the two, or, if they should fail to agree upon a third, then by the President of the International Court of Justice.

(b) The Secretary-General or the United States may ask the General Assembly to request of the International Court of Justice an advisory opinion on any legal question arising in the course of such proceedings. Pending the receipt of the opinion of the Court, an interim decision of the arbitral tribunal shall be observed by both parties. Thereafter, the arbitral tribunal shall render a final decision, having regard to the opinion of the Court.

ARTICLE IX. MISCELLANEOUS PROVISIONS

SECTION 22

(a) The United Nations shall not dispose of all or any part of the land owned by it in the headquarters district without the consent of the United States. If the United States is unwilling to consent to a disposition which the United Nations wishes to make of all or any part of such land, the United States shall buy the same from the United Nations at a price to be determined as provided in paragraph (d) of this section.

(b) If the seat of the United Nations is removed from the headquarters district, all right, title and interest of the United Nations in and to real property in the headquarters district or any part of it shall, on request of either the United Nations or the United States be assigned and conveyed to the United States. In the absence of such a request, the same shall be assigned and conveyed to the sub-division of a state in which it is located or, if such sub-division shall not desire it, then to the state in which it is located. If none of the foregoing desire the same, it may be disposed of as provided in paragraph (a) of this Section.

(c) If the United Nations disposes of all or any part of the headquarters district, the provisions of other sections of this agreement which apply to the headquarters district shall immediately cease to apply to the land and buildings so disposed of.

(d) The price to be paid for any conveyance under this section shall, in default of agreement, be the then fair value of the land, buildings and installations, to be determined under the procedure provided in Section 21.

SECTION 23

The seat of the United Nations shall not be removed from the headquarters district unless the United Nations should so decide.

SECTION 24

This agreement shall cease to be in force if the seat of the United Nations is removed from the territory of the United States, except for such provisions as may be applicable in connection with the orderly termination of the operations of the United Nations at its seat in the United States and the disposition of its property therein.

SECTION 25

Wherever this agreement imposes obligations on the appropriate American authorities, the Government of the United States shall have the ultimate responsibility for the fulfillment of such obligations by the appropriate American authorities.

SECTION 26

The provisions of this agreement shall be complementary to the provisions of the General Convention. In so far as any provisions of this agreement and any provisions of the General Convention relate to the same subject matter, the two provisions shall, wherever possible, be treated as complementary, so that both provisions shall be applicable and neither shall narrow the effect of the other; but in any case of absolute conflict, the provisions of this agreement shall prevail.

SECTION 27

This agreement shall be construed in the light of its primary purpose to enable the United Nations at its headquarters in the United States, fully and efficiently to discharge its responsibilities and fulfill its purposes.

SECTION 28

This agreement shall be brought into effect by an exchange of notes between the Secretary-General, duly authorized pursuant to a resolution of the General

Assembly of the United Nations, and the appropriate executive officer of the United States, duly authorized pursuant to appropriate action of the Congress.

In witness whereof the respective representatives have signed this Agreement and have affixed their seals hereto.

Done in duplicate, in the English and French languages, both authentic, at Lake Success, this twenty-sixth day of June, 1947.

ANNEX 1

The area referred to in Section 1 (*a*) (1) consists of:

(*a*) the premises bounded on the East by the westerly side of Franklin D. Roosevelt Drive, on the West by the easterly side of First Avenue, on the North by the southerly side of East Forty-Eighth Street, and on the South by the northerly side of East Forty-Second Street, all as proposed to be widened, in the Borough of Manhattan, City and State of New York, and

(*b*) an easement over Franklin D. Roosevelt Drive, above a lower limiting plane to be fixed for the construction and maintenance of an esplanade, together with the structures thereon and foundations and columns to support the same in locations below such limiting plane, the entire area to be more definitely defined by supplemental agreement between the United Nations and the United States of America.

ANNEX 2

MAINTENANCE OF UTILITIES AND UNDERGROUND CONSTRUCTION

SECTION 1

The Secretary-General agrees to provide passes to duly authorized employees of the City of New York, the State of New York, or any of their agencies or sub-divisions, for the purpose of enabling them to inspect, repair, maintain, reconstruct and relocate utilities, conduits, mains and sewers within the headquarters district.

SECTION 2

Underground constructions may be undertaken by the City of New York, or the State of New York, or any of their agencies or subdivisions, within the headquarters district only after consultation with the Secretary-General, and under conditions which shall not disturb the carrying out of the functions of the United Nations.

(b) Loan Agreement With the United States for the Construction of the Headquarters, March 23, 1948 [1]

[The present site of the United Nations was acquired through a donation by the Rockefeller family. As further evidence of the interest of the United States in the organization, in 1948 our government extended a $65,000,000 loan for the construction and furnishing of the permanent headquarters. The loan is without interest, and is to be repaid in thirty-two annual installments.]

[1] Treaties and Other International Acts Series 1899, Department of State Publication 3477.

It is hereby agreed by the Government of the United States of America and the United Nations as follows:

(1) Subject to the terms and conditions of this Agreement, the Government of the United States will lend to the United Nations a sum not to exceed in the aggregate $65,000,000. Such sum shall be expended only as authorized by the United Nations for the construction and furnishing of the permanent headquarters of the United Nations in its headquarters district in The City of New York, as defined in the Agreement Between the United States of America and the United Nations Regarding the Headquarters of the United Nations, signed at Lake Success, New York, on June 26, 1947, including the necessary architectural and engineering work, landscaping, underground construction and other appropriate improvements to the land and approaches, and for other related purposes and expenses incident thereto.

(2) Such sum, or parts thereof, will be advanced by the United States through the Secretary of State, to the United Nations upon request of the Secretary-General or other duly authorized officer of the United Nations and upon the certification of the architect or engineer in charge of construction, countersigned by the Secretary-General or other duly authorized officer, that the amount requested is required to cover payments for the purposes set forth in paragraph (1) above which either (a) have been at any time made by the United Nations, or (b) are due and payable, or (c) it is estimated will become due and payable within sixty days from the date of such request. All sums not used by the United Nations for the purposes set forth in paragraph (1) will be returned to the United States through the Secretary of State when no longer required for said purposes. No amounts will be advanced hereunder after July 1, 1951, or such later date, not after July 1, 1955, as may be agreed to by the Secretary of State.

(3) All sums advanced hereunder will be receipted for on behalf of the United Nations by the Secretary-General or other duly authorized officer of the United Nations.

(4) The United Nations will repay, without interest, to the United States the principal amount of all sums advanced hereunder, in annual payments beginning on July 1, 1951, and on the dates and in the amounts indicated, until the entire amount advanced under this agreement has been repaid as follows:

Date	Amount	Date	Amount	Date	Amount
July 1, 1951....	$1,000,000	July 1, 1962...	$2,500,000	July 1, 1973...	$2,500,000
July 1, 1952....	1,000,000	July 1, 1963...	2,500,000	July 1, 1974...	2,500,000
July 1, 1953....	1,500,000	July 1, 1964...	2,500,000	July 1, 1975...	2,500,000
July 1, 1954....	1,500,000	July 1, 1965...	2,500,000	July 1, 1976...	1,500,000
July 1, 1955....	2,000,000	July 1, 1966...	2,500,000	July 1, 1977...	1,500,000
July 1, 1956....	2,000,000	July 1, 1967...	2,500,000	July 1, 1978...	1,500,000
July 1, 1957....	2,000,000	July 1, 1968...	2,500,000	July 1, 1979...	1,500,000
July 1, 1958....	2,000,000	July 1, 1969...	2,500,000	July 1, 1980...	1,500,000
July 1, 1959....	2,000,000	July 1, 1970...	2,500,000	July 1, 1981...	1,500,000
July 1, 1960....	2,500,000	July 1, 1971...	2,500,000	July 1, 1982...	1,000,000
July 1, 1961....	2,500,000	July 1, 1972...	2,500,000		

However, in the event the United Nations does not request the entire sum of $65,000,000 available to it under this Agreement, the amount to be repaid under this paragraph will not exceed the aggregate amount advanced by the United States. All amounts payable to the United States under this paragraph will be paid, out of the ordinary budget of the United Nations, to the Secretary of State of the United States in currency of the United States which is legal tender for public debts on the date such payments are made. All sums repaid to the United States will be receipted for on behalf of the United States by the Secretary of State.

(5) The United Nations may at any time make repayments to the United States of funds advanced hereunder in excess of the annual installments as provided in paragraph (4) hereof.

(6) The United Nations agrees that, in order to give full effect to Section 22 (a) of the Agreement regarding the Headquarters of the United Nations referred to in paragraph (1) above (under which the United Nations shall not dispose of all or any part of the land owned by it in the headquarters district without the consent of the United States), it will not, without the consent of the United States, while any of the indebtedness incurred hereunder is outstanding and unpaid, create any mortgage, lien or other encumbrance on or against any of its real property in the headquarters district as defined in said Agreement. The United Nations also agrees that the United States, as a condition to giving its consent to any such disposition or encumbrance, may require the simultaneous repayment of the balance of all installments remaining unpaid hereunder.

(7) The effective date of this Agreement shall be the date on which the Government of the United States notifies the United Nations that the Congress of the United States, with the approval of the President, has made available the funds necessary to be advanced in accordance with the provisions of this Agreement.

In Witness Whereof, the Government of the United States of America, acting by and through the United States Representative to the United Nations, and the United Nations, acting by and through the Secretary-General, have respectively caused this Agreement to be duly signed in duplicate at Lake Success, New York on this 23rd day of March, 1948.

For the Government of the United States of America:

WARREN R. AUSTIN [SEAL]
United States Representative to the United Nations

For the United Nations:

TRYGVE LIE
Secretary-General

◇◇◇◇◇◇

27. ESTABLISHMENT OF AN INTERIM COMMITTEE OF THE GENERAL ASSEMBLY

Resolution of the General Assembly, November 13, 1947 [1]

[In 1947, the United States Government proposed the establishment of an Interim Committee or "Little Assembly" which was to function while the

[1] The United States and the United Nations: Report by the President to the Congress for the Year 1947, Department of State publication 3024, International Organization and Conference Series III, 1, pp. 159-162.

General Assembly was not in session. It was to be made up of one representative of each member of the United Nations, and was to aid the General Assembly in discharging its duties in the maintenance of international peace, the promotion of international coöperation in the political field, and the peaceful adjustment of situations likely to impair friendly relations among the nations. The Soviet Union argued that the establishment of such an important organ would be a violation of Article 7 of the Charter, which specifically names the principal organs of the United Nations. Although the Soviet Union and its satellites have boycotted the Committee, it has functioned since its establishment in 1947.]

The General Assembly,

Conscious of the responsibility specifically conferred upon it by the Charter in relation to matters concerning the maintenance of international peace and security (Articles 11 and 35), the promotion of international co-operation in the political field (Article 13) and the peaceful adjustment of any situations likely to impair the general welfare or friendly relations among nations (Article 14);

Deeming it necessary for the effective performance of these duties to establish an interim committee to consider such matters during the period between the closing of the present session and the opening of the next regular session of the General Assembly, and report with its conclusions to the General Assembly;

Recognizing fully the primary responsibility of the Security Council for prompt and effective action for the maintenance of international peace and security (Article 24),

Resolves, That

1. There shall be established, for the period between the closing of the present session and the opening of the next regular session of the General Assembly, an Interim Committee on which each Member of the General Assembly shall have the right to appoint one representative;

2. The Interim Committee, as a subsidiary organ of the General Assembly established in accordance with Article 22 of the Charter, shall assist the General Assembly in the performance of its functions by discharging the following duties:

(*a*) To consider and report, with its conclusions, to the General Assembly on such matters as have been referred to it by the General Assembly;

(*b*) To consider and report with its conclusions to the General Assembly on any dispute or any situation which, in virtue of Articles 11 (paragraph 2), 14 or 35 of the Charter, has been proposed for inclusion in the agenda of the General Assembly by any Member of the United Nations or brought before the General Assembly by the Security Council, provided the Committee previously determines the matter to be both important and requiring preliminary study. Such determination shall be made by a majority of two-thirds of the members present and voting, unless the matter is one referred by the Security Council under Article 11 (paragraph 2), in which case a simple majority will suffice;

(*c*) To consider, as it deems useful and advisable, and report with its conclusions to the General Assembly on methods to be adopted to give effect to that part of Article 11 (paragraph 1), which deals with the general principles of co-operation in the maintenance of international peace and security, and to that part of Article 13 (paragraph 1a), which deals with the promotion of international co-operation in the political field;

(*d*) To consider, in connexion with any matter under discussion by the Interim Committee, whether occasion may require the summoning of a special session of the General Assembly and, if it deems that such session is required, so to advise the Secretary-General in order that he may obtain the views of the Members of the United Nations thereon;

(*e*) To conduct investigations and appoint commissions of enquiry within the scope of its duties, as it may deem useful and necessary, provided that decisions to conduct such investigations or enquiries shall be made by a two-thirds majority of the members present and voting. An investigation or enquiry elsewhere than at the headquarters of the United Nations shall not be conducted without the consent of the State or States in whose territory it is to take place;

(*f*) To report to the next regular session of the General Assembly on the advisability of establishing a permanent committee of the General Assembly to perform the duties of the Interim Committee as stated above with any changes considered desirable in the light of experience;

3. In discharging its duties the Interim Committee shall at all times take into account the responsibilities of the Security Council under the Charter for the maintenance of international peace and security as well as the duties assigned by the Charter or by the General Assembly or by the Security Council to other Councils or to any committee or commission. The Interim Committee shall not consider any matter of which the Security Council is seized;

4. Subject to paragraphs 2 (*b*) and 2 (*e*) above, the rules of procedure of the General Assembly shall, so far as they are applicable, govern the proceedings of the Interim Committee and such sub-committees and commissions as it may set up. The Interim Committee shall, however, have authority to adopt such additional rules as it may deem necessary provided that they are not inconsistent with any of the rules of procedure of the General Assembly. The Interim Committee shall be convened by the Secretary-General not later than six weeks following the close of the second regular session of the General Assembly. It shall meet as and when it deems necessary for the conduct of its business;

5. The Secretary-General shall provide the necessary facilities and assign appropriate staff as required for the work of the Interim Committee, its sub-committees and commissions.[1]

---

[1] The Interim Committee was reëstablished by resolutions of the General Assembly of December 3, 1948, and November 21, 1949. See Press Release PGA/100, pt. I, pp. 11-13, and Press Release GA/600, pt. II, pp. 7-8.

◇◇◇◇◇◇

28. UNITING FOR PEACE

Resolution Adopted by the General Assembly, November 3, 1950 [1]

[The Uniting for Peace Resolution is important in the evolution of the United Nations because it alters the basic relationship between the General Assembly and the Security Council in the maintenance of world peace. The resolution is based, in large part, upon the lessons learned in Korea. Its main purpose is to organize the General Assembly so it can convene more quickly and act with greater effectiveness against an aggressor in the event the Security Council is prevented from acting because of the veto. The General Assembly approved the resolution in November 1950 by a vote of 52 to 5 with two abstentions.]

RESOLUTION A

The General Assembly,

RECOGNIZING that the first two stated Purposes of the United Nations are:

"To maintain international peace and security, and to that end: to take effective collective measures for the prevention and removal of threats to the peace, and for the suppression of acts of aggression or other breaches of the peace, and to bring about by peaceful means, and in conformity with the principles of justice and international law, adjustment or settlement of international disputes or situations which might lead to a breach of the peace;

"To develop friendly relations among nations based on respect for the principle of equal rights and self-determination of peoples, and to take other appropriate measures to strengthen universal peace";

REAFFIRMING that it remains to the primary duty of all Members of the United Nations, when involved in an international dispute, to seek settlement of such a dispute by peaceful means through the procedures laid down in Chapter VI of the Charter, and recalling the successful achievements of the United Nations in this regard on a number of previous occasions,

FINDING that international tension exists on a dangerous scale.

RECALLING its resolution 290 (IV) entitled "Essentials of peace," which states that disregard of the Principles of the Charter of the United Nations is primarily responsible for the continuance of international tension, and desiring to contribute further to the objectives of that resolution,

REAFFIRMING the importance of the exercise by the Security Council of its primary responsibility for the maintenance of international peace and security, and the duty of the permanent members to seek unanimity and to exercise restraint in the use of the veto,

REAFFIRMING that the initiative in negotiating the agreements for armed forces provided for in Article 43 of the Charter belongs to the Security Council, and desiring to ensure that, pending the conclusion of such agreements, the United Nations has at its disposal means for maintaining international peace and security,

[1] Department of State Bulletin, November 20, 1950, pp. 823-825.

CONSCIOUS that failure of the Security Council to discharge its responsibilities on behalf of all the Member States, particularly those responsibilities referred to in the two preceding paragraphs, does not relieve Member States of their obligations or the United Nations of its responsibility under the Charter to maintain international peace and security,

RECOGNIZING in particular that such failure does not deprive the General Assembly of its rights or relieve it of its responsibilities under the Charter in regard to the maintenance of international peace and security,

RECOGNIZING that discharge by the General Assembly of its responsibilities in these respects calls for possibilities of observation which would ascertain the facts and expose aggressors; for the existence of armed forces which could be used collectively; and for the possibility of timely recommendation by the General Assembly to Members of the United Nations for collective action which, to be effective, should be prompt,

A.

1. *Resolves* that if the Security Council, because of lack of unanimity of the permanent members, fails to exercise its primary responsibility for the maintenance of international peace and security in any case where there appears to be a threat to the peace, breach of the peace, or act of aggression, the General Assembly shall consider the matter immediately with a view to making appropriate recommendations to Members for collective measures, including in the case of a breach of the peace or act of aggression the use of armed force when necessary, to maintain or restore international peace and security. If not in session at the time, the General Assembly may meet in emergency special session within twenty-four hours of the request therefor. Such emergency special session shall be called if requested by the Security Council on the vote of any seven members, or by a majority of the Members of the United Nations,

2. *Adopts* for this purpose the amendments to its rules of procedure set forth in the annex to the present resolution;

B.

3. *Establishes* a Peace Observation Commission for which the calendar years 1951 and 1952, shall be composed of fourteen Members, namely: China, Colombia, Czechoslovakia, France, India, Iraq, Israel, New Zealand, Pakistan, Sweden, the Union of Soviet Socialist Republics, the United Kingdom of Great Britain and Northern Ireland, the United States of America and Uruguay, and which could observe and report on the situation in any area where there exists international tension the continuance of which is likely to endanger the maintenance of international peace and security. Upon the invitation or with the consent of the State into whose territory the Commission would go, the General Assembly, or the Interim Committee when the Assembly is not in session, may utilize the Commission if the Security Council is not exercising the functions assigned to it by the Charter with respect to the matter in question. Decisions to utilize the Commission shall be made on the affirmative vote of two-thirds of the members present and voting. The Security Council may also utilize the Commission in accordance with its authority under the Charter;

4. *The Commission shall have* authority in its discretion to appoint sub-commissions and to utilize the services of observers to assist it in the performance of its functions;

5. *Recommends* to all governments and authorities that they co-operate with the Commission and assist it in the performance of its functions;

6. *Requests* the Secretary-General to provide the necessary staff and facilities, utilizing, where directed by the Commission, the United Nations Panel of Field Observers envisaged in General Assembly resolution 297 B (IV);

C.

7. *Invites* each Member of the United Nations to survey its resources in order to determine the nature and scope of the assistance it may be in a position to render in support of any recommendations of the Security Council or of the General Assembly for the restoration of international peace and security;

8. *Recommends* to the States Members of the United Nations that each Member maintain within its national armed forces elements so trained, organized and equipped that they could promptly be made available, in accordance with its constitutional processes, for service as a United Nations unit or units, upon recommendation by the Security Council or General Assembly, without prejudice to the use of such elements in exercise of the right of individual or collective self-defence recognized in Article 51 of the Charter;

9. *Invites* the Members of the United Nations to inform the Collective Measures Committee provided for in paragraph 11 as soon as possible of the measures taken in implementation of the preceding paragraph;

10. *Requests* the Secretary-General to appoint, with the approval of the Committee provided for in paragraph 11, a panel of military experts who could be made available, on request, to Member States wishing to obtain technical advice regarding the organization, training, and equipment for prompt service as United Nations units of the elements referred to in paragraph 8;

D.

11. *Establishes* a Collective Measures Committee consisting of fourteen Members, namely: Australia, Belgium, Brazil, Burma, Canada, Egypt, France, Mexico, Philippines, Turkey, the United Kingdom of Great Britain and Northern Ireland, the United States of America, Venezuela and Yugoslavia, and directs the Committee, in consultation with the Secretary-General and with such Member States as the Committee finds appropriate, to study and make a report to the Security Council and the General Assembly, not later than 1 September 1951, on methods, including those in Section C of the present resolution, which might be used to maintain and strengthen international peace and security in accordance with the Purposes and Principles of the Charter, taking account of collective self-defence and regional arrangements (Articles 51 and 52 of the Charter);

12. *Recommends* to all Member States that they co-operate with the Committee and assist it in the performance of its functions;

13. *Requests* the Secretary-General to furnish the staff and facilities necessary for the effective accomplishment of the purposes set forth in sections C and D of the present resolution;

E.

14. THE GENERAL ASSEMBLY, in adopting the proposals set forth above, is fully conscious that enduring peace will not be secured solely by collective security arrangements against breaches of international peace and acts of aggression, but that a genuine and lasting peace depends also upon the observance of all the Principles and Purposes established in the Charter of the United Nations, upon the implementation of the resolutions of the Security Council, the General Assembly and other principal organs of the United Nations intended to achieve the maintenance of international peace and security, and especially upon respect for and observance of human rights and fundamental freedoms for all and on the establishment and maintenance of conditions of economic and social well-being in all countries; and accordingly

15. *Urges* Member States to respect fully, and to intensify, joint action, in co-operation with the United Nations, to develop and stimulate universal respect for and observance of human rights and fundamental freedoms, and to intensify individual and collective efforts to achieve conditions of economic stability and social progress, particularly through the development of underdeveloped countries and areas.

ANNEX

The rules of procedure of the General Assembly are amended in the following respects:

1. The present text of rule 8 shall become paragraph (a) of that rule, and a new paragraph (b) shall be added to read as follows:

"Emergency special sessions pursuant to resolution—(V) shall be convened within twenty-four hours of the receipt by the Secretary-General of a request for such a session from the Security Council, on the vote of any seven members thereof, or of a request from a majority of the Members of the United Nations expressed by vote in the Interim Committee or otherwise, or of the concurrence of a majority of Members as provided in rule 9."

2. The present text of rule 9 shall become paragraph (a) of that rule and a new paragraph (b) shall be added to read as follows:

"This rule shall apply also to a request by any Member for an emergency special session pursuant to resolution—(V). In such a case the Secretary-General shall communicate with other Members by the most expeditious means of communication available."

3. Rule 10 is amended by adding at the end thereof the following:

"In the case of an emergency special session convened pursuant to rule 8 (b), the Secretary-General shall notify the Members of the United Nations at least twelve hours in advance of the opening of the session."

4. Rule 16 is amended by adding at the end thereof the following:

"The provisional agenda of an emergency special session shall be communicated to the Members of the United Nations simultaneously with the communication summoning the session."

5. Rule 19 is amended by adding at the end thereof the following:

"During an emergency special session additional items concerning the matters dealt with in resolution—(V) may be added to the agenda by a two-thirds majority of the Members present and voting."

6. There is added a new rule to precede rule 65 to read as follows:

"Notwithstanding the provisions of any other rule and unless the General Assembly decides otherwise, the Assembly in case of an emergency special session, shall convene in plenary session only and proceed directly to consider the item proposed for consideration in the request for the holding of the session, without previous reference to the General Committee or to any other Committee; the President and Vice-Presidents for such emergency special sessions shall be, respectively, the Chairman of those delegations from which were elected the President and Vice-Presidents of the previous session."

RESOLUTION B

For the purpose of maintaining international peace and security, in accordance with the Charter of the United Nations, and, in particular, with Chapters V, VI and VII of the Charter,

The General Assembly

Recommends to the Security Council:

That it should take the necessary steps to ensure that the action provided for under the Charter is taken with respect to threats to the peace, breaches of the peace or acts of aggression and with respect to the peaceful settlement of disputes or situations likely to endanger the maintenance of international peace and security;

That it should devise measures for the earliest application of Articles 43, 45, 46 and 47 of the Charter of the United Nations regarding the placing of armed forces at the disposal of the Security Council by the States Members of the United Nations and the effective functioning of the Military Staff Committee.

The above dispositions should in no manner prevent the General Assembly from fulfilling its functions under resolution—(V).

RESOLUTION C

The General Assembly,

RECOGNIZING that the primary function of the United Nations Organization is to maintain and promote peace, security and justice among all nations.

RECOGNIZING the responsibility of all Member States to promote the cause of international peace in accordance with their obligations as provided in the Charter,

RECOGNIZING that the Charter charges the Security Council with the primary responsibility for maintaining international peace and security,

REAFFIRMING the importance of unanimity among the permanent members of the Security Council on all problems which are likely to threaten world peace,

RECALLING General Assembly resolution 190 (III) entitled "Appeal to the Great Powers to renew their efforts to compose their differences and establish a lasting peace,"

Recommends to the permanent members of the Security Council that:

(a) They meet and discuss, collectively or otherwise, and, if necessary, with other States concerned, all problems which are likely to threaten international peace and hamper the activities of the United Nations, with a view to their resolving fundamental differences and reaching agreement in accordance with the spirit and letter of the Charter;

(b) They advise the General Assembly and, when it is not in session, the Members of the United Nations, as soon as appropriate, of the results of their consultations.

PART IV

United Nations: Specialized Agencies

[In addition to the principal organs of the United Nations, the Charter provides for the creation of various specialized agencies to handle international problems in the economic, social, cultural, educational, health, and related fields. In each case these agencies have been established by intergovernment agreements and have been brought into relationship with the United Nations in accordance with Article 63 of the Charter. In spite of the

UNITED NATIONS SPECIALIZED AGENCIES

Agency	Headquarters	Members December 31, 1950	Budget, 1950	U. S. Contribution
Food and Agriculture Organization	Rome	66	$ 5,000,000	$ 1,250,000
* Intergovernmental Maritime Consultative Organization	New York			
International Bank for Reconstruction and Development	Washington	49	$ 4,926,171	
International Civil Aviation Organization	Montreal	58	$ 2,810,607	$ 1,000,114
International Labor Organization	Geneva	62	$ 5,983,526	$ 848,058
International Monetary Fund	Washington	49	$ 4,704,315	
International Refugee Organization	Geneva	18	$54,965,909	$25,000,000
International Telecommunication Union	Geneva	82	$ 1,040,000	$ 146,311
Universal Postal Union	Berne	89	$ 322,964	$ 12,056
UN Educational, Scientific and Cultural Organization	Paris	59	$ 8,010,000	$ 2,887,173
World Health Organization	Geneva	74	$ 7,501,500	$ 1,918,220
** World Meteorological Organization	Lausanne	66	$ 270,000	$ 30,000

* Not yet operative (Nov., 1951).
** Since the World Meteorological Organization became operative in 1951, the data on membership and budget is 1951.

political turbulence of the postwar period, they have been able to discharge their functions in a fairly satisfactory manner. The constitutions of five of the more important organizations are included in Part IV of this book. As the table on p. 145 indicates, 11 such agencies are functioning at the present time.]

29. THE CONSTITUTION OF THE INTERNATIONAL LABOUR OR-GANISATION AS AMENDED BY THE CONSTITUTION OF THE INTERNATIONAL LABOUR ORGANISATION INSTRUMENT OF AMENDMENT, OCTOBER 9, 1946 [1]

[The ILO was established in 1919, the U.S. joining in 1934. The organization makes its contribution to world peace by carrying on extensive research on world labor problems and by seeking to improve working and living standards through the adoption of ILO conventions and recommendations. Up to the end of 1950, 98 conventions and 88 recommendations dealing with such subjects as hours of work, wages, conditions of agricultural workers and seamen, industrial safety, and so on, had been approved and submitted to the member states for appropriate action. The ILO constitution is of particular interest because of the coöperation it prescribes between representatives of governments and employers and workers groups. It also contains unique provisions (Article 19) relating to the ratification of ILO conventions.]

PREAMBLE

Whereas universal and lasting peace can be established only if it is based upon social justice;

And whereas conditions of labour exist involving such injustice, hardship and privation to large numbers of people as to produce unrest so great that the peace and harmony of the world are imperilled; and an improvement of those conditions is urgently required: as, for example, by the regulation of the hours of work, including the establishment of a maximum working day and week, the regulation of the labour supply, the prevention of unemployment, the provision of an adequate living wage, the protection of the worker against sickness, disease and injury arising out of his employment, the protection of children, young persons and women, provision for old age and injury, protection of the interests of workers when employed in countries other than their own, recognition of the principle of equal remuneration for work of equal value, recognition of the principle freedom of association, the organisation of vocational and technical education and other measures;

Whereas also the failure of any nation to adopt humane conditions of

[1] The Constitution of the International Labour Organisation . . . , International Labour Office, Washington, D. C., Nov. 1947. Joint Resolution of the Congress, approved June 19, 1934, authorized the President to accept membership for the United States Government in the International Labor Organization, and his acceptance was officially announced Aug. 20, 1934, as effective on that day. The amended constitution was approved by the United States on June 30, 1948, and United States ratification was deposited on Aug. 2, 1948. The protocol bringing into force the agreement establishing official relationship between the ILO and the United Nations, which was approved by the General Assembly, was signed Dec. 20, 1946.

labour is an obstacle in the way of other nations which desire to improve the conditions in their own countries;

The High Contracting Parties, moved by sentiments of justice and humanity as well as by the desire to secure the permanent peace of the world, and with a view to attaining the objectives set forth in this Preamble, agree to the following Constitution of the International Labour Organisation:

CHAPTER I—ORGANISATION

ARTICLE 1

1. A permanent organisation is hereby established for the promotion of the objects set forth in the Preamble to this Constitution and in the Declaration concerning the aims and purposes of the International Labour Organisation adopted at Philadelphia on 10 May 1944 the text of which is annexed to this Constitution.

2. The Members of the International Labour Organisation shall be the States which were Members of the Organisation on 1 November 1945, and such other States as may become Members in pursuance of the provisions of paragraphs 3 and 4 of this Article.

3. Any original Member of the United Nations and any State admitted to membership of the United Nations by a decision of the General Assembly in accordance with the provisions of the Charter may become a Member of the International Labour Organisation by communicating to the Director-General of the International Labour Office its formal acceptance of the obligations of the Constitution of the International Labour Organisation.

4. The General Conference of the International Labour Organisation may also admit Members to the Organisation by a vote concurred in by two-thirds of the delegates attending the session, including two-thirds of the Government delegates present and voting. Such admission shall take effect on the communication to the Director-General of the International Labour Office by the Government of the new Member of its formal acceptance of the obligations of the Constitution of the Organisation.

5. No Member of the International Labour Organisation may withdraw from the Organisation without giving notice of its intention so to do to the Director-General of the International Labour Office. Such notice shall take effect two years after the date of its reception by the Director-General, subject to the Member having at that time fulfilled all financial obligations arising out of its membership. When a Member has ratified any International Labour Convention, such withdrawal shall not affect the continued validity for the period provided for in the Convention of all obligations arising thereunder or relating thereto.

6. In the event of any State having ceased to be a Member of the Organisation, its re-admission to membership shall be governed by the provisions of paragraph 3 or paragraph 4 of this Article as the case may be.

ARTICLE 2

The permanent organisation shall consist of:

(a) a General Conference of representatives of the Members;

(*b*) a Governing Body composed as described in Article 7; and

(*c*) an International Labour Office controlled by the Governing Body.

1. The meetings of the General Conference of representatives of the Members shall be held from time to time as occasion may require, and at least once in every year. It shall be composed of four representatives of each of the Members, of whom two shall be Government delegates and the two others shall be delegates representing respectively the employers and the workpeople of each of the Members.

2. Each delegate may be accompanied by advisers, who shall not exceed two in number for each item on the agenda of the meeting. When questions specially affecting women are to be considered by the Conference, one at least of the advisers should be a woman.

3. Each Member which is responsible for the international relations of non-metropolitan territories may appoint as additional advisers to each of its delegates:

(*a*) persons nominated by it as representatives of any such territory in regard to matters within the self-governing powers of that territory; and

(*b*) persons nominated by it to advise its delegates in regard to matters concerning non-self-governing territories.

4. In the case of a territory under the joint authority of two or more Members, persons may be nominated to advise the delegates of such Members.

5. The Members undertake to nominate non-Government delegates and advisers chosen in agreement with the industrial organisations, if such organisations exist, which are most representative of employers or workpeople, as the case may be, in their respective countries.

*   *   *

1. Every delegate shall be entitled to vote individually on all matters which are taken into consideration by the Conference.

2. If one of the Members fails to nominate one of the non-Government delegates whom it is entitled to nominate, the other non-Government delegate shall be allowed to sit and speak at the Conference, but not to vote.

3. If in accordance with Article 3 the Conference refuses admission to a delegate of one of the Members, the provisions of the present Article shall apply as if that delegate had not been nominated.

*   *   *

1. The Governing Body shall consist of thirty-two persons:

Sixteen representing Governments,

Eight representing the employers, and

Eight representing the workers.

2. Of the sixteen persons representing Governments, eight shall be

appointed by the Members of chief industrial importance, and eight shall be appointed by the Members selected for that purpose by the Government delegates to the Conference, excluding the delegates of the eight Members mentioned above. Of the sixteen Members represented, six shall be non-European States.

3. The Government Body shall as occasion requires determine which are the Members of the Organisation of chief industrial importance and shall make rules to ensure that all questions relating to the selection of the Members of chief industrial importance are considered by an impartial committee before being decided by the Governing Body. Any appeal made by a Member from the declaration of the Governing Body as to which are the Members of chief industrial importance shall be decided by the Conference, but an appeal to the Conference shall not suspend the application of the declaration until such time as the Conference decides the appeal.

4. The persons representing the employers and the persons representing the workers shall be elected respectively by the employers' delegates and the workers' delegates to the Conference. Two employers' representatives and two workers' representatives shall belong to non-European States.

5. The period of office of the Governing Body shall be three years. If for any reason the Governing Body elections do not take place on the expiry of this period, the Governing Body shall remain in office until such elections are held.

* * *

ARTICLE 8

1. There shall be a Director-General of the International Labour Office, who shall be appointed by the Governing Body, and, subject to the instructions of the Governing Body, shall be responsible for the efficient conduct of the International Labour Office and for such other duties as may be assigned to him.

2. The Director-General or his deputy shall attend all meetings of the Governing Body.

ARTICLE 9

1. The staff of the International Labour Office shall be appointed by the Director-General under regulations approved by the Governing Body.

2. So far as is possible with due regard to the efficiency of the work of the Office, the Director-General shall select persons of different nationalities.

3. A certain number of these persons shall be women.

4. The responsibilities of the Director-General and the staff shall be exclusively international in character. In the performance of their duties, the Director-General and the staff shall not seek or receive instructions from any Government or from any other authority external to the Organisation. They shall refrain from any action which might reflect on their position as international officials responsible only to the Organisation.

5. Each Member of the Organisation undertakes to respect the exclusively international character of the responsibilities of the Director-General and the staff and not to seek to influence them in the discharge of their responsibilities.

ARTICLE 10

1. The functions of the International Labour Office shall include the collection and distribution of information on all subjects relating to the international adjustment of conditions of industrial life and labour, and particularly the examination of subjects which it is proposed to bring before the Conference with a view to the conclusion of international Conventions, and the conduct of such special investigations as may be ordered by the Conference or by the Governing Body.

2. Subject to such directions as the Governing Body may give, the Office will—

(a) prepare the documents on the various items of the agenda for the meetings of the Conference;

(b) according to Governments at their request all appropriate assistance within its power in connection with the framing of laws and regulations on the basis of the decisions of the Conference and the improvement of administrative practices and systems of inspection;

(c) carry out the duties required of it by the provisions of this Constitution in connection with the effective observance of Conventions;

(d) edit and issue, in such languages as the Governing Body may think desirable, publications dealing with problems of industry and employment of international interest.

3. Generally, it shall have such other powers and duties as may be assigned to it by the Conference or by the Governing Body.

ARTICLE 11

The Government departments of any of the Members which deal with questions of industry and employment may communicate directly with the Director-General through the representative of their Government on the Governing Body of the International Labour Office or, failing any such representative, through such other qualified official as the Government may nominate for the purpose.

ARTICLE 12

1. The International Labour Organisation shall co-operate within the terms of this Constitution with any general international organisation entrusted with the co-ordination of the activities of public international organisations having specialised responsibilities and with public international organisations having specialised responsibilities in related fields.

2. The International Labour Organisation may make appropriate arrangements for the representatives of public international organisations to participate without vote in its deliberations.

3. The International Labour Organisation may make suitable arrangements for such consultation as it may think desirable with recognised non-governmental international organisations, including international organisations of employers, workers, agriculturists and co-operators.

ARTICLE 13

1. The International Labour Organisation may make such financial and budgetary arrangements with the United Nations as may appear appropriate.

2. Pending the conclusion of such arrangements or if at any time no such arrangements are in force—

(*a*) each of the Members will pay the travelling and subsistence expenses of its delegates and their advisers and of its representatives attending the meetings of the Conference or the Governing Body, as the case may be;

(*b*) all other expenses of the International Labour Office and of the meetings of the Conference or Governing Body shall be paid by the Director-General of the International Labour Office out of the general funds of the International Labour Organisation;

(*c*) the arrangements for the approval, allocation and collection of the budget of the International Labour Organisation shall be determined by the Conference by a two-thirds majority of the votes cast by the delegates present, and shall provide for the approval of the budget and of the arrangements for the allocation of expenses among the Members of the Organisation by a committee of Government representatives.

3. The expenses of the International Labour Organisation shall be borne by the Members in accordance with the arrangements in force in virtue of paragraph 1 or paragraph 2 (*c*) of this Article.

4. A Member of the Organisation which is in arrears in the payment of its financial contribution to the Organisation shall have no vote in the Conference, in the Governing Body, in any committee, or in the elections of members of the Governing Body, if the amount of its arrears equals or exceeds the amount of the contributions due from it for the preceding two full years: Provided that the Conference may by a two-thirds majority of the votes cast by the delegates present permit such a Member to vote if it is satisfied that the failure to pay is due to conditions beyond the control of the Member.

5. The Director-General of the International Labour Office shall be responsible to the Governing Body for the proper expenditure of the funds of the International Labour Organisation.

CHAPTER II—PROCEDURE

ARTICLE 14

1. The agenda for all meetings of the Conference will be settled by the Governing Body, which shall consider any suggestion as to the agenda that may be made by the Government of any of the Members or by any representative organisation recognised for the purpose of Article 3, or by any public international organisation.

2. The Governing Body shall make rules to ensure thorough technical preparation and adequate consultation of the Members primarily concerned, by means of a preparatory Conference or otherwise, prior to the adoption of a Convention or Recommendation by the Conference.

ARTICLE 15

1. The Director-General shall act as the Secretary-General of the Conference, and shall transmit the agenda so as to reach the Members four months before the meeting of the Conference, and, through them, the non-Government delegates when appointed.

2. The reports on each item of the agenda shall be despatched so as to reach the Members in time to permit adequate consideration before the meeting of the Conference. The Governing Body shall make rules for the application of this provision.

ARTICLE 16

1. Any of the Governments of the Members may formally object to the inclusion of any item or items in the agenda. The grounds for such objection shall be set forth in a statement addressed to the Director-General who shall circulate it to all the Members of the Organisation.

2. Items to which such objection has been made shall not, however, be excluded from the agenda, if at the Conference a majority of two-thirds of the votes cast by the delegates present is in favour of considering them.

3. If the Conference decides (otherwise than under the preceding paragraph) by two-thirds of the votes cast by the delegates present that any subject shall be considered by the Conference, that subject shall be included in the agenda for the following meeting.

ARTICLE 17

1. The Conference shall elect a President and three Vice-Presidents. One of the Vice-Presidents shall be a Government delegate, one an employers' delegate and one a workers' delegate. The Conference shall regulate its own procedure and may appoint committees to consider and report on any matter.

2. Except as otherwise expressly provided in this Constitution or by the terms of any Convention or other instrument conferring powers on the Conference or of the financial and budgetary arrangements adopted in virtue of Article 13, all matters shall be decided by a simple majority of the votes cast by the delegates present.

3. The voting is void unless the total number of votes cast is equal to half the number of the delegates attending the Conference.

*   *   *

ARTICLE 19

1. When the Conference has decided on the adoption of proposals with regard to an item in the agenda, it will rest with the Conference to determine whether these proposals should take the form: (a) of an international Convention, or (b) of a Recommendation to meet circumstances where the subject, or aspect of it, dealt with is not considered suitable or appropriate at that time for a Convention.

2. In either case a majority of two-thirds of the votes cast by the delegates present shall be necessary on the final vote for the adoption of the Convention or Recommendation, as the case may be, by the Conference.

3. In framing any Convention or Recommendation of general application the Conference shall have due regard to those countries in which climatic conditions, the imperfect development of industrial organisation, or other special circumstances make the industrial conditions substantially different and shall suggest the modifications, if any, which it considers may be required to meet the case of such countries.

*   *   *

5. In the case of a Convention—

(*a*) the Convention will be communicated to all Members for ratification;

(*b*) each of the Members undertakes that it will, within the period of one year at most from the closing of the session of the Conference, or if it is impossible owing to exceptional circumstances to do so within the period of one year, then at the earliest practicable moment and in no case later than eighteen months from the closing of the session of the Conference, bring the Convention before the authority or authorities within whose competence the matter lies, for the enactment of legislation or other action;

(*c*) Members shall inform the Director-General of the International Labour Office of the measures taken in accordance with this Article to bring the Convention before the said competent authority or authorities, with particulars of the authority or authorities regarded as competent, and of the action taken by them;

(*d*) if the Member obtains the consent of the authority or authorities within whose competence the matter lies, it will communicate the formal ratification of the Convention to the Director General and will take such action as may be necessary to make effective the provisions of such Convention;

(*e*) if the Member does not obtain the consent of the authority or authorities within whose competence the matter lies, no further obligation shall rest upon the Member except that it shall report to the Director-General of the International Labour Office, at appropriate intervals as requested by the Governing Body, the position of its law and practice in regard to the matters dealt with in the Convention, showing the extent to which effect has been given, or is proposed to be given, to any of the provisions of the Convention by legislation, administrative action, collective agreement or otherwise and stating the difficulties which prevent or delay the ratification of such Convention.

6. In the case of a Recommendation—

(*a*) the Recommendation will be communicated to all Members for their consideration with a view to effect being given to it by national legislation or otherwise;

(*b*) each of the Members undertakes that it will, within a period of one year at most from the closing of the session of the Conference, or if it is impossible owing to exceptional circumstances to do so within the period of one year, then at the earliest practicable moment and in no case later than eighteen months after the closing of the Conference, bring the Recommendation before the authority or authorities within whose competence the matter lies for the enactment of legislation or other action;

(*c*) the Members shall inform the Director-General of the International Labour Office of the measures taken in accordance with this Article to bring the Recommendation before the said competent authority or authorities with particulars of the authority or authorities regarded as competent, and of the action taken by them;

(*d*) apart from bringing the Recommendation before the said competent authority or authorities, no further obligation shall rest upon the Members, except that they shall report to the Director-General of the International Labour Office, at appropriate intervals as requested by the Governing Body, the position of the law and practice in their country in regard to the matters dealt with in the Recommendation, showing the extent to which effect has been given, or is proposed to be given, to the provisions of the Recommendation and such modifications of these provisions as it has been found or may be found necessary to make in adopting or applying them.

7. In the case of a federal State, the following provisions shall apply:

(*a*) in respect of Conventions and Recommendations which the federal Government regards as appropriate under its constitutional system for federal action, the obligations of the federal State shall be the same as those of Members which are not federal States;

(*b*) in respect of Conventions and Recommendations which the federal Government regards as appropriate under its constitutional system, in whole or in part, for action by the constituent States, provinces, or cantons rather than for federal action, the federal Government shall—

(i) make, in accordance with its Constitution and the Constitutions of the States, provinces or cantons concerned, effective arrangements for the reference of such Conventions and Recommendations not later than eighteen months from the closing of the session of the Conference to the appropriate federal, State, provincial or cantonal authorities for the enactment of legislation or other action;

(ii) arrange, subject to the concurrence of the State, provincial or cantonal Governments concerned, for periodical consultations between the federal and the State, provincial or cantonal authorities with a view to promoting within the federal State co-ordinated action to give effect to the provisions of such Conventions and Recommendations;

(iii) inform the Director-General of the International Labour Office of the measures taken in accordance with this Article to bring such Conventions and Recommendations before the appropriate federal, State, provincial or cantonal authorities with particulars of the authorities regarded as appropriate and of the action taken by them;

(iv) in respect of each such Convention which it has not ratified, report to the Director-General of the International Labour Office, at appropriate intervals as requested by the Governing Body, the position of the law and practice of the federation and its constituent States, provinces or cantons in regard to the Convention, showing the extent to which effect has been given, or is proposed to be given, to any of the provisions of the Convention by legislation, administrative action, collective agreement, or otherwise;

(v) in respect of each such Recommendation, report to the Director-General of the International Labour Office, at appropriate intervals as requested by the Governing Body, the position of the law and practice of the federation and its constituent States, provinces or cantons in regard to the Recommendation, showing the extent to which effect has been given, or is proposed to be given, to the provisions of the Recommendation and such modifications of these provisions as have been found or may be found necessary in adopting or applying them.

8. In no case shall the adoption of any Convention or Recommendation by the Conference, or the ratification of any Convention by any Member, be deemed to affect any law, award, custom or agreement which ensures more favourable conditions to the workers concerned than those provided for in the Convention or Recommendation.

* * *

ARTICLE 22

Each of the Members agrees to make an annual report to the International Labour Office on the measures which it has taken to give effect to the provisions of Conventions to which it is a party. These reports shall be made in such form and shall contain such particulars as the Governing Body may request.

ARTICLE 23

1. The Director-General shall lay before the next meeting of the Conference a summary of the information and reports communicated to him by Members in pursuance of Articles 19 and 22.

2. Each Member shall communicate to the representative organisations recognised for the purpose of Article 3 copies of the information and reports communicated to the Director-General in pursuance of Articles 19 and 22.

[Articles 24-34, omitted because of space limitations, outline the procedure to be followed in the event a state is charged with failing to live up to·its obligations under a convention to which it is a party.]

CHAPTER III—GENERAL

ARTICLE 35

1. The Members undertake that Conventions which they have ratified in accordance with the provisions of this Constitution shall be applied to the non-metropolitan territories for whose international relations they are responsible, including any trust territories for which they are the administering authority, except where the subject matter of the Convention is within the self-governing powers of the territory or the Convention is inapplicable owing to the local conditions or subject to such modifications as may be necessary to adapt the Convention to local conditions.

2. Each Member which ratifies a Convention shall as soon as possible after ratification communicate to the Director-General of the International Labour Office a declaration stating in respect of the territories other than those referred to in paragraphs 4 and 5 below the extent to which it undertakes that the provisions of the Convention shall be applied and giving such particulars as may be prescribed by the Convention.

3. Each Member which has communicated a declaration in virtue of the preceding paragraph may from time to time, in accordance with the terms of the Convention, communicate a further declaration modifying the terms of any former declaration and stating the present position in respect of such territories.

4. Where the subject matter of the Convention is within the self-governing powers of any non-metropolitan territory the Member responsible for the international relations of that territory shall bring the Convention to the notice of the Government of the territory as soon as possible with a view to the enactment of legislation or other action by such Government. Thereafter the Member, in agreement with the Government of the territory, may communicate to the Director-General of the International Labour Office a declaration accepting the obligations of the Convention on behalf of such territory.

*   *   *

ARTICLE 36

Amendments to this Constitution which are adopted by the Conference by a majority of two-thirds of the votes cast by the delegates present shall take effect when ratified or accepted by two-thirds of the Members of the Organisation including five of the eight Members which are represented on the Governing Body as Members of chief industrial importance in accordance with the provisions of paragraph 3 of Article 7 of this Constitution.

ARTICLE 37

1. Any question or dispute relating to the interpretation of this Constitution or of any subsequent Convention concluded by the Members in pursuance of the provisions of this Constitution shall be referred for decision to the International Court of Justice.

*   *   *

ARTICLE 38

1. The International Labour Organisation may convene such regional conferences and establish such regional agencies as may be desirable to promote the aims and purposes of the Organisation.

2. The powers, functions and procedure of regional conferences shall be governed by rules drawn up by the Governing Body and submitted to the General Conference for confirmation.

CHAPTER IV—MISCELLANEOUS PROVISIONS

ARTICLE 39

The International Labour Organisation shall possess full juridical personality and in particular the capacity—
    (a) to contract:
    (b) to acquire and dispose of immovable and movable property;
    (c) to institute legal proceedings.

ARTICLE 40

1. The International Labour Organisation shall enjoy in the territory of each of its Members such privileges and immunities as are necessary for the fulfilment of its purposes.

2. Delegates to the Conference, members of the Governing Body and the Director-General and officials of the Office shall likewise enjoy such privileges and immunities as are necessary for the independent exercise of their functions in connection with the Organisation.

3. Such privileges and immunities shall be defined in a separate agreement to be prepared by the Organisation with a view to its acceptance by the States Members.

* * *

◇◇◇◇◇◇

30. CONSTITUTION OF THE FOOD AND AGRICULTURE ORGANIZATION, OCTOBER 15, 1945 [1]

[FAO was the first of the new specialized agencies created after World War II. The Organization collects and analyzes information relating to nutrition, agriculture, forestry and fisheries. It also encourages national and international action to improve the conservation and use of land, forest and fishery resources. Current FAO projects include those relating to soil erosion, nutrition, reforestation, irrigation, and the control of various types of pests. Organizationally FAO resembles the other specialized agencies. The constitution provides for a conference which determines the policy of the Organization, a council, and a permanent secretariat headed by a director-general.]

PREAMBLE

The Nations accepting this Constitution, being determined to promote the common welfare by furthering separate and collective action on their part for the purposes of

raising levels of nutrition and standards of living of the peoples under their respective jurisdictions,

securing improvements in the efficiency of the production and distribution of all food and agricultural products,

bettering the condition of rural populations,

and thus contributing toward an expanding world economy,

hereby establish the Food and Agriculture Organization of the United Nations,

[1] Constitution of the Food and Agriculture Organization of the United Nations, Revised Edition, Washington, October 1947. See Original Constitution adopted by the United States and Other Governments, signed at Quebec, Oct. 16, 1945, effective Oct. 16, 1945, Department of State publication 2677, Treaties and Other International Acts Series 1554. Public Law 174, 79th Cong., 1st sess., H. J. Res. 145: Joint Resolution providing for membership of the United States in the Food and Agriculture Organization of the United Nations was approved July 31, 1945. The protocol relating to the entry into force of an agreement, which was approved by the General Assembly, bringing the FAO into official relationship with the United Nations, was signed February 3, 1947.

hereinafter referred to as the "Organization," through which the Members will report to one another on the measures taken and the progress achieved in the fields of action set forth above.

ARTICLE I

FUNCTIONS OF THE ORGANIZATION

1. The Organization shall collect, analyze, interpret, and disseminate information relating to nutrition, food and agriculture.

2. The Organization shall promote and, where appropriate, shall recommend national and international action with respect to

(a) scientific, technological, social, and economic research relating to nutrition, food and agriculture;

(b) the improvement of education and administration relating to nutrition, food and agriculture, and the spread of public knowledge of nutritional and agricultural science and practice;

(c) the conservation of natural resources and the adoption of improved methods of agricultural production;

(d) the improvement of the processing, marketing, and distribution of food and agricultural products;

(e) the adoption of policies for the provision of adequate agricultural credit, national and international;

(f) the adoption of international policies with respect to agricultural commodity arrangements.

3. It shall also be the function of the Organization

(a) to furnish such technical assistance as governments may request;

(b) to organize, in co-operation with the governments concerned, such missions as may be needed to assist them to fulfill the obligations arising from their acceptance of the recommendations of the United Nations Conference on Food and Agriculture; and

(c) generally to take all necessary and appropriate action to implement the purposes of the Organization as set forth in the Preamble.

ARTICLE II

MEMBERSHIP

1. The original Members of the Organization shall be such of the nations specified in Annex I as accept this Constitution in accordance with the provisions of Article XXI.

2. Additional Members may be admitted to the Organization by a vote concurred in by a two-thirds majority of all the members of the Conference and upon acceptance of this Constitution as in force at the time of admission.

ARTICLE III

THE CONFERENCE

1. There shall be a Conference of the Organization in which each Member nation shall be represented by one member.

2. Each Member nation may appoint an alternate, associates, and advisers

to its member of the Conference. The Conference may make rules concerning the participation of alternates, associates, and advisers in its proceedings, but any such participation shall be without the right to vote except in the case of an alternate or associate participating in the place of a member.

3. No member of the Conference may represent more than one Member nation.

4. Each Member nation shall have only one vote. A Member nation which is in arrears in the payment of its financial contributions to the Organization shall have no vote in the Conference if the amount of its arrears equals or exceeds the amount of the contributions due from it for the preceding two full years. The Conference may, nevertheless, permit such a Member nation to vote if it is satisfied that the failure to pay is due to conditions beyond the control of the Member nation.[1]

5. The Conference may invite any public international organization which has responsibilities related to those of the Organization to appoint a representative who shall participate in its meetings on the conditions prescribed by the Conference. No such representative shall have the right to vote.

6. The Conference shall meet at least once in every year.

7. The Conference shall elect its own officers, regulate its own procedure, and make rules governing the convocation of sessions and the determination of agenda.

8. Except as otherwise expressly provided in this Constitution or by rules made by the Conference, all matters shall be decided by the Conference by a simple majority of the votes cast.

ARTICLE IV

FUNCTIONS OF THE CONFERENCE

1. The Conference shall determine the policy and approve the budget of the Organization and shall exercise the other powers conferred upon it by this Constitution.

2. The Conference may by a two-thirds majority of the votes cast make recommendations concerning questions relating to food and agriculture to be submitted to Member nations for consideration with a view to implementation by national action.

3. The Conference may by a two-thirds majority of the votes cast submit conventions concerning questions relating to food and agriculture to Member nations for consideration with a view to their acceptance by the appropriate constitutional procedure.

4. The Conference shall make rules laying down the procedure to be followed to secure:

(*a*) proper consultation with governments and adequate technical preparation prior to consideration by the Conference of proposed recommendations and conventions; and

(*b*) proper consultation with governments in regard to relations between the Organization and national institutions or private persons.

---

[1] The first sentence of Paragraph 4 is part of the original Constitution. The remainder of the paragraph was added as an amendment by the Second Session of the FAO Conference at Copenhagen, September 1946.

5. The Conference may make recommendations to any public international organization regarding any matter pertaining to the purpose of the Organization.

6. The Conference may by a two-thirds majority of the votes cast agree to discharge any other functions consistent with the purposes of the Organization which may be assigned to it by governments or provided for by any arrangement between the Organization and any other public international organization.

ARTICLE V [1]

COUNCIL OF FAO

1. The Conference shall elect a Council of the Food and Agriculture Organization consisting of eighteen Member nations, which will each be represented by one member. The Conference shall appoint an independent Chairman of the Council. The tenure and other conditions of office of the members of the Council shall be subject to rules to be made by the Conference.

2. The Conference may delegate to the Council such powers as it may determine, with the exception of powers set forth in paragraph 2 of Article II, paragraphs 1, 3, 4, 5, and 6 of Article IV, paragraph 1 of Article VII, Article XIII, and Article XX of this Constitution.

3. The Council shall appoint its officers other than the Chairman and, subject to any decisions of the Conference, shall adopt its own rules of procedure.

4. The Council shall establish a Co-ordinating Committee to tender advice on the co-ordination of technical work and the continuity of the activities of the Organization undertaken in accordance with the decisions of the Conference.

ARTICLE VI

COMMITTEES AND CONFERENCES

1. The Conference may establish technical and regional standing committees and may appoint committees to study and report on any matter pertaining to the purpose of the Organization.

2. The Conference may convene general, technical, regional, or other special conferences and may provide for the representation at such conferences in such manner as it may determine, of national and international bodies concerned with nutrition, food and agriculture.

ARTICLE VII

THE DIRECTOR-GENERAL

1. There shall be a Director-General of the Organization who shall be appointed by the Conference by such procedure and on such terms as it may determine.

---

[1] Article V is an amendment to the Constitution, adopted by the Third Session of the FAO Conference at Geneva in September 1947. It replaces the original Article V, which appears in the Appendix.

2. Subject to the general supervision of the Conference and the Council, the Director-General shall have full power and authority to direct the work of the Organization.[1]

3. The Director-General or a representative designated by him shall participate, without the right to vote, in all meetings of the Conference and of the Council and shall formulate for consideration by the Conference and the Council proposals for appropriate action in regard to matters coming before them.[1]

ARTICLE VIII

STAFF

1. The staff of the Organization shall be appointed by the Director-General in accordance with such procedure as may be determined by rules made by the Conference.

2. The staff of the Organization shall be responsible to the Director-General. Their responsibilities shall be exclusively international in character and they shall not seek or receive instructions in regard to the discharge thereof from any authority external to the Organization. The Member nations undertake fully to respect the international character of the responsibilities of the staff and not to seek to influence any of their nationals in the discharge of such responsibilities.

3. In appointing the staff the Director-General shall, subject to the paramount importance of securing the highest standards of efficiency and of technical competence, pay due regard to the importance of selecting personnel recruited on as wide a geographical basis as is possible.

4. Each Member nation undertakes, insofar as it may be possible under its constitutional procedure, to accord to the Director-General and senior staff diplomatic privileges and immunities and to accord to other members of the staff all facilities and immunities accorded to non-diplomatic personnel attached to diplomatic missions, or alternatively to accord to such other members of the staff the immunities and facilities which may hereafter be accorded to equivalent members of the staffs of other public international organizations.

ARTICLE IX

SEAT

The seat of the Organization shall be determined by the Conference.

ARTICLE X

REGIONAL AND LIAISON OFFICES

1. There shall be such regional offices as the Director-General with the approval of the Conference may decide.

2. The Director-General may appoint officials for liaison with particular countries or areas subject to the agreement of the government concerned.

[1] Paragraphs 2 and 3 of Article VII are amendments to the Constitution adopted by the Third Session of the FAO Conference at Geneva, September 1947.

ARTICLE XI

REPORTS BY MEMBERS

1. Each Member nation shall communicate periodically to the Organization reports on the progress made toward achieving the purpose of the Organization set forth in the Preamble and on the action taken on the basis of recommendations made and conventions submitted by the Conference.

2. These reports shall be made at such times and in such form and shall contain such particulars as the Conference may request.

3. The Director-General shall submit these reports, together with analyses thereof, to the Conference and shall publish such reports and analyses as may be approved for publication by the Conference together with any reports relating thereto adopted by the Conference.

4. The Director-General may request any Member nation to submit information relating to the purpose of the Organization.

5. Each member nation shall, on request, communicate to the Organization, on publication, all laws and regulations and official reports and statistics concerning nutrition, food and agriculture.

ARTICLE XII

CO-OPERATION WITH OTHER ORGANIZATIONS

1. In order to provide for close co-operation between the Organization and other public international organizations with related responsibilities, the Conference may, subject to the provisions of Article XIII, enter into agreements with the competent authorities of such organizations defining the distribution of responsibilities and methods of co-operation.

2. The Director-General may, subject to any decisions of the Conference, enter into agreements with other public international organizations for the maintenance of common services, for common arrangements in regard to recruitment, training, conditions of service, and other related matters, and for interchanges of staff.

ARTICLE XIII

RELATION TO ANY GENERAL WORLD ORGANIZATION

1. The Organization shall, in accordance with the procedure provided for in the following paragraph, constitute a part of any general international organization to which may be entrusted the coordination of the activities of international organizations with specialized responsibilities.

2. Arrangements for defining the relations between the Organization and any such general organization shall be subject to the approval of the Conference. Notwithstanding the provisions of Article XX, such arrangements may, if approved by the Conference by a two-thirds majority of the votes cast, involve modification of the provisions of this Constitution: Provided that no such arrangements shall modify the purposes and limitations of the Organization as set forth in this Constitution.

ARTICLE XIV

SUPERVISION OF OTHER ORGANIZATIONS

The Conference may approve arrangements placing other public international organizations dealing with questions relating to food and agriculture under the general authority of the Organization on such terms as may be agreed with the competent authorities of the organization concerned.

ARTICLE XV

LEGAL STATUS

1. The Organization shall have the capacity of a legal person to perform any legal act appropriate to its purpose which is not beyond the powers granted to it by this Constitution.

2. Each Member nation undertakes, insofar as it may be possible under its constitutional procedure, to accord to the Organization all the immunities and facilities which it accords to diplomatic missions, including inviolability of premises and archives, immunity from suit, and exemptions from taxation.

3. The Conference shall make provision for the determination by an administrative tribunal of disputes relating to the conditions and terms of appointment of members of the staff.

ARTICLE XVI

FISH AND FOREST PRODUCTS

In this Constitution the term "agriculture" and its derivatives include fisheries, marine products, forestry, and primary forestry products.

ARTICLE XVII

INTERPRETATION OF CONSTITUTION

Any question or dispute concerning the interpretation of this Constitution or any international convention adopted thereunder shall be referred for determination to an appropriate international court or arbitral tribunal in the manner prescribed by rules to be adopted by the Conference.

ARTICLE XVIII

EXPENSES

1. Subject to the provisions of Article XXV, the Director-General shall submit to the Conference an annual budget covering the anticipated expenses of the Organization. Upon approval of a budget the total amount approved shall be allocated among the Member nations in proportions determined, from time to time, by the Conference. Each Member nation undertakes, subject to the requirements of its constitutional procedure, to contribute to the Organization promptly its share of the expenses so determined.

2. Each Member nation shall, upon its acceptance of this Constitution, pay

as its first contribution its proportion of the annual budget for the current financial year.

3. The financial year of the Organization shall be July 1 to June 30 unless the Conference should otherwise determine.

ARTICLE XIX

WITHDRAWAL

Any Member nation may give notice of withdrawal from the Organization at any time after the expiration of four years from the date of its acceptance of this Constitution. Such notice shall take effect one year after the date of its communication to the Director-General of the Organization subject to the Member nation's having at that time paid its annual contribution for each year of its membership including the financial year following the date of such notice.

ARTICLE XX

AMENDMENT TO CONSTITUTION

1. Amendments to this Constitution involving new obligations for Member nations shall require the approval of the Conference by a vote concurred in by a two-thirds majority of all the members of the Conference and shall take effect on acceptance by two-thirds of the Member nations for each Member nation accepting the amendment and thereafter for each remaining Member nation on acceptance by it.

2. Other amendments shall take effect on adoption by the Conference by a vote concurred in by a two-thirds majority of all the members of the Conference.

ARTICLE XXI

ENTRY INTO FORCE OF CONSTITUTION

1. This Constitution shall be open to acceptance by the nations specified in Annex I.

2. The instruments of acceptance shall be transmitted by each government to the United Nations Interim Commission on Food and Agriculture, which shall notify their receipt to the governments of the nations specified in Annex I. Acceptance may be notified to the Interim Commission through a diplomatic representative, in which case the instrument of acceptance must be transmitted to the Commission as soon as possible thereafter.

3. Upon the receipt by the Interim Commission of twenty notifications of acceptance the Interim Commission shall arrange for this Constitution to be signed in a single copy by the diplomatic representatives, duly authorized thereto, of the nations who shall have notified their acceptance, and upon being so signed on behalf of not less than twenty of the nations specified in Annex I this Constitution shall come into force immediately.

4. Acceptances the notification of which is received after the entry into force of this Constitution shall become effective upon receipt by the Interim Commission or the Organization.

*   *   *

31. ARTICLES OF AGREEMENT OF THE INTERNATIONAL BANK FOR RECONSTRUCTION AND DEVELOPMENT, JULY 22, 1944 (EXCERPTS) [1]

[At the Bretton Woods Conference held in July 1944, two related agencies were set up to cope with postwar international monetary and financial problems. The first of these was the International Monetary Fund, the purpose of which is to assist in the stabilization of national currencies. The second was the International Bank for Reconstruction and Development. As the title indicates, the Bank was designed not only to help finance postwar reconstruction but also to assist in developing the resources and productive capacity of the member states. To this end, the Bank loans money from its own resources and facilitates in various ways the international flow of capital. Through 1950, a total of $1,023,375,000 in loans had been extended to some nineteen states by the Bank. The more important provisions of the Bank's charter follow.]

The Governments on whose behalf the present Agreement is signed agree as follows:

INTRODUCTORY ARTICLE

The International Bank for Reconstruction and Development is established and shall operate in accordance with the following provisions:

ARTICLE I. PURPOSES

The purposes of the Bank are:

(i) To assist in the reconstruction and development of territories of members by facilitating the investment of capital for productive purposes, including the restoration of economies destroyed or disrupted by war, the reconversion of productive facilities to peacetime needs and the encouragement of the development of productive facilities and resources in less developed countries.

(ii) To promote private foreign investment by means of guarantees or participations in loans and other investments made by private investors; and when private capital is not available on reasonable terms, to supplement private investment by providing, on suitable conditions, finance for productive purposes out of its own capital, funds raised by it and its other resources.

(iii) To promote the long-range balanced growth of international trade and the maintenance of equilibrium in balances of payments by

[1] United Nations Monetary and Financial Conference, Bretton Woods, New Hampshire, July 1-22, 1944. Final Act and Related Documents, pp. 68-95, Department of State publication 2187, Conference Series 55; also, Department of State publication 2511, Treaties and Other International Acts Series 1502. Agreement signed at Washington December 27, 1945; effective December 27, 1945. Public Law 171, 79th Cong., 1st sess., H. R. 3314: An Act ("Bretton Woods Agreements Act") to provide for participation of the United States in the International Monetary Fund and the International Bank for Reconstruction and Development was approved July 31, 1945. Agreement establishing official relationship between the Bank and the United Nations was approved by the General Assembly November 15, 1947.

encouraging international investment for the development of the productive resources of members, thereby assisting in raising productivity, the standard of living and conditions of labor in their territories.

(iv) To arrange the loans made or guaranteed by it in relation to international loans through other channels so that the more useful and urgent projects, large and small alike, will be dealt with first.

(v) To conduct its operations with due regard to the effect of international investment on business conditions in the territories of members and, in the immediate post-war years, to assist in bringing about a smooth transition from a wartime to a peacetime economy.

The Bank shall be guided in all its decisions by the purposes set forth above.

ARTICLE II. MEMBERSHIP IN AND CAPITAL OF THE BANK

SECTION 1. MEMBERSHIP

(a) The original members of the Bank shall be those members of the International Monetary Fund which accept membership in the Bank before the date specified in Article XI, Section 2 (e).

(b) Membership shall be open to other members of the Fund, at such times and in accordance with such terms as may be prescribed by the Bank.

SECTION 2. AUTHORIZED CAPITAL

(a) The authorized capital stock of the Bank shall be $10,000,000,000, in terms of United States dollars of the weight and fineness in effect on July 1, 1944. The capital stock shall be divided into 100,000 shares having a par value of $100,000 each, which shall be available for subscription only by members.

(b) The capital stock may be increased when the Bank deems it advisable by a three-fourths majority of the total voting power.

SECTION 3. SUBSCRIPTION OF SHARES

(a) Each member shall subscribe shares of the capital stock of the Bank. The minimum number of shares to be subscribed by the original members shall be those set forth in Schedule A. The minimum number of shares to be subscribed by other members shall be determined by the Bank, which shall reserve a sufficient portion of its capital stock for subscription by such members.

(b) The Bank shall prescribe rules laying down the conditions under which members may subscribe shares of the authorized capital stock of the Bank in addition to their minimum subscriptions.

(c) If the authorized capital stock of the Bank is increased, each member shall have a reasonable opportunity to subscribe, under such conditions as the Bank shall decide, a proportion of the increase of stock equivalent to the proportion which its stock theretofore subscribed bears to the total capital stock of the Bank, but no member shall be obligated to subscribe any part of the increased capital.

SECTION 4. ISSUE PRICE OF SHARES

Shares included in the minimum subscriptions of original members shall be issued at par. Other shares shall be issued at par unless the Bank by a majority of the total voting power decides in special circumstances to issue them on other terms.

SECTION 5. DIVISION AND CALLS OF SUBSCRIBED CAPITAL

The subscription of each member shall be divided into two parts as follows:

(i) twenty percent shall be paid or subject to call under Section 7 (i) of this Article as needed by the Bank for its operations;

(ii) the remaining eighty percent shall be subject to call by the Bank only when required to meet obligations of the Bank created under Article IV, Section 1 (a) (ii) and (iii).

Calls on unpaid subscriptions shall be uniform on all shares.

SECTION 6. LIMITATION ON LIABILITY

Liability on shares shall be limited to the unpaid portion of the issue price of the shares.

SECTION 7. METHOD OF PAYMENT OF SUBSCRIPTIONS FOR SHARES

Payment of subscriptions for shares shall be made in gold or United States dollars and in the currencies of the members as follows:

(i) under Section 5 (i) of this Article, two percent of the price of each share shall be payable in gold or United States dollars, and, when calls are made, the remaining eighteen percent shall be paid in the currency of the member;

(ii) when a call is made under Section 5 (ii) of this Article, payment may be made at the option of the member either in gold, in United States dollars or in the currency required to discharge the obligations of the Bank for the purpose for which the call is made;

(iii) when a member makes payments in any currency under (i) and (ii) above, such payments shall be made in amounts equal in value to the member's liability under the call. This liability shall be a proportionate part of the subscribed capital stock of the Bank as authorized and defined in Section 2 of this Article.

*   *   *

ARTICLE III. GENERAL PROVISIONS RELATING TO LOANS AND GUARANTEES

SECTION 1. USE OF RESOURCES

(a) The resources and the facilities of the Bank shall be used exclusively for the benefit of members with equitable consideration to projects for development and projects for reconstruction alike.

(b) For the purpose of facilitating the restoration and reconstruction of the economy of members whose metropolitan territories have suffered great devastation from enemy occupation or hostilities, the Bank, in determining the conditions and terms of loans made to such members, shall pay special regard to lightening the financial burden and expediting the completion of such restoration and reconstruction.

SECTION 2. DEALINGS BETWEEN MEMBERS AND THE BANK

Each member shall deal with the Bank only through its Treasury, central bank, stabilization fund or other similar fiscal agency, and the Bank shall deal with members only by or through the same agencies.

SECTION 3. LIMITATIONS ON GUARANTEES AND BORROWING OF THE BANK

The total amount outstanding of guarantees, participations in loans and direct loans made by the Bank shall not be increased at any time, if by such increase the total would exceed one hundred percent of the unimpaired subscribed capital, reserves and surplus of the Bank.

SECTION 4. CONDITIONS ON WHICH THE BANK MAY GUARANTEE OR MAKE LOANS

The Bank may guarantee, participate in, or make loans to any member or any political sub-division thereof and any business, industrial, and agricultural enterprise in the territories of a member, subject to the following conditions:

(i) When the member in whose territories the project is located is not itself the borrower, the member or the central bank or some comparable agency of the member which is acceptable to the Bank, fully guarantees the repayment of the principal and the payment of interest and other charges on the loan.

(ii) The Bank is satisfied that in the prevailing market conditions the borrower would be unable otherwise to obtain the loan under conditions which in the opinion of the Bank are reasonable for the borrower.

(iii) A competent committee, as provided for in Article V, Section 7, has submitted a written report recommending the project after a careful study of the merits of the proposal.

(iv) In the opinion of the Bank the rate of interest and other charges are reasonable and such rate, charges and the schedule for repayment of principal are appropriate to the project.

(v) In making or guaranteeing a loan, the Bank shall pay due regard to the prospects that the borrower, and, if the borrower is not a member, that the guarantor, will be in position to meet its obligations under the loan; and the Bank shall act prudently in the interests both of the particular member in whose territories the project is located and of the members as a whole.

(vi) In guaranteeing a loan made by other investors, the Bank receives suitable compensation for its risk.

(vii) Loans made or guaranteed by the Bank shall, except in special circumstances, be for the purpose of specific projects of reconstruction or development.

SECTION 5. USE OF LOANS GUARANTEED, PARTICIPATED IN OR MADE BY THE BANK

(a) The Bank shall impose no conditions that the proceeds of a loan shall be spent in the territories of any particular member or members.

(b) The Bank shall make arrangements to ensure that the proceeds of any loan are used only for the purposes for which the loan was granted, with due attention to considerations of economy and efficiency and without regard to political or other non-economic influences or considerations.

(c) In the case of loans made by the Bank, it shall open an account in the name of the borrower and the amount of the loan shall be credited to this account in the currency or currencies in which the loan is made. The borrower shall be permitted by the Bank to draw on this account only to meet expenses in connection with the project as they are actually incurred.

ARTICLE IV. OPERATIONS

SECTION 1. METHODS OF MAKING OR FACILITATING LOANS

(a) The Bank may make or facilitate loans which satisfy the general conditions of Article III in any of the following ways:

(i) By making or participating in direct loans out of its own funds corresponding to its unimpaired paid-up capital and surplus and, subject to Section 6 of this Article, to its reserves.

(ii) By making or participating in direct loans out of funds raised in the market of a member, or otherwise borrowed by the Bank.

(iii) By guaranteeing in whole or in part loans made by private investors through the usual investment channels.

(b) The Bank may borrow funds under (a) (ii) above or guarantee loans under (a) (iii) above only with the approval of the member in whose markets the funds are raised and the member in whose currency the loan is denominated, and only if those members agree that the proceeds may be exchanged for the currency of any other member without restriction.

*   *   *

SECTION 8. MISCELLANEOUS OPERATIONS

In addition to the operations specified elsewhere in this Agreement, the Bank shall have the power:

(i) To buy and sell securities it has issued and to buy and sell securities which it has guaranteed or in which it has invested, provided that the Bank shall obtain the approval of the member in whose territories the securities are to be bought or sold.

(ii) To guarantee securities in which it has invested for the purpose of facilitating their sale.

(iii) To borrow the currency of any member with the approval of that member.

(iv) To buy and sell such other securities as the Directors by a three-fourths majority of the total voting power may deem proper for the investment of all or part of the special reserve under Section 6 of this Article.

In exercising the powers conferred by this Section, the Bank may deal with any person, partnership, association, corporation or other legal entity in the territories of any member.

*   *   *

SECTION 10. POLITICAL ACTIVITY PROHIBITED

The Bank and its officers shall not interfere in the political affairs of any member; nor shall they be influenced in their decisions by the political character of the member or members concerned. Only economic considerations shall be relevant to their decisions, and these considerations shall be weighed impartially in order to achieve the purposes stated in Article I.

ARTICLE V. ORGANIZATION AND MANAGEMENT

SECTION 1. STRUCTURE OF THE BANK

The Bank shall have a Board of Governors, Executive Directors, a President and such other officers and staff to perform such duties as the Bank may determine.

SECTION 2. BOARD OF GOVERNORS

(a) All the powers of the Bank shall be vested in the Board of Governors consisting of one governor and one alternate appointed by each member in such manner as it may determine. Each governor and each alternate shall serve for five years, subject to the pleasure of the member appointing him, and may be reappointed. No alternate may vote except in the absence of his principal. The Board shall select one of the governors as Chairman.

(b) The Board of Governors may delegate to the Executive Directors authority to exercise any powers of the Board, except the power to:

(i) Admit new members and determine the conditions of their admission;

(ii) Increase or decrease the capital stock;

(iii) Suspend a member;

(iv) Decide appeals from interpretations of this Agreement given by the Executive Directors;

(v) Make arrangements to cooperate with other international organizations (other than informal arrangements of a temporary and administrative character);

(vi) Decide to suspend permanently the operations of the Bank and to distribute its assets;

(vii) Determine the distribution of the net income of the Bank.

*   *   *

SECTION 3. VOTING

(a) Each member shall have two hundred fifty votes plus one additional vote for each share of stock held.

(b) Except as otherwise specifically provided, all matters before the Bank shall be decided by a majority of the votes cast.

SECTION 4. EXECUTIVE DIRECTORS

(a) The Executive Directors shall be responsible for the conduct of the general operations of the Bank, and for this purpose, shall exercise all the powers delegated to them by the Board of Governors.

(b) There shall be twelve Executive Directors, who need not be governors, and of whom:

(i) five shall be appointed, one by each of the five members having the largest number of shares;

(ii) seven shall be elected according to Schedule B by all the Governors other than those appointed by the five members referred to in (i) above.

* * *

Executive directors shall be appointed or elected every two years.

* * *

(e) The Executive Directors shall function in continuous session at the principal office of the Bank and shall meet as often as the business of the Bank may require.

* * *

SECTION 5. PRESIDENT AND STAFF

(a) The Executive Directors shall select a President who shall not be a governor or an executive director or an alternate for either. The President shall be Chairman of the Executive Directors, but shall have no vote except a deciding vote in case of an equal division. He may participate in meetings of the Board of Governors, but shall not vote at such meetings. The President shall cease to hold office when the Executive Directors so decide.

(b) The President shall be chief of the operating staff of the Bank and shall conduct, under the direction of the Executive Directors, the ordinary business of the Bank. Subject to the general control of the Executive Directors, he shall be responsible for the organization, appointment and dismissal of the officers and staff.

(c) The President, officers and staff of the Bank, in the discharge of their offices, owe their duty entirely to the Bank and to no other authority. Each member of the Bank shall respect the international character of this duty and shall refrain from all attempts to influence any of them in the discharge of their duties.

(d) In appointing the officers and staff the President shall, subject to the paramount importance of securing the highest standards of efficiency and of technical competence, pay due regard to the importance of recruiting personnel on as wide a geographical basis as possible.

SECTION 6. ADVISORY COUNCIL

(a) There shall be an Advisory Council of not less than seven persons selected by the Board of Governors including representatives of banking, commercial, industrial, labor, and agricultural interests, and with as wide a national representation as possible. In those fields where specialized international organizations exist, the members of the Council representative of those fields shall be selected in agreement with such organizations. The Council shall advise the Bank on matters of general policy. The Council shall meet annually and on such other occasions as the Bank may request.

(b) Councillors shall serve for two years and may be reappointed. They shall be paid their reasonable expenses incurred on behalf of the Bank.

SECTION 7. LOAN COMMITTEES

The committees required to report on loans under Article III, Section 4, shall be appointed by the Bank. Each such committee shall include an expert selected by the governor representing the member in whose territories the project is located and one or more members of the technical staff of the Bank.

* * *

ARTICLE VI. WITHDRAWAL AND SUSPENSION OF MEMBERSHIP: SUSPENSION OF OPERATIONS

SECTION 1. RIGHT OF MEMBERS TO WITHDRAW

Any member may withdraw from the Bank at any time by transmitting a notice in writing to the Bank at its principal office. Withdrawal shall become effective on the date such notice is received.

SECTION 2. SUSPENSION OF MEMBERSHIP

If a member fails to fulfill any of its obligations to the Bank, the Bank may suspend its membership by decision of a majority of the Governors, exercising a majority of the total voting power. The member so suspended shall automatically cease to be a member one year from the date of its suspension unless a decision is taken by the same majority to restore the member to good standing.

While under suspension, a member shall not be entitled to exercise any rights under this Agreement, except the right of withdrawal, but shall remain subject to all obligations.

SECTION 3. CESSATION OF MEMBERSHIP IN INTERNATIONAL MONETARY FUND

Any member which ceases to be a member of the International Monetary Fund shall automatically cease after three months to be a member of the Bank unless the Bank by three-fourths of the total voting power has agreed to allow it to remain a member.

* * *

ARTICLE VIII. AMENDMENTS

(a) Any proposal to introduce modifications in this Agreement, whether emanating from a member, a governor or the Executive Directors, shall be communicated to the Chairman of the Board of Governors who shall bring the proposal before the Board. If the proposed amendment is approved by the Board the Bank shall, by circular letter or telegram, ask all members whether they accept the proposed amendment. When three-fifths of the members, having four-fifths of the total voting power, have accepted the proposed amendment, the Bank shall certify the fact by a formal communication addressed to all members.

(b) Notwithstanding (a) above, acceptance by all members is required in the case of any amendment modifying

    (i) the right to withdraw from the Bank provided in Article VI, Section 1;

    (ii) the right secured by Article II, Section 3 (c);

    (iii) the limitation on liability provided in Article II, Section 6.

(c) Amendments shall enter into force for all members three months after the date of the formal communication unless a shorter period is specified in the circular letter or telegram.

ARTICLE IX. INTERPRETATION

(a) Any question of interpretation of the provisions of this Agreement arising between any member and the Bank or between any members of the Bank shall be submitted to the Executive Directors for their decision. If the question particularly affects any member not entitled to appoint an executive director, it shall be entitled to representation in accordance with Article V, Section 4 (h).

(b) In any case where the Executive Directors have given a decision under (a) above, any member may require that the question be referred to the Board of Governors, whose decision shall be final. Pending the result of the reference to the Board, the Bank may, so far as it deems necessary, act on the basis of the decision of the Executive Directors.

(c) Whenever a disagreement arises between the Bank and a country which has ceased to be a member, or between the Bank and any member during the permanent suspension of the Bank, such disagreement shall be submitted to arbitration by a tribunal of three arbitrators, one appointed by the Bank, another by the country involved and an umpire who, unless the parties otherwise agree, shall be appointed by the President of the Permanent Court of International Justice or such other authority as may have been prescribed by regulation adopted by the Bank. The umpire shall have full power to settle all questions of procedure in any case where the parties are in disagreement with respect thereto.

ARTICLE X. APPROVAL DEEMED GIVEN

Whenever the approval of any member is required before any act may be done by the Bank, except in Article VIII, approval shall be deemed to have been given unless the member presents an objection within such reasonable period as the Bank may fix in notifying the member of the proposed act.

ARTICLE XI. FINAL PROVISIONS

Schedule A

* * *

SUBSCRIPTIONS

	(millions of dollars)		(millions of dollars)
Australia	200	Iran	24
Belgium	225	Iraq	6
Bolivia	7	Liberia	.5
Brazil	105	Luxembourg	10
Canada	325	Mexico	65
Chile	35	Netherlands	275
China	600	New Zealand	50
Colombia	35	Nicaragua	.8
Costa Rica	2	Norway	50
Cuba	35	Panama	.2
Czechoslovakia	125	Paraguay	.8
* Denmark		Peru	17.5
Dominican Republic	2	Philippine Commonwealth	15
Ecuador	3.2	Poland	125
Egypt	40	Union of South Africa	100
El Salvador	1	Union of Soviet Socialist Republics	1200
Ethiopia	3	United Kingdom	1300
France	450	United States	3175
Greece	25	Uruguay	10.5
Guatemala	2	Venezuela	10.5
Haiti	2	Yugoslavia	40
Honduras	1		
Iceland	1	Total	9100
India	400		

* The quota of Denmark shall be determined by the Bank after Denmark accepts membership in accordance with these Articles of Agreement.

◇◇◇◇◇◇

32. CONSTITUTION OF THE UNITED NATIONS EDUCATIONAL, SCIENTIFIC AND CULTURAL ORGANISATION, NOVEMBER 16, 1945 [1]

[UNESCO's Charter points out that "wars begin in the minds of men." UNESCO's rôle in the UN structure, therefore, is to contribute to world peace by promoting international coöperation in the educational, scientific, and cultural fields, and thus to bring about a better understanding among the peoples of the world. This is, of course, an extremely difficult task, given the present state of world affairs. Some of UNESCO's projects—and it is sometimes accused of sponsoring too many—include the following:

[1] United States National Commission for UNESCO—Report on the First Meeting, September 1946, Department of State publication 2726, United States-United Nations Information Series 14, pp. 11-16. See also, UNESCO and the National Commission: Basic Documents, Department of State publication 3082, International Organization and Conference Series IV, United Nations Educational, Scientific and Cultural Organization 3. Constitution concluded at London November 16, 1945; effective November 4, 1946. Public Law 565, 79th Cong., 2d sess., H. J. Res. 305: Joint Resolution Providing for Membership and Participation by the United States in the UNESCO, approved July 30, 1946. Protocol relating to the entry into force of an agreement bringing the UNESCO into official relationship with the United Nations which was approved by the General Assembly, was signed February 3, 1947.

1. The raising of educational standards;
2. Improving the literacy of people in backward areas;
3. Developing closer relations among peoples through films, radio, press, books, and the exchange of persons;
4. Educational reconstruction in countries devastated by war; and
5. A study of tensions and prejudices that separate people.]

The Governments of the States parties to this Constitution on behalf of their peoples declare

that since wars begin in the minds of men, it is in the minds of men that the defences of peace must be constructed;

that ignorance of each other's ways and lives has been a common cause, throughout the history of mankind, of that suspicion and mistrust between the peoples of the world through which their differences have all too often broken into war;

that the great and terrible war which has now ended was a war made possible by the denial of the democratic principles of the dignity, equality and mutual respect of men, and by the propagation, in their place, through ignorance and prejudice, of the doctrine of the inequality of men and races;

that the wide diffusion of culture, and the education of humanity for justice and liberty and peace are indispensable to the dignity of man and constitute a sacred duty which all the nations must fulfill in a spirit of mutual assistance and concern;

that a peace based exclusively upon the political and economic arrangements of governments would not be a peace which could secure the unanimous, lasting and sincere support of the peoples of the world, and that the peace must therefore be founded, if it is not to fail, upon the intellectual and moral solidarity of mankind.

For these reasons, the States parties to this Constitution, believing in full and equal opportunities for education for all, in the unrestricted pursuit of objective truth, and in the free exchange of ideas and knowledge, are agreed and determined to develop and to increase the means of communication between their peoples and to employ these means for the purposes of mutual understanding and a truer and more perfect knowledge of each other's lives;

In consequence whereof they do hereby create the United Nations Educational, Scientific and Cultural Organisation for the purpose of advancing, through the educational and scientific and cultural relations of the peoples of the world, the objectives of international peace and of the common welfare of mankind for which the United Nations Organisation was established and which its Charter proclaims.

ARTICLE I. PURPOSES AND FUNCTIONS

1. The purpose of the Organisation is to contribute to peace and security by promoting collaboration among the nations through education, science and culture in order to further universal respect for justice, for the rule of law and for the human rights and fundamental freedoms which are affirmed for the peoples of the world, without distinction of race, sex, language or religion, by the Charter of the United Nations.

2. To realise this purpose the Organisation will:

(*a*) collaborate in the work of advancing the mutual knowledge and understanding of peoples, through all means of mass communication and to that end recommend such international agreements as may be necessary to promote the free flow of ideas by word and image;

(*b*) give fresh impulse to popular education and to the spread of culture;

> by collaborating with Members, at their request, in the development of educational activities;

> by instituting collaboration among the nations to advance the ideal of equality of educational opportunity without regard to race, sex or any distinctions, economic or social;

> by suggesting educational methods best suited to prepare the children of the world for the responsibilities of freedom;

(*c*) maintain, increase and diffuse knowledge;

> by assuring the conservation and protection of the world's inheritance of books, works of art and monuments of history and science, and recommending to the nations concerned the necessary international conventions;

> by encouraging cooperation among the nations in all branches of intellectual activity, including the international exchange of persons active in the fields of education, science and culture and the exchange of publications, objects of artistic and scientific interest and other materials of information;

> by initiating methods of international cooperation calculated to give the people of all countries access to the printed and published materials produced by any of them.

3. With a view to preserving the independence, integrity and fruitful diversity of the cultures and educational systems of the States Members of this Organisation, the Organisation is prohibited from intervening in matters which are essentially within their domestic jurisdiction.

ARTICLE II. MEMBERSHIP

1. Membership of the United Nations Organisation shall carry with it the right to membership of the United Nations Educational, Scientific and Cultural Organisation.

2. Subject to the conditions of the agreement between this Organisation and the United Nations Organisation, approved pursuant to Article X of this Constitution, States not members of the United Nations Organisation may be admitted to membership of the Organisation, upon recommendation of the Executive Board, by a two-thirds majority vote of the General Conference.

3. Members of the Organisation which are suspended from the exercise of the rights and privileges of membership of the United Nations Organisation shall, upon the request of the latter, be suspended from the rights and privileges of this Organisation.

4. Members of the Organisation which are expelled from the United Nations Organisation shall automatically cease to be members of this Organisation.

ARTICLE III. ORGANS

The Organisation shall include a General Conference, an Executive Board and a Secretariat.

ARTICLE IV. THE GENERAL CONFERENCE

A. Composition

1. The General Conference shall consist of the representatives of the States Members of the Organisation. The Government of each Member State shall appoint not more than five delegates, who shall be selected after consultation with the National Commission, if established, or with educational, scientific and cultural bodies.

B. Functions

2. The General Conference shall determine the policies and the main lines of work of the Organisation. It shall take decisions on programmes drawn up by the Executive Board.

3. The General Conference shall, when it deems it desirable, summon international conferences on education, the sciences and humanities and the dissemination of knowledge.

4. The General Conference shall, in adopting proposals for submission to the Member States, distinguish between recommendations and international conventions submitted for their approval. In the former case a majority vote shall suffice; in the latter case a two-thirds majority shall be required. Each of the Member States shall submit recommendations or conventions to its competent authorities within a period of one year from the close of the session of the General Conference at which they were adopted.

5. The General Conference shall advise the United Nations Organisation on the educational, scientific and cultural aspects of matters of concern to the latter, in accordance with the terms and procedure agreed upon between the appropriate authorities of the two Organisations.

6. The General Conference shall receive and consider the reports submitted periodically by Member States as provided by Article VIII.

7. The General Conference shall elect the members of the Executive Board and, on the recommendation of the Board, shall appoint the Director-General.

C. Voting

8. Each Member State shall have one vote in the General Conference. Decisions shall be made by a simple majority except in cases in which a two-thirds majority is required by the provisions of this Constitution. A majority shall be a majority of the Members present and voting.

D. Procedure

9. The General Conference shall meet annually in ordinary session; it may meet in extraordinary session on the call of the Executive Board. At each session the location of its next session shall be designated by the General Conference and shall vary from year to year.

10. The General Conference shall, at each session, elect a President and other officers and adopt rules of procedure.

11. The General Conference shall set up special and technical committees and such other subordinate bodies as may be necessary for its purposes.

12. The General Conference shall cause arrangements to be made for public access to meetings, subject to such regulations as it shall prescribe.

E. Observers

13. The General Conference, on the recommendation of the Executive Board and by a two-thirds majority may, subject to its rules of procedure, invite as observers at specified sessions of the Conference or of its commissions representatives of international organisations, such as those referred to in Article XI, paragraph 4.

ARTICLE V. EXECUTIVE BOARD

A. Composition

1. The Executive Board shall consist of eighteen members elected by the General Conference from among the delegates appointed by the Member States, together with the President of the Conference who shall sit *ex officio* in an advisory capacity.

2. In electing the members of the Executive Board the General Conference shall endeavour to include persons competent in the arts, the humanities, the sciences, education and the diffusion of ideas, and qualified by their experience and capacity to fulfil the administrative and executive duties of the Board. It shall also have regard to the diversity of cultures and a balanced geographical distribution. Not more than one national of any Member State shall serve on the Board at any one time, the President of the Conference excepted.

3. The elected members of the Executive Board shall serve for a term of three years, and shall be immediately eligible for a second term, but shall not serve consecutively for more than two terms. At the first election eighteen members shall be elected of whom one third shall retire at the end of the first year and one third at the end of the second year, the order of retirement being determined immediately after the election by the drawing of lots. Thereafter six members shall be elected each year.

4. In the event of the death or resignation of one of its members, the Executive Board shall appoint, from among the delegates of the Member State concerned, a substitute, who shall serve until the next session of the General Conference which shall elect a member for the remainder of the term.

B. Functions

5. The Executive Board, acting under the authority of the General Conference, shall be responsible for the execution of the programme adopted by the Conference and shall prepare its agenda and programme of work.

6. The Executive Board shall recommend to the General Conference the admission of new Members to the Organisation.

7. Subject to decisions of the General Conference, the Executive Board shall adopt its own rules of procedure. It shall elect its officers from among its members.

8. The Executive Board shall meet in regular session at least twice a year and may meet in special session if convoked by the Chairman on his own initiative or upon the request of six members of the Board.

9. The Chairman of the Executive Board shall present to the General Conference, with or without comment, the annual report of the Director-

General on the activities of the Organisation, which shall have been previously submitted to the Board.

10. The Executive Board shall make all necessary arrangements to consult the representatives of international organisations or qualified persons concerned with questions within its competence.

11. The members of the Executive Board shall exercise the powers delegated to them by the General Conference on behalf of the Conference as a whole and not as representatives of their respective Governments.

ARTICLE VI. SECRETARIAT

1. The Secretariat shall consist of a Director-General and such staff as may be required.

2. The Director-General shall be nominated by the Executive Board and appointed by the General Conference for a period of six years, under such conditions as the Conference may approve, and shall be eligible for re-appointment. He shall be the chief administrative officer of the Organisation.

3. The Director-General, or a deputy designated by him, shall participate, without the right to vote, in all meetings of the General Conference, of the Executive Board, and of the committees of the Organisation. He shall formulate proposals for appropriate action by the Conference and the Board.

4. The Director-General shall appoint the staff of the Secretariat in accordance with staff regulations to be approved by the General Conference. Subject to the paramount consideration of securing the highest standards of integrity, efficiency and technical competence appointment to the staff shall be on as wide a geographical basis as possible.

5. The responsibilities of the Director-General and of the staff shall be exclusively international in character. In the discharge of their duties they shall not seek or receive instructions from any government or from any authority external to the Organisation. They shall refrain from any action which might prejudice their position as international officials. Each State Member of the Organisation undertakes to respect the international character of the responsibilities of the Director-General and the staff, and not to seek to influence them in the discharge of their duties.

6. Nothing in this Article shall preclude the Organisation from entering into special arrangements within the United Nations Organisation for common services and staff and for the interchange of personnel.

ARTICLE VII. NATIONAL CO-OPERATING BODIES

1. Each Member State shall make such arrangements as suit its particular conditions for the purpose of associating its principal bodies interested in educational, scientific and cultural matters with the work of the Organisation, preferably by the formation of a National Commission broadly representative of the Government and such bodies.

2. National Commissions or national co-operating bodies, where they exist, shall act in an advisory capacity to their respective delegations to the General Conference and to their Governments in matters relating to the Organisation and shall function as agencies of liaison in all matters of interest to it.

3. The Organisation may, on the request of a Member State, delegate, either temporarily or permanently, a member of its Secretariat to serve on the

National Commission of that State, in order to assist in the development of its work.

ARTICLE VIII. REPORTS BY MEMBER STATES

Each Member State shall report periodically to the Organisation, in a manner to be determined by the General Conference, on its laws, regulations and statistics relating to educational, scientific and cultural life and institutions, and on the action taken upon the recommendations and conventions referred to in Article IV, paragraph 4.

ARTICLE IX. BUDGET

1. The budget shall be administered by the Organisation.
2. The General Conference shall approve and give final effect to the budget and to the apportionment of financial responsibility among the States Members of the Organisation subject to such arrangement with the United Nations as may be provided in the agreement to be entered into pursuant to Article X.
3. The Director-General, with the approval of the Executive Board, may receive gifts, bequests, and subventions directly from governments, public and private institutions, associations and private persons.

ARTICLE X. RELATIONS WITH THE UNITED NATIONS ORGANISATION

This Organisation shall be brought into relation with the United Nations Organisation, as soon as practicable, as one of the specialised agencies referred to in Article 57 of the Charter of the United Nations. This relationship shall be effected through an agreement with the United Nations Organisation under Article 63 of the Charter, which agreement shall be subject to the approval of the General Conference of this Organisation. The agreement shall provide for effective co-operation between the two Organisations in the pursuit of their common purposes, and at the same time shall recognise the autonomy of this Organisation, within the fields of its competence as defined in this Constitution. Such agreement may, among other matters, provide for the approval and financing of the budget of the Organisation by the General Assembly of the United Nations.

ARTICLE XI. RELATIONS WITH OTHER SPECIALIZED ORGANISATIONS AND AGENCIES

1. This Organisation may co-operate with other specialised inter-governmental organisations and agencies whose interests and activities are related to its purposes. To this end the Director-General, acting under the general authority of the Executive Board, may establish effective working relationships with such organisations and agencies and establish such joint committees as may be necessary to assure effective co-operation. Any formal arrangements entered into with such organisations or agencies shall be subject to the approval of the Executive Board.
2. Whenever the General Conference of this Organisation and the competent authorities of any other specialised inter-governmental organisations or agencies whose purposes and functions lie within the competence of this Organisation, deem it desirable to effect a transfer of their resources and activities to this Organisation, the Director-General, subject to the approval

of the Conference, may enter into mutually acceptable arrangements for its purpose.

3. This Organisation may make appropriate arrangements with other inter-governmental organisations for reciprocal representation at meetings.

4. The United Nations Educational, Scientific and Cultural Organisation may make suitable arrangements for consultation and co-operation with non-governmental international organisations concerned with matters within its competence, and may invite them to undertake specific tasks. Such co-operation may also include appropriate participation by representatives of such organisations on advisory committees set up by the General Conference.

ARTICLE XII. LEGAL STATUS OF THE ORGANISATION

The provisions of Articles 104 and 105 of the Charter of the United Nations Organisation concerning the legal status of that Organisation, its privileges and immunities shall apply in the same way to this Organisation.

ARTICLE XIII. AMENDMENTS

1. Proposals for amendments to this Constitution shall become effective upon receiving the approval of the General Conference by a two-thirds majority; provided, however, that those amendments which involve fundamental alterations in the aims of the Organisation or new obligations for the Member States shall require subsequent acceptance on the part of two-thirds of the Member States before they come into force. The draft texts of proposed amendments shall be communicated by the Director-General to the Member States at least six months in advance of their consideration by the General Conference.

2. The General Conference shall have power to adopt by a two-thirds majority rules of procedure for carrying out the provisions of this Article.

ARTICLE XIV. INTERPRETATION

1. The English and French texts of this Constitution shall be regarded as equally authoritative.

2. Any question or dispute concerning the interpretation of this Constitution shall be referred for determination to the International Court of Justice or to an arbitral tribunal, as the General Conference may determine under its rules of procedure.

ARTICLE XV. ENTRY INTO FORCE

1. This Constitution shall be subject to acceptance. The instruments of acceptance shall be deposited with the Government of the United Kingdom.

2. This Constitution shall remain open for signature in the archives of the Government of the United Kingdom. Signature may take place either before or after the deposit of the instrument of acceptance. No acceptance shall be valid unless preceded or followed by signature.

3. This Constitution shall come into force when it has been accepted by twenty of its signatories. Subsequent acceptances shall take effect immediately.

4. The Government of the United Kingdom will inform all members of the United Nations of the receipt of all instruments of acceptance and of the

date on which the Constitution comes into force in accordance with the preceding paragraph.

In faith whereof, the undersigned, duly authorised to that effect, have signed this Constitution in the English and French languages, both texts being equally authentic.

Done in London the sixteenth day of November 1945 in a single copy, in the English and French languages, of which certified copies will be communicated by the Government of the United Kingdom to the Governments of all the Members of the United Nations.

[Here follow the signatures of the heads of the delegations.]

*   *   *

◇◇◇◇◇◇

33. PARTICIPATION IN UNESCO, JULY 30, 1946 [1]

JOINT RESOLUTION Providing for membership and participation by the United States in UNESCO

[Article VII of UNESCO's charter provides for the creation of national commissions in member states so that the principal organizations interested in educational, scientific, and cultural matters can be associated more effectively with the work of UNESCO. The national commission has been very active in the U.S. in furthering the programs and policies of UNESCO. Since this is a relatively new idea in international organization, the law providing for U.S. participation in UNESCO and the establishment of the national commission is reproduced below.]

Resolved by the Senate and House of Representatives of the United States of America in Congress assembled, That the President is hereby authorized to accept membership for the United States in the United Nations Educational, Scientific, and Cultural Organization (hereinafter referred to as the "Organization"), the constitution of which was approved in London on November 16, 1945, by the United Nations Conference for the establishment of an Educational, Scientific, and Cultural Organization, and deposited in the Archives of the Government of the United Kingdom.

SEC. 2. The President by and with the consent of the Senate shall designate from time to time to attend a specified session or specified sessions of the General Conference of the Organization not to exceed five representatives of the United States and such number of alternates not to exceed five as he may determine consistent with the rules of procedure of the General Conference: *Provided, however,* That each such representative and each such alternate must be an American citizen. One of the representatives shall be designated as the senior representative. Such representatives and alternates shall each be entitled to receive compensation at such rates, not to exceed $12,000 per annum, as the President may determine, for such periods as the President may specify, except that no Member of the Senate or House of Rep-

[1] Public Law 565, 79th Cong., 2d sess., H. J. Res. 305.

resentatives or officer of the United States who is designated under this section as a representative of the United States or as an alternate to attend any specified session or specified sessions of the General Conference shall be entitled to receive such compensation. Whenever a representative of the United States is elected by the General Conference to serve on the Executive Board, or is elected President of the General Conference and thus becomes an ex officio adviser to the Executive Board, under provision of article V of the constitution of the Organization, the President may extend the above provisions for compensation to such representative during periods of service in connection with the Executive Board.

SEC. 3. In fulfillment of article VII of the constitution of the Organization, the Secretary of State shall cause to be organized a National Commission on Educational, Scientific, and Cultural Coöperation of not to exceed one hundred members. Such Commission shall be appointed by the Secretary of State and shall consist of (a) not more than sixty representatives of principal national, voluntary organizations interested in educational, scientific, and cultural matters; and (b) not more than forty outstanding persons selected by the Secretary of State, including not more than ten persons holding office under or employed by the Government of the United States, not more than fifteen representatives of the educational, scientific, and cultural interests of State and local governments, and not more than fifteen persons chosen at large. The Secretary of State is authorized to name in the first instance fifty of the principal national voluntary organizations, each of which shall be invited to designate one representative for appointment to the National Commission. Thereafter, the National Commission shall periodically review and, if deemed advisable, revise the list of such organizations designating representatives in order to achieve a desirable rotation among organizations represented. To constitute the initial Commission, one-third of the members shall be appointed to serve for a term of one year, one-third for a term of two years, and one-third or the remainder thereof for a term of three years; from thence on following, all members shall be appointed for a term of three years each, but no member shall serve more than two consecutive terms. The National Commission shall meet at least once annually. The National Commission shall designate from among its members an executive committee, and may designate such other committees as may prove necessary, to consult with the Department of State and to perform such other functions as the National Commission shall delegate to them. No member of the National Commission shall be allowed any salary or other compensation for services: *Provided, however,* That he may be paid his actual transportation expenses, and not to exceed $10 per diem in lieu of subsistence and other expenses, while away from his home in attendance upon authorized meetings or in consultation on request with the Department of State. The Department of State is authorized to provide the necessary secretariat for the Commission.

SEC. 4. That each such member of the National Commission must be an American citizen.

SEC. 5. The National Commission shall call general conferences for the discussion of matters relating to the activities of the Organization, to which conferences organized bodies actively interested in such matters shall be invited to send representatives: *Provided, however,* That the travel and maintenance of such representation shall be without expense to the Government. Such general conferences shall be held annually or biennially, as the National Commission may determine, and in such places as it may designate. They shall be attended so far as possible by the members of the National Commission and by the delegates of the United States to the General Conference of the Organization. The National Commission is further authorized to call special conferences of experts for the consideration of specific matters relating to the Organization by persons of specialized competences. Under such regulations as the Secretary of State may prescribe, the actual transportation expenses of experts attending such conferences shall be borne by the Department of State, and they shall be allowed a per diem of $10 in lieu of subsistence and other expenses, for the period of actual attendance and of necessary travel.

SEC. 6. There is hereby authorized to be appropriated annually to the Department of State, out of any money in the Treasury not otherwise appropriated, such sums as may be necessary for the payment by the United States of its share of the expenses of the Organization as apportioned by the General Conference of the Organization in accordance with article IX of the constitution of the Organization, and such additional sums as may be necessary to pay the expenses of participation by the United States in the activities of the Organization.

*   *   *

SEC. 7. Unless Congress by law authorizes such action, neither the President nor any person or agency shall on behalf of the United States approve any amendment under article XIII of the constitution of the Organization involving any new obligation for the United States.

SEC. 8. In adopting this joint resolution, it is the understanding of the Congress that the constitution of the Organization does not require, nor does this resolution authorize, the disclosure of any information or knowledge in any case in which such disclosure is prohibited by any law of the United States.

Approved July 30, 1946.

◇◇◇◇◇◇

34. CONSTITUTION OF THE WORLD HEALTH ORGANIZATION, JULY 22, 1946 [1]

[The Constitution of WHO (World Health Organization) was drawn up in 1946, although it did not come into effect until 1948. WHO has an exceptionally broad mandate; its objective is "the attainment by all peoples of the highest possible level of health." Among other things, it promotes the improvement of nutrition, housing, sanitation, recreation, and maternal and child health and welfare.

[1] Department of State Bulletin of August 4, 1946, pp. 211-219; also, International Health Conference, New York, N. Y., June 19-July 22, 1946: Report of the U. S. Delegation, Including the Final Act and Related Documents, Department of State publication 2703, Conference Series 91. Agreement establishing formal relationship between the World Health Organization and the United Nations was approved by the General Assembly on November 15, 1947.

At the present writing, WHO has six priority programs relating to malaria, tuberculosis, venereal infection, maternal and child health, nutrition, and environmental hygiene. Like the other specialized agencies, WHO functions under the very loose general supervision of the Economic Council and Social Council.]

The States parties to this Constitution declare, in conformity with the Charter of the United Nations, that the following principles are basic to the happiness, harmonious relations and security of all peoples:

Health is a state of complete physical, mental and social well-being and not merely the absence of disease or infirmity.

The enjoyment of the highest attainable standard of health is one of the fundamental rights of every human being without distinction of race, religion, political belief, economic or social condition.

The health of all peoples is fundamental to the attainment of peace and security and is dependent upon the fullest co-operation of individuals and States.

The achievement of any State in the promotion and protection of health is of value to all.

Unequal development in different countries in the promotion of health and control of disease, especially communicable disease, is a common danger.

Healthy development of the child is of basic importance; the ability to live harmoniously in a changing total environment is essential to such development.

The extension to all peoples of the benefits of medical, psychological and related knowledge is essential to the fullest attainment of health.

Informed opinion and active co-operation on the part of the public are of the utmost importance in the improvement of the health of the people.

Governments have a responsibility for the health of their peoples which can be fulfilled only by the provision of adequate health and social measures.

Accepting these principles, and for the purpose of co-operation among themselves and with others to promote and protect the health of all peoples, the Contracting Parties agree to the present Constitution and hereby establish the World Health Organization as a specialized agency of the United Nations.

CHAPTER I: OBJECTIVE

ARTICLE 1

The objective of the World Health Organization (hereinafter called the Organization) shall be the attainment by all peoples of the highest possible level of health.

CHAPTER II: FUNCTIONS

ARTICLE 2

In order to achieve its objective, the functions of the Organization shall be:

(*a*) to act as the directing and co-ordinating authority on international health work;

(*b*) to establish and maintain effective collaboration with the United Nations, specialized agencies, governmental health administrations, professional groups and such other organizations as may be deemed appropriate;

(*c*) to assist governments, upon request, in strengthening health services;

(*d*) to furnish appropriate technical assistance and, in emergencies, necessary aid upon the request or acceptance of governments;

(*e*) to provide or assist in providing, upon the request of the United Nations, health services and facilities to special groups, such as the peoples of trust territories;

(*f*) to establish and maintain such administrative and technical services as may be required, including epidemiological and statistical services;

(*g*) to stimulate and advance work to eradicate epidemic, endemic and other diseases;

(*h*) to promote, in co-operation with other specialized agencies where necessary, the prevention of accidental injuries;

(*i*) to promote, in co-operation with other specialized agencies where necessary, the improvement of nutrition, housing, sanitation, recreation, economic or working conditions and other aspects of environmental hygiene;

(*j*) to promote co-operation among scientific and professional groups which contribute to the advancement of health;

(*k*) to propose conventions, agreements and regulations, and make recommendations with respect to international health matters and to perform such duties as may be assigned thereby to the Organization and are consistent with its objective;

(*l*) to promote maternal and child health and welfare and to foster the ability to live harmoniously in a changing total environment;

(*m*) to foster activities in the field of mental health, especially those affecting the harmony of human relations;

(*n*) to promote and conduct research in the field of health;

(*o*) to promote improved standards of teaching and training in health, medical and related professions;

(*p*) to study and report on, in co-operation with other specialized agencies where necessary, administrative and social techniques affecting public health and medical care from preventive and curative points of view, including hospital services and social security;

(*q*) to provide information, counsel and assistance in the field of health;

(*r*) to assist in developing an informed public opinion among all peoples on matters of health;

(*s*) to establish and revise as necessary international nomenclatures of diseases, of causes of death and of public health practices;

(*t*) to standardize diagnostic procedures as necessary;

(*u*) to develop, establish and promote international standards with respect to food, biological, pharmaceutical and similar products;

(*v*) generally to take all necessary action to attain the objective of the Organization.

Chapter III: Membership and Associate Membership

Article 3

Membership in the Organization shall be open to all States.

Article 4

Members of the United Nations may become Members of the Organization by signing or otherwise accepting this Constitution in accordance with the provisions of Chapter XIX and in accordance with their constitutional processes.

Article 5

The States whose governments have been invited to send observers to the International Health Conference held in New York, 1946, may become Members by signing or otherwise accepting this Constitution in accordance with the provisions of Chapter XIX and in accordance with their constitutional processes provided that such signature or acceptance shall be completed before the first session of the Health Assembly.

Article 6

Subject to the conditions of any agreement between the United Nations and the Organization, approved pursuant to Chapter XVI, States which do not become Members in accordance with Articles 4 and 5 may apply to become Members and shall be admitted as Members when their application has been approved by a simple majority vote of the Health Assembly.

Article 7

If a Member fails to meet its financial obligations to the Organization or in other exceptional circumstances the Health Assembly many, on such conditions as it thinks proper, suspend the voting privileges and services to which a Member is entitled. The Health Assembly shall have the authority to restore such voting privileges and services.

Article 8

Territories or groups of territories which are not responsible for the conduct of their international relations may be admitted as Associate Members by the Health Assembly upon application made on behalf of such territory or group of territories by the Member or other authority having responsibility for their international relations. Representatives of Associate Members to the Health Assembly should be qualified by their technical competence in the field of health and should be chosen from the native population. The nature and extent of the rights and obligations of Associate Members shall be determined by the Health Assembly.

CHAPTER IV: ORGANS

ARTICLE 9

The work of the Organization shall be carried out by:

(*a*) The World Health Assembly (hereinafter called the Health Assembly);

(*b*) The Executive Board (hereinafter called the Board);

(*c*) The Secretariat.

CHAPTER V: THE WORLD HEALTH ASSEMBLY

ARTICLE 10

The Health Assembly shall be composed of delegates representing Members.

ARTICLE 11

Each Member shall be represented by not more than three delegates, one of whom shall be designated by the Member as chief delegate. These delegates should be chosen from among persons most qualified by their technical competence in the field of health, preferably representing the national health administration of the Member.

ARTICLE 12

Alternates and advisers may accompany delegates.

ARTICLE 13

The Health Assembly shall meet in regular annual session and in such special sessions as may be necessary. Special sessions shall be convened at the request of the Board or of a majority of the members.

*   *   *

ARTICLE 18

The functions of the Health Assembly shall be:

(*a*) to determine the policies of the Organization;

(*b*) to name the Members entitled to designate a person to serve on the Board;

(*c*) to appoint the Director-General;

(*d*) to review and approve reports and activities of the Board and of the Director-General and to instruct the Board in regard to matters upon which action, study, investigation or report may be considered desirable;

(*e*) to establish such committees as may be considered necessary for the work of the Organization;

(*f*) to supervise the financial policies of the Organization and to review and approve the budget;

(*g*) to instruct the Board and the Director-General to bring to the attention of Members and of international organizations, governmental or non-governmental, any matter with regard to health which the Health Assembly may consider appropriate;

(*h*) to invite any organization, international or national, governmental or non-governmental, which has responsibilities related to those of the Organization, to appoint representatives to participate, without right of vote, in its meetings or in those of the committees and conferences convened under its authority, on conditions prescribed by the Health Assembly; but in the case of national organizations, invitations shall be issued only with the consent of the government concerned;

(*i*) to consider recommendations bearing on health made by the General Assembly, the Economic and Social Council, the Security Council or Trusteeship Council of the United Nations, and to report to them on the steps taken by the Organization to give effect to such recommendations;

(*j*) to report to the Economic and Social Council in accordance with any agreement between the Organization and the United Nations;

(*k*) to promote and conduct research in the field of health by the personnel of the Organization, by the establishment of its own institutions or by cooperation with official or non-official institutions of any Member with the consent of its government;

(*l*) to establish such other institutions as it may consider desirable;

(*m*) to take any other appropriate action to further the objective of the Organization.

ARTICLE 19

The Health Assembly shall have authority to adopt conventions or agreements with respect to any matter within the competence of the Organization. A two-thirds vote of the Health Assembly shall be required for the adoption of such conventions or agreements which shall come into force for each Member when accepted by it in accordance with its constitutional processes.

ARTICLE 20

Each Member undertakes that it will, within eighteen months after the adoption by the Health Assembly of a convention or agreement, take action relative to the acceptance of such convention or agreement. Each Member shall notify the Director-General of the action taken and if it does not accept such convention or agreement within the time limit, it will furnish a statement of the reasons for non-acceptance. In case of acceptance, each Member agrees to make an annual report to the Director-General in accordance with Chapter XIV.

ARTICLE 21

The Health Assembly shall have authority to adopt regulations concerning:

(*a*) sanitary and quarantine requirements and other procedures designed to prevent the international spread of disease;

(*b*) nomenclatures with respect to diseases, causes of death and public health practices;

(c) standards with respect to diagnostic procedures for international use;

(d) standards with respect to the safety, purity and potency of biological, pharmaceutical and similar products moving in international commerce;

(e) advertising and labelling of biological, pharmaceutical and similar products moving in international commerce.

ARTICLE 22

Such Regulations adopted pursuant to Article 21 shall come into force for all Members after due notice has been given of their adoption by the Health Assembly except for such Members as may notify the Director-General of rejection or reservations within the period stated in the notice.

ARTICLE 23

The Health Assembly shall have authority to make recommendations to Members with respect to any matter within the competence of the Organization.

CHAPTER VI: THE EXECUTIVE BOARD

ARTICLE 24

The Board shall consist of eighteen persons designated by as many Members. The Health Assembly, taking into account an equitable geographical distribution, shall elect the Members entitled to designate a person to serve on the Board. Each of these Members should appoint to the Board a person technically qualified in the field of health, who may be accompanied by alternates and advisers.

ARTICLE 25

The Members shall be elected for three years and may be re-elected; provided that of the Members elected at the first session of the Health Assembly, the terms of six Members shall be for one year and the terms of six Members shall be for two years, as determined by lot.

ARTICLE 26

The Board shall meet at least twice a year and shall determine the place of each meeting.

ARTICLE 27

The Board shall elect its Chairman from among its Members and shall adopt its rules of procedure.

ARTICLE 28

The functions of the Board shall be:

(a) to give effect to the decisions and policies of the Health Assembly;

(b) to act as the executive organ of the Health Assembly;

(c) to perform any other functions entrusted to it by the Health Assembly;

(*d*) to advise the Health Assembly on questions referred to it by that body and on matters assigned to the Organization by conventions, agreements and regulations;

(*e*) to submit advice or proposals to the Health Assembly on its own initiative;

(*f*) to prepare the agenda of meetings of the Health Assembly;

(*g*) to submit to the Health Assembly for consideration and approval a general programme of work covering a specific period;

(*h*) to study all questions within its competence;

(*i*) to take emergency measures within the functions and financial resources of the Organization to deal with events requiring immediate action. In particular it may authorize the Director-General to take the necessary steps to combat epidemics, to participate in the organization of health relief to victims of a calamity and to undertake studies and research the urgency of which has been drawn to the attention of the Board by any Member or by the Director-General.

ARTICLE 29

The Board shall exercise on behalf of the whole Health Assembly the powers delegated to it by that body.

CHAPTER VII: THE SECRETARIAT

ARTICLE 30

The Secretariat shall comprise the Director-General and such technical and administrative staff as the Organization may require.

ARTICLE 31

The Director-General shall be appointed by the Health Assembly on the nomination of the Board on such terms as the Health Assembly may determine. The Director-General, subject to the authority of the Board, shall be the chief technical and administrative officer of the Organization.

ARTICLE 32

The Director-General shall be ex-officio Secretary of the Health Assembly, of the Board, of all commissions and committees of the Organization and of conferences convened by it. He may delegate these functions.

ARTICLE 33

The Director-General or his representative may establish a procedure by agreement with Members, permitting him, for the purpose of discharging his duties, to have direct access to their various departments, especially to their health administrations and to national health organizations, governmental or non-governmental. He may also establish direct relations with international organizations whose activities come within the competence of the Organization. He shall keep Regional Offices informed on all matters involving their respective areas.

ARTICLE 34

The Director-General shall prepare and submit annually to the Board the financial statements and budget estimates of the Organization.

ARTICLE 35

The Director-General shall appoint the staff of the Secretariat in accordance with staff regulations established by the Health Assembly. The paramount consideration in the employment of the staff shall be to assure that the efficiency, integrity and internationally representative character of the Secretariat shall be maintained at the highest level. Due regard shall be paid also to the importance of recruiting the staff on as wide a geographical basis as possible.

ARTICLE 36

The conditions of service of the staff of the Organization shall conform as far as possible with those of other United Nations organizations.

ARTICLE 37

In the performance of their duties the Director-General and the staff shall not seek or receive instructions from any government or from any authority external to the Organization. They shall refrain from any action which might reflect on their position as international officers. Each Member of the Organization on its part undertakes to respect the exclusively international character of the Director-General and the staff and not seek to influence them.

*   *   *

CHAPTER IX: CONFERENCES

ARTICLE 41

The Health Assembly or the Board may convene local, general, technical or other special conferences to consider any matter within the competence of the Organization and may provide for the representation at such conferences of international organizations and, with the consent of the government concerned, of national organizations, governmental or non-governmental. The manner of such representation shall be determined by the Health Assembly or the Board.

ARTICLE 42

The Board may provide for representation of the Organization at conferences in which the Board considers that the Organization has an interest.

*   *   *

CHAPTER XI: REGIONAL ARRANGEMENTS

ARTICLE 44

(a) The Health Assembly shall from time to time define the geographical areas in which it is desirable to establish a regional organization.

(*b*) The Health Assembly may, with the consent of a majority of the Members situated within each area so defined, establish a regional organization to meet the special needs of such area. There shall not be more than one regional organization in each region.

ARTICLE 45

Each regional organization shall be an integral part of the Organization in accordance with this Constitution.

ARTICLE 46

Each regional organization shall consist of a Regional Committee and a Regional Office.

ARTICLE 47

Regional Committees shall be composed of representatives of the Member states and Associate Members in the region concerned. Territories or groups of territories within the region, which are not responsible for the conduct of their international relations and which are not Associate Members, shall have the right to be represented and to participate in Regional Committees. The nature and extent of the rights and obligations of these territories or groups of territories in Regional Committees shall be determined by the Health Assembly in consultation with the Member or other authority having responsibility for the international relations of these territories and with the Member States in the region.

*   *   *

ARTICLE 50

The functions of the Regional Committee shall be:

(*a*) to formulate policies governing matters of an exclusively regional character;

(*b*) to supervise the activities of the Regional Office;

(*c*) to suggest to the Regional Office the calling of technical conferences and such additional work or investigation in health matters as in the opinion of the Regional Committee would promote the objective of the Organization within the region;

(*d*) to co-operate with the respective regional committees of the United Nations and with those of other specialized agencies and with other regional international organizations having interests in common with the Organization;

(*e*) to tender advice, through the Director-General, to the Organization on international health matters which have wider than regional significance;

(*f*) to recommend additional regional appropriations by the governments of the respective regions if the proportion of the central budget of the Organization allotted to that region is insufficient for the carrying out of the regional functions;

(*g*) such other functions as may be delegated to the Regional Committee by the Health Assembly, the Board or the Director-General.

ARTICLE 51

Subject to the general authority of the Director-General of the Organization, the Regional Office shall be the administrative organ of the Regional Committee. It shall, in addition, carry out within the region, the decisions of the Health Assembly and of the Board.

ARTICLE 52

The head of the Regional Office shall be the Regional Director appointed by the Board in agreement with the Regional Committee.

ARTICLE 53

The staff of the Regional Office shall be appointed in a manner to be determined by agreement between the Director-General and the Regional Director.

ARTICLE 54

The Pan-American sanitary organization represented by the Pan-American Sanitary Bureau and the Pan-American Sanitary Conferences, and all other inter-governmental regional health organizations in existence prior to the date of signature of this Constitution, shall in due course be integrated with the Organization. This integration shall be effected as soon as practicable through common action based on mutual consent of the competent authorities expressed through the organizations concerned.

CHAPTER XII: BUDGET AND EXPENSES

ARTICLE 55

The Director-General shall prepare and submit to the Board the annual budget estimates of the Organization. The Board shall consider and submit to the Health Assembly such budget estimates, together with any recommendations the Board may deem advisable.

ARTICLE 56

Subject to any agreement between the Organization and the United Nations, the Health Assembly shall review and approve the budget estimates and shall apportion the expenses among the Members in accordance with a scale to be fixed by the Health Assembly.

*   *   *

CHAPTER XIII: VOTING

ARTICLE 59

Each Member shall have one vote in the Health Assembly.

ARTICLE 60

(a) Decisions of the Health Assembly on important questions shall be made by a two-thirds majority of the Members present and voting. These questions shall include: the adoption of conventions or agreements; the approval of agreements bringing the Organization into relation with the United Nations and inter-governmental organizations and agencies in accordance with Articles 69, 70, and 72; amendments to this Constitution.

(*b*) Decisions on other questions, including the determination of additional categories of questions to be decided by a two-thirds majority, shall be made by a majority of the Members present and voting.

(*c*) Voting on analogous matters in the Board and in committees of the Organization shall be made in accordance with paragraphs (*a*) and (*b*) of this Article.

*   *   *

CHAPTER XVII: AMENDMENTS

ARTICLE 73

Texts of proposed amendments to this Constitution shall be communicated by the Director-General to Members at least six months in advance of their consideration by the Health Assembly. Amendments shall come into force for all Members when adopted by a two-thirds vote of the Health Assembly and accepted by two-thirds of the Members in accordance with their respective constitutional processes.

*   *   *

PART V

The Inter-American Regional System [1]

~~~~~~

35. HAVANA MEETING OF MINISTERS OF FOREIGN AFFAIRS OF THE AMERICAN REPUBLICS, JULY 21-30, 1940 [2]

[Following the outbreak of World War II, the American republics looked toward closer coöperation in the face of a common danger. At the first meeting of the Foreign Ministers of the American Republics held in Panama in September, 1939, the so-called neutrality zone, designed to keep belligerent activities away from American shores, was agreed upon. At the Havana meeting, further steps were taken to clarify the status of European colonies in the New World and to suppress the activities of foreign agents. The following excerpts are of particular interest in the evolution of inter-American peace machinery; they provide for the peaceful settlement of disputes and call for consultation in connection with any aggression by a non-American state.]

[1] For documents on the earlier evolution of the Inter-American Regional System, see Carnegie Endowment for International Peace, The International Confrences of American States, 1889-1928 and First Supplement, 1933-1940, New York, 1931, 1940; see also the following Pan American Union pamphlets: The Basic Principles of the Inter-American System, Washington, 1943, and The Inter-American System, Washington, 1947.

[2] The following table gives a brief listing of the major Inter-American Conferences:

I. Periodic International Conferences of American States

First—Washington, October 2, 1889-April 19, 1890.
Second—Mexico City, October 22, 1901-January 22, 1902.
Third—Rio de Janeiro, July 21, 1906-August 26, 1906.
Fourth—Buenos Aires, July 12, 1910-August 30, 1910.
Fifth—Santiago, Chile, March 25, 1923-May 3, 1923.
Sixth—Habana, January 16, 1928-February 20, 1928.
Seventh—Montevideo, December 3-26, 1933
Eighth—Lima, December 9-27, 1938
Ninth—Bogotá, March 30-May 2, 1948.

II. Special Conferences on Peace and Security

Inter-American Conference for the Maintenance of Peace, Buenos Aires, December 1-23, 1936.
Inter-American Conference on Problems of War and Peace, Mexico City, February 21-March 8, 1945.
Inter-American Conference for the Maintenance of Continental Peace and Security, Rio de Janeiro, August 15-September 2, 1947.

III. Meetings of Foreign Ministers

First Meeting of the Foreign Ministers of the American Republics, Panama, September 23-October 3, 1939.
Second Meeting of the Foreign Ministers of the American Republics, Habana, July 21-30, 1940.
Third Meeting of the Foreign Ministers of the American Republics, Rio de Janeiro, January 15-28, 1942.
Fourth Meeting of the Foreign Ministers of the American Republics, Washington, March 26-April 7, 1951.

(a) Resolution on the Peaceful solution of conflicts [1]

Whereas:

In behalf of the closest possible unity of the continent, it is imperative that differences existing between some of the American nations be settled,

The Second Meeting of the Ministers of Foreign Affairs of the American Republics

Resolves:

To recommend to the Governing Board of the Pan American Union that it organize, in the American capital deemed most suitable for the purpose, a committee composed of representatives of five countries, which shall have the duty of keeping constant vigilance to insure that states between which any dispute exists or may arise, of any nature whatsoever, may solve it as quickly as possible, and of suggesting, without detriment to the methods adopted by the parties or to the procedures which they may agree upon, the measures and steps which may be conducive to a settlement.

The committee shall submit a report to each meeting of the ministers of foreign affairs and to each international conference of American states regarding the status of such conflicts and the steps which may have been taken to bring about a solution.

(b) Declaration on Reciprocal Assistance and Cooperation for the Defense of the Nations of the Americas [2]

The Second Meeting of the Ministers of Foreign Affairs of the American Republics

Declares:

That any attempt on the part of a non-American state against the integrity or inviolability of the territory, the sovereignty or the political independence of an American state shall be considered as an act of aggression against the states which sign this declaration.

In case acts of aggression are committed or should there be reason to believe that an act of aggression is being prepared by a non-American nation against the integrity or inviolability of the territory, the sovereignty or the political independence of an American nation, the nations signatory to the present declaration will consult among themselves in order to agree upon the measure it may be advisable to take.

All the signatory nations, or two or more of them, according to circumstances, shall proceed to negotiate the necessary complementary agreements so as to organize cooperation for defense and the assistance that they shall lend each other in the event of aggressions such as those referred to in this declaration.

◇◇◇◇◇◇

[1] Report of the Secretary of State on the Second Meeting of the Ministers of Foreign Affairs of the American Republics, Habana, July 21-30, 1940, Department of State publication 1575, Conference Series 48, p. 71.

[2] Report of the Secretary of State on the Second Meeting of the Ministers of Foreign Affairs of the American Republics, Habana, July 21-30, 1940, Department of State publication 1575, Conference Series 48, pp. 71-72.

36. RIO DE JANEIRO MEETING OF THE MINISTERS OF FOREIGN AFFAIRS OF THE AMERICAN REPUBLICS, JANUARY 15-28, 1942 [1]

[Two days after Pearl Harbor, Chile suggested that the third meeting of the Ministers of Foreign Affairs be held to consider the situation and adopt suitable measures. At the meeting forty-one resolutions were approved dealing with the severance of relations with the Axis powers and with various far-reaching measures of coöperation for the common defense of the hemisphere. In view of the fact that the boundary dispute between Peru and Ecuador was still smoldering, the ministers also approved several resolutions dealing with inter-American machinery for the peaceful settlement of disputes. Three of these resolutions are reproduced below.]

XXI

(a) Declaration on Continental Solidarity in Observance of Treaties

Whereas:

1. The concept of solidarity, in addition to embodying altruistic sentiments held in common, includes that of cooperation so necessary to forestall obstacles which may prejudice the maintenance of that principle, or the reestablishment of harmony when weakened or disrupted by the adoption of measures contrary to the dictates of international law and morality;

2. This solidarity must be translated into facts in order to become a living reality; since from a philosophical concept it has developed into an historic affirmation through repeated and frequent reaffirmations in international agreements freely agreed upon;

3. Respect for the pledged word in international treaties rests upon incontestable juridical principles as well as on precepts of morality in accordance with the maxim of canon law: *Pacta sunt servanda;*

4. Such agreements, whether bilateral or multilateral, must not be modified or nullified unilaterally, except as otherwise provided, as in the case of "denunciation" clearly authorized by the parties;

5. Only thus can peace, inspired by the common welfare of the peoples, be founded on an enduring basis, as proclaimed at the Meeting in Habana; and

6. All peaceful relations among peoples would be practically impossible in the absence of strict observance of all pacts solemnly celebrated which have met all the formalities provided for in the laws of the High Contracting Parties in order to render them juridically effective,

The Third Meeting of the Ministers of Foreign Affairs of the American Republics

Declares:

1. That should the Government of an American nation violate an agree-

[1] Report on the Third Meeting of the Ministers of Foreign Affairs of the American Republics, Washington, Pan American Union (Congress and Conference Series No. 36), 1942, pp. 50-53.

ment or a treaty duly perfected by two or more American Republics or should there be reason to believe that a violation which might disturb the peace or solidarity of the Americas is being contemplated, any American State may initiate the consultation contemplated in Resolution XVII of Habana with the object of agreeing upon the measures to be taken.

2. That the Government desiring to initiate the consultation and propose a Meeting of the Ministers of Foreign Affairs of the American Republics, or their representatives, shall communicate with the Governing Board of the Pan American Union specifying in detail the subjects to be considered as well as the approximate date on which the meeting should take place.

Reservation of the Delegation of the Republic of Peru:

"The project voted upon does not refer to the defense of the American Hemisphere against dangers from without the continent and, consequently, it is outside the agenda of this Meeting, the regulations for which, approved by all the Governments, require the unanimous consent of the Ministers of Foreign Affairs of the American Republics.

"In any case, the project voted upon cannot be applied to incidents occurring in connection with conflicts or differences which the interested parties have submitted to a special jurisdiction for settlement or solution."

(b) Declaration on the Good Neighbor Policy

Whereas:

1. Relations among nations, if they are to have foundations which will assure an international order under law, must be based on the essential and universal principle of justice;

2. The standard proclaimed and observed by the United States of America to the effect that its international policy must be founded on that of the "good neighbor" is a general criterion of right and a source of guidance in the relations between States; and this well-conceived policy prescribes respect for the fundamental rights of States as well as cooperation between them for the welfare of international society; and

3. This policy has been one of the elements contributing to the present solidarity of the Americas and their joint cooperation in the solution of outstanding problems of the Continent,

The Third Meeting of the Ministers of Foreign Affairs of the American Republics

Declares:

That the principle that international conduct must be inspired by the policy of the good neighbor is a norm of international law of the American Continent.

(c) Resolution on Condemnation of Inter-American Conflicts

Whereas:

1. A state of war exists between the United States of America and the Axis Powers;

2. The other American Republics, in conformity with inter-American agreements, have declared themselves to be in solidarity with the United States of America; and

3. This consequently implies that all the countries of the Hemisphere should closely unite for the defense of the Continent, which is the defense of each and all the American Republics,

The Third Meeting of the Ministers of Foreign Affairs of the American Republics

Resolves:

To appeal to the spirit of conciliation of the various Governments to settle their conflicts by recourse to the inter-American peace agreements formulated during the course of the recent Pan American conferences, or to any other juridical machinery, and to recognize the meritorious work of the countries which have lent and are lending their collaboration with a view to reaching a pacific solution of the differences existing between American countries and to urge them to continue intensifying their efforts in favor of the noble cause of continental harmony and solidarity.

*   *   *

◇◇◇◇◇◇

37. MEXICO CITY CONFERENCE ON PROBLEMS OF PEACE AND WAR, FEBRUARY 21-MARCH 8, 1945

[Shortly before the United Nations Conference convened at San Francisco, an Inter-American Conference on Problems of War and Peace was held at Mexico City. In the famous Act of Chapultepec, the signatories declared that any attack against the territory, sovereignty, and political independence of an American state should be considered an act of aggression against all; they should consult to determine what to do in the event of such an attack; and that these principles should later be embodied in a permanent treaty. The Conference also approved a resolution which formed the basis for the later reorganization and consolidation of the entire inter-American system. Both of these documents are reproduced in full.]

(a) Act of Chapultepec [1]

*   *   *

Whereas:

The peoples of the Americas, animated by a profound love of justice, remain sincerely devoted to the principles of international law;

It is their desire that such principles, notwithstanding the present difficult circumstances, prevail with even greater force in future international relations;

The inter-American conferences have repeatedly proclaimed certain fundamental principles, but these must be reaffirmed at a time when the juridical bases of the community of nations are being re-established;

[1] Department of State publication 2679, Treaties and Other International Acts Series 1543. For full text of final act, see Report of the Delegation of the United States of America to the Inter-American Conference on Problems of War and Peace, Department of State publication 2497, Conference Series 85.

The new situation in the world makes more imperative than ever the union and solidarity of the American peoples, for the defense of their rights and the maintenance of international peace;

The American states have been incorporating in their international law, since 1890, by means of conventions, resolutions and declarations, the following principles:

a) The proscription of territorial conquest and the non-recognition of all acquisitions made by force (First International Conference of American States, 1890);

b) The condemnation of intervention by one State in the internal or external affairs of another (Seventh International Conference of American States, 1933, and [1] Inter-American Conference for the Maintenance of Peace, 1936); [2]

c) The recognition that every war or threat of war affects directly or indirectly all civilized peoples, and endangers the great principles of liberty and justice which constitute the American ideal and the standard of American international policy (Inter-American Conference for the Maintenance of Peace, 1936);

d) The system of mutual consultation in order to find means of peaceful cooperation in the event of war or threat of war between American countries (Inter-American Conference for the Maintenance of Peace, 1936);

e) The recognition that every act susceptible of disturbing the peace of America affects each and every one of the American nations and justifies the initiation of the procedure of consultation (Inter-American Conference for the Maintenance of Peace, 1936);

f) The adoption of conciliation, unrestricted arbitration, or the application of international justice, in the solution of any difference or dispute between American nations, whatever its nature or origin (Inter-American Conference for the Maintenance of Peace, 1936);

g) The recognition that respect for the personality, sovereignty and independence of each American State constitutes the essence of international order sustained by continental solidarity, which historically has been expressed and sustained by declarations and treaties in force (Eighth International Conference of American States, 1938); [3]

h) The affirmation that respect for and the faithful observance of treaties constitute the indispensable rule for the development of peaceful relations between States, and that treaties can only be revised by agreement of the contracting parties (Declaration of American Principles, Eighth International Conference of American States, 1938);

i) The proclamation that, in case the peace, security or territorial integrity of any American republic is threatened by acts of any nature

[1] Report of the Delegates of the United States of America to the Seventh International Conference of American States, Montevideo, Uruguay, December 3-26, 1933, Department of State publication 666, Conference Series 19.

[2] Report of the Delegation of the United States of America to the Inter-American Conference for the Maintenance of Peace, Buenos Aires, Argentina, December 1-23, 1936, Department of State publication 1088, Conference Series 33.

[3] Report of the Delegation of the United States of America to the Eighth International Conference of American States, Lima, Peru, December 9-27, 1938, Department of State publication 1624, Conference Series 50.

that may impair them, they proclaim their common concern and their determination to make effective their solidarity, coordinating their respective sovereign wills by means of the procedure of consultation, using the measures which in each case the circumstances may make advisable (Declaration of Lima, Eighth International Conference of American States, 1938);

j) The declaration that any attempt on the part of a non-American state against the integrity or inviolability of the territory, the sovereignty or the political independence of an American State shall be considered as an act of aggression against all the American States (Declaration XV of the Second Meeting of the Ministers of Foreign Affairs, Habana, 1940); [1]

The furtherance of these principles, which the American States have constantly practised in order to assure peace and solidarity among the nations of the Continent, constitutes an effective means of contributing to the general system of world security and of facilitating its establishment;

The security and solidarity of the Continent are affected to the same extent by an act of aggression against any of the American States by a non-American State, as by an act of aggression of an American State against one or more American States;

PART I

The Governments Represented at the Inter-American Conference on Problems of War and Peace

Declare:

1. That all sovereign States are juridically equal among themselves.

2. That every State has the right to the respect of its individuality and independence, on the part of the other members of the international community.

3. That every attack of a State against the integrity or the inviolability of the territory, or against the sovereignty or political independence of an American State, shall, comformably to Part III hereof, be considered as an act of aggression against the other States which sign this Act. In any case invasion by armed forces of one State into the territory of another trespassing boundaries established by treaty and demarcated in accordance therewith shall constitute an act of aggression.

4. That in case acts of aggression occur or there are reasons to believe that an aggression is being prepared by any other State against the integrity or inviolability of the territory, or against the sovereignty or political independence of an American State, the States signatory to this Act will consult among themselves in order to agree upon the measures it may be advisable to take.

5. That during the war, and until the treaty recommended in Part II hereof is concluded, the signatories of this Act recognize that such threats and acts of aggression, as indicated in paragraphs 3 and 4 above, constitute an interference with the war effort of the United Nations, calling for such procedures, within the scope of their constitutional powers of a general nature and for

[1] Second Meeting of the Ministers of Foreign Affairs of the American Republics, Habana, July 2-30, 1940, Department of State publication 1575, Conference Series 48, p. 71.

war, as may be found necessary, including: recall of chiefs of diplomatic missions; breaking of diplomatic relations; breaking of consular relations; breaking of postal, telegraphic, telephonic, radio-telephonic relations; interruption of economic, commercial and financial relations; use of armed force to prevent or repel aggression.

6. That the principles and procedure contained in this Declaration shall become effective immediately, inasmuch as any act of aggression or threat of aggression during the present state of war interferes with the war effort of the United Nations to obtain victory. Henceforth, and to the end that the principles and procedures herein stipulated shall conform with the constitutional processes of each Republic, the respective Governments shall take the necessary steps to perfect this instrument in order that it shall be in force at all times.

PART II

The Inter-American Conference on Problems of War and Peace
Recommends:

That for the purpose of meeting threats or acts of aggression against any American Republic following the establishment of peace, the Governments of the American Republics consider the conclusion, in accordance with their constitutional processes, of a treaty establishing procedures whereby such threats or acts may be met by the use, by all or some of the signatories of said treaty, of any one or more of the following measures: recall of chiefs of diplomatic missions; breaking of diplomatic relations; breaking of consular relations; breaking of postal, telegraphic, telephonic, radio-telephonic relations; interruption of economic, commercial and financial relations; use of armed force to prevent or repel aggression.

PART III

The above Declaration and Recommendation constitute a regional arrangement for dealing with such matters relating to the maintenance of international peace and security as are appropriate for regional action in this Hemisphere. The said arrangement, and the pertinent activities and procedures, shall be consistent with the purposes and principles of the general international organization, when established.

This agreement shall be known as the "ACT OF CHAPULTEPEC."

(b) Reorganization, Consolidation and Strengthening of the Inter-American System [1]

Whereas:

The inter-American system and the principles, instruments, agencies, and procedures that give it substance, constitute the living manifestation of the determination of the sovereign American Republics to act together for the fulfillment of the common purposes in the maintenance of peace and security and in the promotion of the well-being of their peoples;

---

[1] Department of State publication 2652, Treaties and Other International Acts Series 1548. See full text of final act, Report of the Delegation of the United States of America to the Inter-American Conference on Problems of War and Peace, Department of State publication 2497, Conference Series 85.

The inter-American system is and has traditionally been inspired by a deep sense of universal cooperation;

The inter-American system, as an expression of the common ideals, the needs, and the will of the community of American Republics, should be further improved and strengthened for the purpose of adjusting and solving inter-American problems;

The inter-American system should, furthermore, maintain the closest relations with the proposed general international organization and assume the appropriate responsibilities in harmony with the principles and purposes of the general international organization,

The Inter-American Conference on Problems of War and Peace

Resolves:

1. That the international Conferences of American States shall meet ordinarily at four-year intervals and shall be the inter-American organ entrusted with the formation of general inter-American policy and the determination of the structure and functions of inter-American instruments and agencies. The next Conference shall meet in Bogotá in 1946.

2. The regular Meetings of the Ministers of Foreign Affairs shall be held annually upon special call by the Governing Board of the Pan American Union, unless there should be held in the same year an International Conference of American States pursuant to the preceding article. The next regular Meeting of the Ministers of Foreign Affairs shall be held in 1947.

The Meetings shall be charged with taking decisions on problems of great urgency and importance concerning the inter-American system and with regard to situations and disputes of every kind which may disturb the peace of the American Republics.

If, under exceptional circumstances, a Minister of Foreign Affairs should be unable to attend, he may be represented by a special delegate.

3. The Governing Board of the Pan American Union shall be composed of one *ad hoc* delegate designated by each of the American Republics, which delegates shall have the rank of Ambassadors and shall enjoy the corresponding privileges and immunities, but shall not be part of the diplomatic mission accredited to the government of the country in which the Pan American Union has its seat. This provision shall take effect at the expiration of the present period of sessions of the existing Board.

4. In addition to its present functions the Governing Board of the Pan American Union

a) Shall take action, within the limitations imposed upon it by the International Conferences of American States or pursuant to the specific direction of the Meetings of Ministers of Foreign Affairs, on every matter that affects the effective functioning of the inter-American system and the solidarity and general welfare of the American Republics;

b) Shall call the regular Meetings of Ministers and Foreign Affairs provided for in Paragraph 1 of Article 2 hereof, and special meetings, when they are requested, to consider exclusively emergency questions. In the latter case the call shall be made upon the vote of an absolute majority of the Board;

c) Shall supervise the inter-American agencies which are or may become related to the Pan American Union, and shall receive and approve annual or special reports from these agencies.

5. The Chairman of the Governing Board of the Pan American Union shall be elected annually and shall not be eligible for re-election for the term immediately following.

The Governing Board of the Pan American Union shall meet at least once each week.

The seat of the Pan American Union and of the Governing Board shall continue to be in Washington.

The Director General of the Pan American Union shall be chosen by the Governing Board for a term of ten years; he shall not be eligible for re-election, nor can he be succeeded by a person of the same nationality.

In the event of a vacancy in the office of Director General of the Pan American Union, a successor shall be appointed who shall hold office until the end of the term and who may be re-elected if the vacancy occurs during the second half of the term.

The first term shall begin on January 1, 1955.

The appointment and replacement of the Assistant Director shall be made in accordance with the above rules, except that the first term shall begin on January 1, 1960.

It is understood that the Governing Board may at any time, by vote of fifteen of its members, remove the Director General or the Assistant Director, on grounds relating to the efficiency of the organization.

6. Until the Ninth International Conference of American States, in accordance with the procedure provided hereinafter, creates or confirms the various agencies of the inter-American system, the following agencies created by the Meetings of Ministers of Foreign Affairs shall continue to function: The Inter-American Juridical Committee, the Emergency Advisory Committee for Political Defense, and the Inter-American Defense Board.

7. In place of the emergency agency now functioning as the Inter-American Financial and Economic Advisory Committee, there is hereby created a permanent Inter-American Economic and Social Council—subsidiary to the Governing Board of the Pan American Union—the members of which shall be designated by the respective Governments, and which shall be empowered:

a) To carry out recommendations of the International Conferences of American States;

b) To serve as the coordinating agency for all official inter-American economic and social activities;

c) To promote social progress and the raising of the standard of living for all the American peoples;

d) To undertake studies and other activities upon its own initiative or upon the request of any American government;

e) To collect and prepare reports on economic and social matters for the use of the American Republics;

f) To maintain liaison with the corresponding agency of the general international organization when established, and with existing or projected international economic and social agencies.

The Governing Board of the Pan American Union is authorized to organize provisionally the Inter-American Economic and Social Council. The permanent organization shall be established by the Ninth International Conference of American States.

8. The Division of Intellectual Cooperation of the Pan American Union shall be maintained for the purpose of strengthening by all means at its command the spiritual bonds between the American nations.

9. The Governing Board of the Pan American Union, availing itself of all Pan American agencies that it deems appropriate, is charged with preparing, beginning May 1, 1945, a draft charter for the improvement and strengthening of the Pan American system. The Governing Board shall submit the draft to the Governments of the Continent prior to December 31, 1945.

The draft charter shall first of all proclaim:

The recognition, by all the American Republics, of international law as the effective rule of their conduct and the pledge of those Governments to observe the standards enunciated in a "Declaration of the Rights and Duties of States" and a "Declaration of the International Rights and Duties of Man"; these shall serve as the definition of the fundamental principles of international law and shall appear as an annex to the charter, so that, without amending it, the Declarations may be revised from time to time to adapt them to the requirements and aspirations of international life.

For the preparation of the first Declaration, the principles already incorporated into the juridical heritage of the inter-American system shall be coordinated, especially those contained in the "Convention on the Rights and Duties of States" approved at the Seventh International Conference of American States;[1] in the "Declaration of Principles of Inter-American Solidarity and Cooperation" adopted at the Inter-American Conference for the Maintenance of Peace;[2] in the "Declaration of the Principles of the Solidarity of America," and the "Declaration of American Principles" adopted at the Eighth International Conference of American States;[3] in the "Declaration on the Maintenance of International Activities in Accordance with Christian Morality"[4] and the declaration relative to "Reciprocal Assistance and Cooperation for the Defense of the Nations of the Americas,"[5] approved at the First and Second Meetings of Ministers of Foreign Affairs, respectively; and in the Declarations on "Continental Solidarity in Observance of Treaties" and "The Good Neighbor Policy," adopted at the Third Meeting of Ministers of Foreign Affairs.[6] The draft declaration on "Reaffirmation of Fundamental Principles of International Law" prepared by the Inter-American Juridical Committee, and any Declaration of Principles that may be adopted by this Conference, shall also be taken into account.

[1] Treaty Series 881; 49 Stat. 3097.
[2] Report of the Delegation of the United States of America to the Inter-American Conference for the Maintenance of Peace, Buenos Aires, Argentina, December 1-23, 1936, Department of State publication 1088, Conference Series 33, pp. 227-228.
[3] Report of the Delegation of the United States of America to the Eighth International Conference of American States, Lima, Peru, December 9-27, 1938, Department of State publication 1624, Conference Series 50, pp. 189-190.
[4] Report of the Delegate of the United States of America to the Meeting of the Foreign Ministers of the American Republics, Held at Panamá September 23-October 3, 1939, Department of State publication 1451, Conference Series 44, p. 60.
[5] Second Meeting of the Ministers of Foreign Affairs of the American Republics, Habana, July 21-30, 1940 (Report of the Secretary of State), Department of State publication 1575, Conference Series 48, pp. 71-72.
[6] Department of State Bulletin, Feb. 7, 1942, publication 1696.

In regard to the second Declaration mentioned above, the text shall be that formulated by the Inter-American Juridical Committee in fulfillment of the request contained in another resolution of the present Conference.

It is the desire of the Inter-American Conference on Problems of War and Peace that there shall be taken into account the Inter-American Commission of Women, which for sixteen years has rendered eminent services to the cause of America and humanity, and that it be included among the organizations which form the Pan American Union, with the same prerogatives and position that have been accorded to other inter-American institutions of a permanent or emergency character that have functioned within or without the Pan American Union.

10. The draft charter shall provide for the strengthening of the inter-American system on the bases of this resolution and by the creation of new agencies or the elimination or adaptation of existing agencies, specifying and coordinating their functions as among themselves and with the world organization.

The draft shall take into account the need of accelerating the consolidation and extension of existing inter-American peace instruments and the simplification and improvement of the inter-American peace structure, and to this end the Governing Board of the Pan American Union shall utilize the services of the Inter-American Juridical Committee. In addition, the draft shall provide for the consolidation and simplification of all other inter-American instruments so that they may be more effective.

11. The American Governments shall send to the Governing Board of the Pan American Union prior to September 1, 1945, all their proposals relating to the preceding articles.

12. The draft charter shall also provide for the establishment of an equitable system for the financial support of the Pan American Union and of all its related agencies.

◇◇◇◇◇◇

38. RIO DE JANEIRO CONFERENCE FOR THE MAINTENANCE OF CONTINENTAL PEACE AND SECURITY, AUGUST 15-SEPTEMBER 2, 1947

[In order to put the Act of Chapultepec on a permanent treaty basis, representatives of the American republics met at Rio de Janeiro in 1947, and drew up what is informally known as the Rio Pact. The Pact, which is the New World predecessor of the North Atlantic Treaty, formalizes the regional collective security system of the western hemisphere. It lays down the principle that an attack against any American state is an attack against all. It also prescribes the collective measures which are to be used in order to cope with any aggression or threat of aggression. Votes on such measures call for a two-thirds majority. There is no veto except that in the case of enforcement action against an aggressor, no state shall be required to use armed force without its consent. As of December 31, 1950, twenty states (all except Guatemala) had ratified the Treaty.]

Inter-American Treaty of Reciprocal Assistance [1]

In the name of their Peoples, the Governments represented at the Inter-American Conference for the Maintenance of Continental Peace and Security, desirous of consolidating and strengthening their relations of friendship and good neighborliness, and

Considering:

That Resolution VIII of the Inter-American Conference on Problems of War and Peace, which met in Mexico City, recommended the conclusion of a treaty to prevent and repeal threats and acts of aggression against any of the countries of America;

That the High Contracting Parties reiterate their will to remain united in an inter-American system consistent with the purposes and principles of the United Nations, and reaffirm the existence of the agreement which they have concluded concerning those matters relating to the maintenance of international peace and security which are appropriate for regional action;

That the High Contracting Parties reaffirm their adherence to the principles of inter-American solidarity and cooperation, and especially to those set forth in the preamble and declarations of the Act of Chapultepec, all of which should be understood to be accepted as standards of their mutual relations and as the juridical basis of the Inter-American System;

That the American States propose, in order to improve the procedures for the pacific settlement of their controversies, to conclude the treaty concerning the "Inter-American Peace System" envisaged in Resolutions IX and XXXIX of the Inter-American Conference on Problems of War and Peace,

That the obligation of mutual assistance and common defense of the American Republics is essentially related to their democratic ideals and to their will to cooperate permanently in the fulfillment of the principles and purposes of a policy of peace;

That the American regional community affirms as a manifest truth that juridical organization is a necessary prerequisite of security and peace, and that peace is founded on justice and moral order and, consequently, on the international recognition and protection of human rights and freedoms, on the indispensable well-being of the people, and on the effectiveness of democracy for the international realization of justice and security,

Have resolved, in conformity with the objectives stated above, to conclude the following Treaty, in order to assure peace, through adequate means, to provide for effective reciprocal assistance to meet armed attacks against any American State, and in order to deal with threats of aggression against any of them:

Article 1. The High Contracting Parties formally condemn war and undertake in their international relations not to resort to the threat or the use of force in any manner inconsistent with the provisions of the Charter of the United Nations or of this Treaty.

Article 2. As a consequence of the principle set forth in the preceding

---

[1] Department of State Bulletin of September 21, 1947, pp. 565-567, 572. Senate document, Executive II, 80th Cong., 1st sess. The treaty was ratified by the President on behalf of the United States on December 19, 1947, and the instrument of ratification was deposited with the Pan American Union in Washington on December 30, 1947.

Article, the High Contracting Parties undertake to submit every controversy which may arise between them to methods of peaceful settlement and to endeavor to settle any such controversy among themselves by means of the procedures in force in the Inter-American System before referring it to the General Assembly or the Security Council of the United Nations.

Article 3.

1. The High Contracting Parties agree that an armed attack by any State against an American State shall be considered as an attack against all the American States and, consequently, each one of the said Contracting Parties undertakes to assist in meeting the attack in the exercise of the inherent right of individual or collective self-defense recognized by Article 51 of the Charter of the United Nations.

2. On the request of the State or States directly attacked and until the decision of the Organ of Consultation of the Inter-American System, each one of the Contracting Parties may determine the immediate measures which it may individually take in fulfillment of the obligation contained in the preceding paragraph and in accordance with the principle of continental solidarity. The Organ of Consultation shall meet without delay for the purpose of examining those measures and agreeing upon the measures of a collective character that should be taken.

3. The provisions of this Article shall be applied in case of any armed attack which takes place within the region described in Article 4 or within the territory of an American State. When the attack takes place outside of the said areas, the provisions of Article 6 shall be applied.

4. Measures of self-defense provided for under this Article may be taken until the Security Council of the United Nations has taken the measures necessary to maintain international peace and security.

Article 4. The region to which this Treaty refers is bounded as follows: beginning at the North Pole; thence due south to a point 74 degrees north latitude, 10 degrees west longitude; thence by a rhumb line to a point 47 degrees 30 minutes north latitude, 50 degrees west longitude; thence by a rhumb line to a point 35 degrees north latitude, 60 degrees west longitude; thence due south to a point in 20 degrees north latitude; thence by a rhumb line to a point 5 degrees north latitude, 24 degrees west longitude; thence due south to the South Pole; thence due north to a point 30 degrees south latitude, 90 degrees west longitude; thence by a rhumb line to a point on the Equator at 97 degrees west longitude; thence by a rhumb line to a point 15 degrees north latitude, 120 degrees west longitude; thence by a rhumb line to a point 50 degrees north latitude, 170 degrees east longitude; thence due north to a point in 54 degrees north latitude; thence by a rhumb line to a point 65 degrees 30 minutes north latitude, 168 degrees 58 minutes 5 seconds west longitude: thence due north to the North Pole.

Article 5. The High Contracting Parties shall immediately send to the Security Council of the United Nations, in conformity with Articles 51 and 54 of the Charter of the United Nations, complete information concerning the activities undertaken or in contemplation in the exercise of the right of self-defense or for the purpose of maintaining inter-American peace and security.

Article 6. If the inviolability or the integrity of the territory or the sovereignty or political independence of any American State should be affected by an aggression which is not an armed attack or by an extra-continental or intra-continental conflict, or by any other fact or situation that might endanger the peace of America, the Organ of Consultation shall meet immediately in order to agree on the measures which must be taken in case of aggression to assist the victim of the aggression or, in any case, the measures which should be taken for the common defense and for the maintenance of the peace and security of the Continent.

Article 7. In the case of a conflict between two or more American States, without prejudice to the right of self-defense in conformity with Article 51 of the Charter of the United Nations, the High Contracting Parties, meeting in consultation shall call upon the contending States to suspend hostilities and restore matters to the *status quo ante bellum,* and shall take in addition all other necessary measures to reestablish or maintain inter-American peace and security and for the solution of the conflict by peaceful means. The rejection of the pacifying action will be considered in the determination of the aggressor and in the application of the measures which the consultative meeting may agree upon.

Article 8. For the purposes of this Treaty, the measures on which the Organ of Consultation may agree will comprise one or more of the following: recall of chiefs of diplomatic missions; breaking of diplomatic relations; breaking of consular relations; partial or complete interruption of economic relations or of rail, sea, air, postal, telegraphic, telephonic, and radiotelephonic or radiotelegraphic communications; and use of armed force.

Article 9. In addition to other acts which the Organ of Consultation may characterize as aggression, the following shall be considered as such:

a. Unprovoked armed attack by a State against the territory, the people, or the land, sea or air forces of another State;

b. Invasion, by the armed forces of a State, of the territory of an American State, through the trespassing of boundaries demarcated in accordance with a treaty, judicial decision, or arbitral award, or, in the absence of frontiers thus demarcated, invasion affecting a region which is under the effective jurisdiction of another State.

Article 10. None of the provisions of this Treaty shall be construed as impairing the rights and obligations of the High Contracting Parties under the Charter of the United Nations.

Article 11. The consultations to which this Treaty refers shall be carried out by means of the Meetings of Ministers of Foreign Affairs of the American Republics which have ratified the Treaty, or in the manner or by the organ which in the future may be agreed upon.

Article 12. The Governing Board of the Pan American Union may act provisionally as an organ of consultation until the meeting of the Organ of Consultation referred to in the preceding Article takes place.

Article 13. The consultations shall be initiated at the request addressed to the Governing Board of the Pan American Union by any of the Signatory States which has ratified the Treaty.

Article 14. In the voting referred to in this Treaty only the representatives of the Signatory States which have ratified the Treaty may take part.

Article 15. The Governing Board of the Pan American Union shall act in all matters concerning this Treaty as an organ of liaison among the Signatory States which have ratified this Treaty and between these States and the United Nations.

Article 16. The decisions of the Governing Board of the Pan American Union referred to in Articles 13 and 15 above shall be taken by an absolute majority of the Members entitled to vote.

Article 17. The Organ of Consultation shall take its decisions by a vote of two-thirds of the Signatory States which have ratified the Treaty.

Article 18. In the case of a situation or dispute between American States, the parties directly interested shall be excluded from the voting referred to in the two preceding Articles.

Article 19. To constitute a quorum in all the meetings referred to in the previous Articles, it shall be necessary that the number of States represented shall be at least equal to the number of votes necessary for the taking of the decision.

Article 20. Decisions which require the application of the measures specified in Article 8 shall be binding upon all the Signatory States which have ratified this Treaty, with the sole exception that no State shall be required to use armed force without its consent.

Article 21. The measures agreed upon by the Organ of Consultation shall be executed through the procedures and agencies now existing or those which may in the future be established.

Article 22. This Treaty shall come into effect between the States which ratify it as soon as the ratifications of two-thirds of the Signatory States have been deposited.

Article 23. This Treaty is open for signature by the American States at the city of Rio de Janeiro, and shall be ratified by the Signatory States as soon as possible in accordance with their respective constitutional processes. The ratifications shall be deposited with the Pan American Union, which shall notify the Signatory States of each deposit. Such notification shall be considered as an exchange of ratifications.

Article 24. The present Treaty shall be registered with the Secretariat of the United Nations through the Pan American Union, when two-thirds of the Signatory States have deposited their ratification.

Article 25. This Treaty shall remain in force indefinitely, but may be denounced by any High Contracting Party by a notification in writing to the Pan American Union, which shall inform all the other High Contracting Parties of each notification of denunciation received. After the expiration of two years from the date of the receipt by the Pan American Union of a notification of denunciation by any High Contracting Party, the present Treaty shall cease to be in force with respect to such State, but shall remain in full force and effect with respect to all the other High Contracting Parties.

Article 26. The principles and fundamental provisions of this Treaty shall be incorporated in the Organic Pact of the Inter-American System.

In witness whereof, the undersigned Plenipotentiaries, having deposited their full powers found to be in due and proper form, sign this Treaty on behalf of their respective Governments, on the dates appearing opposite their signatures.

Done in the City of Rio de Janeiro, in four texts in the English, French, Portuguese and Spanish languages, on the second of September, nineteen hundred forty-seven.

Reservation of Honduras:

The Delegation of Honduras, in signing the present Treaty and in connection with Article 9, section (b), does so with the reservation that the boundary between Honduras and Nicaragua is definitively demarcated by the Joint Boundary Commission of nineteen hundred and nineteen hundred and one, starting from a point in the Gulf of Fonseca, in the Pacific Ocean, to Portillo de Teotecacinte and, from this point to the Atlantic, by the line that His Majesty the King of Spain's arbitral award established on the twenty-third of December of nineteen hundred and six.

*   *   *

STATEMENTS

Argentina:

The Argentine Delegation declares that within the waters adjacent to the South American Continent, along the coasts belonging to the Argentine Republic in the Security Zone, it does not recognize the existence of colonies or possessions of European countries and it adds that it especially reserves and maintains intact the legitimate titles and rights of the Argentine Republic to the Falkland (Malvinas) Islands, the South Georgia Islands, the South Sandwich Islands, and the lands included in the Argentine Antarctic sector, over which the Republic exercises the corresponding sovereignty.

Guatemala:

Guatemala wishes to place on record that it does not recognize any right of legal sovereignty of Great Britain over the territory of Belice, called British Honduras, included in the Security Zone, and that once again, it expressly reserves its rights, which are derived from the Constitution of the Republic, historical documents, juridical arguments and principles of equity which have on appropriate occasions been laid before the universal conscience.

Mexico:

Only because the Delegation of Guatemala has seen fit to make the preceding declaration, the Delegation of Mexico finds it necessary to reiterate that, in case there should occur a change in the status of Belice, there cannot fail to be taken into account the rights of Mexico to a part of the said territory, in accordance with historical and juridical precedents.

Chile:

The Delegation of Chile declares that, within the waters adjacent to the South American Continent, in the extension of coast belonging to the Republic of Chile, comprised within the Security Zone, it does not recognize the existence of colonies or possessions of European countries and it adds that it specially reserves and maintains intact the legitimate title and rights of the Republic of Chile to the lands included in the Chilean Antarctic zone, over which the Republic exercises the corresponding sovereignty.

United States of America:

With reference to the reservations made by other Delegations concerning territories located within the region defined in the Treaty, their boundaries, and questions of sovereignty over them, the Delegation of the United States of America wishes to record its position that the Treaty of Rio de Janeiro has no effect upon the sovereignty, national or international status of any of the territories included in the region defined in Article 4 of the Treaty.

*   *   *

The New York Times

▬▬▬▬   The region defined by Article 4 of the Inter-American Treaty of Reciprocal Assistance, signed at Rio de Janeiro on September 2, 1947

◇◇◇◇◇

39. BOGOTÁ CONFERENCE OF AMERICAN STATES, MARCH 30 TO MAY 2, 1948

Charter of the Organization of American States [1]

[At the Mexico City Conference, it was agreed that the inter-American system needed to be reorganized and consolidated in the interest of greater

[1] Signed at the Ninth International Conference of American States, Bogotá, Mar. 30-May 2, 1948. See Ninth International Conference of American States Bogotá March 30-May 2, 1948, Department of State Publication 3263, released November 1948.

efficiency and to meet the requirements of the postwar period. This was done at the Bogotá Conference, where the Charter of the Organization of American States was signed on April 30, 1948. The Charter is comparable to the United Nations Charter since it serves as the basic constitution of the inter-American system. It establishes the OAS on a permanent treaty basis and defines its rôle as the regional agency of the American republics within the United Nations. The framing of the Charter did not involve any far-reaching changes; rather it represented a consolidation and streamlining of the machinery set up prior to 1948 in the inter-American field.]

In the name of their peoples, the States represented at the Ninth International Conference of American States,

Convinced that the historic mission of America is to offer to man a land of liberty, and a favorable environment for the development of his personality and the realization of his just aspirations;

Conscious that that mission has already inspired numerous agreements, whose essential value lies in the desire of the American peoples to live together in peace, and, through their mutual understanding and respect for the sovereignty of each one, to provide for the betterment of all, in independence, in equality and under law;

Confident that true significance of American solidarity and good neighborliness can only mean the consolidation on this continent, within the framework of democratic institutions, of a system of individual liberty and social justice based on respect for the essential rights of man;

Persuaded that their welfare and their contribution to the progress and the civilization of the world will increasingly require intensive continental cooperation;

Resolved to persevere in the noble undertaking that humanity has conferred upon the United Nations, whose principles and purposes they solemnly reaffirm;

Convinced that juridical organization is a necessary condition for security and peace founded on moral order and on justice; and

In accordance with Resolution IX of the Inter-American Conference on Problems of War and Peace, held at Mexico City,

Have agreed upon the following

CHARTER OF THE ORGANIZATION OF AMERICAN STATES

PART ONE

CHAPTER 1: NATURE AND PURPOSES

ARTICLE 1

The American States establish by this Charter the international organization that they have developed to achieve an order of peace and justice, to promote their solidarity, to strengthen their collaboration, and to defend their sovereignty, their territorial integrity and their independence. Within the United Nations, the Organization of American States is a regional agency.

ARTICLE 2

All American States that ratify the present Charter are Members of the Organization.

ARTICLE 3

Any new political entity that arises from the union of several Member States and that, as such, ratifies the present Charter, shall become a Member of the Organization. The entry of the new political entity into the Organization shall result in the loss of membership of each one of the States which constitute it.

ARTICLE 4

The Organization of American States, in order to put into practice the principles on which it is founded and to fulfill its regional obligations under the Charter of the United Nations, proclaims the following essential purposes:

a) To strengthen the peace and security of the continent;

b) To prevent possible causes of difficulties and to ensure the pacific settlement of disputes that may arise among the Member States;

c) To provide for common action on the part of those States in the event of aggression;

d) To seek the solution of political, juridical and economic problems that may arise among them; and

e) To promote, by cooperative action, their economic, social and cultural development.

CHAPTER II: PRINCIPLES

ARTICLE 5

The American States reaffirm the following principles:

a) International law is the standard of conduct of States in their reciprocal relations;

b) International order consists essentially of respect for the personality, sovereignty and independence of States, and the faithful fulfillment of obligations derived from treaties and other sources of international law;

c) Good faith shall govern the relations between States;

d) The solidarity of the American States and the high aims which are sought through it require the political organization of those States on the basis of the effective exercise of representative democracy;

e) The American States condemn war of aggression: victory does not give rights;

f) An act of aggression against one American State is an act of aggression against all the other American States;

g) Controversies of an international character arising between two or more American States shall be settled by peaceful procedures;

h) Social justice and social security are bases of lasting peace;

i) Economic cooperation is essential to the common welfare and prosperity of the peoples of the continent;

j) The American States proclaim the fundamental rights of the individual without distinction as to race, nationality, creed or sex;

k) The spiritual unity of the continent is based on respect for the cultural values of the American countries and requires their close co-operation for the high purposes of civilization;

l) The education of peoples should be directed toward justice, freedom and peace.

CHAPTER III: FUNDAMENTAL RIGHTS AND DUTIES OF STATES

ARTICLE 6

States are juridically equal, enjoy equal rights and equal capacity to exercise these rights, and have equal duties. The rights of each State depend not upon its power to ensure the exercise thereof, but upon the mere fact of its existence as a person under international law.

ARTICLE 7

Every American State has the duty to respect the rights enjoyed by every other State in accordance with international law.

ARTICLE 8

The fundamental rights of States may not be impaired in any manner whatsoever.

ARTICLE 9

The political existence of the State is independent of recognition by other States. Even before being recognized, the State has the right to defend its integrity and independence, to provide for its preservation and prosperity, and consequently to organize itself as it sees fit, to legislate concerning its interests, to administer its services, and to determine the jurisdiction and competence of its courts. The exercise of these rights is limited only by the exercise of the rights of other States in accordance with international law.

ARTICLE 10

Recognition implies that the State granting it accepts the personality of the new State, with all the rights and duties that international law prescribes for the two States.

ARTICLE 11

The right of each State to protect itself and live its own life does not authorize it to commit unjust acts against another State.

ARTICLE 12

The jurisdiction of States within the limits of their national territory is exercised equally over all the inhabitants, whether nationals or aliens.

ARTICLE 13

Each State has the right to develop its cultural, political and economic life freely and naturally. In this free development, the State shall respect the rights of the individual and the principles of universal morality.

ARTICLE 14

Respect for and the faithful observance of treaties constitute standards for the development of peaceful relations among States. International treaties and agreements should be public.

ARTICLE 15

No State or group of States has the right to intervene, directly or indirectly, for any reason whatever, in the internal or external affairs of any other State. The foregoing principle prohibits not only armed force but also any other form of interference or attempted threat against the personality of the State or against its political, economic and cultural elements.

ARTICLE 16

No State may use or encourage the use of coercive measures of an economic or political character in order to force the sovereign will of another State and obtain from it advantages of any kind.

ARTICLE 17

The territory of a State is inviolable; it may not be the object, even temporarily, of military occupation or of other measures of force taken by another State, directly or indirectly, on any grounds whatever. No territorial acquisitions or special advantages obtained either by force or by other means of coercion shall be recognized.

ARTICLE 18

The American States bind themselves in their international relations not to have recourse to the use of force, except in the case of self-defense in accordance with existing treaties or in fulfillment thereof.

ARTICLE 19

Measures adopted for the maintenance of peace and security in accordance with existing treaties do not constitute a violation of the principles set forth in Articles 15 and 17.

CHAPTER IV: PACIFIC SETTLEMENT OF DISPUTES

ARTICLE 20

All international disputes that may arise between American States shall be submitted to the peaceful procedures set forth in this Charter, before being referred to the Security Council of the United Nations.

ARTICLE 21

The following are peaceful procedures: direct negotiation, good offices, mediation, investigation and conciliation, judicial settlement, arbitration, and those which the parties to the dispute may especially agree upon at any time.

ARTICLE 22

In the event that a dispute arises between two or more American States which, in the opinion of one of them, cannot be settled through the usual diplomatic channels, the Parties shall agree on some other peaceful procedure that will enable them to reach a solution.

ARTICLE 23

A special treaty will establish adequate procedures for the pacific settlement of disputes and will determine the appropriate means for their application, so that no dispute between American States will fail of definitive settlement within a reasonable period.

CHAPTER V: COLLECTIVE SECURITY

ARTICLE 24

Every act of aggression by a State against the territorial integrity or the inviolability of the territory or against the sovereignty or political independence of an American State shall be considered an act of aggression against the other American States.

ARTICLE 25

If the inviolability or the integrity of the territory or the sovereignty or political independence of any American State should be affected by an armed attack or by an act of aggression that is not an armed attack, or by an extracontinental conflict, or by a conflict between two or more American States, or by any other fact or situation that might endanger the peace of America, the American States, in furtherance of the principles of continental solidarity or collective self-defense, shall apply the measures and procedures established in the special treaties on the subject.

CHAPTER VI: ECONOMIC STANDARDS

ARTICLE 26

The Member States agree to cooperate with one another, as far as their sources may permit and their laws may provide, in the broadest spirit of good neighborliness, in order to strengthen their economic structure, develop their agriculture and mining, promote their industry and increase their trade.

ARTICLE 27

If the economy of an American State is affected by serious conditions that cannot be satisfactorily remedied by its own unaided effort, such State may place its economic problems before the Inter-American Economic and Social Council to seek through consultation the most appropriate solution for such problems.

CHAPTER VII: SOCIAL STANDARDS

ARTICLE 28

The Member States agree to cooperate with one another to achieve just and decent living conditions for their entire populations.

ARTICLE 29

The Member States agree upon the desirability of developing their social legislation on the following bases:

a) All human beings, without distinction as to race, nationality, sex, creed or social condition, have the right to attain material well-being and spiritual growth under circumstances of liberty, dignity, equality of opportunity, and economic security;

b) Work is a right and a social duty; it shall not be considered as an article of commerce; it demands respect for freedom of association and for the dignity of the worker; and it is to be performed under conditions that ensure life, health and a decent standard of living, both during the working years and during old age, or when any circumstance deprives the individual of the possibility of working.

CHAPTER VIII: CULTURAL STANDARDS

ARTICLE 30

The Member States agree to promote, in accordance with their constitutional provisions and their material resources, the exercise of the right to education, on the following bases:

a) Elementary education shall be compulsory and, when provided by the State, shall be without cost;

b) Higher education shall be available to all, without distinction as to race, nationality, sex, language, creed or social condition.

ARTICLE 31

With due consideration for the national character of each State, the Member States undertake to facilitate free cultural interchange by every medium of expression.

PART TWO

CHAPTER IX: THE ORGANS

ARTICLE 32

The Organization of American States accomplishes its purposes by means of:

a) The Inter-American Conference;
b) The Meeting of Consultation of Ministers of Foreign Affairs;
c) The Council;
d) The Pan American Union;
e) The Specialized Conferences; and
f) The Specialized Organizations.

CHAPTER X: THE INTER-AMERICAN CONFERENCE

ARTICLE 33

The Inter-American Conference is the supreme organ of the Organization of American States. It decides the general action and policy of the Organization and determines the structure and functions of its Organs, and has the authority to consider any matter relating to friendly relations among the American States. These functions shall be carried out in accordance with the provisions of this Charter and of other inter-American treaties.

ARTICLE 34

All Member States have the right to be represented at the Inter-American Conference. Each State has the right to one vote.

ARTICLE 35

The Conference shall convene every five years at the time fixed by the Council of the Organization, after consultation with the government of the country where the Conference is to be held.

ARTICLE 36

In special circumstances and with the approval of two-thirds of the American Governments, a special Inter-American Conference may be held, or the date of the next regular Conference may be changed.

ARTICLE 37

Each Inter-American Conference shall designate the place of meeting of the next Conference. If for any unforeseen reason the Conference cannot be held at the place designated, the Council of the Organization shall designate a new place.

ARTICLE 38

The program and regulations of the Inter-American Conference shall be prepared by the Council of the Organization and submitted to the Member States for consideration.

CHAPTER XI: THE MEETING OF CONSULTATION OF MINISTERS OF FOREIGN AFFAIRS

ARTICLE 39

The Meeting of Consultation of Ministers of Foreign Affairs shall be held in order to consider problems of an urgent nature and of common interest to the American States, and to serve as the Organ of Consultation.

ARTICLE 40

Any Member State may request that a Meeting of Consultation be called. The request shall be addressed to the Council of the Organization, which shall decide by an absolute majority whether a meeting should be held.

ARTICLE 41

The program and regulations of the Meeting of Consultation shall be prepared by the Council of the Organization and submitted to the Member States for consideration.

ARTICLE 42

If, for exceptional reasons, a Minister of Foreign Affairs is unable to attend the meeting, he shall be represented by a special delegate.

ARTICLE 43

In case of an armed attack within the territory of an American State or within the region of security delimited by treaties in force, a Meeting of Consultation shall be held without delay. Such Meeting shall be called immediately by the Chairman of the Council of the Organization, who shall at the same time call a meeting of the Council itself.

ARTICLE 44

An Advisory Defense Committee shall be established to advise the Organ of Consultation on problems of military cooperation that may arise in connection with the application of existing special treaties on collective security.

ARTICLE 45

The Advisory Defense Committee shall be composed of the highest military authorities of the American States participating in the Meeting of Consultation. Under exceptional circumstances the Governments may appoint substitutes. Each State shall be entitled to one vote.

ARTICLE 46

The Advisory Defense Committee shall be convoked under the same conditions as the Organ of Consultation, when the latter deals with matters relating to defense against aggression.

ARTICLE 47

The Committee shall also meet when the Conference or the Meeting of Consultation or the Governments, by a two-thirds majority of the Member States, assign to it technical studies or reports on specific subjects.

CHAPTER XII: THE COUNCIL

ARTICLE 48

The Council of the Organization of American States is composed of one Representative of each Member State of the Organization, especially appointed by the respective Government, with the rank of Ambassador. The appointment may be given to the diplomatic representative accredited to the Government of the country in which the Council has its seat. During the absence of the titular Representative, the Government may appoint an interim Representative.

ARTICLE 49

The Council shall elect a Chairman and a Vice Chairman, who shall serve for one year and shall not be eligible for election to either of those positions for the term immediately following.

ARTICLE 50

The Council takes cognizance, within the limits of the present Charter and of inter-American treaties and agreements, of any matter referred to it by the Inter-American Conference or the Meeting of Consultation of Ministers of Foreign Affairs.

ARTICLE 51

The Council shall be responsible for the proper discharge by the Pan American Union of the duties assigned to it.

ARTICLE 52

The Council shall serve provisionally as the Organ of Consultation when the circumstances contemplated in Article 43 of this Charter arise.

ARTICLE 53

It is also the duty of the Council:

a) To draft and submit to the Governments and to the Inter-American Conference proposals for the creation of new Specialized Organizations or for the combination, adaptation or elimination of existing ones, including matters relating to the financing and support thereof;

b) To draft recommendations to the Governments, the Inter-American Conference, the Specialized Conferences or the Specialized Organizations, for the coordination of the activities and programs of such organizations, after consultation with them;

c) To conclude agreements with the Inter-American Specialized Organizations to determine the relations that shall exist between the respective agency and the Organization;

d) To conclude agreements or special arrangements for cooperation with other American organizations of recognized international standing;

e) To promote and facilitate collaboration between the Organization of American States and the United Nations, as well as between Inter-American Specialized Organizations and similar international agencies;

f) To adopt resolutions that will enable the Secretary General to perform the duties envisaged in Article 84;

g) To perform the other duties assigned to it by the present Charter.

ARTICLE 54

The Council shall establish the bases for fixing the quota that each Government is to contribute to the maintenance of the Pan American Union, taking into account the ability to pay of the respective countries and their determination to contribute in an equitable manner. The budget, after approval by the Council, shall be transmitted to the Governments at least six months before the first day of the fiscal year, with a statement of the annual quota of each country. Decisions on budgetary matters require the approval of two-thirds of the members of the Council.

ARTICLE 55

The Council shall formulate its own regulations.

ARTICLE 56

The Council shall function at the seat of the Pan American Union.

ARTICLE 57

The following are organs of the Council of the Organization of American States:

a) The Inter-American Economic and Social Council;
b) The Inter-American Council of Jurists; and
c) The Inter-American Cultural Council.

ARTICLE 58

The organs referred to in the preceding article shall have technical autonomy within the limits of this Charter; but their decisions shall not encroach upon the sphere of action of the Council of the Organization.

ARTICLE 59

The organs of the Council of the Organization are composed of representatives of all the Member States of the Organization.

ARTICLE 60

The organs of the Council of the Organization shall, as far as possible, render to the Governments such technical services as the latter may request; and they shall advise the Council of the Organization on matters within their jurisdiction.

ARTICLE 61

The organs of the Council of the Organization shall, in agreement with the Council, establish cooperative relations with the corresponding organs of the United Nations and with the national or international agencies that function within their respective spheres of action.

ARTICLE 62

The Council of the Organization, with the advice of the appropriate bodies and after consultation with the Governments, shall formulate the statutes of its organs in accordance with and in the execution of the provisions of this Charter. The organs shall formulate their own regulations.

A) THE INTER-AMERICAN ECONOMIC AND SOCIAL COUNCIL

ARTICLE 63

The Inter-American Economic and Social Council has for its principal purpose the promotion of the economic and social welfare of the American nations through effective cooperation for the better utilization of their natural resources, the development of their agriculture and industry and the raising of the standards of living of their peoples.

ARTICLE 64

To accomplish this purpose the Council shall:

a) Propose the means by which the American nations may give each other technical assistance in making studies and formulating and executing plans to carry out the purposes referred to in Article 26 and to develop and improve their social services;

b) Act as coordinating agency for all official inter-American activities of an economic and social nature;

c) Undertake studies on its own initiative or at the request of any Member State;

d) Assemble and prepare reports on economic and social matters for the use of the Member States;

e) Suggest to the Council of the Organization the advisability of holding specialized conferences on economic and social matters;

f) Carry on such other activities as may be assigned to it by the Inter-American Conference, the Meeting of Consultation of Ministers of Foreign Affairs, or the Council of the Organization.

ARTICLE 65

The Inter-American Economic and Social Council, composed of technical delegates appointed by each Member State, shall meet on its own initiative or on that of the Council of the Organization.

ARTICLE 66

The Inter-American Economic and Social Council shall function at the seat of the Pan American Union, but it may hold meetings in any American city by a majority decision of the Member States.

B) THE INTER-AMERICAN COUNCIL OF JURISTS

ARTICLE 67

The purpose of the Inter-American Council of Jurists is to serve as an advisory body on juridical matters; to promote the development and codification of public and private international law; and to study the possibility of attaining uniformity in the legislation of the various American countries, insofar as it may appear desirable.

ARTICLE 68

The Inter-American Juridical Committee of Rio de Janeiro shall be the permanent committee of the Inter-American Council of Jurists.

ARTICLE 69

The Juridical Committee shall be composed of jurists of the nine countries selected by the Inter-American Conference. The selection of the jurists shall be made by the Inter-American Council of Jurists from a panel submitted by each country chosen by the Conference. The Members of the Juridical Committee represent all Member States of the Organization. The Council of the Organization is empowered to fill any vacancies that occur during the intervals between Inter-American Conferences and between meetings of the Inter-American Council of Jurists.

ARTICLE 70

The Juridical Committee shall undertake such studies and preparatory work as are assigned to it by the Inter-American Council of Jurists, the Inter-American Conference, the Meeting of Consultation of Ministers of Foreign Affairs, or the Council of the Organization. It may also undertake those studies and projects which, on its own initiative, it considers advisable.

ARTICLE 71

The Inter-American Council of Jurists and the Juridical Committee should seek the cooperation of national committees for the codification of international law, of institutes of international and comparative law, and of other specialized agencies.

ARTICLE 72

The Inter-American Council of Jurists shall meet when convened by the Council of the Organization, at the place determined by the Council of Jurists at its previous meeting.

C) THE INTER-AMERICAN CULTURAL COUNCIL

ARTICLE 73

The purpose of the Inter-American Cultural Council is to promote friendly relations and mutual understanding among the American peoples, in order to strengthen the peaceful sentiments that have characterized the evolution of America, through the promotion of educational, scientific and cultural exchange.

ARTICLE 74

To this end the principal functions of the Council shall be:

a) To sponsor inter-American cultural activities;

b) To collect and supply information on cultural activities carried on in and among the American States by private and official agencies both national and international in character;

c) To promote the adoption of basic educational programs adapted to the needs of all population groups in the American countries;

d) To promote, in addition, the adoption of special programs of training, education and culture for the indigenous groups of the American countries;

e) To cooperate in the protection, preservation and increase of the cultural heritage of the continent;

f) To promote cooperation among the American nations in the fields of education, science and culture, by means of the exchange of materials for research and study, as well as the exchange of teachers, students, specialists and, in general such other persons and materials as are useful for the realization of these ends;

g) To encourage the education of the peoples for harmonious international relations;

h) To carry on such other activities as may be assigned to it by the Inter-American Conference, the Meeting of Consultation of Ministers of Foreign Affairs, or the Council of the Organization.

ARTICLE 75

The Inter-American Cultural Council shall determine the place of its next meeting and shall be convened by the Council of the Organization on the date chosen by the latter in agreement with the Government of the country selected as the seat of the meeting.

ARTICLE 76

There shall be a Committee for Cultural Action of which five States, chosen at each Inter-American Conference, shall be members. The individuals composing the Committee for Cultural Action shall be selected by the Inter-American Cultural Council from a panel submitted by each country chosen by the Conference, and they shall be specialists in education or cultural matters. When the Inter-American Cultural Council and the Inter-American Conference are not in session, the Council of the Organization may fill vacancies that arise and replace those countries that find it necessary to discontinue their cooperation.

ARTICLE 77

The Committee for Cultural Action shall function as the permanent committee of the Inter-American Cultural Council, for the purpose of preparing any studies that the latter may assign to it. With respect to these studies the Council shall have the final decision.

CHAPTER XIII. THE PAN AMERICAN UNION

ARTICLE 78

The Pan American Union is the central and permanent organ of the Organization of American States and the General Secretariat of the Organization. It shall perform the duties assigned to it in this Charter and such other duties as may be assigned to it in other inter-American treaties and agreements.

ARTICLE 79

There shall be a Secretary General of the Organization, who shall be elected by the Council for a ten-year term and who may not be reelected or be succeeded by a person of the same nationality. In the event of a vacancy in the office of Secretary General, the Council shall, within the next ninety days, elect a successor to fill the office for the remainder of the term, who may be reelected if the vacancy occurs during the second half of the term.

ARTICLE 80

The Secretary General shall direct the Pan American Union and be the legal representative thereof.

ARTICLE 81

The Secretary General shall participate with voice, but without vote, in the deliberations of the Inter-American Conference, the Meeting of Consultation of Ministers of Foreign Affairs, the Specialized Conferences, and the Council and its organs.

ARTICLE 82

The Pan American Union, through its technical and information offices, shall, under the direction of the Council, promote economic, social, juridical and cultural relations among all the Member States of the Organization.

ARTICLE 83

The Pan American Union shall also perform the following functions:

a) Transmit *ex officio* to Member States the convocation to the Inter-American Conference, the Meeting of Consultation of Ministers of Foreign Affairs, and the Specialized Conferences;

b) Advise the Council and its organs in the preparation of programs and regulations of the Inter-American Conference, the Meeting of Consultation of Ministers of Foreign Affairs, and the Specialized Conferences;

c) Place, to the extent of its ability, at the disposal of the Government of the country where a conference is to be held, the technical aid and personnel which such Government may request;

d) Serve as custodian of the documents and archives of the Inter-American Conference, of the Meeting of Consultation of Ministers of Foreign Affairs, and, insofar as possible, of the Specialized Conferences;

e) Serve as depository of the instruments of ratification of inter-American agreements;

f) Perform the functions entrusted to it by the Inter-American Conference, and the Meeting of Consultation of Ministers of Foreign Affairs;

g) Submit to the Council an annual report on the activities of the Organization;

h) Submit to the Inter-American Conference a report on the work accomplished by the Organs of the Organization since the previous Conference.

ARTICLE 84

It is the duty of the Secretary General:

a) To establish, with the approval of the Council, such technical and administrative offices of the Pan American Union as are necessary to accomplish its purposes;

b) To determine the number of department heads, officers and employees of the Pan American Union; to appoint them, regulate their powers and duties, and fix their compensation, in accordance with general standards established by the Council.

ARTICLE 85

There shall be an Assistant Secretary General, elected by the Council for a term of ten years and eligible for reelection. In the event of a vacancy in the office of Assistant Secretary General, the Council shall, within the next ninety days, elect a successor to fill such office for the remainder of the term.

ARTICLE 86

The Assistant Secretary General shall be the Secretary of the Council. He shall perform the duties of the Secretary General during the temporary absence or disability of the latter, or during the ninety-day vacancy referred to in Article 79. He shall also serve as advisory officer to the Secretary General, with the power to act as his delegate in all matters that the Secretary General may entrust to him.

ARTICLE 87

The Council, by a two-thirds vote of its members, may remove the Secretary General or the Assistant Secretary General whenever the proper functioning of the Organization so demands.

ARTICLE 88

The heads of the respective departments of the Pan American Union, appointed by the Secretary General, shall be the Executive Secretaries of the Inter-American Economic and Social Council, the Council of Jurists and the Cultural Council.

ARTICLE 89

In the performance of their duties the personnel shall not seek or receive instructions from any government or from any other authority outside the Pan American Union. They shall refrain from any action that might reflect upon their position as international officials responsible only to the Union.

ARTICLE 90

Every Member of the Organization of American States pledges itself to respect the exclusively international character of the responsibilities of the Secretary General and the personnel, and not to seek to influence them in the discharge of their duties.

ARTICLE 91

In selecting its personnel the Pan American Union shall give first consideration to efficiency, competence and integrity; but at the same time importance shall be given to the necessity of recruiting personnel on as broad a geographical basis as possible.

ARTICLE 92

The seat of the Pan American Union is the city of Washington.

CHAPTER XIV: THE SPECIALIZED CONFERENCES

ARTICLE 93

The Specialized Conferences shall meet to deal with special technical matters or to develop specific aspects of inter-American cooperation, when it is so decided by the Inter-American Conference or the Meeting of Consultation of Ministers of Foreign Affairs; when inter-American agreements so provide; or when the Council of the Organization considers it necessary, either on its own initiative or at the request of one of its organs or of one of the Specialized Organizations.

ARTICLE 94

The program and regulations of the Specialized Conferences shall be prepared by the organs of the Council of the Organization or by the Specialized Organizations concerned; they shall be submitted to the Member Governments for consideration and transmitted to the Council for its information.

CHAPTER XV: THE SPECIALIZED ORGANIZATIONS

ARTICLE 95

For the purposes of the present Charter, Inter-American Specialized Organizations are the intergovernmental organizations established by multilateral agreements and having specific functions with respect to technical matters of common interest to the American States.

ARTICLE 96

The Council shall, for the purposes stated in Article 53, maintain a register of the Organizations that fulfill the conditions set forth in the foregoing Article.

ARTICLE 97

The Specialized Organizations shall enjoy the fullest technical autonomy and shall take into account the recommendations of the Council, in conformity with the provisions of the present Charter.

ARTICLE 98

The Specialized Organizations shall submit to the Council periodic reports on the progress of their work and on their annual budgets and expenses.

ARTICLE 99

Agreements between the Council and the Specialized Organizations contemplated in paragraph c) of Article 53 may provide that such Organizations transmit their budgets to the Council for approval. Arrangements may also be made for the Pan American Union to receive the quotas of the contributing countries and distribute them in accordance with the said agreements.

ORGANIZATION OF AMERICAN STATES

The International Organization of the 21 American Republics established by the Charter signed at the Ninth International Conference of American States, Bogotá, Colombia, 1948.

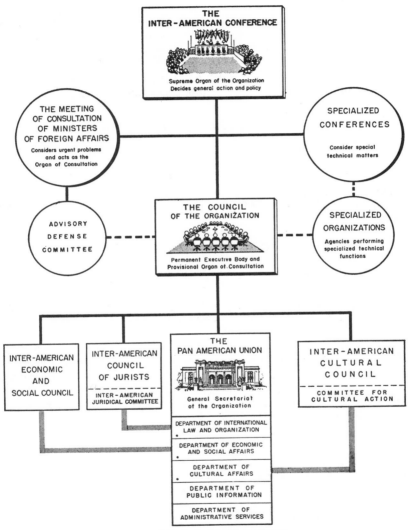

THE INTER-AMERICAN CONFERENCE

Supreme Organ of the Organization
Decides general action and policy

THE MEETING OF CONSULTATION OF MINISTERS OF FOREIGN AFFAIRS

Considers urgent problems and acts as the Organ of Consultation

SPECIALIZED CONFERENCES

Consider special technical matters

ADVISORY DEFENSE COMMITTEE

THE COUNCIL OF THE ORGANIZATION

Permanent Executive Body and Provisional Organ of Consultation

SPECIALIZED ORGANIZATIONS

Agencies performing specialized technical functions

INTER-AMERICAN ECONOMIC AND SOCIAL COUNCIL

INTER-AMERICAN COUNCIL OF JURISTS

INTER-AMERICAN JURIDICAL COMMITTEE

THE PAN AMERICAN UNION

General Secretariat of the Organization

DEPARTMENT OF INTERNATIONAL LAW AND ORGANIZATION

DEPARTMENT OF ECONOMIC AND SOCIAL AFFAIRS

DEPARTMENT OF CULTURAL AFFAIRS

DEPARTMENT OF PUBLIC INFORMATION

DEPARTMENT OF ADMINISTRATIVE SERVICES

INTER-AMERICAN CULTURAL COUNCIL

COMMITTEE FOR CULTURAL ACTION

* *The Directors of these Departments are the Executive Secretaries of the respective Councils.*

ARTICLE 100

The Specialized Organizations shall establish cooperative relations with world agencies of the same character in order to coordinate their activities. In concluding agreements with international agencies of a world-wide character, the Inter-American Specialized Organizations shall preserve their identity and their status as integral parts of the Organization of American States, even when they perform regional functions of international agencies.

ARTICLE 101

In determining the geographic location of the Specialized Organizations the interests of all the American States shall be taken into account.

PART THREE

CHAPTER XVI: THE UNITED NATIONS

ARTICLE 102

None of the provisions of this Charter shall be construed as impairing the rights and obligations of the Member States under the Charter of the United Nations.

CHAPTER XVII: MISCELLANEOUS PROVISIONS

ARTICLE 103

The Organization of American States shall enjoy in the territory of each Member such legal capacity, privileges and immunities as are necessary for the exercise of its functions and the accomplishment of its purposes.

ARTICLE 104

The Representatives of the Governments on the Council of the Organization, the representatives on the organs of the Council, the personnel of their delegations, as well as the Secretary General and the Assistant Secretary General of the Organization, shall enjoy the privileges and immunities necessary for the independent performance of their duties.

ARTICLE 105

The juridical status of the Inter-American Specialized Organizations and the privileges and immunities that should be granted to them and to their personnel, as well as to the officials of the Pan American Union shall be determined in each case through agreements between the respective organizations and the Governments concerned.

ARTICLE 106

Correspondence of the Organization of American States, including printed matter and parcels, bearing the frank thereof, shall be carried free of charge in the mails of the Member States.

ARTICLE 107

The Organization of American States does not recognize any restriction on the eligibility of men and women to participate in the activities of the various Organs and to hold positions therein.

CHAPTER XVIII: RATIFICATION AND ENTRY INTO FORCE

ARTICLE 108

The present Charter shall remain open for signature by the American States and shall be ratified in accordance with their respective constitutional procedures. The original instrument, the Spanish, English, Portuguese and French texts of which are equally authentic, shall be deposited with the Pan American Union, which shall transmit certified copies thereof to the Governments for purposes of ratification. The instruments of ratification shall be deposited with the Pan American Union, which shall notify the signatory States of such deposit.

ARTICLE 109

The present Charter shall enter into force among the ratifying States when two-thirds of the signatory States have deposited their ratifications. It shall enter into force with respect to the remaining States in the order in which they deposit their ratifications.

ARTICLE 110

The present Charter shall be registered with the Secretariat of the United Nations through the Pan American Union.

ARTICLE 111

Amendments to the present Charter may be adopted only at an Inter-American Conference convened for that purpose. Amendments shall enter into force in accordance with the terms and procedure set forth in Article 109.

ARTICLE 112

The present Charter shall remain in force indefinitely, but may be denounced by any Member State upon written notification to the Pan American Union, which shall communicate to all the others each notice of denunciation received. After two years from the date on which the Pan American Union receives a notice of denunciation, the present Charter shall cease to be in force with respect to the denouncing State, which shall cease to belong to the Organization after it has fulfilled the obligations arising from the present Charter.

In witness whereof the undersigned Plenipotentiaries, whose full powers have been presented and found to be in good and due form, sign the present Charter at the city of Bogotá, Colombia, on the dates that appear opposite their respective signatures.

◇◇◇◇◇◇

40. WAGING PEACE IN THE AMERICAS

Address by Secretary Acheson, September 19, 1949 [1]

[This address by Secretary Acheson presents in well-rounded summary form the basic principles which underlie our policy with respect to Latin America. In view of the deep interest of the Latin American countries in economic development, the sections relating to our economic policy and to private capital and public funds are of particular interest.]

I am grateful to the Pan American Society for this welcome opportunity to meet with its distinguished membership and with so many friends from throughout the Western Hemisphere. It is a most appropriate setting in which to discuss the relations within our community of American Republics. There are two reasons in particular why I am glad to be able to discuss this subject tonight. The first is so obvious that we tend to take it for granted. It is that our countries are close neighbors, bound together by a common heritage of struggles for liberty and freedom.

The second reason is that the community between our countries presents us with a unique opportunity to press forward toward the positive objectives of our foreign policy. Much of our effort in other parts of the world has had to be devoted to repairing the destruction caused by war and to strengthening the free nations against aggression. We in this hemisphere have fortunately been spared the terrible destruction of war, and we are relatively remote from any direct threat against our independence. The prospects are, therefore, bright that we can continue to work together in an atmosphere of relative peace and stability. We are in a real sense waging peace in the Americas.

BASIC PRINCIPLES

Before discussing specific policies, it seems well to restate once more the basic principles on which our policy in this hemisphere must rest. They are:

Our essential faith in the worth of the individual;

the preservation of our way of life without trying to impose it on others;

the observance by all governments of ethical standards based on justice and respect for freely accepted international obligations;

protection of the legitimate interests of our people and government, together with respect for the legitimate interests of all other peoples and governments;

the juridical equality of all the American Republics;

nonintervention in the internal or external affairs of any American Republic;

the stimulation of private effort as the most important factor in political, economic, and social purposes;

freedom of information and the development of free exchanges in all fields;

the perfection, with the other American countries, of regional and universal arrangements for maintaining international peace; and

[1] Department of State publication 3647, Inter-American Series 38.

the promotion of the economic, social, and political welfare of the people of the American Republics.

These men are our guiding principles. A statement of the specific policies which rest on these principles can best be made in conjunction with a review of our long-term objective.

NATIONAL AND HEMISPHERE SECURITY

The primary objective of any government is necessarily the security of its territory and people. The Monroe Doctrine is an acknowledgement that the security of this hemisphere is indivisible. With the development of the inter-American system, our countries have jointly created an effective security organization consistent with the Charter of the United Nations.

The Rio de Janeiro treaty of 1947 provides that in case of armed attack on an American Republic, each party pledges itself to assist in meeting the attack. One of the foremost policies of our country in foreign affairs is to fulfill its obligations under the Rio treaty and to seek the maximum cooperation among the American nations in achieving the objective of a secure and peaceful continent.

I stress this point because the security system which has culminated in the Rio treaty is now facing a crucial test.

For more than 2 years the Caribbean area has been disturbed by plots and counterplots. These plots have in themselves been inconsistent with our common commitments not to intervene in each other's affairs. Increasingly, however, denunciations have been succeeded by overt attempts at military adventure. Since 1945 few nations in the Caribbean area have escaped involvement, and at times the entire area has approached a state of political turmoil.

This situation is repugnant to the entire fabric of the inter-American system. The United States could not be faithful to its international obligations if it did not condemn it in the strongest terms. The energies spent in these adventures could much better have been put to use for peaceful purposes and improving the lot of the ordinary citizen. Aggression or plotting against any nation of this hemisphere is of concern to us. Wherever it occurs, or may be threatened, we shall use our strongest efforts, in keeping with our international commitments, to oppose it and to defend the peace of the hemisphere.

Only last Wednesday the Inter-American Peace Committee, meeting at the Pan American Union, set forth the principles and standards that bear on this situation. It is my hope that rigorous adherence to these principles and standards by all American governments will assure peace, not only in the Caribbean area, but also throughout the hemisphere.

We, the nations of this hemisphere, have a responsibility not only to ourselves but also to the rest of the world to live together in peace and harmony. Together we have played an important part in creating the United Nations. We must live up to the responsibilities which we have thus assumed toward the other member nations. This means, among other things, that we must abide by our regional commitments and maintain peace in our own midst. If all of the countries of the hemisphere proceed along these lines, as we in this country intend to do, there is no reason why any nation in the hemisphere should fear aggression.

DEVELOPMENT OF REPRESENTATIVE DEMOCRACY

What I have said, however, should not be construed as blind adherence to the status quo. We oppose aggression; we do not oppose change. Indeed, we welcome and encourage change where it is in the direction of liberty and democracy. We have worked long and persistently in common with our neighbors toward this end.

We would like to see a world in which each citizen participates freely in determining periodically the identity of the members of his government. This is an objective for which we will continue to work, subject always to our common policy of nonintervention.

In the Americas we have had periods of high hope and periods of bitter discouragement as we have seen democratic institutions flourish in some countries, only to see them subverted in others. We always deplore the action of any group in substituting its judgment for that of the electorate. We especially deplore the overthrow by force of a freely elected government. In such situations we do not cease to hope that the people will regain the right to choose their leaders.

We realize, however, that the attainment of the democratic ideal in any country depends fundamentally upon the desires and efforts of the people of that country. The nature of democracy is such that it can be achieved only from within.

Democracy as we endeavor to practice it is a continuing development toward political maturity—not a formula to be imposed upon a nation by a self-appointed ruling class, as is the case with certain other forms of government. Its attainment is essentially a spiritual and personal problem to be solved by the people of each country for themselves.

We are encouraged in our purpose by the realization that the strength of democratic institutions throughout the hemisphere today is measurably greater than a generation ago. In spite of occasional disappointments, we note a steady forward progress. The spirit of democracy is alive and bearing fruit.

RECOGNITION

Our policy with respect to recognizing new governments in the hemisphere is not inconsistent with our encouragement of democracy. We maintain diplomatic relations with other countries primarily because we are all on the same planet and must do business with each other. We do not establish an embassy or legation in a foreign country to show approval of its government. We do so to have a channel through which to conduct essential governmental relations and to protect legitimate United States interests.

When a freely elected government is overthrown and a new and perhaps militaristic government takes over, we do not need to recognize the new government automatically and immediately. We can wait to see if it really controls its territory and intends to live up to its international commitments. We can consult with other governments, as we have often done.

But if and when we do recognize a government under these circumstances, our act of recognition need not be taken to imply approval of it or its policies. It is recognition of a set of facts, nothing more. We may have the gravest reservations as to the manner in which it has come into power. We may deplore its attitude toward civil liberties. Yet our long-range objectives in the promotion of democratic institutions may, in fact, be best served by recognizing it and thus maintaining a channel of communication with the country involved. In this way we are also able to discharge our basic function of protecting the interests of our government and our citizens there. Since recognition is not synonymous with approval, however, our act of recognition need not necessarily be understood as the forerunner of a policy of intimate cooperation with the government concerned.

ECONOMIC POLICY

The economic field offers the greatest opportunity for constructive action. Two sets of problems arise. The first are derived largely from the disruptions of the war, and we hope may be described as short-run problems. The second results from the fact that in wide areas the standard of living is still miserably low. This is a long-run problem, although no less urgent.

It was apparent that the war would be followed by a period of economic stress. In some areas the effectiveness of the economic machine had been destroyed. The effect of the war on various relationships which previously had been the basis of world trade—for example, the reduction in earnings on overseas investment by European countries—raised new issues with respect to achieving equilibrium. Although the heaviest initial impact of this problem fell on Europe, the fundamental disequilibrium has now extended around the world so that for every country the maintenance of trade and the balance of payments has become a major problem of foreign relations. It was obvious in its initial stage that there could be no real recovery in trade without the revival of production in Europe. Therefore, the European Recovery Program must be regarded not merely as a program to meet the individual problems of the European countries but also to revive the flow of goods to and from Europe. We are all aware of the serious character of the present balance-of-payments problems, and it is one to which we must direct our thoughts in the most constructive way possible.

While material well-being is no guaranty that democracy will flourish, a healthy and prosperous people is a far more fertile field for the development of democracy than one which is undernourished and unproductive. That is why we are and must be preoccupied with the long-term problem of economic development.

The record of our economic cooperation in this hemisphere is substantial. It is one of such proved soundness that it forms the precedent and the basis for the more constructive labor ahead.

For 10 years past a large work of technical cooperation has been under way throughout our countries. Our government participates in this work through many of its agencies, such as the Department of Agriculture and the Public Health Service. Our Institute of Inter-American Affairs is cooperating with agencies of the other governments in outstandingly successful programs to improve basic living conditions. Technicians and administrators from the United States and from the host countries work side by side in partnership with each other. They work among the peoples in the remote countryside as well as in the cities. The Institute of Inter-American Affairs has now been authorized by Congress to continue and to expand this work. These programs have furnished the inspiration and the proving ground for the world-wide program of technical cooperation envisaged in Point 4 of President Truman's inaugural address.

In 1935, we created the Export-Import Bank which has become a uniquely successful institution in the field of economic development. The steel mill at Volta Redonda in Brazil is in full operation and a lifelong desire of many Brazilian statesmen and businessmen has become a reality with a plentiful supply of steel products to complement the vigorous growth of industry in that country. At Concepción in Chile we shall soon see the realization of another project which has been brought about by the combination of energy on the part of Chilean leaders and cooperation by the Export-Import Bank in supplying the material needs to bring the idea into fruit. There are constructive evidences throughout the Americas of the good use to which Export-Import credits have been put—in the Artibonite Valley in Haiti, in meat packing plants in Mexico—in highways in many countries, in ships, power systems, public works, agricultural projects, large and small industrial undertakings. The total amount of loans advanced by the Bank to the other American Republics is over 700 million dollars. Defaults on these loans are insignificant.

The International Bank and the International Monetary Fund created at Bretton Woods in 1944 largely on the initiative of the United States, today are actively contributing to economic development and fiscal stability in this hemisphere. The Bank already has made loans to several American nations for basic development, and the Fund has assisted in the solution of currency problems. Through our representation in both institutions, we shall continue our vigorous support of these constructive policies.

These specific programs represent actual deeds—not merely words. Nor are they isolated examples, but rather parts of a broad program of economic cooperation which, while reflecting our national self-interest, can leave no doubt as to our deep and lasting concern with the economic welfare of the other American Republics.

PRIVATE CAPITAL AND PUBLIC FUNDS

Loans of public funds, however, can only be supplementary to the efforts of private capital, both local and foreign. This country has been built by private initiative, and it remains a land of private initiative. The preponderance of our economic strength depends today as in the past upon the technical and financial resources and, even more, upon the abilities and morale of private citizens. I venture to say that the same thing is true of the other American nations.

In providing assistance for economic development, it would be contrary to our traditions to place our government's public funds in direct and wasteful competition with private funds. Therefore, it will be our policy, in general, not to extend loans of public funds for projects for which private capital is available. It is our purpose, also, to emphasize the desirability of loans which increase productivity.

Nor do we necessarily believe that rapid industrialization is good per se. Industrial development is an important factor in raising living standards, and therefore we have cooperated actively to this end. However, we feel that a balance should be achieved between industry, agriculture, and other elements of economic life. In many countries, large and small, the greatest immediate progress toward material well-being may be made through modern and diversified cultivation of the land. Irrigation projects, the use of agricultural machinery, the restoration of old land through fertilizers—these simple measures may do more to raise the standard of living than a dozen new industries.

We have had these principles in mind in elaborating the Point 4 program. Because we believe that the job ahead should be done primarily through private initiative, we have requested Congress to authorize the Export-Import Bank to offer certain guaranties against risks peculiar to foreign private investment.

We hope that the flow of private capital can be stimulated also by the negotiation of treaties to create an atmosphere favorable to increased private investment abroad. We are concerned with two types of treaties: first, treaties to avoid double taxation; second, treaties to define our economic relations and give reasonable assurances to our investors while safeguarding the interests and integrity of the other country.

SPECIAL NEEDS OF COUNTRIES

We believe that this general program can best be developed in full consideration of the special needs of individual countries. The conditions of the various nations of the hemisphere differ widely. Nor can all of our international problems be dealt with in the same way. In the field of economic development we have a common goal of high living standards and increased trade—just as in the political field we have a common goal of security and individual freedom. However, the process of economic development depends upon the efforts and resources of each individual country. There is no common formula. To be sure, the process can be facilitated in various ways by international organizations, such as the United Nations and its specialized agencies and the Organization of American States. But, in the last analysis, it depends upon the energy and resources of the individual countries themselves. The United States is prepared to lend its assistance, both directly and through international bodies, to working out specific programs with individual countries. Possibly this principle might be expanded to the working out of regional programs if two or more countries should seek to plan jointly for economic development.

I cannot stress too strongly that progress will come most rapidly in countries that help themselves vigorously. Economic development, like democracy, cannot be imposed from outside. Positive self-help is also essential to establishing conditions of economic stability and of fair treatment for private investment and the rights of labor. In countries where such conditions are provided, it will follow that we can collaborate more effectively in working out development programs. Public and private capital will be attracted more readily to such countries. While this is dictated by logic rather than emotion, it has been our experience that these conditions are generally founded in countries where constitutional and political democracy exists.

CONCLUSION

These then are our three major objectives—the security of our nation and of the hemisphere; the encouragement of democratic representative institutions; and positive cooperation in the economic field to help in the attainment of our first two objectives.

If I have said nothing new tonight, it may well be because, in a family of nations as in families of individuals we should expect nothing more sensational than growth.

We can take satisfaction in the stability of our policy in the hemisphere. The good-neighbor policy as we practice it today is, for us, an historic, bipartisan, national policy. It has been wrought by Democrats at both ends of Pennsylvania Avenue—President Roosevelt, Secretary Hull, and Senator Connally, and also by Republicans at both ends of the Avenue—President Hoover, Secretary Stimson, and Senator Vandenberg. And this by no means exhausts the distinguished list who have contributed to this great policy.

It is the firm intention of President Truman, as it is of myself as Secretary of State—of the entire personnel of my Department and, I believe, of the people of my country—to work for ever closer relations between the nations of this hemisphere. We seek by positive good will and effort to strengthen the Organization of American States, within the more extensive design of the United Nations, as the most effective expression of law and order in this hemisphere.·

We and the other American Republics have determined and pledged ourselves to carry on our common policy of the Good Neighbor as a living and constantly growing reality.

◇◇◇◇◇

41. ACTION OF THE OAS IN THE MAINTENANCE OF PEACE

Annual Report of the Secretary General of the OAS, Fiscal Year 1949-1950 [1]

[Since the Rio Pact went into force in 1948, it has been invoked in two instances: the first involving a situation between Costa Rica and Nicaragua, the second involving difficulties between Haiti and the Dominican Republic. The following extract from the Annual Report of the Secretary-General of the Organization of American States for 1950 shows clearly how the OAS peace machinery functioned in connection with the Haiti-Dominican Republic controversy and, more important still, it points up the significant lessons which should be learned from that experience.]

If the general atmosphere of optimism toward collective international action is equally advantageous for the United Nations and the OAS, there was good reason before the events I have recounted in the previous chapter for our regional organization to merit a vote of appreciation and an expression of confidence in its effectiveness. Without the drama that inevitably attends all controversies submitted to the United Nations, the OAS brought an expeditious end, by the application of the Treaty of Reciprocal Assistance, to a confused and dangerous situation that threatened a vast region, from the

[1] Organization of American States, *Annual Report of the Secretary General for the fiscal year ending June 30, 1950.* Pan American Union, Washington, D. C., 1950, pp. 14-28.

beginning designated as the *Caribbean area*. I shall not deal here with the historical development of the Organization's intervention in that case, but shall merely point out some of its characteristics and refer to certain conclusions that may now be drawn from this second application of the Inter-American Treaty of Reciprocal Assistance.

As was the case in the situation between Costa Rica and Nicaragua, the Organ of Consultation was called, under article 6 of the Rio Treaty, to consider the two cases presented by Haiti and the Dominican Republic. It was the opinion of the Council of the Organization that it was confronted with *a fact or situation that might endanger the peace of America*, or with *an intracontinental conflict*, or *with an aggression which was not armed attack*, and that under any of these three situations the inviolability, or the integrity of the territory, or the sovereignty, or the political independence of an American State had been affected. By an absolute majority vote, and after hearing the arguments of Haiti, on the one hand, and of the Dominican Republic on the other, the Council decided to convoke the Organ of Consultation, as it had done previously, *sine die*, and to constitute itself provisionally as such, in order to initiate examination of the cases presented. As always happens in situations of conflict that are not armed attack—which is easier to identify by the attendant physical acts—on this occasion the two nations requesting the meeting of consultation did not agree on the facts constituting the ground of the controversy.

PROCEDURE FOR CONVOKING THE ORGAN OF CONSULTATION

The procedure of a judicial trial, whereby facts are established by an examination of charges and defenses, is not the method most in harmony with the spirit and purpose of the Treaty of Reciprocal Assistance, which contemplates political actions of States to defend the victim of aggression and to reestablish peace, actions which are not to be confused with either the peaceful settlement of disputes or with judicial decisions fixing responsibility for crime. Nevertheless, the very nature of the conflicts that have so far been presented to the Organ of Consultation provided for in the Rio Treaty makes it necessary for that organ to be constantly on the alert to resist a natural tendency to turn it into a court, and to surround its essentially executive procedure with the solemnity and complex guarantees accompanying slow judicial action.

It might be said—giving a very strict interpretation to the Treaty that may not always be feasible—that when the Council of the OAS resolves to call the Organ of Consultation it is already fully convinced that facts or situations have occurred that exactly fit the hypotheses contemplated in the Treaty. In order to be assured of this, the Council should, in doubtful cases, undertake an investigation of its own before calling the Organ of Consultation or constituting itself as such provisionally. But does the Treaty authorize an investigation of this nature by the Council? It is evident that any investigation ordered by the Council would be authorized, for it may be one of the measures indicated for the common defense and for the maintenance of continental peace and security. But it is also true that the Council, before convoking the Organ of Consultation, could undertake such in investigation when it is necessary to establish whether or not the case calls for the application of the Treaty.

It has been said that the fact that article 6 of the Treaty provides that *the Organ of Consultation shall meet immediately in order to agree on the measures which must be taken in case of aggression to assist the victim of the aggression or, in any case, the measures which should taken for the common defense and for the maintenance of the peace and security of the Continent* does not permit delay, and that the only function of the Council is to issue the call, automatically, in response to the request of a nation. It is claimed that the Council would be extended political powers by giving it the competence of investigating and judging the question of whether a case is a proper one for the application of the Treaty. Not only is this a very debatable thesis, but experience is showing us that it would be very unfortunate if the Organ of Consultation had to meet to apply the Treaty even when the convocation was made without justification. The Treaty would inevitably lose prestige if it were utilized to air controversies and disputes that might be settled by methods of conciliation or by judicial tribunals. And when it is recalled that the American States have entrusted to this valuable instrument the collective defense of the hemisphere and the maintenance of intercontinental peace, nothing could be more serious or prejudicial than to permit its abuse and cause it to lose both effectiveness and prestige.

So when a case arises involving the application of the Treaty it appears highly important for the Council not to feel obligated to settle it in a summary fashion, and always in favor of the request. Moreover, in cases where there is great confusion because of the sharp disagreement on the facts between two or more parties, it is essential for the Council to anticipate the action—until now taken by the Organ of Consultation—of making an investigation to establish, not the responsibilities or the measures that fall under the competence of the Organ of Consultation, but whether there actually exists one of the situations contemplated in the Treaty. That the Rio Treaty would authorize such a procedure appears clearly from the fact that no provision is made for convening a meeting automatically. The Treaty could have said that the Organ of Consultation was to meet immediately upon the request of a State, but it did not say that. It did say, in article 13, that *"The consultations shall be initiated at the request addressed to the Governing Board of the Pan American Union by any of the Signatory States which has ratified the Treaty,"* and later, in article 16, that *"The decisions of the Governing Board of the Pan American Union referred to in articles 13 and 15 above shall be taken by an absolute majority of the Members entitled to vote."* This does not impose the blind obligation of reaching an agreement (which might be negative, since it is subject to vote), without sufficient information on the subject. And in many cases such information could only be brought out by investigation carried out by the Council.

Preserving the Spirit of the Treaty

It appears clear, therefore, that the Council has the vital function, which it must rigorously perform, of defending the Treaty of Reciprocal Assistance against the natural tendency of every State to attribute to external events that might affect it a motive and a gravity greater than they in reality have. These same events, examined impartially and in the presence of opposing opinions, may not constitute any one of the hypotheses contemplated by the Rio Treaty for the convocation of the Organ of Consultation, although they might very well justify the initiation of peaceful procedures, such as the good offices offered by the Inter-American Peace Committee, or those applicable between States bound by the American Treaty on Pacific Settlement.

On the other hand, the same limited tradition in the application of the Treaty of Reciprocal Assistance offers a good foundation for the interpretation in this manner of its provisions in relation to the function of the Council. In the first case in which recourse was had to the Treaty, on the basis of article 6 (Costa Rica-Nicaragua), the Council proceeded to call the Organ of Consultation and constituted itself provisionally as such with great speed and after a summary presentation of the facts. Subsequent investigation by a Committee showed that the events were not so serious as they at first appeared; but the action was justified by the results obtained. In the second case (Haiti-Dominican Republic, February 16, 1949) the Council decided not to convoke the Organ of Consultation, on the ground that the statements of the parties—in their agreement of peaceful intent by both nations—formed the basis for an understanding between them, and the difference was referred to the Inter-American Peace Committee, whose good offices brought about a fully satisfactory joint declaration. In the last case (the Caribbean situation) the Organ of Consultation was called, and the report of the Committee that investigated the facts on the spot, as well as the conclusions of the Organ, demonstrated that there had been a very serious basis for the application of the Treaty. But the different procedure adopted by the Council proves that it not only has the power to decide upon the application of the Treaty on the basis of the facts presented to it, or which it can learn for itself, but that the Council has been fully conscious of its responsibility in the task of defending the Treaty against improper and prejudicial application.

However, it is still not very clear what the Council can and should do when it finds that a case presented to it for the application of the Rio Treaty does not fall under one of the hypotheses provided in the text. And this is of great importance, because if the Council lacks the authority to recommend some procedure or to assist in the settlement of the controversy, then before folding its arms when there is a possibility that a dispute may become more serious, it would always prefer to open the doors of the Organ of Consultation to perform therein a task of conciliation, and this is definitely not the procedure appropriate for this organ, nor one contemplated by the Treaty. In the Haiti-Dominican Republic case of February 16, 1949, a course was recommended that might very well be converted into inter-American law by the Tenth Conference: the Council could be granted the power to recommend a peaceful procedure—which might be recourse to some other organ, or the use of the methods provided by the American Treaty on Pacific Settlement when the nations involved in the dispute are parties to that agreement. The Council itself might also be given a mediating function permitting it, at any time, to reopen discussion on the convocation of the Organ of Consultation, if the situation should become aggravated. But in any event the Council should not, from an excess of good will so natural in a body that represents the highest ideals of American solidarity and fraternity, systematically assume the powers of an Organ of Consultation to enable it, with authority from the Treaty of Reciprocal Assistance, to settle situations that instrument does not contemplate.

Because, however elastic the interpretation of the Treaty may be, there is not a single expression in it to indicate that it may be applied in cases that do not contain at least the germ of aggression; and the sole act of initiating its procedures would, temporarily at least, characterize as aggression, or as threat of aggression, events, situations and developments that among the American States very rarely, or almost never, have that character.

REASON FOR THE EFFECTIVENESS OF THE OAS

The application of the Rio Treaty in the case known as "The Caribbean Situation" produced well-deserved commendations, and the effectiveness of the OAS was universally praised.

In what did the effectiveness of the Council lie? What are the formulas that achieve such far-reaching remedies for situations that, in any other part of the world, would lead to war? This, and not the anecdotal detail of the facts that produced the state of insecurity in the Caribbean region, is what is important to examine. Certainly there could have been an international war in the Caribbean; disturbances of the peace have been produced with less inflammable material, not only in other parts of the world but right here in America. It is also certain that the danger has disappeared. And that no one in the hemisphere—neither the chancelleries nor public opinion as expressed in the press and on the radio—fails to attribute the good result to the OAS. And in this we can include the public opinion and chancelleries even of the countries affected.

Evidently this effectiveness does not lie, as some suppose, in the machinery created by the American countries to settle their conflicts. It lies in the good faith with which the American States have created that machinery, use it honestly, and pay collective respect to its action, both when it favors their individual interests and when it runs against them. There are no "better" or "worse" international organizations, nor can the failures of an organization always be attributed to its technical defects. When the American States established theirs, they accepted its principles in good faith. All were resolved never again to resort to war as a legitimate instrument of inter-American policy. The American peace machinery operates with disconcerting ease. All the States cooperate to make it function well. Peace is their collective interest. But the States are aware that war is a constant threat, even sometimes against the will of the parties. For this reason, they endow their Organization—which is the sum of all of them—with sufficient powers to contain war, or extinguish it, or nullify its effects. And they pledge themselves, knowing what they do, to respect their Organization.

But that is not all. The American States, as they have demonstrated this time, have an international policy marked by courage and responsibility. They have the courage to call things by their right names. They have the courage and sense of responsibility to hear these things said when they are adverse to themselves. The Committee's report pointed out facts that imply violations of inter-American obligations. None of the States affected by the report's statements tried to evade its responsibility. This is an impressive example of international frankness and loyalty. We can say that it is without precedent in the history of international associations. It is impossible to say which of these two instances was the more important: when five representatives of States

—not five commissioners or five men, but five States—expressed their opinion of the causes and remedies for the situation, without any reticence; or when, one after the other, the States cited in the report and conclusions praised the impartiality and probity of the committee members and refrained from creating the sort of incident we are used to seeing in international meetings whenever anyone must point out that the policy of a certain country is at fault.

The American States demonstrated a maturity of conduct that indicates that the sixty years since they took the first steps to associate themselves honorably in a policy of peace and cooperation have not passed in vain. In these two instances (of the presentation of the report and its discussion in the Council) the tension of the Caribbean area was dissolved, almost automatically. States with such a profound sense of international responsibility and of their obligations within the Organization could not be, never will be a menace to the peace.

IMPLICIT DEFINITION OF AGGRESSION

In the juridical field, this second application of the Treaty of Reciprocal Assistance reveals new and very important points. The Council, acting as Provisional Organ of Consultation, has taken a step in the definition of the concept of aggression that has been sharply debated since the already remote days of the League of Nations. Examining the events that occurred and the intervention by foreign governments in domestic revolutionary situations in certain countries, the Council declared that "Even though the said facts fortunately did not result in the violation of international peace, they did very seriously weaken American solidarity; and if they were to persist or recur, they would give occasion for the application of the procedures of the Inter-American Treaty of Reciprocal Assistance in order to protect the principle of non-intervention and to ensure the inviolability or the integrity of the territory or the sovereignty or the political independence of any American State against aggression on the part of any State or group of States." Actually, this affirmation creates nothing more nor less than the teeth that were lacking in the inter-American treaties and conventions which, in the Committee's judgment, were violated in the cases it investigated. It is almost the same as saying that intervention, as condemned in those treaties and conventions, is one of the acts of aggression that give occasion for applying the measures contemplated by the Treaty of Reciprocal Assistance. No future meeting of the Organ of Consultation, in similar cases, could fail to be guided by this criterion if there should be any doubt as to the application of the Rio de Janeiro Treaty, or if it should be necessary to define the aggressor in the circumstances covered by articles 6, 7, and 9 of that Treaty. Indeed, the Council was acting under the power of article 9, which authorizes it to characterize acts other than armed attack and invasion as acts of aggression.

NON-INTERVENTION AND DEMOCRACY

Another result of this meeting of the Council, acting as Organ of Consultation, was a basic clarification of the supposed conflict between the principle of non-intervention and the principle of democracy. Within the limits of the most rigorous juridical concept, and in defense of the best interests of the American community, the Council once more made it clear that no government or group of governments can feel authorized, in the name of democratic principles, to violate the principle of non-intervention. It recommended that a study be undertaken of the possibilities of stimulating and developing the effective exercise of representative democracy, set forth in article 5 (d) of the Charter, as well as in Article XX of the American Declaration of the Rights and Duties of Man. The relevant section of article 5 of the OAS Charter says that "The solidarity of the American States and the high aims which are sought through it require the political organization of those States on the basis of the effective exercise of representative democracy." And Article XX of the Declaration says that "Every person having legal capacity is entitled to participate in the government of his country, directly or through his representatives, and to take part in popular elections, which shall be by secret ballot, and shall be honest, periodic and free." The American States have evidently acquired an obligation to proceed in conformity with these principles. But even if that obligation went still further and there were some compulsory force to compel its execution, this power would never be given to individual States, for each to put into operation according to its own conception against other governments. We cannot tell whether some day there may be machinery in the Organization to give effect to those principles. But violation of the principle of non-intervention can never be justified as a legitimate individual means of carrying them out.

Another principle that comes out of this meeting reinforced by the approval given to a concept expressed by the Investigating Committee is that no American government may resort to the threat or use of force, even in the name of legitimate self-defense, in any manner inconsistent with the provisions of the UN Charter, the Rio de Janeiro Treaty, and the OAS Charter. Legitimate self-defense implies a previous offensive act. Therefore it is obvious that if it is made into a threat it is not legitimate, nor is it defense. Of course a State can defend itself, if it is attacked, without violating any international commitment. But this right must not be converted into a provocation. Still less when all the resources of collective self-defense are at hand, as they are in the Treaty of Reciprocal Assistance.

CONCLUSION

The effective action of the OAS in the application of the Treaty of Reciprocal Assistance in the cases previously mentioned not only consolidated its prestige in the hemisphere but demonstrated the flexibility and utility of the machinery for collective defense, while it also served to establish precedents that will make still easier the enforcement of the Treaty in the future, if it should unfortunately be necessary to resort to it. At the same time, principally because of the fact that not all American States which are parties to the Treaty of Reciprocal Assistance are also parties, and without reservations, to the American Treaty on Pacific Settlement, there is evident need to maintain the functions now entrusted to the Inter-American Peace Committee. In close connection with those of the Council of the Organization, these functions will help to channel toward pacific settlement controversies or disputes submitted to the Council with a request for application of the Rio Treaty which are found not to contain the elements of the situations contemplated in that instrument.

◇◇◇◇◇◇

42. RESOLUTIONS ADOPTED AT THE FOURTH MEETING OF CONSULTATION OF MINISTERS OF FOREIGN AFFAIRS OF THE AMERICAN REPUBLICS, WASHINGTON, MARCH 26 TO APRIL 7, 1951 [1]

[From 1942 until 1951 there were no meetings of consultation of the Foreign Ministers of the American Republics. The fourth meeting was held in Washington in the spring of 1951 because of the need for action for common defense against the aggressive tactics of international communism. The conference approved thirty-one resolutions and declarations which reaffirmed the solidarity of the new world with respect to the three major items on the agenda: 1) political and military coöperation for the defense of the Americas; 2) strengthening the internal security of the American republics; and 3) emergency economic coöperation. Four of the more important resolutions are reproduced below.]

RESOLUTION I

DECLARATION OF WASHINGTON

WHEREAS:

The present Meeting was called because of the need for prompt action by the Republics of this Hemisphere for common defense against the aggressive activities of international communism;

Such activities, in disregard of the principle of non-intervention, which is deeply rooted in the Americas, disturb the tranquility of the peoples of this Hemisphere and endanger the liberty and democracy on which their institutions are founded;

All the said Republics have stated, in formal acts and agreements, their will to cooperate against any threat to or aggression against the peace, security, and territorial integrity or independence of any one of them;

It will be impossible for such cooperation to be effective unless it is carried out in a true spirit of harmony and conciliation;

In view of the common danger, the present moment is propitious for a reaffirmation of inter-American solidarity;

That danger becomes more serious as a consequence of certain social and economic factors;

In this last connection there is now, more than ever, need for the adoption of measures designed to improve the living conditions of the peoples of this Hemisphere; and,

On the other hand, in any action for the defense of the Hemisphere and its institutions, the essential rights of man, solemnly proclaimed by the American Republics, should not be lost sight of,

The Fourth Meeting of Consultation of Ministers of Foreign Affairs DECLARES:

1. The firm determination of the American Republics to remain stead-

---

[1] Fourth Meeting of Consultation of Ministers of Foreign Affairs of American States, Washington, D. C., March 26-April 7, 1951. Final Act (Provisional text) pp. 6-11, 20-22, 27-28.

fastly united, both spiritually and materially, in the present emergency or in the face of any aggression or threat against any one of them.

2. A reaffirmation of the faith of the American Republics in the efficacy of the principles set forth in the Charter of the Organization of American States and other inter-American agreements to maintain peace and security in the Hemisphere, to defend themselves against any aggression, to settle their disputes by peaceful means, improve the living conditions of their peoples, promote their cultural and economic progress, and ensure respect for the fundamental freedoms of man and the principles of social justice as the bases of their democratic system.

3. Its conviction that strong support of the action of the United Nations is the most effective means of maintaining the peace, security, and well-being of the peoples of the world under the rule of law, justice, and international cooperation.

Resolution II

PREPARATION OF THE DEFENSE OF THE AMERICAN REPUBLICS AND SUPPORT OF THE ACTION OF THE UNITED NATIONS

WHEREAS:

The American Republics, as Members of the United Nations, have pledged themselves to unite their efforts with those of other States to maintain international peace and security, to settle international disputes by peaceful means, and to take effective collective measures to prevent and suppress acts of aggression;

International peace and security have been breached by the acts of aggression in Korea, and the United Nations, despite its efforts to find a peaceful solution, was obliged, pursuant to resolutions of the Security Council and the General Assembly, to take action to restore peace in that area; and

In order to ensure that the United Nations has at its disposal means for maintaining international peace and security, the General Assembly, on November 3, 1950, adopted the resolution entitled 'Uniting for Peace",

The Fourth Meeting of Consultation of Ministers of Foreign Affairs of American States

DECLARES:

That the present world situation requires positive support by the American Republics for: (1) achievement of the collective defense of the Continent through the Organization of American States, and (2) cooperation, within the United Nations Organization, to prevent and suppress aggression in other parts of the world; and

RECOMMENDS:

1. That each of the American Republics should immediately examine its resources and determine what steps it can take to contribute to the defense of the Hemisphere and to United Nations collective security efforts, in order to accomplish the aims and purposes of the "Uniting for Peace" resolution of the General Assembly.

2. That each of the American Republics, without prejudice to attending to national self-defense, should give particular attention to the development and maintenance of elements within its national armed forces so trained,

organized and equipped that they could, in accordance with its constitutional norms, and to the full extent that, in its judgment, its capabilities permit, promptly be made available, (1) for the defense of the Hemisphere, and (2) for service as United Nations unit or units, in accordance with the "Uniting for Peace" resolution.

RESOLUTION III

INTER-AMERICAN MILITARY COOPERATION

WHEREAS:

The military defense of the Continent is essential to the stability of its democratic institutions and the well-being of its peoples;

The American Republics have assumed obligations under the Charter of the Organization of American States and the Inter-American Treaty of Reciprocal Assistance to assist any American States subjected to an armed attack, and to act together for the common defense and for the maintenance of the peace and security of the Continent;

The expansionist activities of international communism require the immediate adoption of measures to safeguard the peace and the security of the Continent;

The present grave international situation imposes on the American Republics the need to develop their military capabilities in order, in conformity with the Inter-American Treaty of Reciprocal Assistance: 1) to assure their individual and collective self-defense against armed attacks; 2) to contribute effectively to action by the Organization of American States against aggression directed against any of them; and, 3) to make provision, as quickly as possible, for the collective defense of the Continent; and

The Ninth International Conference of American States, in its Resolution XXXIV, charged the preparation of collective self-defense against aggression to the Inter-American Defense Board, which, as the only inter-American technical-military organ functioning, is the suitable organ for the preparation of military plans for collective self-defense against aggression,

The Fourth Meeting of Consultation of Ministers of Foreign Affairs RESOLVES:

1. To recommend to the American Republics that they orient their military preparation in such a way that, through self-help and mutual aid, and in accordance with their capabilities and with their constitutional norms, and in conformity with the Inter-American Treaty of Reciprocal Assistance, they can, without prejudice to their individual self-defense and their internal security: a) increase those of their resources and strengthen those of their armed forces best adapted to the collective defense, and maintain those armed forces in such status that they can be immediately available for the defense of the Continent; and, b) cooperate with each other, in military matters, in order to develop the collective strength of the continent necessary to combat aggression against any of them.

2. To charge the Inter-American Defense Board with preparing, as vigorously as possible, and keeping up-to-date, in close liaison with the Governments through their respective Delegations, the military planning of the common defense.

3. That the plans formulated by the Inter-American Defense Board shall be submitted to the Governments for their consideration and decision. To the end of facilitating such consideration and decision, the Delegations of the American Republics to the Inter-American Defense Board shall be in continuous consultation with their Governments on the projects, plans, and recommendations of the Board.

4. To recommend to the Governments of the American Republics: a) that they maintain adequate and continuous representation of their armed forces on the Council of Delegates, on the Staff of the Inter-American Defense Board, and on any other organ of that organization that may be established in the future; b) that they actively support the work of the Board, and consider promptly all the projects, plans, and recommendations of that agency; and c) that they cooperate in the organization, within the Board, of a coordinated system of exchange of appropriate information.

RESOLUTION VIII

STRENGTHENING OF INTERNAL SECURITY

WHEREAS:

The American Republics at the Ninth International Conference.of American States, with specific reference to "the preservation and defense of democracy in America" and using as a basis Resolution VI of the Second Meeting of Consultation, resolved to condemn the methods of every system tending to suppress political and civil rights and liberties, and in particular the action of International Communism or any other totalitarian doctrine, and, consequently, to adopt, within their respective territories and in accordance with their respective constitutional provisions, the measures necessary to eradicate and prevent activities directed, assisted or instigated by foreign governments, organizations or individuals tending to overthrow their institutions by violence, to foment disorder in their domestic political life, or to disturb, by means of pressure, subversive propaganda, threats or by other means, the free and sovereign right of their peoples to govern themselves in accordance with their democratic aspirations;

To supplement those measures of mutual cooperation assuring collective defense as well as the economic and social well-being of the people, upon which the vitality of political institutions so much depends, it is necessary to adopt laws and regulations for internal security;

In their concern to counteract the subversive activity of international Communism, they are imbued with the desire to reaffirm their determination to preserve and strengthen the basic democratic institutions of the peoples of the American Republics, which the agents of international Communism are attempting to abolish through the exploitation and abuse of the democratic freedoms themselves;

Within each one of the American Republics there has been and is being developed through democratic procedures a body of laws designed to assure its political defense;

It is in accordance with the high common and individual interests of the American Republics to ensure that each of them will be able to meet the special and immediate threat of the subversive activities of international Communism; and

Since the said subversive activities recognize no boundaries, the present situation requires, in addition to suitable internal measures, a high degree of international cooperation among the American Republics, looking to the eradiction of any threat of subversive activity endangering democracy and the free way of life in the American Republics,

The Fourth Meeting of Consultation of Ministers of Foreign Affairs RESOLVES:

1. To recommend to the Governments of the American States:

(a) That, mindful of their unity of purpose and taking account of the contents of Resolution VI of the Second Meeting of Consultation in Habana and Resolution XXXII of the Ninth International Conference of American States in Bogotá, each American Republic examine its respective laws and regulations and adopt such changes as it considers necessary to ensure that subversive activities of the agents of international Communism, directed against any of them, may be adequately forestalled and penalized;

(b) That, in accordance with their respective constitutional provisions, they enact those measures necessary to regulate in the countries of the Americas the transit across international boundaries of those foreigners who there is reason to expect will attempt to perform subversive acts against the defense of the American Hemisphere; and

(c) That, in the application of this resolution, they bear in mind the necessity of guaranteeing and defending by the most efficacious means the rights of the individual as well as their firm determination to preserve and defend the basic democratic institutions of the peoples of the American Republics.

2. To instruct the Pan American Union, for the purpose of facilitating the fulfillment of the objectives of this resolution, to assign to the proper Department, which might be the Department of International Law and Organization, with the assistance, if deemed advisable, of experts on the subject, the following duties:

(a) To make technical studies concerning the definition, prevention, and punishment, as crimes, of sabotage and espionage with respect to acts against the American Republics and directed from abroad or against the defense of the Americas;

(b) To make technical studies of general measures by means of which the American Republics may better maintain the integrity and efficacy of the rights of the individual and of the democratic system of their institutions, protecting and defending them from treason and any other subversive acts instigated or directed by foreign powers or against the defense of the Americas;

(c) To make technical studies concerning measures to prevent the abuse of freedom of transit, within the Hemisphere, including clandestine and illicit travel and the misuse of travel documents, aimed at weakening the defense of the Americas.

The Pan American Union shall transmit the reports and conclusions resulting from its studies to the American Governments for their information, through their representatives on the Council of the Organization of American

States, and should any of the said Governments so request and the Council by a simple majority of votes so decide, a specialized conference on the matter shall be called pursuant to the terms of Article 93 of the Charter of the Organization of American States.

RESOLUTION XII

ECONOMIC DEVELOPMENT

WHEREAS:

The present international state of emergency and the dangers it contains for all free countries demand efficacious cooperation among the American Republics for the effective defense of the Hemisphere;

One of the most serious factors in social decline, one that best suits the purposes of aggression, is the existence of low standards of living in many countries that have been unable to attain the benefits of modern techniques;

It is therefore necessary to establish rational bases that will make it possible to maintain the equilibrium and, to the extent that the emergency permits, the development of the economies of the underdeveloped American Republics and to improve the standard of living of their peoples in order to increase their individual and collective capacities for the defense of the Hemisphere and contribute to the strengthening of their internal security; and

The programs of economic development and technical cooperation have proven to be the most successful instruments for strengthening internal economies and improving living standards; and the present emergency situation and the greater needs for defense that it imposes are additional and urgent reasons for increasing international cooperation in this field of activity,

The Fourth Meeting of Consultation of Ministers of Foreign Affairs
DECLARES:

That the economic development of underdeveloped countries should be considered as an essential factor in the total concept of Hemisphere defense, without disregarding the fact that it is the prime duty of the American States in the present emergency to strengthen their defenses and maintain their essential civilian activities; and
RESOLVES:

1. That the American Republics should continue to collaborate actively and with even greater vigor in programs of economic development and programs of technical cooperation with a view to building economic strength and wellbeing in the underdeveloped regions of the Americas and to improving the living levels of their inhabitants.

2. To this end, the American Republics shall supply, subject to the provisions of Resolution No. XVI, the machinery, mechanical equipment, and other materials needed to increase their productive capacity, diversify their production and distribution, facilitating in appropriate cases financial and technical cooperation for carrying out plans for economic development.

3. Such financial and technical collaboration shall be carried forward with the purpose of modernizing agriculture, increasing food production, developing mineral and power resources, increasing industrialization, improv-

ing transportation facilities, raising standards of health and education, encouraging the investment of public and private capital, stimulating employment and raising managerial capacity and technical skills, and bettering the conditions of labor.

4. During the present emergency period, preference among economic development projects should be given in the following order: Projects useful for defense purposes and projects designed to satisfy the basic requirements of the civilian economy; projects already begun, the interruption of which would entail serious losses of materials, money, and effort; and other projects for economic development.

5. Each American state will take steps to coordinate its respective plans and programs for economic development with the emergency economic plans, bearing in mind its own tendencies and possibilities, for the continuity of its development.

Defeated and Occupied Areas [1]

〆〆〆

ITALY

43. DECLARATION OF WAR WITH ITALY, DECEMBER 11, 1941

JOINT RESOLUTION Declaring That a State of War Exists Between Italy and the United States [2]

[The uneasy neutrality of the United States from August 1939 to December 1941 ended with the surprise attack on Pearl Harbor, December 7, 1941. Accordingly on December 8, Congress recognized that a state of war existed with Japan. This was followed by several declarations of war and severances of diplomatic relations, which made the United States a full-fledged partner of the United Nations. On December 11, both Germany and Italy declared war on the United States. Congress met these two declarations in kind.]

Whereas the Government of Italy has formally declared war against the Government and the people of the United States of America: Therefore be it

Resolved by the Senate and House of Representatives of the United States of America in Congress assembled, That the state of war between the United States and the Government of Italy which has thus been thrust upon the United States is hereby formally declared; and the President is hereby authorized and directed to employ the entire naval and military forces of the United States and the resources of the Government to carry on war against the Government of Italy; and, to bring the conflict to a successful termination, all of the resources of the country are hereby pledged by the Congress of the United States.

Approved, December 11, 1941, 3:06 p.m., E.S.T.

◇◇◇◇◇◇

44. ITALIAN MILITARY ARMISTICE [3]

Conditions Presented September 3, 1943

[Italy was the first Axis power to surrender to the United Nations. At the Casablanca Conference, January 26, 1943, President Roosevelt announced

---

[1] Each enemy country or occupied territory in this part is considered in the order in which its surrender occurred or a peace treaty was concluded with the country.

[2] 55 Stat. 707.

[3] United States and Italy 1936-1946: Documentary Record, Department of State publication

that the United Nations would continue to fight until their principal enemies had surrendered unconditionally. Early State Department deliberations favored a negotiated peace with Italy as contrasted with unconditional surrender for Germany and Japan. Actually, however, when the Italian Government capitulated, its surrender was complete and unconditional as the terms of the armistice reproduced below will indicate.]

FAIRFIELD CAMP SICILY
September 3, 1943

The following conditions of an Armistice are presented by

GENERAL DWIGHT D. EISENHOWER
Commander-in-Chief of the Allied Forces,

acting by authority by the Governments of the United States and Great Britain and in the interest of the United Nations, and are accepted by

MARSHALL PIETRO BADOGLIO
Head of the Italian Government

1. Immediate cessation of all hostile activity by the Italian armed forces.

2. Italy will use its best endeavors to deny, to the Germans, facilities that might be used against the United Nations.

3. All prisoners or internees of the United Nations to be immediately turned over to the Allied Commander in Chief, and none of these may now or at any time be evacuated to Germany.

4. Immediate transfer of the Italian Fleet and Italian aircraft to such points as may be designated by the Allied Commander in Chief, with details of disarmament to be prescribed by him.

5. Italian merchant shipping may be requisitioned by the Allied Commander in Chief to meet the needs of his military-naval program.

6. Immediate surrender of Corsica and of all Italian territory, both islands and mainland, to the Allies, for such use as operational bases and other purposes as the Allies may see fit.

7. Immediate guarantee of the free use by the Allies of all airfields and naval ports in Italian territory, regardless of the rate of evacuation of the Italian territory by the German forces. These ports and fields to be protected by Italian armed forces until this function is taken over by the Allies.

8. Immediate withdrawal to Italy of Italian armed forces from all participation in the current war from whatever areas in which they may be now engaged.

9. Guarantee by the Italian Government that if necessary it will employ all its available armed forces to insure prompt and exact compliance with all the provisions of this armistice.

10. The Commander in Chief of the Allied Forces reserves to himself the

2669, European Series 17, pp. 51-52; Armistice with Italy, 1943, Department of State publication 2963, Treaties and Other International Acts Series 1604. See *ibid.* for texts of other documents relating to the Italian Armistice: instrument of surrender of Italy; protocol; memorandum of agreement on the employment and disposition of the Italian fleet and mercantile marine between the Allied Naval Commander in Chief, Mediterranean, acting on behalf of the Allied Commander in Chief and the Italian Minister of Marine; and amendment to agreement between the Naval Commander in Chief, Mediterranean, Allied Forces and the Royal Italian Minister of Marine with respect to the employment of the Italian navy.

right to take any measure which in his opinion may be necessary for the protection of the interests of the Allied Forces for the prosecution of the war, and the Italian Government binds itself to take such administrative or other action as the Commander in Chief may require, and in particular the Commander in Chief will establish Allied Military Government over such parts of Italian territory as he may deem necessary in the military interests of the Allied Nations.

11. The Commander in Chief of the Allied Forces will have a full right to impose measures of disarmament, demobilization, and demilitarization.

12. Other conditions of a political, economic and financial nature with which Italy will be bound to comply will be transmitted at a later date.

The conditions of the present Armistice will not be made public without prior approval of the Allied Commander in Chief. The English will be considered the official text.

MARSHAL PIETRO BADOGLIO
Head of Italian Government.

DWIGHT D. EISENHOWER
General, U. S. Army,
Commander in Chief,
Allied Forces.

By:
GUISEPPE CASTELLANO

Guiseppe Castellano
Brigadier General, attached to
The Italian High Command

By:
WALTER B. SMITH

Walter B. Smith
Major General, U. S. Army,
Chief of Staff

◇◇◇◇◇◇

45. RENEWAL OF DIPLOMATIC RELATIONS WITH ITALY

Statement by the Acting Secretary of State, October 26, 1944 [1]

[The capitulation of Italy and the alignment of that country with the Allied cause in World War II, was followed by the resumption of diplomatic relations several months before the end of the war, and more than two years prior to the signing of the Treaty of Peace. This complete shift in the Italian position placed her in a unique status among the satellite states of Nazi Germany.]

After consultation with the other American Republics, as provided in the resolutions made at Rio de Janeiro in January 1942, it has been agreed that diplomatic relations with the Government of Italy should be resumed. The Governments of Great Britain and the Soviet Union likewise have been consulted.

Consequently, the President will submit to the Senate, after it reconvenes on November 14, 1944, the nomination of the Honorable Alexander C. Kirk as American Ambassador to Italy. Mr. Kirk is presently American Representative on the Advisory Council for Italy in Rome. [2]

[1] Department of State Bulletin of October 29, 1944, p. 491; also, Department of State publication 2669, European Series 17, p. 93. Edward R. Stettinius was Acting Secretary of State.
[2] On December 7, 1944, the Senate confirmed the nomination of Alexander C. Kirk as American Ambassador to Italy.

46. TREATY OF PEACE WITH ITALY, FEBRUARY 10, 1947 [1]

[The peace treaties at the end of World War II may be divided into two categories: (1) the treaties with Italy and the so-called satellite countries of Bulgaria, Finland, Hungary, and Rumania; and (2) the treaties with Germany, Austria, and Japan. The first were signed in Paris December 10, 1947, after some eighteen months of negotiations. The treaties with Germany, Austria, and Japan were long delayed because of the inability of the Great Powers to agree upon the terms.

The Treaty with Italy dispersed the Italian fleet among the victors, reduced the army drastically, eliminated the air force, and brought a temporary end to Italian war-making power. Up to 1952 the Treaty has operated as a limitation on Italy's full participation in the defense of the north Atlantic area. The following summary of the Treaty was prepared for the use of the Senate Committee on Foreign Relations.]

(Summary)

The Preamble gives a brief historical review of Italy's entry into the war, its surrender, and its co-belligerency against Germany as well as expressing the willingness of the Allied and Associated Powers to support its application to become a member of the United Nations and to conclude the present Treaty.

PART I—TERRITORIAL CLAUSES

Section I—Frontiers—Articles 1–5 establish Italy's frontiers, describing the four minor rectifications in the Franco-Italian line and the new lines of the Yugoslav-Italian and Free Territory of Trieste-Italian frontiers as shown on the maps in Annex I, and create boundary commissions for the delimitation of the latter.

Section II—France—Special Clauses—Articles 6-9 provide for the return of archives to France, the establishment of a special railway link and the guarantee to insure Italy electric and water supply from the ceded area of Tenda and Briga, further details of which are given in Annex III.

Section III—Austria—Special Clauses—Article 10 takes note of the Austro-Italian agreement regulating autonomy of South Tyrol, the text of which is given in Annex IV.

Section IV—Yugoslavia—Special Clauses—Articles 11-13 provide for cession to Yugoslavia of Zara and the Dalmatian Islands, delivery of cultural property and guarantee of water supply for Gorizia in accordance with detailed provisions of Annex V.

---

[1] S. Exec. F, G, H, I, 80th Cong., 1st sess., February 27, 28, 1947, pp. 5-10. See also texts of the President's letter of transmittal, report of the Secretary of State, and summaries of texts of treaties with Italy, Bulgaria, Roumania, and Hungary, Department of State Bulletin of March 23 and June 1, 1947; full text of treaty of peace with Italy, Department of State publication 2960, Treaties and Other International Acts Series 1648, also Treaties of Peace with Italy, Bulgaria, Hungary, Roumania, and Finland, Department of State publication 2743, European Series 21. Treaty of peace with Italy signed at Paris February 10, 1947; ratified by the U. S. June 14, 1947; entered into force September 15, 1947.

Section V—Greece—Special Clauses—Article 14 provides for cession of the Dodecanese Islands to Greece, their demilitarization and the withdrawal of troops.

PART II—POLITICAL CLAUSES

Section I—General Clauses—Articles 15-18 contain (a) the assurance of human rights and fundamental freedoms, (b) the guarantees of non-persecution of Allied supporters and abolition of Fascist organizations, and (c) the recognition of the Peace settlements.

Section II—Nationality, Civil and Political Rights—Articles 19-20 grant right of option to persons in territories ceded by Italy and to Yugoslav residents in Italy and assure their human rights and freedoms.

Section III—Trieste—Articles 21-22 set up the Free Territory of Trieste with its integrity and independence to be assured by the Security Council and describe its frontiers with Yugoslavia. Annexes VI, VII, VIII, IX and X refer to this Section. Annex VI contains the statute or charter of the Free Territory to be incorporated in its constitution. The Statute provides for the territory's demilitarization, citizenship of its inhabitants, the democratic organization of its government with legislative authority vested in a popular Assembly and executive power in a Council of Government with special powers conferred upon the Governor appointed by the Security Council, enabling him to protect the integrity and independence of the Territory and human rights of the inhabitants. The statute likewise insures the economic independence of the Territory, makes provision for the operations of its railways and establishes a customs free port with freedom of railway transport to and from the Territory.

Annex VII sets up the rules for the provisional regime until elections can be held in the Free Territory and until the approval of the Security Council can bring the statute into force. During this period the Governor, assisted by a provisional Council of Government appointed by him, has greater powers, and the responsibility for holding free elections Allied forces now in occupation are to be limited to 5,000 each for the United Kingdom, the United States and Yugoslavia and are placed at the disposal of the Governor who shall determine after 90 days whether conditions of internal order require their services for a further period.

Annex VIII sets forth the rules for the operation, under a Director appointed by the Governor, of the Free Port available for use on equal terms by all international commerce, provides for freedom of transit of goods transported by railway and precludes the establishment of any special zones within the Port but guarantees berthing facilities to Italy and Yugoslavia. A special international commission of an advisory character composed of representatives of France, the United Kingdom, the United States, the Union of Socialist Soviet Republics, Yugoslavia, Italy, Czechoslovakia, Poland, Switzerland, Austria and Hungary is created to investigate all matters relating to the operation and administration of the Free Port and to make recommendations thereon.

Annex IX gives technical guarantees for the Free Territory to insure water and electric supply from Italy and Yugoslavia and grants facilities for local frontier trade.

Annex X—Economic and Financial Provisions—provides for an orderly transfer of Italian property to the Free Territory, an adjustment with respect to the Italian public debt, the continuance and reassignment of insurance obligations, and the return of United Nations property, and contains provisions for such matters as property rights including right of removal, restitution, and the disposition of local government property and records.

Section IV—Italian Colonies—Article 23 provides for renunciation of Italian sovereignty over its Colonial possessions and their final disposal under the terms of Annex XI by the United States, the United Kingdom, the Union of Soviet Socialist Republics and France in the light of the wishes and welfare of the inhabitants and the interests of peace and security. Failing agreement within one year, matter is to be referred to the UN Assembly for final solution.

Section V—Special Interests of China—Articles 24-26 liquidate former Italian leases and special rights in China.

Section VI—Albania—Articles 27-32 provide for the final liquidation of the special position, rights and claims of Italy in Albania and for the restoration of property.

Section VII—Ethiopia—Articles 33-38 likewise provide for final liquidation of the special position, rights and claims of Italy in Ethiopia and for the restoration of property.

Section VIII—International Agreements—Articles 39-43 eliminate any special position for Italy as regards mandate system, Congo Basin treaties, Red Sea Islands and the Statute of Tangier and provide for the recognition by Italy of the liquidation of the League of Nations and other similar bodies.

Section IX—Bi-Lateral Treaties—Article 44 provides for the revival of pre-war treaties notified to Italy by the Allied and Associated Power concerned.

PART III—WAR CRIMINALS

Article 45 insures that Italy will take necessary steps looking to the surrender of war criminals and persons accused of treason but gives the Ambassadors at Rome of the great Powers control of the interpretation of this clause.

PART IV—NAVAL, MILITARY AND AIR CLAUSES

Section I—Duration of Application—Article 46 provides that the limitations imposed upon the Italian armed forces remain in effect until modified by agreement either with the Allied and Associated Powers or with the Security Council.

Section II—General Limitations—Articles 47-55 provide for demilitarization of the Franco-Italian frontier, the Italian-Yugoslav frontier, Sardinia, Sicily, and the Mediterranean Islands, as well as for prohibition upon atomic weapons, guided missiles, long-range guns and the limitation on the number of tanks and war material in excess of the amount required for forces limited by the treaty, as well as a prohibition upon service in the armed forces of a former Fascist militia and Republican Army member.

Section III—Limitation of the Italian Navy—Articles 56-60 establish limitations upon the Italian Navy in accordance with the schedule contained in Annex 12-A providing for a small but balanced fleet. The remaining vessels of the Italian Navy are to be placed at the disposal of the four Powers in good condition and provision is made for disposal of submarines, non-operational naval vessels, as well as for prohibition upon the construction of battleships, air-craft carriers, submarines, motor torpedo boats and assault craft and upon replacement construction in excess of the tonnage limit of 67,500 tons. Personnel of the Italian Navy is established at 25,000 officers and men. Naval training is restricted to the above personnel.

Section IV—Limitation of the Army—Articles 61-63 set the limits for the Italian Army at 185,000 and for the Carabinieri at 65,000 and prohibit military training for other persons.

Section V—Limitation of the Air Force—Articles 64-66 limit the Italian Air Force to 200 fighter and 150 transport and other aircraft and to a personnel strength of 25,000 and further prohibit bomber aircraft. Military air training is restricted to the above personnel.

Section VI—Disposal of War Material—Article 67 lays down the rules for disposal of surplus war material.

Section VII—Prevention of German and Japanese Rearmament—Articles 68-70 provide for Italian cooperation in prevention of Axis rearmament.

Section VIII—Prisoners of War—Article 71 requires prompt repatriation of Italian prisoners of war.

Section IX—Mine Clearance—Under Article 72, Italy is invited to join the Mine Clearance Organization and will place its minesweeper forces at the disposal of this body.

Annex XIII contains definitions of terms used in this Part.

PART V—WITHDRAWAL OF ALLIED FORCES

Article 73 calls for withdrawal from Italy of all armed forces of the Allied and Associated Powers within 90 days and the return of goods in their possession.

PART VI—CLAIMS ARISING OUT OF THE WAR

Section I—Reparations—Article 74 sets the figures for Italian reparation at $100,000,000 for the Soviet Union, $5,000,000 for Albania, $25,000,000 for Ethiopia, $105,000,000 for Greece and $125,000,000 to Yugoslavia (total $260,000,000) to be paid over a period of 7 years, which does not, however, start for 2 years except by mutual agreement. Reparation will be made not in cash but from surplus war factory equipment, from Italian assets in Roumania, Bulgaria and Hungary, from capital goods and assets, and from current production. Deliveries are to be scheduled in such a way as to avoid interference with Italy's economic reconstruction and placing a burden on other Allied or Associated Powers. States receiving reparation from current production must provide raw materials required. Specific deliveries are to be determined by mutual agreement, and machinery is established for supervision of reparation. Persons whose property is taken for reparation purposes will be compensated by Italy.

Section II—Restitution by Italy—Article 75 provides for the return in good order of identifiable property removed from territory of any of the United Nations, including monetary gold, and for method of presenting claims.

Section III—Renunciation of Claims by Italy—Articles 76-77 make provision for (a) renunciation by Italy of any claims upon the Allied and Associated Powers for loss or damage from war operations including Prize Court decrees and exercise of belligerent rights, (b) assumption of responsibility for Allied Military currency, (c) eligibility for restitution of Italian property in Germany, and (d) waiver of all Italian claims against Germany.

PART VII—PROPERTY, RIGHTS AND INTERESTS

Section I—United Nations Property in Italy—Article 78 provides for restoration of all legal rights and interests in Italy of the United Nations and their nationals and for restoration of their property in good order. In cases where the property cannot be restored or is damaged, the owner shall receive compensation in Italian lire to the equivalent to ⅔ of the loss. This same responsibility extends to United Nations property in the ceded territories and the Free Territory of Trieste.

Section II—Italian Property in the Territory of the Allied and Associated Powers—Article 79 authorizes the Allied and Associated Powers to take over property of Italy and its nationals in their territories and to apply the property or its proceeds to settlement of claims against Italy not settled by other clauses. The following are exempted from this provision: (a) consular and diplomatic property, (b) property used for religious or charitable purposes, (c) property of persons permitted to reside in the country, where the property is located, or elsewhere in United Nations territory, (d) property rights arising since resumption of trade or from transactions after the Armistice, (e) literary and artistic property rights, and (f) property in ceded territories not taken as reparation.

Section III—Declaration in Respect of Claims—By Article 80 the Allied and Associated Powers declare that their claims against Italy have been settled by other clauses of the Treaty.

Section IV—Debts—Article 81 makes provision for continuance of prewar obligations.

PART VIII—GENERAL ECONOMIC RELATIONS

Article 82 requires that for a period of 18 months Italy shall, on a reciprocal basis, (a) grant most favored nation treatment to United Nations and their nationals, (b) make no arbitrary discrimination against their goods, (c) grant no exclusive or discriminatory rights in respect to commercial aviation and (d) afford equality of opportunity in obtaining international commercial aviation rights and extend the right to fly over Italian territory.

PART IX—SETTLEMENT OF DISPUTES

Article 83 establishes provision for Conciliation Commissions to settle disputes in connection with restitution and restoration of United Nations property.

PART X—MISCELLANEOUS ECONOMIC PROVISIONS

Articles 84 and 85 relate to the scope of application of the economic articles and the legal form of the economic annexes.

PART XI—FINAL CLAUSES

Articles 86 and 87 authorize the Ambassadors in Rome of France, the United Kingdom, the United States and the Soviet Union acting in concert to

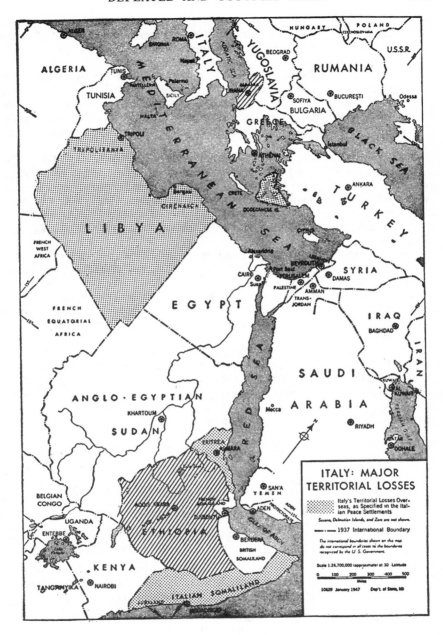

ITALY: MAJOR
TERRITORIAL LOSSES

Italy's Territorial Losses Overseas, as Specified in the Italian Peace Settlements

Sesana, Dalmatian Islands, and Zara are not shown.

——— 1937 International Boundary

*This international boundaries shown on this map
do not correspond in all cases to the boundaries
recognized by the U. S. Government.*

Scale 1:24,700,000 (approximate) at 30° Latitude

0   100   200   300   400   500
Miles

10629 January 1947   Dep't. of State, MB

represent all the Allied Powers in matters relating to the interpretation of the Treaty for a period of 18 months, and, with no time limit, to settle disputes concerning interpretation or execution of the Treaty. If this method fails, provision is made for special commissions for this purpose.

Articles 88-90 provide for accession by other powers, restrict the rights and benefits under the Treaty to those Powers which ratify, and lay down the procedure for signature and the coming into force of the Treaty upon ratification by the Soviet Union, the United Kingdom, the United States and France.

Economic Annexes—not specifically referred to in any Article of the Treaty.

Annex XIV—Economic and Financial Provisions relating to Ceded Territories
These clauses provide for the orderly transfer of Italian property in these areas, an adjustment with respect to the Italian public debt, the continuance and reassignment of insurance obligations and the return of United Nations property and contains provisions for such matters as property rights including right of removal, restitution and the disposition of local government property and records.

Annex XV—Special Provisions relating to Certain Kinds of Property
A.—Industrial, Literary and Artistic Property clauses establish Allied rights and interests in this form of property.

B.—Insurance clauses relate to resumption of insurance business.

Annex XVI—Contracts, Periods of Prescription and Negotiable Instruments
The special clauses relating to the foregoing do not apply as between the United States and Italy.

Annex XVIII—Prize Courts and Judgments
A.—*Prize Courts*—This Section provides for a review of all Italian Prize Court decisions in cases involving ownership rights.

B.—*Judgments*—This Section likewise provides for a review of court judgments after the outbreak of the war when a United Nations national involved was unable to make adequate presentation of his case.

◇◇◇◇◇◇

47. DISPOSAL OF FORMER ITALIAN COLONIES

Resolution of the General Assembly, November 21, 1949 [1]

[Following World War II a bitter struggle ensued over the disposal of the Italian colonies in North Africa because of their strategic value. Annex XI of the Italian Peace Treaty provided that in case the Big Four were unable to agree upon the matter within a year, it was to be referred to the General Assembly of the United Nations for recommendation. The Big Four agreed in advance to accept the Assembly recommendation. Since they were unable to reach agreement, the General Assembly approved a resolution in 1949 providing for the procedure to be followed in disposing of Libya, Italian Somaliland, and Eritrea.]

[1] General Assembly roundup, fourth regular session. Press Release GA/600, Part I, pp. 1-5.

The General Assembly,

In accordance with Annex XI, paragraph 3, of the Treaty of Peace with Italy, 1947, whereby the Powers concerned have agreed to accept the recommendation of the General Assembly on the disposal of the former Italian colonies and to take appropriate measures for giving effect to it,

Having taken note of the report of the Four Power Commission of Investigation, having heard spokesmen of organizations representing substantial sections of opinion in the territories concerned, and having taken into consideration the wishes and welfare of the inhabitants of the territories, the interests of peace and security, the views of the interested Governments and the relevant provisions of the Charter,

A. *With respect to Libya, recommends:*

1. That Libya, comprising Cyrenaica, Tripolitania and the Fezzan, shall be constituted an independent and sovereign State;

2. That this independence shall become effective as soon as possible and in any case not later than 1 January 1952;

3. That a constitution for Libya, including the form of the government, shall be determined by representatives of the inhabitants of Cyrenacia, Tripolitania and the Fezzan meeting and consulting together in a National Assembly;

4. That, for the purpose of assisting the people of Libya in the formulation of the constitution and the establishment of an independent Government, there shall be a United Nations Commissioner in Libya appointed by the General Assembly and a Council to aid and advise him;

5. That the United Nations Commissioner, in consultation with the Council, shall submit to the Secretary-General an annual report and such other special reports as he may consider necessary. To these reports shall be added any memorandum or document that the United Nations Commissioner or a member of the Council may wish to bring to the attention of the United Nations;

6. That the Council shall consist of ten members: namely:

(a) One representative nominated by the Government of each of the following countries: Egypt, France, Italy, Pakistan, the United Kingdom of Great Britain and Northern Ireland and the United States of America;

(b) One representative of the people of each of the three regions of Libya and one representative of the minorities in Libya;

7. That the United Nations Commissioner shall appoint the representatives mentioned in Paragraph 6 (b), after consultation with the administering Powers, the representatives of the Governments mentioned in paragraph 6 (a), leading personalities and representatives of political parties and organizations in the territories concerned;

8. That, in the discharge of his functions, the United Nations Commissioner shall consult and be guided by the advice of the members of his Council, it being understood that he may call upon different members to advise him in respect of different regions or different subjects;

9. That the United Nations Commissioner may offer suggestions to the General Assembly, to the Economic and Social Council and to the

Secretary-General as to the measures that the United Nations might adopt during the transitional period regarding the economic and social problems of Libya;

10. That the administering Powers in co-operation with the United Nations Commissioner:

(a) Initiate immediately all necessary steps for the transfer of power to a duly constituted independent Government;

(b) Administer the territories for the purpose of assisting in the establishment of Libyan unity and independence, co-operate in the formation of governmental institutions and co-ordinate their activities to this end;

(c) Make an annual report to the General Assembly on the steps taken to implement these recommendations;

11. That upon its establishment as an independent State, Libya shall be admitted to the United Nations in accordance with Article 4 of the Charter;

B. *With respect to Italian Somaliland, recommends:*

1. That Italian Somaliland shall be an independent sovereign State;

2. That this independence shall become effective at the end of ten years from the date of the approval of a Trusteeship Agreement by the General Assembly;

3. That during the period mentioned in paragraph 2, Italian Somaliland shall be placed under the International Trusteeship System with Italy as the Administering Authority;

4. That the Administering Authority shall be aided and advised by an Advisory Council composed of representatives of the following States: Colombia, Egypt and the Philippines. The headquarters of the Advisory Council shall be Mogadiscio. The precise terms of reference of the Advisory Council shall be determined in the Trusteeship Agreement and shall include a provision whereby the Trusteeship Council shall invite the States members of the Advisory Council, if they are not members of the Trusteeship Council, to participate without vote in the debates of the Trusteeship Council on any question relating to this territory;

5. That the Trusteeship Council shall negotiate with the Administering Authority the draft of a Trusteeship Agreement for submission to the General Assembly if possible during the present session, and in any case not later than the fifth regular session;

6. That the Trusteeship Agreement shall include an annex containing a declaration of constitutional principles guaranteeing the rights of the inhabitants of Somaliland and providing for institutions designed to ensure the inauguration, development and subsequent establishment of full self-government.

7. That in the drafting of this declaration the Trusteeship Council and the Administering Authority shall be guided by the annexed text proposed by the Indian delegation;

8. That Italy shall be invited to undertake provisional administration of the territory

(a) At a time and pursuant to arrangements for the orderly transfer of administration agreed upon between Italy and the United Kingdom, after the Trusteeship Council and Italy have negotiated the Trusteeship Agreement;

(b) On condition that Italy gives an undertaking to administer the territory in accordance with the provisions of the Charter relating to the International Trusteeship System and to the Trusteeship Agreement pending approval by the General Assembly of a Trusteeship Agreement for the territory;

9. That the Advisory Council shall commence the discharge of its functions when the Italian Government begins its provisional administration;

C. *With respect to Eritrea, recommends:*

1. That a Commission consisting of representatives of not more than five Member States, as follows, Burma, Guatemala, Norway, Pakistan and the Union of South Africa, shall be established to ascertain more fully the wishes and the best means of promoting the welfare of the inhabitants of Eritrea, to examine the question of the disposal of Eritrea and to prepare a report for the General Assembly, together with such proposal or proposals as it may deem appropriate for the solution of the problem of Eritrea;

2. That in carrying out its responsibilities the Commission shall ascertain all the relevant facts, including written or oral information from the present administering Power, from representatives of the population of the territory, including minorities, from Governments and from such organizations and individuals as it may deem necessary. In particular, the Commission shall take into account:

(a) The wishes and welfare of the inhabitants of Eritrea, including the views of the various racial, religious and political groups of the provinces of the territory and the capacity of the people for self-government;

(b) The interests of peace and security in East Africa;

(c) The rights and claims of Ethiopia based on geographical, historical, ethnic or economic reasons, including in particular Ethiopia's legitimate need for adequate access to the sea;

3. That in considering its proposals the Commission shall take into account the various suggestions for the disposal of Eritrea submitted during the fourth regular session of the General Assembly;

4. That the Commission shall assemble at the headquarters of the United Nations as soon as possible. It shall travel to Eritrea and may visit such other places as in its judgment may be necessary in carrying out its responsibilities. The Commission shall adopt its own rules of procedure. Its report and proposal or proposals shall be communicated to the Secretary-General not later than 15 June 1950 for distribution to Member States so as to enable final consideration during the fifth regular session of the General Assembly. The Interim Committee of the General Assembly shall consider the report and proposal, or proposals, of the Commission and report, with conclusions, to the fifth regular session of the General Assembly;

D. *With respect to the above provisions:*

1. *Invites* the Secretary-General to request the necessary facilities from the competent authorities of each of the States in whose territory it may be necessary for the Commission for Eritrea to meet or travel;

2. *Authorizes* the Secretary-General, in accordance with established practice,

(a) To arrange for the payment of an appropriate remuneration to the United Nations Commissioner in Libya;

(b) To reimburse the travelling and subsistence expenses of the members of the Council for Libya, of one representative from each Government represented on the Advisory Council for Somaliland, and of one representative and one alternate from each Government represented on the Commission for Eritrea;

(c) To assign to the United Nations Commissioner in Libya, to the Advisory Council for Somaliland, and to the United Nations Commission for Eritrea such staff and to provide such facilities as the Secretary-General may consider necessary to carry out the terms of the present resolution.

◇◇◇◇◇◇

48. DEPARTURE OF AMERICAN TROOPS FROM ITALY [1]

Statement by the President, December 13, 1947, on Continuing Interest in Preserving a Free and Independent Italy

[Under article 73 of the Peace Treaty the occupying powers agreed to withdraw their troops from Italy ninety days after the treaty came into force. It became effective on September 15, 1947, and the United States Government acted promptly to carry out its obligation.]

Although the United States is withdrawing its troops from Italy in fulfilment of its obligations under the treaty of peace, this country continues its interest in the preservation of a free and independent Italy. If, in the course of events, it becomes apparent that the freedom and independence of Italy upon which the peace settlement is based are being threatened directly or indirectly, the United States, as a signatory of the peace treaty and as a member of the United Nations, will be obliged to consider what measures would be appropriate for the maintenance of peace and security.

[1] Department of State Bulletin, December 21, 1947, p. 1221. For texts of messages exchanged between the United States and Italy, see Department of State Bulletin of December 28, 1947, p. 1269.

◇◇◇◇◇◇

TRIESTE

49. PROVISIONAL ADMINISTRATION OF VENEZIA GIULIA [1]

Agreement Between the United States, the United Kingdom, and Yugoslavia, June 9, 1945

[Victory in World War I resulted in Italy's acquiring or "redeeming" Trieste, which lies at the head of the Adriatic across the main transportation route from Central Eastern Europe to the Mediterranean. Because of its strategic importance, and in spite of its predominantly Italian population, it was sought by Yugoslavia at the end of World War II. Pending a final settlement, the United States, the United Kingdom, and Yugoslavia agreed upon a provisional government for Trieste. This agreement is still in effect among the three governments.]

1. The portion of the territory of Venezia Giulia west of the line on the attached map which includes Trieste, the railways and roads from there to Austria via Gorizia, Caporetto, and Tarvisio, as well as Pola and anchorages on the west coast of Istria will be under the Command and control of the Supreme Allied Commander.

2. All Naval, Military and air forces west of the line on the attached map will be placed under his command from the moment at which this agreement comes into force. Yugoslav forces in the area must be limited to a detachment of regular troops not exceeding 2000 of all ranks. These troops will be maintained by the Supreme Allied Commander's administrative services. They will occupy a district selected by the Supreme Allied Commander west of the dividing line and will not be allowed access to the rest of the area.

3. Using an Allied Military Government, the Supreme Allied Commander will govern the areas west of the line on the attached map, Pola and such other areas on the west coast of Istria as he may deem necessary. A small Yugoslav Mission may be attached to the Headquarters of the Eighth Army as observers. Use will be made of any Yugoslav civil administration which is already set up and which in the view of the Supreme Allied Commander is working satisfactorily. The Allied Military Government will, however, be empowered to use whatever civil authorities they deem best in any particular place and to change administrative personnel at their discretion.

4. Marshal Tito will withdraw the Yugoslav regular forces now in the portion of Venezia Giulia west of the line on the attached map as well as those in the town and vicinity of Pola by 08 hours GMT, June 12th 1945. Arrangements for the retention of the Yugoslav detachment referred to in paragraph 2 will be worked out between the Supreme Allied Commander and the Yugoslav High Command.

5. Any irregular forces in this area will, according to the decision of the Supreme Allied Commander in each case, either hand in their arms to the Allied Military authorities and disband, or withdraw from the area.

6. The Yugoslav Government will return residents of the area whom they

---

[1] Department of State publication 2562, Executive Agreement Series 501.

have arrested or deported with the exception of persons who possessed Yugoslav nationality in 1939, and make restitution of property they have confiscated or removed.

7. This agreement in no way prejudices or affects the ultimate disposal of the parts of Venezia Giulia west of the line. Similarly the military occupation and administration by Yugoslavia of the parts of Venezia Giulia east of the line in no way prejudices or affects the ultimate disposal of that area.

Signed at Belgrade, June 9, 1945.

Dr. Ivan Subasic	R. C. Skrine Stevenson.	Richard C. Patterson Jr.
Minister of Foreign Affairs	*H. B. M. Ambassador*	*U. S. Ambassador*

◇◇◇◇◇◇

BULGARIA

50. DECLARATIONS OF WAR WITH BULGARIA, HUNGARY, AND RUMANIA [1]

Joint Declaration by the Congress, June 5, 1942

[On June 2, 1942, President Roosevelt notified Congress that Bulgaria, Hungary, and Rumania were engaged in military activities against the United Nations, and recommended that Congress recognize that a state of war existed between the United States and these countries. Accordingly three joint resolutions giving effect to the recommendation were passed unanimously on June 5, 1942.]

"JOINT RESOLUTION Declaring that a state of war exists between the Government of Bulgaria and the Government and the people of the United States and making provisions to prosecute the same.[2]

"Whereas the Government of Bulgaria has formally declared war against the Government and the people of the United States of America: Therefore be it

"Resolved by the Senate and House of Representatives of the United States of America in Congress assembled, That the state of war between the United States and the Government of Bulgaria which has thus been thrust upon the United States is hereby formally declared; and the President is hereby authorized and directed to employ the entire naval and military forces of the United States and the resources of the Government to carry on war against the Government of Bulgaria; and, to bring the conflict to a successful termination, all of the resources of the country are hereby pledged by the Congress of the United States.

"Approved, June 5, 1942." [Joint resolutions declaring a state of war with Hungary and Rumania, *mutatis mutandis,* were also approved June 5, 1942.[3]]

[1] Department of State Bulletin, June 6, 1942, pp. 509-510.
[2] Public Law 563, 77th Cong.
[3] Public Laws 564 and 565.

◇◇◇◇◇◇

51. ARMISTICE WITH BULGARIA, OCTOBER 28, 1944

Agreement Between the United States, the Union of Soviet Socialist Republics, and the United Kingdom, on the One Hand, and Bulgaria, on the Other Hand, Concerning an Armistice [1]

[Hostilities between the United States and the satellites of Nazi Germany in World War II came to an end with armistice agreements signed at Moscow as follows: with Rumania, September 12, 1944; with Bulgaria, October 28, 1944; and with Hungary, January 20, 1945. While each agreement differed from the others all were drawn up according to a general pattern. The Bulgarian armistice is reproduced below as an example.]

The Government of Bulgaria accepts the armistice terms presented by the Governments of the United States of America, the Union of Soviet Socialist Republics and the United Kingdom, acting on behalf of all the United Nations at war with Bulgaria.

Accordingly, the representative of the Supreme Allied Commander in the Mediterranean, Lieutenant-General Sir James Gammell, and the representative of the Soviet High Command, Marshal of the Soviet Union F. I. Tolbukhin, duly authorized thereto by the Governments of the United States of America, the Union of Soviet Socialist Republics and the United Kingdom, acting on behalf of all the United Nations at war with Bulgaria, on the one hand, and representatives of the Government of Bulgaria, Mr. P. Stainov, Minister of Foreign Affairs, Mr. D. Terpeshev, Minister without Portfolio, Mr. N. Petkov, Minister without Portfolio, and Mr. P. Stoyanov, Minister of Finance, furnished with due powers, on the other hand, have signed the following terms:

1. (a) Bulgaria, having ceased hostilities with the U. S. S. R. on September 9, and severed relations with Germany on September 6 and with Hungary on September 26, has ceased hostilities against all the other United Nations.

(b) The Government of Bulgaria undertakes to disarm the German armed forces in Bulgaria and to hand them over as prisoners of war.

The Government of Bulgaria also undertakes to intern nationals of Germany and her satellites.

(c) The Government of Bulgaria undertakes to maintain and make available such land, sea and air forces as may be specified for service under the general direction of the Allied (Soviet) High Command. Such forces must not be used on Allied territory except with the prior consent of the Allied Government concerned.

(d) On the conclusion of hostilities against Germany, the Bulgarian armed forces must be demobilized and put on a peace footing under the supervision of the Allied Control Commission.

2. Bulgarian armed forces and officials must be withdrawn within the specified time limit from the territory of Greece and Yugoslavia in accordance with the pre-condition accepted by the Government of Bulgaria on October 11; the Bulgarian authorities must immediately take steps to withdraw from Greek and Yugoslav territory Bulgarians who were citizens of Bulgaria on

---

[1] Agreement signed at Moscow October 28, 1944; effective October 28, 1944. Department of State publication 2305, Executive Agreement Series 437, pp. 1-4, 17.

January 1, 1941, and to repeal all legislative and administrative provisions relating to the annexation or incorporation in Bulgaria of Greek or Yugoslav territory.

3. The Government of Bulgaria will afford to Soviet and other Allied forces freedom of movement over Bulgarian territory in any direction, if in the opinion of the Allied (Soviet) High Command the military situation so requires, the Government of Bulgaria giving to such movements every assistance with its own means of communication, and at its own expense, by land, water and in the air.

4. The Government of Bulgaria will immediately release all Allied prisoners of war and internees. Pending further instructions the Government of Bulgaria will at its own expense provide all Allied prisoners of war and internees, displaced persons and refugees, including nationals of Greece and Yugoslavia, with adequate food, clothing, medical services and sanitary and hygienic requirements, and also with means of transportation for the return of any such persons to their own country.

5. The Government of Bulgaria will immediately release, regardless of citizenship or nationality, all persons held in detention in Bulgaria in connection with their activities in favor of the United Nations, or because of their sympathies with the United Nations' cause or for racial or religious reasons, and will repeal all discriminatory legislation and disabilities arising therefrom.

6. The Government of Bulgaria will cooperate in the apprehension and trial of persons accused of war crimes.

7. The Government of Bulgaria undertakes to dissolve immediately all pro-Hitler or other Fascist political, military, para-military and other organizations on Bulgarian territory conducting propaganda hostile to the United Nations, and not to tolerate the existence of such organizations in future.

8. The publication, introduction and distribution in Bulgaria of periodical or non-periodical literature, the presentation of theatrical performances or films, the operation of wireless stations, post, telegraph and telephone services will take place in agreement with the Allied (Soviet) High Command.

9. The Government of Bulgaria will restore all property of the United Nations and their nationals, including Greek and Yugoslav property, and will make such reparation for loss and damage caused by the war to the United Nations, including Greece and Yugoslavia, as may be determined later.

10. The Government of Bulgaria will restore all rights and interests of the United Nations and their nationals in Bulgaria.

11. The Government of Bulgaria undertakes to return to the Soviet Union, to Greece and Yugoslavia, and to the other United Nations by the dates specified by the Allied Control Commission and in a good state of preservation, all valuables and materials removed during the war by Germany or Bulgaria from United Nations' territory and belonging to state, public or cooperative organizations, enterprises, institutions or individual citizens such as factory and works equipment, locomotives, rolling stock, tractors, motor vehicles, historic monuments, museum treasures and any other property.

12. The Government of Bulgaria undertakes to hand over as booty to the Allied (Soviet) High Command all war material of Germany and her satellites located on Bulgarian territory, including vessels of the fleets of Germany and her satellites located in Bulgarian waters.

13. The Government of Bulgaria undertakes not to permit the removal or expropriation of any form of property (including valuables and currency), belonging to Germany or Hungary or to their nationals or to persons resident in their territories or in territories occupied by them, without the permission of the Allied Control Commission. The Government of Bulgaria will safeguard such property in the manner specified by the Allied Control Commission.

14. The Government of Bulgaria undertakes to hand over to the Allied (Soviet) High Command all vessels belonging to the United Nations which are in Bulgarian ports, no matter at whose disposal these vessels may be, for the use of the Allied (Soviet) High Command during the war against Germany or Hungary in the common interest of the Allies, the vessels to be returned subsequently to their owners.

The Government of Bulgaria will bear full material responsibility for any damage to or destruction of the aforesaid property up to the moment of its transfer to the Allied (Soviet) High Command.

15. The Government of Bulgaria must make regular payments in Bulgarian currency and must supply goods (fuel, foodstuffs, *et cetera*), facilities and services as may be required by the Allied (Soviet) High Command for the discharge of its functions.

16. Bulgarian merchant vessels, whether in Bulgarian or foreign waters, shall be subject to the operational control of the Allied (Soviet) High Command for use in the general interest of the Allies.

17. The Government of Bulgaria will arrange in case of need for the utilization in Bulgarian territory of industrial and transport enterprises, means of communication, power stations, public utility enterprises and installations, stocks of fuel and other materials in accordance with the instructions issued during the armistice by the Allied (Soviet) High Command.

18. For the whole period of the armistice there will be established in Bulgaria an Allied Control Commission which will regulate and supervise the execution of the armistice terms under the chairmanship of the representative of the Allied (Soviet) High Command, and with the participation of representatives of the United States and the United Kingdom.

During the period between the coming into force of the armistice and the conclusion of hostilities against Germany the Allied Control Commission will be under the general direction of the Allied (Soviet) High Command.

19. The present terms will come into force on their signing.

Done at Moscow in quadruplicate, in the Russian, English and Bulgarian languages, the Russian and English texts being authentic.

October 28, 1944.

◇◇◇◇◇◇

52. TREATY OF PEACE WITH BULGARIA, FEBRUARY 10, 1947 [1]

[The treaties between the United Nations and the satellite states of Nazi Germany were all signed on the same day. All had identical preambles similar

[1] S. Exec. F, G, H, I, 80th Cong., 1st sess., February 27, 28, 1947. *See also* texts of the President's letter of transmittal, report of the Secretary of State and summaries of texts of treaties with Italy, Bulgaria, Rumania, and Hungary, Department of State Bulletin of March 23 and June 1, 1947; full text of treaty of peace with Bulgaria, Department of State publication 2973, Treaties and Other International Acts Series 1650, also Treaties of Peace with Italy, Bulgaria,

to that in the Italian Treaty. For the most part the treaties with Bulgaria, Hungary, and Rumania contained the same provisions. The following summaries of the various treaties indicate that they differed only as they were tailored to fit the peculiar conditions of the country involved. This summary of the Bulgarian treaty should be read in conjunction with that of the Rumanian treaty which is reproduced in document No. 54 below.]

(Summary)

The Treaty of Peace with Bulgaria in general contains the same provisions as the Treaty with Rumania. The differences are noted as follows:

Article 1 establishes the frontiers as of January 1, 1941, which include Southern Dobruja transferred from Rumania in August 1940.

No specific clauses relating to non-discrimination against the racial minorities or return of property were deemed necessary in the light of Bulgaria's record of non-persecution.

Article 9 sets the limits for Bulgarian Armed Forces at 55,000 for the Army, 1,800 for anti-aircraft artillery, 3,500 for the Navy, and 5,200 for the Air Force with a 7,250 tons limit for the Navy and 90 aircraft for the Air Force.

Article 12 prohibits the construction on the north side of the Greco-Bulgarian frontier of permanent fortifications and military installations capable of being employed for firing into Greek territory.

Article 20 calls for complete withdrawal of all Allied forces and return of goods in their possession, no exceptions being necessary in this case.

Article 21—Reparation in the amount of $45,000,000 to Greece and $25,-000,000 to Yugoslavia is provided, payable in kind from products of manufacturing and extractive industries and agriculture over a period of eight years, deliveries to be regulated by agreement with Greece and Yugoslavia. Valuation is to be made on basis of 1938 international market prices with a percentage increase.

Article 30 provides that Bulgaria should facilitate railway transit traffic through its territory and negotiate the necessary agreement for this purpose.

Annex VI omits the clauses relating to Prize Courts as inapplicable in this instance.

◇◇◇◇◇

53. RENEWAL OF DIPLOMATIC RELATIONS WITH BULGARIA [1]

Statement by Acting Secretary Lovett, October 1, 1947

[When the United States resumed diplomatic relations with Bulgaria after World War II, differences had already arisen between the two countries over Bulgaria's disregard for human rights and fundamental freedoms. These differences are discussed in Part VIII of this volume. In the statement below, the

---

Hungary, and Finland, Department of State publication 2743, European Series 21. Treaty of peace with Bulgaria signed February 10, 1947, ratified by the United States on June 14, 1947; entered into force September 15, 1947.
[1] Department of State Bulletin of October 12, 1947, p. 746.

Secretary of State announced that the resumption of relations did not indicate United States' condonation of the acts of the Bulgarian Government.]

Last week I was asked whether resumption of diplomatic relations between the United States and Bulgaria might be affected by recent developments in that country. A decision has now been reached in the matter.

With the entry into force on September 15 of the Bulgarian peace treaty and the termination of the state of war between the United States and Bulgaria, the United States Government considers it desirable to accredit a diplomatic representative to supersede the United States Political Representative who has been stationed in Bulgaria during the armistice regime. The Honorable Maynard B. Barnes served as U. S. Political Representative to Bulgaria from December 1944 until his return to this country last spring. In his absence Mr. John Evarts Horner has been Acting U. S. Political Representative in Bulgaria.

The President has appointed Mr. Donald R. Heath, of Topeka, Kansas, as American Minister to Bulgaria. Mr. Heath plans to depart for his new post in the very near future. The appointment of Mr. Heath and the establishment of an American Legation in Sofia is predicated on the intention of the United States to maintain its interest in the welfare of the Bulgarian people, to keep itself informed concerning developments in Bulgaria, and to continue its efforts to protect American interests in that country. The United States Government wishes to make it clear that this step does not reflect either approval or condonation of certain recent actions of the Bulgarian Government. The views of this Government on such matters have been fully set forth.

◇◇◇◇◇◇

54. TREATY OF PEACE WITH RUMANIA, FEBRUARY 10, 1947 [1]

[As stated in the note to document 52 above, the treaties of peace between the satellite states of Nazi Germany and the Allied Powers, which were signed in Paris on February 10, 1947, all followed a common pattern. The Treaty with Rumania is summarized below. The preamble recites the events leading up to the Armistice and promises Allied support for Rumanian application for membership in the United Nations. In addition to the usual articles on frontiers, reparations, and armaments, the Treaty provides for the withdrawal of Allied forces from Rumania within ninety days.]

(Summary)

The Preamble is similar to the preamble of the Italian Treaty, recites the events leading up to the Armistice of September 12, 1944, and expresses the willingness of the Allied and Associated Powers to conclude the present

[1] S. Exec. F, G, H, I, 80th Cong., 1st sess., February 27, 28, 1947, pp. 10-12. See also texts of the President's letter of transmittal, report of the Secretary of State, and summaries of texts of treaties with Italy, Bulgaria, Rumania, and Hungary, Department of State Bulletin of March 23 and June 1, 1947; full text of treaty of peace with Rumania, Department of State publication 2969, Treaties and Other International Acts Series 1649, also, Treaties of Peace with Italy, Bulgaria, Hungary, Rumania, and Finland, Department of State publication 2743, European Series 21. Treaty of peace with Rumania signed at Paris February 10, 1947; ratified by the United States June 14, 1947; entered into force September 15, 1947.

Treaty and to support Rumania's application to become a member of the United Nations.

PART I—FRONTIERS

Articles 1–2 establish Rumania's frontiers as those existing on January 1, 1941, shown on the map contained in Annex I, which confirm the transfer of Southern Dobruja to Bulgaria, recognize Soviet sovereignty over Bessarabia and Northern Bucovina, and restore Transylvania to Rumania.

PART II—POLITICAL CLAUSES

Section I—Articles 3–6 provide (a) the assurances of human rights and fundamental freedoms, (b) guarantees of non-discrimination on account of race, sex, language or religion, (c) non-persecution of racial minorities and United Nations sympathizers, (d) abolition of Fascist organizations, and (e) surrender of war criminals and traitors.

Section II—Article 7–10 contain clauses similar to those in the Italian treaty which provide for the recognition of the peace settlements and of the liquidation of the League of Nations and for the renewal of pre-war Treaties. Provision is also made for the termination of the state of war with Hungary.

PART III—MILITARY, NAVAL AND AIR CLAUSES

Section I—Articles 11–19 (a) establish personnel limitations of 120,000 for the Army, 5,000 for anti-aircraft artillery, 5,000 for the Navy, and 8,000 for the Air Force with a 15,000 tons limit for the Navy and 150 aircraft for the Air Force and limit training to the above personnel, (b) prohibit atomic weapons, guided missiles, sea mines, submarines, M. T. B.s and assault craft, (c) provide for disposal of surplus war material, (d) assure Rumanian co-operation for prevention of German re-armament, and (e) provide that the treaty restrictions remain in force until modified by agreement. *Annexes II and III* contain the standard definitions of the terms used in this Part.

Section II—Article 20 requires prompt repatriation of Rumanian prisoners of war.

PART IV—WITHDRAWAL OF ALLIED FORCES

Article 21 calls for the withdrawal within 90 days of all Allied forces and the return of goods in their possession, subject to the right of the Soviet Union to maintain troops on the line of communication with its occupation forces in Austria.

PART V—REPARATION AND RESTITUTION

Article 22 provides for reparation to the Soviet Union in the amount of $300,000,000 payable in commodities over a period of eight years.

Article 23 provides for the restitution by Rumania of identifiable property removed from United Nations territory and for the method of presenting claims.

PART VI—ECONOMIC CLAUSES

Articles 24–35 contain the standard provisions in respect of (a) United Nations property in Rumania with compensation in local currency for loss or damage equivalent to ⅔ of the value of the property, including a special provision for ships, not needed in the other treaties, (b) Rumanian property in the territory of the Allied and Associated Powers with the same exceptions from sequestration excluding, however, the inapplicable clause relating to ceded territories, (c) Renunciation of Claims including restitution of property in Germany, (d) Debts, (e) General Economic Relations including commercial aviation clauses, (f) Settlement of Economic Disputes, and (g) Miscellaneous Economic Clauses. In addition, the Rumanian Treaty calls for restoration of property and rights of minorities discriminated against in Rumania with fair compensation if restoration impossible and for transfer to appropriate organizations if property unclaimed or heirless. The right of the Soviet Union to German assets in Rumania is specifically recognized. Article 33 relates to settlement by conciliation and arbitration of disputes arising in connection with prices paid by the Rumanian Government for goods delivered for reparations and acquired from an Allied national.

PART VII—DANUBE

Article 36 provides for freedom of navigation on the Danube (the declaration relating to the Conference to be held on this subject having been approved by the Council of Foreign Ministers and published on December 6, 1946).

PART VIII—FINAL CLAUSES

Articles 37–40 contain the provisions relating to the interpretation of the Treaty, settlement of disputes, accession by other States, and the coming into force upon ratification by the United States, the United Kingdom, and the Soviet Union.

Annexes IV, V and VI contain the standard clauses relating to (a) Industrial, Literary and Artistic Property, (b) Insurance, (c) Contracts, Periods of Prescription and Negotiable Instruments, (d) Prize Courts, and (e) Judgments.

◇◇◇◇◇◇

55. RENEWAL OF DIPLOMATIC RELATIONS WITH RUMANIA [1]

Statement by Secretary Marshall, July 23, 1947

[Normal diplomatic relations were resumed with Rumania after the Treaty of Peace had entered into effect. The resumption took the form of an announcement by Secretary Marshall that a United States minister to Rumania had been appointed. As in the case of Bulgaria, the United States made clear that the resumption did not mean the condonation of the Rumanian Government's denial of fundamental rights and freedoms to the Rumanian people.]

With the termination of a state of war between Rumania and the United States imminent, the U. S. Government considers it desirable to accredit a diplomatic representative to Rumania to supersede the U. S. Political Rep-

---

[1] Department of State Bulletin of August 3, 1947, p. 229. The Senate on July 28, 1947, confirmed the nomination of Rudolf E. Schoenfeld to be Envoy Extraordinary and Minister Plenipotentiary of the United States of America to Rumania.

resentative who has been stationed in Rumania during the armistice regime. Mr. Burton Y. Berry served as U. S. Political Representative to Rumania from December 1944 until his return to this country last month. In his absence Mr. Roy M. Melbourne has been Acting U. S. Political Representative in Rumania.

The appointment of Mr. Rudolph E. Schoenfeld as U. S. Minister to Rumania is predicated on the intention of the United States to maintain its interest in the welfare of the Rumanian people, to keep itself informed of developments in Rumania, and to continue its efforts on behalf of American interests there. It does not imply that the U. S. Government condones the actions of the Rumanian Government in denying the Rumanian people fundamental freedoms, regarding which the U. S. position has been set forth on various occasions.

◇◇◇◇◇◇

56. TREATY OF PEACE WITH HUNGARY, FEBRUARY 10, 1947 [1]

[The following summary of the Treaty of Peace with Hungary outlines only the parts in respect to which the terms differ from those of the treaty with Rumania. Perhaps the most important single article is the first, which provides for the return of Transylvania to Rumania and anticipates the award of Sub-Carpathia to the Soviet Union. As in the case of the other satellite peace treaties, the treaty with Hungary also provides for the withdrawal of Allied forces within ninety days.]

(Summary)

Like the Bulgarian Treaty, the Treaty of Peace with Hungary in general contains the same provisions as the Treaty with Rumania. The differences between the Rumanian and Hungarian Treaties are, however, noted as follows:

Article 1 re-establishes the frontiers of Hungary with Austria and with Yugoslavia as those which existed on January 1, 1938. It liquidates the Vienna Award of 1940 and restores Transylvania to Roumania. It establishes a frontier with the Soviet Union in recognition of the transfer of the sub-Carpathian Ukraine from Czechoslovakia to the Soviet Union. It liquidates the Vienna Award of 1938 whereby Hungary received certain territory from Czechoslovakia and restores this territory, together with increased area across the Danube from Bratislava, providing guarantees of human and civic rights for the population of the ceded area.

Article 5 provides that negotiations shall take place between Czechoslovakia and Hungary to settle the problem of the Magyars residing in Czechoslovakia, and that, if no agreement is reached in 6 months, Czechoslovakia shall be entitled to ask the Council of Foreign Ministers to effect a final solution.

Article 11 requires Hungary to deliver certain categories of cultural property and records to Yugoslavia and Czechoslovakia.

[1] S. Exec. F, G, H, I, 80th Cong., 1st sess., February 27, 28, 1947. See also texts of the President's letter of transmittal, report of the Secretary of State, and summaries of texts of treaties with Italy, Bulgaria, Rumania, and Hungary, Department of State Bulletin of March 23 and June 1, 1947; full text of treaty of peace with Hungary, Department of State publication 2974, Treaties and Other International Acts Series 1651; also, Department of State publication 2743, European Series 21. Treaty of peace with Hungary signed at Paris February 10, 1947; ratified by the United States June 14, 1947; effective September 15, 1947.

Article 12 sets the limits for personnel of the Hungarian Army, including frontier troops, anti-aircraft and river flotilla personnel at 65,000 and the personnel of the air force at 5,000 with 90 aircraft.

Article 22 which calls for the withdrawal of all Allied forces within 90 days also contains the reservation in respect of the right of the Soviet Union to maintain troops on line of communication with its occupation forces in Austria.

Article 23 provides for reparation to the Soviet Union in the amount of $200,000,000 and $100,000,000 to Czechoslovakia and Yugoslavia payable in commodities over a period of 8 years.

Article 25 calls for the annulment of the legal consequences of the Vienna Award entailed in the return of territory to Czechoslovakia.

Article 26 contains the standard clauses relating to return of property to the United Nations and their nationals and to compensation in the event of loss or damage and extends these provisions to cover such property in Northern Transylvania during period when it was subject to Hungarian authority.

Article 34 provides that Hungary should facilitate railway transit traffic through its territory and negotiate the necessary agreements for this purpose.

Annex VI omits the clauses relating to Prize Courts as inapplicable.

◇◇◇◇◇◇

57. RENEWAL OF DIPLOMATIC RELATIONS WITH HUNGARY [1]

Statement by the Department of State, September 29, 1945

[The renewal of United States diplomatic relations with Hungary was announced some months after the fighting in Europe ceased. It thus preceded the renewal of diplomatic relations with Bulgaria and Rumania by almost two years. It should be noted that the recognition was accorded only after Hungary had promised on September 25, 1945, to give her people free and untrammeled elections, a representative government, and freedom of political expression.]

Feeling that the provisional government of Hungary is able to take into account the interests of the various elements of the population in performing its functions an as interim government, the United States Government has decided to indicate its willingness to proceed with normalizing its relations with that country.

Accordingly, on September 22, 1945, acting under instructions from the Secretary of State, the United States Representative in Hungary, H. F. Arthur Schoenfeld, delivered a note to the Hungarian Foreign Minister indicating the readiness of this Government to establish diplomatic relations and negotiate a treaty with the provisional government of Hungary if that government would give full assurances for free and untrammeled elections for a representative government and if, in the meantime, it would provide to the full measure of its responsibilities under the armistice regime for freedom of political ex-

[1] Department of State Bulletin, September 30, 1945, p. 478.

pression of democratic parties and right of assembly, such conditions being essential to permit the holding of free elections.

On September 25 the Hungarian Foreign Minister handed the United States Representative in Budapest a note of the same date stating that the Provisional National Government of Hungary was in a position to offer full guaranties to the Government of the United States concerning the conditions set forth in the note of September 22.

FINLAND

58. RENEWAL OF DIPLOMATIC RELATIONS WITH FINLAND

Statement by Secretary Byrnes, August 21, 1945 [1]

[The United States did not go to war with Finland, but broke off diplomatic relations during 1944. The Potsdam Conference set certain contingencies which had to be met before the United States, Britain, and Russia would restore diplomatic relations with Finland. This statement by Secretary Byrnes shows that the United States considered that the contingencies had been properly met by August 1945.]

Paragraph X of the report on the Berlin Conference provided that the three Governments concerned would examine, each separately, the establishment of diplomatic relations with Finland. After studying all available reports the Government of the United States has concluded that the Finnish parliamentary elections of March 1945 were freely conducted and expressed through secret ballot the democratic wishes of the Finnish people. The Finnish Government has been reorganized so as to reflect the results of that election and is now, in the opinion of our Government, broadly representative of all democratic elements in Finnish political life. Accordingly the United States representative in Finland has been instructed to propose to the Finnish Government the establishment of diplomatic relations between the United States and Finland.

[1] Department of State Bulletin, August 26, 1945, p. 283. Although the United States did not declare war on Finland, the Finnish Legation at Washington and the United States Legation at Helsinki were closed in June 1944. Diplomatic relations between the United States and Finland were renewed August 31, 1945. Armistice signed by the Governments of the United Kingdom and the Soviet Union, acting on behalf of the United Nations at war with Finland, and the Government of Finland, September 19, 1944, Department of State Bulletin of February 18, 1945, pp. 261-268; text of treaty of peace with Finland, signed at Paris on February 10, 1947, Department of State publication 2743, European Series 21.

GERMANY [1]

59. DECLARATION OF WAR WITH GERMANY, DECEMBER 11, 1941

JOINT RESOLUTION Declaring That a State of War Exists Between Germany and the United States [2]

[From the time Hitler became Chancellor of the Reich in 1933, the policies of the United States and Nazi Germany came increasingly into conflict. Nevertheless for more than two years after Germany invaded Poland, the United States remained non-belligerent. The Japanese attack on Pearl Harbor, however, was the signal for all Axis powers to declare war upon this country, among them Nazi Germany. On December 11, 1941, Congress recognized the existence of a state of war and authorized the President to use all the United States military and naval forces to bring the war to a successful conclusion.]

Whereas the Government of Germany has formally declared war against the Government and the people of the United States of America: Therefore be it

Resolved by the Senate and House of Representatives of the United States of America in Congress assembled, That the state of war between the United States and the Government of Germany which has thus been thrust upon the United States is hereby formally declared; and the President is hereby authorized and directed to employ the entire naval and military forces of the United States and the resources of the Government to carry on war against the Government of Germany; and, to bring the conflict to a successful termination, all of the resources of the country are hereby pledged by the Congress of the United States.

Approved, December 11, 1941, 3:05 p. m., E. S. T.

◇◇◇◇◇◇

60. THE MORGENTHAU PLAN, 1943

Program To Prevent Germany From Starting a World War III [3]

[Allied governments during World War II gave much thought to the prevention of a recurrence of German militarism. One drastic proposal to ruralize Germany, called the Morgenthau Plan, was advanced by the Secretary of the Treasury, Henry Morgenthau, Jr. President Roosevelt presented the plan to Prime Minister Churchill at Quebec in August 1943, as the basis for a peace

[1] Documents on the problems of war criminals, dismantling and reparations will be found in Part VIII below.

[2] 55 Stat. 796.

[3] This memorandum was printed as the first few pages of Henry Morgenthau, Jr., Germany Is Our Problem, Harper and Brothers Publishers, New York and London, 1945 and is here reproduced with the consent of the publisher. Although it was taken to Quebec by President Roosevelt and Mr. Morgenthau in August 1943 and there provisionally approved by President Roosevelt and Prime Minister Churchill, it never was adopted as the policy of the United States nor was this memorandum ever issued as an official document of the United States. It is included here for handy reference only because so much controversy has raged about it.

settlement with Germany, and both men provisionally approved it. It is significant that President Roosevelt was accompanied to that Conference by Mr. Morgenthau, and not by Mr. Hull, the Secretary of State. The plan met with considerable opposition, however, and did not become official United States policy.]

1. Demilitarization of Germany

It should be the aim of the Allied Forces to accomplish the complete demilitarization of Germany in the shortest possible period of time after surrender. This means completely disarming the German Army and people (including the removal or destruction of all war material), the total destruction of the whole German armament industry, and the removal or destruction of other key industries which are basic to military strength.

2. New Boundaries of Germany

(a) Poland should get that part of East Prussia which doesn't go to the U. S. S. R. and the southern portion of Silesia.

(b) France should get the Saar and the adjacent territories bounded by the Rhine and the Moselle Rivers.

(c) As indicated in 4 below an International Zone should be created containing the Ruhr and the surrounding industrial areas.

3. Partitioning of New Germany

The remaining portion of Germany should be divided into two autonomous, independent states, (1) a South German state comprising Bavaria, Wuerttemberg, Baden and some smaller areas and (2) a North German state comprising a large part of the old state of Prussia, Saxony, Thuringia and several smaller states.

There shall be a custom union between the new South German state and Austria, which will be restored to her pre-1938 political borders.

4. The Ruhr Area

(The Ruhr, surrounding industrial areas, as shown on the map, including the Rhineland, the Keil Canal, and all German territory north of the Keil Canal.)

Here lies the heart of German industrial power. This area should not only be stripped of all presently existing industries but so weakened and controlled that it cannot in the foreseeable future become an industrial area. The following steps will accomplish this:

(a) Within a short period, if possible not longer than 6 months after the cessation of hostilities, all industrial plants and equipment not destroyed by military action shall be completely dismantled and transported to Allied Nations as restitution. All equipment shall be removed from the mines and the mines closed.

(b) The area should be made in international zone to be governed by an international security organization to be established by the United Nations. In governing the area the international organization should be guided by policies designed to further the above stated objective.

5. Restitution and Reparation

Reparations, in the form of future payments and deliveries, should not be demanded. Restitution and reparation shall be effected by the transfer of existing German resources and territories, e. g.,

(a) by restitution of property looted by the Germans in territories occupied by them;

(b) by transfer of German territory and German private rights in industrial property situated in such territory to invaded countries and the international organization under the program of partition;

(c) by the removal and distribution among devastated countries of industrial plants and equipment situated within the International Zone and the North and South German states delimited in the section on partition;

(d) by forced German labor outside Germany; and

(e) by confiscation of all German assets of any character whatsoever outside of Germany.

6. Education and Propaganda

(a) All schools and universities will be closed until an Allied Commission of Education has formulated an effective reorganization program. It is contemplated that it may require a considerable period of time before any institutions of higher education are reopened. Meanwhile the education of German students in foreign universities will not be prohibited. Elementary schools will be reopened as quickly as appropriate teachers and text books are available.

(b) All German radio stations and newspapers, magazines, weeklies, etc. shall be discontinued until adequate controls are established and an appropriate program formulated.

7. Political Decentralization

The military administration in Germany in the initial period should be carried out with a view toward the eventual partitioning of Germany. To facilitate partitioning and to assure its permanence the military authorities should be guided by the following principles:

(a) Dismiss all policy-making officials of the Reich government and deal primarily with local governments.

(b) Encourage the reestablishment of state governments in each of the states (Laender) corresponding to 18 states into which Germany is presently divided and in addition make the Prussian provinces separate states.

(c) Upon the partition of Germany, the various state governments should be encouraged to organize a federal government for each of the newly partitioned areas. Such new governments should be in the form of a confederation of states, with emphasis on states' rights and a large degree of local autonomy.

8. Responsibility of Military for Local German Economy

The sole purpose of the military in control of the German economy shall be to facilitate military operations and military occupation. The Allied Military Government shall not assume responsibility for such economic problems as price controls, rationing, unemployment, production, reconstruction, distribution, consumption, housing, or transportation, or take any measures designed to maintain or strengthen the German economy, except those which are essential to military operations. The responsibility for sustaining the German economy and people rests with the German people with such facilities as may be available under the circumstances.

9. Controls over Development of German Economy

During a period of at least twenty years after surrender adequate controls, including controls over foreign trade and tight restrictions on capital imports, shall be maintained by the United Nations designed to prevent in the newly-established states the establishment or expansion of key industries basic to the German military potential and to control other key industries.

10. Agrarian program

All large estates should be broken up and divided among the peasants and the system of primogeniture and entail should be abolished.

11. Punishment of War Crimes and Treatment of Special Groups

A program for the punishment of certain war crimes and for the treatment of Nazi organizations and other special groups is contained in section 11.

12. Uniforms and Parades

(a) No German shall be permitted to wear, after an appropriate period of time following the cessation of hostilities, any military uniform or any uniform of any quasi military organizations.

(b) No military parades shall be permitted anywhere in Germany and all military bands shall be disbanded.

13. Aircraft

All aircraft (including gliders), whether military or commercial, will be confiscated for later disposition. No German shall be permitted to operate or to help operate any aircraft, including those owned by foreign interests.

14. United States Responsibility

Although the United States would have full military and civilian representation on whatever international commission or commissions may be established for the execution of the whole German program, the primary responsibility for the policing of Germany and for civil administration in Germany should be assumed by the military forces of Germany's continental neighbors. Specifically, these should include Russian, French, Polish, Czech, Greek, Yugoslav, Norwegian, Dutch, and Belgian soldiers.

Under this program United States troops could be withdrawn within a relatively short time.

◇◇◇◇◇◇

61. SURRENDER BY GERMANY [1]

Act of Military Surrender, May 8, 1945

[The fall of Berlin marked the complete collapse of all German military efforts. On May 8, 1945, the German High Command surrendered unconditionally to the Allied Powers. It was not until a month later that the detailed instrument of surrender to be imposed by the victorious powers was agreed upon.]

[1] The Axis in Defeat, Department of State publication 2423, pp. 24-25; also, Department of State publication 2515, Executive Agreement Series 502. See texts of (a) instrument of surrender of all German armed forces in Holland, in northwest Germany including all islands, and in Denmark, May 4, 1945; (b) Act of military surrender signed at Rheims, May 7, 1945, The Axis in Defeat; and (c) instrument of local surrender of German and other forces under the command or control of the German Commander in Chief Southwest, signed at Caserta, Italy, April 29, 1945, The United States and Italy, Department of State publication 2669.

1. We the undersigned, acting by authority of the German High Command, hereby surrender unconditionally to the Supreme Commander, Allied Expeditionary Force and simultaneously to the Supreme High Command of the Red Army all forces on land, at sea, and in the air who are at this date under German control.

2. The German High Command will at once issue orders to all German military, naval and air authorities and to all forces under German control to cease active operations at 2301 hours Central European time on 8th May 1945, to remain in the positions occupied at that time and to disarm completely, handing over their weapons and equipment to the local allied commanders or officers designated by Representatives of the Allied Supreme Commands. No ship, vessel, or aircraft is to be scuttled, or any damage done to their hull, machinery or equipment, and also to machines of all kinds, armament, apparatus, and all the technical means of prosecution of war in general.

3. The German High Command will at once issue to the appropriate commanders, and ensure the carrying out of any further orders issued by the Supreme Commander, Allied Expeditionary Force and by the Supreme High Command of the Red Army.

4. This act of military surrender is without prejudice to, and will be superseded by any general instrument of surrender imposed by, or on behalf of the United Nations and applicable to GERMANY and the German armed forces as a whole.

5. In the event of the German High Command or any of the forces under their control failing to act in accordance with this Act of Surrender, the Supreme Commander, Allied Expeditionary Force and the Supreme High Command of the Red Army will take such punitive or other action as they deem appropriate.

6. This Act is drawn up in the English, Russian and German languages. The English and Russian are the only authentic texts.

Signed at Berlin on the 8. day of May, 1945

FRIEDEBURG   KEITEL   STUMPF
On behalf of the German High Command

IN THE PRESENCE OF:

On behalf of the
Supreme Commander
Allied Expeditionary Force
A. W. TEDDER

On behalf of the
Supreme High Command
of the Red Army
G. ZHUKOV

At the signing also were present as witnesses:

F. DE LATTRE-TASSIGNY
General Commanding in Chief
First French Army

CARL SPAATZ
General, Commanding United
States Strategic Air Forces

◊◊◊◊◊◊

62. AGREEMENT ON REPARATION FROM GERMANY [1]

Establishment of an Inter-Allied Reparation Agency, January 14, 1946

[At Yalta and Potsdam the question of German reparations was the subject of considerable discussion. At Yalta it was agreed that a special commission should be set up at Moscow to deal with the matter. The agreement which follows established the Inter-Allied Reparations Agency and laid down the rules according to which it was to operate. It spelled out the manner in which interested parties were to share in the reparations and provided for the restitution of monetary gold found in Germany by the Allied forces.]

THE GOVERNMENTS OF ALBANIA, THE UNITED STATES OF AMERICA, AUSTRALIA, BELGIUM, CANADA, DENMARK, EGYPT, FRANCE, THE UNITED KINGDOM OF GREAT BRITAIN AND NORTHERN IRELAND, GREECE, INDIA, LUXEMBOURG, NORWAY, NEW-ZEALAND, THE NETHERLANDS, CZECHOSLOVAKIA, THE UNION OF SOUTH AFRICA AND YUGOSLAVIA, in order to obtain an equitable distribution among themselves of the total assets which, in accordance with the provisions of this Agreement and the provisions agreed upon at Potsdam on 1. August 1945 between the Governments of the United States of America, the United Kingdom of Great Britain and Northern Ireland and the Union of Soviet Socialist Republics, are or may be declared to be available as reparation from Germany (hereinafter referred to as German reparation), in order to establish an Inter-Allied Reparation Agency, and to settle an equitable procedure for the restitution of monetary gold,

HAVE AGREED as follows:

PART I. GERMAN REPARATION

ARTICLE 1

Shares in Reparation

A. German reparation (exclusive of the funds to be allocated under Article 8 of Part I of this Agreement), shall be divided into the following categories:

Category A, which shall include all forms of German reparation except those included in Category *B;*

Category B, which shall include industrial and other capital equipment removed from Germany, and merchant ships and inland water transport.

B. Each Signatory Government shall be entitled to the percentage share of the total value of Category A and the percentage share of the total value of Category B set out for that Government in the Table of Shares set forth below:

---

[1] Department of State publication 2966, Treaties and Other International Acts Series 1655. This agreement was opened for signature at Paris, January 14, 1946; entered into force, January 24, 1946. For Final Act and Annex of the Paris Conference on Reparation, November 9-December 21, 1945, see Department of State publication 2584, European Series 12.

Table of shares

Country	Category A	Category B	Country	Category A	Category B
Albania	0.05	0.35	India	2.00	2.90
United States of America	28.00	11.80	Luxembourg	.15	.40
Australia	.70	.95	Norway	1.30	1.90
Belgium	2.70	4.50	New Zealand	.40	.60
Canada	3.50	1.50	Netherlands	3.90	5.60
Denmark	.25	.35	Czechoslovakia	3.00	4.30
Egypt	.05	.20	Union of South Africa(1)	.70	.10
France	16.00	22.80	Yugoslavia	6.60	9.60
United Kingdom	28.00	27.80			
Greece	2.70	4.35	Total	100.00	100.00

(1) The Government of the Union of South Africa has undertaken to waive its claims extent necessary to reduce its percentage share of category B to the figure of 0.1 percent but is entitled, in disposing of German enemy assets within its jurisdiction, to charge the net value of such assets against its percentage share of category A and a percentage share under category B of 1.0 percent.

C. Subject to the provisions of paragraph D below, each Signatory Government shall be entitled to receive its share of merchant ships determined in accordance with Article 5 of Part I of this Agreement, provided that its receipts of merchant ships do not exceed in value its share in Category B as a whole.

Subject to the provisions of paragraph D below, each Signatory Government shall also be entitled to its Category A percentage share in German assets in countries which remained neutral in the war against Germany.

The distribution among the Signatory Governments of forms of German reparation other than merchant ships, inland water transport and German assets in countries which remained neutral in the war against Germany shall be guided by the principles set forth in Article 4 of Part I of this Agreement.

D. If a Signatory Government receives more than its percentage share of certain types of assets in either Category A or Category B its receipts of other types of assets in that Category shall be reduced so as to ensure that it shall not receive more than its share in that Category as a whole.

E. No Signatory Government shall receive more than its percentage share of either Category A or Category B as a whole by surrendering any part of its percentage share of the other Category, except that with respect to German enemy assets within its own jurisdiction, any Signatory Government shall be permitted to charge any excess of such assets over its Category A percentage share of total German enemy assets within the jurisdiction of the Signatory Governments either to its receipts in Category A or to its receipts in Category B or in part to each Category.

F. The Inter-Allied Reparation Agency, to be established in accordance with Part II of this Agreement, shall charge the reparation account of each Signatory Government for the German assets within that Government's jurisdiction over a period of five years. The charges at the date of the entry into force of this Agreement shall be not less than 20 per cent of the net value of such assets (as defined in Article 6 of Part I of this Agreement) as then estimated, at the beginning of the second year thereafter not less than 25 per cent of the balance as then estimated, at the beginning of the third year not less than 33⅓ per cent of the balance as then estimated, at the beginning of the fourth year not less than 50 per cent of the balance as then estimated, at the beginning of the fifth year not less than 90 per cent of the balance as then estimated, and at the end of the fifth year the entire remainder of the total amount actually realized.

G. The following exceptions to paragraphs D and E above shall apply in the case of a Signatory Government whose share in Category B is less than its share in Category A:

(i) Receipts of merchant ships by any such Government shall not reduce its percentage share in other types of assets in Category B, except to the extent that such receipts exceed the value obtained when that Government's Category A percentage is applied to the total value of merchant ships.

(ii) Any excess of German assets within the jurisdiction of such Government over its Category A percentage share of the total of German assets within the jurisdiction of Signatory Government as a whole shall be charged first to the additional share in Category B to which that Government would be entitled if its share in Category B were determined by applying its Category A percentage to the forms of German reparation in Category B.

H. If any Signatory Government renounces its shares or part of its shares in German reparation as set out in the above Table of Shares, or if it withdraws from the Inter-Allied Reparation Agency at a time when all or part of its shares in German reparation remain unsatisfied, the shares or part thereof thus renounced or remaining shall be distributed rateably among the other Signatory Governments.

ARTICLE 2

Settlement of Claims against Germany

A. The Signatory Governments agree among themselves that their respective shares of reparation, as determined by the present Agreement, shall be regarded by each of them as covering all its claims and those of its nationals against the former German Government and its Agencies, of a governmental or private nature, arising out of the war (which are not otherwise provided for), including costs of German occupation, credits acquired during occupation on clearing accounts and claims against the Reichskreditkassen.

B. The provisions of paragraph A above are without prejudice to:

(i) the determination at the proper time of the forms, duration or total amount of reparation to be made by Germany;

(ii) the right which each Signatory Government may have with respect to the final settlement of German reparation; and

(iii) any political, territorial or other demands which any Signatory Government may put forward with respect to the peace settlement with Germany.

C. Notwithstanding anything in the provisions of paragraph A above, the present Agreement shall not be considered as affecting:

(i) the obligation of the appropriate authorities in Germany to secure at a future date the discharge of claims against Germany and German nationals arising out of contracts and other obligations entered into, and rights acquired, before the existence of a state of war between Germany and the Signatory Government concerned or before the occupation of its territory by Germany, whichever was earlier;

(ii) the claims of Social Insurance Agencies of the Signatory Governments or the claims of their nationals against the Social Insurance Agencies of the former German Government; and

(iii) banknotes of the Reichsbank and the Rentenbank, it being understood that their realization shall not have the result of reducing improperly the amount of reparation and shall not be effected without the approval of the Control Council for Germany.

D. Notwithstanding the provisions of Paragraph A of this Article, the Signatory Governments agree that, so far as they are concerned, the Czechoslovak Government will be entitled to draw upon the Giro account of the National Bank of Czechoslovakia at the Reichsbank, should such action be decided upon by the Czechoslovak Government and approved by the Control Council for Germany, in connection with the movement from Czechoslovakia to Germany of former Czechoslovak nationals.

ARTICLE 3

Waiver of Claims Regarding Property Allocated as Reparation.

Each of the Signatory Governments agrees that it will not assert, initiate actions in international tribunals in respect of, or give diplomatic support to claims on behalf of itself or those persons entitled to its protection against any other Signatory Government or its nationals in respect of property received by that Government as reparation with the approval of the Control Council for Germany.

ARTICLE 4

General Principles for the Allocation of Industrial and other Capital Equipment.

A. No Signatory Government shall request the allocation to it as reparation of any industrial or other capital equipment removed from Germany except for use in its own territory or for use by its own nationals outside its own territory.

B. In submitting requests to the Inter-Allied Reparation Agency, the Signatory Governments should endeavour to submit comprehensive programs of requests for related groups of items, rather than requests for isolated items or small groups of items. It is recognized that the work of the Secretariat of the Agency will be more effective, the more comprehensive the programs which Signatory Governments submit to it.

C. In the allocation by the Inter-Allied Reparation Agency of items declared available for reparation (other than merchant ships, inland water transport and German assets in countries which remained neutral in the war against Germany), the following general principles shall serve as guides:

(i) Any item or related group of items in which a claimant country has a substantial prewar financial interest shall be allocated to that country if it so desires. Where two more claimants have such substantial interests in a particular item or group of items, the criteria stated below shall guide the allocation:

(ii) If the allocation between competing claimants is not determined by paragraph (i), attention shall be given, among other relevant factors, to the following considerations:

a. The urgency of each claimant country's needs for the items or item to rehabilitate, reconstruct or restore to full activity the claimant country's economy;

b. The extent to which the item or items would replace property which was destroyed, damaged or looted in the war, or requires replacement because of excessive wear in war production, and which is important to the claimant country's economy;

c. The relation of the item or items to the general pattern of the claimant country's prewar economic life and to programs for its postwar economic adjustment or development;

d. The requirements of countries whose reparation shares are small but which are in need of certain specific items or categories of items.

(iii) In making allocations a reasonable balance shall be maintained among the rates at which the reparation shares of the several claimant Governments are satisfied, subject to such temporary exceptions as are justified by the considerations under paragraph (ii) (*a*) above.

ARTICLE 5

General Principles for the Allocation of Merchant Ships and Inland Water Transport

A. (i) German merchant ships available for distribution as reparation among the Signatory Governments shall be distributed among them in proportion to the respective over-all losses of merchant shipping, on a gross tonnage basis, of the Signatory Governments and their nationals through acts of war. It is recognized that transfers of merchant ships by the United Kingdom and United States Governments to other Governments are subject to such final approvals by the legislatures of the United Kingdom and United States of America as may be required.

(ii) A special committee, composed of representatives of the Signatory Governments, shall be appointed by the assembly of the Inter-Allied Reparation Agency to make recommendations concerning the determination of such losses and the allocation of German merchant ships available for distribution.

(iii) The value of German merchant ships for reparation accounting purposes shall be the value determined by the Tri-partite Merchant Marine Commission in terms of 1938 prices in Germany plus 15 per cent, with an allowance for depreciation.

B. Recognizing that some countries have special need for inland water transport, the distribution of inland water transport shall be dealt with by a special committee appointed by the Assembly of the Inter-Allied Reparation Agency in the event that inland water transport becomes available at a future time as reparation for the Signatory Governments.

The valuation of inland water transport will be made on the basis adopted for the valuation of merchant ships or on an equitable basis in relation to that adopted for merchant ships.

ARTICLE 6

German External Assets

A. Each Signatory Government shall, under such procedures as it may choose, hold or dispose of German enemy assets within its jurisdiction in manners designed to preclude their return to German ownership or control and shall charge against its reparation share such assets (net of accrued taxes, liens, expenses of administration, other *in rem* charges against specific items and legitimate contract claims against the German former owners of such assets).

B. The Signatory Governments shall give to the Inter-Allied Reparation Agency all information for which it asks as to the value of such assets and the amounts realized from time to time by their liquidation.

C. German assets in those countries which remained neutral in the war against Germany shall be removed from German ownership or control and liquidated or disposed of in accordance with the authority of France, the United Kingdom and the United States of America, pursuant to arrangements to be negotiated with the neutrals by these countries. The net proceeds of liquidation or disposition shall be made available to the Inter-Allied Reparation Agency for distribution on reparation account.

D. In applying the provisions of paragraph A above, assets which were the property of a country which is a member of the United Nations or its nationals who were not nationals of Germany at the time of the occupation or annexation of this country by Germany, or of its entry into war, shall not be charged to its reparation account. It is understood that this provision in no way prejudges any questions which may arise as regards assets which were not the property of a national of the country concerned at the time of the latter's occupation or annexation by Germany or of its entry into war.

E. The German enemy assets to be charged against reparation shares shall include assets which are in reality German enemy assets, despite the fact that the nominal owner of such assets is not a German enemy.

Each Signatory Government shall enact legislation or take other appropriate steps, if it has not already done so, to render null and void all transfers made, after the occupation of its territory or its entry into war, for the fraudulent purpose of cloaking German enemy interests, and thus saving them harmless from the effect of control measures regarding German enemy interests.

F. The Assembly of the Inter-Allied Reparation Agency shall set up a Committee of Experts in matters of enemy property custodianship in order to overcome practical difficulties of law and interpretation which may arise. The Committee should in particular guard against schemes which might result in effecting fictitious or other transactions designed to favour enemy interests, or to reduce improperly the amount of assets which might be allocated to reparation.

ARTICLE 7

Captured Supplies

The value of supplies and other materials susceptible of civilian use captured from the German Armed Forces in areas outside Germany and delivered to Signatory Governments shall be charged against their reparation shares in so far as such supplies and materials have not been or are not, in the future either paid for or delivered under arrangements precluding any charge.

It is recognized that transfers of such supplies and materials by the United Kingdom and United States Governments to other Governments are agreed to be subject to such final approval by the legislature of the United Kingdom or the United States of America as may be required.

ARTICLE 8

Allocation of a Reparation Share to Nonrepatriable Victims of German Action

In recognition of the fact that large numbers of persons have suffered heavily at the hands of the Nazis and now stand in dire need of aid to promote their rehabilitation but will be unable to claim the assistance of any Government receiving reparations from Germany, the Governments of the United States of America, France, the United Kingdom, Czechoslovakia and Yugoslavia, in consultation with the Inter-Governmental Committee on Refugees, shall as soon as possible work out in common agreement a plan on the following general lines:

A. A share of reparation consisting of all the non-monetary gold found by the Allied Armed Forces in Germany and in addition a sum not exceeding 25 million dollars shall be allocated for the rehabilitation and resettlement of non-repatriable victims of German action.

B. The sum of 25 million dollars shall be met from a portion of the proceeds of German assets in neutral countries which are available for reparation.

C. Governments of neutral countries shall be requested to make available for this purpose (in addition to the sum of 25 million dollars) assets in such countries of victims of Nazi action who have since died and left no heirs.

D. The persons eligible for aid under the plan in question shall be restricted to true victims of Nazi persecution and to their immediate families and dependents, in the following classes:

(i) Refugees from Nazi Germany or Austria who require aid and cannot be returned to their countries within a reasonable time because of prevailing conditions;

(ii) German and Austrian nationals now resident in Germany or Austria in exceptional cases in which it is reasonable on grounds of humanity to assist such persons to emigrate and providing they emigrate to other countries within a reasonable period;

(iii) Nationals of countries formerly occupied by the Germans who cannot be repatriated or are not in a position to be repatriated within a reasonable time. In order to concentrate aid on the most needy and deserving refugees and to exclude persons whose loyalty to the United Nations is or was doubtful, aid shall be restricted to nationals or former nationals of previously occupied countries who were victims of German concentration camps or of concentration camps established by regimes under Nazi influence but not including persons who have been confined only in prisoners of war camps.

E. The sums made available under paragraphs A and B above shall be administered by the Inter-Governmental Committee on Refugees or by a

United Nations Agency to which appropriate functions of the Inter-Governmental Committee may in the future be transferred. The sums made available under paragraph C above shall be administered for the general purposes referred to in this Article under a program of administration to be formulated by the five Governments named above.

F. The non-monetary gold found in Germany shall be placed at the disposal of the Inter-Governmental Committee on Refugees as soon as a plan has been worked out as provided above.

G. The Inter-Governmental Committee on Refugees shall have power to carry out the purposes of the fund through appropriate public and private field organisations.

H. The fund shall be used, not for the compensation of individual victims, but to further the rehabilitation or resettlement of persons in the eligible classes.

I. Nothing in this Article shall be considered to prejudice the claims which individual refugees may have against a future German Government, except to the amount of the benefits that such refugees may have received from the sources referred to in paragraph A and C above.

PART II. INTER-ALLIED REPARATION AGENCY

ARTICLE 1

Establishment of the Agency

The Governments Signatory to the present Agreement hereby establish an Inter-Allied Reparation Agency (hereinafter referred to as "The Agency"). Each Government shall appoint a Delegate to the Agency and shall also be entitled to appoint an Alternate who, in the absence of the Delegate, shall be entitled to exercise all the functions and rights of the Delegate.

ARTICLE 2

Functions of the Agency

A. The Agency shall allocate German reparation among the Signatory Governments in accordance with the provisions of this Agreement and of any other agreements from time to time in force among the Signatory Governments. For this purpose, the Agency shall be the medium through which the Signatory Governments receive information concerning, and express their wishes in regard to, items available as reparation.

B. The Agency shall deal with all questions relating to the restitution to a Signatory Government of property situated in one of the Western Zones of Germany which may be referred to it by the Commander of that Zone (acting on behalf of his Government), in agreement with the claimant Signatory Government or Governments, without prejudice, however, to the settlement of such questions by the Signatory Governments concerned either by agreement or arbitration.

ARTICLE 3

Internal Organisation of the Agency

A. The organs of the Agency shall be the Assembly and the Secretariat.

B. The Assembly shall consist of the Delegates and shall be presided over by the President of the Agency. The President of the Agency shall be the Delegate of the Government of France.

C. The Secretariat shall be under the direction of a Secretary General, assisted by two Deputy Secretaries General. The Secretary General and the two Deputy Secretaries General shall be appointed by the Governments of France, the United States of America and the United Kingdom. The Secretariat shall be international in character. It shall act for the Agency and not for the individual Signatory Governments.

ARTICLE 4

Functions of the Secretariat

The Secretariat shall have the following functions:

A. To prepare and submit to the Assembly programs for the allocation of German reparation;

B. To maintain detailed accounts of assets available for, and of assets distributed as, German reparation;

C. To prepare and submit to the Assembly the budget of the Agency;

D. To perform such other administrative functions as may be required.

ARTICLE 5

Functions of the Assembly

Subject to the provisions of Articles 4 and 7 of Part II of this Agreement, the Assembly shall allocate German reparation among the Signatory Governments in conformity with the provisions of this Agreement and of any other agreements from time to time in force among the Signatory Governments. It shall also approve the budget of the Agency and shall perform such other functions as are consistent with the provisions of this Agreement.

ARTICLE 6

Voting in the Assembly

Except as otherwise provided in this Agreement, each Delegate shall have one vote. Decisions in the Assembly shall be taken by a majority of the votes cast.

ARTICLE 7

Appeal from Decisions of the Assembly

A. When the Assembly has not agreed to a claim presented by a Delegate that an item should be allocated to his Government, the Assembly shall, at the request of that Delegate and within the time limit prescribed by the Assembly, refer the question to arbitration. Such reference shall suspend the effect of the decision of the Assembly on that item.

B. The Delegates of the Government claiming an item referred to arbitration under paragraph A above shall elect an Arbitrator from among the other Delegates. If agreement cannot be reached upon the selection of an Arbitrator, the United States Delegate shall either act as Arbitrator or appoint as Arbitrator another Delegate from among the Delegates whose Governments are not claiming the item. If the United States Government is one of the claimant Governments, the President of the Agency shall appoint as Arbitrator a Delegate whose Government is not a claimant Government.

ARTICLE 8

Powers of the Arbitrator

When the question of the allocation of any item is referred to arbitration under Article 7 of Part II of this Agreement, the Arbitrator shall have authority to make final allocation of the item among the claimant Governments. The Arbitrator may, at his discretion, refer the item to the Secretariat for further study. He may also, at his discretion, require the Secretariat to resubmit the item to the Assembly.

ARTICLE 9

Expenses

A. The salaries and expenses of the Delegates and of their staffs shall be paid by their own Governments.

B. The common expenses of the Agency shall be met from the funds of the Agency. For the first two years from the date of the establishment of the Agency, these funds shall be contributed in proportion to the percentage shares of the Signatory Governments in Category B and thereafter in proportion to their percentage in Category A.

C. Each Signatory Government shall contribute its share in the budget of the Agency for each budgetary period (as determined by the Assembly) at the beginning of that period; provided that each Government shall, when this Agreement is signed on its behalf, contribute a sum equivalent to not less than its Category B percentage share of £50,000 and shall, within three months thereafter, contribute the balance of its share in the budget of the Agency for the budgetary period in which this Agreement is signed on its behalf.

D. All contributions by the Signatory Governments shall be made in Belgian francs or such other currency or currencies as the Agency may require.

ARTICLE 10

Voting of the Budget

In considering the budget of the Agency for any budgetary period, the vote of each Delegate in the Assembly shall be proportional to the share of the budget for that period payable by his Government.

ARTICLE 11

Official Languages

The official languages of the Agency shall be English and French.

ARTICLE 12

Offices of the Agency

The seat of the Agency shall be in Brussels. The Agency shall maintain liaison offices in such other places as the Assembly, after obtaining the necessary consents, may decide.

ARTICLE 13

Withdrawal

Any Signatory Government, other than a Government which is responsible for the control of a part of German territory, may withdraw from the Agency after written notice to the Secretariat.

ARTICLE 14

Amendments and Termination

This Part II of the Agreement can be amended or the Agency terminated by a decision in the Assembly of the majority of the Delegates voting, provided that the Delegates forming the majority represent Governments whose shares constitute collectively not less than 80 per cent of the aggregate of the percentage shares in category A.

ARTICLE 15

Legal capacity.—Immunities and Privileges

The Agency shall enjoy in the territory of each Signatory Government such legal capacity and such privileges, immunities and facilities, as may be necessary for the exercise of its functions and the fulfilment of its purpose. The representatives of the Signatory Governments and the officials of the Agency shall enjoy such privileges and immunities as are necessary for the independent exercise of their functions in connection with the Agency.

PART III. RESTITUTION OF MONETARY GOLD

SINGLE ARTICLE

A. All the monetary gold found in Germany by the Allied Forces and that referred to in paragraph G below (including gold coins, except those of numismatic or historical value, which shall be restored directly if identifiable) shall be pooled for distribution as restitution among the countries participating in the pool in proportion to their respective losses of gold through looting or by wrongful removal to Germany.

B. Without prejudice to claims by way of reparation for unrestored gold, the portion of monetary gold thus accruing to each country participating in the pool shall be accepted by that country in full satisfatcion of all claims against Germany for restitution of monetary gold.

C. A proportional share of the gold shall be allocated to each country concerned which adheres to this arrangement for the restitution of monetary gold and which can establish that a definite amount of monetary gold belonging to it was looted by Germany or, at any time after March 12th, 1938, was wrongfully removed into German territory.

D. The question of the eventual participation of countries not represented at the Conference (other than Germany but including Austria and Italy) in the above mentioned distribution shall be reserved, and the equivalent of the total shares which these countries would receive, if they were eventually admitted to participate, shall be set aside to be disposed of at a later date in such manner as may be decided by the Allied Governments concerned.

E. The various countries participating in the pool shall supply to the Governments of the United States of America, France and the United Kingdom, as the occupying Powers concerned, detailed and verifiable data regarding the gold losses suffered through looting by, or removal to, Germany.

F. The Governments of the United States of America, France and the United Kingdom shall take appropriate steps within the Zones of Germany occupied by them respectively to implement distribution in accordance with the foregoing provisions.

G. Any monetary gold which may be recovered from a third country to which it was transferred from Germany shall be distributed in accordance with this arrangement for the restitution of monetary gold.

PART IV. ENTRY INTO FORCE AND SIGNATURE.

ARTICLE 1

Entry into force

This Agreement shall be open for signature on behalf of any Government represented at the Paris Conference on Reparation.

As soon as it has been signed on behalf of Governments collectively entitled to not less than 80 p. 100 of the aggregate of shares in Category A of German reparation, it shall come into force among such Signatory Governments.

The Agreement shall thereafter be in force among such Governments and those Governments on whose behalf it is subsequently signed.

ARTICLE 2

Signature

The signature of each contracting Government shall be deemed to mean that the effect of the present Agreement extends to the colonies and overseas territories of such Government, and to territories under its protection or suzerainty or over which it at present exercises a mandate.

In witness whereof, the undersigned, duly authorized by their respective Governments, have signed in Paris the present Agreement in the English and French languages, the two texts being equally authentic, in a single original, which shall be deposited in the Archives of the Government of the French Republic, a certified copy thereof being furnished by that Government to each signatory Government.

[Here follow the signatures of the duly authorized agents of the signatory governments.]

◇◇◇◇◇◇

63. RESTATEMENT OF THE UNITED STATES POLICY ON GERMANY [1]

Address of Secretary Byrnes at Stuttgart, Germany, September 6, 1946
(Excerpts)

*   *   *

[Each of the four major occupying powers had its own concepts of how the government of defeated Germany should be administered. The United States directed its commander in the field to coöperate with all the other occupying powers in setting up the needed central administrative agencies. Conflicting views among the Allies, however, made a clarification of our policy essential. Therefore, during the Paris Peace Conference, Secretary of State Byrnes delivered a most important address at Stuttgart urging the unification of Germany and indicating that we had no intention of withdrawing from Europe.]

In 1917 the United States was forced into the first World War. After that war we refused to join the League of Nations. We thought we could stay out of Europe's wars, and we lost interest in the affairs of Europe. That did not keep us from being forced into a second world war.

We will not again make that mistake.

The American people want peace. They have long since ceased to talk of a hard or soft peace for Germany. This never has been the real issue. What we want is a lasting peace. We will oppose soft measures which invite the breaking of the peace.

In agreeing at Potsdam that Germany should be disarmed and demilitarized and in proposing that the four major powers should by treaty jointly undertake to see that Germany is kept disarmed and demilitarized for a generation, the United States was not unmindful of the responsibility resting upon it and its major Allies to maintain and enforce peace under the law.

*   *   *

The basis of the Potsdam Agreement was that, as part of a combined program of demilitarization and reparations, Germany's war potential should be reduced by elimination and removal of her war industries and the reduction and removal of heavy industrial plants It was contemplated this should be done to the point that Germany would be left with levels of industry capable of maintaining in Germany average European living standards without assistance from other countries.

In fixing the levels of industry no allowance was made for reparations from current production. Reparations from current production would be wholly incompatible with the levels of industry now established under the Potsdam Agreement.

Obviously, higher levels of industry would have had to be fixed if reparations from current production were contemplated. The levels of industry fixed are only sufficient to enable the German people to become self-supporting and

[1] Department of State publication 2616, European Series 13; Department of State Bulletin of September 15, 1946, pp. 496-501.

to maintain living standards approximating the average European living conditions.

That was the principle of reparations to which President Truman agreed at Potsdam. And the United States will not agree to the taking from Germany of greater reparations than was provided by the Potsdam Agreement.

The carrying out of the Potsdam Agreement has, however, been obstructed by the failure of the Allied Control Council to take the necessary steps to enable the Germany economy to function as an economic unit. Essential central German administrative departments have not been established, although they are expressly required by the Potsdam Agreement.

The working out of a balanced economy throughout Germany to provide the necessary means to pay for approved imports has not been accomplished, although that too is expressly required by the Potsdam Agreement.

The United States is firmly of the belief that Germany should be administered as an economic unit and that zonal barriers should be completely obliterated so far as the economic life and activity in Germany are concerned.

*   *   *

A common financial policy is essential for the successful rehabilitation of Germany. Runaway inflation accompanied by economic paralysis is almost certain to develop unless there is a common financial policy directed to the control of inflation. A program of drastic fiscal reform to reduce currency and monetary claims, to revise the debt structure, and to place Germany on a sound financial basis is urgently required.

It is also essential that transportation, communications, and postal services should be organized throughout Germany without regard to zonal barriers. The nation-wide organization of these public services was contemplated by the Potsdam Agreement. Twelve months have passed and nothing has been done.

Germany needs all the food she can produce. Before the war she could not produce enough food for her population. The area of Germany has been reduced. The population in Silesia, for instance, has been forced back into a restricted Germany. Armies of occupation and displaced persons increase demands while the lack of farm machinery and fertilizer reduces supplies. To secure the greatest possible production of food and the most effective use and distribution of the food that can be produced, a central administrative department for agriculture should be set up and allowed to function without delay.

Similarly, there is urgent need for the setting up of a central German administrative agency for industry and foreign trade. While Germany must be prepared to share her coal and steel with the liberated countries of Europe dependent upon those supplies, Germany must be enabled to use her skills and her energies to increase her industrial production and to organize the most effective use of her raw materials.

Germany must be given a chance to export goods in order to import enough to make her economy self-sustaining. Germany is a part of Europe, and recovery in Europe, and particularly in the states adjoining Germany, will be slow indeed if Germany with her great resources of iron and coal is turned into a poorhouse.

*   *   *

The principal purposes of the military occupation were and are to de-militarize and de-Nazify Germany but not to raise artificial barriers to the efforts of the German people to resume their peacetime economic life.

The Nazi war criminals were to be punished for the suffering they brought to the world. The policy of reparations and industrial disarmament prescribed in the Potsdam Agreement was to be carried out. But the purpose of the occupation did not contemplate a prolonged foreign dictatorship of Germany's peacetime economy or a prolonged foreign dictatorship of Germany's internal political life. The Potsdam Agreement expressly bound the occupying powers to start building a political democracy from the ground up.

* * *

The Potsdam Agreement wisely provided that administration of the affairs of Germany should be directed toward decentralization of the political struc-ture and the development of local responsibility. This was not intended to prevent progress toward a central government with the powers necessary to deal with matters which would be dealt with on a nation-wide basis. But it was intended to prevent the establishment of a strong central government dominating the German people instead of being responsible to their democratic will.

It is the view of the American Government that the German people through-out Germany, under proper safeguards, should now be given the primary responsibility for the running of their own affairs.

All that the Allied governments can and should do is to lay down the rules under which German democracy can govern itself. The Allied occupation forces should be limited to the number sufficient to see that those rules are obeyed.

But of course the question for us will be: What force is needed to make certain that Germany does not rearm as it did after the first World War? Our proposal for a treaty with the major powers to enforce for 25 or even 40 years the demilitarization plan finally agreed upon in the peace settlement would have made possible a smaller army of occupation. For enforcement we could rely more upon a force of trained inspectors and less upon infantry.

Security forces will probably have to remain in Germany for a long period. I want no misunderstanding. We will not shirk our duty. We are not withdraw-ing. We are staying here. As long as there is an occupation army in Germany, American armed forces will be part of that occupation army.

The United States favors the early establishment of a provisional German government for Germany. Progress has been made in the American zone in developing local and state self-government in Germany, and the American Government believes similar progress is possible in all zones.

It is the view of the American Government that the provisional government should not be hand-picked by other governments. It should be a German national council composed of the democratically responsible minister presi-dents or other chief officials of the several states or provinces which have been established in each of the four zones.

Subject to the reserved authority of the Allied Control Council, the German National Council should be responsible for the proper functioning of the central administrative agencies. Those agencies should have adequate power to assure the administration of Germany as an economic unit, as was contemplated by the Potsdam Agreement.

The German National Council should also be charged with the preparation of a draft of a federal constitution for Germany which, among other things, should insure the democratic character of the new Germany and the human rights and fundamental freedoms of all its inhabitants.

*   *   *

At Potsdam specific areas which were part of Germany were provisionally assigned to the Soviet Union and to Poland, subject to the final decisions of the Peace Conference. At that time these areas were being held by the Soviet and Polish armies. We were told that Germans in large numbers were fleeing from these areas and that it would in fact, because of the feelings aroused by the war, be difficult to reorganize the economic life of these areas if they were not administered as integral parts in the one case of the Soviet Union and in the other case of Poland.

The heads of government agreed to support at the peace settlement the proposal of the Soviet Government concerning the ultimate transfer to the Soviet Union of the city of Königsberg and the area adjacent to it. Unless the Soviet Government changes its views on the subject we will certainly stand by our agreement.

With regard to Silesia and other eastern German areas, the assignment of this territory to Poland by Russia for administrative purposes had taken place before the Potsdam meeting. The heads of government agreed that, pending the final determination of Poland's western frontier, Silesia and other eastern German areas should be under the administration of the Polish state and for such purposes should not be considered as a part of the Soviet zone of occupation in Germany. However, as the Protocol of the Potsdam Conference makes clear, the heads of government did not agree to support at the peace settlement the cession of this particular area.

The Soviets and the Poles suffered greatly at the hands of Hitler's invading armies. As a result of the agreement at Yalta, Poland ceded to the Soviet Union territory east of the Curzon Line. Because of this, Poland asked for revision of her northern and western frontiers. The United States will support a revision of these frontiers in Poland's favor. However, the extent of the area to be ceded to Poland must be determined when the final settlement is agreed upon.

The United States does not feel that it can deny to France, which has been invaded three times by Germany in 70 years, its claim to the Saar territory, whose economy has long been closely linked with France. Of course, if the Saar territory is integrated with France she should readjust her reparation claims against Germany.

Except as here indicated, the United States will not support any encroachment on territory which is indisputably German or any division of Germany which is not genuinely desired by the people concerned. So far as the United States is aware the people of the Ruhr and the Rhineland desire to remain united with the rest of Germany. And the United States is not going to oppose their desire.

While the people of the Ruhr were the last to succumb to Nazism, without the resources of the Ruhr Nazism could never have threatened the world. Never again must those resources be used for destructive purposes. They must be used to rebuild a free, peaceful Germany and a free, peaceful Europe.

The United States will favor such control over the whole of Germany, including the Ruhr and the Rhineland, as may be necessary for security purposes. It will help to enforce those controls. But it will not favor any controls that would subject the Ruhr and the Rhineland to political domination or manipulation of outside powers.

*   *   *

The United States cannot relieve Germany from the hardships inflicted upon her by the war her leaders started. But the United States has no desire to increase those hardships or to deny the German people an opportunity to work their way out of those hardships so long as they respect human freedom and follow the paths of peace.

The American people want to return the government of Germany to the German people. The American people want to help the German people to win their way back to an honorable place among the free and peace-loving nations of the world.

◇◇◇◇◇

64. ECONOMIC FUSION OF AMERICAN AND BRITISH ZONES OF OCCUPATION

Memorandum of Agreement Between the United States and the United Kingdom, December 2, 1946 [1]

[When, in 1946, the United States and Britain agreed to assign the Saar Basin to France in return for French participation in the establishment of centralized administrative agencies for Germany, the Soviet Union refused to acquiesce. Consequently, the United States offered to join any of the other occupying powers in the administration of their combined zones as a single economic unit. Britain explored the offer, and on December 2, 1946, entered into the agreement with the United States set forth below. The agreement was subsequently extended and revised on December 17, 1947, and June 30, 1949.]

Representatives of the two Governments have met at Washington to discuss the questions arising out of the economic fusion of their zones of occupation in Germany. They have taken as the basis of their discussion the fact that the aim of the two Governments is to achieve the economic unity of Germany as a whole, in accordance with the agreement reached at Potsdam on 2nd August, 1945. The arrangements set out hereunder, for the United States and United Kingdom Zones, should be regarded as the first step towards the achievement of the economic unity of Germany as a whole in accordance with that agreement. The two Governments are ready at any time to enter into discussions

[1] Department of State publication 2740 Treaties and other International Acts Series 1575. Agreement effective January 1, 1947.

with either of the other occupying powers with a view to the extension of these arrangements to their zones of occupation.

On this basis, agreement has been reached on the following paragraphs:—

1. *Date of inception.* This agreement for the economic fusion of the two zones shall take effect on 1st January, 1947.

2. *Pooling of resources.* The two zones shall be treated as a single area for all economic purposes. The indigenous resources of the area and all imports into the area, including food, shall be pooled in order to produce a common standard of living.

3. *German administrative agencies.* The United States and United Kingdom Commanders-in-Chief are responsible for setting up under their joint control the German administrative agencies necessary to the economic unification of the two zones.

4. *Agency for foreign trade.* Responsibility for foreign trade will rest initially with the Joint Export-Import Agency (United States-United Kingdom) or such other agency as may be established by the two Commanders-in-Chief. This responsibility shall be transferred to the German administrative agency for foreign trade under joint supervision to the maximum extent permitted by the restrictions existing in foreign countries at any given period. (All references in this agreement to the Joint Export-Import Agency shall apply to this agency or to any agency established by the two Commanders-in-Chief to succeed it.)

5. *Basis of economic planning.* The aim of the two Governments is the achievement by the end of 1949 of a self-sustaining economy in the area.

6. *Sharing of financial responsibility.* Subject to the provision of the necessary appropriations, the Governments of the United States and the United Kingdom will become responsible on an equal basis for costs of approved imports brought into account after 31st December, 1946 (including stocks on hand financed by the respective Governments), insofar as those cannot be paid for from other sources, in accordance with the following provisions:—

> (a) For this purpose the imports of the area shall be divided into two categories: those imports required to prevent disease and unrest (Category A), which are financed in decreasing amounts by appropriated funds; and those further imports (including raw materials), however financed, which will be required if the economic state of the area is to recover to an extent sufficient to achieve the aim laid down in paragraph 5 of this Agreement (Category B).

*   *   *

> (e) The costs incurred by the two Governments for their two zones before 1st January, 1947, and for the area thereafter, shall be recovered from future German exports in the shortest practicable time consistent with the rebuilding of the German economy on healthy non-aggressive lines.

7. *Relaxation of barriers to trade.* With a view to facilitating the expansion of German exports, barriers in the way of trade with Germany should be removed as rapidly as world conditions permit. To the same end the establishment of an exchange value for the mark should be undertaken as soon as this is practicable; financial reform should be effected in Germany at an early date; and the exchange of full technical and business communications between

Germany and other countries should be facilitated as soon as possible. Potential buyers of German goods should be provided access to both zones to the full extent that facilities permit, and normal business channels should be restored as soon as possible.

8. *Procurement.* The determination of import requirements shall be the responsibility of the Joint Export-Import Agency.

* * *

The two Governments will establish a joint committee in Washington with the following responsibilities:—

(a) In the case of commodities in short supply, to support the requirements of the Joint Export-Import Agency before the appropriate authorities.

(b) To determine, where necessary, sources of supply and to designate procurement agencies having regard to the financial responsibilities and exchange resources of the two Governments.

* * *

9. *Currency and banking arrangements.* The Bipartite Finance Committee (United States-United Kingdom) will be authorized to open accounts with approved banks of the countries in which the Joint Export-Import Agency is operating, provided that agreements are negotiated with those countries for credit balances to be transferred on demand into dollars or sterling. The Bipartite Finance Committee will be authorised to accept payment of balances in either dollars or sterling, whichever, in the judgment of the Joint Export-Import Agency, may be better utilized in financing essential imports.

10. *Food.* The two Governments will support, to the full extent that appropriated and other funds will permit, an increase in the present ration standard to 1800 calories for the normal consumer as soon as the world food supply permits. This standard is accepted as the minimum which will support a reasonable economic recovery in Germany. However, in view of the current world food supply, a ration standard of 1550 calories for the normal consumer must be accepted at present.

11. *Imports for displaced persons.* Subject to any international arrangements which may subsequently be made for the maintenance of displaced persons, the maintenance of displaced persons within both zones from the German economy shall not exceed the maintenance of German citizens from this economy. Supplementary rations and other benefits which may be provided for displaced persons in excess of those available to German citizens must be brought in to Germany without cost to the German economy.

12. *Duration.* It is the intention of the two Governments that this agreement shall govern their mutual arrangements for the economic administration of the area pending agreement for the treatment of Germany as an economic unit or until amended by mutual agreement. It shall be reviewed at yearly intervals.

JAMES F. BYRNES
ERNEST BEVIN
2nd December, 1946.

◇◇◇◇◇◇

65. PROBLEMS RELATING TO REPARATIONS FROM GERMANY

Statements by Secretary Marshall, March 17 and 18, 1947 [1]

[Following the establishment of the Inter-Allied Reparations Agency, all efforts of France, Britain, and the United States to reach an understanding with the U.S.S.R. on the implementation of the Potsdam reparations provisions, which were less generous to the U.S.S.R. than those of Yalta, were thwarted by Soviet obstruction. When the Big Four Foreign Ministers met in Moscow during March, 1947, one of the problems on the agenda was the level of production which German industry was to be permitted to attain. Again no agreement could be reached. On his return from Moscow, Secretary of State Marshall outlined the policy of the United States with respect to reparations and the dismantlement of plants in Germany, and observed that the United States refused "to follow Mr. Molotov in a retreat from Potsdam to Yalta."]

STATUS OF WAR PLANTS IN UNITED STATES ZONE

The United States holds that the provisions of the Potsdam protocol for the delivery of plants for reparations and for the economic unification of Germany to include a common export-import plan must be carried out concurrently. In order that sufficient resources may be retained, as required by the Potsdam protocol, to enable Germany to become self-supporting without external assistance, the economic resources which will be available to Germany after reparations have been removed must be known. The United States has consistently sought an agreement for the establishment of central German administrative agencies to carry out administratively the principles of economic unification. It has also sought the adoption of a common export-import plan: an interim Allied Control Council agreement was secured which called for the formation of such a plan by October 31, 1945. However, this agreement has not been fulfilled.

When persistent efforts to secure economic unification failed, the United States Representative on the Allied Control Council announced the suspension of further dismantling of plants for reparations purposes. This action was required as a protective measure as the United States could not permit the further removal of industrial equipment from the United States zone of Germany in the face of a recurring financial deficit unless it could be assured that the United States zone of Germany would share in the resources of all Germany.

In order that the resumption of reparations may take place promptly when the other provisions of the Potsdam protocol are met, the United States has supported a vigorous program to determine the plants to be made available for reparations and for their prompt valuation. It has continued to dismantle and deliver at the request of the countries to which these plants were assigned 24 major plants included in the program for advance reparations deliveries. It has also dismantled completely 80 of the 117 war plants in its zone and has made the general-purpose equipment in these plants available for allocation

[1] Department of State Bulletin of March 30, 1947, pp. 563-564.

and delivery. It will complete the liquidation of the remaining war plants during the present calendar year.

In addition to the 117 war plants and the 24 plants approved for advance delivery, there are 251 plants in the United States zone approved for valuation under the presently agreed level of industry; 1,593 plants remaining to be valuated were approved only in October and November 1946, and their valuation will be completed on schedule.

The current status of reparations from the three western zones is:

174 plants allocated.

524 additional plants approved by the Coordinating Committee for valuation.

808 plants in the machinery and optic industries approved for valuation, with reservation.

Several hundred additional plants are at various stages of approval in the Allied Control Authority.

A total of 2,000 plants, more or less, have been selected for reparations by the Allied Control Authority.

However, the United States considers that these figures should be regarded as tentative. Specific determination should be made of the plants to be left in Germany to enable it to be self-supporting. This determination should give consideration to population density and to final fixing of boundaries. Experience during the past 20 months has indicated that the redevelopment of a self-supporting Germany is not an easy task. However, the occupying powers cannot be expected to support the German economy indefinitely. While the basic principle to leave a self-supporting economy in Germany established in the Potsdam protocol is sound, the Allied Control Council should re-examine the presently calculated level of industry without delay to determine its adequacy for the purpose. This can be done successfully only if full information is made available in each zone of occupation.

The United States Delegation hopes that agreement may be reached here on the provisions of the Potsdam protocol which have not been carried out, so that reparation deliveries may be resumed.

UNITED STATES POSITION ON THE POTSDAM AGREEMENT [1]

I wish to make completely clear the position that the United States has consistently taken with regard to the relation of the Potsdam agreement on reparations to the Yalta protocol.

Immediately upon his return from Potsdam, before any question was raised as to the scope or meaning of the Potsdam agreement or its relation to the Yalta agreement, President Truman in a public address on August 9, 1945 clearly stated his understanding of the Potsdam agreement. I will read to you exactly what he said: "At the Crimea Conference a basis for fixing reparations had been proposed for initial discussion and study by the Reparations Commission. That basis was a total amount of reparations of 20 billion dollars. Of this sum, one half was to go to Russia, which had suffered more heavily in the loss of life and property than any other country. But at Berlin the idea of attempting to fix a dollar value on the property to be removed from Germany

---

[1] Made on March 18, 1947, and released to the press in Moscow on that date and in Washington on March 19.

was dropped. To fix a dollar value on the share of each nation would be a sort of guaranty of the amount each nation would get—a guaranty which might not be fulfilled. . . . This formula of taking reparations by zones will lead to less friction among the Allies than the tentative basis originally proposed for study at Yalta." [1]

In July 1946 at Paris the question of German reparations was discussed in the Council of Foreign Ministers. At that time Mr. Molotov presented the same arguments regarding the Yalta agreement which he has put forth here.

Secretary Byrnes, who was present at the Yalta Conference and who, as Secretary of State, took an active part in working out the Potsdam Agreement on reparations, stated the view and position of the United States Government that the Potsdam agreement took the place of the preliminary agreement reached at Yalta. Secretary Byrnes pointed out the irrefutable fact and I quote from his statement: "The language read by Mr. Molotov showed what Mr. Roosevelt agreed to was only to study as a basis for discussion the suggestion of the Soviet Government. The language of the protocol shows that the Soviet proposal was passed to the Moscow Reparations Commission as one of the proposals to be considered by the commission." [2] The position of the United States Government regarding reparations is that the agreements at Potsdam supersede the preliminary agreements previously reached at Yalta. We will not follow Mr. Molotov in a retreat from Potsdam to Yalta.

◇◇◇◇◇◇

66. DIRECTIVE TO COMMANDER-IN-CHIEF OF THE UNITED STATES FORCES OF OCCUPATION, JULY 11, 1947, SUPERSEDING JCS 1067/6 OF APRIL 1945 [3]

[Prior to Germany's defeat, the basic surrender directive—the famous JCS 1067/6 finalized in April 1945—was framed by the Joint Chiefs of Staff for the use of the American commander in Germany. It set forth the principles on which Germany was to be administered, principles which were later incorporated into the multilateral agreements for the control of Germany. It was revised and superseded by another directive under date of July 11, 1947. This is reproduced below. The two instruments were very similar, much of the language of the first being taken over in the second.]

I

1. Purpose of this Directive

This directive, issued to you as Commanding General of the United States forces of occupation and as Military Governor in Germany, constitutes a statement of the objectives of your Government in Germany and of the basic

[1] Department of State Bulletin of August 12, 1945, p. 210.

[2] Made on July 11, 1946, at a meeting of the Council of Foreign Ministers in Paris.

[3] Department of State Bulletin, July 27, 1947, pp. 186-193; also Department of State publication 2913, European Series 27.

policies to which your Government wishes you to give effect from the present time forward. It supersedes JCS 1067/6 [1] and its amendments.

2. Authority of Military Government

a. Your authority as Military Governor will be broadly construed and empowers you to take action consistent with relevant international agreements, general foreign policies of this Government and with this directive, appropriate or desirable to attain your Government's objectives in Germany or to meet military exigencies.

b. Pending arrangements for the effective treatment of Germany as an economic and political unit, you will exert every effort to achieve economic unity with other zones.

II

3. United States Policy Toward Germany

The basic interest of the United States throughout the world is just and lasting peace. Such a peace can be achieved only if conditions of public order and prosperity are created in Europe as a whole. An orderly and prosperous Europe requires the economic contributions of a stable and productive Germany as well as the necessary restraints to insure that Germany is not allowed to revive its destructive militarism.

To accomplish the latter purpose the United States Government has proposed to the other Occupying Powers a treaty for the continuing disarmament and demilitarization of Germany and it has committed itself to maintaining a United States army of occupation as long as foreign occupation of Germany continues.

As a positive program requiring urgent action the United States Government seeks the creation of those political, economic and moral conditions in Germany which will contribute most effectively to a stable and prosperous Europe.

III

4. Demilitarization

There should be no relaxation of effort to complete and effectively to maintain the disarmament and the demilitarization of Germany.

IV

5. United States Political Objectives in Germany

It is an objective of the United States Government that there should arise in Germany as rapidly as possible a form of political organization and a manner of political life which, resting on a substantial basis of economic well-being, will lead to tranquillity within Germany and will contribute to the spirit of peace among nations.

Your task, therefore, is fundamentally that of helping to lay the economic and educational bases of a sound German democracy, of encouraging *bona fide* democratic efforts and of prohibiting those activities which would jeopardize genuinely democratic developments.

[1] Department of State Bulletin, October 21, 1945, p. 596.

6. German Self-Government

a. You will continue to promote the development in Germany of institutions of popular self-government and the assumption of direct responsibility by German governmental agencies, assuring them legislative, judicial and executive powers, consistent with military security and the purposes of the occupation.

b. It is the view of your Government that the most constructive development of German political life would be in the establishment throughout Germany of federal German states (*Laender*) and the formation of a central German government with carefully defined and limited powers and functions. All powers shall be vested in the *Laender* except such as are expressly delegated to the Central Government.

c. Your Government does not wish to impose its own historically developed forms of democracy and social organization on Germany and believes equally firmly that no other external forms should be imposed. It seeks the establishment in Germany of a political organization which is derived from the people and subject to their control, which operates in accordance with democratic electoral procedures, and which is dedicated to uphold both the basic civil and human rights of the individual. It is opposed to an excessively centralized government which through a concentration of power may threaten both the existence of democracy in Germany and the security of Germany's neighbors and the rest of the world. Your Government believes finally that, within the principles stated above, the ultimate constitutional form of German political life should be left to the decision of the German people made freely in accordance with democratic processes.

7. Interzonal German Administrative Agencies

Pending the establishment of central German administrative agencies and of a central German government, you will continue, consistent with the objectives of paragraph 6, to make arrangements with other Zonal Commanders for the creation and operation of interzonal German administrative agencies.

8. Political Parties

a. You will adhere to the policy of authorizing and encouraging all political parties whose programs, activities and structure demonstrate their allegiance to democratic principles. Political parties shall be competitive in character, constituted by voluntary associations of citizens in which the leaders are responsible to the members, and with no party enjoying a privileged status.

b. You will likewise give support to the principle that military government and the German authorities should afford non-discriminatory treatment to duly authorized political parties. Every authorized political party should have the right freely to state its views and to present its candidates to the electorate, and you will tolerate no curtailment of nor hindrance to the exercise of that right; if, however, you find that an authorized party is adopting or advocating undemocratic practices or ideas, you may restrict or withdraw its rights and privileges.

c. You will urge in the Control Council the recognition of nationwide political parties and the uniform treatment of all authorized parties in all zones of occupation. You will advocate quadripartite supervision of political activities and of elections throughout Germany as a whole.

9. Denazification

You will implement in your zone the decisions on denazification taken April 23, 1947 by the Council of Foreign Ministers, as may be agreed in ACC.

10. War Crimes

You will make every effort to facilitate and bring to early completion the war crimes program subject to the conclusions and recommendations with respect to organizations and members thereof contained in the judgment of the International Military Tribunal.

11. Courts and Judicial Procedures

a. You will exercise such supervision over German Courts as is necessary to prevent the revival of National Socialist doctrines, to prohibit discrimination on grounds of race, nationality, creed or political belief, to enforce the application of the principles expressed in Control Council Proclamation No. 3 [1] and compliance with the provisions of Control Council and Military Government legislation. You will foster the independence of the German judiciary by allowing the courts freedom in their interpretation and application of the law and by limiting the control measures instituted by Military Government to the minimum consistent with the accomplishment of the aims of the occupation.

b. You will maintain sufficient Military Government Courts to try persons accused of offenses involving the safety and security of United States and Allied personnel and all cases in which the interest of Military Government requires such procedure.

c. You may extend the jurisdiction of the German courts to all cases which do not involve the interests of Military Government or persons under the protective care of Military Government. Any German Tribunal established for the purpose of determining internal restitution claims may exercise jurisdiction over any person irrespective of his status who institutes a proceeding therein.

d. As a basic objective of the occupation is the reestablishment of the rule of law in Germany, you will require all agencies under your control to refrain from arbitrary and oppressive measures. Except when it clearly appears that detention is necessary for the security of the occupying forces, no person will be detained except when he is charged with a specific offense and is subject to trial by a duly constituted tribunal. You will protect the civil rights of persons detained under charges assuring them a fair trial and ample opportunity to prepare their defense. You will by regulation limit arrests for security purposes to cases where overriding considerations of military necessity require such procedure. Persons so detained will be permitted to communicate with their nearest relative or friend unless urgent security considerations require an exception, and you will review their cases periodically to determine whether further detention is warranted. When in your opinion it will be compatible with security considerations, you will eliminate such arrests without prejudice to a revival of the practice in emergencies.

[1] Department of State Bulletin, November 10, 1946, p. 861.

12. Legislation

You will exercise your power of disapproval over German legislation only when such legislation conflicts with the legislation or other policies of Military Government.

13. Movement of Persons

a. You will implement the decisions taken 23 April 1947 by the Council of Foreign Ministers with regard to United Nations displaced persons and population transfers.

b. You will, in cooperation with IRO, facilitate the emigration to other countries of those displaced persons unwilling to be repatriated.

c. Pending the movement of displaced persons you will retain overall responsibility for their appropriate care, maintenance and protection. You will utilize the IRO to the maximum possible extent in assisting you to discharge this responsibility.

d. The term displaced persons as used above refers to displaced persons and refugees as defined in the IRO Constitution.

e. You will hold the German authorities responsible for the care and disposition of nationals of former enemy countries not otherwise provided for herein and you will continue to facilitate their repatriation.

f. You will require that persons of German extraction who have been transferred to Germany be granted German nationality with full civil and political rights except in cases of recognized disqualifications under German law. You will take such measures as you may deem appropriate to assist the German authorities in effecting a program of resettlement.

g. You will continue to permit the exchange of Germans seeking permanent residence between the United States Zone and other zones on a reciprocal basis. You will permit free movement for temporary purposes to the greatest possible extent consistent with security considerations and with interzonal or quadripartite agreement.

h. You will continue to receive those Germans whose presence abroad is deemed by your Government to be contrary to the national interest. You will likewise permit the re-entry of German and former German nationals who desire to return permanently but in view of restricted facilities you will give priority to those who are willing and able to contribute to the peaceful reconstruction of Germany.

i. You will permit only those Germans to leave Germany who are included in categories approved by Allied agreements or your Government's instructions.

14. Prisoners of War

In carrying out the decision of the Council of Foreign Ministers of 23 April 1947, you will press in the Control Council for the earliest possible return of all German prisoners of war still located in the territories of the Allied Powers and in all other territories.

V

15. General Economic Objectives

The economic objectives of the United States Government in Germany are:

 a. to eliminate industry used solely to manufacture and to reduce industry used chiefly to support the production of arms, ammunition and implements of war;

 b. to exact from Germany reparation for the losses suffered by United Nations as a consequence of German aggression; and

 c. to encourage the German people to rebuild a self-supporting State devoted to peaceful purposes, integrated into the economy of Europe.

Although the economic rehabilitation of Germany, within the framework of these objectives, is the task and responsibility of the German people, you should provide them general policy guidance, assist in the development of a balanced foreign trade and ensure that German efforts are consistent with, and contribute to the fulfillment of your Government's objectives.

16. Economic Disarmament and Reparation

 a. Your Government continues to desire the general fulfillment of the principles of the Potsdam Agreement regarding reparation and industrial disarmament.

 b. Your Government believes that the level of industry eventually agreed upon for Germany as a basis for reparation removals, while eliminating excess industrial capacity which has been used by Germany for the purpose of making war, should not permanently limit Germany's industrial capacity. The German people after the period of reparation removals should not be denied the right, consistent with continued disarmament, to develop their resources for the purpose of achieving higher standards of living.

 c. Your Government does not agree to reparation from Germany greater than that provided by the Potsdam Agreement. Nor does your Government agree to finance the payment of reparation by Germany to other United Nations by increasing its financial outlay in Germany or by postponing the achievement of a self-sustaining German economy. Your Government reaffirms the principle that the proceeds of authorized exports shall be used in the first place for the payment of authorized imports.

 d. You will attempt to obtain Control Council recognition of the principle of compensation for property taken for reparation or where it has been necessary to destroy property under the agreements for economic disarmament, such compensation to constitute a charge against the German economy as a whole. Except in prohibited industries, you will endeavor to ensure, to the greatest extent practicable, that no plant in which there is foreign ownership or control is removed for reparation as long as German-owned plants are available for that purpose.

 e. You will continue to assist in the location of cloaked German-owned assets abroad and where possible you will assist in their liquidation.

17. Restitution

 a. You will proceed, consistent with agreements on restitution reached in the Control Council, to restore such identifiable property other than gold and transport essential to minimum German economy to the government of the country from which it was taken. You will not consent to any extensive program for the replacement of looted or displaced property which has been destroyed or cannot be located whenever such replacement can be accomplished only at the expense of reparation, a self-sustaining German economy, or the cultural heritage of the German people.

b. You will turn over monetary gold uncovered in Germany to the Tripartite Gold Commission in Brussels for distribution in accordance with the terms of the Paris Act on Reparation.[1]

c. In accordance with JCS 1570/9, you will make available for the rehabilitation and resettlement of non-repatriable victims of German action valuable personal property looted from Nazi victims which is not restitutable.

d. It is the policy of your Government that persons and organizations deprived of their property as a result of National Socialist persecution should either have their property returned or be compensated therefor and that persons who suffered personal damage or injury through National Socialist persecution should receive indemnification in German currency. With respect to heirless and unclaimed property subject to internal restitution you will designate appropriate successor organizations.

18. *Economic Unity and Recovery*

a. Your Government is desirous of securing agreement in the Control Council to the treatment of Germany as an economic unit, the formulation of common policies in all matters affecting Germany as a whole, and the establishment of central Germany administrative agencies for the purpose of implementing such common policies in the fields of finance, transport, communications, agriculture, economics (including industry and foreign trade) and such other fields as the Control Council may consider necessary and appropriate.

b. Your Government likewise desires to secure the adoption of a production and foreign trade program for Germany as a whole which should be directed toward an increasing standard of living in Germany and the attainment at the earliest practicable date of a self-sustaining German economy. Such a program should give highest priority to increased production of coal, food and export goods; provide for such allocation and distribution of German indigenous output and approved imports throughout Germany as are necessary to carry out the production program and attain the agreed standard of living; ensure full payment for all goods and services exported from Germany (other than reparation or restitution) in approved imports or in foreign exchange which can be utilized for the payment of approved imports, and provide for the pooling of all export proceeds to be made available, first to meet the import needs of Germany as a whole for such time and in such amount as may hereafter be determined, and secondly to compensate the occupying powers for past expenditures pursuant to terms and conditions to be established hereafter, priority in the latter case being given to payment of costs sustained for essential imports in direct proportion to the expenditures made by the occupying powers.

---

[1] Department of State Bulletin, January 27, 1946, p. 114.

c. In cases where the restoration of normal international commercial relations between Germany and the rest of Europe would involve an increase of US dollar expenditures for the government of Germany, or a delay in the attainment of a self-supporting German economy at an appropriate standard of living, funds for German expenditures shall be increased, or the German economy compensated through provision by the US of sufficient relief monies to the country or countries so benefited to enable them to pay Germany. You will consult other European countries and international organizations representing such countries in matters of German production and trade mentioned above, and ensure that emphasis is given, in the selection of items for export, to goods needed by European countries for their economic recovery and rehabilitation insofar as these countries may provide in payment needed imports for Germany, or foreign exchange which can pay for such imports. Proposed transactions of a substantial nature which would lead to a restoration of general European trade or normal international commercial relations or restore normal trade exchanges between Germany and other European countries but which would not conform to the principles stated in this paragraph should be referred to the US Govt for decision.

d. You will support the removal of existing trade barriers and will encourage the return of foreign trade to normal trade channels.

19. *Finance*

a. Your government views the reorganization of German finances on a sound basis and the attainment of financial stability in Germany as among the main factors essential to German economic recovery along democratic and peaceful lines. To that end, you will endeavor to have the Control Council adopt uniform financial policies in conformity with the principles and the objectives set forth in this directive.

b. Pending agreement in the Control Council, or until receipt of further directive from your government, you will continue to be guided by the following policies in your zone:

(1) you will control, within the scope of your authority, all financial transactions of an international character in order to keep Nazi influence out of the field of finance and prevent outward movements of capital from Germany;

(2) you will exercise general supervision over German public expenditures and measures of taxation in order to insure that they are consistent with the objectives of the Military Government;

(3) you will take such action as may be necessary to prevent the establishment of a centralized German banking system and an undue concentration of financial power, but will encourage the establishment of a central authority for the production, issuance and control of currency and for technical banking supervision. You will also encourage the Germans to reestablish normal banking facilities within the limitation prescribed above and within the present blocking of assets and accounts under Military Government Law No. 52;

(4) you will use the resources of the German economy to the maximum extent possible in order to reduce expenditures from appropriated funds of your government. You are authorized, as provided in the Pots-

dam Agreement, to use the proceeds of exports to pay for imports which you deem essential, subject to strict accounting and auditing procedures;

(5) you will continue to aid economic recovery by collection of full payment for exports of German goods and services; and

(6) you will continue to prevent non-essential imports.

c. You will press for the adoption by the Control Council of a program for financial reform which provides for a substantial and appropriate reduction in outstanding currency and monetary claims, including public and private debt; for the equitable sharing of the costs of war and defeat; and for ancillary measures including adjustments in the wage-price structure necessary to the restoration of balance between the financial structure and the economic realities.

d. (1) You will maintain such accounts and records as may be necessary to reflect the financial operations of the Military Government (U. S.) in Germany, including also such operations undertaken jointly by you with the Military Government in the British and other zones of occupation in Germany.

(2) You will take measures necessary for calculating occupation costs distinguishing those now incurred within Germany and supported by the German economy, and external occupation costs for eventual settlement with Germany. You will endeavor to agree on a definition of occupation costs of both types within the Control Council and to limit and control internal occupation costs on a quadripartite basis.

20. Agriculture

a. In accordance with the decision of 23 April 1947 of the Council of Foreign Ministers, you will ensure the carrying out and completion of land reform in your zone in 1947.

b. You will require the appropriate German authorities to adopt and implement policies and practices which will:

Maximize the production and provide for the effective collection and distribution of agricultural products.

c. You will require the appropriate German authorities to adopt and implement similar policies and practices in respect to forestry and fishing resources.

21. Economic Institutions

a. Pending agreement among the occupying powers you will in your zone prohibit all cartels and cartel-like organizations, and effect a dispersion of ownership and control of German industry through the dissolution of such combines, mergers, holding companies and interlocking directorates which represent an actual or potential restraint of trade or may dominate or substantially influence the policies of governmental agencies. You will not, however, prohibit governmental regulation of prices or monopolies subject to government regulation, in fields where competition is impracticable. In so far as possible, you will coordinate your action in this field with the commanders of other zones of occupation.

b. You will permit the formation and functioning of cooperatives provided they are voluntary in membership, and are organized along democratic lines and do not engage in activities prohibited under the above paragraph.

c. While it is your duty to give the German people an opportunity to learn of the principles and advantages of free enterprise, you will refrain from interfering in the question of public ownership of enterprises in Germany, except to ensure that any choice for or against public ownership is made freely through the normal processes of democratic government. No measure of public ownership shall apply to foreign-owned property unless arrangements which are satisfactory to your Government have been made for the compensation of foreign owners. Pending ultimate decision as to the form and powers of the central German Government, you will permit no public ownership measure which would reserve that ownership to such central government.

d. Pending agreement among the occupying powers, you will limit new foreign investment in your zone of Germany and will continue to ensure that all property, however owned, and all production and manpower in your zone are subject in all respects to the decisions and directives of the Control Council, and to Military Government and German law.

e. (1) You will permit the organization, operation, and free development of trade unions provided that their leaders are responsible to the membership and their aims and practices accord with democratic principles. Any federation of trade unions shall not impair the financial and organizational autonomy of member unions. You will encourage the trade unions to support programs of adult education and to foster an understanding of democratic processes among their members. You will permit trade unions to act in the interests of their members and to bargain collectively regarding wages, hours and working conditions within the framework of such wage and price controls as it may be necessary to maintain.

(2) Trade unions may represent the occupational, economic and social interests of their members in accordance with the authority contained in their constitutions. Their basic functions may include participation with appropriate authorities in the establishment and development of a peaceful economy.

f. You will permit the organization and functioning of work councils on a democratic basis for the representation of the interests of employees in individual enterprises and will not prohibit the cooperation of trade unions therewith.

g. You will also permit the establishment of machinery for the voluntary settlement of industrial disputes.

VI

22. *Cultural Objectives*

Your Government holds that the reeducation of the German people is an integral part of policies intended to help develop a democratic form of government and to restore a stable and peaceful economy; it believes that there should be no forcible break in the cultural unity of Germany, but recognizes the spiritual value of the regional traditions of Germany and wishes to foster them; it is convinced that the manner and purposes of the reconstruction of the national German culture have a vital significance for the future of Germany.

It is, therefore, of the highest importance that you make every effort to secure maximum coordination between the occupying powers of cultural objectives designed to serve the cause of peace. You will encourage German initiative and responsible participation in this work of cultural reconstruction and you will expedite the establishment of these international cultural relations which will overcome the spiritual isolation imposed by National Socialism on Germany and further the assimilation of the German people into the world community of nations.

23. Education

a. In recognition of the fact that evil consequences to all free men flow from the suppression and corruption of truth and that education is a primary means of creating a democratic and peaceful Germany, you will continue to encourage and assist in the development of educational methods, institutions, programs and materials designed to further the creation of democratic attitudes and practices through education. You will require the German *Laender* authorities to adopt and execute educational programs designed to develop a healthy, democratic educational system which will offer equal opportunity to all according to their qualifications.

b. You will continue to effect the complete elimination of all National Socialist, militaristic and aggressively nationalistic influences, practices and teachings from the German educational system.

24. Religious Affairs

a. You will, in the United States Area of Occupation, continue to assure freedom of religion. You will assure protection of religious activity and support these principles in the deliberations of the Control Council.

b. You will give freedom to the Germans to decide all questions concerning the constitution, the religious activity and the amalgamation of purely ecclesiastical bodies.

c. You will continue to take such action as may be necessary to prevent the revival of National Socialist and militaristic activity under the cloak of a religious program or organization.

25. Monuments, Fine Arts, and Archives

a. You will respect, and permit German authorities to protect and preserve, the property of all cultural institutions dedicated to religion, charity, education, the arts and sciences, historic monuments and historic archives, together with their collections and endowments. You will apply the same principle to all other property of cultural value, whether publicly or privately owned, except for institutions and monuments specifically devoted to the perpetuation of National Socialism or to the glorification of the German militaristic tradition.

b. You are authorized to make such use of German records and archives as may be appropriate.

26. Public Information

a. You will, in the United States Area of Occupation, supervise, encourage and assist in the development by the Germans of media of public information designed to advance the political and cultural objectives stated in this directive.

b. You will arrange through the Allied Control Council for the implementation of the decision of 23 April 1947 of the Council of Foreign Ministers on the free exchange of information and democratic ideas by all media in all of Germany.

c. You will develop and maintain organizations and facilities for the operation of media of information, including those sponsored by Military Government, designed to further the objectives of your Government.

27. *Reestablishment of International Cultural Relations*

In furtherance of the program of the reorientation of the German people and the revival of international cultural relations, you will permit and assist the travel into and out of Germany of persons useful for this program within the availability of your facilities. You will also permit and assist, to the extent of your facilities, the free flow of cultural materials to and from Germany.

◇◇◇◇◇◇

67. LEVEL-OF-INDUSTRY TALKS, AUGUST 22-27, 1947 [1]

Revised Plan for Level of Industry in the United States and United Kingdom Zones of Germany, August 29, 1947

[After the war the Allies initially planned a very low level of industry for Germany. It became increasingly evident however that unless the occupying powers were ready to accept responsibility for support of Germany in perpetuity, they would have to allow it to produce enough to support its people. On July 15, 1947, the United States initiated a drastic revision of the original plans by issuing a directive which would have permitted a substantial increase in industrial production in its zone. The occupying powers, however, disagreed with the United States position. In August 1947, a conference among the interested parties resulted in agreement to raise the level of industry in the British and American zones.]

PREAMBLE

In March, 1946, the four occupying powers, acting through the allied control authority, adopted a plan for reparations and the level of post-war German economy. The objectives of the plan were to eliminate Germany's war potential, to provide reparations and yet to leave within Germany the necessary plants and equipment to permit the rebuilding of a viable peaceful economy.

Experience has shown the necessity for revision of the plan which was based on specific assumptions that have not been fulfilled. Neither the bizonal area nor all of Germany can regain economic health under the plan as it now stands. Moreover, it has become increasingly apparent that under present conditions Germany cannot contribute her indispensable part to the economic rehabilitation of Europe as a whole.

The revised plan continues to observe the same objectives as the original plan.

[1] Released to the press simultaneously in Washington, London, and Paris on August 28, 1947. Printed from telegraphic text. Department of State Bulletin, Sept. 7, 1947, pp. 467-472.

Consideration has been given throughout to the necessity for ensuring that the bizonal plan can be assimilated into a plan for Germany as a whole. The offer to the other occupying powers to join the bizonal area in developing a unified German economy still stands. The plan has been developed with due regard to the hope that this offer will be accepted.

I. General Considerations

The industrial capacity retained under the March 1946 plan was estimated to provide production equal to 55% of 1938, which would have been about 70-75% of 1936 production. The effect of the new plan will be to return sufficient capacity in the bizonal area to approximate the level of industry prevailing in Germany in 1936, a year that was not characterized by either boom or depressed conditions.

A. The old plan provided for very sharp cuts in production capacities in the metals, machinery and chemical industries, from which the bulk of reparations were to be obtained. It is impossible to provide a self-sustaining economy in the bizonal area without materially increasing the levels in these industries. Substantially the entire difference between the original and revised plan is in these reparations industries since the original plan already provided for maximum, and in some cases unrealistic, levels for the non-reparations industries. Under the revised plan, capacities in the metals, machinery, and chemical industries will be sufficient to permit production at levels averaging about 5 or 10% less than in 1936. As compared with the war year 1944, the proposed level represents a reduction of 55 to 60%.

B. It must be borne in mind that the bizonal area already has a population at least six million more than in 1936 and by 1952 it may be expected to have a population from 8 to 10 millions greater than pre-war. On the basis of an expected population of 42 to 44 million in the bizonal area in 1952, the per capita production capacity provided in the new plan would be approximately 75% of 1936.

C. In developing the bizonal plan, the overriding requirement has been to provide the level of industry necessary to make the area self-supporting. In determining the levels for the specific industries, for example, steel and machinery, the requirements for experts, for the internal needs of the bizonal area and for trade with the rest of Germany have been taken into account. In evaluating the requirements for trade with the rest of Germany and of imports, account had to be taken of removals of capital equipment from the other zones and Berlin. The potential output of particular industries, therefore, allows for the needs of the rest of Germany through trade, and the capacities retained for this purpose represent requirements of the bizonal area. In other words, the bizonal area, in order to be self-supporting, must obtain the products in which it is deficient either as imports from outside Germany or in trade from the rest of Germany.

II. Requirement for a Balanced Economy

In addition to pre-war foreign trade, the bizonal area must produce a surplus over its internal requirements for trading with the remainder of Germany; this particularly affects requirements for the industrial capacity of steel and steel products, which are the most needed and, therefore, the most dependable trade commodities required by the rest of Germany in exchange for key products essential to the bizonal economy.

A. *Change in price relationships.* World food and raw material prices have increased more rapidly than the prices of manufactured goods since 1936 and this situation seems likely to continue. Consequently, the bizonal area must be prepared to exchange in foreign trade proportionately larger quantities of industrial products in return for necessary food and raw material imports.

B. *Imports in the general way.* The bizonal area accounted for the whole of Germany pre-war food deficit, as the remainder of Germany was about self-sufficient in food stuffs. It is estimated that imports of food, seed and fertilizer sufficient to make possible an essential diet will amount to 1.00 to 1.25 billion dollars at current prices.

1. Industrial imports from the other countries to the bizonal area were approximately RM 1.5 billion, in 1936, which represents at least 1.0 billion dollars at current trade prices. But the altered character of German trade will make it possible to reduce this figure.

2. The invisible items in Germany's foreign trade were approximately balanced before the war. The present calculations, which make no provision for invisibles on either side of the account, may be optimistic.

3. The foregoing considerations lead to the conclusion that the total bizonal requirements from outside of Germany will approximate at least 2.0 billion dollars at current prices. Repayment of advances by the occupying powers would be an addition to these estimates.

C. *Exports.* The 1936 exports from the bizonal area were approximately RM 2.6 billion, which is estimated to represent about 1.75 billion dollars at current prices.

1. These estimates, therefore, indicate that, in addition to trade requirements for the rest of Germany, the bizonal economy will need to export to other countries at least 15% more in volume than in 1936. Since trade between the bizonal area and the rest of Germany is subject to greater uncertainty than former internal trade, the result may be to increase still further the need for trade with other countries.

2. Before the war, the broad fields of metals, machinery, and chemicals accounted for two-thirds of the total exports. Production of textiles, ceramics, and consumer goods can be raised, but the extent to which additional sales above pre-war levels can be sold on the export markets is difficult to predict. Exports from the unrestricted industries would need to be increased approximately 90% if the higher export requirements were provided entirely from the unrestricted industries, which is obviously impracticable. Therefore, the level of exports from the restricted industries will need to be greater than pre-war.

*   *   *

IV. PROHIBITED INDUSTRIES

The production of aluminium, beryllium, vanadium, and magnesium is prohibited under the pervious level of industry plan. No plants in these industries will be made available for reparations purposes pending further review. No change is proposed in the arrangements made under the previous

Industry or branch of industry	Unit	Estimated 1936 production	Revised level	Existing capacity	Revised level as % of 1936	Revised production as % of existing capacity
STEEL	Million tons	14.9	10.7	¹ 19.2	72	56
PRIMARY NON-FERROUS METALS (production):						
Copper, crude	Thousand tons	128	128	134	....	96
Copper, refined	"	....	215	231	....	93
Zinc, refined	"	....	180	180	....	100
Lead, refined	"	....	141	141	....	100
Semi-fabricating and casting:						
Copper and zinc	"	596	535	605	90	88
Lead	"	72.5	52.2	52.2	72	100
MECHANICAL ENGINEERING MACHINERY:						
Heavy machinery	Million rm. (measured in 1936 prices)	619	500	775	80	65
Light machinery	Million rm.	769	916	1,195	119	77
Machine tools	"	206	170	259	83	65
AUTOMOBILES AND TRACTORS:						
Passenger cars	Thousand units	....	160	190	....	84
Commercial vehicles	"	....	61.5	65	....	95
Agricultural and road tractors	"	....	² 19.5	16.5	....	Over 100
FINE MECHANICS AND OPTICS	Million rm. (measured in 1936 prices)	180	248.7	307.7	138	81
ELECTRICAL EQUIPMENT	Million rm.	830	1,237	1,291	149	96
CEMENT	Million tons	7	³ 8.9	¹ 11.4	127	100
CHEMICALS—total	Million rm. (measured in 1936 prices)	2,325	2,271	4,194	98	54
BASIC CHEMICALS	Million rm.	270	283	288	105	98
Synthetic ammonia	"	95	118	118	124	100
Inorganic chemicals	"	180	180	240	100	75
Misc. chemicals (incl. military explosives)	"	1,095	1,066	2,821	97	38
Organic chemicals	"	160	160	225	100	71
Dyestuffs	"	180	173	176	96	98
Pharmaceuticals	"	270	228	263	84	87
Tar distillation	"	75	63	63	84	100

¹ Related capacity.
² Existing capacity is less than proposed level.
³ Production.

322

plan in regard to ball bearings, synthetic ammonia, synthetic rubber, and synthetic gasoline and oil.

◇◇◇◇◇◇

68. LONDON MEETING OF THE COUNCIL OF FOREIGN MINISTERS, NOVEMBER 25 TO DECEMBER 15, 1947: STATEMENT BY SECRETARY MARSHALL [1]

Soviet Disagreement on Fundamental Principles for Germany, December 15, 1947 [2]

[As we have noted above in Part II of this volume, the November 1947 meeting of the Council of Foreign Ministers, which dealt primarily with the German peace settlement, was not successful. The following excerpt from Secretary Marshall's report on the Conference is valuable because it summarizes the main disagreements between the Western powers and the Soviet Union over German issues.]

We have reached quite evidently a fundamental difference regarding the question of reparations. Mr. Molotov's last statement seemed to me a repetition of statements which we largely felt were without foundation. Now at the expense of some repetition of the views Mr. Bevin has just stated, I would like to review the situation as it is seen by the United States Delegation.

The United States hoped there would emerge from this Conference the beginnings of a united and self-respecting Germany which could find its way back to peace and freedom and achieve its own well-being and redemption through cooperative effort with other European countries.

The United States had even higher hopes for an Austrian settlement.

It will be useful, I think, at this point to see just where we are.

We have failed to reach agreement on a treaty for Austria because the Soviet Union has demanded for itself properties and special privileges in Austria in an amount and to an extent which far exceed any rightful claims and which far exceed what a free Austria can afford. If Soviet claims were admitted, it would be at the price of Austrian independence and in violation of past agreements.

At Moscow the United States, the United Kingdom and France, although differing in some details, found a common basis for agreement on the essential unagreed article in the Austrian treaty—the problem of German assets. The Soviet Union was in disagreement. To resolve our differences we appointed a treaty commission which for five months conferred in Vienna last summer. Again three delegations found a common approach. Again the Soviet Union was in disagreement. At the present meeting the French Delegation presented a new proposal for a concrete settlement which sought to avoid the problems that had prevented agreement. To three delegations that proposal appeared to present a practical basis for settlement. On December 4 it was rejected by Mr. Molotov, who added that he had no new proposals to make on the

[1] Department of State Bulletin, December 28, 1947, p. 1247.
[2] Department of State Bulletin, December 28, 1947, pp. 1247-1248.

subject. Thus the Soviet Delegation has persistently blocked agreement by reason of its unjustified demands on Austria.

As regards Germany, taking first the subject of frontiers, we have been unable to agree on what we mean by Germany. Three delegations are in accord that the Saar territory should be detached from Germany and economically integrated with France. The Soviet Union does not agree.

With respect to the eastern boundary of Germany, the Potsdam protocol clearly provided that the "final delineation of the western frontier of Poland should await the peace settlement".

The United States believes that an effort should be made to establish a frontier which, while it would compensate Poland, would not become a formidable economic barrier preventing Germany access to food and raw materials from this eastern area upon which it has heavily depended.

Three of the delegations agree that boundary commissions be at once established to examine frontier questions. The Soviet Union rejects this proposal. So we neither agree on what Germany is to be nor do we agree on establishing commissions to study these vital boundary problems.

In examining the discussions on economic principles, we have progressed only in agreeing to procedures without substance.

We have failed to reach agreement on sharing of the financial burdens. An ostensible agreement on the equitable distribution of indigenous resources is deprived of all meaning by the Soviet demand for a continuation of present Soviet withdrawals of current German production for reparations.

The Soviet Union has refused to furnish vitally necessary information with respect to reparations removals. Thus we have been asked to reach agreement while information essential to such agreement is withheld by the Soviet representatives.

The Soviet Delegation has refused to agree to the relinquishment of property interests in Germany unilaterally seized under guise of reparations. As matters now stand a large share of the produce of the eastern zone of Germany is drawn off for the Soviet account. An important part of its industry has been placed in a gigantic Soviet trust which enjoys special privilege and which is put above German law, presumably in perpetuity.

These Soviet practices in eastern Germany have prevented Germany from playing its part in the recovery of Europe. In fact they have greatly increased the necessity for the outside aid provided by the United States and the United Kingdom to enable western Germany to live. Nevertheless, the Soviet representatives have chosen to charge that this aid has as its purpose to use western Germany as a "strategic base against the democratic states of Europe" and to advance "expansionist aims." Apart from the complete absurdity of these charges, to discontinue this aid to some 40 million Germans in the U. S. and U. K. zones until they have become self-supporting would doom them to mass starvation.

The Soviet Union demands reparations for itself and Poland of 10 billion dollars at 1938 values, which is at least 15 billion dollars today. These reparation payments to an undisclosed degree would take the form of current production over 20 years. This demand is not in accordance with the Potsdam agreement. It is utterly impossible of achievement on practical economic grounds. It implies the establishment of an economic power so comprehensive that it would be in reality a power of life and death over any German government.

It was accepted by all at Moscow that full agreement on economic principles was essential to the establishment of political unification. We are unable to agree on what shall be the area of the German economy; we cannot agree how to make German resources available to Germany as a whole, a condition prerequisite to the revival of German economy; we are confronted with a demand for reparations in excess of the Potsdam agreement which would make a German government subservient to its reparations creditor. It is therefore clear that agreement can be reached only under conditions which would not only enslave the German people but would seriously retard the recovery of all Europe.

If real economic unity could have been established, the United States would have been ready for the German people to be immediately accorded, under agreed controls, self-government with the authority, responsibility, and initiative this entails. But free government cannot succeed under conditions of economic serfdom. True political and economic unity would require a free movement of goods, persons, and ideas throughout Germany and the establishment of a rule of law and political freedom which the occupying powers themselves would respect.

A German government of any type established to function in present conditions and under the supervision of a control council reflecting these basic disagreements would be powerless. In such circumstances a German government would be only a façade, and its establishment would subtract from rather than add to a real union of the German people. It is useless to debate the characteristics of a German government when actual governmental power would be elsewhere.

The simple fact is, the present division of Germany has been caused by the policies and practices of the occupying powers themselves. Only the occupying powers can create German unity in the present circumstances. That is why the United States has consistently pressed for certain fundamental decisions by the occupying powers themselves as the absolutely essential first step for the achievement of a unified Germany.

Three delegations at this conference have registered their willingness to take these decisions here and now. The Soviet Union alone refuses to agree.

In view of these facts, it seems impossible at this time to make practical progress. Therefore, I reluctantly conclude that no useful purpose would be served by a debate on the other points on our agenda; and I suggest that the Council of Foreign Ministers might now consider adjournment of this session.

◇◇◇◇◇◇

69. AGREEMENTS ON GERMANY BY THE UNITED STATES, THE UNITED KINGDOM, AND FRANCE, APRIL 8, 1949 [1]

[By the fall of 1947 the United States had reached the conclusion that a strong central government and a self-sustaining German economy were vital to a sound European economy and to the security of that continent. But the

[1] Department of State Bulletin, April 17, 1949, pp. 499-501.

French were apprehensive of Soviet threats that the U.S.S.R. would not tolerate a united Western Germany. Finally on April 8, 1949, the French agreed to brave the Russian threats and consented to the uniting of Western Germany. The occupying powers resolved their differences, merged the French zone with the Bizone thus constituting a new Trizone, proclaimed an Occupation Statute, and paved the way for the establishment of a government for Western Germany.]

(a) Communiqué

The Foreign Ministers of the United States, United Kingdom, and France have discussed in Washington the whole range of issues now pending in connection with Germany and have arrived at complete agreement.

The text of an occupation statute in a new and simpler form has been approved and is being transmitted to the German Parliamentary Council at Bonn. Agreement was reached on the basic principles to govern the exercise of Allied powers and responsibilities and also the tripartite Allied control machinery. The Foreign Ministers confirmed and approved agreements on the subject of plant dismantling, prohibited and restricted industries, and the establishment of an International Ruhr Authority, all of which were recently negotiated in London.

The occupation statute will define the powers to be retained by the occupation authorities upon the establishment of the German Federal Republic and set forth basic procedures for the operation of Allied supervision. Subject only to the limitations of the statute, the German Federal State and the participating Laender will have full legislative, executive, and judicial powers, in accordance with the basic law and with their respective constitutions. The statute aims to permit the German people to exercise democratic self-government. Provision is made for a review of the terms of the statute after a year in force.

With the establishment of the German Federal Republic, there will be a marked change in the organization to carry out occupation responsibilities. Military Government as such will be terminated, and the functions of the Allied authorities will become mainly supervisory. Each of the Allied establishments in Germany will come under the direction of a High Commissioner, aside from the occupation forces which will remain headed by military commanders. The three High Commissioners together will constitute an Allied High Commission, which will be the supreme Allied agency of control. In order to permit the German Federal Republic to exercise increased responsibility for domestic affairs and to reduce the burden of occupation costs, staff personnel shall be kept to a minimum.

The German Government authorities will be at liberty to take administrative and legislative action, and such action will have validity if not disapproved by Allied authorities. There will be certain limited fields in which the Allies will reserve the right to take direct action themselves or to direct German authorities to take action. However, these fields will be limited, and aside from security matters, the exercise of direct powers by the Allies is regarded in many instances as self-liquidating in nature.

It was agreed that a major objective of the three Allied Governments was to encourage and facilitate the closest integration, on a mutually beneficial basis, of the German people, under a democratic federal state within the framework of a European association. In this connection it is understood that the German Federal Republic will negotiate a separate bilateral ECA agreement with the United States and should participate as a full member in the Organization for European Economic Cooperation, thus becoming a responsible partner in the European Recovery Program.

(b) Proclamation of Occupation Statute

In the exercise of the supreme authority which is retained by the Governments of France, the United States and the United Kingdom,

We, GENERAL PIERRE KOENIG, Military Governor and Commander-in-Chief of the French Zone of Germany,

General LUCIUS D. CLAY, Military Governor and Commander-in-Chief of the United States Zone of Germany, and

General SIR BRIAN HUBERT ROBERTSON, Military Governor and Commander-in-Chief of the British Zone of Germany,

DO HEREBY JOINTLY PROCLAIM THE FOLLOWING OCCUPATION STATUTE:

1. During the period in which it is necessary that the occupation continue, the Governments of France, the United States and the United Kingdom desire and intend that the German people shall enjoy self-government to the maximum possible degree consistent with such occupation. The Federal State and the participating Laender shall have, subject only to the limitations in this Instrument, full legislative, executive and judicial powers in accordance with the Basic Law and with their respective constitutions.

2. In order to ensure the accomplishment of the basic purposes of the occupation, powers in the following fields are specifically reserved, including the right to request and verify information and statistics needed by the occupation authorities:

(a) disarmament and demilitarization, including related fields of scientific research, prohibitions and restrictions on industry and civil aviation;

(b) controls in regard to the Ruhr, restitution, reparations, decartelization, deconcentration, nondiscrimination in trade matters, foreign interests in Germany and claims against Germany;

(c) foreign affairs, including international agreements made by or on behalf of Germany;

(d) displaced persons and the admission of refugees;

(e) protection, prestige, and security of Allied forces, dependents, employees, and representatives, their immunities and satisfaction of occupation costs and their other requirements;

(f) respect for the Basic Law and the Land constitutions;

(g) control over foreign trade and exchange;

(h) control over internal action, only to the minimum extent necessary to ensure use of funds, food and other supplies in such manner as to reduce to a minimum the need for external assistance to Germany;

(i) control of the care and treatment in German prisons of persons charged before or sentenced by the courts or tribunals of the occupying powers or occupation authorities; over the carrying out of sentences imposed on them; and over questions of amnesty, pardon or release in relation to them.

3. It is the hope and expectation of the Governments of France, the United States and the United Kingdom that the occupation authorities will not have occasion to take action in fields other than those specifically reserved above. The occupation authorities, however, reserve the right, acting under instructions of their Governments, to resume, in whole or in part, the exercise of full authority if they consider that to do so is essential to security or to preserve democratic government in Germany or in pursuance of the international obligations of their governments. Before so doing, they will formally advise the appropriate German authorities of their decision and of the reasons therefor.

4. The German Federal Government and the governments of the Laender shall have the power, after due notification to the occupation authorities, to legislate and act in the fields reserved to these authorities, except as the occupation authorities otherwise specifically direct, or as such legislation or action would be inconsistent with decisions or actions taken by the occupation authorities themselves.

5. Any amendment of the Basic Law will require the express approval of the occupation authorities before becoming effective. Land constitutions, amendments thereof, all other legislation, and any agreements made between the Federal State and foreign governments, will become effective twenty-one days after official receipt by the occupation authorities unless previously disapproved by them, provisionally or finally. The occupation authorities will not disapprove legislation unless in their opinion it is inconsistent with the Basic Law, a Land Constitution, legislation or other directives of the occupation authorities themselves or the provisions of this Instrument, or unless it constitutes a grave threat to the basic purposes of the occupation.

6. Subject only to the requirements of their security, the occupation authorities guarantee that all agencies of the occupation will respect the civil rights of every person to be protected against arbitrary arrest, search or seizure; to be represented by counsel; to be admitted to bail as circumstances warrant; to communicate with relatives; and to have a fair and prompt trial.

7. Legislation of the occupation authorities enacted before the effective date of the Basic Law shall remain in force until repealed or amended by the occupation authorities in accordance with the following provisions:

(a) legislation inconsistent with the foregoing will be repealed or amended to make it consistent herewith;

(b) legislation based upon the reserved powers, referred to in paragraph 2 above, will be codified;

(c) legislation not referred to in (a) and (b) will be repealed by the occupation authorities on request from appropriate German authorities.

8. Any action shall be deemed to be the act of the occupation authorities under the powers herein reserved, and effective as such under this Instrument, when taken or evidenced in any manner provided by any agreement between them. The occupation authorities may in their discretion effectuate their decisions either directly or through instructions to the appropriate German authorities.

9. After 12 months and in any event within 18 months of the effective date of this Instrument the occupying powers will undertake a review of its provisions in the light of experience with its operation and with a view to extending the jurisdiction of the German authorities in the legislative, executive and judicial fields.

(c) *Trizonal Fusion Agreement for Western Germany* [1]

The Governments of the United Kingdom, France and the United States agree to enter into a trizonal fusion agreement prior to the entry into effect of the Occupation Statute. The representatives of the three occupying powers will make the necessary arrangements to establish tripartite control machinery for western zones of Germany, which will become effective at the time of the establishment of a provisional German government. The following provisions agreed by the Governments of the United Kingdom, France and the United States shall form the basis of those arrangements:

1. An Allied High Commission composed of one High Commissioner of each occupying power or his representative shall be the supreme Allied agency of control.

2. The nature and extent of controls exercised by the Allied High Commission shall be in harmony with the Occupation Statute and international agreements.

3. In order to permit the German Federal Republic to exercise increased responsibilities over domestic affairs and to reduce the burden of occupation costs, staff personnel shall be kept to a minimum.

4. In the exercise of the powers reserved to the Occupation Authorities to approve amendments to the Federal Constitution, the decisions of the Allied High Commission shall require unanimous agreement.

5. In cases in which the exercise of, or failure to exercise, the powers reserved under paragraph 2 (*g*) of the Occupation Statute would increase the need for assistance from United States Government appropriated funds, there shall be a system of weighted voting. Under such system the representatives of the Occupation Authorities will have a voting strength proportionate to the funds made available to Germany by their respective governments. This provision shall not, however, reduce the present United States predominant voice in JEIA and JFEA while these organizations, or any successor organization to them, continue in existence and are charged with the performance of any of their present functions. No action taken hereunder shall be contrary to any inter-government agreement among the signatories or to the principles of non-discrimination.

6. On all other matters action shall be by majority vote.

7. (*a*) If a majority decision alters or modifies any inter-governmental agreement which relates to any of the subjects listed in paragraph 2 (*a*) and 2 (*b*) of the Occupation Statute, any dissenting High Commissioner may appeal to his Government. This appeal shall serve to suspend the decision pending agreement between the three governments.

(*b*) If a High Commissioner considers that a majority decision conflicts with any inter-governmental agreement which relates to any of the subjects in

1 Department of State Bulletin, May 8, 1949, pp. 589-590. Release to the press April 26, 1949.

paragraph 2 (*a*) and 2 (*b*) of the Occupation Statute or with the fundamental principles for the conduct of Germany's external relations or with matters essential to the security, prestige, and requirements of the occupying forces, he may appeal to his Government. Such an appeal shall serve to suspend action for 30 days, and thereafter unless two of the Governments indicate that the grounds do not justify further suspension.

(*c*) If such appeal is from an action of the Allied High Commission either declining to disapprove or deciding to disapprove German legislation, such legislation shall be provisionally disapproved for the duration of the appeal period.

8. A High Commissioner who considers that a decision made by less than unanimous vote involving any other matter reserved by the Occupation Statute is not in conformity with basic tripartite policies regarding Germany or that a Land constitution, or an amendment thereto, violates the Basic Law, may appeal to his government. An appeal in this case shall serve to suspend action for a period not to exceed twenty-one days from the date of the decision unless all three governments agree otherwise. If such appeal is from an action of the Allied High Commission either declining to disapprove or deciding to disapprove German legislation, such legislation shall be provisionally disapproved for the duration of the appeal period.

9. All powers of the Allied High Commission shall be uniformly exercised in accordance with tripartite policies and directives. To this end in each Land the Allied High Commission shall be represented by a single Land Commissioner who shall be solely responsible to it for all tripartite affairs. In each Land the Land Commissioner shall be a national of the Allied Power in whose zone the Land is situated. Outside his own zone each High Commissioner will delegate an observer to each of the Land Commissioners for purposes of consultation and information. Nothing in this paragraph shall be construed to limit the functions of bodies established pursuant to inter-governmental agreement.

10. To the greatest extent possible, all directives and other instruments of control shall be addressed to the federal and/or Land authorities.

11. The Trizonal Fusion Agreement will continue in force until altered by agreement among the governments.

70. LIMITATIONS ON CERTAIN INDUSTRIES IN GERMANY [1]

Agreement by United States, United Kingdom, and France, April 13, 1949

[Following World War II, the victorious powers agreed that all German munitions and war plants were to be destroyed or removed. Those industries, which served both war and peace purposes, were to be limited in number and capacity. ECA, shortly after it came into existence in 1948, appointed an Industrial Advisory Committee to examine the progress of the dismantling of industrial plants and the relationship of such dismantling to German recovery.

[1] Department of State Bulletin, April 24, 1949, pp. 526-531.

On January 12, 1949, the Committee made its report and recommendations; and most of the latter found their way into the following agreement concluded by the U. S., the U. K. and France. This agreement sets forth in specific terms the prohibitions and limitations under which German industries were to operate.]

The Departments of State and Army made public the text of an agreement which was announced on April 13 by the Military Governors of the United States, the United Kingdom, and France, in Germany, regarding limitations to be placed upon certain industries in Germany in the interest of security. The agreement embodies recommendations recently formulated by representatives of the three Governments in London and approved by the three Foreign Ministers on April 8, 1949, in Washington, as part of the general agreement which they reached regarding Germany, in order to permit the establishment of a German Federal Government which could form a part of the European community.

The question of prohibited and restricted industries was considered by the three Governments in conjunction with the review of the reparation dismantling program to bring that program into harmony with the European Recovery Program. In consequence, coordinated agreements were reached by the three Governments on both subjects. A separate announcement was made with regard to reparations.

Pursuant to instructions received from their respective governments to conclude the agreement hereinafter set forth, concerning prohibited and limited industries in the United States, United Kingdom and French Occupied Areas of Germany (hereinafter referred to for the purposes of this Agreement as Germany), the United States, United Kingdom and French Military Governors and Commanders-in-Chief hereby promulgate the following agreement, effective forthwith:

Article I

The prohibitions laid down in this Agreement shall remain in force until the peace settlement.

The limitations laid down in this Agreement shall remain in force until 1st January, 1953, or until the peace settlement, whichever is the earlier, and thereafter as may be agreed.

Should no peace settlement have been concluded by 30th June, 1952, the Military Governors shall forthwith review these limitations in the light of the conditions then prevailing, taking into account the requirements of security of the Allied Powers, the state and effectiveness of the arrangements made to preserve security, and the requirements of European Recovery. Should the Military Governors be unable within 90 days from 30th June, 1952, to reach agreement on the limitations which in the absence of an earlier peace settlement shall be continued after 1st January, 1953, the matter shall be considered forthwith by the three Governments.

Article II

Action within the discretion of the Military Governors under the terms of the Agreement shall be taken by unanimous decision.

Article III

The production or manufacture of the following substances and war materials shall be prohibited, and all plants and equipment for their production or manufacture not already removed or destroyed shall, as soon as possible, be removed from Germany or destroyed.

(*a*) The items listed in Schedule A to Control Council Law No. 43 (at Annex A)

(*b*) Primary Magnesium

(*c*) Beryllium

Article IV

The production, import, export, transport, storage, use and possession of radioactive materials will be the subject of legislation by the Military Governors.

Article V

1. The production of synthetic rubber and butadiene shall be prohibited.

2. In order to give effect to the foregoing prohibitions, facilities for copolymerization, facilities for research and testing of synthetic rubber, and facilities for the production of butadiene at the Huls, Ludwigshafen and Leverkusen plants shall be removed or destroyed.

Article VI

1. The production of petrol, oil and lubricants directly or indirectly from coal or brown coal by the Bergius hydrogenation process, the Fischer-Tropsch synthesis, or analogous processes, shall be prohibited except, temporarily, to the extent inseparable from the production of hydrocarbon waxes for the manufacture of synthetic fatty acids for the production of washing materials.

2. The synthesis of hydrocarbon waxes by the Fischer-Tropsch process shall be permitted only so long as the supply of fats and oils available in Germany is inadequate for the manufacture of sufficient washing materials without the use of synthetic fatty acids, and in any event not beyond 31st December, 1949.

3. The Fischer-Tropsch plants not now engaged in the synthesis of hydrocarbon waxes shall, as soon as possible, be removed from Germany or destroyed. The two Fischer-Tropsch plants engaged in the synthesis of hydrocarbon waxes shall, as soon as possible after production ceases, be removed from Germany or destroyed.

4. All Bergius plants except the Wesseling plant shall, as soon as possible, be removed from Germany or destroyed. The whole Wesseling plant shall be retained, and may be used for the refining of natural petroleum, for the hydrogenation of heavy residues from such refining and for the synthesis of ammonia and methanol.

Article VII

The manufacture of electronic valves shall be limited to a list to be drawn up by experts and published by the Military Governors of permitted types that shall not exceed either 10 watts dissipation or 250 megacycles frequency, subject to the authority of the Military Governors, acting upon the advice of the Military Security Board, to permit by license the manufacture of types exceeding 10 watts dissipation (but not exceeding 250 megacycles frequency) in case of necessity.

Article VIII

1. The capacity of the following industries shall be limited as stated below:

(a) *Steel,* to that remaining after the removal of reparations;

(b) *Electric arc and high frequency furnace steel* furnace capacity, to that remaining after the removal of reparations;

(c) *Primary Aluminium,* to that sufficient to produce 85,000 tons of primary aluminum a year;

(d) *Shipbuilding,* to that remaining after the removal as reparations of the following yards in addition to those four that have already been made available for reparations:

CIND 1206 Germania Werft, Kiel

CIND 1235 Deutsche Werke, Kiel

CIND 1287 Deutsche Werft Reiherstieg, Hamburg;

(e) *Ball and Roller Bearings,* to that remaining after the removal as reparations of plant and equipment calculated to leave in Germany capacity sufficient to produce 33 million units a year on a one-shift basis, or present capacity, whichever is the less;

(f) *Synthetic Ammonia,* to that remaining after the removal of reparations;

(g) *Chlorine,* to that remaining after the removal of reparations;

(h) *Styrene,* to 20,000 tons annual working capacity.

2. In order that the total authorised capacity of the industries limited in paragraph 1 above shall not be exceeded, no enterprise shall be permitted, (except under license from the Military Governors, acting upon the advice of the Military Security Board) to increase the productive capacity of any of its plant or equipment that is engaged or partly engaged in any of the industries listed in this article, whether it is proposed to effect the increase by the extension of existing facilities, the construction of new facilities, or the addition of new equipment. The construction of new plant and equipment, and the replacement or reconstruction of that removed or destroyed shall likewise be prohibited except under license from the Military Governors, acting upon the advice of the Military Security Board. The Military Security Board will ensure that obsolete or wornout plant or equipment the replacement of which by new has been licensed is removed from Germany or destroyed.

Article IX

1. The production of steel shall be limited to 11.1 million ingot tons a year.

2. The production of primary aluminum shall be limited to 85,000 tons of primary aluminum a year. No specific limitation shall be placed on imports of bauxite and alumina; they shall, however, be controlled to prevent stockpiling in excess of a number of months' supply, to be determined by the Military Governors.

3. The production of styrene shall be limited to 20,000 tons a year.

Article X

1. The manufacture of the following shall be prohibited:

(a) *Machine tools* or other manufacturing equipment specifically designed for the production of weapons, ammunition or other implements of war.

(b) Attachments, devices, tools or other objects having no normal, peace-time use and specifically designed to convert or adapt machine tools or other manufacturing equipment to the production of weapons, ammunition or other implements of war.

2. The manufacture of the types of machine tools listed at Annex B shall be prohibited except under licence from the Military Governors, acting upon the advice of the Military Security Board, which licence will normally be granted unless the Military Governors have reason to think that the tools are not intended for peaceful production.

Article XI

1. The construction of ships whose size or speed does not exceed the limits contained in the following table shall be permitted in Germany, provided that no ocean-going ships shall be constructed until a German coastal fleet adequate for the requirements for European and German recovery has been reconstituted. (It has been estimated that Germany will require for this purpose 517,000 G. R. T., including 360,000 G. R. T. of dry cargo ships.)

Dry cargo ships   12 knots 7,200 G. R. T.
Tankers   12 knots 7,200 G. R. T.
Small craft   12 knots 650 G. R. T.
    (including fishing vessels and ships other than cargo-carrying craft)
Coastal vessels   12 knots 2,700 G. R. T.

2. Notwithstanding the above provisions, Germany shall be permitted during the period of this Agreement to acquire abroad up to 100,000 G. R. T. of tankers of not more than 14 knots speed and 10,700 G. R. T., being not less than 16,000 dwt; and up to 300,000 G. R. T. of dry cargo ships of not more than 12 knots speed and 7,200 G. R. T.

3. In order to provide guidance for the Military Governors, a committee of experts is to be constituted by the Governments of the United States, the United Kingdom and France with instructions to prepare, within three months, a report outlining the types of ships, excluding ships primarily for passengers, which may be required by Germany, although they exceed in one respect or another the limits in paragraph 1 above. The committee shall also determine those features of design, construction, propulsion machinery, etc., which would facilitate use for or conversion for war purposes or which do not conform to normal merchant marine practice and should therefore be prohibited. The recommendations of the committee shall be transmitted to the Military Governors for action in accordance with the procedure outlined in the following paragraph.

4. The Military Governors, acting upon the advice of the Military Security Board, may permit by licence the construction or acquisition of ships exceeding in some respects the limitations on speed and tonnage shown in paragraph 1 above, in order to provide for ships having special purposes or functions. The Military Governors shall take into account the requirements of security and the necessity that ships shall be capable of operating economically in the trades or routes for which they are intended.

5. Notwithstanding anything contained herein to the contrary, the Military Governors, acting upon the advice of the Military Security Board, may authorise under licence the construction of vessels having a greater speed than

12 knots that are shown to be essential for such purposes as the prevention of smuggling and illegal fishing, frontier control, fire fighting, or for the use of pilots or the civil police.

6. The Military Governors shall promulgate the legislation necessary to give effect to the foregoing provisions; and upon the coming into effect of such legislation the operation of the relevant provisions of Control Council Directives Nos. 33, 37, 44 and 45 shall be suspended. Until the promulgation of such legislation, the building of any ships other than those permitted under the relevant provisions of Control Council Directives Nos. 33, 37, 44 and 45 shall remain prohibited.

Article XII

Nothing in this Agreement shall be interpreted as impairing or reducing the powers with which the Military Security Board is vested.

◇◇◇◇◇◇

71. AGREEMENT FOR AN INTERNATIONAL AUTHORITY FOR THE RUHR, SIGNED APRIL 28, 1949 [1]

[The control of the vast industrial resources of the Ruhr was the subject of considerable controversy among the victorious powers from VE (Victory in Europe) day on. The U.S.S.R. wished to share both in the production of the area and its control. The London agreement of April 28, 1949, established an international authority for the Ruhr in which Belgium, France, Luxembourg, the Netherlands, the United Kingdom, the United States, and Germany were to participate. Due to differences over reparations and the whole German problem, the Soviet Union was not a party to the final arrangements.]

Whereas international security and general economic recovery require:
>that the resources of the Ruhr shall not in the future be used for the purpose of aggression but shall be used in the interests of peace;
>that access to the coal, coke and steel of the Ruhr, which was previously subject to the exclusive control of Germany, be in the future assured on an equitable basis to the countries cooperating in the common economic good;

Whereas it is desirable for the political and economic well being of the countries of Europe cooperating in the common economic good, including a democratic Germany, that there be close association of their economic life;

Whereas it is important that trade between the countries mentioned in the preceding paragraph should be facilitated by lowering trade barriers and by any other means;

Now therefore, in furtherance of the foregoing purposes and in order to establish an international control in the Ruhr in conformity with the agreed statement of principles contained in Annex C to the Report signed in London on the first day of June, 1948 at the conclusion of the Six Power Talks on

[1] Department of State Bulletin, January 9. 1949, pp. 46-52.

Germany, the Governments of Belgium, France, Luxembourg, the Netherlands, the United Kingdom of Great Britain and Northern Ireland and the United States of America have agreed as follows:

PART I: THE AUTHORITY

ARTICLE 1

There is hereby established an International Authority for the Ruhr, hereinafter referred to as the *"Authority"*, the composition, powers and functions of which are set forth herein.

ARTICLE 2

The members of the Authority shall be the Signatory Governments and Germany.

ARTICLE 3

The Authority shall consist of a Council composed of representatives of the Signatory Governments and, subject to the provisions of Article 4, of Germany. The Council shall be assisted by a Secretariat, headed by an Executive Secretary. The members shall also appoint alternate representatives.

ARTICLE 4

(a) When a German Government is established, it may appoint a delegate to the Authority with the right to attend meetings of the Council. At such time as the German Government becomes entitled to cast the votes allocated

ADMINISTRATIVE DIVISIONS OF GERMANY

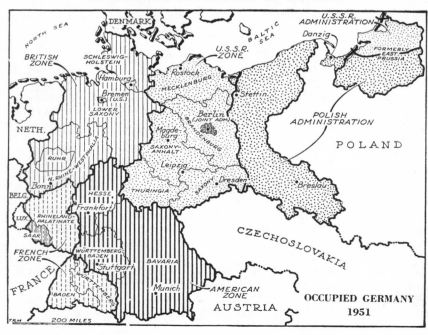

OCCUPIED GERMANY
1951

to Germany, as provided in Article 9 (c), it may appoint a representative on the Council and an alternate.

(b) The Occupation Authorities concerned shall be represented at the Council by one of their nationals jointly designated by them, until such time as the votes allocated to Germany are cast by the German representative.

ARTICLE 5

The Headquarters of the Authority shall be at such place in Land North Rhine-Westphalia as the Council may determine.

* * *

PART II: INTERNAL ORGANIZATION AND PROCEDURE

* * *

ARTICLE 9

(a) The voting rights of the several members of the Authority in its Council shall be:

Belgium	1 vote
France	3 votes
Germany	3 votes
Luxembourg	1 vote
The Netherlands	1 vote
The United Kingdom	3 votes
The United States	3 votes

(b) Eight favorable votes shall be sufficient for every decision of the Authority, except as provided in Articles 13, 14, 17 and 24.

(c) The votes allocated to Germany shall be cast as a unit by the joint representative of the Occupation Authorities concerned appointed as provided in Article 4, until the Occupying Powers concerned determine that the German Government, by accession or by other means, has assumed the responsibilities placed upon Germany by the present Agreement. Thereafter such votes shall be cast by the German representative.

* * *

ARTICLE 11

The annual budget shall be prepared by the Executive Secretary for approval by the Council.

ARTICLE 12

The Authority shall conduct its business in English, French and German, of which English and French shall be the official languages. Authoritative German texts of documents shall be provided as necessary.

* * *

PART III: FUNCTIONS

ARTICLE 14

(a) The Authority shall make a division of coal, coke and steel from the Ruhr as between German consumption and export. Such division shall:—

(i) ensure adequate access to supplies of these products by countries co-operating in the common economic good, taking into account the essential needs of Germany;

(ii) be in accordance with the terms of any agreement among the Occupying Powers with respect to the allocation of coal, coke or steel, which is in force at the time the division is made;

(iii) be consistent with the objectives set forth in the Convention for European Economic Cooperation and with any program approved, or decision taken, by the Organization for European Economic Co-operation, which is applicable to the period for which such division is made.

(b) The export allocations of the Authority shall be in terms of minimum amounts of coal, coke and finished or semi-finished steel to be made available from the Ruhr for export. The Authority shall have the power to express these export allocations in terms of various qualities or types of coal, coke and finished or semi-finished steel. Exceptionally, the Authority may make an allocation of pig-iron if at any time it decides by twelve affirmative votes that such an allocation is necessary in order to ensure adequate access to supplies of pig-iron. In making export allocations of finished or semi-finished steel, the Authority shall be bound by, and shall act within, any agreements relating to the level of steel production in Germany which are in force at the time and to which the Occupying Powers concerned are party.

(c) Before the Authority begins to exercise its functions under this Article, it will agree with the Occupation Authorities concerned on a procedure for co-ordinating the decisions of the Authority with the preparation of proposed programs and plans for submission to the Organization for European Economic Co-operation. This procedure shall be reviewed at any time at the request of any member, and in any case at the end of the Control Period or at such earlier time as may be agreed upon by the Occupying Powers.

ARTICLE 15

The Authority shall have the right to examine transport, price and trade practices, quotas, tariffs, and other governmental measures or commercial arrangements instituted or permitted by the German authorities which affect the coal, coke or steel of the Ruhr. If the Authority determines that such practices, measures or arrangements are artificial or discriminatory and are of such a nature as:—

(i) to impede access by other countries to the coal, coke or steel of the Ruhr,

(ii) to distort the movements of Ruhr coal, coke or steel in international trade, or

(iii) otherwise to prejudice the accomplishment of the purposes of the present Agreement,

the Authority shall decide that such practices, measures or arrangements shall be appropriately modified or terminated. In making its determinations under this Article the Authority shall have due regard for the requirements of international peace and security, for Germany's obligations under the Convention for European Economic Co-operation, and for the need of the German authorities to afford legitimate protection to the commercial and financial position of Germany in international trade.

ARTICLE 16

(a) During the Control Period, or until such earlier time as may be agreed upon by the Occupying Powers, the Authority shall bring to the attention of the Occupation Authorities concerned measures which would ensure, and after such period or time the Authority shall itself ensure, in conformity with any international agreements relating to the protection of foreign interests in Germany in force at the time, to which the Signatory Governments are party,

(i) the safeguard and protection of foreign interests in coal, coke and steel enterprises in the Ruhr, and

(ii) the protection of such enterprises involving foreign interests from the application of discriminatory measures in any sector of their activity; provided that when and to the extent that the protection of such foreign interests or enterprises is entrusted to any agency created or designated by any international agreement to which the Signatory Governments are party, the functions of the Authority in this matter shall cease.

(b) At the end of the Control Period, or at such earlier time as may be agreed upon by the Occupying Powers, the functions of the Authority referred to in paragraph (a) of this Article shall, unless they have previously ceased, be reviewed by the Signatory Governments, taking into account the desirability of transferring these functions to a separate agency or of extending them to the Aachen area.

ARTICLE 17

(a) During the Control Period, or until such earlier time as may be agreed upon by the Occupying Powers, the Occupation Authorities concerned will maintain such powers as may be necessary to enforce the disarmament of Germany, including power to control the supply of Ruhr coal, coke and steel to any industry which may be prohibited or limited in the interests of security by agreement among the Occupying Powers or under the terms of any international agreement to which they may become party.

(b) At the end of the Control Period, or at such earlier time as may be agreed upon by the Occupying Powers, the powers referred to in paragraph (a) of this Article shall be transferred to such international body as may be designated for these purposes by the peace settlement or by any international agreement to which the Signatory Governments are party, and the Authority shall cooperate with that international body in such ways as shall be prescribed by the peace settlement or international agreement. If no such international body is established, these powers shall be transferred to the Authority to be exercised by the representatives of the Signatory Governments thereon.

ARTICLE 18

(a) At the end of the Control Period, or at such earlier time as may be agreed upon by the Occupying Powers, such of the existing powers of the Occupation Authorities as are necessary to ensure:

(i) that there shall not be allowed to develop, or be restored, any pattern of ownership in the Ruhr coal, coke or steel industries, or trade and marketing agreements among such industries, which would constitute excessive concentration of economic power;

(ii) that persons who have been, or may be, found to have furthered the aggressive designs of the National Socialist Party do not hold positions of ownership or control in the Ruhr coal, coke or steel industries or the trade and marketing organizations of such industries; and

(iii) that adequate information is made available for the purposes specified in sub-paragraphs (i) and (ii) above, will be transferred to the Authority or to the Military Security Board or its successor or to some other body created by international agreement and charged with ensuring the achievement of these objectives with respect to these and other industries in Germany. The Authority shall cooperate with any other body to which such powers may be transferred.

(b) In conjunction with the first meeting of the special representatives of the members contemplated in Article 27, if practicable, but in any event before the end of the Control Period, the Signatory Governments will determine, in the light of the experience of the Occupation Authorities;

(i) which of the existing powers of the Occupation Authorities are to be continued for the purposes provided for in paragraph (a) of this Article;

(ii) whether such powers will be transferred to the Authority, the Military Security Board or its successor, or some other body created by international agreement;

(iii) the manner in which such powers will be exercised if transferred to the Authority; and,

(iv) in the event of powers being so transferred to another body, the manner in which the Authority will cooperate with such other body.

ARTICLE 19

(a) At the end of the Control Period, or at such earlier time as may be agreed upon by the Occupying Powers, only such of the existing powers of the Occupation Authorities over the direction and management of the Ruhr coal, coke or steel industries as are necessary to ensure:

(i) that the general policies and general programs relating to production, development and investment in those industries are in conformity with the purposes stated in the preamble to the present Agreement and

(ii) that adequate information concerning such policies and programs be made available,

will be transferred to the Authority, to the Military Security Board or its successor, or to some other body created by international agreement.

(b) In conjunction with the first meeting of the special representatives of the members contemplated in Article 27, if practicable, but in any event before the end of the Control Period, the Signatory Governments will determine, in the light of the experience of the Occupation Authorities:

(i) which of the existing powers of the Occupation Authorities are to be continued for the purposes provided in paragraph (a) of this Article;

(ii) which of these powers will be exercised by the Authority, by the Military Security Board or its successor, or by some other body created by international agreement;

(iii) the manner in which powers transferred to the Authority will be exercised; and

(iv) the relationship of the Authority with the Military Security Board or its successor, or with any other body to which the powers mentioned in paragraph (a) of this Article may be transferred.

PART IV: INFORMATION AND INVESTIGATION

ARTICLE 20

In order that the Authority may properly perform its functions and in order that it may determine whether its decisions are being appropriately carried out, the Authority shall have the right:

(i) to obtain periodical reports, and such additional reports as it considers necessary, on production, distribution and consumption of Ruhr coal, coke and steel, including such forecasts of production, distribution and consumption as may be necessary to enable it to perform its functions under Article 14;

(ii) to obtain such information as it considers necessary concerning supplies of coal, coke and steel available to Germany from sources other than the Ruhr, and concerning exports from Germany of such products from sources other than the Ruhr; and

(iii) to make in the Ruhr any investigations, including the examination of witnesses, which it considers necessary to verify the information obtained under this Article or other Articles of the present agreement, and to determine the manner in which its decisions are being carried out, provided that similar investigations may also be made in other parts of Germany under a special procedure to be established in accordance with Article 13.

In the exercise of these rights, the Authority may make enquiries of individuals, including public officials, and public or private organizations, enterprises and firms, and may examine records and installations.

PART V: EXECUTION OF FUNCTIONS

ARTICLE 21

(a) During the Control Period, or until such earlier time or times as may be agreed upon by the Occupying Powers, the Authority shall transmit its decisions under Articles 14 and 15 and its recommendations under Article 16 to the Occupation Authorities concerned.

(b) After the Control Period, or after such earlier time or times as may be agreed upon by the Occupying Powers, the Authority shall transmit its decisions under Articles 14 and 15 and its directions under Article 16 to the German Government.

ARTICLE 22

During the Control Period, or until such earlier time or times as may be agreed upon by the Occupying Powers, the Occupation Authorities concerned will:

(i) ensure that the decisions of the Authority under Article 14 are carried out except in so far as, in the judgment of the Occupation Authorities concerned, they require modification in order to make them consistent either with any agreement between two or more of the Occupying Powers relating to financial assistance to Germany which is in force at the time, or with any Agreement among the Occupying Powers with respect to the allocation of coal, coke or steel which is in force at the time;

(ii) ensure that the decisions of the Authority under Article 15 are carried out;

(iii) inform the Authority of measures taken as the result of its recommendations under Article 16;

(iv) take such action as is necessary to enable the Authority to exercise the rights provided for in Article 20; and

(v) ensure the enjoyment of the privileges and immunities provided for in Article 28.

ARTICLE 23

After the Control Period, or after such earlier time or times as may be agreed upon by the Occupying Powers, the German Government shall:

(i) ensure that the decisions of the Authority under Articles 14 and 15 and the directions of the Authority under Article 16 are carried out, and that any powers transferred to the Authority under Articles 17, 18 and 19 can be effectively exercised;

(ii) take such action as is necessary to enable the Authority to exercise the rights provided for in Article 20; and

(iii) ensure the enjoyment of the privileges and immunities provided for in Article 28.

PART VI: DEFAULT

ARTICLE 24

(a) Should the German Government fail to take any action as required by Article 23 of the present Agreement, the representatives of the Signatory Governments on the Authority may serve notice in writing upon the German Government, which notice shall afford the German Government an opportunity, within a time determined by such representatives to be reasonable, to appear and present reasons why it should not be declared in default.

(b) If the German Government does not present reasons satisfactory to the representatives of the Signatory Governments, such representatives may declare the German Government in default and in that event shall inform the German Government in writing of their decision. Such representatives shall then make recommendations as to the necessary and appropriate measures to be applied.

(c) Should the representatives of the Signatory Governments decide that the German Government is taking, or permitting, action which if permitted to continue might frustrate the proper exercise of the functions of the Authority, and that it is expedient that such action should be suspended pending further investigation by the Authority and the formulation of a decision or direction, such representatives may serve preliminary notice in writing upon the German Government that such action shall be suspended, with immediate effect, for such a period as may seem appropriate, pending further consideration by the Authority.

(d) The German Government may, within fifteen days of the service of the preliminary notice in accordance with the provisions of paragraph (c) of this Article, request that the notice be set aside, and in that event shall be afforded a hearing at such time and place as may be determined by the representatives of the Signatory Governments. If the German Government fails to comply with the preliminary notice after:—

(i) a hearing has been held and such representatives have notified that Government that their decision has been maintained;

(ii) having failed to appear for a hearing at the time and place established; or

(iii) fifteen days have elapsed and no request that the notice be set aside has been made,

such representatives may without further formality declare the German Government in default and in that event shall inform that Government in writing of their decision. Such representatives shall then make recommendations as to the necessary measures to be applied.

(e) All decisions under this Article shall be reached by a majority of the votes allocated to the representatives of the Signatory Governments.

(f) During the Control Period, the recommendations provided for in paragraphs (b) and (d) of this Article shall be made to the Occupation Authorities.

(g) After the end of the Control Period, the recommendations provided for in paragraphs (b) and (d) of this Article will be made to the Signatory Governments. The measures recommended will be applied in accordance with the relevant provisions of the peace settlement or any international agreement to which the Signatory Governments are party.

PART VII: GENERAL PROVISIONS

ARTICLE 25

The Authority may establish such formal or informal relationship with the United Nations and its subsidiary bodies, and with the Specialized Agencies and with other intergovernmental bodies, as may facilitate the performance of its functions.

ARTICLE 26

The Powers of the Authority will not be exercised for the purpose of protecting the commercial or competitive interests of any country, nor for the purpose of preventing peaceful technological development or increased deficiency.

ARTICLE 27

(a) One year after entering upon its functions and thereafter at annual intervals the Authority shall make a written report to the members on every aspect of its work. After the receipt by the members of such annual report there shall be held, unless all the Signatory Governments decide otherwise, a meeting of special representatives of the members for the purpose of reviewing the report and the work of the Authority.

(b) Except as provided in paragraph (c) of this Article, any two or more members of the Authority which, at any time, believe that the course of action or the policies initiated by the Authority are inconsistent with the purposes of the present Agreement, may give notice in writing to this effect to all other members of the Authority specifying the particulars which they consider to constitute such inconsistency. Upon receipt of such notice, the members shall consult together with respect to the complaint and shall take such action as may be required in the circumstances to accomplish a solution of the matter, including, where appropriate, such arbitration or judicial settlement as may be agreed by such members.

(c) A notice of complaint with respect to a course of action or policies initiated by the Authority for reasons of disarmament, demilitarization or denazification may only be given when supported by two members of the Authority other than Germany.

(d) Nothing in this Article shall be construed to affect the provisions of Articles 13 or 33 of the present Agreement.

Part VIII: Privileges and Immunities

article 28

(a) The Authority and its assets, income and other property shall enjoy in Germany the same privileges, immunities and facilities as are provided for the United Nations by the General Convention on Privileges and Immunities of the United Nations.

(b) During the Control Period, or until such earlier time as may be agreed upon by the Occupying Powers, the representatives of the Signatory Governments and their staffs and members of the staff of the Authority other than German nationals, and the dependents of such persons, shall enjoy in Germany the same privileges and immunities as are enjoyed by the official personnel of the Occupation Authorities. Thereafter all such persons shall enjoy in Germany the same privileges and immunities as are provided for persons of comparable status by the General Convention on Privileges and Immunities of the United Nations.

(c) German nationals on the staff of the Authority shall be immune from legal process in respect of words spoken or written and all acts performed by them in their official capacity.

* * *

Part X: Final Clauses

article 30

The present Agreement shall come into force as soon as it has been signed on behalf of the Government of Belgium, the Government of France, the Government of Luxembourg, the Government of the Netherlands, the Government of the United Kingdom of Great Britain and Northern Ireland and the Government of the United States of America.

ARTICLE 31

As soon as a German Government has been established, it may accede to the present Agreement by executing an instrument containing such undertakings with respect to the assumption of the responsibilities of the German Government under the Agreement and such other provisions as may be agreed by the Signatory Governments.

ARTICLE 32

The present Agreement shall, subject to the provisions of Article 33, continue in force until the coming into effect of a peace settlement for Germany and thereafter as provided in such peace settlement.

ARTICLE 33

The present Agreement may be amended by the agreement of all the Signatory Governments on the recommendation of the Authority. As long as the special relation of the Occupying Powers towards Germany continues, the present Agreement may be terminated by those Powers, subject to prior consultation with the other Signatory Governments. Thereafter it may be terminated by the agreement of all the Signatory Governments.

ARTICLE 34

The English and French texts of the present Agreement are authentic.

*　　*　　*

ANNEX

In Regierungsbezirk Duesseldorf:
 (1) Landkreis Dinslaken
 (2)   "   Duesseldorf-Mettmann
 (3)   "   Essen
 (4)   "   Geldern
 (5)   "   Krefeld-Uerdingen
 (6)   "   Moers
 (7)   "   Rees
 (8) Stadtkreis Duesseldorf
 (9)   "   Duisburg-Hamborn
 (10)   "   Muelheim
 (11)   "   Neuss
 (12)   "   Oberhausen
 (13)   "   Remscheid
 (14)   "   Solingen
 (15)   "   Wuppertal

In Regierungsbezirk Muenster:
 (1) Landkreis Beckum
 (2)   "   Luedinghausen
 (3)   "   Recklinghausen
 (4) Stadtkreis Bottrop
 (5)   "   Gelsenkirchen
 (6)   "   Gladbeck
 (7)   "   Recklinghausen

In Regierungsbezirk Arnsberg:
 (1) Landkreis Ennepe-Ruhrkreis
 (2)   "   Iserlohn
 (3)   "   Unna
 (4) Stadtkreis Bochum
 (5)   "   Castrop-Rauxel
 (6)   "   Dortmund
 (7)   "   Hagen
 (8)   "   Hamm
 (9)   "   Herne
 (10)   "   Iserlohn
 (11)   "   Luenen
 (12)   "   Wanne-Eickel
 (13)   "   Wattenscheid
 (14)   "   Witten

◇◇◇◇◇◇

72. MODIFICATION OF DISMANTLING IN GERMANY [1]

Agreement Between the United States, United Kingdom, and France,
November 24, 1949

[Even before the formation of the German Federal Republic, vigorous voices of protest were raised both in Germany and America, against the dismantling of certain German industrial plants. On November 22, 1949, the Allied Commissioners met with President Adenauer at Bonn and a broad understanding on German matters was reached. As outlined in the agreement announced by the Western governments two days later, the understandings included 'not only the liberalization of the dismantling program, but several other matters such as relaxation of restrictions on German shipbuilding, greater participation by Germany in international organization, and the prevention of any re-creation of armed forces in Germany.]

Following upon the meeting of the three Foreign Ministers in Paris on November 9 and 10 the United Kingdom, French, and United States High Commissioners were authorized to discuss with the Federal Chancellor the letters which he had addressed to them on the subject of dismantling with a view to a final settlement of this problem. The instructions to the High Commissioners also covered a wider field and required them to examine with the Chancellor other points to be included in a general settlement. Discussions took place accordingly on November 15, 17 and 22 on the Petersberg.

The discussions were animated throughout by the desire and the determination of both parties that their relations should develop progressively upon a basis of mutual confidence. Meanwhile, their primary objective is the incorporation of the Federal Republic as a peaceful member of the European community and to this end German association with the countries of Western Europe in all fields should be diligently pursued by means of her entry into the appropriate international bodies and the exchange of commercial and consular representation with other countries. Both the High Commissioners and the Chancellor appreciate that progress toward this objective must depend upon the establishment of a true sense of security in Western Europe, and they have addressed themselves particularly to this end. In all these matters they have been encouraged to find a wide community of ideas and intention and they have in particular agreed upon the following:

I. The High Commission and the Federal Government are agreed to promote the participation of Germany in all these international organizations through which German experience and support can contribute to the general welfare. They record their satisfaction at the various steps already achieved in this direction citing German participation in OEEC, the desire expressed on both sides that the Federal Republic should be promptly admitted to the Council of Europe as an associate member and the proposed signature of a bilateral agreement with the Government of the United States of America covering ECA assistance.

[1] Department of State Bulletin of December 5, 1949, pp. 863a-864a.

II. The Federal Government, appreciating the desirability of the closest possible cooperation by Germany in the rehabilitation of Western European economy, declares its intention of applying for membership in the International Authority for the Ruhr in which, at present, the Federal Government is only represented by an observer, it being understood between both parties that German accession will not be subject to any special conditions under article 31 of the agreement for the establishment of the Authority.

III. The Federal Government further declares its earnest determination to maintain the demilitarization of the Federal territory and to endeavor by all means in its power to prevent the re-creation of Armed Forces of any kind. To this end the Federal Government will cooperate fully with the High Commission in the work of the Military Security Board.

IV. It is further agreed between them that the Federal Government shall now initiate the gradual reestablishment of consular and commercial relations with those countries where such relations appear advantageous.

V. The Federal Government affirms its resolve as a freely elected democratic body to pursue unreservedly the principles of freedom, tolerance, and humanity which unite the nations of Western Europe and to conduct its affairs according to those principles. The Federal Government is firmly determined to eradicate all traces of Nazism from German life and institutions and to prevent the revival of totalitarianism in this or any form. It will seek to liberalize the structure of government and to exclude authoritarianism.

VI. In the field of decartelization and monopolistic practices the Federal Government will take legislative action corresponding to decisions taken by the High Commission in accordance with article 2 (B) of the Occupation Statute.

VII. The High Commission has communicated to the Chancellor the terms of an agreement reached by the three powers for the relaxation of the present restrictions on German shipbuilding.

The main provisions now agreed are as follows:

The construction of ocean-going ships excluding those primarily designed for passengers, and tankers up to 7,200 tons, fishing vessels up to 650 tons and coastal vessels up to 2,700 tons not exceeding 12 knots service speed may begin forthwith. The number of such ships to be constructed shall not be limited.

The Federal Government may, with the approval of the High Commission, acquire or construct before December 31, 1950, six special ships exceeding these limitations of size and speed. Further particulars on this point were communicated to the Chancellor.

The Federal Chancellor raised the question of the construction and repair of ships in German shipyards for export. The High Commissioners informed him that this matter was not discussed by the Committee of Experts and that they were not in a position to give him a final decision on it. However, they will meanwhile authorize German shipyards to construct for export ships of the types and within such limits of numbers as are applicable to construction for the German economy; they will authorize repair of foreign ships without restriction.

VIII. On the question of dismantling, the High Commission has reviewed the present position in the light of the assurances given by the Federal Government and has agreed to the following modification of the programme. The following plants will be removed from the reparations list and dismantling of their equipment will cease forthwith.

A. *Synthetic Oil and Rubber Plants*

Farbenfabriken Bayer, Leverkusen

Chemische Werke Huels (except for certain research equipment)

Gelsenberg Benzin, A. G.

Hydrierwerke Scholven, A. G.

Ruhroel G. M. B. H., Bottrop

Ruhrchemie, A. G.

Gewerkschaft Victor

Krupp Treibstoff G. M. B. H.

Steinkohlenbergwerke

Dortmunder paraffin

Essener Steinkohle A. G.

B. *Steel Plants*

August Thyssen Hutte, Duisberg, Hamborn

Huttenwerke Siegerland, Charlottenhutte

Deutsche Edelstahlwerke, Krefeld

August Thyssen Hutte, Niederreinische Hutte

Klockner Werke, Duesseldorf

Ruhrstahl A. G. Heinrichschutte, Hattingen

Bochummer Verein Gusstahlwerke, Bochum

Except that electric furnaces not essential to the functioning of the works will continue to be dismantled or destroyed.

C. Further dismantling at the I. G. Farben plant at Ludwigshafen will not take place except for the removal of the equipment for the production of synthetic ammonia and methanol to the extent provided for in the reparations programme.

D. All dismantling in Berlin will cease and work on the affected plants will be again rendered possible.

It is understood that equipment already dismantled will be made available to IARA except in the case of Berlin. The present modification of the reparations list will not affect the existing prohibitions and restrictions upon the production of certain materials. Dismantled plants may be reconstructed or re-equipped only as permitted by the Military Security Board and those plants at which dismantling has been stopped will be subject to suitable control to ensure that the limitation on the production of steel (11.1 million tons per annum) is not exceeded.

IX. The question of the termination of the state of war was discussed. Although such termination may be as consistent with the spirit of this protocol, it presents considerable legal and practical difficulties which need to be examined.

X. The High Commissioners and the Federal Chancellor have signed this protocol with the joint determination to carry into effect the purposes stated in the preamble hereof and with the hope that their understandings will constitute a notable contribution to the incorporation of Germany into a peaceful and stable European community of nations.

Initialled:
B. H. ROBERTSON   J. J. McCLOY
A. FRANCOIS-PONCET   K. ADENAUER

◇◇◇◇◇◇

73. CHARTER OF THE ALLIED HIGH COMMISSION FOR GERMANY, JUNE 20, 1949 [1]

[The final step in the implementation of the London agreement of June 7, 1948, relating to the political and economic organization of Western Germany, was taken over a year later with the adoption of the Charter of the Allied High Commission for Germany. The Charter set up a new High Commission of three members and transferred to that body the authority previously exercised by the commanders-in-chief of the occupying powers. This is the instrument under which Allied authority is still being exercised in Germany.]

I. ESTABLISHMENT OF ALLIED HIGH COMMISSION AND TRANSFER OF CONTROL

1. An Allied High Commission (hereinafter referred to as the High Commission) is hereby established for the exercise of Supreme Allied Authority in the Federal Republic of Germany. The High Commission shall be headed by three High Commissioners, one designated by each of the three powers signatory hereto.

2. As from the date of entry into force of the Occupation Statute all authority with respect to the control of Germany or over any governmental authority thereof, vested in or exercised by the respective Commanders-in-Chief of the forces of occupation of the three powers in Germany, from whatever source derived and however exercised, will be transferred to the three High Commissioners respectively, to be exercised in accordance with the provisions hereof and of the Occupation Statute.

3. The forces of occupation of the three powers in Germany shall remain stationed in their respective zones of occupation. Command of the forces of occupation in each zone and control of their related military establishments shall remain with the respective Commanders of the forces of occupation in such zones.

4. Legislation of the occupation authorities enacted before the effective date of the Occupation Statute shall remain in force until repealed or amended or otherwise replaced as provided in the Occupation Statute.

II. FUNCTIONS OF THE HIGH COMMISSION

1. The High Commission shall exercise control over the Federal Government and the Governments of its constituent Laender as provided in the Occupation Statute. In the exercise of the powers reserved to the occupation authorities under said Statute, the High Commission shall reach its decisions

[1] Department of State Bulletin, July 11, 1949, pp. 25-28, 38.

in accordance with the provisions of the "Agreement as to Tripartite Controls" among the Three Powers dated 8 April 1949 and attached hereto and made a part of this instrument as Annex A. These decisions shall constitute a joint exercise of the authority of all the three High Commissioners.

2. The High Commission shall act only through the Federal or appropriate Land Government except where direct action or legislation by the High Commission is necessary or appropriate for the due exercise of any of the powers reserved to the occupation authorities under the Occupation Statute.

3. The Headquarters of the High Commission shall be at the seat of the German Federal Government which, together with a surrounding area to be defined, will constitute a special area directly under the High Commission and excluded from any individual zone of occupation. The necessary special arrangements in connection with the definition and administration of this area in as far as they concern the Allies will be determined subsequently by the High Commission.

III. ORGANIZATION OF THE HIGH COMMISSION

1. The organization of the High Commission at its headquarters shall be tripartite in character and shall consist of:

A. An Allied Council (hereinafter referred to as "The Council") composed of the three High Commissioners. Each High Commissioner shall nominate a Deputy or permanent representative who will take his place on the Council in his absence. The Deputies or permanent representatives of the respective High Commissioners acting together may function as an Executive Committee of the Council if the Council so decides;

B. Such committees or bodies as the Council may from time to time establish. These committees and bodies shall advise the Council in their respective spheres and shall exercise such executive functions as the Council may delegate to them. The number, functions, and organization of such committees or bodies may be changed, adjusted, or eliminated entirely by the Council in light of experience. Subject to the above, in order to ensure continuity of operation, the Council initially shall be assisted by Committees respectively for Political Affairs, Foreign Trade and Exchange, Finance, Economics, Law and by the Military Security Board. Each Committee shall be assisted by such associated staff as it may require and as the Council approves.

C. Allied General Secretariat.

2. *The Council*

A. The Council shall constitute the supreme authority of the High Commission. The Council shall meet as frequently as it considers necessary and at any time upon the request of any of its members. The Chairmanship of the Council and its various committees shall be held in monthly rotation by each of its members. The Council shall fix the time and place of its meetings and shall establish appropriate rules and procedures for the conduct of its business. Decisions of the Council shall be reached in accordance with Annex A hereof.

3. *Committees*

The composition of each Committee and its terms of reference shall be fixed by the Council. Initially, such Committees, together with their respective terms of reference, shall be as follows:

A. The Political Affairs Committee, consisting of the three Political Advisers to the respective High Commissioners will be concerned with all political and foreign affairs of the German Federal and Land Governments coming with the competence of the Council.

B. A Foreign Trade and Exchange Committee consisting of the respective Economic and Finance Advisers of each of the High Commissioners.

(1) The Committee shall observe the economic, financial and foreign trade policies of the German authorities and shall advise the Council if such policies or any action taken or proposed to be taken pursuant thereto is likely to have such adverse effect on the foreign trade or foreign exchange resources of the German Government as is likely to increase its need for external assistance.

(2) The members of the Committee shall automatically be members of the Board of Directors of the Joint Export-Import Agency (hereinafter referred to as "JEIA") and in conjunction with the other Directors shall be charged with the orderly liquidation of JEIA at the earliest practicable date. The Committee shall assume any control functions presently exercised by JEIA as may warrant retention when the liquidation of JEIA is completed.

(3) It is understood that the German Federal Republic will become party to the convention for European Economic Cooperation and will execute a bilateral agreement with the Government of the United States. It is further understood that thereafter the functions of the High Commission in respect of the matters referred to in (I) will be appropriately modified.

C. The Economics Committee, consisting of the three Economics Advisers to the respective High Commissioners, shall observe the general economic policies of the German authorities and shall advise the Council as to the exercise of its powers in this connection reserved under the Occupation Statute. The Committee shall advise the Council on all matters relating to the Decartelization and Deconcentration of German industry.

D. The Finance Committee, consisting of the three Finance Advisers to the respective High Commissioners, shall observe the general financial policies of the German authorities, and shall advise the Council as to the exercise of its powers in this connection reserved under the Occupation Statute. To the extent necessary within the limits of the provisions of the Occupation Statute the Finance Committee shall succeed to and shall assume the functions heretofore exercised by the Allied Bank Commission.

E. The Law Committee, consisting of the Legal Advisers to the respective High Commissioners, shall advise the Council and its committees on all legal and judicial affairs arising out of the work of the High Commission.

F. The Military Security Board shall deal with all matters of demilitarization, disarmament, industrial prohibitions and limitations, and scientific research, in accordance with its existing terms of reference.

4. *Committee Staffs and Subordinate Groups*

A. Within numerical limitations established by the Council, each of the committees designated pursuant to paragraph 3 of this Article III shall establish such tripartite subordinate committees or other groups as may be necessary to the performance of its functions and as the Council may approve.

B. Except as specifically otherwise provided in subparagraph *C* of this paragraph 4, personnel for such subordinate committees or groups shall be appointed by each of the High Commissioners on a basis of parity among the three Allied nations. They may include military personnel. The number, functions and organization of such subordinate committees or groups may be changed, adjusted or eliminated entirely by the Council in the light of experience. Each subordinate committee or group shall be answerable to the committee responsible for its creation and shall report to the Council through such committee. Each subordinate agency shall be physically located at the headquarters of the High Commission except as may be otherwise determined by the Council.

C. The subordinate committees and groups established pursuant to subparagraph *A* of this paragraph 4 shall include:

(1) Joint Export-Import Agency which, until liquidated as provided in subparagraph *B* of paragraph 3 hereof, shall function under its existing terms of reference with an integrated staff and shall report to the Committee on Foreign Trade and Exchange through its Director General who, together with the Deputy Directors-General, shall be members of the Board of Directors of JEIA.

(2) The Decartelization and Industrial Deconcentration Group, the Coal Control Group and the Steel Control Group, all of which shall report through the Economics Committee.

(3) The Combined Travel Board which shall report through the Political Affairs Committee.

(4) Civil Aviation Board which shall report as determined by the Council.

(5) Information and Cultural Affairs Subcommittee which shall report through the Political Affairs Committee.

(6) A subcommittee on foreign interests which shall report as determined by the Council.

5. *Allied General Secretariat*

The High Commission shall be served by a Tripartite General Secretariat. The Secretariat will receive and dispatch all communications to or from the High Commission, prepare the agenda and materials for the meetings of the Council and shall keep the minutes of their meetings. The Secretariat or its appropriate branches shall act as the channel of communication between the High Commission and the agencies of the Federal Government, and between the Council and the several Land Commissioners with respect to matters affecting said Land Governments. The Secretariat shall maintain the records of the High Commission and be responsible for such other tasks as the Council may decide.

IV. LAND COMMISSIONERS

1. All powers of the High Commission shall be uniformly exercised in the constituent Laender of the Federal Republic, in accordance with tripartite policies and the directions of the Council.

2. To achieve uniformity in the exercise of its powers, the High Commission shall be represented at the seat of government of each of the constituent Laender by an Allied Land Commissioner who shall be solely responsible to the Council for ensuring due compliance on the part of the Land authorities with the Council's decisions and directives. The Land Commissioner shall report and be solely responsible to the Council for all matters of tripartite concern in the Land and shall be the exclusive channel of communication and liaison between the Council and the Land Government with respect to such matters.

3. In particular, each Land Commissioner shall be responsible to the Council for:

A. Initial consideration and prompt transmittal to the Council of Land legislation, together with his recommendations thereon;

B. observing and ensuring due compliance on the part of the Land Government with the provisions of the Federal and Land constitutions, the Occupation Statute and the laws of the occupation authorities in force;

C. providing information as required by the Military Security Board and giving all necessary assistance to the inspectorate of the Military Security Board and such other bodies as may be authorized by the Council;

D. the preparation of such periodic or special reports as the Council may request.

4. Each Land Commissioner and the members of his staff shall be nationals of the Power in whose zone the Land is situated, and shall be appointed by and administratively responsible to the High Commissioner designated by such Power. Each Land Commissioner shall be accountable exclusively to his High Commissioner and shall be his channel of communication and liaison with the Land Government with respect to:

A. All matters which are listed in Article V, paragraph 2;

B. conduct of all relationships between the forces of occupation stationed in the Land and the governmental agencies thereof except to the extent that direct communications and relations may be authorized by him.

5. Each High Commissioner shall designate an observer together with a small personal staff to be agreed in each case by the High Commissioners concerned, to each of the Land Commissioners outside of his own Zone for purposes of consultation and information.

V. INDIVIDUAL RESPONSIBILITIES OF THE HIGH COMMISSIONERS

1. Each High Commissioner shall maintain at the seat of government of each of the Laender in his zone a Land Commissioner with the minimum staff and facilities required for the purposes set forth in Articles IV and V hereof. He shall ensure the due implementation by each of said Land Commissioners

of the decisions and directions of the Council. He shall also ensure that all powers of the High Commission are uniformly exercised within said Laender in accordance with tripartite policy and the decisions of the Council.

2. Each High Commissioner shall be responsible to his government with respect to the Laender of his zone for the matters in fields reserved to the occupation authorities listed below. Nevertheless, so far as possible, he shall coordinate the general policies which he may pursue in these fields with those of the other High Commissioners and exercise these powers in accordance with such tripartite legislation or policies as the Council may adopt.

A. Maintenance of law and order if the responsible German authorities are unable to do so;

B. ensuring the protection, prestige, security and immunities of the Allied forces of occupation, of the Allied occupation authorities, their dependents, employees and official representatives;

C. the delivery of reparations and restitutable property;

D. care and administration of displaced persons;

E. the disposition of war criminals;

F. administration of justice in cases falling within the jurisdiction of Allied courts;

G. control of the care and treatment in German prisons of persons charged before or sentenced by the courts or tribunals of the occupation authorities, over the carrying out of sentences imposed on them and over question of amnesty, pardon or release in relation to them.

3. Each High Commissioner shall be individually responsible for the formulation annually in accordance with tripartite policies and criteria, of a budget of occupation costs and other requirements within his zone. Such budget shall be formulated and submitted to the Council on a date to be determined by it for consideration and approval by the Council and for consolidation in a total budget of the occupation authorities for transmission to the German Government. Each High Commissioner shall be responsible to the Council for control of the approved budget for his zone in accordance with accounting standards and procedures established by the Council.

VI. DECISIONS OF THE COUNCIL

1. Formal decisions and directions of the Council affecting the Federal Government or any agency thereof shall be in writing and shall be communicated to the Chancellor by or on behalf of the Council.

2. Formal communications involving matters of lesser import or of a routine character may be addressed to the Minister concerned by the appropriate organ of the Council.

3. Formal decisions or directions of the Council affecting a Land Government or any agency thereof shall be in writing and shall be communicated to its Minister President through the Land Commissioner, in the name of the Council.

4. Formal decisions of the Council shall be recorded in an official gazette maintained by the High Commission at the Allied seat of control in Germany, which shall be published in the English, French, and German languages. Publication of any such decision in the official gazette of the High Commission shall be conclusive evidence that the recorded action or decision was taken

pursuant to the powers vested in the occupation authorities under the Occupation Statute.

VII. INTERNATIONAL AUTHORITY FOR THE RUHR

The High Commission shall take all necessary steps to give effect to Article XXII of the agreement establishing the International Authority for the Ruhr of April 28, 1949.

VIII. FOREIGN MISSIONS IN GERMANY

The necessary liaison with the governments of other nations especially interested will be ensured by the appointment by such governments of appropriate missions to the Council of the High Commission having access, by procedures to be determined, to its subordinate bodies and to the German Government.

IX. UNITED NATIONS ORGANIZATIONS IN GERMANY

United Nations organizations and specialized agencies may operate in the Federal Republic of Germany on such terms as may be agreed by the Council.

X. OFFICIAL LANGUAGES

The official languages of the High Commission shall be English and French. Authoritative German texts of documents shall be provided as necessary.

IN WITNESS WHEREOF the foregoing agreement has been duly executed by the respective representatives thereunto duly authorized of the Governments of the United Kingdom of Great Britain, the United States of America and the Republic of France, in triplicate in the French and English languages, each text being equally authentic and shall come into effect on the date of the entry into force of the Occupation Statute.

PARIS

20th June, 1949.

[Signed at Paris by Secretary of State Acheson, Foreign Minister Bevin, and Foreign Minister Schuman on behalf of their governments.]

74. CHANGED STATUS OF U. S. HIGH COMMISSIONER IN GERMANY, SEPTEMBER 21, 1949 [1]

[Prior to the establishment of the new federal republic of Germany, a constitutional assembly was convened at Bonn from September 1948 to May 1949. The instrument it produced was adopted by the voters of Western Germany in the elections of August 14, 1949. On September 7th, the two houses of the new German Parliament met for the first time, and eight days later they elected Konrad Adenauer the first chancellor of the new republic. As the document below illustrates, the birth of the new republic terminated military government in the U. S. zone in Germany and changed the status and the mission of our high commissioner there.]

[1] Department of State Bulletin, October 3, 1949, pp. 512-513.

Effective September 21, 1949, the Allied High Commissioners in Germany have been formally advised of the formation of the Federal Republic of Germany and have proclaimed that the Occupation Statute is now in force.

Under the terms of Executive Order No. 10062, dated June 6, 1949, "The United States High Commissioner for Germany, hereinafter referred to as the High Commissioner, shall be the supreme United States authority in Germany. The High Commissioner shall have the authority, under the immediate supervision of the Secretary of State (subject, however, to consultation with and ultimate direction by the President), to exercise all of the governmental functions of the United States in Germany (other than the command of troops), including representation of the United States on the Allied High Commission for Germany and the exercise of appropriate functions of a Chief of Mission within the meaning of the Foreign Service Act of 1946."

By the same Executive Order, the United States High Commissioner for Germany was designated also as "the United States Military Governor with all the powers thereof including those vested in the United States Military Governor under all international agreements" until such time as the Military Government of the United States zone of Germany shall have been terminated. Effective September 21, 1949, the Military Government of the United States zone of Germany was terminated. Therefore, by virtue of these events, the United States High Commissioner for Germany no longer exercises the role of the United States Military Governor.

The role of the United States High Commissioner for Germany as the ECA representative for Germany is outlined in Executive Order No. 10063, dated June 13, 1949, as follows:

"1. During his tenure of office as United States High Commissioner for Germany, Mr. John J. McCloy, under the immediate supervision of the Administrator for Economic Cooperation and the coordination of the United States Special Representative for Europe (subject, however, to consultation with and ultimate direction by the President), shall be the representative of the said Administrator and the said Special Representative in all their relations and actions with respect to Germany.

"2. Mr. McCloy, in performing the duties set forth in paragraph one hereof, shall be assisted by a Chief of Special Mission who shall be appointed by the Administrator for Economic Cooperation and who shall be acceptable to Mr. McCloy. The Chief of Special Mission shall have the rank of Minister and shall act under the immediate supervision and direction of Mr. McCloy."

The United States High Commissioner for Germany is the Honorable John J. McCloy. The British High Commissioner for Germany is General Sir Brian Robertson. The French High Commissioner for Germany is His Excellency André Francois-Poncet.

◇◇◇◇◇◇

AUSTRIA [1]

75. ZONES OF OCCUPATION AND THE ADMINISTRATION OF THE CITY OF VIENNA

Agreement Between the United States, the Union of Soviet Socialist Republics and the United Kingdom and the Provisional Government of the French Republic, July 9, 1945 [2]

[At the end of World War I, the centuries-old Hapsburg Empire of Austria-Hungary was broken up into several new states, which left Austria truncated. Small and vulnerable to aggression, the new Austria remained an independent state until March 11, 1938, when it was incorporated by a Nazi putsch into Hitler's Third Reich. When Germany was defeated in World War II, Austria was again resurrected by the Allies and dealt with as a separate state. In the document which follows the four victorious powers defined the zones which they were to occupy and provided for the establishment of an inter-Allied Governing Authority.]

1. The Governments of the United States of America, the Union of Soviet Socialist Republics and the United Kingdom of Great Britain and Northern Ireland and the Provisional Government of the French Republic have agreed that the territory of Austria within her frontiers as they were on 31st December, 1937, will be occupied by armed forces of the United States of America, the Union of Soviet Socialist Republics, the United Kingdom and the French Republic.

2. For the purposes of occupation, Austria will be divided as follows into four zones, one of which will be allotted to each of the four Powers, and a special Vienna area which will be jointly occupied by armed forces of the four Powers:

North-Eastern (*Soviet*) *Zone*	The province of Lower Austria with the exception of the City of Vienna, that part of the province of Upper Austria situated on the left bank of the Danube, and the province of Burgenland which existed prior to the Decree of 1st October, 1938,[3] concerning boundary changes in Austria, will be occupied by armed forces of the Union of Soviet Socialist Republics.
North-Western (*United States*) *Zone*	The province of Salzburg and that part of the province of Upper Austria situated on the

---

[1] Austria had been forcibly incorporated into Hitler Germany before the outbreak of World War II and thus had lost autonomy for the time being. Since there was no Austria, the United States was not at war with Austria.

[2] Department of State publication 2861, Treaties and Other International Acts Series 1600. Agreement signed July 9, 1945; entered into force July 24, 1945.

[3] "Gesetz Uber Gebietsveränderungen im Lande Österreich Vom I. Oktober 1938." Translation: "The Law concerning territorial changes in Austria since October 1, 1938." [*Reichsgesetzblatt*, Part 1, pp. 1333 ff. (1938).]

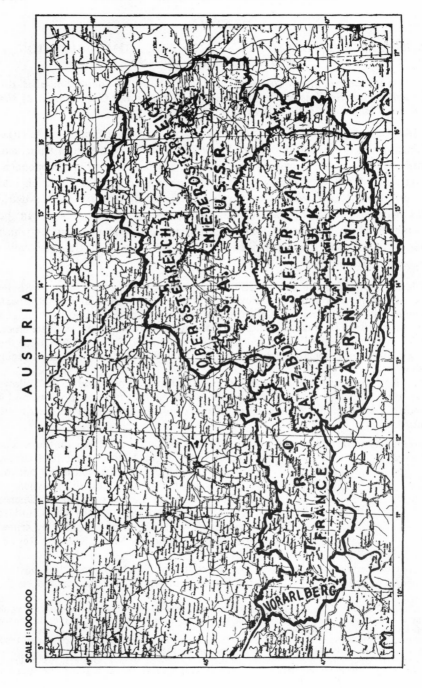

right bank of the Danube will be occupied by armed forces of the United States.

Western (French) Zone   The provinces of Tirol and Vorarlberg will be occupied by armed forces of the French Republic.

Southern (United Kingdom) Zone   The province of Carinthia, including Ost Tirol, and the province of Styria, except the area of the Burgenland as it existed before the Decree of 1st October, 1938, will be occupied by armed forces of the United Kingdom.

City of Vienna

The territory of the City of Vienna will be divided into the following parts   .   .   .   :—

The districts of Leopoldstadt, Brigittenau, Floridsdorf, Wieden and Favoriten will be occupied by armed forces of the Soviet Union;

The districts of Neubau, Josefstadt, Hernals, Alsergrund, Währing and Döbling will be occupied by armed forces of the United States of America;

The districts of Mariahilf, Penzing, Funfhaus (including the district of Rudolfsheim) and Ottakring will be occupied by armed forces of the French Republic;

The districts of Hietzing, Margareten, Meidling, Landstrasse and Simmering will be occupied by armed forces of the United Kingdom.

The district of Innere Stadt will be occupied by armed forces of the four Powers.

3. Boundaries between the zones of occupation, with the exception of the boundaries of the City of Vienna and of the province of Burgenland, will be those obtaining after the coming into effect of the Decree of 1st October, 1938, concerning boundary changes in Austria. The boundaries of the City of Vienna and of the province of Burgenland will be those which existed on 31st December, 1937.

4. An inter-Allied Governing Authority (Komendatura), consisting of four Commandants appointed by their respective Commanders-in-Chief, will be established to direct jointly the administration of the City of Vienna.

5. The Tulln airdrome, together with all installations and facilities pertaining thereto, will be under the administrative and operational control of the armed forces of the United States of America. The Schwechat airdrome, together with all installations and facilities pertaining thereto, will be under the administrative and operational control of the armed forces of the United Kingdom for the joint use of the British and French armed forces. The armed forces and officials of the occupying Powers will enjoy free and unimpeded access to the airdromes assigned to their respective occupancy and use.

6. The present Agreement has been drawn up in quadruplicate in the English, Russian and French languages. All three texts are authentic.

7. The present Agreement will come into force as soon as it has been approved by the four Governments.[1]

The above text of the Agreement between the Governments of the United States of America, the Union of Soviet Socialist Republics and the United Kingdom and the Provisional Government of the French Republic on the Zones of Occupation in Austria and the Administration of the City of Vienna has been prepared and unanimously adopted by the European Advisory Commission at a meeting held on 9th July, 1945.

Representative of the Government of the United States of America on the European Advisory Commission:

JOHN G. WINANT.

Representative of the Government of the United Kingdom on the European Advisory Commission:

RONALD I. CAMPBELL

Representative of the Government of the Union of Soviet Socialist Republics on the European Advisory Commission:

F. T. GOUSEV.

Representative of the Provisional Government of the French Republic on the European Advisory Commission:

R. MASSIGLI

LANCASTER HOUSE,
   LONDON, S. W. 1.
9th July 1945.

◇◇◇◇◇◇

76. RECOGNITION OF AUSTRIAN GOVERNMENT, JANUARY 7, 1946 [2]

[Shortly after the German surrender, a new Austrian government was organized along democratic lines under the supervision of the Allied Council. In according recognition to this new Austrian government, the United States made it clear that it did not thereby terminate its occupation of Austria.]

In accordance with the resolution of December 18, 1945 of the Allied Council in Austria, the members of the Council unanimously recommended to their respective governments that the Austrian Government formed by Chancellor Leopold Figl as a result of the mandate received in the elections of November 25, 1945 be recognized by the states represented on the Council. The recognition of the Austrian Government has been approved by the President, and the United States member of the Allied Council has been instructed to notify the Austrian Government to this effect. The President has in addition sent the following telegram to Dr. Karl Renner on the occasion of his election to the presidency of the Austrian Republic:

"I wish to extend to you my sincere congratulations on your election as President of the Austrian Republic and my best wishes in your task of com-

[1] Notices of approval dated as follows: by the United Kingdom July 12, 1945; by France July 16, 1945; by the Union of Soviet Socialist Republics July 21, 1945; and by the United States of America July 24, 1945.

[2] Department of State Bulletin, January 20, 1946, p. 81.

pleting the liberation of Austria and the revival of an independent and democratic state. I can assure you that the people of the United States will wish to assist Austria in this endeavor."

The recognition of the Austrian Government by the United States in no way affects the supreme authority of the Allied Council. The Council will continue to operate in carrying out the Allied objectives in Austria. As the Council proceeds with its task of eliminating Nazi influences and institutions in Austria, and assisting in the reconstruction of democratic life, it is hoped that a large-scale reduction may be made in the number of occupation troops of the four states and that Austria may progressively acquire the status of an independent state. The United States Government also hopes that an Austrian agent will arrive soon in Washington to discuss matters of mutual interest which do not affect the supreme authority of the Allied Council.

◇◇◇◇◇◇

77. CONTROL MACHINERY IN AUSTRIA [1]

Agreement Between the United Kingdom, the United States of America, the Union of Soviet Socialist Republics and the French Republic, June 28, 1946

[After the war, disagreement among the occupying powers resulted in a divided Austria with an Eastern Austrian zone set against the three Western zones. At the outset, agreement was reached to establish an Allied Commission consisting of representatives of all the four occupying powers. This commission, among other things, was to complete the separation of Austria from Germany, bring about demilitarization and disarmament, and help in various ways to re-establish the Austrian government on a sound and democratic basis. It should be noted, however, that while the control machinery has operated effectively in the Western Zones of Austria, it has not been effective in the Soviet Zone.]

*   *   *

ARTICLE 1

The authority of the Austrian Government shall extend fully throughout Austria, subject only to the following reservations;

(*a*) The Austrian Government and all subordinate Austrian authorities shall carry out such directions as they may receive from the Allied Commission:

(*b*) In regard to the matters specified in Article 5 below neither the Austrian Government nor any subordinate Austrian authority shall take action without the prior written consent of the Allied Commission.

ARTICLE 2

(*a*) The Allied organization in Austria shall consist of
(*i*) an Allied Council, consisting of four High Commissioners, one appointed by each of the Four Powers;

[1] Department of State Bulletin, July 28, 1946, pp. 175-178.

(*ii*) an Executive Committee, consisting of one high ranking representative of each of the High Commissioners;

(*iii*) Staffs appointed respectively by the Four Powers, the whole organization being known as the Allied Commission for Austria.

(*b*) (*i*) The authority of the Allied Commission in matters affecting Austria as a whole shall be exercised by the Allied Council or the Executive Committee or the Staffs appointed by the Four Powers when acting jointly.

(*ii*) The High Commissioners shall within their respective zones ensure the execution of the decisions of the Allied Commission and supervise the execution of the directions of the central Austrian authorities.

(*iii*) The High Commissioners shall also ensure within their respective zones that the actions of the Austrian provincial authorities deriving from their autonomous functions do not conflict with the policy of the Allied Commission.

(*c*) The Allied Commission shall act only through the Austrian Government or other appropriate Austrian authorities except:

(*i*) to maintain law and order if the Austrian authorities are unable to do so;

(*ii*) if the Austrian Government or other appropriate Austrian authorities do not carry out directions received from the Allied Commission;

(*iii*) where, in the case of any of the subjects detailed in Article 5 below, the Allied Commission acts directly.

(*d*) In the absence of action by the Allied Council, the four several High Commissioners may act independently in their respective zones in any matter covered by subparagraphs (*i*) and (*ii*) of paragraph (*c*) of this Article and by Article 5, and in any matter in respect of which power is conferred on them by the agreement to be made under Article 8 (*a*) of the agreement.

(*e*) Forces of occupation furnished by the Four Powers will be stationed in the respective zones of occupation in Austria and Vienna as defined in the Agreement on Zones of Occupation in Austria and the administration of the City of Vienna, signed in the European Advisory Commission on 9th July, 1945. Decisions of the Allied Council which require implementation by the forces of occupation will be implemented by the latter in accordance with instructions from their respective High Commissioners.

ARTICLE 3

The primary tasks of the Allied Commission for Austria shall be:

(*a*) To ensure the enforcement in Austria of the provisions of the Declaration on the Defeat of Germany signed at Berlin on 5th June, 1945;

(*b*) To complete the separation of Austria from Germany, and to maintain the independent existence and integrity of the Austrian State, and pending the final definition of its frontiers to ensure respect for them as they were on 31st December, 1937;

(*c*) To assist the Austrian Government to recreate a sound and democratic national life based on an efficient administration, stable economic and financial conditions and respect for law and order;

(*d*) To assist the freely elected Government of Austria to assume as quickly as possible full control of the affairs of state in Austria;

(*e*) To ensure the institution of a progressive long-term educational program designed to eradicate all traces of Nazi ideology and to instill into Austrian youth democratic principles.

ARTICLE 4

(*a*) In order to facilitate the full exercise of the Austrian Government's authority equally in all zones and to promote the economic unity of Austria, the Allied Council will from the date of signature of this Agreement ensure the removal of all remaining restrictions on the movement within Austria of persons, goods, or other traffic, except such as may be specifically prescribed by the Allied Council or required in frontier areas for the maintenance of effective control of international movements. The zonal boundaries will then have no other effect than as boundaries of the spheres of authority and responsibility of the respective High Commissioners and the location of occupation troops.

(*b*) The Austrian Government may organize a customs and frontier administration, and the Allied Commission will take steps as soon as practicable to transfer to it customs and travel control functions concerning Austria which do not interfere with the military needs of the occupation forces.

ARTICLE 5

The following are the matters in regard to which the Allied Commission may act directly as provided in Article 2 (*c*) (*iii*) above:

(*i*) Demilitarization and disarmament (military, economic, industrial, technical and scientific).

(*ii*) The protection and security of the Allied forces in Austria, and the fulfilment of their military needs in accordance with the Agreement to be negotiated under Article 8 (*a*).

(*iii*) The protection, care and restitution of property belonging to the Governments of any of the United Nations or their nationals.

(*iv*) The disposal of German property in accordance with the existing agreements between the Allies.

(*v*) The care and evacuation of, and exercise of judicial authority over prisoners of war and displaced persons.

(*vi*) The control of travel into and out of Austria until Austrian travel controls can be established.

(*vii*) (*a*) The tracing, arrest and handing-over of any person wanted by one of the Four Powers or by the International Court for War Crimes and Crimes against Humanity.

(*b*) The tracing, arrest and handing-over of any person wanted by other United Nations for the crimes specified in the preceding paragraph and included in the lists of the United Nations Commission for War Crimes.

The Austrian Government will remain competent to try any other person accused of such crimes and coming within its jurisdiction, subject to the Allied Council's right of control over prosecution and punishment for such crimes.

ARTICLE 6

(*a*) All legislative measures, as defined by the Allied Council, and international agreements which the Austrian Government wishes to make except agreements with one of the 4 Powers, shall, before they take effect or are published in the State Gazette be submitted by the Austrian Government to the Allied Council. In the case of constitutional laws, the written approval of the Allied Council is required, before any such law may be published and put into effect. In the case of all other legislative measures and international agreements it may be assumed that the Allied Council has given its approval if within thirty-one days of the time of receipt by the Allied Commission it has not informed the Austrian Government that it objects to a legislative measure or an international agreement. Such legislative measure or international agreement may then be published and put into effect. The Austrian Government will inform the Allied Council of all international agreements entered into with one or more of the 4 Powers.

(b) The Allied Council may at any time inform the Austrian Government or the appropriate Austrian authority of its disapproval of any of the Legislative measures or administrative actions of the Government or of such authority, and may direct that the action in question shall be cancelled or amended.

ARTICLE 7

The Austrian Government is free to establish diplomatic and consular relations with the Governments of the United Nations. The establishment of diplomatic and consular relations with other Governments shall be subject to the prior approval of the Allied Council. Diplomatic Missions in Vienna shall have the right to communicate directly with the Allied Council. Military Missions accredited to the Allied Council shall be withdrawn as soon as their respective Governments establish diplomatic relations with the Austrian Government, and in any case within two months of the signature of this agreement.

ARTICLE 8

(a) A further agreement between the Four Powers shall be drawn up and communicated to the Austrian Government as soon as possible, and within three months of this day's date defining the immunities of the members of the Allied Commission and of the forces in Austria of the Four Powers and the rights they shall enjoy to ensure their security and protection and the fulfilment of their military needs.

(b) Pending the conclusion of the further agreement required by Article 8 (a) the existing rights and immunities of members of the Allied Commission and of the forces in Austria of the Four Powers, deriving either from the Declaration on the Defeat of Germany or from the powers of a Commander-in-Chief in the field, shall remain unimpaired.

ARTICLE 9

(a) Members of the Allied Council, the Executive Committee and other staffs appointed by each of the Four Powers as part of the Allied Commission may be either civilian or military.

(b) Each of the Four Powers may appoint as its High Commissioner either the Commander-in-Chief of its forces in Austria or its diplomatic or political representative in Austria or such other official as it may care to nominate.

(*c*) Each High Commissioner may appoint a deputy to act for him in his absence.

(*d*) A High Commissioner may be assisted in the Allied Council by a political adviser and/or a military adviser who may be respectively the diplomatic or political representative of his Government in Vienna or the Commander-in-Chief of the forces in Austria of his Government.

(*e*) The Allied Council shall meet at least twice in each month or at the request of any member.

ARTICLE 10

(*a*) Members of the Executive Committee shall, when necessary, attend meetings of the Allied Council;

(*b*) The Executive Committee shall act on behalf of the Allied Council in matters delegated to it by the Council;

(*c*) The Executive Committee shall ensure that the decisions of the Allied Council and its own decisions are carried out;

(*d*) The Executive Committee shall coordinate the activities of the Staffs of the Allied Commission.

ARTICLE 11

(*a*) The staffs of the Allied Commission in Vienna shall be organized in Divisions matching one or more of the Austrian Ministries or Departments with the addition of certain Divisions not corresponding to any Austrian Ministry or Department. The List of Divisions is given in Annex I to this Agreement; this organization may be changed at any time by the Allied Council;

(*b*) The Divisions shall maintain contact with the appropriate Departments of the Austrian Government and shall take such action and issue such directions as are within the policy approved by the Allied Council or the Executive Committee;

(*c*) The Divisions shall report as necessary to the Executive Committee;

(*d*) At the Head of each Division there shall be four Directors, one from each of the Four Powers, to be collectively known as the Directorate of that Division. Directors of Divisions or their representatives may attend meetings of the Allied Council or of the Executive Committee in which matters affecting the work of their Divisions are being discussed. The four officials acting as the head of each Division may appoint such temporary subcommittees as they deem desirable.

ARTICLE 12

The decisions of the Allied Council, Executive Committee, and other constituted bodies of the Allied Commission shall be unanimous.

The Chairmanship of the Allied Council, Executive Committee and Directorates shall be held in rotation.

ARTICLE 13

The existing Inter-Allied Command in Vienna, formerly known as the Kommendatura, shall continue to act as the instrument of the Allied Commission for affairs concerning Vienna as a whole until its functions in connection with civil administration can be handed over to the Vienna Municipality. These will be handed over progressively and as rapidly as possible. The form of supervision which will then be applied will be decided by the Allied Council. Meanwhile the Vienna Inter-Allied Command shall have the same relation to the Municipal Administration of Vienna as the Allied Commission has to the Austrian Government.

ARTICLE 14

The present Agreement shall come into operation as from this day's date and shall remain in force until it is revised or abrogated by agreement between the Four Powers. On the coming into effect of the present Agreement the Agreement signed in the European Advisory Commission on 4th July 1945, shall be abrogated. The Four Powers shall consult together not more than six months from this day's date with a view to its revision.

In witness whereof the present Agreement has been signed on behalf of each of the Four Powers by its High Commissioners in Austria.

Done this twenty-eighth day of June 1946 at Vienna in quadruplicate in English, in French and in Russian each text being equally authentic. A translation into German shall be agreed between the four High Commissioners and communicated by them as soon as possible to the Austrian Government.

For the Government of the United Kingdom:
Lieutenant General J. S. STEELE
For the Government of the United States of America:
General MARK W. CLARK
For the Government of the Union of Soviet Socialist Republics:
Colonel General L. V. KAURASOV
For the Government of the French Republic:
General de Corps d'Armee M. E. BETHOUART

◇◇◇◇◇◇

JAPAN [1]

78. DECLARATION OF WAR WITH JAPAN, DECEMBER 8, 1941

JOINT RESOLUTION Declaring That a State of War Exists Between Japan and the United States [2]

[On December 7, 1941, the Japanese air force, in a surprise attack, bombed and sank a major part of the United States Pacific fleet anchored in Pearl Harbor, Hawaii. This same stratagem, used by the Japanese in the Russo-Japanese War, had given the Japanese a tremendous advantage over Russia when it enabled them to sink the entire Russian Far Eastern fleet before a formal declaration of war was made. On December 8, the United States

---

[1] For more comprehensive treatment of this subject, including documents, see Occupation of Japan: Policy and Progress, Department of State publication 2671, Far Eastern Series 17; Activities of the Far Eastern Commission: Report by the Secretary General, Department of State publication 2888, Far Eastern Series 24; Supreme Commander for the Allied Powers, Two Years of Occupation, General Headquarters, August 1947.

[2] 55 Stat. 795.

Congress answered with a joint resolution declaring that a state of war existed between the two countries.]

Whereas the Imperial Government of Japan has committed unprovoked acts of war against the Government and the people of the United States of America: Therefore be it

Resolved by the Senate and House of Representatives of the United States of America in Congress assembled, That the state of war between the United States and the Imperial Government of Japan which has thus been thrust upon the United States is hereby formally declared; and the President is hereby authorized and directed to employ the entire naval and military forces of the United States and the resources of the Government to carry on war against the Imperial Government of Japan; and, to bring the conflict to a successful termination, all of the resources of the country are hereby pledged by the Congress of the United States.

Approved, December 8, 1941, 4:10 p. m., E. S. T.

◇◇◇◇◇◇

79. INSTRUMENT OF SURRENDER, SEPTEMBER 2, 1945 [1]

[More than four years of bitter fighting elapsed before Japan was ready to surrender to the Allied powers. During that time, the Japanese occupied most of the Far Eastern possessions of the Western countries as far as the borders of India. Although Japan offered to surrender on August 10, 1945, (and she is reported to have made peace overtures considerably before that time) the formal signing ceremony of the unconditional surrender instrument did not take place until September 2, 1945, in Tokyo Harbor on the U.S.S. *Missouri.*]

We, acting by command of and in behalf of the Emperor of Japan, the Japanese Government and the Japanese Imperial General Headquarters, hereby accept the provisions set forth in the declaration issued by the heads of the Governments of the United States, China and Great Britain on 26 July 1945, at Potsdam, and subsequently adhered to by the Union of Soviet Socialist Republics, which four powers are hereafter referred to as the Allied Powers.

We hereby proclaim the unconditional surrender to the Allied Powers of the Japanese Imperial General Headquarters and of all Japanese armed forces and all armed forces under Japanese control wherever situated.

We hereby command all Japanese forces wherever situated and the Japanese people to cease hostilities forthwith, to preserve and save from damage all ships, aircraft, and military and civil property and to comply with all requirements which may be imposed by the Supreme Commander for the Allied Powers or by agencies of the Japanese Government at his direction.

We hereby command the Japanese Imperial General Headquarters to issue

[1] Terms signed at Tokyo Bay, September 2, 1945; effective September 2, 1945; Department of State publication 2504, Executive Agreement Series 493, also, The Axis in Defeat, Department of State publication 2423, pp. 36-37. See Potsdam Declaration, July 26, 1945 printed under I. Wartime Documents. See also Axis in Defeat for texts of Japanese offer of surrender, August 10, 1945; Japanese acceptance of Potsdam Declaration, August 14, 1945; Imperial Rescript (Proclamation), September 1-2, 1945; and President Truman's radio address, September 1, 1945.

at once orders to the Commanders of all Japanese forces and all forces under Japanese control wherever situated to surrender unconditionally themselves and all forces under their control.

We hereby command all civil, military and naval officials to obey and enforce all proclamations, orders and directives deemed by the Supreme Commander for the Allied Powers to be proper to effectuate this surrender and issue by him or under his authority and we direct all such officials to remain at their posts and to continue to perform their non-combatant duties unless specifically relieved by him or under his authority.

We hereby undertake for the Emperor, the Japanese Government and their successors to carry out the provisions of the Potsdam Declaration in good faith, and to issue whatever orders and take whatever action may be required by the Supreme Commander for the Allied Powers or by any other designated representative of the Allied Powers for the purpose of giving effect to that Declaration.

STRATEGIC POSITIONS OF JAPAN AND KOREA

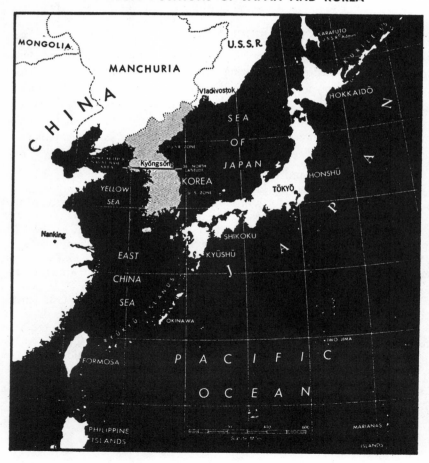

We hereby command the Japanese Imperial Government and the Japanese Imperial General Headquarters at once to liberate all allied prisoners of war and civilian internees now under Japanese control and to provide for their protection, care, maintenance and immediate transportation to places as directed.

The authority of the Emperor and the Japanese Government to rule the state shall be subject to the Supreme Commander for the Allied Powers who will take such steps as he deems proper to effectuate these terms of surrender.

Signed at Tokyo Bay, Japan, at 0947 on the second day of September, 1945.

[Signatures to document, signed on the U. S. S. *Missouri,* are of Foreign Minister Mamoru Shigemitsu and Gen. Yoshijiro Umezu of the Imperial General Staff, and for the United Nations the signatures are of Gen. Douglas MacArthur for the Allied Powers, Admiral Chester W. Nimitz for the United States, Gen. Hsu Yung-ch'ang for China, Admiral Sir Bruce A. Fraser for the United Kingdom, Lt. Gen. Kuzma Derevyanko for the Soviet Union, Gen. Sir Thomas Blamey for Australia, Col. L. Moore Cosgrave for Canada, Gen. Jacques Le Clerc for France, Admiral C. E. L. Helfrich for the Netherlands, and Air Vice Marshal Leonard M. Isitt for New Zealand.]

◇◇◇◇◇

80. TRANSFER OF JAPANESE INDUSTRIAL FACILITIES TO DEVASTATED COUNTRIES

Statement by Frank R. McCoy, United States Member of Far Eastern Commission, April 3, 1947 [1]

[For more than a year after the close of the war in the Pacific, the Far Eastern Commission was unable to lay down a policy for the allocation of Japanese reparations because of basic disagreement among the interested parties. In order to prevent further delay, the United States, in April, 1947, resorted to its power to act unilaterally in Japan on urgent matters and issued the following interim directive. This directive instructed the Supreme Commander of the Allied Powers to distribute as reparations 30 per cent of the Japanese industrial facilities declared to be surplus to Japan's needs.]

*   *   *

This directive will provide that the four specified countries immediately receive out of the Japanese industrial facilities which the Far Eastern Commission has already decided to be available for removals, certain items capable of immediate employment for relief purposes. Those four countries have been assigned percentages which clearly do not prejudice their own or any other country's interest in final national percentage shares of Japanese repara-

[1] Department of State Bulletin of April 13, 1947, pp. 674-675. Made on April 3, 1947, and released to the press on that date. General McCoy is United States member of the Far Eastern Commission.

tions. China will receive 15 percent of such facilities; the Philippines, 5 percent; the Netherlands, for the Indies, 5 percent; and the United Kingdom, for Burma, Malaya, and its colonial possessions in the Far East, 5 percent. The United States will receive nothing for itself under the advance transfers program.

*   *   *

The start of actual reparations removals from Japan has now been delayed for over a year. All members of the Far Eastern Commission agree as to the urgency of commencing such removals. Consistent with the Far Eastern Commission's Terms of Reference, the United States Government, therefore, has decided to send to the Supreme Comamnder as an interim directive the paper on *Advance Transfers of Japanese Reparations,* with an accompanying paper, *Reparations Allocations Procedures for Industrial Facilities in Japan,* which is largely a set of administrative regulations. This interim directive, which will deal only with these two papers, will be placed before the Commission for review in accordance with the Terms of Reference of the Far Eastern Commission, and the Commission will continue to consider this as well as all other aspects of the reparations problem.

◇◇◇◇◇◇

81. SELECTION OF PLANTS FOR REPARATIONS REMOVALS, DESTRUCTION, OR RETENTION IN JAPAN [1]

Policy Decision Approved by the Far Eastern Commission, May 22, 1947

[Beginning in May 1946, the Far Eastern Commission issued directives providing for the transfer of surplus equipment to claimant states in proportion to the destruction the claimants had suffered from Japanese aggression. One of the most difficult issues in resolving the reparations problem was how much Japanese industry could be destroyed or removed in the form of reparations. The following important policy decision by the Far Eastern Commission provided that purely wartime industries were to be destroyed; a fair balance should be achieved between the claimants; the peacetime needs of the Japanese economy should be respected; large monopolies should be dissolved; and priorities were to be established for the plants to be dismantled.]

1. Within those amounts of industrial capacity determined by the Far Eastern Commission for retention in Japan, for destruction, or for removal as reparations, the Supreme Commander for the Allied Powers should, in selecting specific plants, machinery, equipment, and other facilities, give consideration to the following:

   a. Security and industrial disarmament requirements: facilities which have been employed in primary and secondary war industries and facilities in war-

---

[1] Department of State Bulletin of June 22, 1947, p. 1201. Also Activities of the Far Eastern Commission: Report by the Secretary General, Department of State publication 2888, Far Eastern Series 24. Policy decision approved by the Far Eastern Commission on May 22, 1947.

supporting industries, the operation of which was directly and closely related to war industries, should be removed in preference to those not so employed.

b. The achievement of a fair balance between:

(1) The general preferences of reparations claimants for plants, machinery, equipment and other facilities

(a) Of modern and efficient design and manufacture.

(b) In good working condition and capable of being removed from Japan with minimum loss of value and efficiency

(c) In consolidated or integrated units

(d) Of special value or need to claimant countries, and

(2) The legitimate needs, as determined by the Far Eastern Commission, of Japan's peacetime economy for similar equipment having due regard for the geographical location of individual plants in reference to markets, raw materials, manpower, fuel supply, and complementary facilities; for variations in specific products as among types, sizes and other variable characteristics; and for the feasibility of repair and rehabilitation in Japan.

c. The occupation policies of dissolving large industrial and banking corporations which have exercised control over a great part of Japanese trade and industry.

d. Consistent with the provisions of paragraph *a, b,* and *c,* the following order of preference in the selection of particular plants, machinery and equipment for removal:

(1) Plants and equipment owned by the "Zaibatsu" concerns and other big industrial and financial concerns and companies

(2) Plants and equipment owned by other Japanese nationals, the Japanese Government, and by nationals and Governments of the countries which were allies of Japan

(3) Plants and equipment owned by nationals and Governments of the neutral countries.

2. Property of nationals of Members of the United Nations should be dealt with in accordance with FEC-226/1 (Destruction or Removal of United Nations' Property in Japan, Serial No. 76, approved 24 April 1947.)[1]

❖❖❖❖❖

82. BASIC POST-SURRENDER POLICY FOR JAPAN, JUNE 19, 1947 [2]

[The occupation of Japan by the Allied powers was guided during the first two years by directives issued by the United States Government to the American commander-in-chief, who was the Supreme Commander for the Allied Powers for the Occupation and Control of Japan (SCAP). The Far Eastern Commission, which was charged with final determination of the occupation

---

[1] Department of State Bulletin, May 18, 1947, p. 986.

[2] Department of State Bulletin, August 3, 1947, pp. 216-221. Adopted on June 19, 1947, by the Far Eastern Commission, which gave final approval to a set of fundamental principles which had been under continuing examination since the organization of the Commission. The Commission's basic post-surrender policy for Japan will be effective until such time as the treaty of peace comes into force. A directive based upon this policy decision has been forwarded to the Supreme Commander for the Allied Powers for implementation.

policy, did not issue a directive until 1947 because of basic disagreement among its members. Its directive, when finally issued on June 19, 1947, paralleled closely the two preceding United States directives. The instrument, which is reproduced in full below, laid down in broad outline the basic principles which were to guide the occupation forces in the administration of Japan.]

PREAMBLE

WHEREAS on September 2, 1945, Japan surrendered unconditionally to the Allied Powers and is now under military occupation by forces of these Powers under the command of General of the Army Douglas MacArthur, Supreme Commander for the Allied Powers, and

WHEREAS representatives of the following nations, namely, Australia, Canada, China, France, India, the Netherlands, New Zealand, the Philippines, the U.S.S.R., the United Kingdom, and the United States of America, which were engaged in the war against Japan, have on the decision of the Moscow Conference of Foreign Ministers met together at Washington as a Far Eastern Commission, to formulate the policies, principles and standards in conformity with which the fulfillment by Japan of its obligations under the Terms of Surrender may be accomplished;

THE NATIONS COMPOSING THIS COMMISSION, with the object of fulfilling the intentions of the Potsdam Declaration, of carrying out the instrument of surrender and of establishing international security and stability,

CONSCIOUS that such security and stability depend first, upon the complete destruction of the military machine which has been the chief means whereby Japan has carried out the aggressions of past decades; second, upon the establishment of such political and economic conditions as would make impossible any revival of militarism in Japan; and third, upon bringing the Japanese to a realization that their will to war, their plan of conquest, and the methods used to accomplish such plans, have brought them to the verge of ruin,

RESOLVED that Japan cannot be allowed to control her own destinies again until there is on her part a determination to abandon militarism in all its aspects and a desire to live with the rest of the world in peace, and until democratic principles are established in all spheres of the political, economic, and cultural life of Japan;

ARE THEREFORE AGREED:

To ensure the fulfillment of Japan's obligations to the Allied Powers;

To complete the task of physical and spiritual demilitarization of Japan by measures including total disarmament, economic reform designed to deprive Japan of power to make war, elimination of militaristic influences, and stern justice to war criminals, and requiring a period of strict control; and

To help the people of Japan in their own interest as well as that of the world at large to find means whereby they may develop within the framework of a democratic society an intercourse among themselves and with other countries along economic and cultural lines that will enable them to satisfy their reasonable individual and national needs and bring them into permanently peaceful relationship with all nations;

AND HAVE ADOPTED the following basic objectives and policies in dealing with Japan:

PART I—ULTIMATE OBJECTIVES

1. The ultimate objectives in relation to Japan, to which policies for the post-surrender period for Japan should conform, are:

a. To insure that Japan will not again become a menace to the peace and security of the world.

b. To bring about the earliest possible establishment of a democratic and peaceful government which will carry out its international responsibilities, respect the rights of other states, and support the objectives of the United Nations. Such government in Japan should be established in accordance with the freely expressed will of the Japanese people.

2. These objectives will be achieved by the following principal means:

a. Japan's sovereignty will be limited to the islands of Honshu, Hokkaido, Kyushu, Shikoku and such minor outlying islands as may be determined.

b. Japan will be completely disarmed and demilitarized. The authority of the militarists and the influence of militarism will be totally eliminated. All institutions expressive of the spirit of militarism and aggression will be vigorously suppressed.

c. The Japanese people shall be encouraged to develop a desire for individual liberties and respect for fundamental human rights, particularly the freedoms of religion, assembly and association, speech and the press. They shall be encouraged to form democratic and representative organizations.

d. Japan shall be permitted to maintain such industries as will sustain her economy and permit the exaction of just reparations in kind, but not those which would enable her to rearm for war. To this end access to, as distinguished from control of, raw materials should be permitted. Eventual Japanese participation in world trade relations will be permitted.

PART II—ALLIED AUTHORITY

1. MILITARY OCCUPATION

There will be a military occupation of the Japanese home islands to carry into effect the surrender terms and further the achievement of the ultimate objectives stated above. The occupation shall have the character of an operation in behalf of the Powers that have participated in the war against Japan. The principle of participation in the occupation of Japan by forces of these nations is affirmed.

The occupation forces will be under the command of a Supreme Commander designated by the United States.

2. RELATIONSHIP TO JAPANESE GOVERNMENT

The authority of the Emperor and the Japanese Government will be subject to the Supreme Commander, who will possess all powers necessary to effectuate the surrender terms and to carry out the policies established for the conduct of the occupation and the control of Japan.

The Supreme Commander will exercise his authority through Japanese governmental machinery and agencies, including the Emperor, but only to the extent that this satisfactorily furthers the objectives and policies stated herein. According to the judgment and discretion of the Supreme Commander, the Japanese Government may be permitted to exercise the normal powers of government in matters of domestic administration, or the Supreme Commander may in any case direct action to be taken without making use of the agencies of the Japanese Government.

After appropriate preliminary consultation with the representatives of the Allied Powers in the Allied Council for Japan, the Supreme Commander may, in cases of necessity, take decisions concerning the removal of individual ministers of the Japanese Government, or concerning the filling of vacancies created by the resignation of individual cabinet members. Changes in the governmental machinery, or a change in the Japanese Government as whole, will be made in accordance with the principles laid down in the Terms of Reference of the Far Eastern Commission.

The Supreme Commander is not committed to support the Emperor or any other Japanese governmental authority. The policy is to use the existing form of government in Japan and not to support it. Changes in the pre-surrender form of the Emperor institution and in the form of government in the direction of modifying or removing its feudal and authoritarian character and of establishing a democratic Japan are to be encouraged.

3. PROTECTION OF UNITED NATIONS INTERESTS

It shall be the duty of the Supreme Commander to protect the interests, assets, and rights of all Members of the United Nations and their nationals. Where such protection conflicts with the fulfillment of the objectives and policies of the occupation, the government of the nation concerned shall be informed through diplomatic channels and shall be consulted on the question of proper adjustment.

4. PUBLICITY AS TO POLICIES

The peoples of the nations which have participated in the war against Japan, the Japanese people, and the world at large shall be kept fully informed of the objectives and policies of the occupation, and of progress made in their fulfillment.

PART III—POLITICAL

1. DISARMAMENT AND DEMILITARIZATION

Disarmament and demilitarization are the initial tasks of the military occupation and shall be carried out promptly and with determination. Every effort shall be made to bring home to the Japanese people the part played by those who have deceived and misled them into embarking on world conquest, and those who collaborated in so doing.

Japan is not to have any army, navy, airforce, secret police organization, or any civil aviation, or gendarmerie, but may have adequate civilian police forces. Japan's ground, air and naval forces shall be disarmed and disbanded, and the Japanese Imperial General Headquarters, the General Staff and all secret police organizations shall be dissolved. Military and naval material, military and naval vessels and military and naval installations, and military, naval and civilian aircraft, wherever situated, shall be surrendered to the appropriate Allied commanders in their zones of capitulation of the Japanese troops and shall be disposed of in accordance with decisions of the Allied Powers already adopted or which may be adopted. Inventories shall be made and inspections authorized to insure complete execution of these provisions.

High officials of the Japanese Imperial General Headquarters and General Staff, other high military and naval officials of the Japanese Government, leaders of ultra-nationalist and militarist organizations and other important exponents of militarism and aggression will be taken into custody and held for future disposition. Persons who have been active exponents of militarism and militant nationalism will be removed and excluded from public office and from any other position of public or substantial private responsibility. Ultra-nationalistic or militaristic social, political, professional and commercial societies and institutions will be dissolved and prohibited.

The restoraton, even in a disguised form, of any anti-democratic and militaristic activity shall be prevented, particularly on the part of former Japanese career military and naval officers, gendarmerie, and former members of dissolved militaristic, ultra-nationalistic and other anti-democratic organizations.

Militaristic, ultra-nationalistic and anti-democratic doctrines and practices, including para-military training, shall be eliminated from the educational system. Former career military and naval officers, both commissioned and non-commissioned, and all other exponents of militaristic, ultra-nationalistic and anti-democratic doctrines and practices shall be excluded from supervisory and teaching positions.

2. WAR CRIMINALS

Stern justice shall be meted out to all war criminals, including those who visited cruelties upon prisoners of war or other nationals of Members of the United Nations. Persons charged by the Supreme Commander, or appropriate United Nations agencies with being war criminals shall be arrested, tried and, if convicted, punished. Those wanted by another of the United Nations for offenses against its nationals, shall, if not wanted for trial or as witnesses or otherwise by the Supreme Commander, be turned over to the custody of such other nation.

3. ENCOURAGEMENT OF DESIRE FOR INDIVIDUAL LIBERTIES AND DEMOCRATIC PROCESSES

Freedom of worship and observance of all religions shall be proclaimed and guaranteed for the future. It should also be made plain to the Japanese that ultra-nationalistic, militaristic and anti-democratic organizations and movements will not be permitted to hide behind the cloak of religion.

The Japanese people shall be afforded opportunity and encouraged to become familiar with the history, institutions, culture and the accomplishments of the democracies.

Obstacles to the revival and strengthening of democratic tendencies among the Japanese people shall be removed.

Democratic political parties, with rights of assembly and public discussion, and the formation of trade unions shall be encouraged, subject to the necessity for maintaining the security of the occupying forces.

Laws, decrees, and regulations which establish discrimination on grounds of race, nationality, creed or political opinion shall be abrogated; those which conflict with the objectives and policies outlined in this document shall be repealed, suspended or amended as required, and agencies charged specifically with their enforcement shall be abolished or appropriately modified. Persons unjustly confined by Japanese authority on political grounds shall be released. The judicial, legal and police systems shall be reformed as soon as practicable to conform to the policies set forth herein and it shall be the duty of all judicial, legal and police officers to protect individual liberties and civil rights.

PART IV—ECONOMIC

1. ECONOMIC DEMILITARIZATION

The existing economic basis of Japanese military strength must be destroyed and not be permitted to revive.

Therefore, a program will be enforced containing the following elements, among others: the immediate cessation and future prohibition of production of all goods designed for the equipment, maintenance, or use of any military force or establishment; the imposition of a ban upon facilities for the production or repair of implements of war, including naval vessels and all forms of aircraft; the institution of a system of inspection and control designed to prevent concealed or disguised military preparation; the elimination in Japan of those industries or branches of production which would provide Japan with the capacity to rearm for war; and the prohibition of specialized research and instruction contributing directly to the development of war-making power. Research for peaceful ends, will be permitted, but shall be strictly supervised by the Supreme Commander to prevent its use for war purposes. Japan shall be restricted to the maintenance of these industries which will sustain the level of economy and standard of living fixed in accordance with principles determined by the Far Eastern Commission, and consistent with the Potsdam Declaration.

The eventual disposition of those existing production facilities within Japan which are to be eliminated in accord with this program, as between transfer abroad for the purpose of reparations, scrapping, and conversion to other uses, will be determined, after inventory, in accordance with the principles laid down by the Far Eastern Commission or pursuant to the Terms of Reference of the Far Eastern Commission. Pending decision, no such facilities either suitable for transfer abroad or readily convertible for civilian use, shall be destroyed except in emergency situations.

2. PROMOTION OF DEMOCRATIC FORCES

Organizations of labor in industry and agriculture, organized on a democratic basis, shall be encouraged. Other organizations in industry and agriculture, organized on a democratic basis, shall be encouraged if they will contribute to furthering the democratization of Japan or other objectives of the occupation.

Policies shall be laid down with the object of insuring a wide and just distribution of income and of the ownership of the means of production and trade.

Encouragement shall be given to those forms of economic activity, organization and leadership deemed likely to strengthen the democratic forces in Japan and to prevent economic activity from being used in support of military ends.

To this end it shall be the policy of the Supreme Commander:

a. To prohibit the retention in important positions in the economic field of individuals who because of their past associations or for other reasons cannot be trusted to direct Japanese economic effort solely towards peaceful and democratic ends; and

b. To require a program for the dissolution of the large industrial and banking combinations accompanied by their progressive replacement by organizations which would widen the basis of control and ownership.

3. RESUMPTION OF PEACEFUL ECONOMIC ACTIVITY

The policies of Japan have brought down upon the people great economic destruction and confronted them with economic difficulty and suffering. The plight of Japan is the direct outcome of its own behavior, and the Allies will not undertake the burden of repairing the damage. It can be repaired only if the Japanese people renounce all military aims and apply themselves diligently and with single purpose to the ways of peaceful living. It will be necessary for them to undertake physical reconstruction and basically to reform the nature and direction of their economic activities and institutions. In accordance with assurances contained in the Potsdam Declaration, the Allies have no intention of imposing conditions which would prevent the accomplishment of these tasks in due time.

Japan will be expected to provide goods and services to meet the needs of the occupying forces to the extent that this can, in the judgment of the Supreme Commander, be effected without causing starvation, wide-spread disease and acute physical distress.

The Japanese authorities will be expected, and if necessary directed, to maintain, develop and enforce programs, subject to the approval of the Supreme Commander, which are designed to serve the following purposes:

a. To avoid acute economic distress.

b. To assure just and impartial distribution of available supplies.

c. To meet the requirements for reparations deliveries.

d. To make such provision for the needs of the Japanese population as may be deemed reasonable in accordance with principles formulated by the Far Eastern Commission in the light both of supplies available and of obligations to other peoples of the United Nations and territories formerly occupied by Japan.

4. REPARATIONS AND RESTITUTIONS

Reparations

For acts of aggression committed by Japan and for the purpose of equitable reparation of the damage caused by her to the Allied Powers and in the interests of destruction of the Japanese war potential in those industries which could lead to Japan's rearmament for waging war, reparations shall be exacted from Japan through the transfer˙of such existing Japanese capital equipment and facilities or such Japanese goods as exist or may in future be produced and which under policies set forth by the Far Eastern Commission· or pursuant to the Terms of Reference of the Far Eastern Commission should be made available for this purpose. The reparations shall be in such a form as would not endanger the fulfillment of the program of demilitarization of Japan and which would not prejudice the defraying of the cost of the occupation and the maintenance of the minimum civilian standard of living. The shares of particular countries in the total sum of the reparations from Japan shall be determined on a broad political basis, taking into due account the scope of material and human destruction and damage suffered by each claimant country as a result of the preparation and execution of Japanese aggression, and taking also into due account each country's contribution to the cause of the defeat of Japan, including the extent and duration of its resistence [sic] to Japanese aggression.

Restitution

Full and prompt restitution will be required of all identifiable property, looted, delivered under duress, or paid for in worthless currency.

5. FISCAL, MONETARY, AND BANKING POLICIES

While the Japanese authorities will remain responsible for the management and direction of the domestic fiscal, monetary, and credit policies, this responsibility is subject to the approval and review of the Supreme Commander, and wherever necessary to his direction.

6. INTERNATIONAL TRADE AND FINANCIAL RELATIONS

Eventual Japanese participation in world trade relations shall be permitted. During occupation and under suitable controls and subject to the prior requirements of the peoples of countries which have participated in the war against Japan, Japan will be permitted to purchase from foreign countries raw materials and other goods that it may need for peaceful purposes. Japan will also be permitted under suitable controls to export goods to pay for approved imports. Exports other than those directed to be shipped on reparations account or as restitution may be made only to those recipients who agree to provide necessary imports in exchange or agree to pay for such exports in foreign exchange usable in purchasing imports. The proceeds of Japanese exports may be used after the minimum civilian standard of living has been secured to pay for the costs of non-military imports necessary for the occupation which have already been made since the surrender.

Control is to be maintained over all imports and exports of goods and foreign exchange and financial transactions. The Far Eastern Commission shall formulate the policies and principles governing exports from and imports to Japan. The Far Eastern Commission will formulate the policies to be followed in the exercise of these controls.

7. JAPANESE PROPERTY LOCATED ABROAD

The clauses herein on reparations and references to this subject are without prejudice to the views of Governments on the overseas assets issue.

8. EQUALITY OF OPPORTUNITY FOR FOREIGN ENTERPRISE WITHIN JAPAN

All business organizations of any of the United Nations shall have equal opportunity in the overseas trade and commerce of Japan. Within Japan equal treatment shall be accorded to all nationals of the United Nations.

9. IMPERIAL HOUSEHOLD PROPERTY

Imperial Household property shall not be exempt from any action necessary to carry out the objectives of the occupation.

83. EXAMINATION OF MATTERS RELATING TO JAPANESE REPARATIONS

Report on the Economic Position and Prospects of Japan and Korea (Johnston Report), April 26, 1948 (Excerpts) [1]

[In the spring of 1948, a group of American businessmen (the Johnston committee) made an independent study of the economics of Japan and Korea and recommended a more lenient reparations policy. Their report, brief excerpts of which are reproduced below, emphasized the principle that industrial plants necessary for the recovery of Japan should not be dismantled and that only excess capacity should be removed. Any other course, argued the committee, would result in the United States footing the reparations bill.]

REPARATIONS

Reparations policy toward Japan has been in the process of development since the surrender in August 1945. Reports of the Pauley Committee, the National Engineers Council, the Special Committee on Japanese Reparations (Strike Report), the Economic Analysis of the State Department, reparations studies of SCAP, studies made by the members of the Far Eastern Commission and finally the comprehensive report of Overseas Consultants, Inc., all of which have contributed to a better understanding and clarification of the problem.

These reports differ in many respects, yet all are in agreement on these two premises:

(1) Japan's industries must be so demilitarized as to prevent it ever again becoming a threat to the peace of the world.

(2) Japan should be left sufficient industrial capacity so that it will have an opportunity to develop an economy which will provide a tolerable standard of living.

In seeking to determine the amount and character of industrial plants re-

[1] Department of Army press release, May 19, 1948.

quired to meet the objective stated in (2) above, various estimates were offered. The earlier estimates differed so widely that the occupying authorities .decided that there was need for an all-inclusive and detailed analysis of the Japanese plant and its potential. Consequently, in June 1947, Overseas Consultants, Inc., an organization of eleven distinguished industrial engineering and appraisal companies, was formed and engaged by the Secretary of War to make such an analysis.

*   *   *

The Committee has given careful consideration to studies and recommendations made by the various groups heretofore, and, after carefully considering on-the-scene data, recommends that:

(1) External assets formerly owned by Japan be formally released to the countries holding jurisdiction over the territories in which these assets were located at the time of the Japanese surrender.

(2) There be made available as reparations from the home islands of Japan the machinery and industrial equipment in all government-owned arsenals except for (a) such equipment as is deemed necessary by SCAP for the Japanese economy or for occupation use, and (b) such non-armament facilities (fertilizer, fuel, oil storage, etc.) as were exempted from the interim reparation program by the FEC policy decision of 13 May 1946.

(3) There be made available for reparations certain other plants and equipment in amounts as listed by industries at the end of this section.

(4) These recommendations be made effective at the earliest possible moment by appropriate directives to SCAP, which directives should include (a) percentage shares of the total to be allotted to each FEC nation or a limiting date prior to which those nations should settle the division between them of the total available items, (b) a limiting date for the acceptance by each nation of the items allocated to it, and (c) a statement that these directives supersede all previous directives on the same subject.

(5) No industrial equipment in addition to that included in these recommendations be made available for reparations: Provided, however, that SCAP should be authorized to substitute for any item specified in those recommendations any other item of equivalent productive capacity.

If the above recommendations for a final reparations settlement are carried out, the amount of plant equipment and the number of machine tools available for reparations will be reduced below the level recommended by Overseas Consultants, Inc. Our major purpose in recommending this reduction is to retain for the rehabilitation of Japan's peacetime industry a substantial number of machine tools of modern design. Only by retaining such tools can the peacetime industry of Japan quickly be rehabilitated on an efficient basis. In view of the developments of the last two years and the continuing deficit economy, there is, in our opinion, a cumulative urgency for the rapid rehabilitation of Japan's industry.

Paramount to all other considerations is the need for prompt and final action. Further delay in the settlement of the reparation problem will not help the claimant nations and will hurt Japan greatly.

RECOMMENDED REMOVALS FOR REPARATIONS

Industry	Annual capacity		Value (1939 yen)
Nitric acid	Metric tons	82,000	8,000,000
Synthetic rubber	Metric tons	750	10,000,000
Shipbuilding	Gross tons	152,300	50,000,000
Aluminum and magnesium fabricating	Metric tons	50,000	21,688,000
Magnesium reduction	Metric tons	480	12,559,000
Subtotal			102,247,000
Primary war facilities			560,000,000
Total			662,247,000

NOTE.—Only those primary war facilities in government owned arsenals should be made available for reparations. Those facilities within the government owned arsenals designated by the Supreme Commander for the Allied Powers, as essentials for the rehabilitation of Japan's industrial economy, should be exempted.

84. ACTIVITIES OF THE FAR EASTERN COMMISSION, JULY 10, 1947 TO DECEMBER 23, 1948

Second Report by the Secretary General [1]

[In the autumn of 1945, the United States proposed a Far Eastern Advisory Commission to formulate Allied policy for Japan. It was established over the Soviet Union's protest, since the latter desired a control commission for Japan similar to those of Germany and Austria. In December 1945, at the Moscow Conference, a compromise arrangement was reached and a Far Eastern Commission created. This Commission, which, at the time this book goes to press, is still located in Washington, determines and fixes occupation policies which are transmitted through the United States Government to the Supreme Commander in Tokyo. The Commission's second annual report, which is the most comprehensive to date, reflects the nature of the problems which have been encountered in the occupation of Japan.]

REVIEW

A year and a half has passed since the first public report on the activities of the Far Eastern Commission made its appearance.[2] That document summarized developments in the Commission from its inception on February 26, 1946, to July 10, 1947. During that year and a half a total of 41 formal decisions on matters relating to Allied policy for the occupation of Japan were adopted. Since July 10, 1947, 13 more policy decisions—some on matters previously reported as under discussion, some on issues not then mentioned—have been approved. Still other matters previously reported as under discussion have not as yet been finally settled by Commission action.

The broad policy objectives to which the work of the Far Eastern Commission must of necessity conform are set forth in the Potsdam Declaration. Roughly, they are three—disarmament, democratization, and the determina-

[1] Department of State Documents and State Papers, January 1949, pp. 615-622.
[2] Activities of the Far Eastern Commission, Department of State publication 2888 (1947).

tion of a self-sustaining economy for Japan. Except for the Basic Post-Surrender Policy for Japan, which was a general statement of Allied policy covering a variety of points, Commission decisions previously reported have generally fallen under one or another of these three main headings. Disarmament, for example, although not yet the subject of a separate policy decision last year, was touched upon in the Basic Post-Surrender Policy. In addition, several decisions on reparations and economic matters had distinct disarmament implications in so far as they placed limitations on Japanese industrial capacity. With respect to democratization, the Commission's accomplishments included policies relating to Japan's new Constitution, educational reform, and the development of trade-union activity. Commission activity in the field of economic readjustment and recovery included an "interim" reparations removal program, the designation of the period 1930-34 as a yardstick for determining Japan's proper peacetime standard of living, and several policies looking toward the revival of Japanese trade. Outside the scope of these three main headings the Commission's work also touched on a number of miscellaneous subjects, including war criminals, aliens in Japan, and the prohibition of Japanese research in atomic energy.

Also mentioned in a very general way in the earlier report were several subjects still under consideration; specifically, these included disarmament, reduction of industrial war potential, a revised policy on the restitution of looted property, percentage reparations shares, and peacetime levels for certain specified Japanese industries.

DISARMAMENT OF JAPAN

Of the 13 policies adopted by the Far Eastern Commission since July 1947, several represent agreement on subjects previously reported as under consideration. This is true in the case of disarmament, the first of the three major headings under which Commission action can still be most easily considered. A policy decision on disarmament, entitled "Prohibition of Military Activity in Japan and Disposition of the Japanese Military Equipment," was adopted on February 12, 1948.[1]

Under the terms of this decision, possession by Japanese of arms, ammunition, and implements of war is prohibited, except that the Supreme Commander for the Allied Powers (SCAP) may authorize the use of small arms by Japanese civil police agencies. In addition, the development, manufacture, or exportation of arms, ammunition, and implements of war is prohibited, and the importation of such items is restricted to the number and kind required by Japanese civil police. Manufacture of aircraft and naval vessels and reconversion of commercial vessels for military purposes are prohibited. Japan is forbidden any military or "para-military" organizations, including, of course, a ministry of war. Provisions against the subsequent revival of Japanese military activity are also included; any revival of the "Japanese Army, Navy, gendarmerie, secret police and their administrative organs" is banned, and military records are to be "confiscated and transferred to the Supreme Commander for the Allied Powers for subsequent destruction. No further records of this nature should be compiled or maintained by the Japanese." All organizations of a military or ultra-nationalistic nature are forbidden and their

[1] DOCUMENTS AND STATE PAPERS, May 1948, p. 99.

"revival or establishment in any form, including a disguised form," prohibited. This provision is intended to apply as well to "any other associations composed wholly or substantially of ex-officers of the Japanese Army and Navy and gendarmerie, ostensibly created for legitimate purposes, but which are, in reality, disguised forms of military or para-military organizations, or which have some other disguised subversive purpose." Military drills or similar training in schools are prohibited and career officers are barred not only from public office but also from teaching, except in so far as SCAP may otherwise specifically authorize.

In connection with disarmament, mention might also be made of a policy adopted on August 14, 1947, on "Reduction of Japanese Industrial War Potential," another subject previously reported as under discussion.[1] This policy, which will be handled in detail below, lays the framework for the destruction or reduction of those portions of Japan's industries which contributed to her war-making strength.

ATTENDANCE AT INTER-GOVERNMENTAL CONFERENCES

A policy decision adopted on June 9, 1948, entitled "Attendance at Inter-Governmental Conferences,"[2] has a direct bearing on the occupation objective of democratization. This decision, incidentally, is on a subject not mentioned in the previous report. It permits members of SCAP's staff, upon appropriate invitation, to serve as observers at inter-governmental conferences, provided their attendance is considered to be in the interest of the occupation, and also makes it possible for technical personnel of Japanese nationality to accompany these observers if their presence is necessary and if the country acting as host to the conference in question has no objection.

PRINCIPLES FOR JAPANESE FARMERS' ORGANIZATIONS

A second policy decision, adopted on December 9, 1948, also bears on the objective of strengthening democratic tendencies. Entitled "Principles for Japanese Farmers' Organizations"[3] it specifies that Japanese farmers are to

---

[1] Department of State Bulletin of September 14, 1947, p. 513.

[2] ATTENDANCE AT INTER-GOVERNMENTAL CONFERENCES (FEC Policy Decision, 9 June 1948). The Far Eastern Commission decides as a matter of policy that:

1. Upon receipt of an appropriate invitation SCAP may appoint members of his staff as observers at inter-governmental conferences, attendance at which he deems to be in the interest of the occupation.

2. Members of SCAP's staff attending an inter-governmental conference on invitation as provided in paragraph 1, may be accompanied by Japanese technical personnel when deemed necessary by SCAP, and when the attendance of Japanese personnel is acceptable to the country acting as host to the conference.

[3] PRINCIPLES FOR JAPANESE FARMERS' ORGANIZATIONS (FEC Policy Decision, 9 December 1948)

General principles

1. Japanese farmers should be encouraged to form themselves into farmers' organizations, including unions and cooperatives of all kinds, for their mutual economic and social benefit, and for the purpose of preserving and improving conditions of agricultural work and otherwise assisting the legitimate interests of farmers.

2. Farmers' organizations and their members should be assured of and encouraged to observe in the conduct of their operations the fundamental freedoms guaranteed by Chapter III ("Rights and Duties of the People") of the Constitution of Japan.

3. Any existing laws or parts thereof which are contrary to the provisions stated in this policy should be abrogated, and any organizations established thereunder abolished.

4. This policy should be put into effect gradually, due regard being paid to the immediate

be "encouraged to form themselves into farmers' organizations, including unions and cooperatives of all kinds, for their mutual economic and social benefit, and for the purpose of preserving and improving conditions of agricultural work and otherwise assisting the legitimate interests of farmers." This policy further provides that Japanese farmers' organizations "should be assured of and encouraged to observe in the conduct of their operations the fundamental freedoms guaranteed" by the Constitution and that any existing laws which are contrary to the provisions of this policy "should be abrogated, and any organizations established thereunder abolished."

Under this policy the organizing of farmer's cooperatives is to be pro-

---

economic needs of the country and the need to prevent avoidable dislocation of food control measures.

Farmers' Cooperatives

5. Farmers' cooperatives should be a means whereby those who are actively concerned in obtaining their living by working on the land or in pursuits closely connected therewith can combine for their mutual advantage.

6. The right of farmers to organize themselves into cooperatives should be assured and protected by law and the freedom of farmers to join or abstain from joining cooperatives should be provided by law. Any farmers' cooperative should have the power to make rules admitting to membership any person who is not a genuine farmer, which rules may or may not exclude non-farmers from voting. Measures should be taken, however, to prevent cooperatives becoming controlled by any banking, trade, industrial, or other non-farmer companies and interests.

7. Farmers' cooperatives should not be subject to any adversely discriminatory taxation, nor to any discriminatory restrictions upon their engaging in any economic activity related to their own agricultural pursuits and for the benefit of members.

8. Farmers' cooperatives should be subject to the laws relating to juridical persons, but should not, in their internal management and operation, be subject to any control, interference, or supervision by any administrative organ of the Japanese Government, nor should they be subject to dissolution by administrative order. Where it is alleged that cooperatives have violated the law, or their articles of incorporation or by-laws, remedial action should be sought and taken through the courts of law and not through government decree or administrative decision.

9. Farmers' cooperatives should be free from any obligation to take part in, or from any responsibility for, the enforcement of government measures, except that they should comply with government measures to the same extent as any other Japanese national or organization under Japanese Government jurisdiction.

10. Farmers' cooperatives should be encouraged and assisted by the Japanese Government in providing education for their members, both generally in an understanding of democratic processes and particularly in cooperative practices and agricultural techniques. The Japanese Government should, as far as possible, assist cooperative officials in obtaining information on cooperative activities in other countries. These objectives should be given due weight when allocations of paper supplies and import of foreign publications are made.

11. Japanese should be free to choose the forms of organization of their cooperatives. Cooperatives should be allowed to associate themselves in regional or national bodies, with representation in such bodies in proportion to the membership of the individual cooperatives. Emphasis, however, should be placed on the importance of a solid local basis for the future of cooperative activity in Japan.

12. The director and officials, other than administrative officers, of farmers' cooperatives should be elected at regular stated intervals by the farmers concerned by secret ballot and democratic methods. Each member should have one vote. It should be the responsibility of the cooperatives to ensure that all their activities are democratically conducted.

13. No member should hold office in a cooperative if (1) he is engaged in activities which are likely substantially to compete with the activities of the cooperative, or (2) he is subject to the purge directive of January 4, 1946, or subject to subsequent purge directives by the Supreme Commander for the Allied Powers.

14. The Japanese Government, in so far as practicable, should make available to farmers' cooperatives technical advisory and other services and should ensure that credit is available to them on reasonable terms.

15. Farmers' cooperatives should be encouraged to participate in voluntary measures to promote the objectives of the occupation.

Farmers' Unions

16. The Principles for Japanese Trade Unions (Fec-045/5) should, with the necessary modifications, be applicable to farmers' unions.

tected by law. When cooperatives are established they are to be free from any discriminatory taxation or restrictions on their economic activities, from any administrative control by organs of the Japanese Government, and from any special responsibility for the enforcement of Government measures. The Government, on the other hand, should make available to cooperatives, where practicable, credit on reasonable terms, technical advisory services, and information on cooperative activities abroad.

Farmers' cooperatives should be democratically organized and operated, and Japanese should be free to choose the forms of organization of their cooperatives and should be encouraged to provide education for their members in the understanding of democratic processes. No person subject to "purge" directives or engaged in activities competitive with those of the cooperatives should be allowed to hold office in a cooperative. Steps should be taken "to prevent cooperatives becoming controlled by any banking, trade, industrial, or other non-farmer companies and interests."

The policy further provides that the principles already adopted by the commission for Japanese Trade Unions [1] should, with necessary modifications, be applicable to farmers unions.

REDUCTION OF JAPANESE INDUSTRIAL WAR POTENTIAL

With regard to the third main policy objective, determination of a peaceful and viable economy for Japan, several important decisions, some on matters previously reported under discussion, have been adopted during the year.

Mention has already been made of the policy "Reduction of Japanese Industrial War Potential." Generally speaking the principal economic task of the occupation is to fix the productive capacity of Japan's major industries at a level which will prevent her from again becoming a threat to world peace but which is high enough to provide her with a viable peaceful economy. The decision on "Reduction of Japanese Industrial War Potential" was an important step forward in accomplishing this task.

The policy describes measures necessary to insure that Japan shall not retain industrial capacity for manufacture of armaments or capacity to provide a foundation on which armament industries could be quickly rebuilt. A distinction is made between industrial facilities which were directly engaged in the production of combat weapons (defined as "primary and secondary war facilities")—for example, arsenals and aircraft plants—and industries, such as iron and steel, light metals, automobiles, and synthetic rubber, which are capable of important military as well as peaceful uses (defined as "war-supporting industries"). Primary and secondary war facilities which are "functionally limited to use in connection with combat equipment end-products" are to be destroyed. The "war-supporting" industries which are listed in the policy are to be reduced to levels no greater than necessary to "meet the peaceful needs of the Japanese people." The policy further provides that primary and secondary war facilities and excess capacity in the war-supporting industries should, when it is not provided that they should be destroyed, be made available for removal as reparations.

[1] Activities of the Far Eastern Commission, Department of State, Publication 2888 (1947), appendix 37, p. 91.

After the reductions and removals provided for have been accomplished, any reestablishment of primary war industries is prohibited throughout the period of the occupation. This prohibition extends to the "manufacture or assembly of civil aircraft; and [to] the participation by the Japanese Government or Japanese nationals in the ownership or airborne operation of civil aircraft"; and also to "the building of merchant vessels above a size to be determined by the Far Eastern Commission." As far as war-supporting industries are concerned, however, there is a stipulation that in the case of seven specified industries [1] such peacetime levels as may separately be established will hold valid "until the end of the present phase of the occupation of Japan or until 1 October 1949, whichever is the earlier, pending a decision as to the long-term disarmament controls."

One other item in this important policy decision deserves mention. The Supreme Commander is given a general authorization "to except temporarily from the provisions of this paper particularly primary war facilities, secondary war facilities, and facilities in war-supporting industries, in so far as such facilities are required to meet the needs of the occupation."

ISSUES AWAITING DECISION

As has been said above, the policy on reduction of industrial war potential was an important step forward, but it left several important decisions to be made. The most important is the determination of specific levels in the war-supporting industries. In a previous policy decision the Commission had selected the 1930-34 standard of living as .the most appropriate by which to measure Japan's peaceful needs in 1950, by which year it was hoped economic conditions in Japan might approach the normal. It was proposed in this same policy decision to make an estimate of the nature and size of the industrial structure required to satisfy those needs, account being taken of such factors as technological developments, the balance of payments, and employment. With the adoption of the paper on "Reduction of Japanese Industrial War Potential," the Commission had defined the particular war-supporting industries in which capacity in excess of that necessary to meet the peaceful needs of the Japanese people, as defined by the Far Eastern Commission, should be made available for removal as reparations. The task of determining actual capacity levels in these industries still remains to be completed.

As stated above, the policy also prohibits building of merchant vessels above a size to be determined by the Far Eastern Commission. So far the Commission has not reached a decision on this matter.

Finally, though the policy provides that excess industrial facilities in Japan should be made available for removal as reparations, the completion of such removals awaits a decision on the shares which claimant countries are to receive.

*   *   *

◇◇◇◇◇◇

[1] Iron and steel, light metals, metal working machinery, shipbuilding, oil refining and storage, synthetic oil, and synthetic rubber.

85. JAPANESE REPARATIONS AND LEVEL OF INDUSTRY [1]

Statement by Frank R. McCoy, U. S. Representative on the Far Eastern Commission, May 12, 1949

[The report of the Johnston Committee—a group of American businessmen who went to Japan in 1948—concluded that the Japanese economy was operating at a heavy deficit, much of which was being borne by the American taxpayer. It emphasized the point that Japan should be permitted to retain an adequate industrial capacity to enable it to provide a tolerable standard of living for its people. The following statement of the United States representative on the Far Eastern Commission announced that these were also the views of our government; and that the United States would no longer use its interim directive powers to make possible further reparations removals from Japan.]

*   *   *

In our discussions of the matter here in the Commission, we have proceeded from the agreement contained in the Potsdam Declaration that reparations would be exacted from Japan and that they should be in a form which would not impair the ability of the Japanese people to support themselves. From the earliest days of the Far Eastern Commission, the United States has been guided by a desire that the victims of Japanese aggression receive as reparations such of Japan's resources as was possible without jeopardizing Japan's ability to meet its own peaceful needs. The United States has felt, further, that in order that the nations devastated by Japan might receive reparation while their need was greatest, in order that there might be removed from the mind of the Japanese Government and people uncertainty regarding the reparations question, and in order that as many as possible of Japan's postwar obligations might be disposed of during the period of the occupation, a reparations program should be worked out and put into effect at the earliest practical moment.

*   *   *

I should like to emphasize at this point that the action of my government, and, it is assumed, of the other member governments, in participating in the policy decisions which have been taken by the Commission on the question of reparations was predicated upon two basic assumptions, namely, that the resources to be removed from Japan as reparations were clearly excess to the peaceful needs of a self-supporting Japanese economy, and that there would be a shares schedule acceptable to and agreed upon by the Far Eastern Commission countries which would determine in what proportions available reparations should be divided.

As I have already stated, and as the Commission well knows, the second of these assumptions has not been realized, and there seems little prospect of

[1] Department of State Bulletin of May 22, 1949, pp. 667-670. Made before the Commission on May 12, 1949, and released to the press in Washington on the same date.

its being realized. As regards the first assumption, that reparations removals should be limited to facilities clearly excess to the needs of a self-supporting Japanese economy, successive studies during the past 18 months of Japan's future industrial requirements have necessitated progressive upward adjustments of earlier estimates of these requirements.

*   *   *

The United States has, since the time of the Japanese surrender, carried the burden of preventing such disease and unrest in Japan as might jeopardize the purposes of the occupation. The critical economic conditions with which, it is now apparent, Japan is faced, and the prospect of continuing deficits in Japan's international payments for some years to come, render measures of Japanese economic recovery of utmost importance. It is inescapable that if the basic purposes of the occupation are to be achieved, the Japanese people must be enabled to support themselves at a tolerable standard of living. No one could reasonably suggest that Japan should be abandoned to economic despair. So to abandon Japan would be to undo the costly victory in the Pacific.

*   *   *

In view of the above considerations, the United States is forced to the following conclusions:

(a) The deficit Japanese economy shows little prospect of being balanced in the near future and, to achieve eventual balance, will require all resources at its disposal.

(b) The burden of removing further reparations from Japan could detract seriously from the occupation objective of stabilizing the Japanese economy and permitting it to move toward self-support.

(c) There is little or no prospect of Far Eastern Commission agreement on a reparations-shares schedule despite the repeated initiatives by the United States over the past 3 years to assist the Commission in reaching such an agreement. Without agreement on a shares schedule the existing Far Eastern Commission policy decisions regarding reparations are incapable of implementation.

(d) Japan has already paid substantial reparations through expropriation of its former overseas assets and, in smaller degree, under the Advance Transfer Program.

In light of these conclusions the United States Government is impelled to rescind its interim directive of April 4, 1947, bringing to an end the Advance Transfer Program called for by that directive. It is impelled also to withdraw its proposal of November 6, 1947, on Japanese reparations shares, and I am so informing the Secretary-General. Finally, the United States Government takes this occasion to announce that it has no intention of taking further unilateral action under its interim directive powers to make possible additional reparations removals from Japan.

*   *   *

The United States Government plans shortly to submit to the FEC for its consideration proposals for the rescission or amendment of existing and pending FEC reparations and level-of-industry policy papers so as to bring FEC policies on these matters, should the proposals be approved by the Commission, into conformity with the position which I have set forth. My government earnestly hopes that the other member governments will appreciate the considerations underlying this position and will be able to concur in the new United States proposals.

◇◇◇◇◇◇

86. ESSENTIALS OF A PEACE WITH JAPAN

Address by John Foster Dulles, March 31, 1951 [1]

[The turbulent situation in the Far East during 1950 and 1951, particularly as it pertained to the Korean affair and the Communist control of China, made desirable a speedy return of Japan to normal peacetime conditions. Preliminary negotiations for a peace treaty were carried on by the United States for several months before the nature of the terms was made public. In an address at Whittier College, Ambassador Dulles, who had been charged by the President with the responsibility for carrying on negotiations with respect to the treaty, outlined the main provisions of the treaty as they had been developed up to that time by our government. Excerpts from Mr. Dulles' address are reproduced below.]

*　　*　　*

Two principal postwar goals of the Soviet Communists are Japan and Germany. If Russia's rulers could exploit the industrial and human potential of either Japan or Germany, it would be a sad day for peace. That would involve such a shift in the balance of world power that these new imperialists might calculate that they could start a general war with good prospect of success. They know that Japan, even alone, was able seriously to menace the free world in the Pacific and they imagine vast possibilities out of a combination, under their direction, of the Asiatic power of Russia, China, and Japan.

Fortunately the Japanese people do not want that combination, which would make them the front line of a new aggression which in the end would mean disaster far greater than that which they have already suffered. They are in a mood to reject militarism in all of its aspects, and they want fellowship with the nations which genuinely seek peace through collective security in accordance with the principles of the United Nations. Thus there is the opportunity to make a Japanese peace which will not only end the old war but give new strength and hope to those who strive to prevent another war.

*　　*　　*

We contemplate a simple document, limited to the essentials of peace.

*　　*　　*

[1] Department of State Publication 4171; Far Eastern Series 40. The peace treaty with Japan was signed in San Francisco September 8, 1951.

TERRITORY

The treaty proper would prescribe the territory over which the Japanese will hereafter be sovereign. It is contemplated generally speaking that Japan's sovereignty should be limited in accordance with the agreed surrender terms. That would mean sovereignty over the four home islands and minor adjacent islands. There would be a renunciation by Japan of all rights, titles, and claims to Korea, Formosa, the Pescadores, and the Antarctic area. Also the treaty might contemplate that in the Ryukyu and Bonin islands there could be United Nations trusteeship and continuing United States administrative responsibility.

The South Sakhalin and Kurile Islands were allotted to Russia at Yalta and are actually in Russian possession. Any peace-treaty validation of Russia's title should, we suggest, be dependent upon Russia's becoming a party to that treaty.

SECURITY

The security of Japan itself should, we think, be worked out through individual and collective self-defense arrangements authorized by the United Nations Charter. Thus the peace treaty itself need only affirm that, upon the coming into force of the peace, Japan would in fact possess what the Charter of the United Nations refers to as the "inherent right" of sovereign nations in these respects.

*　　*　　*

JAPAN'S SECURITY

Since Japan is now thoroughly disarmed and materially and legally unable to maintain armed forces, there is need for provisional security measures. Accordingly, with the authority of the President, and following conversations with committees of Congress, I stated publicly in Japan that, if the Japanese wanted it, the United States would sympathetically consider the retention of United States armed forces in and about Japan, so that the coming into force of a treaty of peace would not leave Japan a vacuum of power and, as such, an easy prey to such aggression as has already shown itself in nearby Korea. This suggestion of mine was warmly welcomed by the Japanese Government and the people generally so that it is now in order to study the implementation of such an arrangement.

Since Japan is an island, its security is strongly influenced by sea and air power—power which the United States is in a position to exercise in the Pacific. The defense of Japan need not require, either now from the United States or ultimately from Japan, as large ground forces as might be thought to be necessary if Japan had common land boundaries with militaristic powers.

PACIFIC SECURITY

Bound up with the problem of Japan's security is the broader problem of security in the Pacific. Japan should hereafter make some contribution of its own to security, but this should never be the pretext for militarism that could be an aggressive threat. Thus the problem has a dual aspect.

No nation able to make a dependable contribution to security should get a "free ride." In our Senate, the Vandenberg Resolution has laid down for the United States the basic proposition that collective-security arrangements should be based upon "continuous and effective self-help and mutual aid." The United Nations Charter also establishes that all peace-loving states should stand ready to contribute armed forces, assistance, and facilities for the purpose of maintaining international peace and security. That is one aspect of the problem. The other side of the problem is that Japan should never again develop armament which could be an offensive threat or serve other than to promote peace and security in accordance with the purposes and principles of the United Nations Charter. The peace we seek is one which will for all time liberate Japan's neighbors and indeed the Japanese people from the nightmare of militarism.

When we were in Canberra, Australia, our mission had significant discussions on this subject with the Governments of Australia and New Zealand. They made convincingly clear the attitude of their peoples on this subject. Now we are working actively to find the ways to secure the desired results.

We believe that out of our discussions, which are now well advanced, there will emerge a series of arrangements which on the one hand will enable the Japanese to make their own indispensable contribution to preventing their nation's being forced into the service of the new imperialism that ominously threatens from the mainland and which on the other hand will effectively assure that there will be no unbridled rearmament which could become an. offensive threat.

The United States is able and daily growing more able to exert a mighty influence for peace and to make peace in the Pacific more secure than it has ever been before. We can see the way to remove the pall of fear which results from Japan's past conduct and from the present Communist menace. But that is not a task which we would or should undertake single-handed and alone. In the Pacific, as elsewhere, security is a cooperative enterprise. Those who wish to cooperate for security can share the protection of immense deterrent power which, in the words of the United Nations Charter, "shall not be used, save in the common interest."

Since the arrangements for peace and security in the Pacific will in part be outside of the peace treaty and since the whole problem is not yet fully explored, we consider that any presently suggested treaty provisions are to be supplemented in the light of the outcome of the promising exchanges of views which are now taking place and to which we attach the utmost importance. No one should assume that the United States takes this problem lightly or that we shall accept a solution that will be illusory.

REPARATIONS

As regards reparations, the United States does not question the inherent justice of the proposition that Japan should make good the damage done to others by its aggression. Reparation is, however, not merely a matter of what is just but of what is economically practicable, without disastrous consequences. We have closely examined this problem. Considerable industrial machinery has already been removed from Japan and given to countries having reparation claims. Also there is substantial Japanese property within allied countries which, as indicated, should be applicable to the satisfaction of claims. It is, however, not easy to see the possibility of Japan's providing future reparation out of her remaining capital assets or as a surplus from her current economic activity over coming years.

One of the gravest problems which confront Japan, and it equally concerns the reparation creditors, is whether Japan, deprived of its formerly owned sources of raw material and with a population of 85 million on four relatively small and barren islands, can maintain the standard of living and employment necessary to prevent widespread social unrest. This, if it occurred, would inevitably give rise to dangerous expansionist and explosive tendencies, which Japan's Communist neighbors would joyously exploit.

The United States, to prevent social and economic unrest within Japan since the occupation began, has advanced about 2 billion dollars for relief and economic assistance. That is a realistic measure of how seriously the United States views this problem and its responsibility as principal occupying power. However, the United States is not prepared after the occupation ends to continue indefinitely such economic relief. Neither is it willing in effect to pay Japanese reparations by putting into Japan what reparation creditors would take out. The United States considers indeed that its postwar advances have a certain priority status.

We doubt that it is practicable to get the essential over-all and long-range results which are sought, if the treaty also seeks to extract reparation payments other than in terms of the Japanese assets already received from Japan or within the territory of the Allied Powers. However, the United States has not closed its mind on this subject, and it is, with an open mind, actively exchanging views with countries which were most grievously damaged by Japanese aggression.

ECONOMIC DISABILITIES

Some suggestions have been made as to imposing upon the Japanese economic disabilities as, for example, requiring a dismantling of a part of Japan's industrial plants, particularly her shipbuilding capacity. As experience in Germany has shown, such provisions cannot be carried out without arousing great public bitterness. If the peace treaty required the first postwar Japanese Government physically to decimate Japan's industrial equipment, it would impose an almost inhuman burden, and the consequences would almost surely be against the best interests of the Allied Powers.

*   *   *

A PEACE OF RECONCILIATION

From the foregoing it can be seen that the Japanese peace settlement we seek, while it would confirm the cut-back of Japan's territory to her home islands, would contemplate that Japan would be a sovereign and sustaining member of the free world. She would contribute in due course to collective security in accordance with her means but without developing armament which could be an offensive threat. Also, from an economic standpoint, Japan would be expected to get along without such subsidies as the United States has been providing during the occupation. On the other hand Japan would be restored to a position of equality, free of burdensome and discriminatory conditions. In essence the peace would be one of reconciliation.

That is not the kind of peace which victors usually grant to a vanquished nation which has committed armed aggression on a vast scale. It is not surprising that some, made bitter and distrusting by Japan's past conduct, would like to impose upon Japan continuing burdens and restrictions. Some of these taken separately seem to have justification, and perhaps no one of them alone would be of decisive historical significance. In the aggregate, however, they would fundamentally change the character of the peace settlement.

The major objective of any Japanese peace treaty is to bring the Japanese people hereafter to live with others as good neighbors. That does not require that the Japanese people should be pampered. It does mean that the victors should not take advantage of Japan's present helpless state to impose for the future unequal conditions. It means that the peace settlement should restore the vanquished to a position of dignity and equality among the nations.

The peace would be a peace of trust, not because the past justifies trust but because the act of extending trust usually evokes an effort to merit trust. It would be a peace of opportunity, in that it would afford the Japanese people the same opportunity to develop peacefully their domestic economy and their international relations as are enjoyed by most of the other free nations of the world.

UNITED STATES RESPONSIBILITY

In proposing that kind of peace, the United States assumes a serious responsibility, for the results cannot be guaranteed. We have, however, a duty to exercise our best judgment as to the kind of peace which will endure. Circumstances have made our duty inescapable.

In the great war in the Pacific, we had valiant allies who, through long, hard years, poured out life and treasure according to their means. But the United States possessed most of the means required for victory in the Pacific. The United States has carried the responsibility of occupation, and the accomplishments of General MacArthur as Supreme Commander represent a moral investment to which his countrymen cannot honorably be indifferent. The United States has contributed the economic aid which has prevented the postwar misery which would have exposed Japan to capture by communism. The United States is the member of the free world which possesses large present and prospective military power in the western Pacific, and today we are the principal contributor to the United Nations effort in Korea, which fends off danger to Japan, to our Pacific allies, as well as to ourselves.

These are some of the circumstances which require the United States to exercise an initiative for peace; to do so while there is still time; and to shape that initiative with all of the wisdom and all of the vision that is available. For a misjudgment as to timing or as to substance can bring incalculable disaster to all mankind.

The United States does not consider that it has any monopoly of responsibility nor any monopoly of experience, wisdom, and enlightenment that are required. We have no desire to "go it alone," nor have we the slightest thought of dictating. We continuously have sought and shall seek the views of others, and indeed our present suggestions are a composite, not deriving from any single source. They reflect the ideas of many, and the United Kingdom and Australia are two important sources of actual language that we accept. However, in the last analysis the United States cannot, in justice to our own people or indeed to others, become cosponsor of a peace settlement which in our judgment, made after ample consideration without arrogance and in humbleness of spirit, would throw unnecessary and intolerable burdens of a military or economic character upon the United States and jeopardize the lasting peace that the war was fought to win.

NO VETO

Happily the exchanges of views which have taken place have, with one exception, been altogether cordial, and no basic disagreements have developed. The Government of the Soviet Union is perhaps an exception. For 3 months its representative joined with us in full and frank discussions. But now that a peace treaty with Japan seems actually to be in the offing, the Soviet leaders seem to have taken fright. The Soviet Government has publicly announced that it will not resume discussions with us.

When peace is far off, the Russian leaders speak lovingly of peace. But when peace comes near, they shun peace like the plague.

We continue to hope that the Soviet leaders will join in a treaty of peace which would cost them nothing and which would start a relaxing of tensions which would be felt all around the globe. We are ready to give scrupulously full consideration to any views they may express. We shall steadily urge that they join in the Japanese peace.

Fortunately, however, Soviet participation is not indispensable. The Soviet Union has no legal power to veto. It has no moral due bills, for its vast takings in Manchuria, Port Arthur, Dairen, Sakhalin, and the Kuriles repay it a thousandfold for its 6 days of nominal belligerency. Japan, unlike Germany and Austria, is not divided by zones of occupation.

In relation to Japan there is the opportunity to show which of the Allies of World War II now have the genuine will for peace. There is the opportunity for them to make peace so righteous that the example will hearten and uplift men everywhere. That is the opportunity; and to its challenge we are determined worthily to respond.

◇◇◇◇◇

KOREA [1]

87. THE INDEPENDENCE OF KOREA

Statement by the President, September 18, 1945 [2]

[At the Cairo and Potsdam conferences the Allied Powers promised the Korean people independence and self-government. After the defeat of Japan, the United States, as one of the two occupying powers, established a military

---

[1] For more comprehensive treatment of this subject, including documents, see Korea's Independence, Department of State publication 2933, Far Eastern Series 18; Korea's Independence: Current Developments, Office of Public Affairs, Department of State, March 1948. The latter publication contains a Chronology of Events, December 1943 to February 2, 1948.

[2] Department of State Bulletin, September 23, 1945, p. 435. See (a) Cairo Declaration of December 1, 1943, (b) Potsdam Declaration of July 26, 1945, and (c) the Soviet-Anglo-American Communiqué of December 27, 1945 (Establishment of the Joint U. S.- U. S. S. R. Commission) printed under I. Wartime Documents, (a) and (b), and II. Post-War Conferences (c).

government south of the 38th parallel, while the U.S.S.R. established a similar government north of the parallel. In his statement of September 18, 1945, President Truman expressed the rejoicing of the American people over the liberation of Korea; but noted the difficult tasks that lay ahead, which he said could only be accomplished through the joint efforts of the Korean people and the Allies.]

The surrender of the Japanese forces in Seoul, ancient Korean capital, heralds the liberation of a freedom-loving and heroic people. Despite their long and cruel subjection under the warlords of Japan, the Koreans have kept alive their devotion to national liberty and to their proud cultural heritage. This subjection has now ended. The Japanese warlords are being removed. Such Japanese as may be temporarily retained are being utilized as servants of the Korean people and of our occupying forces only because they are deemed essential by reason of their technical qualifications.

In this moment of liberation we are mindful of the difficult tasks which lie ahead. The building of a great nation has now begun with the assistance of the United States, China, Great Britain, and the Soviet Union, who are agreed that Korea shall become free and independent.

The assumption by the Koreans themselves of the responsibilities and functions of a free and independent nation and the elimination of all vestiges of Japanese control over Korean economic and political life will of necessity require time and patience. The goal is in view, but its speedy attainment will require the joint efforts of the Korean people and of the Allies.

The American people rejoice in the liberation of Korea as the Taegook-kee, the ancient flag of Korea, waves again in the Land of the Morning Calm.

88. MEETINGS OF JOINT COMMISSION FOR KOREA, MAY 21 TO OCTOBER 18, 1947 [1]

United States and Soviet Views on Consultative Groups

[When the Joint U.S.-U.S.S.R. Commission created at Moscow in December 1945 was unable to reach agreement on the economic and administrative coördination of the two zones of occupation in Korea, the 38th parallel became the boundary between the Soviet and American areas of occupation. A dispute arose over which Korean groups were to be consulted relative to the elections to be held in Korea and the kind of government to be established. The State Department requested the Joint Commission to prepare a report setting forth the areas of disagreement between the two occupying powers. Excerpts from that report follow.]

The U.S.-Soviet Joint Commission held its forty-second meeting, 1330, 14 July 1947, Duk Soo Palace, Seoul, Korea. General Brown was chairman. The Joint Commission has continued the discussion of a disagreement,

[1] Department of State Bulletin, August 10, 1947, pp. 294-297.

which arose in the thirty-seventh meeting and extended through to the forty-second meeting, on the list of parties and organizations to be invited for initial consultation.

*   *   *

There are two basic issues involved:

The first issue is whether one delegation may unilaterally exercise veto power and exclude from consultation any party or social organization that it does not approve. The Soviet Delegation wishes to exercise such veto power. The American Delegation maintains that this is an arbitrary position and is contrary to the agreement of the Foreign Ministers. Furthermore, it is impractical in application because it could be used to exclude parties and social organizations to such a degree that consultation would not represent a fair sample of Korean opinion. The U.S. position is that exclusion from consultation can only be by mutual agreement of both Delegations as specifically stated in the Marshall-Molotov letters. The U.S. Delegation has many times offered to review systematically the whole list of applicants and consider any and all objections by either Delegation to various parties and organizations in order to make a decision as to which should be excluded through mutual agreement. The Soviet Delegation has repeatedly refused such proposals.

The second issue is in regard to membership of a party or organization in the so-called anti-trusteeship committee or similar organization. The Soviet Delegation has not brought specific charges against any one party that it has actually fomented or instigated active opposition to the Joint Commission or the Moscow decision after signing the declaration, but has arbitrarily accused all the member parties of bad faith and imply that they are guilty even before they have been indicted. The U.S. position is that no party or social organization can be assumed guilty of acting in bad faith until it has been indicted and proved guilty of actions which do in fact incite and foment active opposition to the Joint Commission, the Moscow decision, or either of the Allies.

The American Delegation has consistently upheld and will continue to insist on complete implementation of the Marshall-Molotov Agreements which guarantee wide-scale participation of Korean democratic parties and social organizations in consultation and freedom of expression of opinion by all Koreans.

The Joint Commission is continuing its meetings in an attempt to resolve these basic differences.

◇◇◇◇◇

89. UNITED STATES PROPOSAL FOR FOUR-POWER CONVERSATIONS ON KOREA

Letter From Acting Secretary Lovett to Soviet Minister Molotov, August 28, 1947 [1]

[As time elapsed and the occupying powers repeatedly failed to agree, it became plain that the Joint U.S.-U.S.S.R. Commission would not be able to

---

[1] Department of State Bulletin, September 7, 1947, pp. 473-475. The letter was delivered by Ambassador W. Bedell Smith at the Soviet Foreign Office on August 28, 1947.

fulfil the aspirations of the Korean people for free and independent statehood. Therefore, on August 28, 1947, Acting Secretary of State Lovett proposed to Foreign Minister Molotov that a four-power conference (the United States, Britain, China, and Soviet Russia) be held with respect to Korea. His note outlined seven proposals according to which the Korean people in both zones would be enabled to establish an independent united Korea under a free and democratic constitution.]

*   *   *

For almost two years the Government of the United States has devoted its utmost efforts to carrying out the terms of the Moscow Agreement on Korea. The present stalemate in the Joint Commission negotiations and the failure of that Commission to accomplish even the first task of its mission have made it abundantly clear to all that bilateral negotiations on the subject of consultation with Korean political parties and organizations will only serve to delay the implementation of this agreement and defeat its announced purpose of bringing about early independence for Korea. The United States Government cannot in good conscience be a party to any such delay in the fulfillment of its commitment to Korean independence and proposes that the four powers adhering to the Moscow Agreement meet to consider how that agreement may be speedily carried out.

The United States Government therefore submits for the consideration of your government the enclosed outlines of proposals designed to achieve the aims of the Moscow Agreement on Korea. The United States Government proposes that these suggestions be considered at an early date by the powers adhering to that Agreement. It is therefore hoped that the Soviet Chargé d'Affaires at Washington or an authorized deputy may be designated to participate in four-power conversations on this problem at Washington beginning on September 8, 1947.

It is believed that the Joint Commission's report on the status of its deliberations might be helpful in consideration of the United States proposals during these four-power conversations. The United States Delegation has accordingly been instructed to endeavor to reach agreement with the Soviet Delegation on a joint report to be submitted not later than September 5, 1947.

Copies of this letter are being transmitted to the Foreign Ministers of the United Kingdom and China together with invitations to participate in the four-power conversations referred to above.[1]

Please accept [etc.]

ROBERT A. LOVETT

UNITED STATES PROPOSALS REGARDING KOREA

1. In both the U.S.S.R. and U.S. zones of Korea there shall be held early elections to choose wholly representative provisional legislatures for each zone. Voting shall be by secret, multi-party ballot on a basis of universal suffrage

---

[1] Copies of the letter to Foreign Minister Molotov have been delivered to the Foreign Offices of Great Britain and China under cover of notes inviting the representatives of those two Governments in Washington to participate in the four-power consultations referred to in the letter.

and elections shall be held in accordance with the laws adopted by the present Korean legislatures in each zone.

2. These provisional zonal legislatures shall choose representatives in numbers which reflect the proportion between the populations of the two zones, these representatives to constitute a national provisional legislature. This legislature shall meet at Seoul to establish a provisional government for a united Korea.

3. The resulting Provisional Government of a united Korea shall meet in Korea with representatives of the four Powers adhering to the Moscow Agreement on Korea to discuss with them what aid and assistance is needed in order to place Korean independence on a firm economic and political foundation and on what terms this aid and assistance is to be given.

4. During all the above stages the United Nations shall be invited to have observers present so that the world and the Korean people may be assured of the wholly representative and completely independent character of the actions taken.

5. The Korean Provisional Government and the Powers concerned shall agree upon a date by which all occupation forces in Korea will be withdrawn.

6. The provisional legislatures in each zone shall be encouraged to draft provisional constitutions which can later be used as a basis for the adoption by the national provisional legislature of a constitution for all Korea.

7. Until such time as a united, independent Korea is established, public and private Korean agencies in each zone shall be brought into contact with international agencies established by or under the United Nations and the presence of Korean observers at official international conferences shall be encouraged in appropriate cases.

◇◇◇◇◇◇

90. INDEPENDENCE OF KOREA

[When the Soviet Union declined the American invitation to a four-power conference on Korea, the United States became convinced that further direct discussions with Soviet Russia within the framework of the Moscow directive would be futile. In his address before the General Assembly on September 17, 1947, Secretary Marshall pointed out the basic issue involved and announced the intention of the United States to request action by the Assembly on the problem of Korean independence. Subsequently, on November 14, 1947, the Assembly adopted a resolution which called for elections in Korea by not later than March 1, 1948; participation of the Korean people in the consideration of the Korean question; establishment of a nine-nation United Nations Temporary Commission on Korea (UNTCOK); and withdrawal of occupying forces from Korea as soon as possible after the establishment of a new national government.]

(a) Address by Secretary Marshall Before the General Assembly, September 17, 1947 (Excerpts) [1]

I turn now to the question of the independence of Korea. At Cairo in December 1943, the United States, the United Kingdom, and China joined in declaring that in due course Korea should become free and independent. This multilateral pledge was reaffirmed in the Potsdam Declaration of July 1945 and subscribed to by the Union of Soviet Socialist Republics when it entered the war against Japan. In Moscow in December of 1945, the Foreign Ministers of the U.S.S.R., the United Kingdom, and the United States concluded an agreement designed to bring about the independence of Korea. This agreement was later adhered to by the Government of China. It provided for the establishment of a Joint U.S.-U.S.S.R. Commission to meet in Korea and, through consultations with Korean democratic parties and social organizations, to decide on methods for establishing a provisional Korean government. The Joint Commission was then to consult with that provisional government on methods of giving aid and assistance to Korea, any agreement reached being submitted for approval to the four powers adhering to the Moscow Agreement.

For about two years the United States Government has been trying to reach agreement with the Soviet Government, through the Joint Commission and otherwise, on methods of implementing the Moscow Agreement and thus bringing about the independence of Korea. The United States representatives have insisted that any settlement of the Korean problem must in no way infringe the fundamental democratic right of freedom of opinion. That is still the position of my Government. Today the independence of Korea is no further advanced than it was two years ago. Korea remains divided at the 38th parallel with Soviet forces in the industrial north and United States forces in the agricultural south. There is little or no exchange of goods or services between the two zones. Korea's economy is thus crippled.

The Korean people, not former enemies but a people liberated from 40 years of Japanese oppression, are still not free. This situation must not be allowed to continue indefinitely. In an effort to make progress the United States Government recently made certain proposals designed to achieve the purposes of the Moscow Agreement and requested the powers adhering to that Agreement to join in discussion of these proposals. China and the United Kingdom agreed to this procedure. The Soviet Government did not. Furthermore, the United States and Soviet Delegations to the Joint Commission have not even been able to agree on a joint report on the status of their deliberations. It appears evident that further attempts to solve the Korean problem by means of bilateral negotiations will only serve to delay the establishment of an independent, united Korea.

It is therefore the intention of the United States Government to present the problem of Korean independence to this session of the General Assembly. Although we shall be prepared to submit suggestions as to how the early

[1] Korea's Independence, Department of State Publication 2933, Far Eastern Series 18. The Secretary of State announced on September 17, 1947, that the United States was placing the problem of Korean Independence before the General Assembly and on September 23, 1947, the General Assembly voted to place that problem upon its agenda.

attainment of Korean independence might be effected, we believe that this is a matter which now requires the impartial judgment of the other members. We do not wish to have the inability of two powers to reach agreement delay any further the urgent and rightful claims of the Korean people to independence.

(b) *Resolutions Adopted at the Second Regular Session of the General Assembly, November 14, 1947* [1]

I

INASMUCH AS the Korean question which is before the General Assembly is primarily a matter for the Korean people itself and concerns its freedom and independence, and

RECOGNIZING that this question cannot be correctly and fairly resolved without the participation of representatives of the indigenous population;

The General Assembly

1. *Resolves* that elected representatives of the Korean people be invited to take part in the consideration of the question;

2. *Further resolves* that in order to facilitate and expedite such participation and to observe that the Korean representatives are in fact duly elected by the Korean people and not mere appointees by military authorities in Korea, there be forthwith established a United Nations Temporary Commission on Korea, to be present in Korea, with right to travel, observe and consult throughout Korea.

II

The General Assembly,

RECOGNIZING the urgent and rightful claims to independence of the people of Korea;

BELIEVING that the national independence of Korea should be re-established and all occupying forces then withdrawn at the earliest practicable date;

RECALLING its previous conclusion that the freedom and independence of the Korean people cannot be correctly or fairly resolved without the participation of representatives of the Korean people, and its decision to establish a United Nations Temporary Commission on Korea (hereinafter called the "Commission") for the purpose of facilitating and expediting such participation by elected representatives of the Korean people:

1. *Decides* that the Commission shall consist of representatives of Australia, Canada, China, El Salvador, France, India, Philippines, Syria, Ukrainian Soviet Socialist Republic;

2. *Recommends* that the elections be held not later than 31 March 1948 on the basis of adult suffrage and by secret ballot to choose representatives with whom the Commission may consult regarding the prompt attainment of the freedom and independence of the Korean people and which representatives, constituting a National Assembly, may establish a National Government of Korea. The number of representatives from each voting area or zone

[1] The United States and the United Nations: Report by the President to the Congress for the Year 1947, Department of State publication 3024. International Organization and Conference Series III, 1, pp. 157-159.

should be proportionate to the population, and the elections should be under the observation of the Commission;

3. *Further recommends* that as soon as possible after the elections, the National Assembly should convene and form a National Government and notify the Commission of its formation;

4. *Further recommends* that immediately upon the establishment of a National Government, that Government should, in consultation with the Commission: (*a*) constitute its own national security forces and dissolve all military or semi-military formations not included therein, (*b*) take over the functions of government from the military commands and civilian authorities of north and south Korea, and (*c*) arrange with the occupying Powers for the complete withdrawal from Korea of their armed forces as early as practicable and if possible within ninety days;

5. *Resolves* that the Commission shall facilitate and expedite the fulfilment of the foregoing programme for the attainment of the national independence of Korea and withdrawal of occupying forces, taking into account its observations and consultations in Korea. The Commission shall report, with its conclusions, to the General Assembly and may consult with the Interim Committee with respect to the application of this resolution in the light of developments;

6. *Calls upon* the Member States concerned to afford every assistance and facility to the Commission in the fulfilment of its responsibilities;

7. *Calls upon* all Members of the United Nations to refrain from interfering in the affairs of the Korean people during the interim period preparatory to the establishment of Korean independence, except in pursuance of the decisions of the General Assembly; and thereafter, to refrain completely from any and all acts derogatory to the independence and sovereignty of Korea.

91. UNITED STATES POSITION ON WITHDRAWAL OF OCCUPATION FORCES FROM KOREA, SEPTEMBER 20, 1948 [1]

[The UN Commission on Korea (UNTCOK) was not able to affect a settlement of the Korean problem (as one of its reports stated) because of "the negative attitude of the Soviet authorities." Nevertheless the Russian Government continued to urge that United States troops be withdrawn from Korea. Our government in this statement issued by the Department of State replied that the withdrawal of troops was only one facet of the question of the independence of Korea.]

It has been the consistent view of this government that the best interests of the Korean people would be served by the withdrawal of all occupying forces from Korea at the earliest practicable date. This same view was embodied in the United Nations General Assembly resolution of November 14, 1947, in which provision was made for such withdrawal as soon as practicable after the establishment of the Korean Government which it was the intention of

[1] Korea 1945-1948. Department of State Publication No. 3305, Washington, D. C., 1948, p. 116.

that resolution to bring into being. Had the Soviet Union cooperated in carrying out the provisions of the resolution of November 14, 1947, the question of troop withdrawal from Korea would doubtless have been already resolved.

The United States Government regards the question of the withdrawal of occupying forces as but one facet of the entire question of the unity and independence of Korea. The General Assembly of the United Nations has taken cognizance of this larger question as evidenced by the resolution referred to above, and it may be expected to give further consideration to the matter at its forthcoming meeting.

◇◇◇◇◇◇

92. UNITED STATES RECOGNITION OF THE REPUBLIC OF KOREA, JANUARY 1, 1949 [1]

[Elections were held in South Korea under the auspices of the UN Korean Commission (UNTCOK) on May 10, 1948, and shortly thereafter a new Korean government was established. By its resolution of December 12, 1948 the General Assembly approved the work of the Commission, and on January 1, 1949, the United States accorded the new Republic of Korea *de jure* recognition. Since the Soviet Union refused to coöperate with the Commission, and no elections were held in North Korea, our recognition extended only to South Korea.]

On December 12, 1948, the United Nations General Assembly adopted a resolution approving the conclusions of the report of the United Nations Temporary Commission on Korea and declaring in part "that there has been established a lawful government (the Government of the Republic of Korea), having effective control and jurisdiction over that part of Korea where the Temporary Commission was able to observe and consult and in which the great majority of the people of all Korea reside; that this Government is based on elections which were a valid expression of the free will of the electorate of that part of Korea and which were observed by the Temporary Commission; and that this is the only such Government in Korea." The resolution of December 12 concluded with the recommendation that member states and other nations take the foregoing facts into consideration in establishing their relations with the Government of Korea.

In the light of this action by the General Assembly, and taking into account the facts set forth in the statement issued by this Government on August 12, 1948, concerning the new Korean Government, the United States Government has decided to extend full recognition to the Government of the Republic of Korea. Incidental to this step it is anticipated that, by agreement with that Government, the Mission of the United States Special Representative in Korea will in the near future be raised to Embassy rank.

In conformity with the General Assembly resolution of December 12, the United States Government will endeavor to afford every assistance and facility to the new United Nations Commission on Korea established thereunder in its

[1] Department of State Bulletin, Vol. 20, No. 497, Jan. 9, 1949, pp. 59-60.

efforts to help the Korean people and their lawful Government to achieve the goal of a free and united Korea.

◇◇◇◇◇

93. THE PROBLEM OF THE INDEPENDENCE OF KOREA [1]

Resolution of the General Assembly, October 21, 1949

[All efforts to unify Korea after the 1948 elections were unsuccessful. The UN Commission (UNTCOK) reported in August 1949 that the United States military forces had left South Korea, but the Commission had been unable to establish contact with the northern zone with the result that no report could be made of the conditions north of the 38th parallel. Therefore the UN Assembly voted on October 21, 1949, to continue the Commission (henceforth designated as UNCOK) in existence, and instructed the Commission to persist in its efforts to bring about the unification of Korea.]

THE GENERAL ASSEMBLY

HAVING REGARD to its resolutions 112 (II) of 14 November 1947 and 195 (III) of 12 December 1948 concerning the problem of the independence of Korea,

HAVING CONSIDERED the report of the United Nations Commission on Korea, and having taken note of the conclusions reached therein,

MINDFUL of the fact that, due to difficulties referred to in the report of the Commission, the objectives set forth in the resolutions referred to have not been fully accomplished, and in particular that the unification of Korea and the removal of barriers to economic, social and other friendly intercourse caused by the division of Korea have not yet been achieved,

HAVING NOTED that the Commission has observed and verified the withdrawal of United States occupation forces, but that it has not been accorded the opportunity to observe or verify the reported withdrawal of Soviet occupation forces,

RECALLING its declaration of 12 December 1948 that there has been established a lawful government (the Government of the Republic of Korea) having effective control and jurisdiction over that part of Korea where the United Nations Temporary Commission on Korea was able to observe and consult and in which the great majority of the people of Korea reside; that this Government is based on elections which were a valid expression of the free will of the electorate of that part of Korea and which were observed by the Temporary Commission; and that this is the only such Government in Korea;

CONCERNED lest the situation described by the Commission in its report menace the safety and well-being of the Republic of Korea and of the people of Korea and lead to open military conflict in Korea,

1. *Resolves* that the United Nations Commission on Korea shall continue being with the following membership: Australia, China, El Salvador, France,

[1] General Assembly Roundup, Fourth Regular Session, Press Release GA/600, 10 December 1949.

India, Philippines and Turkey and, having in mind the objectives set forth in the General Assembly resolutions of 14 November 1947 and 12 December 1948 and also the status of the Government of the Republic of Korea as defined in the latter resolution, shall:

(a) Observe and report any developments which might lead to or otherwise involve military conflict in Korea;

(b) Seek to facilitate the removal of barriers to economic, social and other friendly intercourse caused by the division of Korea; and make available its good offices and be prepared to assist, whenever in its judgment a favorable opportunity arises, in bringing about the unification of Korea in accordance with the principles laid down by the General Assembly in the resolution of 14 November 1947;

(c) Have authority, in order to accomplish the aims defined under subparagraphs (a) and (b) of the present paragraph, in its discretion to appoint observers, and to utilize the services and good offices of one or more persons whether or not representatives on the Commission;

(d) Be available for observation and consultation throughout Korea in the continuing development of representative government based on the freely-expressed will of the people including elections of national scope;

(e) Verify the withdrawal of Soviet occupation forces insofar as it is in a position to do so;

2. DECIDES that the Commission:

(a) Shall meet in Korea within thirty days from the date of the present resolution;

(b) Shall continue to maintain its seat in Korea;

(c) Is authorized to travel, consult and observe throughout Korea;

(d) Shall continue to determine its own procedures;

(e) May consult with the Interim Committee of the General Assembly (if it be continued) with respect to the discharge of its duties in the light of developments and within the terms of the present resolution;

(f) Shall render a report to the next regular session of the General Assembly and to any prior special session which might be called to consider the subject matter of the present resolution, and shall render such interim reports as it may deem appropriate to the Secretary-General for transmission to Members;

(g) Shall remain in existence pending a new decision by the General Assembly;

3. CALLS UPON Member States, the Government of the Republic of Korea, and all Koreans to afford every assistance and facility to the Commission in the fulfilment of its responsibilities, and to refrain from any acts derogatory to the purposes of the present resolution;

4. REQUESTS the Secretary-General to provide the Commission with adequate staff and facilities, including technical advisers and observers as required; and authorizes the Secretary-General to pay the expenses and *per diem* of a representative and alternate from each of the States members of the Commission and of such persons as may be appointed in accordance with paragraph 1(c) of the present resolution.

◇◇◇◇◇◇

94. FAR EASTERN ECONOMIC ASSISTANCE ACT OF 1950, AS AMENDED [1]

Public Law 447, Eighty-first Congress, Second Session, as Amended by Section 107 of Title I of Public Law 535, Eighty-first Congress, Second Session

[During the period of military occupation, relief and economic assistance were furnished South Korea by the United States from funds of the army program for Government and Relief in the Occupied Areas (GARIOA). When the United States military forces withdrew from Korea on July 1, 1949, relief and rehabilitation had already been turned over to the Economic Coöperation Administration (ECA) by an executive order dated January 5, 1949. Early the following year, Congress included further aid for Korea in the Far Eastern Economic Assistance Act of 1950; and subsequently Congress provided aid for still another year in the Foreign Economic Assistance Act of 1950. The former act, which is reproduced below as amended, authorized $60,000,000 in assistance (which was one-half the first year's program) and laid down the conditions under which our assistance was to be granted. An additional $100,000,000 was provided for the fiscal year ending June 30, 1951.]

AN ACT To provide economic assistance to certain areas of the Far East

Be it enacted by the Senate and House of Representatives of the United States of America in Congress assembled, That this Act be cited as the "Far Eastern Economic Assistance Act of 1950."

SEC. 2. To enable the President until June 30, 1950, to obligate funds heretofore appropriated for assistance in certain areas of China, section 12 of Public Law 47, Eighty-first Congress, is amended by striking out "February 15, 1950" and inserting in lieu thereof "June 30, 1950."

SEC. 3. (a) The Administrator for Economic Cooperation is hereby authorized to furnish assistance to the Republic of Korea in conformity with—

(1) the provisions of the Economic Cooperation Act of 1948, as amended, wherever such provisions are applicable and not inconsistent with the intent and purposes of this section 3; and

(2) the agreement on aid between the United States of America and the Republic of Korea signed December 10, 1948, or any supplementary or succeeding agreement which shall not substantially alter the basic obligations of either party.

(b) Notwithstanding the provisions of any other law, the Administrator shall immediately terminate aid under this section in the event of the formation in the Republic of Korea of a coalition government which includes one or more members of the Communist Party or of the party now in control of the government of northern Korea.

(c) Notwithstanding the provisions of any other law, the Administrator is authorized to make available to the Republic of Korea merchant vessels of

[1] United States, House of Representatives, Committee on Foreign Affairs, *Economic Cooperation Act of 1948 as amended,* Committee Print, 1950, pp. 33-34.

tonnage not in excess of two thousand five hundred gross tons each, in a number not to exceed ten at any one time, with a stipulation that such vessels shall be operated only in east Asian waters and must be returned forthwith upon demand of the Administrator and in any event not later than June 30, 1952.[1] Any agency of the United States Government owning or operating any such vessel is authorized to make such vessel available to the Administrator for the purposes of this section upon his application, notwithstanding the provisions of any other law and without reimbursement by the Administrator and title to any such vessel so supplied shall remain in the United States Government.

(d) In order to carry out the provisions of this section 3, there is hereby authorized to be appropriated to the President, in addition to sums already appropriated, not to exceed $60,000,000 for the fiscal year ending June 30, 1950, and $100,000,000 for the fiscal year ending June 30, 1951.

(e) Notwithstanding the provisions of any other law, until such time as an appropriation shall be made pursuant to subsection (d) of this section, the Reconstruction Finance Corporation is authorized and directed to make advances not to exceed in the aggregate $30,000,000 to carry out the provisions of this section, in such manner, at such times, and in such amounts as the Administrator shall request, and no interest shall be charged on advances made by the Treasury to the Reconstruction Finance Corporation for this purpose. The Reconstruction Finance Corporation shall be repaid without interest for advances made by it hereunder, from funds made available for the purposes of this section 3.

SEC. 4. The authorization for appropriations in this Act is limited to the period ending June 30, 1951, in order that any subsequent authorizations may be separately passed on, and is not to be construed as an express or implied commitment to provide further authorizations or appropriations.

Approved February 14, 1950.

◇◇◇◇◇◇

95. NORTH KOREAN ATTACK AGAINST SOUTH KOREA

Report of the UN Commission on Korea to the Secretary-General, June 25, 1950 [2]

[Efforts at unifying the two zones of Korea failed and rumors of the massing of troops along the north of the 38th parallel were widespread early in the summer of 1950. On June 25th, the North Korean government launched a full-scale attack, which obviously had been long and carefully prepared, against the Republic of Korea (R.O.K.). The UN Commission, which was still in existence and on the spot, reported the attack to the Secretary General of the UN urging that the matter be brought to the immediate attention of the Security Council.]

[1] Sec. 107(a) of Public Law 535 changed the date in this sentence from June 30, 1951, as originally provided, to June 30, 1952.

[2] UN doc. S/1496. Printed from telegraphic text. Department of State Publication 3922, Far Eastern Series 34, July 1950, p. 12.

Government of Republic of Korea states that about 04:00 hrs. 25 June attacks were launched in strength by North Korean forces all along the 38th parallel. Major points of attack have included Ongjin Peninsula, Kaesong area and Chunchon and east coast where seaborne landings have been reported north and south of Kanknung. Another seaborne landing reported imminent under air cover in Pohang area on southeast coast. The latest attacks have occurred along the parallel directly north of Seoul along shortest avenue of approach. Pyongyang radio allegation at 13:35 hrs. of South Korean invasion across parallel during night declared entirely false by President and Foreign Minister in course of conference,with Commission members and principal secretary. Allegations also stated Peoples Army instructed repulse invading forces by decisive counterattack and placed responsibility for consequences on South Korea. Briefing on situation by President included statement thirty-six tanks and armoured cars used in northern attacks at four points. Following emergency Cabinet meeting Foreign Minister issuing broadcast to people of South Korea encouraging resistance against dastardly attack. President expressed complete willingness for Commission broadcast urging cease-fire and for communication to United Nations to inform of gravity of situation. Although North Korean declaration of war rumoured at 11:00 hrs. over Pyongyang radio, no confirmation available from any source. President not treating broadcast as official notice. United States Ambassador, appearing before Commission, stated his expectation Republican Army would give good account of itself.

At 17:15 hrs. four yak-type aircraft strafed civilian and military air fields outside Seoul destroying planes, firing gas tanks and attacking jeeps. Yongdungpo railroad station on outskirts also strafed.

Commission wishes to draw attention of Secretary-General to serious situation developing which is assuming character of full-scale war and may endanger the maintenance of international peace and security. It suggests that he consider possibility of bringing matter to notice of Security Council. Commission will communicate more fully considered recommendation later.

96. POSITION OF THE UNITED STATES WITH RESPECT TO KOREAN AGGRESSION

Statement to the Security Council by Ernest A. Gross, Deputy Representative of the United States to the United Nations, June 25, 1950 [1]

[When the North Koreans launched their attack, the United States immediately took the lead in urging vigorous action by the United Nations in order to carry out its responsibilities with respect to the maintenance of peace. Our representative made a statement in the Security Council, in which he summarized the postwar developments in Korea and recommended a resolution for adoption by the Council. On the same day, June 25, 1950, the

---

[1] UN doc. S/PV.473. Department of State Publication 3922, Far Eastern Series 34, July 1950, pp. 13-15.

Council approved the proposed resolution without change. The historic statement of Ambassador Gross is reproduced below.]

At 4 o'clock in the morning of Sunday, 25 June, Korean time, armed forces from North Korea commenced an unprovoked assault against the territory of the Republic of Korea. This assault was launched by ground forces along the 38th parallel and the Ongjin, Kaesong, and Chunchon sectors, and by amphibious landings in the east coast in the vicinity of Kangnung. In addition, North Korean aircraft have attacked and strafed Kimpo airport in the outskirts of the capital city of Seoul.

The facts and a general outline of the situation have now been reported by the United Nations Commission on Korea, and are reflected in document S/1496, to which the President has referred. Under these circumstances, this wholly illegal and unprovoked attack by North Korean forces, in the view of my Government, constitutes a breach of the peace and an act of aggression. This is clearly a threat to international peace and security. As such, it is of grave concern to my Government.

It is a threat which must inevitably be of grave concern to the Governments of all peace-loving and freedom-loving nations. A full-scale attack is now going forward in Korea. It is an invasion upon a State which the United Nations itself, by action of its General Assembly, has brought into being. It is armed aggression against the Government elected under United Nations supervision. Such an attack strikes at the fundamental purposes of the United Nations Charter. Such an attack openly defies the interest and authority of the United Nations. Such an attack, therefore, concerns the vital interest which all the Member nations have in the Organization. The history of the Korean problem is well known to the members of the Council. At this critical hour I shall not review that history in detail.

May I be permitted to recall just a few of the milestones in the development of the Korean situation? A Joint Commission of the United States of America and the Union of Soviet Socialist Republics sought unsuccessfully, for two years, to agree at ways and means of bringing to Korea the independence which we assumed would automatically come when Japan was defeated. This two-year deadlock prevented 38 million people in Korea from getting the independence which it was agreed was their right. My Government, thereupon, sought to hold a Four Power Conference, at which China and the United Kingdom would join the United States and the Soviet Union in seeking agreement on the independence of Korea. The Soviet Union rejected that proposal.

The United States then asked the General Assembly to consider the problem. The Soviet Union opposed that suggestion. The General Assembly, in resolution 112 (II) of 14 November 1947, created the United Nations Temporary Commission on Korea. By that resolution, the General Assembly recommended the holding of elections not later than 31 March 1948 to choose representatives with whom the Commission might consult regarding the prompt attainment of freedom and independence for the Korean people. These elected representatives would constitute a national assembly and establish a national government of Korea. The General Assembly further recommended that, upon the establishment of a national government, that government should, in consultation with the Commission, constitute its own national security forces and dissolve all military or semi-military formations not included therein. The General Assembly recommended that the national government should take over the functions of government from the Military Command and from the civilian authorities of the North and South, and arrange with the occupying Powers for the complete withdrawal from Korea of their armed forces, as early as practicable and, if possible, within ninety days.

Elections were held in South Korea and the Commission observed them. A Government in South Korea was set up as a result of the elections observed by the Commission. The Commission was unable to enter North Korea because of the attitude of the Soviet Union.

The United Nations Temporary Commission on Korea, in its report to the third session of the General Assembly, stated that not all the objectives set forth for it had been fully accomplished and that, in particular, unification of Korea had not yet been achieved. Notwithstanding the frustrations and the difficulties which the Temporary Commission had experienced in Korea, the General Assembly, at its third session, in resolution 195 (III) continued the Commission's existence and requested it to go on with its efforts to bring North and South Korea together.

One aspect of resolution 195 (III) adopted by the third session of the General Assembly should, I feel, be particularly emphasized. The General Assembly declared that a lawful government had been established in Korea as a result of the elections observed by the Commission, and declared further that this was the only lawful government in Korea. This is a most significant fact. The General Assembly declared further that the Government of Korea was based on elections which were a valid expression of the free will of the electorate of that part of Korea, and which were observed by the United Nations Commission. In the light of this declaration, my Government, on 1 January 1949, extended recognition to the Government of the Republic of Korea, and more than thirty States have, since that time, also accorded recognition to that Government.

The United Nations Commission worked toward the United Nations objectives of the withdrawal of occupying forces from Korea, the removal of the barriers between the regions of the North and the South and the unification of that country under a representative government freely determined by its people.

In 1949, as in 1948, the Commission's efforts to attain access to North Korea, which included direct intercourse with the Northern authorities and endeavours to negotiate through the Government of the U.S.S.R. were fruitless. The Commission was unable to make progress either towards the unification of Korea or toward the reduction of barriers between the Republic of Korea and the Northern authorities. The Commission reported to the General Assembly that the border of the 38th parallel was becoming a scene of increasingly frequent exchanges of fire and armed raids, and that this constituted a serious barrier to friendly intercourse among the people of Korea.

The Commission observed the withdrawal of United States forces, which was completed on 19 June 1949. Although it signified its readiness to verify the fact of the withdrawal of the occupation forces of the Soviet Union from

North Korea, the Commission received no response to its message to the U.S.S.R., and, therefore, could take no action.

At its fourth session, the General Assembly, in resolution 293 (IV) adopted on 21 October 1949, again directed the Commission to "seek to facilitate the removal of barriers to economic, social and other friendly intercourse caused by the division of Korea." The General Assembly also authorized the Commission "in its discretion to appoint observers, and to utilize the services and good offices of one or more persons, whether or not representatives on the Commission."

The United Nations Commission on Korea is presently in Seoul, and we have now received its latest report.

I have submitted a draft resolution [S/1497] which notes the Security Council's grave concern at the invasion of the Republic of Korea by the armed forces of North Korea. This draft resolution calls upon the authorities in the north to cease hostilities and to withdraw their armed forces to the border along the 38th parallel. It requests that the United Nations Commission on Korea observe the withdrawal of the North Korean forces to the 38th parallel and keep the Security Council informed on the implementation and execution of the resolution. The draft resolution also calls upon all Members of the United Nations to render every assistance to the United Nations in the carrying out of this resolution, and to refrain from giving assistance to the North Korean authorities.

*   *   *

⟡⟡⟡⟡⟡⟡

97. FIRST SECURITY COUNCIL RESOLUTION ON KOREA, JUNE 25, 1950 [1]

[The first resolution of the Security Council with respect to the Korean invasion was speedily adopted by a vote of 9 to 0 and became a landmark in UN history. The resolution noted that the armed invasion constituted a breach of peace, called upon the North Koreans to cease hostilities and withdraw north of the 38th parallel, and urged the UN members to give effect to the resolution and to refrain from assisting the North Koreans. The Soviet Union, which had boycotted the Security Council for several months, was absent from the meeting and did not vote.]

The Security Council
Recalling the finding of the General Assembly in its resolution of 21 October 1949 that the Government of the Republic of Korea is a lawfully established government "having effective control and jurisdiction over that part of Korea where the United Nations Temporary Commission on Korea was able to observe and consult and in which the great majority of the people of Korea reside; and that this Government is based on elections which were a valid expression of the free will of the electorate of that part of Korea and which

[1] UN doc. S/1501. Department of State Publication 3922, Far Eastern Series 34, July 1950, p. 16.

were observed by the Temporary Commission; and that this is the only such Government in Korea";

Mindful of the concern expressed by the General Assembly in its resolutions of 12 December 1948 and 21 October 1949 of the consequences which might follow unless Member States refrained from acts derogatory to the results sought to be achieved by the United Nations in bringing about the complete independence and unity of Korea; and the concern expressed that the situation described by the United Nations Commission on Korea in its report menaces the safety and well being of the Republic of Korea and of the people of Korea and might lead to open military conflict there;

Noting with grave concern the armed attack upon the Republic of Korea by forces from North Korea,

Determines that this action constitutes a breach of the peace,

I. *Calls* for the immediate cessation of hostilities; and

Calls upon the authorities of North Korea to withdraw forthwith their armed forces to the thirty-eighth parallel;

II. *Requests* the United Nations Commission on Korea

(a) To communicate its fully considered recommendations on the situation with the least possible delay;

(b) To observe the withdrawal of the North Korean forces to the thirty-eighth parallel; and

(c) To keep the Security Council informed on the execution of this resolution;

III. *Calls upon* all Members to render every assistance to the United Nations in the execution of this resolution and to refrain from giving assistance to the North Korean authorities.

◇◇◇◇◇◇

98. SECOND SECURITY COUNCIL RESOLUTION ON KOREA, JUNE 27, 1950 [1]

[After two days of uninterrupted fighting, it became apparent that the North Koreans had no intention of heeding the Security Council resolution to cease hostilities and withdraw north of the 38th parallel. Therefore the Council adopted a second resolution by a vote of 7 to 1, in which it recommended that the UN members furnish South Korea with such assistance as was required to repel the attack and restore peace. This resolution was also a landmark because it circumvented the difficulties which the United Nations had encountered in attempting to establish an international force to be placed at the disposal of the Council. Again as in the case of the adoption of the first resolution, the Soviet Union was absent from the Council meeting.]

The Security Council,

Having determined that the armed attack upon the Republic of Korea by forces from North Korea constitutes a breach of the peace,

Having called for an immediate cessation of hostilities, and

[1] Department of State publication 3922, Far Eastern Series 34, July 1950, p. 24.

Having called upon the authorities of North Korea to withdraw forthwith their armed forces to the 38th parallel, and

Having noted from the report of the United Nations Commission for Korea that the authorities in North Korea have neither ceased hostilities nor withdrawn their armed forces to the 38th parallel and that urgent military measures are required to restore international peace and security, and

Having noted the appeal from the Republic of Korea to the United Nations for immediate and effective steps to secure peace and security,

Recommends that the Members of the United Nations furnish such assistance to the Republic of Korea as may be necessary to repel the armed attack and to restore international peace and security in the area.

◇◇◇◇◇◇

99. UNITED STATES RESPONSE TO SECURITY COUNCIL RESOLUTIONS ON KOREA

Statement by President Truman, June 27, 1950 [1]

[In accordance with the UN call for troops in Korea, President Truman, after consultation with Congressional leaders, announced that the United States would help the South Koreans with air and sea power. He also announced that the U.S. Seventh Fleet would prevent any attack on Formosa, and in return he called upon the Chinese Nationalists in Formosa to refrain from air and sea attack upon the Chinese mainland. In addition he promised further military assistance for both the Philippines and Indo-China. It should be noted that the President's statement was issued in the morning of June 27, 1950 while the resolution of the Security Council calling upon UN members for assistance was not passed until the afternoon of the same day.]

In Korea the Government forces, which were armed to prevent border raids and to preserve internal security, were attacked by invading forces from North Korea. The Security Council of the United Nations called upon the invading troops to cease hostilities and to withdraw to the 38th parallel. This they have not done but on the contrary have pressed the attack. The Security Council called upon all members of the United Nations to render every assistance to the United Nations in the execution of this resolution. In these circumstances I have ordered United States air and sea forces to give the Korean Government troops cover and support.

The attack upon Korea makes it plain beyond all doubt that Communism has passed beyond the use of subversion to conquer independent nations and will now use armed invasion and war. It has defied the orders of the Security Council of the United Nations issued to preserve international peace and security. In these circumstances the occupation of Formosa by Communist forces would be a direct threat to the security of the Pacific area and to United States forces performing their lawful and necessary functions in that area.

Accordingly I have ordered the Seventh Fleet to prevent any attack on

[1] Department of State Publication 3922, Far Eastern Series 34, p. 18.

Formosa. As a corollary of this action I am calling upon the Chinese Government on Formosa to cease all air and sea operations against the mainland. The Seventh Fleet will see that this is done. The determination of the future status of Formosa must await the restoration of security in the Pacific, a peace settlement with Japan, or consideration by the United Nations.

I have also directed that United States Forces in the Philippines be strengthened and that military assistance to the Philippine Government be accelerated.

I have similarly directed acceleration in the furnishing of military assistance to the forces of France and the Associated States in Indochina and the dispatch of a military mission to provide close working relations with those forces.

I know that all members of the United Nations will consider carefully the consequences of this latest aggression in Korea in defiance of the Charter of the United Nations. A return to the rule of force in international affairs would have far-reaching effects. The United States will continue to uphold the rule of law.

I have instructed Ambassador Austin, as the Representative of the United States to the Security Council, to report these steps to the Council.

◇◇◇◇◇◇

100. VALIDITY OF SECURITY COUNCIL'S ACTION

[The validity of the Security Council's resolution of June 27 calling for an end to the North Korean aggression was challenged by the Soviet Union because the latter was absent when the vote was taken; and because the representatives of Nationalist China were not considered legally competent to cast the Chinese vote in the Council. The United States answered the Soviet allegations by noting that a series of precedents going back to 1946 had established that an abstention by a permanent member of the Council did not constitute a veto. Therefore, our Government argued, the Council's resolution of June 27 was valid since none of the permanent members had voted against it. Statements issued by the two governments follow.]

(a) The Deputy Minister of Foreign Affairs of the Union of Soviet Socialist Republics to the Secretary-General, June 29, 1950 [1]

The Soviet Government has received from you the text of the Security Council resolution of 27 June 1950 calling the attention of Members of the United Nations to the necessity of intervening in Korean affairs in the interests of the South Korean authorities. The Soviet Government notes that this resolution was adopted by six votes, the seventh vote being that of the Kuomintang representative Dr. Tingfu F. Tsiang who has no legal right to represent China, whereas the United Nations Charter requires that a Security Council resolution must be adopted by seven votes including those of the five permanent members of the Council namely the United States, the United Kingdom, France, the Union of Soviet Socialist Republics and China. As is known,

[1] Department of State Publication 3922, Far Eastern Series 34, July 1950, p. 56.

moreover, the above resolution was passed in the absence of two permanent members of the Security Council, the Union of Soviet Socialist Republics and China, whereas under the United Nations Charter a decision of the Security Council on an important matter can only be made with the concurring votes of all five permanent members of the Council, viz. the United States, the United Kingdom, France, the Union of Soviet Socialist Republics and China. In view of the foregoing it is quite clear that the said resolution of the Security Council on the Korean question has no legal force.

A. GROMYKO

(b) Statement by the Department of State, June 30, 1950 [1]

SOVIET ALLEGATION OF ILLEGALITY OF UNITED NATIONS SECURITY COUNCIL ACTION WITH RESPECT TO KOREA

In its reply to the United Nations and to the United States, the U.S.S.R. alleges that the action of the Security Council with respect to Korea was illegal, since the action taken did not have the concurring votes of all the permanent members. In its reply of June 29 to the U.S. communication of June 27 asking the U.S.S.R. to use its influence with the North Korean authorities to cease hostilities, the U.S.S.R. made the same point and contended further that the action of the Council was illegal because the representative of China participating in this action was not the representative of the Peiping regime.

With respect to article 27 of the Charter dealing with Security Council voting, it is provided that substantive questions be decided by an affirmative vote of seven members including the concurring votes of the permanent members.

By a long series of precedents, however, dating back to 1946, the practice has been established whereby abstention by permanent members of the Council does not constitute a veto.

In short, prior to the Soviet allegations, every member of the United Nations, including the U.S.S.R., accepted as legal and binding decisions of the Security Council made without the concurrence, as expressed through an affirmative vote of all permanent members of the Council.

As to the Soviet claim concerning the Chinese vote, the Rules of Procedure of the Security Council provide the machinery for the seating of an accredited representative of the Security Council. No affirmative action has been taken which, by any stretch of the imagination, could give force to the contention of the U.S.S.R. that a representative of the Peiping regime should be regarded as the representative of China on the Security Council. The credentials of the representative of the National Government of China were approved by the Council and the Soviet attempt at a later date to withdraw this approval was defeated. Therefore, the vote of the Nationalist representative on June 25 and 27 was the official vote of China.

A list of some of the more important precedents involving action by the Security Council on substantive matters taken without the concurrence of an affirmative vote by the Soviet Union follow:

[1] Department of State Press Release 702. Department of State Publication 3922, Far Eastern Series 34, pp. 61-63.

Palestine Case:

On April 16, 1948, the Soviet Union abstained on a resolution which called for a truce in Palestine.

On May 22, 1948, the Soviet Union abstained on a resolution for a "cease-fire" in Palestine.

On July 15, 1948, the Soviet Union abstained on a resolution ordering a "cease-fire" in Palestine and giving instructions to the Mediator there.

On November 4, 1948, the Soviet Union abstained on a resolution calling upon all governments concerned to withdraw beyond positions they held in Palestine on October 14, 1948.

In none of these instances has the Soviet Union challenged the legality of the action taken by the Security Council.

Kashmir Case:

On January 17, 1948, the Soviet Union abstained on a resolution calling upon the parties concerned to avoid actions aggravating the situation.

On January 20, 1948, the Soviet Union abstained on a resolution for setting up a UN Commission for India and Pakistan and which gave that Commission broad terms of reference.

On April 21, 1948, the Soviet Union abstained on a resolution expanding the terms of reference of the UN Commission for India and Pakistan and which set the terms for bringing about a "cease-fire" and the conditions for the holding of a plebiscite.

On June 3, 1948, the Soviet Union abstained on a resolution which affirmed the previous resolution and ordered the UN Commission to proceed to the area.

In none of these instances has the Soviet Union challenged the legality of the action taken by the Security Council.

Indonesian Case:

On December 24, 1948, the Soviet Union abstained on a resolution calling upon the parties to cease hostilities and ordering the release of Indonesian officials. In that case the French also abstained.

On January 28, 1949, the Soviet Union abstained on a number of paragraphs of a resolution setting up the UN Commission for Indonesia with wide powers.

In none of these instances has the Soviet Union challenged the legality of the action taken by the Security Council.

Furthermore the Soviet Union has never questioned the legality of action taken by the Security Council in which it voted with the majority but on which other permanent members of the Council abstained.

This has occurred in at least three substantive decisions:

1. In the action of the Council on December 28, 1948, in which a resolution was passed calling on the Netherlands to set free political prisoners in Indonesia (a resolution incidentally introduced by the representative of China). France and the U.K. abstained on this resolution.

2. In the action of the Council on March 4, 1949, recommending to the

General Assembly that Israel be admitted to UN membership. The U.K. abstained on this resolution.

3. In the action of the Council on· March 5, 1948, recommending consultation of the permanent members of the Council in connection with the Palestine situation. The U.K. abstained on this resolution.

The voluntary absence of a permanent member from the Security Council is clearly analogous to abstention.

Furthermore article 28 of the Charter provides that the Security Council shall be so organized as to be able to function continuously. This injunction is defeated if the absence of a representative of a permanent member is construed to have the effect of preventing all substantive action by the Council.

No one of the 10 members of the Council participating in the meetings of June 25 and June 27 raised any question regarding the legality of the action— not even the member who dissented on June 27.

◇◇◇◇◇◇

101. ESTABLISHMENT OF A UNIFIED UN FORCE IN KOREA

[The third resolution of the Security Council relating to the Korean affair was adopted by a vote of 7 to 0 on July 7, 1950. Again the Soviet Union was absent. The resolution noted the prompt and vigorous assistance furnished by the United States, called upon all other members to provide military forces to a unified command and requested the United States to designate a commander of these forces. In answer to this request, President Truman on the next day appointed General Douglas MacArthur as the military commander and directed him to use the United Nations flag with the flags of the participating nations.]

(a) Third Security Council Resolution on Korea, July 7, 1950 [1]

"The Security Council,

"HAVING DETERMINED that the armed attack upon the Republic of Korea by forces from North Korea constitutes a breach of the peace.

"HAVING RECOMMENDED that the members of the United Nations furnish such assistance to the Republic of Korea as may be necessary to repel armed attack and to restore international peace and security in the area,

"1. *Welcomes,* the prompt and vigorous support which Governments and peoples of the United Nations have given to its resolutions of 25 and 27 June 1950 to assist the Republic of Korea in defending itself against armed attack and thus to restore international peace and security in the area;

"2. *Notes* that members of the United Nations have transmitted to the United Nations offers of assistance for the Republic of Korea;

"3. *Recommends* that all members providing military forces and other assistance pursuant to the aforesaid Security Council resolutions make such forces and other assistance available to a unified command under the United States;

[1] Department of State Bulletin, July 17, 1950, p. 83.

"4. *Requests* the United States to designate the commander of such forces;

"5. *Authorizes* the unified command at its discretion to use the United Nations flag in the course of operations against North Korean forces concurrently with the flags of the various nations participating;

"6. *Requests* the United States to provide the Security Council with reports as appropriate on the course of action taken under the unified command."

(b) Statement by the President Designating General MacArthur as Commanding General, July 8, 1950 [1]

The Security Council of the United Nations, in its resolution of July 7, 1950, has recommended that all members providing military forces and other assistance pursuant to the Security Council resolutions of June 25 and 27, make such forces and other assistance available to a unified command under the United States.

The Security Council resolution also requests that the United States designate the commander of such forces, and authorizes the unified command at its discretion to use the United Nations flag in the course of operations against the North Korean forces concurrently with the flags of the various nations participating.

I am responding to the recommendation of the Security Council and have designated General Douglas MacArthur as the Commanding General of the military forces which the members of the United Nations place under the unified command of the United States pursuant to the United Nations' assistance to the Republic of Korea in repelling the unprovoked armed attack against it.

I am directing General Douglas MacArthur, pursuant to the Security Council resolution, to use the United Nations flag in the course of operations against the North Korean forces concurrently with the flags of the various nations participating.

102. AIMS AND OBJECTIVES IN RESISTING AGGRESSION IN KOREA

Address by President Truman, September 1, 1950 [2]

[For several weeks after the beginning of their invasion of South Korea, the North Korean armies forced the United Nations troops to retreat. Against this background on September 1, 1950, President Truman addressed the American people on the aims and objectives of the United States in Korea. He promised continued support for the United Nations, expressed the hope that the Chinese would not be drawn into the affair, disclaimed any United States desire for territory, and stated that we were fighting only for peace in Korea.]

[1] Department of State Bulletin, July 17, 1950, p. 83.
[2] Department of State Bulletin, September 11, 1950, pp. 407-410.

Tonight, I want to talk to you about Korea, about why we are there, and what our objectives are.

As I talk with you, thousands of families in this land of ours have a son, or a brother, or a husband fighting in Korea. I know that your thoughts and hopes are constantly with them—and so are mine.

These men of ours are engaged once more in the age-old struggle for human liberty. Our men, and the men of other free nations, are defending with their lives the cause of freedom in the world. They are fighting for the proposition that peace shall be the law of this earth.

We must and shall support them with every ounce of our strength and with all our hearts. We shall put aside all else for this supreme duty.

No cause has ever been more just or more important.

For the first time in all history, men of many nations are fighting under a single banner to uphold the rule of law in the world. This is an inspiring fact.

If the rule of law is not upheld, we can look forward only to the horror of another world war and ultimate chaos. For our part, we do not intend to let that happen.

TWO COURSES FACED BY FREE WORLD

Two months ago, Communist imperialism turned from the familiar tactics of infiltration and subversion to a brutal attack on the small Republic of Korea. When that happened, the free and peace-loving nations of the world faced two possible courses.

One course would have been to limit our action to diplomatic protests, while the Communist aggressors went ahead and swallowed up their victim. That would have been the course of appeasement. If the history of the 1930's teaches us anything, it is that appeasement of dictators is the sure road to world war. If aggression were allowed to succeed in Korea, it would be an open invitation to new acts of aggression elsewhere.

The other course is the one which the free world chose. The United Nations made its historic decision to meet military aggression with armed force. The effects of that decision will be felt far beyond Korea. The firm action taken by the United Nations is our best hope of achieving world peace.

It is your liberty and mine which is involved. What is at stake is the free way of life—the right to worship as we please, the right to express our opinions, the right to raise our children in our own way, the right to choose our jobs, the right to plan our own future, and the right to live without fear. All these are bound up in the present action of the United Nations to put down aggression in Korea.

We cannot hope to maintain our own freedom if freedom elsewhere is wiped out. That is why the American people are united in support of our part in this task.

During the last 5 years, we have worked day in and day out to achieve a just and lasting peace. We have given every possible proof of our desire to live at peace with all nations. We have worked for liberty and self-government for people the world over. Most nations have joined with us in this effort, but the Soviet Union and the nations it controls have unceasingly hampered all efforts to achieve a just peace.

The Soviet Union has repeatedly violated its pledges of international cooperation. It has destroyed the independence of its neighbors. It has sought to disrupt those countries it could not dominate. It has built up tremendous armed forces far beyond the needs of its own defense.

Communist imperialism preaches peace but practices aggression.

In these circumstances, the free nations have been compelled to take measures to protect themselves against the aggressive designs of the Communists.

The United Nations was able to act as it did in Korea because the free nations in the years since World War II have created a common determination to work together for peace and freedom.

Every American can be justly proud of the role that our country has played in bringing this about.

RECORD TO CREATE UNITY AMONG FREE NATIONS

We have taken the lead in step after step to create unity and strength among the free nations. The record of these steps is impressive. Let me recall some of them to you.

In 1945, we helped to bring the United Nations into existence at San Francisco.

In 1946, the United States gave its full support to the successful action taken by the United Nations to protect Iran against Communist invasion.

In 1947, we began our military and economic aid to Greece and Turkey, which has helped those countries to keep their independence against Communist attacks and threats.

Also in 1947, by the treaty of Rio de Janeiro, we joined with the other American nations to guarantee the safety of the Western Hemisphere.

In 1948, the Marshall Plan checked the danger of Communist subversion in Europe; and, since that time, it has brought the free nations more closely together in a strong economic framework.

The Berlin airlift, in 1948 and 1949, defeated the Soviet effort to drive the free nations out of the democratic outpost of western Berlin.

The North Atlantic Treaty, in 1949, served notice that the nations of the North Atlantic community would stand together to preserve their freedom.

Today, in 1950, we are going ahead with an enlarged program for military aid to strengthen the common defense of free nations.

Step by step, these achievements in the struggle between freedom and Communist imperialism have brought the free nations closer together.

When the Communist movement turned to open, armed aggression in Korea, the response of the free nations was immediate.

Fifty-three of the fifty-nine members of the United Nations joined in meeting the challenge. Thirty have already pledged concrete aid to the United Nations to put down this aggression.

Thus far, the brunt of the fighting has fallen upon the armed forces of the Republic of Korea and the United States. In addition, naval forces from Australia, Canada, France, Great Britain, the Netherlands, and New Zealand have been and are now in action under the United Nations command. Fighting planes from Australia, Canada, and Great Britain have joined the operation.

Ground forces have been offered by Thailand, the Philippines, Turkey, Australia, France, and other countries. Some British troops have landed in Korea and more are on their way. All of these will serve under the flag of the

United Nations and under the United Nations Commander, General Mac-Arthur.

Our own men, with their gallant Korean comrades, have held the breach. In less than 8 weeks, five divisions of United States troops have moved into combat, some of them from bases more than 6,000 miles away. More men are on the way. Fighting in difficult country, under every kind of hardship, American troops have held back overwhelming numbers of the Communist invaders. Our naval and air forces have been carrying the attack to the military bases and supply lines of the aggressors.

Our men have fought with grim gallantry. All of us, especially those of us who are old soldiers, know how worthy they are of a place on that long and honored roll of those who created and preserved liberty for our country.

The soldiers of the Republic of Korea have been fighting fiercely for their own freedom.

The determination of the South Koreans to maintain their independence is shown not only by the valor of their soldiers in the battle line but also by countless supporting activities of the whole population. They are giving every possible assistance to the United Nations forces.

These United Nations troops are still outnumbered. But their hard valiant fight is bringing results. We hold a firm base of about 3,500 square miles. For weeks, the enemy has been hammering, now at one spot, now at another, sometimes at many points at once. He has been beaten back each time with heavy loss.

The enemy is spending his strength recklessly in desperate attacks. We believe the invasion has reached its peak. The task remaining is to crush it. Our men are confident, the United Nations command is confident, that it will be crushed. The power to do this is being gathered in Korea.

Right now, the battle in Korea is the front line in the struggle between freedom and tyranny. But the fighting there is part of a larger struggle to build a world in which a just and lasting peace can be maintained.

That is why we in the United States must increase our own defensive strength over and above the forces we need in Korea. That is why we must continue to work with other free nations to increase our combined strength.

The Congress is now acting on my request to increase our program of arms aid to other free countries. These nations are greatly increasing their own efforts. Our aid is not a substitute but is an addition to what they themselves do.

In Western Europe alone, there are over 200 million people. Next to ours, their industry is the world's greatest workshop. They are joining with us to develop collective forces for mutual defense—our defense as well as their own.

U.S.—KEY ELEMENT IN STRENGTH

The armed forces of the United States are a key element in the strength of the free world. In view of the threats of aggression which now face us, we shall have to increase these forces, and we shall have to maintain larger forces for a long time to come.

We have had about 1½ million men and women on active duty in our Army,

Navy, and Air Force. Our present plans call for increasing this number to close to 3 million, and further increases may be required.

In addition to increasing the size of our armed forces, we must step up sharply the production of guns, tanks, planes, and other military equipment. We shall also have to increase our stockpile of essential materials, and expand our industrial capacity to produce military supplies.

We have the ability and the resources to meet the demands which confront us. Our industry and agriculture have never been stronger or more productive. We will use as much of this economic strength as is needed to defend ourselves and establish peace.

Hitler and the Japanese generals miscalculated badly, 10 years ago, when they thought we would not be able to use our economic power effectively for the defeat of aggression.

Let would-be aggressors make no such mistake today.

We now have over 62 million men and women employed—more than we have ever had before. Our farmers are producing over 20 percent more than they were in 1940. The productive capacity of our manufacturing industry is 60 percent greater than it was 10 years ago, when the Axis dictators threatened the world.

We must now divert a large share of this productive power to defense purposes. To do this will require hard work and sacrifice by all of us. I know all of us are prepared to do whatever is necessary in the cause of peace and freedom. We have never yet failed to give all that is needed in that cause, and we never will.

In order to increase our defense effort rapidly enough to meet the danger that we face, we shall have to make many changes in our way of living and working here at home. We shall have to give up many things we enjoy. We shall all have to work harder and longer. To prevent inflation and runaway prices, we shall have to impose certain restrictions upon ourselves.

The Congress has today completed action on legislation to enable us to channel the necessary effort to defense production, to increase our productive capacity, and to hold down inflation.

After this legislation is signed, I intend to talk to you again, to explain what your Government proposes to do, and how each citizen can play his part in this national effort.

As we move forward to arm ourselves more quickly in the days ahead and as we strive with the United Nations for victory in Korea, we must keep clearly in mind what we believe in and what we are trying to do. We also want the rest of the world to understand clearly our aims and our hopes.

STATEMENT OF U.S. AIMS AND POLICY

First: We believe in the United Nations. When we ratified its Charter, we pledged ourselves to seek peace and security through this world organization. We kept our word when we went to the support of the United Nations in Korea 2 months ago. We shall never go back on that pledge.

Second: We believe the Koreans have a right to be free, independent, and united—as they want to be. Under the direction and guidance of the United Nations, we, with others, will do our part to help them enjoy that right. The United States has no other aim in Korea.

Third: We do not want the fighting in Korea to expand into a general war. It will not spread unless Communist imperialism draws other armies and governments into the fight of the aggressors against the United Nations.

Fourth: We hope in particular that the people of China will not be misled or forced into fighting against the United Nations and against the American people, who have always been and still are their friends. Only the Communist imperialism, which has already started to dismember China, could gain from China's involvement in war.

Fifth: We do not want Formosa or any part of Asia for ourselves. We believe that the future of Formosa, like that of any other territory in dispute, should be settled peacefully. We believe that it should be settled by international action and not by the decision of the United States or of any other state alone. The mission of the Seventh Fleet is to keep Formosa out of the conflict. Our purpose is peace, not conquest.

Sixth: We believe in freedom for all the nations of the Far East. That is one of the reasons why we are fighting under the United Nations for the freedom of Korea. We helped the Philippines become independent, and we have supported the national aspirations to independence of other Asian countries. Russia has never voluntarily given up any territory it has acquired in the Far East; it has never given independence to any people who have fallen under its control. We not only want freedom for the peoples of Asia but we also want to help them secure for themselves better health, more food, better clothes and homes, and the chance to live their own lives in peace. The things we want for the people of Asia are the same things we want for the people of the rest of the world.

Seventh: We do not believe in aggressive or preventive war. Such war is the weapon of dictators, not of free democratic countries like the United States. We are arming only for defense against aggression. Even though Communist imperialism does not believe in peace, it can be discouraged from new aggression if we and other free peoples are strong, determined, and united.

Eighth: We want peace and we shall achieve it. Our men are fighting for peace today in Korea. We are working for peace constantly in the United Nations and in all the capitals of the world. Our workers, our farmers, our businessmen, all our vast resources, are helping now to create the strength which will make peace secure.

We want peace not only for its own sake but because we want all the peoples of the world, including ourselves, to be free to devote their full energies to making their lives richer and happier. We shall give what help we can to make this universal human wish come true.

We invite all the nations of the world, without exception, to join with us in this great work.

The events in Korea have shown us again all the misery and horrors of war. The North Koreans have learned that the penalties of armed conflict fall as heavily on those who act as tools for the Communist dictatorship as they do on its victims. There will be no profit for any people who follow the Communist dictatorship down its dark and bloody path.

Against the futile and tragic course of dictatorship, we uphold, for all people, the way of freedom—the way of mutual cooperation and international peace. We assert that mankind can find progress and advancement along the path of peace. At this critical hour in the history of the world, our country has been called upon to give of its leadership, its efforts, and its resources, to maintain peace and justice among nations. We have responded to that call. We will not fail.

The task which has fallen upon our beloved country is a great one. In carrying it out, we ask God to purge us of all selfishness and meanness and to give us strength and courage for the days ahead.

◇◇◇◇◇◇

103. PLANS FOR REHABILITATION OF KOREA

Resolution of the General Assembly, October 7, 1950 [1]

[In October, 1950, a United Nations victory in Korea seemed sufficiently assured in order to justify making plans for the rehabilitation of that war-torn country and to provide for its return to normal conditions. On October 7, the General Assembly adopted a resolution which recommended the establishment of a unified, independent, democratic government in Korea and the withdrawal of UN forces as far as was consistent with the attainment of this objective. The Assembly resolved to set up a seven-power commission to have charge of the unification and rehabilitation of Korea. It also called upon the Economic and Social Council to speed up studies for the long-term recovery of that country.]

The General Assembly,

Having regard to its resolutions of 14 November 1947 (112 (II)), of 12 December 1948 (195 (III)) and of 21 October 1949 (293 (IV)),

Having received and considered the report of the United Nations Commission on Korea,

Mindful of the fact that the objectives set forth in the resolutions referred to above have not been fully accomplished and, in particular, that the unification of Korea has not yet been achieved, and that an attempt has been made by an armed attack from North Korea to extinguish by force the Government of the Republic of Korea,

Recalling the General Assembly declaration of 12 December 1948 that there has been established a lawful government (the Government of the Republic of Korea) having effective control and jurisdiction over that part of Korea where the United Nations Temporary Commission on Korea was able to observe and consult and in which the great majority of the people of Korea reside; that this Government is based on elections which were a valid expression of the free will of the electorate of that part of Korea and which were observed by the Temporary Commission; and that this is the only such Government in Korea,

Having in mind that United Nations armed forces are at present operating in Korea in accordance with the recommendations of the Security Council of 27 June 1950, subsequent to its resolution of 25 June 1950, that Members

[1] UN doc. A/1435, 7 October 1950.

of the United Nations furnish such assistance to the Republic of Korea as may be necessary to repel the armed attack and to restore international peace and security in the area,

Recalling that the essential objective of the resolutions of the General Assembly referred to above was the establishment of a unified, independent and democratic Government of Korea,

1. *Recommends* that

(a) All appropriate steps be taken to ensure conditions of stability throughout Korea;

(b) All constituent acts be taken, including the holding of elections, under the auspices of the United Nations, for the establishment of a unified, independent and democratic Government in the sovereign State of Korea;

(c) All sections and representative bodies of the population of Korea, South and North, be invited to co-operate with the organs of the United Nations in the restoration of peace, in the holding of elections and in the establishment of a unified Government;

(d) United Nations forces should not remain in any part of Korea otherwise than so far as necessary for achieving the objectives specified in subparagraphs (a) and (b) above;

(e) All necessary measures be taken to accomplish the economic rehabilitation of Korea;

2. *Resolves* that

(a) A Commission consisting of Australia, Chile, Netherlands, Pakistan, Philippines, Thailand and Turkey, to be known as the United Nations Commission for the Unification and Rehabilitation of Korea, be established to (i) assume the functions hitherto exercised by the present United Nations Commission in Korea; (ii) represent the United Nations in bringing about the establishment of a unified, independent and democratic government of all Korea; (iii) exercise such responsibilities in connexion with relief and rehabilitation in Korea as may be determined by the General Assembly after receiving the recommendations of the Economic and Social Council. The United Nations Commission for the Unification and Rehabilitation of Korea should proceed to Korea and begin to carry out its functions as soon as possible;

(b) Pending the arrival in Korea of the United Nations Commission for the Unification and Rehabilitation of Korea, the Governments of the States represented on the Commission should form an interim committee composed of representatives meeting at the seat of the United Nations to consult with and advise the United Nations Unified Command in the light of the above recommendations; the interim committee should begin to function immediately upon the approval of the present resolution by the General Assembly;

(c) The Commission shall render a report to the next regular session of the General Assembly and to any prior special session which might be called to consider the subject matter of the present resolution, and shall render such interim reports as it may deem appropriate to the Secretary-General for transmission to Members;

The General Assembly furthermore,

Mindful of the fact that at the end of the present hostilities the task of rehabilitating the Korean economy will be of great magnitude,

3. *Requests* the Economic and Social Council, in consultation with the specialized agencies, to develop plans for relief and rehabilitation on the termination of hostilities and to report to the General Assembly within three weeks of the adoption of the present resolution by the General Assembly;

4. *Also recommends* the Economic and Social Council to expedite the study of long-term measures to promote the economic development and social progress of Korea, and meanwhile to draw the attention of the authorities which decide requests for technical assistance to the urgent and special necessity of affording such assistance to Korea;

5. *Expresses* its appreciation of the services rendered by the members of the United Nations Commission on Korea in the performance of their important and difficult task;

6. *Requests* the Secretary-General to provide the Commission with adequate staff and facilities, including technical advisers as required; and authorizes the Secretary-General to pay the expenses and *per diem* of a representative and alternate from each of the States members of the Commission.

◇◇◇◇◇

104. WAKE ISLAND CONFERENCE BETWEEN PRESIDENT TRUMAN AND GENERAL MAC ARTHUR

Statement of President Truman, October 15, 1950 [1]

[When the North Korean attack was turned back in the early fall of 1950, President Truman met General MacArthur on Wake Island to discuss the Far Eastern situation, developments in Korea, and the possibilities of an early peace with Japan. On his return to the United States the President issued this communiqué in which he commented upon the complete unanimity of views between General MacArthur and himself. The President expressed confidence that the dangers ahead could be surmounted because of our devotion to peace, the unity of the UN members, and the growing strength and determination of the United States.]

I have met with General of the Army Douglas MacArthur for the purpose of getting first-hand information and ideas from him. I did not wish to take him away from the scene of action in Korea any longer than necessary, and, therefore, I came to meet him at Wake. Our conference has been highly satisfactory.

The very complete unanimity of view which prevailed enabled us to finish our discussions rapidly in order to meet General MacArthur's desire to return at the earliest possible moment. It was apparent that the excellent coordination which has existed between Washington and the field, to which General MacArthur paid tribute, greatly facilitated the discussion.

After I had talked with General MacArthur privately, we met together

[1] Department of State Bulletin, October 23, 1950, p. 643.

with our advisers. These joint talks were then followed by technical consultations in which the following participated:

General MacArthur and Ambassador John Muccio; Mr. Averell Harriman, Special Assistant to the President; Secretary of the Army Frank Pace; General of the Army Omar N. Bradley, Chairman, Joint Chiefs of Staff; Admiral Arthur W. Radford, Commander in Chief of the Pacific Fleet; Assistant Secretary of State Dean Rusk; and Ambassador-at-large Philip C. Jessup.

Primarily, we talked about the problems in Korea which are General MacArthur's most pressing responsibilities. I asked him for information on the military aspects.

I got from him a clear picture of the heroism and high capacity of the United Nations forces under his command. We also discussed the steps necessary to bring peace and security to the area as rapidly as possible in accordance with the intent of the resolution of the United Nations General Assembly and in order to get our armed forces out of Korea as soon as their United Nations mission is completed.

We devoted a good deal of time to the major problem of peaceful reconstruction of Korea which the United Nations is facing and to the solution of which we intend to make the best contribution of which the United States is capable.

This is a challenging task which must be done properly if we are to achieve the peaceful goals for which the United Nations has been fighting.

The success which has attended the combined military effort must be supplemented by both spiritual and material rehabilitation. It is essentially a task of helping the Koreans to do a job which they can do for themselves better than anyone else can do it for them.

The United Nations can, however, render essential help with supplies and technical advice as well as with the vital problem of rebuilding their educational system.

Meanwhile, I can say I was greatly impressed with what General MacArthur and Ambassador Muccio told me about what has already been done and is now being done to bring order out of chaos and to restore to the Korean people the chance for a good life in peace.

For example, the main rail line from Inchon to Suwon was opened to rail traffic in less than 10 days after the Inchon landing. The rail line from Pusan to the west bank of the Han River opposite Seoul was open to one-way rail traffic about October 8. Bridge and highway reconstruction is progressing rapidly. Power and the water supply in Seoul were reestablished within a week after the reentry into the capital.

General MacArthur paid a particularly fine tribute to the service being rendered in Korea by Ambassador Muccio.

I asked General MacArthur also to explain at first hand his views on the future of Japan with which I was already generally familiar through his written reports. As already announced, we are moving forward with preliminary negotiations for a peace treaty to which Japan is entitled.

General MacArthur and I look forward with confidence to a new Japan which will be both peaceful and prosperous.

I also asked General MacArthur to tell me his ideas on the ways in which the United States can most effectively promote its policies of assisting the

United Nations to promote and maintain international peace and security throughout the Pacific area.

On all these matters, I have found our talks most helpful and I am very glad to have had this chance to talk them over with one of America's great soldier-statesmen, who is also now serving in the unique position of the first Commander in Chief of United Nations peace forces.

We are fully aware of the dangers which lie ahead, but we are confident that we can surmount these dangers with three assets which we have:

first, unqualified devotion to peace;

second, unity with our fellow peace-loving members of the United Nations;

third, our determination and growing strength.

105. CHINESE COMMUNIST INTERVENTION IN KOREA

Communiqué by General MacArthur, November 6, 1950 [1]

[As the tide of battle turned against the North Koreans in October 1950, a fresh element was injected into the conflict. It had been rumored for some time previously that Chinese troops were on the move to the Korean borders. The rumor was confirmed by this communiqué which General MacArthur issued on November 6, 1950. In it he stated that while the North Korean military forces had been destroyed, final victory would have to be postponed because a new and fresh army backed by large alien reserves faced the UN forces.]

The military position of the United Nations forces in the western sector of North Korea is now sufficiently stabilized and information on enemy unit identifications adequately evaluated to permit me to put the situation growing out of the last few days' operations in proper perspective.

The Korean war was brought to a practical end with the closing of the trap on enemy elements north of Pyongyang and seizure of the east coastal area, resulting in raising the number of enemy prisoners of war in our hands to well over 135,000, which, with other losses amounting to over 200,000, brought casualties to 335,000, representing a fair estimate of North Korean total military strength.

The defeat of the North Koreans and destruction of their armies was thereby decisive. In the face of this victory of United Nations arms, the Communists committed one of the most offensive acts of international lawlessness of historic record by moving without any notice of belligerency elements of alien Communist forces across the Yalu River into North Korea and massing a great concentration of possible reinforcing divisions with adequate supply behind the privileged sanctuary of the adjacent Manchurian border.

A possible trap was thereby surreptitiously laid, calculated to encompass the destruction of the United Nations forces engaged in restoring order and the processes of civil government in the North Korean border area.

[1] Department of State Bulletin, November 13, 1950, p. 763.

This potential danger was avoided with minimum losses only by the timely detection and skillful maneuvering of the United Nations commander responsible for that sector who, with great perspicacity and skill, completely revised the movement of his forces in order to achieve the greater integration of tactical power necessitated by the new situation, and avert any possibility of a great military reverse.

The present situation, therefore, is this:

While the North Korean forces with which we were initially engaged have been destroyed or rendered impotent for military action, a new and fresh army now faces us, backed up by a possibility of large alien reserves, and adequate supply within easy reach to the enemy but beyond the limits of our present sphere of military action.

Whether and to what extent these reserves will be moved forward to reinforce units now committed remains to be seen and is a matter of the gravest international significance.

Our present mission is limited to the destruction of those forces now arrayed against us in North Korea, with a view to achieving the United Nations' objective to bring unity and peace to the Korean nation and people.

DOUGLAS MACARTHUR,
General of the Army, United States Army,
Commander-in-Chief.

◇◇◇◇◇◇

106. COMMUNIST INTERVENTION IN KOREA

Statement by Ambassador Warren R. Austin before the Security Council,
November 28, 1950 [1]

[During the fall of 1950, in hopes of reaching a solution of the Chinese intervention in Korea, the Chinese Communist Government was invited to share in the deliberations of the Security Council. The invitation was accepted on November 11. On November 28th, the Communist delegation accused the United States of "criminal armed aggression" against China. In the statement which follows the United States representative refuted the charge, pointed to the long-standing friendship of the United States for the people of China, and noted the subservience of the Chinese Communists to Moscow. He concluded with the thought that the people of the world were anxiously watching to see whether the Chinese Communist Government would elect peace or war in the Far East.]

The Mission of the United States of America is glad that the Security Council has decided to bracket, for purposes of discussion, the two questions of the complaint of aggression against the Republic of Korea and the complaint of armed invasion of Taiwan (Formosa). These two agenda items are distinct, but they are closely related aspects of one great problem. It is no

[1] UNITED STATES DELEGATION TO THE GENERAL ASSEMBLY Press Release 1083/Rev. 1 November 28, 1950.

exaggeration to say that that problem is the gravest one now confronting the world.

*   *   *

The Security Council will undoubtedly wish to hear the latest news from the United Nations front in Korea. Last week the forces of the United Nations opened a general attack designed to finish their assigned task of repulsing aggression and restoring international peace and security in the area. This attack has been repulsed in circumstances which make it clear that Chinese Communist armed forces totaling more than 200,000 men are now engaged in North Korea. They are supported by heavy reinforcements moving forward from behind the international boundary. It now appears doubtful that the war in Korea can be quickly concluded.

It also appears clear beyond any doubt that what all the free world hoped was an intervention for limited purposes is in fact aggression open and notorious. It will be recalled that yesterday I used that word, "aggression," and then withdrew it, saying that I would not use it; I would use only the word, "intervention," until the facts came to our knowledge which would justify the use of the word, "aggression." I now employ it here in this Council, and before all the world, by direction of my Government.

The consequences of these facts must be faced squarely by the people of the world, and more particularly, by this Council. Because such consequences are potentially so grave, I considered it essential to review the recent history of events in the Far East. This is particularly necessary in view of the presence here for the first time of a representative of the Peiping regime.

The statements—that is, the written statements to which we referred yesterday—from Peiping bear a close family resemblance to the statements made here by representatives of the Soviet Union and reveal the same lack of contact with reality. The recent history of Korea, as understood by the vast majority of governments and the vast bulk of peoples in the world, shows that, first, the United States, and then, the United Nations, have bent their efforts ever since the end of the war with Japan to establish a free and independent Korea. When the United States was unable to gain the agreement of the Soviet Union in eliminating the 38th Parallel as a military frontier, my Government asked the United Nations to take up the case.

The General Assembly from 1947 onwards maintained a commission in Korea charged with the creation of an independent, democratic and unified Government. That commission was denied access above the 38th Parallel first by the Soviet Union as the occupying Power and then by the Soviet-installed North Korean regime. They even refused to accept and sign for communications from the United Nations Commission on Korea. South of the Parallel, the Commission supervised two elections and certified the establishment of a democratic government—a government accepted by the General Assembly of the United Nations as the only valid and lawful government in Korea.

This same United Nations Commission on Korea found on 24 June of this year that the Army of the Republic of Korea "is organized entirely for defense and is in no condition to carry out attacks on a large scale against forces of the north."

The next day the forces of the north marched into the territory of the Republic. On the following day, the Commission declared that "judging from actual progress of operations northern regime is carrying out well-planned, concerted and full-scale invasion of South Korea." This was a unanimous finding by representatives of Australia, China, El Salvador, France, India, the Philippines and Turkey. Perhaps you have noticed that no representative of the United States was on that Commission.

In the face of this breach of the peace, the Security Council immediately called upon the authorities of North Korea to cease hostilities and to withdraw their armed forces. It also called upon "all members to render every assistance to the United Nations in the execution of this resolution and to refrain from giving assistance to the North Korean authorities." That is a quotation from the resolution of the Security Council. The North Korean authorities ignored this order and pressed their attack. On 27 June, the President of the United States, heeding the Security Council's call "to render every assistance to the United Nations," ordered United States air and sea forces to give the Korean Government troops cover and support. That same day, the Security Council, noting that the authorities in North Korea had ignored its previous order and that "urgent military measures are required to restore international peace and security," recommended that the members "furnish such assistance to the Republic of Korea as may be necessary to repel the armed attack and to restore international peace and security in the area."

This resolution received the prompt endorsement and support of fifty-three Members of the United Nations. The Governments and peoples of these fifty-three countries can hardly be pleased by the numerous Soviet and Chinese Communist statements declaring that the United Nations action in Korea is a United States aggression. They also have sons who serve and die.

The multi-national effort in Korea now includes, among the forces either in operation or on the way there, ground troops from thirteen countries, naval forces from ten, combat air forces from four, and military transport from seven. Moreover, non-military supplies in substantial quantities have been contributed by twenty-six countries.

Because of the sacrifices of the fighting men of many nations and the splendid support given the United Nations operations by the vast majority of Members, the attackers from the north were repulsed. The military campaign seemed last month to be nearing its conclusion. The free peoples of the United Nations felt that their hopes for Korea were about to be realized: that Korea should be free, unified and independent of outside influence from any great Power, on or off the continent, and that the people of Korea should be free to choose their own future and to control their own destinies. In anticipation of victory, the General Assembly had adopted resolutions calling for the withdrawal of all United Nations forces as soon as order was restored to the country, and providing for relief and reconstruction to start the people of Korea, both north and south, well on the road to peace and prosperity.

That prospect was suddenly beclouded by the entrance into Korea on a large scale of Chinese Communist forces. Previous to that time, the regime at Peiping had refrained from such open military support of the North Korean aggression. The regime had persistently strengthened the hand of the aggressor with moral encouragement. It had sent military supplies and equipment on a considerable scale. Most important, it had relieved approximately 140,000 combat troops of Korean origin from its own armies and had allowed the recruitment for the North Korean armies of Koreans living in Manchuria. But those things were then done covertly. Now the Peiping regime openly sends its fighting units in large numbers across the border from Manchuria to join battle with the United Nations. These forces immediately attacked the United Nations forces. They were organized, equipped and supplied as fighting units. Their supply bases and reinforcement depots were protected by the Manchurian frontier—a frontier which the United Nations forces respected despite the serious disabilities which this practice laid upon their operations.

Did the Chinese Communists go into Korea, as they allege in the paper to which I called attention yesterday, on a sentimental journey?

The Chinese Communists know that their influence in North Korea was in the ratio of one to ninety-nine compared with Soviet influence. They know that the Peiping Government had so little respect for the North Korean regime as an independent and sovereign government that it refused to establish a Chinese Communist Embassy in Pyongyang until 10 July 1950, after the North Korean aggression began, though the Peiping regime was established in October 1949 and the North Korean regime had established an Embassy at Peiping in February 1950.

In the circumstances, one asks our visitors: Was the aggression really in the interest of the Chinese people, as has been proclaimed, or was it on behalf of the great Russian power which has already taken so many benefits away from Manchuria at the expense of the Chinese people?

Let us look at the recent history of Formosa. When the President of the United States ordered United States air and sea forces to support the troops of the Republic of Korea, he pointed out that the aggression upon the Republic of Korea endangered international peace and security, and that "in these circumstances, the occupation of Formosa by Communist forces would be a direct threat to the security of the Pacific area and to United States Forces performing their necessary and lawful functions in that area." How plain it is to see that that was true. We see it clearly this morning.

The President went on to say:

"Accordingly, I have ordered the Seventh Fleet to prevent any attack on Formosa. As a corollary of this action, I am calling upon the Chinese Government on Formosa to cease all air and sea operations against the mainland. The Seventh Fleet will see that this is done. The determination of the future status of Formosa must await the restoration of security in the Pacific, a peace settlement with Japan, or consideration by the United Nations."

In a subsequent message to the Congress of the United States on 19 July 1950, the President pointed out that this action "was a matter of elementary security." He added:

"In order that there may be no doubt in any quarter about our intentions regarding Formosa, I wish to state that the United States has no territorial ambitions whatever concerning that island, nor do we seek for ourselves any special position or privilege on Formosa. The present military neutralization of Formosa is without prejudice to political questions affecting that island. Our desire is that Formosa not become embroiled in hostilities disturbing to the peace of the Pacific and that all questions affecting Formosa be settled by peaceful means as envisaged in the Charter of the United Nations. With peace re-established, even the most complex political questions are susceptible of solution. In the presence of brutal and unprovoked aggression, however, some of these questions may have to be held in abeyance in the interest of the essential security of all."

That is the end of the extract from the President's speech.

These are the facts about Korea and Formosa as they are understood by my Government. It is quite clear from the statements so far made on behalf of the Chinese Communist regime to which I alluded yesterday that it does not share this view of the facts. Mr. Malik says that a representative of the Ministry of Foreign Affairs at Peiping stated on 11 November:

"The real facts are that the United States of America has invaded Chinese territory, violated Chinese sovereignty and is threatening China's security."

The statement went on to say:

"Filled with righteous indignation, the Chinese people are voluntarily helping the Korean people to repulse aggression and its acts are completely natural and just."

The authorities at Peiping have further charged the United States with aggression against Formosa, invasion of that island, and the imposition of a United States blockade. The United States is further charged with deliberate violations of Chinese territorial air and with the repeated bombing of Chinese towns and villages. Finally, the United States is charged with turning the United Nations into an instrument to conceal United States aggression—an instrument which, it is also charged, has been used illegally since two permanent members are alleged to have been absent from the Security Council when the decisions were taken to support the Republic of Korea and to establish the Unified Command.

Obviously, there is a gaping void between the facts as seen by most of the world and the facts as claimed by the authorities of Peiping. One of our hopes is that from these Security Council discussions will come some measure of agreement as to the facts, some understanding by the representatives of the Chinese Communist regime of the aims and purposes of the United Nations. The 53 Members of the United Nations who have supported the Organization's action in Korea must be dismayed when they read and hear these unbridled and unjustified attacks upon the United Nations and its efforts to stop armed aggression in Korea and restore peace and security in the Far East. My Government is dismayed, and it deplores these attacks the more because of the long and close friendship between the people of China and the people of the United States.

The preservation of China's territorial and administrative entity has been a major tenet of American policy ever since relations were first established between the two Governments in 1844 by the Treaty of Wanghia—more than 150 years ago. The American record of support to the Chinese Government against the imperialist pressures of Russia and Japan is well known.

The "Open Door Notes" of Secretary of State John Hay, in 1899, awoke the world's conscience to an appreciation of the menace of Russian imperialist pressure on Manchuria. United States efforts to support Chinese sovereignty over Manchuria have never relaxed since that time. This policy was not relaxed when Russian imperialism was replaced by Japanese imperialism in 1905; this policy was not relaxed when Japanese imperialism was replaced in turn by the new Soviet imperialism in 1945.

The purpose of the United States, during the last half century, to aid China in developing her independence, free from foreign control, and, particularly, in maintaining the stability of international relations in the Far East has been demonstrated in the several alternating attempts of Russia and Japan to violate the integrity of China in Manchuria.

Many examples could be given of the continuity of American policy in this respect. For instance, in 1902, the United States circularized the powers, protesting that Russian pressure against Manchuria and threats to Chinese control there were contrary to the Open Door Policy. Again in 1904 and 1905, during the Russo-Japanese War, the United States Secretary of State, John Hay, appealed to both belligerents to respect the neutrality and administrative entity of China and circularized the powers in the interest of the integrity of China and the Open Door in the Orient.

In the Root-Takahira Agreement of 1908, the United States agreed with Japan to uphold the Open Door in China and to support, by pacific means, the independence and integrity of China. In 1908, the United States Secretary of State, Elihu Root, circularized the powers in an effort to strengthen the Open Door principle and to discourage Russian and Japanese commercial penetration into Manchuria at the expense of China's territorial integrity and political independence.

In 1915, the United States opposed Japan's Twenty-one Demands and, in affirming its traditional policy towards China, stated that it could not recognize any agreement that would impair the political and territorial integrity of China. The Open Door Principle was reaffirmed again in 1917 by the Lansing-Ishii Agreement. At the Washington Conference of 1921-22, the United States assisted in bringing about a settlement of the Shantung controversy between China and Japan and took a leading role in the negotiations which led to the Nine-Power Treaty. Referring to Japanese aggression in Manchuria in 1932, the United States Secretary of State, Henry L. Stimson, informed the Japanese and Chinese Governments that the United States Government did not:

> ". . . intend to recognize any treaty or agreement entered into between those two Governments, or agents thereof, which may impair the treaty rights of the United States or its citizens in China, including those which relate to the sovereignty, the independence, or the territorial and administrative integrity of the Republic of China or to the international policy relative to China, commonly known as the 'Open Door Policy' ".

All during the 1930's, the United States continued to manifest the gravest concern over Japanese aggression against China, and it was United States opposition to Japan's expansionism which led to Pearl Harbor.

The record of American friendship for China during the war and postwar period is recent history. On two occasions in 1943 the United States obtained international acknowledgment of China's position as a great power. This was first done in the Moscow Declaration of Four Nations on General Security on 30 October 1943. It was also done in the Cairo Declaration of 1 December

1943. It was done still again in 1945 at the San Francisco Conference where the United States insisted, over Soviet objections, that China be included as one of the great powers in the organization of the peace by making it one of the sponsoring powers of the United Nations and one of the permanent members of the Security Council.

American friendship for China also was shown by the large quantities of economic aid given to China. From 1937 to V-J Day, the United States sent to China economic aid valued at $670,000,000. After the V-J Day, it sent an additional $1,009,000,000 in economic aid. In other words, during the past thirteen years the United States has sent aid to China at a rate considerably greater than a hundred million dollars a year. These figures do not include Lend-Lease and military aid. They include only assistance and commodities required for the reconstruction of the war-devastated economy of China. They were composed of such things as rice, cotton, petroleum, ships, emergency relief aid, industrial machinery, technical assistance and so forth.

A joint United States-Chinese programme for rural reconstruction was entered upon in 1945 and continued for as long a period of time as possible in Szechuán and Chekiang Provinces; it still goes on in Taiwan. This was for the benefit principally of Chinese farmers.

Need I say that such friendly assistance meant much to China and the Chinese people? And I am speaking of that vast number of Chinese people— five hundred million of them. It is not towards them that I point when I speak of aggression: I refer to the Chinese Communists when I speak of aggression. Let us maintain for ever that wonderful friendship which has existed, and still exists, between the people of the United States and the people of China. To the people of China, our assistance meant much.

For instance, during 1948, more than half the rice and flour ration requirements of Shanghai, Nanking, Tsingtao, Tientsin and Peiping were met by United States-financed imports. Similarly, 40 per cent of the cotton requirements of the great textile mills in Shanghai, Tsingtao and Tientsin were supplied by United States resources. The mills of China were kept alive to furnish employment to the Chinese people. Almost all of China's petroleum requirements were thus met.

Millions of Chinese will not forget that they ate, worked, travelled and were clothed during the harsh years following the war largely because of United States assistance. The rice alone which we sent to China in 1948 and 1949 filled the rice bowls of ten million Chinese. In view of China's vast problems, it cannot be questioned that much more was needed. But I submit that this attitude toward the Chinese people and their true interests contrasts favourably with the Barter Agreement concluded by the Soviet Union with local authorities in Manchuria last year, under which, despite critical food shortages in China, food was taken from the rice bowls of the Chinese and shipped to the Soviet Union.

The traditional friendship of the United States for China also has proved itself on a non-governmental level.

Does this sound like a bloodthirsty aggressor? Can it be that any Chinese really is the author of that contumely, that false charge against the people of the United States?

United States medical work, which was begun in 1835, is today an integral part of China's daily life. United States medical missions have supported 203 hospitals, 82 nursing schools, and a number of other medical institutions such as schools for the training of midwives. United States contributions have been a major source of support for 320 orphanages maintained by the Catholic Church in China.

One-eighth of all the college graduates in China have received education at one or more of the thirteen colleges established by American Protestant missions. The names of these institutions and the benevolent character of their work is well known to the great masses of the Chinese people; I feel confident that it is well known to the Chinese Communists. Some of those who were here had the benefit of education in some of those institutions. They include Yenching University, Peiping; Cheeloo University, Tsinan. I want you to notice how they are spread out over the Flowery Kingdom. The others are: West China University, Chengtu; Hua Chung University, Wuchang; University of Nanking; Ginling College, Nanking; University of Shanghai; Hangchow University; Soochow University; St. John's University, Shanghai; Fukien Christian University; Hwa Nan College, Fuchow; Lingnan University, Canton.

There are, in addition to these colleges, such outstanding American-endowed institutions of higher learning as the Peiping Union Medical College; Yale-in-China, Changsha, Hunan; Catholic University of Peiping; Tsinghua University, Peiping; Nankai University of Economics, Tsientsin. Some of these universities are well known to the whole world, not merely to the Chinese. They are not evidences of a bloodthirsty aggressor.

At least 15,000 Chinese students have received their college degrees from American-supported institutions in China. Another 10,000 have received their college educations in the United States. Can it be that all those golden threads that connect the Chinese people and the American people culturally have been sundered? Moreover, it is estimated that over 250,000 Chinese students have graduated from primary and middle schools maintained in China with American funds. Thousands upon thousands of Chinese and Americans share a community of experience and a compatibility that cannot be erased by evil propaganda.

The American people treasure their relations with the people of China. They enjoyed, with the Chinese, the relinquishment by their Government of the extra-territorial rights of the United States in China under the treaty signed in Washington on 11 January 1943. The friendship of the American people for the Chinese people has weathered storms in the past. It is the earnest hope of my Government that it will weather the storms of the present.

I should like now to put some questions to the Chinese Communist representative; first, a group of questions relating to Korea and second a group of questions relating to Formosa.

With regard to Korea:

Can the representative tell us how many Chinese Communist troops have entered Korea and are there now?

What is the organization of these troops?

It is quite clear to the United Nations forces that they are in fact organized into units. The units have been identified and their numbers cited in the special report of the Unified Command to the Security Council of 5 November. The news this morning makes it quite clear that Chinese Communist forces in

Korea are organized on an army, corps and divisional basis. Does the representative still maintain that these forces are composed only of volunteers?

Will the representative tell the Security Council how long the Peiping regime has been planning and preparing this aggression? It is apparent to anyone that an operation of this kind is not organized in a few days or weeks. It must be true that these troops were trained and equipped as a disciplined fighting force over a long period and that their attack was carefully prepared. Was all this being done while the Peiping radio was protesting the peaceful intentions of the Peiping regime?

If the representative persists in telling us that the intervention was entirely voluntary, can he explain to us the voluntary manner in which their supplies have been organized, dispatched across the frontier and distributed?

Will he tell us whether the aircraft which have attacked from bases in Manchuria were also "volunteers"?

How could private Chinese citizens come into possession of jet planes?

Can the representative tell us what was his Government's estimate of United Nations objectives which brought it to decide to commit this aggression?

What led his Government to ignore and set aside the reiterated statements by the United Nations bodies and by my own Government that there were no designs on Chinese territory or legitimate interests?

If his Government was aware of these reassurances but did not believe them, what more could the Security Council conceivably do to reassure the Peiping authorities that the United Nations does not in fact have any such evil designs?

The representative is doubtless familiar with the pending resolution before the Council. This resolution reaffirms the General Assembly resolution of 7 October, which declares that "United Nations forces should not remain in any part of Korea otherwise than so far as necessary for achieving the objectives of stability throughout Korea and the establishment of a unified, independent and free government in the sovereign State of Korea." The resolution also affirms that it is the policy of the United Nations to hold the Chinese frontier inviolate and fully to protect Chinese and Korean interests in the frontier zone. It requests the United Nations Commission for the Unification and Rehabilitation of Korea "to consider urgently and to assist in the settlement of many problems relating to conditions on the Korean frontier in which States or authorities on the other side of the frontier have an interest."

Can the representative tell us why his Government does not consider it preferable to rely upon the Commission for the peaceful settlement of any problems relating to the frontier, and why instead of that it has continued to resort to force?

I should like to ask the representative: what are his Government's interests relative to Korea?

The United Nations has made it clear that once order has been restored, all forces will be withdrawn from Korea. My own Government has stated repeatedly that it has no intention of maintaining bases in Korea, and that its sole interest in Korea is the interest shared by 53 Members of the United Nations, namely, the establishment of a unified country independent of outside influence, living in peace with its neighbours.

Can the representative tell us whether his Government feels that it can live in peace and good neighbourly relations with this kind of Korea, or will it feel secure only if Korea is controlled by a Communist government?

My next question with regard to Korea is not the least important. It is this: will the authorities at Peiping respond to the central paragraph of the draft resolution before the Council? By the way, this resolution should be acted upon as promptly as is convenient. Note how simple it is for a peace-loving country to carry out what is stated therein. That paragraph reads as follows:

> "The Security Council calls upon all States and authorities ... to refrain from assisting or encouraging the North Korean authorities, to prevent their nationals or individuals or units of their armed forces from giving assistance to North Korean forces and to cause the immediate withdrawals of such nationals, individuals, or units which might presently be in Korea."

Well, we have been told that the Soviet Union would vote against that resolution. If so, we understand that means a veto of the resolution. But, nevertheless, it represents the conscience of the people of the world. And does this Peiping regime recognize the conscience of the people of the world as something that it ought to give weight to?

But even if that resolution should be vetoed, there is another resolution which was not vetoed by the Soviet Union, just because the Soviet Union did not see fit to be present in the Security Council when it was passed. That resolution is dated 25 June 1950, and one paragraph therein has the same moral character as this paragraph in the pending resolution that I have referred to. The paragraph of the resolution passed on 25 June 1950 reads as follows: "The Security Council calls upon all Members to render every assistance to the United Nations in the execution of this resolution and to refrain from giving assistance to the North Korean authorities." This is one sure way that would help to prevent a general war.

I repeat my question: will the authorities at Peiping heed this judgment of the United Nations, or will they defy the United Nations, thus further endangering international peace and security?

The answer to this question may determine whether the Korean conflict will be brought to a speedy end, or whether it will rage on, thus heightening the danger that it may spread and involve neighbouring areas.

Will there be peace or war in the Far East?

With regard to the Chinese Communist complaint of violations of the Chinese territorial air by United Nations aircraft, I should like to remind the representative that when these complaints were first made the United States admitted the possibility that unfortunate mistakes might have occurred in the heat and confusion of modern aerial war. My Government went on to say that it stood ready to make payment to the Secretary-General of the United Nations for appropriate transmission to the injured party of compensation for such damages as might be adjudged fair and equitable as the result of an appropriate investigation. My Government even proposed a method of investigation which commended itself to a majority of the members of this Council: namely, the appointment of a commission to investigate the allegations on the spot. We pledged ourselves in advance to abide by the findings of this commission, which would have consisted of representatives of the Governments of India and of Sweden. The Soviet Union representative vetoed this proposal. Since then, the Chinese Communists have intervened on a large scale in Korea and have caused great damage to the United Nations and to Korea.

The Unified Command has nevertheless maintained in force its instructions strictly prohibiting United Nations aircraft from crossing the Korean frontier, and has taken every precaution to avoid any violation of Chinese territory. This continues to be the case despite the extensive use of Chinese territory as a base for both ground and air operations against the United Nations Forces in Korea.

With regard to Formosa, it is clear from the statements I have already cited that United States action in connexion with Formosa is not "blood-thirsty aggression," invasion, or blockade. I have already quoted statements by the President of the United States showing that the despatch of the Seventh Fleet to the Formosa Strait was designed to neutralize Formosa and to prevent the extension of the Korean conflict. The Government of China that is recognized by my Government and by a majority of the Members of the United Nations is in effective control of the island of Formosa.

The representative of China stated in the Security Council on 25 August 1950:

> "I need only one minute to make a statement, and that statement is contained in one sentence. There has been no United States aggression against the island of Taiwan (Formosa)." (S/PV.490,p.18)

Again on 29 August, he said:

> "My Government knows of no aggression on the part of the United States. My Government has no complaint to make. We have not heard even a whisper of a demand on the part of the United States for any territorial or economic concessions on the island of Taiwan, or for any special political privileges on that Island. There is absolutely no case whatever." (S/PV.492,p.5)

The United States has stationed no combat ground or air forces on Formosa. There are forty-four United States military personnel on Formosa, not combat units but military attaches and liaison personnel. This is hardly an invasion in the understood sense of the word. As for the charge of blockade, the plain fact is that no United States naval vessel has interfered in any way with the entry into or departure from any Formosan port of any vessel. The sole mission of the United States Seventh Fleet is to prevent any attack from the mainland on Formosa or from Formosa upon the mainland. My Government has stated repeatedly that this action in no way compromises the future status of Formosa.

The President of the United States stated on 27 August: "The actual status of the island is that it is territory taken from Japan by the victories of the Allies Forces in the Pacific. Like other such territories, its legal status cannot be fixed until there is international action to determine its future." Further to this, the Secretary of State of the United States wrote on 21 September to the Secretary-General of the United Nations: "The Government of the United States has made it abundantly clear that the measures it has taken with respect to Formosa were without prejudice to the long-term political status of

Formosa, and that the United States has no territorial ambitions and seeks no special position or privilege with respect to Formosa."

In view of these facts, we should like to ask the representative:

What are the intentions of the regime he represents towards Formosa?

Will that regime pledge itself to accept a peaceful settlement of the question, or does it intend to risk the grave disturbance of international peace and security by a war-like act?

The United Nations objectives in the Far East, as everywhere in the world, are to maintain international peace and security. The United Nations way with disputes is to seek every means of settling them peacefully, through mediation, conciliation, and agreement by negotiation. But the United Nations is not to be coerced.

It has indicated by its action in Korea and by its adoption of the resolution "Uniting for Peace" at this session of the General Assembly that it is determined to repulse and prevent aggression. Its forces are now fighting in Korea to achieve this objective. The United Nations has not hesitated in the past and does not hesitate now to give assurances of its peaceful intentions. But such assurances must be mutual if they are to be effective.

The Chinese Communist regime, by its actions as well as by its statements, has caused grave doubts to arise in the minds of people all over the world. What the United Nations now seeks is an assurance of the peaceful intent of the regime at Peiping. More important than that assurance, it seeks deeds which will demonstrate that its intent is genuine.

Only if these deeds are forthcoming can China's neighbours and the people of the world feel assured that peace and security will prevail in the Far East.

◇◇◇◇◇

107. THE TRUMAN-ATTLEE CONFERENCE

Communiqué, December 8, 1950 [1]

[On November 27, 1950, the Chinese Communists in Korea began an offensive with the avowed purpose of driving the UN forces off the peninsula. In the light of the early UN reverses some apprehension was felt in the United States lest some UN members should attempt a negotiated truce, which in effect might mean the abandonment of Korea by the UN. Against this backdrop Prime Minister Attlee visited President Truman in Washington to discuss the outstanding problems in international affairs confronting Britain and the United States. On December 8, the following communiqué was issued by the two leaders, in which they asserted complete agreement that there should be no appeasement or rewarding of aggression in the Far East or elsewhere.]

Since Prime Minister Attlee arrived in Washington on December 4, six meetings between the President and Mr. Attlee have been held. Among those who participated as advisers to the President were the Secretary of State Dean

[1] Department of State Bulletin, December 18, 1950, p. 959-961.

Acheson, the Secretary of the Treasury John W. Snyder, the Secretary of Defense Gen. George C. Marshall, the Secretary of the Interior Oscar L. Chapman, the Secretary of Commerce Charles Sawyer, the Chairman of the Joint Chiefs of Staff General of the Army Omar N. Bradley, W. Averell Harriman, the Chairman of the National Security Resources Board, W. Stuart Symington, and Ambassador-designate Walter S. Gifford. Mr. Attlee's advisers included the British Ambassador, Sir Oliver S. Franks, Field Marshal Sir William Slim, Chief of the Imperial General Staff, Marshal of the Royal Air Force Lord Tedder, Sir Roger Makins, and R. H. Scott of the Foreign Office and Sir Edwin Plowden, Chief of the Economic Planning Staff.

At the conclusion of their conferences, the President and the Prime Minister issued the following joint statement:

We have reviewed together the outstanding problems facing our two countries in international affairs. The objectives of our two nations in foreign policy are the same: to maintain world peace and respect for the rights and interests of all peoples, to promote strength and confidence among the freedom-loving countries of the world, to eliminate the causes of fear, want and discontent, and to advance the democratic way of life.

We first reviewed the changed aspect of world affairs arising from the massive intervention of Chinése Communists in Korea. We have discussed the problems of the Far East and the situation as it now presents itself in Europe. We have surveyed the economic problems and the defense programs of our respectives countries, and particularly the existing and threatened shortages of raw materials. We have considered the arrangements for the defense of the Atlantic community, and our future course in the United Nations.

The unity of objectives of our two countries underlay all the discussions. There is no difference between us as to the nature of the threat which our countries face or the basic policies which must be pursued to overcome it. We recognize, that many of the problems which we have discussed can only be decided through the procedures of the United Nations or the North Atlantic Treaty Organization.

The peoples of the United States and the United Kingdom will act together with resolution and unity to meet the challenge to peace which recent weeks have made clear to all.

The situation in Korea is one of great gravity and far-reaching consequences. By the end of October, the forces of the United Nations had all but completed the mission set for them by the United Nations "to repel the armed attack and to restore international peace and security in the area." A free and unified Korea—the objective which the United Nations has long sought—was well on the way to being realized. At that point Chinese Communist forces entered Korea in large numbers, and on November 27 launched a large-scale attack on the United Nations troops. The United Nations forces have the advantage of superior air power and naval support, but on the ground they are confronted by a heavy numerical superiority.

The United Nations forces were sent into Korea on the authority and at the recommendation of the United Nations. The United Nations has not changed the mission which it has entrusted to them and the forces of our two countries will continue to discharge their responsibilities.

We were in complete agreement that there can be no thought of appeasement or of rewarding aggression, whether in the Far East or elsewhere. Lasting peace and the future of the United Nations as an instrument for world peace depend upon strong support for resistance against aggression.

For our part we are ready, as we have always been, to seek an end to the hostilities by means of negotiation. The same principles of international conduct should be applied to this situation as are applied, in accordance with our obligations under the Charter of the United Nations, to any threat to world peace. Every effort must be made to achieve the purposes of the United Nations in Korea by peaceful means and to find a solution of the Korean problem on the basis of a free and independent Korea. We are confident that the great majority of the United Nations takes the same view. If the Chinese on their side display any evidence of a similar attitude, we are hopeful that the cause of peace can be upheld. If they do not, then it will be for the peoples of the world, acting through the United Nations, to decide how the principles of the Charter can best be maintained. For our part, we declare in advance our firm resolve to uphold them.

We considered two questions regarding China which are already before the United Nations. On the question of the Chinese seat in the United Nations, the two Governments differ. The United Kingdom has recognized the Central People's Government and considers that its representatives should occupy China's seat in the United Nations. The United States has opposed and continues to oppose the seating of the Chinese Communist representatives in the United Nations. We have discussed our difference of view on this point and are determined to prevent it from interfering with our united effort in support of our common objectives.

On the question of Formosa, we have noted that both Chinese claimants have insisted upon the validity of the Cairo Declaration and have expressed reluctance to have the matter considered by the United Nations. We agree that the issues should be settled by peaceful means and in such a way as to safeguard the interests of the people of Formosa and the maintenance of peace and security in the Pacific, and that consideration of this question by the United Nations will contribute to these ends.

The free nations of Asia have given strong support to the United Nations and have worked for world peace. Communist aggression in Korea increases the danger to the security and independence of these nations. We reaffirm our intention to continue to help them.

The pressure of Communist expansion existed in Europe and elsewhere long before the aggression against Korea, and measures were taken to meet it. The need to strengthen the forces of collective security had already been recognized and action for this purpose is under way. Clearly, decisions regarding the Far East have their repercussions and effects elsewhere. In considering the necessities of the Far Eastern situation, we have kept in mind the urgency of building up the strength of the whole free world. We are in complete agreement on the need for immediate action by all the North Atlantic Treaty countries to intensify their efforts to build up their defenses and to strengthen the Atlantic community.

We recognize that adequate defense forces are essential if war is to be prevented.

Accordingly, we have reached the following conclusions:

1. The military capabilities of the United States and the United Kingdom should be increased as rapidly as possible.

2. The two countries should expand the production of arms which can be used by the forces of all the free nations that are joined together in common defense. Together with those other nations the United States and the United Kingdom should continue to work out mutual arrangements by which all will contribute appropriately to the common defense.

We agreed that as soon as the plan now nearing completion in the North Atlantic Treaty Organization for an effective integrated force for the defense of Europe is approved, a Supreme Commander should be appointed. It is our joint desire that this appointment shall be made soon.

In addition to these decisions on increasing our military strength, we have agreed that the maintenance of healthy civilian economies is of vital importance to the success of our defense efforts. We agreed that, while defense production must be given the highest practicable priority in the case of raw materials whose supply is inadequate, the essential civilian requirements of the free countries must be met so far as practicable. In order to obtain the necessary materials and to devote them as rapidly as possible to these priority purposes, we have agreed to work closely together for the purpose of increasing supplies of raw materials. We have recognized the necessity of international action to assure that basic raw materials are distributed equitably in accordance with defense and essential civilian needs. We discussed certain immediate problems of raw materials shortages and consideration of these specific matters will continue. We are fully conscious of the increasing necessity of preventing materials and items of strategic importance from flowing into the hands of those who might use them against the free world.

In the circumstances which confront us throughout the world our nations have no other choice but to devote themselves with all vigor to the building up of our defense forces. We shall do this purely as a defensive measure. We believe that the Communist leaders of the Soviet Union and China could, if they chose, modify their conduct in such a way as to make these defense preparations unnecessary. We shall do everything that we can, through whatever channels are open to us, to impress this view upon them and to seek a peaceful solution of existing issues.

The President stated that it was his hope that world conditions would never call for the use of the atomic bomb. The President told the Prime Minister that it was also his desire to keep the Prime Minister at all times informed of developments which might bring about a change in the situation.

In this critical period, it is a source of satisfaction to us that the views of our Governments on basic problems are so similar. We believe that this identity of aims will enable our Governments to carry out their determination to work together to strengthen the unity which has already been achieved among the free nations and to defend those values which are of fundamental importance to the people we represent.

◇◇◇◇◇◇

108. CEASE-FIRE IN KOREA

[The Chinese offensive of December 1950 forestalled any quick UN victory in Korea. A move for a negotiated peace then developed in the UN with the result that the General Assembly set up a three-man committee with the task of finding a satisfactory basis for a cease-fire agreement. On January 13, 1951, the Assembly recommended a cease-fire on the basis of the withdrawal of all foreign troops from Korea and the establishment of a committee consisting, among others, of Britain, the United States, the U.S.S.R., and Red China. It would have been the purpose of this committee to achieve a settlement of Far Eastern problems including the disposal of Formosa and the representation of China in the UN. In spite of certain criticisms in the United States that the cease-fire proposal was "appeasement," our government accepted it. The Chinese Communist Government rejected it, however, and it failed to be adopted.]

(a) *Resolution of the General Assembly, adopted December 14, 1950* [1]

The General Assembly,
VIEWING with grave concern the situation in the Far East,
ANXIOUS that immediate steps should be taken to prevent the conflict in Korea spreading to other areas and to put an end to the fighting in Korea itself and that further steps should then be taken for a peaceful settlement of existing issues in accordance with the purposes and principles of the United Nations,
Requests the President of the General Assembly to constitute a group of three persons including himself to determine the basis on which a satisfactory cease-fire in Korea can be arranged and to make recommendations to the General Assembly as soon as possible.

(b) *Principles for a Cease-Fire Adopted by the General Assembly,*
January 13, 1951 [2]

SUPPLEMENTARY REPORT OF THE GROUP ON CEASE-FIRE IN KOREA

The objective shall be the achievement, by stages, of the programme outlined below for a cease-fire in Korea, for the establishment of a free and united Korea, and for a peaceful settlement of Far Eastern problems.

1. In order to prevent needless destruction of life and property, and while other steps are being taken to restore peace, a cease-fire should be immediately arranged. Such an arrangement should contain adequate safeguards for ensuring that it will not be used as a screen for mounting a new offensive.

2. If and when a cease-fire occurs in Korea, either as a result of a formal arrangement or, indeed, as a result of a lull in hostilities pending some such

[1] Department of State Bulletin, December 25, 1950, p. 1005. Submitted to Committee I by Afghanistan, Burma, Egypt, India, Indonesia, Iran, Iraq, Lebanon, Pakistan, Philippines, Saudi Arabia, Syria, and Yemen. The three representatives appointed to serve on the committee were Lester B. Pearson (Canada), Nasrollah Entezam (Iran), President of the General Assembly, and Sir Benegal N. Rau (India).
[2] UN doc. A/C.1/645, Department of State Bulletin, January 29, 1951, p. 164.

arrangement, advantage should be taken of it to pursue consideration of further steps to be taken for the restoration of peace.

3. To permit the carrying out of the General Assembly resolution that Korea should be a unified, independent, democratic, sovereign State with a constitution and a government based on free popular elections, all non-Korean armed forces will be withdrawn, by appropriate stages, from Korea, and appropriate arrangements, in accordance with United Nations principles, will be made for the Korean people to express their own free will in respect of their future government.

4. Pending the completion of the steps referred to in the preceding paragraph, appropriate interim arrangements, in accordance with United Nations principles, will be made for the administration of Korea and the maintenance of peace and security there.

5. As soon as agreement has been reached on a cease-fire, the General Assembly shall set up an appropriate body which shall include representatives of the Governments of the United Kingdom, the United States of America, the Union of Soviet Socialist Republics, and the People's Republic of China with a view to the achievement of a settlement, in conformity with existing international obligations and the provisions of the United Nations Charter, of Far Eastern problems, including, among others, those of Formosa (Taiwan) and of representation of China in the United Nations.

109. THE McCLELLAN RESOLUTIONS, JANUARY 23, 1951

[Chinese Communist intervention in the Korean conflict aroused deep resentment in the United States. This resentment was reflected in the Congress where steps were taken to encourage the United Nations to move more vigorously against the aggressor. On January 23, 1951, the Senate unanimously passed the two so-called McClellan resolutions urging that the United Nations should brand Communist China an aggressor, and that the government of the latter should not be permitted to represent China in the United Nations. Similar action was taken by the House of Representatives.]

(a) Resolution [1]

Resolved, That it is the sense of the Senate that the United Nations should immediately declare Communist China an aggressor in Korea.

(b) Resolution [2]

Resolved, That it is the sense of the Senate that the Communist China Government should not be admitted to membership in the United Nations as the representative of China.

---

[1] S. Res. 35, 82nd Cong., 1st sess.
[2] S. Res. 36, 82nd Cong., 1st sess.

110. CHINESE INTERVENTION IN KOREA BRANDED AGGRESSION

Resolution of the General Assembly, February 1, 1951 [1]

[After the Chinese intervention in the Korean conflict, members of the United Nations were divided on how the situation should be met. The majority, led by the United States, wished to declare the Chinese Government an aggressor. The Soviet bloc was unalterably opposed to such a declaration, and a number of other states, notably Britain, were unwilling at that time to join in such a declaration because they believed that a moral condemnation of the Communists without sanctions would be ineffective. Finally, after an understanding had been reached that the United States would not press for drastic punitive action, the General Assembly adopted the following resolution declaring the Chinese Communist Government to be engaged in aggression in Korea.]

The General Assembly,

Noting that the Security Council, because of lack of unanimity of the permanent members, has failed to exercise its primary responsibility for the maintenance of international peace and security in regard to Chinese Communist intervention in Korea,

Noting that the Central People's Government of the People's Republic of China has not accepted United Nations proposals to bring about a cessation of hostilities in Korea with a view to peaceful settlement, and that its armed forces continue their invasion of Korea and their large-scale attacks upon United Nations forces there,

1. *Finds* that the Central People's Government of the People's Republic of China, by giving direct aid and assistance to those who were already committing aggression in Korea and by engaging in hostilities against United Nations forces there, has itself engaged in aggression in Korea;

2. *Calls upon* the Central People's Government of the People's Republic of China to cause its forces and nationals in Korea to cease hostilities against the United Nations forces and to withdraw from Korea;

3. *Affirms* the determination of the United Nations to continue its action in Korea to meet the aggression;

4. *Calls upon* all States and authorities to continue to lend every assistance to the United Nations action in Korea;

5. *Calls upon* all States and authorities to refrain from giving any assistance to the aggressors in Korea;

6. *Requests* a Committee composed of the members of the Collective Measures Committee as a matter of urgency to consider additional measures to be employed to meet this aggression and to report thereon to the General Assembly, it being understood that the Committee is authorized to defer its report if the Good Offices Committee referred to in the following paragraph reports satisfactory progress in its efforts;

[1] UN doc. A/1771, 1 February 1951.

7. *Affirms* that it continues to be the policy of the United Nations to bring about a cessation of hostilities in Korea and the achievement of United Nations objectives in Korea by peaceful means, and requests the President of the General Assembly to designate forthwith two persons who would meet with him at any suitable opportunity to use their good offices to this end.

◇◇◇◇◇◇

111. THE RECALL OF GENERAL MAC ARTHUR

[During his conduct of the campaign in Korea, General Douglas MacArthur took exception to the military restrictions under which he was required to operate. At times he was reported to advocate the bombing of Chinese bases in Manchuria, the establishment of a blockade of the Chinese coast, and the use of Chinese Nationalist forces based on Formosa for diversionary attacks on the mainland of China. Some of these suggestions seemed to be in flat contradiction of announced United States policy. On April 10, 1951, President Truman announced that because General MacArthur was not able to give the policies of the United States his full support he (the President) had decided to make a change in command. On the evening of the next day President Truman broadcast a speech on the Far Eastern situation in which he supported his action and explained the relationship between the recall of General MacArthur and our over-all foreign policy.]

(a) *Statement by the President, April 10, 1951* [1]

With deep regret I have concluded that General of the Army Douglas MacArthur is unable to give his wholehearted support to the policies of the United States Government and of the United Nations in matters pertaining to his official duties. In view of the specific responsibilities imposed upon me by the Constitution of the United States and the added responsibility which has been entrusted to me by the United Nations, I have decided that I must make a change of command in the Far East. I have, therefore, relieved General MacArthur of his commands and have designated Lt. Gen. Matthew B. Ridgway as his successor.

Full and vigorous debate on matters of national policy is a vital element in the constitutional system of our free democracy. It is fundamental, however, that military commanders must be governed by the policies and directives issued to them in the manner provided by our laws and Constitution. In time of crisis, this consideration is particularly compelling.

General MacArthur's place in history as one of our greatest commanders is fully established. The nation owes him a debt of gratitude for the distinguished and exceptional service which he has rendered his country in posts of great responsibility. For that reason I repeat my regret at the necessity for the action I feel compelled to take in his case.

[1] White House Press Release, April 10, 1951.

(b) Preventing a New World War

Address by President Truman, April 11, 1951 [1]

I want to talk plainly to you tonight about what we are doing in Korea and about our policy in the Far East.

In the simplest terms, what we are doing in Korea is this: We are trying to prevent a third world war.

I think most people in this country recognized that fact last June. And they warmly supported the decision of the Government to help the Republic of Korea against the Communist aggressors. Now, many persons, even some who applauded our decision to defend Korea, have forgotten the basic reason for our action.

It is right for us to be in Korea. It was right last June. It is right today.

I want to remind you why this is true.

THE COMMUNIST THREAT TO FREEDOM

The Communists in the Kremlin are engaged in a monstrous conspiracy to stamp out freedom all over the world. If they were to succeed, the United States would be numbered among their principal victims. It must be clear to everyone that the United States cannot—and will not—sit idly by and await foreign conquest. The only question is: When is the best time to meet the threat and how?

The best time to meet the threat is in the beginning. It is easier to put out a fire in the beginning when it is small than after it has become a roaring blaze.

And the best way to meet the threat of aggression is for the peace-loving nations to act together. If they don't act together, they are likely to be picked off, one by one.

If they had followed the right policies in the 1930's—if the free countries had acted together, to crush the aggression of the dictators, and if they had acted in the beginning, when the aggression was small—there probably would have been no World War II.

If history has taught us anything, it is that aggression anywhere in the world is a threat to peace everywhere in the world. When that aggression is supported by the cruel and selfish rulers of a powerful nation who are bent on conquest, it becomes a clear and present danger to the security and independence of every free nation.

This is a lesson that most people in this country have learned thoroughly. This is the basic reason why we joined in creating the United Nations. And since the end of World War II we have been putting that lesson into practice —we have been working with other free nations to check the aggressive designs of the Soviet Union before they can result in a third world war.

That is what we did in Greece, when that nation was threatened by the aggression of international communism.

The attack against Greece could have led to general war. But this country came to the aid of Greece. The United Nations supported Greek resistance.

[1] Department of State Bulletin, April 16, 1951, pp. 603-605.

With our help, the determination and efforts of the Greek people defeated the attack on the spot.

Another big Communist threat to peace was the Berlin blockade. That too could have led to war. But again it was settled because free men would not back down in an emergency.

THE COMMUNIST PLAN FOR CONQUEST

The aggression against Korea is the boldest and most dangerous move the Communists have yet made.

The attack on Korea was part of a greater plan for conquering all of Asia.

I would like to read to you from a secret intelligence report which came to us after the attack. It is a report of a speech a Communist army officer in North Korea gave to a group of spies and saboteurs last May, one month before South Korea was invaded. The report shows in great detail how this invasion was part of a carefully prepared plot. Here is part of what the Communist officer, who had been trained in Moscow, told his men: "Our forces," he said, "are scheduled to attack South Korean forces about the middle of June. . . . The coming attack on South Korea marks the first step toward the liberation of Asia."

Notice that he used the word "liberation." That is Communist double-talk meaning "conquest."

I have another secret intelligence report here. This one tells what another Communist officer in the Far East told his men several months before the invasion of Korea. Here is what he said: "In order to successfully undertake the long awaited world revolution, we must first unify Asia. . . . Java, Indo-China, Malaya, India, Tibet, Thailand, Philippines, and Japan are our ultimate targets. . . . The United States is the only obstacle on our road for the liberation of all countries in southeast Asia. In other words, we must unify the people of Asia and crush the United States."

That is what the Communist leaders are telling their people, and that is what they have been trying to do.

They want to control all Asia from the Kremlin.

This plan of conquest is in flat contradiction to what we believe. We believe that Korea belongs to the Koreans, that India belongs to the Indians—that all the nations of Asia should be free to work out their affairs in their own way. This is the basis of peace in the Far East and everywhere else.

The whole Communist imperialism is back of the attack on peace in the Far East. It was the Soviet Union that trained and equipped the North Koreans for aggression. The Chinese Communists massed 44 well-trained and well-equipped divisions on the Korean frontier. These were the troops they threw into battle when the North Korean Communists were beaten.

STOPPING SHORT OF GENERAL WAR

The question we have had to face is whether the Communist plan of conquest can be stopped without general war. Our Government and other countries associated with us in the United Nations believe that the best chance of stopping it without general war is to meet the attack in Korea and defeat it there.

That is what we have been doing. It is a difficult and bitter task.

But so far it has been successful.

So far, we have prevented World War III.

So far, by fighting a limited war in Korea, we have prevented aggression from succeeding and bringing on a general war. And the ability of the whole free world to resist Communist aggression has been greatly improved.

We have taught the enemy a lesson. He has found out that aggression is not cheap or easy. Moreover, men all over the world who want to remain free have been given new courage and new hope. They know now that the champions of freedom can stand up and fight and that they will stand up and fight.

Our resolute stand in Korea is helping the forces of freedom now fighting in Indochina and other countries in that part of the world. It has already slowed down the timetable of conquest.

In Korea itself, there are signs that the enemy is building up his ground forces for a new mass offensive. We also know that there have been large increases in the enemy's available air forces.

If a new attack comes, I feel confident it will be turned back. The United Nations fighting forces are tough and able and well equipped. They are fighting for a just cause. They are proving to all the world that the principle of collective security will work. We are proud of all these forces for the magnificent job they have done against heavy odds. We pray that their efforts may succeed, for upon their success may hinge the peace of the world.

The Communist side must now choose its course of action. The Communist rulers may press the attack against us. They may take further action which will spread the conflict. They have that choice, and with it the awful responsibility for what may follow. The Communists also have the choice of a peaceful settlement which could lead to a general relaxation of tensions in the Far East. The decision is theirs, because the forces of the United Nations will strive to limit the conflict if possible.

We do not want to see the conflict in Korea extended. We are trying to prevent a world war—not to start one. The best way to do that is to make it plain that we and the other free countries will continue to resist the attack.

THE BEST COURSE TO FOLLOW

But you may ask: Why can't we take other steps to punish the aggressor? Why don't we bomb Manchuria and China itself? Why don't we assist Chinese Nationalist troops to land on the mainland of China?

If we were to do these things we would be running a very grave risk of starting a general war. If that were to happen, we would have brought about the exact situation we are trying to prevent.

If we were to do these things, we would become entangled in a vast conflict on the continent of Asia and our task would become immeasurably more difficult all over the world.

What would suit the ambitions of the Kremlin better than for our military forces to be committed to a full-scale war with Red China?

It may well be that, in spite of our best efforts, the Communists may spread the war. But it would be wrong—tragically wrong—for us to take the initiative in extending the war.

The dangers are great. Make no mistake about it. Behind the North Koreans and Chinese Communists in the front lines stand additional millions of

Chinese soldiers. And behind the Chinese stand the tanks, the planes, the submarines, the soldiers, and the scheming rulers of the Soviet Union.

Our aim is to avoid the spread of the conflict.

The course we have been following is the one best calculated to avoid an all-out war. It is the course consistent with our obligation to do all we can to maintain international peace and security. Our experience in Greece and Berlin shows that it is the most effective course of action we can follow.

First of all, it is clear that our efforts in Korea can blunt the will of the Chinese Communists to continue the struggle. The United Nations forces have put up a tremendous fight in Korea and have inflicted very heavy casualties on the enemy. Our forces are stronger now than they have been before. These are plain facts which may discourage the Chinese Communists from continuing their attack.

Second, the free world as a whole is growing in military strength every day. In the United States, in Western Europe, and throughout the world, free men are alert to the Soviet threat and are building their defenses. This may discourage the Communist rulers from continuing the war in Korea—and from undertaking new acts of aggression elsewhere.

If the Communist authorities realize that they cannot defeat us in Korea, if they realize it would be foolhardy to widen the hostilities beyond Korea, then they may recognize the folly of continuing their aggression. A peaceful settlement may then be possible. The door is always open.

Then we may achieve a settlement in Korea which will not compromise the principles and purposes of the United Nations.

I have thought long and hard about this question of extending the war in Asia. I have discussed it many times with the ablest military advisers in the country. I believe with all my heart that the course we are following is the best course.

I believe that we must try to limit the war to Korea for these vital reasons: to make sure that the precious lives of our fighting men are not wasted; to see that the security of our country and the free world is not needlessly jeopardized; and to prevent a third world war.

AVOIDING CONFUSION OVER U.S. POLICY

A number of events have made it evident that General MacArthur did not agree with that policy. I have therefore considered it essential to relieve General MacArthur so that there would be no doubt or confusion as to the real purpose and aim of our policy.

It was with the deepest personal regret that I found myself compelled to take this action. General MacArthur is one of our greatest military commanders. But the cause of world peace is more important than any individual.

The change in commands in the Far East means no change whatever in the policy of the United States. We will carry on the fight in Korea with vigor and determination in an effort to bring the war to a speedy and successful conclusion.

The new commander, Lt. Gen. Matthew Ridgway, has already demonstrated that he has the great qualities of military leadership needed for this task.

We are ready, at any time, to negotiate for a restoration of peace in the area. But we will not engage in appeasement. We are only interested in real peace.

Real peace can be achieved through a settlement based on the following factors:

One: the fighting must stop.

Two: concrete steps must be taken to insure that the fighting will not break out again.

Three: there must be an end to the aggression.

A settlement founded upon these elements would open the way for the unification of Korea and the withdrawal of all foreign forces.

In the meantime, I want to be clear about our military objective. We are fighting to resist an outrageous aggression in Korea. We are trying to keep the Korean conflict from spreading to other areas. But at the same time we must conduct our military activities so as to insure the security of our forces. This is essential if they are to continue the fight until the enemy abandons its ruthless attempt to destroy the Republic of Korea.

That is our military objective—to repel attack and to restore peace.

In the hard fighting in Korea, we are proving that collective action among nations is not only a high principle but a workable means of resisting aggression. Defeat of aggression in Korea may be the turning point in the world's search for a practical way of achieving peace and security.

The struggle of the United Nations in Korea is a struggle for peace.

The free nations have united their strength in an effort to prevent a third world war.

That war can come if the Communist rulers want it to come. But this Nation and its allies will not be responsible for its coming.

We do not want to widen the conflict. We will use every effort to prevent that disaster. And in so doing we know that we are following the great principles of peace, freedom, and justice.

<><><><><><>

112. ADDRESS OF GENERAL OF THE ARMY DOUGLAS MAC-ARTHUR BEFORE A JOINT MEETING OF THE CONGRESS, APRIL 19, 1951 [1]

[President Truman's dismissal of General MacArthur brought to a head a fundamental disagreement in the United States relative to the conduct of hostilities in Korea. As a result, General MacArthur was invited to address the two houses of Congress in a joint meeting. In his historic speech on that occasion, April 19, 1951, he asserted that the free world could not appease nor surrender to communism in Asia without simultaneously undermining its efforts to halt communist advances in Europe. He warned against letting Formosa fall to the Chinese red government and maintained that not only the United States Joint Chiefs of Staff but practically every responsible military leader concerned with the Korean campaign shared his (MacArthur's) views

[1] *Congressional Record* (daily edition), April 19, 1951, pp. 4233-4235.

as to the bombing of supply centers in Manchuria, the blockading of the China coast, and the effective utilization of the Chinese Nationalist troops on Formosa.]

Mr. President, Mr. Speaker, distinguished Members of the Congress, I stand on this rostrum with a sense of deep humility and great pride; humility in the wake of those great American architects of our history who have stood here before me; pride in the reflection that this forum of legislative debate represents human liberty in the purest form yet devised.

Here are centered the hopes, and aspirations, and faith of the entire human race.

I do not stand here as advocate for any partisan cause, for the issues are fundamental and reach quite beyond the realm of partisan consideration. They must be resolved on the highest plane of national interest if our course is to prove sound and our future protected. I trust, therefore, that you will do me the justice of receiving that which I have to say as solely expressing the considered viewpoint of a fellow American. I address you with neither rancor nor bitterness in the fading twilight of life with but one purpose in mind, to serve my country.

The issues are global and so interlocked that to consider the problems of one sector oblivious to those of another is but to court disaster for the whole.

While Asia is commonly referred to as the gateway to Europe, it is no less true that Europe is the gateway to Asia, and the broad influence of the one cannot fail to have its impact upon the other.

There are those who claim our strength is inadequate to protect on both fronts, that we cannot divide our effort. I can think of no greater expression of defeatism. If a potential enemy can divide his strength on two fronts, it is for us to counter his effort.

The Communist threat is a global one. Its successful advance in one sector threatens the destruction of every other sector. You cannot appease or otherwise surrender to communism in Asia without simultaneously undermining our efforts to halt its advance in Europe.

Beyond pointing out these general truisms, I shall confine my discussion to the general areas of Asia. Before one may objectively assess the situation now existing there, he must comprehend something of Asia's past and the revolutionary changes which have marked her course up to the present. Long exploited by the so-called colonial powers, with little opportunity to achieve any degree of social justice, individual dignity, or a higher standard of life such as guided our own noble administration of the Philippines, the peoples of Asia found their opportunity in the war just past to throw off the shackles of colonialism and now see the dawn of new opportunity and heretofore unfelt dignity and the self-respect of political freedom.

Mustering half of the earth's population and 60 percent of its natural resources, these peoples are rapidly consolidating a new force, both moral and material, with which to raise the living standard and erect adaptations of the design of modern progress to their own distinct cultural environments. Whether one adheres to the concept of colonization or not, this is the direction of Asian progress and it may not be stopped. It is a corollary to the shift of the world economic frontiers, as the whole epi-center of world affairs rotates back toward the area whence it started. In this situation it becomes vital that our own country orient its policies in consonance with this basic evolutionary condition rather than pursue a course blind to the reality that the colonial era is now past and the Asian peoples covet the right to shape their own free destiny. What they seek now is friendly guidance, understanding, and support, not imperious direction, the dignity of equality, not the shame of subjugation. Their prewar standard of life, pitifully low, is infinitely lower now in the devastation left in war's wake. World ideologies play little part in Asian thinking and are little understood. What the peoples strive for is the opportunity for a little more food in their stomachs, a little better clothing on their backs, a little firmer roof over their heads, and the realization of a normal nationalist urge for political freedom. These political-social conditions have but an indirect bearing upon our own national security, but do form a backdrop to contemporary planning which must be thoughtfully considered if we are to avoid the pitfalls of unrealism.

Of more direct and immediate bearing upon our national security are the changes wrought in the strategic potential of the Pacific Ocean in the course of the past war. Prior thereto, the western strategic frontier of the United States lay on the littoral line of the Americas with an exposed island salient extending out through Hawaii, Midway, and Guam to the Philippines. That salient proved not an outpost of strength but an avenue of weakness along which the enemy could and did attack. The Pacific was a potential area of advance for any predatory force intent upon striking at the bordering land areas.

All this was changed by our Pacific victory. Our strategic frontier then shifted to embrace the entire Pacific Ocean which became a vast moat to protect us as long as we held it. Indeed, it acts as a protective shield for all of the Americas and all free lands of the Pacific Ocean area. We control it to the shores of Asia by a chain of islands extending in an arc from the Aleutians to the Marianas held by us and our free allies.

From this island chain we can dominate with sea and air power every Asiatic port from Vladivostok to Singapore and prevent any hostile movement into the Pacific. Any predatory attack from Asia must be an amphibious effort. No amphibious force can be successful without control of the sea lanes and the air over those lanes in its avenues of advance. With naval and air supremacy and modest ground elements to defend bases, any major attack from continental Asia toward us or our friends of the Pacific would be doomed to failure. Under such conditions the Pacific no longer represents menacing avenues of approach for a prospective invader—it assumes instead the friendly aspect of a peaceful lake. Our line of defense is a natural one and can be maintained with a minimum of military effort and expense. It envisions no attack against anyone nor does it provide the bastions essential for offensive operations, but properly maintained would be an invincible defense against aggression.

The holding of this littoral defense line in the western Pacific is entirely dependent upon holding all segments thereof, for any major breach of that line by an unfriendly power would render vulnerable to determined attack every other major segment. This is a military estimate as to which I have yet to find a military leader who will take exception.

For that reason I have strongly recommended in the past as a matter of military urgency that under no circumstances must Formosa fall under Communist control.

Such an eventuality would at once threaten the freedom of the Philippines and the loss of Japan, and might well force our western frontier back to the coasts of California, Oregon, and Washington.

To understand the changes which now appear upon the Chinese mainland, one must understand the changes in Chinese character and culture over the past 50 years. China up to 50 years ago was completely nonhomogeneous, being compartmented into groups divided against each other. The war-making tendency was almost nonexistent, as they still followed the tenets of the Confucian ideal of pacifist culture. At the turn of the century, under the regime of Chan So Lin, efforts toward greater homogeneity produced the start of a nationalist urge. This was further and more successfully developed under the leadership of Chiang Kai-shek, but has been brought to its greatest fruition under the present regime, to the point that it has now taken on the character of a united nationalism of increasingly dominant aggressive tendencies. Through these past 50 years, the Chinese people have thus become militarized in their concepts and in their ideals. They now constitute excellent soldiers with competent staffs and commanders. This has produced a new and dominant power in Asia which for its own purposes is allied with Soviet Russia, but which in its own concepts and methods has become aggressively imperialistic with a lust for expansion and increased power normal to this type of imperialism. There is little of the ideological concept either one way or another in the Chinese make-up. The standard of living is so low and the capital accumulation has been so thoroughly dissipated by war that the masses are desperate and avid to follow any leadership which seems to promise the alleviation of local stringencies. I have from the beginning believed that the Chinese Communists' support of the North Koreans was the dominant one. Their interests are at present parallel to those of the Soviet, but I believe that the aggressiveness recently displayed not only in Korea, but also in Indochina and Tibet and pointing potentially toward the south, reflects predominantly the same lust for the expansion of power which has animated every would-be conqueror since the beginning of time.

The Japanese people since the war have undergone the greatest reformation recorded in modern history. With a commendable will, eagerness to learn, and marked capacity to understand, they have, from the ashes left in war's wake, erected in Japan an edifice dedicated to the primacy of individual liberty and personal dignity, and in the ensuing process there has been created a truly representative government, committed to the advance of political morality, freedom of economic enterprise and social justice. Politically, economically, and socially Japan is now abreast of many free nations of the earth and will not again fail the universal trust. That it may be counted upon to wield a profoundly beneficial influence over the course of events in Asia is attested by the magnificent manner in which the Japanese people have met the recent challenge of war, unrest, and confusion surrounding them from the outside, and checked communism within their own frontiers without the slightest slackening in their forward progress. I sent all four of our occupation divisions to the Korean battle front without the slightest qualms as to the effect of the resulting power vacuum upon Japan. The results fully justified my faith. I know of no nation more serene, orderly, and industrious—nor in which higher hopes can be entertained for future constructive service in the advance of the human race.

Of our former wards, the Philippines, we can look forward in confidence that the existing unrest will be corrected and a strong and healthy nation will grow in the longer aftermath of war's terrible destructiveness. We must be patient and understanding and never fail them, as in our hour of need they did not fail us. A Christian nation, the Philippines stand as a mighty bulwark of Christianity in the Far East, and its capacity for high moral leadership in Asia is unlimited.

On Formosa, the Government of the Republic of China has had the opportunity to refute by action much of the malicious gossip which so undermined the strength of its leadership on the Chinese mainland.

The Formosan people are receiving a just and enlightened administration with majority representation on the organs of government; and politically, economically, and socially appear to be advancing along sound and constructive lines.

With this brief insight into the surrounding areas I now turn to the Korean conflict. While I was not consulted prior to the President's decision to intervene in the support of the Republic of Korea, that decision from a military standpoint proved a sound one. As I say, a brief and sound one as we hurled back the invaders and decimated his forces. Our victory was complete and our objectives within reach when Red China intervened with numerically superior ground forces. This created a new war and an entirely new situation, a situation not contemplated when our forces were committed against the North Korean invaders, a situation which called for new decisions in the diplomatic sphere to permit the realistic adjustment of military strategy. Such decisions have not been forthcoming.

While no man in his right mind would advocate sending our ground forces into continental China—and such was never given a thought—the new situation did urgently demand a drastic revision of strategic planning if our political aim was to defeat this new enemy as we had defeated the old.

Apart from the military need as I saw it to neutralize sanctuary, protection given to the enemy north of the Yalu, I felt that military necessity in the conduct of the war made necessary:

First, the intensification of our economic blockade against China.

Second, the imposition of a naval blockade against the China coast.

Third, removal of restrictions on air reconnaissance of China's coastal areas and of Manchuria.

Fourth, removal of restrictions on the forces of the Republic of China on Formosa with logistical support to contribute to their effective operation against the Chinese mainland.

For entertaining these views all professionally designed to support our forces committed to Korea and bring hostilities to an end with the least possible delay and at a saving of countless American and Allied lives, I have been severely criticized in lay circles, principally abroad, despite my understanding that from a military standpoint the above views have been fully shared in past by practically every military leader concerned with the Korean campaign, including our own Joint Chiefs of Staff.

I called for reinforcements, but was informed that reinforcements were not available. I made clear that if not permitted to utilize the friendly Chinese force of some 600,000 men on Formosa; if not permitted to blockade the China coast to prevent the Chinese Reds from getting succor from without; and if there were to be no hope of major reinforcements, the position of the command from the military standpoint forbade victory. We could hold in Korea by constant maneuver and at an approximate area where our supply line advantages were in balance with the supply line disadvantages of the enemy, but we could hope at best for only an indecisive campaign, with its terrible and constant attrition upon our forces if the enemy utilized his full military potential. I have constantly called for the new political decisions essential to a solution. Efforts have been made to distort my position. It has been said in effect that I was a warmonger. Nothing could be further from the truth. I know war as few other men now living know it, and nothing to me is more revolting. I have long advocated its complete abolition as its very destructiveness on both friend and foe has rendered it useless as a means of settling international disputes. Indeed, on the 2d of September 1945, just following the surrender of the Japanese Nation on the battleship *Missouri,* I formally cautioned as follows:

"Men since the beginning of time have sought peace. Various methods through the ages have been attempted to devise an international process to prevent or settle disputes between nations. From the very start, workable methods were found insofar as individual citizens were concerned, but the mechanics of an instrumentality of larger international scope have never been successful. Military alliances, balances of power, leagues of nations, all in turn failed, leaving the only path to be by way of the crucible of war. The utter destructiveness of war now blots out this alternative. We have had our last chance. If we will not devise some greater and more equitable system, Armageddon will be at our door. The problem basically is theological and involves a spiritual recrudescence and improvement of human character that will synchronize with our almost matchless advances in science, art, literature, and all material and cultural developments of the past 2,000 years. It must be of the spirit if we are to save the flesh."

But once war is forced upon us, there is no other alternative than to apply every available means to bring it to a swift end. War's very object is victory—not prolonged indecision. In war, indeed, there can be no substitute for victory.

There are some who for varying reasons would appease Red China. They are blind to history's clear lesson. For history teaches with unmistakable emphasis that appeasement but begets new and bloodier war. It points to no single instance where the end has justified that means—where appeasement has led to more than a sham peace. Like blackmail, it lays the basis for new and successively greater demands, until, as in blackmail, violence becomes the only other alternative. Why, my soldiers asked of me, surrender military advantages to an enemy in the field? I could not answer. Some may say to avoid spread of conflict into an all-out war with China; others, to avoid Soviet intervention. Neither explanation seems valid. For China is already engaging with the maximum power it can commit and the Soviet will not necessarily mesh its actions with our moves. Like a cobra, any new enemy will more likely strike whenever it feels that the relativity in military or other potential is in its favor on a world-wide basis.

The tragedy of Korea is further heightened by the fact that as military action is confined to its territorial limits, it condemns that nation, which it is our purpose to save, to suffer the devastating impact of full naval and air bombardment, while the enemy's sanctuaries are fully protected from such attack and devastation. Of the nations of the world, Korea alone, up to now, is the sole one which has risked its all against communism. The magnificence of the courage and fortitude of the Korean people defies description. They have chosen to risk death rather than slavery. Their last words to me were "Don't scuttle the Pacific."

I have just left your fighting sons in Korea. They have met all tests there and I can report to you without reservation they are splendid in every way. It was my constant effort to preserve them and end this savage conflict honorably and with the least loss of time and a minimum sacrifice of life. Its growing bloodshed has caused me the deepest anguish and anxiety. Those gallant men will remain often in my thoughts and in my prayers always.

I am closing my 52 years of military service. When I joined the Army even before the turn of the century, it was the fulfillment of all my boyish hopes and dreams. The world has turned over many times since I took the oath on the plain at West Point, and the hopes and dreams have long since vanished. But I still remember the refrain of one of the most popular barrack ballads of that day which proclaimed most proudly that—

"Old soldiers never die; they just fade away." And like the old soldier of that ballad, I now close my military career and just fade away—an old soldier who tried to do his duty as God gave him the light to see that duty.

Good-by.

PART VII

Other Areas of Special Interest to the United States

CANADA

113. HYDE PARK AGREEMENT

Statement on Exchange of Defense Materials With Canada,
April 20, 1941 [1]

[After the outbreak of World War II, the governments of the New World took a number of important steps to strengthen their mutual defense. On August 18, 1940, President Roosevelt and Prime Minister MacKenzie King of Canada set up a permanent Joint Board of Defense to direct and plan the common defense of North America. This was followed in 1941 by the Hyde Park Agreement calling for the joint mobilization of the economic resources of the two countries.]

Among other important matters, the President and the Prime Minister discussed measures by which the most prompt and effective utilization might be made of the productive facilities of North America for the purposes both of local and hemisphere defense and of the assistance which in addition to their own programs both Canada and the United States are rendering to Great Britain and the other democracies.

It was agreed as a general principle that in mobilizing the resources of this continent each country should provide the other with the defense articles which it is best able to produce, and, above all, produce quickly, and that production programs should be coordinated to this end.

While Canada has expanded its productive capacity manyfold since the beginning of the war, there are still numerous defense articles which it must obtain in the United States, and purchases of this character by Canada will be even greater in the coming year than in the past. On the other hand, there is existing and potential capacity in Canada for the speedy production of certain kinds of munitions, strategic materials, aluminum, and ships, which are urgently required by the United States for its own purposes.

While exact estimates cannot yet be made, it is hoped that during the next 12 months Canada can supply the United States with between $200,000,000 and $300,000,000 worth of such defense articles. This sum is a small fraction of the total defense program of the United States, but many of the articles to

---

[1] Department of State Bulletin of April 26, 1941, pp. 494-495. This statement was released at the conclusion of a conference between President Roosevelt and Prime Minister MacKenzie King of Canada at Hyde Park, New York.

be provided are of vital importance. In addition, it is of great importance to the economic and financial relations between the two countries that payment by the United States for these supplies will materially assist Canada in meeting part of the cost of Canadian defense purchases in the United States.

Insofar as Canada's defense purchases in the United States consist of component parts to be used in equipment and munitions which Canada is producing for Great Britain, it was also agreed that Great Britain will obtain these parts under the Lease-Lend Act and forward them to Canada for inclusion in the finished article.

The technical and financial details will be worked out as soon as possible in accordance with the general principles which have been agreed upon between the President and the Prime Minister.

◇◇◇◇◇◇

114. COLLABORATION FOR SECURITY PURPOSES [1]

Continuance of United States Canadian Permanent Joint Board on Defense, February 12, 1947

[Following the war the United States and Canada continued their close collaboration in the security field. The inability of the United Nations to bring an end to threats to world peace particularly emphasized the need for continuing the Joint Board of Defense, which had been created on August 10, 1940. The announcement that the Board would go on functioning indefinitely was made on February 12, 1947, thus underlining the identity of interests between the two countries in defense matters.]

Announcement was made in Ottawa and Washington on February 12 of the results of discussions which have taken place in the Permanent Joint Board on Defense on the extent to which the wartime cooperation between the armed forces of the United States and Canada should be maintained in this post-war period. In the interest of efficiency and economy, each Government has decided that its national defense establishment shall, to the extent authorized by law, continue to collaborate for peacetime joint security purposes. The collaboration will necessarily be limited and will be based on the following principles:

1. Interchange of selected individuals so as to increase the familiarity of each country's defense establishment with that of the other country.

2. General cooperation and exchange of observers in connection with exercises and with the development and tests of material of common interest.

3. Encouragement of common designs and standards in arms, equipment, organization, methods of training, and new developments. As certain United Kingdom standards have long been in use in Canada, no radical change is contemplated or practicable and the application of this principle will be gradual.

4. Mutual and reciprocal availability of military, naval, and air facilities in each country; this principle to be applied as may be agreed in specific instances. Reciprocally each country will continue to provide with a minimum

1 Department of State Bulletin of February 23, 1947, p. 361.

of formality for the transit through its territory and its territorial waters of military aircraft and public vessels of the other country.

5. As an underlying principle all cooperative arrangements will be without impairment of the control of either country over all activities in its territory.

While in this, as in many other matters of mutual concern, there is an identity of view and interest between the two countries, the decision of each has been taken independently in continuation of the practice developed since the establishment of the Joint Defense Board in 1940.[1] No treaty, executive agreement, or contractual obligation has been entered into. Each country will determine the extent of its practical collaboration in respect of each and all of the foregoing principles. Either country may at any time discontinue collaboration on any or all of them. Neither country will take any action inconsistent with the Charter of the United Nations. The Charter remains the cornerstone of the foreign policy of each.

An important element in the decision of each Government to authorize continued collaboration was the conviction on the part of each that in this way their obligations under the Charter of the United Nations for the maintenance of international peace and security could be fulfilled more effectively. Both Governments believe that this decision is a contribution to the stability of the world and to the establishment through the United Nations of an effective system of world-wide security. With this in mind each Government has sent a copy of this statement to the Secretary-General of the United Nations for circulation to all its members.

In August 1940, when the creation of the Board was jointly announced by the late President Roosevelt and Prime Minister King, it was stated that the Board "shall commence immediate studies relating to sea, land, and air problems including personnel and matériel. It will consider in the broad sense the defense of the north half of the Western Hemisphere." In discharging this continuing responsibility the Board's work led to the building up of a pattern of close defense cooperation. The principles announced on February 12 are in continuance of this cooperation. It has been the task of the Governments to assure that the close security relationship between Canada and the United States in North America will in no way impair but on the contrary will strengthen the cooperation of each country within the broader framework of the United Nations.

◇◇◇◇◇◇

115. PRINCIPLES FOR ECONOMIC COOPERATION WITH CANADA

Exchange of notes between the United States and Canada, October 26, 1950 [2]

[As East-West tensions increased, Canada and the United States found it necessary to coordinate their efforts in the economic as well as the security field. To that end a new understanding was reached between the two countries

[1] Department of State Bulletin of August 24, 1940, p. 154. See also Department of State Bulletin of November 8, 1941, p. 360, and February 4, 1945, p. 162.
[2] Department of State Bulletin, November 6, 1950, pp. 742-3.

in the fall of 1950, so that a maximum production of goods necessary for the common defense might be achieved. This is an excellent example of an important agreement concluded between two countries by an exchange of diplomatic notes.]

U.S. Note to Canada

I have the honor to refer to recent discussions between representatives of our two Governments for the general purpose of reaching an agreement to the end that the economic efforts of the two countries be coordinated for the common defense and that the production and resources of both countries be used for the best combined results. Their deliberations were based on concepts of economic cooperation which were inherent in the Hyde Park Agreement of 1941 and which are still valid today. They formulated and agreed to the "Statement of Principles for Economic Cooperation" annexed hereto, which is intended to guide, in the light of these basic concepts, the activities of our respective Governments.

If this attached statement is agreeable to your Government, this note and your reply to that effect will constitute an agreement between our two Governments on this subject.

DEAN G. ACHESON
Secretary of State

Canadian Reply

I have your note of today with regard to the recent discussions between representatives of our two Governments for the purpose of reaching an agreement to the end that the economic efforts of the two countries be coordinated for the common defense and that the production and resources of both countries be used for the best combined results. I am glad to confirm that the "statement of Principles for Economic Cooperation", which was annexed to your note, is acceptable to my Government. Your note and this reply will, therefore, constitute an agreement between our two Governments on this subject.

HUME WRONG
Ambassador of Canada

Statement of Principles for Economic Cooperation

The United States and Canada have achieved a high degree of cooperation in the field of industrial mobilization during and since World War II through the operation of the principles embodied in the Hyde Park Agreement of 1941, through the extension of its concepts in the post-war period and more recently through the work of the Joint Industrial Mobilization Planning Committee. In the interests of mutual security and to assist both Governments to discharge their obligations under the United Nations Charter and the North Atlantic Treaty, it is believed that this field of common action should be further extended. It is agreed, therefore, that our two Governments shall cooperate in all respects practicable, and to the extent of their respective executive powers, to the end that the economic efforts of the two countries be coordinated for the common defense and that the production and resources of both countries be used for the best combined results.

The following principles are established for the purpose of facilitating these objectives:

1. In order to achieve an optimum production of goods essential for the common defense, the two countries shall develop a coordinated program of requirements, production, and procurement.

2. To this end, the two countries shall, as it becomes necessary, institute coordinated controls over the distribution of scarce raw materials and supplies.

3. Such United States and Canadian emergency controls shall be mutually consistent in their objectives, and shall be so designed and administered as to achieve comparable effects in each country. To the extent possible, there shall be consultation to this end prior to the institution of any system of controls in either country which affects the other.

4. In order to facilitate essential production, the technical knowledge and productive skill involved in such production within both countries shall, where feasible, be freely exchanged.

5. Barriers which impede the flow between Canada and the United States of goods essential for the common defense effort should be removed as far as possible.

6. The two Governments, through their appropriate agencies, will consult concerning any financial or foreign exchange problems which may arise as a result of the implementation of this agreement.

◇◇◇◇◇◇

CHINA [1]

116. UNITED STATES POLICY TOWARD CHINA [2]

Statement by President Truman, December 16, 1945

[During World War II, Allied leaders envisioned a postwar Far East in which China—not Japan—should be the dominant power. With the surrender of Japan, however, civil war between the Nationalist régime and the communists in China continued on an enlarged scale and it became apparent that China did not possess the unity necessary to enable it to become a stabilizing force in the Far East. In his policy statement of December 16, 1945, President Truman reiterated the American position that a united and democratic China was essential for world peace. While he pointed out that the United States continued to recognize the Nationalist government as the only legal government in China, he urged that a cessation of hostilities be arranged and that the major political elements work together to bring about the unification of China.]

The Government of the United States holds that peace and prosperity of the world in this new and unexplored era ahead depend upon the ability of

[1] For a more complete account of Sino-American diplomacy, see United States Relations with China, Department of State Publication 3573, released August 1949.

[2] Department of State Bulletin of December 16, 1945, pp. 945-946.

the sovereign nations to combine for collective security in the United Nations Organization.

It is the firm belief of this Government that a strong, united, and democratic China is of the utmost importance to the success of this United Nations Organization and for world peace. A China disorganized and divided either by foreign aggression, such as that undertaken by the Japanese, or by violent internal strife is an undermining influence to world stability and peace, now and in the future. The United States Government has long subscribed to the principle that the management of internal affairs is the responsibility of the peoples of the sovereign nations. Events of this century, however, would indicate that a breach of peace anywhere in the world threatens the peace of the entire world. It is thus in the most vital interest of the United States and all the United Nations that the people of China overlook no opportunity to adjust their internal differences promptly by methods of peaceful negotiation.

The Government of the United States believes it essential:

(1) That a cessation of hostilities be arranged between the armies of the National Government and the Chinese Communists and other dissident Chinese armed forces for the purpose of completing the return of all China to effective Chinese control, including the immediate evacuation of the Japanese forces.

(2) That a national conference of representatives of major political elements be arranged to develop an early solution to the present internal strife—a solution which will bring about the unification of China.

The United States and the other United Nations have recognized the present National Government of the Republic of China as the only legal government in China. It is the proper instrument to achieve the objective of a unified China.

The United States and the United Kingdom by the Cairo Declaration in 1943 and the Union of Soviet Socialist Republics by adhering to the Potsdam Declaration of last July and by the Sino-Soviet treaty and agreements of August 1945 are all committed to the liberation of China, including the return of Manchuria to Chinese control. These agreements were made with the National Government of the Republic of China.

In continuation of the constant and close collaboration with the National Government of the Republic of China in the prosecution of this war, in consonance with the Potsdam Declaration, and to remove possibility of Japanese influence remaining in China, the United States has assumed a definite obligation in the disarmanent and evacuation of the Japanese troops. Accordingly the United States has been assisting and will continue to assist the National Government of the Republic of China in effecting the disarmament and evacuation of Japanese troops in the liberated areas. The United States Marines are in north China for that purpose.

The United States recognizes and will continue to recognize the National Government of China and cooperate with it in international affairs and specifically in eliminating Japanese influence from China. The United States is convinced that a prompt arrangement for a cessation of hostilities is essential to the effective achievement of this end. United States support will not extend to United States military intervention to influence the course of any Chinese internal strife.

The United States has already been compelled to pay a great price to restore the peace which was first broken by Japanese aggression in Manchuria. The maintenance of peace in the Pacific may be jeopardized, if not frustrated unless Japanese influence in China is wholly removed and unless China takes her place as a unified, democratic, and peaceful nation. This is the purpose of the maintenance for the time being of United States military and naval forces in China.

The United States is cognizant that the present National Government of China is a "one-party government" and believes that peace, unity, and democratic reform in China will be furthered if the basis of this Government is broadened to include other political elements in the country. Hence, the United States strongly advocates that the national conference of representatives of major political elements in the country agree upon arrangements which would give those elements a fair and effective representation in the Chinese National Government. It is recognized that this would require modification of the one-party "political tutelage" established as an interim arrangement in the progress of the nation toward democracy by the father of the Chinese Republic, Dr. Sun Yat-sen.

The existence of autonomous armies such as that of the Communist army is inconsistent with, and actually makes impossible, political unity in China. With the institution of a broadly representative government, autonomous armies should be eliminated as such and all armed forces in China integrated effectively into the Chinese National Army.

In line with its often expressed views regarding self-determination, the United States Government considers that the detailed steps necessary to the achievement of political unity in China must be worked out by the Chinese themselves and that intervention by any foreign government in these matters would be inappropriate. The United States Government feels, however, that China has a clear responsibility to the other United Nations to eliminate armed conflict within its territory as constituting a threat to world stability and peace— a responsibility which is shared by the National Government and all Chinese political and military groups.

As China moves toward peace and unity along the lines described above, the United States would be prepared to assist the National Government in every reasonable way to rehabilitate the country, improve the agrarian and industrial economy, and establish a military organization capable of discharging China's national and international responsibilities for the maintenance of peace and order. In furtherance of such assistance, it would be prepared to give favorable consideration to Chinese requests for credits and loans under reasonable conditions for projects which would contribute toward the development of a healthy economy throughout China and healthy trade relations between China and the United States.

◇◇◇◇◇◇

117. UNITED STATES POLICY TOWARD CHINA

Statement by President Truman, December 18, 1946 [1]

[The continuation of civil strife in China, intensified by growing nationalism and agrarian discontent, caused the United States to exert further efforts to

[1] Department of State Bulletin of December 29, 1946, pp. 1179-1183.

bring about a cessation of hostilities. In January 1946, President Truman sent General George C. Marshall to serve as his personal representative to help the Chinese leaders achieve peace and unity. When Mr. Truman made his second policy statement on China he explained the situation which confronted General Marshall when he arrived in China and the various steps he took to try to bring about an end to the civil war. Mr. Truman again reaffirmed support of Chiang Kai-shek and indicated that sympathetic consideration would be given to further requests for aid.]

Last December I made a statement of this Government's views regarding China. We believed then, and do now, that a united and democratic China is of the utmost importance to world peace, that a broadening of the base of the National Government to make it representative of the Chinese people will further China's progress toward this goal, and that China has a clear responsibility to the other United Nations to eliminate armed conflict within its territory as constituting a threat to world stability and peace. It was made clear at Moscow last year that these views are shared by our Allies, Great Britain and the Soviet Union. On December 27, Mr. Byrnes, Mr. Molotov, and Mr. Bevin issued a statement which said, in part:

"The three Foreign Secretaries exchanged views with regard to the situation in China. They were in agreement as to the need for a unified and democratic China under the National Government, for broad participation by democratic elements in all branches of the National Government, and for a cessation of civil strife. They affirmed their adherence to the policy of non-interference in the internal affairs of China." [1]

The policies of this Government were also made clear in my statement of last December. We recognized the National Government of the Republic of China as the legal government. We undertook to assist the Chinese Government in reoccupation of liberated areas and in disarming and repatriating the Japanese invaders. And finally, as China moved toward peace and unity along the lines mentioned, we were prepared to assist the Chinese economically and in other ways.

I asked General Marshall to go to China as my representative. We had agreed upon my statement of the United States Government's views and policies regarding China as his directive. He knew full well in undertaking the mission that halting civil strife, broadening the base of the Chinese Government, and bringing about a united, democratic China were tasks for the Chinese themselves. He went as a great American to make his outstanding abilities available to the Chinese.

During the war the United States entered into an agreement with the Chinese Government regarding the training and equipment of a special force of 39 divisions. That training ended V-J Day and the transfer of the equipment had been largely completed when General Marshall arrived.

The United States, the United Kingdom, and the Union of Soviet Socialist Republics all committed themselves to the liberation of China, including the return of Manchuria to Chinese control. Our Government had agreed to assist the Chinese Government in the reoccupation of areas liberated from the

[1] See under Part II: Conferences on the Peace Settlement.

Japanese, including Manchuria, because of China's lack of shipping and transport planes. Three armies were moved by air and eleven by sea to central China, Formosa, north China, and Manchuria. Most of these moves had been made or started when General Marshall arrived.

The disarming and evacuation of Japanese progressed slowly—too slowly. We regarded our commitment to assist the Chinese in this program as of overwhelming importance to the future peace of China and the whole Far East. Surrendered but undefeated Japanese armies and hordes of administrators, technicians, and Japanese merchants, totalling about 3,000,000 persons, had to be removed under the most difficult conditions. At the request of the Chinese Government we had retained a considerable number of American troops in China, and immediately after V-J Day we landed a corps of Marines in north China. The principal task of these forces was to assist in the evacuation of Japanese. Only some 200,000 had been returned to Japan by the time General Marshall arrived.

General Marshall also faced a most unpropitious internal situation on his arrival in China. Communications throughout the country were badly disrupted due to destruction during the war and the civil conflicts which had broken out since. This disruption was preventing the restoration of Chinese economy, the distribution of relief supplies, and was rendering the evacuation of Japanese a slow and difficult process. The wartime destruction of factories and plants, the war-induced inflation in China, the Japanese action in shutting down the economy of occupied China immediately after V-J Day, and finally the destruction of communications combined to paralyze the economic life of the country, spreading untold hardship to millions, robbing the victory over the Japanese of significance to most Chinese, and seriously aggravating all the tensions and discontents that existed in China.

Progress toward solution of China's internal difficulties by the Chinese themselves was essential to the rapid and effective completion of most of the programs in which we had already pledged our assistance to the Chinese Government. General Marshall's experience and wisdom were available to the Chinese in their efforts to reach such solutions.

Events moved rapidly upon General Marshall's arrival. With all parties availing themselves of his impartial advice, agreement for a country-wide truce was reached and announced on January 10th. A feature of this agreement was the establishment of a unique organization—the Executive Headquarters in Peiping. It was realized that due to poor communications and the bitter feelings on local fronts, generalized orders to cease fire and withdraw might have little chance of being carried out unless some authoritative executive agency, trusted by both sides, could function in any local situation.

The headquarters operated under the leaders of three commissioners—one American who served as chairman, one Chinese Government representative, and one representative of the Chinese Communist Party. Walter S. Robertson, Chargé d'Affaires of the American Embassy in China, served as chairman until his return to this country in the fall. In order to carry out its function in the field, Executive Headquarters formed a large number of truce teams, each headed by one American officer, one Chinese Government officer, and one Chinese Communist officer. They proceeded to all danger spots where fighting was going on or seemed impending and saw to the implementation of the truce terms, often under conditions imposing exceptional hardships and requiring courageous action. The degree of cooperation attained between Government and Communist officers in the headquarters and on the truce teams was a welcome proof that, despite two decades of fighting, these two Chinese groups could work together.

Events moved forward with equal promise on the political front. On January 10, the Political Consultative Conference began its sessions with representatives of the Kuomintang or Government Party, the Communist Party and several minor political parties participating. Within three weeks of direct discussion these groups had come to a series of statesmanlike agreements on outstanding political and military problems. The agreements provided for an interim government of a coalition type with representation of all parties for revision of the draft constitution along democratic lines prior to its discussion and adoption by a national assembly, and for reduction of the Government and Communist armies and their eventual amalgamation into a small, modernized, truly national army, responsible to a civilian government.

In March General Marshall returned to this country. He reported on the important step the Chinese had made toward. peace and unity in arriving at these agreements.[1] He also pointed out that these agreements could not be satisfactorily implemented and given substance unless China's economic disintegration were checked and particularly unless the transportation system could be put in working order. Political unity could not be built on economic

[1] Department of State Bulletin, March 24, 1946, p. 484.

chaos. This Government had already authorized certain minor credits to the Chinese Government in an effort to meet emergency rehabilitation needs as it was doing for other war devastated countries throughout the world. A total of approximately $66,000,000 was involved in six specific projects, chiefly for the purchase of raw cotton, and for ships and railroad repair material. But these emergency measures were inadequate. Following the important forward step made by the Chinese in the agreements as reported by General Marshall, the Export-Import Bank earmarked a total of $500,000,000 for possible additional credits on a project by project basis to Chinese Government agencies and private enterprises. Agreement to extend actual credits for such projects would obviously have to be based upon this Government's policy as announced December 15, 1945. So far, this $500,000,000 remains earmarked, but unexpended.

While comprehensive large-scale aid has been delayed, this Government has completed its wartime lend-lease commitments to China. Lend-lease assistance was extended to China to assist her in fighting the Japanese, and later to fulfil our promise to assist in reoccupying the country from the Japanese. Assistance took the form of goods and equipment and of services. Almost half the total made available to China consisted of services, such as those involved in air- and water-transportation of troops. According to the latest figures reported, lend-lease assistance to China up to V-J Day totaled approximately $870,000,000. From V-J Day to the end of February, shortly after General Marshall's arrival, the total was approximately $600,000,000 —mostly in transportation costs. Thereafter, the program was reduced to the fulfilment of outstanding commitments, much of which was later suspended.

A considerable quantity of civilian goods has also been made available by our agreement with China for the disposal of surplus property which enabled us to liquidate a sizable indebtedness and to dispose of large quantities of surplus material. During the war the Chinese Government furnished Chinese currency to the United States Army for use in building its installations, feeding the troops, and other expenses. By the end of the war this indebtedness amounted to something like 150,000,000,000 Chinese dollars. Progressive currency inflation in China rendered it impossible to determine the exact value of the sum in United States currency.

China agreed to buy all surplus property owned by the United States in China and on seventeen Pacific Islands and bases with certain exceptions. Six months of negotiations preceded the agreement finally signed in August.[1] It was imperative that this matter be concluded in the Pacific as had already been done in Europe, especially in view of the rapid deterioration of the material in open storage under tropical conditions, and the urgent need for the partial alleviation of the acute economic distress of the Chinese people, which it was hoped this transaction would permit. Aircraft, all non-demilitarized combat material, and fixed installations outside of China were excluded. Thus, no weapons which could be used in fighting a civil war were made available through this agreement.

The Chinese Government canceled all but 30,000,000 United States dollars of our indebtedness for the Chinese currency, and promised to make available the equivalent of 35,000,000 United States dollars for use in paying United

[1] Department of State Bulletin of September 22, 1946, p. 548.

States governmental expenses in China and acquiring and improving buildings and properties for our diplomatic and consular establishments. An additional sum of 20,000,000 United States dollars is also designated for the fulfilment of a cultural and educational program.

Before General Marshall arrived in China for the second time, in April, was evidence that the truce agreement was being disregarded. The sincere and unflagging efforts of Executive Headquarters and its truce teams have succeeded in many instances in preventing or ending local engagements, and thus saved thousands of lives. But fresh outbreaks of civil strife continued to occur, reaching a crisis of violence in Manchuria, with the capture of Changchun by the Communists, and where the presence of truce teams had not been fully agreed to by the National Government.

A change in the course of events in the political field was equally disappointing. Negotiations between the Government and the Communists have been resumed again and again, but they have as often broken down. Although hope for final success has never disappeared completely, the agreements made in January and February have not been implemented, and the various Chinese groups have not since that time been able to achieve the degree of agreement reached at the Political Consultative Conference.

There has been encouraging progress in other fields, particularly the elimination of Japanese from China. The Chinese Government was responsible under an Allied agreement for the disarmament of all Japanese military personnel and for the repatriation of all Japanese civilians and military personnel from China, Formosa, and French Indo-China north of the sixteenth degree of latitude. Our Government agreed to assist the Chinese in this task. The scope of the job was tremendous. There were about 3,000,000 Japanese, nearly one half of them Army or Navy personnel, to be evacuated. Water and rail transportation had been destroyed or was immobilized. Port facilities were badly damaged and overcrowded with relief and other supplies. The Japanese had to be disarmed, concentrated, and then transported to the nearest available port. In some instances this involved long distances. At the ports they had to be individually searched and put through a health inspection. All had to be inoculated. Segregation camps had to be established at the ports to cope with the incidence of epidemic diseases such as Asiatic cholera. Finally, 3,000,000 persons had to be moved by ship to Japan.

American forces helped in the disarmament of Japanese units. Executive Headquarters and its truce teams were able to make the complicated arrangements necessary to transfer Japanese across lines and through areas involved in civil conflict on their way to ports of embarkation. American units also participated in the inspections at the port, while American medical units supervised all inoculation and other medical work. Finally, American and Japanese ships under the control of General MacArthur in Japan, and a number of United States Navy ships under the Seventh Fleet transported this enormous number of persons to reception ports in Japan.

At the end of last year, approximately 200,000 Japanese had been repatriated. They were leaving Chinese ports at a rate of about 2,500 a day. By March of this year, rapidly increased efforts on the part of the American forces and the Chinese authorities involved had increased this rate to more than 20,000 a day. By November, 2,986,438 Japanese had been evacuated and the program was considered completed. Except for indeterminate numbers in certain parts of Manchuria, only war criminals and technicians retained on an emergency basis by the Chinese Government remain. That this tremendous undertaking has been accomplished despite conflict, disrupted communications, and other difficulties will remain an outstanding example of successful American-Chinese cooperation toward a common goal.

Much has been said of the presence of United States armed forces in China during the past year. Last fall these forces were relatively large. They had to be. No one could prophesy in advance how well the Japanese forces in China would observe the surrender terms. We had to provide forces adequate to assist the Chinese in the event of trouble. When it became obvious that the armed Japanese would not be a problem beyond the capabilities of the Chinese Armies to handle, redeployment was begun at once.

The chief responsibility of our forces was that of assisting in evacuation of Japanese. This task was prolonged by local circumstances. Provision of American personnel for the Executive Headquarters and its truce teams has required a fairly large number of men, particularly since the all important network of radio and other communications was provided entirely by the United States. The Executive Headquarters is located at Peiping, a hundred miles from the sea, and in an area where there was the possibility of local fighting. Hence, another responsibility was to protect the line of supply to and from headquarters. Another duty our forces undertook immediately upon the Japanese surrender was to provide the necessary protection so that coal from the great mines northeast of Tientsin could reach the sea for shipment to supply the cities and railroads of central China. This coal was essential to prevent the collapse of this industrial area. Our Marines were withdrawn from this duty last September. Other units of our forces were engaged in searching for the bodies or graves of American soldiers who had died fighting the Japanese in China. Still others were required to guard United States installations and stores of equipment, and to process these for return to this country or sale as surplus property.

At peak strength a year ago we had some 113,000 soldiers, sailors, and marines in China. Today this number is being reduced to less than 12,000, including some 2,000 directly concerned with the operations of Executive Headquarters, and will be further reduced to the number required to supply and secure the American personnel of Executive Headquarters and the air field and stores at Tsingtao.

Thus during the past year we have successfully assisted in the repatriation of the Japanese and have subsequently been able to bring most of our own troops home. We have afforded appropriate assistance in the reoccupation of the country from the Japanese. We have undertaken some emergency measures of economic assistance to prevent the collapse of China's economy and have liquidated our own wartime financial account with China.

It is a matter of deep regret that China has not yet been able to achieve unity by peaceful methods. Because he knows how serious the problem is, and how important it is to reach a solution, General Marshall has remained at his post even though active negotiations have been broken off by the Communist Party. We are ready to help China as she moves toward peace and genuine democratic government.

The views expressed a year ago by this Government are valid today. The plan for political unification agreed to last February is sound. The plan for military unification of last February has been made difficult of implementation by the process of the fighting since last April, but the general principles involved are fundamentally sound.

China is a sovereign nation. We recognize that fact and we recognize the National Government of China. We continue to hope that the Government will find a peaceful solution. We are pledged not to interfere in the internal affairs of China. Our position is clear. While avoiding involvement in their civil strife, we will persevere with our policy of helping the Chinese people to bring about peace and economic recovery in their country.

As ways and means are presented for constructive aid to China, we will give them careful and sympathetic consideration. An example of such aid is the recent agricultural mission to China under Dean Hutchison of the University of California, sent at the request of the Chinese Government. A joint Chinese-American agricultural collaboration commission was formed which included the Hutchison mission.[1] It spent over four months studying rural problems. Its recommendations are now available to the Chinese Government, and so also is any feasible aid we can give in implementing those recommendations. When conditions in China improve, we are prepared to consider aid in carrying out other projects, unrelated to civil strife, which would encourage economic reconstruction and reform in China and which, in so doing, would promote a general revival of commercial relations between American and Chinese businessmen.

We believe that our hopes for China are identical with what the Chinese people themselves most earnestly desire. We shall therefore continue our positive and realistic policy toward China, which is based on full respect for her national sovereignty and on our traditional friendship for the Chinese people, and is designed to promote international peace.

◇◇◇◇◇◇

118. THE SITUATION IN CHINA

Statement by General George C. Marshall, January 7, 1947 [2]

[After prolonged efforts which lasted more than a year, General Marshall terminated his mission to China disappointed over the hopes of bringing the warring factions together. On his return to the United States, he issued the following statement condemning both sides for their failure to coöperate in bringing peace and order to China. He criticized the Communists for their unwillingness to compromise and deplored the attitude of what he called "irreconcilable groups" within the Kuomintang.]

The President has recently given a summary of the developments in China during the past year and the position of the American Government toward

[1] Department of State Bulletin of June 16, 1946, p. 1054.
[2] Department of State Bulletin of January 19, 1947, pp. 83-85.

China.[1] Circumstances now dictate that I should supplement this with impressions gained at first hand.

In this intricate and confused situation, I shall merely endeavor here to touch on some of the more important considerations—as they appeared to me—during my connection with the negotiations to bring about peace in China and a stable democratic form of government.

In the first place, the greatest obstacle to peace has been the complete, almost overwhelming suspicion with which the Chinese Communist Party and the Kuomintang regard each other.

On the one hand, the leaders of the Government are strongly opposed to a communistic form of government. On the other, the Communists frankly state that they are Marxists and intend to work toward establishing a communistic form of government in China, though first advancing through the medium of a democratic form of government of the American or British type.

The leaders of the Government are convinced in their minds that the Communist-expressed desire to participate in a government of the type endorsed by the Political Consultative Conference last January had for its purpose only a destructive intention. The Communists felt, I believe, that the Government was insincere in its apparent acceptance of the PCC resolutions for the formation of the new government and intended by coercion of military force and the action of secret police to obliterate the Communist Party. Combined with this mutual deep distrust was the conspicuous error by both parties of ignoring the effect of the fears and suspicions of the other party in estimating the reason for proposals or opposition regarding the settlement of various matters under negotiation. They each sought only to take counsel of their own fears. They both, therefore, to that extent took a rather lopsided view of each situation and were susceptible to every evil suggestion or possibility. This complication was exaggerated to an explosive degree by the confused reports of fighting on the distant and tremendous fronts of hostile military contact. Patrol clashes were deliberately magnified into large offensive actions. The distortion of the facts was utilized by both sides to heap condemnation on the other. It was only through the reports of American officers in the field teams from Executive Headquarters that I could get even a partial idea of what was actually happening, and the incidents were too numerous and the distances too great for the American personnel to cover all of the ground. I must comment here on the superb courage of the officers of our Army and Marines struggling against almost insurmountable and maddening obstacles to bring some measure of peace to China.

I think the most important factors involved in the recent break-down of negotiations are these: On the side of the National Government, which is in effect the Kuomintang, there is a dominant group of reactionaries who have been opposed, in my opinion, to almost every effort I have made to influence the formation of a genuine coalition government. This has usually been under the cover of political or party action, but since the Party was the Government, this action, though subtle or indirect, has been devastating in its effect. They were quite frank in publicly stating their belief that cooperation by the Chinese Communist Party in the government was inconceivable and that only a policy

---

[1] See preceding document.

of force could definitely settle the issue. This group includes military as well as political leaders.

On the side of the Chinese Communist Party there are, I believe, liberals as well as radicals, though this view is vigorously opposed by many who believe that the Chinese Communist Party discipline is too rigidly enforced to admit of such differences of viewpoint. Nevertheless, it has appeared to me that there is a definite liberal group among the Communists, especially of young men who have turned to the Communists in disgust at the corruption evident in the local governments—men who would put the interest of the Chinese people above ruthless measures to establish a Communist ideology in the immediate future. The dyed-in-the-wool Communists do not hesitate at the most drastic measures to gain their end as, for instance, the destruction of communications in order to wreck the economy of China and produce a situation that would facilitate the overthrow or collapse of the Government, without any regard to the immediate suffering of the people involved. They completely distrust the leaders of the Kuomintang and appear convinced that every Government proposal is designed to crush the Chinese Communist Party. I must say that the quite evidently inspired mob actions of last February and March, some within a few blocks of where I was then engaged in completing negotiations, gave the Communists good excuse for such suspicions.

However, a very harmful and immensely provocative phase of the Chinese Communist Party procedure has been in the character of its propaganda. I wish to state to the American people that in the deliberate misrepresentation and abuse of the action, policies, and purposes of our Government this propaganda has been without regard for the truth, without any regard whatsoever for the facts, and has given plain evidence of a determined purpose to mislead the Chinese people and the world and to arouse a bitter hatred of Americans. It has been difficult to remain silent in the midst of such public abuse and wholesale disregard of facts, but a denial would merely lead to the necessity of daily denials; an intolerable course of action for an American official. In the interest of fairness, I must state that the Nationalist Government publicity agency has made numerous misrepresentations, though not of the vicious nature of the Communist propaganda. Incidentally, the Communist statements regarding the Anping incident which resulted in the death of three Marines and the wounding of twelve others were almost pure fabrication, deliberately representing a carefully arranged ambuscade of a Marine convoy with supplies for the maintenance of Executive Headquarters and some UNRRA supplies as a defense against a Marine assult. The investigation of this incident was a tortuous procedure of delays and maneuvers to disguise the true and privately admitted facts of the case.

Sincere efforts to achieve settlement have been frustrated time and again by extremist elements of both sides. The agreements reached by the Political Consultative Conference a year ago were a liberal and forward-looking charter which then offered China a basis for peace and reconstruction. However, irreconcilable groups within the Kuomintang, interested in the preservation of their own feudal control of China, evidently had no real intention of implementing them. Though I speak as a soldier, I must here also deplore the dominating influence of the military. Their dominance accentuates the weakness of civil government in China. At the same time, in pondering the situation in China, one must have clearly in mind not the workings of small Communist groups or committees to which we are accustomed in America but rather of millions of people and an army of more than a million men.

I have never been in a position to be certain of the development of attitudes in the innermost Chinese Communist circles. Most certainly, the course which the Chinese Communist Party has pursued in recent months indicated an unwillingness to make a fair compromise. It has been impossible even to get them to sit down at a conference table with Government representatives to discuss given issues. Now the Communists have broken off negotiations by their last offer which demanded the dissolution of the National Assembly and a return to the military positions of January 13 which the Government could not be expected to accept.

Between this dominant reactionary group in the Government and the irreconcilable Communists who, I must state, did not so appear last February, lies the problem of how peace and well-being are to be brought to the long-suffering and presently inarticulate mass of the people of China. The reactionaries in the Government have evidently counted on substantial American support regardless of their actions. The Communists by their unwillingness to compromise in the national interest are evidently counting on an economic collapse to bring about the fall of the Government, accelerated by extensive guerrilla action against the long lines of rail communications—regardless of the cost in suffering to the Chinese people.

The salvation of the situation, as I see it, would be the assumption of leadership by the liberals in the Government and in the minority parties, a splendid group of men, but who as yet lack the political power to exercise a controlling influence. Successful action on their part under the leadership of Generalissimo Chiang Kai-shek would, I believe, lead to the unity through good government.

In fact, the National Assembly has adopted a democratic constitution which in all major respects is in accordance with the principles laid down by the all-party Political Consultative Conference of last January. It is unfortunate that the Communists did not see fit to participate in the Assembly since the constitution that has been adopted seems to include every major point that they wanted.

Soon the Government in China will undergo major reorganization pending the coming into force of the constitution following elections to be completed before Christmas Day 1947. Now that the form for a democratic China has been laid down by the newly adopted constitution, practical measures will be the test. It remains to be seen to what extent the Government will give substance to the form by a genuine welcome of all groups actively to share in the responsibility of government.

The first step will be the reorganization of the State Council and the executive branch of Government to carry on administration pending the enforcement of the constitution. The manner in which this is done and the amount of representation accorded to liberals and to non-Kuomintang members will be significant. It is also to be hoped that during this interim period the door will remain open for Communists or other groups to participate if they see fit to assume their share of responsibility for the future of China.

It has been stated officially and categorically that the period of political tutelage under the Kuomintang is at an end. If the termination of one-party rule is to be a reality, the Kuomintang should cease to receive financial support from the Government.

I have spoken very frankly because in no other way can I hope to bring the people of the United States to even partial understanding of this complex problem. I have expressed all these views privately in the course of negotiations; they are well known, I think, to most of the individuals concerned. I express them now publicly, as it is my duty, to present my estimate of the situation and its possibilities to the American people who have a deep interest in the development of conditions in the Far East promising an enduring peace in the Pacific.

◇◇◇◇◇◇

119. FACT-FINDING MISSION TO CHINA

Report by Ambassador Wedemeyer, September 19, 1947 [1]

[One of the most controversial documents in recent history is the report of Lieutenant General Albert C. Wedemeyer, who was sent by President Truman on a fact-finding mission to China shortly after General Marshall returned to this country. On September 18, 1947, General Wedemeyer reported to President Truman and made a number of important recommendations relative to our China policy. Although he recognized the weakness of the Nationalist régime, he urged that the United States provide the recognized government with moral, economic, and military aid at the earliest practicable moment. This report was not released to the public until August 1949 when the China part reproduced below appeared in the so-called White Book on China issued by the State Department.]

Part I—General Statement

China's history is replete with examples of encroachment, arbitrary action, special privilege, exploitation, and usurpation of territory on the part of foreign powers. Continued foreign infiltration, penetration or efforts to obtain spheres of influence in China, including Manchuria and Taiwan (Formosa), could be interpreted only as a direct infringement and violation of China's sovereignty and a contravention of the principles of the Charter of the United Nations. It is mandatory that the United States and those other nations subscribing to the principles of the Charter of the United Nations should combine their efforts to insure the unimpeded march of all peoples toward goals that recognize the dignity of man and his civil rights and, further, definitely provide the opportunity to express freely how and by whom they will be governed.

Those goals and the lofty aims of freedom-loving peoples are jeopardized today by forces as sinister as those that operated in Europe and Asia during the ten years leading to World War II. The pattern is familiar—employment of subversive agents; infiltration tactics; incitement of disorder and chaos to disrupt normal economy and thereby to undermine popular confidence in

[1] United States Relations with China, Department of State Publication 3573, Far Eastern Series 30 pp. 764 to 815. The portion of the report relating to Korea was not released until May 1951.

government and leaders; seizure of authority without reference to the will of the people—all the techniques skillfully designed and ruthlessly implemented in order to create favorable conditions for the imposition of totalitarian ideologies. This pattern is present in the Far East particularly in the areas contiguous to Siberia.

If the United Nations is to have real effect in establishing economic stability and in maintaining world peace, these developments merit high priority on the United Nations' agenda for study and action. Events of the past two years demonstrate the futility of appeasement based on the hope that the strongly consolidated forces of the Soviet Union will adopt either a conciliatory or a cooperative attitude, except as tactical expedients. Soviet practice in the countries already occupied or dominated completes the mosaic of aggressive expansion through ruthless secret police methods and through an increasing political and economic enslavement of peoples. Soviet literature, confirmed repeatedly by Communist leaders, reveals a definite plan for expansion far exceeding that of Nazism in its ambitious scope and dangerous implications. Therefore in attempting a solution to the problem presented in the Far East, as well as in other troubled areas of the world, every possible opportunity must be used to seize the initiative in order to create and maintain bulwarks of freedom.

Notwithstanding all the corruption and incompetence that one notes in China, it is a certainty that the bulk of the people are not disposed to a Communist political and economic structure. Some have become affiliated with Communism in indignant protest against oppressive police measures, corrupt practices and mal-administration of National Government officials. Some have lost all hope for China under existing leadership and turn to the Communists in despair. Some accept a new leadership by mere inertia.

Indirectly, the United States facilitated the Soviet program in the Far East by agreeing at the Yalta Conference to Russian re-entry into Manchuria, and later by withholding aid from the National Government. There were justifiable reasons for these policies. In the one case we were concentrating maximum Allied strength against Japanese in order to accelerate crushing defeat and thus save Allied lives. In the other we were withholding unqualified support from a government within which corruption and incompetence were so prevalent that it was losing the support of its own people. Further, the United States had not yet realized that the Soviet Union would fail to cooperate in the accomplishment of world-wide plans for post-war rehabilitation. Our own participation in those plans has already afforded assistance to other nations and peoples, friends and former foes alike, to a degree unparalleled in humanitarian history.

Gradually it has become apparent that the World War II objectives for which we and others made tremendous sacrifices are not being fully attained, and that there remains in the world a force presenting even greater dangers to world peace than did the Nazi militarists and the Japanese jingoists. Consequently the United States made the decision in the Spring of 1947 to assist Greece and Turkey with a view to protecting their sovereignties, which were threatened by the direct or inspired activities of the Soviet Union. Charges of unilateral action and circumvention of the United Nations were made by members of that organization. In the light of its purposes and principles such criticisms seemed plausible. The United States promptly declared its intention of referring the matter to the United Nations when that organization would be ready to assume responsibility.

It follows that the United Nations should be informed of contemplated action with regard to China. If the recommendations of this report are approved, the United States should suggest to China that she inform the United Nations officially of her request to the United States for material assistance and advisory aid in order to facilitate China's post-war rehabilitation and economic recovery. This will demonstrate that the United Nations is not being circumvented, and that the United States is not infringing upon China's sovereignty, but contrary-wise is cooperating constructively in the interest of peace and stability in the Far East, concomitantly in the world.

The situation in Manchuria has deteriorated to such a degree that prompt action is necessary to prevent that area from becoming a Soviet satellite. The Chinese Communists may soon gain military control of Manchuria and announce the establishment of a government. Outer Mongolia, already a Soviet satellite, may then recognize Manchuria and conclude a "mutual support agreement" with a *de facto* Manchurian government of the Chinese Communists. In that event, the Soviet Union might accomplish a mutual support agreement with Communist-dominated Manchuria, because of her current similar agreement with Outer Mongolia. This would create a difficult situation for China, the United States and the United Nations. Ultimately it could lead to a Communist-dominated China.

The United Nations might take immediate action to bring about cessation of hostilities in Manchuria as a prelude to the establishment of a Guardianship or Trusteeship. The Guardianship might consist of China, Soviet Russia, the United States, Great Britain and France. This should be attempted promptly and could be initiated only by China. Should one of the nations refuse to participate in Manchurian Guardianship, China might then request the General Assembly of the United Nations to establish a Trusteeship, under the provisions of the Charter.

Initially China might interpret Guardianship or Trusteeship as an infringement upon her sovereignty. But the urgency of the matter should encourage a realistic view of the situation. If these steps are not taken by China, Manchuria may be drawn into the Soviet orbit, despite United States aid, and lost, perhaps permanently, to China.

The economic deterioration and the incompetence and corruption in the political and military organizations in China should be considered against an all-inclusive background lest there be disproportionate emphasis upon defects. Comity requires that cognizance be taken of the following:

Unlike other Powers since V-J Day, China has never been free to devote full attention to internal problems that were greatly confounded by eight years of war. The current civil war has imposed an overwhelming financial and economic burden at a time when resources and energies have been dissipated and when, in any event, they would have been strained to the utmost to meet the problems of recovery.

The National Government has consistently, since 1927, opposed Communism. Today the same political leader and same civil and military officials are determined to prevent their country from becoming a Communist-dominated State or Soviet satellite.

Although the Japanese offered increasingly favorable surrender terms during the course of the war, China elected to remain steadfast with her Allies. If China had accepted surrender terms, approximately a million Japanese would have been released for employment against American forces in the Pacific.

I was assured by the Generalissimo that China would support to the limit of her ability an American program for the stabilization of the Far East. He stated categorically that, regardless of moral encouragement of material aid received from the United States, he is determined to oppose Communism and to create a democratic form of government in consonance with Doctor Sun Yat-sen's principles. He stated further that he plans to make sweeping reforms in the government including the removal of incompetent and corrupt officials. He stated that some progress has been made along these lines but, with spiraling inflation, economic distress and civil war, it has been difficult to accomplish fully these objectives. He emphasized that, when the Communist problem is solved, he could drastically reduce the Army and concentrate upon political and economic reforms. I retain conviction that the Generalissimo is sincere in his desire to attain these objectives. I am not certain that he has today sufficient determination to do so if this requires absolute overruling of the political and military cliques surrounding him. Yet, if realistic United States aid is to prove effective in stabilizing the situation in China and in coping with the dangerous expansion of Communism, that determination must be established.

Adoption by the United States of a policy motivated solely toward stopping the expansion of Communism without regard to the continued existence of an unpopular repressive government would render any aid ineffective. Further, United States prestige in the Far East would suffer heavily, and wavering elements might turn away from the existing government to Communism.

In China [and Korea], the political, economic and psychological problems are inextricably mingled. All of them are complex and are becoming increasingly difficult of solution. Each has been studied assiduously in compliance with your directive. Each will be discussed in the course of this report. However, it is recognized that a continued global appraisal is mandatory in order to preclude disproportionate or untimely assistance to any specific area.

The following three postulates of the United States foreign policy are pertinent to indicate the background of my investigations, analyses and report:

The United States will continue support of the United Nations in the attainment of its lofty aims, accepting the possible development that the Soviet Union or other nations may not actively participate.

Moral support will be given to nations and peoples that have established political and economic structures compatible with our own, or that give convincing evidence of their desire to do so.

Material aid may be given to those same nations and peoples in order to accelerate post-war rehabilitation and to develop economic stability, provided:

That such aid shall be used for the purposes intended.

That there is continuing evidence that they are taking effective steps to help themselves, or are firmly committed to do so.

That such aid shall not jeopardize American economy and shall conform to an integrated program that involves other international commitments and contributes to the attainment of political, economic and psychological objectives of the United States.

PART II—CHINA

POLITICAL

Although the Chinese people are unanimous in their desire for peace at almost any cost, there seems to be no possibility of its realization under existing circumstances. On one side is the Kuomintang, whose reactionary leadership, repression and corruption have caused a loss of popular faith in the Government. On the other side, bound ideologically to the Soviet Union, are the Chinese Communists, whose eventual aim is admittedly a Communist state in China. Some reports indicate that Communist measures of land reform have gained for them the support of the majority of peasants in areas under their control, while others indicate that their ruthless tactics of land distribution and terrorism have alienated the majority of such peasants. They have, however, successfully organized many rural areas against the National Government. Moderate groups are caught between Kuomintang misrule and repression and ruthless Communist totalitarianism. Minority parties lack dynamic leadership and sizable following. Neither the moderates, many of whom are in the Kuomintang, nor the minority parties are able to make their influence felt because of National Government repression. Existing provincial opposition leading to possible separatist movements would probably crystallize only if collapse of the Government were imminent.

Soviet actions, contrary to the letter and spirit of the Sino-Soviet Treaty of 1945 and its related documents, have strengthened the Chinese Communist position in Manchuria, with political, economic and military repercussions on the National Government's position both in Manchuria and in China proper, and have made more difficult peace and stability in China. The present trend points toward a gradual disintegration of the National Government's control, with the ultimate possibility of a Communist-dominated China.

Steps taken by the Chinese Government toward governmental reorganization in mid-April 1947 aroused hopes of improvement in the political situation. However, the reorganization resulted in little change. Reactionary influences continue to mold important policies even though the Generalissimo remains the principal determinative force in the government. Since the April reorganization, the most significant change has been the appointment of General Chen Cheng to head the civil and military administration of Manchuria. Projected steps include elections in the Fall for the formation of a constitutional government, but, under present conditions, they are not expected to result in a government more representative than the present regime.

ECONOMIC

Under the impact of civil strife and inflation, the Chinese economy is disintegrating. The most probable outcome of present trends would be, not

sudden collapse, but a continued and creeping paralysis and consequent decline in the authority and power of the National Government. The past ten
years of war have caused a serious deterioration of transportation and communication facilities, mines, utilities and industries. Notwithstanding some
commendable efforts and large amounts of economic aid, their overall capabilities are scarcely half those of the pre-war period. With disruption of transportation facilities and the loss of much of North China and Manchuria, important
resources of those rich areas are no longer available for the rehabilitation
and support of China's economy.

Inflation in China has been diffused slowly through an enormous population
without causing the immediate dislocation which would have occurred in a
highly industrialized economy. The rural people, 80 per cent of the total
Chinese population of 450 million, barter food-stuffs for local handicraft
products without suffering a drastic cut in living standards. Thus, local economies exist in many parts of China, largely insulated from the disruption of urban
industry. Some local economies are under the control of Communists, and some
are loosely under the control of provincial authorities.

The principal cause of the hyper-inflation is the long-continued deficit
in the national budget. Present revenue collections, plus the profits of national-
ized enterprises, cover only one-third of governmental expenditures, which
are approximately 70 percent military, and an increasing proportion of the
budget is financed by the issuance of new currency. In the first six months
of 1947 note-issue was tripled but rice prices increased seven-fold. Thus prices
and governmental expenditures spiral upwards, with price increases occurring
faster than new currency can be printed. With further price increases, budget
revisions will undoubtedly be necessary. The most urgent economic need of
Nationalist China is a reduction of the military budget.

China's external official assets amounted to $327 million (U.S.) on July 30,
1947. Privately-held foreign exchange assets are at least $600 million and
may total $1500 million, but no serious attempt has been made to mobilize
these private resources for rehabilitation purposes. Private Chinese assets
located in China include probably $200 million in gold, and about $75 million
in U.S. currency notes. Although China has not exhausted her foreign official
assets, and probably will not do so at the present rates of imports and exports
until early 1949, the continuing deficit in her external balance of payments
is a serious problem.

Disparity between the prices of export goods in China and in world markets
at unrealistic official exchange rates has greatly penalized exports, as have
disproportionate increases in wages and other costs. Despite rigorous trade
and exchange controls, imports have greatly exceeded exports, and there
consistently has been a heavy adverse trade balance.

China's food harvests this year are expected to be significantly larger
than last year's fairly good returns. This moderately encouraging situation
with regard to crops is among the few favorable factors which can be found
in China's current economic situation.

Under inflationary conditions, long-term investment is unattractive for both
Chinese and foreign capital. Private Chinese funds tend to go into short-term
advances, hoarding of commodities, and capital flight. The entire psychology

is speculative and inflationary, preventing ordinary business planning and handicapping industrial recovery.

Foreign business enterprises in China are adversely affected by the inefficient and corrupt administration of exchange and import controls, discriminatory application of tax laws, the increasing role of government trading agencies and the trend towards state ownership of industries. The Chinese Government has taken some steps toward improvement but generally has been apathetic in its efforts. Between 1944 and 1947, the anti-inflationary measure on which the Chinese Government placed the most reliance was the public sale of gold borrowed from the United States. The intention was to absorb paper currency, and thus reduce the effective demand for goods. Under the circumstance of continued large deficits, however, the only effect of the gold sales program was to retard slightly the price inflation and dissipate dollar assets.

A program to stabilize the economic situation was undertaken in February 1947. The measures included a wage freeze, a system of limited rationing to essential workers in a few cities, and the sale of government bonds. The effect of this program has been slight, and the wage freeze has been abandoned. In August 1947, the unrealistic official rate of exchange was replaced, for proceeds of exports and remittances, by a free market in foreign exchange. This step is expected to stimulate exports, but it is too early to determine whether it will be effective.

The issuance of a new silver currency has been proposed as a future measure to combat inflation. If the government continued to finance budgetary deficits by unbacked note issue, the silver would probably go into hoards and the price inflation would continue. The effect would be no more than that of the gold sales in 1944-1947, namely, a slight and temporary retardation of the inflationary spiral. The proposal could be carried out, moreover, only through a loan from the United States of at least $200 million in silver.

In the construction field, China has prepared expansive plans for reconstruction of communications, mines and industries. Some progress has been made in implementing them, notably in the partial rehabilitation of certain railroads and in the textile industry. Constructive results have been handicapped by a lack of funds, equipment and experienced management, supervisory and technical personnel.

On August 1, 1947, the State Council approved a "Plan for Economic Reform." This appears to be an omnibus of plans covering all phases of Chinese economic reconstruction but its effectiveness cannot yet be determined.

SOCIAL—CULTURAL

Public education has been one of the chief victims of war and social and economic disruption. Schoolhouses, textbooks and other equipment have been destroyed and the cost of replacing any considerable portion cannot now be met. Teachers, like other public servants, have seen the purchasing power of a month's salary shrink to the market value of a few days' rice ration. This applies to the entire educational system, from primary schools, which provide a medium to combat the nation's grievous illiteracy, to universities, from which must come the nation's professional men, technicians and administrators. The universities have suffered in an additional and no less serious respect—traditional academic freedom. Students participating in protest demonstrations have been severely and at times brutally punished by National Government agents without pretense of trial or public evidence of the sedition charged. Faculty members have often been dismissed or refused employment with no evidence of professional unfitness, patently because they were politically objectionable to government officials. Somewhat similarly, periodicals have been closed down "for reasons of military security" without stated charges, and permitted to reopen only after new managements have been imposed. Resumption of educational and other public welfare activities on anything like the desired scale can be accomplished only by restraint of officialdom's abuses, and when the nation's economy is stabilized sufficiently to defray the cost of such vital activities.

MILITARY

The over-all military position of the National Government has deteriorated in the past several months and the current military situation favors Communist forces. The Generalissimo has never wavered in his contention that he is fighting for national independence against forces of an armed rebellion nor has he been completely convinced that the Communist problem can be resolved except by the force of arms. Although the Nationalist Army has a preponderance of force, the tactical initiative rests with the Communists. Their hit-and-run tactics, adapted to their mission of destruction at points or in areas of their own selection, give them a decided advantage over Nationalists, who must defend many critical areas including connecting lines of communication. Obviously large numbers of Nationalist troops involved in such defensive roles are immobilized whereas Communist tactics permit almost complete freedom of action. The Nationalists' position is precarious in Manchuria, where they occupy only a slender finger of territory. Their control is strongly disputed in Shantung and Hopei Provinces where the Communists make frequent dislocating attacks against isolated garrisons.

In order to improve materially the current military situation, the Nationalist forces must first stabilize the fronts and then regain the initiative. Further, since the Government is supporting the civil war with approximately seventy per cent of its national budget, it is evident that steps taken to alleviate the situation must point toward an improvement in the effectiveness of the armed forces with a con-comitant program of social, political and economic reforms, including a decrease in the size of the military establishment. Whereas some rather ineffective steps have been taken to reorganize and revitalize the command structure, and more sweeping reforms are projected, the effectiveness of the Nationalist Army requires a sound program of equipment and improved logistical support. The present industrial potential of China is inadequate to support military forces effectively. Chinese forces under present conditions cannot cope successfully with internal strife or fulfill China's obligations as a member of the family of nations. Hence outside aid, in the form of munitions (most urgently ammunition) and technical assistance, is essential before any plan of operations can be undertaken with a reasonable prospect of success. Military advice is now available to the Nationalists on a General Staff level through American military advisory groups. The Generalissimo expressed to me repeatedly a strong desire to have this advice and supervision extended in scope to include field forces, training centers and particularly logistical agencies.

Extension of military aid by the United States to the National Government might possibly be followed by similar aid from the Soviet Union to the Chinese Communists, either openly or covertly—the latter course seems more likely. An arena of conflicting ideologies might be created as in 1935 in Spain. There is always the possibility that such developments in this area, as in Europe and in the Middle East, might precipitate a third world war.

PART IV—CONCLUSIONS

The peaceful aims of freedom-loving peoples in the world are jeopardized today by developments as portentous as those leading to World War II.

The Soviet Union and her satellites give no evidence of a concilatory or cooperative attitude in these developments. The United States is compelled, therefore, to initiate realistic lines of action in order to create and maintain bulwarks of freedom, and to protect United States strategic interests.

The bulk of the Chinese are not disposed to Communism and they are not concerned with ideologies. They desire food, shelter and the opportunity to live in peace.

CHINA

The spreading internecine struggle within China threatens world peace. Repeated American efforts to mediate have proved unavailing. It is apparent that positive steps are required to end hostilities immediately. The most logical approach to this very complex and ominous situation would be to refer the matter to the United Nations.

A China dominated by Chinese Communists would be inimical to the interests of the United States, in view of their openly expressed hostility and active opposition to those principles which the United States regards as vital to the peace of the world.

The Communists have the tactical initiative in the overall military situation. The Nationalists' position in Manchuria is precarious, and in Shantung and Hopei Provinces strongly disputed. Continued deterioration of the situation may result in the early establishment of a Soviet satellite government in Manchuria and ultimately in the evolution of a Communist-dominated China.

China is suffering increasingly from disintegration. Her requirements for rehabilitation are large. Her most urgent needs include governmental reorganization and reforms, reduction of the military budget and external assistance.

A program of aid, if effectively employed, would bolster opposition to Communist expansion, and would contribute to gradual development of stability in China.

Due to excesses and oppressions by government police agencies basic freedoms of the people are being jeopardized. Maladministration and corruption cause a loss of confidence in the Government. Until drastic political and economic reforms are undertaken United States aid can not accomplish its purpose.

Even so, criticism of results achieved by the National Government in efforts for improvement should be tempered by a recognition of the handicaps imposed on China by eight years of war, the burden of her opposition to Communism, and her sacrifices for the Allied cause.

A United States program of assistance could best be implemented under the supervision of American advisors in specified economic and military fields. Such a program can be undertaken only if China requests advisory aid as well as material assistance.

PART V—RECOMMENDATIONS

It is recommended:

That the United States Government provide as early as practicable moral, advisory, and material support to China in order to contribute to the early establishment of peace in the world in consonance with the enunciated principles of the United Nations, and concomitantly to protect United States strategic interests against militant forces which now threaten them.

That United States policies and actions suggested in this report be thoroughly integrated by appropriate government agencies with other international commitments. It is recognized that any foreign assistance extended must avoid jeopardizing the American economy.

CHINA

That China be advised that the United States is favorably disposed to continue aid designed to protect China's territorial integrity and to facilitate her recovery, under agreements to be negotiated by representatives of the two governments, with the following stipulations:

That China inform the United Nations promptly of her request to the United States for increased material and advisory assistance.

That China request the United Nations to make immediate action to bring about a cessation of hostilities in Manchuria and request that Manchuria be placed under a Five-Power Guardianship or, failing that, under a Trusteeship in accordance with the United Nations Charter.

That China make effective use of her own resources in a program for economic reconstruction and initiate sound fiscal policies leading to reduction of budgetary deficits.

That China give continuing evidence that the urgently required political and military reforms are being implemented.

That China accept American advisors as responsible representatives of the United States Government in specified military and economic fields to assist China in utilizing United States aid in the manner for which it is intended.

◇◇◇◇◇◇

120. CHINA AID ACT OF 1948 [1]

* * *

[During the war United States aid to China totaled in the neighborhood of one and one-half billion dollars. In the post-war period the United States furnished Chiang with an additional two billion dollars' worth of aid of various types. As long as there was a hope of the Nationalist Government surviving, the United States continued to furnish assistance. In the China Aid Act of 1948 provision was made for the administration of our economic aid by the Economic Cooperation Administration. In 1949 and again in 1950 legislation was passed making available the unexpended balance of these funds for use in China or the general area of China.]

Be it enacted by the Senate and House of Representatives of the United States of America in Congress assembled, That this Act may be cited as the 'Foreign Assistance Act of 1948".

TITLE IV

SEC. 401. This title may be cited as the "China Aid Act of 1948".

SEC. 402. Recognizing the intimate economic and other relationships between the United States and China, and recognizing that disruption following in the wake of war is not contained by national frontiers, the Congress finds that the existing situation in China endangers the establishment of a lasting peace, the general welfare and national interest of the United States, and the attainment of the objectives of the United Nations. It is the sense of the Congress that the further evolution in China of principles of individual liberty, free institutions, and genuine independence rests largely upon the continuing development of a strong and democratic national government as the basis for the establishment of sound economic conditions and for stable international economic relationships. Mindful of the advantages which the United States has enjoyed through the existence of a large domestic market with no internal trade barriers, and believing that similar advantages can accrue to China, it is declared to be the policy of the people of the United States to encourage the Republic of China and its people to exert sustained common efforts which will speedily achieve the internal peace and economic stability in China which are essential for lasting peace and prosperity in the world. It is further declared to be the policy of the people of the United States to encourage the Republic of China in its efforts to maintain the genuine independence and the administrative integrity of China, and to sustain and strengthen principles of individual liberty and free institutions in China through a program of assistance based on self-help and cooperation: *Provided,* That no assistance to China herein contemplated shall seriously impair the economic stability of the United States. It is further declared to be the policy of the United States that assistance provided by the United States under this title should at all times be dependent upon cooperation by the Republic of China and its people in furthering the program:

[1] Public Law 472, 80th Cong., 2d sess., S. 2202.

Provided further, That assistance furnished under this title shall not be construed as an express or implied assumption by the United States of any responsibility for policies, acts, or undertakings of the Republic of China or for conditions which may prevail in China at any time.

SEC. 403. Aid provided under this title shall be provided under the applicable provisions of the Economic Cooperation Act of 1948 which are consistent with the purposes of this title. It is not the purpose of this title that China, in order to receive aid hereunder, shall adhere to a joint program for European recovery.

SEC. 404. (a) In order to carry out the purposes of this title, there is hereby authorized to be appropriated to the President for aid to China a sum not to exceed $338,000,000 to remain available for obligation for the period of one year following the date of enactment of this Act.

(b) There is also hereby authorized to be appropriated to the President a sum not to exceed $125,000,000 for additional aid to China through grants, on such terms as the President may determine and without regard to the provisions of the Economic Cooperation Act of 1948, to remain available for obligation for the period of one year following the date of enactment of this Act.

SEC. 405. An agreement shall be entered into between China and the United States containing those undertakings by China which the Secretary of State, after consultation with the Administrator for Economic Cooperation, may deem necessary to carry out the purposes of this title and to improve commercial relations with China.

SEC. 406. Notwithstanding the provisions of any other law, the Reconstruction Finance Corporation is authorized and directed, until such time as an appropriation is made pursuant to section 404, to make advances, not to exceed in the aggregate $50,000,000, to carry out the provisions of this title in such manner and in such amounts as the President shall determine. From appropriations authorized under section 404, there shall be repaid without interest to the Reconstruction Finance Corporation the advances made by it under the authority contained herein. No interest shall be charged on advances made by the Treasury to the Reconstruction Finance Corporation in implementation of this section.

SEC. 407. (a) The Secretary of State, after consultation with the Administrator, is hereby authorized to conclude an agreement with China establishing a Joint Commission on Rural Reconstruction in China, to be composed of two citizens of the United States appointed by the President of the United States and three citizens of China appointed by the President of China. Such Commission shall, subject to the direction and control of the Administrator, formulate and carry out a program for reconstruction in rural areas of China, which shall include such research and training activities as may be necessary or appropriate for such reconstruction: *Provided,* That assistance furnished under this section shall not be construed as an express or implied assumption by the United States of any responsibility for making any further contributions to carry out the purposes of this section.

(b) Insofar as practicable, an amount equal to not more than 10 per centum of the funds made available under subsection (a) of section 404 shall be used to carry out the purposes of subsection (a) of this section. Such amount may be in United States dollars, proceeds in Chinese currency from the sale of commodities made available to China with funds authorized under subsection (a) of section 404, or both.

Approved April 3, 1948.

◇◇◇◇◇◇

121. A SUMMARY OF AMERICAN-CHINESE RELATIONS

Letter From the Secretary of State to the President, July 30, 1949, Transmitting "United States Relations With China, With Special Reference to the Period 1944 to 1949" [1]

[As the Nationalist Government lost control of the situation in China, criticisms of our China policy mounted in the United States. President Truman and Secretary Acheson were censured for what strong supporters of the Chiang régime described as a lack of policy. On the ground that much of this criticism was due to a lack of information about the actual situation in the Far East, the State Department, in August 1949, released its important white book on China. The introduction to this collection of state papers summarizes the developments which led to the collapse of the Nationalist government, and justifies our policy toward China. Secretary Acheson pointed out that the result of the civil war was beyond the contro! of the United States. At the same time he argued that we should encourage all developments in China by which the democratic elements there might reassert themselves and throw off the yoke of communism.]

THE PRESIDENT: In accordance with your wish, I have had compiled a record of our relations with China, special emphasis being placed on the last five years. This record is being published and will therefore be available to the Congress and to the people of the United States.

Although the compilation is voluminous, it necessarily covers a relatively small part of the relations between China and the United States. Since the beginning of World War II, these relations have involved many Government departments and agencies. The preparation of the full historical record of that period is by no means yet complete. Because of the great current interest in the problems confronting China, I have not delayed publication until the complete analysis could be made of the archives of the National Military Establishment, the Treasury Department, the Lend-Lease Administration, the White House files and many other official sources. However, I instructed those charged with the compilation of this document to present a record which would reveal the salient facts which determined our policy toward China during this period and which reflect the execution of that policy. This is a frank record of an extremely complicated and most unhappy period in the life of a great country to which the United States has long been attached by ties of closest friendship. No available item has been omitted because it contains statements critical of our policy or might be the basis of future criticism. The

[1] The letter transmitting the so-called China White Paper of 1949, Department of State publication 3573 pp. III-XVII.

inherent strength of our system is the responsiveness of the Government to an informed and critical public opinion. It is precisely this informed and critical public opinion which totalitarian governments, whether Rightist or Communist, cannot endure and do not tolerate.

The interest of the people and the Government of the United States in China goes far back into our history. Despite the distance and broad differences in background which separate China and the United States, our friendship for that country has always been intensified by the religious, philanthropic and cultural ties which have united the two peoples, and has been attested by many acts of good will over a period of many years, including the use of the Boxer indemnity for the education of Chinese students, the abolition of extraterritoriality during the Second World War, and our extensive aid to China during and since the close of the war. The record shows that the United States has consistently maintained and still maintains those fundamental principles of our foreign policy toward China which include the doctrine of the Open Door, respect for the administrative and territorial integrity of China, and opposition to any foreign domination of China. It is deplorable that respect for the truth in the compilation of this record makes it necessary to publish an account of facts which reveal the distressing situation in that country. I have not felt, however, that publication could be withheld for that reason.

The record should be read in the light of conditions prevailing when the events occurred. It must not be forgotten, for example, that throughout World War II we were allied with Russia in the struggle to defeat Germany and Italy, and that a prime object of our policy was to bring Russia into the struggle against Japan in time to be of real value in the prosecution of the war. In this period, military considerations were understandably predominant over all others. Our most urgent purpose in the Far East was to defeat the common enemy and save lives of our own men and those of our comrades-in-arms, the Chinese included. We should have failed in our manifest duty had we pursued any other course.

In the years since V-J Day, as in the years before Pearl Harbor, military considerations have been secondary to an earnest desire on our part to assist the Chinese people to achieve peace, prosperity and internal stability. The decisions and actions of our Government to promote these aims necessarily were taken on the basis of information available at the time. Throughout this tragic period, it has been fully realized that the material aid, the military and technical assistance, and the good will of the United States, however abundant, could not of themselves put China on her feet. In the last analysis, that can be done only by China herself.

Two factors have played a major role in shaping the destiny of modern China.

The population of China during the eighteenth and nineteenth centuries doubled, thereby creating an unbearable pressure upon the land. The first problem which every Chinese Government has had to face is that of feeding this population. So far none has succeeded. The Kuomintang attempted to solve it by putting many land-reform laws on the statute books. Some of these laws have failed, others have been ignored. In no small measure, the predicament in which the National Government finds itself today is due to its failure to provide China with enough to eat. A large part of the Chinese Communists' propaganda consists of promises that they will solve the land problem.

The second major factor which has shaped the pattern of contemporary China is the impact of the West and of Western ideas. For more than three thousand years the Chinese developed their own high culture and civilization, largely untouched by outside influences. Even when subjected to military conquest the Chinese always managed in the end to subdue and absorb the invader. It was natural therefore that they should come to look upon themselves as the center of the world and the highest expression of civilized mankind. Then in the middle of the nineteenth century the heretofore impervious wall of Chinese isolation was breached by the West. These outsiders brought with them aggressiveness, the unparalleled development of Western technology, and a high order of culture which had not accompanied previous foreign incursions into China. Partly because of these qualities and partly because of the decay of Manchu rule, the Westerners, instead of being absorbed by the Chinese, introduced new ideas which played an important part in stimulating ferment and unrest.

By the beginning of the twentieth century, the combined force of overpopulation and new ideas set in motion that chain of events which can be called the Chinese revolution. It is one of the most imposing revolutions in recorded history and its outcome and consequences are yet to be foreseen. Out of this revolutionary whirlpool emerged the Kuomintang, first under the leadership of Dr. Sun Yat-sen, and later Generalissimo Chiang Kai-shek, to assume the direction of the revolution. The leadership of the Kuomintang was not challenged until 1927 by the Chinese Communist Party which had been organized in the early twenties under the ideological impetus of the Russian revolution. It should be remembered that Soviet doctrine and practice had a measurable effect upon the thinking and principles of Dr. Sun Yat-sen, particularly in terms of economics and party organization, and that the Kuomintang and the Chinese Communists cooperated until 1927 when the Third International demanded a predominant position in the Government and the army. It was this demand which precipitated the break between the two groups. To a large extent the history of the period between 1927 and 1937 can be written in terms of the struggle for power between the Kuomintang and the Chinese Communists, with the latter apparently fighting a losing battle. During this period the Kuomintang made considerable progress in its efforts to unify the country and to build up the nation's financial and economic strength. Somewhere during this decade, however, the Kuomintang began to lose the dynamism and revolutionary fervor which had created it, while in the Chinese Communists the fervor became fanaticism.

Perhaps largely because of the progress being made in China, the Japanese chose 1937 as the departure point for the conquest of China proper, and the goal of the Chinese people became the expulsion of a brutal and hated invader. Chinese resistance against Japan during the early years of the war compelled the unqualified admiration of freedom-loving peoples throughout the world. Until 1940 this resistance was largely without foreign support. The tragedy of these years of war was that physical and human devastation to a large extent destroyed the emerging middle class which historically has been the backbone and heart of liberalism and democracy.

In contrast also to the unity of the people of China in the war against Japan were the divided interests of the leaders of the Kuomintang and of the Chinese Communists. It became apparent in the early forties that the leaders of the Government, just as much as the Communist leaders, were still as preoccupied with the internal struggle for power as they were with waging war against Japan. Once the United States became a participant in the war, the Kuomintang was apparently convinced of the ultimate defeat of Japan and saw an opportunity to improve its position for a show-down struggle with the Communists. The Communists, for their part, seemed to see in the chaos of China an opportunity to obtain that which had been denied them before the Japanese war, namely, full power in China. This struggle for power in the latter years of the war contributed largely to the partial paralysis of China's ability to resist.

It was precisely here that two of the fundamental principles of United States policy in regard to China—noninterference in its internal affairs and support of its unity and territorial integrity—came into conflct and that one of them also conflicted with the basic interests of the Allies in the war against Japan. It seemed highly probable in 1943 and 1944 that, unless the Chinese could subordinate their internal interests to the larger interest of the unified war effort against Japan, Chinese resistance would become completely ineffective and the Japanese would be able to deprive the Allies of valuable bases, operating points and manpower in China at a time when the outcome of the war against Japan was still far from clear. In this situation and in the light of the paramount necessity of the most vigorous prosecution of the war, in which Chinese interests were equally at stake with our own, traditional concepts of policy had to be adapted to a new and unprecedented situation.

After Pearl Harbor we expanded the program of military and economic aid which we had inaugurated earlier in 1941 under the Lend-Lease Act. That program, described in chapter I of the attached record, was far from reaching the volume which we would have wished because of the tremendous demands on the United States from all theaters of a world-wide war and because of the difficulties of access to a China all of whose ports were held by the enemy. Nevertheless it was substantial.

Representatives of our Government, military and civilian, who were sent to assist the Chinese in prosecuting the war soon discovered that, as indicated above, the long struggle had seriously weakened the Chinese Government not only militarily and economically, but also politically and in morale. The reports of United States military and diplomatic officers reveal a growing conviction through 1943 and 1944 that the Government and the Kuomintang had apparently lost the crusading spirit that won them the people's loyalty during the early years of the war. In the opinion of many observers they had sunk into corruption, into a scramble for place and power, and into reliance on the United States to win the war for them and to preserve their own domestic supremacy. The Government of China, of course, had always been a one-party rather than a democratic government in the Western sense. The stresses and strains of war were now rapidly weakening such liberal elements as it did possess and strengthening the grip of the reactionaries who were indistinguishable from the war lords of the past. The mass of the Chinese people were coming more and more to lose confidence in the Government.

It was evident to us that only a rejuvenated and progressive Chinese Government which could recapture the enthusiastic loyalty of the people could and would wage an effective war against Japan. American officials repeatedly brought their concern with this situation to the attention of the Generalissimo and he repeatedly assured them that it would be corrected. He made, however, little or no effective effort to correct it and tended to shut himself off from Chinese officials who gave unpalatable advice. In addition to a concern over the effect which this atrophy of the central Chinese administration must have upon the conduct of the war, some American observers, whose reports are also quoted in the attached record, were concerned over the effect which this deterioration of the Kuomintang must have on its eventual struggle, whether political or military, with the Chinese Communists. These observers were already fearful in 1943 and 1944 that the National Government might be so isolating itself from the people that in the postwar competition for power it would prove itself impotent to maintain its authority. Nevertheless, we continued for obvious reasons to direct all our aid to the National Government.

This was of course the period during which joint prosecution of the war against Nazi Germany had produced a degree of cooperation between the United States and Russia. President Roosevelt was determined to do what he could to bring about a continuance in the post-war period of the partnership forged in the fire of battle. The peoples of the world, sickened and weary with the excesses, the horrors, and the degradation of the war, shared this desire. It has remained for the postwar years to demonstrate that one of the major partners in this world alliance seemingly no longer pursues this aim, if indeed it ever did.

When Maj. Gen. Patrick J. Hurley was sent by President Roosevelt to Chungking in 1944 he found what he considered to be a willingness on the part of the National Government and the Chinese Communists to lay aside their differences and cooperate in a common effort. Already they had been making sporadic attempts to achieve this result.

Previously and subsequently, General Hurley had been assured by Marshal Stalin that Russia had no intention of recognizing any government in China except the National Government with Chiang Kai-shek as its leader. It may be noted that during the late war years and for a time afterwards Marshal Stalin reiterated these views to American officials. He and Molotov expressed the view that China should look to the United States as the principal possible source of aid. The sentiments expressed by Marshal Stalin were in large part incorporated in the Sino-Soviet treaty of 1945.

From the wartime cooperation with the Soviet Union and from the costly campaigns against the Japanese came the Yalta Agreement. The American Government and people awaited with intense anxiety the assault on the main islands of Japan which it was feared would cost up to a million American casualties before Japan was conquered. The atomic bomb was not then a reality and it seemed impossible that the war in the Far East could be ended without this assault. It thus became a primary concern of the American Government to see to it that the Soviet Union enter the war against Japan at the earliest possible date in order that the Japanese Army in Manchuria might not be returned to the homeland at the critical moment. It was considered vital not only that the Soviet Union enter the war but that she do so before our invasion of Japan, which already had been set for the autumn of 1945.

At Yalta, Marshal Stalin not only agreed to attack Japan within two or three months after V–E Day but limited his "price" with reference to Manchuria substantially to the position which Russia had occupied there prior to 1904. We for our part, in order to obtain this commitment and thus to bring the war to a close with a consequent saving of American, Chinese and other Allied lives, were prepared to and did pay the requisite price. Two facts must not, however, be lost sight of in this connection. First, the Soviet Union when she finally did enter the war against Japan, could in any case have seized all the territories in question and considerably more regardless of what our attitude might have been. Second, the Soviets on their side in the Sino-Soviet Treaty arising from the Yalta Agreement, agreed to give the National Government of China moral and material support and moreover formalized their assurances of noninterference in China's internal affairs. Although the unexpectedly early collapse of Japanese resistance later made some of the provisions of the Yalta Agreement seem unnecessary, in the light of the predicted course of the war at that time they were considered to be not only justified but clearly advantageous. Although dictated by military necessity, the Agreement and the subsequent Sino-Soviet Treaty in fact imposed limitations on the action which Russia would, in any case, have been in a position to take.

For reasons of military security, and for those only, it was considered too dangerous for the United States to consult with the National Government regarding the Yalta Agreement or to communicate its terms at once to Chungking. We were then in the midst of the Pacific War. It was felt that there was grave risk that secret information transmitted to the Nationalist capital at this time would become available to the Japanese almost immediately. Under no circumstances, therefore, would we have been justified in incurring the security risks involved. It was not until June 15, 1945, that General Hurley was authorized to inform Chiang Kai-shek of the Agreement.

In conformity with the Russian agreement at Yalta to sign a treaty of friendship and alliance with Nationalist China, negotiations between the two nations began in Moscow in July 1945. During their course, the United States felt obliged to remind both parties that the purpose of the treaty was to implement the Yalta Agreement—no more, no less—and that some of the Soviet proposals exceeded its provisions. The treaty, which was signed on August 14, 1945, was greeted with general satisfaction both in Nationalist China and in the United States. It was considered that Russia had accepted definite limitations on its activities in China and was committed to withhold all aid from the Chinese Communists. On September 10, however, our embassy in Moscow cautioned against placing undue confidence in the Soviet observance of either the spirit or letter of the treaty. The subsequent conduct of the Soviet Government in Manchuria has amply justified this warning.

When peace came the United States was confronted with three possible alternatives in China: (1) it could have pulled out lock, stock and barrel; (2) it could have intervened militarily on a major scale to assist the Nationalists to destroy the Communists; (3) it could, while assisting the Nationalists to assert their authority over as much of China as possible, endeavor to avoid a civil war by working for a compromise between the two sides.

The first alternative would, and I believe American public opinion at the time so felt, have represented an abandonment of our international responsibilities and of our traditional policy of friendship for China before we had made a determined effort to be of assistance. The second alternative policy, while it may look attractive theoretically and in retrospect, was wholly impracticable. The Nationalists had been unable to destroy the Communists during the 10 years before the war. Now after the war the Nationalists were, as indicated above, weakened, demoralized, and unpopular. They had quickly dissipated their popular support and prestige in the areas liberated from the Japanese by the conduct of their civil and military officials. The Communists on the other hand were much stronger than they had ever been and were in control of most of North China. Because of the ineffectiveness of the Nationalist forces which was later to be tragically demonstrated, the Communists probably could have been dislodged only by American arms. It is obvious that the American people would not have sanctioned such a colossal commitment of our armies in 1945 or later. We therefore came to the third alternative policy whereunder we faced the facts of the situation and attempted to assist in working out a *modus vivendi* which would avert civil war but nevertheless preserve and even increase the influence of the National Government.

As the record shows, it was the Chinese National Government itself which, prior to General Hurley's mission, had taken steps to arrive at a working agreement with the Communists. As early as September 1943 in addressing the Kuomintang Central Executive Committee, the Generalissimo said, "we should clearly recognize that the Communist problem is a purely political problem and should be solved by political means." He repeated this view on several occasions. Comprehensive negotiations between representatives of the Government and of the Communists, dealing with both military cooperation and civil administration, were opened in Sian in May 1944. These negotiations, in which Ambassador Hurley later assisted at the invitation of both parties between August 1944 and September 1945, continued intermittently during a year and a half without producing conclusive results and culminated in a comprehensive series of agreements on basic points on October 11, 1945, after Ambassador Hurley's departure from China and before General Marshall's arrival. Meanwhile, however, clashes between the armed forces of the two groups were increasing and were jeopardizing the fulfillment of the agreements. The danger of widespread civil war, unless the negotiations could promptly be brought to a successful conclusion, was critical. It was under these circumstances that General Marshall left on his mission to China at the end of 1945.

As the account of General Marshall's mission and the subsequent years in chapters V and VI of the underlying record reveals, our policy at that time was inspired by the two objectives of bringing peace to China under conditions which would permit stable government and progress along democratic lines, and of assisting the National Government to establish its authority over as wide areas of China as possible. As the event proved, the first objective was unrealizable because neither side desired it to succeed: The Communists because they refused to accept conditions which would weaken their freedom to proceed with what remained consistently their aim, the communization of all China: the Nationalists because they cherished the illusion, in spite of repeated advice to the contrary from our military representatives, that they could destroy the Communists by force of arms.

The second objective of assisting the National Government, however, we pursued vigorously from 1945 to 1949. The National Government was the recognized government of a friendly power. Our friendship, and our right under international law alike, called for aid to the Government instead of to the Communists who were seeking to subvert and overthrow it. The extent of our aid to Nationalist China is set forth in detail in chapters V, VI, VII and VIII of the record and need not be repeated here. The National Government had in 1945, and maintained until the early fall of 1948, a marked superiority in manpower and armament over their rivals. Indeed during that period, thanks very largely to our aid in transporting, arming and supplying their forces, they extended their control over a large part of North China and Manchuria. By the time General Marshall left China at the beginning of 1947, the Nationalists were apparently at the very peak of their military successes and territorial expansion. The following year and a half revealed, however, that their seeming strength was illusory and that their victories were built on sand.

The crisis had developed around Manchuria, traditional focus of Russian and Japanese imperialism. On numerous occasions, Marshal Stalin had stated categorically that he expected the National Government to take over the occupation of Manchuria. In the truce agreement of January 10, 1946, the Chinese Communists agreed to the movement of Government troops into Manchuria for the purpose of restoring Chinese sovereignty over this area. In conformity with this understanding the United States transported sizable government armies to the ports of entry into Manchuria. Earlier the Soviet Army had expressed a desire to evacuate Manchuria in December 1945, but had remained an additional two or three months at the request of the Chinese Government. When the Russian troops did begin their evacuation, the National Government found itself with extended lines of communications, limited rolling stock and insufficient forces to take over the areas being evacuated in time to prevent the entry of Chinese Communist forces, who were already in occupation of the countryside. As the Communists entered, they obtained the large stocks of matériel from the Japanese Kwantung Army which the Russians had conveniently "abandoned." To meet this situation the National Government embarked on a series of military campaigns which expanded the line of its holdings to the Sungari River. Toward the end of these campaigns it also commenced hostilities within North China and succeeded in constricting the areas held by the Communists.

In the spring of 1946 General Marshall attempted to restore peace. This effort lasted for months and during its course a seemingly endless series of proposals and counterproposals were made which had little effect upon the course of military activities and produced no political settlement. During these negotiations General Marshall displayed limitless patience and tact and a willingness to try and then try again in order to reach agreement. Increasingly he became convinced, however, that twenty years of intermittent civil war between the two factions, during which the leading figures had remained the same, had created such deep personal bitterness and such irreconcilable differences that no agreement was possible. The suspicions and the lack of confidence were beyond remedy. He became convinced that both parties were merely sparring for time, jockeying for military position and catering temporarily to what they believed to be American desires. General Marshall concluded that there was no hope of accomplishing the objectives of his mission.

Even though for all practical purposes General Marshall, by the fall of 1946, had withdrawn from his efforts to assist in a peaceful settlement of the civil war, he remained in China until January 1947. One of the critical points of dispute between the Government and the Communists had been the convocation of the National Assembly to write a new constitution for China and to bring an end to the period of political tutelage and of one-party government. The Communists had refused to participate in the National Assembly unless there were a prior military settlement. The Generalissimo was determined that the Assembly should be held and the program carried out. It was the hope of General Marshall during the late months of 1946 that his presence in China would encourage the liberal elements in non-Communist China to assert themselves more forcefully than they had in the past and to exercise a leavening influence upon the absolutist control wielded by the reactionaries and the militarists. General Marshall remained in China until the Assembly had completed its work. Even though the proposed new framework of government appeared satisfactory, the evidence suggested that there had been little shift in the balance of power.

In his farewell statement, General Marshall announced the termination of his efforts to assist the Chinese in restoring internal peace. He described the deep-seated mutual suspicion between the Kuomintang and the Chinese Communist Party as the greatest obstacle to a settlement. He made it clear that the salvation of China lay in the hands of the Chinese themselves and that, while the newly adopted constitution provided the framework for a democratic China, practical measures of implementation by both sides would be the decisive test. He appealed for the assumption of leadership by liberals in and out of the Government as the road to unity and peace. With these final words he returned to Washington to assume, in January 1947, his new post as Secretary of State.

As the signs of impending disaster multiplied, the President in July 1947, acting on the recommendation of the Secretary of State, instructed Lt. Gen. Albert C. Wedemeyer to survey the Chinese scene and make recommendations. In his report, submitted on September 19, 1947, the General recommended that the United States continue and expand its policy of giving aid to Nationalist China, subject to these stipulations:

1. That China inform the United Nations of her request for aid.

2. That China request the United Nations to bring about a truce in Manchuria and request that Manchuria be placed under a Five-Power guardianship or a trusteeship.

3. That China utilize her own resources, reform her finances, her Government and her armies, and accept American advisers in the military and economic fields.

General Wedemeyer's report, which fully recognized the danger of Communist domination of all China and was sympathetic to the problems of the National Government, nevertheless listed a large number of reforms which he considered essential if that Government were to rehabilitate itself.

It was decided that the publication at that time of a suggestion for the alienation of a part of China from the control of the National Government, and for placing that part under an international administration to include Soviet Russia, would not be helpful. In this record, the full text of that part of General Wedemeyer's report which deals with China appears as an annex to chapter VI.

The reasons for the failures of the Chinese National Government appear in some detail in the attached record. They do not stem from any inadequacy of American aid. Our military observers on the spot have reported that the Nationalist armies did not lose a single battle during the crucial year of 1948 through lack of arms or ammunition. The fact was that the decay which our observers had detected in Chungking early in the war had fatally sapped the powers of resistance of the Kuomintang. Its leaders had proved incapable of meeting the crisis confronting them, its troops had lost the will to fight, and its Government had lost popular support. The Communists, on the other hand, through a ruthless discipline and fanatical zeal, attempted to sell themselves as guardians and liberators of the people. The Nationalist armies did not have to be defeated; they disintegrated. History had proved again and again that a regime without faith in itself and an army without morale cannot survive the test of battle.

The record obviously can not set forth in equal detail the inner history and development of the Chinese Communist Party during these years. The principal reason is that, while we had regular diplomatic relations with the National Government and had the benefit of voluminous reports from our representatives in their territories, our direct contact with the Communists was limited in the main to the mediation efforts of General Hurley and General Marshall.

Fully recognizing that the heads of the Chinese Communist Party were ideologically affiliated with Moscow, our Government nevertheless took the view, in the light of the existing balance of forces in China, that peace could be established only if certain conditions were met. The Kuomintang would have to set its own house in order and both sides would have to make concessions so that the Government of China might become, in fact as well as in name, the Government of all China and so that all parties might function within the constitutional system of the Government. Both internal peace and constitutional development required that the progress should be rapid from one party government with a large opposition party in armed rebellion, to the participation of all parties, including the moderate non-communist elements, in a truly national system of government.

None of these conditions has been realized. The distrust of the leaders of both the Nationalist and Communist Parties for each other proved too deep-seated to permit final agreement, notwithstanding temporary truces and apparently promising negotiations. The Nationalists furthermore, embarked in 1946 on an over-ambitious military campaign in the face of warnings by General Marshall that it not only would fail but would plunge China into economic chaos and eventually destroy the National Government. General Marshall pointed out that though Nationalist armies could, for a period, capture Communist-held cities, they could not destroy the Communist armies. Thus every Nationalist advance would expose their communications to attack by Communist guerrillas and compel them to retreat or to surrender their armies together with the munitions which the United States has furnished them. No estimate of a military situation has ever been more completely confirmed by the resulting facts.

The historic policy of the United States of friendship and aid toward the people of China was, however, maintained in both peace and war. Since V–J Day, the United States Government has authorized aid to Nationalist China in the form of grants and credits totaling approximately 2 billion dollars, an amount equivalent in value to more than 50 percent of the monetary expenditures of the Chinese Government and of proportionately greater magnitude in relation to the budget of that Government than the United States has provided to any nation of Western Europe since the end of the war. In addition to these grants and credits, the United States Government has sold the Chinese Government large quantities of military and civilian war surplus property with a total procurement cost of over 1 billion dollars, for which the agreed realization to the United States was 232 million dollars. A large proportion of the military supplies furnished the Chinese armies by the United States since V–J Day has, however, fallen into the hands of the Chinese Communists through the military ineptitude of the Nationalist leaders, their defections and surrenders, and the absence among their forces of the will to fight.

It has been urged that relatively small amounts of additional aid—military and economic—to the National Government would have enabled it to destroy communism in China. The most trustworthy military, economic, and political information available to our Government does not bear out this view.

A realistic appraisal of conditions in China, past and present, leads to the conclusion that the only alternative open to the United States was full-scale intervention in behalf of a Government which had lost the confidence of its own troops and its own people. Such intervention would have required the expenditure of even greater sums than have been fruitlessly spent thus far, the command of Nationalist armies by American officers, and the probable participation of American armed forces—land, sea, and air—in the resulting war. Intervention of such a scope and magnitude would have been resented by the mass of the Chinese people, would have diametrically reversed our historic policy, and would have been condemned by the American people.

It must be admitted frankly that the American policy of assisting the Chinese people in resisting domination by any foreign power or powers is now confronted with the gravest difficulties. The heart of China is in Communist hands. The Communist leaders have foresworn their Chinese heritage and have publicly announced their subservience to a foreign power, Russia, which during the last 50 years, under czars and Communists alike, has been most assiduous in its efforts to extend its control in the Far East. In the recent past, attempts at foreign domination have appeared quite clearly to the Chinese people as external aggression and as such have been bitterly and in the long run successfully resisted. Our aid and encouragement have helped them to resist. In this case, however, the foreign domination has been masked behind the facade of a vast crusading movement which apparently has seemed to many Chinese to be wholly indigenous and national. Under these circumstances, our aid has been unavailing.

The unfortunate but inescapable fact is that the ominous result of the civil war in China was beyond the control of the government of the United States. Nothing that this country did or could have done within the reasonable limits of its capabilities could have changed that result; nothing that was left undone by this country has contributed to it. It was the product of internal Chinese forces, forces which this country tried to influence but could not. A decision was arrived at within China, if only a decision by default.

And now it is abundantly clear that we must face the situation as it exists in fact. We will not help the Chinese or ourselves by basing our policy on wishful thinking. We continue to believe that, however tragic may be the immediate future of China and however ruthlessly a major portion of this great people may be exploited by a party in the interest of a foreign imperialism, ultimately the profound civilization and the democratic individualism of China will re-assert themselves and she will throw off the foreign yoke. I consider that we should encourage all developments in China which now and in the future work toward this end.

In the immediate future, however, the implementation of our historic policy of friendship for China must be profoundly affected by current developments. It will necessarily be influenced by the degree to which the Chinese people come to recognize that the Communist regime serves not their interests but those of Soviet Russia and the manner in which, having become aware of the facts, they react to this foreign domination. One point, however, is clear. Should the Communist regime lend itself to the aims of Soviet Russian imperialism and attempt to engage in aggression against China's neighbors, we and the other members of the United Nations would be confronted by a situation violative of the principles of the United Nations Charter and threatening international peace and security.

Meanwhile our policy will continue to be based upon our own respect for the Charter, our friendship for China, and our traditional support for the Open Door and for China's independence and administrative and territorial integrity.

Respectfully yours,

DEAN ACHESON

◇◇◇◇◇◇

122. THREATS TO THE POLITICAL INDEPENDENCE AND TERRITORIAL INTEGRITY OF CHINA

Resolution of the General Assembly, December 8, 1949 [1]

[Chinese representatives in the United Nations charged the U.S.S.R. with violations of the UN Charter because the Soviet Union was aiding the Chinese communists and obstructing the efforts of the National Government to bring order to China. In response the General Assembly passed this resolution on December 8, 1949. It called upon all states to respect the political independence of China, the right of the Chinese people to choose freely their own government, and the integrity of existing treaties with China. The General Assembly also asked all states to refrain from seeking spheres of influence or special privileges in China, and referred any charges relating to the violation

[1] General Assembly Roundup, Fourth Regular Session, Press Release GA/600, Part I, pp. 13-14.

of the above principles to the Interim Committee of the Assembly for further study.]

I

WHEREAS the peoples of the United Nations have expressed in the Charter of the United Nations their determination to practice tolerance and to live together in peace with one another as good neighbors and to unite their strength to maintain international peace and security, and to that end the Members of the United Nations have obligated themselves to carry out the purposes and principles set forth in the Charter,

WHEREAS it is a purpose of the United Nations to develop friendly relations among nations based on respect for the principles of equal rights and self-determination of peoples,

WHEREAS the organization of the United Nations is based on the principle of the sovereign equality of all its members and on respect for international agreements, and

WHEREAS the Charter calls upon all Members to refrain in their international relations from the threat or use of force against the territorial integrity or political independence of any State, or in any other manner inconsistent with the purposes of the United Nations,

THE GENERAL ASSEMBLY,

DESIRING to promote the stability of international relations in the Far East

CALLS UPON ALL STATES:

1. To respect the political independence of China and to be guided by the principles of the United Nations in their relations with China:

2. To respect the right of the people of China now and in the future to choose freely their political institutions and to maintain a government independent of foreign control;

3. To respect existing treaties relating to China; and

4. To refrain from (a) seeking to acquire spheres of influence or to create foreign controlled regimes within the territory of China; (b) seeking to obtain special rights or privileges within the territory of China..

II

THE GENERAL ASSEMBLY,

CONSIDERING that item 68 regarding threats to the political independence and territorial integrity of China and to the peace of the Far East, resulting from Soviet violations of the Sino-Soviet Treaty of Friendship and Alliance of 14 August 1945, and from Soviet violations of the Charter of the United Nations is of special importance, involves the fundamental principles of the Charter and the prestige of the United Nations and requires further examination and study,

CONSIDERING further the resolution on the promotion of the stability of international relations in the Far East,

DECIDES to refer that item *and any other charges of violations of the principles contained in that resolution* to the Interim Committee of the General Assembly for continuous examination and study in the light of the resolution mentioned above, and to report to the next session of the General Assembly with recommendations, or to bring it to the attention of the Secretary-General in order to report to the Security Council if it deems it necessary to do so as a result of the examination or of the state of the matter submitted to it for study.

◇◇◇◇◇◇

123. UNITED STATES POSITION ON FORMOSA

Statement by President Truman, January 5, 1950 [1]

[Following the flight of the Chinese Nationalist régime to Formosa, the Chinese Communists demanded control of that island on the ground that they were the legal government of China. Meanwhile, many strong voices in the United States insisted that this country should continue to support Chiang. Against this background President Truman issued the following Formosa statement, in which he made clear that the United States had no intention of utilizing our armed forces to interfere in the existing situation. This policy was, of course, modified as a result of the Korean aggression in June 1950.]

The United States Government has always stood for good faith in international relations. Traditional United States policy toward China, as exemplified in the Open Door policy, called for international respect for the territorial integrity of China. This principle was recently reaffirmed in the UN General Assembly resolution of December 8, 1949, which, in part, calls on all states

> To refrain from (a) seeking to acquire spheres of influence or to create foreign controlled regimes within the territory of China; (b) seeking to obtain special rights or privileges within the territory of China.

A specific application of the foregoing principles is seen in the present situation with respect to Formosa. In the Joint Declaration at Cairo on December 1, 1943, the President of the United States, the British Prime Minister and the President of China stated that it was their purpose that territories Japan had stolen from China, such as "Formosa", should be restored to the Republic of China. The United States was a signatory to the Potsdam Declaration of July 26, 1945, which declared that the terms of the Cairo Declaration should be carried out. The provisions of this Declaration were accepted by Japan at the time of its surrender. In keeping with these declarations, Formosa was surrendered to Generalissimo Chiang Kai-shek and for the past four years the United States and the other Allied Powers have accepted the exercise of Chinese authority over the Island.

The United States has no predatory designs on Formosa or on any other Chinese territory. The United States has no desire to obtain special rights or privileges or to establish military bases on Formosa at this time. Nor does it have any intention of utilizing its armed forces to interfere in the present situation. The United States Government will not pursue a course which will lead to involvement in the civil conflict in China.

Similarly, the United States Government will not provide military aid or ad-

1 White House Press Release, January 5, 1950.

vice to Chinese forces on Formosa. In the view of the United States Government, the sources on Formosa are adequate to enable them to obtain the items which they might consider necessary for the defense of the Island. The United States Government proposes to continue under existing legislative authority the present ECA program of economic assistance.

◇◇◇◇◇◇

GREECE [1]

124. CONSIDERATION OF GREEK PROBLEM BY THE SECURITY COUNCIL DURING THE YEAR 1946

(a) Summary Statement of U. S. Position in the Security Council on the Greek Case [2]

[At the end of World War II, communist guerrillas supported by Yugoslavia, Albania, and Bulgaria created disorder in Greece and carried depredation across the borders. These guerrilla activities threatened to draw Greece behind the Iron Curtain. The Soviet Union brought the Greek situation to the attention of the Security Council when it complained of the presence of British troops in Greece and charged the British with responsibility for the Greek disorders. On December 16, 1946, the Security Council passed a resolution reproduced in (b) which follows, establishing a commission of investigation which was directed to proceed to the spot not later than January 1947, and there to determine the facts and to make any recommendations it deemed wise to prevent a repetition of border violations and disturbances.]

CASE BROUGHT BY THE U.S.S.R.

The first Greek case was brought to the Security Council's attention on January 21, 1946 by a letter from the chairman of the Soviet Delegation to the General Assembly, in which it was charged that the presence of British troops in Greece constituted interference with that country's internal affairs and contributed to tension fraught with grave consequences to the maintenance of international peace.

The United States Representative stated that he did not believe that the presence of British troops in Greece could be regarded as constituting a situation likely to endanger international peace and security within the meaning of the Charter; accordingly the United States felt that without such a finding the Security Council was without Charter authority to recommend procedures or methods of adjustment. The Council finally accepted a proposal, originally put forward by the United States Representative, that its president should read a

---

[1] Material relating to aid for Greece and Turkey will be found in Part VIII, Current International Issues.

[2] The United States and the United Nations: Report by the President to the Congress for the Year 1946, Department of State Publication 2735, the United States and the United Nations Report Series 7, pp. 35-36. A comprehensive summary of the Greek situation may be found in Greece and the United Nations, 1946-1949, Department of State publication 3645, released October 1949.

statement affirming that the Council had taken note of the statements made during the discussion and that the matter should be considered closed.

CASE BROUGHT BY THE UKRAINIAN S.S.R.

On August 24, 1946 the Ukrainian S.S.R. complained of internal conditions in Greece and incidents along the Greek-Albanian frontier, allegedly provoked by Greek armed forces. After full discussion in the Council the United States Representative proposed that the Security Council establish a commission to investigate the facts relating to border incidents along the whole northern frontier of Greece, with authority to call upon Albania, Bulgaria, Greece, and Yugoslavia for information.

This resolution received eight affirmative votes but failed of adoption because of the negative vote of the Union of Soviet Socialist Republics. Accordingly, the Council took no action at the time.

(b) Resolution on the Greek Question, Establishing a Commission of Investigation, December 16, 1946 [1]

WHEREAS, there have been presented to the Security Council oral and written statements by the Greek, Yugoslav, Albanian and Bulgarian Governments relating to disturbed conditions in northern Greece along the frontier between Greece on the one hand and Albania, Bulgaria and Yugoslavia on the other, which conditions, in the opinion of the Council, should be investigated before the Council attempts to reach any conclusions regarding the issues involved.

Resolves:

That the Security Council under Article 34 of the Charter establish a Commission of Investigation to ascertain the facts relating to the alleged border violations along the frontier between Greece on the one hand and Albania, Bulgaria and Yugoslavia on the other.

That the Commission be composed of a representative of each of the members of the Security Council as it will be constituted in 1947.

That the Commission shall proceed to the area not later than 15 January 1947, and shall submit to the Security Council at the earliest possible date a report of the facts disclosed by its investigation. The Commission shall, if it deems it advisable or if requested by the Security Council, make preliminary reports to the Security Council.

That the Commission shall have authority to conduct its investigation in northern Greece and in such places in other parts of Greece, in Albania, Bulgaria and Yugoslavia as the Commission considers should be included in its investigation in order to elucidate the causes and nature of the above-mentioned border violations and disturbances.

That the Commission shall have authority to call upon the Governments, officials and nationals of those countries, as well as such other sources as the Commission deems necessary, for information relevant to its investigation.

That the Security Council request the Secretary-General to communicate with the appropriate authorities of the countries named above in order to facilitate the Commission's investigation in those countries.

[1] UN Doc. S/339, May 2, 1947. Republication of S/P. V. 87/Annex B. The United Nations and the Problem of Greece, Department of State publication 2909, Near Eastern Series 9, p. 51.

That each representative on the Commission be entitled to select the personnel necessary to assist him and that, in addition, the Security Council request the Secretary-General to provide such staff and assistance to the Commission as it deems necessary for the prompt and effective fulfillment of its task.

That a representative of each of the Governments of Greece, Albania, Bulgaria and Yugoslavia be invited to assist in the work of the Commission in a liaison capacity.

That the Commission be invited to make any proposals that it may deem wise for averting a repetition of border violations and disturbances in these areas.

◇◇◇◇◇◇

125. REPORT TO THE SECURITY COUNCIL BY THE COMMISSION OF INVESTIGATION CONCERNING GREEK FRONTIER INCIDENTS, MAY 27, 1947 (EXCERPTS) [1]

(a) Part III: Conclusions

[The Security Council's Special Investigation Commission created on December 16, 1946, proceeded to the Balkans, conducted its on-the-spot investigation in spite of the obstacles thrown in its way by Albania, Bulgaria, and Yugoslavia, and made the following report on May 27, 1947. The Commission reported that Yugoslavia, and to a lesser degree Albania and Bulgaria, had supported guerrilla warfare in Greece. The Commission recommended: (1) the re-establishment of normal relations between Greece and her neighbors; (2) the creation of effective machinery for the control of the Greek frontiers; (3) the establishment of a small commission or a commissioner to police the frontiers; and (4) the setting up of refugee camps in order to control and regulate the flow of people across the borders in question.]

SECTION A

ALBANIA, BULGARIA AND YUGOSLAVIA AND THE GUERILLAS IN GREECE

1. *Introduction*

The charge of the Greek Government that its northern neighbours were supporting the guerilla warfare in Greece was directed jointly against Albania, Bulgaria and Yugoslavia. The evidence submitted, however, related primarily to Yugoslavia intervention in this regard, and only to a lesser degree to that of Albania and Bulgaria. Although the Liaison Representatives repeatedly denied these charges, and attacked the credibility of the witnesses who testified in their support, little direct evidence was brought forward to disprove them. On the basis of the facts ascertained by the Commission, it is its conclusion that Yugoslavia, and to a lesser extent, Albania, and Bulgaria, have supported the guerilla warfare in Greece.

2. *Yugoslavia*

a. The Commission heard a considerable amount of evidence by direct testi-

[1] UN Doc. S/360, May 27, 1947. Vol. I, Part III, chap. 1, pp. 167-182. Department of State Bulletin of July 6, 1947, pp. 18-24.

mony and by deposition that assistance had been rendered in Yugoslavia to the guerillas, taking the form of training refugees from Greece within the borders of Yugoslavia, recruiting and dispatching them to Greece for action with the guerillas' units there, as well as supplying them for this purpose with arms, supplies, transport, guides, hospitalization, etc., and providing an avenue of escape for guerillas fleeing from Greek Government forces.

b. The Commission heard the testimony of several witnesses that in the spring of 1946 a special course for guerilla leaders was established in the refugee camp at Bulkes in Yugoslavia, which was designed to give theoretical and practical training to refugees from Greece in guerilla warfare. There was presented to the Commission a copy of a military manual for training in guerilla tactics and several witnesses testified that it was used as the text book in the Bulkes school. Indeed, one witness, a Greek refugee, testified that he was one of the authors of the manual when it was written in the summer of 1945. The evidence indicated that during the spring and at least through the summer of 1946 actual training in partisan warfare was given to selected personnel among the refugees at the Bulkes camp. Furthermore, the Commission heard evidence which demonstrated that at least some of the refugees who had received military training returned to Greece and participated in the operations of the guerilla bands. Certain witnesses testified that they had served in the Yugoslav Army and had later been released so that they might return to Greece and join the guerillas.

c. The Commission was provided with considerable evidence indicating that preparatory to returning to Greece, Greek refugees at the Bulkes camp and in other places in Yugoslavia were provided with arms and other military supplies, clothing and food. Other refugees testifying before the Commission stated that in crossing the frontier to or from Greece, transportation was provided them in Yugoslavia, that they were conducted by Yugoslav guides, including Yugoslav soldiers, and that they were provided with a network of liaison agents who facilitated the crossings. According to the evidence Yugoslav frontier guards permitted guerilla bands to escape into Yugoslavia when pursued by the Greek army. This was clearly demonstrated to the Commission by its investigation of the incidents at Sourmena and Idhomeni.

d. In addition, the evidence showed that as part of the pattern of assistance to the guerilla movement, arrangements were made for the transportation of guerillas wounded in Greece into Yugoslavia where hospitalization was provided. Three witnesses testified that they themselves had transported wounded guerillas on donkeys to or across the Yugoslav border.

e. At the time of its visit to the camp at Bulkes on April 2, 1947, the Commission was unable to find evidence of military activities or of the military training which had theretofore been carried on.

f. There is no doubt, however, that at the Bulkes camp the refugees from Greece were subjected to political indoctrination and propaganda looking toward the overthrow of the Greek Government. Witnesses uniformly testified that on March 25, 1946, Greece's Independence Day, the leader of the Greek Communist Party, Zachariades, visited the camp at Bulkes and made a speech urging the refugees to prepare themselves to return to Greece "when the Greek people will need them." The evidence also indicated that the refugees at Bulkes heard similar propaganda from other official personnel, including the Yugoslav

Minister of Education for Viovodina, and a Bulgarian Commission of several officers, who paid visits to the camp. While at Bulkes Novi Sad, Djevdjelija and Strumitsa, the Commission witnessed political demonstrations antagonistic to the present Greek Government, which indicated that political activity among the refugees continued to be sanctioned.

3. *Albania*

a) In the case of Albania, evidence presented to the Commission indicated that at Rubig, a village about 50 miles north of Pirana, a camp for Greek refugees had·been in existence from the Spring of 1945 to October 1945. During that period the refugees there received political instruction as well as practical and theoretical military training. A military training manual, written in Greek at Rubig, similar to the one used at Bulkes, was presented in evidence to the Commission. Moreover, the Commission heard testimony that one manual, which was published in Albania, was mimeographed on paper furnished by the Albanian Press Ministry.

b) Witnesses testified before the Commission that after the Varkiza Agreement of February 12, 1945, former members of ELAS (the military arm of EAM) were advised by KKE (the Communist Party of Greece) or their ELAS comrades, to cross into Albania, as well as into Bulgaria and Yugoslavia, to avoid persecution. The evidence indicated that officers of the KKE made arrangements with Albanian security authorities for the reception, transportation, feeding and housing of refugees. Witnesses testified that before returning to Greece they were supplied in Albania with food, clothing, military equipment and transportation to the border. Evidence was also brought forward that refugees were given assistance by Albanian military personnel in their efforts to cross the frontier between Greece and Albania.

c) The evidence presented to the Commission indicated that there was no military or other training of Greek refugees in Albania after October 1945 when the refugees in the camp at Rubig were transferred to Bulkes in Yugoslavia. However, the evidence indicated that as late as November 1946 Albanian assistance to the Greek guerrillas continued in the form of providing arms and ammunition, as well as making available routes of entry, guides and liaison assistance for guerrilla groups returning to Greece from both Albania and Yugoslavia.

4. *Bulgaria*

a) The evidence submitted to the Commission regarding Bulgarian aid to the Greek guerrilla movement indicated that Greek guerrillas, in groups and individually were assisted in crossing Bulgarian territory from Yugoslavia to Greece, and that sizeable Greek guerrilla groups had on a number of occasions taken refuge on Bulgarian soil, with the assistance of Bulgarian authorities. Evidence was also presented to show that, in certain instances, Greek guerrillas were given arms in or near Sofia while on their way to Greece from Yugoslavia, and that hospital facilities were offered to Greek guerrillas who were transferred for this purpose to Bulgarian territory.

b) The Commission feels that the weight of the evidence indicates that aid was provided the Greek guerrillas by the Bulgarian Government in the form of assistance in entering and leaving Bulgarian territory, provision of transportation for guerrillas crossing Bulgaria to and from Yugoslavia, and hospitalization of guerrillas wounded in Greece. Less evidence was provided the Commission, however, as to the arming and equipping of guerrillas.

SECTION B
MOVEMENT TO DETACH MACEDONIA FROM GREECE

5. a) The Greek government charged that support was being given by the Yugoslav and Bulgarian Government, through propaganda and otherwise, looking towards the detachment of the province of Macedonia from Greece and its incorporation together with Bulgarian and Yugoslavian Macedonia into the Federative People's Republic of Yugoslavia.

b) Evidence was introduced in the Commission, consisting of these quotations from speeches by responsible Yugoslav and Bulgarian statesmen and from the government-controlled press, which indicated that these governments adopted a policy of support for a separate Macedonian state within the Yugoslav federation, and exploited the aspirations of Slavo-Macedonians in Greece for an autonomous Macedonia. This exploitation had the natural consequence of fomenting dissatisfaction and disturbances among the Slavo-Macedonians.

c) In addition, the Commission heard witnesses who testified that there was in Yugoslavia an organization known as NOF (National Liberation Front), one of whose objects was to detach Greek Macedonia from Greece and to incorporate it into the federation of Yugoslavia. These witnesses testified that the activities of NOF were directed from its headquarters in Skoplje and during its most active phase through a special "Aegean Bureau" in Bitolj (Monastir). The program of NOF included propaganda supporting the Macedonian movement.

d) In explanation of the organization called NOF, it was stated that it was in fact no more than the name of the Greek EAM in Slavic translation. Both the Yugoslav and Bulgarian Representatives denied, however, that NOF was engaged in activities of the type described in the Greek charge. Although certain witnesses testified to the Commission that they had not heard of this aspect of the functions of NOF, the references to NOF's relationship to the Macedonian movement were so numerous and so uniform as to leave little doubt on this point in the minds of the Commission.

e) Furthermore it is quite clear that Bulgaria also supported the movement for the unification of the three parts of Macedonia as a republic within the Yugoslav federation. As late as November 16, 1946, an article in the official Communist paper *Rabotnichesko Delo* welcomed the creation of the Republic of Macedonia within the Yugoslav Federation, and asserted that "unification of other parts of the Macedonian nation can take place only on the basis of this republic. Such unification is in the interests of the future peaceful development of Bulgaria in close cooperation with Yugoslavia."

(f) In explaining the attitude of his Government with regard to the Macedonian question the Yugoslav Liaison Representative stated that Yugoslavia could not be indifferent to the "terrible state" of the Slav minority in Macedonia. He stated that Yugoslavia's interest was in assisting this minority in its achievement of full political and cultural rights and that this was to be achieved within the framework of the Charter of the United Nations.

g) It was pointed out to the Commission, and not disputed, that after the

Varkiza Agreement over 20,000 Greek citizens had fled into Yugoslavia, (either directly or through Albania or Bulgaria) and approximately 5,000 into Bulgaria, a substantial proportion in each case being of Slavo-Macedonian origin. Evidence was also presented in support of the charge that Greece has sanctioned persecution of its Slavo-Macedonian minorities. Furthermore, the Commission heard some testimony that the Slavic dialect spoken by the Slavo-Macedonians who comprise about 85,000 persons was not taught in schools, and that in certain areas the use of this dialect by Greek nationals had on occasions been prohibited.

h) The Commission is of the opinion that such treatment has resulted in unrest and discontent on the part of the Slavic minority in Greek Macedonia and has provided fertile breeding ground for separatist movements. This does not, of course, absolve the Northern neighbours from their responsibility for their support of the Macedonian movement.

i) Although it is undoubtedly true, as pointed out by the Yugoslav Liaison Representative that during the war the Axis occupying authorities had themselves supported a Macedonian autonomist movement in an effort to create controversy among the Balkan states, it seems equally clear that since the war the Yugoslav and Bulgarian governments, by speeches of responsible officials and articles in the press, have themselves revived and promoted a separatist movement among the Slavo-Macedonians in Greece.

*   *   *

(b) Part IV: Proposals Made in Pursuance of the Final Paragraph of the Security Council's Resolution of 19 December 1946 [1]

*   *   *

The following are the Commission's proposals:

A. The Commission proposes to the Security Council that it should recommend to the governments of Greece on the one hand and Albania, Bulgaria and Yugoslavia on the other, to do their utmost to establish normal good neighbourly relations, to abstain from all action direct or indirect which is likely to increase or maintain the tension and unrest in the border areas, and rigorously to refrain from any support, overt or covert, of elements in neighbouring countries aiming at the overthrow of the lawful governments of those countries. Should subjects of complaint arise these should be made not the object of propaganda campaigns, but referred either through diplomatic channels to the Government concerned, or should this resource fail, to the appropriate organ of the United Nations. In the light of the situation investigated by it the Commission believes that, in the area of its investigation future cases of support of armed bands formed on the territory of one State and crossing into the territory of another State, or of refusal by a government in spite of the demands of the State, concerned to take all possible measures on its own territory to deprive such bands of any aid or protection, should be considered by the Security Council as a threat to the peace within the meaning of the Charter of the United Nations.

B. With a view to provide effective machinery for the regulation and con-

[1] UN Doc. S/360, May 27, 1947, Vol. I, Part IV, chap. 1, pp. 246-251.

trol of their common frontiers, the Commission proposes that the Security Council recommend to the governments concerned that they enter into new conventions along the lines of the Greco-Bulgarian Convention of 1931, taking into account the needs of the present situation.

C. For the purpose of restoring normal conditions along the frontiers between Greece on the one hand and Albania, Bulgaria and Yugoslavia on the other, and thereby assisting in the establishment of good neighbourly relations, the Commission recommends the establishment of a body with the following composition and functions:

a) The body should be established by the Security Council in the form of either a small Commission or a single Commissioner. If the body is a small Commission it should be composed of representatives of Governments. If the body is to consist of a Commissioner he and his staff should be nationals of States who are neither permanent members of the Security Council nor have any direct connection or interest in the affairs of the four countries concerned.

b) The Commission or Commissioner should have the staff necessary to perform their functions including persons able to act as border observers and to report on the observance of the frontier conventions referred to in recommendation (B), the state of the frontier area, and cognate matters.

c) The Commission or Commissioner should have the right to perform their functions on both sides of the border and the Commission or Commissioner should have the right to direct access to the four Governments of Albania, Bulgaria, Yugoslavia and Greece. The functions and duties of the Commission or the Commissioner should be:

(i) To investigate any frontier violations that occur;

(ii) To use its good offices for the settlement, by the means mentioned in Article 33 of the Charter, of:

a. Controversies arising from frontier violations;

b. Controversies directly connected with the application of the Frontier Conventions envisaged in (B);

c. Complaints regarding conditions on the border which may be brought by one Government against another.

(iii) To use its good offices to assist the Governments concerned in the negotiation and conclusion of the frontier conventions envisaged in recommendation (B).

(iv) To study and make recommendations to the governments concerned with respect to such additional bilateral agreements between them for the pacific settlement of disputes relating to frontier incidents or conditions on the frontier, as the Commission considers desirable.

(v) To assist in the implementation of Recommendation D below; to receive reports from the four governments with respect to persons who have fled from any one of such countries to any of the others; to maintain a register for their confidential use of all such persons and to assist in the repatriation of those who wish to return to their homes, and in connection with these functions to act in concert with the appropriate agency of the United Nations.

(vi) To report to the Security Council every three months, or whenever they think fit.

It is recommended that this body should be established for a period of at least two years, before the expiry of which the necessity for its continued existence should be reviewed by the Security Council.

D. The Commission recognises that owing the deep-rooted causes of the present disturbances and to the nature of the frontiers it is physically impossible to control the passage of refugees across the border. As the presence of these refugees in any of the four countries is a disturbing factor each Government should assume the obligation to remove them as far from which they came as it is physically and practically possible.

These refugees should be placed in camps or otherwise segregated. The governments concerned should undertake to ensure that they should not be permitted to indulge in any political or military activity.

The Commission would also strongly recommend that if it is practicable the camps containing the refugees should be placed under the supervision of some international body authorised by the United Nations to undertake the task.

In order to ensure that only genuine refugees return, their return to their country of origin shall not take place except after (1) arrangement with the government of such country and (2) notification to the Commission or Commissioner or to the international United Nations body if such is established. The Commission would here point out the desirability of the governments concerned encouraging the return of refugees to their homes.

E. The Commission proposes that the Security Council recommend to the governments concerned that they study the practicability of concluding agreements for the voluntary transfer of minorities. In the meantime minorities in any of the countries concerned desiring to emigrate should be given all facilities to do so by the government of the State in which they at present reside. The arrangements of any such transfers could be supervised by the Commission or Commissioner who would act as a registration authority for any person desiring to emigrate.

◇◇◇◇◇◇

126. ESTABLISHING THE UNITED NATIONS SPECIAL COMMITTEE ON THE BALKANS (UNSCOB)

Resolution Adopted by the General Assembly, October 21, 1947 [1]

[The efforts of the Security Council to establish a special committee on the Balkans, which had been recommended by the Investigation Commission, were vetoed by the Soviet Union, first on July 12, 1947, and twice thereafter. Greek frontier incidents continued without interruption, and it was plain to see that, if they were to be stopped by the United Nations, it would have to be accomplished through some other organ than the Security Council. Therefore, on October 21, 1947, the United States resorted to the General Assembly and introduced the following resolution which called upon Albania, Bulgaria, and Yugoslavia to stop aiding the Greek guerrillas. The resolution also pro-

[1] The United States and the United Nations: Report by the President to the Congress for the Year 1947, Department of State publication 3024, International Organization and Conference Series III, 1, pp. 155-157.

vided for the establishment of a United Nations Special Committee on the Balkans (UNSCOB) and set forth its terms of reference.]

1. WHEREAS

The peoples of the United Nations have expressed in the Charter of the United Nations their determination to practise tolerance and to live together in peace with one another as good neighbours and to unite their strength to maintain international peace and security; and to that end the Members of the United Nations have obligated themselves to carry out the purposes and principles of the Charter,

2. The General Assembly of the United Nations,

HAVING CONSIDERED the record of the Security Council proceedings in connection with the complaint of the Greek Government of 3 December 1946, including the report submitted by the Commission of Investigation established by the Security Council resolution of 19 December 1946 and information supplied by the Subsidiary Group of the Commission of Investigation subsequent to the report of the Commission;

3. TAKING ACCOUNT of the report of the Commission of Investigation which found by a majority vote that Albania, Bulgaria and Yugoslavia had given assistance and support to the guerrillas fighting against the Greek Government;

4. *Calls upon* Albania, Bulgaria and Yugoslavia to do nothing which could furnish aid and assistance to the said guerrillas;

5. *Calls upon* Albania, Bulgaria and Yugoslavia on the one hand and Greece on the other to co-operate in the settlement of their disputes by peaceful means, and to that end recommends:

(1) That they establish normal diplomatic and good neighbourly relations among themselves as soon as possible;

(2) That they establish frontier conventions providing for effective machinery for the regulation and control of their common frontiers and for the pacific settlement of frontier incidents and disputes;

(3) That they co-operate in the settlement of the problems arising out of the presence of refugees in the four States concerned through voluntary repatriation wherever possible and that they take effective measures to prevent the participation of such refugees in political or military activity;

(4) That they study the practicability of concluding agreements for the voluntary transfer of minorities.

6. *Establishes* a Special Committee:

(1) To observe the compliance by the four Governments concerned with the foregoing recommendations;

(2) To be available to assist the four Governments concerned in the implementation of such recommendations;

7. *Recommends* that the four Governments concerned co-operate with the Special Committee in enabling it to carry out these obligations;

8. *Authorizes* the Special Committee, if in its opinion further consideration of the subject matter of this resolution by the General Assembly prior to its next regular session is necessary for the maintenance of international peace and security, to recommend to the Members of the United Nations that a special session of the General Assembly be convoked as a matter of urgency;

9. *Decides* that the Special Committee

Shall consist of representatives of Australia, Brazil, China, France, Mexico, the Netherlands, Pakistan, the United Kingdom and the United States of America, seats being held open for Poland and the Union of Soviet Socialist Republics;

10. *Shall have* its principal headquarters in Salonika and with the co-operation of the four Governments concerned shall perform its functions in such places and in the territories of the four States concerned as it may deem appropriate;

11. *Shall render* a report to the next regular session of the General Assembly and to any prior special session which might be called to consider the subject matter of this resolution, and shall render such interim reports as it may deem appropriate to the Secretary-General for transmission to the Members of the Organization; in any reports to the General Assembly the Special Committee may make such recommendations to the General Assembly as it deems fit;

12. *Shall determine* its own procedure, and may establish such sub-committees as it deems necessary;

13. *Shall commence* its work within thirty days after the final decision of the General Assembly on this resolution, and shall remain in existence pending a new decision of the General Assembly;

14. The General Assembly,

Requests the Secretary-General to assign to the Special Committee staff adequate to enable it to perform its duties, and to enter into a standing arrangement with each of the four Governments concerned to assure the Special Committee, so far as it may find it necessary to exercise its functions with their territories, of full freedom of movement and all necessary facilities for the performance of its functions.

◇◇◇◇◇◇

127. CESSATION OF ACTIVITIES OF GREEK GUERRILLAS [1]

Statement by Secretary Acheson, October 17, 1949

[United Nations efforts at bringing about a settlement of the Greek civil war went on continually throughout 1948 and 1949. A decisive development occurred when Marshal Tito broke with the Soviet bloc and subsequently terminated Yugoslav aid to the Greek guerrillas. In October 1949, Secretary Acheson reported that organized Greek guerrilla activities had practically ceased. He expressed scepticism that the guerrilla cease-fire order had been given to save Greece from destruction and indicated that it was due to the desire of the guerrillas to save their own skins.]

As a result of the Greek Army offensives in October in the Grammos-Vitsi areas, Greek Government forces now for the first time since the war command the northern borders of Greece. Guerrilla forces operating within Greece amount to approximately two thousand, scattered in small groups over the entire country. In most cases, these groups are mainly concerned with self-

[1] Department of State Bulletin of October 31, 1949, p. 658.

protection and raiding for food and are continually being pursued and harassed. There has been a noticeable trend of the leaders and some of the members of these groups to work their way toward Albania.

Most of the guerrillas who fled from Greece as the result of the Grammos-Vitsi campaigns entered Albania. There are approximately eight thousand five hundred guerrillas located in Albania. There is estimated to be about three thousand guerrillas in Bulgaria. Some of these guerrillas in Bulgaria entered the country as the result of recent operations in northeastern Greece, but the majority of them have been in Bulgaria over a period of time as a part of guerrilla operations and hospitalization which has taken place in Bulgaria. There is no objective information available to the Department giving evidence that the guerrillas in either Albania or Bulgaria have been disarmed or interned.

According to the United Nations Special Committee, the Yugoslav Government has closed the Greek borders, precluding the entry of fleeing guerrillas, and has not recently lent support to these forces. In general, the closed border appears to have been effective, except in a few cases in which some guerrilla forces have entered Yugoslavia where the terrain is very rugged and sparsely manned by the Yugoslavs. It is not believed that there is a large number of guerrillas now remaining in Yugoslavia.

Unconfirmed reports have indicated that guerillas located in Albania are being moved by sea or air from Albania to Bulgaria, Rumania, and possibly other satellite countries. The Department is in possession of no information indicating the purpose of this reported redisposition.

The "cease fire" guerrilla announcement is, in any case, a practical recognition of the state of affairs existing at this time. The stated purpose of the announcement, in order to "save Greece from destruction," must be viewed with some scepticism in as much as during guerrilla operations in force in Greece, they engaged to the fullest extent possible in the destruction of the Greek economy and resorted to every crime against humanity, including murder, arson, kidnapping, wholesale slaughter, abrogation of all liberties, and terrorizing whole areas. Now that these guerrillas who are located in Greece are forced to devote their activities to self-preservation and the majority of the guerrilla forces, because they are located outside of Greece, can no longer indulge in bringing about ruin and disaster, it is natural that they would attempt to make political salvage by attributing their defeat to the tardily announced desire "to save Greece from destruction."

128. DISCUSSION OF THE GREEK CASE IN THE GENERAL ASSEMBLY

Statement by Benjamin V. Cohen, U.S. Alternate Representative, November 17, 1949 [1]

[When the General Assembly met in the fall of 1949, the Greek case still remained on the agenda. Even though the guerrilla activities had diminished considerably, there remained a potential danger which continued to menace the security of Greece and the stability of its government. The United States delegate noted this condition in his statement to the General Assembly on November 17, 1949. After tracing the background of the situation, he said that the United States would support the continuing of the Special Committee for another year, and he urged that the neighbors of Greece cooperate in the return of Greek children to their homes as soon as possible.]

* * *

The difficulties in Greece go back to the struggle in the winter of 1944-45 between the Liberation Government of Greece and EAM, the Greek Communist popular-front organization created during the Axis occupation. EAM viciously attacked the Liberation Government as being collaborationist, monarcho-Fascist, undemocratic, and sought by force to overthrow it. Supporters of the government charged the Communists as being more pro-Soviet than Greek and recalled that the Communist leaders had shown little interest in the defense of Greek freedom until the Soviet Union was attacked. The struggle led to many excesses and much bitterness. The bitterness was exacerbated by the widespread feeling in Greece, which subsequent events clearly confirmed, that the Communists were more concerned to seize power on behalf of the Soviet-dominated world Communist movement than to restore it to the Greek people. That does not, however, mean that all those working with the EAM were so motivated. There were patriotic Greeks who had cooperated with EAM during the Axis occupation because of the active part the Communists had taken in the resistance movement.

The hostilities of 1944-45 were terminated shortly after the appointment of the greatly respected Archbishop Damaskinos as regent by an armistice agreement, known as the Varkiza agreement, concluded on February 12, 1945, between the Greek Government and EAM. The agreement provided for a broad amnesty, the disarmament of the regular Communist forces, a plebiscite on the monarchy, and an election under international supervision. Following the armistice, there were complaints from the start by both sides concerning truce violations. The Communists demanded an immediate election. There was a revival of bitter attacks upon the Government accompanied by the recurrence of guerrilla operations.

In the winter of 1945-46 when conditions were still tense within Greece, the Soviet Union sought through the Security Council to have the remaining

[1] Released to the press by the U.S. delegation to the General Assembly on November 17, 1949. Department of State Bulletin of November 28, 1949, pp. 813-816.

British military forces withdrawn from Greece. The Government of Greece appeared before the Council and stated that the British troops were in Greece at its request and that their presence there was necessary to the maintenance of public order and to prevent the renewal of civil war. The Security Council refused to request the withdrawal of the British forces.

PARLIAMENTARY ELECTIONS

During the winter of 1945-46, the Greek Government began preparations for parliamentary elections and asked that the four great powers observe these elections as contemplated by the Yalta and Varkiza agreement. Britain, France, and the United States responded to this request, but the Soviet Union refused on the ground that international supervision of the election would constitute an interference in the internal affairs of Greece. Thereupon, the Greek Communists also shifted their line and opposed the holding of the election. Some of the center parties opposed the holding of the election, fearing that the bitter feeling in the country against the Communists would react in favor of the more conservative parties. But the Regent, Archbishop Damaskinos, and the Government insisted that a free election was necessary for the maintenance of the authority of the Government, and, despite the Communist boycott, the election was held on March 31, 1946.

The election of 1946 was held under the close scrutiny of more than 1,000 American, British, and French observers. The Allied Mission to observe the Greek election estimated that the proportion of qualified voters who abstained for "party reasons" was about 15 per cent. The Allied Mission in its report concluded:

That notwithstanding the present political emotions in Greece, conditions were such as to warrant the holding of elections, that the election proceedings were on the whole free and fair, and that the general outcome represents a true and valid verdict of the Greek people.

Though the election of 1946, like most elections, may not have been a perfect register of the popular will or of the comparative strength of different parties, it did afford a much freer expression of the popular will than was afforded in any of the postwar elections in other countries of southeastern Europe. The election did unquestionably give convincing proof that the Communist popular-front groups did not enjoy the confidence of the Greek people and in no way represented the Greek people as a whole.

The Communists were unwilling to accept the election or to confine their struggle with their political opponents to peaceful political opposition. Guerrilla warfare did not cease but increased. The interest of the Cominform countries in the guerrilla activities was scarcely concealed. In the summer of 1946, the Ukraine brought charges in the Security Council that Greek policy was disturbing the peace in the Balkans. The Security Council, apparently regarding this as a case of the pot calling the kettle black, refused to intervene.

It soon became evident that the guerrilla activities were being supported and aided by the northern neighbors of Greece, not sporadically or casually, but actively and deliberately in accordance with an internationally concerted Communist plan. It was then, in December 1946, that the Greek Government drew the attention of the Security Council to the danger to the peace arising from the assistance being given by Greece's northern neighbors to the Greek guerrillas.

APPEAL FOR AMERICAN AID

It was in March 1947, that the Greek Government first appealed to the United States Government for material aid in maintaining her political independence and territorial integrity. American assistance from the start not only was conditioned on the continuing consent of the Greek Government, but was also expressly made subject to termination whenever the Security Council or General Assembly should find that action taken or assistance furnished by the United Nations made the continuance of American assistance unnecessary or undesirable. And what is more, we expressly waived our right of veto should the question of American assistance come before the Security Council.

American aid was extended to Greece, as American lend-lease aid was extended to other Allies during the war, to protect our common interest in the preservation of freedom in the world. It will be recalled that the United States extended more than 50 billion dollars' worth in lend-lease to our Allies during the war, and more than 11 billion of that amount went to the Soviet Union. That aid safeguarded and did not compromise the independence of the Soviet Union or of any of the other Allies. American aid has not been used and will not be used to compromise the independence of Greece.

American aid to Greece has not been given to support any particular party or faction. Our aid has been given to safeguard the independence of Greece from the efforts of the Cominform to impose the Communist system by force upon the people of Greece. This is its sole purpose. American aid to Greece does not threaten the legitimate interests in Greece of any foreign power, nor does it in any way threaten the security of Greece's northern neighbors or of any other power. No American combat troops have ever been sent to Greece, and there is not a single American military, naval, or air base in the country.

The investigations of the Security Council confirmed the facts regarding the activities of the Cominform countries in support of the Greek guerrillas, but the Council was unable to act because of the Soviet veto. It was then in the fall of 1947 that the United States first brought the Greek case to the attention of the General Assembly.

GENERAL ASSEMBLY ACTION

Both in 1947 and 1948, the General Assembly found that the aid given to the Greek guerrillas by the northern neighbors of Greece was a threat to the peace and a violation of the Charter. In 1947, the General Assembly created the Special Committee on the Balkans for purposes of observation and conciliation and in 1948, continued the committee with special stress upon its conciliatory functions. This year the Political Committee recommends to the Assembly that the Assembly again condemn the aid being given to the Greek guerrillas in violation of the Charter, particularly by Albania and Bulgaria, and ask that such aid be terminated. Meanwhile it recommends that the Assembly call upon all states to cease all arms shipments to Albania and Bulgaria and to take into account in their relations with such states the extent to which they abide by the recommendations of the Assembly. The Political Committee also recommends that the Assembly continue the Special Committee for another year.

The Political Committee further recommends that the Assembly call upon the northern neighbors of Greece harboring Greek nationals as a result of guerrillas' operations against Greece to facilitate the peaceful repatriation of all such individuals who wish to return and live in accordance with the law of the land. The recommendation expressly refers to peaceful repatriation and does not suggest that any individual be required to return who does not wish to return. The Political Committee also recommends that the Assembly authorize the Secretary-General to arrange through the Special Committee or other appropriate United Nations or international agencies the extension of any feasible assistance to the governments concerned in making and carrying out arrangements for the repatriation to Greece or resettlement elsewhere of Greek guerrillas and other Greek nationals who have been involved in the guerrilla warfare. It is our hope now that the struggle between the guerrillas and the Greek Government has abated and that the Special Committee or the Red Cross or some other international group may, with the cooperation of Greece and her northern neighbors, arrange for the repatriation of Greece or their resettlement elsewhere of the Greek nationals who have been involved in the guerrilla warfare. . . .

ATTITUDE OF COMINFORM STATES

The Cominform states have talked loud and long in the committee about a so-called terror in Greece. One cannot but express the hope that these states may in their own countries move toward those ideals of tolerance for dissident groups that they have preached with such eloquence to the Greeks. The Greek Government has had a good reason, as I have shown, to suspect that the Cominform's interest in Greece has not always been an interest in Greek freedom of Greek tolerance. The Greeks have had good reason to suspect the Cominform bearing gifts.

*   *   *

There is no iron curtain between the Greek stage and world opinion. The members of this Assembly are, therefore, informed as to the true state of affairs inside Greece from their own diplomatic representatives and their own nationals, official or otherwise, who are free to travel in Greece where they choose. The members of this Assembly are thus aware that if conditions in Greece are somewhat less than perfect, this fact is primarily the legacy of a cruel occupation and the fruit of the bitter guerrilla warfare fomented and supported by Greece's Cominform neighbors.

There have been no executions in Greece since the announcement of the leniency legislation on September 30. There have been, however, in the meantime a number of reports of executions and death sentences in the Cominform countries. The violent remarks of the delegations of the Cominform countries seem almost calculated to goad the Greek government to follow the Cominform's own pattern of terror. We cannot accept the Cominform's pleas for the blanket repeal of death sentences in Greece, while Greek independence is still threatened, as bona fide pleas for mercy and greater tolerance.

The effect of the remarks of the Cominform delegations in the Political

Committee, whatever their intention, was not to further peace in Greece or peace between Greece and her northern neighbors. The effect of their remarks was to incite and revive efforts to overthrow the Greek Government, in line with past Cominform policy. Their pleas seemed designed to stir up passions and even to incite to further violence the extremists on both sides of the languishing hostilities in Greece.

*   *   *

Whatever may be the shortcomings of the Greek Government, we cannot support the proposals made by the Soviet Union in the Political Committee which are based on the assumption which in our judgment is contrary to the facts that external threats to Greek independence arise from the repressive measures of the Greek Government. It is our view that the stringent security measures in Greece, concerning which the Soviet Union complains, are a direct result of the external threats to Greek independence. We believe that those measures will and certainly should be relaxed and eliminated when the external threats to Greek independence are removed.

Some of the Cominform delegations have also insisted that the difficulties between Greece and her northern neighbors are due to aggressive territorial designs of Greece. Such a suggestion is in our judgment without the slightest basis in fact. The observations conducted by the Special Committee over the last 2 years reveal that, while there have been some minor and unavoidable frontier violations on the part of Greece in repulsing guerrilla fighting along the frontier, there is no evidence whatsoever of aggressive designs by Greece upon the territory of her northern neighbors. Following the war, Greece did claim the right to submit to the Council of Foreign Ministers certain historic claims. But Greece has repeatedly declared that she does not seek any change in her frontiers except by peaceful means. Greece has made it clear to the Conciliation Committee that she will respect her Charter obligations and that she will unqualifiedly accept the Conciliation Committee's suggestion that she and her northern neighbors agree not to use force or the threat of force to change existing boundaries.

*   *   *

DANGER IN BALKANS REDUCED

Thanks, however, to the courage of the Greeks and to the support given to Greece by states which do respect the Charter and the recommendations of the General Assembly, the danger to peace in the Balkans has been substantially reduced. It has even been announced that the guerrilla forces have temporarily grounded their arms. That does not mean that vigilance on the part of the United Nations is not necessary to see that they do not again take up their arms. It is, however, happily becoming apparent that the Charter and the recommendations of the General Assembly cannot be treated as if they were mere scraps of paper.

The Special Committee on the Balkans has also reported that one of Greece's northern neighbors which in the past has contributed substantial aid to the Greek guerrillas has virtually stopped that aid. That action is significant not only for its bearing on the Greek case, but it is, I think, also significant of a growing appreciation among states that those who wish the protection of the United Nations must respect the purposes and principles set forth in the Charter and the considered opinions of the Assembly regarding the fulfillment of those purposes and principles.

* * *

GREEK CHILDREN

Before closing, I should like to add only a few words regarding the resolution on the Greek children. . . . The Political Committee has unanimously recommended that the Assembly again urge all states harboring Greek children to cooperate with the International Red Cross to arrange for the early return of these children to their homes. It is the hope of the United States delegation that the Assembly without dissent will make this appeal on behalf of the Greek children and that all states concerned will act promptly to carry out this humanitarian task.

◇◇◇◇◇◇

129. THREATS TO THE POLITICAL INDEPENDENCE AND TERRITORIAL INTEGRITY OF GREECE

Resolution of the General Assembly, November 19, 1949 [1]

[In its resolution of November 19, 1949, the General Assembly followed the recommendations put forth by the United States and certain other countries, with respect to the Greek situation, and authorized the continuation of the Special Committee on the Balkans. The resolution further urged the reestablishment of normal relations between Greece and her neighbors; and it called upon countries bordering Greece to cooperate with the International Red Cross to expedite the return of the Greek children held in involuntary captivity abroad.]

A

The GENERAL ASSEMBLY,

HAVING CONSIDERED the reports of the United Nations Special Committee on the Balkans established by General Assembly resolution 109 (II) and continued by General Assembly resolution 193 (III), including the additional facts and the recommendations in its supplementary report of 10 September 1949, and in particular its unanimous conclusions that:

(i) Albania and Bulgaria have continued to give moral and material assistance to the Greek guerrilla movement, Albania being the principal source of material assistance;

(ii) There has been an increase in the support afforded to the guerrillas from certain States not bordering upon Greece, particularly Romania,

HAVING NOTED the report of the Conciliation Committee established by the

1 UN Doc. A/1117. Department of State Bulletin of December 5, 1949, pp. 852a-853a.

First Committee of the General Assembly in its resolution of 29 September 1949;

1. *Considers* that the active assistance given to the Greek guerrillas by Albania in particular, by Bulgaria and by certain other States, including Romania, in disregard of the Assembly's recommendations, is contrary to the purpose and principles of the United Nations Charter and endangers peace in the Balkans;

2. *Considers* that further foreign assistance to the Greek guerrillas resulting in the launching of new armed action against Greece from adjacent territory would seriously increase the gravity of the danger to the peace and would justify the Special Committee in recommending, pursuant to paragraph 8 of resolution 109 (II), the convocation, as a matter of urgency, of a special session of the General Assembly in order to give consideration to further steps necessary for the removal of this danger to the peace;

3. *Calls upon* Albania, Bulgaria and the other States concerned to cease forthwith rendering any assistance or support to the guerrillas in fighting against Greece, including the use of their territories as a base for the preparation or launching of armed actions;

4. *Recommends* to all Members of the United Nations and to all other States:

(a) To refrain from any action designed to assist directly or through any other Government any armed group fighting against Greece;

(b) To refrain from the direct or indirect provision of arms or other materials of war to Albania and Bulgaria until the Special Committee or another competent United Nations organ has determined that the unlawful assistance of these States to the Greek guerrillas has ceased;

(c) To take into account, in their relations with Albania and Bulgaria, the extent to which those two countries henceforth abide by the recommendations of the General Assembly in their relations with Greece;

5. *Again calls upon* Albania, Bulgaria and Yugoslavia to co-operate with Greece in the settlement of their differences by peaceful means in accordance with the provisions of Article 2, paragraph 3 of the Charter, and to that end recommends:

(a) That, in view of the existence of diplomatic relations between the Governments of Greece and Yugoslavia, further efforts be made by those Governments through diplomatic channels to resolve the differences between them;

(b) That Albania and Bulgaria on the one hand, and Greece on the other, establish normal diplomatic and good neighbourly relations, and endeavour through diplomatic channels to resolve differences;

(c) That they renew previously operative conventions or conclude new ones providing effective machinery for the regulation and control of their common frontiers and for the peaceful adjustment of frontier incidents;

6. *Calls upon* Albania, Bulgaria and Yugoslavia to co-operate with the Special Committee in enabling it to carry out its functions, in particular the functions in accordance with paragraph 10 (c) of resolution 193 (III) and paragraphs 10, 11, and 13 of the present resolution, and upon Greece to continue to co-operate towards the same end;

7. *Approves* the reports of the Special Committee and continues it in being in accordance with all the terms of reference contained in the present resolution and in General Assembly resolutions 109 (II) and 193 (III), which are hereby continued in effect;

8. *Again instructs* the Special Committee to continue to be available to assist the four Governments concerned in the implementation of the Assembly's resolutions, in particular to promote the restoration of normal relations between Greece and her northern neighbours and the maintenance of international peace and security in the Balkans, and for this purpose continues the authorization to the Special Committee in its discretion, to appoint and utilize the services and good offices of one or more persons whether or not members of the Special Committee;

9. *Notes* the report of the Special Committee, which states that the Governments of Albania, Bulgaria and Yugoslavia have publicly announced that Greek guerrillas who have entered their respective territories have been disarmed and interned, and calls upon all States harbouring Greek guerrillas to co-operate with the Special Committee or other appropriate international agency for verification of the disarming and disposition of the Greek guerrillas who have entered their respective territories;

10. *Calls upon* all States harbouring Greek nationals as a result of the Greek guerrillas' operations against Greece to facilitate the peaceful repatriation to Greece of all such individuals who desire to return and live in accordance with the law of the land;

11. *Authorizes* the Secretary-General to arrange, through the Special Committee or other appropriate United Nations or international agency, the extension of any feasible assistance to the Governments concerned in making and carrying out arrangements for the repatriation to Greece or resettlement elsewhere of Greek guerrillas and other Greek nationals who have been involved in the guerrilla warfare.

B

The GENERAL ASSEMBLY,

NOTING the report submitted by the International Committee of the Red Cross and the League of Red Cross Societies on the question of the repatriation of Greek children (A/1014), and expressing warm appreciation of the efforts made by the two international Red Cross organizations to facilitate the implementation of General Assembly resolution 193 (III) C,

NOTING that the Greek children have not as yet been returned to their homes in accordance with the resolution of the General Assembly, and recognizing the necessity of further efforts for the full implementation of this resolution.

1. *Instructs* the Secretary-General to request the International Committee of the Red Cross and the League of Red Cross Societies to continue their efforts in this humanitarian cause to lend them all appropriate assistance in carrying out their task;

2. *Urges* all the Members of the United Nations and other States harbouring the Greek children to make all necessary arrangements, in consultation and co-operation with the international Red Cross organizations, for the early

return to their homes of the children in accordance with the aforementioned resolution;

3. *Invites* the international Red Cross organizations to report to the Secretary-General for the information of the Members of the United Nations, on the progress being made in the implementation of the present resolution.

◇◇◇◇◇◇

130. THREATS TO THE POLITICAL INDEPENDENCE AND TERRITORIAL INTEGRITY OF GREECE

Resolutions adopted by the General Assembly on 1 December 1950 [1]

[In spite of resolutions adopted by the General Assembly, Bulgaria and Albania continued to hold captured Greek soldiers prisoners and refused to repatriate thousands of Greek children whom they were holding captive. As a consequence, the Fifth General Assembly kept in existence the United Nations Special Committee on the Balkans, and made several recommendations with the purpose of reëstablishing normal relations between Greece and her neighbors.]

A.

The General Assembly,

Having considered the unanimous conclusions of the United Nations Special Committee on the Balkans concerning those members of the Greek armed forces who were captured by the Greek guerrillas and taken into countries north of Greece,

Having noted that, with the sole exception of Yugoslavia, the other States concerned are still detaining these members of the Greek armed forces without justification under commonly accepted international practice,

1. *Recommends* the repatriation of all those among them who express the wish to be repatriated;

2. *Calls upon* the States concerned to take the necessary measures for the speedy implementation of the present resolution;

3. *Instructs* the Secretary-General to request the International Committee of the Red Cross and the League of Red Cross Societies to ensure liaison with the national Red Cross organizations of the States concerned, with a view to implementing the present resolution.

B.

The General Assembly,

Having considered the report of the United Nations Special Committee on the Balkans and having noted that, although a certain improvement has taken place in the situation on the northern frontiers of Greece, there nevertheless remains a threat to the political independence and territorial integrity of Greece,

1. *Approves* the report of the United Nations Special Committee on the Balkans;

[1] Fifth Session, General A 1584, 2 December 1950.

2. *Continues* the Special Committee in being until the sixth session of the General Assembly, in accordance with the terms of reference and administrative arrangements contained in General Assembly resolutions 109 (II), 193 (III) and 288 (IV), unless meanwhile the Special Committee recommends to the Interim Committee its own dissolution;

3. *Authorizes* the Interim Committee to act on such recommendation as it thinks proper.

C.

The General Assembly,

Noting with grave concern the reports of the International Committee of the Red Cross and the League of Red Cross Societies and of the Secretary-General, and particularly the statement that "not a single Greek child has yet been returned to his native land and, except for Yugoslavia, no country harbouring Greek children has taken definite action to comply with the resolutions unanimously adopted in two successive years by the General Assembly",

Recognizing that every possible effort should be made to restore the children to their homes, in a humanitarian spirit detached from political or ideological considerations,

Expressing its full appreciation of the efforts made by the International Committee of the Red Cross and the League of Red Cross Societies and by the Secretary-General to implement General Assembly resolutions 193 C (III) and 288 B (IV),

1. *Requests* the Secretary-General and the International Committee of the Red Cross and the League of Red Cross Societies to continue their efforts in accordance with the aforementioned resolutions;

2. *Urges* all States harbouring the Greek children to make all the necessary arrangements, in co-operation with the Secretary-General and the international Red Cross organizations, for the early return of the Greek children to their parents and, whenever necessary, to allow the international Red Cross organizations free access to their territories for this purpose;

3. *Establishes* a Standing Committee, to be composed of the representatives of Peru, the Philippines and Sweden, to act in consultation with the Secretary-General, and to consult with the representatives of the States concerned, with a view to the early repatriation of the children;

4. *Requests* the International Committee of the Red Cross and the League of Red Cross Societies to co-operate with the Standing Committee;

5. *Requests* the Secretary-General to report from time to time to Member States on the progress made in the implementation of the present resolution, and requests the international Red Cross organizations and the Secretary-General to submit reports to the General Assembly at its sixth session.

✧✧✧✧✧✧

INDIA, PAKISTAN

131. NEW DOMINIONS OF INDIA AND PAKISTAN [1]

Telegrams from President Truman Extending Good Wishes,
August 14, 1947

[The announcement made by Prime Minister Attlee on February 20, 1947, that Britain would relinquish her rule over India after 350 years marked a significant turning point in history. British India, formed from scores of states bound together by many different ties, was nevertheless divided into two great cultures and religions. It was therefore logical upon the attainment of independence that the country should become two separate and independent states, namely Hindu India and Moslem Pakistan. On August 14, 1947, the President of the United States extended the greetings and the recognition of this country in separate telegrams sent to each of the two new governments.]

To Lord Louis Mountbatten, Governor General of the Dominion of India

On this memorable occasion, I extend to you, to Prime Minister Jawaharlal Nehru, and to the people of the Dominion of India the sincere best wishes of the Government and the people of the United States of America. We welcome India's new and enhanced status in the world community of sovereign independent nations, assure the new Dominion of our continued friendship and good will, and reaffirm our confidence that India, dedicated to the cause of peace and to the advancement of all peoples, will take its place at the forefront of the nations of the world in the struggle to fashion a world society founded in mutual trust and respect. India faces many grave problems, but its resources are vast, and I am confident that its people and leadership are equal to the tasks ahead. In the years to come the people of this great new nation will find the United States a constant friend. I earnestly hope that our friendship will in the future, as in the past, continue to be expressed in close and fruitful cooperation in international undertakings and in cordiality in our relations one with the other.

HARRY S. TRUMAN
President of the United States of America

To Mohammed Ali Jinnah, Governor General of the Dominion of Pakistan

On this auspicious day which marks the emergence among the family of nations of the new Dominion of Pakistan, I extend on behalf of the American people sincere best wishes to you, and through you, to Prime Minister Liaquat Ali Khan and the people of Pakistan. To you who have labored so steadfastly for this day, and to the other leaders and the people of Pakistan fall profound responsibilities. I wish to assure you that the new Dominion embarks on its course with the firm friendship and good will of the United States of America. The American Government and people anticipate a long history of close and cordial relations with your country. We rejoice with you in the prospect for rapid progress toward the advancement of the welfare of the people of Pakis-

[1] Department of State Bulletin of August 24, 1947, p. 396.

tan, and look forward to the constructive participation of the new Dominion in world affairs for the welfare of all mankind.

HARRY S. TRUMAN
President of the United States of America

132. INDIA-PAKISTAN QUESTION IN THE UNITED NATIONS

Resolution of the Security Council, April 21, 1948 [1]

[When India and Pakistan achieved their independence, some areas, notably Kashmir (Jammu and Kashmir), Nepal and Hyderabad, were not included in the territory of either state. Both India and Pakistan sought to incorporate Kashmir into their respective realms and the dispute could not be settled without outside help. India brought the matter to the attention of the Security Council, which by its resolution of April 21, 1948 promptly established a commission to work out a solution. The resolution called upon the disputing parties to restore peace and order and urged that a plebiscite be held on the question of the accession of Kashmir to India or Pakistan.]

The Security Council,

Having considered the complaints of the Government of India concerning the dispute over the State of Jammu and Kashmir, having heard the representative of India in support of that complaint and the reply and counter complaints of the representative of Pakistan,

Being strongly of opinion that the early restoration of peace and order in Jammu and Kashmir is essential and that India and Pakistan should do their utmost to bring about a cessation of all fighting,

Noting with satisfaction that both India and Pakistan desire that the question of the accession of Jammu and Kashmir to India or Pakistan should be decided through the democratic method of a free and impartial plebiscite,

Considering that the continuation of the dispute is likely to endanger international peace and security;

Reaffirms the Council's Resolution of January 17th,

Resolves that the membership of the Commission established by the Resolution of the Council of January 20th, 1948, shall be increased to five and shall include in addition to the membership mentioned in that Resolution, representative of ———— and ———— and that if the membership of the Commission has not been completed within ten days from the date of the adoption of this Resolution the President of the Council may designate such other Member or Members of the United Nations as are required to complete the membership of five,

Instructs the Commission to proceed at once to the Indian subcontinent

---

[1] UN Doc. S/726, April 22, 1948. Submitted jointly by the Representatives of Belgium, Canada, China, Colombia, the United Kingdom, and the United States. Adopted at the 286th meeting of the Security Council on April 21, 1948. Department of State Bulletin of May 30, 1948, pp. 698-700.

and there place its good offices and mediation at the disposal of the Governments of India and Pakistan with a view to facilitating the taking of the necessary measures, both with respect to the restoration of peace and order and to the holding of a plebiscite by the two Governments, acting in co-operation with one another and with the Commission and further instructs the Commission to keep the Council informed of the action taken under the Resolution, and to this end,

Recommends to the Governments of India and Pakistan the following measures as those which in the opinion of the Council are appropriate to bring about a cessation of the fighting and to create proper conditions for a free and impartial plebiscite to decide whether the State of Jammu and Kashmir is to accede to India or Pakistan.

A. Restoration of Peace and Order

1. The Government of Pakistan should undertake to use its best endeavours:

(*a*) To secure the withdrawal from the State of Jammu and Kashmir of tribesmen and Pakistani nationals not normally resident therein who have entered the State for the purposes of fighting and to prevent any intrusion into the State of such elements and any furnishing of material aid to those fighting in the State.

(*b*) To make known to all concerned that the measures indicated in this and the following paragraphs provide full freedom to all subjects of the State, regardless of creed, caste, or party, to express their views and to vote on the question of the accession of the State, and that therefore they should co-operate in the maintenance of peace and order.

2. The Government of India should:

(*a*) When it is established to the satisfaction of the Commission set up in accordance with the Council's Resolution of 20 January that the tribesmen are withdrawing and that arrangements for the cessation of the fighting have become effective, put into operation in consultation with the Commission a plan for withdrawing their own forces from Jammu and Kashmir and reducing them progressively to the minimum strength required for the support of the civil power in the maintenance of law and order,

(*b*) Make known that the withdrawal is taking place in stages and announce the completion of each stage;

(*c*) When the Indian forces shall have been reduced to the minimum strength mentioned in (*a*) above, arrange in consultation with the Commission for the stationing of the remaining forces to be carried out in accordance with the following principles:

(i) That the presence of troops should not afford any intimidation or appearance of intimidation to the inhabitants of the State,

(ii) That as small a number as possible should be retained in forward areas,

(iii) That any reserve of troops which may be included in the total strength should be located within their present Base area.

3. The Government of India should agree that until such time as the Plebiscite Administration referred to below finds it necessary to exercise the powers of direction and supervision over the State forces and police provided

for in Paragraph 8 they will be held in areas to be agreed upon with the Plebiscite Administrator.

4. After the plan referred to in paragraph 2 (*a*) above has been put into operation, personnel recruited locally in each district should so far as possible be utilized for the reestablishment and maintenance of law and order with due regard to protection of minorities, subject to such additional requirements as may be specified by the Plebiscite Administration referred to in paragraph 7.

5. If these local forces should be found to be inadequate, the Commission, subject to the agreement of both the Government of India and the Government of Pakistan, should arrange for the use of such forces of either Dominion as it deems effective for the purpose of pacification.

B. PLEBISCITE

6. The Government of India should undertake to ensure that the Government of the State invite the major political groups to designate responsible representatives to share equitably and fully in the conduct of the administration at the Ministerial level, while the plebiscite is being prepared and carried out.

7. The Government of India should undertake that there will be established in Jammu and Kashmir a Plebiscite Administration to hold a plebiscite as soon as possible on the question of the accession of the State to India or Pakistan.

8. The Government of India should undertake that there will be delegated by the State to the Plebiscite Administration such powers as the latter considers necessary for holding a fair and impartial plebiscite including, for that purpose only, the direction and šupervision of the State forces and police.

9. The Government of India should at the request of the Plebiscite Administration make available from the Indian forces such assistance as the Plebiscite Administration may require for the performance of its functions.

10. (*a*) The Government of India should agree that a nominee of the Secretary-General of the United Nations will be appointed to be the Plebiscite Administrator.

(*b*) The Plebiscite Administrator, acting as an officer of the State of Jammu and Kashmir, should have authority to nominate his Assistants and other subordinates and to draft regulations governing the Plebiscite. Such nominees should be formally appointed and such draft regulations should be formally promulgated by the State of Jammu and Kashmir.

(*c*) The Government of India should undertake that the Government of Jammu and Kashmir will appoint fully qualified persons nominated by the Plebiscite Administrator to act as special magistrates within the State judicial system to hear cases which in the opinion of the Plebiscite Administrator have a serious bearing on the preparation for and the conduct of a free and impartial plebiscite.

(*d*) The terms of service of the Administrator should form the subject of a separate negotiation between the Secretary-General of the United Nations and the Government of India. The Administrator should fix the terms of service for his Assistants and subordinates.

(*e*) The Administrator should have the right to communicate direct with the Government of the State and with the Commission of the Security Council and, through the Commission with the Security Council, with the Governments of India and Pakistan and with their Representatives with the Commission. It would be his duty to bring to the notice of any or all of the foregoing (as he in his discretion may decide) any circumstances arising which may tend, in his opinion, to interfere with the freedom of the plebiscite.

11. The Government of India should undertake to prevent and to give full support to the Administrator and his staff in preventing any threat, coercion or intimidation, bribery or other undue influence on the voters in the plebiscite, and the Government of India should publicly announce and should cause the Government of the State to announce this undertaking as an international obligation binding on all public authorities and officials in Jammu and Kashmir.

12. The Government of India should themselves and through the Government of the State declare and make known that all subjects of the State of Jammu and Kashmir, regardless of creed, caste or party, will be safe and free in expressing their views and in voting on the question of the accession of the State and that there will be freedom of the Press, speech and assembly and freedom of travel in the State, including freedom of lawful entry and exit.

13. The Government of India should use and should ensure that the Government of the State also use their best endeavours to effect the withdrawal from the State of all Indian nationals other than those who are normally resident therein or who on or since 15 August 1947 have entered it for a lawful purpose.

14. The Government of India should ensure that the Government of the State release all political prisoners and take all possible steps so that:

(*a*) all citizens of the State who have left it on account of disturbances are invited, and are free, to return to their homes and to exercise their rights as such citizens;

(*b*) there is no victimization;

(*c*) minorities in all parts of the State are accorded adequate protection.

15. The Commission of the Security Council should at the end of the plebiscite certify to the Council whether the plebiscite has or has not been really free and impartial.

C. GENERAL PROVISIONS

16. The Governments of India and Pakistan should each be invited to nominate a Representative to be attached to the Commission for such assistance as it may require in the performance of its task.

17. The Commission should establish in Jammu and Kashmir such observers as it may require of any of the proceedings in pursuance of the measures indicated in the foregoing paragraphs.

18. The Security Council Commission should carry out the tasks assigned to it herein.

◇◇◇◇◇◇

133. UN COMMISSION FOR INDIA AND PAKISTAN

Third Interim Report, December 5, 1949 (Excerpts) [1]

[The United Nations Commission charged with investigating the Kashmir dispute made several reports on its work during the year and a half following its creation. The third report, excerpts of which appear below, stated that the dispute could be settled, and it recommended that each of the disputants be urged to observe the cease-fire agreements which they had entered into. The commission also recommended the appointment of a single individual, whose function it would be to bring the disputing parties together and make certain that conditions were established which would be conducive to a fair plebiscite in Kashmir. Any issues that could not be settled between the parties or by plebiscite were to be settled by arbitration.]

VI. Conclusions

277. The Commission has endeavoured in the previous chapters to present an objective and factual report on its activities in the sub-continent from February to September 1949.

278. The roots of the Kashmir dispute are deep; strong undercurrents—political, economic, religious—in both Dominions have acted, and do act, against an easy and prompt solution of this outstanding dispute between India and Pakistan. These currents which at this early stage of national formation are often antagonistic and account to a considerable degree for the misgivings, reluctance and hesitancy, which the Commission felt were often present in the negotiations and which restricted both Governments in the concessions which they might otherwise have been prepared to make to facilitate agreement. The Commission, however, has no doubt that both Governments are keenly conscious of their duties and responsibilities as members of the United Nations, and that both desire a final and peaceful solution of the Kashmir question.

279. In drafting the report the Commission has therefore intentionally avoided comment on its own appreciation of the broad and complex background of the relations between the two countries, significant as the overall relations unquestionably are in the greater understanding of any one issue. It has felt it wise to restrict itself to the specific problems arising out of the implementation of the agreement entered into by India and Pakistan under the Resolutions of 13 August 1948 and 5 January 1949. The Commission must note, however, that the issues of the disposal of Azad Forces, the withdrawal of troops, and the defence and administration of the Northern Area, have made of the Truce an end in itself; the difficulty in disposing of them to the satisfaction of both Governments has been, if they are judged independently of other implications and exclusively as preliminaries to a plebiscite, out of proportion to their real importance.

280. The agreements in the Resolutions represent an advance toward a final settlement. The Commission has all along been reassured by the repre-

[1] United Nations, Security Council, S/1430, 9 December 1949.

sentatives of both Governments that they are willing to meet their obligations. As a consequence of that advance the primary and immediate objective of the Security Council was fulfilled with the cessation of hostilities on 1 January 1949 and in the Karachi Agreement of July when the cease-fire line was demarcated. That it is not the intention of either Government to resort to the use of force is proven by their efforts to observe the cease-fire and their mutual co-operation in correcting and minimizing such minor incidents as did occur during the months before a line had been demarcated on the ground.

281. The function of investigating the facts with which the Commission was invested by the Security Council has also been completed. The protracted negotiations of the past have provided thorough knowledge of the facts of the case. This is a positive achievement. The main issues which have prevented the Governments of India and Pakistan from progressing more rapidly toward a settlement of their dispute over Kashmir, and the conditions which they believe should regulate the putting into effect of their commitments, are now in sharp focus. The Commission trusts that United Nations action in the future should prove more effective with the foundation which this investigation provides.

282. The Commission employed a variety of methods in its efforts to bring about agreement of the two parties to the implementation of their undertakings. During the past months it has conducted separate negotiations with representatives of the two Governments, it has sponsored joint talks, and has submitted to them the Commission's own proposals based on frequent consultations, and lastly, suggested arbitration of their differences with respect to the Truce.

283. The period of investigation has been completed. Within the framework of its terms of reference, following in its endeavours the provisions contained in its Resolutions of 13 August 1948 and 5 January 1949, the Commission feels that the possibilities of mediation open to it have been exhausted. Over a prolonged period, in a changing and dynamic situation and restricted by a long-standing related clarification which proved to be a real impediment to reaching agreement, the framework of the resolution of 13 August has become inadequate in the light of the factual conditions in the State. The Commission has been unable, therefore, to mediate much beyond what is today a rather outmoded pattern. The State of Jammu and Kashmir has not been demilitarized, as was envisaged in Part II of the Resolution of 13 August, and until this is achieved the conditions necessary to the holding of a plebiscite cannot begin to be established. As has been seen from those parts of the report entitled Withdrawal of Forces and the Azad Kashmir Forces, the Commission believes that the problem of demilitarization must be treated as a whole, and that the distinctions relative to demilitarization which exist in the division of the problem into Truce and Plebiscite periods as visualized in the original plan of demilitarization has proved one of the most difficult obstacles in achieving agreement on the problem. It is evident that the presence of large numbers of troops in the State is not conducive to the creation of a peaceful atmosphere. The demilitarization of the State is essential to permit the holding of a free and unfettered plebiscite.

284. It is imperative that a settlement of the Kashmir issue be reached and the Commission believes that it can be reached. To this end, conditions should be established at an early date which will make possible the holding of

a plebiscite whereby the wishes of the people of the State regarding the future of the State may be freely ascertained.

285. The Commission doubts whether a five-member body is the most flexible and desirable instrument to continue in the task. In the Commission's view, a single person can now more effectively conduct the negotiations which, to be successful, must be carried out in active and constant consultation with the two parties. The designation of a single person with broad authority and undivided responsibility offers a more practical means of finding the balance and compromise necessary to advance the settlement of the dispute.

286. Finally, the Commission feels that, since the Government of Pakistan accepted the suggestion that the issues relating to the Truce be settled by arbitration, and that the Government of India has stated that it does not object to the principle of arbitration as provided for in the Charter, further consideration should be given to the use of this procedure.

*   *   *

VII. RECOMMENDATIONS

1. That the Security Council should ask the two Governments to take all necessary precautions to secure that their agreements regarding the cease-fire be faithfully observed; also that the two Governments be enjoined to abstain from any measure liable to augment tension in the State of Jammu and Kashmir pending the final settlement of the future of the State.

2. That the Security Council designate as its representative a single individual whose terms of reference will be defined after the consultations envisaged in point 3, below, and who would proceed to the Sub-continent with broad authority from the Council to endeavour to bring the two Governments together on all unresolved issues; the representative designated to take into account the objectives pursued by the resolution of the Commission, already agreed to by both Governments, for the establishment of conditions conducive to the holding of a plebiscite in the State of Jammu and Kashmir whereby the will of the people as to the future of the State may be freely and impartially ascertained.

3. That the Security Council should consult with representatives of the two Governments in order to arrive at terms of reference for its representative —including consultation regarding the scope of his authority to settle eventually by arbitration, those issues involved in the demilitarization of the State of Jammu and Kashmir as may remain outstanding which impede the creation of conditions for the holding of the plebiscite.

INDONESIA [1]

134. SELECTED RESOLUTIONS OF THE SECURITY COUNCIL ON THE INDONESIAN CASE DURING THE YEAR 1947

(a) Cease Fire Order, August 1, 1947 [2]

[When the Japanese drove the Western powers out of their holdings in the Far East during World War II, they swept the Dutch out of the East Indies. On their return after the Japanese defeat, the Dutch found a strong independence movement had developed in the Islands. On March 25, 1947, the Netherlands government signed the so-called Linggadjati Agreement in which the Dutch contracted to have the Allied troops withdrawn from the Republic of Indonesia by January 1, 1949. But a dispute arose over the application of the Agreement, and on July 31, 1947, as a result of hostilities in Indonesia, the Security Council found it necessary to begin the consideration of the Indonesian case. On the next day the Council adopted a cease-fire order, and on August 27, it established a Good Offices Committee for Indonesia.]

The Security Council
NOTING with concern the hostilities in progress between the armed forces of the Netherlands and the Republic of Indonesia,
Calls upon the parties
(a) to cease hostilities forthwith, and
(b) to settle their disputes by arbitration or by other peaceful means and keep the Security Council informed about the progress of the settlement.

(b) Resolution on Good Offices Committee for Indonesia, August 25, 1947 [3]

The Security Council
Resolves to tender its good offices to the parties in order to assist in the pacific settlement of their dispute in accordance with paragraph (b) of the

[1] For more complete documentation of the Indonesian Question, see Work of the United Nations Good Offices Committee in Indonesia, Department of State publication 3108, International Organization and Conference Series III, 4; Department of State Bulletin of March 14, 1948, pp. 323-336.

[2] The United States and the United Nations: Report by the President to the Congress for the year 1947, Department of State publication 3024, International Organization and Conference Series III, 1, pp. 242-245. The Linggadjati agreement of November 1946 provided for the de facto recognition of the authority of the Republic in Java, Madura, and Sumatra; the establishment by January 1, 1949, of a sovereign, democratic, federal United States of Indonesia (U. S. I.), composed of the Republic and at least two other states to be formed in Borneo and the eastern islands; and the linking of the U. S. I. to the Netherlands in a Netherlands-Indonesian Union. Although the agreement was finally signed by both governments in March 1947, negotiations aimed at its implementation failed and on July 21, 1947, the Dutch began "police action" that brought under their control economically important areas of Java, Madura, and Sumatra and reduced the Republic to three noncontiguous areas—central Java, westernmost Java, and parts of Sumatra.
The conflict was brought to the attention of the Security Council of the United Nations by Australia and India.

[3] The Netherlands designated Belgium and the Republic of Indonesia designated Australia to

Resolution of the Council of 1 August 1947. The Council expresses its readiness, if the parties so request, to assist in the settlement through a committee of the Council consisting of three members of the Council, each party selecting one, and the third to be designated by the two so selected.

✧✧✧✧✧✧

135. TRUCE (RENVILLE) AGREEMENT BETWEEN THE NETHERLANDS AND INDONESIA, JANUARY 17, 1948 [1]

[The Security Council's Good Offices Committee for Indonesia experienced difficulty in getting under way; finally it succeeded in bringing the Dutch and Indonesians to an Agreement, which was signed on board the U. S. S. Renville on January 17, 1948. The agreement provided for a military truce and laid down the principles to be applied to the interested parties and the area in question pending a final settlement.]

The Government of the Kingdom of the Netherlands and the Government of the Republic of Indonesia, referred to in this agreement as the parties, hereby agree as follows:

1. That a stand fast and cease fire order be issued separately and simultaneously by both parties immediately upon the signing of this agreement and to be fully effective within forty-eight hours. This order will apply to the troops of both parties along the boundary lines of the areas described in the proclamation of the Netherlands Indies Government on 29 August 1947, which shall be called the *status quo* line, and in the areas specified in the following paragraph.

2. That in the first instance and for the time being, demilitarized zones be established in general conformity with the above-mentioned *status quo* line; these zones as a rule will comprise the territories between this *status quo* line and, on one side, the line of the Netherlands forward positions and, on the other side, the line of the Republican forward positions, the average width of each of the zones being approximately the same.

3. That the establishment of the demilitarized zones in no way prejudices the rights, claims or position of the parties under the resolutions of the Security Council of 1, 25, and 26 August and 1 November 1947.

4. That upon acceptance of the foregoing by both parties, the Committee will place at the disposal of both parties its military assistants who will be instructed to assume, in the first instance, responsibility for determining whether any incident requires enquiry by the higher authorities of either or both parties.

5. That, pending a political settlement, the responsibility for the main-

---

serve on the Good Offices Committee, and the United States was selected as the third member. The Committee arrived in Batavia on October 27, 1947 and held numerous meetings with representatives of the Netherlands Government and the Republic of Indonesia. Press release 49 of January 20, 1948: "... Dutch and Indonesian delegations have accepted the proposals of the Security Council's Committee of Good Offices as a basis for the settlement of the Dutch-Indonesian dispute ..."

[1] UN Doc. S/649, February 10, 1948. The agreement was signed at the fourth meeting of the Committee of Good Offices with the parties on January 17, 1948, aboard the U. S. S. *Renville*.

tenance of law and order and of security of life and property in the demilitarized zones will remain vested in the civil police forces of the respective parties. (The term civil police does not exclude the temporary use of military personnel in the capacity of civil police, it being understood that the police forces will be under civil control.) The Committee's military assistants will be available to advise the appropriate authorities of the parties and to serve in such other proper capacities as may be requested. Among other, they should;

(a) call upon pools of police officers established by each party in its demilitarized zone to accompany the military assistants in their endeavours and moves throughout that demilitarized zone. Police officers of one party will not move into and throughout the demilitarized zone of the other party unless accompanied by a military assistant of the Committee of Good Offices and a police officer of that other party.

(b) promote co-operation between the two police forces.

6. That trade and intercourse between all areas should be permitted as far as possible; such restrictions as may be necessary will be agreed upon by the parties with the assistance of the Committee and its representatives if required.

7. That this agreement shall include all the following points already agreed to in principle by the parties:

(a) To prohibit sabotage, intimidation and reprisals and other activities of a similar nature against individuals, groups of individuals, and property, including destruction of property of any kind and by whomsoever owned, and to utilize every means at their command to this end.

(b) To refrain from broadcasts or any other form of propaganda aimed at provoking or disturbing troops and civilians.

(c) To initiate broadcasts and institute other measures to inform all troops and civilians of the delicate situation and the necessity for strict compliance with the provisions sub (a) and (b).

(d) Full opportunity for observation by military and civil assistants made available to the Committee of Good Offices.

(e) To cease immediately the publication of a daily operational communique or any other information about military operations unless by prior mutual agreement in writing, except weekly publication of lists of individuals (giving names, numbers and home addresses) who have been killed or have died as a result of injuries received in action.

(f) To accept the principle of the release of prisoners by each party and to commence discussions with a view to the most rapid and convenient implementation thereof, the release in principle to be without regard to the number of prisoners held by either party.

8. That, on the acceptance of the foregoing, the Committee's military assistants will immediately conduct enquiries to establish whether and where, especially in West Java, elements of the Republican military forces continue to offer resistance behind the present forward positions of the Netherlands forces. If the enquiry establishes the existence of such forces, these would withdraw as quickly as practicable, and in any case within twenty-one days, as set out in the following paragraph.

9. That all forces of each party in any area accepted as a demilitarized zone or in any area on the other party's side of a demilitarized zone, will,

under the observation of military assistants of the Committee and with arms and warlike equipment, move peacefully to the territory on the party's own side of the demilitarized zones. Both parties undertake to facilitate a speedy and peaceful evacuation of the forces concerned.

10. This agreement shall be considered binding unless one party notifies the Committee of Good Offices and the other party that it considers the truce regulations are not being observed by the other party and that this agreement should therefore be terminated.

For the Government of the Kingdom of the Netherlands
RADEN ABDULKADIR WIDJOJOATMODJO,
Chairman of the delegation
For the Government of the Republic of Indonesia
DR. AMIR SJARIFUDDIN,
Chairman of the delegation

The signatures appearing above were hereunto subscribed this 17th day of January 1948, on board the U. S. S. *Renville,* in the presence of the representatives on the United Nations Security Council Committee of Good Offices on the Indonesian question, and the Committee Secretary, whose signatures are hereunto subscribed as witnesses:

Chairman: MR. JUSTICE RICHARD C. KIRBY (Australia)
Representatives: MR. PAUL VAN ZEELAND (Belgium)
                 DR. FRANK P. GRAHAM (United States)
Secretary: MR. T. G. NARAYANAN

◇◇◇◇◇◇

136. POLITICAL SETTLEMENT IN INDONESIA [1]

(a) *Basic Principles for the Negotiations Between the Netherlands and the Republic of Indonesia, January 17, 1948*

[On the same day the Renville Agreement was entered into, the Dutch and Indonesian Governments accepted a number of basic principles to be followed in reaching a final solution of their dispute. Four in particular were taken from the earlier Linggadjati Agreement: (1) the Indonesian people should be independent; (2) the Dutch and Indonesian people were to coöperate with each other; (3) the new state was to be sovereign, federal, constitutional, and democratic; and (4) the United States of Indonesia should be part of the Kingdom of the Netherlands. Because these principles were so important in working out the differences between the two governments, they are reproduced in full below, together with the statement made by our representative on the Security Council relating to the work of the Good Offices Committee.]

The Committee of Good Offices has been informed by the delegation of the Kingdom of the Netherlands and by the delegation of the Republic of Indonesia that, the truce agreement having been signed, their Governments

---

[1] UN Doc. S/649, February 10, 1948, p. 111. These principles were accepted at the fourth meeting of the Committee of Good Offices with the parties on January 17, 1948.

accept the following principles on which the political discussions will be based:

1. That the assistance of the Committee of Good Offices be continued in the working out and signing of an agreement for the settlement of the political dispute in the islands of Java, Sumatra and Madura, based upon the principles underlying the Linggadjati Agreement.

2. It is understood that neither party has the right to prevent the free expression of popular movements looking toward political organizations which are in accord with the principles of the Linggadjati Agreement. It is further understood that each party will guarantee the freedom of assembly, speech and publication at all times provided that his guarantee is not construed so as to include the advocacy of violence or reprisals.

3. It is understood that decisions concerning changes in administration of territory should be made only with the full and free consent of the populations of those territories and at a time when the security and freedom from coercion of such populations will have been ensured.

4. That on the signing of the political agreement provision be made for the gradual reduction of the armed forces of both parties.

5. That as soon as practicable after the signing of the truce agreement, economic activity, trade, transportation and communications be restored through the co-operation of both parties, taking into consideration the interests of all the constitutent parts of Indonesia.

6. That provision be made for a suitable period of not less than six months nor more than one year after the signing of the agreement, during which time uncoerced and free discussion and consideration of vital issues will proceed. At the end of this period, free elections will be held for self-determination by the people of their political relationship to the United States of Indonesia.

7. That a constitutional convention be chosen according to democratic procedure to draft a constitution for the United States of Indonesia.

8. It is understood that if, after signing the agreement referred to in item 1, either party should ask the United Nations to provide an agency to observe conditions at any time up to the point at·which sovereignty is transferred from the Government of the Netherlands to the Government of the United States of Indonesia, the other party will take this request in serious consideration.

The following four principles are taken from the Linggadjati Agreement:

9. Independence for the Indonesian peoples.

10. Co-operation between the peoples of the Netherlands and Indonesia.

11. A sovereign state on a federal basis under a constitution which will be arrived at by democratic processes.

12. A union between the United States of Indonesia and other parts of the Kingdom of the Netherlands under the King of the Netherlands.

Confirmed for the Government of the Kingdom of the Netherlands

RADEN ABDULKADIR WIDJOJOATMODJO
Chairman of the delegation

Confirmed for the Government of the Republic of Indonesia

DR. AMIR SJARIFUDDIN
Chairman of the delegation

The representatives on the United Nations Security Council Committee of Good Offices on the Indonesian Question, and the Committee Secretary, whose signatures are hereunto subscribed on this 17th day of January 1948, on board the U. S. S. *Renville,* testify that the above principles are agreed to as basis for the political discussions.

Chairman: MR. JUSTICE RICHARD C. KIRBY (Australia)
Representatives: MR. PAUL VAN ZEELAND (Belgium)
DR. FRANK P. GRAHAM (United States)
Secretary: T. G. NARAYANAN

(b) *Additional Principles for the Negotiations Between the Netherlands and the Republic of Indonesia, January 19, 1948* [1]

The Committee of Good Offices is of the opinion that the following principles, among others, form a basis for the negotiations towards a political settlement:

1. Sovereignty throughout the Netherlands Indies is and shall remain with the Kingdom of the Netherlands until, after a stated interval, the Kingdom of the Netherlands transfers its sovereignty to the United States of Indonesia. Prior to the termination of such stated interval, the Kingdom of the Netherlands may confer appropriate rights, duties and responsibilities on a provisional federal government of the territories of the future United States of Indonesia. The United States of Indonesia, when created, will be a sovereign and independent State in equal partnership with the Kingdom of the Netherlands in a Netherlands-Indonesian Union at the head of which shall be the King of the Netherlands. The status of the Republic of Indonesia will be that of a state within the United States of Indonesia.

2. In any provisional federal government created prior to the ratification of the constitution of the future United States of Indonesia, all states will be offered fair representation.

3. Prior to the dissolution of the Committee of Good Offices, either party may request that the services of the Committee be continued to assist in adjusting differences between the parties which relate to the political agreement and which may arise during the interim period. The other party will interpose no objection to such a request; this request would be brought to the attention of the Security Council of the United Nations by the Government of the Netherlands.

4. Within a period of not less than six months or more than one year from the signing of this agreement, a plebiscite will be held to determine whether the populations of the various territories of Java, Madura and Sumatra wish their territory to form part of the Republic of Indonesia or of another state within the United States of Indonesia, such plebiscite to be conducted under observation by the Committee of Good Offices should either party, in accordance with the procedure set forth in paragraph 3 above, request the services of the Committee in this capacity. The parties may agree that another method for ascertaining the will of the populations may be employed in place of a plebiscite.

[1] UN Doc. S/649, February 10, 1948. These principles were submitted by the Committee of Good Offices at the fourth meeting of the Committee of Good Offices with the parties on January 17, 1948, and accepted at the fifth meeting of the Committee with the parties on January 19, 1948.

5. Following the delineation of the states in accordance with the procedure set forth in paragraph 4 above, a constitutional convention will be convened, through democratic procedures, to draft a constitution for the United States of Indonesia. The representation of the various states in the convention will be in proportion to their populations.

6. Should any state decide not to ratify the constitution and desire, in accordance with the principles of articles 3 and 4 of the Linggadjati Agreement, to negotiate a special relationship with the United States of Indonesia and the Kingdom of the Netherlands, neither party will object.

(c) Statement to the Security Council by the United States Representative on the Good Offices Committee on Indonesia, February 17, 1948 [1]

We were always aware of the wisdom in the statements of both the former Prime Minister of the Republic and the Netherlands Ambassador to the United States that there would be reciprocal relations between progress in the effectuation of the truce and progress in the settlement of the political dispute. Accordingly, on Christmas Day, our Committee unanimously adopted a draft plan—on an informal basis—including truce proposals and democratic political principles which were submitted informally to the parties as an integrated and balanced whole. The Republic, though expressing disappointment in what it considered a rigid truce plan, with a status quo line which for a time would continue to include behind Dutch lines former Republican areas containing millions of people, accepted the plan as a whole for its political principles of freedom and democracy, independence and union. The Netherlands, holding the Christmas message on its continuing informal basis, as counter proposals, accepted most of the suggestions, rejected parts, and accepted other parts with modifications. The Netherlands then made these proposals formal with indications that if not accepted by the Republic, it would not be bound by the twelve political principles. These twelve principles provided, among other things, for the continuance of the assistance of the Committee of Good Offices in the working out of the settlement of the political dispute in Java, Sumatra and Madura; for civil and political liberties; that there would be no interference with the expression of popular movements, looking toward the formation of states in accordance with the principles of the Linggadjati agreement; that changes in the administration of territory would be made only with the full and free consent of the population of the territory at a time of security and freedom from coercion; that, on the signing of the political agreement, there would be gradual reduction of the armed forces of both parties; that, on the signing of the truce agreement, there would be resumption of trade, transportation and communication through the co-operation of the parties; that there would be a period of not less than six months nor more than one year after the signing of the agreement during which uncoerced and free discussion of vital issues should proceed and that at the end of such period free elections would be held for self-determination by the people of their political relations to the United States of Indonesia;

[1] Work of the United Nations Good Offices Committee in Indonesia, Department of State publication 3108, International Organization and Conference Series III, 4, pp. 9-10; Department of State Bulletin of March 14, 1948, pp. 331-332. Made on February 17, 1948, and released to the press by the U. S. Mission to the United Nations on the same date. This is a partial text.

provision for the convening of a Constitutional Convention by democratic procedure; provision for serious consideration by one party of the request of the other party for an agency of the United Nations to observe conditions between the signing of the agreement and the transfer of sovereignty from the Netherlands to the United States of Indonesia; provisions for the independence of the Indonesian people and cooperation between the peoples of the Netherlands and Indonesia; provision for a sovereign nation on a federal basis under a constitution to be arrived at by democratic procedures; and provision for the Union of the United States of Indonesia and the other parts of the Kingdom of the Netherlands under the King of the Netherlands.

While deeply appreciative of the fact that the twelve political principles contained many basic provisions for freedom, democracy, independence and cooperation, the Republic was most deeply concerned that there was no guarantee of international observation between the signing of the agreement and the transfer of sovereignty; that there was no provision for the representation of the Republic in the interim government, and that there was no mention of the Republic by name in any of the twelve principles.

Aware of the limitations inherent in a Committee of Good Offices, and in the desperate circumstances of the probable breakdown of negotiations, the Committee decided to make still another new approach to the parties. The Committee suggested for the informal consideration of the parties six additional political principles in addition to the twelve. Pending consideration of the six principles by both parties, the Republic was pondering the acceptance or rejection of the status quo military line and the democratic political principles in which were missing several guarantees of deep concern to the Republic. It soon appeared that the content of the six additional principles, if accepted by the Netherlands, would be decisive as to acceptance by the Republic of the combined plans as, in effect—though not formally—an integrated and balanced whole.

In the six principles were the three things of deep concern to the Republic; specific references to the Republic of Indonesia by name as one of the States in the United States of Indonesia, fair representation of all states in the interim government, and, if either party requested, the guarantee of international observation in the period between the signing of the political agreement and the transfer of the recognized historical sovereignty of the Netherlands to the United States of Indonesia. In addition were two new political principles. One of these provisions was that not sooner than six months and not later than one year after the signing of the agreement, plebiscites would be held under international observation for the self-determination of the people of the various territories of Java, Sumatra and Madura as to whether they would form a part of the Republic of Indonesia or another State of the United States of Indonesia. The other basically democratic provision was that the representation in the Constitutional Convention would be in proportion to population which should mean that the new United States of Indonesia would not only be free and independent but would also be democratic in structure, leadership, function and services of, for and by the people of Indonesia.

To accept would transfer the struggle from a military demarcation line, which would soon disappear, to a democratic political line which would endure. The underground struggle of bitterness and hatred, killings and destruction, would be brought above ground for good will, production, the possible conversion of military budgets for long range constructive programs of education, health, and welfare of all the people of Indonesia. Acceptance would mean the cooperation of the Netherlands, the Republicans and the non-Republicans in the formation of the sovereign, free and independent United States of Indonesia in the union of equal nations in the United Nations.

In consideration of these things, the Netherlands and the Republic accepted unconditionally the truce, the twelve principles and the six Members of the Committee expressed their personal faith to the representatives of the Netherlands that the Republic would, with increasing effectiveness, keep the truce in good faith and good will, and furthermore, than a considerable proportion of the able and dedicated Indonesian leaders were in the Republic. They also expressed to representatives of the Republic their personal faith that the sovereignty of the Netherlands in the interim period would not be used to fix in the new clothes of freedom the old body of colonialism, but rather that the Netherlands would act in good faith, and that the Republic would not lose its existing status as one of the two parties in the Indonesian question on the agenda of the Security Council of the United Nations, and that the Security Council through the Committee of Good Offices would be available to assist the parties to the present agreement in reaching an early long-term settlement. Members of the Committee advised both parties to subordinate all claims and issues which would soon disappear or be absorbed in the permanent settlement to the three main objectives of keeping the truce, restoring economic production and trade through mutual cooperation, and, not the least important of all, the negotiation of the political settlement.

The many and complex difficulties of the truce, the need for sincere and patient care and follow through, the high stakes of mutual cooperation in keeping the truce, all these challenged the leaders, the armies and the people to do their persistent best, with good faith and good will and to send the word everywhere that peace has come and that it is now the patriot's duty to keep the peace and make secure the life and property of all people. The whole world is looking on to encourage and sustain the leaders, who carry by day and by night this heavy responsibility for themselves and the people whom they now lead as hopefully in peace as they formerly led bravely in battle.

◇◇◇◇◇◇

137. RESOLUTION BY THE SECURITY COUNCIL ON THE INDONESIAN QUESTION, JANUARY 28, 1949 [1]

[Following the Renville Agreement, the Dutch accused the Indonesians of not keeping their promises, attacked Jogjakarta on December 18, 1948, and interned the Republican leaders. The United Nations Good Offices Committee declared the Dutch to be in violation of the Renville Agreement, and on January 28, 1949, the Security Council called upon the Netherlands government to cease military action and to free the prisoners they were holding.

[1] Department of State Bulletin of February 27, 1949, pp. 250-251. UN Doc. S/1234, January 28, 1949.

The resolution approved by the Council urged the disputing parties to co-operate in carrying out the Linggadjati and Renville Agreements. It also reconstituted the Committee of Good Offices as the new United Nations Commission for Indonesia and assigned it the task of bringing about a satisfactory settlement of the dispute.]

The Security Council,

RECALLING its resolutions of 1 August 1947, 25 August 1947, and 1 November 1947, with respect to the Indonesian Question:

TAKING NOTE with approval of the Reports submitted to the Security Council by its Committee of Good Offices for Indonesia;

CONSIDERING that its resolutions of 24 December 1948 and 28 December 1948 have not been fully carried out;

CONSIDERING that continued occupation of the territory of the Republic of Indonesia by the armed forces of the Netherlands is incompatible with the restoration of good relations between the parties and with the final achievement of a just and lasting settlement of the Indonesian dispute;

CONSIDERING that the establishment and maintenance of law and order throughout Indonesia is a necessary condition to the achievement of the expressed objectives and desires of both parties;

NOTING with satisfaction that the parties continue to adhere to the principles of the Renville Agreement and agree that free and democratic elections should be held throughout Indonesia for the purpose of establishing a constituent assembly at the earliest practicable date, and further agree that the Security Council should arrange for the observation of such elections by an appropriate agency of the United Nations; and that the representative of the Netherlands has expressed his government's desire to have such elections held not later than 1 October 1949;

NOTING also with satisfaction that the Government of the Netherlands plans to transfer sovereignty to the United States of Indonesia by 1 January 1950, if possible, and, in any case, during the year 1950,

CONSCIOUS of its primary responsibility for the maintenance of international peace and security, and in order that the rights, claims and position of the parties may not be prejudiced by the use of force;

1. *Calls* upon the Government of the Netherlands to insure the immediate discontinuance of all military operations, calls upon the Government of the Republic simultaneously to order its armed adherents to cease guerrilla warfare, and calls upon both parties to co-operate in the restoration of peace and the maintenance of law and order throughout the area affected.

2. *Calls upon* the Government of the Netherlands to release immediately and unconditionally all political prisoners arrested by them since 17 December 1948 in the Republic of Indonesia; and to facilitate the immediate return of officials of the Government of the Republic of Indonesia to Jogjakarta in order that they may discharge their responsibilities under paragraph 1 above and in order to exercise their appropriate functions in full freedom, including administration of the Jogjakarta area, which shall include the city of Jogjakarta and its immediate environs. The Netherlands authorities shall afford to the Government of the Republic of Indonesia such facilities as may reasonably

be required by that Government for its effective function in the Jogjakarta area and for communication and consultation with all persons in Indonesia.

3. *Recommends* that, in the interest of carrying out the expressed objectives and desires of both parties to establish a federal, independent, and sovereign United States of Indonesia at the earliest possible date, negotiations be undertaken as soon as possible by representatives of the Government of the Netherlands and representatives of the Republic of Indonesia with the assistance of the Commission referred to in paragraph 4 below on the basis of the principles set forth in the Linggadjati and Renville Agreements, and taking advantage of the extent of agreement reached between the parties regarding the proposals submitted to them by the United States representative on the Committee of Good Offices on 10 September 1948; and in particular on the basis that:

(a) The establishment of the Interim Federal Government which is to be granted the powers of internal government in Indonesia during the interim period before the transfer of sovereignty shall be the result of the above negotiations and shall take place not later than 15 March 1949;

(b) The elections which are to be held for the purpose of choosing representatives to an Indonesian Constituent Assembly should be completed by 1 October 1949; and

(c) The transfer of sovereignty over Indonesia by the Government of the Netherlands to the United States of Indonesia should take place at the earliest possible date and in any case not later than 1 July 1950;

Provided that if no agreement is reached by one month prior to the respective dates referred to in sub-paragraphs (a), (b), and (c) above, the Commission referred to in paragraph 4 (a) below or such other United Nations agency as may be established in accordance with paragraph 4 (c) below, shall immediately report to the Security Council with its recommendations for a solution of the difficulties.

4. (a) The Committee of Good Offices shall henceforth be known as the United Nations Commission for Indonesia. The Commission shall act as the representative of the Security Council in Indonesia and shall have all of the functions assigned to the Committee of Good Offices by the Security Council since 18 December, and the functions conferred on it by the terms of this resolution. The Commission shall act by majority vote, but its reports and recommendations to the Security Council shall present both majority and minority views if there is a difference of opinion among the members of the Commission.

(b) The Consular Commission is requested to facilitate the work of the United Nations Commission for Indonesia by providing military observers and other staff and facilities to enable the Commission to carry out its duties under the Council's resolutions of 24 and 28 December 1948 as well as under the present resolution, and shall temporarily suspend other activities.

(c) The Commission shall assist the parties in the implementation of this resolution, and shall assist the parties in the negotiations to be undertaken under paragraph 3 above and is authorized to make recommendations to them or to the Security Council on matters within its competence. Upon agreement being reached in such negotiations the Commission shall make recommendations to the Security Council as to the nature, powers, and functions of the United Nations agency which should remain in Indonesia to assist in the implementation of the provisions of such agreement until sovereignty is transferred by the Government of the Netherlands to the United States of Indonesia.

(d) The Commission shall have authority to consult with representatives of areas in Indonesia other than the Republic, and to invite representatives of such areas to participate in the negotiations referred to in paragraph 3 above.

(e) The Commission or such other United Nations agency as may be established in accordance with its recommendation under paragraph 4 (c) above is authorized to observe on behalf of the United Nations the elections to be held throughout Indonesia and is further authorized, in respect of the Territories of Java, Madura and Sumatra, to make recommendations regarding the conditions necessary (a) to ensure that the elections are free and democratic and (b) to guarantee freedom of assembly, speech and publication at all times, provided that such guarantee is not construed so as to include the advocacy of violence or reprisals.

(f) The Commission should assist in achieving the earliest possible restoration of the civil administration of the Republic. To this end it shall, after consultation with the parties, recommend the extent to which, consistent with reasonable requirements of public security and the protection of life and property, areas controlled by the Republic under the Renville Agreement (outside of the Jogjakarta area) should be progressively returned to the administration of the Government of the Republic of Indonesia, and shall supervise such transfers. The recommendations of the Commission may include provision for such economic measures as are required for the proper functioning of the administration and for the economic well-being of the population of the areas involved in such transfers. The Commission shall, after consultation with the parties, recommend which if any Netherlands forces shall be retained temporarily in any area (outside of the Jogjakarta area) in order to assist in the maintenance of law and order. If either of the parties fails to accept the recommendations of the Commission mentioned in this paragraph, the Commission shall report immediately to the Security Council with its further recommendations for a solution of the difficulties.

(g) The Commission shall render periodic reports to the Council, and special reports whenever the Commission deems necessary.

(h) The Commission shall employ such observers, officers and other persons as it deems necessary.

5. *Requests* the Secretary-General to make available to the Commission such staff, funds and other facilities as are required by the Commission for the discharge of its function.

6. *Calls upon* the Government of the Netherlands and the Republic of Indonesia to co-operate fully in giving effect to the provisions of this resolution.

◇◇◇◇◇◇

138. AGREEMENT BETWEEN THE NETHERLANDS AND THE REPUBLIC OF INDONESIA [1]

Letter From the Netherlands' Representative to President of Security Council, May 7, 1949

[On March 1, 1949, the United Nations Commission for Indonesia suggested that the most effective way of bringing about a settlement of the Indonesian question was to bring the two parties together for direct negotiations. On March 29, the Dutch accepted the Commission's invitation and agreed to meet with the Republican leaders in Batavia. Two weeks later, the talks opened, and on May 7 an agreement was reached providing for the return of the Republican Government to Jogjakarta, the termination of guerrilla warfare, and the holding of a round table conference at The Hague. The text of the understanding is reproduced below.]

SIR, I have the honour to inform you that today, 7 May, the Delegations of the Netherlands and of the Republic of Indonesia met in Batavia, under the auspices and in the presence of the United Nations Commission for Indonesia, and made the following formal statements, endorsed by their respective governments.

The statement of the Chairman of the Republican Delegation, Dr. Mohammed Rum, reads as follows:

"As Chairman of the Republican Delegation I am authorized by President Sukarno and Vice President Mohammed Hatta to give their personal assurances they favour, in conformity with the Security Council's Resolution of January 28th, 1949 and its directive of March 23rd:

1. The issuance of an order to the Republican armed adherents to cease guerrilla warfare,

2. Co-operation in restoration of peace and the maintenance of law and order, and

3. Participation in a round table conference at The Hague with a view to accelerate the unconditional transfer of real and complete sovereignty to the United States of Indonesia.

President Sukarno and Vice President Hatta undertake that they will urge the adoption of such a policy by the Government of the Republic of Indonesia as soon as possible after its restoration at Djokjakarta."

The statement of the Chairman of the Netherlands Delegation, Dr. J. H. van Roijen, reads as follows:

"1. The Netherlands Delegation is authorized to state that, in view of the undertaking just announced by Dr. Mohammed Rum, it agrees to the return of the Republican Government to Djokjakarta. The Netherlands Delegation agrees further to the setting up of one or more joint committees under the auspices of the United Nations Commission for Indonesia, for such purposes as:

A. to make the necessary investigations and preparations preliminary to the return of the Republican Government to Djokjakarta;

[1] Department of State Bulletin of May 22, 1949, pp. 653-654. UN Doc. S/1319.

B. to study and advise on the measures to be taken in order to effectuate the cessation of guerrilla warfare and the co-operation in the restoration and maintenance of law and order.

2. The Netherlands Government agrees that the Republican Government shall be free and facilitated to exercise its appropriate functions in an area of the residency of Djokjakarta and that this is a step taken in the light of the Security Council's directive of March 23rd, 1949.

3. The Netherlands Government re-affirms its willingness to insure the immediate discontinuance of all military operations and to release immediately and unconditionally all political prisoners arrested by them since December 17th, 1948 in the Republic of Indonesia.

4. Without prejudice to the right of self-determination of the Indonesian peoples as recognized by Linggadjati and the Renville principles, the Netherlands Government will refrain from the establishment or recognition of Negaras or Daerahs on territory under Republican control prior to December 19th, 1948, and from the expansion of Negaras and Daerahs affecting said territory.

5. The Netherlands Government favours the existence of the Republic as a state to take its place in the United States of Indonesia. When a provisional representative body for the whole of Indonesia is to be established and it consequently becomes necessary to determine the number of representatives from the Republic to said body, this number will be one half of the total membership exclusive of the Republican's membership.

6. Consonant with the intent of the Security Council's ruling of March 23rd, 1949, on the subject of the proposed round table conference at The Hague to the end that the negotiations contemplated by the resolution of January 28th, 1949, may be held as soon as possible, the Netherlands Government is fully prepared to do its utmost that this conference take place immediately after the return of the Republican Government to Djokjakarta. At this conference discussions will take place as to the way in which to accelerate the unconditional transfer of real and complete sovereignty to the United States of Indonesia in accordance with the Renville principles.

7. In the light of the necessary co-operation in the restoration of peace and the maintenance of law and order, the Netherlands Government agrees that in all those areas outside the residency of Djokjakarta where civil, police and other officials of the Government of Indonesia are not operating at present, the Republican civil, police and other officials, where still operating, will remain in function.

It is understood that the Netherlands authorities shall afford to the Republican Government such facilities as may reasonably be required by that Government for communication and consultation with all persons in Indonesia, including those serving in civil and military services of the Republic, and that the technical details will have to be worked out by the parties under the auspices of the United Nations Commission for Indonesia."

I would highly appreciate it if you would have the contents of this letter circulated to the Members of the Security Council.

I have [etc.]

J. W. M. SNOUCK HURGRONJE.

◇◇◇◇◇◇

139. THE HAGUE ROUND TABLE CONFERENCE ON INDONESIA [1]

Draft Charter of Transfer of Sovereignty, November 2, 1949

[The round table discussions which had been agreed upon by the Dutch and Indonesians on May 7, 1949, opened at The Hague on August 25. On October 15 a military pact was consummated; on October 24 the size of the debt of the Indonesian Republic was fixed; and on October 29 a provisional constitution for Indonesia was signed. The conference ended on November 1, and was followed the next day by the signing of the document reproduced below, which transferred sovereignty to the United States of Indonesia. Subsequently, the Dutch lived up to their agreement with the Indonesians to withdraw their troops from the Islands by July 1950.]

ARTICLE 1

1. The Kingdom of the Netherlands unconditionally and irrevocably transfers complete sovereignty over Indonesia to the Republic of the United States of Indonesia and thereby recognizes said Republic of the United States of Indonesia as an independent and sovereign State.

2. The Republic of the United States of Indonesia accepts said sovereignty on the basis of the provisions of its Constitution which as a draft has been brought to the knowledge of the Kingdom of the Netherlands.

3. The transfer of sovereignty shall take place at the latest on 30 December 1949.

ARTICLE 2

With regard to the residency of New Guinea it is decided:

a. in view of the fact that it has not yet been possible to reconcile the views of the parties on New Guinea, which remain, therefore, in dispute,

b. in view of the desirability of the Round Table Conference concluding successfully on 2 November 1949,

c. in view of the important factors which should be taken into account in settling the question of New Guinea,

d. in view of the limited research that has been undertaken and completed with respect to the problems involved in the question of New Guinea,

e. in view of the heavy tasks with which the Union partners will initially be confronted, and

f. in view of the dedication of the parties to the principle of resolving by peaceful and reasonable means any differences that may hereafter exist or arise between them,

that the status quo of the residency of New Guinea shall be maintained with the stipulation that within a year from the date of transfer of sovereignty to

[1] Round Table Conference, Results as accepted in the Second Plenary Meeting, held on 2 November 1949 in the "Ridderzaal" at the Hague, published by the Secretariat of the Round Table Conference. This publication also includes the Draft Union Statute with attached agreements, the Draft Agreement on transitional measures with attached agreements, Exchange of Letters, and an English translation of the Constitution of the Republic of the United States of Indonesia.

the Republic of the United States of Indonesia the question of the political status of New Guinea be determined through negotiations between the Republic of the United States of Indonesia and the Kingdom of the Netherlands.

◇◇◇◇◇◇

140. INDEPENDENCE OF INDONESIA [1]

Statement by Secretary Acheson, November 3, 1949

[The United States played a very important part in bringing about the settlement of the Indonesian question through the machinery of the United Nations. It was therefore natural that immediately upon the conclusion of the round table conference and the granting of independence to the United States of Indonesia, the United States should recognize the new government. The Secretary of State on November 3, 1949, in a formal statement summarized the main steps of the new state towards independence and welcomed it into the family of nations.]

Upon this most auspicious occasion, the successful termination of the round-table conference at The Hague, this government wishes to congratulate the Netherlands and Indonesian representatives on the high statesmanship which both have exhibited in the course of the Conference. The conferees, in finding a settlement of those differences, both political and economic, which have separated them some years, have accorded the Indonesian people full independence and sovereignty, at the same time preserving interests of the Netherlands in the Indonesian Archipelago which are legitimate and just. The new and sovereign Republic of United Indonesia is to join the Netherlands in the Netherlands-Indonesian Union, a voluntary association of equal partners thus offering the world a bright prospect for practical collaboration between East and West. It is the firm expectation of this Government that the agreements reached at the Conference will mark a renewed growth of Dutch-Indonesian friendship and cooperation, which in our opinion will surely further the welfare of both nations.

By its courageous action against a subversive Communist movement last September, the Indonesian Republic has demonstrated its genuine nationalist character. The Indonesian Federalists have joined with the Indonesian Republic in compounding a genuine all-Indonesian nationalist position at The Hague Conference. The Government of the Netherlands, under whose auspices the round-table conference has been held, has during the course of negotiations demonstrated full fidelity to its principle of independence for Indonesia and faith in the integrity of the new state.

The dispute has been before the Security Council since July 1947. The United Nations Good Offices Committee, the name of which was subsequently changed to United Nations Commission for Indonesia, was formed through the selection of Belgium by the Netherlands, of Australia by the Indonesian Republic, and the selection by Australia and Belgium of the United States as the third member. The United States' contribution to the solution of the

[1] Department of State Bulletin of November 14, 1949, pp. 752, 753.

Indonesian problem has been made through the discharge of its responsibility as a member of the United Nations Commission for Indonesia.

Negotiations, under the auspices of the Committee of Good Offices, which were suspended in 1948, were resumed on April 14, 1949 under the auspices of the United Nations Commission for Indonesia which was created by the Security Council resolution of January 28, 1949. This same resolution called upon both parties for a cease fire order, for a release of all political prisoners, and for the restoration of the Republican Government of Jogjakarta, to be followed by staged withdrawals of Netherlands forces from areas occupied by them after December 18, and made several recommendations to the parties. The parties agreed on May 7 to the restoration of the Republican Government to the Residency of Jogjakarta, the issuance of a cease fire, the release of Republican prisoners by the Dutch, and the holding of a conference at The Hague leading to a definite political settlement.

The new Republic of United Indonesia will be faced with great tasks and must assume heavy responsibilities. It can count upon the sympathy and support of all who believe in democracy and the right of self-government. For its part, the United States Government is engaged in study of ways and means by which it may be of assistance, should such assistance be requested.

The United States will be gratified to welcome into the community of free nations the United Republic of Indonesia and looks forward to Indonesia's membership in the United Nations which the Netherlands has undertaken to propose. With their record of genuine nationalism, the Indonesian people may be expected successfully to resist all efforts of aggressive foreign dictatorships to subvert their newly won independence.

◇◇◇◇◇

PALESTINE, ISRAEL

141. REPORT OF THE ANGLO-AMERICAN COMMITTEE OF INQUIRY [1]

Excerpts From the Report, April 20, 1946

[Jewish demands for an independent homeland grew more and more insistent during World War II. Meanwhile, the British mandate over Palestine became progressively more difficult to administer as tensions between the Arabs and the Jews increased. In 1945, following consultation between the

---

[1] Department of State Bulletin of May 12, 1946, pp. 783-787. See also Anglo-American Committee of Inquiry: Report to the United States Government and His Majesty's Government in the United Kingdom; Lausanne, Switzerland, April 20, 1946, Department of State publication 2536, Near Eastern Series 2.

The text of the report and the President's statement were released to the press by the White House on April 30, 1946.

The report, as submitted to the Governments of the United States and the United Kingdom, was signed at Lausanne, Switzerland, on April 20, 1946. The following signatures were attached to the report: Joseph C. Hutcheson, American Chairman; John E. Singleton, British Chairman; Frank Aydelotte (U. S.), Frank W. Buxton (U. S.), W. F. Crick (U. K.), R. H. S. Crossman (U. K.), Bartley C. Crum (U. S.), Frederick Leggett (U. K.), R. E. Manningham-Buller (U. K.), James G. McDonald (U. S.), Morrison (U. K.), William Phillips (U. S.), Leslie L. Rood, American Secretary, Evan M. Wilson, American Secretary, H. G. Vincent, British Secretary, and H. Beeley, British Secretary.

United States and Great Britain, an Anglo-American Commission of Inquiry was appointed to examine the political, social, and economic conditions in Palestine; to study the position of the Jews in Europe; and to recommend such remedial action as the Commission deemed desirable. The following unanimous report contains ten specific recommendations designed to make it possible for both Jews and Arabs to live in peace in Palestine. The report was agreed upon only after much compromise, but it failed to please either the Arabs or the Jews.]

*   *   *

CHAPTER I

RECOMMENDATIONS [1]

The European Problem.

Recommendation No. 1. We have to report that such information as we received about countries other than Palestine gave no hope of substantial assistance in finding homes for Jews wishing or impelled to leave Europe.

But Palestine alone cannot meet the emigration needs of the Jewish victims of Nazi and Fascist persecution; the whole world shares responsibility for them and indeed for the resettlement of all "displaced persons".

We therefore recommend that our Governments together, and in association with other countries, should endeavor immediately to find new homes for all such "displaced persons", irrespective of creed or nationality, whose ties with their former communities have been irreparably broken.

Though immigration will solve the problems of some victims of persecution, the overwhelming majority, including a considerable number of Jews, will continue to live in Europe. We recommend therefore that our Governments endeavor to secure that immediate effect is given to the provision of the United Nations Charter calling for "universal respect for, and observance of, human rights and fundamental freedoms for all without distinction as to race, sex, language, or religion".

Refugee Immigration Into Palestine.

Recommendation No. 2. We recommend (a) that 100,000 certificates be authorized immediately for the admission into Palestine of Jews who have been the victims of Nazi and Fascist persecution; (b) that these certificates be awarded as far as possible in 1946 and that actual immigration be pushed forward as rapidly as conditions will permit.

Principles of Government: no Arab, no Jewish State.

Recommendation No. 3. In order to dispose, once and for all, of the exclusive claims of Jews and Arabs to Palestine, we regard it as essential that a clear statement of the following principles should be made:

I. That Jew shall not dominate Arab and Arab shall not dominate Jew in Palestine. II. That Palestine shall be neither a Jewish state nor an Arab state. III. That the form of government ultimately to be established, shall, under

[1] In the report each of these recommendations is followed by comments.

international guarantees, fully protect and preserve the interests in the Holy Land of Christendom and of the Moslem and Jewish faiths.

Thus Palestine must ultimately become a state which guards the rights and interests of Moslems, Jews and Christians alike; and accords to the inhabitants, as a whole, the fullest measure of self-government, consistent with the three paramount principles set forth above.

Mandate and United Nations Trusteeship.

Recommendation No. 4. We have reached the conclusion that the hostility between Jews and Arabs and, in particular, the determination of each to achieve domination, if necessary by violence, make it almost certain that, now and for some time to come, any attempt to establish either an independent Palestinian state or independent Palestinian states would result in civil strife such as might threaten the peace of the world. We therefore recommend that, until this hostility disappears, the government of Palestine be continued as at present under mandate pending the execution of a trusteeship agreement under the United Nations.

Equality of Standards.

Recommendation No. 5. Looking towards a form of ultimate self-government, consistent with the three principles laid down in recommendation No. 3, we recommend that the mandatory or trustee should proclaim the principle that Arab economic, educational and political advancement in Palestine is of equal importance with that of the Jews; and should at once prepare measures designed to bridge the gap which now exists and raise the Arab standard of living to that of the Jews; and so bring the two peoples to a full appreciation of their common interest and common destiny in the land where both belong.

Future Immigration Policy.

Recommendation No. 6. We recommend that pending the early reference to the United Nations and the execution of a trusteeship agreement, the mandatory should administer Palestine according to the mandate which declares with regard to immigration that "The administration of Palestine, while ensuring that the rights and position of other sections of the population are not prejudiced, shall facilitate Jewish immigration under suitable conditions."

Land Policy.

Recommendation No. 7. (a) We recommend that the land transfer regulations of 1940 be rescinded and replaced by regulations based on a policy of freedom in the sale, lease or use of land, irrespective of race, community or creed; and providing adequate protection for the interests of small owners and tenant cultivators. (b) We further recommend that steps be taken to render nugatory and to prohibit provisions in conveyances, leases and agreements relating to land which stipulate that only members of one race, community or creed may be employed on or about or in connection therewith. (c) We recommend that the Government should exercise such close supervision over the Holy Places and localities such as the Sea of Galilee and its vicinity as will protect them from desecration and from uses which offend the conscience of religious people; and that such laws as are required for this purpose be enacted forthwith.

Economic Development.

Recommendation No. 8. Various plans for large-scale agricultural and industrial development in Palestine have been presented for our consideration; these projects, if successfully carried into effect, could not only greatly enlarge the capacity of the country to support an increasing population, but also raise the living standards of Jew and Arab alike.

We are not in a position to assess the soundness of these specific plans; but we cannot state too strongly that, however technically feasible they may be, they will fail unless there is peace in Palestine. Moreover their full success requires the willing cooperation of adjacent Arab states, since they are not merely Palestinian projects. We recommend therefore that the examination, discussion and execution of these plans be conducted, from the start and throughout, in full consultation and cooperation not only with the Jewish agency but also with the governments of the neighboring Arab states directly affected.

Education.

Recommendation No. 9. We recommend that, in the interests of the conciliation of the two peoples and of general improvement of the Arab standard of living, the educational system of both Jews and Arabs be reformed including the introduction of compulsory education within a reasonable time.

The Need for Peace in Palestine.

Recommendation No. 10. We recommend that, if this report is adopted, it should be made clear beyond all doubt to both Jews and Arabs that any attempt from either side, by threats of violence, by terrorism, or by the organization or use of illegal armies to prevent its execution, will be resolutely suppressed.

Furthermore, we express the view that the Jewish agency should at once resume active cooperation with the mandatory in the suppression of terrorism and of illegal immigration, and in the maintenance of that law and order throughout Palestine which is essential for the good of all, including the new immigrants.

[Here follow Chapters II through X under the headings of: "The Position of the Jews in Europe"; "The Political Situation in Palestine"; "Geography and Economics"; "The Jewish Attitude"; "The Arab Attitude"; "Christian Interests in Palestine"; "Jews, Arabs and Government"; "Public Security"; and "General".]

◇◇◇◇◇◇

142. IMMIGRATION INTO PALESTINE

Statement by President Truman, October 4, 1946 [1]

[The Anglo-American Committee of Inquiry recommended the immediate admission of 100,000 Jews into Palestine, but British regulations permitted the admission of only 1500 Jews a month. Many people in the United States favored the more liberal policy proposed by the Committee of Inquiry. In the following statement President Truman advocated the admission of 100,000 Jewish refugees into Palestine at the earliest possible moment. He also summarized the background of the problem of Palestine and urged its speedy solution.]

* * *

On June 11, I announced the establishment of a Cabinet Committee on Palestine and Related Problems, composed of the Secretaries of State, War, and Treasury, to assist me in considering the recommendations of the Anglo-American Committee of Inquiry.[2] The alternates of this Cabinet Committee, headed by Ambassador Henry F. Grady, departed for London on July 10, 1946, to discuss with British Government representatives how the Report might best be implemented. The alternates submitted on July 24, 1946 a report, commonly referred to as the "Morrison plan", advocating a scheme of provincial autonomy which might lead ultimately to a bi-national state or to partition. However, opposition to this plan developed among members of the major political parties in the United States—both in the Congress and throughout the country. In accordance with the principle which I have consistently tried to follow, of having a maximum degree of unity within the country and between the parties on major elements of American foreign policy, I could not give my support to this plan.

I have, nevertheless, maintained my deep interest in the matter and have repeatedly made known and have urged that steps be taken at the earliest possible moment to admit 100,000 Jewish refugees to Palestine.

In the meantime, this Government was informed of the efforts of the British Government to bring to London representatives of the Arabs and Jews, with a view to finding a solution to this distressing problem. I expressed the hope that as a result of these conversations a fair solution of the Palestine problem could be found.[3] While all the parties invited had not found themselves able to attend, I had hoped that there was still a possibility that representatives of the Jewish Agency might take part. If so, the prospect for an agreed and constructive settlement would have been enhanced.

The British Government presented to the Conference the so-called "Morrison plan" for provincial autonomy and stated that the Conference was open to other proposals. Meanwhile, the Jewish Agency proposed a solution of the Palestine problem by means of the creation of a viable Jewish state in control of its own immigration and economic policies in an adequate area of Palestine

[1] Department of State Bulletin of October 13, 1946, pp. 669-670.
[2] For text of the Executive order establishing the Committee, see Department of State Bulletin of June 23, 1946, p. 1089.
[3] Department of State Bulletin of August 25, 1946, p. 380.

instead of in the whole of Palestine. It proposed furthermore the immediate issuance of certificates for 100,000 Jewish immigrants. This proposal received wide-spread attention in the United States, both in the press and in public forums. From the discussion which has ensued it is my belief that a solution along these lines would command the support of public opinion in the United States. I cannot believe that the gap between the proposals which have been put forward is too great to be bridged by men of reason and good-will. To such a solution our Government could give its support.

In the light of the situation which has now developed I wish to state my views as succinctly as possible:

1. In my views of the fact that winter will come on before the Conference can be resumed I believe and urge that substantial immigration into Palestine cannot await a solution to the Palestine problem and that it should begin at once. Preparations for this movement have already been made by this Government and it is ready to lend its immediate assistance.

2. I state again, as I have on previous occasions, that the immigration laws of other countries, including the United States, should be liberalized with a view to the admission of displaced persons. I am prepared to make such a recommendation to the Congress and to continue as energetically as possible collaboration with other countries on the whole problem of displaced persons.

3. Furthermore, should a workable solution for Palestine be devised, I would be willing to recommend to the Congress a plan for economic assistance for the development of that country.

In the light of the terrible ordeal which the Jewish people of Europe endured during the recent war and the crisis now existing, I cannot believe that a program of immediate action along the lines suggested above could not be worked out with the cooperation of all people concerned. The Administration will continue to do everything it can to this end.

143. UNITED STATES POSITION ON PALESTINE QUESTION [1]

Statement by Herschel V. Johnson, United States Deputy Representative to the United Nations, October 11, 1947 [2]

[On April 2, 1947, Britain brought the question of Palestine to the attention of the United Nations and asked that it be placed on the agenda of the next regular session of the General Assembly. The position of the United States on this important matter was set forth in the statement of its Deputy Representative at the meeting of the *ad hoc* Committee on Palestine of the General As-

[1] Department of State Bulletin of October 19, 1947, pp. 761-762. The question of Palestine was brought before the United Nations by the Government of the United Kingdom in a letter to the Secretary-General dated April 2, 1947, which requested the Secretary-General to place the question of Palestine on the agenda of the General Assembly at its next regular session.

[2] Statement made at meeting of the *ad hoc* Committee on Palestine of the General Assembly on October 11, 1947, and released to the press by the United States Mission to the United Nations on the same date. Herschel V. Johnson was the United States Deputy Representative to the United Nations.

sembly held on October 11, 1947. One may note that among the observations and proposals made at that time, our country supported the partition of Palestine between the Arabs and the Jews, and also urged a more liberal immigration policy for Palestine.]

1. The problem of the future government of Palestine confronts the General Assembly of the United Nations with a heavy and complex responsibility. The General Assembly, having assumed responsibility for making recommendations to the United Kingdom on the subject, must do everything within its power to evolve a practical solution consistent with the principles laid down in the United Nations Charter.

* * *

6. The United States Delegation supports the basic principles of the unanimous recommendations and the majority plan which provides for partition and immigration. It is of the opinion, however, that certain amendments and modifications would have to be made in the majority plan in order more accurately to give effect to the principles on which that plan is based. My delegation believes that certain geographical modifications must be made. For example Jaffa should be included in the Arab State because it is predominantly an Arab city.

My delegation suggests that the General Assembly may wish to provide that all the inhabitants of Palestine, regardless of citizenship or place of residence, be guaranteed access to ports and to water and power facilities on a non-discriminatory basis; that constitutional guarantees, including guarantees regarding equal economic opportunity, be provided for Arabs and Jews alike, and that the powers of the Joint Economic Board be strengthened. Any solution which this Committee recommends should not only be just, but also workable and of a nature to command the approval of world opinion.

7. The United States Delegation desires to make certain observations on the carrying out of such recommendations as the General Assembly may make regarding the future government of Palestine. The General Assembly did not, by admitting this item to its agenda, undertake to assume responsibility for the administration of Palestine during the process of transition to independence. Responsibility for the government of Palestine now rests with the mandatory power. The General Assembly, however, would not fully discharge its obligation if it did not take carefully into account the problem of implementation.

8. Both the majority report and the statement of the United Kingdom representative in this Committee raise the problem of carrying into effect the recommendations of the General Assembly. We note, for example, that the majority report indicates several points at which the majority thought the United Nations could be of assistance. It was suggested that the General Assembly approve certain steps involved in the transitional period, that the United Nations guarantee certain aspects of the settlement concerning Holy Places and minority rights, that the Economic and Social Council appoint three members of the Joint Economic Board, and that the United Nations accept responsibility as administering authority of the City of Jerusalem under an international trusteeship.

9. The United States is willing to participate in a UN program to ·assist

the parties involved in the establishment of a workable political settlement in Palestine. We refer to assistance through the UN in meeting economic and financial problems and the problem of internal law and order during the transition period. The latter problem might require the establishment of a special constabulary or police force recruited on a volunteer basis by the UN. We do not refer to the possibility of violation by any member of its obligations to refrain in its international relations from the threat or use of force. We assume that there will be Charter observance.

10. In the final analysis the problem of making any solution work rests with the people of Palestine. If new political institutions are to endure, they must provide for early assumption by the people themselves of the responsibility for their own domestic order. Acts of violence against constituted authority and against rival elements of the local population have appeared in Palestine over a period of many years and have greatly increased the difficulties of finding a workable solution to this complex problem. Certain elements have restored to force and terror to obtain their own particular aims. Obviously, this violence must cease if independence is to be more than an empty phrase in the Holy Land.

11. Mr. Chairman, we must now consider how this committee is to take the next step in dealing with this question. If the committee favors the principles of the majority plan, we should establish a subcommittee to work out the details of a program which we could recommend to the GA [General Assembly].

12. The recommendations reached by the GA will represent the collective opinion of the world. The problem has thus far defied solution because the parties primarily at interest have been unable to reach a basis of agreement. This is a problem in the solution of which world opinion can be most helpful.

❖❖❖❖❖

144. PARTITION OF PALESTINE

Resolution of the General Assembly, November 29, 1947 [1]

[On May 15, 1947, the General Assembly established a United Nations Special Committee on Palestine (UNSCOP) with eleven members, and assigned to it the duties of investigating the problem of Palestine and of making recommendations for a settlement. The Committee visited the territory in dispute and the neighboring countries. Subsequently, the Committee issued a report on August 31, 1947, in which it recommended the division of Palestine into a Jewish and an Arab state. The two parts were to be joined in an economic union while the holy places and Jerusalem were to be internationalized. These proposals found favor neither with Jews nor with Arabs. Nevertheless, they were the basis for the General Assembly's partition plan as set forth in its resolution of November 29, 1947.]

[1] The United States and the United Nations: Report by the President to the Congress for the year 1947, Department of State publication 3024, International Organization and Conference Series III, 1, pp. 164-187.

The General Assembly,

HAVING MET in special session at the request of the Mandatory Power to constitute and instruct a Special Committee to prepare for the consideration of the question of the future government of Palestine at the second regular session;

HAVING CONSTITUTED a Special Committee and instructed it to investigate all questions and issues relevant to the problem of Palestine, and to prepare proposals for the solution of the problem; and

HAVING RECEIVED AND EXAMINED the report of the Special Committee (document A/364) including a number of unanimous recommendations and a plan of partition with economic union approved by the majority of the Special Committee;

Considers that the present situation in Palestine is one which is likely to impair the general welfare and friendly relations among nations;

Takes note of the declaration by the Mandatory Power that it plans to complete its evacuation of Palestine by 1 August 1948;

Recommends to the United Kingdom, as the Mandatory Power for Palestine, and to all other Members of the United Nations the adoption and implementation, with regard to the future government of Palestine, of the Plan of Partition with Economic Union set out below;

Requests that

(*a*) The Security Council take the necessary measures as provided for in the Plan for its implementation;

(*b*) The Security Council consider if circumstances during the transitional period require such consideration, whether the situation in Palestine constitutes a threat to the peace. If it decides that such a threat exists and in order to maintain international peace and security, the Security Council should supplement the authorization of the General Assembly by taking measures, under Articles 39 and 41 of the Charter, to empower the United Nations Commission, as provided in this resolution, to exercise in Palestine the functions which are assigned to it by this resolution;

(*c*) The Security Council determine as a threat to the peace, breach of the peace or act of aggression, in accordance with Article 39 of the Charter, any attempt to alter by force the settlement envisaged by this resolution;

(*d*) The Trusteeship Council be informed of the responsibilities envisaged for it in this Plan;

Calls upon the inhabitants of Palestine to take such steps as may be necessary on their part to put this Plan into effect;

Appeals to all Governments and all peoples to refrain from taking any action which might hamper or delay the carrying out of these recommendations; and

Authorizes the Secretary-General to reimburse travel and subsistence expenses of the members of the Commission referred to in Part I, Section B, paragraph 1 below on such basis and in such form as he may determine most appropriate in the circumstances, and to provide to the Commission the necessary staff to assist in carrying out the functions assigned to the Commission by the General Assembly.

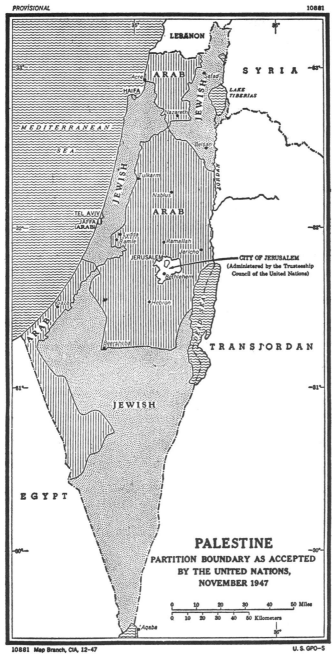

PALESTINE

PARTITION BOUNDARY AS ACCEPTED
BY THE UNITED NATIONS,
NOVEMBER 1947

Plan of Partition with Economic Union

PART I. FUTURE CONSTITUTION AND GOVERNMENT OF PALESTINE

A. TERMINATION OF MANDATE, PARTITION AND INDEPENDENCE

1. The Mandate for Palestine shall terminate as soon as possible but in any case not later than 1 August 1948.

2. The armed forces of the Mandatory Power shall be progressively withdrawn from Palestine, the withdrawal to be completed as soon as possible but in any case not later than 1 August 1948.

The Mandatory Power shall advise the Commission, as far in advance as possible, of its intention to terminate the Mandate and evacuate each area.

The Mandatory Power shall use its best endeavours to ensure that an area situated in the territory of the Jewish State, including a seaport and hinterland adequate to provide facilities for a substantial immigration, shall be evacuated at the earliest possible date and in any event not later than 1 February 1948.

3. Independent Arab and Jewish States and the Special International Regime for the City of Jerusalem, set forth in Part III of this Plan, shall come into existence in Palestine two months after the evacuation of the armed forces of the Mandatory Power has been completed but in any case not later than 1 October 1948. The boundaries of the Arab State, the Jewish State, and the City of Jerusalem shall be as described in Parts II and III below.

*   *   *

B. STEPS PREPARATORY TO INDEPENDENCE

1. A Commission shall be set up consisting of one representative of each of five Member States. The Members represented on the Commission shall be elected by the General Assembly on as broad a basis, geographically and otherwise, as possible.

2. The administration of Palestine shall, as the Mandatory Power withdraws its armed forces, be progressively turned over to the Commission, which shall act in conformity with the recommendations of the General Assembly, under the guidance of the Security Council. The Mandatory Power shall to the fullest possible extent co-ordinate its plans for withdrawal with the plans of the Commission to take over and administer areas which have been evacuated.

In the discharge of this administrative responsibility the Commission shall have authority to issue necessary regulations and take other measures as required.

The Mandatory Power shall not take any action to prevent, obstruct or delay the implementation by the Commission of the measures recommended by the General Assembly.

3. On its arrival in Palestine the Commission shall proceed to carry out measures for the establishment of the frontiers of the Arab and Jewish States and the City of Jerusalem in accordance with the general lines of the recommendations of the General Assembly on the partition of Palestine. Nevertheless, the boundaries as described in Part II of this Plan are to be modified in such a way that village areas as a rule will not be divided by state boundaries unless pressing reasons make that necessary.

4. The Commission, after consultation with the democratic parties and other public organizations of the Arab and Jewish States, shall select and establish in each State as rapidly as possible a Provisional Council of Government. The activities of both the Arab and Jewish Provisional Councils of Government shall be carried out under the general direction of the Commission.

If by 1 April 1948 a Provisional Council of Government cannot be selected for either of the States, or, if selected, cannot carry out its functions, the Commission shall communicate that fact to the Security Council for such action with respect to that State as the Security Council may deem proper, and to the Secretary-General for communication to the Members of the United Nations.

5. Subject to the provision of these recommendations, during the transitional period the Provisional Councils of Government, acting under the Commission, shall have full authority in the areas under their control, including authority over matters of immigration and land regulations.

*   *   *

8. The Provisional Council of Government of each State shall, within the shortest time possible, recruit an armed militia from the residents of that State, sufficient in number to maintain internal order and to prevent frontier clashes.

This armed militia in each State shall, for operational purposes, be under the command of Jewish or Arab officers resident in that State, but general political and military control, including the choice of the militia's High Command, shall be exercised by the Commission.

9. The Provisional Council of Government of each State shall, not later than two months after the withdrawal of the armed forces of the Mandatory Power, hold elections to the Constituent Assembly which shall be conducted on democratic lines.

*   *   *

10. The Constituent Assembly of each State shall draft a democratic Constitution for its State and choose a provisional government to succeed the Provisional Council of Government appointed by the Commission. The Constitutions of the State shall embody chapters 1 and 2 of the Declaration provided for in Section C below and include *inter alia* provisions for:

(a) Establishing in each State a legislative body elected by universal suffrage and by secret ballot on the basis of proportional representation, and an executive body responsible to the legislature.

(b) Settling all international disputes in which the State may be involved by peaceful means in such a manner that international peace and security, and justice, are not endangered.

(c) Accepting the obligation of the State to refrain in its international relations from the threat or use of force against the territorial integrity or political independence of any State, or in any other manner inconsistent with the purposes of the United Nations.

(d) Guaranteeing to all persons equal and non-discriminatory rights in civil, political economic and religious matters and the enjoyment of human rights and fundamental freedoms, including freedom of religion, language, speech and publication, education, assembly and association.

(*e*) Preserving freedom of transit and visit for all residents and citizens of the other State in Palestine and the City of Jerusalem, subject to considerations of national security, provided that each State shall control residence within its borders.

11. The Commission shall appoint a Preparatory Economic Commission of three members to make whatever arrangements are possible for economic co-operation, with a view to establishing, as soon as practicable, the Economic Union and the Joint Economic Board, as provided in Section D below.

12. During the period between the adoption of the recommendations on the question of Palestine by the General Assembly and the termination of the Mandate, the Mandatory Power in Palestine shall maintain full responsibility for administration in areas from which it has not withdrawn its armed forces. The Commission shall assist the Mandatory Power in the carrying out of these functions. Similarly the Mandatory Power shall co-operate with the Commission in the execution of its functions.

*   *   *

C. DECLARATION

1. A Declaration shall be made to the United Nations by the Provisional Government of each proposed State before independence. It shall contain *inter alia* the following clauses:

General Provision

The stipulations contained in the Declaration are recognized as fundamental laws of the State and no law, regulation or official action shall conflict or interfere with these stipulations, nor shall any law, regulation or official action prevail over them.

Chapter 1. Holy Places, Religious Buildings and Sites

1. Existing rights in respect of Holy Places and religious buildings or sites shall not be denied or impaired.

2. In so far as Holy Places are concerned, the liberty of access, visit and transit shall be guaranteed, in conformity with existing rights, to all residents and citizens of the other State and of the City of Jerusalem, as well as to aliens, without distinction as to nationality, subject to requirements of national security, public order and decorum.

Similarly, freedom of worship shall be guaranteed in conformity with existing rights, subject to the maintenance of public order and decorum.

3. Holy Places and religious buildings or sites shall be preserved. No act shall be permitted which may in any way impair their sacred character. If at any time it appears to the Government that any particular Holy Place, religious building or site is in need of urgent repair, the Government may call upon the community or communities concerned to carry out such repair. The Government may carry it out itself at the expense of the community or communities concerned if no action is taken within a reasonable time.

4. No taxation shall be levied in respect of any Holy Place, religious build-

ing or site which was exempt from taxation on the date of the creation of the State.

* * *

Chapter 2. Religious and Minority Rights

1. Freedom of conscience and the free exercise of all forms of worship, subject only to maintenance of public order and morals, shall be ensured to all.

2. No discrimination of any kind shall be made between the inhabitants on the ground of race, religion, language or sex.

3. All persons within the jurisdiction of the State shall be entitled to equal protection of the laws.

4. The family law and personal status of the various minorities and their religious interests, including endowments, shall be respected.

5. Except as may be required for the maintenance of public order and good government, no measure shall be taken to obstruct or interfere with the enterprise of religious or charitable bodies of all faiths or to discriminate against any representative or member of these bodies on the ground of his religion or nationality.

6. The State shall ensure adequate primary and secondary education for the Arab and Jewish minority respectively, in its own language and its cultural traditions.

The right of each community to maintain its own schools for the education of its own members in its own language, while conforming to such educational requirements of a general nature as the State may impose, shall not be denied or impaired. Foreign educational establishments shall continue their activity on the basis of their existing rights.

7. No restrictions shall be imposed on the free use by any citizen of the State of any language in private intercourse, in commerce, in religion, in the press or in publications of any kind, or at public meetings.[1]

8. No expropriation of land owned by an Arab in the Jewish State (by a Jew in the Arab State)[2] shall be allowed except for public purposes. In all cases of expropriation full compensation so fixed by the Supreme Court shall be paid previous dispossession.

Chapter 3. Citizenship, International Conventions and Financial Obligations

1. Citizenship.—Palestinian citizens residing in Palestine outside the City of Jerusalem, as well as Arabs and Jews who, not holding Palestinian citizenship, reside in Palestine outside the City of Jerusalem shall, upon the recognition of independence, become citizens of the State in which they are resident and enjoy full civil and political rights. Persons over the age of eighteen years may opt within one year from the date of recognition of independence of the State in which they reside for citizenship of the other State, providing that no Arab residing in the area of the proposed Arab State shall have the right

[1] The following stipulation shall be added to the Declaration concerning the Jewish State: "In the Jewish State adequate facilities shall be given to Arabic-speaking citizens for the use of their language, either orally or in writing, in the legislature, before the Courts and in the administration."

[2] In the Declaration concerning the Arab State, the words "by an Arab in the Jewish State" should be replaced by the words "by a Jew in the Arab State."

to opt for citizenship in the proposed Jewish State and no Jew residing in the proposed Jewish State shall have the right to opt for citizenship in the proposed Arab State. The exercise of this right of option will be taken to include the wives and children under eighteen years of age of persons so opting.

Arabs residing in the area of the proposed Jewish State and Jews residing in the area of the proposed Arab State who have signed a notice of intention to opt for citizenship of the other State shall be eligible to vote in the elections to the Constituent Assembly of that State, but not in the elections to the Constituent Assembly of the State in which they reside.

*   *   *

D. ECONOMIC UNION AND TRANSIT

1. The Provisional Council of Government of each State shall enter into an Undertaking with respect to Economic Union and Transit. This Undertaking shall be drafted by the Commission provided for in Section B, paragraph 1, utilizing to the greatest possible extent the advice and co-operation of representative organizations and bodies from each of the proposed States. It shall contain provisions to establish the Economic Union of Palestine and provide for other matters of common interest. If by 1 April 1948 the Provisional Councils of Government have not entered into the Undertaking, the Undertaking shall be put into force by the Commission.

The Economic Union of Palestine

2. The objectives of the Economic Union of Palestine shall be:
(*a*) A customs union.
(*b*) A joint currency system providing for a single foreign exchange rate.
(*c*) Operation in the common interest on a non-discriminatory basis of railways, interstate highways, postal, telephone and telegraphic services, and ports and airports involved in international trade and commerce.
(*d*) Joint economic development, especially in respect of irrigation, land reclamation and soil conservation.
(*e*) Access for both States and for the City of Jerusalem on a non-discriminatory basis to water and power facilities.

3. There shall be established a Joint Economic Board, which shall consist of three representatives of each of the two States and three foreign members appointed by the Economic and Social Council of the United Nations. The foreign members shall be appointed in the first instance for a term of three years; they shall serve as individuals and not as representatives of States.

4. The functions of the Joint Economic Board shall be to implement either directly or by delegation the measures necessary to realize the objectives of the Economic Union. It shall have all powers of organization and administration necessary to fulfil its functions.

5. The States shall bind themselves to put into effect the decisions of the Joint Economic Board. The Board's decisions shall be taken by a majority vote.

*   *   *

11. There shall be a common customs tariff with complete freedom of trade between the States, and between the States and the City of Jerusalem.

* * *

Freedom of Transit and Visit

18. The Undertaking shall contain provisions preserving freedom of transit and visit for all residents or citizens of both States and of the City of Jerusalem, subject to security considerations; provided that each State and City shall control residence within their borders.

* * *

F. ADMISSION TO MEMBERSHIP IN THE UNITED NATIONS

When the independence of either the Arab or the Jewish State as envisaged in this Plan has become effective and the Declaration and Undertaking, as envisaged in this Plan, have been signed by either of them, sympathetic consideration should be given to its application for admission to membership in the United Nations in accordance with Article 4 of the Charter of the United Nations.

* * *

PART III. CITY OF JERUSALEM

A. The City of Jerusalem shall be established as a *corpus separatum* under a Special International Regime and shall be administered by the United Nations. The Trusteeship Council shall be designated to discharge the responsibilities of the Administering Authority on behalf of the United Nations.

B. The City of Jerusalem shall include the present municipality of Jerusalem plus the surrounding villages and towns, the most eastern of which shall be Abu Dis; the most southern, Bethlehem; the most western, Ein Karim (including also the built-up area of Motsa) and the most northern, Shu'fat, as indicated on the attached sketch-map (Annex B).

C. The Trusteeship Council shall within five months from the approval of the present plan elaborate and approve a detailed Statute of the City which shall contain *inter alia* the substance of the following provisions:

1. Government Machinery: Special Objectives

The Administering Authority in discharging its administrative obligations shall pursue the following special objectives:

(*a*) To protect and to preserve the unique spiritual and religious interests located in the City of the three great monotheistic faiths throughout the world, Christian, Jewish and Moslem; to this end to ensure that order and peace, and especially religious peace, reign in Jerusalem.

(*b*) To foster co-operation among all the inhabitants of the City in their own interests as well as in order to encourage and support the peaceful development of the mutual relations between the two Palestinian peoples throughout the Holy Land; to promote the security, well-being and any constructive measures of development of the residents, having regard to the special circumstances and customs of the various peoples and communities.

2. Governor and Administrative Staff

A Governor of the City of Jerusalem shall be appointed by the Trusteeship Council and shall be responsible to it. He shall be selected on the basis of special qualifications and without regard to nationality. He shall not, however, be a citizen of either State in Palestine.

The Governor shall represent the United Nations in the City and shall exercise on their behalf all powers of administration including the conduct of external affairs. He shall be assisted by an administrative staff classed as international officers in the meaning of Article 100 of the Charter and chosen whenever practicable from the residents of the City and of the rest of Palestine on a non-discriminatory basis. A detailed plan for the organization of the administration of the City shall be submitted by the Governor to the Trusteeship Council and duly approved by it.

* * *

4. Security Measures

(a) The City of Jerusalem shall be demilitarized, its neutrality shall be declared and preserved, and no para-military formations, exercises or activities shall be permitted within its borders.

(b) Should the administration of the City of Jerusalem be seriously obstructed or prevented by the non-co-operation or interference of one or more sections of the population, the Governor shall have authority to take such measures as may be necessary to restore the effective functioning of the administration.

(c) To assist in the maintenance of internal law and order and especially for the protection of the Holy Places and religious buildings and sites in the City, the Governor shall organize a special police force of adequate strength, the members of which shall be recruited outside of Palestine. The Governor shall be empowered to direct such budgetary provision as may be necessary for the maintenance of this force.

* * *

10. Official Languages

Arabic and Hebrew shall be the official languages of the City. This will not preclude the adoption of one or more additional working languages, as may be required.

11. Citizenship

All the residents shall become *ipso facto* citizens of the City of Jerusalem unless they opt for citizenship of the State of which they have been citizens or, if Arabs or Jews, have filed the notice of intention to become citizens of the Arab or Jewish State respectively, according to Part I, section B, paragraph 9 of this Plan.

The Trusteeship Council shall make arrangements for Consular protection of the citizens of the City outside its territory.

12. Freedoms of Citizens

1. Subject only to the requirements of public order and morals, the inhabitants of the City shall be ensured the enjoyment of human rights and

fundamental freedoms, including freedom of conscience, religion and worship, language, education, speech and press, assembly and association, and petition.

2. No discrimination of any kind shall be made between the inhabitants on the grounds of race, religion, language or sex.

3. All persons within the City shall be entitled to equal protection of the laws.

4. The family law and personal status of the various persons and communities and their religious interests, including endowments, shall be respected.

5. Except as may be required for the maintenance of public order and good government, no measure shall be taken to obstruct or interfere with the enterprise of religious or charitable bodies of all faiths or to discriminate against any representative or member of these bodies on the ground of his religion or nationality.

6. The City shall ensure adequate primary and secondary education for the Arab and Jewish community respectively, in its own language and its cultural traditions.

The right of each community to maintain its own schools for the education of its own members in its own language, while conforming to such educational requirements of a general nature as the City may impose, shall not be denied or impaired. Foreign educational establishments shall continue their activity on the basis of their existing rights.

7. No restriction shall be imposed on the free use by any inhabitant of the City of any language in private intercourse, in commerce, in religion, in the press or in publications of any kind, or at public meetings.

13. Holy Places

1. Existing rights in respect of Holy Places and religious buildings or sites shall not be denied or impaired.

2. Free access to the Holy Places and religious buildings or sites and the free exercise of worship shall be secured in conformity with existing rights and subject to the requirements of public order and decorum.

*   *   *

D. DURATION OF THE SPECIAL REGIME

The Statute elaborated by the Trusteeship Council on the aforementioned principles shall come into force not later than 1 October 1948. It shall remain in force in the first instance for a period of ten years, unless the Trusteeship Council finds it necessary to undertake a re-examination of these provisions at an earlier date. After the expiration of this period the whole scheme shall be subject to re-examination by the Trusteeship Council in the light of the experience acquired with its functioning. The residents of the City shall be then free to express by means of a referendum their wishes as to possible modifications of the regime of the City.

*   *   *

◇◇◇◇◇◇

145. UNITED STATES POSITION ON PALESTINE [1]

*Statement by Ambassador Warren R. Austin, U. S. Representative
in the Security Council, March 19, 1948 (Excerpts)* [2]

[When it became apparent that the Arabs and the Jews could not reach an agreement based on the General Assembly's partition plan, the United States expressed the view that the four permanent members of the Security Council should make it clear they did not intend to let the situation in Palestine get out of hand. The United States further suggested that Palestine be placed under a temporary trusteeship of the Security Council. These views were presented by the American representative to the Security Council on March 19, 1948. While his remarks are not reproduced here, it is interesting to note that President Truman in a statement delivered six days later reiterated the trusteeship proposal. However, the United Nations failed to adopt this American suggestion.]

The resolution adopted by the Security Council on 5 March 1948 requested the permanent members of the Security Council "to consult and to inform the Security Council regarding the situation with respect to Palestine. . . ."

The plan proposed by the General Assembly was an integral plan which would not succeed unless each of its parts could be carried out. There seems to be general agreement that the plan cannot now be implemented by peaceful means. From what has been said in the Security Council and in consultations among the several members of the Security Council, it is clear that the Security Council is not prepared to go ahead with efforts to implement this plan in the existing situation. We had a vote on that subject and only five votes could be secured for that purpose.

The Security Council now has before it clear evidence that the Jews and Arabs of Palestine and the mandatory power cannot agree to implement the General Assembly plan of partition through peaceful means. The announced determination of the mandatory power to terminate the mandate on 15 May 1948, if carried out by the United Kingdom, would result, in the light of information now available, in chaos, heavy fighting and much loss of life in Palestine. The United Nations cannot permit such a result. The loss of life in the Holy Land must be brought to an immediate end. The maintenance of international peace is at stake.

The United States fully subscribes to the conclusion reached by the four permanent members that the Security Council should make it clear to the parties and governments concerned that the Security Council is determined not to permit the situation in Palestine to threaten international peace and, further, that the Security Council should take further action by all means available to it to bring about the immediate cessation of violence and the restoration of peace and order in Palestine.

Under the Charter, the Security Council has both an inescapable responsibility and full authority to take the steps necessary to bring about a cease-fire

[1] Department of State Bulletin, March 28, 1948, pp. 402-408.
[2] Made in the Security Council on March 19, 1948 (UN Doc. S/P. V. 271 March 19, 1948).

in Palestine and a halt to the incursions being made into that country. The powers of articles 39, 40, 41 and 42 are very great, and the Security Council should not hesitate to use them—all of them—if necessary to bring about peace.

In addition, my Government believes that a temporary trusteeship for Palestine should be established under the Trusteeship Council of the United Nations to maintain the peace and to afford the Jews and Arabs of Palestine, who must live together, further opportunity to reach an agreement regarding the future government of that country. Such a United Nations trusteeship would, of course, be without prejudice to the character of the eventual political settlement, which we hope can be achieved without long delay. In our opinion, the Security Council should recommend the establishment of such a trusteeship to the General Assembly and to the mandatory power. This would require an immediate special session of the General Assembly, which the Security Council might call under the terms of the Charter. Pending the meeting of the special session of the General Assembly, we believe that the Security Council should instruct the Palestine Commission to suspend its efforts to implement the proposed partition plan.

I shall now read three propositions which are being submitted by the United States. I am not making any representation for any other one of the permanent members. The United States propositions are contained in a paper entitled "Additional Conclusions and Recommendations Concerning Palestine", which has been circulated to the members. It reads as follows:

"1. The plan proposed by the General Assembly is an integral plan which cannot succeed unless each of its parts can be carried out. There seems to be general agreement that the plan cannot now be implemented by peaceful means.

"2. We believe that further steps must be taken immediately not only to maintain the peace but also to afford a further opportunity to reach an agreement between the interested parties regarding the future government of Palestine. To this end we believe that a temporary trusteeship for Palestine should be established under the Trusteeship Council of the United Nations. Such a United Nations trusteeship would be without prejudice to the rights, claims or position of the parties concerned or to the character of the eventual political settlement, which we hope can be achieved without long delay. In our opinion, the Security Council should recommend the establishment of such a trusteeship to the General Assembly and to the mandatory power. This would require an immediate special session of the General Assembly, which the Security Council should request the Secretary-General to convoke under article 20 of the Charter.

"3. Pending the meeting of the proposed special session of the General Assembly, we believe that the Security Council should instruct the Palestine Commission to suspend its efforts to implement the proposed partition plan."

Draft resolutions which would give effect to the above suggestions will be circulated shortly for the consideration of the Security Council.

◇◇◇◇◇◇

146. APPOINTMENT OF UN MEDIATOR IN PALESTINE

Resolution of the General Assembly, May 14, 1948 [1]

[While the settlement of the Palestine problem was under discussion in the United Nations, the Arabs and the Jews were engaged in bitter fighting. The debate before the General Assembly in April and May of 1947 showed conclusively that the proposal for a trusteeship for Palestine would not be accepted. With this as a background, the General Assembly on May 14, 1948, adopted the following resolution, which provided for the appointment of a United Nations mediator to seek an end to the conflict. On May 20, 1948, Count Folke Bernadotte, President of the Swedish Red Cross, was appointed as the mediator.]

The General Assembly,
Taking account of the present situation in regard to Palestine,

I

Strongly affirms its support of the efforts of the Security Council to secure a truce in Palestine and calls upon all Governments, organizations and persons to co-operate in making effective such a truce;

II

1. *Empowers* a United Nations Mediator in Palestine, to be chosen by a committee of the General Assembly composed of representatives of China, France, the Union of Soviet Socialist Republics, the United Kingdom and the United States of America, to exercise the following functions:

(*a*) To use his good offices with the local and community authorities in Palestine to:

(*i*) Arrange for the operation of common services necessary to the safety and well-being of the population of Palestine;

(*ii*) Assure the protection of the Holy Places, religious buildings and sites in Palestine;

(*iii*) Promote a peaceful adjustment of the future situation in Palestine;

(*b*) To co-operate with the Truce Commission for Palestine appointed by the Security Council in its resolution of 23 April 1948;

(*c*) To invite, as seems to him advisable, with a view to the promotion of the welfare of the inhabitants of Palestine, the assistance and cooperation of appropriate specialized agencies of the United Nations, such as the World Health Organization, of the International Red Cross, and of other governmental or non-governmental organizations of a humanitarian and non-political character;

2. *Instructs* the United Nations Mediator to render progress reports monthly, or more frequently as he deems necessary, to the Security Council and to the Secretary-General for transmission to the Members of the United Nations;

3. *Directs* the United Nations Mediator to conform in his activities with

[1] UN Doc. 186 (S-2), May 14, 1948.

the provisions of this resolution, and with such instructions as the General Assembly or the Security Council may issue;

4. *Authorizes* the Secretary-General to pay the United Nations Mediator an emolument equal to that paid to the President of the International Court of Justice, and to provide the Mediator with the necessary staff to assist in carrying out the functions assigned to the Mediator by the General Assembly;

III

Relieves the Palestine Commission from the further exercise of responsibilities under resolution 181 (II) of 29 November 1947.

◇◇◇◇◇◇

147. RECOGNITION OF ISRAEL AS AN INDEPENDENT STATE

(a) Statement by President Truman, May 14, 1948 [1]

[On May 14, 1948, the United States proclaimed that it recognized the *de facto* control then being exercised by the Provisional Government over Israel. On the following day, the Agent of the Provisional Government asked for full *de jure* recognition, but it was not until January 31, 1949, after democratic elections had been held in Israel, that a press release from the White House stated that this government had accorded Israel the requested recognition. It is interesting to note that our *de facto* recognition of Israel was extended on the same day the new state proclaimed its independence.]

This Government has been informed that a Jewish state has been proclaimed in Palestine, and recognition has been requested by the provisional government thereof.

The United States recognizes the provisional government as the *de facto* authority of the new State of Israel.

(b) Statement by President Truman, January 31, 1949 [2]

On October 24, 1948, the President stated that when a permanent government was elected in Israel, it would promptly be given *de jure* recognition. Elections for such a government were held on January 25th. The votes have now been counted, and this Government has been officially informed of the results. The United States Government is therefore pleased to extend *de jure* recognition to the Government of Israel as of this date.

◇◇◇◇◇◇

---

[1] Department of State Bulletin, May 23, 1948, p. 673.
[2] Press release issued by the White House for publication at 4.00 p.m., January 31, 1949.

148. CONCLUSIONS FROM PROGRESS REPORT OF THE UN MEDIATOR ON PALESTINE, SEPTEMBER 16, 1948 [1]

(a) Mediation Effort

[The appointment of the mediator for Palestine and the issuance of a cease-fire order by the Security Council produced an uneasy peace in Palestine, which was climaxed by the assassination of the mediator in Jerusalem on September 17, 1948. On the day before his death, the mediator, Count Bernadotte, signed a Progress Report in which, among other things, he outlined the seven basic premises on which he had conducted his work, as well as the conclusions which he believed would provide the basis for an equitable and workable settlement of the controversy.]

VIII. CONCLUSIONS

1. Since I presented my written Suggestions to the Arab and Jewish authorities on 27 June, I have made no formal submission to either party of further suggestions or proposals for a definitive settlement.[2] Since that date, however, I have held many oral discussions in the Arab capitals and Tel Aviv, in the course of which various ideas on settlement have been freely exchanged. As regards my original Suggestions, I hold to the opinion that they offered a general framework within which a reasonable and workable settlement might have been reached, had the two parties concerned been willing to discuss them. They were flatly rejected, however, by both parties. Since they were put forth on the explicit condition that they were purely tentative, were designed primarily to elicit views and counter-suggestions from each party, and, in any event, could be implemented only if agreed upon by both parties, I have never since pressed them. With respect to one basic concept in my Suggestions, it has become increasingly clear to me that however desirable a political and economic union might be in Palestine, the time is certainly not now propitious for the effectuation of any such scheme.

2. I do not consider it to be within my province to recommend to the Members of the United Nations a proposed course of action on the Palestine question. That is a responsibility of the Members acting through appropriate organs. In my role as United Nations Mediator, however, it was inevitable that I should accumulate information and draw conclusions from my experience which might well be of assistance to Members of the United Nations in charting the future course of United Nations action on Palestine. I consider it my duty, therefore, to acquaint the Members of the United Nations, through the medium of this report, with certain of the conclusions on means of peaceful adjustment which have evolved from my frequent consultations with Arab and Jewish authorities over the past three and one-half months and from my personal appraisal of the present Palestinian scene. I do not suggest that these conclusions would provide the basis for a proposal which would readily win

[1] Excerpts from UN Doc. A/648 (part one, p. 29; part two, p. 23 and part three, p. 11), September 18, 1948. Department of State Bulletin of October 3, 1948, pp. 436-440. The report was signed Folke Bernadotte in Rhodes on September 16, 1948.
[2] Bulletin of July 25, 1948, p. 105.

the willing approval of both parties. I have not, in the course of my intensive efforts to achieve agreement between Arabs and Jews, been able to devise any such formula. I am convinced, however, that it is possible at this stage to formulate a proposal which, if firmly approved and strongly backed by the General Assembly, would not be forcibly resisted by either side, confident as I am, of course, that the Security Council stands firm in its resolution of 15 July that military action shall not be employed by either party in the Palestine dispute. It cannot be ignored that the vast difference between now and last November is that a war has been started and stopped and that in the intervening months decisive events have occurred.

SEVEN BASIC PREMISES

3. The following seven basic premises form the basis for my conclusions:

Return to peace

(a) Peace must return to Palestine and every feasible measure should be taken to ensure that hostilities will not be resumed and that harmonious relations between Arab and Jew will ultimately be restored.

The Jewish State

(b) A Jewish State called Israel exists in Palestine and there are no sound reasons for assuming that it will not continue to do so.

Boundary determination

(c) The boundaries of this new State must finally be fixed either by formal agreement between the parties concerned or failing that, by the United Nations.

Continuous frontiers

(d) Adherence to the principle of geographical homogeneity and integration, which should be the major objective of the boundary arrangements, should apply equally to Arab and Jewish territories, whose frontiers should not, therefore, be rigidly controlled by the territorial arrangements envisaged in the resolution of 29 November.

Right of repatriation

(e) The right of innocent people, uprooted from their homes by the present terror and ravages of war, to return to their homes, should be affirmed and made effective, with assurance of adequate compensation for the property of those who may choose not to return.

Jerusalem

(f) The City of Jerusalem, because of its religious and international significance and the complexity of interest involved, should be accorded special and separate treatment.

International responsibility

(g) International responsibility should be expressed where desirable and necessary in the form of international guarantees, as a means of allaying existing fears, and particularly with regard to boundaries and human rights.

SPECIFIC CONCLUSIONS

4. The following conclusions, broadly outlined, would, in my view, considering all the circumstances, provide a reasonable, equitable and workable basis for settlement:

(a) Since the Security Council, under pain of Chapter VIII sanctions, has forbidden further employment of military action in Palestine as a means of settling the dispute, hostilities should be pronounced formally ended either by mutual agreement of the parties or, failing that, by the United Nations. The existing indefinite truce should be superseded by a formal peace, or at the minimum, an armistice which would involve either complete withdrawal and demobilization of armed forces or their wide separation by creation of broad demilitarized zones under United Nations supervision.

(b) The frontiers between the Arab and Jewish territories, in the absence of agreement between Arabs and Jews, should be established by the United Nations and delimited by a technical boundaries commission appointed by and responsible to the United Nations, with the following revisions in the boundaries broadly defined in the resolution of the General Assembly of 29 November in order to make them more equitable, workable and consistent with existing realities in Palestine.

    (i) The area known as the Negev, south of a line running from the sea near Majdal east southeast to Faluja (both of which places would be in Arab territory), should be defined as Arab territory;

    (ii) The frontier should run from Faluja north northeast to Ramleh and Lydda (both of which places would be in Arab territory), the frontier at Lydda then following the line established in the General Assembly resolution of 29 November;

    (iii) Galilee should be defined as Jewish territory.

(c) The disposition of the territory of Palestine not included within the boundaries of the Jewish State should be left to the Governments of the Arab States in full consultation with the Arab inhabitants of Palestine, with the recommendation, however, that in view of the historical connection and common interests of Transjordan and Palestine, there would be compelling reasons for merging the Arab territory of Palestine with the territory of Transjordan, subject to such frontier rectifications regarding other Arab States as may be found practicable and desirable.

(d) The United Nations, by declaration or other appropriate means, should undertake to provide special assurance that the boundaries between the Arab and Jewish territories shall be respected and maintained, subject only to such modifications as may be mutually agreed upon by the parties concerned.

(e) The port of Haifa, including the oil refineries and terminal and without prejudice to their inclusion in the sovereign territory of the Jewish State or the administration of the city of Haifa, should be declared a free port, with assurances of free access for interested Arab countries and an undertaking on their part to place no obstacle in the way of oil deliveries by pipeline to the Haifa refineries, whose distribution would continue on the basis of the historical pattern.

(f) The airport of Lydda should be declared a free airport with assurance of access to it and employment of its facilities for Jerusalem and interested Arab countries.

(g) The City of Jerusalem, which should be understood as covering the area defined in the resolution of the General Assembly of 29 November, should be treated separately and should be placed under effective United Nations control with maximum feasible local autonomy for its Arab and Jewish communities, with full safeguards for the protection of the Holy Places and sites and free access to them, and for religious freedom.

(h) The right of unimpeded access to Jerusalem, by road, rail or air, should be fully respected by all parties.

(i) The right of Arab refugees to return to their homes in Jewish-controlled territory at the earliest possible date should be affirmed by the United Nations, and their repatriation, resettlement and economic and social rehabilitation, and payment of adequate compensation for the property of those choosing not to return, should be supervised and assisted by the United Nations conciliation commission described in paragraph (k) below.

(j) The political, economic, social and religious rights of all Arabs in the Jewish territory of Palestine and of all Jews in the Arab territory of Palestine should be fully guaranteed and respected by the authorities. The conciliation commission provided for in the following paragraph should supervise the observance of this guarantee. It should also lend its good offices, on the invitation of the parties, to any efforts toward exchanges of populations with a view to eliminating troublesome minority problems, and on the basis of adequate compensation for property owned.

(k) In view of the special nature of the Palestine problem and the dangerous complexities of Arab-Jewish relationships, the United Nations should establish a Palestine conciliation commission. This commission, which should be appointed for a limited period, should be responsible to the United Nations and act under its authority. The commission, assisted by such United Nations personnel as may prove necessary should undertake

  (i) To employ its good offices to make such recommendations to the parties or to the United Nations, and to take such other steps as may be appropriate, with a view to ensuring the continuation of the peaceful adjustment of the situation in Palestine;

  (ii) Such measures as it might consider appropriate in fostering the cultivation of friendly relations between Arabs and Jews;

  (iii) To supervise the observance of such boundary, road, railroad, free port, free airport, minority rights and other arrangements as may be decided upon by the United Nations;

  (iv) To report promptly to the United Nations any development in Palestine likely to alter the arrangements approved by the United Nations in the Palestine settlement or to threaten the peace of the area.

*   *   *

(b) Assistance to Refugees

VI. Conclusions

1. Conclusions which may be derived from the experience to date are summarized as follows:

(a) As a result of the conflict in Palestine there are approximately 360,000 Arab refugees and 7,000 Jewish refugees requiring aid in that country and adjacent States.

(b) Large numbers of these are infants, children, pregnant women and nursing mothers. Their condition is one of destitution and they are "vulnerable groups" in the medical and social sense.

(c) The destruction of their property and the loss of their assets will render most of them a charge upon the communities in which they have sought refuge for a minimum period of one year (through this winter and until the end of the 1949 harvest).

(d) The Arab inhabitants of Palestine are not citizens or subjects of Egypt, Iraq, Lebanon, Syria and Transjordan, the States which are at present providing them with a refuge and the basic necessities of life. As residents of Palestine, a former mandated territory for which the international community has a continuing responsibility until a final settlement is achieved, these Arab refugees understandably look to the United Nations for effective assistance.

(e) The temporary alleviation of their condition, which is all that my disaster relief programme can promise them now, is quite inadequate to meet any continuing need, unless the resources in supplies and personnel available are greatly increased. Such increased resources might indirectly be of permanent value in establishing social services in the countries concerned, or improving greatly existing services. This applies particularly to general social administrative organizations, maternal and child care services, the training of social workers and the improvement of food economics.

(f) The refugees, on return to their homes, are entitled to adequate safeguards for their personal security, normal facilities for employment, and adequate opportunities to develop within the community without racial, religious or social discrimination.

(g) So long as large numbers of the refugees remain in distress, I believe that responsibility for their relief should be assumed by the United Nations in conjunction with the neighbouring Arab States, the Provisional Government of Israel, the specialized agencies, and also all the voluntary bodies or organizations of a humanitarian and non-political character.

2. In concluding this part of my report, I must emphasize again the desperate urgency of this problem. The choice is between saving the lives of many thousands of people now or permitting them to die. The situation of the majority of these hapless refugees is already tragic, and to prevent them from being overwhelmed by further disaster and to make possible their ultimate rehabilitation, it is my earnest hope that the international community will give all necessary support to make the measures I have outlined fully effective. I believe that for the international community to accept its share of responsibility for the refugees of Palestine is one of the minimum conditions for the success of its effort to bring peace to that land.

◇◇◇◇◇◇

149. CREATION OF A CONCILIATION COMMISSION FOR PALESTINE

Resolution of the General Assembly, December 11, 1948 [1]

[In his Progress Report, made public after his assassination, Count Bernadotte recommended that the General Assembly establish a Conciliation Commission for Palestine. Accordingly, the Assembly by resolution on December 11, 1948, created the recommended commission, which it directed to assume such powers of the acting mediator as it might find desirable and necessary to bring about a settlement of the issues in Palestine.]

THE GENERAL ASSEMBLY,

HAVING CONSIDERED FURTHER the situation in Palestine,

1. *Expresses* its deep appreciation of the progress achieved through the good offices of the late United Nations Mediator in promoting a peaceful adjustment of the future situation of Palestine, for which cause he sacrificed his life; and

Extends its thinks to the Acting Mediator and his staff for their continued efforts and devotion to duty in Palestine;

2. *Establishes* a Conciliation Commission consisting of three States Members of the United Nations which shall have the following functions:

(a) To assume, insofar as it considers necessary in existing circumstances, the functions given to the United Nations Mediator on Palestine by the resolution of the General Assembly of 14 May 1948;

(b) To carry out the specific functions and directives given to it by the present resolution and such additional functions and directives as may be given to it by the General Assembly or by the Security Council;

(c) To undertake, upon the request of the Security Council, any of the functions now assigned to the United Nations Mediator on Palestine or to the United Nations Truce Commission by resolutions of the Security Council; upon such request to the Conciliation Commission by the Security Council with respect to all the remaining functions of the United Nations Mediator on Palestine under Security Council resolutions, the office of the Mediator shall be terminated;

3. *Decides* that a Committee of the Assembly, consisting of China, France, the Union of Soviet Socialist Republics, the United Kingdom and the United States of America, shall present, before the end of the first part of the present session of the General Assembly, for the approval of the Assembly, a proposal concerning the names of the three States which will constitute the Conciliation Commission;

4. *Requests* the Commission to begin its functions at once, with a view to the establishment of contact between the parties themselves and the Commission at the earliest possible date;

5. *Calls upon* the Governments and authorities concerned to extend the scope of the negotiations provided for in the Security Council's resolution of 16 November 1948 and to seek agreement by negotiations conducted either

[1] United States participation in the United Nations: Report by the President to the Congress for the year 1948, Department of State publication 3437, pp. 195-198.

with the Conciliation Commission or directly with a view to the final settlement of all questions outstanding between them;

6. *Instructs* the Conciliation Commission to take steps to assist the Governments and authorities concerned to achieve a final settlement of all questions outstanding between them;

7. *Resolves* that the Holy Places—including Nazareth—religious building and sites in Palestine should be protected and free access to them assured, in accordance with existing rights and historical practice; that arrangements to this end should be under effective United Nations supervision; that the United Nations Conciliation Commission, in presenting to the fourth regular session of the General Assembly its detailed proposal for a permanent international regime for the territory of Jerusalem, should include recommendations concerning the Holy Places in that territory; that with regard to the Holy Places in the rest of Palestine the Commission should call upon the political authorities of the areas concerned to give appropriate formal guarantees as to the protection of the Holy Places and access to them; and that these undertakings should be presented to the General Assembly for approval;

8. *Resolves* that, in view of its association with three world religions, the Jerusalem area, including the present municipality of Jerusalem *plus* the surrounding villages and towns, the most eastern of which shall be Abu Dis; the most southern, Bethlehem; the most western, Ein Karim (including also the built-up area of Motsa); and the most northern, Shufat, should be accorded special and separate treatment from the rest of Palestine and should be placed under effective United Nations control;

Requests the Security Council to take further steps to ensure the demilitarization of Jerusalem at the earliest possible date;

Instructs the Conciliation Commission to present to the fourth regular session of the General Assembly detailed proposals for a permanent international regime for the Jerusalem area which will provide for the maximum local autonomy for distinctive groups consistent with the special international status of the Jerusalem area;

The Conciliation Commission is authorized to appoint a United Nations representative who shall co-operate with the local authorities with respect to the interim administration of the Jerusalem area;

9. *Resolves* that, pending agreement on more detailed arrangements among the Governments and authorities concerned, the freest possible access to Jerusalem by road, rail or air should be accorded to all inhabitants of Palestine;

Instructs the Conciliation Commission to report immediately to the Security Council, for appropriate action by that organ, any attempt by any party to impede such access;

10. *Instructs* the Conciliation Commission to seek arrangements among the Governments and authorities concerned which will facilitate the economic development of the area, including arrangements for access to ports and airfields and the use of transportation and communication facilities;

11. *Resolves* that the refugees wishing to return to their homes and live at peace with their neighbours should be permitted to do so at the earliest practicable date, and that compensation should be paid for the property of those choosing not to return and for loss of or damage to property which, under

principles of international law or in equity, should be made good by the Governments or authorities responsible;

Instructs the Conciliation Commission to facilitate the repatriation, resettlement and economic and social rehabilitation of the refugees and the payment of compensation, and to maintain close relations with the Director of the United Nations Relief for Palestine Refugees and, through him, with the appropriate organs and agencies of the United Nations;

12. *Authorizes* the Conciliation Commission to appoint such subsidiary bodies and to employ such technical experts, acting under its authority, as it may find necessary for the effective discharge of its functions and responsibilities under the present resolution;

The Concilation Commission will have its official headquarters at Jerusalem. The authorities responsible for maintaining order in Jerusalem will be responsible for taking all measures necessary to ensure the security of the Commission. The Secretary-General will provide a limited number of guards for the protection of the staff and premises of the Commission;

13. *Instructs* the Concilation Commission to render progress reports periodically to the Secretary-General for transmission to the Security Council and to the Members of the United Nations;

14. *Calls upon* all Governments and authorities concerned to co-operate with the Conciliation Commission and to take all possible steps to assist in the implementation of the present resolution;

15. *Requests* the Secretary-General to provide the necessary staff and facilities and to make appropriate arrangements to provide the necessary funds required in carrying out the terms of the present resolution.

150. REPORT ON STATUS OF THE ARMISTICE NEGOTIATIONS AND TRUCE IN PALESTINE, JULY 21, 1949 (EXCERPTS) [1]

[Prior to the appointment of the mediator for Palestine, the Security Council adopted a resolution dated April 1, 1948, calling for a truce in Palestine and requesting the Jews and Arabs to cease all military activities and to stop any activities that might prejudice the final settlement. On July 7, 1948, the Council resolved to continue the truce, which action was shortly followed by the assassination of Bernadotte and the opening of hostilities in the Negev. This fighting was brought to an end in April 1949. On July 21, 1949, the acting mediator, Ralph J. Bunche, made the following report in which he noted that the armistice agreement reached between the Arabs and Jews made the truce no longer necessary. He also recommended a resolution for Council adoption, which would terminate the functions of the mediator and

[1] UN Doc. S/1357, dated July 26, 1949. Transmitted with a letter dated July 21, 1949, from the UN Acting Mediator on Palestine, Ralph J. Bunche, to the Secretary-General, Trygve Lie, Department of State Bulletin of August 15, 1949, pp. 223-226. For text of the Israeli-Syrian armistice agreement, see Bulletin of August 8, 1949, p. 177; for texts of Israeli agreements with Egypt, Lebanon, and Hashemite Jordan Kingdom, see Documents and State Papers of May 1949, p. 798.

transfer to the Concilation Commission the duty of seeing that the UN cease-fire order was observed.]

III. CONCLUSIONS

1. The practical application of the Security Council's truce in Palestine has now been superseded by effective armistice agreements voluntarily negotiated by the parties in the transition from truce to permanent peace. Since all of these agreements are self-enforcing and establish the necessary machinery for their supervision, with the assistance of the United Nations Chief of Staff of the Truce Supervision and United Nations observers at his command, it would seem unnecessary longer to impose upon the States concerned the restrictive conditions of the Security Council truce. The Security Council resolution of 15 July 1948 imposed not only a truce and the conditions relating thereto, but ordered the Governments and authorities concerned, pursuant to Article 40 of the Charter of the United Nations, to desist from further military action.

2. In view of the existing state of affairs in Palestine, the Security Council might consider it advisable to review the situation in the light of the new conditions and to take appropriate action. Such action might declare it unnecessary to prolong the truce provided for in the Security Council resolution of 15 July 1948. It might, at the same time, reaffirm the order in that resolution to the Governments and authorities concerned, pursuant to Article 40 of the Charter of the United Nations, to desist from further military action, and might also call upon the parties to the dispute to continue to observe an unconditional cease-fire. Action along some such lines would be consistent with the realities of the present situation and would at the same time fully safe-guard the basic objective of the Security Council that fighting in Palestine shall not be resumed.

3. In conclusion, I would respectively call to the attention of the Security Council my communication to the Council of 17 January 1949 (S/1215). In my view, the action which the Council might now properly take should also provide, in accordance with the resolution of the General Assembly of 11 December 1948 (S/807), for the termination or transfer to the United Nations Palestine Conciliation Commission of such functions as now remain to the position of Mediator under Security Council resolutions. With the armistice agreements concluded, there is no longer any useful function to be performed by the Mediator. Any further activity by me would inevitably impinge upon the work of the Palestine Conciliation Commission. This could create only confusion and duplication of effort and would serve no useful purpose whatsoever. Under the terms of the several armistice agreements, I have no responsibility for their implementation or supervision, since this responsibility, by mutual agreement, is assumed by the parties themselves. With the truce obsolete, the armistice agreements concluded and the Palestine Conciliation Commission conducting peace negotiations, the mission of the Mediator has been fulfilled. I am happy to have had this great opportunity to serve the United Nations and the cause of peace in Palestine and in this, my final report, wish to thank the Security Council for the indispensable support which it has given to me in my efforts to discharge the responsibilities entrusted to me.

4. Finally, it is clear to me that the success or failure of any mediation or conciliation effort in a situation such as that presented by Palestine must

depend very largely upon the measure of support afforded by the United Nations. If the voice of the United Nations is strong and clear, it can be the decisive factor in the mediatory effort to resolve the conflict. The most effective instrument at the disposal of a mediator or conciliator is the assurance of prompt and vigorous support and action by the United Nations.

5. I have taken the liberty of attaching to this report, as an annex, a memorandum suggesting the general lines of the action which the Security Council might now consider it appropriate to take.

(Signed) RALPH J. BUNCHE

Acting Mediator

ANNEX

The Security Council,

HAVING NOTED with satisfaction the several armistice agreements concluded by means of negotiations between the parties involved in the conflict in Palestine in pursuance of its resolution of 16 November 1948 (S/1080);

Expresses the hope that the Governments and authorities concerned, having undertaken by means of the negotiations now being conducted by the Palestine Conciliation Commission, to fulfill the request of the General Assembly in its resolution of 11 December 1948 to extend the scope of the armistice negotiations and to seek agreement by negotiations concluded either with the Conciliation Commission or directly, will at an early date achieve agreement on the final settlement of all questions outstanding between them;

Declares that the armistice agreements as an important step in the transition from truce to permanent peace in Palestine, render unnecessary the prolongation of the truce as provided in the resolution of the Security Council of 15 July 1948 (S/902);

Reaffirms the order set forth in its resolution of 15 July 1948 to the Governments and authorities concerned, pursuant to Article 40 of the Charter of the United Nations, to desist from further military action, and calls upon them to continue to observe an unconditional cease-fire;

Requests the Conciliation Commission, with the assistance of the United Nations Chief of Staff of the Truce Supervision Organization, to undertake the observance of the cease-fire in Palestine, and terminates all remaining functions of the United Nations Mediator on Palestine under Security Council resolutions;

Requests the Secretary-General to continue in existence such of the present Truce Supervision Organization as the Conciliation Commission, in consultation with the Chief of Staff, may require in maintaining the cease-fire and as may be necessary in assisting the parties to the armistice agreements in the supervision of the application and observance of the terms of those agreements.

151. JOINT RESOLUTION ON PALESTINE REFUGEES, MARCH 24, 1949

Authorization of contribution by the United States [1]

[Hostilities in Palestine made homeless some 800,000 Arabs and approximately 7,000 Jews. The Arabs were driven out of the territory newly acquired by the Jews, while the Jewish refugees consisted of those who were no longer welcome in the Arab areas. The mediator asked the United Nations members to help with the problem. On November 19, 1948, the Assembly adopted a voluntary relief plan for the refugees and called upon the United Nations members for donations. The United States answered with a contribution not to exceed $16,000,000, voted by Congress on March 24, 1948.]

Resolved by the Senate and House of Representatives of the United States of America in Congress assembled, That there is hereby authorized to be appropriated to the President, out of any money in the Treasury not otherwise appropriated, not to exceed $16,000,000 as a special contribution by the United States to the United Nations for the purposes set forth in the resolution of the General Assembly of the United Nations of November 19, 1948, providing for the relief of Palestine refugees.

SEC. 2. Notwithstanding the provision of any other law, the Reconstruction Finance Corporation is authorized and directed, until such time as an appropriation shall be made pursuant to section 1, to make advances to the President, not to exceed in the aggregate $8,000,000, to carry out the provisions of this joint resolution. From appropriations authorized under section 1, there shall be repaid to the Reconstruction Finance Corporation, without interest, the advances made by it under authority contained herein. No interest shall be charged on advances made by the Treasury to the Reconstruction Finance Corporation in implementation of this section.

Approved March 24, 1949.

◇◇◇◇◇◇

152. ASSISTANCE TO PALESTINE REFUGEES

Resolution of the General Assembly, December 8, 1949 [2]

[It was hoped that in providing the Palestinian refugees with aid, constructive relief programs producing permanent improvements in the economy of the region might be undertaken. On December 8, 1949, the General Assembly established the United Nations Relief and Works Agency for Palestine Refugees

---

[1] Public Law 25, 81st Cong., 1st sess., S. J. Res. 36.
[2] UN Doc. A/1237, December 9, 1949. By this resolution the United Nations Relief for Palestine Refugees was discontinued and its assets and functions were transferred to the newly established United Nations Relief and Works Agency for Palestine Refugees in the Near East, which combined relief to refugees with a works program.

in the Near East to carry out relief programs for the refugees in coöperation with the interested governments. Part of the Assembly resolution follows.[1]]

The General Assembly,

Recalling its resolutions 212 (III) of 19 November 1948 and 194 (III) of 11 December 1948, affirming in particular the provisions of paragraph 11 of the latter resolution,

Having examined with appreciation the first interim report of the United Nations Economic Survey Mission for the Middle East (A/1106) and the report of the Secretary-General on assistance to Palestine refugees (A/1060 and A/1060/Add. 1),

1. *Expresses* its appreciation to the Governments which have generously responded to the appeal embodied in its resolution 212 (III), and to the appeal of the Secretary-General, to contribute in kind or funds to the alleviation of the conditions of starvation and distress amongst the Palestine refugees;

2. *Expresses* also its gratitude to the International Committee of the Red Cross, to the League of Red Cross Societies and to the American Friends Service Committee for the contribution they have made to this humanitarian cause by discharging, in the face of great difficulties, the responsibility they voluntarily assumed for the distribution of relief supplies and the general care of the refugees; and welcomes the assurance they have given the Secretary-General that they will continue their co-operation with the United Nations until the end of March 1950 on a mutually acceptable basis;

3. *Commends* the United Nations International Children's Emergency Fund for the important contribution which it has made towards the United Nations programme of assistance; and commends those specialized agencies which have rendered assistance in their respective fields, in particular the World Health Organization, the United Nations Educational, Scientific and Cultural Organization and the International Refugee Organization;

4. *Expresses* its thanks to the numerous religious, charitable and humanitarian organizations which have materially assisted in bringing relief to Palestine refugees;

5. *Recognizes* that, without prejudice to the provisions of paragraph 11 of the General Assembly resolution 194 (III) of 11 December 1948, continued assistance for the relief of the Palestine refugees is necessary to prevent conditions of starvation and distress among them and to further conditions of peace and stability, and that constructive measures should be undertaken at an early date with a view to the termination of international assistance for relief;

6. *Considers that,* subject to the provisions of paragraph 9 (d) of the present resolution, the equivalent of approximately $33,700,000 will be required for direct relief and works programmes for the period 1 January to 31 December 1950 of which the equivalent of $20,200,000 is required for direct relief and $13,500,000 for works programmes; that the equivalent of approximately $21,200,000 will be required for works programmes from 1 January to 30 June 1951, all inclusive of administrative expenses; and that direct relief should be terminated not later than 31 December 1950 unless otherwise determined by the General Assembly at its fifth regular session;

[1] On December 2, 1950 the Assembly by resolution voted to continue the work of the Agency, laying down instructions for its operation.

7. *Establishes* the "United Nations Relief and Works Agency for Palestine Refugees in the Near East":

(a) To carry out in collaboration with local governments the direct relief and works programmes as recommended by the Economic Survey Mission;

(b) To consult with the interested Near Eastern Governments concerning measures to be taken by them preparatory to the time when international assistance for relief and works projects is no longer available;

8. *Establishes* an Advisory Commission consisting of representatives of France, Turkey, the United Kingdom of Great Britain and Northern Ireland and the United States of America, with power to add not more than three additional members from contributing Governments, to advise and assist the Director of the United Nations Relief and Works Agency for Palestine Refugees in the Near East in the execution of the programme; the Director and the Advisory Commission shall consult with each Near Eastern Government concerned in the selection, planning and execution of projects;

9. *Requests* the Secretary-General to appoint the Director of the United Nations Relief and Works Agency for Palestine Refugees in the Near East in consultation with the Governments represented on the Advisory Commission;

(a) The Director shall be the chief executive officer of the United Nations Relief and Works Agency for Palestine Refugees in the Near East responsible to the General Assembly for the operation of the programme;

(b) The Director shall select and appoint his staff in accordance with general arrangements made in agreement with the Secretary-General, including such of the staff rules and regulations of the United Nations as the Director and the Secretary-General shall agree are applicable, and to the extent possible utilize the facilities and assistance of the Secretary-General;

(c) The Director shall, in consultation with the Secretary-General and the Advisory Committee on Administrative and Budgetary Questions, establish financial regulations for the United Nations Relief and Works Agency for Palestine Refugees in the Near East;

(d) Subject to the financial regulations established pursuant to clause (c) of the present paragraph, the Director, in consultation with the advisory Commission, shall apportion available funds between direct relief and works projects in their discretion, in the event that the estimates in paragraph 6 require revision;

10. *Requests* the Director to convene the Advisory Commission at the earliest practicable date for the purpose of developing plans for the organization and administration of the programme, and of adopting rules of procedure;

11. *Continues* the United Nations Relief for Palestine Refugees as established under General Assembly resolution 212 (III) until 1 April 1950, or until such date thereafter as the transfer referred to in paragraph 12 is effected, and requests the Secretary-General in consultation with the operating agencies to continue the endeavour to reduce the numbers of rations by progressive stages in the light of the findings and recommendations of the Economic Survey Mission;

12. *Instructs* the Secretary-General to transfer to the United Nations Relief and Works Agency for Palestine Refugees in the Near East the assets

and liabilities of the United Nations Relief for Palestine Refugees by 1 April 1950, or at such date as may be agreed by him and the Director of the United Nations Relief and Works Agency for Palestine Refugees in the Near East;

13. *Urges* all Members of the United Nations and non-members to make voluntary contributions in funds or in kind to ensure that the amount of supplies and funds required is obtained for each period of the programme as set out in paragraph 6; contributions in funds may be made in currencies other than the United States dollar in so far as the programme can be carried out in such currencies;

14. *Authorizes* the Secretary-General, in consultation with the Advisory Committee on Administrative and Budgetary Questions, to advance funds deemed to be available for this purpose and not exceeding $5,000,000 from the Working Capital Fund to finance operations pursuant to the present resolution, such sum to be repaid not later than 31 December 1950 from the voluntary governmental contributions requested under paragraph 13 above;

15. *Authorizes* the Secretary-General, in consultation with the Advisory Committee on Administrative and Budgetary Questions, to negotiate with the International Refugee Organization for an interest-free loan in an amount not to exceed the equivalent of $2,800,000 to finance the programme subject to mutually satisfactory conditions for repayment;

16. *Authorizes* the Secretary-General to continue the Special Fund established under General Assembly resolution 212 (III) and to make withdrawals therefrom for the operation of the United Nations Relief for Palestine Refugees and, upon the request of the Director, for the operations of the United Nations Relief and Works Agency for Palestine Refugees in the Near East;

17. *Calls upon* the Governments concerned to accord to the United Nations Relief and Works Agency for Palestine Refugees in the Near East the privileges, immunities, exemptions and facilities which have been granted to the United Nations Relief for Palestine Refugees, together with all other privileges, immunities, exemptions and facilities necessary for the fulfilment of its functions;

18. *Urges* the United Nations International Children's Emergency Fund, the International Refugee Organization, the World Health Organization, the United Nations Educational, Scientific and Cultural Organization, the Food and Agricultural Organization and other appropriate agencies and private groups and organizations, in consultation with the Director of the United Nations Relief and Works Agency for Palestine Refugees in the Near East, to furnish assistance within the framework of the programme;

19. *Requests* the Director of the United Nations Relief and Works Agency for Palestine Refugees in the Near East:

(a) To appoint a representative to attend the meeting of the Technical Assistance Board as observer so that the technical assistance activities of the United Nations Relief and Works Agency for Palestine Refugees in the Near East may be co-ordinated with the technical assistance programmes of the United Nations and specialized agencies referred to in Economic and Social Council resolution 222 (IX) A of 15 August 1949;

(b) To place at the disposal of the Technical Assistance Board full information concerning any technical assistance work which may be done by the

United Nations Relief and Works Agency for Palestine Refugees in the Near East, in order that it may be included in the reports submitted by the Technical Assistance Board to the Technical Assistance Committee of the Economic and Social Council;

20. *Directs* the United Nations Relief and Works Agency for Palestine Refugees in the Near East to consult with the United Nations Conciliation Commission for Palestine in the best interests of their respective tasks, with particular reference to paragraph 11 of General Assembly resolution 194 (III) of 11 December 1948;

21. *Requests* the Director to submit to the General Assembly of the United Nations an annual report on the work of the United Nations Relief and Works Agency for Palestine Refugees in the Near East, including an audit of funds, and invites him to submit to the Secretary-General such other reports as the United Nations Relief and Works Agency for Palestine Refugees in the Near East may wish to bring to the attention of Members of the United Nations, or its appropriate organs;

22. *Instructs* the United Nations Conciliation Commission for Palestine to transmit the final report of the Economic Survey Mission, with such comments as it may wish to make, to the Secretary-General for transmission to the Members of the United Nations and to the United Nations Relief and Works Agency for Palestine Refugees in the Near East.

◇◇◇◇◇

153. INTERNATIONAL REGIME FOR THE JERUSALEM AREA AND PROTECTION OF THE HOLY PLACES

Resolution of the General Assembly, December 9, 1949 [1]

[Great concern was felt throughout the world lest Jerusalem and the holy places, so precious to millions of people of many faiths, should be injured or destroyed by hostilities in Palestine. There was also reluctance to have the holy places permanently linked to either the Arab or the Jewish state. The UNSCOP and other reports proposed placing Jerusalem under international administration. This pleased neither the Arabs nor the Jews. Nevertheless, the General Assembly on December 9, 1949, resolved to ask the Trusteeship Council to draw up a plan and statute for the internationalization of the city.]

The General Assembly,

Having regard to its resolutions 181 (II) of 29 November 1947 and 194 (III) of 11 December 1948,

Having studied the reports of the United Nations Conciliation Commission for Palestine set up under the latter resolution,

I. *Decides*

In relation to Jerusalem,

Believing that the principles underlying its previous resolutions concerning this matter, and in particular its resolution of 29 November 1947, represent a just and equitable settlement of the question,

[1] UN Doc. A/1245, December 10, 1949.

1. To reinstate, therefore, its intention that Jerusalem should be placed under a permanent international regime, which should envisage appropriate guarantees for the protection of the Holy Places, both within and outside Jerusalem and to confirm specifically the following provisions of General Assembly resolution 181 (II) [1] (1) The City of Jerusalem shall be established as a *corpus separatum* under a special international regime and shall be administered by the United Nations; (2) The Trusteeship Council shall be designated to discharge the responsibilities of the Administering Authority . . .; and (3) The City of Jerusalem shall include the present municipality of Jerusalem plus the surrounding villages and towns, the most eastern of which shall be Abu Dis; the most southern, Bethlehem; the most western, Ein Karim (including also the built-up area of Motsa); and the most northern, Shu'fat, as indicated on the attached sketch-map (annex B);

2. To request for this purpose that the Trusteeship Council at its next session, whether special or regular, complete the preparation of the Statute of Jerusalem (T/118/Rev. 2), omitting the now inapplicable provisions, such as articles 32 and 39, and, without prejudice to the fundamental principles of the international regime for Jerusalem set forth in General Assembly resolution 181 (II) introducing therein amendments in the direction of its greater democratization, approve the Statute, and proceed immediately with its implementation. The Trusteeship Council shall not allow any actions taken by any interested Government or Governments to divert it from adopting and implementing the Statute of Jerusalem;

II. *Calls upon* the State concerned, to make formal undertakings, at an early date and in the light of their obligations as Members of the United Nations, that they will approach these matters with good will, and be guided by the terms of the present resolution.

◇◇◇◇◇

154. TRIPARTITE DECLARATION REGARDING SECURITY IN THE NEAR EAST [2]

Three-Power Statement, May 25, 1950

[The issues between the Arabs and the Jews contained seeds of war in the Near East, which made the supplying of arms and war materials to either side a grave international problem. On May 25, 1950, France, Great Britain, and the United States announced that they had taken measures to stabilize the situation in that area by agreement among themselves not to furnish arms to a state which intended to use those arms for aggression upon another state. The three countries also agreed to take action both from within and outside of the United Nations to prevent any Near Eastern state from violating established frontiers or armistice lines.]

[1] See UN Doc. A/519.
[2] Department of State Bulletin, June 5, 1950, p. 886.

The Governments of the United Kingdom, France, and the United States, having had occasion during the recent Foreign Ministers meeting in London to review certain questions affecting the peace and stability of the Arab states and of Israel, and particularly that of the supply of arms and war material to these states, have resolved to make the following statements:

1. The three Governments recognize that the Arab states and Israel all need to maintain a certain level of armed forces for the purposes of assuring their internal security and their legitimate self-defense and to permit them to play their part in the defense of the area as a whole. All applications for arms or war material for these countries will be considered in the light of these principles. In this connection the three Governments wish to recall and affirm the terms of the statements made by their representatives on the Security Council on August 4, 1949, in which they declared their opposition to the development of an arms race between the Arab states and Israel.

2. The three Governments declare that assurances have been received from all the states in question, to which they permit arms to be supplied from their countries, that the purchasing state does not intend to undertake any act of aggression against any other state. Similar assurances will be requested from any other state in the area to which they permit arms to be supplied in the future.

3. The three Governments take this opportunity of declaring their deep interest in and their desire to promote the establishment and maintenance of peace and stability in the area and their unalterable opposition to the use of force or threat of force between any of the states in that area. The three Governments, should they find that any of these states was preparing to violate frontiers or armistice lines, would, consistently with their obligations as members of the United Nations, immediately take action, both within and outside the United Nations, to prevent such violation.

◇◇◇◇◇

PHILIPPINES

155. INDEPENDENCE OF THE PHILIPPINES

Proclamation by President Truman, July 4, 1946 [1]

[The movement on the part of colonial peoples towards independence is one of the striking phenomena of our times. This movement was given considerable impetus in 1934 when Congress provided for the withdrawal of the United States from the Philippines after a ten-year transitional period. President Truman's proclamation of Philippine independence was issued on the fourth of July after the end of the war in the Far East. This action has been widely acclaimed by many nations in the postwar era as setting an example for the other colonial powers to follow.]

WHEREAS the United States of America by the Treaty of Peace with Spain of December 10, 1898, commonly known as the Treaty of Paris, and by the

[1] Department of State Bulletin of July 14, 1946, p. 66.

Treaty with Spain of November 7, 1900, did acquire sovereignty over the Philippines, and by the Convention of January 2, 1930, with Great Britain did delimit the boundary between the Philippine Archipelago and the State of North Borneo; and

WHEREAS the United States of America has consistently and faithfully during the past forty-eight years exercised jurisdiction and control over the Philippines and its people; and

WHEREAS it has been the repeated declaration of the legislative and executive branches of the Government of the United States of America that full independence would be granted the Philippines as soon as the people of the Philippines were prepared to assume this obligation; and

WHEREAS the people of the Philippines have clearly demonstrated their capacity for self-government; and

WHEREAS the Act of Congress approved March 24, 1934, known as the Philippine Independence Act, directed that, on the 4th Day of July immediately following a ten-year transitional period leading to the independence of the Philippines, the President of the United States of America should by proclamation withdraw and surrender all rights of possession, supervision, jurisdiction, control, or sovereignty of the United States of America in and over the territory and people of the Philippines, except certain reservations therein or thereafter authorized to be made, and, on behalf of the United States of America, should recognize the independence of the Philippines:

Now, THEREFORE, I, Harry S. Truman, President of the United States of America, acting under and by virtue of the authority vested in me by the aforesaid act of Congress, do proclaim that, in accord with and subject to the reservations provided for in the applicable statutes of the United States,

The United States of America hereby withdraws and surrenders all rights of possession, supervision, jurisdiction, control, or sovereignty now existing and exercised by the United States of America in and over the territory and people of the Philippines; and,

On behalf of the United States of America, I do hereby recognize the independence of the Philippines as a separate and self-governing nation and acknowledge the authority and control over the same of the government instituted by the people thereof, under the constitution now in force.

IN WITNESS WHEREOF, I have hereunto set my hand and caused the seal of the United States to be affixed.

DONE at the City of Washington this Fourth day of July in the year of our Lord, nineteen hundred and forty-six, and of the Independence [SEAL]   of the United States of America the one hundred and seventy-first.

HARRY S. TRUMAN

By the President:
DEAN ACHESON
  Acting Secretary of State.

◇◇◇◇◇◇

156. GENERAL RELATIONS

Treaty Between the United States and the Republic of the Philippines, July 4, 1946 [1]

[This treaty is the international act which establishes the independence of the Philippines. It also deals with certain mutual problems between the two countries which naturally arise when sovereignty passes to a dependent people, such as claims against the two governments, responsibility for debts, diplomatic privileges and immunities, and so on. Of particular importance is Article I which grants to the United States the right to retain bases in the Philippines necessary for the protection of the two countries.]

The United States of America and the Republic of the Philippines, being animated by the desire to cement the relations of close and long friendship existing between the two countries, and to provide for the recognition of the independence of the Republic of the Philippines as of July 4, 1946 and the relinquishment of American sovereignty over the Philippine Islands, have agreed upon the following articles:

ARTICLE I

The United States of America agrees to withdraw and surrender, and does hereby withdraw and surrender, all right of possession, supervision, jurisdiction, control or sovereignty existing and exercised by the United States of America in and over the territory and the people of the Philippine Islands, except the use of such bases, necessary appurtenances to such bases, and the rights incident thereto, as the United States of America, by agreement with the Republic of the Philippines, may deem necessary to retain for the mutual protection of the United States of America and of the Republic of the Philippines. The United States of America further agrees to recognize, and does hereby recognize, the independence of the Republic of the Philippines as a separate self-governing nation and to acknowledge, and does hereby acknowledge, the authority and control over the same of the Government instituted by the people thereof, under the Constitution of the Republic of the Philippines.

ARTICLE II

The diplomatic representatives of each country shall enjoy in the territories of the other the privileges and immunities derived from generally recognized international law and usage. The consular representatives of each country, duly provided with exequatur, will be permitted to reside in the territories of the other in the places wherein consular representatives are by local laws permitted to reside; they shall enjoy the honorary privileges and the immunities accorded to such officers by general international usage; and they shall not be treated in a manner less favorable than similar officers of any other foreign country.

[1] Department of State publication 2712, Treaties and Other International Acts, Series 1568. Signed at Manila July 4, 1946; effective October 22, 1946.

ARTICLE III

Pending the final establishment of the requisite Philippine Foreign Service establishments abroad, the United States of America and the Republic of the Philippines agree that at the request of the Republic of the Philippines the United States of America will endeavor in so far as it may be practicable, to represent through its Foreign Service the interests of the Republic of the Philippines in countries where there is no Philippine representation. The two countries further agree that any such arrangements are to be subject to termination when in the judgment of either country such arrangements are no longer necessary.

ARTICLE IV

The Republic of the Philippines agrees to assume, and does hereby assume, all the debts and liabilities of the Phillipine Islands, its provinces, cities, municipalities and instrumentalities, which shall be valid and subsisting on the date hereof. The Republic of the Philippines will make adequate provision for the necessary funds for the payment of interest on and principal of bonds issued prior to May 1, 1934 under authority of an Act of Congress of the United States of America [1] by the Philippine Islands, or any province, city or municipality therein, and such obligations shall be a first lien on the taxes collected in the Philippines.

ARTICLE V

The United States of America and the Republic of the Philippines agree that all cases at law concerning the Government and people of the Philippines which, in accordance with Section 7 (6) of the Independence Act of 1934,[2] are pending before the Supreme Court of the United States of America at the date of the granting of the independence of the Republic of the Philippines shall continue to be subject to the review of the Supreme Court of the United States of America for such period of time after independence as may be necessary to effectuate the disposition of the cases at hand. The contracting parties also agree that following the disposition of such cases the Supreme Court of the United States of America will cease to have the right of review of cases originating in the Philippine Islands.

ARTICLE VI

In so far as they are not covered by existing legislation, all claims of the Government of the United States of America or its nationals against the Government of the Republic of the Philippines and all claims of the Government of the Republic of the Philippines and its nationals against the Government of the United States of America shall be promptly adjusted and settled. The property rights of the United States of America and the Republic of the Philippines shall be promptly adjusted and settled by mutual agreement, and all existing property rights of citizens and corporations of the United States of America in the Republic of the Philippines and of citizens and corporations of the Republic of the Philippines in the United States of America shall be

[1] 48 Stat. 456.
[2] 48 Stat. 462.

acknowledged, respected and safeguarded to the same extent as property rights of citizens and corporations of the Republic of the Philippines and of the United States of America respectively. Both Governments shall designate representatives who may in concert agree on measures best calculated to effect a satisfactory and expeditious disposal of such claims as may not be covered by existing legislation.

ARTICLE VII

The Republic of the Philippines agrees to assume all continuing obligations assumed by the United States of America under the Treaty of Peace between the United States of America and Spain concluded at Paris on the 10th day of December, 1898,[1] by which the Philippine Islands were ceded to the United States of America, and under the Treaty between the United States of America and Spain concluded at Washington on the 7th day of November, 1900.[2]

ARTICLE VIII

This Treaty shall enter into force on the exchange of instruments of ratification.

This Treaty shall be submitted for ratification in accordance with the constitutional procedures of the United States of America and of the Republic of the Philippines; and instruments of ratification shall be exchanged and deposited at Manila.

Signed at Manila this fourth day of July, one thousand nine hundred forty-six.

FOR THE GOVERNMENT OF THE UNITED STATES OF AMERICA:
[SEAL]   PAUL V. McNUTT

FOR THE GOVERNMENT OF THE REPUBLIC OF THE PHILIPPINES:
[SEAL]   MANUEL ROXAS

◇◇◇◇◇◇

157. THE PHILIPPINE REHABILITATION ACT OF 1946 (EXCERPTS) [3]

Be it enacted by the Senate and House of Representatives of the United States of America in Congress assembled, That this Act may be cited as the "Philippine Rehabilitation Act of 1946".

[After Philippine independence was granted, the United States continued to extend assistance of various types to the new Philippine government. During the five years following the war, it is estimated that our aid amounted to approximately $2,000,000,000. Much of this was in the form of compensation for damages incurred during the war, surplus property grants, and the res-

---

[1] Treaty Series 343; 30 Stat. 1754.
[2] Treaty Series 345; 31 Stat. 1942.
[3] Public Law 370, 79th Cong., 2d sess., S. 1610, as amended by Public Law 597, 79th Cong. 2d sess.

toration of public property and essential public services as provided in the Philippine Rehabilitation Act of 1946.]

TITLE I—COMPENSATION FOR WAR DAMAGE

SEC. 101. (a) There is hereby established a Philippine War Damage Commission (in this title referred to as the "Commission"). The Commission shall consist of three members, to be appointed by the President of the United States, by and with the advice and consent of the Senate. One of the members of the Commission shall be a Filipino. The members of the Commission shall receive compensation at the rate of $12,000 a year. The terms of office of the members of the Commission shall expire at the time fixed in subsection (d) for winding up the affairs of the Commission. A vacancy in the membership of the Commission shall not impair the authority of the remaining two members of the Commission to exercise all of its functions. Vacancies occurring in the membership of the Commission shall be filled in the same manner as in the case of the original selection. Members of the Commission shall receive their necessary traveling and other expenses incurred in connection with their duties as such members, or a per diem allowance in lieu thereof, to be fixed by the Commission without regard to the limitation prescribed in any existing law.

*   *   *

(d) The Commission shall, so far as practicable, give consideration to, but need not await, or be bound by, the recommendations of the Filipino Rehabilitation Commission (created by the Act approved June 29, 1944) with respect to Philippine war damage. The Commission shall wind up its affairs not later than two years after the expiration of the time for filing claims under this title if possible, but, in no event later than five years from the enactment of this Act.

SEC. 102. (a) The Commission is hereby authorized to make compensation to the extent hereinafter provided on account of physical loss or destruction of or damage to property in the Philippines occurring after December 7, 1941 (Philippine time), and before October 1, 1945, as a result of one or more of the following perils: (1) Enemy attack; (2) action taken by or at the request of the military, naval, or air forces of the United States to prevent such property from coming into the possession of the enemy; (3) action taken by enemy representatives, civil or military, or by the representatives of any government cooperating with the enemy; (4) action by the armed forces of the United States or other forces cooperating with the armed forces of the United States in opposing, resisting or expelling the enemy from the Philippines; (5) looting, pillage, or other lawlessness or disorder accompanying the collapse of civil authority determined by the Commission to have resulted from any of the other perils enumerated in this section or from control by enemy forces: *   *   *   *Provided further,* That no claim shall be approved in an aggregate amount which exceeds whichever of the following amounts, as determined by the Commission, is less: (a) The actual cash value, at the time of loss, of property lost or destroyed and the amount of the actual damage to other property of the claimant which was damaged as a direct result of the causes enumerated in this section; (b) the cost of repairing or rebuilding such lost or damaged property, or replacing the same with other property of like or similar quality: *Provided further,* That in case the aggregate amount of the claims which would be payable to any one claimant under the foregoing provisions exceeds $500, the aggregate amount of the claims approved in favor of such claimant shall be reduced by 25 per centum of the excess over $500.

* * *

SEC. 104. (a) No claim shall be paid unless approved by the Commission or its authorized representatives, and on account of each claim so approved the Commission may make immediate payment of (1) so much of the approved amount of the claim as does not exceed five hundred dollars or one thousand Philippine pesos, plus (2) such percentage, not in excess of 80 per centum of the remainder of the approved amount of the claim as the Commission shall make applicable to all approved claims, due consideration having been given to the total funds available for distribution. After the time for filing claims has expired, the Commission shall determine the amount of money available for the further payment of claims. Such funds shall be applied pro rata toward the payment of the unpaid balances of the amounts authorized to be paid pursuant to section 102 of this title.

* * *

SEC. 105. Not later than six months after its organization, and every six months thereafter, the Commission shall make a report to the Congress concerning operations under this title.

SEC. 106. (a) There is hereby authorized to be appropriated, out of any money in the Treasury not otherwise appropriated, the amount of $400,000,-000 for the purposes of paying compensation to the extent authorized by this title, and of such sum, not to exceed $4,000,000 shall be available to pay the expenses of the Commission.

(b) Any money or bullion received by the United States from the Japanese Government or the Japanese people by way of reparations or indemnity on account of war losses in the Philippines—

(1) shall be covered into the Treasury of the United States until the value of said money or bullion so covered into the Treasury is equal to the sum of the amounts appropriated for the payment of compensation under this title and the amounts appropriated for carrying out the purposes of title III of this Act;

(2) when the amounts covered into the Treasury under clause (1) are equal to the amounts so appropriated, the excess over the amounts so appropriated shall be used, first, to satisfy in full the balance unpaid of any approved claims under this title; second, toward the payment of any amount by which any claim was reduced under Section 102 (a) hereof; third, toward the satisfaction of any approved claim of the Government of the Commonwealth of the Philippines (or the Republic of the Philippines), its provinces, cities, municipalities, and instrumentalities, not compensated under this Act; and

(3) the balance shall be covered into the Treasury of the United States.

* * *

(d) Nothing in this Act shall prejudice the right of any claimant not covered by this Act to recover damages from the Japanese Government or the Japanese people, by way of reparations or indemnity on account of the war, for losses not, or not fully, compensated for hereunder.

* * *

TITLE II—DISPOSAL OF SURPLUS PROPERTY

SEC. 201. In order to expedite the disposition of surplus property of the United States in the Philippines and to aid in repairing and replacing buildings (including hospitals, educational, and charitable institutions furnishing essential health, educational, and welfare services), works, utilities, equipment, or other property, owned by the Commonwealth of the Philippines, provincial governments, chartered cities or municipalities, or other governmental units in the Philippines, in cases where such government-owned buildings, works, utilities, equipment, or other property have been damaged, lost, or destroyed in the war, and otherwise to aid in facilitating the normal operations of existing governmental units in the Philippines, the Department of State, the disposal agency for the Philippines designated under the Surplus Property Act of 1944, acting through the Foreign Liquidation Commissioner (hereinafter referred to as the "Commissioner"), is hereby authorized to transfer to the Commonwealth of the Philippines, provincial governments, chartered cities or municipalities, without reimbursement, property of the United States now or hereafter located in the Philippines and declared surplus under the Surplus Property Act of 1944, upon such terms and conditions, including the use or disposition of such property by the Commonwealth of the Philippines, as the Commissioner may deem appropriate to carry out the purposes of this title.

* * *

SEC. 204. No military weapons, munitions, or toxic gas shall be transferred or otherwise disposed of under section 201.

SEC. 205. The fair value of the property transferred to the Commonwealth of the Philippines (Republic of the Philippines) provincial governments, chartered cities or municipalities under section 201, as estimated by the Commissioner, shall not exceed $100,000,000 in the aggregate.

* * *

TITLE III—RESTORATION AND IMPROVEMENT OF PUBLIC PROPERTY AND ESSENTIAL PUBLIC SERVICES

SEC. 301. As a manifestation of good will to the Filipino people, there are hereby authorized to be appropriated, out of any money in the Treasury not otherwise appropriated, (1) the sum of $120,000,000, to be allocated from time to time, but not later than the fiscal year 1950, by the President of the United States among the various programs set forth in sections 302, 303, 304, and 305, and (2) such additional sums as may be necessary to carry out the purposes of sections 306 to 311, inclusive.[1]

* * *

[1] Omitted sections 302-311 deal with restoration and improvement of public roads, port and harbor facilities, public health services, inter-island commerce and navigation, etc.

TITLE VI—GENERAL PROVISIONS

SEC. 601. No payments under title I of this Act in excess of $500 shall be made until an executive agreement shall have been entered into between the President of the United States and the President of the Philippines, and such agreement shall have become effective according to its terms, providing for trade relations between the United States and the Philippines, and which agreement shall also provide for the same offenses, and penalties upon conviction, thereof, as are set forth in section 107 and section 108 of title I of this Act.

*   *   *

◇◇◇◇◇

158. MILITARY BASES

Agreement Between the United States and the Republic of the Philippines, March 14, 1947 [1]

[Both the Philippines and the United States realized it would be unwise to grant independence to the islands unless satisfactory arrangements were made to protect the mutual security interests of the two countries in that area. To this end, the Agreement of March 14, 1947, grants to the United States the right to use certain military, naval, and air bases in the Philippines. The Agreement, which is to remain in force for ninety-nine years, defines in some detail the rights and duties of the two governments with respect to these bases.]

WHEREAS, the war in the Pacific has confirmed the mutuality of interest of the United States of America and the Republic of the Philippines in matters relating to the defense of their respective territories and that mutuality of interest demands that the Governments of the two countries take the necessary measures to promote their mutual security and to defend their territories and areas;

WHEREAS, the Governments of the United States of America and of the Republic of the Philippines are desirous of cooperating in the common defense of their two countries through arrangements consonant with the procedures and objectives of the United Nations; and particularly through a grant to the United States of America by the Republic of the Philippines, in the exercise of its title and sovereignty, of the use, free of rent, in furtherance of the mutual interest of both countries, of certain lands of the public domain;

WHEREAS, the Government of the Republic of the Philippines has requested United States assistance in providing for the defense of the Philippines and in developing for such defense effective Philippine Armed Forces;

WHEREAS, pursuant to this request the Government of the United States of America has, in view of its interest in the welfare of the Philippines indicated its intention of dispatching a military mission to the Philippines and of

---

[1] Department of State press release 193, March 14, 1947. Agreement accepted by the United States on June 16, 1947; by the Philippines on January 21, 1948.

extending to her appropriate assistance in the development of the Philippine defense forces;

WHEREAS, a Joint Resolution of the Congress of the United States of America of June 29, 1944, authorized the President of the United States of America to acquire bases for the mutual protection of the Philippines and of the United States of America; and

WHEREAS, Joint Resolution No. 4 of the Congress of the Philippines, approved July 28, 1945, authorized the President of the Republic of the Philippines to negotiate with the President of the United States of America for the establishment of bases provided for in the Joint Resolution of the Congress of the United States of America of June 29, 1944, with a view to insuring the territorial integrity of the Philippines, the mutual protection of the Philippines and the United States of America, and the maintenance of peace in the Pacific;

THEREFORE the Governments of the United States of America and of the Republic of the Philippines agree upon the following terms for the delimitation, establishment, maintenance and operation of military bases in the Philippines:

ARTICLE I

GRANT OF BASES

1. The Government of the Republic of the Philippines (hereinafter referred to as the Philippines) grants to the Government of the United States of America (hereinafter referred to as the United States) the right to retain the use of the bases in the Philippines listed in Annex A attached hereto.

2. The Philippines agrees to permit the United States, upon notice to the Philippines, to use such of those bases listed in Annex B as the United States determines to be required by military necessity.

3. The Philippines agrees to enter into negotiations with the United States at the latter's request, to permit the United States to expand such bases, to exchange such bases for other bases, to acquire additional bases, or relinquish rights to bases, as any of such exigencies may be required by military necessity.

4. A narrative description of the boundaries of the bases to which this Agreement relates is given in Annex A and Annex B. An exact description of the bases listed in Annex A, with metes and bounds, in conformity with the narrative descriptions will be agreed upon between the appropriate authorities of the two Governments as soon as possible. With respect to any of the bases listed in Annex B, an exact description with metes and bounds, in conformity with the narrative description of such bases, will be agreed upon if and when such bases are acquired by the United States.

ARTICLE II

MUTUAL COOPERATION

1. It is mutually agreed that the armed forces of the Philippines may serve on United States bases and that the armed forces of the United States may serve on Philippine military establishments whenever such conditions appear beneficial as mutually determined by the armed forces of both countries.

2. Joint outlined plans for the development of military bases in the Philippines may be prepared by military authorities of the two Governments.

3. In the interests of international security any bases listed in Annexes A and B may be made available to the Security Council of the United Nations on its call by prior mutual agreement between the Philippines and the United States.

ARTICLE III

DESCRIPTION OF RIGHTS

1. It is mutually agreed that the United States shall have the rights, power and authority within the bases which are necessary for the establishment, use, operation and defense thereof or appropriate for the control thereof and all the rights, power and authority within the limits of territorial waters and air space adjacent to, or in the vicinity of, the bases which are necessary to provide access to them, or appropriate for their control.

2. Such rights, power and authority shall include, *inter alia,* the right, power and authority:

   (a) to construct (including dredging and filling), operate, maintain, utilize, occupy, garrison and control the bases;

   (b) to improve and deepen the harbors, channels, entrances and anchorages, and to construct or maintain necessary roads and bridges affording access to the bases;

   (c) to control (including the right to prohibit) in so far as may be required for the efficient operation and safety of the bases, and within the limits of military necessity, anchorages, moorings, landings, takeoffs, movements and operation of ships and waterborne craft, craft and other vehicles on water, in the air or on land comprising or in the vicinity of the bases;

   (d) the right to acquire, as may be agreed between the two Governments, such rights of way, and to construct thereon, as may be required for military purpose, wire and radio communications facilities, including submarine and subterranean cables, pipe lines and spur tracks from railroads to bases, and the right, as may be agreed upon between the two Governments to construct the necessary facilities;

   (e) to construct, install, maintain, and employ on any base any type of facilities, weapons, substance, device, vessel or vehicle on or under the ground, in the air or on or under the water that may be requisite or appropriate, including meteorological systems, aerial and water navigation lights, radio and radar apparatus and electronic devices of any desired power, type of emission and frequency.

3. In the exercise of the above-mentioned rights, power and authority, the United States agrees that the powers granted to it will not be used unreasonably or, unless required by military necessity determined by the two Governments so as to interfere with the necessary rights of navigation, aviation, communication, or land travel within the territories of the Philippines. In the practical application outside the bases of the rights, power and authority granted in this Article there shall be, as the occasion requires, consultation between the two Governments.

ARTICLE IV

SHIPPING AND NAVIGATION

1. It is mutually agreed that United States public vessels operated by or for the War or Navy Departments, the Coast Guard or the Coast and Geodetic Survey, and the military forces of the United States, military and naval aircraft and Government-owned vehicles, including armor, shall be accorded free access to and movement between ports and United States bases throughout the Philippines, including territorial waters, by land, air and sea. This right shall include freedom from compulsory pilotage and all toll charges. If, however, a pilot is taken, pilotage shall be paid for at appropriate rates. In connection with entrance into Philippine ports by United States public vessels appropriate notification under normal conditions shall be made to the Philippine authorities.

2. Lights and other aids to navigation of vessels and aircraft placed or established in the bases and territorial waters adjacent thereto or in the vicinity of such bases shall conform to the system in use in the Philippines. The position, characteristics and any alterations in the light or other aids shall be communicated in advance to the appropriate authorities of the Philippines.

3. Philippine commercial vessels may use the bases on the same terms and conditions as United States commercial vessels.

4. It is understood that a base is not a part of the territory of the United States for the purpose of coastwise shipping laws so as to exclude Philippine vessels from trade between the United States and the bases.

ARTICLE V

EXEMPTION FROM CUSTOMS AND OTHER DUTIES

No import, excise consumption or other tax, duty or impost shall be charged on material, equipment, supplies or goods, including food stores and clothing, for exclusive use in the construction, maintenance, operation or defense of the bases, consigned to, or destined for, the United States authorities and certified by them to be for such purposes.

ARTICLE VI

MANEUVER AND OTHER AREAS

The United States shall, subject to previous agreement with the Philippines, have the right to use land and coastal sea areas of appropriate size and location for periodic maneuvers, for additional staging areas, bombing and gunnery ranges, and for such intermediate airfields as may be required for safe and efficient air operations. Operations in such areas shall be carried on with due regard and safeguards for the public safety.

ARTICLE VII

USE OF PUBLIC SERVICES

It is mutually agreed that the United States may employ and use for United States military forces any and all public utilities, other services and facilities, airfields, ports, harbors, roads, highways, railroads, bridges, viaducts, canals, lakes, rivers and streams in the Philippines under conditions no less favorable than those that may be applicable from time to time to the military forces of the Philippines.

ARTICLE VIII

HEALTH MEASURES OUTSIDE BASES

It is mutually agreed that the United States may construct, subject to agreement by the appropriate Philippine authorities, wells, water catchment areas or dams to insure an ample supply of water for all base operations and personnel. The United States shall likewise have the right, in cooperation with the appropriate authorities of the Philippines, to take such steps as may be mutually agreed upon to be necessary to improve health and sanitation in areas contiguous to the bases, including the right, under such conditions as may be mutually agreed upon, to enter and inspect any privately owned property. The United States shall pay just compensation for any injury to persons or damage to property that may result from action taken in connection with this Article.

ARTICLE IX

SURVEYS

It is mutually agreed that the United States shall have the right after appropriate notification has been given to the Philippines, to make topographic, hydrographic, and coast and geodetic surveys and aerial photographs in any part of the Philippines and water adjacent thereto. Copies with title and triangulation data of any surveys or photomaps made of the Philippines shall be furnished to the Philippines.

* * *

ARTICLE XIII

JURISDICTION

1. The Philippines consents that the United States shall have the right to exercise jurisdiction over the following offenses:

(a) Any offense committed by any person within any base; except where the offender and the offended parties are both Philippine citizens, not members of the Armed Forces of the United States on active duty or the offense is against the security of the Philippines, and the offender is a Philippine citizen;

(b) Any offense committed outside the bases by any member of the Armed Forces of the United States in which the offended party is also a member of the Armed Forces of the United States; and

(c) Any offense committed outside the bases by any member of the Armed Forces of the United States against the security of the United States.

2. The Philippines shall have the right to exercise jurisdiction over all other offenses committed outside the bases by any member of the Armed Forces of the United States.

3. Whenever for special reasons the United States may desire not to exercise the jurisdiction reserved to it in paragraphs 1 and 6 of this Article, the officer holding the offender in custody shall so notify the fiscal (prosecuting attorney) of the city or province in which the offense has been committed within ten days after his arrest, and in such a case the Philippines shall exercise jurisdiction.

4. Whenever for special reasons the Philippines may desire not to exercise the jurisdiction reserved to it in paragraph 2 of this Article, the fiscal (prosecuting attorney) of the city or province where the offense has been committed shall so notify the officer holding the offender in custody within ten days after his arrest, and in such a case the United States shall be free to exercise jurisdiction. If any offense falling under paragraph 2 of this Article is committed by any member of the Armed Forces of the United States

(a) while engaged in the actual performance of a specific military duty, or

(b) during a period of national emergency declared by either Government and the fiscal (prosecuting attorney) so finds from the evidence, he shall immediately notify the officer holding the offender in custody that the United States is free to exercise jurisdiction. In the event the fiscal (prosecuting attorney) finds that the offense was not committed in the actual performance of a specific military duty, the offender's commanding officer shall have the right to appeal from such finding to the Secretary of Justice within ten days from the receipt of the decision of the fiscal and the decision of the Secretary of Justice shall be final.

5. In all cases over which the Philippines exercise jurisdiction the custody of the accused, pending trial and final judgment, shall be entrusted without delay to the commanding officer of the nearest base, who shall acknowledge in writing that such accused has been delivered to him for custody pending trial in a competent court of the Philippines and that he will be held ready to appear and will be produced before said court when required by it. The commanding officer shall be furnished by the fiscal (prosecuting attorney) with a copy of the information against the accused upon the filing of the original in the competent court.

6. Notwithstanding the foregoing provisions, it is mutually agreed that in time of war the United States shall have the right to exercise exclusive jurisdiction over any offenses which may be committed by members of the Armed Forces of the United States in the Philippines.

7. The United States agrees that it will not grant asylum in any of the bases to any person fleeing from the lawful jurisdiction of the Philippines. Should any such person be found in any base, he will be surrendered on demand to the competent authorities of the Philippines.

8. In every case in which jurisdiction over an offense is exercised by the United States, the offended party may institute a separate civil action against the offender in the proper court of the Philippines to enforce the civil liability which under the laws of the Philippines may arise from the offense.

*   *   *

ARTICLE XV

SECURITY LEGISLATION

The Philippines agrees to take such steps as may from time to time be agreed to be necessary with a view to the enactment of legislation to insure the adequate security and protection of the United States bases, equipment and other property and the operations of the United States under this Agreement, and the punishment of persons who may contravene such legislation. It is mutually agreed that appropriate authorities of the two Governments will also consult from time to time in order to insure that laws and regulations of the United States and of the Philippines in relation to such matters shall, so far as may be possible, be uniform in character.

*   *   *

ARTICLE XXV

GRANT OF BASES TO A THIRD POWER

1. The Philippines agrees that it shall not grant, without prior consent of the United States, any bases or any rights, power, or authority whatsoever, in or relating to bases, to any third power.

2. It is further agreed that the United States shall not, without the consent of the Philippines, assign, or underlet, or part with the possession of the whole or any part of any base, or of any right, power or authority granted by this Agreement, to any third power.

ARTICLE XXVI

DEFINITION OF BASES

For the purposes of this Agreement, bases are those areas named in Annex A and Annex B and such additional areas as may be acquired for military purposes pursuant to the terms of this Agreement.

ARTICLE XXVII

VOLUNTARY ENLISTMENT OF PHILIPPINE CITIZENS

It is mutually agreed that the United States shall have the right to recruit citizens of the Philippines for voluntary enlistment into the United States Armed Forces for a fixed term of years, and to train them and to exercise the same degree of control and discipline over them as is exercised in the case of other members of the United States Armed Forces. The number of such enlistments to be accepted by the Armed Forces of the United States may from time to time be limited by agreement between the two Governments.

ARTICLE XXVIII

UNITED STATES RESERVE ORGANIZATIONS

It is mutually agreed that the United States shall have the right to enroll and train all eligible United States citizens residing in the Philippines in the reserve organizations of the Armed Forces of the United States, which include the Officers Reserve Corps and the Enlisted Reserve Corps, except that prior consent of the Philippines shall be obtained in the case of such persons who are employed by the Philippines or any municipal or provincial government thereof.

ARTICLE XXIX

TERM OF AGREEMENT

The present Agreement shall enter into force upon its acceptance by the two Governments and shall remain in force for a period of ninety-nine years subject to extension thereafter as agreed by the two Governments.

Signed in Manila, P. I., in duplicate this 14th day of March, 1947.

On behalf of the Government of the United States of America:

PAUL V. McNUTT,
United States Ambassador to The Republic of the Philippines.

On behalf of the Government of the Republic of the Philippines:

MANUEL A. ROXAS,
President of the Republic of the Philippines.

ANNEX "A"

Clark Field Airbase, Pampanga
Fort Stotsenberg, Pampanga
Mariveles Military Reservation, POL Terminal & Training Area, Bataan
Camp John Hay Leave and Recreation Center, Baguio
Army Communications System with the deletion of all stations in the Port of Manila Area.
U. S. AF Cemetery No. 2, San Francisco, Delmonte, Rizal
Angeles General Depot, Pampanga
Leyte-Samar Naval Base including shore installations and air bases
Subic Bay, No. West Shore Naval Base Zambales Province and the existing naval reservation at Olongapo and the existing Baguio naval reservation
Tawi Tawi Naval Anchorage and small adjacent land areas
Canacao—Sangley Point Navy Base, Cavite Province
Bagobantay Transmitter Area, Quezon City, and associated radio receiving and control sites, Manila Area
Tarumpitao Point (Loran Master Transmitter Station) (Palawan)
Talampulan Island, C. G. #354 (Loran) (Palawan)
Naule Point (Loran Station) (Zambales)
Castillejos, C. G. #356 (Zambales)

ANNEX "B"

Mactan Island Army and Navy Airbase
Florida Blanca Airbase, Pampanga
Aircraft Service Warning Net
Camp Wallace, San Fernando, La Union
Puerta Princesa Army and Navy Air Base including Navy Section Base and Air Warning Sites, Palawan

Tawi Tawi Naval Base, Sulu Archipelago
Aparri Naval Air Base.

◇◇◇◇◇◇

159. REPORT BY THE ECONOMIC SURVEY MISSION TO THE PHILIPPINES [1] (THE BELL REPORT), OCTOBER 9, 1950

[From 1948 to 1950, the economic situation in the Philippines deteriorated rapidly. As a result, the President of the Philippine Republic requested President Truman to send a United States mission to the Philippines to study that country's economic and financial problems and to recommend measures that would enable it to become self-supporting. The Mission, under Mr. Daniel Bell, formerly Under-Secretary of the Treasury, surveyed on the spot various aspects of the Philippine economy including agriculture, industry, finances, trade and public administration. The findings and recommendations of the Mission—including a $250,000,000 program of financial assistance from the United States—are summarized below.]

*   *   *

URGENT ECONOMIC PROBLEMS

The basic economic problem in the Philippines is inefficient production and very low incomes. While a substantial recovery was made in production after the liberation, agricultural and industrial output is still below the prewar level. In the past ten years, however, the population has increased by 25 percent. Although home production has been supplemented by large imports, the standard of living of most people is lower than before the war. In Manila, real wages of industrial workers are about the same or slightly higher than in 1941; but in the provinces, real wages in agriculture are lower than before the war. For many agricultural workers, wages are wholly inadequate, in some instances less than one peso (50 cents) a day.

The finances of the Government have become steadily worse and are now critical. The treasury has a large and mounting deficit, with taxes covering little more than 60 per cent of the expenditures. Obligations have been allowed to accumulate, warrants have been issued for which funds are not available, and school teachers have not been paid in some provincial areas. The new taxes voted by the special session of Congress cannot meet the budget needs and the cash position of the Treasury is becoming steadily worse. If the Central Bank is used to cover the large deficit of the Government it may lead to a new outburst of inflation, the burden of which will fall on those struggling for a living in a land of very high prices and very low incomes.

The international payments position of the country is seriously distorted and a balance has been maintained in recent months only by imposing strict import and exchange controls. The country has had an excessive volume of

[1] Report to the President of the United States by the Economic Survey Mission to the Philippines, Washington, D. C., October 9, 1950, Government Printing Office, pp. 1-5.

imports, which hitherto could be paid for out of very large dollar receipts from United States Government disbursements and accumulated dollar balances. These balances have been drawn down and receipts from the United States Government have been declining sharply. Greater difficulty will probably be experienced in the future in paying for imports. In the meantime, the volume of exports is less than before the war and can be expected to grow only gradually. Unless foreign exchange receipts are increased or excessive dependence on imports decreased, import and exchange controls will have to become even more restrictive.

CAUSES OF THE DIFFICULTIES

While production in general has been restored to almost the prewar level, little of fundamental importance was done to increase productive efficiency and to diversify the economy. In agriculture, the area under cultivation was brought to the prewar level, and the livestock population partially restored. But almost nothing was done to open new lands for the increased population, to improve the methods of cultivation, or to better the position of farm workers and tenants. In industry, production was restored very much in the prewar pattern. While some new enterprises have been started, particularly in the past year, there has been little real progress in opening new work opportunities and in strengthening the economy. The country still relies too heavily on the export of a few basic agricultural crops—coconut, sugar and hemp—which provide a meager livelihood to most of the people engaged in their production.

The failure to expand production and to increase productive efficiency is particularly disappointing because investment was exceptionally high and foreign exchange receipts were exceptionally large during most of the post-liberation period. Too much of the investment went into commerce and real estate instead of the development of agriculture and industry; investment undertaken by Government corporations has unfortunately been ineffective. A considerable part of the large foreign exchange receipts were dissipated in imports of luxury and non-essential goods, in the remittance of high profits, and in the transfer of Philippine capital abroad. The opportunity to increased productive efficiency and to raise the standard of living in the Philippines in the postwar period has thus been wasted because of misdirected investment and excessive imports for consumption.

The inequalities in income in the Philippines, always large, have become even greater during the past few years. While the standard of living of the mass of people has not reached the prewar level, the profits of businessmen and the incomes of large landowners have risen very considerably. Wages and farm income remain lower than the economy can afford because of the unequal bargaining power of workers and tenants on the one hand, and employers and landowners on the other. Under such conditions any policy that keeps prices high has the effect of transferring real income from the poor to the rich. This is what has happened in the Philippines, where prices on the average are three and a half times as high as prewar. The inflationary conditions which have made this possible were caused by large budgetary deficits and an excessive creation of credit, much of it for the Government and Government corporations.

As a consequence of the inflationary conditions, along with insufficient production, the demand for foreign exchange to pay for imports, and to remit profits and transfer funds abroad has exceeded the current foreign exchange receipts from exports and United States Government disbursements. The foreign exchange reserves of the country, although still considerable have been greatly reduced, confidence in the currency has been shaken, and a breakdown in international payments has been averted only by stringent import and exchange controls. The generally unfavorable economic and political environment and the fear of discrimination in the administration of import and exchange controls have the effect of discouraging foreign investment in the Philippines.

The high hopes of the Philippine people that with peace and independence, they could look forward to economic progress and a rising standard of living have not been realized. Because of the deteriorating economic situation, there is a widespread feeling of disillusion. Most agricultural and industrial workers have no faith that their economic position can or will be improved. Businessmen fear a collapse of the peso. The uncertainties created by these doubts are strengthened by the recent tendency toward unemployment resulting from the slowing up of construction and the sharp curtailment of imports. The economy shows little inherent capacity to overcome the difficulties with which it is faced.

There are officials in the Philippine Government who are aware of the dangers in this pervading economic unbalance between production and needs, between prices and wages, between Government expenditures and taxes, between foreign exchange payments and receipts. Some of them understand the reasons why these difficulties arose; but the measures that could halt the deterioration have not been put into effect. Inefficiency and even corruption in the Government service are widespread. Leaders in agriculture and in business have not been sufficiently aware of their responsibility to improve the economic position of the lower income groups. The public lacks confidence in the capacity of the Government to act firmly to protect the interests of all the people. The situation is being exploited by the Communist-led Hukbalahap movement to incite lawlessness and disorder.

The Government has thus far attempted to deal with some of these emerging problems through import and exchange controls and through price controls. Such measures are directed to the symptoms rather than the causes of economic disorder. At best, they are measures that can only delay a breakdown in the economy; they cannot remedy the fundamental ills from which the country suffers. A permanent solution to these problems will be found only through a determined effort on the part of the people and the Government of the Philippines, with the aid and encouragement of the United States, to increase production and improve productive efficiency, to raise the level of wages and farm income, and to open new opportunities for work and for acquiring land.

RECOMMENDATIONS

The Mission recommends that the following measures be taken:

1. That the finances of the Government be placed on a sound basis in order to avoid further inflation; that additional tax revenues be raised immediately in as equitable a manner as possible to meet the expenditures of

the Government; that the tax structure be revised to increase the proportion of taxes collected from high incomes and large property holdings; that the tax collecting machinery be overhauled to secure greater efficiency in tax collection; that a credit policy be adopted which will encourage investment in productive enterprises; and that fiscal, credit and investment policy be better co-ordinated to prevent inflation.

2. That agricultural production be improved by applying known methods of increasing the yield from all basic crops; that the Department of Agriculture and Natural Resources be adequately supplied with funds and the agricultural extension service expanded; that the agricultural college at Los Banos be rehabilitated and the central experiment station located there, with other stations at appropriate places throughout the country; that rural banks be established to provide production credit for small farmers; that the opening of new lands for settlement in homesteads be expedited and the clearance of land titles promptly assured; that a program of land redistribution be undertaken through the purchase of large estates for resale to small farmers; and that measures be undertaken to provide tenants with reasonable security on their land and an equitable share of the crops they produce.

3. That steps be taken to diversify the economy of the country by encouraging new industries; that adequate power and transportation facilities be provided as needed for further economic development; that a Philippine Development Corporation be established to co-ordinate all government corporations and enterprises and liquidate those that are ineffective; that financial assistance be made available to productive enterprises by the Corporation acting in cooperation with private banks; that the natural resources of the country be systematically explored to determine their potentialities for economic development; and that the present laws and practices with respect to the use of the public domain be re-examined.

4. That to avoid a further deterioration in the international payments position and to reduce the excessive demand for imports, a special emergency tax of 25 percent be levied for a period not to exceed two years on imports of all goods other than rice, corn, flour, canned fish, canned milk and fertilizer; that if such an emergency import levy is not possible under the Trade Agreement with the United States, either very heavy excise taxes should be imposed or a tax of 25 percent should be levied on all sales of exchange; that, as a safety measure, the present exchange and import controls be retained but their administration be simplified and liberalized and the full remittance of current earnings be permitted; that a Treaty of Friendship, Commerce and Navigation be concluded between the Philippines and the United States and the present Trade Agreement re-examined in the light of the new conditions.

5. That an adequate program of public health and improved education be undertaken, and better facilities for urban housing be provided; that the right of workers to organize free trade unions to protect their economic interests be established through appropriate legislation; that abuses in present employment practices depriving the workers of their just earnings be eliminated by legislation making mandatory direct payment of wages and retroactive monetary awards to workers; that a minimum wage for agricultural and other workers be established to provide subsistence standards of living.

6. That public administration be improved and reorganized so as to

insure honesty and efficiency in Government; that the civil service be placed on a merit basis and civil service salaries raised to provide a decent standard of living; that the Philippine Government remove barriers to the employment of foreign technicians and take steps to improve training facilities for technicians in the Philippines; and that in accordance with the request of the Philippine Government, the United States send a Technical Mission to assist the Philippine Government in carrying out its agricultural and industrial development, fiscal controls, public administration, and labor and social welfare program.

7. That the United States Government provide financial assistance of $250 million through loans and grants, to help in carrying out a five-year program of economic development and technical assistance; that this aid be strictly conditioned on steps being taken by the Philippine Government to carry out the recommendations outlined above, including the immediate enactment of tax legislation and other urgent reforms; that expenditure of the United States funds under this recommendation, including pesos derived from United States loans and grants, be subject to continued supervision and control of the Technical Mission; that the use of funds provided by the Philippine Government for economic and social development be co-ordinated with the expenditure of the United States funds made available for this purpose; and that an agreement be made for final settlement of outstanding financial claims between the United States and the Philippines including funding of the Reconstruction Finance Corporation loan of $60 million.

*   *   *

No one must expect that even so comprehensive a program as this will quickly or automatically remove all the ills of the Philippine economy. What it can do is to provide an environment in which the people of the Philippines can work out a reasonable solution of their problems. What they ultimately achieve will be determined primarily by their own efforts and by the devotion of the Philippine Government to the interests of all people. The nation has the physical and human resources to accomplish this task with help from the United States. In' the few years since independence, the Philippines has taken a leading position in world affairs and in the United Nations. With thorough measures to deal with its economic problems, it can take its rightful place as a prosperous and stable nation.

◇◇◇◇◇◇

SPAIN

160. RELATIONS WITH SPAIN

Letter From President Roosevelt to the American Ambassador to Spain, March 10, 1945 [1]

[Our relations with Spain have been the subject of considerable controversy in this country ever since the Franco régime came to power in 1936. The natural antipathy of the Western democracies toward totalitarian govern-

[1] Department of State Bulletin of September 30, 1945, p. 466.

ment ripened into deep suspicion and distrust during World War II when Franco extended aid and comfort to our Axis enemies. This letter, written by President Roosevelt, outlined our policy toward Spain in the spring of 1945 and emphasized that the maintenance of diplomatic relations with Spain in no way implied approval of the Franco régime.]

MARCH 10, 1945

MY DEAR MR. ARMOUR:

In connection with your new assignment as Ambassador to Madrid I want you to have a frank statement of my views with regard to our relations with Spain.

Having been helped to power by Fascist Italy and Nazi Germany, and having patterned itself along totalitarian lines the present regime in Spain is naturally the subject of distrust by a great many American citizens who find it difficult to see the justification for this country to continue to maintain relations with such a regime. Most certainly we do not forget Spain's official position with and assistance to our Axis enemies at a time when the fortunes of war were less favorable to us, nor can we disregard the activities, aims, organizations, and public utterances of the Falange, both past and present. These memories cannot be wiped out by actions more favorable to us now that we are about to achieve our goal of complete victory over those enemies of ours with whom the present Spanish regime identified itself in the past spiritually and by its public expressions and acts.

The fact that our Government maintains formal diplomatic relations with the present Spanish regime should not be interpreted by anyone to imply approval of that regime and its sole party, the Falange, which has been openly hostile to the United States and which has tried to spread its fascist party ideas in the Western Hemisphere. Our victory over Germany will carry with it the extermination of Nazi and similar ideologies.

As you know, it is not our practice in normal circumstances to interfere in the internal affairs of other countries unless there exists a threat to international peace. The form of government in Spain and the policies pursued by that Government are quite properly the concern of the Spanish people. I should be lacking in candor, however, if I did not tell you that I can see no place in the community of nations for governments founded on fascist principles.

We all have the most friendly feelings for the Spanish people and we are anxious to see a development of cordial relations with them. There are many things which we could and normally would be glad to do in economic and other fields to demonstrate that friendship. The initiation of such measures is out of the question at this time, however, when American sentiment is so profoundly opposed to the present regime in power in Spain.

Therefore, we earnestly hope that the time may soon come when Spain may assume the role and the responsibility which we feel it should assume in the field of international cooperation and understanding.

Very sincerely yours,

FRANKLIN D. ROOSEVELT

◇◇◇◇◇◇

161. RELATIONS WITH PRESENT SPANISH GOVERNMENT

Statement by the United States, the United Kingdom, and France, March 4, 1946 [1]

[In 1945 and 1946, a tremendous amount of pressure was put on the Franco régime by the victorious powers, particularly by the Soviet bloc. At the San Francisco Conference, at Potsdam, and at the first meeting of the General Assembly in London, the participating governments condemned the Franco government and declared that Spain should not be admitted to the United Nations so long as Franco remained in control. The three-power statement of March 4, 1946, was a part of the studied campaign to promote the establishment of a more liberal régime in Spain through diplomatic pressure.]

The Governments of France, the United Kingdom, and the United States of America have exchanged views with regard to the present Spanish Government and their relations with that regime. It is agreed that so long as General Franco continues in control of Spain, the Spanish people cannot anticipate full and cordial association with those nations of the world which have, by common effort, brought defeat to German Nazism and Italian Fascism, which aided the present Spanish regime in its rise to power and after which the regime was patterned.

There is no intention of interfering in the internal affairs of Spain. The Spanish people themselves must in the long run work out their own destiny. In spite of the present regime's repressive measures against orderly efforts of the Spanish people to organize and give expression to their political aspirations, the three Governments are hopeful that the Spanish people will not again be subjected to the horrors and bitterness of civil strife.

On the contrary, it is hoped that leading patriotic and liberal-minded Spaniards may soon find means to bring about a peaceful withdrawal of Franco, the abolition of the Falange, and the establishment of an interim or caretaker government under which the Spanish people may have an opportunity freely to determine the type of government they wish to have and to choose their leaders. Political amnesty, return of exiled Spaniards, freedom of assembly and political association and provision for free public elections are essentials. An interim government which would be and would remain dedicated to these ends should receive the recognition and support of all freedom-loving peoples.

Such recognition would include full diplomatic relations and the taking of such practical measures to assist in the solution of Spain's economic problems as may be practicable in the circumstances prevailing. Such measures are not now possible. The question of the maintenance or termination by the Governments of France, the United Kingdom, and the United States of diplomatic relations with the present Spanish regime is a matter to be decided in the light of events and after taking into account the efforts of the Spanish people to achieve their own freedom.

◇◇◇◇◇

[1] Department of State Bulletin of March 17, 1946, p. 412.

162. RELATIONS BETWEEN SPAIN AND THE UNITED NATIONS

(a) Resolution of General Assembly, February 9, 1946 [1]

[Post-war feeling against Franco reached its peak in December, 1946, when the General Assembly approved a resolution by a 34 to 6 vote recommending that Franco Spain be debarred from membership in the specialized agencies of the UN. It also recommended that all UN members recall their ambassadors and ministers from Madrid. Although the United States voted for final passage of the resolution, there was some difference of opinion in the U. S. delegation as to whether this was a logical course for the UN to pursue. The text of the resolution, together with the resolution adopted earlier in London, is reproduced in full below.]

1. The Assembly recalls that the San Francisco Conference adopted a resolution according to which paragraph 2 of Article 4 of Chapter II of the United Nations Charter "cannot apply to States whose regimes have been installed with the help of armed forces of countries which have fought against the United Nations so long as these regimes are in power".

2. The Assembly recalls that at the Potsdam Conference the Governments of the United Kingdom, the United States of America and the Soviet Union stated that they would not support a request for admission to the United Nations of the present Spanish Government "which, having been founded with the support of the Axis Powers, in view of its origins, its nature, its record, and its close association with the aggressor States, does not possess the necessary qualifications to justify its admission".

3. The Assembly, in endorsing these two statements, recommends that the Members of the United Nations should act in accordance with the letter and the spirit of these statements in the conduct of their future relations with Spain.

(b) Resolution of General Assembly, December 12, 1946 [2]

The peoples of the United Nations, at San Francisco, Potsdam and London condemned the Franco regime in Spain and decided that as long as that regime remains, Spain may not be admitted to the United Nations.

The General Assembly, in its resolution of 9 February 1946, recommended that the Members of the United Nations should act in accordance with the letter and spirit of the declarations of San Francisco and Potsdam.

[1] The United States and the United Nations: Report of the. U. S. Delegation to the First Part of the First Session of the General Assembly of the United Nations, London, England, January 10-February 14, 1946. Department of State publication 2484, United States-United Nations Report Series 1, p. 46. At that time, the United States did not have an Ambassador in Spain, because Norman Armour, who had been Ambassador, had resigned, and to the time of preparation of this collection of documents, in December 1949, no one had been appointed to take his place.

[2] The United States and the United Nations: Report by the President to the Congress for the year 1946, Department of State publication 2735, United States-United Nations Report Series 7, pp. 98-100.

The peoples of the United Nations assure the Spanish people of their enduring sympathy and of the cordial welcome awaiting them when circumstances enable them to be admitted to the United Nations.

The General Assembly recalls that in May and June 1946, the Security Council conducted an investigation of the possible further action to be taken by the United Nations. The Sub-Committee of the Security Council charged with the investigation found unanimously:

"(a) In origin, nature, structure and general conduct, the Franco regime is a Fascist regime patterned on, and established largely as a result of aid received from Hitler's Nazi Germany and Mussolini's Fascist Italy.

"(b) During the long struggle of the United Nations against Hitler and Mussolini, Franco, despite continued Allied protests, gave very substantial aid to the enemy Powers. First, for example, from 1941 to 1945, the Blue Infantry Division, the Spanish Legion of Volunteers and the Salvador Air Squadron fought against Soviet Russia on the Eastern front. Second, in the summer of 1940, Spain seized Tangier in breach of international statute, and as a result of Spain maintaining a large army in Spanish Morocco large numbers of Allied troops were immobilized in North Africa.

"(c) Incontrovertible documentary evidence establishes that Franco was a guilty party with Hitler and Mussolini in the conspiracy to wage war against those countries which eventually in the course of the world war became banded together as the United Nations. It was part of the conspiracy that Franco's belligerency should be postponed until a time to be mutually agreed upon."

THE GENERAL ASSEMBLY,

CONVINCED that the Franco Fascist Government of Spain, which was imposed upon the Spanish people with the aid of the Axis Powers and which gave material assistance to the Axis Powers in the war, does not represent the Spanish people, and by its continued control of Spain is making impossible the participation of the Spanish people with the peoples of the United Nations in international affairs;

RECOMMENDS that the Franco Government of Spain be debarred from membership in international agencies established by or brought into relationship with the United Nations, and from participation in conference or other activities which may be arranged by the United Nations or by these agencies, until a new and acceptable government is formed in Spain.

FURTHER DESIRING to secure the participation of all peace-loving peoples, including the people of Spain, in the community of nations,

RECOMMENDS that if, within a reasonable time, there is not established a government which derives its authority from the consent of the governed, committed to respect freedom of speech, religion and assembly and to the prompt holding of an election in which the Spanish people, free from force and intimidation and regardless of party, may express their will, the Security Council consider the adequate measures to be taken in order to remedy the situation;

RECOMMENDS that all Members of the United Nations immediately recall from Madrid their ambassadors and ministers plenipotentiary accredited there.

THE GENERAL ASSEMBLY FURTHER RECOMMENDS that the States Members of the Organization report to the Secretary-General and to the next session of the Assembly what action they have taken in accordance with this recommendation.[1]

◇◇◇◇◇◇

163. UNITED STATES SPANISH POLICY

Letter From Secretary Acheson to Senator Connally, January 18, 1950 [2]

[As the tensions between the U.S.S.R. and the West increased, a strong sentiment for coöperation with Spain rapidly developed in the United States. Many members of Congress, pointing to the strategic importance of Spain, insisted that our ambassador be returned to Madrid, and that financial aid be extended to Spain. In his letter of January 18, 1950, Secretary Acheson pointed out that, in line with the principle that the maintenance of full diplomatic relations with a government does not imply approval of the régime, our government would favor the return of ambassadors to Madrid and would not interpose any political objections to the extension of loans to Spain. Mr. Acheson's letter presents an excellent review of a most difficult problem.]

The Honorable TOM CONNALLY,
United States Senate.

MY DEAR SENATOR CONNALLY: In response *to* your letter of January 16 and following my consultation with the Foreign Relations Committee I am pleased to send you a more detailed statement on United States policy toward Spain, particularly as it affects the problem of sending an Ambassador to Spain. I am sending a similar letter to Senator Vandenberg, Judge Kee, and Dr. Eaton.

The Spanish question has been magnified by controversy to a position among our present-day foreign-policy problems which is disproportionate to its intrinsic importance. Organized propaganda and pressures have kept this controversy alive both here and abroad and have served to stimulate more emotional feeling than rational thinking. Thus far, we have succeeded in dealing with this question on a broad bipartisan basis through our distinguished delegations to the United Nations. A clarification of some of the issues might help now to put this question in its proper framework in relation to the broader aspects of our policy.

Since the end of the war there have been a number of international actions with respect to Spain. It was agreed at the Potsdam Conference in the summer of 1945 and at the San Francisco Conference of the United Nations that same year that Spain could not be a member of the United Nations as long as the present Government remains in power. This position was endorsed

---

[1] This resolution was reaffirmed by the Assembly in 1947.

[2] Department of State Press Release 54, January 19, 1950. This is one of the documents referred to in the foreword, which even though it appeared after December 31, 1949, had such a significance for American foreign policy and this collection of documents that an exception was made, and it is included to round out the material on Spain.

by the first session of the General Assembly of the United Nations in London in February 1946.

In April 1946 the Security Council discussed fully relations with the Spanish Government, and again in December the matter was debated by the General Assembly at even greater length. The Resolution which finally passed the General Assembly recommended that the Franco Government be barred from membership in specialized agencies of the UN and that all members of the United Nations immediately recall from Madrid their Ambassadors and Ministers Plenipotentiary accredited there.

This matter was discussed again by the General Assembly in November 1947. In the voting on various resolutions the two-thirds rule resulted in the refusal to reaffirm the 1946 Resolution. However, the Resolution was not repealed.

In May 1949 the General Assembly undertook a further discussion of the Spanish question, but no change was made in the Resolution.

The United States has opposed moves in the United Nations to bring about a break in diplomatic relations with or to impose economic sanctions against Spain. This position is based on the Security Council view that the existence of the Franco Regime in Spain is not a threat to peace, and on our view that such outside pressures would either unite the Spanish people against the development of democratic freedoms or would precipitate the Spanish people themselves toward civil war with unknown but inevitably costly consequences.

Entirely aside from its views concerning the present regime in Spain, the United States has long questioned the wisdom and efficacy of the actions recommended in the 1946 Resolution. At the time that Resolution was debated, the United States Delegation, because of its reservations on the sections dealing with Chiefs of Mission and with Security Council action abstained in the vote in the Political Committee. It voted for the Resolution in the plenary session of the General Assembly "in the interests of harmony and of obtaining the closest possible approach to unanimity in the General Assembly on the Spanish problem."

Experience since that time has served to confirm our doubts about these recommendations. They were intended as a gesture of disapproval and an attempt to bring about a change in the Spanish Government. In retrospect it is now clear, however, that this action has not only failed in its intended purpose but has served to strengthen the position of the present regime. This action of the United Nations and discussions of the Spanish question in subsequent sessions of the General Assembly have all been represented in Spain as foreign interference in Spanish affairs. The Spanish reaction has been no different from that to be expected from any proud people.

Although some members of the United Nations no longer observe the recommendation with respect to Chiefs of Mission and have returned Ambassadors or Ministers to Madrid, the recommendation has not been amended or repealed by the General Assembly. Since the support and strengthening of the United Nations is a fundamental principle of our foreign policy, and since we attach importance as a matter of policy to compliance with United Nations recommendations, we are continuing to adhere to the 1946 Resolution so long as it remains in effect.

The question arises, therefore, whether the Resolution itself should be changed. Political considerations which have created general reluctance to accept Spain as a partner in the close cooperation among the Western European nations also apply to this situation. This is a problem which requires consideration by many nations and is not a matter which can be solved by the United States alone.

This is not a problem of recognition, as it has frequently been portrayed. The 1946 Resolution on Spain does not call for a break in diplomatic relations with Spain. The United States formally recognized the present Spanish Government on April 1, 1939, and we have had continuous diplomatic relations ever since. Three American Ambassadors had been accredited to that Government before the 1946 Resolution was passed. When the Resolution came into force, the United States abided by the recommendation that Ambassadors be withdrawn by refraining from appointing another Ambassador to fill a vacancy which existed at that time.

In our view, the withdrawal of Ambassadors from Spain as a means of political pressure was a mistaken departure from established principle. It is traditional practice, once a state has been formally recognized, to exchange Ambassadors or Ministers and is usually without political significance. At the Ninth International Conference of American States in Bogota, this principle was incorporated in Resolution 35 which states in part that "the establishment or maintenance of diplomatic relations with a government does not imply any judgment upon the domestic policy of that government." However, the withdrawal of Ambassadors from Spain disregarded this principle. By attaching moral significance to the *refusal* to maintain full diplomatic relations with Spain, this action has also implied moral significance to the *maintenance* of full diplomatic relations through the return of Ambassadors. This situation inevitably led to confusion in public opinion both here and abroad. On the one hand, the question of returning Ambassadors to Spain has tended to become identified with the larger issue of whether it is desirable to have closer relations with the present Spanish Government. On the other hand, public bewilderment has been increased over the inconsistency of accrediting Ambassadors to such countries as those in Eastern Europe whose regimes we do not condone while, at the same time, refusing to appoint an Ambassador to Spain.

At the General Assembly last spring a majority of the members who voted on the Latin American resolution relating to Spain expressed a wish to revise the 1946 Resolution in such a way as to permit members to exercise freedom of action in determining whether to return Ambassadors or Ministers to Madrid. It is the opinion of this Government that the anomalous situation with respect to Spain should be resolved. The United States is therefore prepared to vote for a resolution in the General Assembly which will leave members free to send an Ambassador or Minister to Spain if they choose. We would do this for the reasons I have already stated and in the hope that this aspect of the Spanish issue would no longer be available to be used by hostile propaganda to create unnecessary divisions within the United Nations and among our own people. Our vote would in no sense signify approval of the regime in Spain. It would merely indicate our desire, in the interests of orderly international intercourse, to return to normal practice in exchanging diplomatic representation.

We have stated on a number of occasions that we would favor the amendment of the 1946 Resolution of the General Assembly to permit specialized agencies to admit Spain to membership if, in the opinion of the specialized agencies, Spanish membership would contribute to the effective work of these organizations. We believe that membership in these agencies should be determined, to the extent practicable, on the technical and nonpolitical basis. It has already been discovered on a number of occasions that the work of these specialized organizations has been impaired through the inability of Spain to accept the obligations and restraints, as well as the privileges of their activities.

These conclusions by the United States Government do not imply any change in the basic attitude of this Government toward Spain.

The policy of the United States toward Spain is based on the recognition of certain essential facts. First, there is no sign of an alternative to the present Government.

Second, the internal position of the present regime is strong and enjoys the support of many who, although they might prefer another form of government or chief of state, fear that chaos and civil strife would follow a move to overthrow the Government.

Third, Spain is a part of Western Europe which should not be permanently isolated from normal relations with that area. There are, however, certain obstacles to the achievement of this. Spain, for reasons associated with the nature, origin, and history of the present Spanish Government, is still unacceptable to many of the Western European nations as an associate in such cooperative projects as the European Recovery Program and the Council of Europe. We believe that this is a matter in which the Western European nations must have a leading voice. These programs, which require for their success the closest possible cooperation between the participants, are directed to the strengthening and development of the democratic way of life as opposed to the threats to it posed by Communist expansion. This is a policy which we and the Western European nations have agreed upon. It is not merely a negative reaction to Communism. It is, rather, a positive program to support and strengthen democratic freedoms politically, economically, and militarily. In that context the participation of the present Spanish Government, unless and until there has been some indication of evolution toward more democratic government in Spain, would weaken rather than strengthen the collective effort to safeguard and strengthen democracy.

We are therefore continuing our efforts in a frank and friendly manner to persuade the Spanish Government that its own interest in participating in the international community, and particularly in the Western European community, requires steps toward democratic government which offers the best hope for the growth of basic human rights and fundamental freedoms in Spain. It requires cooperation on the part of all parties and, as must be evident, it is not fundamentally a matter which can be successfully brought about by American action. The decisions as to what steps can and should be taken is obviously one for Spaniards alone. At the same time, it is difficult to envisage Spain as a full member of the free Western community without substantial advances in such directions as increased civil liberties and as religious freedom and the freedom to exercise the elementary rights of organized labor. It is significant that one of the first acts of the new International Confederation of Free Trade Unions was to pass a resolution condemning the present government of Spain, and opposing any assistance to Spain "until such time as democratic and full trade-union rights have been restored and the workers are once more able to make their contribution to the country's recovery."

United States economic policy toward Spain is directed to the development of mutually beneficial economic relations. This policy is based on purely economic, as distinct from political, grounds. We believe that private business and banking arrangements and trade activities with Spain should be conducted on a free and normal basis. The Department interposes no political objections and restrictions on such activities.

So far as economic assistance from this Government is concerned, Spain is free to apply to and consult with the Export-Import Bank for credits for specific projects on the same basis as any other country. While the United States Government definitely does not favor the extension of a general balance of payments loan to the Spanish Government to use as it sees fit, it is quite prepared to acquiesce in the extension of credits to Spain covering specific and economically justifiable projects. It has been made clear to all Spaniards, both private and official, that Spanish applications for such projects will be considered on the same basis as those from any other country and the final decision will be made, in accordance with the Bank's regular policy, not only on the basis of the need for the credit and the suitability of the particular purpose to be served, but also on whether there is a reasonable prospect of repayment.

The successful development of mutually beneficial economic relations between the United States and Spain is entirely dependent upon the equal cooperation of both parties. Unfortunately, however, little progress has been made. The United States sincerely desires to facilitate normal business and trade with Spain but ultimate success depends on the cooperation of the Spanish Government in taking constructive steps to promote its trade and to attract foreign investment. In order to assist in the development of these activities, the negotiation of a new Treaty of Friendship, Commerce, and Navigation was offered by the United States. To date, the Spanish Government has indicated no interest in such arrangements. Efforts have also been made to encourage the Spanish Government to simplify its export and import controls and its foreign exchange system, which is based upon a multiplicity of rates, in order to establish an exchange rate which would permit Spanish goods to compete, particularly in the dollar market. Furthermore, efforts have been made to encourage the Spanish Government to lift the restriction of 25 percent on the participation of foreign investors in any Spanish enterprise and to accord better treatment to existing foreign investments, both of which are today distinct hindrances to the flow of investment to Spain. We have, in connection with these problems, pointed out to interested Spaniards and to the Spanish Government that the present critical situation in the Spanish dollar balance of payments seems to derive from difficulties many of which it is believed could be substantially rectified by action of the Spanish Government. To date, however, that Government has taken little action along these lines. In the Department's opinion the next steps to be taken in furthering mutually beneficial economic relations between Spain and the United States are up to the Spanish Government.

Sincerely yours,   (Signed)   DEAN ACHESON.

164. WITHDRAWAL OF UN SANCTIONS AGAINST SPAIN

Resolution of the General Assembly adopted on November 4, 1950 [1]

[After four years of agitation, the General Assembly finally revoked the diplomatic sanctions which it had imposed against Spain in its 1946 resolution. The vote on the measure was 38 to 10 with 12 abstentions. Shortly thereafter, the United States resumed full diplomatic relations with Spain by the appointment of Stanton Griffis as Ambassador to Madrid.]

The General Assembly,

Considering that: the General Assembly during the second part of its first session in 1946 adopted several recommendations concerning Spain, one of which provided that Spain be debarred from membership in international agencies established by or brought into relationship with the United Nations, and another that Member States withdraw their Ambassadors and Ministers from Madrid;

The establishment of diplomatic relations and the exchange of Ambassadors and Ministers with a government does not imply any judgment upon the domestic policy of that government;

The specialized agencies of the United Nations are technical and largely non-political in character and have been established in order to benefit the peoples of all nations, and that, therefore, they should be free to decide for themselves whether the participation of Spain in their activities is desirable in the interest of their work.

Resolves:

1. To revoke the recommendation for the withdrawal of Ambassadors and Ministers from Madrid, contained in General Assembly Resolution 39 (1) of 12 December 1946; and

2. To revoke the recommendation intended to debar Spain from membership in international agencies established by or brought into relationship with the United Nations, which recommendation is a part of the same resolution adopted by the General Assembly in 1946 concerning relations of Members of the United Nations with Spain.

[1] Department of State Bulletin, November 13, 1950, p. 772.

TURKISH STRAITS [1]

165. UNITED STATES POSITION ON TURKISH STRAITS

(a) *Exchange of Notes Between the Soviet Charge D'Affaires and Acting Secretary Acheson, August 7, 1946* [2]

[The Montreux Convention of 1936 was the most recent of a series of international conventions since 1841, concerned with the regulation of the Turkish Straits and the Sea of Marmora. It lays down the provisions which control the use of the Straits—under the general supervision of Turkey—in time of peace and in wartime. At the Potsdam Conference it was agreed that the Montreux Convention should be revised; but differences soon developed over the nature of the revisions. In the following correspondence the Soviet Union proposed to place the Straits under the control of the Black Sea Powers, which would include Russia. The United States rejected the proposal because other powers in addition to the Black Sea states are interested in using the Straits. The United States also urged that Turkey should continue to remain responsible for the administration and defense of the Straits. Up to January 1, 1951, there had been no further important developments on this matter.]

EMBASSY OF THE UNION OF SOVIET SOCIALIST REPUBLICS,
Washington, D. C., August 7, 1946.

SIR:

By direction of the Soviet Government I have the honor to communicate to you the following:

As is known, the Berlin Conference of the Three Powers on the question of the Montreux Convention adopted a resolution, whereby the three governments declared that the said convention should be revised, since it does not correspond to present conditions. At the same time the three governments agreed that this question was to be the subject of direct negotiations between each of the Three Powers and the Turkish Government. In accordance with this, the Soviet Government on August 7 of this year addressed to the Turkish Government a note which is transcribed below:

"The Ministry of Foreign Affairs of the USSR has the honor to inform the Turkish Government of the following:

"Events which occurred during the past war clearly indicated that the regime of the Black Sea Straits, established by the Straits Convention, signed in 1936 at Montreux, does not meet the interests of the safety of the Black Sea Powers and does not insure conditions under which the use of these Straits for purposes inimical to the Black Sea Powers would be prevented.

"It will suffice to mention a series of incidents during this war, when the Axis Powers directed their warships and auxiliary craft through the Straits

[1] For more thorough treatment see The Problems of the Turkish Straits, Department of State publication 2752, Near East Series 5.

[2] Department of State, Bulletin of September 1, 1946, pp. 420-422. Copies of Acting Secretary Acheson's note have also been transmitted to the Governments of the United Kingdom, France, Turkey, Greece, Yugoslavia, and Rumania, which were among the signatories of the Montreux Convention of July 20, 1936, See The Problems of the Turkish Straits, Department of State publication 2752, Near East Series 5.

into the Black Sea and out of the Black Sea, which in turn gave rise to the corresponding steps and protests registered by the Soviet Government with the Turkish Government.

"On July 9, 1941 the German command sent the German patrol boat 'Seefalke' through the Straits into the Black Sea, which was a gross violation of the Straits Convention and called forth a protest to the Turkish Government on the part of the Soviet Government.

"In August 1941, Turkish authorities gave the Italian auxiliary war vessel 'Tarvizio' permission to pass through the Straits into the Black Sea, which likewise called forth a representation on the part of the Soviet Government, calling to the attention of the Turkish Government the fact that the passage of the Italian auxiliary vessel into the Black Sea would appear to be a violation of the Straits Convention.

"On November 4, 1942, the Soviet Government again called to the attention of the Turkish Government the fact that Germany planned to send to the Black Sea through the Straits auxiliary warships under the guise of merchant vessels with a total displacement of 140,000 tons. These vessels were intended for the transfer of military forces and war materials of the Axis countries into the Black Sea. In its representation, the Soviet Government emphasized the fact that 'the admission of the aforementioned vessels through the Straits into the Black Sea would be an obvious violation of the Convention regarding the regime of the Straits concluded in Montreux, inasmuch as these vessels are left at the disposal of the German Government and are in reality auxiliary warships.'

"In June 1944, the Soviet Government registered a protest against the fact that toward the end of May and early in June of 1944 there took place a series of passages through the Straits from the Black Sea into Aegean Sea of German warships and auxiliary warships of varying tonnage of the 'Ems' (8 vessels) and 'Kriegtransport' (5 vessels) types, which had taken part in the naval operations in the Black Sea.

"It is obvious from the aforementioned facts that at the time of the past war with Germany and her allies, the Straits Convention did not prevent the enemy powers from using the Straits for military purposes against the U. S. S. R. and other allied powers, with the Turkish Government not being able to escape the responsibility for this situation.

"In view of this, the Soviet Government suggested to the Berlin Conference of the Three Powers—Great Britain, the United States of America and the Soviet Union, which took place in July and August 1945, to discuss the question that the regime of the Straits, established by the Montreux Convention, does not conform to present conditions and that it is necessary to establish a new regime of the Straits. As is known, the Berlin Conference of the Three Powers adopted a resolution consisting of the following:

"*a*) The three governments declared that the Convention regarding the Straits, concluded in Montreux, should be revised, as it does not meet the conditions of the present time;

"*b*) The three governments agreed that as the proper course the said question would be subject of direct negotiations between each of the three powers and the Turkish Government.

"The Soviet Government is also acquainted with the contents of the note of November 2, 1945 of the Government of the United States of America and with the note of the British Government of November 21, 1945 addressed to the Government of Turkey on this question.

"For its own part, the Soviet Government proposes to establish for the Straits a new regime, proceeding from the following principles:

"1) The Straits should be always open to the passage of merchant ships of all countries.

"2) The Straits should be always open to the passage of warships of the Black Sea Powers.

"3) Passage through the Straits for warships not belonging to the Black Sea Powers shall not be permitted except in cases specially provided for.

"4) The establishment of a regime of the Straits, as the sole sea passage, leading from the Black Sea and to the Black Sea, should come under the competence of Turkey and other Black Sea Powers.

"5) Turkey and the Soviet Union, as the powers most interested and capable of guaranteeing freedom to commercial navigation and security in the Straits, shall organize joint means of defense of the Straits, for the prevention of the utilization of the Straits by other countries for aims hostile to the Black Sea Powers.

"The Soviet Government is informing the governments of the United States of America and Great Britain regarding the present declaration."

The Soviet Union has directed me to bring this to the knowledge of the Government of the United States of America.

Accept [etc.]

FEDOR OREKHOV

Acting Secretary of State DEAN ACHESON,
Department of State, Washington.

August 19, 1946.

SIR:

I acknowledge receipt of your note of August 7, 1946, which sets forth the text of the note addressed on the same day by the Government of the Union of Soviet Socialist Republics to the Government of the Republic of Turkey and express the appreciation of this Government for the courtesy of the Soviet Government in making this information available.

It will be recalled that the American Embassy in Moscow made available to the Soviet Government in November 1945 a copy of the note which the American Embassy delivered to the Turkish Government on November 2, 1945.[1]

This Government has given careful study to the views expressed by the Soviet Government in its note to the Turkish Government. It would appear from a comparison of this Government's note of November 2, 1945, with the Soviet note to the Turkish Government of August 7, 1946, that the views of the Governments of the United States and of the Soviet Union, while not in entire accord, are in general agreement with regard to the three following proposals set forth in the Soviet note:

"1. The Straits should be always open to the passage of merchant ships of all countries.

[1] Substance of note printed in Department of State Bulletin of November 11, 1945, p. 766.

"2. The Straits should be always open to the passage of warships of the Black Sea Powers.

"3. Passage through the Straits for warships not belonging to the Black Sea powers shall not be permitted except in cases specially provided for."

The fourth proposal set forth in the Soviet note does not appear to envisage a revision of the Montreux Convention, as suggested in our note to the Turkish Government of November 2, 1945, but rather the establishment of a new régime which would be confined to Turkey and the other Black Sea powers. It is the view of this Government that the régime of the Straits is a matter of concern not only to the Black Sea powers but also to other powers, including the United States. This Government cannot, therefore, agree with the Soviet view that the establishment of the régime of the Straits should come under the competence of the Black Sea powers to the exclusion of other powers.

The fifth proposal set forth in the note of the Soviet Government was that Turkey and the Soviet Union should organize joint means of defense of the Straits. It is the firm opinion of this Government that Turkey should continue to be primarily responsible for the defense of the Straits. Should the Straits become the object of attack or threat by an aggressor, the resulting situation would constitute a threat to international security and would clearly be a matter for action on the part of the Security Council of the United Nations.

It is observed that the note of the Soviet Government contains no reference to the United Nations. The position of the Government of the United States is that the régime of the Straits should be brought into appropriate relationship with the United Nations and should function in a manner entirely consistent with the principles and aims of the United Nations.

The Government of the United States reaffirms its willingness to participate in a conference called to revise the Montreux Convention.

Accept [etc.]

DEAN ACHESON
Acting Secretary of State

(b) Note Delivered by W. Bedell Smith, United States Ambassador to the U.S.S.R., to the Soviet Foreign Office on October 9, 1946 [1]

I have the honor to inform Your Excellency that my Government has studied carefully the contents of the note of the Soviet Union to Turkey of September 24 relating to the regime of the Straits.

In pursuance of its policy of making clear to all interested parties its views on matters relating to the Straits, my Government has instructed me to inform you that after examining the note referred to above it continues to adhere to the position outlined in its note of August 19, 1946 to the Soviet Government.

It will be recalled that in the Protocol of the proceedings of the Potsdam Conference, signed by the U.S.S.R., Great Britain and the United States, the three Governments recognized that the Convention on the Straits concluded at Montreux should be revised as failing to meet present-day conditions. It was further agreed in the Protocol that as the next step the matter should be the subject of direct conversations between each of the three Governments and the Turkish Government.

[1] Department of State Bulletin of October 20, 1946, p. 722.

It has been the understanding of my Government that the three Governments, in agreeing with one another that the regime of the Straits should be brought into accord with present-day conditions by means of a revision of the Montreux Convention, mutually recognized that all three signatories of the Protocol have an interest in the regime of the Straits and in any changes which might be made in that regime. My Government furthermore informed the Soviet Government in its note of August 19, that in its view the regime of the Straits is a matter of concern not only to the Black Sea powers but also to other powers, including the United States. The Soviet Government, nevertheless, in its note of September 24, apparently continues to take the position set forth in its note of August 7 to Turkey that "the establishment of a regime of the Straits . . . should come under the competence of Turkey and the other Black Sea powers". My Government does not consider that it was contemplated at the Potsdam Conference that the direct conversations which might take place between any one of the three signatory governments and the Turkish Government with regard to the regime of the Convention of the Straits concluded at Montreux should have the effect of prejudicing the participation of the other two signatory powers in the revision of the regime of the Straits. On the contrary, my Government considers that the Potsdam Agreement definitely contemplated only an exchange of views with the Turkish Government as a useful preliminary to a conference of all the interested powers, including the United States, to consider the revision of the Montreux Convention. As stated in its note of August 19, my Government stands ready to participate in such a conference.

My Government also feels that it would be lacking in frankness if it should fail to point out again at this time, in the most friendly spirit, that in its opinion the Government of Turkey should continue to be primarily responsible for the defense of the Straits and that should the Straits become the object of attack or threat of attack by an aggressor, the resulting situation would be a matter for action on the part of the Security Council of the United Nations.

UNION OF SOVIET SOCIALIST REPUBLICS

166. COOPERATION FOR PEACE

Message by President Truman to the President of the Presidium of the Supreme Soviet of the Union of Soviet Socialist Republics, November 7, 1945 [1]

[In 1945, the Soviet Union as our ally was highly regarded in this country. Since the end of hostilities, however, public opinion in the United States has undergone a great change, due in large measure to the aggressive and expansionist tactics of the Soviet leaders. The following message of President Truman reflects how ready the American people were in 1945 to live amicably with the Soviet Union.]

[1] Department of State Bulletin of November 11, 1945, p. 768.

It gives me great pleasure on this national anniversary of the Union of Soviet Socialist Republics to send to Your Excellency and to the people of the Soviet Union the congratulations and best wishes of the people of the United States, as well as my own personal greetings and felicitations.'

Through the joint efforts of our two peoples and their valiant armed forces, in alliance with the other peoples of the United Nations, the forces of aggression in Europe and Asia which constituted so dangerous a threat to the freedom and prosperity of the peoples of the world have been totally defeated in a long and bloody struggle. The years ahead offer an unexampled opportunity for achieving peaceful progress and improving the lot of the common man. The recent entry into effect of the United Nations Charter is a happy augury for cooperation between our two peoples and the other free nations of the world in the quest for firm, lasting and universal peace.

I am confident that the challenge presented as a result of our joint victory over the common enemy will be successfully and constructively met through the continued cooperation of our two peoples during the coming years of peace in the same spirit which animated them during the past four years of war.

HARRY S. TRUMAN

◇◇◇◇◇◇

167. SMITH-MOLOTOV EXCHANGE [1]

(a) Statement of Ambassador Walter Bedell Smith, to Foreign Minister Molotov, May 4, 1948

[During 1946 and 1947 tensions between the Soviet Union and the United States continued to increase. In an effort to clarify the position of the United States, Ambassador Walter Bedell Smith on May 4, 1948, presented to the Soviet Foreign Minister the views of the United States with respect to Russian-American relations. He informed Mr. Molotov that the people of the United States stood united behind the policies of their government, and that they did not harbor any aggressive intentions or designs against the U.S.S.R., as Soviet propaganda was constantly asserting.

Mr. Molotov answered by pointing out what he called the "unfriendly character of the policy of the Government of the United States with regard to the Union of Soviet Socialist Republics," and stated that the United States was pursuing a hostile policy of encirclement and warlike threats. In his reply, Ambassador Smith argued that the whole history of the United States was a complete refutation of these charges.]

Two years ago during my initial conversation with Generalissimo Stalin and yourself, I stated as clearly as possible my estimate of the inevitable reaction of the American people to the continuance of a policy by the Soviet Government which would appear to have as its purpose the progressive extension of the area of Soviet power. At that time I pointed out that it would

---

[1] Department of State Bulletin, May 23, 1948, pp. 679-686. May 4 Ambassador Walter Bedell Smith called on V. M. Molotov, Soviet Minister for Foreign Affairs, and made to him this oral statement on behalf of the United States Government.

be a grave misinterpretation of the fundamentally pacific character of the American people to believe that they would not react strongly and vigorously to the progressive domination by one country of its neighbors and the clear threat to the world community which such actions would imply.

I emphasized at that time that the United States had no desire whatever to see the world divided into two major groupings, nor to divert a large part of its income to the maintenance of a military establishment which such a world situation would necessitate in elementary self-defense. It seemed apparent then that such a line of policy as that described would lead inevitably to a crystallization of the non-Soviet areas of the world, whose people would quite understandably feel themselves progressively threatened by such developments. It seemed also inevitable in such a case that the United States, as the strongest nation in this community, would be forced to take a leading part in this movement and to divert a large portion of its energy, which by preference our people would prefer to utilize for assistance in the reconstruction of the ravages of the war, to the maintenance of a military establishment adequate to meet the developing world situation.

Unhappily the apprehensions I felt at that time have been realized.

Since that date, Soviet policies in eastern Europe have produced the reaction which was predicted. The situation which has resulted is obviously one of great seriousness.

The European community and the United States have become alarmed at the implications of Soviet policy, and are drawing closer together in mutual self-protection, but only in self-protection.

It is for this reason that my Government desires me to outline to you with complete clarity and frankness the position of the United States Government.

There should be no mistake about the determination of the United States to play its part in these cooperative movements for recovery and self-defense. The concern and the determination of the people of the United States have been intensified by the inexplicable hostility of the Soviet Government to the European Recovery Program—a measure which in its inception and subsequent development is so obviously only a measure of American assistance for reconstruction on a cooperative basis without menace or threat to anyone.

The situation which has been produced by the actions of the Soviet Government or by political groups obviously under its control, and the natural and inevitable reaction on the part of other countries, including the United States, to these actions is obviously one of great seriousness.

My Government has no idea what conclusions the Soviet Government has reached concerning the present attitude of the United States. It has noted that the pictures of this attitude given by the Soviet press is dangerously distorted and erroneous. Whether, or in what degree, the members of the Soviet Government themselves believe this distorted version my Government has no means of estimating. For this reason I wish to make plain certain points on which my Government considers it extremely important that there be no misunderstanding at this time.

1. The policies of the United States Government in international questions have been made amply clear in recent months and weeks. They have the support of the overwhelming majority of the American people. They will continue to be vigorously and firmly prosecuted.

It would be a grave error if others were to assume that domestic considerations, such as the forthcoming elections, would in any way weaken the determination of the United States to support what it believes to be right. The American people have always known how to separate domestic and foreign policy at the proper moment.

Similarly, my Government is aware that Communist organizations here and there have been disseminating propaganda to the effect that a forthcoming economic crisis in the United States will soon produce a radical change in American policies. It is hoped that no one will be so foolish as to forfeit the chances of progress toward world stability for the sake of an economic prognostication which has been proven wrong time and time again. Even those who persist in believing such a prognostication must, at the very least, realize that an economic crisis would not affect in any way our basic productive capacity nor our concept of the basic factors underlying our foreign policy.

It must be emphasized that the present state of world affairs involves issues which the people of the United States consider to be vital to United States national security and to world peace. No one should deceive himself as to the seriousness of United States policy with respect to these issues.

2. On the other hand, my Government wishes to make it unmistakably clear that the United States has no hostile or aggressive designs whatever with respect to the Soviet Union. Assertions to the contrary are falsehoods which can result only from complete misunderstanding or malicious motives. United States policies have been so devised that they cannot possibly affect adversely the interests of a Soviet Union which seeks to live at peace with its neighbors and to refrain from attempts to exercise undue influence, directly or indirectly, in their affairs.

In fact, many of the elements of United States foreign policy to which the Soviet press takes such strong exception today would never have come into existence if it had not been necessary for the United States to aid other countries to defend their own political integrity from attempts, on the part of Communist minorities, to seize power and to establish regimes subservient to foreign interests. Should these attempts cease, the necessity for some of the manifestations of United States foreign policy, which are apparently unwelcome in Moscow, would cease with them.

The present state of United States-Soviet relations is a source of grievous disappointment to the American people and to the United States Government. As far as we are concerned, it represents a painful and undesired alternative toward which we have been driven, step by step, by the pressure of Soviet and world Communist policy. We still do not despair by any means of a turn of events which will permit us to find the road to a decent and reasonable relationship between our two countries, with a fundamental relaxation of those tensions which today exercise so unhappy an influence on international society everywhere. As far as the United States is concerned, the door is always wide open for full discussion and the composing of our differences.

My Government earnestly hopes that the members of the Soviet Government will not take lightly the position of the United States Government, as here expressed. They have it in their power to alleviate many of the situations which today weigh so heavily on all international life. It is our earnest hope that they will take advantage of these possibilities. If they do, they will not find us lacking in readiness and eagerness to make our own contribution to a stabilization of world conditions entirely compatible with the security of the Soviet peoples.

(b) Translation of the Statement of Foreign Minister Molotov to Ambassador Smith, May 9, 1948

The Soviet Government has familiarized itself with the declaration of the Ambassador of the United States of America, Mr. Smith, dated May 4, 1948, in connection with the present state of Soviet-American relations. The Soviet Government shares the desire, expressed in this statement by the Government of the United States of America, to better these relations, and is in agreement with the proposal to proceed with this aim toward a discussion and settlement of the difference existing between us.

At the same time the Soviet Government considers it necessary to state that it cannot agree with the Government of the United States of America that the reason for the present unsatisfactory conditions of Soviet-American relations and the tension in the international situation is a result of the policy of the Union of Soviet Socialist Republics in eastern Europe and to the increased influence there of the Union of Soviet Socialist Republics.

As concerns the relations of the Union of Soviet Socialist Republics with bordering as well as other countries of Europe, the Soviet Government notes with satisfaction that in fact these relations following the war have significantly improved.

As is known, this has found expression through the conclusion of treaties of friendship and mutual assistance between the Union of Soviet Socialist Republics and these countries which are directed exclusively against the repetition of aggression on the part of Germany and its possible allies and which, contrary to the statement of the Ambassador of the United States of America in Moscow, Mr. Smith, do not include any secret protocols. The countries overrun by German aggression are particularly interested in the conclusion of these agreements.

It is common knowledge that the United States of America also is carrying out the policy of strengthening its relations with bordering countries, for example, with Canada, Mexico, and also with other countries of America, and this is fully understandable. It is likewise understandable that the Soviet Union also is conducting a policy of strengthening its relations with bordering and other countries of Europe. The Union of Soviet Socialist Republics will pursue in the future as well its policy of strengthening friendly relationships with these countries of Europe.

In the declaration of the Government of the United States of America it is stated that certain of the external political measures of the United States of America in other countries, which have evoked the dissatisfaction of the Union of Soviet Socialist Republics, are explained by the excessive influence of the Union of Soviet Socialist Republics in the internal affairs of these countries. The Soviet Government is unable to agree with this kind of explanation.

In the countries of eastern Europe which are under consideration, following the war, as is well known, there took place serious democratic reforms which are a means of defense against the threat of a new war and which created favorable conditions for the growth of friendly relations between these countries and the Union of Soviet Socialist Republics. It would be absolutely incorrect to attribute the democratic reforms which have taken place here to interference of the Soviet Union in the internal affairs of these countries. This would mean ignoring the indubitable fact that the above-mentioned reforms are a natural result of the victory of democratic forces over Nazism and Fascism and are regarded by the peoples of eastern Europe as guaranties against the threat of a new war. In this connection, the emergence of Communists in positions of leadership is completely understandable, since the people of these lands consider Communists the most effective fighters against a new war.

No one has the right to dispute the fact that the carrying through of democratic reforms is an internal affair of each state. However, from the above-mentioned communication of the Government of the United States it is clear that it holds another viewpoint and tolerates on its own part interference in the internal affairs of other states which cannot but call forth serious objections on the part of the Soviet Government. Events in Greece are not the only example of such interference in the internal affairs of other states.

The Government of the United States of America explains the present unsatisfactory state of Soviet-American relations also by the position of the Soviet Government on the question of the so-called European Recovery Program.

At the same time it is absolutely clear that if the question of the economic recovery of the European countries has been set up, not as has been done in the indicated program but on the basis of normal conditions of international economic cooperation within the framework of the United Nations organization and with the necessary regard of the national rights and sovereignty of states, there would be no reason for the Soviet Socialist Republics' negative attitude toward the ERP, all the more since the Union of Soviet Socialist Republics, as one of the states which suffered most, economically, in the war, is fully interested in the development of postwar international economic cooperation.

At the same time the Soviet Government thinks it necessary to state that the present unsatisfactory condition of Soviet-American relations and the tense state of the international situation are the result of the recent policy of the Government of the United States of America.

The creation of such a tense situation has been fostered in the first place by such steps of the Government of the United States of America as the increasing development of a network of naval and air bases in all parts of the world, including territories adjacent to the Union of Soviet Socialist Republics, about which the press and a series of official representatives of the United States of America frankly declare that the establishment of these bases has the aim of the encirclement of the Union of Soviet Socialist Republics. Such measures cannot be explained by the interests of self-defense. It is likewise impossible to overlook the fact that the present atmosphere of international relations is poisoned by warlike threats of all kinds directed against the Union of Soviet Socialist Republics, issuing from certain circles closely connected with the Government of the United States of America. In contrast to this, the Soviet Government is conducting a consistently peaceful policy with respect to the

United States of America and other states, is not establishing military bases in other countries and is not emitting any kind of threat toward anyone at all.

Further, there was recently formed a military union of western countries, including England, France, Belgium, Holland, and Luxembourg. At a time when all the treaties of mutual assistance concluded by the Soviet Union with the eastern countries, as well as with England and France, have as their aim the prevention of a new aggression on the part of Germany and are not directed against any allied state, the newly founded military alliance of the five western states, as is clear from the treaty, has in view not only Germany but may equally be directed against those states which were allies in the second world war. In all the English, French, and American press it is openly said that this union is directed against the Union of Soviet Socialist Republics. Furthermore, it cannot be overlooked that the formation of the stated military union was possible only thanks to the patronage of the Government of the United States of America. It is clear that the military treaty of the five western states can in no way be regarded as a treaty of self-defense.

The unfriendly character of the policy of the Government of the United States of America with regard to the Union of Soviet Socialist Republics has its effect also in the realm of Soviet-American commerce. In accordance with the commercial agreement concluded between our two states, the Government of the United States of America is obliged not to apply in regard to the export of goods from the United States of America to the Union of Soviet Socialist Republics any more burdensome regulations or formalities than are applied in regard to any third country. However, the policy now conducted by the Government of the United States of America ignores this obligation and is in complete contradiction to the Soviet-American commercial agreement, setting up discrimination in regard to the Union of Soviet Socialist Republics, regardless of the fact that the Union of Soviet Socialist Republics is fulfilling in good faith its obligations under the aforementioned agreement. As a result thereof, the export into the Union of Soviet Socialist Republics of American goods is disrupted, goods on which the Union of Soviet Socialist Republics has paid deposits or even the full cost, a fact which injures the American firms concerned as well. The intolerability of such a situation is completely evident.

At the present time the Government of the United States of America declares that the United States has no hostile or aggressive intentions with regard to the Union of Soviet Socialist Republics, and expresses the hope of the possibility of finding a way to the establishment of good and reasonable relations between our two countries, together with a fundamental relaxation of the tension in international relations, and expresses its readiness to cooperate in such a stabilization of world conditions as would correspond as well to the interests of the security of the Soviet people.

The Soviet Government can only welcome this declaration of the Government of the United States of America, for, as is known, it has always carried on a peace-loving policy and one of collaboration with regard to the United States of America which has always met with unanimous approval and support on the part of the peoples of the Union of Soviet Socialist Republics. The Government of the Union of Soviet Socialist Republics declares that in the future as well it intends to carry out this policy with complete consistency.

The Soviet Government also expresses the hope for the possibility of finding the means to eliminate present disagreements and to establish between our countries good relations which would correspond to the interests of our peoples, as well as to the consolidation of universal peace.

(c) Additional Comments by Ambassador Walter Bedell Smith to Foreign Minister Molotov's Reply, May 9, 1948

At the conclusion of Mr. Molotov's statement I said I would comment briefly. With regard to remarks about "development of United States bases", our "policy of encirclement and our warlike threats", I had only to say that our entire history was refutation of any suspicion of a policy which involved aggressive war. As I stated during our previous conversation, the drawing together of the western European countries and the support which was being given them by the United States was a direct reflection of the apprehensions and fears which had been aroused by the expansionist policy of the Union of Soviet Socialist Republics, and that while I had no right to disbelieve his statements, I could not refrain from paraphrasing Mr. Vyshinski's comment that facts spoke for themselves.

The United States was secure in its honesty of purpose with regard to ERP. Our people were, as stated previously, completely unable to understand implications placed on that program by the Union of Soviet Socialist Republics. The United States appreciates and fully understands the desire and indeed the necessity of close and friendly relations between the Union of Soviet Socialist Republics and its neighbors, but that here again facts spoke for themselves, and I was fully familiar with events which followed the acceptance by Czechoslovakia of the invitation to the ERP conference in Paris and subsequent reversal of this acceptance during the immediately following visit of Masaryk and Gottwald to Moscow. A country like my own which permitted complete freedom of political thought and expression did not oppose Communism because of its Marxian ideology but purely and simply because we had seen repeated instances of Communist minorities coming into power by illegal means and against the will of the majority of the population in the countries referred to. The United States remained convinced that these minority *coups d'état* would have been quite impossible without the moral and physical support of the Union of Soviet Socialist Republics.

With respect to trade agreements, there was nothing the United States would like better under conditions of reasonable and honest understanding than to participate in expanding trade with the Union of Soviet Socialist Republics and to contribute to the economic recovery of the Soviet states which had suffered during the war. If proof were desired of our previous feelings in this respect it could be found in fact that under lend-lease we had shipped to the Union of Soviet Socialist Republics enormous values in basic industrial plants which when shipped obviously would not be in production in time to contribute to the war effort. Our change in views with regard to trade was again a direct reflection of the Soviet expansionist policies referred to in my previous conversation.

I did not wish to indulge in a contest of words which might be interpreted as the "pot calling the kettle black", but I had recently reviewed some of our past agreements with the Union of Soviet Socialist Republics, particularly the

Roosevelt-Litvinov agreement, and that I would remind him of what I am sure he already knows, i. e., that the only provision of this agreement which had not been violated by the Union of Soviet Socialist Republics was that permitting the presence of an American clergyman in Moscow.

However, these were matters which it would be profitless for us to pursue to the exclusion of the major issues. I had, I believed, made completely clear the policies of the United States and the reasons which prompted the adoption of these policies. I appreciated Mr. Molotov's statement of the policies of his Government, which I would communicate at once to Washington.

◇◇◇◇◇◇

168. BASIC ISSUES BETWEEN THE UNITED STATES AND RUSSIA

(a) Comment by State Department on Stalin Statement, May 18, 1948 [1]

[In an effort to find a solution for the outstanding problems existing between the Soviet Union and the United States, Henry Wallace, the former Vice President of the United States, addressed an open letter to Premier Stalin in the spring of 1948. Premier Stalin observed in reply that a peaceful solution of the differences was possible. The State Department took occasion to comment on the Stalin reply by setting forth the major areas of difference between the two countries. This document constitutes a useful background summary in any study of Soviet-American relations.]

The Department has seen the press reports of a statement by Premier Stalin in response to an "open letter" from Mr. Wallace. Premier Stalin's opinion that a peaceful settlement of outstanding problems is possible and necessary in the interests of a general peace is encouraging, but the specific issues listed in Premier Stalin's statement are not bilateral issues between this country and the Soviet Union. They are of intimate and compelling interest to many countries and have been under negotiation for the past two years or more in bodies where other countries were represented, such as the United Nations and the Council of Foreign Ministers. For example, the U.N. Atomic Energy Commission and its Sub-Committees have held over 200 meetings and the Commission just yesterday reported its inability to reach an agreement because of the adamant opposition of two of its members—the Soviet Union and the Ukraine—to proposals which were acceptable to the other nine nations represented on the Commission. A similar situation exists with regard to other issues mentioned in Premier Stalin's statement.

(b) Further Comments by State Department on the Stalin Statement, May 19, 1948 [2]

The Department of State today made the following information available to the press in connection with the Stalin statement:

[1] Department of State Press Release, No. 390, May 18, 1948.
[2] Department of State Press Release No. 392, May 19, 1948.

1. Reduction of Armaments

The problem of the regulation of conventional armaments was discussed in the 1946 General Assembly of the United Nations, and has since been under consideration in the Commission for Conventional Armaments of the Security Council.

2. Atomic Energy

In the field of atomic energy, agreement on an effective plan for international control has so far been blocked by the Soviet Union.

The presentation of the Third Report of the Commission marks the recognition of an impasse which has existed practically since the negotiations began almost two years and 220 meetings ago. Fourteen out of seventeen of the nations which are now or have been represented on the Commission are agreed on the basic and indispensable requirements of an international control plan; the Soviet Union, Poland and the Ukraine have been the only members of the Commission to disagree.

Despite its unceasing efforts, the Commission has now been forced to declare that: "It has been unable to secure the agreement of the Soviet Union to even those elements of effective control considered essential from the technical point of view, let alone their acceptance of the nature and extent of participation in the world community required of all nations in this field by the First and Second Reports of the Atomic Energy Commission." In this situation, the Commission has concluded that for the present no useful purpose could be served by carrying on negotiations at the Commission level and has referred the whole problem to the Security Council with a recommendation that it be forwarded to the General Assembly.

The conclusion that further work at the Commission level would be futile does not mean that the efforts to achieve international control of atomic energy are to be terminated, but it does mean that the Commission has recognized the factors necessary to bring about agreement on an effective system for the international control of atomic energy are outside the competence of the Commission. The United Nations is still confronted with the problem of international control of atomic energy and the United States Government is still ready to participate in genuinely effective control.

3. German Peace Settlement

By common agreement the question of a German peace settlement is one for the Council of Foreign Ministers. The Council has held two long meetings devoted to this subject. Soviet opposition to virtually every proposition put forward by the United States, Great Britain and France has thus far blocked all progress on this question.

4. Japanese Peace Settlement

In July 1947 the United States proposed to the ten other members of the Far Eastern Commission that a preliminary conference be held to discuss a peace treaty for Japan, the voting procedure of such a conference to be by two-thirds majority. Eight States indicated general agreement with this proposal. The Soviet Union held that the peace treaty problems should be considered by the Council of Foreign Ministers, composed in this instance of the United Kingdom, China, the U. S. S. R., and the United States. China proposed that the peace treaty be considered by a conference of the eleven Far Eastern Commission countries and that decisions be taken by a majority which must include the four powers named above. It has so far been impossible to resolve the conflict between these widely different concepts as to the basis on which the Japanese peace treaty conference should be convened.

5. Evacuation of Troops from China

As of March 31, 1948 there were stationed in China, of the armed forces of the United States, 1,496 army personnel and 4,125 navy and marine personnel. These forces remain in China at the request of the National Government.

6. Evacuation of Troops from Korea

With respect to the suggestion that United States and Soviet occupation forces be withdrawn from Korea, the United Nations General Assembly, by Resolution of November 14, 1947, recommended a plan for the early achievement of Korean independence, to be followed promptly by the withdrawal of all foreign armed forces.

The General Assembly constituted a United Nations Commission to assist in this program. The Ukraine was elected to membership on the Commission but refused to serve. The U. S. S. R. denied the United Nations Commission entry into the northern zone of Korea. It has not only refused to collaborate in any way in the implementation of the United Nations plan but has attempted to proceed unilaterally with a plan of its own which threatens to lead to civil war among the Koreans themselves.

7. Respect for National Sovereignty and Non-Interference in Domestic Affairs

The facts bearing on this subject are too voluminous for recapitulation here. The actions and policies of the two Governments in this respect are a matter of public record, and speak for themselves.

8. Military Bases

The policy of the United States in this respect has been governed by the unanimous resolution of the United Nations General Assembly of December 14, 1946, which makes the retention of armed forces on the territories of members conditional upon the freely and publicly expressed consent of such members. In accordance with Article 103 of the Charter, the United States has made it a practice to register with the United Nations the instruments of agreements. It is of interest to note that the United States has proposed in the Security Council that armed forces acting under the Security Council have unlimited rights of passage and rights to use bases wherever located. The U. S. S. R. has rejected this proposal.

9. International Trade

The representatives of twenty-three countries attended the session of the Preparatory Committee for the United Nations conference on trade and employment which was held in Geneva in the summer of 1947. The representatives of fifty-six nations participated in the final conference on trade and employment held in Havana, Cuba from November 1947 to March 1948. This Conference agreed upon the charter for an international trade organization, one of the main purposes of which is the elimination of all forms of discrimination in international trade. The Soviet Government declined to participate in either of these meetings.

10. Assistance to War-Devastated Countries

The aid being extended by the United States to other countries on a worldwide scale, through both United Nations channels and others, should be an adequate answer to this point. In the case of the European Recovery Program, in which the U. S. S. R. declined to participate, the proposal to create a new organization came from the participating European countries.

11. Human Rights

The United Nations turned to the question of human rights as one of its first tasks and its work in this field is well advanced. The Human Rights Commission, under the chairmanship of Mrs. Eleanor Roosevelt, may shortly recommend a draft declaration and covenant on human rights to the Economic and Social Council and to the General Assembly. Since both the U. S. S. R. and the United States are active members of the Human Rights Commission, it is difficult to see how this matter could be advanced in any other forum. It lies in the nature of this subject that it is imminently a multilateral and international problem and both the Soviet Union and the United States have, in the United Nations Commission, a wholly adequate forum in which to put forward their views.

<><><><><>

169. SOVIET VIOLATIONS OF TREATY OBLIGATIONS

Document Submitted by the Department of State to the Senate Foreign Relations Committee, June 2, 1948 [1]

[According to Marxist principles, agreements between communist and so-called capitalist governments are binding only so long as the instruments serve communist purposes. In line with this philosophy, the Soviet Union has often violated the terms of agreements which they have entered into with the Western Powers. How extensive and numerous these breaches were was not apparent to the general public until the Senate Committee on Foreign Relations in 1948 requested a list of Soviet Treaty violations from the State Department. While the list has been considerably expanded since it was first published, the following document illustrates the nature of the problem.]

[1] Senate Report No. 1440, 80th Congress, 2d session, June 2, 1948.

Text of Resolution

[S. Res. 213, 80th Cong., 2d sess.]

Whereas the President of the United States declared in his address to the Congress on March 17, 1948, that one nation has "persistently ignored and violated" agreements which "could have furnished a basis for a just peace"; and

Whereas such violations have been proclaimed the cause for international disturbances which have led to the requested consideration by this Congress of drastic legislation affecting the peoples of this Nation: Therefore be it

Resolved, That the President of the United States be, and is hereby, requested to furnish to the Congress full and complete information on the specific violations of agreements by the nation referred to in the President's address on March 17, 1948, before the Congress; . . .

Document Submitted by the Department of State

I. GERMANY

Agreements	*Violations*
1. The final delimitation of German-Polish frontier should await the peace settlement (Potsdam protocol, VIII, B).	1. U. S. S. R. has repeatedly maintained that the Oder-Neisse line constitutes the definitive German-Polish frontier and has approved incorporation of territory east of this line into Poland.
2. Payment of reparations to leave enough resources to enable German people to subsist without external assistance. Reparation claims of U. S. S. R. to be met by removals of capital goods and appropriation of external assets. Economic controls in Germany to be limited to those essential to curb German war potential and insure equitable distribution of essential goods among zones (Potsdam protocol, II, B, 15, 19; III, 1).	2. U. S. S. R. has taken large amounts of reparations from current production, has absorbed a substantial part of German industry in Soviet zone into Soviet state-owned concerns, and has otherwise exploited and drained German resources in a manner not authorized by Potsdam protocol or other agreements.
3. Economic Directorate of ACA agreed, May 24, 1946, that each member would submit report on reparations removals from its zone.	3. U. S. S. R. has refused to submit report on any reparations removals from its zone.
4. Germany to be treated as a single economic unit (Potsdam protocol, II, B, 14).	4. U. S. S. R. has consistently obstructed all four-power attempts to implement this principle and has carried out a unilateral economic policy in its own zone. In particular it has refused to cooperate in es-

I. Germany—Continued

Agreements	Violations
	tablishing a common export-import program for Germany as a whole, and in permitting "equitable distribution of essential commodities between zones so as to produce a balanced economy throughout Germany and reduce the need for imports."
5. All democratic political • parties to be allowed and encouraged throughout Germany (Potsdam protocol, II, A, 9).	5. Soviet authorities have restricted the freedom of action of non-Communist parties by depriving them of equal facilities with the SED, interfering in their internal affairs, coercing their leaders dictating party

THE COMMUNIST DRIVE WESTWARD SINCE 1939

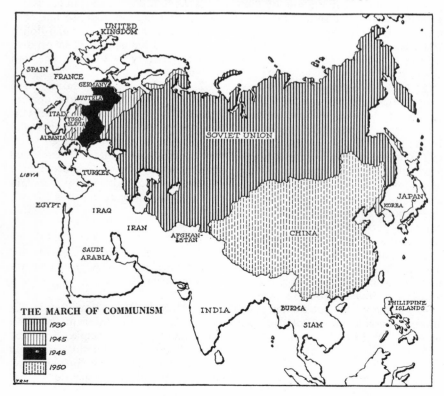

1. GERMANY—Continued

Agreements	*Violations*
	actions, and in general denying them the autonomy essential to democratic political organizations. They have denied the Social Democratic Party the right to operate in the Soviet zone as an independent organization.
6. Control Council agreed to prevent German political leaders or press from making statements criticizing allied decisions or aimed at disrupting allied unity or creating hostile German attitude toward any of occupying powers (Control Council Directive No. 40).	6. Soviet authorities have permitted and encouraged scurrilous propagandistic campaign by the Soviet zone press and political leaders directed against the western powers, and particularly the United States.
7. The Allied Control Authority has authorized the free exchange of printed matter and films in the different zones and Berlin (Control Council Directive No. 55).	7. Soviet authorities have repeatedly barred such materials originating in other zones from the Soviet zone or Soviet sector of Berlin.
8. Freedom of speech and press are guaranteed (Potsdam protocol, II, A, 10). Germany is to be prepared for eventual reconstruction of political life on democratic basis (Potsdam protocol, II, A, 3).	8. Soviet authorities have instituted a system of suppression, intimidation and terrorism through military, police, and party authorities that nullifies any genuine freedom of speech and press. A totalitarian system of police control is being built up which suppresses basic human rights and legal processes and indulges in arbitrary seizures of property, arrests, deportation, forced labor and other practices which are incompatible with democratic principles.
9. German external assets in Finland, eastern Austria, Hungary, Bulgaria, and Rumania, to be vested in the German External Property Commission (Control Council Law No. 5).	9. U. S. S. R. has directly appropriated German external assets in these countries without unvesting and assignment by the German External Property Commission as required by Control Council Law No. 5.
10. Quadripartite legislation has been enacted to provide for tax uniformity and stabilization of wages in all zones (Control Council Laws Nos. 12 and 61; Control Council Directive No. 14).	10. Soviet authorities have permitted the land governments of Brandenburg and Saxony-Anhalt to grant partial tax exemptions to large groups of wage and salary earners in violation of this legislation. This move

I. GERMANY—Continued

Agreements   *Violations*

is intended to stop the exodus of skilled workers to the western zones, encourage qualified workers to take jobs in Soviet-owned factories, and make propaganda for the improving living standards of Soviet-zone workers.

II. AUSTRIA

1. The Allied Council would insure the removal of all restrictions on movement within Austria of persons, goods, or other traffic; economic unity to be promoted (new control agreement of June 28, 1946, art. 4, a).

2. Obligation to open the way for the Austrian people to find economic security (Moscow declaration). Obligation of Allied Council (i. e. occupying powers) to assist Austrian Government to recreate a sound national life based on stable economic and financial conditions (new control agreement, art. 3, c).

3. Obligation to assist Austrian Government to recreate a sound national life based on stable economic and financial conditions; to assist Austrian Government to assume full control of affairs of state in Austria; to facilitate full exercise of Austrian Government's authority equally in all zones; to promote the economic unity of Austria (new control agreement, arts. 3, c; 3, d; and 4, a).

4. Obligations with respect to stable economic and financial conditions, free movement within Austria as a whole, and economic unity (new control agreement, arts. 3, c; 4, a).

5. Obligation to assist Austrian Government to recreate a sound and democratic national life based on

1. Soviet-instituted system of licensing specified categories of goods for shipment from eastern to other zones (December 1947) impedes free movement of goods and traffic throughout Austria as a whole.

2. Properties seized by Soviets as oil in 1945, land in February 1946, industrial plants in April 1946, and later exceed what might reasonably be construed as legitimate German assets under the Potsdam protocol. Removals of equipment and materials under guise of "German assets" and "war booty."

3. Withholding of certain food and industrial production from Austrian economy and from application of Austrian law.

4. Soviets designate certain railroad cars as "war booty," prohibit their movement from Soviet to other zones, and propose Austrians "repurchase" these cars (April 1948).

5. Soviet interference with Austrian efforts to maintain law and order through arbitrary arrest of

II. AUSTRIA—Continued

Agreements	*Violations*
respect for law and order (new control agreement, art. 3, c).	abduction of Austrians (i. e., abduction of transport official from a train in December 1947).
6. Obligations with respect to law and order, assumption by Austrian Government of full control of affairs of state, full exercise of Austrian Government's authority equally in all zones (new control agreement, arts. 3, c; 3, d; and 4, a).	6. Confiscation in eastern zone and Soviet sector of Vienna of certain issues of the United States-sponsored Wiener Kurier and other publications; threats to distributors of such publications.
7. Obligation with respect to full exercise of Austrian Government's authority equally in all zones (new control agreement, art. 4, a).	7. Local Soviet military authorities insist that 17 nonelected Communist mayors remain in office in Soviet zone against authority of provincial and national governments.

III. EASTERN AND SOUTHEASTERN EUROPE

POLAND

"This Polish Provisional Government of National Unity shall be pledged to the holding of free and unfettered elections as soon as possible on the basis of universal suffrage and secret ballot. In these elections all democratic and anti-Nazi parties shall have the right to take part and to put forward candidates" (Crimean Conference, February 12, 1945).

"The three powers note that the Polish Provisional Government in accordance with the decisions of the Crimea Conference has agreed to the holding of free and unfettered elections as soon as possible on the basis of universal suffrage and secret ballot in which all democratic and anti-Nazi parties shall have the right to take part and to put forward candidates * * *" (Potsdam agreement, August 2, 1945).

On several occasions prior to the elections and following persistent reports of reprehensible methods employed by the Government against the democratic opposition, this Government reminded the Polish Provisional Government of its obligations under the Yalta and Potsdam agreements and was joined on these occasions by the British Government. On January 5, 1947, the British and Soviet Governments were asked to associate themselves with this Government in approaching the Poles on this subject, and the British Government made similar representations to the Soviet Government reiterating the request that the Soviet Government support the British and American Governments in calling for a strict fulfillment of Poland's obligations. The Soviet Government refused to participate in the proposed approach to the Polish Government. The British and American represen-

III. Eastern and Southeastern Europe—Continued

POLAND—continued

Agreements   *Violations*

tations were summarily rejected by the Polish Government as "undue interference" in the internal affairs of Poland.

Of the 444 deputies elected to the parliament in the elections of January 19, 1947, the Polish Peasant Party (reliably reported to represent a large majority of the population) obtained only 28 places, thus demonstrating the efficiency with which the government had prepared the ground. On January 28, the Department of State issued a release to the press stating that reports received from our Embassy in Poland immediately prior to and subsequent to the elections, based upon the observations of American officials, confirmed the fears which this Government had expressed that the election would not be free.

HUNGARY

1. Under the armistice agreement an Allied Control Commission was established under the chairmanship of the U. S. S. R. and with participation of the United States and United Kingdom (armistice agreement, January 1945, art. 18 and annex F).

2. The three heads of the Governments of the Union of Soviet Socialist Republics, the United States, and United Kingdom declared their mutual agreement to concert during the temporary period of instability in liberated Europe the policies of their three Governments in assisting the peoples liberated from the domination of Nazi Germany and the peoples of the former Axis satellite states of Europe to solve by democratic means

1. The U. S. S. R. representative on the ACC for Hungary consistently acted unilaterally in the name of the ACC without consultation with or notice to his United States and United Kingdom colleagues, thus denying them any semblance of effective participation in the work of the ACC.

2. Contrary to the Yalta agreement, the U. S. S. R., acting through the Hungarian Communist Party and its own agencies and armed forces in Hungary, far from concerting its policy toward assisting the Hungarian people to solve their problems by democratic means, unilaterally subverted the will of the Hungarian people to totalitarianism in negation of fundamental freedoms. For example—

III. EASTERN AND SOUTHEASTERN EUROPE—Continued

HUNGARY—continued

Agreements	Violations
their pressing political and economic problems (Yalta agreement, February 1945).	(1) General Sviridov, Deputy Soviet Chairman of the ACC, without consulting the United States and United Kingdom ACC representatives, dissolved Catholic youth organization, June 1946.
	(2) Soviet armed forces arrested Bela Kovacs, member of Parliament and former secretary general of Smallholders Party, February 1947.
	(3) General Sviridov precipitated a political crisis enabling the Communist minority to force the resignation of Prime Minister Nagy, May-June 1947.
	(4) The Soviet Government refused repeated United States proposals that it join in tripartite examination of Hungary's economic situation with a view to assisting Hungary to solve its pressing economic problems, 1946.
	(5) Discriminatory economic agreements were forced upon Hungary, including the establishment of joint Soviet-Hungarian companies, 1945-47.
	(6) The Soviet ACC contended that only the occupational forces who control the airfields can permit the Hungarian Government to negotiate air agreements. Notwithstanding, the Soviets formed a Hungarian-Soviet civil air transport company. The Soviets also permitted the Hungarian Government to negotiate agreements with certain other countries but not with the United States or Britain.
3. Upon the cessation of hostilities, it was agreed at Potsdam that the United States, United Kingdom and Union of Soviet Socialist Republics would consult with a view to revising the procedures of the Allied	3. Despite repeated requests, the U. S. S. R. declined to discuss the revision of procedures for the ACC's as agreed at Potsdam. Instead, the U. S. S. R. continued to act unilaterally in the name of the ACC's in

III. Eastern and Southeastern Europe—Continued

Hungary—continued

Agreements	*Violations*
Control Commissions for Rumania, Bulgaria, and Hungary to provide for effective participation by the United States and United Kingdom in the work of those bodies (Potsdam protocol XI, August 1945).	matters of substance without consultation with, or notice to the United States and United Kingdom members. For example—

Control Commissions for Rumania, Bulgaria, and Hungary to provide for effective participation by the United States and United Kingdom in the work of those bodies (Potsdam protocol XI, August 1945).

matters of substance without consultation with, or notice to the United States and United Kingdom members. For example—

(1) Instructions were issued by the Soviet High Command regarding the size of the Hungarian Army without consulting the British or United States representatives.

(2) The Soviet deputy chairman of the ACC ordered the Hungarian Government without the knowledge of the United States to disband certain Catholic youth organizations in June-July 1946. He also recommended dismissal of certain Government officials.

(3) In the fall of 1946 permission was given by the Soviet element of the Allied Control Commission, without consulting the Americans or British, for the formation of the Hungarian Freedom Party.

(4) Early in 1947 the Hungarian police were ordered by the Soviet chairman in the name of the Allied Control Commission to suppress the publication of Ciano's diary.

(5) In early 1947 the Soviet chairman stated he had personally given approval to the Hungarian Government to resume diplomatic relations with certain countries in the name of the Allied Control Commission and without prior discussion with the British or Americans.

(6) In May 1947 the ACC chairman refused the United States permission to visit Hungarian Army units.

(7) The Soviets refused to permit free movement of the American element of the Allied Control Commission.

III. Eastern and Southeastern Europe—Continued

Hungary—continued

Agreements   *Violations*

(8) The Soviets refused to transmit to the American representative data on the arrest by the Soviet Army of Bela Kovacs.

BULGARIA

1. By the terms of the armistice agreement an Allied Control Commission under Soviet direction during the period of hostilities but with the United States and United Kingdom participation was established (armistice agreement, October 1944, art. XVIII).

2. Bulgaria was obligated to restore United Nations property to make reparation for war damage as later determined, to restore all United Nations rights and interests, and to make available to Greece and Yugoslavia immediately on reparation account foodstuffs in quantities to be agreed by the United States, United Kingdom, and Union of Socialist Soviet Republics (armistice agreement, October 1944, arts. IX, X, XI, and par. 1 of protocol).

3. The three heads of the Governments of the Union of Soviet Socialist Republics, the United States and United Kingdom declared their mutual agreement to concert during the temporary period of instability in liberated Europe the policies of their three Governments in assisting the peoples liberated from the domination of Nazi Germany and the peoples of the former Axis satellite states of Europe to solve by democratic means their pressing political and economic problems.

1. The Soviet chairman of the ACC repeatedly took unilateral action in the name of the ACC and without consultation with his United States or United Kingdom colleagues, thus effectively negating the United States and United Kingdom participation in that body.

2. The U. S. S. R. has aided and abetted the Bulgarian Government in failing to fulfill these provisions of the armistice to varying degrees. The Soviets have refused to consider with the United States and United Kingdom Bulgaria's obligation to restore and restitute United Nations property and interests and, while deliveries of foodstuffs were made to the Yugoslavs unilaterally, the U. S. S. R. has blocked three-power consideration of amounts to be shipped to Greece. None has been shipped to that country.

3. The Soviet Government has consistently refused to concert policies with the United States and United Kingdom to assist the people of Bulgaria to solve their political and economic problems democratically. On the contrary the Soviet Government, through the local Communist Party, has unilaterally subverted representative democratic processes in Bulgaria and assisted in denying the Bulgarian people the exercise of fundamental freedoms. For example, in 1945 the Soviets unilaterally interfered in the internal affairs of Bul-

III. EASTERN AND SOUTHEASTERN EUROPE—Continued
BULGARIA—continued

Agreements	Violations
	garia's largest political party by demanding and obtaining the replacement of Dr.· G. M. Dimitrov as Secretary General of the Agrarian Union.
4. The United Kingdom, United States, and Union of Soviet Socialist Republics stated they had no doubt that representatives of the allied press would enjoy full-freedom to report to the world upon developments in Bulgaria (Potsdam communique X, August 1945).	4. The Soviet Chairman of the ACC consistently thwarted American press coverage of Bulgarian developments by negative or extremely dilatory action on United States Government requests for entry permits for reputable American correspondents. Conversely, representatives of the Daily Worker and other left-wing periodicals were permitted to enter Bulgaria without difficulties.
5. Upon the termination of hostilities, agreement was reached at Potsdam that consultations should be held with a view to revising the procedures of the Allied Control Commissions for Rumania, Bulgaria, and Hungary to provide for effective three-power participation in the Commissions (Potsdam protocol XI, August 1945).	5. The Union of Soviet Socialist Republics refused repeated United States and United Kingdom requests to consult as agreed, and continued to operate the ACC's unilaterally without effective participation of or even, on occasion, knowledge of the United States and United Kingdom members.
6. The U. S. S. R. undertook to give friendly advice to the Bulgarian Government regarding the desirability of the inclusion in the government of two representatives of democratic groups, "who (a) are truly representative of the groups of the parties which are not participating in the Government, and (b) are really suitable and will work loyally with the Government" (Moscow Conference, December 1945).	6. The Soviet authorities, despite the Moscow agreement, aided and abetted a minority Bulgarian Communist regime in thwarting the implementation of the agreement and prevented the broadening of the Bulgarian Government envisaged therein.

RUMANIA

1. The three heads of the Governments of the Union of Soviet Socialist Republics, the United States, and United Kingdom declared their mutual agreement to concert during the	1. Contrary to its agreement at Yalta, the U. S. S. R., acting through the Rumanian Communist Party and its own agencies and armed forces in Rumania, systematically and unilater-

III. Eastern and Southeastern Europe—Continued

rumania—continued

Agreements	*Violations*
temporary period of instability in liberated Europe the policies of their three Governments in assisting the peoples liberated from the domination of Nazi Germany and the peoples of the former Axis satellite states of Europe to solve by democratic means their pressing political and economic problems (Yalta agreement on liberated Europe, February 1945).	ally subverted the democratic will of the Rumanian people to totalitarianism in negation of their fundamental freedoms. Major examples of such U. S. S. R. actions may be cited as follows:

Violations (continued):

(1) Unilateral intervention by Soviet occupation authorities and by Vishinsky (February-March 1945) in effecting the overthrow of Premier Radescu's interim representative government and the installation of a Communist-controlled regime. Refusal in this connection to concert either with the United States representatives in Rumania or on a governmental level.

(2) Unilateral support of Premier Groza's retention of office in defiance of the King's demand for his resignation and the United States request for tripartite consultation in response to the King's appeal (August 1945).

(3) Direct and indirect unilateral interference by the Soviet occupation authorities in the election campaign of 1946, extending to the use of Soviet troops to break up meetings of the opposition and the arbitrary exercise of censorship.

(4) Preclusive exploitation of the Rumanian economy from 1944 onward, through (a) armistice extractions many times in excess of the requirements of the armistice agreement and in large measure unauthorized by that agreement, (b) through the establishment of Soviet-controlled joint companies covering the principal economic activities of Rumania, and (c) through commercial agreements the knowledge of whose terms was repeatedly refused to the other two Yalta powers.

III. Eastern and Southeastern Europe—Continued

RUMANIA—continued

Agreements	*Violations*
	(5) Rejection of a proposal by the United States and United Kingdom in December 1946 for setting up a joint commission to study the economic situation in Rumania.
	(6) Unilateral intervention, from March 1945 onward, in Rumanian commercial negotiations with countries outside the Soviet orbit.
2. Upon the cessation of hostilities, it was agreed at Potsdam that the Allied Control Commission procedure should be revised to provide for effective United States and United Kingdom participation in the work of those bodies (Potsdam protocol XI, revised Allied Control Commission procedure in Rumania, Bulgaria, and Hungary).	2. Despite repeated requests, the U. S. S. R. refused to consult with a view to accomplishing the procedural revision agreed to at Potsdam and continued unilaterally to operate the ACC in Rumania without effective participation by the United States and United Kingdom. Examples of such actions may be cited as follows:
	(1) Issuance of directives to Rumanian authorities by Soviet element of ACC, throughout armistice period, without agreement of United States and United Kingdom representatives, sometimes in the face of United States and United Kingdom protests, often without even notification or discussion. Many of these directives were prejudicial to United States interests.
	(2) Obstructive handling, throughout armistice period, of clearances to enter Rumania for official United States personnel and aircraft.
3. The three Governments stated that they had no doubt that, in view of the changed conditions resulting from the termination of the war in Europe, representatives of the allied press would enjoy full freedom to report to the world upon developments in Rumania.	3. In contravention of this agreement, the Soviet chairman of the Control Commission, by the usurpation of authority, delayed and withheld entry permits to Rumania for accredited United States correspondents, ejected several correspondents from that country on fabricated charges, and censored United States press dispatches. These obstructive tactics, which continued throughout

III. Eastern and Southeastern Europe—Continued

RUMANIA—continued

Agreements	Violations
	the armistice period, were particularly in evidence prior to the Rumanian elections of November 1946.

IV. Korea

1. Reestablishment of movement of persons, motor, rail transport and coastwise shipping between the zones of north and south Korea (agreement of Joint United States and Union of Soviet Socialist Republics Conference, January-February 1946).

1. The Soviet command in north Korea has since 1946 refused to discuss or implement the agreements reached on these matters, resisting efforts toward reestablishing the natural economic unity of the country. Concessions to economic coordination have been made only on a barter basis. No regularized movement of persons or transport has been established beyond that allowing the limited supply by the United States of its outposts that are accessible only by roads through Soviet-occupied territory.

2. Consultation by the Joint United States and Union of Soviet Socialist Republics Commission with "Korean democratic parties and social organizations" in the preparation of proposals for the formation of a provisional Korean government (Moscow agreement, December 27, 1945, III, 2).

2. The U. S. S. R. delegation on the Joint Commission consistently refused to allow such consultation except under unilateral interpretations of the phrase, "democratic parties and social organizations," which interpretation, in each case, would exclude all but pro-Soviet political groups.

3. That the Joint United States and Union of Soviet Socialist Republics Commission would consult with political groups "truly democratic in their aims and methods", who would declare their willingness to "uphold the aims of the Moscow Decision," "abide by the decisions of the Joint Commission in * * * the formation of a provisional Korean government * * *" (Joint Commission communiqué No. 5, April 18, 1946).

3. The U. S. S. R. delegation refused to consult with groups adhering to communiqué No. 5 if the representatives of the group had ever expressed opposition to the provision for placing Korea under the period of trusteeship envisaged in the Moscow agreement.

4. That a signature of the communiqué No. 5 (later included in decision No. 12) will be accepted as

4. The U. S. S. R. delegation refused to adhere to the agreement when an attempt was made to sched-

IV. KOREA—Continued

Agreements	*Violations*
a declaration of good faith with respect to upholding fully the Moscow agreement and will make the signatory party or organization eligible for consultation by the Joint Commission; that such signatories who, after signing the communiqué, foment or instigate active opposition to the Joint Commission, the two powers, or the Moscow agreement, can be declared ineligible for consultation only by mutual agreement of the two delegations on the Joint Commission (exchange of letters between Secretary Marshall and Foreign Minister Molotov, May 2 through May 12, 1947, citing the November 26, 1946, December 24, 1946, exchange of letters between the Soviet and American commanders).	ule the party consultations. The U. S. S. R. delegation unilaterally asserted that, despite the signature of communiqué No. 5, and despite assurances of cooperation with the Commission, and a pledge to refrain from fomenting or instigating active opposition, the members of a so-called anti-trusteeship committee could not be consulted by the Joint Commission.

V. MANCHURIA

1. "The high contracting parties agree to render each other every possible economic assistance in the postwar period with a view to facilitating and accelerating reconstruction in both countries and to contributing to the cause of world prosperity" (Sino-Soviet treaty and agreements of August 14, 1945, art. VI).	1. "Industry * * * (in the three eastern provinces, also known as Manchuria) * * * was directly damaged to the extent of $858,000,000 during Soviet occupancy * * * the greatest part of the damage to the Manchurian industrial complex * * * was primarily due to Soviet removals of equipment."—Department of State press release No. 907 of December 13, 1947, citing Pauley report.
2. "* * * In accordance with the spirit of the aforementioned treaty, and in order to put into effect its aims and purposes, the Government of the U. S. S. R. agrees to render to China moral support and aid in military supplies and other material resources, such support and aid to be entirely given to the National Government as the central government of China. "2. In the course of conversations * * * the Government of the	2. The Chinese Government has failed to receive from the U. S. S. R. since August 14, 1945, the promised military supplies and other material resources. But when Russian troops withdrew from Manchuria, "Chinese Communists in that area appeared with Japanese arms in very substantial quantities * * * the natural assumption is that they were taken with the acquiescence, at least, of the Russians."—Quotation is from testi-

V. MANCHURIA—Continued

Agreements	*Violations*
U. S. S. R. regarded the three eastern provinces (i. e. Manchuria) as part of China" (note of V. M. Molotov, August 14, 1945, relating to the treaty of friendship and alliance).	mony of W. W. Butterworth at hearing before the Committee on Appropriations, United States Senate, December 17, 1947.
3. "The administration of Dairen shall belong to China" (agreement concerning Dairen of August 14, 1945).	3. Chinese Government troops attempting to enter Manchuria subsequent to the Japanese surrender were denied the right to land at Dairen by the Soviet authorities there and were forced to utilize less advantageous landing points.
	Due in large part to Soviet obstructionism, China has up to the present time been unable to establish a Chinese Government administration at Dairen.

170. UNITED STATES PROTEST ON SOVIET BLOCKADE OF BERLIN [1]

Note From Secretary Marshall to Ambassador Panyushkin, July 6, 1948

[The Russians, incensed by the merger of the economic zones of Western Germany, protested twice, once in February and later in March of 1948. They proceeded to retaliate by halting rail and barge traffic into Berlin. When the Western Allies on June 18 announced a new currency for Western Germany excluding Berlin, Russia promptly halted all rail, passenger, and road traffic between the Western and the Eastern zones. On July 6, Secretary Marshall in a note to Ambassador Panyushkin asserted that the United States was in Berlin by right of occupation and entitled to free access to its zone. He demanded that the free movement of goods and persons should be restored between the various sectors of Berlin.]

EXCELLENCY: The United States Government wishes to call to the attention of the Soviet Government the extremely serious international situation which has been brought about by the actions of the Soviet Government in imposing restrictive measures on transport which amount now to a blockade against the sectors in Berlin occupied by the United States, United Kingdom and France. The United States Government regards these measures of blockade as a clear violation of existing agreements concerning the administration of Berlin by the four occupying powers.

The rights of the United States as a joint occupying power in Berlin derive

[1] Department of State Bulletin, July 18, 1948, pp. 85-86.

from the total defeat and unconditional surrender of Germany. The international agreements undertaken in connection therewith by the Governments of the United States, United Kingdom, France and the Soviet Union defined the zones in Germany and the sectors in Berlin which are occupied by these powers. They established the quadripartite control of Berlin on a basis of friendly cooperation which the Government of the United States earnestly desires to continue to pursue.

These agreements implied the right of free access to Berlin. This right has long been confirmed by usage. It was directly specified in a message sent by President Truman to Premier Stalin on June 14, 1945, which agreed to the withdrawal of United States forces to the zonal boundaries, provided satisfactory arrangements could be entered into between the military commanders, which would give access by rail, road and air to United States forces in Berlin. Premier Stalin replied on June 16 suggesting a change in date but no other alteration in the plan proposed by the President. Premier Stalin then gave assurances that all necessary measures would be taken in accordance with the plan. Correspondence in a similar sense took place between Premier Stalin and Mr. Churchill. In accordance with this understanding, the United States, whose armies had penetrated deep into Saxony and Thuringia, parts of the Soviet zone, withdrew its forces to its own area of occupation in Germany and took up its position in its own sector in Berlin. Thereupon the agreements in regard to the occupation of Germany and Berlin went into effect. The United States would not have so withdrawn its troops from a large area now occupied by the Soviet Union had there been any doubt whatsoever about the observance of its agreed right of free access to its sector of Berlin. The right of the United States to its position in Berlin thus stems from precisely the same source as the right of the Soviet Union. It is impossible to assert the latter and deny the former.

It clearly results from these undertakings that Berlin is not a part of the Soviet zone, but is an international zone of occupation. Commitments entered into in good faith by the zone commanders, and subsequently confirmed by the Allied Control Authority, as well as practices sanctioned by usage, guarantee the United States together with other powers, free access to Berlin for the purpose of fulfilling its responsibilities as an occupying power. The facts are plain. Their meaning is clear. Any other interpretation would offend all the rules of comity and reason.

In order that there should be no misunderstanding whatsoever on this point, the United States Government categorically asserts that it is in occupation of its sector in Berlin with free access thereto as a matter of established right deriving from the defeat and surrender of Germany and confirmed by formal agreements among the principal Allies. It further declares that it will not be induced by threats, pressures or other actions to abandon these rights. It is hoped that the Soviet Government entertains no doubts whatsoever on this point.

This Government now shares with the Governments of France and the United Kingdom the responsibility initially undertaken at Soviet request on July 7, 1945, for the physical well-being of 2,400,000 persons in the western sectors of Berlin. Restrictions recently imposed by the Soviet authorities in Berlin have operated to prevent this Government and the Governments of the

United Kingdom and of France from fulfilling that responsibility in an adequate manner.

The responsibility which this Government bears for the physical well-being and the safety of the German population in its sector of Berlin is outstandingly humanitarian in character. This population includes hundreds of thousands of women and children, whose health and safety are dependent on the continued use of adequate facilities for moving food, medical supplies and other items indispensable to the maintenance of human life in the western sectors of Berlin. The most elemental of these human rights which both our Governments are solemnly pledged to protect are thus placed in jeopardy by these restrictions. It is intolerable that any one of the occupying authorities should attempt to impose a blockade upon the people of Berlin.

The United States Government is therefore obliged to insist that in accordance with existing agreements the arrangements for the movement of freight and passenger traffic between the western zones and Berlin be fully restored. There can be no question of delay in the restoration of these essential services, since the needs of the civilian population in the Berlin area are imperative.

Holding these urgent views regarding its rights and obligations in the United States sector of Berlin, yet eager always to resolve controversies in the spirit of fair consideration for the viewpoints of all concerned, the Government of the United States declares that duress should not be invoked as a method of attempting to dispose of any disagreements which may exist between the Soviet Government and the Government of the United States in respect of any aspect of the Berlin situation.

Such disagreements if any should be settled by negotiation or by any of the other peaceful methods provided for in Article 33 of the Charter in keeping with our mutual pledges as copartners in the United Nations. For these reasons the Government of the United States is ready as a first step to participate in negotiations in Berlin among the four Allied Occupying Authorities for the settlement of any question in dispute arising out of the administration of the city of Berlin. It is, however, a prerequisite that the lines of communication and the movement of persons and goods between the United Kingdom, the United States and the French sectors in Berlin and the Western Zones shall have been fully restored.

Accept [etc.]

G. C. MARSHALL

His Excellency
ALEXANDER S. PANYUSHKIN,
Ambassador of the Union of Soviet Socialist Republics.

◇◇◇◇◇◇

171. INFORMAL CONVERSATIONS ON BERLIN BLOCKADE

Statement by the Department of State, April 26, 1949 [1]

[Following the imposition of the Berlin blockade the people of Western Berlin were fed and provided with fuel for many months by the Allied air lift. Meanwhile, representatives of the Western Powers conferred from time to time with representatives of the Soviet Union in an effort to break the deadlock. The following document summarizes the conversations which took place on this subject between Jacob Malik, Soviet Representative to the Security Council, and U. S. Ambassador Philip C. Jessup.]

Since the imposition by the Soviet Government of the blockade of the city of Berlin the three Western Governments have consistently sought to bring about the lifting of that blockade on terms consistent with their rights, duties, and obligations as occupying powers in Germany. It was in conformity with this policy that the Western Governments initiated conversations in Moscow last summer. Following their breakdown, the matter was referred in September 1948 to the Security Council of the United Nations.

All these efforts ended in failure, and the three Western Governments made it plain that they were not prepared to continue discussions in the light of the Soviet attitude.

Since that time the Western Governments have looked consistently for any indication of a change in the position of the Soviet Government and have been anxious to explore any reasonable possibility in that direction through contacts with Soviet officials.

In this connection the Department of State noted with particular interest that on January 30, 1949, Premier Stalin made no mention of the currency question in Berlin in his reply to questions asked him by an American journalist. Since the currency question had hitherto been the announced reason for the blockade, the omission of any reference to it by Premier Stalin seemed to the Department to indicate a development which should be explored.

With these considerations in mind, Mr. Jessup, then the U. S. Deputy Representative on the Security Council, took occasion, in a conversation on February 15 with Mr. Malik, the Soviet Representative on the Security Council, to comment on the omission by Premier Stalin of any reference to the currency question. Since this question had been the subject of much discussion in the Security Council and in the Experts Committee appointed under the auspices of the Council, Mr. Jessup inquired whether the omission had any particular significance.

One month later, on March 15, Mr. Malik informed Mr. Jessup that Premier Stalin's omission of any reference to the currency problem in regard to Berlin was "not accidental," that the Soviet Government regarded the currency question as important but felt that it could be discussed at a meeting of the Council of Foreign Ministers if a meeting of that body could be arranged to review the whole German problem.

Mr. Jessup inquired whether this meant that the Soviet Government had

[1] Department of State Bulletin, May 8, 1949, pp. 590-591.

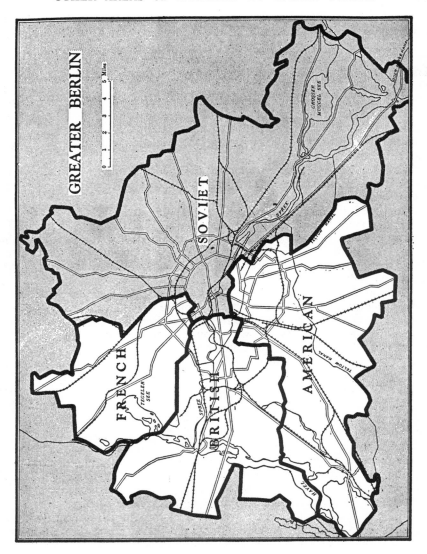

in mind a Foreign Ministers' meeting while the blockade of Berlin was in progress or whether it indicated that the blockade would be lifted in order to permit the meeting to take place.

The information as to the Soviet Government's attitude revealed in these informal contracts was immediately conveyed to the British and French Governments.

On March 21 Mr. Malik again asked Mr. Jessup to visit him to inform him that if a definite date could be set for the meeting of the Council of Foreign Ministers, the restrictions on trade and transportation in Berlin could be lifted reciprocally and that the lifting of the blockade could take place in advance of the meeting.

Taking advantage of the presence of the Foreign Ministers of Great Britain and France in Washington, the recent developments in regard to the Soviet attitude were discussed with them.

An agreed position was reached among the three Western Powers. In order that there should be no misunderstanding in the mind of the Soviet Government in regard to this position, a statement was read to Mr. Malik by Mr. Jessup on April 5. The purpose of this statement, which represented the agreed position of the three Western Powers, was to make clear that the points under discussion were the following:

1. Reciprocal and simultaneous lifting of the restrictions imposed by the Soviet Union since March 1, 1948, on communications, transportation, and trade between Berlin and the Western zones of Germany and the restrictions imposed by the Three Powers on communications, transportation, and trade to and from the Eastern zone of Germany.

2. The fixing of a date to be determined for a meeting of the Council of Foreign Ministers.

The Western Powers wished to be sure that these two points were not conditioned in the understanding of the Soviet Government on any of the other points which in the past had prevented agreement upon the lifting of the blockade.

The statement summarized the understanding of the three Governments of the position which the Soviet Government took concerning the proposal of lifting the blockade and the meeting of the Council of Foreign Ministers. Its purpose was to make unmistakably clear that the position of the Soviet Government was as now stated in the release of the Tass Agency.

On April 10 Mr. Malik again asked Mr. Jessup to call upon him at that time and again stated the position of the Soviet Government. From this statement it appeared that there were still certain points requiring clarification.

As a result of this meeting, further discussions took place between the three Governments, which have resulted in a more detailed formulation of their position, which will be conveyed by Mr. Jessup to Mr. Malik.

If the present position of the Soviet Government is as stated in the Tass Agency release as published in the American press, the way appears clear for a lifting of the blockade and a meeting of the Council of Foreign Ministers. No final conclusion upon this can be reached until further exchanges of view with Mr. Malik.

◇◇◇◇◇◇

172. LIFTING OF BERLIN BLOCKADE

(a) *Letter From French, United Kingdom, and United States Representatives to United Nations Secretary-General, May 4, 1949* [1]

[Not until May 4, 1949, was it possible for the disputing powers to reach agreement on the lifting of the Berlin blockade. The announcement was made in a letter to the United Nations Security Council from the United States, Britain, and France, and also in a communiqué of the same date. The agreement provided for the lifting on May 12, 1949 of the restrictions imposed by both sides and for the meeting of the Council of Foreign Ministers on May 23, 1949.]

EXCELLENCY:

We, the Representatives of France, the United Kingdom and the United States on the Security Council, have the honor to request that you bring to the attention of the Members of the Security Council the fact that our Governments have concluded an agreement with the Government of the Union of Soviet Socialist Republics providing for the lifting of the restrictions which have been imposed on communications, transportation and trade with Berlin. A copy of the communiqué indicating the agreement reached between us is enclosed.

Accept, Excellency, the renewed assurances of our highest consideration.

JEAN CHAUVEL
Representative of France
ALEXANDER CADOGAN
Representative of the United Kingdom
WARREN R. AUSTIN
Representative of the United States

(b) *Communiqué, May 5, 1949* [2]

The Governments of France, the Union of Soviet Socialist Republics, the United Kingdom, and the United States have reached the following agreement:

1. All the restrictions imposed since March 1, 1948, by the Government of the Union of Soviet Socialist Republics on communications, transportation, and trade between Berlin and the Western zones of Germany and between the Eastern zone and the Western zones will be removed on May 12, 1949.

2. All the restrictions imposed since March 1, 1948, by the Governments of France, the United Kingdom, and the United States, or any one of them, on communications, transportation, and trade between Berlin and the Eastern zone and between the Western and Eastern zones of Germany will also be removed on May 12, 1949.

3. Eleven days subsequent to the removal of the restrictions referred to in paragraphs one and two, namely, on May 23, 1949, a meeting of the Council of Foreign Ministers will be convened in Paris to consider questions

---

[1] Department of State Bulletin of May 15, 1949, p. 631. UN Doc. S/1316.
[2] Known as the New York agreement.

relating to Germany and problems arising out of the situation in Berlin, including also the question of currency in Berlin.

◇◇◇◇◇◇

173. "ESSENTIALS OF PEACE"

(a) Statement by Ambassador Warren R. Austin, November 14, 1949 [1]

[During the Fourth General Assembly the Soviet Union launched a particularly vicious propaganda campaign against the West. Mr. Vishinsky denounced Great Britain and the United States "for their preparations for a new war" and requested the five great powers to conclude a pact for the strengthening of peace. Speaking for the United States, Ambassador Austin pointed out that the basic principles essential for peace are to be found in the United Nations Charter; and that the causes of international tension are to be found largely in the disregard of the Soviet Union for those principles. Mr. Austin's speech represents a well-reasoned summary record of the Soviet Union's unwillingness to coöperate with the Western powers.]

*   *   *

In this General Assembly, the Soviet Union delegation, on the instruction of its government, charges that preparations for a new war are now being conducted in a number of countries and in particular in the United States and the United Kingdom. In its warmongering charges the Soviet Union departs from previous attacks upon "certain circles" and directs its accusations against governments, charging them with organizing aggressive blocs and pursuing aggressive aims. Today, we have listened to the representative of the Soviet Union expressing claims that propaganda for a new war is aided and abetted by the governments of the United States and the United Kingdom. These charges are coupled with a proposal for a new treaty among the five permanent members of the Security Council. The proposal is epitomized in the item on the agenda reading: "Condemnations of the preparations for a new war and the conclusion of a Five Power pact for the strengthening of peace."

The purport of the speech of the representative of the Soviet Union was to offer proof that the United States and the United Kingdom are interested in breaking the peace of the world. All of us deeply regret that the skill and energy employed by the Soviet Union to produce propaganda proposals are not employed in an effort at harmony. Name-calling does not promote constructive collaboration. Provocation does not contribute to friendly coöperation.

We find in this resolution ingredients of all the Soviet Union's provocative proposals of the last 4 years artfully put together so that adoption of any

[1] Statement made before Committee I on November 14, 1949, and released to the press by the United States delegation to the United Nations on the same date. Department of State Bulletin of November 28, 1949, pp. 801-808.

part of it could be claimed by its sponsor to be a condemnation of the United States, the United Kingdom, and other states not named.

*   *   *

The *Ad Hoc* Committee has before it the report of the Atomic Energy Commission, which affords the benefit of 4 years' effort to achieve an effective, enforceable system of international control that would not only prohibit the destructive use of atomic energy but would safeguard complying states against the hazards of violations and evasions. That Committee also has before it a report on the consultations in progress among the six permanent members of the Atomic Energy Commission.

I am sure the Committee will agree that this vital issue needs to be considered in that setting rather than in relation to a vague paragraph that seeks to avoid effective control by deceptively promising prohibition.

I should, therefore, only like, at this time, to point out that this innocent, sweet-sounding paragraph constitutes continued resistance to the will of the General Assembly. It contains virtually the same ideas that were rejected by the Assembly at its last session by an overwhelming vote. It ignores the Assembly's finding that effective prohibition can be achieved only by placing all dangerous quantities of atomic materials and all facilities for making or using them in the hands of an international cooperative. This Soviet paragraph is a propaganda maneuver which I feel sure the Committee will want to reject in favor of the detailed, earnest study being given this subject in the *Ad Hoc* Committee. I believe we can be confident of the *Ad Hoc* Committee's ability to handle this issue constructively, and certainly we will not take the hazard of two committees opposed to each other in their views on the same subject.

ARTIFICIAL OLIVE BRANCH

The trickery of the paragraph on atomic energy is combined with slanderous accusations in the first paragraph to introduce a proposal for a five-power pact. By its own terms, this Soviet draft resolution is revealed to be an artificial olive branch surrounded by thorns. This talk of peace sounds more like war.

A proposal honestly intended as a "measure for strengthening peace" would never be placed in such a setting. Its sham and pretense is exposed by the fact that the five permanent members of the Security Council have already, by the Charter, obligated themselves to strengthen peace. In this speech we listened to this morning, that atmosphere carried through in the phrase which I think I am quoting correctly, "The threat of war has come into the public field."

Under the Charter, the five permanent members of the Security Council have particular responsibility for maintaining peace and security. Their particular responsibility was recognized when they were accorded special voting privileges. The fact that one of these five—the Soviet Union—has ignored that particular responsibility and has abused that special privilege has been the principal barrier to constructive cooperation.

The principle of unanimity of the five permanent members of the Security

Council is based on the assumption that they will cooperate toward a common goal of peace. But the Soviet Union has twisted that principle into a weapon of obstruction and sabotage of world peace.

At Yalta, at Potsdam, in the Allied Control Council, in the Council of Foreign Ministers, and in the long negotiations for peace treaties, the unanimity principle has been used by the Soviet Union, not to promote agreement but to relay settlements and to force concessions. And in the Security Council, a long list of vetoes provides evidence that Soviet cooperation is available only on Soviet terms and only for Soviet purposes.

Does the Soviet representative contend that a new pact would initiate a reversal of such policies? If it would, then such a pact is unnecessary. If it would not, then such a pact would be a futility.

Confidence in Soviet pledges has been undermined by the experience of the past few years. To find cause for concern, it is not necessary to recall the Friendship Pact with Nazi Germany, or the Soviet nonaggression pacts with Finland, Latvia, Esthonia, and Lithuania. We need only look at the long, unhappy list of broken Soviet pledges that has grown since we have been engaged in the common effort to create the United Nations.

You will recall the promises that free elections would be held in Poland, in Bulgaria, Hungary, and Rumania. In the case of Rumania it was the present Soviet spokesman who went to Bucharest and delivered an ultimatum that the existing government should be replaced with a hand-picked pro-Soviet government within 2 hours and 5 minutes. This action occurred within 3 weeks after Premier Stalin had agreed with President Roosevelt and Prime Minister Churchill that their governments would "jointly assist" these 3 ex-enemy countries to form governments "broadly representative of all democratic elements" and pledged to hold free elections.

This melancholy pattern, I regret to say, has continued and spread.

A Soviet agreement to withdraw troops from Iran at the end of the war was only fulfilled because the non-Soviet members of the Security Council stood together in demanding that the pledge finally be honored.

U. S. S. R. POWER-GRABBING ACTIONS

The depredation of Manchuria, the forced partition of Korea, guerrilla warfare waged against Greece, the threats to Turkey, the obliteration of freedom in Czechoslovakia, the ruthless destruction of all democratic opposition in Bulgaria, Hungary, and Rumania, and now, the subjugation of Poland to the point where a Marshal of the Red Army has been installed as that partitioned country's Minister of Defense—all these are power-grabbing actions by the Soviet Union that peaceful words cannot hide.

Less than a year ago my Government and others at this table were faced with the threat of force in an effort to drive us out of our position in Berlin, which we held by virtue of an agreement with the Soviet Union. In that case, even starvation was employed as a weapon of Soviet policy. We and others here stood firm against such tactics and they failed.

Our efforts at this Assembly to promote compliance with the treaties of peace with Hungary, Bulgaria, and Rumania have stimulated the Soviet spokesman to a vigorous demonstration of his highly developed art of denunciation. He has provided us with further evidence of Soviet disregard of ratified agreements which no longer fit the convenience of Soviet policy.

Since this Assembly began, we have seen still other treaties of friendship and alliance with Yugoslavia denounced and repudiated not only by the Soviet Union but by the other states which it still controls. These pressure tactics have been augmented by troop movements, border incidents, and an unrelenting rain of epithets.

*   *   *

SOVIET POLICIES SHIFT PEACE PATHS

Faced with these facts, the peace-loving nations have been compelled to seek other paths toward their goal of peace. They have had to face squarely the problem posed by Soviet insistence that everybody is out of step but the Cominform. The aggressively reactionary Soviet policies that have prevented the Cominform states from cooperating with the rest of the world have forced the rest of the world to promote collective security without them.

These collective efforts to strengthen international peace and security are the real objects of the Soviet Union's attack. You are asked to condemn the United States, the United Kingdom, and an unspecified number of other states because they are partners in such agreements as the Treaty of Rio de Janeiro, the North Atlantic Treaty, and the Mutual Defense Assistance Act. The Soviet Union thus wants you to condemn agreements which seek to advance the objectives of the United Nations. The existence of these agreements is a reassurance to all states having a similar aim and a similar purpose. Their purpose is peace.

None of the safeguards we have erected will ever be used unless there is a clear violation of peace which the Security Council is unable to prevent. None of these safeguards alter our hope that the Soviet Union will sometime join with the other members of the United Nations to strengthen collective security. That has been our hope since the first day we began planning the organization of the United Nations. It remains our hope today.

CONGRESS EXPRESSES U.S. INTENT

Only the Cominform countries have chosen to misinterpret the intent of our efforts. Cominform spokesmen branded the North Atlantic Treaty as an aggressive alliance even before it was drafted. They have clung to their preconceptions despite the assurances given on behalf of the American people. But, I urge them to consider these Congressional declarations—the Congress of the United States expresses the public policy of the United States, the policy of the people.

The Senate Foreign Relations Committee, in presenting the North Atlantic Treaty to the United States Senate for ratification, made these statements which stand as an official declaration of intent:

"The basic objective of the treaty is to assist in achieving the primary purpose of the United Nations—the maintenance of peace and security.

"It has been conceived within the framework of the United Nations Charter with all the solemn obligations against aggressive action which that document imposes upon its members.

"If it can be called an alliance, it is an alliance only against war itself."

The Mutual Defense Assistance Act which is designed to support the aims of the North Atlantic Treaty, as passed by both Houses of our Congress and approved by President Truman, opens with these declarations:

"The Congress of the United States reaffirms the policy of the United States to achieve international peace and security through the United Nations so that armed force shall not be used except in the common interest.

"In furnishing such military assistance, it remains the policy of the United States to continue to exert maximum efforts to obtain agreements to provide the United Nations with armed forces as contemplated in the Charter, agreements to achieve universal control of weapons of mass destruction, and universal regulation and reduction of armaments, including armed forces, under adequate safeguards to protect complying nations against violation and evasion."

Thus is declared the determination of the 150 million people of my country to do their part "to save succeeding generations from the scourge of war." No policy, no emotion stirs the American people so profoundly. The representative of the Soviet Union needs shed no more crocodile tears for the American taxpayers.

Their policy and their desire is to cooperate with all states—I repeat, Mr. Chairman, with all states—in the building of a universal system of collective security within the United Nations.

* * *

UNITED STATES COOPERATION WITH U. S. S. R.

Solving this problem of security on a universal basis within the United Nations requires increasing cooperation among all the member states. The United States believes in such cooperation and believes that through the United Nations it ultimately can be achieved. I should like to point out, particularly to the Cominform representatives, some evidence of our belief in cooperation and to assure them that in spite of the disappointing experiences of the past few years, we hold firmly to that belief.

During the war we sent a military mission to Moscow to transmit military and technological information to the Soviet forces. That service continued throughout the war despite a complete lack of reciprocal treatment from the Soviet Union.

Millions of dollars of medical supplies and civilian goods sent from this country by unofficial relief agencies, supplemented UNRRA aid valued at 250 million dollars.

Military and civilian supplies sent to the Soviet Union under Lend-Lease totalled approximately 11 billion dollars. This included equipment that has been invaluable to Soviet reconstruction—for example, electric power generating equipment totalling a million and a half kilowatts capacity, four huge aviation gasoline refineries, a 10-million dollar tire plant, thousands of machine tools, 50 million dollars worth of construction machinery, nearly 2,000 locomotives, and 427,000 trucks—approximately half as many trucks as the Soviet Union had produced in its entire history before the Nazi invasion.

Despite this intimate experience with American economic assistance—from which the Soviet Union emerged with its sovereignty unimpaired—Cominform spokesmen tell the world that the sole purpose and certain result of such assistance is economic and political domination by the United States.

The Soviet Union was invited to participate in the Committee of European Economic Cooperation which met in Paris in July 1947 to consider Secretary Marshall's proposal to implement European recovery with American aid. The main response to this offer of economic cooperation was a violent propaganda offensive against the European Recovery Program, and the establishment of the Cominform for the declared purpose of sabotaging and wrecking that program.

Our efforts to obtain political cooperation have shared the same fate as our efforts at economic cooperation.

When Soviet spokesmen expressed fear of a revival of German and Japanese military power, Secretary Byrnes offered the Soviet Union a mutual-guarantee past against German and Japanese aggression to extend for 25 or even 40 years. This offer was repeated by Secretary Marshall. The Soviet Government rejected the offer.

SOVIET REFUSES COOPERATION

We have sought from the beginning to advocate and encourage full Soviet participation in all the work of the United Nations. Secretary Hull flew to Moscow in October 1943, to interest the Soviet Government in the idea of a postwar security organization. President Roosevelt devoted the closing weeks of his life to the same cause. Byelorussia and the Ukraine—as much a part of the Soviet Union as California and Texas are of the United States—sit at this table today in testimony of our earnest desire, and the desire of other states here, to secure Soviet participation in the work of the United Nations.

Most of us here are working together to build a more peaceful and a more productive world through such agencies as the Food and Agriculture Organization, the World Health Organization, the International Bank, the International Monetary Fund, the International Refugee Organization, the International Civil Aviation Organization, the International Labor Organization, the International Trade Organization, and the United Nations Educational, Scientific and Cultural Organization.

The Soviet Union is not participating in any of these peace-making partnerships. All of us know that the Soviet Union's non-participation is entirely a matter of its own choice. And I am sure I speak for all of us in saying that Soviet participation in these constructive efforts would be welcomed as evidence that it is ready to contribute to peace and progress.

In all this somber picture, nothing concerns us more fundamentally than the barriers that prevent the peoples under Soviet domination from having contact with the rest of the world. Free exchange of knowledge, ideas, and information among the peoples of the world is a basic requirement of peace. How can there be enduring peace unless peoples come to know each other, to recognize each other's faults, to appreciate each other's virtues, to find a basis for understanding? How can there be understanding when the Russian peoples' knowledge of the non-Soviet world comes solely from government owned and controlled organs that pour out the same abuse, misrepresentation, and distortion that characterize the speeches of the Cominform delegates here?

*   *   *

History has left all of our countries—including my own—a legacy of barriers that hamper free interchange among peoples. Most of us are working together to tear down these barriers. But the Soviet Government has persisted in erecting a "spite fence" that blocks the Russian people from good neighborly relations with the rest of the world community.

Again and again, during the past four years, we have tried to promote cultural and educational exchange with the Soviet Union. In October 1945, the United States asked the Soviet Government to consider sending the Red Army Chorus or other similar groups to the United States for a tour. We expressed a desire to institute an exchange of ballet groups, theater groups, and orchestras, of holding reciprocal exhibits of art, architecture, and handicraft as a means of increasing mutual understanding. Nothing happened. The following month, Ambassador Harriman asked Mr. Vishinsky to consider the possibilities of initiating an exchange of students. He received no reply.

In 1946, invitations were extended to Soviet professors by the United States Office of Education, Princeton University, and the Rockefeller Foundation. The Universities of Texas, Amherst, Columbia, Cornell, and other institutions, as well as private citizen groups, offered scholarships to Soviet students. Princeton, Massachusetts Institute of Technology, and several others offered to exchange scientific personnel. Most of these invitations were not even acknowledged. None were accepted.

An invitation to exchange medical specialists accompanied by an offer of a penicillin plant was never answered.

War veterans receiving government funds for college study were authorized to use those funds for study in Soviet institutions. All applicants have been rejected.

The Boston Symphony Orchestra extended an invitation to the conductor of the Leningrad Philharmonic but received no answer. Twice the orchestra offered to tour the Soviet Union at its own expense but received no reply. A Soviet ballet company was invited to tour the United States. Nothing happened.

The private and public groups making these and many similar offers refused to be discouraged.

STALIN'S WORDS CONTRARY TO ACTIONS

When Marshal Stalin told an American visitor in December 1946 that he was unequivocally in favor of a wider exchange of ideas, students, teachers, artists, and tourists, Ambassador Smith quickly followed up the opportunity. For example, he presented to Mr. Vishinsky a specific proposal for a visit to the United States by 50 Soviet scholars in various field of science and cultural studies.[1] All he ever received in reply was a simple acknowledgement.

[1] See, Cultural Relations Between the United States and the Soviet Union, Department of State publication 3480.

In sharp contrast to Marshal Stalin's interview, the Soviet Government six months later, in June 1947, began a campaign to place every sort of legal obstacle, backed with the threat of heavy punishment in the way of contacts between the Russian people and foreigners. This campaign began with promulgation of the Secrecy Act of June 1947 and has proceeded with increasing intensity ever since. It has been part of an organized effort to persuade the Russian people that cultural relations with people from the non-Soviet world endangers the Soviet state. In such an atmosphere a mere gesture of friendship toward a Soviet citizen threatens his well-being.

Efforts to speak to the Russian people over the radio have been met by the most intensive jamming of the airwaves ever attempted in peace time. Quarantined from contact with the outside world, the Russian people are receiving from the official press and radio a mixture of hatred, abuse, and untruth that gives little evidence of a desire for understanding and cooperation.

Information coming from the Soviet Union has been subjected to strict censorship. Correspondents from the United States have been restricted to such a point that now only one newspaper and two press associations continue to maintain regular representatives in the Soviet Union. Correspondents from other non-Cominform countries are sharing a similar fate.

I cite these facts at length because they expose the root of our problem. There is no incompatibility between economic systems. The world is full of differing social and cultural institutions. But only in the area of the Cominform is interchange forbidden and branded as evil and traitorous.

If all the peoples of the United Nations could begin to meet and to talk with one another, we would be on the way toward solving the many problems that beset the world community. I am sure the people of the Soviet Union, no less than the people of the United States, want cooperation and peace. The refusal of the Soviet Government to let their people meet with others is perhaps the greatest single tragedy of our time.

Without the understanding that can come only from a free interchange among peoples, agreements among governments rest on unfirm foundations. A government which does not trust its own people can hardly be expected to trust others. Good neighborliness and peace can not grow in an atmosphere of suspicion and distrust.

MEASURES FOR STRENGTHENING PEACE

If the Soviet Government wishes to undertake measures for strengthening peace, the means are at its instant command. Stop your campaign of hate against the non-Cominform world. Forsake your doctrine that the non-Cominform world is your enemy. Let your people meet with ours and discuss together our common problems. Lift your iron curtain and you will strengthen peace.

The interest of the individual human being in peaceful progress was recognized by all of us when we signed a Charter which begins by declaring the determination of "we, the *peoples* of the United Nations . . . to save succeeding generations from the scourge of war."

* * *

Action to fulfill these obligations, agreements, pledges, and promises is what the world requires now. That means respect for international obligations. That means noninterference in the internal affairs of other states through indirect aggression or through subverting their governments by manipulating minority groups and similar devices. That means respect for the rights of others. That means belief in the dignity of man and respect for the rights and freedoms of the individual.

The great majority of the members of the United Nations are making progress toward peace. The great majority of the nations are tackling patiently the serious problems besetting the world. The great majority of the nations are sharing their resources and technical skills to promote economic stability and progress. The great majority of the nations are exchanging ideas, information, and people to promote understanding.

The path toward peace must be traveled step by step. There are no superhighways. Patient, persistent efforts to solve each of the numerous and varied problems brought to the United Nations for settlement is required. We gain strength from those we solve to concentrate on those whose solutions have escaped us.

* * *

JOINT RESOLUTION: "ESSENTIALS OF PEACE"

My government, therefore, has joined with the United Kingdom in sponsoring a resolution which directs attention to the basic requirements for enduring peace. By this resolution, we seek to erect a standard to which all believers in peace and all supporters of the United Nations may repair. This resolution seeks to mobilize support for genuine efforts to settle disputes among nations and to promote understanding between them and their peoples.

Our resolution is put forward in full recognition that there is no substitute for performance by members of their treaty obligations. Good citizenship in the world community requires faithful adherence, in deed as well as in words, to the "Essentials of Peace."

By adopting this resolution the General Assembly would declare that the Charter of the United Nations is the most solemn pact of peace in history and lays down basic principles necessary for an enduring peace. It clearly recognizes that disregard of these principles is primarily responsible for international tension, and asserts the urgent necessity of actions by member states in accordance with these principles in the spirit of cooperation on which the United Nations was founded.

Based on these realistic grounds, the resolution sets forth in detail the individual and collective actions that are essential if principles are to be put into practice.

The resolution calls upon all nations to refrain from threatening or using force contrary to the Charter; to refrain from any threats or acts, direct or indirect, aimed at impairing the freedom, independence, or integrity of any State, or at fomenting civil strife and subverting the will of the people in any State.

It calls upon all nations to carry out in good faith their international agreements and to afford all United Nations bodies full cooperation and free access in the performance of tasks assigned to them under the Charter.

The close link between human freedom, human well-being, and world peace is recognized in two paragraphs which call upon all nations to promote the dignity and worth of the human person, full freedom for the peaceful expression of political opposition, full opportunity for the exercise of religious freedom, full respect for other fundamental human rights expressed in the Universal Declaration of Human Rights; and to promote nationally and internationally efforts to achieve and sustain higher standards of living for all peoples.

Every member of the United Nations is called upon to participate fully in the work of the organization. The five permanent members are especially urged to broaden progressively their cooperation and to exercise restraint in the use of the veto in order to make the Security Council a more effective instrument for maintaining peace.

Finally, it calls upon every nation to cooperate in supporting United Nations efforts to settle outstanding problems; to cooperate in attaining effective international regulation and reduction of conventional armaments; and to agree to the exercise of national sovereignty jointly with other nations to the extent necessary to attain international control of atomic energy which would make effective the prohibition of atomic weapons and assure the use of atomic energy for peaceful purposes only.

This resolution is, of course, incompatible with the Soviet resolution which should be rejected. No part of the Soviet resolution is worthy either of amendment or adoption. It should be rejected as an attempt to slander, obstruct, and deceive.

I have placed before this Committee the Soviet Union's record of noncooperation. And now, I place before you, on behalf of the Governments of the United Kingdom and the United States, a resolution on "Essentials of Peace."

If the Soviet Union is ready to perform these essentials, then a Five-Power pact is not needed. If it is not, then, I repeat, Mr. Chairman, the pact is a hollow proposal.

The resolution the United Kingdom and the United States have placed before you seeks fulfillment of the pledges we have made to support and defend the Charter of the United Nations. Your overwhelming response to this resolution would give new life to those pledges. It would give new strength to the United Nations and new hope to all mankind. In the fervent hope that its adoption will stimulate in every nation a re-dedication to the principles of peace, we place before you this resolution on "Essentials of Peace."

(b) Resolution of the General Assembly, December 1, 1949 [1]

[This resolution was adopted following the most comprehensive debate ever staged in the United Nations on the purposes and policies of Soviet communism. It does not establish any new principles or new standards. It

---

[1] UN Doc. A/1167, December 1, 1949. This resolution is the same as the U.S.-U.K. Joint Resolution introduced into the Assembly on November 14, 1949.

does, however, reflect the attitude of the great majority of nations as to the basic standards of international conduct which states must adhere to if peace is to be achieved. The resolution, which was approved in place of the proposals advanced by the Soviet Union, was accepted by a vote of 53 to 5 with one abstention.]

The General Assembly

1. *Declares* that the Charter of the United Nations, the most solemn pact of peace in history, lays down basic principles necessary for an enduring peace; that disregard of these principles is primarily responsible for the continuance of international tension; and that it is urgently necessary for all Members to act in accordance with these principles in the spirit of co-operation on which the United Nations was founded;

Calls upon every nation

2. *To refrain* from threatening or using force contrary to the Charter;
3. *To refrain* from any threats or acts, direct or indirect, aimed at impairing the freedom, independence or integrity of any State, or at fomenting civil strife and subverting the will of the people in any State;
4. *To carry out* in good faith its international agreements;
5. *To afford* all United Nations bodies full co-operation and free access in the performance of the tasks assigned to them under the Charter;
6. *To promote,* in recognition of the paramount importance of preserving the dignity and worth of the human person, full freedom for the peaceful expression of political opposition, full opportunity for the exercise of religious freedom and full respect for all the other fundamental rights expressed in the Universal Declaration of Human Rights;
7. *To promote* nationally and through international co-operation, efforts to achieve and sustain higher standards of living for all peoples;
8. *To remove* the barriers which deny to peoples the free exchange of information and ideas essential to international understanding and peace;

Calls upon every Member

9. *To participate* fully in all the work of the United Nations;

Calls upon the five permanent members of the Security Council

10. *To broaden* progressively their co-operation and to exercise restraint in the use of the veto in order to make the Security Council a more effective instrument for maintaining peace;

Calls upon every nation

11. *To settle* international disputes by peaceful means and to co-operate in supporting United Nations efforts to resolve outstanding problems;
12. *To co-operate* to attain the effective international regulation of conventional armaments; and
13. *To agree* to the exercise of national sovereignty jointly with other nations to the extent necessary to attain international control of atomic energy

which would make effective the prohibition of atomic weapons and assure the use of atomic energy for peaceful purposes only.

—From New York Times.

◇◇◇◇◇◇

174. McMAHON RESOLUTION EXPRESSING FRIENDSHIP FOR RUSSIA [1]

SENATE CONCURRENT RESOLUTION AGREED TO BY CONGRESS, JUNE, 1951

[Many issues between the Soviet Union and the United States in 1951 remained unresolved. A substantial number of Congressmen and Senators were convinced that the difficulties lay not in the ill will of the Russian people

[1] S. Con. Res. 11, 82nd Cong., 1st sess. Passed by the Senate May 4, 1951 and by the House June 4, 1951; Conference report agreed to June 18 by the Senate and June 26 by the House.

for the United States, but rather in the machinations of the Soviet leaders. Accordingly, in June 1951, Congress approved Senate Concurrent Resolution 11, which reaffirmed the historical friendship of the United States for all people, including the people of the Soviet Union; expressed America's desire to live in friendship with all people; and requested the President to call upon the Soviet Government to make the contents of the resolution known to the Russian people.]

WHEREAS the goal of the American people is now, and ever has been, a just and lasting peace; and

WHEREAS the deepest wish of our Nation is to join with all other nations in preserving the dignity of man, and in observing those moral principles which alone lend meaning to his existence; and

WHEREAS in proof of this the United States has offered to share all that is good in atomic energy, asking in return only safeguards against the evil in the atom; and

WHEREAS this Nation has likewise given of its substance and resources to help those peoples ravaged by war and poverty; and

WHEREAS terrible danger to all free peoples compels the United States to undertake a vast program of armaments expenditures; and

WHEREAS we rearm only with reluctance and would prefer to devote our energies to peaceful pursuits: Now, therefore, be it

Resolved by the Senate (the House of Representatives concurring), That the Members of this Congress reaffirm the historic and abiding friendship of the American people for all other peoples, including the peoples of the Soviet Union, by declaring—

That the American people deeply regret the artificial barriers which separate them from the peoples of the Union of Soviet Socialist Republics, and which keep the Soviet peoples from learning of America's desire to live in friendship with all other peoples, and to work with them in advancing the ideal of human brotherhood; and

That the American people desire neither war with the Soviet Union nor the terrible consequences of such a war; and

That, although they are firmly determined to defend their freedom and security, the American people welcome all honorable efforts to compose the differences standing between them and the Soviet Government; and

That the Congress request the President of the United States to call upon the Government of the Union of Soviet Socialist Republics to acquaint the people of the Soviet Union with the contents of this resolution.

PART VIII

Current International Issues

ʊʊ

WAR CRIMINALS

175. PROSECUTION AND PUNISHMENT OF THE MAJOR WAR CRIMINALS OF THE EUROPEAN AXIS

(a) *Agreement for the Establishment of an International Military Tribunal, August 8, 1945* [1]

[One of the most widely debated postwar actions of the Allied Powers was the trial of the Nazi war criminals. At Yalta and later at the Potsdam Conference the great powers affirmed their intention "to bring these criminals to swift and sure justice." Six days after the Conference, the following document, which provided the bases for achieving this objective, was agreed to. The tribunal it provided for was later constituted and sat at Nuremberg. That tribunal subsequently tried twenty-two high-ranking Nazi leaders whom it sentenced on September 30 and October 1, 1946—twelve to death and seven to imprisonment, while three were acquitted. (On October 16, 1946, eleven were executed and one committed suicide.) Having pronounced sentence, the tribunal went out of existence on October 1, 1946.]

AGREEMENT BY THE GOVERNMENT OF THE UNITED STATES OF AMERICA, THE PROVISIONAL GOVERNMENT OF THE FRENCH REPUBLIC, THE GOVERNMENT OF THE UNITED KINGDOM OF GREAT BRITAIN AND NORTHERN IRELAND AND THE GOVERNMENT OF THE UNION OF SOVIET SOCIALIST REPUBLICS FOR THE PROSECUTION AND PUNISHMENT OF THE MAJOR WAR CRIMINALS OF THE EUROPEAN AXIS.

WHEREAS the United Nations have from time to time made declarations of their intention that War Criminals shall be brought to justice;

AND WHEREAS the Moscow Declaration of the 30th October 1943 on German atrocities in Occupied Europe stated that those German Officers and men and members of the Nazi Party who have been responsible for or have taken a consenting part in atrocities and crimes will be sent back to the countries in which their abominable deeds were done in order that they may be judged and

---

[1] Department of State publication 2461, Executive Agreement Series 472. See also Report of Robert H. Jackson to the President, and the Indictment, Department of State publication 2420, European Series 10.

punished according to the laws of these liberated countries and of the free Governments that will be created therein:

AND WHEREAS this Declaration was stated to be without prejudice to the case of major criminals whose offenses have no particular geographical location and who will be punished by the joint decision of the Government of the Allies;

NOW THEREFORE the Government of the United States of America, the Provisional Government of the French Republic, the Government of the United Kingdom of Great Britain and Northern Ireland and the Government of the Union of Soviet Socialist Republics (hereinafter called "the Signatories") acting in the interests of all the United Nations and by their representatives duly authorized thereto have concluded this Agreement.

Article 1.

There shall be established after consultation with the Control Council for Germany an International Military Tribunal for the trial of war criminals whose offenses have no particular geographical location whether they be accused individually or in their capacity as members of organizations or groups or in both capacities.

Article 2.

The constitution, jurisdiction and functions of the International Military Tribunal shall be those set out in the Charter annexed to this Agreement, which Charter shall form an integral part of this Agreement.

Article 3.

Each of the Signatories shall take the necessary steps to make available for the investigation of the charges and trial the major war criminals detained by them who are to be tried by the International Military Tribunal. The Signatories shall also use their best endeavors to make available for investigation of the charges against and the trial before the International Military Tribunal such of the major war criminals as are not in the territories of any of the signatories.

Article 4.

Nothing in this Agreement shall prejudice the provisions established by the Moscow Declaration concerning the return of war criminals to the countries where they committed their crimes.

Article 5.

Any Government of the United Nations may adhere to this Agreement by notice given through the diplomatic channel to the Government of the United Kingdom, who shall inform the other signatory and adhering Governments of each such adherence.

Article 6.

Nothing in this Agreement shall prejudice the jurisdiction or the powers of any national or occupation court established or to be established in any allied territory or in Germany for the trial of war criminals.

Article 7.

This Agreement shall come into force on the day of signature and shall remain in force for the period of one year and shall continue thereafter, subject to the right of any Signatory to give, through the diplomatic channel, one month's notice of intention to terminate it. Such termination shall not prejudice any proceedings already taken or any findings already made in pursuance of this Agreement.

(*b*) *Charter of the International Military Tribunal, August 8, 1945* [1]

I. CONSTITUTION OF THE INTERNATIONAL MILITARY TRIBUNAL

Article 1.

In pursuance of the Agreement signed on the 8th day of August 1945 by the Government of the United States of America, the Provisional Government of the French Republic, the Government of the United Kingdom of Great Britain and Northern Ireland and the Government of the Union of Soviet Socialist Republics, there shall be established an International Military Tribunal (hereinafter called "the Tribunal) for the just and prompt trial and punishment of the major war criminals of the European Axis.

Article 2.

The Tribunal shall consist of four members, each with an alternate. One member and one alternate shall be appointed by each of the Signatories. The alternates shall, so far as they are able, be present at all sessions of the Tribunal. In case of illness of any member of the Tribunal or his incapacity for some other reason to fulfill his functions, his alternate shall take his place.

Article 3.

Neither the Tribunal, its members nor their alternates can be challenged by the prosecution, or by the Defendants or their Counsel. Each signatory may replace its member of the Tribunal or his alternate for reasons of health or for other good reasons, except that no replacement may take place during a Trial, other than by an alternate.

Article 4.

(a) The presence of all four members of the Tribunal or the alternate for any absent member shall be necessary to constitute the quorum.

(b) The members of the Tribunal shall, before any trial begins, agree among themselves upon the selection from their number of a President, and the President shall hold office during that trial, or as may otherwise be agreed by a vote of not less than three members. The principle of rotation of presidency for successive trials is agreed. If, however, a session of the Tribunal takes place on the territory of one of the four Signatories, the representative of that Signatory on the Tribunal shall preside.

(c) Save as aforesaid the Tribunal shall take decisions by a majority vote

[1] Department of State publication 2461, Executive Agreements Series 472.

and in case the votes are evenly divided, the vote of the President shall be decisive: provided always that convictions and sentences shall only be imposed by affirmative votes of at least three members of the Tribunal.

Article 5.

In case of need and depending on the number of the matters to be tried, other Tribunals may be set up; and the establishment, functions, and procedure of each Tribunal shall be identical, and shall be governed by this Charter.

II. JURISDICTION AND GENERAL PRINCIPLES

Article 6.

The Tribunal established by the Agreement referred to in Article 1 hereof for the trial and punishment of the major war criminals of the European Axis countries shall have the power to try and punish persons who, acting in the interests of the European Axis countries, whether as individuals or as members of organizations, committed any of the following crimes.

The following acts, or any of them, are crimes coming within the jurisdiction of the Tribunal for which there shall be individual responsibility:

(a) CRIMES AGAINST PEACE: namely, planning, preparation, initiation or waging of a war of aggression, or a war in violation of international treaties, agreements or assurances, or participation in a common plan or conspiracy for the accomplishment of any of the foregoing;

(b) WAR CRIMES: namely, violations of the laws or customs of war. Such violations shall include, but not be limited to, murder, ill-treatment or deportation to slave labor or for any other purpose of civilian population of or in occupied territory, murder or ill-treatment of prisoners of war or persons on the seas, killing of hostages, plunder of public or private property, wanton destruction of cities, towns or villages, or devastation not justified by military necessity.

(c) CRIMES AGAINST HUMANITY: namely, murder, extermination, enslavement, deportation, and other inhumane acts committed against any civilian population, before or during the war; [1] or persecutions on political, racial or religious grounds in execution of or in connection with any crime within the jurisdiction of the Tribunal, whether or not in violation of the domestic law of the country where perpetrated.

Leaders, organizers, instigators and accomplices participating in the formulation or execution of a common plan or conspiracy to commit any of the foregoing crimes are responsible for all acts performed by any persons in execution of such a plan.

Article 7.

The official position of defendants, whether as Heads of State or responsible officials in Government Departments, shall not be considered as freeing them from responsibility or mitigating punishment.

[1] The contracting governments signed a protocol at Berlin on Oct. 6, 1945 which provides that this semicolon in the English text should be changed to a comma.

Article 8.

The fact that the Defendant acted pursuant to order of his Government or of a superior shall not free him from responsibility, but may be considered in mitigation of punishment if the Tribunal determines that justice so requires.

Article 9.

At the trial of any individual member of any group or organization the Tribunal may declare (in connection with any act of which the individual may be convicted) that the group or organization of which the individual was a member was a criminal organization.

After receipt of the Indictment the Tribunal shall give such notice as it thinks fit that the prosecution intends to ask the Tribunal to make such declaration and any member of the organization will be entitled to apply to the Tribunal for leave to be heard by the Tribunal upon the question of the criminal character of the organization. The Tribunal shall have power to allow or reject the application. If the application is allowed, the Tribunal may direct in what manner the applicants shall be represented and heard.

Article 10.

In cases where a group or organization is declared criminal by the Tribunal, the competent national authority of any Signatory shall have the right to bring individuals to trial for membership therein before national, military or occupation courts. In any such case the criminal nature of the group or organization is considered proved and shall not be questioned.

Article 11.

Any person convicted by the Tribunal may be charged before a national, military or occupation court, referred to in Article 10 of this Charter, with a crime other than of membership in a criminal group or organization and such court may, after convicting him, impose upon him punishment independent of and additional to the punishment imposed by the Tribunal for participation in the criminal activities of such group or organization.

Article 12.

The Tribunal shall have the right to take proceedings against a person charged with crimes set out in Article 6 of this Charter in his absence, if he has not been found or if the Tribunal, for any reason, finds it necessary, in the interests of justice, to conduct the hearing in his absence.

Article 13.

The Tribunal shall draw up rules for its procedure. These rules shall not be inconsistent with the provisions of this Charter.

III. Committee for the Investigation and Prosecution of Major War Criminals

Article 14.

Each Signatory shall appoint a Chief Prosecutor for the investigation of the charges against and the prosecution of major war criminals.

The Chief Prosecutors shall act as a committee for the following purposes:

(a) to agree upon a plan of the individual work of each of the Chief Prosecutors and his staff,

(b) to settle the final designation of major war criminals to be tried by the Tribunal,

(c) to approve the Indictment and the documents to be submitted therewith,

(d) to lodge the Indictment and the accompanying documents with the Tribunal,

(e) to draw up and recommend to the Tribunal for its approval draft rules of procedure, contemplated by Article 13 of this Charter. The Tribunal shall have power to accept, with or without amendments, or to reject, the rules so recommended.

The Committee shall act in all the above matters by a majority vote and shall appoint a Chairman as may be convenient and in accordance with the principle of rotation: provided that if there is an equal division of vote concerning the designation of a Defendant to be tried by the Tribunal, or the crimes with which he shall be charged, that proposal will be adopted which was made by the party which proposed that the particular Defendant be tried, or the particular charges be preferred against him.

Article 15.

The Chief Prosecutors shall individually, and acting in collaboration with one another, also undertake the following duties:

(a) investigation, collection and production before or at the Trial of all necessary evidence,

(b) the preparation of the Indictment for approval by the Committee in accordance with paragraph (c) of Article 14 hereof,

(c) the preliminary examination of all necessary witnesses and of the Defendants,

(d) to act as prosecutor at the Trial,

(e) to appoint representatives to carry out such duties as may be assigned to them,

(f) to understand such other matters as may appear necessary to them for the purposes of the preparation for and conduct of the Trial.

It is understood that no witness or Defendant detained by any Signatory shall be taken out of the possession of that Signatory without its assent.

IV. Fair Trial for Defendants

Article 16.

In order to ensure fair trial for the Defendants, the following procedure shall be followed:

(a) The Indictment shall include full particulars specifying in detail the charges against the Defendants. A copy of the Indictment and of all the documents lodged with the Indictment, translated into a language which he understands, shall be furnished to the Defendant at a reasonable time before the Trial.

(b) During any preliminary examination or trial of a Defendant he shall have the right to give any explanation relevant to the charges made against him.

(c) A preliminary examination of a Defendant and his Trial shall be conducted in, or translated into, a language which the Defendant understands.

(d) A defendant shall have the right to conduct his own defense before the Tribunal or to have the assistance of Counsel.

(e) A defendant shall have the right through himself or through his Counsel to present evidence at the Trial in support of his defense, and to cross-examine any witness called by the Prosecution.

V. Powers of the Tribunal and Conduct of the Trial

Article 17.

The Tribunal shall have the power
(a) to summon witnesses to the Trial and to require their attendance and testimony and to put questions to them,
(b) to interrogate any Defendant,
(c) to require the production of documents and other evidentiary material,
(d) to administer oaths to witnesses,
(e) to appoint officers for the carrying out of any task designated by the Tribunal including the power to have evidence taken on commission.

Article 18.

The Tribunal shall
(a) confine the Trial strictly to an expeditious hearing of the issues raised by the charges,
(b) take strict measures to prevent any action which will cause unreasonable delay, and rule out irrelevant issues and statements of any kind whatsoever,
(c) deal summarily with any contumacy, imposing appropriate punishment, including exclusion of any Defendant or his Counsel from some or all further proceedings, but without prejudice to the determination of the charges.

Article 19.

The Tribunal shall not be bound by technical rules of evidence. It shall adopt and apply to the greatest possible extent of expeditious and non-technical procedure, and shall admit any evidence which it deems to have probative value.

Article 20.

The Tribunal may require to be informed of the nature of any evidence before it is offered so that it may rule upon the relevance thereof.

Article 21.

The Tribunal shall not require proof of facts of common knowledge but shall take judicial notice thereof. It shall also take judicial notice of official governmental documents and reports of the United Nations, including the acts and documents of the committees set up in the various allied countries for the investigation of war crimes, and the records and findings of military or other Tribunals of any of the United Nations.

Article 22.

The permanent seat of the Tribunal shall be in Berlin. The first meetings of the members of the Tribunal and of the Chief Prosecutors shall be held at Berlin in a place to be designated by the Control Council for Germany. The first trial shall be held at Nuremberg, and any subsequent trials shall be held at such places as the Tribunal may decide.

Article 23.

One or more of the Chief Prosecutors may take part in the prosecution at each Trial. The function of any Chief Prosecutor may be discharged by him personally, or by any person or persons authorized by him.

The function of Counsel for a Defendant may be discharged at the Defendant's request by any Counsel professionally qualified to conduct cases before the Courts of his own country, or by any other person who may be specially authorized thereto by the Tribunal.

Article 24.

The proceedings at the Trial shall take the following course:
(a) The Indictment shall be read in court.
(b) The Tribunal shall ask each Defendant whether he pleads "guilty" or "not guilty".
(c) The prosecution shall make an opening statement.
(d) The Tribunal shall ask the prosecution and the defense what evidence (if any) they wish to submit to the Tribunal, and the Tribunal shall rule upon the admissibility of any such evidence.
(e) The witnesses for the Prosecution shall be examined and after that the witnesses for the Defense. Thereafter such rebutting evidence as may be held by the Tribunal to be admissible shall be called by either the Prosecution or the Defense.
(f) The Tribunal may put any question to any witness and to any Defendant, at any time.
(g) The Prosecution and the Defense shall interrogate and may cross-examine any witnesses and any Defendant who gives testimony.
(h) The Defense shall address the court.
(i) The Prosecution shall address the court.
(j) Each Defendant may make a statement to the Tribunal.
(k) The Tribunal shall deliver judgment and pronounce sentence.

Article 25.

All official documents shall be produced, and all court proceedings conducted, in English, French and Russian, and in the language of the Defendant. So much of the record and of the proceedings may also be translated into the language of any country in which the Tribunal is sitting, as the Tribunal considers desirable in the interests of justice and public opinion.

VI. Judgment and Sentence

Article 26.

The judgment of the Tribunal as to the guilt or the innocence of any Defendant shall give the reasons on which it is based, and shall be final and not subject to review.

Article 27.

The Tribunal shall have the right to impose upon a Defendant, on conviction, death or such other punishment as shall be determined by it to be just.

Article 28.

In addition to any punishment imposed by it, the Tribunal shall have the right to deprive the convicted person of any stolen property and order its delivery to the Control Council for Germany.

Article 29.

In case of guilt, sentences shall be carried out in accordance with the orders of the Control Council for Germany, which may at any time reduce or otherwise alter the sentences, but may not increase the severity thereof. If the Control Council for Germany, after any Defendant has been convicted and sentenced, discovers fresh evidence which, in its opinion, would found a fresh charge against him, the Council shall report accordingly to the Committee established under Article 14 hereof, for such action as they may consider proper, having regard to the interests of justice.

VII. Expenses

Article 30.

The expenses of the Tribunal and of the Trials, shall be charged by the Signatories against the funds allotted for maintenance of the Control Council for Germany.

◇◇◇◇◇◇

176. CHARTER OF THE INTERNATIONAL MILITARY TRIBUNAL FOR THE FAR EAST, JANUARY 19, 1946 [1]

[The policy of the Allied Powers toward Japanese war criminals was publicly stated in section ten of the "Proclamation defining Terms for Japanese Surrender" as follows:

> We do not intend that the Japanese shall be enslaved as a race or destroyed as a nation, but stern justice shall be meted out to all war criminals, including those who have visited cruelties upon our prisoners . . .

[1] Trial of Japanese War Criminals, Department of State publication 2613, Far Eastern Series 12, pp. 39-44. This publication also contains texts of the Opening Statement by Joseph B. Keenan, Chief of Counsel, and the Indictment. The Charter was approved by the Supreme Commander for the Allied Powers on January 19, 1946; it was amended by order of the Supreme Commander, General Headquarters, APO 500, April 26, 1946, General Orders No. 20. The amendments have been incorporated herewith.

The charter which follows set up an eleven-man tribunal for the trial of Japanese war criminals and established the procedure under which it was to operate. The tribunal began its sessions on May 3, 1946, and pronounced sentence on November 12, 1948. Of the twenty-five defendants, seven were condemned to death by hanging, and the rest to imprisonment for long terms or life. As in the case of the Nuremberg tribunal, the Tokyo tribunal ceased to function after pronouncing sentence on November 12, 1948.]

I. CONSTITUTION OF TRIBUNAL

Article 1. Tribunal Established. The International Military Tribunal for the Far East is hereby established for the just and prompt trial and punishment of the major war criminals in the Far East. The permanent seat of the Tribunal is in Tokyo.

Article 2. Members. The tribunal shall consist of not less than six members nor more than eleven members, appointed by the Supreme Commander for the Allied Powers from the names submitted by the Signatories to the Instrument of Surrender, India, and the Commonwealth of the Philippines.

Article 3. Officers and Secretariat.

(*a*) *President.* The Supreme Commander for the Allied Powers shall appoint a Member to be President of the Tribunal.

(*b*) *Secretariat.*

(1) The Secretariat of the Tribunal shall be composed of a General Secretary to be appointed by the Supreme Commander for the Allied Powers and such assistant secretaries, clerks, interpreters, and other personnel as may be necessary.

(2) The General Secretary shall organize and direct the work of the Secretariat.

(3) The Secretariat shall receive all documents addressed to the Tribunal, maintain the records of the Tribunal, provide necessary clerical services to the Tribunal and its Members, and perform such other duties as may be designated by the Tribunal.

Article 4. Convening and Quorum, Voting and Absence.

(*a*) *Convening and Quorum.* When as many as six members of the Tribunal are present, they may convene the Tribunal in formal session. The presence of a majority of all members shall be necessary to constitute a quorum.

(*b*) *Voting.* All decisions and judgments of this Tribunal, including convictions and sentences, shall be by a majority vote of those Members of the Tribunal present. In case the votes are evenly divided, the vote of the President shall be decisive.

(*c*) *Absence.* If a member at any time is absent and afterwards is able to be present, he shall take part in all subsequent proceedings; unless he declares in open court that he is disqualified by reason of insufficient familiarity with the proceedings which took place in his absence.

II. JURISDICTION AND GENERAL PROVISIONS

Article 5. Jurisdiction Over Persons and Offenses. The Tribunal shall have the power to try and punish Far Eastern war criminals who as individuals or as members of organizations are charged with offenses which include Crimes against Peace.

The following acts, or any of them, are crimes coming within the jurisdiction of the Tribunal for which there shall be individual responsibility:

(*a*) *Crimes against Peace:* Namely, the planning, preparation, initiation or waging of a declared or undeclared war of aggression, or a war in violation of international law, treaties, agreements or assurances, or participation in a common plan or conspiracy for the accomplishment of any of the foregoing;

(*b*) *Conventional War Crimes:* Namely, violations of the laws or customs of war;

(*c*) *Crimes against Humanity:* Namely, murder, extermination, enslavement, deportation, and other inhumane acts committed against any civilian population, before or during the war, or persecutions on political or racial grounds in execution of or in connection with any crime within the jurisdiction of the Tribunal, whether or not in violation of the domestic law of the country where perpetrated. Leaders, organizers, instigators and accomplices participating in the formulation or execution of a common plan or conspiracy to commit any of the foregoing crimes are responsible for all acts performed by any person in execution of such plan.

Article 6. Responsibility of Accused. Neither the official position, at any time, of an accused, nor the fact that an accused acted pursuant to order of his government or of a superior shall, of itself, be sufficient to free such accused from responsibility for any crime with which he is charged, but such circumstances may be considered in mitigation of punishment if the Tribunal determines that justice so requires.

Article 7. Rules of Procedure. The Tribunal may draft and amend rules of procedure consistent with the fundamental provisions of this Charter.

Article 8. Counsel.

(*a*) *Chief of Counsel.* The Chief of Counsel designated by the Supreme Commander for the Allied Powers is responsible for the investigation and prosecution of charges against war criminals within the jurisdiction of this Tribunal, and will render such legal assistance to the Supreme Commander as is appropriate.

(*b*) *Associate Counsel.* Any United Nation with which Japan has been at war may appoint an Associate Counsel to assist the Chief of Counsel.

III. FAIR TRIAL FOR ACCUSED

Article 9. Procedure for Fair Trial. In order to insure fair trial for the accused the following procedure shall be followed:

(*a*) *Indictment.* The indictment shall consist of a plain, concise, and adequate statement of each offense charged. Each accused shall be furnished, in adequate time for defense, a copy of the indictment, including any amendment, and of this Charter, in a language understood by the accused.

(*b*) *Language.* The trial and related proceedings shall be conducted in English and in the language of the accused. Translations of documents and other papers shall be provided as needed and requested.

(*c*) *Counsel for Accused.* Each accused shall have the right to be represented by counsel of his own selection, subject to the disapproval of such counsel at any time by the Tribunal. The accused shall file with the General

Secretary of the Tribunal the name of his counsel. If an accused is not represented by counsel and in open court requests the appointment of counsel, the Tribunal shall designate counsel for him. In the absence of such request the Tribunal may appoint counsel for an accused if in its judgment such appointment is necessary to provide for a fair trial.

(*d*) *Evidence for Defense.* An accused shall have the right, through himself or through his counsel (but not through both), to conduct his defense, including the right to examine any witness, subject to such reasonable restrictions as the Tribunal may determine.

(*e*) *Production of Evidence for the Defense.* An accused may apply in writing to the Tribunal for the production of witnesses or of documents. The application shall state where the witness or document is thought to be located. It shall also state the facts proposed to be proved by the witness of the document and the relevancy of such facts to the defense. If the Tribunal grants the application the Tribunal shall be given such aid in obtaining production of the evidence as the circumstances require.

Article 10. Applications and Motions before Trial. All motions, applications, or other requests addressed to the Tribunal prior to the commencement of trial shall be made in writing and filed with the General Secretary of the Tribunal for action by the Tribunal.

IV. Powers of Tribunal and Conduct of Trial

Article 11. Powers. The Tribunal shall have the power

(*a*) To summon witnesses to the trial, to require them to attend and testify, and to question them,

(*b*) To interrogate each accused and to permit comment on his refusal to answer any question,

(*c*) To require the production of documents and other evidentiary material,

(*d*) To require of each witness an oath, affirmation, or such declaration as is customary in the country of the witness, and to administer oaths,

(*e*) To appoint officers for the carrying out of any task designated by the Tribunal, including the power to have evidence taken on commission.

Article 12. Conduct of Trial. The Tribunal shall

(*a*) Confine the trial strictly to an expeditious hearing of the issues raised by the charges,

(*b*) Take strict measures to prevent any action which would cause any unreasonable delay and rule out irrelevant issues and statements of any kind whatsoever,

(*c*) Provide for the maintenance of order at the trial and deal summarily with any contumacy, imposing appropriate punishment, including exclusion of any accused or his counsel from some or all further proceedings, but without prejudice to the determination of the charges,

(*d*) Determine the mental and physical capacity of any accused to proceed to trial.

Article 13. Evidence.

(*a*) *Admissibility.* The Tribunal shall not be bound by technical rules of evidence. It shall adopt and apply to the greatest possible extent expeditious and non-technical procedure, and shall admit any evidence which it deems to have probative value. All purported admissions or statements of the accused are admissible.

(*b*) *Relevance*. The Tribunal may require to be informed of the nature of any evidence before it is offered in order to rule upon the relevance.

(*c*) *Specific evidence admissible*. In particular, and without limiting in any way the scope of the foregoing general rules, the following evidence may be admitted:

(1) A document, regardless of its security classification and without proof of its issuance or signature, which appears to the Tribunal to have been signed or issued by any officer, department, agency or member of the armed forces of any government.

(2) A report which appears to the Tribunal to have been signed or issued by the International Red Cross or a member thereof, or by a doctor of medicine or any medical service personnel, or by an investigator or intelligence officer, or by any other person who appears to the Tribunal to have personal knowledge of the matters contained in the report.

(3) An affidavit, deposition or other signed statement.

(4) A diary, letter or other document, including sworn or unsworn statements which appear to the Tribunal to contain information relating to the charge.

(5) A copy of a document or other secondary evidence of its contents, if the original is not immediately available.

(*d*) *Judicial Notice*. The Tribunal shall neither require proof of facts of common knowledge, nor of the authenticity of official government documents and reports of any nation nor of the proceedings, records, and findings of military or other agencies of any of the United Nations.

(*e*) *Records, Exhibits and Documents*. The transcript of the proceedings, and exhibits and documents submitted to the Tribunal, will be filed with the General Secretary of the Tribunal and will constitute part of the Record.

Article 14. Place of Trial. The first trial will be held at Tokyo and any subsequent trials will be held at such places as the Tribunal decides.

Article 15. Course of Trial Proceedings. The proceedings at the Trial will take the following course:

(*a*) The indictment will be read in court unless the reading is waived by all accused.

(*b*) The Tribunal will ask each accused whether he pleads "guilty" or "not guilty."

(*c*) The prosecution and each accused (by counsel only, if represented) may make a concise opening statement.

(*d*) The prosecution and defense may offer evidence and the admissibility of the same shall be determined by the Tribunal.

(*e*) The prosecution and each accused (by counsel only, if represented) may examine each witness and each accused who gives testimony.

(*f*) Accused (by counsel only, if represented) may address the Tribunal.

(*g*) The prosecution may address the Tribunal.

(*h*) The Tribunal will deliver judgment and pronounce sentence.

V. Judgment and Sentence

Article 16. Penalty. The Tribunal shall have the power to impose upon an accused, on conviction, death or such other punishment as shall be determined by it to be just.

Article 17. Judgment and Review. The judgment will be announced in open court and will give the reasons on which it is based. The record of the trial will be transmitted directly to the Supreme Commander for the Allied Powers for his action thereon. A sentence will be carried out in accordance with the order of the Supreme Commander for the Allied Powers, who may at any time reduce or otherwise alter the sentence except to increase its severity.

By command of General MacArthur:

RICHARD J. MARSHALL
Major General, General Staff
Corps, Chief of Staff.

OFFICIAL:

B M FITCH
Brigadier General, AGD,
Adjutant General.

◇◇◇◇◇◇

177. AFFIRMATION OF THE PRINCIPLES OF INTERNATIONAL LAW RECOGNIZED BY THE CHARTER OF THE NUREMBERG TRIBUNAL [1]

Resolution of the General Assembly, December 11, 1946

[The Nuremberg trials were attacked by some people not only because they applied international criminal law to offenses which were not defined by international law as crimes at the time they were committed, but also because up to that time generally speaking international law had been applied only to states and not to individuals. The resolution adopted by the General Assembly on December 11, 1946, possessed peculiar importance in that it reaffirmed the principles of international law as stated by the Nuremberg charter. In effect it meant that crimes against humanity were the proper subject of international law and that international law in this respect, at least, was applicable to individuals as well as to states.]

THE GENERAL ASSEMBLY,

RECOGNIZES the obligation laid upon it by Article 13, paragraph 1, subparagraph a. of the Charter, to initiate studies and make recommendations for the purpose of encouraging the progressive development of international law and its codification; and

TAKES NOTE of the Agreement for the establishment of an International Military Tribunal for the prosecution and punishment of the major war

[1] The United States and the United Nations: Report by the President to the Congress for the year 1946, Department of State publication 2735, The United States and the United Nations Report Series 7, pp. 129-130.

criminals of the European Axis signed in London on 8 August 1945, and of the Charter annexed thereto, and of the fact that similar principles have been adopted in the Charter of the International Military Tribunal for the trial of the major war criminals in the Far East, proclaimed at Tokyo on 19 January 1946.

THEREFORE

AFFIRMS the principles of international law recognized by the Charter of the Nuremberg Tribunal and the judgment of the Tribunal;

DIRECTS the Committee on the codification of international law established by the resolution of the General Assembly of December 1946, to treat as a matter of primary importance plans for the formulation, in the context of a general codification of offenses against the peace and security of mankind, or of an International Criminal Code, of the principles recognized in the Charter of the Nuremberg Tribunal and in the judgment of the Tribunal.

◇◇◇◇◇

FORMER JAPANESE MANDATED ISLANDS

178. SUBMISSION OF UNITED STATES DRAFT TRUSTEESHIP AGREEMENT FOR JAPANESE MANDATED ISLANDS

Statement by Warren R. Austin, United States Representative to the United Nations, February 26, 1947 [1]

[When World War II came to an end, the United States remained in control of several island chains which our forces had wrested from the Japanese. Among these were the Marshalls, the Marianas, and the Carolines which had been held by Japan as mandates under the League of Nations. On February 26, 1947, Ambassador Warren Austin submitted to the Security Council our government's proposal to place these three island groups under United Nations trusteeship. His speech made clear that even though the islands were to be designated as "strategic areas" in order to protect our strategic interests there, our government would continue to stress the welfare of the inhabitants of those territories.]

Mr. President, the United States, like other nations adhering to the United Nations Declaration of January 1, 1942, subscribed to the Atlantic Charter principle that "their countries seek no aggrandizement, territorial or other."

It was for the purpose of making clear that the United States adheres unswervingly to this principle that the President of the United States on November 6, 1946 declared our intentions regarding Pacific islands whose control by Japan enabled her to attack the United States. The President said:

"The United States is prepared to place under trusteeship, with the United States as the administering authority, the Japanese Mandated Islands and any Japanese islands for which it assumes responsibility as a result of the second

[1] Statement made by Warren R. Austin, United States Representative to the United Nations, before the Security Council on February 26, 1947; Department of State Bulletin of March 9, 1947, pp. 416-419. See Draft Trusteeship Agreement for the Japanese Mandated Islands, Department of State publication 2784, Far Eastern Series 20.

World War. In so far as the Japanese Mandated Islands are concerned, this Government is transmitting for information to the other members of the Security Council (Australia, Brazil, China, Egypt, France, Mexico, the Netherlands, Poland, the Union of Soviet Socialist Republics, and the United Kingdom) and to New Zealand and the Philippines a draft of a strategic area trusteeship agreement which sets forth the terms upon which this Government is prepared to place those islands under trusteeship. At an early date we plan to submit this draft agreement formally to the Security Council for its approval."

Final disposition of islands belonging to Japan must, of course, await the peace settlement with Japan. The draft trusteeship agreement submitted to the Security Council for its approval relates only to the former Japanese Mandated Islands, which never belonged to Japan but were a part of the League of Nations mandate system. The United States has consistently and strongly supported the position of the General Assembly that former mandated territories should be placed under the trusteeship system as soon as possible.

The General Assembly, at the first part of its first session, called on "those members of the United Nations which are now administering territories held under mandate" to undertake practical steps for the implementation of article 79 of the Charter. Since the United States was, and is, occupying the territory formerly mandated to Japan, the United States desired to play its part in attaining the objectives of the General Assembly resolution, namely that trusteeship agreements for all former mandated territories should be concluded promptly and the trusteeship system organized as soon as possible.

The Japanese Mandated Islands—the Marshalls, Marianas, and Carolines—consist of some 98 islands and island clusters with a total land mass of only 846 square miles, a total population of only about 48,000 native inhabitants, and negligible indigenous economic resources.

The tremendous strategic value of the Mandated Islands to Japan is evident, however, in the way these islands were used in carrying out its basic plan of aggression. Before Japan entered the war on December 7, 1941, she had established fortified positions, naval bases and air bases in the islands of the Japanese Mandates. As a whole, the islands formed a deep, well-defended barrier between the United States and Guam, the Philippines, and its British and Dutch Allies in the Far East.

* * *

Tens of thousands of American lives, vast expenditures of treasure, and years of bitter fighting were necessary to drive the Japanese aggressors back from these islands. These islands constitute an integrated strategic physical complex vital to the security of the United States.

The American people are firmly resolved that this area shall never again be used as a springboard for aggression against the United States or any other member of the United Nations.

Most of the strategically important areas of the world, including those in the Pacific, are at present under the exclusive sovereignty of various of the larger nations. The United States, however, is proposing trusteeship rather than annexation as the basis for its administration of these highly strategic islands.

* * *

The first of the four basic objectives of the trusteeship system set forth in article 76 of the Charter is "to further international peace and security." Since the area of the former Japanese Mandated Islands is of paramount strategic importance, the United States proposes, in accordance with article 82 of the Charter, that the trust territory be designated a strategic area.

* * *

In conformity with the provisions of the Charter for strategic areas the trust territory will contain bases. Many atolls in the territory have potential value as base sites or as anchorages. Few such sites, however, are being developed and maintained at present.

The United States will administer this strategic trust territory in accordance with the provisions of the Charter. In particular, the United States will administer the territory in accordance with the obligations contained in article 2, paragraph 4, to "refrain . . . from the threat or use of force against the territorial integrity or political independence of any state, or in any other manner inconsistent with the Purposes of the United Nations."

The United States as administering authority will insure that this trust territory shall play its part in the maintenance of international peace and security in accordance with its obligation under article 1 of the Charter—"to take effective collective measures for the prevention and removal of threats to the peace, and for the suppression of acts of aggression or other breaches of the peace." Its administration will also be in accordance with article 84 of the Charter, relating to the part to be played by trust territories "in carrying out the obligations towards the Security Council" of the administering authority.

The United States intends, therefore, to include this trust territory as fully as those territories under its sovereignty in the special agreement or agreements it will conclude with the Security Council for the provision to the United Nations of "armed forces, assistance, and facilities, including rights of passage, necessary for the purpose of maintaining international peace and security" as envisaged under article 43 of the Charter.

* * *

The United States draft agreement provides that the administering authority may from time to time specify certain areas as closed for security reasons. This provision will not, of course, prejudice the full application to the entire trust territory of all international control and inspection measures that become part of a system of international control of atomic energy, other weapons of mass destruction, and conventional armaments.

The United States is willing to submit to international supervision, as provided in the agreement, the political, economic, social, and educational development of the inhabitants of the trust territory. It is equally willing to submit military and naval installations to whatever degree of supervision and control may be provided by agreements for the international control of armaments and armed forces.

* * *

Although this is a strategic area vital to that system of international peace and security to which articles 73 and 76 refer, the United States draft agreement goes beyond the requirements of the Charter in strategic areas: It provides that articles 87 and 88—relating to reports, petitions, visits, and questionnaires in non-strategic trusteeship areas—shall be applicable to the whole of this trust territory, except that the administering authority may determine the extent of applicability in any areas which may from time to time be specified by the administering authority as closed for security reasons. This exception has been made in recognition of the fact that an administering authority of a strategic trust territory should have the authority necessary to safeguard the installations established in the discharge of its responsibilities for the maintenance of international peace and security.

*   *   *

Articles 6 and 7 of the draft trusteeship agreement submitted to the Security Council contain strong provisions relating to the political, economic, social, and educational advancement of the inhabitants of this territory and to guaranties of their basic human rights. These are the fundamental objectives of the trusteeship system, aside from the strengthening of international peace and security. The United States is glad to invite the members of the Security Council to make a searching examination of the provisions contained in these articles not only in relation to the requirements of the Charter but in relation to the comparable provisions of the trusteeship agreements approved by the General Assembly last December. The United States believes these articles, taken together with other provisions of the draft agreement, provide a maximum degree of protection for the welfare and advancement of the inhabitants of these islands.

The United States believes it has fulfilled the requirements of article 79 of the Charter, first by transmitting copies of a draft trusteeship agreement for the former Japanese Mandated Islands to all members of the United Nations which, in the view of the Government of the United States, may have special interests in these islands, and now by formally submitting the draft agreement to the Security Council for its approval.

The United States Government does not consider that there is any barrier to the placing of these islands under trusteeship in accordance with the Charter whenever the Security Council approves the draft agreement.

As a result of the war, Japan has ceased to exercise, or to be entitled to exercise, any authority in these islands. The islands were entrusted to Japan under mandate from the League of Nations following the first World War. In utter disregard of the mandate Japan used the territories for aggressive warfare, contrary to the law of nations, against the United States and others of the United Nations. By Japan's criminal acts of aggression, she forfeited the right and capacity to be the mandatory of the islands. The termination of Japan's status as mandatory in the islands has been frequently affirmed, as in the Cairo Declaration of 1943, subsequently reaffirmed in the Potsdam Declaration and in the instrument of surrender accepted by the powers responsible for Japan's defeat.

All authority in these islands is now exercised by the United States. The United States in repelling Japanese aggression occupied, and is in possession of, the former Japanese Mandated Islands. This Government is not aware that any other member of the United Nations has asserted any claim for trusteeship of these islands. All the members which may have special interests in the islands have been sent copies of the draft agreement which the United States, as the responsible administering authority in the islands, has submitted to the Security Council.

Under the above circumstances, it is the view of this Government that the conclusion of a trusteeship agreement, pursuant to the Charter, for the former Japanese Mandated Islands clearly can take effect at this time and does not depend upon, and need not await, the general peace settlement with Japan.

* * *

◇◇◇◇◇◇

179. TRUSTEESHIP AGREEMENT FOR THE FORMER JAPANESE MANDATED ISLANDS

Resolution of the Security Council, April 2, 1947 [1]

[This is an unusual document. In the first place, it is an international agreement between the United States and the Security Council designating the United States as the administering authority of the Marshalls, the Carolines, and the Mariana Islands. In the second place, it provides for the only "strategic area" trust territory yet established under the United Nations trusteeship system. In effect, this means that the United States may from time to time specify certain areas in the islands as closed for security reasons. Even in such instances, however, the United States in administering the territory remains obligated to apply the basic objectives of the United Nations trusteeship system as set forth in Article 76 of the Charter.]

PREAMBLE

WHEREAS Article 75 of the Charter of the United Nations provides for the establishment of an international trusteeship system for the administration and supervision of such territories as may be placed thereunder by subsequent agreements; and

WHEREAS under Article 77 of the said Charter the trusteeship system may be applied to territories now held under mandate; and

WHEREAS on 17 December 1920 the Council of the League of Nations confirmed a mandate for the former German islands north of the equator to Japan, to be administered in accordance with Article 22 of the Covenant of the League of Nations; and

WHEREAS Japan, as a result of the Second World War, has ceased to exercise any authority in these islands;

Now, THEREFORE, the Security Council of the United Nations, having satisfied itself that the relevant articles of the Charter have been complied with, hereby resolves to approve the following terms of trusteeship for the Pacific Islands formerly under mandate to Japan.

[1] Department of State publication 2992, Treaties and Other International Acts Series 1665.

ARTICLE 1

The Territory of the Pacific Islands, consisting of the islands formerly held by Japan under mandate in accordance with Article 22 of the Covenant of the League of Nations, is hereby designated as a strategic area and placed under the trusteeship system established in the Charter of the United Nations. The Territory of the Pacific Islands is hereinafter referred to as the trust territory.

ARTICLE 2

The United States of America is designated as the administering authority of the trust territory.

ARTICLE 3

The administering authority shall have full powers of administration, legislation, and jurisdiction over the territory subject to the provisions of this agreement, and may apply to the trust territory, subject to any modifications which the administering authority may consider desirable, such of the laws of the United States as it may deem appropriate to local conditions and requirements.

ARTICLE 4

The administering authority, in discharging the obligations of trusteeship in the trust territory, shall act in accordance with the Charter of the United Nations, and the provisions of this agreement, and shall, as specified in Article 83 (2) of the Charter, apply the objectives of the international trusteeship system, as set forth in Article 76 of the Charter, to the people of the trust territory.

ARTICLE 5

In discharging its obligations under Article 76 (a) and Article 84, of the Charter, the administering authority shall ensure that the trust territory shall play its part, in accordance with the Charter of the United Nations, in the maintenance of international peace and security. To this end the administering authority shall be entitled:

1. to establish naval, military and air bases and to erect fortifications in the trust territory;

2. to station and employ armed forces in the territory; and

3. to make use of volunteer forces, facilities and assistance from the trust territory in carrying out the obligations towards the Security Council undertaken in this regard by the administering authority, as well as for the local defense and the maintenance of law and order within the trust territory.

ARTICLE 6

In discharging its obligations under Article 76 (b) of the Charter, the administering authority shall:

1. foster the development of such political institutions as are suited to the trust territory and shall promote the development of the inhabitants of the trust territory toward self-government or independence, as may be appro-

priate to the particular circumstances of the trust territory and its peoples and the freely expressed wishes of the peoples concerned; and to this end shall give to the inhabitants of the trust territory a progressively increasing share in the administrative services in the territory; shall develop their participation in government; shall give due recognition to the customs of the inhabitants in providing a system of law for the territory; and shall take other appropriate measures toward these ends;

2. promote the economic advancement and self-sufficiency of the inhabitants, and to this end shall regulate the use of natural resources; encourage the development of fisheries, agriculture, and industries; protect the inhabitants against the loss of their lands and resources; and improve the means of transportation and communication;

3. promote the social advancement of the inhabitants, and to this end shall protect the rights and fundamental freedoms of all elements of the population without discrimination; protect the health of the inhabitants; control the traffic in arms and ammunition, opium and other dangerous drugs, and alcohol and other spirituous beverages; and institute such other regulations as may be necessary to protect the inhabitants against social abuses; and

4. promote the educational advancement of the inhabitants, and to this end shall take steps toward the establishment of a general system of elementary education; facilitate the vocational and cultural advancement of the population; and shall encourage qualified students to pursue higher education, including training on the professional level.

ARTICLE 7

In discharging its obligations under Article 76 (c), of the Charter, the administering authority shall guarantee to the inhabitants of the trust territory freedom of conscience, and, subject only to the requirements of public order and security, freedom of speech, of the press, and of assembly; freedom of worship, and of religious teaching; and freedom of migration and movement.

ARTICLE 8

1. In discharging its obligations under Article 76 (d) of the Charter, as defined by Article 83 (2) of the Charter, the administering authority, subject to the requirements of security, and the obligation to promote the advancement of the inhabitants, shall accord to nationals of each Member of the United Nations and to companies and associations organized in conformity with the laws of such Member, treatment in the trust territory no less favourable than that accorded therein to nationals, companies and associations of any other United Nation except the administering authority.

2. The administering authority shall ensure equal treatment to the Members of the United Nations and their nationals in the administration of justice.

3. Nothing in this Article shall be so construed as to accord traffic rights to aircraft flying into and out of the trust territory. Such rights shall be subject to agreement between the administering authority and the state whose nationality such aircraft possesses.

4. The administering authority may negotiate and conclude commercial and other treaties and agreements with Members of the United Nations and other states, designed to attain for the inhabitants of the trust territory treat-

ment by the Members of the United Nations and other states no less favourable than that granted by them to the nationals of other states. The Security Council may recommend, or invite other organs of the United Nations to consider and recommend, what rights the inhabitants of the trust territory should acquire in consideration of the rights obtained by Members of the United Nations in the trust territory.

ARTICLE 9

The administering authority shall be entitled to constitute the trust territory into a customs, fiscal, or administrative union or federation with other territories under United States jurisdiction and to establish common services between such territories and the trust territory where such measures are not inconsistent with the basic objectives of the International Trusteeship System and with the terms of this agreement.

ARTICLE 10

The administering authority, acting under the provisions of Article 3 of this agreement, may accept membership in any regional advisory commission, regional authority, or technical organization, or other voluntary association of states, may co-operate with specialized international bodies, public or private, and may engage in other forms of international co-operation.

ARTICLE 11

1. The administering authority shall take the necessary steps to provide the status of citizenship of the trust territory for the inhabitants of the trust territory.

2. The administering authority shall afford diplomatic and consular protection to inhabitants of the trust territory when outside the territorial limits of the trust territory or of the territory of the administering authority.

ARTICLE 12

The administering authority shall enact such legislation as may be necessary to place the provisions of this agreement in effect in the trust territory.

ARTICLE 13

The provisions of Articles 87 and 88 of the Charter shall be applicable to the trust territory, provided that the administering authority may determine the extent of their applicability to any areas which may from time to time be specified by it as closed for security reasons.

ARTICLE 14

The administering authority undertakes to apply in the trust territory the provisions of any international conventions and recommendations which may be appropriate to the particular circumstances of the trust territory and which would be conducive to the achievement of the basic objectives of Article 6 of this agreement.

ARTICLE 15

The terms of the present agreement shall not be altered, amended or terminated without the consent of the administering authority.

Article 16

The present agreement shall come into force when approved by the Security Council of the United Nations and by the Government of the United States after due constitutional process.

Certified corrected true copy

For the Security Council Affairs Department

D. Protitch

D. Protitch

Director in charge of Security Council Affairs Department

180. APPROVAL OF TRUSTEESHIP AGREEMENT

(a) *JOINT RESOLUTION Authorizing the President to Approve the Trusteeship Agreement for the Territory of the Pacific Islands, July 18, 1947* [1]

[The decision in the Executive Branch to place the Japanese mandated islands under United Nations trusteeship was reached only after considerable discussion and controversy. Once those differences had been ironed out, Congress approved the agreement without extensive debate. It will be noted that the agreement was submitted to both houses in the form of a joint resolution rather than as a treaty, which requires a two-thirds vote by the Senate alone.]

Whereas the United States submitted to the Security Council of the United Nations for its approval in accordance with article 83 of the Charter of the United Nations a proposed trusteeship agreement for the Pacific islands formerly mandated to Japan under which the United States would be prepared to administer those islands under trusteeship in accordance with the Charter of the United Nations; and

Whereas the Security Council on April 2, 1947, approved unanimously the trusteeship agreement with amendments acceptable to the United States; and

Whereas the said agreement, having been approved by the Security Council, will come into force upon approval by the Government of the United States after due constitutional process: Therefore be it

Resolved by the Senate and House of Representatives of the United States of America in Congress assembled, That the President is hereby authorized to approve, on behalf of the United States, the trusteeship agreement between the United States of America and the Security Council of the United Nations for the former Japanese mandated islands (to be known as the Territory of the Pacific Islands) which was approved by the Security Council at the seat of the United Nations, Lake Success, Nassau County, New York, on April 2, 1947.

Approved July 18, 1947.

[1] Public Law 204, 80th Cong., 1st sess., H. J. Res. 232.

(b) Provisions for Interim Administration for Trust Territory: Executive Order 9875, July 18, 1947 [1]

[On the same day Congress approved the trusteeship agreement, the President terminated the military government in the islands and delegated responsibility for the civil administration of the area to the Secretary of the Navy on an interim basis. On July 1, 1951, at the President's direction, jurisdiction over the administration of the area passed to the Department of the Interior.]

WHEREAS the Trust Territory of the Pacific Islands (hereinafter referred to as the trust territory) has been placed under the trusteeship system established' in the Charter of the United Nations by means of a trusteeship agreement (hereinafter referred to as the agreement), approved by the Security Council of the United Nations on April 2, 1947, and by the United States Government on July 18, 1947, after due constitutional process; and

WHEREAS the United States of America, under the terms of the agreement, is designated as the administering authority of the trust territory and has assumed obligations for the government thereof; and

WHEREAS it is necessary to establish an interim administration of the trust territory, pending the enactment of appropriate legislation by the Congress of the United States providing for the future government thereof:

NOW, THEREFORE, by virtue of the authority vested in me as President of the United States, it is ordered as follows:

1. The military government in the former Japanese Mandated Islands is hereby terminated, and the authority and responsibility for the civil administration of the trust territory, on an interim basis, is hereby delegated to the Secretary of the Navy.

2. The Secretary of the Navy shall, subject to such policies as the President may from time to time prescribe, and, when appropriate, in collaboration with other departments or agencies of the Federal Government, carry out the obligations which the United States, as the administering authority of the trust territory, has assumed under the terms of the agreement and the Charter of the United Nations: *Provided, however,* that the authority granted to the United States under Article 13 of the agreement to close any areas for security reasons and to determine the extent to which Articles 87 and 88 of the Charter of the United Nations shall be applicable to such closed areas shall be exercised jointly by the Secretary of the Navy and the Secretary of State: *And Provided further,* that all relations between departments or agencies of the Federal Government and appropriate organs of the United Nations with respect to the trust territory shall be conducted through the Secretary of State.

3. This order, subject to subsequent modification, shall be effective as of this date and shall remain effective until a designation is made of the civilian department or agency which is to have permanent responsibility for the government of the trust territory.

THE WHITE HOUSE   HARRY S. TRUMAN
July 18, 1947   ◇◇◇◇◇◇

[1] Ex. Or. 9875 (12 Federal Register 4837).

181. ANNUAL REPORT OF UNITED STATES ON TRUST TERRITORY OF THE PACIFIC ISLANDS, FEBRUARY 18, 1949

[It is obvious that one of the great advantages of the trusteeship system lies in the publication and consideration of the regular reports which the administering authorities must submit to the United Nations. This summary of the first annual report submitted by the United States reveals some of the problems which we have encountered in the trust territory and the progress which has been made in the economic, educational, and health fields.]

(a) Letter of Transmittal [1]

February 18, 1949

I have the honour to inform you that the Government of the United States is transmitting under separate cover four hundred copies of a report on the first year of the administration of the Trust Territory of the Pacific Islands under the Trusteeship Agreement which entered into force on July 18, 1947.

This report on the administration of the Trust Territory of the Pacific Islands is submitted in pursuance of Article 13 of the Trusteeship Agreement which states that the provisions of Articles 87 and 88 of the Charter shall be applicable to the trust territory, provided that the Administering Authority may determine the extent of their applicability to any areas which may from time to time be specified by it as closed for security reasons.

The United States Government is aware that the Security Council is at present seized of the question of the "procedure in application of Articles 87 and 88 of the Charter with regard to the Pacific Islands under strategic trusteeship of the United States", but does not consider that it is thereby relieved of an obligation to report to the United Nations on the administration of the trust territory.

As a matter of convenience, the Provisional Questionnaire formulated by the Trusteeship Council has been utilized in the preparation of the report. The decision of the United States Government to prepare this report and to transmit it to the United Nations and the use of the Provisional Questionnaire in this connection are without prejudice to the question before the Security Council.

WARREN R. AUSTIN
Representative of the
United States of America

(b) Summary of the Report [2]

Political advancement—The Navy Department's policy with respect to self-government is stated, in part: "It is desired that the inhabitants of the island territories be granted the highest degree of self-government that they are capable of assimilating. They shall be encouraged and assisted to assume as much

[1] Department of State Bulletin of March 6, 1949, pp. 293, 294.
[2] Trust Territory of the Pacific Islands (OPNAV-P22-100E). Prepared by the Navy Department, July 1948.

as possible of the management of their own affairs and the conduct of their own government on . . .". The report details the degree to which native leaders are taking part in local governmental functions and explains the steps being taken to develop administrative, educational and professional skills.

Economic Advancement—Japanese occupation and the war years left many islands in a state of chaotic devastation. Islands untouched by hostilities found their economic life severely restricted, the report states. The chief agency of commercial life in the trust area is the Island Trading Company, a United States Government Corporation whose entire stock is held by the Deputy High Commissioner of the Trust Territory in his official capacity. All profits are held in trust for the benefit of the natives. The Island Trading Company carries on the trade of the area, buying the products of the region for sale to outer markets, and importing the goods needed for consumption in the islands.

"During the past year the economic situation in the Trust Territory has been greatly improved by various factors, and two in particular: first, an encouraging growth of interest in economic pursuits on the part of the inhabitants; second, a very advantageous market in the United States and throughout the world for copra and trochus shells," the report says.

U.S. funds appropriated for the Territory for the fiscal year ended June 30, 1948, amounted to $1,123,810, apportioned $151,178 to general administration, $88,433 to legal and public safety functions, $225,432 to public education, $76,312 to commerce, industry, and agriculture, $392,751 to medical care, public health, and sanitation, and $189,704 to public works.

The report states that the mineral resources of the region are sparse and that the only two mining operations are the phosphate and bauxite operations in the Palau area.

Social Advancement—The report describes the hamlet-like clusters of homes and farmsteads that make up the typical communities of the islands. Population is increasing, with the birth rate nearly double the death rate. A bill of rights has been promulgated, and essential freedoms preserved. Slavery does not exist, and cruel and unusual punishments are forbidden, although crime is not a major problem. A few cases of migration of natives are reported, including the evacuation of Bikini and Eniwetok atolls to make way for scientific experimentation. Labor problems in the Western sense are unknown, the report explaining that "as of January 1, 1948, subsistence farming and fishing took up most of the islanders' time; scarcely 3,000 were gainfully employed for wages in Western-style jobs." Two thirds of these were on the administration payroll, and the others were employed in "light business enterprises."

In the field of public health, the incidence of yaws was reduced during the year from practically 90 percent to an estimated 5 percent, and that of intestinal parasites was cut from 20 percent to 5 percent. Substantial reductions also were achieved in the incidence of filariasis and other endemic diseases.[1] A system of frequent inspections has helped raise standards of sanitation. Research programs in tropical medicine are in progress. There are six dispensaries on the islands each with from 50 to 75 beds, three subdispensaries with from 8 to 25 beds, and 87 subdispensaries without facilities for in-patient

---

[1] Definite steps has been taken to examine, treat, and/or isolate as necessary tuberculin patients. This disease is one of the chief concerns of the administering authority.

care. In addition, for difficult cases, the 250-bed general hospital at Guam is available, seven logistic ships serve as mobile clinics, and a medical survey ship carries complete X-ray and laboratory equipment. A leper colony has been established on Tinian.

Educational Advancement—A free public-school system has been instituted with approximately 250 teachers and more than 9,000 students in 130 elementary and intermediate schools in the period March-July 1948. Exclusive of cost-free items supplied to the school system, education in fiscal 1948 cost roughly $18 per capita. Adult and vocational education programs also have been undertaken. The Pacific Island Teacher Training School on Guam, offering two consecutive courses of six and nine months, is training native instructors for the school system.

An important change in tariff policy with relation to the Trust Territory has taken place since the end of the one-year period covered by the report. Tariff duties in effect during that period are given in detail, being simply an extension to the Trust Territory of the import arrangements applied to Guam with respect to articles "not produced, processed or manufactured in the United States, its possessions or the Trust Territory". This action was permitted under article 8 (1) of the trusteeship agreement. Subsequently, by order dated November 30, 1948, this tariff schedule was cancelled. Therefore, import duties on products entering the Trust Territory no longer exist.

◇◇◇◇◇◇

VOTING PROCEDURE IN THE SECURITY COUNCIL

182. FOUR POWER STATEMENT AT SAN FRANCISCO ON VOTING IN SECURITY COUNCIL, JUNE 7, 1945 [1]

[According to Article 27 of the United Nations Charter, decisions of the Security Council on substantive or non-procedural matters are to be taken by an affirmative vote of seven members, including the concurring votes of the five permanent members. This is the so-called principle of unanimity, better known as the veto provision because it permits any of the Great Powers, by its negative vote, to prevent substantive action by the Council. During the San Francisco Conference, the Great Powers, in response to criticisms and questions raised by the smaller states, issued a statement which explained the voting procedure provided for under Article 27 and attempted to justify it. While the statement was not approved by the Conference and therefore has no binding legal effect, it is of considerable importance in understanding the philosophy back of Article 27.]

Specific questions covering the voting procedure in the Security Council have been submitted by a Sub-Committee of the Conference Committee on Structure and Procedures of the Security Council to the Delegations of the four Governments sponsoring the Conference—the United States of America,

[1] U. S. Senate Committee on Foreign Relations, the Charter of the United Nations, hearings, 1945, pp. 213-215.

the United Kingdom of Great Britain and Northern Ireland, the Union of Soviet Socialist Republics, and the Republic of China. In dealing with these questions, the four Delegations desire to make the following statement of their general attitude towards the whole question of unanimity of permanent members in the decisions of the Security Council.

1. The Yalta voting formula recognizes that the Security Council, in discharging its responsibilities for the maintenance of international peace and security, will have two broad groups of functions. Under Chapter VIII, the Council will have to make decisions which involve its taking direct measures in connection with settlement of disputes, adjustment of situations likely to lead to disputes, determination of threats to the peace, removal of threats to the peace, and suppression of breaches of the peace. It will also have to make decisions which do not involve the taking of such measures. The Yalta formula provides that the second of these two groups of decisions will be governed by a procedural vote—that is, the vote of any seven members. The first group of decisions will be governed by a qualified vote—that is, the vote of seven members, including the concurring votes of the five permanent members, subject to the proviso that in decisions under section A and a part of section C of chapter VIII parties to a dispute shall abstain from voting.

2. For example, under the Yalta formula a procedural vote will govern the decisions made under the entire section D of chapter VI. This means that the Council will, by a vote of any seven of its members, adopt or alter its rules of procedure; determine the method of selecting its president; organize itself in such a way as to be able to function continuously; select the times and places of its regular and special meetings; establish such bodies or agencies as it may deem necessary for the performance of its functions; invite a member of the Organization not represented on the Council to participate in its discussions when that Member's interests are specially affected; and invite any state when it is a party to a dispute being considered by the Council to participate in the discussion relating to that dispute.

3. Further, no individual member of the Council can alone prevent consideration and discussion by the Council of a dispute or situation brought to its attention under paragraph 2, section A, chapter VIII. Nor can parties to such dispute be prevented by these means from being heard by the Council. Likewise, the requirement for unanimity of the permanent members cannot prevent any member of the Council from reminding the members of the Organization of their general obligations assumed under the Charter as regards peaceful settlement of international disputes.

4. Beyond this point, decisions and actions by the Security Council may well have major political consequences and may even initiate a chain of events which might, in the end, require the Council under its responsibilities to invoke measures of enforcement under section B, chapter VIII. This chain of events begins when Council decides to make an investigation, or determines that the time has come to call upon states to settle their differences, or makes recommendations to the parties. It is to such decisions and actions that unanimity of the permanent members applies, with the important proviso, referred to above, for abstention from voting by parties to a dispute.

5. To illustrate: In ordering an investigation, the Council has to consider whether the investigation—which may involve calling for reports, hearing

witnesses, dispatching a commission of inquiry, or other means—might not further aggravate the situation. After investigation, the Council must determine whether the continuance of the situation or dispute would be likely to endanger international peace and security. If it so determines, the Council would be under obligation to take further steps. Similarly, the decision to make recommendations, even when all parties request it to do so, or to call upon parties to a dispute to fulfill their obligations under the Charter, might be the first step on a course of action from which the Security Council could withdraw only at the risk of failing to discharge its responsibilities.

6. In appraising the significance of the vote required to take such decisions or actions, it is useful to make comparison with the requirements of the League Covenant with reference to decisions of the League Council. Substantive decisions of the League of Nations Council could be taken only by the unanimous vote of all its members, whether permanent or not, with the exception of parties to a dispute under article XV of the League Covenant. Under article XI, under which most of the disputes brought before the League were dealt with and decisions to make investigations taken, the unanimity rule was invariably interpreted to include even the votes of the parties to a dispute.

7. The Yalta voting formula substitutes for the rule of complete unanimity of the League Council a system of qualified majority voting in the Security Council. Under this system nonpermanent members of the Security Council individually would have no veto. As regards the permanent members, there is no question under the Yalta formula of investing them with a new right; namely, the right to veto, a right which the permanent members of the League Council always had. The formula proposed for the taking of action in the Security Council by a majority of seven would make the operation of the Council less subject to obstruction than was the case under the League of Nations rule of complete unanimity.

8. It should also be remembered that under the Yalta formula the five major powers could not act by themselves, since even under the unanimity requirement any decisions of the Council would have to include the concurring votes of at least two of the nonpermanent members. In other words, it would be possible for five nonpermanent members as a group to exercise a veto. It is not to be assumed, however, that the permanent members, any more than the nonpermanent members, would use their veto power willfully to obstruct the operation of the Council.

9. In view of the primary responsibilities of the permanent members they could not be expected, in the present condition of the world, to assume the obligation to act in so serious a matter as the maintenance of international peace and security in consequence of a decision in which they had not concurred. Therefore, if majority voting in the Security Council is to be made possible, the only practicable method is to provide, in respect of nonprocedural decisions, for unanimity of the permanent members plus the concurring votes of at least two of the nonpermanent members.

10. For all these reasons, the four sponsoring governments agreed on the Yalta formula and have presented it to this Conference as essential if an international organization is to be created through which all peace-loving nations can effectively discharge their common responsibilities for the maintenance of international peace and security.

II

In the light of the considerations set forth in part 1 of this statement, it is clear what the answers to the questions submitted by the subcommittee should be, with the exception of question 19. The answer to that question is as follows:

1. In the opinion of the delegations of the sponsoring governments, the Draft Charter itself contains an indication of the application of the voting procedures to the various functions of the Council.

2. In this case, it will be unlikely that there will arise in the future any matters of great importance on which a decision will have to be made as to whether a procedural vote would apply. Should, however, such a matter arise the decision regarding the preliminary question as to whether or not such a matter is procedural must be taken by a vote of seven members of the Security Council, including the concurring votes of the permanent members.

◇◇◇◇◇◇

183. VOTING PROCEDURE IN THE SECURITY COUNCIL

[During the first year of the UN, it became painfully apparent that the Soviet Union's excessive use of the veto was seriously impairing the functioning of the Security Council. The General Assembly debated this problem at considerable length, both in 1946 and 1947. As a result of these deliberations, two resolutions were adopted urging restraint upon the Great Powers in their use of the veto and requesting the Interim Committee of the General Assembly to study the whole problem.]

(a) Resolution of the General Assembly, December 13, 1946 [1]

THE GENERAL ASSEMBLY,

MINDFUL of the purposes and principles of the Charter of the United Nations, and having taken notice of the divergencies which have arisen in regard to the application and interpretation of Article 27 of the Charter:

EARNESTLY REQUESTS the permanent members of the Security Council to make every effort, in consultation with one another and with fellow members of the Security Council, to ensure that the use of the special voting privilege of its permanent members does not impede the Security Council in reaching decisions promptly;

RECOMMENDS to the Security Council the early adoption of practices and procedures, consistent with the Charter, to assist in reducing the difficulties in the application of Article 27 and to ensure the prompt and effective exercise by the Security Council of its functions; and

FURTHER RECOMMENDS that, in developing such practices and procedures, the Security Council take into consideration the views expressed by Members

---

[1] The United States and the United Nations: Report by the President to the Congress for the Year 1946, Department of State publication 2735, the United States and the United Nations Report Series 7, p. 98.

of the United Nations during the second part of the first session of the General Assembly.

(b) Resolution of the General Assembly, November 21, 1947 [1]

The General Assembly, in the exercise of its power to make recommendations relating to the powers and functions of any organs of the United Nations (Article 10 of the Charter):

Requests the Interim Committee of the General Assembly, in accordance with paragraph 2 (a) of the resolution of the General Assembly of 13 November 1947, establishing that Committee, to:

1. Consider the problem of voting in the Security Council, taking into account all proposals which have been or may be submitted by Members of the United Nations to the second session of the General Assembly or to the Interim Committee;

2. Consult with any committee which the Security Council may designate to co-operate with the Interim Committee in the study of the problem;

3. Report, with its conclusions, to the third session of the General Assembly, the report to be transmitted to the Secretary-General not later than 15 July 1948, and by the Secretary-General to the Member States and to the General Assembly;

Requests the permanent members of the Security Council to consult with one another on the problem of voting in the Security Council in order to secure agreement among them on measures to ensure the prompt and effective exercise by the Security Council of its functions.

◇◇◇◇◇◇

184. UNITED STATES PROPOSALS ON THE VETO QUESTION, MARCH 10, 1948 [2]

[On March 10, 1948, the U.S. submitted to the Interim Committee a list of thirty-one types of Security Council decisions which our government believed should not be subject to the veto. Included in the thirty-one categories are a number of items, such as decisions relating to the time and place of Security Council meetings, which are purely procedural and which have never required the unanimous vote of the permanent members. Other types of decisions, such as those relating to the peaceful settlement of disputes and the admission of new members, have been subject to the veto. The list is substantially that approved by the General Assembly in 1949.]

I. STUDY OF CATEGORIES OF SECURITY COUNCIL DECISIONS

A. The Interim Committee should study the categories of decisions which the Security Council is required to make in carrying out the functions entrusted to it under the Charter and the Statute of the International Court of

[1] The United States and the United Nations: Report by the President to the Congress for the year 1947, Dept. of State Publication 3024.
[2] U. N. Document A/AC.18/41, Mar. 10, 1948.

Justice, and should report to the General Assembly those categories of decisions which in its judgment, in order to ensure the effective exercise by the Security Council of its responsibilities under the Charter, should be made by an affirmative vote of seven members of the Security Council, whether or not such categories are regarded as procedural or non-procedural. (A provisional proposed list of such categories is attached.)

B. The Interim Committee should recommend to the General Assembly:

1. That the General Assembly accept the conclusions of the Interim Committee's report, and

2. That the General Assembly as a first step, recommend to the permanent members of the Security Council that they mutually agree that such voting procedures be followed and that steps be taken to make their agreement effective.

II. Consultations Among Permanent Members

The Interim Committee should recommend to the General Assembly that, in order to improve the functioning of the Security Council, the General Assembly recommend to the permanent members of the Security Council that wherever feasible consultations should take place among them concerning important decisions to be taken by the Security Council.

PROVISIONAL LIST OF CATEGORIES OF SECURITY COUNCIL DECISIONS WHICH THE UNITED STATES PROPOSES SHOULD BE MADE BY AN AFFIRMATIVE VOTE OF SEVEN MEMBERS, WHETHER OR NOT SUCH CATEGORIES ARE REGARDED AS PROCEDURAL OR NON-PROCEDURAL

1. Decisions with respect to admission of States to membership in the United Nations, pursuant to Article 4, paragraph 2.

2. Decisions to bring a question relating to the maintenance of international peace and security before the General Assembly pursuant to Article 11, paragraph 2.

3. Decisions to request the recommendation of the General Assembly concerning a matter relating to the maintenance of international peace and security being dealt with by the Security Council, pursuant to Article 12, paragraph 1.

4. Decisions to cease dealing with a matter relating to the maintenance of international peace and security pursuant to Article 12, paragraph 2.

5. Decisions with respect to the consent of the Security Council to the notifications made by the Secretary-General under Article 12, paragraph 2.

6. Decisions with respect to the request directed by the Security Council to the Secretary-General that he convoke a special session of the General Assembly under Article 20.

7. Submission of annual and special reports from the Security Council to the General Assembly pursuant to Article 24, paragraph 3.

8. Decisions of the Security Council as to whether a matter is procedural within the meaning of Article 27, paragraph 2.

9. Determination of the parties to a dispute and the existence of a dispute

for the purpose of deciding whether a member of the Security Council shall be required to abstain from voting, pursuant to Article 27, paragraph 3.

10. Decisions concerning the manner of the organization of the Security Council pursuant to Article 28, paragraph 1.

11. Decisions concerning the time and place of its regular and periodic meetings pursuant to Article 28, paragraph 2 and Article 28, paragraph 3.

12. Establishment of subsidiary organs pursuant to Article 29.

13. The election of a President pursuant to Article 30.

14. Adoption of rules of procedure pursuant to Article 30.

15. Decisions to permit the participation of members of the United Nations in the discussion of any question where the Council considers that the interests of the member are specially affected pursuant to Article 31.

16. Decisions to invite a Member State which is not a member of the Security Council or a State not a member of the United Nations which is a party to a dispute under consideration by the Council to participate without vote in the discussion relating to the dispute pursuant to Article 32.

17. Decisions with respect to conditions for the participation of a State which is not a member of the United Nations in the Security Council discussions in accordance with Article 32.

18. Decisions to consider and discuss a matter brought to the attention of the Council.

19. Decisions to call upon the parties to a dispute to settle their dispute by peaceful means of their own choice pursuant to Article 33, paragraph 2.

20. Decisions to investigate a dispute or a situation which might lead to international friction or give rise to a dispute, pursuant to Article 34.

21. Decisions to recommend appropriate procedures or methods of adjustment of a dispute or situation endangering the maintenance of international peace and security, pursuant to Article 36, paragraph 1.

22. Decisions of the Security Council pursuant to Article 36, paragraph 3, to recommend to the parties to a legal dispute that the dispute should be referred by the parties to the International Court of Justice in accordance with provisions of the Statute of the Court.

23. Decisions to make recommendations at the request of all parties to a dispute with a view to its pacific settlement, pursuant to Article 38.

24. Decisions to request assistance from the Economic and Social Council pursuant to Article 65.

25. Reference of a legal question to the International Court of Justice for an advisory opinion pursuant to Article 96, paragraph 1.

26. Decision to convoke a conference to review the Charter prior to the tenth annual session of the General Assembly pursuant to Article 109, paragraph 1.

27. Decision to convoke a conference to review the Charter subsequent to the tenth annual session of the General Assembly pursuant to Article 109, paragraph 3.

28. Election of judges of the International Court of Justice pursuant to

Article 4, paragraph 1, Article 10, paragraph 1, of the Statute of the Court. (Article 10, paragraph 2, of the Statute).

29. Decisions of the Security Council determining the conditions under which a State which is a party to the present Statute of the International Court of Justice, but which is not a member of the United Nations, may participate in electing the members of the Court pursuant to Article 4, paragraph 3, of the Statute of the Court.

30. Appointment of conferees in connection with election of judges of the International Court of Justice pursuant to Article 12 of the Statute of the Court. (Article 10, paragraph 2, of the Statute).[1]

31. Determination of the date of election of judges of the International Court of Justice pursuant to Article 14 of the Statute of the Court.

185. U.S. POSITION ON VOTING IN THE SECURITY COUNCIL

Statement by Warren R. Austin, United States Representative to the United Nations, April 13, 1949 [2]

[The results of the Interim Committee's study of the veto problem came before the General Assembly in the form of a resolution sponsored by the U.S., U.K., China, and France. In his speech urging the passage of the resolution, Ambassador Warren Austin explained how the voting provisions could be made to work satisfactorily without destroying the basic principle of unanimity.]

The General Assembly has before it at this time a resolution relating to the voting procedures of the Security Council approved by the *Ad Hoc* Political Committee on December 10, 1948, in Paris.[3]

* * *

The results of the study are now before us. Even a superficial perusal of the resolution of the *Ad Hoc* Committee must disclose that it is not designed to alter fundamentally the unanimity principle as it is embodied in the Charter. A very great majority of the members of the United Nations have expressed the view either explicitly or implicitly that the unanimity principle is and should remain a fundamental principle of the Charter. A majority of the members of the United Nations are opposed to any effort being made at this time to amend the Charter.

On the other hand, there is a large majority of the members of the United Nations who are making an anxious effort to design ways and means of giving life to the unanimity principle and making it work so that the Security Council can carry out its function effectively. The working of this principle requires an effort on the part of all members of the United Nations and particularly

---

[1] These decisions are made by "an absolute majority of votes in the General Assembly and in the Security Council."

[2] Department of State Bulletin, April 24, 1949, pp. 512-515.

[3] Department of State Bulletin, January 23, 1949, p. 99.

the permanent members of the Security Council to reconcile their divergent views on the basis of tolerance and mutual understanding.

The resolution before us sets us on the path toward this objective. It represents a policy of gradual liberalization of the voting procedures of the Security Council through processes of interpretation and application of the principles of the Charter and through agreement of the members of the Security Council. We rely on processes of discussion, definition, regulation, and practice to move us forward toward our objective and not upon revolutionary change. We recommend restraint and self-discipline to member nations in accordance with the letter and spirit of the Charter as an appropriate means of giving life to the unanimity principle and keeping it within proper bounds.

In our view the proposals now before us are most moderate. They are designed to be within the limits of what is practicable under prevailing world conditions. We firmly believe that if the members of the United Nations would cooperate in carrying out the program presented in these proposals we would quickly see substantial improvement in the effectiveness of the Security Council's operations. You will recall that efforts by the Assembly along similar lines in 1946 have resulted in a substantial improvement. I refer to the suggestions made by several members of the Assembly during the debates that abstention of a permanent member of the Security Council should not be considered a veto. That practice was adopted by common consent in the Security Council and has now become a well-accepted Security Council procedure. I believe all of you will agree that the adoption of this practice has substantially added to the effectiveness of the Security Council. A number of important decisions of the Council during the past two years has been approved with one or more of the permanent members abstaining. At least one Security Council decision under chapter VII and one decision recommending a state for membership has been approved with a permanent member abstaining.

Let us now look at this resolution in more detail. The work of the Interim Committee [1] on which the resolution is based revealed the great potentialities which can be progressively realized under the present Charter if there can be general agreement upon a moderate course. By adoption of this resolution, the Assembly would make an important decision to the effect that 34 specified and described decisions of the Security Council are procedural. This effect would principally arise out of the first paragraph—"Recommends to the members of the Security Council that, without prejudice to other decisions which the Security Council may deem procedural, the decisions set forth in the attached Annex be deemed procedural and that the members of the Security Council conduct their business accordingly:"

The principal criteria for placing these 34 items in the category of decisions deemed procedural were—

(a) Decisions under procedure provisions of the Charter;
(b) Decisions relating to the internal procedure of the United Nations;
(c) Decisions relating to internal functioning of the Security Council;
(d) Decisions analogous to the foregoing;
(e) Decisions which implement procedural decisions.

[1] Documents and State Papers, August 1948, p. 340.

In short, the Interim Committee, after a thorough study, concluded that these decisions are procedural in the light of the express language of the Charter, and of sound Charter interpretation.

This first paragraph is concerned with the reversal of a tendency toward an unwarranted extension of the veto to areas where its application was never contemplated by the Charter. Its purpose is, also, to eliminate undisciplined use of the veto contrary to the assumptions and understanding under which the privileged vote was accorded to the permanent members. This first paragraph is simply an interpretation of the Charter according to its letter and spirit. It amounts to saying to the Security Council: "The proper interpretation of the Charter forbids stultification of the Security Council in the cases described." In a word, the effect of this paragraph of the resolution is to keep certain enumerated types of decision in the category of procedural. Its main objective, of course, is to give life to the purposes and principles of the United Nations in accordance with which the Security Council must act in the discharge of its duties.

*   *   *

This first paragraph does not abridge the unanimity rule of voting. On the contrary, it gives it life—vitality. As I have said, it would make the Security Council efficient with respect to matters in which it is sometimes now stultified. It is proposed at this time because the three years of practice in the Security Council has developed an unforeseen and willful use of the veto based on minority interpretation, contrary to majority decision.

Now I shall advance to paragraph 2 of the resolution. It contains a recommendation to the permanent members of the Security Council that they seek agreement among themselves upon what possible decisions of the Security Council they might forbear to exercise their veto when seven affirmative votes are cast in the Council in support of such decisions. In seeking agreement, the permanent members are to give favorable consideration to the list of decisions compiled by the Interim Committee. The theory upon which the Interim Committee prepared this list was that if the permanent members could agree to refrain from using their veto with reference to such decisions, the Security Council would be able to perform its responsibilities more promptly and effectively. The types of decision dealt with here thus differ from those contained in the first recommendation because some of them are unquestionably of substance while as to others there may be differing views upon whether they are substantive or procedural. Indeed, the Interim Committee has indicated clearly that the insertion of decisions in this list was not governed by the criterion of their procedural or nonprocedural character. The most important decisions contained in this list are not procedural, such as, for example, the decision on the admission of a new member and certain pacific settlement matters under chapter VI of the Charter. In this connection, I would recall that the United States is on record as favoring a liberalization of the voting procedure of the Security Council through elimination by whatever means that may be appropriate of the unanimity requirement with respect to applications for membership and to matters arising under chapter VI of the Charter.

Neither the first nor the second recommendation in the resolution before us violates the spirit of the statement of the four sponsoring powers at San Francisco. During the debate there upon the voting formula, a questionnaire was addressed to the sponsoring powers by the smaller powers. The sponsoring powers thereupon undertook to make a joint interpretation of the voting formula, insofar as such an interpretation of a basic constitutional provision could appropriately be made in advance of its adoption, and in the absence of any practical experience as to the operation of the Organization or of the Security Council. This statement is not a treaty, nor was it intended to be any part of the treaty which is the Charter. By its own words it is characterized as a "statement of their general attitude toward the whole question of unanimity of permanent members in the decisions of the Security Council." It was connected with the act of agreement upon the Charter and is therefore entitled to great weight in that connection. It is nevertheless inferior to the Charter and must be subservient to its principles and purposes. Certainly its natural meaning should not be extended by willful obstruction.

The four-power statement contained an expression of hope that there would not arise matters of great importance upon which a decision would have to be made as to whether a procedural vote would apply. Experience since San Francisco has shown that this optimistic expectation has not been realized, and the first recommendation is based on a recognition of this fact. This recommendation should be of assistance to the Security Council in determining whether or not a question is procedural. The four-power statement made it clear that the enumeration of procedural questions which it contained was not exclusive. Furthermore, it in no way foreclosed advance agreement as to what questions should be considered procedural. It did not say that a question should be considered nonprocedural simply because one of the permanent members so regards it. The four-power statement cannot enjoy a position of supremacy over the Charter.

The four-power statement contained another explicit assumption, which has proved contrary to fact; that the permanent members would not use their privileged vote "willfully to obstruct the operation of the Council." The powers participating in the statement thus recognized that self-restraint upon the part of the permanent members was necessary and to be expected if the Security Council was to function as intended. If this be true it would seem quite proper for the Assembly in light of experience to recommend to the permanent members that if they are unable, after genuine effort, to achieve unanimity among themselves on certain decisions not immediately concerning their vital interests they should agree among themselves not to exercise the veto in those decisions. Such agreement among the permanent members is the objective of the second recommendation.

For the reasons I have stated, the four-power statement in the view of my Government constitutes no barrier to such agreement. The parties to that statement are free to explore, as this resolution attempts to do, how better voting procedures can be put into operation.

The third recommendation of the draft resolution suggests to the permanent members a "code of conduct" which they should observe in connection with their privileged vote. They are to consult together whatever feasible and to exercise their veto only when they consider a question of vital importance, taking into account the interests of the United Nations as a whole, and to state upon what ground they consider this condition to be present.

All permanent members are on record as favoring consultations. We believe that these consultations should take place whenever there is a possibility of obtaining constructive results. These consultations should take place not only with reference to specific matters before the Council; above all, the method of consultation should be applied as one of the means of implementing the recommendations contained in the draft resolution.

This resolution was sponsored by four permanent members and aroused the support of an impressive number of member states. The vote in the *Ad Hoc* Committee of the General Assembly was yeas 33, nays 6, abstentions 4.

It ought to gain strength in the vote of the General Assembly. Its purpose and natural tendency is to make the United Nations more effective in its vital functions.

◇◇◇◇◇◇

186. ASSEMBLY PROPOSAL ON VOTING IN THE SECURITY COUNCIL [1]

Resolution of the General Assembly, April 14, 1949

[On April 14, 1949, the General Assembly approved the report of the Interim Committee by an overwhelming vote. The Assembly resolution emphasized two main ways of meeting the veto problem: (1) by increasing the categories of votes to which the veto does not apply; and (2) by encouraging consultation among the Great Powers. It is to be noted that the resolution is in the form of a *recommendation* to the members of the Security Council, and has no binding effect unless it is accepted by them. To date, there has been no indication that the Soviet Union would agree.]

The General Assembly,

Having considered the report of its Interim Committee on the problem of voting in the Security Council, and

Exercising the authority conferred upon it by Article 10 of the Charter to discuss any question within the scope of the Charter or relating to the functions of any organ of the United Nations and to make recommendations to the Members of the United Nations and to the Security Council thereon,

1. *Recommends* to the members of the Security Council that, without prejudice to any other decisions which the Security Council may deem procedural, the decisions set forth in the attached annex be deemed procedural and that the members of the Security Council conduct their business accordingly;

2. *Recommends* to the permanent members of the Security Council that they seek agreement among themselves upon what possible decisions by the Security Council they might forbear to exercise their veto, when seven affirmative votes have already been cast in the Council, giving favourable considera-

[1] Official Records of the Third Session of the General Assembly, Part II, 5 April-18 May 1949, p. 7.

tion to the list of such decisions contained in conclusion 2 of part IV of the report of the Interim Committee;

3. *Recommends* to the permanent members of the Security Council, in order to avoid impairment of the usefulness and prestige of the Council through excessive use of the veto:

(*a*) To consult together wherever feasible upon important decisions to be taken by the Security Council;

(*b*) To consult together wherever feasible before a vote is taken if their unanimity is essential to effective action by the Security Council;

(*c*) If there is not unanimity, to exercise the veto only when they consider the question of vital importance, taking into account the interest of the United Nations as a whole, and to state upon what ground they consider this condition to be present;

4. *Recommends* to the Members of the United Nations that in agreements conferring functions on the Security Council such conditions of voting within that body be provided as would to the greatest extent feasible exclude the application of the rule of unanimity of the permanent members.

Hundred and ninety-fifth plenary meeting, 14 April 1949.

INTERNATIONAL CONTROL OF ATOMIC ENERGY

187. THREE POWER PROPOSAL FOR CONTROL OF ATOMIC ENERGY

Joint Declaration by the President of the United States, the Prime Minister of the United Kingdom, and the Prime Minister of Canada, November 15, 1945 [1]

[The bombing of Hiroshima and Nagasaki during the closing months of World War II confronted us all with a terrible challenge. If the nations could coöperate to prevent the use of atomic energy for destructive purposes and promote its use for peaceful ends, man might enter an era of peace and prosperity hitherto unknown. If not, civilization might well suffer an overwhelming disaster in a third world war far more terrible than the last had been.

The challenge was worth a serious effort. On November 15, 1945, shortly after the close of World War II, representatives of the three countries possessing the knowledge essential to the use of atomic energy, agreed to coöperate in the establishment of a United Nations commission to deal with the matter. The scope of the problem, together with the terms of reference of the proposed commission, are outlined below in the communiqué issued by the President of the United States and the Prime Ministers of Canada and the United Kingdom at the conclusion of their meeting.]

1. We recognize that the application of recent scientific discoveries to the methods and practice of war has placed at the disposal of mankind means of

[1] Department of State Publication 2520, Treaties and Other International Acts Series 1504.

destruction hitherto unknown, against which there can be no adequate military defence, and in the employment of which no single nation can in fact have a monopoly.

2. We desire to emphasize that the responsibility for devising means to ensure that the new discoveries shall be used for the benefit of mankind, instead of as a means of destruction, rests not on our nations alone, but upon the whole civilized world. Nevertheless, the progress that we have made in the development and use of atomic energy demands that we take an initiative in the matter, and we have accordingly met together to consider the possibility of international action:—

    (a) To prevent the use of atomic energy for destructive purposes

    (b) To promote the use of recent and future advances in scientific knowledge, particularly in the utilization of atomic energy, for peaceful and humanitarian ends.

3. We are aware that the only complete protection for the civilized world from the destructive use of scientific knowledge lies in the prevention of war. No system of safeguards that can be devised will of itself provide an effective guarantee against production of atomic weapons by a nation bent on aggression. Nor can we ignore the possibility of the development of other weapons, or of new methods of warfare, which may constitute as great a threat to civilization as the military use of atomic energy.

4. Representing as we do, the three countries which possess the knowledge essential to the use of atomic energy, we declare at the outset our willingness, as a first contribution, to proceed with the exchange of fundamental scientific information and the interchange of scientists and scientific literature for peaceful ends with any nation that will fully reciprocate.

5. We believe that the fruits of scientific research should be made available to all nations, and that freedom of investigation and free interchange of ideas are essential to the progress of knowledge. In pursuance of this policy, the basic scientific information essential to the development of atomic energy for peaceful purposes has already been made available to the world. It is our intention that all further information of this character that may become available from time to time shall be similarly treated. We trust that other nations will adopt the same policy, thereby creating an atmosphere of reciprocal confidence in which political agreement and cooperation will flourish.

6. We have considered the question of the disclosure of detailed information concerning the practical industrial application of atomic energy. The military exploitation of atomic energy depends, in large part, upon the same methods and processes as would be required for industrial uses.

We are not convinced that the spreading of the specialized information regarding the practical application of atomic energy, before it is possible to devise effective, reciprocal, and enforceable safeguards acceptable to all nations, would contribute to a constructive solution of the problem of the atomic bomb. On the contrary we think it might have the opposite effect. We are, however, prepared to share, on a reciprocal basis with others of the United Nations, detailed information concerning the practical industrial application of atomic energy just as soon as effective enforceable safeguards against its use for destructive purposes can be devised.

7. In order to attain the most effective means of entirely eliminating the use of atomic energy for destructive purposes and promoting its widest use for industrial and humanitarian purposes, we are of the opinion that at the earliest practicable date a Commission should be set up under the United Nations Organization to prepare recommendations for submission to the Organization.

The Commission should be instructed to proceed with the utmost dispatch and should be authorized to submit recommendations from time to time dealing with separate phases of its work.

In particular the Commission should make specific proposals:

(a) For extending between all nations the exchange of basic scientific information for peaceful ends,

(b) For control of atomic energy to the extent necessary to ensure its use only for peaceful purposes,

(c) For the elimination from national armaments of atomic weapons and of all other major weapons adaptable to mass destruction,

(d) For effective safeguards by way of inspection and other means to protect complying states against the hazards of violations and evasions.

8. The work of the Commission should proceed by separate stages, the successful completion of each one of which will develop the necessary confidence of the world before the next stage is undertaken. Specifically it is considered that the Commission might well devote its attention first to the wide exchange of scientists and scientific information, and as a second stage to the development of full knowledge concerning natural resources of raw materials.

9. Faced with the terrible realities of the application of science to destruction, every nation will realize more urgently than before the overwhelming need to maintain the rule of law among nations and to banish the scourge of war from the earth. This can only be brought about by giving wholehearted support to the United Nations Organization, and by consolidating and extending its authority, thus creating conditions of mutual trust in which all peoples will be free to devote themselves to the arts of peace. It is our firm resolve to work without reservation to achieve these ends.

The City of Washington
THE WHITE HOUSE
November 15, 1945

HARRY S. TRUMAN
President of the United States
C. R. ATTLEE
Prime Minister of the United Kingdom
W. L. MACKENZIE KING
Prime Minister of Canada

◊◊◊◊◊◊

188. ESTABLISHMENT OF A COMMISSION ON ATOMIC ENERGY

Resolution of the General Assembly, January 24, 1946 [1]

[The proposal of the United States, the United Kingdom and Canada to establish an atomic energy commission was almost immediately approved by the UN. In a display of unanimity almost unheard of since, the General Assembly at its first session, held in London in 1946, agreed to set up the new organ by a vote of 52 to 0. Two points might be noted in connection with the Assembly's resolution: (1) the commission was to be accountable for its work to the Security Council; and (2) the terms of reference of the commission as approved by the Assembly were precisely those suggested by the three powers in their communiqué of November 15, 1945, including the reference to other major weapons adaptable to mass destruction.]

Resolved by the General Assembly of the United Nations to establish a commission, with the composition and competence set out hereunder, to deal with the problems raised by the discovery of atomic energy and other related matters:—

1. *Establishment of the Commission*

A Commission is hereby established by the General Assembly with the terms of reference set out under Section V below.

2. *Relations of the Commission with the Organs of the United Nations*

(*a*) The Commission shall submit its reports and recommendations to the Security Council, and such reports and recommendations shall be made public unless the Security Council, in the interest of peace and security, otherwise directs. In the appropriate cases the Security Council should transmit these Reports to the General Assembly and the members of the United Nations, as well as to the Economic and Social Council and other organs within the framework of the United Nations.

(*b*) In view of the Security Council's primary responsibility under the Charter of the United Nations for the maintenance of international peace and security, the Security Council shall issue directions to the Commission in matters affecting security. On these matters the Commission shall be accountable for its work to the Security Council.

3. *Composition of the Commission*

The Commission shall be composed of one representative from each of those States, represented on the Security Council, and Canada when that State is not a member of the Security Council. Each representative on the Commission may have such assistance as he may desire.

[1] The United States and the United Nations: Report of the United States Delegation to the First Part of the First Session of the General Assembly of the United Nations, London, England, January 10-February 14, 1946, Department of State publication 2484, United States-United Nations Report Series 1, pp. 33-34.

4. *Rules of Procedure*

The Commission shall have whatever staff it may deem necessary, and shall make recommendations for its rules of procedure to the Security Council, which shall approve them as a procedural matter.

5. *Terms of Reference of the Commission*

The Commission shall proceed with the utmost despatch and enquire into all phases of the problem, and make such recommendations from time to time with respect to them as it finds possible. In particular the Commission shall make specific proposals:

(*a*) For extending between all nations the exchange of basic scientific information for peaceful ends;

(*b*) For control of atomic energy to the extent necessary to ensure its use only for peaceful purposes;

(*c*) For the elimination from national armaments of atomic weapons and of all other major weapons adaptable to mass destruction;

(*d*) For effective safeguards by way of inspection and other means to protect complying States against the hazards of violations and evasions.

The work of the Commission should proceed by separate stages, the successful completion of each of which will develop the necessary confidence of the world before the next stage is undertaken.

The Commission shall not infringe upon the responsibilities of any organ of the United Nations, but should present recommendations for the consideration of those organs in the performance of their tasks under the terms of the United Nations Charter.

◇◇◇◇◇◇

189. UNITED STATES PROPOSALS FOR CONTROL OF ATOMIC ENERGY

Statement by Bernard M. Baruch, United States Representative to the Atomic Energy Commission, June 14, 1946 [1]

[Some five months after the establishment of the Atomic Energy Commission, Bernard M. Baruch set forth the basic elements of the United States plan for the international control of atomic energy. Among other things, he proposed the creation of an International Atomic Development Authority with extensive powers over all phases of the development and use of atomic energy. The ideas he presented then, in the main still reflect the American point of view.]

*   *   *

The United States proposes the creation of an International Atomic Development Authority, to which should be entrusted all phases of the development and use of atomic energy, starting with the raw material and including—

---

[1] The International Control of Atomic Energy: Growth of a Policy, Department of State publication 2702, pp. 138-147. This publication contains a summary record of the official declarations and proposals relating to the International control of atomic energy made between August 6, 1945 and October 15, 1946.

1. Managerial control or ownership of all atomic-energy activities potentially dangerous to world security.
2. Power to control, inspect, and license all other atomic activities.
3. The duty of fostering the beneficial uses of atomic energy.
4. Research and development responsibilities of an affirmative character
intended to put the Authority in the forefront of atomic knowledge
and thus to enable it to comprehend, and therefore to detect, misuse of atomic energy. To be effective, the Authority must itself be
the world's leader in the field of atomic knowledge and development and thus supplement its legal authority with the great power
inherent in possession of leadership in knowledge.

I offer this as a basis for beginning our discussion.

But I think the peoples we serve would not believe—and without faith
nothing counts—that a treaty, merely outlawing possession or use of the
atomic bomb, constitutes effective fulfilment of the instructions to this Commission. Previous failures have been recorded in trying the method of simple
renunciation, unsupported by effective guaranties of security and armament
limitation. No one would have faith in that approach alone.

*   *   *

When an adequate system for control of atomic energy, including the
renunciation of the bomb as a weapon, has been agreed upon and put into
effective operation and condign punishments set up for violations of the rules
of control which are to be stigmatized as international crimes, we propose
that—

1. Manufacture of atomic bombs shall stop;
2. Existing bombs shall be disposed of pursuant to the terms of the
treaty, and
3. The Authority shall be in possession of full information as to the
know-how for the production of atomic energy.

Let me repeat, so as to avoid misunderstanding: my country is ready to
make its full contribution toward the end we seek, subject, of course, to our
constitutional processes, and to an adequate system of control becoming fully
effective, as we finally work it out.

Now as to violations: in the agreement, penalties of as serious a nature as
the nations may wish and as immediate and certain in their execution as
possible, should be fixed for:

1. Illegal possession or use of an atomic bomb;
2. Illegal possession, or separation, of atomic material suitable for use
in an atomic bomb;
3. Seizure of any plant or other property belonging to or licensed by
the Authority;
4. Wilful interference with the activities of the Authority;
5. Creation or operation of dangerous projects in a manner contrary to,
or in the absence of, a license granted by the international control
body.

It would be a deception, to which I am unwilling to lend myself, were I
not to say to you and to our peoples, that the matter of punishment lies at
the very heart of our present security system. It might as well be admitted,

here and now, that the subject goes straight to the veto power contained in the Charter of the United Nations so far as it relates to the field of atomic energy. The Charter permits penalization only by concurrence of each of the five great powers—Union of Soviet Socialist Republics, the United Kingdom, China, France and the United States.

I want to make very plain that I am concerned here with the veto power only as it affects this particular problem. There must be no veto to protect those who violate their solemn agreements not to develop or use atomic energy for destructive purposes.

*   *   *

But before a country is ready to relinquish any winning weapons it must have more than words to reassure it. It must have a guarantee of safety, not only against the offenders in the atomic area but against the illegal users of other weapons—bacteriological, biological, gas—perhaps—why not?—against war itself.

*   *   *

I now submit the following measures as representing the fundamental features of a plan which would give effect to certain of the conclusions which I have epitomized.

1. *General.* The Authority should set up a thorough plan for control of the field of atomic energy, through various forms of ownership, dominion, licenses, operation, inspection, research and management by competent personnel. After this is provided for, there should be as little interference as may be with the economic plans and the present private, corporate and state relationships in the several countries involved.

2. *Raw Materials.* The Authority should have as one of its earliest purposes to obtain and maintain complete and accurate information on world supplies of uranium and thorium and to bring them under its dominion. The precise pattern of control for various types of deposits of such materials will have to depend upon the geological, mining, refining, and economic facts involved in different situations.

The Authority should conduct continuous surveys so that it will have the most complete knowledge of the world geology of uranium and thorium. Only after all current information on world sources of uranium and thorium is known to us all can equitable plans be made for their production, refining, and distribution.

3. *Primary Production Plants.* The Authority should exercise complete managerial control of the production of fissionable materials. This means that it should control and operate all plants producing fissionable materials in dangerous quantities and must own and control the product of these plants.

4. *Atomic Explosives.* The Authority should be given sole and exclusive right to conduct research in the field of atomic explosives. Research activities in the field of atomic explosives are essential in order that the Authority may keep in the forefront of knowledge in the field of atomic energy and fulfil the objective of preventing illicit manufacture of bombs. Only by maintaining its position as the best-informed agency will the Authority be able to determine the line between intrinsically dangerous and non-dangerous activities.

5. *Strategic Distribution of Activities and Materials.* The activities entrusted exclusively to the Authority because they are intrinsically dangerous to security should be distributed throughout the world. Similarly, stockpiles of raw materials and fissionable materials should not be centralized.

6. *Non-Dangerous Activities.* A function of the Authority should be promotion of the peacetime benefits of atomic energy.

Atomic research (except in explosives), the use of research reactors, the production of radioactive tracers by means of non-dangerous reactors, the use of such tracers, and to some extent the production of power should be open to nations and their citizens under reasonable licensing arrangements from the Authority. Denatured materials, whose use we know also requires suitable safeguards, should be furnished for such purposes by the Authority under lease or other arrangement. Denaturing seems to have been overestimated by the public as a safety measure.

7. *Definition of Dangerous and Non-Dangerous Activities.* Although a reasonable dividing line can be drawn between dangerous and non-dangerous activities, it is not hard and fast. Provision should, therefore, be made to assure constant reexamination of the questions and to permit revision of the dividing line as changing conditions and new discoveries may require.

8. *Operations of Dangerous Activities.* Any plant dealing with uranium or thorium after it once reaches the potential of dangerous use must be not only subject to the most rigorous and competent inspection by the Authority, but its actual operation shall be under the management, supervision, and control of the Authority.

9. *Inspection.* By assigning intrinsically dangerous activities exclusively to the Authority, the difficulties of inspection are reduced. If the Authority is the only agency which may lawfully conduct dangerous activities, then visible operation by others than the Authority will constitute an unambiguous danger signal. Inspection will also occur in connection with the licensing functions of the Authority.

10. *Freedom of Access.* Adequate ingress and egress for all qualified representatives of the Authority must be assured. Many of the inspection activities of the Authority should grow out of, and be incidental to, its other functions. Important measures of inspection will be associated with the tight control of raw materials, for this is a keystone of the plan. The continuing activities of prospecting, survey, and research in relation to raw materials will be designed not only to serve the affirmative development functions of the Authority, but also to assure that no surreptitious operations are conducted in the raw materials field by nations or their citizens.

11. *Personnel.* The personnel of the Authority should be recruited on a basis of proven competence but also so far as possible on an international basis.

12. *Progress by Stages.* A primary step in the creation of the system of control is the setting forth, in comprehensive terms, of the functions, responsibilities, powers and limitations of the Authority. Once a Charter for the Authority has been adopted, the Authority and the system of control for which it will be responsible will require time to become fully organized and effective. The plan of control will, therefore, have to come into effect in successive stages. These should be specifically fixed in the Charter or means should be

otherwise set forth in the Charter for transitions from one stage to another, as contemplated in the resolution of the United Nations Assembly which created this Commission.

13. *Disclosures.* In the deliberations of the United Nations Commission on Atomic Energy, the United States is prepared to make available the information essential to a reasonable understanding of the proposals which it advocates. Further disclosures must be dependent, in the interests of all, upon the effective ratification of the treaty. When the Authority is actually created, the United States will join the other nations in making available the further information essential to that organization for the performance of its functions. As the successive stages of international control are reached, the United States will be prepared to yield, to the extent required by each stage, national control of activities in this field to the Authority.

14. *International Control.* There will be questions about the extent of control to be allowed to national bodies, when the Authority is established. Purely national authorities for control and development of atomic energy should to the extent necessary for the effective operation of the Authority be subordinate to it. This is neither an endorsement nor a disapproval of the creation of national authorities. The Commission should evolve a clear demarcation of the scope of duties and responsibilities of such national authorities.

* * *

◇◇◇◇◇◇

190. U. S. S. R. PROPOSALS FOR CONTROL

Statement by Andrei A. Gromyko, U. S. S. R. Representative to the Atomic Energy Commission, June 19, 1946 [1]

[On June 19, 1946, when the Soviet Union presented its proposal for the control of atomic energy, it became obvious that there were several sharp differences between the Russian and American plans. Mr. Gromyko called first for the conclusion of a convention outlawing the production and use of atomic weapons and the destruction of existing stockpiles of atomic bombs. He also proposed the creation of two commissions, one on the exchange of scientific information, and the other on the prevention of the use of atomic energy to the detriment of mankind. But he made no reference to anything like the International Development Authority Mr. Baruch had proposed.]

MR. GROMYKO (Soviet Union (*translated from Russian*):

As one of the primary measures for the fulfilment of the resolution of the General Assembly of 24 January 1946, the Soviet delegation proposes that consideration be given to the question of concluding an international convention prohibiting the production and employment of weapons based on the use of atomic energy for the purpose of mass destruction. The object of such a convention should be the prohibition of the production and employment

[1] The International Control of Atomic Energy: Growth of a Policy, Department of State publication 2702, pp. 209-216.

of atomic weapons, the destruction of existing stocks of atomic weapons and the condemnation of all activities undertaken in violation of this convention. The elaboration and conclusion of a convention of this kind would be, in the opinion of the Soviet delegation, only one of the primary measures to be taken to prevent the use of atomic energy to the detriment of mankind. This act should be followed by other measures aiming at the establishment of methods to ensure the strict observance of the terms and obligations contained in the above-mentioned convention, the establishment of a system of control over the observance of the convention and the taking of decisions regarding the sanctions to be applied against the unlawful use of atomic energy. The public opinion of the whole civilized world has already rightly condemned the use in warfare of asphyxiating, poisonous and other similar gases, as well as all similar liquids and substances, and likewise bacteriological means, by concluding corresponding agreements for the prohibition of their use.

In view of this, the necessity of concluding a convention prohibiting the production and employment of atomic weapons is even more obvious. Such a convention would correspond in an even greater degree to the aspirations of the peoples of the whole world.

The conclusion of such a convention and the elaboration of a system of measures providing for the strict fulfilment of its terms, the establishment of control over the observance of the obligations imposed by the convention, and the establishment of sanctions to be applied against violators of the convention will, in the opinion of the Soviet delegation, be a serious step forward on the way towards the fulfilment of the tasks that lie before the Atomic Energy Commission, and fully corresponds to the aspirations and conscience of the whole of progressive humanity.

The necessity for the States to assume the obligation not to produce or employ atomic weapons is also dictated by the fact that the character of this weapon is such that its employment brings untold misery above all to the peaceful population. The results of its employment are incompatible with the generally accepted standards and ideas riveted in the consciousness of humanity in the course of many centuries to the effect that the rules of warfare must not allow the extermination of innocent civilian populations.

The situation existing at the present time, which has been brought about by the discovery of the means of applying atomic energy and using them for the production of atomic weapons, precludes the possibility of normal scientific co-operation between the States of the world. At the very basis of the present situation, which is characterized by the absence of any limitation in regard to the production and employment of atomic weapons, there are reasons which can only increase the suspicion of some countries in regard to others and give rise to political instability. It is clear that the continuation of such a situation is likely to bring only negative results in regard to peace.

Moreover, the continuation of the present situation means that the latest scientific attainments in this field will not be a basis for joint scientific efforts among the countries for the object of discovering ways of using atomic energy for peaceful purposes. Hence there follows only one correct conclusion, namely, the necessity of an exchange of scientific information between countries and the necessity of joint scientific efforts directed toward a broadening of the possibilities of the use of atomic energy only in the interests of promoting the material welfare of the peoples and developing science and culture. The success of the work of the Commission will be determined in a large measure by the extent to which it succeeds in solving this important task.

The proposal for a wide exchange of scientific information is timely because such a scientific discovery, as the discovery of methods of using atomic energy, cannot remain for an indefinite time the property of only one country or small group of countries. It is bound to become the property of a number of countries. This confirms the necessity of a wide exchange of scientific information on the problem in question, and the necessity of drawing up corresponding measures in this field, including measures of organization.

I have stated the general considerations regarding the tasks and the character of the activities of the Atomic Energy Commission. In order to develop these general statements, on the instructions of my Government, I will place before the Commission for consideration two concrete proposals which, in the opinion of the Soviet Government, may constitute a basis for the adoption by the Commission of recommendations to the Security Council and play an important role in the strengthening of peace.

* * *

DRAFT INTERNATIONAL CONVENTION TO PROHIBIT THE PRODUCTION AND EMPLOYMENT OF WEAPONS BASED ON THE USE OF ATOMIC ENERGY FOR THE PURPOSE OF MASS DESTRUCTION

[Here follows a list of signatory states.]

* * *

Article 1. The high contracting parties solemnly declare that they are unanimously resolved to prohibit the production and employment of weapons based on the use of atomic energy, and for this purpose assume the following obligations:

(*a*) not to use atomic weapons in any circumstances whatsoever;

(*b*) to prohibit the production and storing of weapons based on the use of atomic energy;

(*c*) to destroy, within a period of three months from the day of the entry into force of the present convention, all stocks of atomic energy weapons whether in a finished or unfinished condition.

Article 2. The high contracting parties declare that any violation of article 1 of the present convention is a most serious international crime against humanity.

Article 3. The high contracting parties shall, within a period of six months from the day of the entry into force of the present convention, pass legislation providing severe penalties for violators of the statutes of the present convention.

Article 4. The present convention shall be of indefinite duration.

Article 5. The present convention shall be open for the adhesion of any State whether a Member or non-member of the United Nations.

Article 6. The present convention shall come into force after its approval by the Security Council and after the ratification and delivery of ratification documents to the Secretary-General for safe keeping by one half of the signatory States, including all the Member States of the United Nations named in Article 23 of the Charter of the Organization.

Article 7. After the entry into force of the present convention it shall be binding on all States whether Members or non-members of the United Nations.

*   *   *

I will read the text of the second proposal.

CONCERNING THE ORGANIZATION OF THE WORK OF THE ATOMIC ENERGY COMMISSION

In accordance with the resolution of the General Assembly of 24 January 1946 regarding the establishment of a commission to deal with problems raised by the discovery of atomic energy and other related matters, and in particular with article 5 of the said resolution relating to the terms of reference of the Commission, the Soviet delegation deems it necessary to propose the following plan of organization of the work of the Commission for the initial stage of its activity.

I. ESTABLISHMENT OF COMMITTEES OF THE COMMISSION

In pursuance of the aim indicated in the resolution of the General Assembly "to proceed with the utmost despatch and inquire into all phases of the problems," it appears to be necessary to set up two committees which as auxiliary organs of the Commission would ensure a thorough examination of the problem of atomic energy and the elaboration of recommendations, which the Commission must make in fulfilment of the resolution of the General Assembly and other organs of the United Nations.

It is proposed that the following committees should be set up:

Committee for the exchange of scientific information

This committee shall be set up for the purpose of carrying out the aims indicated in point (*a*) of item 5 of the resolution of the General Assembly of 24 January 1946.

The tasks of the committee shall include the elaboration of recommendations concerning practical measures for organizing the exchange of information:

(1) concerning the contents of scientific discoveries connected with the splitting of the atomic nucleus and other discoveries connected with obtaining and using atomic energy;

(2) concerning the technology and the organization of technological processes for obtaining and using atomic energy;

(3) concerning the organization and methods of industrial production of atomic energy and the use of this energy;

(4) concerning the forms, sources and locations of the raw materials necessary for obtaining atomic energy.

Committee for the prevention of the use of atomic energy to the detriment of mankind

This committee shall be set up to carry out the aims set forth in points (*b*), (*c*), and (*d*) of item 5 of the resolution of the General Assembly.

The task of the committee shall be to elaborate recommendations:

(1) concerning the drafting of an international convention for outlawing weapons based on the use of atomic energy and prohibiting the production and use of such weapons and all other similar kinds of weapons capable of being used for mass destruction;

(2) concerning the quest for and establishment of measures to prohibit the production of weapons based on the use of atomic energy and to prevent the use of atomic weapons and all other main kinds of weapons capable of being used for mass destruction;

(3) concerning the measures, systems and organization of control over the use of atomic energy and over the observance of the terms of the above-mentioned international convention for the outlawing of atomic weapons;

(4) concerning the elaboration of a system of sanctions to be applied against the unlawful use of atomic energy.

II. COMPOSITION OF THE COMMITTEES

Each committee shall be composed of one representative of each State represented in the Commission. Each representative may have assistants.

III. RULES OF PROCEDURE OF THE COMMITTEES

The rules of procedure of the committees shall be drawn up by the Commission.

The proposal for the conclusion of a convention and the proposal for the organization of the work of the Commission are both capable of being put into practice at the present time.

The convention would be a definite and important step towards the creation of an effective system of control over atomic energy. This measure would have an immense moral and political significance and would contribute to the strengthening of political stability in the world and of friendly relations between the peoples.

The creation of the two committees that I have proposed, with the terms of reference laid down in the proposal, will mean the adoption of a concrete plan of work of the Commission for the initial stage of its activities, and at the same time, the adoption of the necessary organizational forms for carrying out its work which will facilitate the speedy preparation by the Commission of proposals concerning the wide exchange of scientific information, as well as concerning matters relating to the prevention of the use of atomic energy to the detriment of mankind.

The activity of the Atomic Energy Commission can bring about the desired results only when it is in full conformity with the principles of the Charter of the United Nations which are laid down as the basis of the activity of the Security Council, because the Commission is an organ of this Organization, working under the instructions of the Security Council and responsible to the same.

Attempts to undermine the principles, as established by the Charter, of the activity of the Security Council, including unanimity of the members of the Security Council in deciding questions of substance, are incompatible with the interests of the United Nations, who created the international organization for the preservation of peace and security. Such attempts must be rejected.

*　　*　　*

◇◇◇◇◇◇

191. FINDINGS OF ATOMIC ENERGY COMMISSION INCORPORATED IN ITS FIRST REPORT TO THE SECURITY COUNCIL, DECEMBER 31, 1946 [1]

[Less than one year after its creation, the Atomic Energy Commission submitted its first report to the Security Council. The report emphasized the point that it is technically possible to set up an effective international system of inspection and control so as to make certain that atomic energy would be used only for peaceful ends. The findings of the Atomic Energy Commission, which correspond closely to the proposals submitted by Mr. Baruch on June 14, 1946, are reproduced below. The U.S.S.R. abstained from voting on the first report.]

Based upon the proposals and information presented to the Commission, upon the hearings, proceedings, and deliberations of the Commission to date, and upon the proceedings, discussions, and reports of its several committees and subcommittees, all as set forth in this report, the Commission has made the following additional findings of a general nature:

1. That scientifically, technologically, and practically, it is feasible

(*a*) to extend among "all nations the exchange of basic scientific information" on atomic energy "for peaceful ends",

(*b*) to control "atomic energy to the extent necessary to insure its use only for peaceful purposes",[2]

(*c*) to accomplish "the elimination from national armaments of atomic weapons",[2] and

(*d*) to provide "effective safeguards by way of inspection and other means to protect complying states against the hazards of violations and evasions".[2]

2. That effective control of atomic energy depends upon effective control

---

[1] The United States and the United Nations: Report of the President to the Congress for the year 1946, Department of State publication 2735, the United States and the United Nations Report Series 7, pp. 190-194. For the text of The First Report of the United Nations Atomic Energy Commission to the Security Council, December 31, 1946, see Department of State publication 2737, the United States and the United Nations Report Series 8. While containing certain language modifications, these General Findings and Recommendations are, in all essentials, the same as those put forward for the approval of the Commission by the United States Representative on December 5, 1946, and on December 17, 1946.

[2] Commission's Term of Reference, art. V, Resolution of the General Assembly, January 24, 1946. [Footnoting is that of the original document.]

of the production and use of uranium, thorium, and their nuclear fuel derivatives. Appropriate mechanisms of control to prevent their unauthorized diversion or clandestine production and use and to reduce the dangers of seizure—including one or more of the following types of safeguards: accounting, inspection, supervision, management, and licensing—must be applied through the various stages of the processes from the time the uranium and thorium ores are severed from the ground to the time they become nuclear fuels and are used. . . . Ownership by the international control agency of mines and of ores still in the ground is not to be regarded as mandatory.

3. That, whether the ultimate nuclear fuels be destined for peaceful or destructive uses, the productive processes are identical and inseparable up to a very advanced state of manufacture. Thus, the control of atomic energy to insure its use for peaceful purposes, the elimination of atomic weapons from national armaments, and the provision of effective safeguards to protect complying States against the hazards of violations and evasions must be accomplished through a single unified international system of control and inspection designed to carry out all of these related purposes.

4. That the development and use of atomic energy are not essentially matters of domestic concern of the individual nations, but rather have predominantly international implications and repercussions.

5. That an effective system for the control of atomic energy must be international, and must be established by an enforceable multilateral treaty or convention which in turn must be administered and operated by an international organ or agency within the United Nations, possessing adequate power and properly organized, staffed, and equipped for the purpose.

Only by such an international system of control and inspection can the development and use of atomic energy be freed from nationalistic rivalries with consequent risks to the safety of all peoples. Only by such a system can the benefits of widespread exchange of scientific knowledge and of the peaceful uses of atomic energy be assured. Only such a system of control and inspection would merit and enjoy the confidence of the people of all nations.

6. That international agreement to outlaw the national production, possession, and use of atomic weapons is an essential part of any such international system of control and inspection. An international treaty or convention to this effect, if standing alone, would fail (a) "to ensure" the use of atomic energy "only for peaceful purposes" [1] and (b) to provide "for effective safeguards by way of inspection and other means to protect complying States against the hazards of violations and evasions," [1] and thus would fail to meet the requirements of the terms of reference of the Commission. To be effective such agreement must be embodied in a treaty or convention providing for a comprehensive international system of control and inspection and including guarantees and safeguards adequate to insure the carrying out of the terms of the treaty or convention and "to protect complying States against the hazards of violations and evasions." [1]

Based upon the findings of the Commission, . . . the Commission makes the following recommendations to the Security Council with respect to certain of the matters covered by the terms of reference of the Commission, which

[1] Commission's Terms of Reference, article V, Resolution of the General Assembly, January 24, 1946. [Footnoting is that of the original document.]

recommendations are interdependent and not severable, embodying the fundamental principles and indicating the basic organizational mechanisms necessary to attain the objectives set forth in the General Findings, paragraph 1 (a)—(d) above.

1. There should be a strong and comprehensive international system of control and inspection aimed at attaining the objectives set forth in the Commission's terms of reference.

2. Such an international system of control and inspection should be established and its scope and functions defined by a treaty or convention in which all of the nations Members of the United Nations should be entitled to participate on fair and equitable terms.

The international system of control and inspection should become operative only when those Members of the United Nations necessary to assure its success by signing and ratifying the treaty or convention have bound themselves to accept and support it.

Consideration should be given to the matter of participation by non-members of the United Nations.

3. The treaty or convention should include, among others, provisions

(a) Establishing, in the United Nations, an international control agency (hereinafter called "the agency") possessing powers and charged with responsibility necessary and appropriate for the prompt and effective discharge of the duties imposed upon it by the terms of the treaty or convention. Its rights, powers, and responsibilities, as well as its relations to the several organs of the United Nations, should be clearly established and defined by the treaty or convention. Such powers should be sufficiently broad and flexible to enable the authority to deal with new developments that may hereafter rise in the field of atomic energy. The treaty shall provide that the rule of unanimity of the permanent Members, which in certain circumstances exists in the Security Council, shall have no relation to the work of the agency. No government shall possess any right of veto over the fulfilment by the agency of the obligations imposed upon it by the treaty nor shall any government have the power, through the exercise of any right of veto or otherwise, to obstruct the course of control or inspection.

The agency shall promote among all nations the exchange of basic scientific information on atomic energy for peaceful ends, and shall be responsible for preventing the use of atomic energy for destructive purposes, and for the control of atomic energy to the extent necessary to insure its use only for peaceful purposes.

The agency should have positive research and developmental responsibilities in order to remain in the forefront of atomic knowledge so as to render the agency more effective in promoting the beneficial uses of atomic energy and in eliminating its destructive ones. The exclusive right to carry on atomic research for destructive purposes should be vested in the agency.

Research in nuclear physics having a direct bearing on the use of atomic energy should be subject to appropriate safeguards established by the international control agency in accordance with the treaty or convention. Such safeguards should not interfere with the prosecution of pure scientific research, or the publication of its results, provided no dangerous use or purpose is involved.

Decisions of the agency pursuant to the powers conferred upon it by the treaty or convention should govern the operations of national agencies for atomic energy. In carrying out its prescribed functions, however, the agency should interfere as little as necessary with the operations of national agencies for atomic energy, or with the economic plans and the private, corporate, and State relationships in the several countries.

(*b*) Affording the duly accredited representatives of the agency unimpeded rights of ingress, egress, and access for the performance of their inspections and other duties into, from, and within the territory of every participating nation, unhindered by national or local authorities.

(*c*) Prohibiting the manufacture, possession, and use of atomic weapons by all nations parties thereto and by all persons under their jurisdiction.

(*d*) Providing for the disposal of any existing stocks of atomic weapons and for the proper use of nuclear fuels adaptable for use in weapons.

(*e*) Specifying the means and methods of determining violations of its terms, setting forth such violations as shall constitute international crimes, and establishing the nature of the measures of enforcement and punishment to be imposed upon persons and upon nations guilty of violating the terms of the treaty or convention.

The judicial or other processes for determination of violations of the treaty or convention, and of punishments therefor, should be swift and certain. Serious violations of the treaty shall be reported immediately by the agency to the nations parties to the treaty, to the General Assembly, and to the Security Council. Once the violations constituting international crimes have been defined and the measures of enforcement and punishment therefor agreed to in the treaty or convention, there shall be no legal right, by veto or otherwise, whereby a wilful violator of the terms of the treaty or convention shall be protected from the consequences of violation of its terms.

The enforcement and punishment provisions of the treaty or convention would be ineffectual if, in any such situations, they could be rendered nugatory by the veto of a State which had voluntarily signed the treaty.

4. In consideration of the problem of violation of the terms of the treaty or convention, it should also be borne in mind that a violation might be of so grave a character as to give rise to the inherent right of self-defense recognized in article 51 of the Charter of the United Nations.

5. The treaty or convention should embrace the entire program for putting the international system of control and inspection into effect and should provide a schedule for the completion of the transitional process over a period of time, step by step in an orderly and agreed sequence leading to the full and effective establishment of international control of atomic energy. In order that the transition may be accomplished as rapidly as possible and with safety and equity to all, this Commission should supervise the transitional process, as prescribed in the treaty or convention, and should be empowered to determine when a particular stage or stages have been completed and subsequent ones are to commence.

◇◇◇◇◇◇

192. SECOND REPORT OF THE ATOMIC ENERGY COMMISSION, SEPTEMBER 11, 1947 (EXCERPT) [1]

Part II: Operational and Developmental Functions of the International Control Agency

[In 1946, the Atomic Energy Commission approved the broad outline of an international control plan which it incorporated in its first report. In 1947, it developed specific proposals in its second report showing how effective controls could be carried out. This part of the report deals with the powers of the proposed international control agency and some of the security problems involved in atomic control. The U.S.S.R. voted against the Commission's second report.]

CHAPTER 1: GENERAL INTRODUCTION

PREFATORY NOTE

THE FIRST REPORT "led to the conclusion that a single international control agency must be responsible for the system of safeguards and control". The Commission recognized at that time that it had "not discussed the general characteristics of such an agency or its exact powers in the way, for example, of development, research, or the international planning of atomic energy production. Nor has it considered how the various safeguards would be administered in practice as part of an over-all system." Moreover, the Commission recognized that the findings (given in the First Report) which represented safeguards against diversion of material at each stage taken separately "do not represent a plan for atomic energy control but only some of the elements which should be incorporated in any complete or effective plan."

Moving forward from this basis, the Atomic Energy Commission has now considered some of the broader aspects of the over-all problem of the control of atomic energy so as to ensure its use for peaceful purposes only, and it has considered the interrelation of various measures of safeguard required in the interests of international security to prevent nuclear fuel in "dangerous" quantities being accumulated or seized by any nation.

THE PROBLEM OF SECURITY

(a) *The Purpose of Control.* In studying the operational and developmental functions of the international agency and its relation to the planning, co-ordination, and direction of the production of nuclear fuels and of the use of atomic energy for peaceful purposes, the establishment of security was deemed the paramount requirement to be fulfilled. An attempt was, therefore, made to state the principles of a system of operative control which would have the following objectives:

---

[1] For full report, see The Second Report of the United Nations Atomic Energy Commission to the Security Council, September 11, 1947, Department of State publication 2932, The United States and the United Nations Report Series 11.

1. to give the international control agency the means of preventing preparation for atomic warfare,
2. to lessen the possibility of one nation or group of nations achieving potential supremacy in the field of atomic energy,
3. to give warning to complying states of any breach of the treaty, and
4. to dispel suspicions and false accusations.

In working out the application of these principles, it was found necessary to study additional considerations of security which were not within the scope of the First Report and thus in some cases to provide for more comprehensive and stricter measures of control than those recommended in that Report, in particular with regard to certain particular phases of the production or use of atomic energy.

(b) *Additional Considerations of Security.* These considerations may be summarized as follows: On the one hand, the international control agency might have full powers to take any decisions relating to the planning, coordination, and direction of the development of atomic energy. On the other hand, the nations might be left free to develop their programmes of production of atomic energy for peaceful purposes (on condition that the precautionary measures provided for in the First Report were applied to each operation). An intermediate solution between these two extremes might also be adopted.

It was considered that, in choosing between these policies, the elimination of national rivalries in the field of production, distribution, and stockpiling of nuclear fuels, and the determination of over-all production rates are of paramount importance to security.

(c) *Nature of the Dangers.* The First Report has already made it clear that nuclear fuels can easily be manufactured into weapons. It is recognized that the peaceful application of atomic energy in the future will require large-scale facilities for the production of nuclear fuel, facilities utilizing large quantities of nuclear fuel, and reserve stockpiles of nuclear fuel. To some extent, this will be true even before the utilization of atomic power. It is important to remember that at present the science and technique of the production of nuclear fuel is far in advance of that of its use for peaceful purposes, that is to say, nuclear fuels can be produced in quantities which far exceed their present possible uses in medicine, research, and industry. Even now, reactors producing radioactive isotopes on a useful scale for application in research and industry may involve dangerous quantities of key substances or nuclear fuels. Development work in connection with power generation may also require a number of installations, each using dangerous quantities of material. The materials present in these installations could be readily utilized for military purposes. It is clear, therefore, that general security will depend largely upon the production rate of these substances, upon their distribution, and upon their location.

(d) *Mining.* Mining constitutes the first stage of production. If the right to decide upon the rate of extraction were left in the hands of individual nations, there would be a risk that one country might retain reserves of ore in its soil or might deliberately accumulate stockpiles, to the disadvantage of others; or that a single country would acquire dangerous quantities of source material by purchase.

(e) *Processing and Utilization Facilities.* It is essential to bring under international regulation decisions regarding the distribution, number, and type of facilities in which nuclear fuels are produced or utilized. A lack of balance in the location of these facilities would affect general security by introducing a corresponding lack of balance in military potentials.

(f) *Dangers of Seizure.* A still more immediate danger would result from the initial advantage which might be gained by a nation or a group of nations through seizure of production facilities or of stockpiles of these materials, particularly in the case of separated or purified nuclear fuel, since it would be possible to manufacture weapons from these materials with small facilities and slight additional effort. The seizure of stockpiles, production facilities, and facilities utilizing nuclear fuel will always be a danger of such magnitude that seizure should be recognized by all nations to mean that a most serious violation of the treaty has taken place and that the nation is about to embark on atomic warfare. It is of vital importance that production facilities, facilities utilizing nuclear fuel, and stockpiles should be distributed amongst nations in such a way as to minimize the military advantage that their seizure would provide for a nation which has aggressive intentions. A well-planned distribution could not in itself prevent atomic war, but the objective should be to decrease the incentive for any one nation or group of nations to attempt to secure a military advantage by seizure. This problem will be examined more fully at a later stage.

(g) *Conclusion.* The dangers have, however, been recognized as sufficiently great to warrant the conclusion that, if the right to decide upon the number and size of such facilities and upon the size of the stockpiles of source material and nuclear fuel situated on their territory were left to nations, the control measures provided for in the First Report would not, if applied alone, eliminate the possibility of one nation or group of nations achieving potential military supremacy, or, through seizure, actual military supremacy.

POWERS AND FUNCTIONS OF THE AGENCY

(a) *Statement of Proposals.* The dangers attached to decisions regarding the matters covered in the preceding paragraph being acknowledged, it follows that the right to take these decisions cannot be left in the hands of nations. It is, therefore, proposed that:

1. in addition to its duties in regard to the management of facilities producing or utilizing nuclear fuels and to the application of measures for safeguarding these fuels as provided in the First Report, the international agency should have, under the conditions described below, the duty of implementing the terms of the treaty or convention in respect to the production, distribution, and stock-piling of nuclear fuels and the distribution and utilization of dangerous facilities utilizing or producing nuclear fuels; and that
2. the agency should have, subject to the conditions described below, the duty of implementing the terms of the treaty or convention in respect to mining quotas and the transfer and processing of source material.

(b) *Production Policy.* With regard to proposal 1 above, however, it is recommended that the agency should not be authorized to define the policy to be pursued in the production and use of atomic energy but that the principles governing this policy should be established by international agreement, and it should be the duty and responsibility of the agency to implement such an agreement. It was decided not to give the agency the right to decide this policy, because the signatory nations would rightly require that policies which substantially affect world security should be defined in the treaty or convention. Perhaps the most striking example is provided by the production of nuclear fuel. If the agency were free to decide the rate of production of nuclear fuel and were to embark upon a policy of production exceeding recognized or actual beneficial uses (see specific proposal XII of chapter 5), the conditions of world security would be greatly affected. Moreover, the possible exercise of these powers might cause serious conflicts within the agency, since the establishment of quotas for distribution constitutes a most difficult task. The treaty or convention establishing the agency should lay down fairly strictly the general principles to be followed in deciding such questions and should even go so far, in certain cases, as to prescribe a numerical quota. Any modification of these principles should be subject to a revision procedure, the rules of which should be laid down in the treaty or convention. At the same time, sufficient freedom should be left to the agency to allow it to deal satisfactorily with the changes in conditions that are inevitable in such a rapidly developing field.

The object to be aimed at in the foregoing recommendations is to eliminate, as far as practicable, the possibility that a nation or group of nations might obtain potential military supremacy.

In considering what should be the initial mandate to be given to the agency, recognition was given to the conflict between the requirements of security and those of preparing for large-scale application of peaceful developments. It is recommended, therefore, that the disposition to be included initially in the treaty or convention should make it mandatory for the agency to keep the production of nuclear fuel in a form suitable for ready conversion to weapon use, at the minimum required for efficient operating procedures necessitated by actual beneficial uses, including research and development.

(c) *Reactors.* The above considerations, regarding the production and stockpiling of nuclear fuels, also apply to the utilization of nuclear fuels when dangerous facilities are involved. The agency should, therefore, have the duty of implementing the terms of the treaty or convention with respect to the type and location of reactors which fall within the category of dangerous facilities.

When the technique of the industrial utilization of atomic power has been sufficiently developed, the international agency, within the limits imposed by security, should make power available on a fair and equitable basis to any nation which may require it. In the determination of the type and location of facilities, the agency will have power to determine distribution by nations in accordance with quotas, provisions, and principles set up in the treaty or convention, whereas the location and type of any particular facility within a nation will be decided by the nation concerned in agreement with the agency. The agency's rights pertaining to determining location within a nation will be limited to such specific factors pertaining to international security as may be specified in the treaty or convention.

(d) *Mining Policy.* The agency should be prepared to provide the requirements for nuclear fuels. This is one of the considerations which should be taken into account in determining mining quotas. Here again, it is not thought that the agency should have an entirely free hand in the allocation of these quotas. It is not feasible to effect a strategic redistribution of uranium and thorium ores as they are found in nature. Hence, it is recommended that the treaty or convention should embody the principle that comparable national deposits throughout the world should, insofar as practical considerations permit, be depleted proportionately.

(e) *Dangerous Activities or Facilities* are those which are of military significance in the production of atomic weapons. The word "dangerous" is used in the sense of potentially dangerous to world security. In determining from time to time what are dangerous activities and dangerous facilities, the international agency shall comply with the provisions of the treaty or convention which will provide that the agency shall take into account the quantity and quality of materials in each case, the possibility of diversion, the ease with which the materials can be used or converted to produce atomic weapons, the total supply and distribution of such materials in existence, the design and operating characteristics of the facilities involved, the ease of altering those facilities, possible combinations with other facilities, scientific and technical advances which have been made, and the degree to which the agency has achieved security in the control of atomic energy. All facilities not falling in the category of being dangerous as defined above will be referred to in this text as non-dangerous.

(f) *Research and Development.* The foregoing consideration is one of the arguments in favour of giving the agency the power to conduct research and development work. Another argument is the necessity of knowing whether regeneration is possible, since this a factor upon which the evaluation of world resources and, consequently, the whole field of peaceful application, largely depend. It is also necessary that the agency should know to what extent the use of denatured fuels would affect the possibility of utilizing atomic energy, both from the economic and from the practical point of view. Although it is considered that most of the research and the facilities in which it is conducted will be classified as non-dangerous, it is essential that the agency should have scientific knowledge of all matters relating to atomic energy. These are merely examples of the arguments in support of the generally acknowledged thesis that the agency, in order to give security and to perform its task, must have full knowledge, not only of the results achieved but also (since the subject is perpetually developing) of all innovations as they occur. It must be able to recognize all clandestine operations, even though these may be of a new and unfamiliar character.

It is considered, however, that it would be detrimental to all concerned (and to the agency itself) if private or national work on research and development should stop. The principle is, therefore, proposed that national research and development activities should be limited in scope only insofar as is necessary for reasons of security.

It is by no means considered that the agency should hamper individual or national research, but rather that its policy should be to encourage such research. It will appear that, in the field of useful application, there would be nothing in the proposals that would prevent work on problems of a national character, except, however, that nations or individuals should be forbidden to use nuclear fuel for the perfecting, production or assembly of any atomic weapon whatsoever, and should be forbidden to use dangerous quantities of nuclear fuel; all use of nuclear fuel in non-dangerous quantities should be subject to proper safeguards when necessary.

(g) *Ownership.* In the following chapters, the expression "ownership by the international agency" is frequently used with reference to source materials, nuclear fuels, and dangerous facilities. It is important to understand the reasons which have led to the conclusion that "ownership" should be vested in the international agency in respect to materials and certain facilities and to understand the sense in which this expression is used.

The First Report contained an examination of the controls necessary at the separate stages of production and use of atomic energy and left the co-ordination of controls and the general requirements of international security for subsequent study. Such study has established the necessity for international control and allocation of the quantities and locations of uranium and thorium which are to be separated from their place in nature, the time and place of the further processing and purification of source materials, and the size, use, and disposition of working stocks and stocks in transit. Without such comprehensive international control of the flow of source materials from the first point where they are capable of being diverted, there would be a serious risk of the diversion of source material or of the accumulation of stocks with a view to subsequent diversion or seizure. The basic policies and provisions governing the exercise of this international control and direction must be specified in the treaty or convention and implemented by the international agency. To administer these controls effectively, the international agency, acting as trustee for all the signatory nations jointly in accordance with the policies set forth in the treaty or convention, must be given indisputable control of the source materials promptly after their separation from their natural deposits.

If ownership of source material, after separation from its place of deposit in nature, were to remain with the nation, it might be left open to doubt as to whose decision would prevail in regard to the disposition of this material. International security requires that there be no doubt that, within the terms of the treaty or convention, the right of decision in these matters must lie with the international agency.

It has, therefore, been decided that ownership of source material must not be vested in the nation or any individual under the terms of the treaty or convention. No nation or person would, therefore, be able lawfully to possess or dispose of source material after it had been mined. The mere possession or movement of any such material without the consent of the agency would be unambiguous evidence of violation of the treaty or convention.

With regard to nuclear fuel and to facilities producing or utilizing nuclear fuel, it is proposed that, in the interests of international security, the treaty or convention and the agency, in implementing the terms of the treaty or convention, must determine the number of facilities to be established in each nation and the agency must manage their operation. On the other hand, since nuclear fuel and all such facilities would necessarily have to be located on some national territory, the question arises whether international security would permit that nations should have any proprietary rights or right of decision arising therefrom with regard to nuclear fuel or to the facilities located on their territory. If national or private ownership were permitted, it might be argued that the nations might lay a claim to source material, nuclear fuel, or dangerous facilities located on their territory in such a way as to endanger international security. It was, therefore, concluded that it is necessary for the international agency to have, in addition to those duties of management as defined in the First Report, the duty to make and to carry out decisions in implementation of the quotas, provisions, and principles set up in the treaty or convention, regarding the production, distribution, and stockpiling of nuclear fuel and the distribution and utilization of dangerous facilities involving nuclear fuel. This duty to make decisions will be exercised in accordance with the principles embodied in the treaty or convention. If national or private ownership were permitted, it would lead to controversy and make it impossible for the agency, in accordance with quotas, provisions, and principles set up in the treaty or convention, to exercise sufficient control to ensure security. It was, therefore, concluded that nations or persons should not own source material, nuclear fuel, or dangerous facilities.

If ownership of these materials and facilities is to be denied to nations or persons under the terms of the treaty or convention, it might seem to follow that such ownership must of necessity be attributed to the agency. On the other hand, the agency will be very closely controlled by the terms of the treaty or convention precisely in respect to those decisions which normally go with ownership, namely, the rights of disposition. This fact might be expressed by saying that the agency would hold all dangerous materials and facilities in trust for the signatory states and would be responsible for ensuring that the provisions of the treaty or convention in regard to their disposition are executed. It is in this sense that the phrase "ownership by the agency" is to be understood in what follows. There can, of course, be no question that any nation or person has any right in any circumstances to dispose of or to possess these materials or facilities.

It will be seen from the chapters which follow that ownership by the agency of source materials or nuclear fuels includes the exclusive right to move or lease the materials, the right to use and to produce energy from them, and the same rights for all products formed from them. Ownership also includes the principle that no disposition of material can be made without the permission of the agency. It is proposed that the agency should acquire ownership, for a price to be agreed, of source material from the time it is removed from its place of deposit in nature or, in case of source material containing other important constituents, from the time those constituents have been extracted. The agency will not be permitted to sell these materials but could lease them for authorized uses.

Likewise, ownership by the agency of dangerous facilities includes the right of the agency to make decisions regarding their allocation, construction, and operation, within the terms of the treaty or convention. The useful and non-dangerous products of these plants would be made available to the nations under fair and equitable arrangements. The location and type within a nation will be decided by agreement with the nation concerned. Ownership by the agency of facilities within a nation includes rights of possession, operation, and disposition subject to the terms of the treaty or convention. The agency could not sell dangerous facilities. Ownership by the agency of a power plant would not include the right to shut down such a plant at will. Ownership does include the responsibility to operate facilities in such a way as not to endanger health and the responsibility for any damage.

While vesting ownership in the agency, in the sense of a trust exercised on behalf of signatory states jointly, in order that the agency should have the final right of decision in regard to the disposition of source materials, nuclear fuels, and the operation of dangerous facilities, it was also realized that the nations could not be expected to agree to give unlimited discretionary powers to an international agency. The following chapters, therefore, set out in detail the provisions which are to govern the location, mining, production, distribution, and use of source material and nuclear fuel, as well as dangerous facilities. It would then be the duty and responsibility of the international agency to implement these provisions in accordance with the terms of the treaty or convention.

These chapters, coupled with the First Report, give an outline of the major provisions from the point of view of security that must be incorporated in a plan for the control of atomic energy. It is recognized, however, that the treaty or convention which would put such a system of control into effect cannot cover all the situations that might arise between the signatory states and the agency. It must be stated at this time that, whatever legal issues might arise in this connection, nations cannot have any proprietary rights or rights of decision arising therefrom over source materials, nuclear fuels, or dangerous facilities located within their territory.

(*h*) *Clandestine Activities*. The study of the problem of security in the light of the additional considerations described at the beginning of this chapter does not affect the problem of the detection of clandestine activities. The measures provided for in the following chapters, therefore, represent only an elaboration of those recommended in the First Report. The purpose of these measures is to give the agency the duties and the powers in order to deter nations which might be tempted to conduct clandestine operations, to seek out and to detect such clandestine activities if a nation were to conduct them, and to dispel suspicions and false accusations.

It is obvious that no feeling of security could be established in the world if nations could reserve the right to prohibit access to certain parts of their territory. Nevertheless, it is also impracticable to subject the whole of the territories of the contracting nations to detailed inspection for, apart from the obvious political disadvantages, no international agency could ever be in a position to fulfil such a task. Thus, the exercise of the right, which the international agency must possess, of determining on the spot whether a nation is conducting clandestine preparations for atomic warfare, would be subject to various procedures, according to the nature of the territory or the building inspected, and these procedures would be designed to guarantee nations and individuals against abuses on the part of the agency and to conform, as far as possible, with national legal procedures.

It is recognized that these procedures will have to be considered from a juridical standpoint in order that they might be defined in legal terms capable of juridical interpretation, it being understood that the substance of the proposals should not be altered.

◇◇◇◇◇◇

193. THIRD REPORT OF THE ATOMIC ENERGY COMMISSION, MAY 17, 1948 [1]

[The third report of the Atomic Energy Commission revealed what the world had feared for some time—after twenty-two months of negotiations the Commission had reached an impasse in its work. The impasse stemmed from two facts reported by the Commission: (1) the full coöperation of the U.S.S.R. is essential for any effective system of atomic control; and (2) the Soviet Union rejected the plan approved by the majority of the Commission on the ground that it constituted an "unwarranted infringement of national sovereignty." The Commission recommended, therefore, that negotiations in the Atomic Energy Commission be suspended.]

The Atomic Energy Commission reports that it has reached an impasse.

In almost two years of work the Commission has accomplished much and has succeeded in making clear the essentials of a plan for the control of atomic energy, in fulfillment of the objectives of the resolution of the General Assembly of 24 January 1946. Nevertheless, it considers that it cannot now prepare a draft treaty "incorporating its ultimate proposals" as urged by the resolution of the Security Council of 10 March 1947.

The difficulties which confront the Commission were first evidenced when the plan under consideration by most of the governments members of the Commission was rejected by the USSR, "either as a whole or in its separate parts," on the ground that such a plan constituted an unwarranted infringement of national sovereignty. For its part, the USSR insisted that a convention outlawing atomic weapons and providing for the destruction of existing weapons must precede any control agreement. The majority of the Commission considered that such a convention, without safeguards, would offer no protection against non-compliance.

This initial divergency of view did not deter the Commission from pursuing its task in the hope that the disagreements might be resolved as a result of further studies. Accordingly, the Commission decided to defer the consideration of the political aspects of the problem until it had first determined whether control of atomic energy was practicable from a technical point of view. In September 1946 the Scientific and Technical Committee reported unanimously that

"we do not find any basis in the available scientific facts for supposing that effective control is not technologically feasible."

During the remainder of 1946, the Commission continued to study the technical and scientific aspects of control and adopted the broad outlines of

---

[1] AEC/P.V.15, May 7, 1948. This document is the Three Power declaration which was presented to the Commission on May 7 and adopted as the body of a Third Report at the Commission's meeting on May 17, 1948. The fully assembled Third Report contains the proceedings of the Commission and a series of annexed documents.

a control plan set forth in the General Findings and Recommendations of the First Report. In 1947 it elaborated specific proposals in a Second Report which show, on many points, how control could be carried out.

The USSR abstained from voting on the First Report and voted against the Second Report.

In February 1947, the USSR submitted Amendments and Additions to the General Findings and Recommendations of the First Report, and in June 1947, it submitted control proposals of its own. The discussion of the USSR Amendments and Additions did not lead the Commission to revise its General Findings and Recommendations. The USSR proposals of June 1947 have been analyzed in detail. In April 1948 they were rejected by a 9-2 vote, in the following terms:

"They ignore the existing technical knowledge of the problem of atomic energy control, do not provide an adequate basis for the effective international control of atomic energy and the elimination from national armaments of atomic weapons, and, therefore, do not conform to the terms of reference of the Atomic Energy Commission."

The analysis of the technical requirements of atomic energy control has been pursued as far as is possible. Unfortunately, this analysis has not led to agreement even on the technical aspects of control. During more than 200 meetings of the Atomic Energy Commission and its various committees, the USSR has had time to study the technical knowledge available to the Commission, to review its own position in the light of such knowledge, and to appreciate that the admittedly far-reaching proposals sponsored by the majority are based on the scientific and technical facts. But the USSR has not changed its fundamental position.

Thus, after twenty-two months of work, the Commission finds itself confronted by virtually the same deadlock that stultified its initial discussions. The Government of the USSR itself acknowledges the deadlock. It is now apparent that this deadlock cannot be broken at the Commission level.

Both political and technical considerations demand that no important areas of the world be outside the control system. It is therefore evident that the full co-operation of the USSR is indispensable for the establishment of a system of control which would prevent an atomic armaments race.

Whether the functions and powers of the International Control Agency as elaborated by the majority are politically acceptable or not, they provide the technically necessary basis for an effective control of atomic energy. The question is not whether those measures are now acceptable but whether governments now want effective international control.

The problems which have not been elaborated in detail, i. e., organization and administration, financing, strategic balance, prohibitions and enforcement, and the stages of transition from the present situation to one of full international control, are of a different nature. These questions do not affect the basic nature of the problem of control. Some questions, such as stages, which only concern the period of transition to full international control, will be conditional on future technological developments and the conditions of world security. The same considerations apply to the question of the strategic balance to be established in the location of nuclear materials and nuclear reactors between one part of the globe and another. Others, such as organization and administration of the agency—on which inconclusive discussions have recently taken place—and the question of the agency's finances, depend almost entirely on the existence of prior agreement on the nature and extent of the control system. Indeed, until agreement on the basic principles of control has been reached, the elaboration of proposals to cover these remaining topics would be unrealistic and would serve no useful purpose. On the other hand, given such agreement, solutions to these problems could be worked out.

The discovery of atomic energy has confronted the world with a new situation. The Atomic Energy Commission has studied and made recommendations on the international control of atomic energy to meet this situation. It has rejected proposals which do not meet the known facts of the problem.

By concentrating on the technical facts which, irrespective of any political situation, must be met by any satisfactory plan of control, the Commission has prepared findings and recommendations which, in the view of the majority, will stand as the basis of any further study of this subject. This is a substantial achievement. These findings and recommendations are summarized in Annex 2 as the best evidence both of the scope of the problem and of the realism with which it has been faced.

In addition to thus summarizing what it has done, the Commission has a duty to set forth the reasons why it has not achieved more, for it is important that Governments and peoples may understand the findings it has made, the lessons it has drawn from the difficulties it has met, and the conclusions it has reached.

General conclusions and recommendations.—The mandate given by the General Assembly is clear evidence that all Members of the United Nations share the conviction that, unless effective international control is established, there can be no lasting security against atomic weapons for any nation, whatever its size, location, or power.

The First and Second Reports of the Commission show how and to what extent the world must adapt itself if it wants to be protected against the misuse of its new discovery. Ways and means to eliminate the dangers of diversion, clandestine activities, and the seizure of atomic materials and facilities have been studied at length. Specific proposals have been put forward, together with principles for the governance of national policies and of the policies to be pursued by the International Control Agency itself.

The principles submitted in the two Reports of the Commission provide an alternative to the armaments race that results from the absence of international control and which would not be prevented by the establishment of an inadequate system of control. These principles require that atomic energy must not be developed on the basis of national interests and needs, means and resources; but that its planning and operation should be made a common enterprise in all its phases.

Only if traditional economic and political practices are adapted to the overriding requirements of international security can these proposals be implemented. Traditional conceptions of the economic exploitation of the resources of nature for private or national advantage would then be replaced in this field by a new pattern of co-operation in international relations.

Furthermore, secrecy in the field of atomic energy is not compatible with lasting international security. Co-operative development and complete dissemination of information alone promise to remove fears and suspicion that nations are conducting secret activities.

The unprecedented character of its conclusions has not deterred the majority of the Commission from adopting them, since the scientific and technical evidence makes such conclusions inescapable. Past experience has shown that unless there is a novel approach to the problem of controlling a force so readily adaptable to warfare, atomic weapons—notwithstanding their vastly superior destructive power—will continue just as uncontrolled as other weapons have been and still are, and the threat of atomic war will remain.

The majority of the Commission is fully aware of the impact of its plan on traditional prerogatives of national sovereignty. But in the face of the realities of the problem it sees no alternative to the voluntary sharing by nations of their sovereignty in this field to the extent required by its proposals. It finds no other solution which will meet the facts, prevent national rivalries in this most dangerous field, and fulfil the Commission's terms of reference.

The new pattern of international co-operation and the new standards of openness in the dealings of one country with another that are indispensable in the field of atomic energy might, in practice, pave the way for international co-operation in broader fields, for the control of other weapons of mass destruction, and even for the elimination of war itself as an instrument of national policy.

However, in the field of atomic energy, the majority of the Commission has been unable to secure the agreement of the Soviet Union to even those elements of effective control considered essential from the technical point of view, let alone their acceptance of the nature and extent of participation in the world community required of all nations in this field by the first and second reports of the Atomic Energy Commission. As a result, the Commission has been forced to recognize that agreement on effective measures for the control of atomic energy is itself dependent on co-operation in broader fields of policy.

The failure to achieve agreement on the international control of atomic energy arises from a situation that is beyond the competence of this Commission. In this situation, the Commission concludes that no useful purpose can be served by carrying on negotiations at the Commission level.

The Atomic Energy Commission, therefore, recommends that, until such time as the General Assembly finds that this situation no longer exists, or until such time as the sponsors of the General Assembly resolution of 24 January 1946, who are the permanent members of the Atomic Energy Commission, find, through prior consultation, that there exists a basis for agreement on the international control of atomic energy, negotiations in the Atomic Energy Commission be suspended.

In accordance with its terms of reference, the Atomic Energy Commission submits this report and recommendation to the Security Council for consideration, and recommends that they be transmitted, along with the two previous reports of the Commission, to the next regular session of the General Assembly as a matter of special concern.

◇◇◇◇◇◇

194. REPORTS OF ATOMIC ENERGY COMMISSION [1]

Resolution of the General Assembly, November 4, 1948

[Although the third report of the Atomic Energy Commission recommended that negotiations in the Commission be suspended, the General Assembly, at the insistence of the smaller states, refused to admit that a solution to the atomic problem could not be found. At its Paris session in the fall of 1948, the Assembly called upon the Atomic Energy Commission to resume its meetings and requested the Great Powers and Canada to enter into further consultations to determine whether some basis for agreement existed.]

The General Assembly,

HAVING EXAMINED the first, second and third reports of the Atomic Energy Commission which have been transmitted to it by the Security Council in accordance with the terms of General Assembly resolution 1 (I) of 24 January 1946,

1. *Approves* the General Findings (part II C) and Recommendations (part III) of the first report and the Specific Proposals of part II of the second report of the Commission as constituting the necessary basis for establishing an effective system of international control of atomic energy to ensure its use only for peaceful purposes and for the elimination from national armaments of atomic weapons in accordance with the terms of reference of the Atomic Energy Commission;

2. *Expresses* its deep concern at the impasse which has been reached in the work of the Atomic Energy Commission as shown in its third report and regrets that unanimous agreement has not yet been reached;

3. *Requests* the six sponsors of the General Assembly resolution of 24 January 1946, which are the permanent members of the Atomic Energy Commission, to meet together and consult in order to determine if there exists a basis for agreement on the international control of atomic energy to ensure its use only for peaceful purposes and for the elimination from national armaments of atomic weapons, and to report to the General Assembly the results of their consultation not later than its next regular session:

4. Meanwhile,

The General Assembly,

Calls upon the Atomic Energy Commission to resume its sessions, to survey its programme of work, and to proceed to the further study of such of the subjects remaining in the programme of work as it considers to be practicable and useful.

◇◇◇◇◇◇

[1] United States Participation in the United Nations: Report by the President to Congress for the year 1948, State Department Publication 3437, pp. 134-185.

195. ATOMIC EXPLOSION IN THE U. S. S. R.

Statement by President Truman, September 23, 1949 [1]

[On September 23, 1949, President Truman announced that there was evidence that an atomic explosion had recently occurred in the Soviet Union. This announcement drastically upset the calculations of many of our leaders who assumed that our monopoly of atomic weapons would last at least until 1952. If there was any hope left by 1949 that an international control system could be agreed upon *before* Russia discovered the secret of the atomic bomb, that hope was dispelled.]

I believe the American people to the fullest extent consistent with the national security are entitled to be informed of all developments in the field of atomic energy. That is my reason for making public the following information.

We have evidence that within recent weeks an atomic explosion occurred in the U. S. S. R.

Ever since atomic energy was first released by man, the eventual development of this new force by other nations was to be expected. This probability has always been taken into account by us.

Nearly four years ago I pointed out that "scientific opinion appears to be practically unanimous that the essential theoretical knowledge upon which the discovery is based is already widely known. There is also substantial agreement that foreign research can come abreast of our present theoretical knowledge in time." And, in the three-nation declaration of the President of the United States and the Prime Ministers of the United Kingdom and of Canada, dated November 15, 1945. It was emphasized that no single nation could, in fact, have a monopoly of atomic weapons.

This recent development emphasizes once again, if indeed such emphasis were needed, the necessity for that truly effective and enforceable international control of atomic energy which this Government and the large majority of the members of the United Nations support.

196. FIVE POWER STATEMENT ON ATOMIC ENERGY [2]

Statement by the Representatives of Canada, China, France, the United Kingdom, and the United States, October 25, 1949

[In accordance with the mandate of the General Assembly expressed on November 4, 1948, the Great Powers and Canada held a number of consultations to determine whether there existed any basis for agreement on the international control of atomic energy. The statement presented here represents the joint views of the United States, the United Kingdom, Canada,

[1] Department of State Bulletin, October 3, 1949, p. 487.
[2] Department of State Bulletin, November 7, 1949, pp. 686-690. U. N. Doc. A/1050.

France, and China on the first ten consultative meetings. It is reproduced in full because it presents in succinct form the issues between the East and West and points out the basic obstacles in the way of agreement.]

On 24 October 1949, the representatives of Canada, China, France, the Union of Soviet Socialist Republics, the United Kingdom and the United States of America agreed to send to the Secretary-General of the United Nations, for transmission to the General Assembly, the following interim report on the consultations of the six permanent members of the Atomic Energy Commission:

"In paragraph 3 of General Assembly resolution 191 (III) of 4 November 1948, the representatives of the Sponsoring Powers, who are the Permanent Members of the Atomic Energy Commission, namely, Canada, China, France, the Union of Soviet Socialist Republics, the United Kingdom of Great Britain and Northern Ireland and the United States of America, were requested to hold consultations 'in order to determine if there exist a basis for agreement on the international control of atomic energy to ensure its use only for peaceful purposes, and for the elimination from national armaments of atomic weapons'.

"The first meeting took place on 9 August 1949. The consultations have not yet been concluded and are continuing but, in order to inform the General Assembly of the position which has so far been reached, the six Sponsoring Powers have decided to transmit to it the summary records of the first ten meetings."

It was agreed by the group that any of the representatives of the Governments taking part in these consultations retained the right to submit to the Assembly their observations on the course of the consultations so far. The representatives of Canada, China, France, the United Kingdom and the United States accordingly submit to the General Assembly this statement, which represents their joint views, in the hope that it may assist the Assembly in its consideration of this problem.

BASIS OF DISCUSSION

It was found desirable to approach these consultations from the viewpoint of general principles rather than specific proposals which had been the basis of most of the discussion in the United Nations Atomic Energy Commission. To this end, the representative of the United Kingdom offered a list of topics as a basis for discussion. Included in this paper was a Statement of Principles relating to each topic (Annex I). It was pointed out that the United Kingdom Statement of Principles was based on the plan approved by the General Assembly,[1] but at the same time covered the essential topics with which any plan for the prohibition of atomic weapons and the control of atomic energy would have to deal. The list of topics was then adopted as the basis for discussion. The representatives of Canada, China, France, the United Kingdom and the United States made it clear that their Governments accepted the Statement of Principles set forth in this paper and considered them essential to any plan of effective prohibition of atomic weapons and effective control of atomic energy for peaceful purposes. They expressed the readiness of their

[1] See Official Records, AEC., Fourth Year, Special Supplement No. 1.

Governments to consider any alternative proposals which might be put forward, but emphasized that they would continue to support the plan approved by the General Assembly unless and until proposals were made which would provide equally or more effective and workable means of control and prohibition.

PROHIBITION OF ATOMIC WEAPONS

At the request of the Soviet representative, the question of the prohibition of atomic weapons was taken up first. The texts which served as a basis for the discussion were point four of the Statement of Principles, and a Soviet amendment submitted to replace that text (Annex II). In the course of the discussion, the Soviet representative declared that the representatives of all six Sponsoring Powers were in agreement in recognizing that atomic weapons should be prohibited, and he therefore drew the conclusion that his amendment should be accepted. The other representatives pointed out that it had always been agreed that the production, possession or use of atomic weapons by all nations must be prohibited. But it was also agreed that prohibition could only be enforced by means of an effective system of control. This was recognized even in the Soviet amendment, but the remainder of the amendment contained a repetition of the earlier Soviet proposals for control which were deemed inadequate.

The Soviet representative insisted that two separate conventions, one on prohibition and the other on control, should be put into effect simultaneously. The other representatives maintained that the important point to be resolved was what constitutes effective control, and that this control had to embrace all uses of atomic materials in dangerous quantities. In their view the Soviet proposals would not only fail to provide the security required but they would be so inadequate as to be dangerous. They would delude the peoples of the world into thinking that atomic energy was being controlled when in fact it was not. On the other hand, under the approved plan, the prohibition of the use of atomic weapons would rest not only on the pledge of each nation, but no nation would be permitted to possess the materials with which weapons could be made. Furthermore, the Soviet Government took an impracticable stand as regards the question of timing or stages by which prohibition and control would be brought into effect.

STAGES FOR PUTTING INTO EFFECT PROHIBITION AND CONTROL

On this topic, the Soviet representative maintained that the entire system of prohibition and control must be put into effect simultaneously over the entire nuclear industry.

The representatives of the other Powers pointed out that this would be physically impossible. The development of atomic energy is the world's newest industry, and already is one of the most complicated. It would not be reasonable to assume that any effective system of control could be introduced and enforced overnight. Control and prohibition must, therefore, go into effect over a period of time and by a series of stages.

The plan approved by the General Assembly on 4 November 1948 does not attempt to define what the stages should be, the order in which they should be put into effect, or the time which the whole process of transition would take. The reason for this is that no detailed provisions on stages could be drawn up until agreement is reached on what the control system should be, and the provisions would also depend on the state of development of atomic energy in the various countries at the time agreement is reached. Until then, detailed study of the question of stages would be unrealistic.

Meanwhile, the approved plan covers the question of stages in so far as it can usefully be carried at present. The plan provides that the schedule of stages of application of control and prohibition over all the many phases of the entire nuclear industry is to be written into the treaty, with the United Nations Atomic Energy Commission as the body to supervise their orderly implementation. No other commitment or position on this question is contained in the approved plan.

CONTROL

(a) *Means of Control*

The Soviet representative insisted, as in the past, that any plan of control, to be acceptable to the Soviet Union, must be based on the Soviet proposals for control, originally put forward in June 1947 (Document AEC/24, 11 June 1947), which provide for periodic inspection of nationally owned plants producing or using atomic materials, when declared to an international control organ by the Governments concerned.

The representatives of Canada, China, France, the United Kingdom and the United States recalled that the nuclear fuels produced or used in such plants are the very nuclear explosives used in the manufacture of weapons. A new situation therefore was created in the field of armaments where the conversion of a peaceful industry into a war industry could take place rapidly and without warning.

In dealing with such materials a system of control depending merely on inspection would be ineffective. For ordinary chemical or mineral substances and their processing inspection might provide adequate guarantees, but atomic development presented special problems which could not be solved in this way. Materials used in the development of atomic energy were highly radioactive and could not, therefore, be handled except by remote control. The process of measuring atomic fuels was extremely intricate and, at the present stage of our knowledge, subject to appreciable error. It would be impracticable to rely on the inspection of plants and impossible to check the actual amounts of atomic materials inside piles or reactors against the amounts shown in the records.

A system of inspection alone would not prevent the clandestine diversion of atomic materials to war purposes from plants designed for peaceful use and would provide no guarantee that, in spite of any treaty, a nation which was determined to continue the secret manufacture of atomic weapons would be prevented from doing so. A plan based on periodic inspection, on which the Soviet Union insists, would be even less adequate than one based on continuous inspection.

The Soviet representative dismissed these arguments as exaggerated or non-existent.

Since there was evidence that an atomic explosion had been produced in the Soviet Union, the Soviet representative was asked whether he had any new evidence derived from Soviet experience to support his contention that periodic inspection would be sufficient to assure control. No answer has yet been received to this question.

The five Powers remain convinced that any system of inspection alone would be inadequate and that in order to provide security the International Control Agency must itself operate and manage dangerous facilities and must hold dangerous atomic materials and facilities for making or using dangerous quantities of such materials in trust for Member States.

(b) *Ownership*

During the consultations, the question of ownership, which has often been represented as the real obstacle to agreement on control, was the subject of an extended exchange of views.

The Soviet representative argued that international management and operation were equivalent to international ownership; and that neither international ownership nor international management and operation was essential to control. He stated that his Government would not accept either.

The representatives of the other Sponsoring Powers refuted the interpretation put by the Soviet representative on ownership, management and operation. For the reasons given they believed that the management and operation of dangerous facilities must be entrusted to the International Agency. Management and operation were clearly among the more important rights conferred by ownership. Since effective control would be impossible unless these rights were exercised by the Agency, the nations on whose territories such facilities were situated would have to renounce important rights normally conferred by ownership. This did not necessarily mean the complete devolution of the rights of ownership to the Agency; for example, the Agency would not have the right arbitrarily to close atomic power plants; it would have to conform to national legislation as regards public health and working conditions; it could not construct plants at will but only in agreement with the nation concerned. Moreover, the Agency would not be free to determine the production policy for nuclear fuel since this would follow provisions to be laid down in advance in the treaty. The treaty would also determine the quotas for production and consumption of atomic fuel. Finally, the Agency would hold materials and facilities in trust and would not therefore be able to manage or dispose of them arbitrarily or for its own profit but only for the benefit of Member States.

There might well be other rights which would normally be conferred by ownership and which were not specifically mentioned in the approved plan. Their disposition would follow a simple principle. If there were rights, the exercise of which could impair the effectiveness of control, individual nations would be required to renounce them. Otherwise they might retain them.

If individual nations agreed to renounce national ownership of dangerous atomic materials and the right of managing and operating plants making or using them, in favor of an International Agency acting for the international community, such agreement would be on the basic principle, and there would be no need to quarrel over terminology.

(c) *Sovereignty*

A further argument put forward by the Soviet representative was that to confer on any international agency the powers suggested in the Statement of Principles would constitute a gross infringement of national sovereignty and would permit the International Agency to interfere in the internal economy of individual nations.

In answer to this argument it was pointed out that any plan for international prohibition and control must involve some surrender of sovereignty. The representatives of the other Powers argued that it was indefensible to reject a plan for the international control of atomic energy on the purely negative ground that it would infringe national sovereignty. The ideal of international co-operation and, indeed, the whole concept on which the United Nations was based would be meaningless if States insisted on the rigid maintenance of all their sovereign rights. The question was not one of encroachment on sovereignty, but of assuring the security of the world, which could only be attained by the voluntary association of nations in the exercise of certain rights of sovereignty in an open and co-operating world community.

The Soviet representative remarked that, while some representatives had stated that their Governments were prepared to waive sovereignty provided that the majority plan was accepted, the Government of the U. S. S. R. would not agree to do so.

BASIC OBSTACLES IN THE WAY OF AGREEMENT

It appears from these consultations that, as in the past, the Soviet Union will not negotiate except on the basis of the principles set forth in the Soviet proposals of June 1947.

The essential points in the Soviet control proposals, and the reasons for their rejection by the other five Powers, as brought out in the consultations, are as follows:

The Soviet Union proposes that nations should continue to own explosive atomic materials.

> The other five Powers feel that under such conditions there would be no effective protection against the sudden use of these materials as atomic weapons.

The Soviet Union proposes that nations continue, as at present, to own, operate and manage facilities making or using dangerous quantities of such materials.

> The other Five powers believe that, under such conditions, it would be impossible to detect or prevent the diversion of such materials for use in atomic weapons.

The Soviet Union proposes a system of control depending on periodic inspection of facilities the existence of which the national Government concerned reports to the international agency, supplemented by special investigations on suspicion of treaty violations.

> The other five Powers believe that periodic inspection would not prevent the diversion of dangerous materials and that the special investigations envisaged would be wholly insufficient to prevent clandestine activities.

Other points of difference, including Soviet insistence on the right to veto the recommendations of the International Control Agency, have not yet been discussed in the consultations.

Conclusions

These consultations have not yet succeeded in bringing about agreement between the U. S. S. R. and the other five Powers, but they have served to clarify some of the points on which there is disagreement.

It is apparent that there is a fundamental difference not only on methods but also on aims. All of the Sponsoring Powers other than the U. S. S. R. put world security first and are prepared to accept innovations in traditional concepts of international co-operation, national sovereignty and economic organization where these are necessary for security. The Government of the U. S. S. R. put its sovereignty first and is unwilling to accept measures which may impinge upon or interfere with its rigid exercise of unimpeded state sovereignty.

If this fundamental difference could be overcome, other differences which have hitherto appeared insurmountable could be seen in true perspective, and reasonable ground might be found for their adjustment.

ANNEX I

List of Topics and Statement of Principles Prepared by the Representative of the United Kingdom of Great Britain and Northern Ireland

1. International system of control:

(a) There should be a strong and comprehensive international system for the control of atomic energy and the prohibition of atomic weapons, aimed at attaining the objectives set forth in the resolution of the General Assembly of 24 January 1946. Such an international system should be established, and its scope and functions defined by an enforceable multilateral treaty in which all nations should participate on fair and equitable terms.

(b) Policies concerning the production and use of atomic energy which substantially affect world security should be governed by principles established in the treaty. Production and other dangerous facilities should be distributed in accordance with quotas and provisions laid down in the treaty.

2. International Control Agency:

(a) There should be established, within the framework of the Security Council, an international control agency, deriving its powers and status from the treaty under which it is established. The Agency should possess powers and be charged with responsibility necessary and appropriate for the prompt and effective discharge of the duties imposed upon it by the terms of the treaty. Its powers should be sufficiently broad and flexible to enable it to deal with new developments that may hereafter arise in the field of atomic energy.

(b) The personnel of the Agency should be recruited on an international basis.

(c) The duly accredited representatives of the Agency should be afforded unimpeded rights of ingress, egress and access for the performance of their inspections and other duties into, from and within the territory of every participating nation, unhindered by national or local authorities.

3. Exchange of information:

(a) The Agency and the participating nations should be guided by the general principle that there should be no secrecy concerning scientific and technical information on atomic energy.

(b) The Agency should promote among all nations the exchange of basic scientific information on atomic energy for peaceful ends.

4. Prohibition of atomic weapons:

(a) International agreement to outlaw the national production and use of atomic weapons is an essential part of this international system of control.

(b) The manufacture, possession and use of atomic weapons by all nations and by all persons under their jurisdiction should be forbidden.

(c) Any existing stocks of atomic weapons should be disposed of, and proper use should be made of nuclear fuel for peaceful purposes.

5. Development of atomic energy:

(a) The development and use of atomic energy even for peaceful purposes are not exclusively matters of domestic concern of individual nations, but rather have predominantly international implications and repercussions. The development of atomic energy must be made an international co-operative enterprise in all its phases.

(b) The Agency should have positive research and developmental responsibilities in order to remain in the forefront of atomic knowledge so as to render itself more effective in promoting the beneficial uses of atomic energy and in eliminating the destructive ones.

(c) The Agency should obtain and maintain information as complete and accurate as possible concerning world supplies of source material.

6. Control over atomic materials and facilities:

(a) The Agency should hold all atomic source materials, nuclear fuels and dangerous facilities in trust for the participating nations and be responsible for ensuring that the provisions of the treaty in regard to their disposition are executed.

(b) The Agency should have the exclusive right to operate and manage all dangerous atomic facilities.

(c) In any matters affecting security, nations cannot have any proprietary right or rights of decision arising therefrom over atomic source materials, nuclear fuels or dangerous facilities located within their territories.

(d) The Agency must be given indisputable control of the source materials promptly after their separation from their natural deposits, and on taking possession should give fair and equitable compensation determined by agreement with the nation concerned.

(e) Activities related to atomic energy, which are nondangerous to security, such as mining and milling of source material, and research, may be operated by nations or persons under license from the Agency.

7. *Means of detecting and preventing clandestine activities:*

The Agency should have the duty of seeking out any clandestine activities or facilities involving source material or nuclear fuel; to this end it should have the power to require reports on relevant matters, to verify these reports and obtain such other information as it deems necessary by direct inspection or other means, all subject to appropriate limitations.

8. *Stages:*

The treaty should embrace the entire programme for putting the international system of control into effect, and should provide a schedule for the completion of the transitional process over a period of time, step by step, in an orderly and agreed sequence leading to the full and effective establishment of international control of atomic energy and prohibition of atomic weapons.

ANNEX II

Amendments Submitted by the Representative of the Union of Soviet Socialist Republics to Point 4 of the List of Topics Prepared by the Representative of the United Kingdom of Great Britain and Northern Ireland

4. *Prohibition of atomic weapons:*

(a) An international convention outlawing the production, use and possession of atomic weapons is an essential part of any system of international control of atomic energy. In order to be effective such a convention should be supplemented by the establishment of a universal system of international control, including inspection to ensure that the provisions of the convention are carried out and "to protect States observing the convention from possible violations and evasions".

(b) The Atomic Energy Commission should forthwith proceed to prepare a draft convention for the prohibition of atomic weapons and a draft convention on control of atomic energy, on the understanding that both conventions should be concluded and brought into effect simultaneously.

(c) Atomic weapons should not be used in any circumstances. The production, possession and use of atomic weapons by any State, agency or person whatsoever should be prohibited.

(d) All existing stocks of finished and unfinished atomic weapons should be destroyed within three months of the date of entry into force of the convention for the prohibition of atomic weapons. Nuclear fuel contained in the said atomic weapons should be used for peaceful purposes.

◇◇◇◇◇◇

197. CONTINUING EFFORT TO REACH AGREEMENT ON ATOMIC ENERGY CONTROL

Resolution of the General Assembly, November 23, 1949 [1]

[Once again in 1949 the General Assembly, functioning as the conscience of the world, refused to give up trying to find a solution to the atomic energy problem. This resolution exhorts all nations to do everything within their power to bring about the effective prohibition of atomic weapons and calls upon the Great Powers to continue their consultations. But at Lake Success there was little hope that the resolution would achieve its purpose.]

THE GENERAL ASSEMBLY,

RECALLING its resolutions 1 (I) of 24 January 1946, 41 (I) of 14 December 1946 and 191 (III) of 4 November 1948,

AWARE that atomic energy, if used for peace, will lead to the increase of human welfare, but if used for war may bring about the destruction of civilization,

ANXIOUS to free humanity from the dangers which will continue to exist as long as States retain under their individual control the development and operation of atomic energy facilities,

CONVINCED that an international co-operative effort can avoid these dangers and can hasten the development of the peaceful uses of atomic energy for the benefit of all peoples,

1. URGES all nations to join in such a co-operative development and use of atomic energy for peaceful ends;

2. CALLS upon Governments to do everything in their power to make possible, by the acceptance of effective international control, the effective prohibition and elimination of atomic weapons;

3. REQUESTS the permanent members of the United Nations Atomic Energy Commission to continue their consultations, to explore all possible avenues and examine all concrete suggestions with a view to determining whether they might lead to an agreement securing the basic objectives of the General Assembly in this question, and to keep the Atomic Energy Commission and the General Assembly informed of their progress;

4. RECOMMENDS that all nations, in the use of their rights of sovereignty, join in mutual agreement to limit the individual exercise of those rights in the control of atomic energy to the extent required, in the light of the foregoing considerations, for the promotion of world security and peace, and recommends that all nations agree to exercise such rights jointly.

❖❖❖❖❖

[1] General Assembly roundup, Fourth regular session, Press release GA/600, Part II, p. 11.

REGULATION AND REDUCTION OF ARMAMENTS

198. PRINCIPLES GOVERNING THE GENERAL REGULATION AND REDUCTION OF ARMAMENTS

Resolution of the General Assembly, December 14, 1946 [1]

[Although the Security Council has responsibility in the United Nations system for the formulation of plans for the regulation of armaments, the General Assembly may make recommendations about such matters under Article 11 of the Charter. The First Assembly did just that. After a lengthy debate, it adopted a resolution setting forth a number of important principles governing the general regulation and reduction of armaments. While the resolution is a hodge-podge of compromises, it does make clear that any reduction of armaments will depend upon various other factors such as: (1) the control of atomic energy; (2) the development of an adequate system of collective security; (3) the size and location of national armed forces; and (4) the establishment of an international system of inspection and control.]

1. In pursuance of Article 11 of the Charter and with a view to strengthening international peace and security in conformity with the Purposes and Principles of the United Nations,

THE GENERAL ASSEMBLY,

RECOGNIZES the necessity of an early general regulation and reduction of armaments and armed forces.

2. Accordingly,

THE GENERAL ASSEMBLY,

RECOMMENDS that the Security Council give prompt consideration to formulating the practical measures, according to their priority, which are essential to provide for the general regulation and reduction of armaments and armed forces and to assure that such regulation and reduction of armaments and armed forces will be generally observed by all participants and not unilaterally by only some of the participants. The plans formulated by the Security Council shall be submitted by the Secretary-General to the Members of the United Nations for consideration at a special session of the General Assembly. The treaties or conventions approved by the General Assembly shall be submitted to the signatory States for ratification in accordance with Article 26 of the Charter.

3. As an essential step towards the urgent objective of prohibiting and eliminating from national armaments atomic and all other major weapons adaptable now and in the future to mass destruction, and the early establishment of international control of atomic energy and other modern scientific

[1] The United States and the United Nations: Report by the President to the Congress for the Year 1946, Department of State publication 2735. The United States and the United Nations Report Series 7. pp. 95-97. The wording of this resolution follows closely that of the draft proposal of the United States delegation on the regulation and reduction of armaments presented to the General Assembly on November 13, 1946.

discoveries and technical developments to ensure their use only for peaceful purposes.

THE GENERAL ASSEMBLY,

URGES the expeditious fulfilment by the Atomic Energy Commission of its terms of reference as set forth in Section 5 of the General Assembly Resolution of 24 January 1946.

4. In order to ensure that the general prohibition, regulation and reduction of armaments are directed towards the major weapons of modern warfare and not merely towards the minor weapons,

THE GENERAL ASSEMBLY,

RECOMMENDS that the Security Council expedite consideration of the reports which the Atomic Energy Commission will make to the Security Council and that it facilitate the work of that Commission, and also that the Security Council expedite consideration of a draft convention or conventions for the creation of an international system of control and inspection, these conventions to include the prohibition of atomic and all other major weapons adaptable now and in the future to mass destruction and the control of atomic energy to the extent necessary to ensure its use only for peaceful purposes.

5. THE GENERAL ASSEMBLY,

FURTHER RECOGNIZES that essential to the general regulation and reduction of armaments and armed forces is the provision of practical and effective safeguards by way of inspection and other means to protect complying States against the hazards of violations and evasions. Accordingly,

THE GENERAL ASSEMBLY,

RECOMMENDS to the Security Council that it give prompt consideration to the working out of proposals to provide such practical and effective safeguards in connection with the control of atomic energy and the general regulation and reduction of armaments.

6. To ensure the adoption of measures for the early general regulation and reduction of armaments and armed forces, for the prohibition of the use of atomic energy for military purposes and the elimination from national armaments of atomic and all other major weapons adaptable now or in the future to mass destruction, and for the control of atomic energy to the extent necessary to ensure its use only for peaceful purposes.

THERE SHALL BE ESTABLISHED,

within the framework of the Security Council, which bears the primary responsibility for the maintenance of international peace and security, an international system, as mentioned in paragraph 4, operating through special organs, which organs shall derive their powers and status from the convention or conventions under which they are established.

7. THE GENERAL ASSEMBLY, regarding the problem of security as closely connected with that of disarmament,

RECOMMENDS the Security Council to accelerate as much as possible the placing at its disposal of the armed forces mentioned in Article 43 of the Charter;

It RECOMMENDS the Members to undertake the progressive and balanced withdrawal, taking account of the needs of occupation, of their armed forces stationed in ex-enemy territories, and the withdrawal without delay of armed forces stationed in the territories of Members without their consent freely and publicly expressed in treaties or agreements consistent with the Charter and not contradicting international agreements;

It FURTHER RECOMMENDS a corresponding reduction of national armed forces, and a general progressive and balanced reduction of national armed forces.

8. Nothing herein contained shall alter or limit the resolution of the General Assembly passed on 24 January 1946, creating the Atomic Energy Commission.

9. THE GENERAL ASSEMBLY,

CALLS upon all Members of the United Nations to render every possible assistance to the Security Council and the Atomic Energy Commission in order to promote the establishment and maintenance of international peace and collective security with the least diversion for armaments of the world's human and economic resources.

◇◇◇◇◇◇

199. IMPLEMENTATION OF ASSEMBLY RESOLUTIONS ON THE REGULATION AND REDUCTION OF ARMAMENTS

Resolution of the Security Council, February 13, 1947 [1]

[On February 13, 1947, the Security Council responded to the resolution of the General Assembly. In particular, it approved the creation of a Commission for Conventional Armaments to serve as a companion body to the Atomic Energy Commission. This second Commission the Council charged with the responsibility of working out proposals for the general regulation and reduction of armaments and armed forces. Through these two subsidiary agencies the Council hoped that progress could be made in both fields simultaneously.]

The Security Council, having accepted the resolution of the General Assembly of 14 December 1946 and recognizing that the general regulation and reduction of armaments and armed forces constitute a most important measure for strengthening international peace and security, and that the implementation of the resolution of the General Assembly on this subject is one of the most urgent and important tasks before the Security Council,

Resolves:

1. to work out the practical measures for giving effect to the resolutions of the General Assembly on 14 December 1946 concerning, on the one hand,

<hr>

[1] The United States and the United Nations: Report by the President to the Congress for the Year 1947, Department of State publication 3024, International Organization and Conference Series III, 1, pp. 250-252.

the general regulation and reduction of armaments and armed forces, and the establishment of international control to bring about the reduction of armaments and armed forces and, on the other hand, information concerning the armed forces of the United Nations;

2. to consider as soon as possible the report submitted by the Atomic Energy Commission and to take suitable decisions in order to facilitate its work;

3. to set up a Commission consisting of representatives of the Members of the Security Council with instructions to prepare and to submit to the Security Council within the space of not more than three months, the proposals:

(a) for the general regulation and reduction of armaments and armed forces and

(b) for practical and effective safeguards in connection with the general regulation and reduction of armaments

which the Coommission may be in a position to formulate in order to ensure the implementation of the above-mentioned resolutions of the General Assembly of 14 December 1946, insofar as these resolutions relate to armaments within the Commission's jurisdiction.

The Commission shall submit a plan of work to the Council for approval.

Those matters which fall within the competence of the Atomic Energy Commission as determined by the General Assembly Resolution of 24 January 1946 and 14 December 1946 shall be excluded from the jurisdiction of the Commission hereby established.

The title of the Commission shall be the Commission for Conventional Armaments.

The Commission shall make such proposals as it may deem advisable concerning the studies which the Military Staff Committee and possibly other organs of the United Nations might be asked to undertake.

4. to request the Military Staff Committee to submit to it, as soon as possible and as a matter of urgency, the recommendations for which it has been asked by the Security Council on 16 February 1946 in pursuance of Article 43 of the Charter, and as a first step, to submit to the Security Council not later than 30 April 1947, its recommendations with regard to the basic principles which should govern the organization of the United Nations Armed Force.

◇◇◇◇◇◇

200. PLAN OF WORK ADOPTED BY THE COMMISSION FOR CONVENTIONAL ARMAMENTS, JULY 8, 1947 [1]

[The Commission for Conventional Armaments was convened on March 24, 1947. Its first task was to prepare a plan of work. The plan which finally emerged was an American proposal and generally reflects our position that the regulation of armaments depends upon the establishment of those basic conditions in the world which are essential to international peace and security.

[1] The United States and the United Nations: Report by the President to the Congress for the Year 1947. Department of State publication 3024, International Organization and Conference Series III, 1, p. 252.

While the plan of work was later approved by the Security Council, Poland and the Soviet Union abstained from the vote.]

1. Consideration of and recommendation to the Security Council concerning armaments and armed forces which fall within the jurisdiction of the Commission for Conventional Armaments.

2. Consideration and determination of general principles in connection with the regulation and reduction of armaments and armed forces.

3. Consideration of practical and effective safeguards by means of an international system of control operating through special organs (and by other means) to protect complying states against the hazards of violations and evasions.

4. Formulation of practical proposals for the regulation and reduction of armaments and armed forces.

5. Extension of the principles and proposals set forth in paragraphs 2, 3, and 4 above to states which are not Members of the United Nations.

6. Submission of a report or reports to the Security Council including, if possible, a draft convention.

It is proposed that under the six headings listed above, all of the references by the various delegations suggested for the Plan of Work will be considered.

It is also understood that this Plan of Work does not limit the freedom of individual delegations to make additional suggestions at a later time.

◇◇◇◇◇◇

201. UNITED STATES POSITION ON REGULATION OF CONVENTIONAL ARMAMENTS

Address by Secretary Marshall, September 17, 1947 (Excerpt) [1]

[The position of the United States with respect to the regulation of conventional armaments has been stated on numerous occasions in various United Nations organs since 1946. Nowhere, however, has it been put more succinctly than in the brief excerpt which follows from General Marshall's address before the Second General Assembly in New York.]

The United States also recognizes the importance of regulating conventional armaments. We regret that much more progress has not been made in this field. From this rostrum it is very easy to pay lip service to the sincere aspirations of all peoples for the limitation and reduction of armed forces. This is a serious matter which should not be the subject of demagogic appeals and irresponsible propaganda. I say frankly to the General Assembly that it is the conviction of my Government that a workable system for the regulation of armaments cannot be put into operation until conditions of international confidence prevail. We have consistently and repeatedly made it clear that the regulation of armaments presupposes enough international understanding to make possible the settlement of peace terms with Germany and Japan, the implementation

[1] The United States and the United Nations: Report by the President to the Congress for the Year 1947. Department of State publication 3024, International Organization and Conference Series III, 1, p. 265.

of agreements putting military forces and facilities at the disposal of the Security Council, and an international arrangement for the control of atomic energy.

Nevertheless, we believe it is important not to delay the formulation of a system of arms regulation for implementation when conditions permit. The Security Council has accepted a logical plan of work for the Commission for Conventional Armaments. We believe that the Commission should proceed vigorously to develop a system for the regulation of armaments in the business-like manner outlined in its plan of work.

◇◇◇◇◇◇

202. FORMULATION OF PROPOSALS FOR REGULATION AND REDUCTION OF ARMAMENTS AND ARMED FORCES [1]

Resolution of the Commission for Conventional Armaments, August 12, 1948

[In accordance with its plan of work adopted on July 8, 1947, the Commission gave much of its attention in 1948 to the preparation of a statement of principles to govern the formulation of proposals relating to the regulation and reduction of conventional armaments and armed forces. The resolution which emerged was adopted by a 9 to 2 vote, with the Ukraine and the U.S.S.R. in opposition. It will be noted that the Commission emphasized that the development of an atmosphere of international security is a first prerequisite to the reduction of armaments.]

The Commission for Conventional Armaments recommends that the following principles should govern the formulation of practical proposals for the establishment of a system for the regulation and reduction of armaments and armed forces:

1. A system for the regulation and reduction of armaments and armed forces should provide for the adherence of all States. Initially it must include at least all States having substantial military resources.

2. A system of regulation and reduction of armaments and armed forces can only be put into effect in an atmosphere of international confidence and security. Measures for the regulation and reduction of armaments which would follow the establishment of the necessary degree of confidence might in turn be expected to increase confidence and so justify further measures of regulation and reduction.

3. Examples of conditions essential to such confidence and security are:

(*a*) The establishment of an adequate system of agreements under Article 43 of the Charter. Until the agreed forces are pledged to the Security Council an essential step in establishing a system of collective security will not have been taken.

(*b*) The establishment of international control of atomic energy. It is a basic assumption of the work of the Commission for Conventional Armaments

---

[1] U. N. document S/C.3/31, August 15, 1948. Adopted at the thirteenth meeting of the Commission for Conventional Armaments on August 12, 1948.

that the Atomic Energy Commission will make specific proposals for the elimination from national armaments of atomic weapons and other weapons of mass destruction.

(c) The conclusion of the peace settlements with Germany and Japan. Conditions of international peace and security will not be fully established until measures have been agreed upon which will prevent these States from undertaking aggressive action in the future.

4. A system for the regulation and reduction of armaments and armed forces, in order to make possible the least diversion for armaments of the world's human and economic resources pursuant to Article 26 of the Charter of the United Nations, must limit armaments and armed forces to those which are consistent with and indispensable to the maintenance of international peace and security. Such armaments and armed forces should not exceed those necessary for the implementation of members' obligations and the protection of their rights under the Charter of the United Nations.

5. A system for the regulation and reduction of armaments and armed forces must include an adequate system of safeguards, which by including an agreed system of international supervision will ensure the observance of the provisions of the treaty or convention by all parties thereto. A system of safeguards cannot be adequate unless it possesses the following characteristics:

(a) it is technically feasible and practical;

(b) it is capable of detecting promptly the occurrence of violations;

(c) it causes the minimum interference with, and imposes the minimum burdens on, any aspects of the life of individual nations.

6. Provision must be made for effective enforcement action in the event of violations.

◇◇◇◇◇◇

203. DEFINITION OF ARMAMENTS

Resolution of the Commission for Conventional Armaments, August 12, 1948 [1]

[Following the creation of the Commission for Conventional Armaments, the proper division of work between it and the Commission on Atomic Energy became the subject of some controversy. The resolution adopted by the former Commission on August 12, 1948, resolved the main jurisdictional differences which may have existed between the two agencies by defining what is meant by "conventional armaments" and "weapons of mass destruction."]

The Commission for Conventional Armaments resolves to advise the Security Council:

1. that it considers that all armaments and armed forces, except atomic weapons and weapons of mass destruction, fall within its jurisdiction and that weapons of mass destruction should be defined to include atomic explosive weapons, radio active material weapons, lethal chemical and biological weapons, and any weapons developed in the future which have characteristics

[1] Department of State Bulletin, August 29, 1948, p. 268.

comparable in destructive effect to those of the atomic bomb or other weapons mentioned above.

2. that it proposes to proceed with its work on the basis of the above definition.

◇◇◇◇◇◇

204. ARMS CENSUS

[Largely for propaganda purposes the Soviet Union has proposed, on several occasions, that all states reduce their armed forces by one-third. Due to the rapid demobilization of the West immediately after the war any such fractional reduction of armaments would be advantageous to the Soviet Union. The Western powers, which only recently began building up their strength as a deterrent to Soviet aggression have maintained, in any event, that no such proposal could seriously be considered until complete and verified information is available relating to the conventional arms and armed forces of each state— including the Soviet Union. These two resolutions, adopted by the Third and Fourth General Assemblies, urge that steps be taken to secure such information.]

(a) Resolution of the General Assembly, November 19, 1948 [1]

The General Assembly,

Desiring to establish relations of confident collaboration between the States within the framework of the Charter and to make possible a general reduction of armaments in order that humanity may in future be spared the horrors of war and that the peoples may not be overwhelmed by the continually increasing burden of military expenditure.

Considering that no agreement is attainable on any proposal for the reduction of conventional armaments and armed forces so long as each State lacks exact and authenticated information concerning the conventional armaments and armed forces of other States, so long as no convention has been concluded regarding the types of military forces to which such reduction would apply, and so long as no organ of control has been established,

Considering that the aim of the reduction of conventional armaments and armed forces can only be attained in an atmosphere of real and lasting improvement in international relations, which implies in particular the application of control of atomic energy involving the prohibition of the atomic weapon,

But noting on the other hand that this renewal of confidence would be greatly encouraged if States were placed in possession of precise and verified data as to the level of their respective conventional armaments and armed forces,

Recommends the Security Council to pursue the study of the regulation and reduction of conventional armaments and armed forces through the agency

---

[1] United Nations, Official Records of the Third Session of the General Assembly, Part I, Resolutions, pp. 17, 18.

of the Commission for Conventional Armaments in order to obtain concrete results as soon as possible;

Trusts that the Commission for Conventional Armaments, in carrying out its plan of work, will devote its first attention to formulating proposals for the receipt, checking and publication, by an international organ of control within the framework of the Security Council, of full information to be supplied by Member States with regard to their effectives and their conventional armaments;

Invites the Security Council to report to the Assembly no later than its next regular session on the effect given to the present recommendation, with a view to enabling it to continue its activity with regard to the regulation of armaments in accordance with the purposes and principles defined by the Charter;

Invites all nations in the Commission for Conventional Armaments to co-operate to the utmost of their power in the attainment of the above-mentioned objectives.

Hundred and sixty-third plenary meeting, 19 November 1948.

(b) Resolution of the General Assembly, December 15, 1949 [1]

THE GENERAL ASSEMBLY,

RECALLING its resolution 192 (III) of 19 November 1948, and in particular its recommendation that the Commission for Conventional Armaments, in carrying out its plan of work, devote its first attention to the formulation of proposals for the receipt, checking and publication, by international organ of control within the framework of the Security Council, of full information to be supplied by Member States with regard to their effectives and their conventional armaments,

Having examined the records of the discussions in the Security Council and in the Commission for Conventional Armaments regarding the implementation of the above-mentioned recommendation,

1. APPROVES the proposals formulated by the Commission for Conventional Armaments for the submission by Member States of full information on their conventional armaments and armed forces and the verification thereof, as constituting the necessary basis for the implementation of the above-mentioned recommendation;

2. CONSIDERS that the early submission of this information would constitute as essential step towards a substantial reduction of conventional armaments and armed forces and that, on the other hand, no agreement is likely to be reached on this matter so long as each State lacks exact and authenticated information concerning the conventional armaments and armed forces of other States;

3. NOTES that unanimity among the permanent members of the Security Council, which is essential for the implementation of the above-mentioned proposals, has not yet been achieved;

4. RECOMMENDS therefore that the Security Council, despite the lack of unanimity among its permanent members on this essential feature of its work,

[1] General Assembly Roundup, Fourth Regular Session, Press Release GA/600, Part II, pp. 15-16.

continue its study of the regulation and reduction of conventional armaments and armed forces through the agency of the Commission for Conventional Armaments in accordance with its plan of work, in order to make such progress as may be possible;

5. CALLS UPON all members of the Security Council to co-operate to this end.

◇◇◇◇◇◇

ARMED FORCES FOR THE UNITED NATIONS

205. GENERAL PRINCIPLES GOVERNING THE USE OF ARMED FORCES MADE AVAILABLE BY UN MEMBERS

Report by the Military Staff Committee, 30 April 1947 [1]

[Under Article 43 of the Charter, members of the United Nations agreed to make available to the Security Council, in accordance with special agreements, armed forces necessary for the purpose of maintaining peace and security. Thus far, however, the United Nations Military Staff Committee has been unable to devise plans acceptable to the Great Powers, and Article 43 remains a dead letter. In its first report, the Military Staff Committee pointed out that the Great Powers were unable to agree on such important matters as: (1) the size of the forces to be furnished; (2) the proportion of ground, air, and naval forces to be provided; and (3) the Supreme Command. This extract from the Military Staff Committee's report is a good summary of the areas of agreement and disagreement between the East and the West.]

I. PURPOSE OF ARMED FORCES

Article 1

Armed Forces made available to the Security Council by Member Nations of the United Nations are intended for the maintenance of the restoration of international peace and security in cases:

a. of existence of any threat to international peace;

b. of any breach of international peace and security;

c. of any act of aggression,

when measures undertaken by the Security Council in accordance with Article 41 of the United Nations Charter would be inadequate or have proved to be inadequate and when the threat to international peace and security is such that it necessitates the employment of these armed forces.

Article 2

These Armed Forces may not be employed for purposes inconsistent with the purposes, principles and spirit of the United Nations Charter as defined in its Preamble and Chapter I.

[1] U.N. doc. S/336, 30 April 1947, pp. 3-25.

II. Composition of Armed Forces

Article 3

Armed Forces made available to the Security Council by Member Nations of the United Nations in accordance with Article 43 of the Charter shall be composed of units (formations) of national armed forces, land, sea and air which are normally maintained as components of armed forces of Member Nations of the United Nations.

Article 4

These Armed Forces shall be made available to the Security Council from the best trained and equipped units (formations) of Member Nations of the United Nations.

III. Overall Strength of Armed Forces

Article 5

The moral weight and the potential power behind any decision to employ the Armed Forces made available to the Security Council by Member Nations of the United Nations in enforcement action will be very great, and this fact will directly influence the size of the Armed Forces required.

Article 6

The Armed Forces made available to the Security Council by Member Nations of the United Nations shall be limited to a strength sufficient to enable the Security Council to take prompt action in any part of the world for the maintenance or the restoration of international peace and security as envisaged in Article 42 of the Charter.

Article 7

Accepted by the Chinese, French, U.K. and U.S. Delegations.

An estimate of the overall strength of the Armed Forces and the strength of the Services, land, sea and air, constituting those forces will be made by the Security Council with the assistance of the Military Staff Committee, and used as a basis for negotiating the Special Agreements referred to in Article 43 of the Charter. The final decision regarding the overall strength required will be made by the Security Council as a result of these negotiations.

The U.S.S.R. Delegation accepts Article 7 conditionally. The final acceptance of Article 7 by the U.S.S.R. Delegation will depend on the acceptance by the other Delegations of the Principle of Equality regarding strength and composition of Armed Forces contributed by the five Permanent Members of the Security Council, as stated in the proposal by the U.S.S.R. Delegation for Article 11.

Article 8

Accepted by the Chinese, French, U.K. and U.S. Delegations.

In order to adapt the overall strength of the Armed Forces to international conditions, this overall strength and the strength of the Services constituting these Forces, may be changed on the initiative of the Security Council by additional agreements between the Security Council and the Member Nations of the United Nations.

The U.S.S.R. Delegation accepts Article 8 conditionally. The final acceptance of Article 8 by the U.S.S.R. Delegation will depend on the acceptance by the other Delegations of the Principle of Equality regarding strength and composition of Armed Forces contributed by the five Permanent Members of the Security Council, as stated in the proposal by the U.S.S.R. Delegation for Article 11.

IV. CONTRIBUTION OF ARMED FORCES BY MEMBER NATIONS

Article 9

All Member Nations shall have the opportunity as well as the obligation to place armed forces, facilities and other assistance at the disposal of the Security Council on its call and in accordance with their capabilities and the requirements of the Security Council.

Article 10

In order to facilitate the early establishment of the Armed Forces made available to the Security Council, the Permanent Members of the Security Council shall contribute initially the major portion of these Forces. As the contribution of other Nations of the United Nations become available they shall be added to the forces already contributed.

Article 11

Accepted by the Chinese, French, U.K. and U.S. Delegations.

Each of the five Permanent Members of the Security Council will make a comparable initial overall contribution to the Armed Forces made available to the Security Council by Member Nations of the United Nations. In view of the differences in size and composition of national forces of each Permanent Member and in order to further the ability of the Security Council to constitute balanced and effective combat forces for operations, these contributions

Accepted by the U.S.S.R. Delegation.

Permanent Members of the Security Council shall make available armed forces (land, sea and air) on the Principle of Equality regarding the overall strength and the composition of these forces. In individual instances, deviations from this principle are permitted by special decisions of the Security Council, if such a desire is expressed by a Permanent Member of the Security Council.

may differ widely as to the strength
of the separate components, land,
sea and air.

Article 12

The size and composition of contributions of individual Member Nations will be determined on the initiative of the Security Council, and on the advice of the Military Staff Committee, in the process of negotiations with each Member Nation in accordance with Article 43 of the Charter.

Article 13

No Member Nation of the United Nations shall be urged to increase the strength of its armed forces or to create a particular component thereof for the specific purpose of making a contribution to the Armed Forces made available to the Security Council by Member Nations of the United Nations.

Article 14

Contributions by Member Nations of the United Nations, other than the Permanent Members of the Security Council, may not necessarily be represented by armed forces. Such other Member Nations which may be unable to furnish armed forces may fulfill their obligation to the United Nations by furnishing facilities and other assistance in accordance with agreements reached with the Security Council.

Article 15

Proposals for changes in the size or composition of contributions of a Member Nation or a group of Nations may be initiated by the Security Council or by the Member Nation or group of Nations. Any change in contributions will be effected by additional agreements between the Security Council and the respective Member Nation or group of Nations.

Article 16

Accepted by the Chinese, French, U.K. and U.S. Delegations.

Accepted by the U.S.S.R. Delegation.

The strength and composition of national air force contributions made available to the Security Council shall be determined as set forth in Article 12 above taking into account the obligations arising from Article 45 of the Charter.

The strength and composition of national air force contingents made available to the Security Council by Member Nations for action envisaged in Article 45 of the Charter are determined by the Security Council, with the assistance of the Military Staff Committee, within the limits of a Special agreement or Agreements referred to in Article 43 of the Charter.

Article 17

Accepted by the Chinese and French Delegations.

Not accepted by the U.S.S.R., U.K. and U.S. Delegations.

In case of self-defense (Article 51 of the Charter) and of national emergencies, Member Nations will have the right to make use of Armed Forces, which they have made available to the Security Council in conformity with the terms of special agreements. They undertake, however, to assume anew all of their obligations within the shortest possible space of time.

V. Employment of Armed Forces

Article 18

The Armed Forces made available to the Security Council by Member Nations of the United Nations will be employed, in whole or in part, only by the decision of the Security Council and only for the period necessary for the fulfillment of the tasks envisaged in Article 42 of the Charter.

Article 19

In view of the military advantages which would accrue, the employment of the Armed Forces under Article 42 of the Charter should, whenever possible, be initiated in time to forestall or to suppress promptly a breach of the peace or an act of aggression.

Article 20

Accepted by the Chinese, French, U.K. and U.S. Delegations.

Accepted by the U.S.S.R. Delegation.

After the Armed Forces, including line of communication forces, made available to the Security Council have carried out the tasks with which they have been entrusted by the Security Council under Article 42 of the Charter, they shall be withdrawn as soon as possible to the general locations governed by the Special Agreement or Agreements provided for by Article 43 of the Charter. The time for the beginning and completion of the withdrawal shall be fixed by the Security Council.

The Armed Forces will be withdrawn to their own territories and territorial waters within a time-limit of thirty to ninety days after they have fulfilled the measures envisaged in Article 42 of the Charter, unless otherwise decided by the Security Council. This time-limit should be provided for in Agreements concluded under Article 43 of the Charter.

Article 21

Not accepted by the Chinese, French, U.K. and U.S. Delegations.

Accepted by the U.S.S.R. Delegation.

If for any reasons these Armed Forces remain in territories or territorial waters granted for the use of such forces, under agreements between the Security Council and other Member Nations of the United Nations for the passage, stationing or action of these forces, they should be withdrawn to their own territories or territorial waters not later than thirty days after the expiration of the period indicated in Article 20, unless otherwise decided by the Security Council. This time-limit should be provided for in Agreements concluded under Article 43 of the Charter.

VI. Degree of Readiness of Armed Forces

Article 22

The degree of readiness of the Armed Forces made available by individual Member Nations of the United Nations is fixed by the Security Council, on the advice of the Military Staff Committee, as a result of the negotiations in concluding the Special Agreements with those Member Nations under Article 43 of the Charter.

Article 23

The degree of readiness of the Armed Forces should be maintained at a level which will enable these Forces to start in good time with the fulfillment of the Security Council measures envisaged in Article 42 of the Charter.

Article 24

These Armed Forces should be either maintained in readiness for combat or brought up to readiness for combat within the time-limits to be specified in the Special Agreements.

Article 25

Accepted by the Chinese, French, U.K. and U.S. Delegations.

Accepted by the U.S.S.R. Delegation.

The degree of readiness of national air force contingents should be maintained at a level which will enable the United Nations to take urgent military measures in accordance with

The degree of readiness of national air force contingents made available to the Security Council by Member Nations for action envisaged in Article 45 of the Charter are determined the provisions of Article 45 of the Charter.

by the Security Council, with the assistance of the Military Staff Committee, within the limits of a Special Agreement or Agreements referred to in Article 43 of the Charter.

VII. Provision of Assistance and Facilities, Including Rights of Passage, For Armed Forces

Article 26

Accepted by the Chinese, U.K. and U.S. Delegations.

Accepted by the French Delegation.

Accepted by the U.S.S.R. Delegation.

The Special Agreements between the Security Council and Member Nations under Article 43 of the Charter shall include the following:
a. A general guarantee of rights of passage and of the use of such of the Member Nation's available bases as are required by Armed Forces operating under the Security Council;
b. Specific provisions covering details of bases and other assistance and facilities, including rights of passage, which Member Nations agree to make available to the Security Council on its call. Such specific provisions may be contained in the original agreement or in subsequent agreements under Article 43 of the Charter to be concluded at the appropriate time.

Special Agreements envisaged in Article 43 of the Charter will indicate bases, assistance and facilities, including the right of passage, which the Member Nations will put at the disposal of the Security Council on its call.

In case of necessity, Member Nations undertake, on call of the Security Council and through additional Special Agreements, to make available to it, other bases, assistance and facilities which would have proved necessary to the operations undertaken.

Specific Agreements, concluded at the appropriate time, between the Security Council and the Member Nation concerned, will indicate the duration and the other conditions involved in the exercise of rights thus extended to the Armed Forces operating under the direction of the Security Council.

Special Agreements envisaged in Article 43 of the Charter will indicate assistance and facilities, including the rights of passage, which the Member Nations will make available to the Security Council on its call and in accordance with specific agreements concluded between the Security Council and the Member Nations concerned.

Specific Agreements, concluded at the appropriate time between the Security Council and the Member Nation concerned, will indicate the duration and the other conditions involved in the exercise of rights thus extended to the Armed Forces operating under the direction of the Security Council.

Article 27

Accepted by the Chinese, French, U.K. and U.S. Delegations.

Not accepted by the U.S.S.R. Delegation.

A Member Nation will retain its national sovereignty, and its control and command, over bases and other facilities placed at the disposal of the Security Council.

Article 28

Accepted by the Chinese, French, U.K. and U.S. Delegations.

Not accepted by the U.S.S.R. Delegation.

If additional contributions from Permanent Members of the Security Council are requested when enforcement action under Chapter VII of the Charter is under consideration, those contributions should also be of comparable size taking into account the value of assistance and facilities as well as armed forces which any of the above Member Nations may provide.

VIII. LOGISTICAL SUPPORT OF ARMED FORCES

Article 29

Member Nations of the United Nations which, in accordance with Special Agreements, have placed armed forces at the disposal of the Security Council on its call for the carrying out of measures envisaged in Article 42 of the Charter, will provide their respective forces with all necessary replacements in personnel and equipment and with all necessary supplies and transport.

Article 30

Each Member Nation will at all times maintain a specified level of reserves to replace initial personnel, transport, equipment, spare parts, ammunition and all other forms of supply for the forces which it has agreed to place at the disposal of the Security Council on its call. This reserve level will be prescribed in the Special Agreements under Article 43 of the Charter.

Article 31

Accepted by the Chinese, U.K. and U.S. Delegations.

Accepted by the French and U.S.S.R. Delegations.

Member Nations, in the event of inability to discharge to the full extent

Deviations from the principle stated in Article 29 above shall be permitted their responsibilities under Article 29 above, may invoke the aid of the Security Council, which, on the advice of the Military Staff Committee, will negotiate with other appropriate Member Nations for the provision such assistance as it deems necessary. The agreement of Member Nations concerned must be obtained by the Security Council before the deficiencies in the contribution of one Member Nation can be made up by transfers from the contribution of another Member Nation.

in individual instances at the request of a Member Nation, by special decisions of the Security Council on the advice of the Military Staff Committee, if this Member Nation desires to have supplies and transport made available to it for the proper provision of the Armed Forces placed by this Member Nation at the disposal of the Security Council.

IX. GENERAL LOCATION OF ARMED FORCES

Article 32

Accepted by the Chinese, U.K. and U.S. Delegations.

Accepted by the French Delegation.

Accepted by the U.S.S.R. Delegation.

Armed Forces made available to the Security Council by Member Nations when not employed by the Security Council will, within the terms of Special Agreements referred to in Article 43 of the Charter, be based at the discretion of Member Nations in any territories or waters to which they have legal right of access.

When they are not employed by the Security Council, the Armed Forces which the Member Nation undertakes to make available to the Security Council, on its call, are stationed in the general locations governed by the Special Agreement or Agreements concluded between the Security Council and the Member Nation under Article 43 of the Charter:

(1) either within the national borders of the Member Nation or the territories or waters under its jurisdiction;

(2) or within the territory or waters of ex-enemy nations

Armed Forces made available to the Security Council by Member Nations of the United Nations shall be garrisoned within the frontiers of the contributing Member Nations' own territories or territorial waters, except in cases envisaged in Article 107 of the Charter.

under Article 107 of the Charter or under the terms of the Peace Treaties;

(3) or within the territory or waters of other Nations where Armed Forces have access under international agreements registered with the United Nations Secretariat and published by it in accordance with Article 102 of the Charter;

(4) or in certain strategic areas specified by the Security Council and which have been the subject of specific agreements between the Security Council and the Member Nation under Articles 82 and 83 of the Charter.

Article 33

Accepted by the Chinese, French, U.K. and U.S. Delegations.

Not accepted by the U.S.S.R. Delegation.

The locations of these Armed Forces should be so distributed geographically as to enable the Security Council to take prompt action in any part of the world for the maintenance or restoration of international peace and security.

Article 34

Accepted by the Chinese, French, U.K. and U.S. Delegations.	Not accepted by the U.S.S.R. Delegation.

Any displacement of forces likely to modify their availability as governed by the Special Agreement or Agreements shall be brought to the notice of the Security Council.

Article 35

The Armed Forces made available to the Security Council by Member Nations of the United Nations, on its call, for the fulfillment of measures envisaged in Article 42 of the Charter will be based, during the carrying out of these measures, in areas designated by the Security Council.

X. STRATEGIC DIRECTION AND COMMAND OF ARMED FORCES

Article 36

The Armed Forces which Member Nations of the United Nations agree to make available to the Security Council shall be under the exclusive command of the respective contributing Nations, except when operating under the Security Council.

Article 37

When these forces are called upon for the fulfillment of measures envisaged in Article 42 of the Charter, they shall come under the control of the Security Council.

Note: The word "control" is translated into French as *autorité* and into Russian as подчинение.

Article 38

During the period these armed forces are employed by the Security Council, the Military Staff Committee shall be responsible, under the Security Council, for their strategic direction. The time and place at which the Military Staff Committee will assume or relinquish strategic direction will be designated by the Security Council.

Article 39

The command of national contingents will be exercised by Commanders appointed by the respective Member Nations. These contingents will retain their national character and will be subject at all times to the discipline and regulations in force in their own national armed forces.

Article 40

The Commanders of national contingents will be entitled to communicate directly with the authorities of their own country on all matters.

Article 41

Accepted by the Chinese, U.S.S.R., and U.S. Delegations.	Accepted by the French and U.K. Delegations.

An overall Commander or overall Commanders of Armed Forces made available to the Security Council may be appointed by the latter, on the advice of the Military Staff Committee, for the period of employment of these forces by the Security Council.	A supreme Commander or supreme Commanders of Armed Forces made available to the Security Council may be appointed by the latter, on the advice of the Military Staff Committee, for the period of employment of these forces by the Security Council. Commanders-in-Chief of land, sea or air forces acting under the supreme Commander or Commanders mentioned above may be appointed by the Security Council on the advice of the Military Staff Committee.

◇◇◇◇◇◇

206. THE WORK OF THE MILITARY STAFF COMMITTEE

Letter From the Chairman of the Military Staff Committee to the President of the Security Council, August 6, 1948 [1]

[Following its first report, the Military Staff Committee has continued to disagree on the fundamentals necessary to implement Article 43. This letter reflects the difficult atmosphere in which the Military Staff Committee has carried on its work, and indicates the nature of the stalemate which still exists.]

SIR,

In order that the Security Council may be fully advised concerning the work in the Military Staff Committee, the United Kingdom, the United States, Chinese and French Delegations have requested the Chairman to submit the following statement to you. Such divergent views as the USSR Delegation may desire to call to your attention will be submitted when received from that Delegation.

In its letter dated 2 July 1948, issued as MS/405 on 6 July 1948, the Military Staff Committee reported to you that, owing to the divergencies of view which still prevailed on some of the General Principles, it had not been in a position to undertake the final determination of the Overall Strength and Composition of the Armed Forces, and thus achieve further progress in this matter towards the conclusion of the special agreements required by Article 43 of the Charter.

Since the dispatch of that letter, the Military Staff Committee met to discuss the pursuance of the tasks entrusted to it, as set out in its Programme of Work (Ref: MS/271/M44, dated 16 May 1947, an excerpt of which is enclosed as Annex).

[1] United Nations document, S/956, 9 August 1948.

Inasmuch as unanimity could not be achieved on the question of the Overall Strength and Composition of the United Nations Armed Forces (Item I of the Programme of Work), it was, a priori, impossible to consider Items II and III of the Programme of Work, dealing with the contributions by Member Nations.

The consideration of Item IV of the Programme of Work, i. e., Preparation of a Draft Standard Form of Special Agreement was then envisaged.

However, there again, the five Delegations were unable to agree unanimously that such a study could be undertaken before the Military Staff Committee had received instructions from the Security Council concerning the divergencies noted on some of the General Principles.

In reporting to you the existence of this latest stalemate, the Military Staff Committee has the honour to call, once more, the attention of the Security Council to the fact that the Military Staff Committee considers it urgent to resolve the disagreement which prevails on some of the General Principles, and of which the Security Council had been apprised as early as 30 April 1947 (MS/264).

HUMAN RIGHTS

207. UNIVERSAL DECLARATION OF HUMAN RIGHTS

Resolution of General Assembly, December 10, 1948 [1]

[The Declaration of Human Rights is one of the historic landmarks in the evolution of the idea that people everywhere—because they are human beings —are entitled to certain social, economic, civil, and political rights. The declaration was the product of two years of work by the UN Commission on Human Rights. From a legal point of view it is a statement of goals and principles and by itself has no binding effect upon the governments of the world. Therefore a companion Convention on Human Rights has been under preparation by the United Nations. The Convention, when signed and ratified by a sufficient number of states will be binding upon the contracting parties.]

---

[1] Adopted by the General Assembly, December 10, 1948. See press release PGA/100, pt. IV, 11-16. On February 16, 1946, the United Nations created a Commission on Human Rights as one of the subsidiary organs of the Economic and Social Council. On December 11, 1946, the General Assembly referred the draft Declaration on Fundamental Human Rights and Freedoms, submitted by Panama, to the Council for reference to the Commission. (See U. N. Document A/234.) For United States proposals regarding an International Bill of Rights, see Department of State Bulletin of February 16, 1947, pp. 277-278. For more specific proposals by the United States at the first session of Commission on Human Rights, June 9-25, 1947, see U. N. Document E/CN.4/AC.1/8, June 11, 1947. For a United States proposal for a Declaration of Human Rights, see Department of State Press Release 937, November 28, 1947. This proposal was developed by an interdepartmental committee which included representatives from the Departments of State, Justice, Labor, and Interior, and the Federal Security Agency. It was discussed at a conference of representatives of approximately 150 nongovernmental organizations held at the Department of State on October 31, 1947, and was revised to take account of the views expressed at this conference. This proposal was submitted by Mrs. Franklin D. Roosevelt, United States Representative on the Commission on Human Rights, at its second session, held at Geneva, Switzerland, December 1-19, 1947. For first drafts of the International Covenant on Human Rights and International Declaration on Human Rights, see United Nations Bulletin, January 15, 1948, pp. 1-5.

PREAMBLE

WHEREAS recognition of the inherent dignity and of the equal and inalienable rights of all members of the human family is the foundation of freedom, justice and peace in the world,

WHEREAS disregard and contempt for human rights have resulted in barbarous acts which have outraged the conscience of mankind, and the advent of a world in which human beings shall enjoy freedom of speech and belief and freedom from fear and want has been proclaimed as the highest aspiration of the common people,

WHEREAS it is essential, if man is not to be compelled to have recourse, as a last resort, to rebellion against tyranny and oppression, that human rights should be protected by the rule of law,

WHEREAS it is essential to promote the development of friendly relations between nations,

WHEREAS the peoples of the United Nations have in the Charter reaffirmed their faith in fundamental human rights, in the dignity and worth of the human person and in the equal rights of men and women and have determined to promote social progress and better standards of life in larger freedom,

WHEREAS Member States have pledged themselves to achieve, in co-operation with the United Nations, the promotion of universal respect for and observance of human rights and fundamental freedoms,

WHEREAS a common understanding of these rights and freedoms is of the greatest importance for the full realization of this pledge,

Now therefore

The General Assembly,

Proclaims this Universal Declaration of Human Rights as a common standard of achievement for all peoples and all nations, to the end that every individual and every organ of society, keeping this Declaration constantly in mind, shall strive by teaching and education to promote respect for these rights and freedoms and by progressive measures, national and international, to secure their universal and effective recognition and observance, both among the peoples of Member States themselves and among the peoples of territories under their jurisdiction.

ARTICLE 1. All human beings are born free and equal in dignity and rights. They are endowed with reason and conscience and should act towards one another in a spirit of brotherhood.

ARTICLE 2. Everyone is entitled to all the rights and freedoms set forth in this Declaration, without distinction of any kind, such as race, colour, sex, language, religion, political or other opinion, national or social origin, property, birth or other status.

Furthermore, no distinction shall be made on the basis of the political, jurisdictional or international status of the country or territory to which a person belongs, whether it be independent, trust, non-self-governing or under any other limitation of sovereignty.

ARTICLE 3. Everyone has the right to life, liberty and the security of person.

ARTICLE 4. No one shall be held in slavery or servitude; slavery and the slave trade shall be prohibited in all their forms.

ARTICLE 5. No one shall be subjected to torture or to cruel, inhuman or degrading treatment or punishment.

ARTICLE 6. Everyone has the right to recognition everywhere as a person before the law.

ARTICLE 7. All are equal before the law and are entitled without any discrimination to equal protection of the law. All are entitled to equal protection against any discrimination in violation of this Declaration and against any incitement to such discrimination.

ARTICLE 8. Everyone has the right to an effective remedy by the competent national tribunals for acts violating the fundamental rights granted him by the constitution or by law.

ARTICLE 9. No one shall be subjected to arbitrary arrest, detention or exile.

ARTICLE 10. Everyone is entitled in full equality to a fair and public hearing by an independent and impartial tribunal, in the determination of his rights and obligations and of any criminal charge against him.

ARTICLE 11. *1*. Everyone charged with a penal offence has the right to be presumed innocent until proved guilty according to law in a public trial at which he has had all the guarantees necessary for his defence.

2. No one shall be held guilty of any penal offence on account of any act or omission which did not constitute a penal offence, under national or international law, at the time when it was committed. Nor shall a heavier penalty be imposed than the one that was applicable at the time the penal offence was committed.

ARTICLE 12. No one shall be subjected to arbitrary interference with his privacy, family, home or correspondence, nor to attacks upon his honour and reputation. Everyone has the right to the protection of the law against such interference or attacks.

ARTICLE 13. *1*. Everyone has the right to freedom of movement and residence within the borders of each state.

2. Everyone has the right to leave any country, including his own, and to return to his country.

ARTICLE 14. *1*. Everyone has the right to seek and to enjoy in other countries asylum from persecution.

2. This right may not be invoked in the case of prosecutions genuinely arising from non-political crimes or from acts contrary to the purposes and principles of the United Nations.

ARTICLE 15. *1*. Everyone has the right to a nationality.

2. No one shall be arbitrarily deprived of his nationality nor denied the right to change his nationality.

ARTICLE 16. *1*. Men and women of full age, without any limitation due to race, nationality or religion, have the right to marry and to found a family. They are entitled to equal rights as to marriage, during marriage and at its dissolution.

2. Marriage shall be entered into only with the free and full consent of the intending spouses.

3. The family is the natural and fundamental group unit of society and is entitled to protection by society and the State.

ARTICLE 17. *1.* Everyone has the right to own property alone as well as in association with others.

2. No one shall be arbitrarily deprived of his property.

ARTICLE 18. Everyone has the right to freedom of thought, conscience and religion; this right includes freedom to change his religion or belief, and freedom, either alone or in community with others and in public or private, to manifest his religion or belief in teaching, practice, worship and observance.

ARTICLE 19. Everyone has the right to freedom of opinion and expression; this right includes freedom to hold opinions without interference and to seek, receive and impart information and ideas through any media and regardless of frontiers.

ARTICLE 20. *1.* Everyone has the right to freedom of peaceful assembly and association.

2. No one may be compelled to belong to an association.

ARTICLE 21. *1.* Everyone has the right to take part in the Government of his country, directly or through freely chosen representatives.

2. Everyone has the right of equal access to public service in his country.

3. The will of the people shall be the basis of the authority of government; this will shall be expressed in periodic and genuine elections which shall be by universal and equal suffrage and shall be held by secret vote or by equivalent free voting procedures.

ARTICLE 22. Everyone, as a member of society, has the right to social security and is entitled to realization, through national effort and international co-operation and in accordance with the organization and resources of each State, of the economic, social and cultural rights indispensable for his dignity and the free development of his personality.

ARTICLE 23. *1.* Everyone has the right to work, to free choice of employment, to just and favourable conditions of work and to protection against unemployment.

2. Everyone, without any discrimination, has the right to equal pay for equal work.

3. Everyone who works has the right to just and favourable remuneration insuring for himself and his family an existence worthy of human dignity, and supplemented, if necessary, by other means of social protection.

4. Everyone has the right to form and to join trade unions for the protection of his interests.

ARTICLE 24. Everyone has the right to rest and leisure, including reasonable limitation of working hours and periodic holidays with pay.

ARTICLE 25. *1.* Everyone has the right to a standard of living adequate for the health and well-being of himself and of his family, including food, clothing, housing and medical care and necessary social services, and the right to security in the event of unemployment, sickness, disability, widowhood, old age or other lack of livelihood in circumstances beyond his control.

2. Motherhood and childhood are entitled to special care and assistance. All children, whether born in or out of wedlock, shall enjoy the same social protection.

ARTICLE 26. *1.* Everyone has the right to education. Education shall be free, at least in the elementary and fundamental stages. Elementary education shall be compulsory. Technical and professional education shall be made generally available and higher education shall be equally accessible to all on the basis of merit.

2. Education shall be directed to the full development of the human personality and to the strengthening of respect for human rights and fundamental freedoms. It shall promote understanding, tolerance and friendship among all nations, racial or religious groups, and shall further the activities of the United Nations for the maintenance of peace.

3. Parents have a prior right to choose the kind of education that shall be given to their children.

ARTICLE 27. 1. Everyone has the right freely to participate in the cultural life of the community, to enjoy the arts and to share in scientific advancement and its benefits.

2. Everyone has the right to the protection of the moral and material interests resulting from any scientific, literary or artistic production of which he is the author.

ARTICLE 28. Everyone is entitled to a social and international order in which the rights and freedoms set forth in this Declaration can be fully realized.

ARTICLE 29. 1. Everyone has duties to the community in which alone the free and full development of his personality is possible.

2. In the exercise of his rights and freedoms, everyone shall be subject only to such limitations as are determined by law solely for the purpose of securing due recognition and respect for the rights and freedoms of others and of meeting the just requirements of morality, public order and the general welfare in a democratic society.

3. These rights and freedoms may in no case be exercised contrary to the purposes and principles of the United Nations.

ARTICLE 30. Nothing in this Declaration may be interpreted as implying for any State, group or person any right to engage in any activity or to perform any act aimed in the destruction of any of the rights and freedoms set forth herein.

◇◇◇◇◇◇

208. RESOLUTION OF THE GENERAL ASSEMBLY RELATING TO THE CRIME OF GENOCIDE, AND TEXT OF THE CONVENTION, DECEMBER 9, 1948 [1]

[The atrocities practiced upon subject peoples by totalitarian states both before and during World War II aroused public opinion throughout the world. Consequently one of the first acts of the UN General Assembly was to condemn this practice by declaring in December 1946 that genocide—which includes various types of acts committed with intent to destroy, in whole or in part, a national, ethnical, racial, or religious group—was a crime against international law. At the same time, an *ad hoc* committee was appointed to

---

[1] Press Release PGA/100, pt. VII, pp. 12-16. On June 16, 1949, President Truman transmitted this convention to the Senate for its advice and consent to ratification. The Senate had not taken final action at the time these documents went to press. See Department of State Bulletin, July 4, 1949, pp. 844-847.

prepare a draft convention incorporating the principles of the declaration. Finally, on December 9, 1948, the Assembly adopted the Genocide Convention, which was ratified subsequently and adhered to by a sufficient number of states to put it into effect early in 1951. At that time, the United States had not yet ratified the Convention and therefore was not bound by its terms.]

THE GENERAL ASSEMBLY

APPROVES the annexed Convention on the Prevention and Punishment of the Crime of Genocide and proposes it for signature and ratification or accession in accordance with its article XI.

ANNEX

CONVENTION ON THE PREVENTION AND PUNISHMENT OF THE CRIME OF GENOCIDE

THE CONTRACTING PARTIES,

HAVING CONSIDERED the declaration made by the General Assembly of the United Nations in its resolution 96 (I) dated 11 December 1946 that genocide is a crime under international law, contrary to the spirit and aims of the United Nations and condemned by the civilized world;

RECOGNIZING that at all periods of history genocide has inflicted great losses on humanity; and

BEING CONVINCED that, in order to liberate mankind from such an odious scourge, international co-operation is required;

HEREBY AGREE AS HEREINAFTER PROVIDED:

ARTICLE I

The Contracting Parties confirm that genocide, whether committed in time of peace or in time of war, is a crime under international law which they undertake to prevent and to punish.

ARTICLE II

In the present Convention, genocide means any of the following acts committed with intent to destroy, in whole or in part, a national, ethnical, racial or religious group, as such:

    (a) Killing members of the group;
    (b) Causing serious bodily or mental harm to members of the group;
    (c) Deliberately inflicting on the group conditions of life calculated to bring about its physical destruction in whole or in part;
    (d) Imposing measures intended to prevent births within the group;
    (e) Forcibly transferring children of the group to another group.

ARTICLE III

The following acts shall be punishable:

    (a) Genocide;
    (b) Conspiracy to commit genocide;
    (c) Direct and public incitement to commit genocide;

(d) Attempt to commit genocide;

(e) Complicity in genocide.

ARTICLE IV

Persons committing genocide or any of the other acts enumerated in article III shall be punished, whether they are constitutionally responsible rulers, public officials or private individuals.

ARTICLE V

The Contracting Parties undertake to enact, in accordance with their respective Constitutions, the necessary legislation to give effect to the provisions of the present Convention and, in particular, to provide effective penalties for persons guilty of genocide or any of the other acts enumerated in Article III.

ARTICLE VI

Persons charged with genocide or any of the other acts enumerated in article III shall be tried by a competent tribunal of the State in the territory of which the act was committed, or by such international penal tribunal as may have jurisdiction with respect to those Contracting Parties which shall have accepted its jurisdiction.

ARTICLE VII

Genocide and the other acts enumerated in article III shall not be considered as political crimes for the purpose of extradition.

The Contracting Parties pledge themselves in such cases to grant extradition in accordance with their laws and treaties in force.

ARTICLE VIII

Any Contracting Party may call upon the competent organs of the United Nations to take such action under the Charter of the United Nations as they consider appropriate for the prevention and suppression of acts of genocide or any of the other acts enumerated in article III.

ARTICLE IX

Disputes between the Contracting Parties relating to the interpretation, application or fulfillment of the present Convention, including those relating to the responsibility of a State for genocide or any of the other acts enumerated in article III, shall be submitted to the International Court of Justice at the request of any of the parties to the dispute.

ARTICLE X

The present Convention, of which the Chinese, English, French, Russian and Spanish texts are equally authentic, shall bear the date of 9 December 1948.

ARTICLE XI

The present Convention shall be open until 31 December 1949 for signature on behalf of any Member of the United Nations and of any non-member State to which an invitation to sign has been addressed by the General Assembly.

The present Convention shall be ratified, and the instruments of ratification shall be deposited with the Secretary-General of the United Nations.

After 1 January 1950 the present Convention may be acceded to on behalf of any Member of the United Nations and of any non-member State which has received an invitation as aforesaid.

Instruments of accession shall be deposited with the Secretary-General of the United Nations.

ARTICLE XII

Any Contracting Party may at any time, by notification addressed to the Secretary-General of the United Nations, extend the application of the present Convention to all or any of the territories for the conduct of whose foreign relations that Contracting Party is responsible.

ARTICLE XIII

On the day when the first twenty instruments of ratification or accession have been deposited, the Secretary-General shall draw up a process-verbal and transmit a copy of it to each Member of the United Nations and to each of the non-member States contemplated in article XI.

The present Convention shall come into force on the ninetieth day following the date of deposit of the twentieth instrument of ratification or accession.

Any ratification or accession effected subsequent to the latter date shall become effective on the ninetieth day following the deposit of the instrument of ratification or accession.

ARTICLE XIV

The present Convention shall remain in effect for a period of ten years as from the date of its coming into force.

It shall thereafter remain in force for successive periods of five years for such Contracting Parties as have not denounced it at least six months before the expiration of the current period.

Denunciation shall be effected by a written notification addressed to the Secretary-General of the United Nations.

ARTICLE XV

If, as a result of denunciations, the number of Parties to the present Convention should become less than sixteen, the Convention shall cease to be in force as from the date on which the last of these denunciations shall become effective.

ARTICLE XVI

A request for the revision of the present Convention may be made at any time by any Contracting Party by means of a notification in writing addressed to the Secretary-General.

The General Assembly shall decide upon the steps, if any, to be taken in respect of such request.

ARTICLE XVII

The Secretary-General of the United Nations shall notify all Members of the United Nations and the non-member States contemplated in article XI of the following:

(a) Signatures, ratifications and accessions received in accordance with article XI;

(b) Notifications received in accordance with article XII;

(c) The date upon which the present Convention comes into force in accordance with article XIII;

(d) Denunciations received in accordance with article XIV;

(e) The abrogation of the Convention in accordance with article XV;

(f) Notifications received in accordance with article XVI.

ARTICLE XVIII

The original of the present Convention shall be deposited in the archives of the United Nations.

A certified copy of the Convention shall be transmitted to all Members of the United Nations and to the non-member States contemplated in article XI.

ARTICLE XIX

The present Convention shall be registered by the Secretary-General of the United Nations on the date of its coming into force.

◇◇◇◇◇◇

209. VIOLATION OF HUMAN RIGHTS AND FUNDAMENTAL FREEDOMS IN BULGARIA, HUNGARY, AND RUMANIA

[At Yalta and Potsdam it was agreed that democratic governments should be established in Bulgaria, Hungary, and Rumania. The treaties of peace with those countries contained guarantees of fundamental rights and human freedom. After the new governments were established, these promises were violated and the United States delivered protests to all three countries. Each country denied the accusations and complained that the United States was attempting to interfere in the former's domestic affairs. Since the notes followed a common pattern, only those exchanged with Bulgaria are reproduced here by way of example.]

(a) Note From the United States to Bulgaria, March 29, 1949 [1]

The Legation of the United States of America presents its compliments to the Ministry of Foreign Affairs of Bulgaria and, acting under the instructions of the United States Government, has the honor to refer to Article 2 of the Treaty of Peace with Bulgaria, and to the Bulgarian Government's record with respect to fulfillment of its obligations under that Article to protect human rights and the fundamental freedoms.

Article 2 of the Treaty of Peace reads as follows:

"Bulgaria shall take all measures necessary to secure to all persons under Bulgarian jurisdiction, without distinction as to race, sex, language or reli-

[1] Department of State Bulletin, April 10, 1949, pp. 450-453.

gion, the enjoyment of human rights and of the fundamental freedoms, including freedom of expression, of press and publication, of religious worship, of political opinion and of public meeting."

Since the entry into force on September 15, 1947 of the Treaty of Peace with Bulgaria, the United States Government, as a signatory of that instrument, has observed closely developments in Bulgaria with a view to ascertaining whether the Bulgarian Government has been fulfilling its obligations under the Treaty. The United States Government attaches particular importance to the obligations, set forth in the aforementioned Article, which require the Bulgarian Government to secure to all persons under Bulgarian jurisdiction the enjoyment of human rights and of the fundamental freedoms. On the basis of its observations during this period, the United States Government concludes that the Bulgarian Government, although it has had ample opportunity to carry out its commitments in good faith, has deliberately and systematically denied to the Bulgarian people, by means of privative measures and oppressive acts, the exercise of the very rights and freedoms which it has pledged to secure to them under Article 2 of the Treaty. The disregard shown by the Bulgarian Government for the rights and liberties of persons under its jurisdiction, as illustrated below, has indeed become so notorious as to evoke the condemnation of free peoples everywhere.

Through the exercise of police power the Bulgarian Government has deprived large numbers of its citizens of their basic human rights, assured to them under the Treaty of Peace. These deprivations have been manifested by arbitrary arrests, systematic perversion of the judicial process, and the prolonged detention in prisons and camps, without public trial, or persons whose views are opposed to those of the regime.

Similarly, the Bulgarian Government has denied to persons living under its jurisdiction, as individuals and as organized groups including democratic political parties, the fundamental freedoms of political opinion and of public meeting. It has dissolved the National Agrarian Union, the Bulgarian Socialist Party and other groups, and has imprisoned many of their leaders. With the Treaty of Peace barely in effect and in the face of world opinion, the Bulgarian Government ordered the execution of Nikola Petkov, National Agrarian Union leader, who dared to express democratic political opinions, which did not correspond to those of the Bulgarian Government. Proceedings were instituted against those deputies who did not agree with its policies, with the result that no vestige of parliamentary opposition now remains, an illustration of the effective denial of freedom of political opinion in Bulgaria.

By restrictions on the press and on other publications, the Bulgarian Government has denied to persons under its jurisdiction the freedom of expression guaranteed to them under the Treaty of Peace. By laws, administrative acts, and the use of force and intimidation on the part of its officials, the Bulgarian Government has made it impossible for individual citizens openly to express views not in conformity to those officially prescribed. Freedom of the press does not exist in Bulgaria.

By legislation, by the acts of its officials, and by "trials" of religious leaders, the Bulgarian Government has acted in contravention of the express provision of the Treaty of Peace in respect of freedom of worship. Recent measures directed against the Protestant denominations in Bulgaria, for example, are clearly incompatible with the Bulgarian Government's obligation to secure freedom of religious worship to all persons under its jurisdiction.

The Bulgarian Government bears full responsibility not only for acts committed since the effective date of the Treaty of Peace which are in contravention of Article 2, but also for its failure to redress the consequences of acts committeed prior to that date which have continued to prejudice the enjoyment of human rights and of the fundamental freedoms. The United States Government, mindful of its responsibilities under the Treaty of Peace, has drawn attention on appropriate occasions to the flagrant conduct of the Bulgarian authorities in this regard. The Bulgarian Government, however, has failed to modify its conduct in conformity with the stipulations of the Treaty.

In the circumstances, the United States Government, as a signatory of the Treaty of Peace, finds that the Bulgarian Government has repeatedly violated the provisions of Article 2 of that Treaty. In as much as the obligation of the Government of Bulgaria to secure to all persons under Bulgarian jurisdiction the enjoyment of human rights and fundamental freedoms is expressly stipulated in the Treaty, no specious argument that the matters raised in the present note are purely of a domestic character can be accepted. The United States Government, accordingly, calls upon the Bulgarian Government to adopt prompt remedial measures in respect of the violations referred to above and requests the Bulgarian Government to specify the steps which it is prepared to take in implementing fully the terms of Article 2 of the Treaty of Peace.

*   *   *

(b) Bulgarian Note to the United States, April 21, 1949 [1]

The Ministry of Foreign Affairs of the People's Republic of Bulgaria has the honor to inform the Legation of the United States that it has taken cognizance of the tenor of the Legation's Note No. 130.

The Government of the People's Republic of Bulgaria has always carried out and will carry out in a most conscientious manner the clauses of the Peace Treaty and this not only because this Government is signatory to the said Treaty, but also because its policy, expression of the will of the overwhelming majority of the Bulgarian people, is, by its inherent nature, profoundly democratic, and corresponds fully to the letter and spirit of Articles 2, 3, 4, and 5 of the Peace Treaty.

1. Even before the entry into force of the Peace Treaty, the Bulgarian Government had undertaken all measures dependent on it (its will) for the guaranteeing of the fundamental civil liberties as well as the political rights of Bulgarian citizens, without distinction of race, nationality, sex or creed:

(a) This Government convoked, on the basis of universal, secret, equal and direct suffrage, a Grand National Assembly which elaborated the constitutional law of the country, and this Constitution did not only consecrate in a solemn manner the fundamental rights and freedoms of Bulgarian citizens —rights and freedoms which are subject matter of Article 2 of the Peace Treaty but also guaranteed their effective exercise.

[1] Department of State Bulletin, June 12, 1949, pp. 755-759.

(*b*) At the same time, this Government took the necessary measures for the definitive liquidation of the fascist regime and the elimination of every attempt to frustrate the nation of its democratic rights and freedoms. These measures of the Government were in conformance with the text itself of Article 4 of the Treaty, and moreover, the new Bulgarian Constitution which came into force on December 5, 1947, guaranteed to the Bulgarian people the necessary right and power to condemn to failure all attempts of fascist or anti-democratic restoration in Bulgaria. In the presence of such well-known facts, it is strange that the Government of the United States could formulate against Bulgaria accusations of non-observance and violation of the political clauses of the Peace Treaty, and of Article 2 of the said Treaty in particular.

2. Similarly, it is surprising that the Government of the United States has deemed it necessary to support its accusations of the Peace Treaty in force since September 15, 1947 by evoking facts going back to the Armistice period, at a time when the three great Powers disposed of measures to exercise a wide control over the administration of the country.

3. On the other hand, the note of the United States Government relates to certain facts and acts of the Bulgarian Government, such as trials, etc., which have taken place after the entry into force of the Peace Treaty. The Bulgarian Government having taken all measures to ensure the compliance with all the political clauses of the Peace Treaty, and notably after Bulgaria had been granted the most democratic Constitution in the world, and the people had been guaranteed legal power to exercise and defend its rights and freedoms, the Bulgarian Government, as government of a sovereign state, cannot agree to permit other states the appreciation of its acts, for which it is solely responsible to the National Assembly. This Government can even less agree to suffer the criticism of foreign powers, in so far as the activities of Bulgarian courts are concerned, being (in existence) by virtue of the Constitution and functioning in public in accordance with the most modern and most democratic of laws.

The Bulgarian Government will repel every attempt of interference in the domestic affairs of Bulgaria and will consider as an unfriendly act any attempt to force it to accept treatment as a state whose internal acts would be subject to judgment by foreign powers.

4. As regards the essence of the accusations formulated in the note of the United States Government, the Bulgarian Government, without wishing to discuss their compass, rejects them energetically. Under the regime of people's democracy in Bulgaria, the toiling masses of towns and villages which constitute the immense majority of the nation, enjoy not only on paper but also in fact all fundamental political rights and freedoms of man. Restrictions on the exercise of the freedom of meeting or of association, of the freedom of speech or of press, do not exist and are not applied in Bulgaria excepting in the cases provided by the laws against infringers and in the interest itself of public security, maintenance of order, and public morals of the people.

In conclusion, the Government of the People's Republic of Bulgaria considers the note of the Honorable Legation of the United States as unfounded, and its tenor, rendered public by the United States Government immediately after it had been delivered and long before the present reply, as unfriendly propaganda, incompatible with the principles of international law, and of a nature to encourage the pro-fascist and hostile elements in the country.

The Ministry of Foreign Affairs of the People's Republic of Bulgaria avails itself of this opportunity to reiterate to the Honorable Legation of the United States the assurance of its high consideration.

◇◇◇◇◇◇

210. RESOLUTION BY THE GENERAL ASSEMBLY, APRIL 30, 1949 [1]

[When Bulgaria and Hungary continued to violate their treaty pledges with respect to human rights and fundamental freedoms, Britain sent notes of protest to the three governments similar to those delivered by the United States. The results were the same. Consequently, the United States and Britain laid the problem at the door of the United Nations, and the General Assembly passed the following resolution calling upon Bulgaria and Hungary to observe their treaties of peace.]

The General Assembly,

CONSIDERING that one of the purposes of the United Nations is to achieve international co-operation in promoting and encouraging respect for human rights and fundamental freedoms for all, without distinction as to race, sex, language or religion,

CONSIDERING that the Governments of Bulgaria and Hungary have been accused, before the General Assembly, of acts contrary to the purposes of the United Nations and to their obligations under the Peace Treaties to ensure to all persons within their respective jurisdictions the enjoyment of human rights and fundamental freedoms,

1. EXPRESSES its deep concern at the grave accusations made against the Governments of Bulgaria and Hungary regarding the suppression of human rights and fundamental freedoms in those countries;

2. NOTES with satisfaction that steps have been taken by several States signatories to the Peace Treaties with Bulgaria and Hungary regarding these accusations, and expresses the hope that measures will be diligently applied, in accordance with the Treaties, in order to ensure respect for human rights and fundamental freedoms;

3. MOST URGENTLY DRAWS the attention of the Governments of Bulgaria and Hungary to their obligations under the Peace Treaties, including the obligation to co-operate in the settlement of all these questions;

4. *Decides* to retain the question on the agenda of the fourth regular session of the General Assembly of the United Nations.

[1] U. N. doc. A/851 Adopted April 30, 1949.

◇◇◇◇◇◇

211. UNITED STATES NOTE TO BULGARIA INVOKING PEACE TREATY CLAUSES TO SETTLE DISPUTE ON VIOLATING HUMAN FREEDOMS, MAY 31, 1949 [1]

UNITED STATES NOTE TO BULGARIA, MAY 31, 1949

[The treaties of peace with Bulgaria, Hungary, and Rumania provided that in the event of a dispute over the interpretation of any of the treaty provisions, the matter was to be referred to American, British, and Soviet representatives for consideration. On May 31, 1949, the United States notified Bulgaria, Hungary, and Rumania that it was invoking the procedure provided in the treaties to settle the dispute over the violation of fundamental human rights by those countries. The text of the note to Bulgaria is reproduced here by way of example.]

The Legation of the United States of America presents its compliments to the Ministry of Foreign Affairs of Bulgaria and, acting under the instructions of the United States Government, has the honor to reply to the Ministry's note of April 21, 1949 concerning the question of Bulgaria's compliance with the obligations of Article 2 of the Treaty of Peace.

The United States Government, taking note of the Bulgarian Government's rejection of the statements made in the Legation's note of April 2, 1949, concerning Bulgaria's disregard of its obligations under Article 2, finds it necessary to place on record its view that the Bulgarian Government has not given a satisfactory reply to the specific charges set forth in the Legation's note. The Bulgarian Government has also failed to furnish the United States Government with the requested information as to measures which the Bulgarian Government is prepared to adopt in order to remedy the situation caused by the violation of its obligations under Article 2 and to implement fully the terms of that Article. The remaining portions of the Bulgarian Government's note of April 21 consist of allegations against the United States which are demonstrably false and irrelevant to the matter at hand.

The United States Government accordingly considers that a dispute has arisen concerning the interpretation and execution of the Treaty of Peace which the Bulgarian Government has shown no disposition to join in settling by direct diplomatic negotiations.

The American Minister has therefore been instructed by his Government to refer the dispute to his British and Soviet colleagues for consideration jointly with himself in accordance with the provisions of Article 23 of the Treaty of Peace. Copies of his letters to the Ambassador of the Union of Soviet Socialist Republics and to the British Minister inviting them to meet for this purpose are enclosed.

◇◇◇◇◇◇

[1] Department of State Bulletin, June 12, 1949, pp. 755-759.

212. RESOLUTION OF THE GENERAL ASSEMBLY, OCTOBER 22, 1949 [1]

[British and American efforts to invoke the terms of the treaties of peace with Bulgaria, Hungary, and Rumania by having the Heads of Missions (British, Soviet, and United States) in the satellite countries examine the accusations, failed because the Soviet Union would not coöperate. In the hope of solving this dilemma the General Assembly passed a resolution, on October 22, 1949, expressing its concern over the accusations made against Bulgaria, Hungary, and Rumania, and sought the opinion of the International Court of Justice on the legal issues involved.]

WHEREAS the United Nations pursuant to Article 55 of the Charter shall promote universal respect for, and observance of, human rights and fundamental freedoms for all without distinction as to race, sex, language, or religion,

WHEREAS the General Assembly at the Second Part of its third regular session considered the question of the observance in Bulgaria and Hungary of human rights and fundamental freedoms,

WHEREAS the General Assembly, on 30 April 1949, adopted resolution 272 (III) concerning this question in which it expressed its deep concern at the grave accusations made against the Governments of Bulgaria and Hungary regarding the suppression of human rights and fundamental freedoms in those countries; noted with satisfaction that steps had been taken by several States signatories to the Peace Treaties with Bulgaria and Hungary regarding these accusations; expressed the hope that measures would be diligently applied, in accordance with the Treaties, in order to ensure respect for human rights and fundamental freedoms; and most urgently drew the attention of the Governments of Bulgaria and Hungary to their obligations under the Peace Treaties, including the obligation to co-operate in the settlement of the question,

WHEREAS the General Assembly has resolved to consider also at the fourth regular session the question of the observance in Rumania of human rights and fundamental freedoms,

WHEREAS certain of the Allied and Associated Powers signatories to the Treaties of Peace with Bulgaria, Hungary and Rumania have charged the Governments of those countries with violations of the Treaties of Peace and have called upon those Governments to take remedial measures,

WHEREAS the Governments of Bulgaria, Hungary and Rumania have rejected the charges of Treaty violations,

WHEREAS the Governments of the Allied and Associated Powers concerned have sought unsuccessfully to refer the question of Treaty violations to the Heads of Mission in Sofia, Budapest and Bucharest, in pursuance of certain provisions in the Treaties of Peace,

WHEREAS the Governments of these Allied and Associated Powers have called upon the Governments of Bulgaria, Hungary and Rumania to join in

[1] Contained in U. N. document A/1023.

appointing Commissions pursuant to the provisions of the respective Treaties of Peace for the settlement of disputes concerning the interpretation or execution of these Treaties,

WHEREAS the Governments of Bulgaria, Hungary and Rumania have refused to appoint their representatives to the Treaty Commissions, maintaining that they were under no legal obligation to do so,

WHEREAS the Secretary-General of the United Nations is authorized by the Treaties of Peace, upon request by either party to a dispute, to appoint the third member of a Treaty Commission if the parties fail to agree upon the appointment of the third member,

WHEREAS it is important for the Secretary-General to be advised authoritatively concerning the scope of his authority under the Treaties of Peace,

The General Assembly

1. *Expresses* its continuing interest in and its increased concern at the grave accusations made against Bulgaria, Hungary and Rumania.

2. *Records* its opinion that the refusal of the Governments of Bulgaria, Hungary and Rumania to co-operate in its efforts to examine the grave charges with regard to the observance of human rights and fundamental freedoms justifies this concern of the General Assembly about the state of affairs prevailing in Bulgaria, Hungary and Rumania in this respect;

3. *Decides* to submit the following questions to the International Court of Justice for an advisory opinion:

"I. Do the diplomatic exchanges between Bulgaria, Hungary and Rumania on the one hand and certain Allied and Associated Powers signatories to the Treaties of Peace on the other, concerning the implementation of article 2 in the Treaties with Bulgaria and Hungary and article 3 in the Treaty with Rumania, disclose disputes subject to the provisions for the settlement of disputes contained in article 36 of the Treaty of Peace with Bulgaria, article 40 of the Treaty of Peace with Hungary, and article 38 of the Treaty of Peace with Rumania?"

In the event of an affirmative reply to question I:

"II. Are the Governments of Bulgaria, Hungary and Rumania obligated to carry out the provisions of the articles referred to in question I, including the provisions for the appointment of their representatives to the Treaty Commissions?"

In the event of an affirmative reply to question II and if within thirty days from the date when the Court delivers its opinion the Governments concerned have not notified the Secretary-General that they have appointed their representatives to the Treaty Commission, and the Secretary-General has so advised the International Court of Justice:

"III. If one party fails to appoint a representative to a Treaty Commission under the Treaties of Peace with Bulgaria, Hungary and Rumania where that party is obligated to appoint a representative to the Treaty Commission, is the Secretary-General of the United Nations authorized to appoint the third member of the Commission upon the request of the other party to a dispute according to the provisions of the respective Treaties?"

In the event of an affirmative reply to question III:

"IV. Would a Treaty Commission composed of a representative of one party and a third member appointed by the Secretary-General of the United

Nations constitute a commission, within the meaning of the relevant Treaty articles, competent to make a definitive and binding decision in settlement of a dispute?"

4. *Requests* the Secretary-General to make available to the International Court of Justice the relevant exchanges of diplomatic correspondence communicated to the Secretary-General for circulation to the Members of the United Nations and the records of the General Assembly proceedings on this question;

5. *Decides* to retain on the agenda of the fifth regular session of the General Assembly the question of the observance of human rights and fundamental freedoms in Bulgaria, Hungary and Rumania, with a view to ensuring that the charges are appropriately examined and dealt with.

◇◇◇◇◇◇

213. CONDEMNATION OF BULGARIA, HUNGARY, AND RUMANIA ON HUMAN RIGHTS ISSUE

Resolution of the General Assembly, adopted November 3, 1950 [1]

[In spite of protests and in the face of mounting disapproval of public opinion throughout the world, the ruling communist cliques in Hungary, Rumania, and Bulgaria continued to maintain and extend their hold upon their respective countries by fresh and uninterrupted violations of the fundamental rights and human freedom sections of the peace treaties. At the end of 1950, the situation being in no way improved, the General Assembly of the United Nations passed a resolution condemning the wilful refusal of the three countries to observe their peace treaty obligations.]

The General Assembly,

CONSIDERING that one of the purposes of the United Nations is to achieve international co-operation in promoting and encouraging respect for human rights and fundamental freedoms for all without distinction as to race, sex, language or religion.

HAVING REGARD to General Assembly resolutions 272 (III) and 294 (IV) concerning the question of the observance in Bulgaria, Hungary and Rumania of human rights and fundamental freedoms, and to its decision in the latter resolution to submit certain questions to the International Court of Justice for an advisory opinion,

1. *Takes note* of the advisory opinion delivered by the International Court of Justice on 30 March 1950 and 18 July 1950 to the effect that:

(*a*) The diplomatic exchanges between Bulgaria, Hungary and Rumania on the one hand, and certain Allied and Associated Powers signatories to the Treaties of Peace on the other, concerning the implementation of article 2 of the Treaties with Bulgaria and Hungary and article 3 of the Treaty with Rumania, disclose disputes subject to the provisions for the settlement of disputes contained in article 36 of the Treaty of Peace with Bulgaria, article 40

[1] Department of State Bulletin, November 27, 1950, p. 872.

of the Treaty of Peace with Hungary, and article 38 of the Treaty of Peace with Rumania;

(*b*) The Governments of Bulgaria, Hungary and Rumania are obligated to carry out the provisions of those articles of the Treaties of Peace which relate to the settlement of disputes, including the provisions for the appointment of representatives to the Treaty Commissions;

(*c*) If one party fails to appoint a representative to a Treaty Commission under the Treaties of Peace with Bulgaria, Hungary and Rumania where that party is obligated to appoint a representative to the Treaty Commission, the Secretary-General of the United Nations is not authorized to appoint the third member of the Commission upon the request of the other party to a dispute;

2. *Condemns* the wilful refusal of the Governments of Bulgaria, Hungary and Rumania to fulfill their obligation under the provisions of the Treaties of Peace to appoint representatives to the Treaty Commissions, which obligation has been confirmed by the International Court of Justice;

3. *Is of the opinion* that the conduct of the Governments of Bulgaria, Hungary, and Rumania in this matter is such as to indicate that they are aware of breaches being committed of those articles of the Treaties of Peace under which they are obligated to secure the enjoyment of human rights and fundamental freedoms in their countries; and that they are callously indifferent to the sentiments of the world community;

4. *Notes* with anxiety the continuance of serious accusations on these matters against the Governments of Bulgaria, Hungary, and Rumania, and that the three Governments have made no satisfactory refutation of these accusations;

5. *Invites* Members of the United Nations, and in particular those which are parties to the Treaties of Peace with Bulgaria, Hungary, and Rumania, to submit to the Secretary-General all evidence which they now hold or which may become available in future in relation to this question;

6. *Likewise invites* the Secretary-General to notify the Members of the United Nations of any information he may receive in connexion with this question.

◇◇◇◇◇◇

214. YALTA COMMITMENTS UNFULFILLED IN BULGARIA, HUNGARY, AND RUMANIA

Statement by President Truman upon Ratification of Peace Treaties, June 14, 1947 [1]

[At the time the treaties of peace with Bulgaria, Hungary, and Rumania were ratified, it was apparent that these countries had failed to establish truly democratic governments in accordance with the terms of the Yalta agreement. In spite of that fact, as President Truman pointed out, the United States proceeded to ratification in order to end the state of war and to effect the withdrawal of Russian troops.]

[1] Department of State Bulletin, June 22, 1947, p. 1214.

At the time of ratification of the treaties establishing peace with Hungary, Rumania, and Bulgaria, I feel I must publicly express regret that the governments of those countries not only have disregarded the will of the majority of the people but have resorted to measures of oppression against them. Ever since the liberation of these countries from the Nazi yoke and the commitments undertaken by the three Allies at Yalta, I had hoped that governments truly representative of the people would be established there. Such governments do not exist today in those three countries.

It is, however, in the interests of the Hungarian, Rumanian, and Bulgarian peoples to terminate the state of war which has existed between their governments and the United States for over five years. The establishment of peace will mean that all occupation forces (not including Soviet units needed to maintain lines of communication to the Soviet zone of occupation in Austria) will be withdrawn from these countries and armistice Control Commissions terminated.

◇◇◇◇◇◇

215. ARREST, SENTENCE, AND EXECUTION OF BULGARIAN OPPOSITION LEADER, NIKOLA PETKOV

Statement by the Department of State, September 23, 1947 [1]

[United States efforts in the early postwar period to bring about free elections and to achieve representation for opposition parties in the governments of the Soviet satellite states proved futile. Of particular concern to our government were the so-called political trials, one of the most notorious of which was that of Nikola Petkov, the opposition leader in Bulgaria. Both the trial and the sentence were carried out over the protests of Britain and the United States. In the following statement the State Department branded the whole performance a travesty on justice. While similar trials were held in Rumania, Hungary, and the other satellite states, only the Petkov affair is touched upon here by way of example.]

The Department of State has received confirmation from the Acting Political Representative in Sofia that Nikola Petkov was executed on September 23.

Mr. Petkov was one of the four Bulgarian signers of the Bulgarian armistice. As the leader of the Agrarian Party, the largest political party in Bulgaria, he played an active and leading role in the establishment of a coalition government in September 1944, following the overthrow of the Bulgarian Nazi regime. Subsequently, in July 1945, Mr. Petkov and the majority of his party withdrew from the minority-controlled organ which that Government became. Since July 1945 he has been the acknowledged leader of the opposition. He was arrested on charges of conspiracy against the government on June 8, 1947.

Mr. Petkov's trial was a travesty on justice. Two of the attorneys selected by Petkov were seized by the militia. The court refused to permit the appearance of numerous witnesses requested by the defense. The court likewise denied a request by the defense for a postponement to permit study of the

[1] Department of State Bulletin, October 5, 1947, pp. 702-703.

pre-trial record. The presiding judge actively participated in the prosecution. On August 16, 1947, the court pronounced Mr. Petkov guilty of "having inspired certain Bulgarian Army officers to found a military union which conspired to overthrow the Fatherland Front Government," et cetera. Mr. Petkov was sentenced to death.

Mindful of its obligations under the Yalta agreement in regard to assisting the peoples of the former Axis satellite states to solve by democratic means their pressing political problems, the United States Government requested the Soviet acting deputy chairman of the Allied Control Commission to instruct the Bulgarian Government, without prejudice to the right of Mr. Petkov to appeal, to suspend the sentence passed upon him until the Commission had had full opportunity to review the case. This and subsequent approaches to the Allied Control Commission were rejected by the Soviet acting deputy chairman on the grounds that such review would constitute "interference in Bulgarian internal affairs". On August 23 the American Embassy at Moscow informed the Soviet Foreign Office that the United States Government could not accept the position taken by the Soviet Representative on the Allied Control Commission and requested immediate consultation at a government level among the three Yalta Powers in order that they might reach concerted policies in regard to the matter. This approach and a later one of August 30 to the Soviet Foreign Office were likewise rejected on similar reasoning. The United States Government also communicated its views concerning the Petkov case to the highest Bulgarian authorities.

The timing and conduct of the trial and its relationship to other repressive measures undertaken by the Bulgarian authorities make it abundantly clear that the trial constituted but one of a series of measures undertaken by the Communist-dominated Fatherland Front government to remove from the Bulgarian scene all save a purely nominal opposition and to consolidate, despite its professions to the contrary, a totalitarian form of government. The trial of Nikola Petkov recalls to memory another trial which occurred in Leipzig 14 years ago. In that earlier trial a Bulgarian defendant evoked world-wide admiration for his courageous defiance of the Nazi bully who participated in his prosecution. Today that defendant has assumed another role, and it is now the courage of another Bulgarian whose steadfast opposition to forces of oppression has evoked world-wide admiration. In bringing Nikola Petkov to trial the Bulgarian regime placed itself on trial in the minds of many Bulgarians and of freedom-supporting peoples outside Bulgaria. In the court of world opinion that regime has shown itself wanting with respect to elementary principles of justice and the rights of man.

◇◇◇◇◇◇

216. POLITICAL DEVELOPMENTS IN CZECHOSLOVAKIA [1]

Statement by Warren R. Austin, U. S. Representative in Security Council,
April 12, 1948

[Czechoslovakia was the last of the European satellite countries to be forcibly brought under the complete domination of Moscow. The coup of February 22 to 25, 1948, by which this was accomplished, was promptly brought to the attention of the Security Council. On April 12, 1948, the United States representative in the Council asserted that it was with the aid of the Soviet Government that communist minorities in all the satellite governments had finally been able to achieve power. Part of his statement was devoted to the techniques used by the communists in engineering their successful revolts.]

* * *

As has been pointed out in the Security Council discussions, the Czechoslovak story assumes added significance where compared with developments that have taken place throughout eastern and central Europe. In Hungary, Bulgaria, Rumania, and Poland, while details varied, the general pattern was the same. Like Czechoslovakia, all these countries have been occupied by the Soviet armies. The chief steps were the acquisition by the Communists of key posts in the Cabinet; control of the police; control of the armies; control of the media of mass communications; and finally control of or subversion of the judiciary. In none of these countries did the Communists enjoy popular support sufficient to warrant their commanding position in the government. In such countries where truly free elections were held they received as little as 17 percent of the total vote, and the largest vote they received was 38 percent.

There is a striking uniformity in techniques applied by the Communists in their fight against the majority. In all five countries they concentrated their propaganda barrage against one non-Communist party after another. The familiar pattern of accusation of conspiracy against the state and of hostility to the Soviet Union was used.

Let us think of the trial of the Bulgarian peasant leader, Petkov; the trial of Maniu of Rumania; the arrest of the popular peasant leader, Kovács, in Hungary; the trials of opposition leaders in Poland; and, finally, in Czechoslovakia the charges of conspiracy against Vladimir Krajina, one of the outstanding underground leaders in the resistance against the Germans.

The remarkably similar methods lead of course to remarkably similar results. In all five countries we are now confronted with regimes controlled unquestionably and totally by the Communist parties. The policies of these regimes would seem to follow without deviation the interests of the Soviet Union.

As was the case previously in the other four countries, the new Czechoslovak regime has now cast aside the entire substance of parliamentary practice. All effective opposition leaders are removed, the opposition journalists

[1] Department of State Bulletin, April 25, 1948, pp. 536-539.

deprived of their freedom to write, the traditional autonomy of the 600-year-old Charles University of Prague brutally violated by the dismissal of its duly elected head followed by a purge of a substantial number of its professors.

The uniformity and the smooth operation of the pattern raises the logical question whether or not there is any coordination from a central point for the implementation of this pattern. It is not significant that the top Communists in Hungary such as the Deputy Prime Minister, Rakosi, and the economic czar, Vas, Foreign Minister Pauker in Rumania, Prime Minister Dimitrov and Foreign Minister Kolarov of Bulgaria, and the entire leadership of Czechoslovakia, including Premier Gottwald, Cabinet Ministers Fierlinger, Kopecky, Nejedly, and the Secretary General of the Communist Party, Slansky, have all spent years of active work in Moscow and have been in close association with both the Soviet Communist leaders as well as the Communist leaders in other countries and that some of them have even become Soviet citizens?

To complete the similarity of the patterns in all those countries, is it a mere coincidence as I pointed out on Tuesday that the Soviet Deputy Foreign Minister Vyshinsky appeared in Bucharest at the crucial moment and another Soviet Deputy Foreign Minister, Zorin, was present in Prague at the time of the February coup?

What is the significance of the fact after the Czechoslovak Government had indicated its readiness to participate in the Marshall Plan this decision was reversed as a result of a telephone call to Prague from Moscow where the Czechoslovak Prime Minister and Foreign Minister had been summoned? Is it not significant that the Communist Party of Czechoslovakia as well as the Communist Parties of other European countries, including all the countries of eastern Europe joined with the Soviet Communist Party in the Cominform in October 1947? Is it also not significant that shortly thereafter the Communist Party in Czechoslovakia became more aggressive? The leading role of the Soviet Communist Party in the Cominform is a matter of common knowledge.

All of these circumstances lead to the basic question: Has the Government of Czechoslovakia been subverted with the assistance, direct or indirect, of an outside power? Has a threat of the use of force or of other pressure or interference by an outside power been directed against the political independence of Czechoslovakia? If the answer is in the affirmative then we are confronted with a situation which very definitely is outside of article 2 (7) and concerns the Security Council.

We have heard many contradictory statements in the course of this discussion. The Council must ascertain the truth. It should never condemn nor approve blindly. This was a consideration in my previous proposal that the Council should invite the Representative of the new Czechoslovak Government to the table.[1]

This invitation has now been rejected.[2] Why? The rejection is based on

[1] Department of State Bulletin, April 18, 1948, p. 517.

[2] "A letter dated April 8, 1948, to the Secretary-General from Dr. Vladimir Houdek, representative of Czechoslovakia to the U. N. (see U. N. Document S/718 of April 10, 1948), follows:

"Sir: Referring to your letter dated April 6, 1948, and upon instructions from my Government, I have the honour to bring the following to your attention:

"The discussion of internal matters before the Security Council is in contradiction to the

the thesis that article 2 (7) applies. This, as I have said previously, is a matter for determination by this Council. The new Czech regime and the Soviet Union are attempting to decide that question for the Security Council, to dictate their unilateral and prejudiced opinion on this point to the Council. This is a high-handed and arbitrary way of behaving which would be surprising had it not come from these regimes. This refusal to participate does not give me a feeling of confidence that all is well. If these regimes had a clear conscience, surely they would seize eagerly the opportunity of presenting their side of the case to the Council. They would not oppose the Council's learning the facts by taking evidence. This refusal makes me feel more than ever that it is important for the Security Council to get to the bottom of this situation.

We have also now been told that there are groups of men outside of Czechoslovakia who were leaders in the political life of this country prior to the coup. The Representative of Chile has made a suggestion for the creation by the Council of a subcommittee to hear the stories of these leaders who were in Czechoslovakia when the coup occurred and presumably should have firsthand knowledge of the events at that time and those which led up to the coup. My Government feels the Council would not be discharging fully its obligations if it did not hear these people. It feels that the creation of a sub-group to receive such testimony and to obtain other available information and to report back to the full Council on it is a convenient and feasible procedure.

We feel the subcommittee should consist of representatives of five states of the Council. In our view the terms of reference should be very simple. The subcommittee should be authorized to hear the testimony of these Czech political leaders and to report on this testimony to the Security Council.

My Government feels that it is essential that such information be obtained in order that the Council will be better able to decide what further steps should be taken on this matter. I should add that we would not consider the activity of such a sub-group to be in any way an investigation. The proposal before us has the full support of my Government.

---

provisions of the Charter. Such matters are exclusively within the domestic jurisdiction of any state. The Czechoslovak Government therefore rejects with indignation the unfounded complaint which has been put before the Security Council.

"Czechoslovakia has been and will remain a peace-loving state and wishes to maintain friendly relations with peace-loving nations on the basis of mutual respect in accordance with the purposes and principles of the United Nations. The discussion on the changes in the composition of the Czechoslovak Government based on slanderous allegations has confirmed our conviction that it is only a pretext to stir up the hostile campaign against the Soviet Union and other states of eastern Europe with which Czechoslovakia has strong bonds of friendship. Such action is in flagrant contradiction to one of the fundamental tasks of the United Nations which is to promote friendly relations between nations in order to strengthen international peace and security.

"Since the discussion of internal matters of Czechoslovakia in the Security Council is contrary to the basic principles of the Charter, inspired by the aim of protecting the sovereignty and independence of states, the Czechoslovak Government does not find it possible to take in any way part in such discussion."

217. UNITED STATES POSITION ON ELECTORAL PROCEDURES AND SUPPRESSION OF OPPOSITION IN HUNGARY

Statement by the Department of State, August 17, 1947 [1]

[Under various agreements concluded by the Allies, the people of the defeated governments of Eastern Europe were promised free governments and elections; but, when the so-called "people's democracies" were installed in those countries, they were neither free nor democratic. The communist cliques used every conceivable trick to consolidate their hold upon Eastern Europe. The following statement is submitted by way of example. In it the State Department severely criticized the practices resorted to by the communists at the polls.]

The United States Government, a member of the Allied Control Commission for Hungary, is seriously concerned by reports from Budapest of widespread abuses of the already restrictive provisions of the new Hungarian electoral law, under which national elections will be held on August 31. The United States Government, which has taken note of the assurances of free elections voiced publicly by the Hungarian Prime Minister and other Hungarian officials, is prompted in this matter by its desire that freedoms guaranteed by the treaty of peace with Hungary, already ratified by both the United States and Hungary, shall not be denied the Hungarian people.

Aside from the unwarranted interference of the minority Communist Party with the right of other parties to prepare freely their own lists of candidates, abuses of the Hungarian electoral law center in the wholesale disfranchisement of voters by the Communist-controlled electoral organs on flimsy and illegal pretexts. According to the non-Communist Hungarian press, exclusion from the electorate has now reached 70 percent in some districts. Some estimates indicate that 20 percent of the electorate, or roughly one million Hungarian citizens, have already been deprived of their right to vote.

The overwhelming majority of Hungarian citizens thus far disfranchised are non-Communists. The charges on which potential voters have lost their suffrage rights border on the grotesque: citizens of the Jewish faith have been disqualified on the accusation of having been members of Nazi organizations; old women, of being prostitutes; factory workers, of belonging to the former landed nobility. Thousands of persons have arbitrarily been classified as mentally deranged. Appeals against disfranchisement are permitted by law, but the burden of proof rests upon the citizens and the right of review is in the hands of the Communist-controlled political police. Moreover, only eight days are allowed for the review of all appeals—a period clearly inadequate, in view of the large number of cases, for judicious consideration of the evidence.

The Communist arrangement of supervising the lists of candidates prepared by other political parties, obtained through pressure, is obviously intended to assure the Communist Party and its collaborators control of the new legislature regardless of the outcome of the balloting.

In as much as the Hungarian Government, under article 2 of the treaty of

---

[1] Department of State Bulletin, August 24, 1947, pp. 392-393.

peace, has assumed the obligation of securing to all persons under Hungarian jurisdiction the enjoyment of human rights and the fundamental freedoms, including freedom of political opinion, the United States Government has instructed the American Minister in Budapest to seek an interview with the Hungarian Prime Minister and to urge him to take all necessary steps on behalf of his Government to correct the prevailing electoral abuses. It is understood that the British Government is similarly instructing its Minister in Budapest.

◇◇◇◇◇◇

218. TRIAL OF JOZSEF CARDINAL MINDSZENTY BY HUNGARY

[World opinion was shocked at the trials and imprisonment of Archbishop Stepinac in Yugoslavia, Cardinal Mindszenty and Bishop Ordass in Hungary, and leading Protestant clergymen in Bulgaria. The resort to police-state methods and the utter disregard for human decency brought forth protests both from the United States and other countries. In the two statements which follow, the Secretary of State and the Senate of the United States registered their protests and horror over these forced confessions and other notorious practices involved in these trials.]

(a) Statement by Secretary Acheson, February 9, 1949 [1]

The trial of Jozsef Cardinal Mindszenty, upon whom the Hungarian Government has now imposed a sentence of life imprisonment, confirms the Government and people of the United States in the views expressed by the Acting Secretary of State on December 29, 1948.[2] By this conscienceless attack upon religious and personal freedom, as well as by the persecution of Lutheran Bishop Lajos Ordass and other respected Church leaders, the Soviet-controlled Hungarian authorities seek to discredit and coerce religious leadership in Hungary in order to remove this source of moral resistance to Communism.

In their conduct of the case of Cardinal Mindszenty, the Hungarian authorities do not appear to have omitted any of the usual methods practiced by a police state. Such proceedings constitute not the administration of justice but wanton persecution. They have evoked universal condemnation, and the Hungarian Government must bear full responsibility for its action.

The cases of Cardinal Mindszenty and other Hungarian Church leaders are not isolated developments. During the past two years, with governmental power entirely in the hands of the minority Communist party, the people of Hungary have been increasingly denied the exercise of fundamental human rights and freedoms. Parliamentary opposition, an element indispensable to the democratic process, has been ruthlessly eliminated, the totalitarian con-

---

[1] Department of State Bulletin, February 20, 1949, pp. 230-231.

[2] In a press conference on December 29, 1948, Acting Secretary Lovett denounced as a sickening sham the arrest of Jozsef Cardinal Mindszenty by the Hungarian Government on espionage charges. Mr. Lovett declared the action as obviously based on false charges and culminated a long series of oppressive actions in Hungary against personal freedom—and now religious freedom. He commented at the press conference that such behavior was one of the things that makes achievement of a peace a hope rather than a reality. He commented that this action is all that is needed to indicate the attitude of the Hungarian Government toward the liberties to which the rest of the world attaches the greatest importance.

trols of state and party have been laid like a deadening hand upon every phase of daily personal existence, and the Hungarian people have been divested of any real independence.

The people of the United States and, without question, peoples of other freedom-loving nations, are sickened and horrified by these developments and fully comprehend the threat they constitute to free institutions everywhere.

(b) Resolution of the United States Senate, April 11, 1949 [1]

Whereas the persecution of Cardinal Mindszenty and Bishop Ordass in Hungary, of Archbishop Stepinac in Yugoslavia, and of Protestant clergymen in Bulgaria, evidences the abridgement and violation of fundamental human freedoms guaranteed in the treaties of peace and reaffirmed in the United Nations Charter: Now, therefore, be it

Resolved, That it is the sense of the Senate that these actions should be strongly protested in the United Nations or by whatever other means may be appropriate.

❧❧❧❧❧❧

219. UNITED STATES POLICY TOWARD POLAND [2]

Statement by Secretary Stettinius, December 18, 1944

[Shortly after the German invasion of Poland, the Polish government and many of its leaders fled to London. There they established a government in exile and continued to participate in the war against the Axis powers. The following statement of policy by the Secretary of State, made prior to the Yalta Conference, indicated the desire of the United States government to restore Poland to full independence after the war was over. The statement laid stress on "the right of the Polish people to determine their internal existence as they see fit."]

The United States Government's position as regards Poland has been steadfastly guided by full understanding and sympathy for the interests of the Polish people. This position has been communicated on previous occasions to the interested governments, including the Government of Poland. It may be summarized as follows:

1. The United States Government stands unequivocally for a strong, free, and independent Polish state with the untrammeled right of the Polish people to order their internal existence as they see fit.

2. It has been the consistently held policy of the United States Government that questions relating to boundaries should be left in abeyance until the termination of hostilities. As Secretary Hull stated in his address of April 9, 1944, "This does not mean that certain questions may not and should not in the meantime be settled by friendly conference and agreement." In the case of the future frontiers of Poland, if a mutual agreement is reached by the United Nations directly concerned, this Government would have no objec-

1 S. Res. 102, 81st Cong. 1st sess.
2 Department of State Bulletin, December 24, 1944, p. 836.

tion to such an agreement which could make an essential contribution to the prosecution of the war against the common enemy. If, as a result of such agreement, the Government and people of Poland decide that it would be in the interests of the Polish state to transfer national groups, the United States Government in cooperation with other governments will assist Poland, in so far as practicable, in such transfers. The United States Government continues to adhere to its traditional policy of declining to give guarantees for any specific frontiers. The United States Government is working for the establishment of a world security organization through which the United States together with other member states would assume responsibility for the preservation of general security.

3. It is the announced aim of the United States Government, subject to legislative authority, to assist the countries liberated from the enemy in repairing the devastation of war and thus to bring to their peoples the opportunity to join as full partners in the task of building a more prosperous and secure life for all men and women. This applies to Poland as well as the other United Nations.

The policy of the United States Government regarding Poland outlined above has as its objective the attainment of the announced basic principles of United States foreign policy.

◇◇◇◇◇◇

220. UNITED STATES POSITION ON THE CONDUCT OF POLISH ELECTIONS

Statement by the Department of State, January 28, 1947 [1]

[At the Potsdam Conference provision was made for "free and unfettered elections in Poland as soon as possible on the basis of universal suffrage and secret ballot." Under Soviet aegis the Polish communist party was permitted to take over control of Poland and to freeze out representatives of minority parties. In January 1947 a bogus election was held returning a communist majority as had been planned. The election was an outright violation of the Yalta and Potsdam agreements and the United States registered vigorous protest as may be seen from the following summary statement issued by the Department of State.]

On January 19 a general election was held in Poland, the results of which are expected to be announced shortly. The United States Government has followed closely the developments leading up to this event in accordance with the commitments it accepted at the Yalta and Potsdam Conferences. On numerous occasions it has expressed its concern over the course of events in Poland, which increasingly indicated that the election would not be conducted in such manner as to allow a free expression of the will of the Polish people. On August 19 and November 22, 1946, formal notes were addressed to the Polish Provisional Government on this subject. On January 5 this Government brought the situation in Poland to the attention of the British and Soviet

[1] Department of State Bulletin, February 9, 1947, p. 251.

Governments and expressed the hope that those Governments would associate themselves with the Government of the United States in an approach to the Polish Provisional Government of National Unity. This proposal was rejected by the Soviet Government.[1] On January 9 this Government delivered a further note to the Polish Provisional Government which stated among other things that if the repressive activities on the part of the Provisional Government did not cease immediately there was little likelihood that elections could be held in accordance with the terms of the Potsdam agreement. The British Government has also protested to the Polish Provisional Government the violation of its election pledges.

The reports received from the United States Embassy in Poland in the period immediately prior to the elections as well as its subsequent reports based upon the observations of American officials who visited a number of Polish voting centers confirmed the fears which this Government had expressed that the election would not be free. These reports were corroborated by the general tenor of the dispatches from foreign correspondents in Poland. It is clear that the Provisional Government did not confine itself to the suppression of the so-called "underground" but employed wide-spread measures of coercion and intimidation against democratic elements which were loyal to Poland although not partisans of the Government "bloc". In these circumstances the United States Government cannot consider that the provisions of the Yalta and Potsdam agreements have been fulfilled.

The United States Government has made it clear that it has no desire to intervene in the internal affairs of Poland. By virtue of the responsibility which devolved upon it as one of the principal powers engaged in liberating the countries of Europe from Nazi occupation it undertook, together with the British and Soviet Governments, to secure for the long-suffering Polish people the opportunity to select a government of their own choosing. It was in connection with this undertaking that this Government agreed to the decisions respecting Poland that were taken at the Yalta Conference, including the decision to recognize the Polish Provisional Government of National Unity. These decisions with respect to Poland, which were accepted by the Polish Provisional Government in their entirety, formed part of a series of agreements between the United States, British, and Soviet Governments. The United States Government considers that the Polish Provisional Government has failed to carry out its solemn pledges.

The United States Government intends to maintain its interest in the welfare of the Polish people. While retaining full liberty of action to determine its future attitude toward the government of Poland, this Government will continue to keep itself informed of developments in Poland through its diplomatic mission in Warsaw.

◇◇◇◇◇◇

[1] Department of State Bulletin, January 26, 1947, p. 164.

221. RECOGNITION OF RUMANIAN GOVERNMENT

Statement by the Department of State, February 5, 1946 [1]

[In December 1945, the representatives of Britain, the U.S.S.R., and the United States reached an agreement on a broadly representative government for Rumania, which should include members of the Peasant and Liberal parties. The Government so reorganized gave assurances that it would conduct free and unfettered elections, and promised it would grant the Rumanian people freedom of press, religion, speech, and association. In according the new government of Rumania recognition, the United States stated in a note transmitted to the Rumanian government on February 5, 1946, that it did so on the basis of these assurances.]

*   *   *

"The Government of the United States of America has taken note of the communication of January 8, 1946, addressed to Ambassador William Averell Harriman by the President of the Council of Ministers, Dr. Petru Groza, enclosing a declaration of the Rumanian Government, made at a meeting of the Council of Ministers on January 8. According to this declaration the Council of ministers considered it indispensable that—

"*One*. General elections should be held in the shortest time possible.

"*Two*. The freedom of these elections shall be assured. They shall be held on the basis of universal suffrage and secret ballot with the participation of all democratic and anti-Fascist parties which shall have the right to present candidates.

"*Three*. Freedom of the press, speech, religion and assembly shall be assured.

"The Government of the United States has been advised of the conversation which took place on January 9th between the President of the Council of Ministers, and the American and British Ambassadors. It has taken note of the oral explanation of the aforementioned declaration which the President of the Council of Ministers made to the American and British Ambassadors in this conversation to the effect that:

"*One*. All political parties represented in the Rumanian Government shall have the right to participate in the elections and to put forward candidates.

"*Two*. The examination of the balloting procedure and counting of the ballots shall take place in the presence of representatives of all the political parties represented in the Government.

"*Three*. All political parties represented in the Government shall be accorded equitable broadcasting facilities for the presentation of their political views.

"*Four*. All political parties represented in the Government shall have equal rights to print, publish and distribute their own newspapers and political publications. Newsprint shall be distributed to them on a fair and equitable basis.

[1] Department of State Bulletin, February 17, 1946, pp. 256-257.

"Five. All political parties represented in the Government shall have the right to organize associations and hold meetings. They shall be allowed premises for this purpose.

"Six. The Council of Ministers will consult with the representatives of the political parties in order to reach agreement concerning the grant of freedom of the press and speech as well as on questions relating to the drafting of the electoral law and the conduct of the elections.

* * *

"On the basis of the assurances contained in the declaration of the Rumanian Government and on the understanding that the oral statement of the President of the Council of Ministers, as set forth above, reflects the intentions of the Rumanian Government, the Government of the United States is prepared to recognize the Government of Rumania."

◇◇◇◇◇◇

222. UNITED STATES POSITION ON THE CONDUCT OF RUMANIAN ELECTIONS IN 1946

Statement by the Department of State, November 26, 1946 [1]

[The Rumanian elections of November 19, 1946 were conducted according to the familiar police-state pattern, including the crushing of opposition and the denying of the ballot to large sections of the population. The elections were manipulated so as to produce by force, fraud, and intimidation a complete endorsement of the existing government's policies. The United States refused to consider that the elections had met the conditions agreed upon at Yalta and Potsdam by the Big Three. That was the import of the State Department announcement which follows.]

At the Crimea conference in 1945 the Governments of the United States, the Union of Soviet Socialist Republics, and the United Kingdom agreed jointly to assist the people of liberated Europe with a view to the earliest possible establishment through free elections of governments responsive to the will of those people. Subsequently, pursuant to agreement reached at Moscow in December 1945 between the same powers, representatives of the three Governments met in Rumania and obtained assurances from the Rumanian Government that the latter would hold free and unfettered elections as soon as possible on the basis of universal and secret ballot.

The Rumanian Government held elections on November 19, 1946. The Department of State has now received extensive reports concerning the conduct of those elections, and the information contained therein makes it abundantly clear that, as a result of manipulations of the electoral registers, the procedures followed in conducting the balloting and the counting of votes, as well as by intimidation through terrorism of large democratic elements of the electorate, the franchise was on that occasion effectively denied to important sections of the population. Consequently, the United States Govern-

[1] Department of State Bulletin, December 8, 1946, pp. 1057-1058.

ment, cannot regard those elections as a compliance by the Rumanian Government with the assurances it gave the United States, United Kingdom, and Union of Soviet Socialist Republics Government in implementation of the Moscow decision.

◇◇◇◇◇◇

223. VIOLATIONS OF TREATY OF PEACE BY RUMANIA

Letter From the United States Minister to Rumania to Rumanian Ministry of Foreign Affairs, February 2, 1948 [1]

[During the two years which followed United States recognition of the Rumanian Government, the latter wiped out all opposition and persecuted those who had the courage to stand for democratic processes in Rumania. On February 2, 1948, the United States Minister in Rumania delivered a letter to the Rumanian Ministry of Foreign Affairs in which our government stated that there never had existed, nor did there then exist in Rumania, the human rights and fundamental freedoms which the Rumanian Government had promised in the peace treaty to secure for all people under its jurisdiction.]

* * *

In January 1946, in compliance with the Moscow Agreement, representatives of the National Peasant and National Liberal Parties were included in the Rumanian Government. The Rumanian Council of Ministers thereupon made a solemn written declaration that free general elections would be held in the shortest possible time, on the basis of universal suffrage and secret ballot, in which all democratic and anti-Fascist parties would have a right to participate and to present candidates. Likewise, the declaration of the Rumanian Government pledged that freedom of the press, speech, religion and assembly would be assured. In an oral amplification of this declaration, the President of the Rumanian Council of Ministers, Petru Groza, made explicit the application of these assurances to all the parties represented in the reorganized Government, thereby acknowledging the National Peasant Party headed by Mr. Iuliu Maniu, the National Liberal Party led by Mr. Constantin Bratianu, and the Social Democratic Party under the direction of Mr. Constantin Petrescu as democratic and anti-Fascist.

The Rumanian Premier also gave explicit assurances that these parties would be entitled (1) to participate in the elections and to put forward candidates, (2) to have representatives present for the examination of the balloting procedure and the counting of the ballots, (3) to be accorded equitable broadcasting facilities for the presentation of their political views, (4) to have equal opportunity to print and distribute their own newspapers and political publications and to obtain newsprint on a fair and equitable basis, (5) to organize associations, to hold meetings and to be allowed premises for this purpose, and (6) to be consulted by the Council of Ministers in order to reach agreement concerning the assured freedoms of press and speech as well as on the drafting of an electoral law and on the conduct of the elections.

[1] Department of State Bulletin, February 15, 1948, pp. 216-218.

However, notwithstanding the categorical nature of these international commitments the Rumanian Government undertook virtually at once to subvert them, and throughout 1946 steadily violated their spirit and letter. All manner of chincanery, and extreme physical violence was employed by or with the consent of the Rumanian Government to reduce the legitimate political activity of any elements not subservient to the controlling minority. Every one of the assurances given was either ignored or sabotaged. The representatives of the Peasant and Liberal Parties were effectively excluded from decisions of the Government and from any real voice in the preparation of the elections. Broadcasting facilities were wholly denied to all but the minority Government bloc. Through the inequitable distribution of newsprint, the denial of freedom to print, publish and distribute and by various other artifices and official censorship, the legitimate opposition press was relegated to a point of virtual extinction. Party meetings of the opposition were prevented by violence. Government officials, employing compulsion and forgery, wrested the control of the Social Democratic Party from the majority of its members.

During nine months which preceded the general elections, numerous eligible candidates were dis'_arred from participation and large sections of the rightful electorate were disenfranchised. The balloting in the election was accompanied by intimidation, by preventing voters from reaching the polls, by multiple voting, by denying legitimate opposition representatives their assured right to be present at the counting, and by distortion of the final returns.

* * *

In February 1947, the Rumanian Government signed a Treaty of Peace with representatives of the Allied and Associated Powers which, under Article 3, obligated Rumania to take all measures necessary to secure to all persons under Rumanian jurisdiction the enjoyment of human rights and of the fundamental freedoms, including freedom of expression, of press and publication, of religious worship, of political opinion and of public meeting.

Despite this development, in the spring and summer following its signature of this Treaty, the Rumanian Government, through its police authorities, intensified its systematic and brutal campaign to eliminate all political opposition. Nation-wide manhunts were conducted on a mass scale resulting in the arbitrary arrest and incarceration of thousands of opposition and non-party persons.

* * *

Reports reaching the United States Government over a period of several months demonstrated convincingly that the political prisoners apprehended as a result of the mass arrests in Rumania were being subjected by the Rumanian authorities not only to physical conditions of starvation and disease but in some instances to methods designed to extract "confessions" in anticipation of forthcoming trials. The United States Government in a public statement on August 15, 1947 took note of this inhuman treatment of Rumanian political prisoners and the methods employed to predetermine their conviction —methods which had already been clearly revealed by the Rumanian mass trials of allegedly subversive organizations which had taken place in November 1946.

On September 15, 1947 the Treaty of Peace with Rumania came into force with its consequent obligation upon the Rumanian Government to secure the specified rights and freedoms to all people under its jurisdiction. Nevertheless, in October and November 1947, the Rumanian authorities tried, convicted and sentenced for treason Mr. Iuliu Maniu and other members of the National Peasant Party of Rumania. The transparent political motivation of this "judicial process" was manifest. The recent threats by the Rumanian authorities against the National Liberal and Independent Socialist Parties, which have been reduced to impotence, give further evidence of the Rumanian Government's intent to wipe out the last vestiges of democratic opposition in Rumania.

By its actions over a period of almost three years since March 1945, the Rumanian Government placed the legitimate and patriotic opposition elements in Rumania in a position of seeming to constitute a clandestine, subversive movement. Activities on their part to bring about, through constitutional means, a democratic alteration in the Government of Rumania so that it might be broadly representative of the Rumanian people were construed as subversive and treasonable. Associations or communications about Rumanian conditions with two of the Powers which had rights and responsibilities in Rumania by virtue of the Yalta, Potsdam, and Moscow Agreements, the Rumanian Armistice and the Rumanian Peace treaty, were made to appear as conspiracy.

The trial of Mr. Maniu and his co-defendants, which was concluded on November 11, 1947, itself was specifically prejudiced in the following respects which, by generally recognized standards of civilized procedure, precluded the free exercise of justice:

1) The possibility of an impartial trial was excluded by the appointment of a presiding judge known to be thoroughly compromised by improper acts as a military judge during the recent war and lacking in judicial integrity.

2) The defendants were effectively deprived of their right to be represented by counsel of their own choice which, except for intimidation, might have been available.

3) Defense of the accused by the appointed counsel was inadequate, despite an apparently spirited summation in the single instance of Maniu.

4) Excessive restrictions were placed upon the preparation of the defense, on the testimony of the defendants and on the interrogation of state witnesses by or for the defendants.

5) A violent campaign of excitation against the defendants was conducted before and during the trial through the officially controlled press, labor, professional and Government organizations, which not only had the effect of intimidating witnesses and influencing the judges but which also by its scope and nature revealed that it was inspired, directed and assisted by the Rumanian Government for the evident purpose of supporting a pre-arranged verdict.

Aside from the lack of validity of a trial carried out under such conditions, the prosecution failed to substantiate the charges of treasonable activities, upon which the defendants were found guilty, by evidence other than that of highly questionable "confessions" which had been drawn from certain defendants following their arrest.

The United States Government considers it necessary to state that in its view the actions of the Rumanian Government recited in this note make it clear that there have not existed, and do not now exist in Rumania those human rights and fundamental freedoms which the Rumanian Government is obligated by the Treaty of Peace to secure to all persons under its jurisdiction.

INFORMATION AND EDUCATIONAL EXCHANGE

224. UNITED STATES INFORMATION AND EDUCATIONAL EXCHANGE ACT, 1948 [1]

AN ACT To promote the better understanding of the United States among the peoples of the world and to strengthen cooperative international relations

[Peace, freedom, and justice are determined in the hearts and minds of men. Accurate knowledge of essential facts is basic to the judgments on which these conditions rest. Government and private industry are now coöperating to spread the truth about this country abroad and to combat the distorted concepts spread by communist propaganda. The popularly known Smith-Mundt Act, reproduced below, authorized the State Department with the aid of advisory commissions of experts to convey to the world the facts about the United States through radio, press, exchange of persons and technical skills, libraries, and other known means of communication.]

Be it enacted by the Senate and House of Representatives of the United States of Amercia in Congress assembled,

TITLE I—SHORT TITLE, OBJECTIVES, AND DEFINITIONS

SHORT TITLE

SECTION 1. This Act may be cited as the "United States Information and Educational Exchange Act of 1948".

OBJECTIVES

SEC. 2. The Congress hereby declares that the objectives of this Act are to enable the Government of the United States to promote a better understanding of the United States in other countries, and to increase mutual understanding between the people of the United States and the people of other countries. Among the means to be used in achieving these objectives are—

(1) an information service to disseminate abroad information about the United States, its people, and policies promulgated by the Congress, the President, the Secretary of State and other responsible officials of Government having to do with matters affecting foreign affairs;

(2) an educational exchange service to cooperate with other nations in—

---

[1] Public Law 402, 80th Cong. 2d sess., H. R. 3342. Popularly known as the Smith-Mundt bill. See also Sen. Rept. No. 811, January 7, 1948.

(a) the interchange of persons, knowledge, and skills;
(b) the rendering of technical and other services;
(c) the interchange of developments in the field of education, the arts, and sciences.

UNITED NATIONS

SEC. 3. In carrying out the objectives of this Act, information concerning the participation of the United States in the United Nations, its organizations and functions, shall be emphasized.

DEFINITIONS

SEC. 4. When used in this Act, the term—

(1) "Secretary" means the Secretary of State.

(2) "Department" means the Department of State.

(3) "Government agency" means any executive department, board, bureau, commission, or other agency of the Federal Government, or independent establishment, or any corporation wholly owned (either directly or through one or more corporations) by the United States.

TITLE II—INTERCHANGE OF PERSONS, KNOWLEDGE AND SKILLS

PERSONS

SEC. 201. The Secretary is authorized to provide for interchanges on a reciprocal basis between the United States and other countries of students, trainees, teachers, guest instructors, professors, and leaders in fields of specialized knowledge or skill and shall wherever possible provide these interchanges by using the services of existing reputable agencies which are successfully engaged in such activity. The Secretary may provide for orientation courses and other appropriate services for such persons from other countries upon their arrival in the United States, and for such persons going to other countries from the United States. When any country fails or refuses to cooperate in such program on a basis of reciprocity the Secretary shall terminate or limit such program, with respect to such country, to the extent he deems to be advisable in the interests of the United States. The persons specified in this section shall be admitted as nonimmigrant visitors for business under clause 2 of section 3 of the Immigration Act of 1924, as amended (43 Stat. 154; 8 U. S. C. 203), for such time and under such conditions as may be prescribed by regulations promulgated by the Secretary of State and the Attorney General. A person admitted under this section who fails to maintain the status under which he was admitted or who fails to depart from the United States at the expiration of the time for which he was admitted, or who engages in activities of a political nature detrimental to the interests of the United States, or in activities not consistent with the security of the United States, shall, upon the warrant of the Attorney General, be taken into custody and promptly deported pursuant to section 14 of the Immigration Act of 1924 (43 Stat. 162, 8 U. S. C. 214). Deportation proceedings under this section shall be summary and the findings of the Attorney General as to matters of fact shall be conclusive. Such persons shall not be eligible for suspension of deportation under clause 2 of subdivision (c) of section 19 of the Immigration Act of February 5, 1917 (54 Stat. 671, 56 Stat. 1044; 8 U. S. C. 155).

BOOKS AND MATERIALS

SEC. 202. The Secretary is authorized to provide for interchanges between the United States and other countries of books and periodicals, including government publications, for the translation of such writings, and for the preparation, distribution, and interchange of other educational materials.

INSTITUTIONS

SEC. 203. The Secretary is authorized to provide for assistance to schools, libraries, and community centers abroad, founded or sponsored by citizens of the United States, and serving as demonstration centers for methods and practices employed in the United States. In assisting any such schools, however, the Secretary shall exercise no control over their educational policies and shall in no case furnish assistance of any character which is not in keeping with the free democratic principles and the established foreign policy of the United States.

TITLE III—ASSIGNMENT OF SPECIALISTS

PERSONS TO BE ASSIGNED

SEC. 301. The Secretary is authorized, when the government of another country is desirous of obtaining the services of a person having special scientific or other technical or professional qualifications, from time to time to assign or authorize the assignment for service, or in cooperation with such government, any citizen of the United States in the employ or service of the Government of the United States who has such qualifications, with the approval of the Government agency in which such person is employed or serving. No person shall be assigned for service to or in cooperation with the government of any country unless (1) the Secretary finds that such assignment is necessary in the national interest of the United States, or (2) such government agrees to reimburse the United States in an amount equal to the compensation, travel expenses, and allowances payable to such person during the period of such assignment in accordance with the provisions of section 302, or (3) such government shall have made an advance of funds, property, or services as provided in section 902. Nothing in this Act, however, shall authorize the assignment of such personnel for service relating to the organization, training, operation, development, or combat equipment of the armed forces of a foreign government.

STATUS AND ALLOWANCES

SEC. 302. Any citizen of the United States, while assigned for service to or in cooperation with another government under the authority of this Act, shall be considered, for the purpose of preserving his rights, allowances, and privileges as such, an officer or employee of the Government of the United States and of the Government agency from which assigned and he shall continue to receive compensation from that agency. He may also receive, under such regulations as the President may prescribe, representation allowances similar to those allowed under section 901 (3) of the Foreign Service Act of 1946 (60 Stat. 999). The authorization of such allowances and other benefits and the payment thereof out of any appropriations available therefor shall be considered as meeting all the requirements of section 1765 of the Revised Statutes.

ACCEPTANCE OF OFFICE UNDER ANOTHER GOVERNMENT

SEC. 303. Any citizen of the United States while assigned for service to or in cooperation with another government under authority of this Act may, at the discretion of his Government agency, with the concurrence of the Secretary, and without additional compensation therefor, accept an office under the government to which he is assigned, if the acceptance of such an office in the opinion of such agency is necessary to permit the effective performance of duties for which he is assigned, including the making or approving on behalf of such foreign government the disbursement of funds provided by such government or of receiving from such foreign government funds for deposit and disbursement on behalf of such government, in carrying our programs undertaken pursuant to this Act: *Provided, however,* That such acceptance of office shall in no case involve the taking of an oath of allegiance to another government.

TITLE IV—PARTICIPATION BY GOVERNMENT AGENCIES

GENERAL AUTHORITY

SEC. 401. The Secretary is authorized, in carrying on any activity under the authority of this Act, to utilize, with the approval of the President, the services, facilities, and personnel of the other Government agencies. Whenever the Secretary shall use the services, facilities, or personnel of any Government agency for activities under authority of this Act, the Secretary shall pay for such performance out of funds available to the Secretary under this Act, either in advance, by reimbursement, or direct transfer. The Secretary shall include in each report submitted to the Congress under section 1008 a statement of the services, facilities, and personnel of other Government agencies utilized in carrying on activities under the authority of this Act, showing the names and salaries of the personnel utilized, or performing services utilized, during the period covered by such report, and the amounts paid to such other agencies under this section as payment for such performance.

TECHNICAL AND OTHER SERVICES

SEC. 402. A Government agency, at the request of the Secretary, may perform such technical or other services as such agency may be competent to render for the government of another country desirous of obtaining such services, upon terms and conditions which are satisfactory to the Secretary and to the head of the Government agency, when it is determined by the Secretary that such services will contribute to the purposes of this Act. However, nothing in this Act shall authorize the performance of services relating to the organization, training, operation, development, or combat equipment of the armed forces of a foreign government.

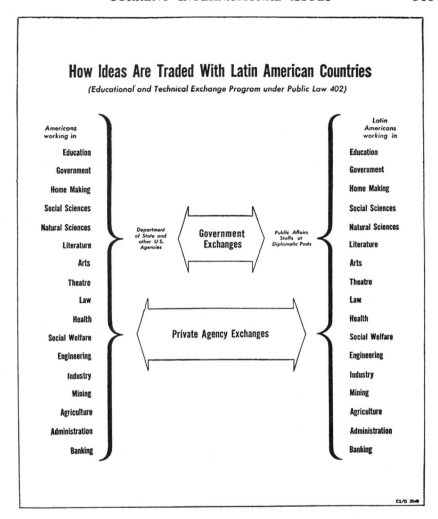

How Ideas Are Traded With Latin American Countries

(Educational and Technical Exchange Program under Public Law 402)

Americans working in | Latin Americans working in

Education
Government
Home Making
Social Sciences
Natural Sciences
Literature
Arts
Theatre
Law
Health
Social Welfare
Engineering
Industry
Mining
Agriculture
Administration
Banking

Department of State and other U.S. Agencies

Government Exchanges

Public Affairs Staffs at Diplomatic Posts

Private Agency Exchanges

CS/G 3048

POLICY GOVERNING SERVICES

SEC. 403. In authorizing the performance of technical and other services under this title, it is the sense of the Congress (1) that the Secretary shall encourage through any appropriate Government agency the performance of such services to foreign governments by qualified private American individuals and agencies, and shall not enter into the performance of such services to any foreign government where such services may be performed adequately by qualified private American individuals and agencies and such qualified individuals and agencies are available for the performance of such services; (2) that if such services are rendered by a Government agency, they shall demonstrate the technical accomplishments of the United States, such services being of an advisory, investigative, or instructional nature, or a demonstration of a technical process; (3) that such services shall not include the construction of public works or the supervision of the construction of public works, and that, under authority of this Act, a Government agency shall render engineering services related to public works only when the Secretary shall determine that the national interest demands the rendering of such services by a Government agency, but this policy shall not be interpreted to preclude the assignment of individual specialists as advisers to other governments as provided under title III of this Act, together with such incidental assistance as may be necessary for the accomplishment of their individual assignments.

TITLE V—DISSEMINATING INFORMATION ABOUT THE UNITED STATES ABROAD

GENERAL AUTHORIZATION

SEC. 501. The Secretary is authorized, when he finds it appropriate, to provide for the preparation, and dissemination abroad, of information about the United States, its people, and its policies, through press, publications, radio, motion pictures, and other information media, and through information centers and instructors abroad. Any such press release or radio script, on request, shall be available in the English language at the Department of State, at all reasonable times following its release as information abroad, for examination by representatives of United States press associations, newspapers, magazines, radio systems, and stations, and, on request, shall be made available to Members of Congress.

POLICIES GOVERNING INFORMATION ACTIVITIES

SEC. 502. In authorizing international information activities under this Act, it is the sense of the Congress (1) that the Secretary shall reduce such Government information activities whenever corresponding private information dissemination is found to be adequate; (2) that nothing in this Act shall be construed to give the Department a monopoly in the production or sponsorship on the air of short-wave broadcasting programs, or a monopoly in any other medium of information.

TITLE VI—ADVISORY COMMISSIONS TO FORMULATE POLICIES

SEC. 601. There are hereby created two advisory commissions, (1) United States Advisory Commission on Information (hereinafter in this title referred to as the Commission on Information) and (2) United States Advisory Commission on Educational Exchange (hereinafter in this title referred to as the Commission on Educational Exchange) to be constituted as provided in section 602. The Commissions shall formulate and recommend to the Secretary policies and programs for the carrying out of this Act: *Provided, however,* That the commissions created by this section shall have no authority over the Board of Foreign Scholarships or the program created by Public Law 584 of the Seventy-ninth Congress, enacted August 1, 1946, or the United States National Commission for UNESCO.

MEMBERSHIP OF THE COMMISSIONS; GENERAL PROVISIONS

SEC. 602. (a) Each Commission shall consist of five members, not more than three of whom shall be from any one political party. Members shall be appointed by the President, by and with the advice and consent of the Senate. No person holding any compensated Federal or State office shall be eligible for appointment.

(b) The members of the Commission on Information shall represent the public interest, and shall be selected from a cross section of professional, business, and public service backgrounds.

(c) The members of the Commission on Educational Exchange shall represents the public interest and shall be selected from a cross section of educational, cultural, scientific, technical, and public service backgrounds.

(d) The term of each member appointed under subsection (a) of this section shall be three years, except that the terms of office of such members first taking office on each Commission shall expire, as designated by the President at the time of appointment, two at the end of one year, two at the end of two years, and one at the end of three years from the date of the enactment of this Act. Any member appointed to fill a vacancy occurring prior to the expiration of the term for which his predecessor is appointed shall be appointed for the remainder of such term. Upon the expiration of his term of office any member may continue to serve until his successor is appointed and has qualified.

(e) The President shall designate a chairman for each Commission from among members of the Commission.

(f) The members of the Commissions shall receive no compensation for their services as such members but shall be entitled to reimbursement for travel and subsistence in connection with attendance of meetings of the Commissions away from their places of residences, as provided in subsection (6) of section 801 of this Act.

(g) The Commissions are authorized to adopt such rules and regulations as they may deem necessary to carry out the authority conferred upon them by this title.

(h) The Department is authorized to provide the necessary secretarial and clerical assistance for the Commissions.

RECOMMENDATIONS AND REPORTS

SEC. 603. The Commissions shall meet not less frequently than once each month during the first six months after their establishment, and thereafter at such intervals as the Commissions find advisable, and shall transmit to the Secretary a quarterly report, and to the Congress a semiannual report of all programs and activities carried on under the authority of this Act, including appraisals, where feasible, as to the effectiveness of the several programs, and such recommendations as shall have been made by the Commissions to the Secretary for effectuating the purposes and objectives of this Act and the action taken to carry out such recommendations.

TITLE VII—APPROPRIATIONS

GENERAL AUTHORIZATION

SEC. 701. Appropriations to carry out the purposes of this Act are hereby authorized.

TRANSFER OF FUNDS

SEC. 702. The Secretary shall authorize the transfer to other Government agencies for expenditure in the United States and in other countries, in order to carry out the purposes of this Act, any part of any appropriations available to the Department for carrying out the purposes of this Act, for direct expenditure or as a working fund, and any such expenditures may be made under the specific authority contained in this Act or under the authority governing the activities of the Government agency to which a part of any such appropriation is transferred, provided the activities come within the scope of this Act.

*   *   *

TITLE IX—FUNDS PROVIDED BY OTHER SOURCES

REIMBURSEMENT

SEC. 901. The Secretary shall, when he finds it in the public interest, request and accept reimbursement from any cooperating governmental or private source in a foreign country, or from State or local governmental institutions or private sources in the United States, for all or part of the expenses of any portion of the program undertaken hereunder. The amounts so received shall be covered into the Treasury as miscellaneous receipts.

ADVANCE OF FUNDS

SEC. 902. If any other government shall express the desire to provide funds, property, or services to be used by this Government, in whole or in part, for the expenses of any specific part of the program undertaken pursuant to this Act, the Secretary is authorized, when he finds it in the public interest, to accept such funds, property, or services. Funds so received may be established as a special deposit account in the Treasury of the United States, to be available for the specified purpose, and to be used for reimbursement of appropriations or direct expenditure, subject to the provisions of this Act. Any unexpended balance of the special deposit account and other property received under this section and no longer required for the purposes for which provided shall be returned to the government providing the funds or property.

◇◇◇◇◇◇

225. FULBRIGHT ACT, 1946 [1]

*Encouraging Educational Exchange between the United States
and Other Countries*

[Next to the Smith-Mundt program the largest United States educational exchange arrangement is carried out under the Fulbright Act. Funds from the sales of surplus war property abroad belonging to the United States are used for the financing of studies and research of American students in foreign lands, and for the transportation of citizens of other countries, who wish to attend educational institutions in the United States. The selection of the recipients is in the charge of the so-called ten man Board of Foreign Scholarships appointed by the President.]

Be it enacted by the Senate and House of Representatives of the United States of America in Congress assembled, That section 10 of the Surplus Property Act of 1944, as amended, is hereby amended by adding a new subsection (c) to read as follows:

"(c) Except as provided in subsection (b) of this section, the Department of State shall be the sole disposal agency for surplus property located outside the continental United States, Hawaii, Alaska (including the Aleutian Islands), Puerto Rico, and the Virgin Islands, and with respect to such property the Secretary of State shall exercise the functions heretofore conferred upon the Surplus Property Administrator by Public Law 181, Seventy-ninth, Congress. The Secretary of State shall, subject to the provisions of the War Mobilization and Reconversion Act of 1944, have sole responsibility for carrying out the provisions of the Surplus Property Act of 1944, with respect to surplus property located outside the continental United States, Hawaii, Alaska (including the Aleutian Islands), Puerto Rico, and the Virgin Islands."

SEC. 2. Section 32 (b) of such Act, as amended, is hereby amended to read as follows:

"(b) (1) The provisions of this Act shall be applicable to disposition of property within the United States and elsewhere, but the Secretary of State may exempt from some or all of the provisions hereof dispositions of property located outside of the continental United States, Hawaii, Alaska (including the Aleutian Islands), Puerto Rico, and the Virgin Islands, whenever he deems that such provisions would obstruct the efficient and economic disposition of such property in accordance with the objectives of this Act. In addition to the authority conferred by section 15 of this Act, the Department of State may dispose of surplus property located outside the continental United States, Hawaii, Alaska (including the Aleutian Islands), Puerto Rico, and the Virgin Islands, for foreign currencies or credits, or substantial benefits or the discharge of claims resulting from the compromise, or settlement of such claims by any Government agency in accordance with the law, whenever the Secretary of State determines that it is in the interest of the United States to do so and upon such terms and conditions as he may deem proper. Any foreign currencies or credits acquired by the Department of State pursuant

[1] Public Law 584, 79th Cong., 2d sess., S. 1636.

to this subsection shall be administered in accordance with procedures that may from time to time be established by the Secretary of the Treasury and, if and when reduced to United States currency, shall be covered into the Treasury as miscellaneous receipts.

"(2) In carrying out the provisions of this section, the Secretary of State is hereby authorized to enter into an executive agreement or agreements with any foreign government for the use of currencies, or credits for currencies, of such government acquired as a result of such surplus property disposals, for the purpose of providing, by the formation of foundations or otherwise, for (A) financing studies, research, instruction, and other educational activities of or for American citizens in schools and institutions of higher learning located in such foreign country, or of the citizens of such foreign country in American schools and institutions of higher learning located outside the continental United States, Hawaii, Alaska (including the Aleutian Islands), Puerto Rico, and the Virgin Islands, including payment for transportation, tuition, maintenance, and other expenses incident to scholastic activities; or (B) furnishing transportation for citizens of such foreign country who desire to attend American schools and institutions of higher learning in the continental United States, Hawaii, Alaska (including the Aleutian Islands), Puerto Rico, and the Virgin Islands, and whose attendance will not deprive citizens of the United States of an opportunity to attend such schools and institutions: *Provided however,* That no such agreement or agreements shall provide for the use of an aggregate amount of the currencies, or credits for currencies, of any one country in excess of $20,000,000 or for the expenditure of the currencies, or credits for currencies of any one foreign country in excess of $1,000,000 annually at the official rate of exchange for such currencies, unless otherwise authorized by Congress, nor shall any such agreement relate to any subject other than the use and expenditure of such currencies or credits for currencies for the purposes herein set forth: *Provided further,* That for the purpose of selecting students and educational institutions qualified to participate in this program, and to supervise the exchange program authorized herein, the President of the United States is hereby authorized to appoint a Board of Foreign Scholarships, consisting of ten members, who shall serve without compensation, composed of representatives of cultural, educational, student and war veterans groups, and including representatives of the United States Office of Education, the United States Veterans' Administration, State educational institutions, and privately endowed educational institutions: *And Provided further,* That in the selection of American citizens for study in foreign countries under this paragraph preference shall be given to applicants who shall have served in the military or naval forces of the United States during World War I or World War II, and due consideration shall be given to applicants from all geographical areas of the United States. The Secretary of State shall transmit to the Congress not later than the 1st day of March of each year a report of operations under this paragraph during the preceding calendar year. Such report shall include the text of any agreements which have been entered into hereunder during the preceding calendar year, and shall specify the names and addresses of American citizens who are attending schools or institutions of higher learning in foreign countries pursuant to such agreements, the names and locations of such schools and institutions, and th⁼

amounts of the currencies or credits for currencies expended for any of the purposes under this paragraph in each such foreign country during the preceding calendar year."
Approved August 1, 1946.

226. FULBRIGHT AGREEMENT WITH ITALY [1]

[The annual exchange of students and technically skilled people in the educational, cultural, and scientific fields between the United States and nearly sixty countries involves between 6,000 and 7,000 people. At least twenty-five of our federal agencies participate in the exchanges. The formal arrangements between the United States and the participating countries are made in executive agreements, which lay the bases for the programs and provide for their administration. A typical agreement, that with Italy, is reproduced below.]

AGREEMENT

between the Government of the United States of America and the Government of the Italian Republic for financing certain educational exchange programs.

The GOVERNMENT OF THE UNITED STATES OF AMERICA and the GOVERNMENT OF THE ITALIAN REPUBLIC

Desiring to promote further mutual understanding between the peoples of the United States of America and of Italy by a wider exchange of knowledge and professional talents;

Considering that the Secretary of State of the United States of America may enter into an agreement for financing certain educational exchange programs from currencies or credits for currencies acquired pursuant to the Memorandum of Agreement dated September 9, 1946 or any supplement or modification thereof (hereinafter collectively referred to as the *Memorandum*).

Have agreed as follows:

Article 1

The Government of the Italian Republic shall deposit, subsequent to 30 days from December 18th 1948, with the Treasurer of the United States of America on such dates as the Government of the United States of America shall specify, amounts of Italian currency until an aggregate amount of Italian currency equivalent to $5,000,000 (United States currency) shall have been so deposited, provided, however, that in no event shall a total amount of Italian currency in excess of the equivalent of $1,000,000 (United States currency) be deposited during any single calendar year. The amount of currency so deposited shall reduce the amount that would otherwise be payable

[1] Department of State, Treaties and Other International Acts Series 1864.

in dollars by the Government of the Italian Republic to the Government of the United States of America in accordance with the *Memorandum*.

The rate of exchange between Italian currency and United States currency to be used in determining the amount of Italian currency to be deposited from time to time pursuant to this agreement shall be determined in accordance with the *Memorandum,* or any supplement or modification thereof.

Article 2

The amounts thus made available to the Treasurer of the United States of America shall not be subject to the domestic and local laws of the United States of America as they relate to the use and expenditure of currencies and credits for currencies for the purposes set forth in the present agreement, and shall be considered as property constituted pursuant to a transaction entered into in accordance with the *Memorandum* and are therefore not subject in the Italian Republic to any tax, duty, or other assessment under paragraph 8 of the *Memorandum*. Such amounts shall be used for the purposes of:

1. Financing studies, research, instruction and other educational activities of or for citizens of the United States of America in schools and institutions of higher learning located in the Italian Republic or of citizens of the Italian Republic in United States schools and institutions of higher learning located outside the continental United States, Hawaii, Alaska (including the Aleutian Islands), Puerto Rico and the Virgin Islands, including payment for transportation, maintenance, tuition and other expenses, incident to scholastic activities; or

2. Furnishing transportation for citizens of the Italian Republic who desire to attend United States schools and institutions of higher learning in the continental United States, Hawaii, Alaska (including the Aleutian Islands), Puerto Rico and the Virgin Islands, and whose attendance will not deprive citizens of the United States of America of an opportunity to attend such schools and institutions.

Article 3

In order to promote the integrated development of the educational program, there shall be established a joint Commission, to be known as the American Commission for Cultural Exchange with Italy (hereinafter designated "the Commission") which will receive funds made available to the Government of the United States of America under the *Memorandum*. The funds so made available shall be placed at the disposal of the Commission by deposit in the Italian Republic in the name of the Treasurer of the Commission.

Article 4

The Commission shall exercise all powers necessary for carrying out the educational program, including the following:

(*a*) authorize the disbursement of the funds and the making of grants and advances therefrom;

(*b*) plan, adopt and carry out programs which, in the territory of the Italian Republic, shall be executed in collaboration with the Government of the Italian Republic;

(*c*) recommend to the Board of Foreign Scholarships, provided for in the United States Surplus Property Act of 1944, as amended, students, teachers, professors, research scholars, resident in the Italian Republic, and institutions situated in the Italian Republic, qualified in the opinion of the Commission to participate in the programs in accordance with the aforesaid Act;

(*d*) recommend to the aforesaid Board of Foreign Scholarships such qualifications for the selection of participants in the programs as it may deem necessary;

(*e*) provide for periodic audits of the accounts of the Commission as directed by auditors selected by the Secretary of State of the United States of America;

(*f*) engage an executive officer, administrative and clerical staff and fix and authorize the payment of salaries and wages thereof out of the funds made available.

Article 5

All expenditures authorized by the Commission shall be made in accordance with budgets to be approved by the Secretary of State of the United States of America pursuant to such regulations he may prescribe, and the Commission shall not authorize any commitments or create any obligation in excess of the part of the funds actually placed at its disposal at the time of the authorization.

Article 6

The Commission shall consist of twelve members, six of whom shall be citizens of the United States of America, six of whom shall be citizens of the Italian Republic.

Of the citizens of the United States of America, a minimum of three shall be officers of the United States Foreign Service Establishments in the Italian Republic; one of them shall serve as Treasurer. The principal officer in charge of the Diplomatic Mission of the United States of America in the Italian Republic shall be Honorary Chairman of the Commission. He shall have the power of appointment and removal of the United States citizens on the Commission, and deciding vote in case of tie. The citizens of the Italian Republic on the Commission shall be appointed and may be removed by the Government of the Italian Republic. A Chairman with voting power shall be elected by the Commission from among its members.

The members shall serve from the time of their appointment until one year from the following December 31st, and shall be eligible for reappointment. Vacancies by reason of resignation, transfer of residence outside the territory of the Italian Republic, expiration of term of service or otherwise, shall be filled in accordance with the above procedure. The members shall serve without compensation, but the Commission may authorize the payment of the necessary expenses of the members in attending the meetings of the Commission.

The Commission shall adopt such rules and appoint such committees as it deems necessary for the conduct of its affairs.

Article 7

Reports shall be made annually on the activities of the Commission to the Secretary of State of the United States of America and the Government of the Italian Republic. Such reports shall be submitted in such form and detail as may be required by the Secretary of State.

Article 8

The principal office of the Commission shall be in Rome, but meetings of the Commission and any of its committees may be held in such other places as the Commission may from time to time determine, and the activities of any of the Commission officers or staff may be carried on at such places as may be approved by the Commission, within the limit of any rules, regulations and restrictions in force in territories under the authority of the Italian Republic.

Article 9

Wherever in the present agreement, the term "Secretary of State of the United States of America" is used, it shall be understood to mean the Secretary of State of the United States of America or any officer or employee of the Government of the United States of America designated by him to act on his behalf.

Article 10

The Government of the United States of America and the Government of the Italian Republic shall make every effort to facilitate the exchange of persons programs authorized in this agreement and to resolve problems which may arise in the operation thereof.

Article 11

The present agreement shall enter into force on the date of its signature. It shall be reviewed at the expiration of a period of three years. It may also be reviewed at any prior time at the instance of one or the other Government.

IN WITNESS WHEREOF the undersigned, being duly authorized thereto by their respective Governments, have signed the present agreement.

DONE in Rome, this 18th day of December 1948 in duplicate in the English and Italian languages both equally authentic.

For the	*For the*
Government of the United States	*Italian Government*
of America	
JAMES CLEMENT DUNN	SFORZA

◇◇◇◇◇◇

FOREIGN AID AND RECONSTRUCTION

227. AID TO GREECE AND TURKEY

Message From the Greek Prime Minister and the Minister for Foreign Affairs to the President and the Secretary of State, March 3, 1947 [1]

[During the winter of 1947, the British Government encountered serious economic difficulties which made it necessary to restrict its financial commitments abroad. The consequent withdrawal of British aid from Greece, coupled with the increasing activities of communist-inspired guerillas, forced the Greek Government to turn to the United States for additional assistance in order to survive as a free nation. It will be noted, in the text of the message which follows, that the Greeks requested aid for military purposes as well as for relief and rehabilitation.]

SIR: I have the honor, on instructions of my Government, to convey the following urgent message to His Excellency the President of the United States and to Your Excellency:

"Owing to the systematic devastation of Greece, the decimation and debilitation of her people and the destruction of her economy through four invasions and protracted enemy occupation, as well as through disturbances in the wake of war, and despite the valuable assistance rendered by our Allies during and after the war for which the Greek people feel profoundly grateful, further and immediate assistance has unfortunately become vital. It is impossible to exaggerate the magnitude of the difficulties that beset those survivors in Greece who are devoting themselves to the restoration of their country. Such means of survival as remained to the Greek people after the enemy withdrew have now been exhausted so that today Greece is without funds to finance the import even of those consumption goods that are essential for bare subsistence. In such circumstances the Greek people cannot make progress in attacking the problems of reconstruction, though substantial reconstruction must be begun if the situation in Greece is not to continue to be critical.

"The Greek Government and people are therefore compelled to appeal to the Government of the United States and through it to the American people for financial, economic and expert assistance. For Greece to survive she must have:

"1. The financial and other assistance which will enable her immediately to resume purchases of the food, clothing, fuel, seeds and the like that are indispensable for the subsistence of her people and that are obtainable only from abroad.

"2. The financial and other assistance necessary to enable the civil and military establishments of the Government to obtain from abroad the means of restoring in the country the tranquillity and feeling of security indispensable to the achievement of economic and political recovery.

---

[1] First Report to Congress on Assistance to Greece and Turkey, Department of State publication 2957, Near Eastern Series 11, pp. 28-29. Delivered by the Chargé d'Affaires of Greece at Washington on March 3, 1947, and released to the press on March 4.

"3. Aid in obtaining the financial and other assistance that will enable Greece and the Greek people to create the means for self-support in the future. This involves problems which unhappily cannot be solved unless we surmount the crisis immediately confronting us.

"4. The aid of experienced American administrative, economic and technical personnel to assure the utilization in an effective and up-to-date manner of the financial and other assistance given to Greece, to help to restore a healthy condition in the domestic economy and public administration and to train the young people of Greece to assume their responsibilities in a reconstructed economy.

"The need is great. The determination of the Greek people to do all in their power to·restore Greece as a self-supporting, self-respecting democracy is also great; but the destruction in Greece has been so complete as to rob the Greek people of the power to meet the situation by themselves. It is because of these circumstances that they turn to America for aid.

"It is the profound hope of the Greek Government that the Government of the United States will find a way to render to Greece without delay the assistance for which it now appeals.

"Signed: D. MAXIMOS, Prime Minister, C. TSALDARIS, Deputy Prime Minister and Minister for Foreign Affairs."

Accept, Sir, the renewed assurances of my highest consideration.

PAUL ECONOMOU-GOURAS

His Excellency GEORGE C. MARSHALL
Secretary of State
Washington, D. C.

◇◇◇◇◇◇

228. RECOMMENDATIONS ON GREECE AND TURKEY (TRUMAN DOCTRINE)

Message of the President to the Congress, March 12, 1947 [1]

[March 12, 1947, marks a significant turning point in the postwar history of American policy. When the President on that day appeared before a joint session of Congress and requested assistance for Greece and Turkey, he launched the United States upon a positive program of resisting the expansionist tactics of international communism. He declared that it must be our policy to "support free peoples who are resisting attempted subjugation by armed minorities or by outside pressures." In some quarters, this statement which soon became known as the Truman Doctrine, was considered as important as the Monroe Doctrine. The full text of President Truman's historic speech follows.]

MR. PRESIDENT, MR. SPEAKER, MEMBERS OF THE CONGRESS OF THE UNITED STATES:

[1] Department of State Bulletin, Supplement of May 4, 1947, pp. 829-832. Delivered by the President before a joint session of Congress on March 12, 1947, and released to the press by the White House on the same date.

The gravity of the situation which confronts the world today necessitates my appearance before a joint session of the Congress.

The foreign policy and the national security of this country are involved.

One aspect of the present situation, which I wish to present to you at this time for your consideration and decision, concerns Greece and Turkey.

The United States has received from the Greek Government an urgent appeal for financial and economic assistance. Preliminary reports from the American Economic Mission now in Greece and reports from the American Ambassador in Greece corroborate the statement of the Greek Government that assistance is imperative if Greece is to survive as a free nation.

I do not believe that the American people and the Congress wish to turn a deaf ear to the appeal of the Greek Government.

Greece is not a rich country. Lack of sufficient natural resources has always forced the Greek people to work hard to make both ends meet. Since 1940 this industrious and peace-loving country has suffered invasion, four years of cruel enemy occupation, and bitter internal strife.

When forces of liberation entered Greece they found that the retreating Germans had destroyed virtually all the railways, roads, port facilities, communications, and merchant marine. More than a thousand villages had been burned. Eighty-five percent of the children were tubercular. Livestock, poultry, and draft animals had almost disappeared. Inflation had wiped out practically all savings.

As a result of these tragic conditions, a militant minority, exploiting human want and misery, was able to create political chaos which, until now, has made economic recovery impossible.

Greece is today without funds to finance the importation of those goods which are essential to bare subsistence. Under these circumstances the people of Greece cannot make progress in solving their problems of reconstruction. Greece is in desperate need of financial and economic assistance to enable it to resume purchases of food, clothing, fuel, and seeds. These are indispensable for the subsistence of its people and are obtainable only from abroad. Greece must have help to import the goods necessary to restore internal order and security so essential for economic and political recovery.

The Greek Government has also asked for the assistance of experienced American administrators, economists, and technicians to insure that the financial and other aid given to Greece shall be used effectively in creating a stable and self-sustaining economy and in improving its public administration.

The very existence of the Greek state is today threatened by the terrorist activities of several thousand armed men, led by Communists, who defy the Government's authority at a number of points, particularly along the northern boundaries. A commission appointed by the United Nations Security Council is at present investigating disturbed conditions in northern Greece and alleged border violations along the frontier between Greece on the one hand and Albania, Bulgaria, and Yugoslavia on the other.

Meanwhile, the Greek Government is unable to cope with the situation. The Greek Army is small and poorly equipped. It needs supplies and equipment if it is to restore authority to the Government throughout Greek territory.

Greece must have assistance if it is to become a self-supporting and self-respecting democracy.

The United States must supply that assistance. We have already extended to Greece certain types of relief and economic aid, but these are inadequate.

There is no other country to which democratic Greece can turn.

No other nation is willing and able to provide the necessary support for a democratic Greek Government.

The British Government, which has been helping Greece, can give no further financial or economic aid after March 31. Great Britain finds itself under the necessity of reducing or liquidating its commitments in several parts of the world, including Greece.

We have considered how the United Nations might assist in this crisis. But the situation is an urgent one requiring immediate action, and the United Nations and its related organizations are not in a position to extend help of the kind that is required.

It is important to note that the Greek Government has asked for our aid in utilizing effectively the financial and other assistance we may give to Greece, and in improving its public administration. It is of the utmost importance that we supervise the use of any funds made available to Greece, in such a manner that each dollar spent will count toward making Greece self-supporting, and will help to build an economy in which a healthy democracy can flourish.

No government is perfect. One of the chief virtues of a democracy, however, is that its defects are always visible and under democratic processes can be pointed out and corrected. The Government of Greece is not perfect. Nevertheless it represents 85 percent of the members of the Greek Parliament who were chosen in an election last year. Foreign observers, including 692 Americans, considered this election to be a fair expression of the views of the Greek people.

The Greek Government has been operating in an atmosphere of chaos and extremism. It has made mistakes. The extension of aid by this country does not mean that the United States condones everything that the Greek Government has done or will do. We have condemned in the past, and we condemn now, extremist measures of the right or the left. We have in the past advised tolerance, and we advise tolerance now.

Greece's neighbor, Turkey, also deserves our attention.

The future of Turkey as an independent and economically sound state is clearly no less important to the freedom-loving peoples of the world than the future of Greece. The circumstances in which Turkey finds itself today are considerably different from those of Greece. Turkey has been spared the disasters that have beset Greece. And during the war the United States and Great Britain furnished Turkey with material aid.

Nevertheless, Turkey now needs our support.

Since the war Turkey has sought additional financial assistance from Great Britain and the United States for the purpose of effecting that modernization necessary for the maintenance of its national integrity.

That integrity is essential to the preservation of order in the Middle East.

The British Government has informed us that, owing to its own difficulties, it can no longer extend financial or economic aid to Turkey.

As in the case of Greece, if Turkey is to have the assistance it needs, the United States must supply it. We are the only country able to provide that help.

I am fully aware of the broad implications involved if the United States extends assistance to Greece and Turkey, and I shall discuss these implications with you at this time.

One of the primary objectives of the foreign policy of the United States is the creation of conditions in which we and other nations will be able to work out a way of life free from coercion. This was a fundamental issue in the war with Germany and Japan. Our victory was won over countries which sought to impose their will, and their way of life, upon other nations.

To insure the peaceful development of nations, free from coercion, the United States has taken a leading part in establishing the United Nations. The United Nations is designed to make possible lasting freedom and independence for all its members. We shall not realize our objectives, however, unless we are willing to help free peoples to maintain their free institutions and their national integrity against aggressive movements that seek to impose upon them totalitarian regimes. This is no more than a frank recognition that totalitarian regimes imposed upon free peoples, by direct or indirect aggression, undermine the foundations of international peace and hence the security of the United States.

The peoples of a number of countries of the world have recently had totalitarian regimes forced upon them against their will. The Government of the United States has made frequent protests against coercion and intimidation, in violation of the Yalta agreement, in Poland, Rumania, and Bulgaria. I must also state that in a number of other countries there have been similar developments.

At the present moment in world history nearly every nation must choose between alternative ways of life. The choice is too often not a free one.

One way of life is based upon the will of the majority, and is distinguished by free institutions, representative government, free elections, guaranties, of individual liberty, freedom of speech and religion, and freedom from political oppression.

The second way of life is based upon the will of a minority forcibly imposed upon the majority. It relies upon terror and oppression, a controlled press and radio, fixed elections, and the suppression of personal freedoms.

I believe that it must be the policy of the United States to support free peoples who are resisting attempted subjugation by armed minorities or by outside pressures.

I believe that we must assist free peoples to work out their own destinies in their own way.

I believe that our help should be primarily through economic and financial aid which is essential to economic stability and orderly political processes.

The world is not static, and the *status quo* is not sacred. But we cannot allow changes in the *status quo* in violation of the Charter of the United Nations by such methods as coercion, or by such subterfuges as political infiltration. In helping free and independent nations to maintain their freedom, the United States will be giving effect to the principles of the Charter of the United Nations.

It is necessary only to glance at a map to realize that the survival and integrity of the Greek nation are of grave importance in a much wider situation. If Greece should fall under the control of an armed minority, the effect upon its neighbor, Turkey, would be immediate and serious. Confusion and disorder might well spread throughout the entire Middle East.

Moreover, the disappearance of Greece as an independent state would have a profound effect upon those countries in Europe whose peoples are struggling against great difficulties to maintain their freedoms and their independence while they repair the damages of war.

It would be an unspeakable tragedy if these countries, which have struggled so long against overwhelming odds, should lose that victory for which they sacrificed so much. Collapse of free institutions and loss of independence would be disastrous not only for them but for the world. Discouragement and possibly failure would quickly be the lot of neighboring peoples striving to maintain their freedom and independence.

Should we fail to aid Greece and Turkey in this fateful hour, the effect will be far-reaching to the West as well as to the East.

We must take immediate and resolute action.

I therefore ask the Congress to provide authority for assistance to Greece and Turkey in the amount of $400,000,000 for the period ending June 30, 1948. In requesting these funds, I have taken into consideration the maximum amount of relief assistance which would be furnished to Greece out of the $350,000,000 which I recently requested that the Congress authorize for the prevention of starvation and suffering in countries devastated by the war.

In addition to funds, I ask the Congress to authorize the detail of American civilian and military personnel to Greece and Turkey, at the request of those countries, to assist in the tasks of reconstruction, and for the purpose of supervising the use of such financial and material assistance as may be furnished. I recommend that authority also be provided for the instruction and training of selected Greek and Turkish personnel.

Finally, I ask that the Congress provide authority which will permit the speediest and most effective use, in terms of needed commodities, supplies, and equipment, of such funds as may be authorized.

If further funds, or further authority, should be needed for purposes indicated in this message, I shall not hesitate to bring the situation before the Congress. On this subject the Executive and Legislative branches of the Government must work together.

This is a serious course upon which we embark.

I would not recommend it except that the alternative is much more serious.

The United States contributed $341,000,000,000 toward winning World War II. This is an investment in world freedom and world peace.

The assistance that I am recommending for Greece and Turkey amounts to little more than one-tenth of one percent of this investment. It is only common sense that we should safeguard this investment and make sure that it was not in vain.

The seeds of totalitarian regimes are nurtured by misery and want. They spread and grow in the evil soul of poverty and strife. They reach their full growth when the hope of a people for a better life has died.

We must keep that hope alive.

The free peoples of the world look to us for support in maintaining their freedoms.

If we falter in our leadership, we may endanger the peace of the world—and we shall surely endanger the welfare of our own Nation.

Great responsibilities have been placed upon us by the swift movement of events.

I am confident that the Congress will face these responsibilities squarely.

229. AN ACT TO PROVIDE FOR ASSISTANCE TO GREECE AND TURKEY, 1947 [1]

[When the President suddenly announced the Truman Doctrine on March 12, 1947, he clearly ran the risk of having Congress reject his proposal to extend aid to Greece and Turkey. In that event, American prestige would have suffered a serious setback abroad. Congress responded, however, and on May 22, 1947, approved by a large majority in both houses, the bill providing $400 million in aid to Greece and Turkey was passed. One of the main contributions Congress made to the legislation was to clarify the rôle of the United Nations to the program.]

Whereas the Governments of Greece and Turkey have sought from the Government of the United States immediate financial and other assistance which is necessary for the maintenance of their national integrity and their survival as free nations; and

Whereas the national integrity and survival of these nations are of importance to the security of the United States and of all freedom-loving peoples and depend upon the receipt at this time of assistance; and

Whereas the Security Council of the United Nations has recognized the seriousness of the unsettled conditions prevailing on the border between Greece on the one hand and Albania, Bulgaria, and Yugoslavia on the other, and, if the present emergency is met, may subsequently assume full responsibility for this phase of the problem as a result of the investigation which its commission is currently conducting; and

Whereas the Food and Agriculture Organization mission for Greece recognized the necessity that Greece receive financial and economic assistance and recommended that Greece request such assistance from the appropriate agencies of the United Nations and from the Governments of the United States and the United Kingdom; and

Whereas the United Nations is not now in a position to furnish to Greece and Turkey the financial and economic assistance which is immediately required; and

Whereas the furnishing of such assistance to Greece and Turkey by the United States will contribute to the freedom and independence of all members of the United Nations in conformity with the principles and purposes of the Charter: Now, therefore,

[1] Public Law 75, 80th Cong., 1st sess. This act has been implemented by additional appropriations annually since 1947.

Be it enacted by the Senate and House of Representatives of the United States of America in Congress assembled, That, notwithstanding the provisions of any other law, the President may from time to time when he deems it in the interest of the United States furnish assistance to Greece and Turkey, upon request of their governments, and upon terms and conditions determined by him—

(1) by rendering financial aid in the form of loans, credits, grants, or otherwise, to those countries;

(2) by detailing to assist those countries any persons in the employ of the Government of the United States; and the provisions of the Act of May 25, 1938 (52 Stat. 442), as amended, applicable to personnel detailed pursuant to such Act, as amended, shall be applicable to personnel detailed pursuant to this paragraph: *Provided, however,* That no civilian personnel shall be assigned to Greece or Turkey to administer the purposes of this Act until such personnel have been investigated by the Federal Bureau of Investigation;

(3) by detailing a limited number of members of the military services of the United States to assist those countries, in an advisory capacity only; and the provisions of the Act of May 19, 1926 (44 Stat. 565), as amended, applicable to personnel detailed pursuant to such Act, as amended, shall be applicable to personnel detailed pursuant to this paragraph;

(4) by providing for (A) the transfer to, and the procurement for by manufacture or otherwise and the transfer to, those countries of any articles, services, and information, and (B) the instruction and training of personnel of those countries; and

(5) by incurring and defraying necessary expenses, including administrative expenses and expenses for compensation of personnel, in connection with the carrying out of the provisions of this Act.

*   *   *

SEC. 3. As a condition precedent to the receipt of any assistance pursuant to this Act, the government requesting such assistance shall agree (a) to permit free access of United States Governnment officials for the purpose of observing whether such assistance is utilized effectively and in accordance with the undertakings of the recipient government; (b) to permit representatives of the press and radio of the United States to observe freely and to report fully regarding the utilization of such assistance; (c) not to transfer, without the consent of the President of the United States, title to or possession of any article or information transferred pursuant to this Act nor to permit, without such consent, the use of any such article or the use or disclosure of any such information by or to anyone not an officer, employee, or agent of the recipient government; (d) to make such provisions as may be required by the President of the United States for the security of any article, service, or information received pursuant to this Act; (e) not to use any part of the proceeds of any loan, credit, grant, or other form of aid rendered pursuant to this Act for the making of any payment on account of the principal or interest on any loan made to such government by any other foreign government; and (f) to give full and continuous publicity within such country as to the purpose, source, character, scope, amounts, and progress of the United States economic assistance carried on therein pursuant to this Act.

SEC. 4. (a) Notwithstanding the provisions of any other law, the Reconstruction Finance Corporation is authorized and directed, until such time as

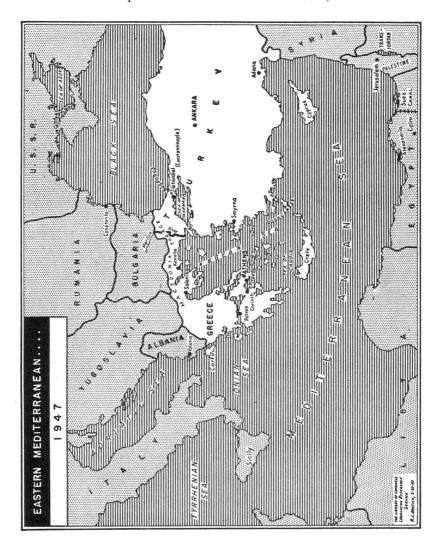

an appropriation shall be made pursuant to subsection (b) of this section, to make advances, not to exceed in the aggregate $100,000,000, to carry out the provisions of this Act, in such manner and in such amounts as the President shall determine.

(b) There is hereby authorized to be appropriated to the President not to exceed $400,000,000 to carry out the provisions of this Act. From appropriations made under this authority there shall be repaid to the Reconstruction Finance Corporation the advances made by it under subsection (a) of this section.

SEC. 5. The President may from time to time prescribe such rules and regulations as may be necessary and proper to carry out any of the provisions of this Act; and he may exercise any power or authority conferred upon him pursuant to this Act through such department, agency, independent establishment, or officer of the Government as he shall direct.

The President is directed to withdraw any or all aid authorized herein under any of the following circumstances:

(1) If requested by the Government of Greece or Turkey, respectively, representing a majority of the people of either such nation;

(2) If the Security Council finds (with respect to which finding the United States waives the exercise of any veto) or the General Assembly finds that action taken or assistance furnished by the United Nations makes the continuance of such assistance unnecessary or undesirable;

(3) If the President finds that any purposes of the Act have been substantially accomplished by the action of any other inter-governmental organizations or finds that the purposes of the Act are incapable of satisfactory accomplishment; and

(4) If the President finds that any of the assurances given pursuant to section 3 are not being carried out.

SEC. 6. Assistance to any country under this Act may, unless sooner terminated by the President, be terminated by concurrent resolution by the two Houses of the Congress.

SEC. 7. The President shall submit to the Congress quarterly reports of expenditures and activities, which shall include uses of funds by the recipient governments, under authority of this Act.

SEC. 8. The chief of any mission to any country receiving assistance under this Act shall be appointed by the President, by and with the advice and consent of the Senate, and shall perform such functions relating to the administration of this Act as the President shall prescribe.

Approved May 22, 1947.

◇◇◇◇◇◇

230. THE EUROPEAN RECOVERY PROGRAM

Remarks by Secretary Marshall, June 5, 1947 [1]

[After the war the United States continued to extend assistance to many of the devastated countries. But by and large this aid was piecemeal in nature; a palliative rather than a cure for Europe's basic economic ills. The germ of the Marshall Plan idea for a four-year program of aid to Europe (which was anticipated in an earlier speech by Under-Secretary Acheson) is to be found in this speech delivered by Secretary Marshall at Harvard on June 5, 1947.

[1] Department of State Bulletin, June 15, 1947, pp. 1159-1160. Made on the occasion of commencement exercises at Harvard University on June 5, 1947, and released to the press on the same date.

He pointed out that substantial aid would have to be granted by the United States in order to avert economic and political chaos in Europe. At the same time, he placed the initiative for the formulation of a joint program squarely in the hands of the European countries.]

I need not tell you gentlemen that the world situation is very serious. That must be apparent to all intelligent people. I think one difficulty is that the problem is one of such enormous complexity that the very mass of facts presented to the public by press and radio make it exceedingly difficult for the man in the street to reach a clear appraisement of the situation. Furthermore, the people of this country are distant from the troubled areas of the earth and it is hard for them to comprehend the plight and consequent reactions of the long-suffering peoples, and the effect of those reactions on their governments in connection with our efforts to promote peace in the world.

In considering the requirements for the rehabilitation of Europe, the physical loss of life, the visible destruction of cities, factories, mines, and railroads was correctly estimated, but it has become obvious during recent months that this visible destruction was probably less serious than the dislocation of the entire fabric of European economy. For the past 10 years conditions have been highly abnormal. The feverish preparation for war and the more feverish maintenance of the war effort engulfed all aspects of national economies. Machinery has fallen into disrepair or is entirely obsolete. Under the arbitrary and destructive Nazi rule, virtually every possible enterprise was geared into the German war machine. Long-standing commercial ties, private institutions, banks, insurance companies, and shipping companies disappeared, through loss of capital, absorption through nationalization, or by simple 'destruction. In many countries, confidence in the local currency has been severely shaken. The breakdown of the business structure of Europe during the war was complete. Recovery has been seriously retarded by the fact that two years after the close of hostilities a peace settlement with Germany and Austria has not been agreed upon. But even given a more prompt solution of these difficult problems, the rehabilitation of the economic structure of Europe quite evidently will require a much longer time and greater effort than had been foreseen.

There is a phase of this matter which is both interesting and serious. The farmer has always produced the foodstuffs to exchange with the city dweller for the other necessities of life. This division of labor is the basis of modern civilization. At the present time it is threatened with breakdown. The town and city industries are not producing adequate goods to exchange with the food-producing farmer. Raw materials and fuel are in short supply. Machinery is lacking or worn out. The farmer or the peasant cannot find the goods for sale which he desires to purchase. So the sale of his farm produce for money which he cannot use seems to him an unprofitable transaction. He, therefore, has withdrawn many fields from crop cultivation and is using them for grazing. He feeds more grain to stock and finds for himself and his family an ample supply of food, however short he may be on clothing and the other ordinary gadgets of civilization. Meanwhile people in the cities are short of food and fuel. So the governments are forced to use their foreign money and credits to procure these necessities abroad. This process exhausts funds which are urgently needed for reconstruction. Thus a very serious situation is rapidly developing which bodes no good for the world. The modern system of the division of labor upon which the exchange of products is based is in danger of breaking down.

The truth of the matter is that Europe's requirements for the next three or four years of foreign food and other essential products—principally from America—are so much greater than her present ability to pay that she must have substantial additional help or face economic, social, and political deterioration of a very grave character.

The remedy lies in breaking the vicious circle and restoring the confidence of the European people in the economic future of their own countries and of Europe as a whole. The manufacturer and the farmer throughout wide areas must be able and willing to exchange their products for currencies the continuing value of which is not open to question.

Aside from the demoralizing effect on the world at large and the possibilities of disturbances arising as a result of the desperation of the people concerned, the consequences to the economy of the United States should be apparent to all. It is logical that the United States should do whatever it is able to do to assist in the return of normal economic health in the world, without which there can be no political stability and no assured peace. Our policy is directed not against any country or doctrine but against hunger, poverty, desperation, and chaos. Its purpose should be the revival of a working economy in the world so as to permit the emergence of political and social conditions in which free institutions can exist. Such assistance, I am convinced, must not be on a piecemeal basis as various crises develop. Any assistance that this Government may render in the future should provide a cure rather than a mere palliative. Any government that is willing to assist in the task of recovery will find full cooperation, I am sure, on the part of the United States Government. Any government which maneuvers to block the recovery of other countries cannot expect help from us. Furthermore, governments, political parties, or groups which seek to perpetuate human misery in order to profit therefrom politically or otherwise will encounter the opposition of the United States.

It is already evident that, before the United States Government can proceed much further in its efforts to alleviate the situation and help start the European world on its way to recovery, there must be some agreement among the countries of Europe as to the requirements of the situation and the part those countries themselves will take in order to give proper effect to whatever action might be undertaken by this Government. It would be neither fitting nor efficacious for this Government to undertake to draw up unilaterally a program designed to place Europe on its feet economically. This is the business of the Europeans. The initiative, I think, must come from Europe. The role of this country should consist of friendly aid in the drafting of a European program and of later support of such a program so far as it may be practical for us to do so. The program should be a joint one, agreed to by a number, if not all, European nations.

An essential part of any successful action on the part of the United States is an understanding on the part of the people of America of the character of the problem and the remedies to be applied. Political passion and prejudice should have no part. With foresight, and a willingness on the part of our people to face up to the vast responsibility which history has clearly placed upon our country, the difficulties I have outlined can and will be overcome.

◇◇◇◇◇◇

231. PROGRAM FOR U. S. AID TO EUROPEAN RECOVERY

Message of the President to the Congress, December 19, 1947 [1]

[Responding to Secretary Marshall's address of June 5, 1947, representatives of various European countries met in Paris in July to draw up a coöperative program of European recovery. The sixteen nations which formed the Committee of European Economic Coöperation were: Austria, Belgium, Denmark, France, Greece, Iceland, Ireland, Italy, Luxembourg, the Netherlands, Norway, Portugal, Sweden, Switzerland, Turkey, and the United Kingdom. In September, the Committee submitted its findings to the United States. On the basis of these findings, which were carefully studied by the Executive Branch, the President presented the Marshall Plan to Congress for its consideration. That portion of the President's message which deals with the basic elements of the program are reproduced below.]

To the Congress of the United States:

*　　*　　*

THE RECOVERY PROGRAM PROPOSED BY THE EUROPEAN COUNTRIES

The report of the European Committee was transmitted to the Government of the United States late in September. The report describes the present economic situation of Europe and the extent to which the participating countries can solve their problem by individual and joint efforts. After taking into account these recovery efforts, the report estimates the extent to which the sixteen countries will be unable to pay for the imports they must have.

The report points out that the people of Western Europe depend for their support upon international trade. It has been possible for some 270 million people, occupying this relatively small area, to enjoy a good standard of living only by manufacturing imported raw materials and exporting the finished products to the rest of the world. They must also import foodstuffs in large volume, for there is not enough farm land in Western Europe to support its population even with intensive cultivation and with favorable weather. They cannot produce adequate amounts of cotton, oil and other raw materials. Unless these deficiencies are met by imports, the productive centers of Europe can function only at low efficiency, if at all.

In the past these necessary imports were paid for by exports from Europe, by the performance of services such as shipping and banking, and by income from capital investments abroad. All these elements of international trade were so badly disrupted by the war that the people of Western Europe have been unable to produce in their own countries, or to purchase elsewhere, the goods

---

[1] Department of State Bulletin, December 28, 1947, pp. 1233-1243.

essential to their livelihood. Shortages of raw materials, productive capacity, and exportable commodities have set up vicious circles of increasing scarcities and lowered standards of living.

The economic recovery of Western Europe countries depends upon breaking through these vicious circles by increasing production to a point where exports and services can pay for the imports they must have to live. The basic problem in making Europe self-supporting is to increase European production.

The sixteen nations presented in their report a recovery program designed to enable them, and Western Germany, to become economically self-supporting within a period of four years and thereafter to maintain a reasonable minimum standard of living for their people without special help from others. The program rests upon four basic points:

(1) A strong production effort by each of the participating countries.

(2) Creation of internal financial stability by each country.

(3) Maximum and continuing cooperation among the participating countries.

(4) A solution of the problem of the participating countries' trading deficit with the American continents, particularly by increasing European exports.

The nations represented on the European Committee agreed at Paris to do everything in their power to achieve these four aims. They agreed to take definite measures leading to financial, economic and monetary stability, the reduction of trade barriers, the removal of obstacles to the free movement of persons within Europe, and a joint effort to use their common resources to the best advantage.

These agreements are a source of great encouragement. When the representatives of sixteen sovereign nations, with diverse peoples, histories and institutions, jointly determine to achieve closer economic ties among themselves and to break away from the self-defeating actions of narrow nationalism, the obstacles in the way of recovery appear less formidable.

The report takes into account the productive capacities of the participating nations and their ability to obtain supplies from other parts of the world. It also takes into account the possibilities of obtaining funds through the International Bank for Reconstruction and Development, through private investment, and in some instances by the sale of existing foreign assets. The participating countries recognized that some commodities, particularly food, will remain scarce for years to come, and the diet they have set as their goal for 1951 is less adequate in most cases than their pre-war diet. The report assumes that many countries will continue restrictions on the distribution of shortage items such as food, clothing and fuel.

When all these factors had been considered, the European Committee concluded that there will still be a requirement for large quantities of food, fuel, raw materials and capital equipment for which the financial resources of the participating countries will be inadequate. With successful execution of the European recovery program, this requirement will diminish in each of the four years ahead, and the Committee anticipated that by 1952 Europe could again meet its needs without special aid.

*   *   *

PROGRAM FOR UNITED STATES AID

In the light of all these factors, an integrated program for United States aid to European recovery has been prepared for submission to the Congress.

In developing this program, certain basic considerations have been kept in mind:

First, the program is designed to make genuine recovery possible within a definite period of time, and not merely to continue relief indefinitely.

Second, the program is designed to insure that the funds and goods which we furnish will be used most effectively for European recovery.

Third, the program is designed to minimize the financial cost to the United States, but at the same time to avoid imposing on the European countries crushing financial burdens which they could not carry in the long run.

Fourth, the program is designed with due regard for conserving the physical resources of the United States and minimizing the impact on our economy of furnishing aid to Europe.

Fifth, the program is designed to be consistent with other international relationships and responsibilities of the United States.

Sixth, the administration of the program is designed to carry out wisely and efficiently this great enterprise of our foreign policy.

I shall discuss each of these basic considerations in turn.

Recovery—Not Relief

The program is designed to assist the participating European countries in obtaining imports essential to genuine economic recovery which they cannot finance from their own resources. It is based on the expectation that with this assistance European recovery can be substantially completed in about four years.

The aid which will be required from the United States for the first fifteen months—from April 1, 1948, to June 30, 1949—is now estimated at $6.8 billion.

These funds represent careful estimates of the cost of the goods and services which will be required during this period to start Europe on the road to genuine economic recovery. The European requirements as they were stated in the Paris report have been closely reviewed and scaled downward where they appeared to include non-essentials or where limited supplies will prevent their full satisfaction.

The requirements of the remaining three years of the program are more difficult to estimate now, but they are expected to decrease year by year as progress is made toward recovery. Obviously, price changes, weather and crop conditions and other unpredictable factors will influence the over-all cost of our aid. Nevertheless, the inherent nature of this enterprise and the long-range planning necessary to put it into effect on both sides of the Atlantic require that this Government indicate its plans for the duration and the general magnitude of the program, without committing itself to specific amounts in future years. The best estimates we can now make indicate that appropriations of about $10.2 billion will be required for the last three years.

I recommend that legislation providing for United States aid in support of the European recovery program authorize the appropriation of $17 billion from April 1, 1948, to June 30, 1952. Appropriation for the period from April 1, 1948, to June 30, 1949, should be made in time for the program to be put into effect by April 1, 1948. Appropriations for the later years should be considered subsequently by the Congress on an annual basis.

The funds we make available will enable the countries of Europe to purchase goods which will achieve two purposes—to lift the standard of living in Europe closer to a decent level, and at the same time to enlarge European capacity for production. Our funds will enable them to import grain for current consumption, and fertilizer and agricultural machinery to increase their food production. They will import fuel for current use, and mining machinery to increase their coal output. In addition they will obtain raw materials, such as cotton, for current production, and some manufacturing and transportation equipment to increase their productive capacity.

The industrial goods we supply will be primarily to relieve critical shortages at a few strategic points which are now curtailing the great productive powers of Europe's industrial system.

The fundamental objective of further United States aid to European countries is to help them achieve economic self-support and to contribute their full share to a peaceful and prosperous world. Our aid must be adequate to this end. If we provide only half-hearted and half-way help, our efforts will be dissipated and the chances for political and economic stability in Europe are likely to be lost.

Insuring Proper Use of United States Aid

A second basic consideration with regard to this program is the means by which we can insure that our aid will be used to achieve its real purposes—that our goods and our dollars will contribute most effectively to European recovery. Appropriate agreements among the participating countries and with the United States are essential to this end.

At the Paris conference the European nations pledged themselves to take specific individual and cooperative actions to accomplish genuine recovery. While some modification or amplification of these pledges may prove desirable, mutual undertakings of this nature are essential. They will give unity of purpose and effective coordination to the endeavors of the peoples of the sixteen nations.

In addition, each of the countries receiving aid will be expected to enter into an agreement with the United States affirming the pledges which it has given to the other participating countries, and making additional commitments.

Under these agreements, each country would pledge itself to take the following actions, except where they are inapplicable to the country concerned:

(1) To promote increased industrial and agricultural production in order to enable the participating country to become independent of abnormal outside economic assistance.

(2) To take financial and monetary measures necessary to stabilize its currency, establish or maintain a proper rate of exchange, and generally to restore or maintain confidence in its monetary system.

(3) To cooperate with other participating countries to reduce barriers to trade among themselves and with other countries, and to stimulate an increasing interchange of goods and services.

(4) To make efficient use, within the framework of a joint program for European recovery, of the resources of the participating country, and to take the necessary steps to assure efficient use in the interest of European economic recovery of all goods and services made available through United States aid.

(5) To stimulate the production of specified raw materials, as may be mutually agreed upon, and to facilitate the procurement of such raw materials by the United States for stockpiling purposes from the excess above the reasonable domestic usage and commercial export requirements of the source country.

(6) To deposit in a special account the local currency equivalent of aid furnished in the form of grants, to be used only in a manner mutually agreed between the two governments.

(7) To publish domestically and to furnish to the United States appropriate information concerning the use made of our aid and the progress made under the agreements with other participating countries and with the United States.

The United States will, of course, retain the right to determine whether aid to any country is to be continued if our previous assistance has not been used effectively.

Financial Arrangements

A third basic consideration in formulating the program of United States aid relates to the financial arrangements under which our aid is to be provided.

One of the problems in achieving the greatest benefit from United States aid is the extent to which funds should be made available in the form of grants as contrasted with loans. It is clear that we should require repayment to the extent that it is feasible and consistent with the objectives of the program, in order that no unnecessary burden be imposed upon the people of the United States. It is equally clear that we should not require repayment where it would impose paralyzing financial obligations on the people of Europe and thus defeat the basic purpose of making Europe self-supporting.

Recovery for Europe will not be achieved until its people are able to pay for their necessary imports with foreign exchange obtained through the export of goods and services. If they were to have additional burdens to bear in the form of interest and amortization payments in future years, they would have to plan for an even higher level of exports to meet these obligations. This would necessarily increase the requirements of the recovery program, and delay the achievement of economic stability.

It is also important that an increasing portion of the financial needs of Europe be met by dollar loans from the International Bank, and by the revival of private financing. This prospect would be seriously jeopardized if the United States, as part of the recovery program, were to impose all that the traffic will bear in the form of debt obligations.

I recommend that our aid should be extended partly in the form of grants and partly in the form of loans, depending primarily upon the capacity of each country to make repayments, and the effect of additional international debt upon the accomplishment of genuine recovery. No grants should be made to countries able to pay cash for all imports or to repay loans.

At a later date it may prove desirable to make available to some of the

European countries special loans to assist them in attaining monetary stability. I am not now requesting authorization for such loans, since it is not possible at this time to determine when or to what extent such loans should be made.

As economic conditions in Europe improve and political conditions become more stable, private financing can be expected to play an increasingly important role. The recommended program of United States aid includes provisions to encourage private financing and investments.

Impact of the United States Economy

A fourth basic consideration is the effect of further aid for Europe upon the physical resources of the United States and upon our economy.

The essential import requirements of the 270 million people of Western Europe cover a wide range of products. Many of these requirements can be met by the United States and other countries without substantial difficulty. However, a number of the commodities which are most essential to European recovery are the same commodities for which there is an unsatisfied demand in the United States.

Sharing these commodities with the people of Europe will require some self-denial by the people of the United States. I believe that our people recognize the vital importance of our aid program and are prepared to share their goods to insure its success.

While the burden on our people should not be ignored or minimized, neither should it be exaggerated. The program of aid to Europe which I am recommending is well within our capacity to undertake.

Its total cost, though large, will be only about five percent of the cost of our effort in the recent war.

It will cost less than three percent of our national income during the life of the program.

As an investment toward the peace and security of the world and toward the realization of hope and confidence in a better way of life for the future, this cost is small indeed.

A committee under the chairmanship of the Secretary of the Interior was appointed last summer to study the effect of a foreign aid program upon the natural resources of our country. Its study has shown that our resources can safely meet the demands of a program such as I am now recommending. Such demands could not, however, be supplied indefinitely. Our program of aid to Europe recognizes this fact. Our exports to Europe will decrease during the succeeding years of the program as trade is revived along realistic patterns which will make available from other sources an increasing share of Europe's requirements.

Actually, our position with respect to some raw materials of which we have inadequate domestic resources will be improved since, under our program of aid to Europe, an increased amount of these materials will be made available to us.

During recent months the Council of Economic Advisers made an intensive study of the impact of foreign aid on our domestic economy. The Council concluded that a program of the size now contemplated is well within our productive capacity and need not produce a dangerous strain on our economy.

At the same time, a group of distinguished private citizens under the chairmanship of the Secretary of Commerce considered the extent and nature of foreign aid which the United States can and should provide. The conclusion of this group was that a program of the scope I am recommending is a proper, wise and necessary use of United States resources.

The reports submitted to me by the Council of Economic Advisers and the committees under the chairmanship of the Secretary of the Interior and the Secretary of Commerce all emphasized that specific measures should be taken to prevent our foreign aid program from imposing unnecessary burdens on our economy.

If the United States were to supply from its own production all the essential commodities needed to meet European requirements, unnecessary scarcities and unnecessary inflationary pressures would be created within our economy. It is far wiser to assist in financing the procurement of certain of these commodities from other countries, particularly the other food-producing countries in the Western Hemisphere. The funds we make available to aid European recovery therefore should not be restricted to purchases within the United States.

Under the proposed program of aid to Europe, the total exports to the whole world from this country during the next year are expected to be no greater than our total exports during the past twelve months.

This level of exports will nevertheless have an important impact on our markets. The measures I have already proposed to the Congress to fight general domestic inflation will be useful, as well, in cushioning the impact of the European aid program.

The effect of aid to Europe upon our economy, as well as its financial cost, will be significantly affected by the arrangements we make for meeting shipping requirements.

The interest of the United States will be served best by permitting the sale or temporary transfer of some of our war-built merchant ships to the European countries. Because of world steel shortages, the sale or temporary transfer of ships should be linked with a reduction or deferment of the projected shipbuilding schedules of the participating countries. These arrangements should be consistent with their long-range merchant marine requirements. They should also be consistent with our long-range objectives of maintaining an adequate merchant marine and shipbuilding industry for the United States.

Making these vessels available to the European countries will materially reduce the cost of United States aid both by lowering shipping costs and by reducing the use of scarce materials for new ship construction overseas.

Relationship to Other International Questions

A fifth basic consideration is the relationship of our aid to the European recovery program to other international questions.

I have already mentioned that the requirements and resources of Western Germany were included in the considerations of the sixteen countries at Paris. Our program of United States aid also includes Western Germany.

The productive capacity of the highly industrialized areas of Western Germany can contribute substantially to the general cooperative effort required for European recovery. It is essential that this productive capacity be effectively utilized, and it is especially important that the coal production of the Ruhr continue to increase rapidly.

Every precaution must of course be taken against a resurgence of military power in Germany. The United States has made clear on many occasions its determination that Germany shall never again threaten to dominate Europe or endanger the peace of the world. The inclusion of Western Germany in the European recovery program will not weaken this determination.

As an occupying power in Western Germany, the United States has a responsibility to provide minimum essentials necessary to prevent disease and unrest. Separate appropriations will be requested for this purpose for the period through June 30, 1949.

Above this minimum level, amounts needed to assist in the rehabilitation of Western Germany are included in the over-all estimates for aid to European recovery.

Another significant area of the world which has been considered in developing the recovery program is Eastern Europe. A number of the governments of Eastern Europe which were invited to participate in the work of the Paris Conference on Economic Cooperation chose not to do so. Their failure to join in the concerted effort for recovery makes this effort more difficult and will undoubtedly prolong their own economic difficulties.

This should not, however, prevent the restoration of trade between Eastern and Western Europe to the mutual advantage of both areas. Both the report of the sixteen nations and the program now submitted to the Congress are based on the belief that over the next few years the normal pattern of trade between Eastern and Western Europe will be gradually restored. As this restoration of trade is achieved, the abnormal demands on the Western Hemisphere, particularly for food and fuel, should diminish.

The relationship between this program and the United Nations deserves special emphasis because of the central importance in our foreign policy of support of the United Nations. Our support of European recovery is in full accord with our support of the United Nations. The success of the United Nations depends upon the independent strength of its members and their determination and ability to adhere to the ideals and principles embodied in the Charter. The purposes of the European recovery program are in complete harmony with the purposes of the Charter—to insure a peaceful world through the joint efforts of free nations. Attempts by any nation to prevent or sabotage European recovery for selfish ends are clearly contrary to these purposes.

It is not feasible to carry out the recovery program exclusively through the United Nations. Five of the participating countries are not yet Members of the United Nations. Furthermore, some European Members are not participating in the program.

We expect, however, that the greatest practicable use will be made of the facilities of the United Nations and its related agencies in the execution of the program. This view is shared by all the participating countries.

Our intention to undertake a program of aid for European recovery does not signify any lessening of our interest in other areas of the world. Instead, it is the means by which we can make the quickest and most effective contribution to the general improvement of economic conditions throughout the world. The workshops of Europe, with their great reservoir of skilled workers, must produce the goods to support peoples of many other nations.

I wish to make especially clear that our concentration on the task in Western Europe at this time will not lessen our long-established interest in economic cooperation with our neighbors in the Western Hemisphere. We are first of all a member of an American community of nations, in which cooperative action, similar to that which the European nations are now undertaking, is required to increase production, to promote financial stability, and to remove barriers to trade. Fortunately we in the Americas are further advanced along this road, but we must not overlook any opportunity to make additional progress. The European recovery program will require procurement of supplies in many nations of this hemisphere. This will act as a stimulant to production and business activity and promote the reestablishment of world trade upon which the prosperity of all of us depends.

While our present efforts must be devoted primarily to Western Europe, as the most important area in the world at this time for the future of peace, we also have a special concern for the war torn areas of Asia. In Japan and Korea, the United States has supplied extensive aid to support life and commence reconstruction. Since the war's end, we have provided China with varied and important assistance which has aided that nation substantially.

The United States should continue to do all it appropriately can to assist in the restoration of economic stability as a basis for recovery in the Far East. Extensive study has been given during the last few months to the means by which we might best aid in meeting the special needs for relief and rehabilitation in China. I expect to make recommendations on that subject to the Congress during its next session.

*   *   *

CONCLUSION

In proposing that the Congress enact a program of aid to Europe, I am proposing that this Nation contribute to world peace and to its own security by assisting in the recovery of sixteen countries which, like the United States, are devoted to the preservation of free institutions and enduring peace among nations.

It is my belief that United States support of the European recovery program will enable the free nations of Europe to devote their great energies to the reconstruction of their economies. On this depends the restoration of a decent standard of living for their peoples, the development of a sound world economy, and continued support for the ideals of individual liberty and justice.

In providing aid to Europe we must share more than goods and funds. We must give our moral support to those nations in their struggle to rekindle the fires of hope and strengthen the will of their peoples to overcome their adversities. We must develop a feeling of teamwork in our common cause of combating the suspicions, prejudices, and fabrications which undermine cooperative effort, both at home and abroad.

This joint undertaking of the United States and a group of European nations, in devotion to the principles of the Charter of the United Nations, is proof that free men can effectively join together to defend their free institutions against totalitarian pressures, and to promote better standards of life for all their peoples.

I have been heartened by the widespread support which the citizens of the United States have given to the concept underlying the proposed aid to European recovery. Workers, farmers, businessmen and other major groups have all given evidence of their confidence in its noble purpose and have shown their willingness to give it full support.

I know that the Members of the Congress have already given much thoughtful consideration to the grave issues now before us. I know that the Congress will, as it should, consider with great care the legislation necessary to put the program into effect. This consideration should proceed as rapidly as possible in order that the program may become effective by April 1, 1948. It is for this reason that I am presenting my recommendations to the Congress now, rather than awaiting its reconvening in January.

I recommend this program of United States support for European recovery to the Congress in full confidence of its wisdom and necessity as a major step in our Nation's quest for a just and lasting peace.

HARRY S. TRUMAN

THE WHITE HOUSE
December 19, 1947

◇◇◇◇◇◇

232. ECONOMIC COOPERATION ACT OF 1948, AS AMENDED [1]

[The Economic Coöperation Act of 1948 was written by a Democratic Administration and a Republican Congress. Few laws in our nation's history have been subjected to such thorough study. The Act originally contemplated a four-year program, although it contained an authorization for funds for only one year. The law clearly demonstrates the close relationship between foreign policy and domestic policy, for it deals with such domestic problems as shipping, agricultural surpluses, private enterprise, and so on. The authorizations and appropriations approved for the ECA and other foreign economic aid since 1948, are shown in the table on pp. 852, 853.]

TITLE I

SEC. 101. This title may be cited as the "Economic Cooperation Act of 1948."

FINDINGS AND DECLARATION OF POLICY

SEC. 102. (a) Recognizing the intimate economic and other relationships between the United States and the nations of Europe, and recognizing that disruption following in the wake of war is not contained by national frontiers, the Congress finds that the existing situation in Europe endangers the establishment of a lasting peace, the general welfare and national interest of the

---

[1] Title I of Public Law 472, Eightieth Congress, as Amended by Public Law 47, Eighty-First Congress, First Session, and Sections 102 Through 106 of Title I of Public Law 535, Eighty-First Congress, Second Session.

United States, and the attainment of the objectives of the United Nations. The restoration or maintenance in European countries of principles of individual liberty, free institutions, and genuine independence rests largely upon the establishment of sound economic conditions, stable international economic relationships, and the achievement by the countries of Europe of a healthy economy independent of extraordinary outside assistance. The accomplishment of these objectives calls for a plan of European recovery, open to all such nations which cooperate in such plan, based upon a strong production effort, the expansion of foreign trade, the creation and maintenance of internal financial stability, and the development of economic cooperation, including all possible steps to establish and maintain equitable rates of exchange and to bring about the progressive elimination of trade barriers. Mindful of the advantages which the United States has enjoyed through the existence of a large domestic market with no internal barriers to trade or to the free movement of persons, and believing that similar advantages can accrue to the countries of Europe, it is declared to be the policy of the people of the United States to encourage these countries through their joint organization to exert sustained common efforts to achieve speedily that economic cooperation in Europe which is essential for lasting peace and prosperity. It is further declared to be the policy of the people of the United States to encourage the further unification of Europe, and to sustain and strengthen principles of individual liberty, free institutions, and genuine independence in Europe through assistance to those countries of Europe which participate in a joint recovery program based upon self-help and mutual cooperation: *Provided,* That no assistance to the participating countries herein contemplated shall seriously impair the economic stability of the United States. It is further declared to be the policy of the United States that continuity of assistance provided by the United States should, at all times, be dependent upon continuity of cooperation among countries participating in the program.

PURPOSES OF TITLE

(b) It is the purpose of this title to effectuate the policy set forth in subsection (a) of this section by furnishing material and financial assistance to the participating countries in such a manner as to aid them, through their own individual and concerted efforts, to become independent of extraordinary outside economic assistance within the period of operations under this title, by—

(1) promoting industrial and agricultural production, increased productivity, maximum employment, and freedom from restrictive business practices in the participating countries;

(2) furthering the restoration or maintenance of the soundness of European currencies, budgets, and finances; and

(3) facilitating and stimulating the growth of international trade of participating countries with one another and with other countries by appropriate measures including reduction of barriers which may hamper such trade.

PARTICIPATING COUNTRIES

SEC. 103. (a) As used in this title, the term "participating country" means—

(1) any country, together with dependent areas under its administration, which signed the report of the Committee of European Economic Cooperation at Paris on September 22, 1947; and

(2) any other country (including any of the zones of occupation of Germany, any areas under international administration or control, and the Free Territory of Trieste or either of its zones) wholly or partly in Europe, together with dependent areas under its administration;

provided such country adheres to, and for so long as it remains an adherent to, a joint program for European recovery designed to accomplish the purposes of this title.

* * *

ESTABLISHMENT OF ECONOMIC COOPERATION ADMINISTRATION

SEC. 104. (a) There is hereby established, with its principal office in the District of Columbia, an agency of the Government which shall be known as the Economic Cooperation Administration, hereinafter referred to as the Administration. The Administration shall be headed by an Administrator for Economic Cooperation, hereinafter referred to as the Administrator, who shall be appointed by the President, by and with the advice and consent of the Senate, and who shall receive compensation at the rate of $20,000 per annum. The Administrator shall be responsible to the President and shall have a status in the executive branch of the Government comparable to that of the head of an executive department. Except as otherwise provided in this title, the administration of the provisions of this title is hereby vested in the Administrator and his functions shall be performed under the control of the President.

(b) There shall be in the Administration a Deputy Administrator for Economic Cooperation who shall be appointed by the President, by and with the advice and consent of the Senate, and shall receive compensation at the rate of $17,500 per annum. The Deputy Administrator for Economic Cooperation shall perform such functions as the Administrator shall designate, and shall be Acting Administrator for Economic Cooperation during the absence or disability of the Administrator or in the event of a vacancy in the office of Administrator.

* * *

(e) Any department, agency, or establishment of the Government (including, whenever used in this title, any corporation which is an instrumentality of the United States) performing functions under this title is authorized to employ, for duty within the continental limits of the United States, such personnel as may be necessary to carry out the provisions and purposes of this title, and funds available pursuant to section 114 of this title shall be available for personal services in the District of Columbia and elsewhere without regard to section 14 (a) of the Federal Employees Pay Act of 1946 (60 Stat. 219). Of such personnel employed by the Administration, not to exceed one hundred may be compensated without regard to the provisions of the Classification Act of 1923, as amended, of whom not more than twenty-five may be compensated at a rate in excess of the highest rate authorized by such Act, but not in excess of $15,000 per annum. Experts and consultants or organizations thereof, as authorized by section 15 of the Act of August 2, 1946 (U. S. C., title 5, sec. 55a), may be employed by the Administration, and individuals so employed may be compensated at rates not in excess of $50 per diem and while away from their homes or regular places of business, they may be paid actual travel expenses and not to exceed $10 per diem in lieu of subsistence and other expenses while so employed.

* * *

GENERAL FUNCTIONS OF ADMINISTRATOR

SEC. 105. (a) The Administrator, under the control of the President, shall in addition to all other functions vested in him by this title—

(1) review and appraise the requirements of participating countries for assistance under the terms of this title;

(2) formulate programs of United States assistance under this title, including approval of specific projects which have been submitted to him by the participating countries;

(3) provide for the efficient execution of any such programs as may be placed in operation; and

(4) terminate provision of assistance or take other remedial action as provided in section 118 of this title.

(b) In order to strengthen and make more effective the conduct of the foreign relations of the United States—

(1) the Administrator and the Secretary of State shall keep each other fully and currently informed on matters, including prospective action, arising within the scope of their respective duties which are pertinent to the duties of the other;

(2) whenever the Secretary of State believes that any action, proposed action, or failure to act on the part of the Administrator is inconsistent with the foreign-policy objectives of the United States, he shall consult with the Administrator and, if differences of view are not adjusted by consultation, the matter shall be referred to the President for final decision;

(3) whenever the Administrator believes that any action, proposed action, or failure to act on the part of the Secretary of State in performing functions under this title is inconsistent with the purposes and provisions of this title, he shall consult with the Secretary of State and, if differences of view are not adjusted by consultation, the matter shall be referred to the President for final decision.

(c) The Administrator and the department, agency, or officer in the executive branch of the Government exercising the authority granted to the President by the Export Control Act of 1949, shall keep each other fully and currently informed on matters, including prospective action, arising within the scope of their respective duties which are pertinent to the duties of the other. Whenever the Administrator believes that any action, proposed action, or failure to act on the part of such department, agency, or officer in performing functions under this title is inconsistent with the purposes and provisions of this title, he shall consult with such department, agency, or officer and, if differences of view are not adjusted by consultation, the matter shall be referred to the President for final decision.

*   *   *

PUBLIC ADVISORY BOARD

SEC. 107. (a) There is hereby created a Public Advisory Board, (hereinafter referred to as the "Board"), which shall advise and consult with the Administrator with respect to general or basic policy matters arising in connection with the Administrator's discharge of his responsibilities. The Board shall consist of the Administrator, who shall be Chairman, and not to exceed twelve additional members to be appointed by the President, by and with the advice and consent of the Senate, and who shall be selected from among citizens of the United States of broad and varied experience in matters affecting the public interest, other than officers and employees of the United States (including any agency or instrumentality of the United States) who, as such, regularly receive compensation for current services. The Board shall meet at least once a month and at other times upon the call of the Administrator or when three or more members of the Board request the Administrator to call a meeting. Not more than a majority of two of the members shall be appointed to the Board from the same political party. Members of the Board, other than the Administrator, shall receive, out of funds made available for the purposes of this title, a per diem allowance of $50 for each day spent away from their homes or regular places of business, for the purpose of attendance at meetings of the Board, or at conferences held upon the call of the Administrator, and in necessary travel, and while so engaged, they may be paid actual travel expenses and not to exceed $10 per diem in lieu of subsistence and other expenses.

(b) The Administrator may appoint such other advisory committees as he may determine to be necessary or desirable to effectuate the purposes of this title.,

UNITED STATES SPECIAL REPRESENTATIVES ABROAD

SEC. 108. There shall be a United States Special Representative in Europe who shall (a) be appointed by the President, by and with the advice and consent of the Senate, (b) be entitled to receive the same compensation and allowances as a chief of mission, class 1, within the meaning of the Act of August 13, 1946 (60 Stat. 999), and (c) have the rank of ambassador extraordinary and plenipotentiary. He shall be the representative of the Administrator, and shall also be the chief representative of the United States Government to any organization of participating countries which may be established by such countries to further a joint program for European recovery, and shall discharge in Europe such additional responsibilities as may be assigned to him with the approval of the President in furtherance of the purposes of this title. He may also be designated as the United States representative on the Economic Commission for Europe. He shall receive his instructions from the Administrator and such instructions shall be prepared and transmitted to him in accordance with procedures agreed to between the Administrator and the Secretary of State in order to assure appropriate coordination as provided by subsection (b) of section 105 of this title. He shall coordinate the activities of the chiefs of special missions provided for in section 109 of this title. He shall keep the Administrator, the Secretary of State, the chiefs of the United States diplomatic missions, and the chiefs of the special missions provided for in section 109 of this title currently informed concerning his activities. He shall consult with the chiefs of all such missions, who shall give him such cooperation as he may require for the performance of his duties under this title. There shall be a Deputy United States Special Representative in Europe who shall (a) be appointed by the President, by and with the advice and consent of the Senate, (b) be entitled to receive the same compensation and allowances as a chief of mission, class 3, within the meaning of the Act of August 13, 1946 (60 Stat. 999), and (c) have the rank of ambassador extraordinary and plenipotentiary. The Deputy United States Special Representative shall perform such functions as the United States Special Representative shall designate, and shall be Acting United States Special Representative during the absence or disability of the United States Special Representative or in the event of a vacancy in the office of United States Special Representative.

SPECIAL ECA MISSIONS ABROAD

SEC. 109. (a) There shall be established for each participating country, except as provided in subsection (d) of this section, a special mission for economic cooperation under the direction of a chief who shall be responsible for assuring the performance within such country of operations under this title. The chief shall be appointed by the Administrator, shall receive his instructions from the Administrator, and shall report to the Administrator on the performance of the duties assigned to him. The chief of the special mission shall take rank immediately after the chief of the United States diplomatic mission in such country; and the chief of the special mission shall be entitled to receive the same compensation and allowances as a chief of mission, class 3, or a chief of mission, class 4, within the meaning of the Act of August 13, 1946 (60 Stat. 999), or compensation and allowances in accordance with section 110 (a) of this title, as the Administrator shall determine to be necessary or appropriate.

(b) The chief of the special mission shall keep the chief of the United· States diplomatic mission fully and currently informed on matters, including prospective action, arising within the scope of the operations of the special mission and the chief of the diplomatic mission shall keep the chief of the special mission fully and currently informed on matters relative to the conduct of the duties of the chief of the special mission. The chief of the United States diplomatic mission will be responsible for assuring that the operations of the special mission are consistent with the foreign-policy objectives of the United States in such country and to that end whenever the chief of the United States diplomatic mission believes that any action, proposed action, or failure to act on the part of the special mission is inconsistent with such foreign-policy objectives, he shall so advise the chief of the special mission and the United

States Special Representative in Europe. If differences of view are not adjusted by consultation, the matter shall be referred to the Secretary of State and the Administrator for decision.

* * *

NATURE AND METHOD OF ASSISTANCE

SEC. 111. (a) The Administrator may, from time to time, furnish assistance to any participating country by providing for the performance of any of the functions set forth in paragraphs (1) through (5) of this subsection when he deems it to be in furtherance of the purposes of this title, and upon the terms and conditions set forth in this title and such additional terms and conditions consistent with the provisions of this title as he may determine to be necessary and proper.

(1) Procurement from any source, including Government stocks on the same basis as procurement by Government agencies under Public Law 375 (Seventy-ninth Congress) for their own use, of any commodity which he determines to be required for the furtherance of the purposes of this title. As used in this title, the term "commodity" means any commodity, material, article, supply, or goods necessary for the purposes of this title.

(2) Processing, storing, transporting, and repairing any commodities, or performing any other services with respect to a participating country which he determines to be required for accomplishing the purposes of this title. The Administrator shall, in providing for the procurement of commodities under authority of this title, take such steps as may be necessary to assure, as far as is practicable, that at least 50 per centum of the gross tonnage of commodities procured out of funds made available under this title and transported to or from the United States on ocean vessels, computed separately for dry bulk carriers, dry cargo liner and tanker services, is so transported on United States flag vessels to the extent such vessels are available at market rates for United States flag vessels; and, in the administration of this provision, the Administrator shall, insofar as practicable and consistent with the purposes of this title, endeavor to secure a fair and reasonable participation by United States flag vessels in cargoes by geographic area.

(3) Procurement of and furnishing technical information and assistance.

(4) Transfer of any commodity or service, which transfer shall be signified by delivery of the custody and right of possession and use of such commodity, or otherwise making available any such commodity, or by rendering a service to a participating country or to any agency or organization representing a participating country.

(5) The allocation of commodities or services to specific projects designed to carry out the purposes of this title, which have been submitted to the Administrator by participating countries and have been approved by him.

(b) In order to facilitate and maximize the use of private channels of trade, subject to adequate safeguards to assure that all expenditures in connection with such procurement are within approved programs in accordance with terms and conditions established by the Administrator, he may provide for the performance of any of the functions described in subsection (a) of this section—

* * *

(3) by making, under rules and regulations to be prescribed by the Administrator, guaranties to any person of investments in connection with projects, including expansion, modernization, or development of existing enterprises, approved by the Administrator and the participating country concerned as furthering the purposes of this title (including guaranties of investments in enterprises producing or distributing informational media consistent with the national interests of the United States: *Provided,* That the amount of such guaranties made in any fiscal year does not exceed $10,000,000), which guaranties shall terminate not later than fourteen years from the date of enactment of this Act: *Provided,* That—

(i) the guaranty to any person shall not exceed the amount of dollars invested in the project by such person with the approval of the Administrator plus actual earnings or profits on said project to the extent provided by such guaranty;

(ii) the Administrator shall charge a fee in an amount determined by him not exceeding 1 per centum per annum of the amount of each guaranty under clause (1) of subparagraph (v), and not exceeding 4 per centum per annum of the amount of each guaranty under clause (2) of such subparagraph, and all fees collected hereunder shall be available for expenditure in discharge of liabilities under guaranties made under this paragraph until such time as all such liabilities have been discharged or have expired, or until all such fees have been expended in accordance with the provisions of this paragraph; and

* * *

(v) the guaranty to any person shall be limited to assuring one or both of the following: (1) The transfer into United States dollars of other currencies, or credits in such currencies received by such person, as earnings or profits from the approved project, as repayment or return of the investment therein, in whole or in part, or as compensation for the sale or disposition of all or any part thereof; and (2) the compensation in United States dollars for loss of all or any part of the investment in the approved project which shall be found by the Administrator to have been lost to such person by reason of expropriation or confiscation by action of the government of a participating country. When any payment is made to any person pursuant to a guaranty as hereinbefore described, the currency, credits, asset, or investment on account of which such payment is made shall become the property of the United States Government, and the United States Government shall be subrogated to any right, title, claim, or cause of action existing in connection therewith.

It being the intent of the Congress that the guaranty herein authorized should be used to the maximum practicable extent and so administered as to increase the participation of private enterprise in achieving the purposes of this Act, the Administrator is authorized to issue guaranties up to a total of $200,000,000: *Provided,* That any funds allocated to a guaranty and remaining after all liability of the United States assumed in connection therewith has been released, discharged, or otherwise terminated, shall be available for allocation to other guaranties, the foregoing limitation notwithstanding. Any payments made to discharge liabilities under guaranties issued under paragraph (3) of this subsection shall be paid out of fees collected under subparagraph (ii) of paragraph (3) of this subsection as long as such fees are available, and thereafter shall be paid out of funds realized from the sale of notes which shall be issued under authority of paragraph (2) of subsection (c) of this section when necessary to discharge liabilities under any such guaranty.

(c) (1) The Administrator may provide assistance for any participating country, in the form and under the procedures authorized in subsections (a) and (b), respectively, of this section, through grants or upon payment in cash, or on credit terms, or on such other terms of payment as he may find appropriate, including payment by the transfer to the United States (under such terms and in such quantities as may be agreed to between the Administrator and the participating country) of materials which are required by the United States as a result of deficiencies or potential deficiencies in its own resources. In determining whether such assistance shall be through grants or upon terms of payment, and in determining the terms of payment, he shall act in consultation with the National Advisory Council on International Monetary and Financial Problems, and the determination whether or not a participating country should be required to make payment for any assistance furnished to such country in furtherance of the purposes of this title, and the terms of such payment, if required, shall depend upon the character and purpose of the assistance and upon whether there is reasonable assurance of repayment considering the capacity of such country to make such payments without jeopardizing the accomplishment of the purposes of this title.

(2) When it is determined that assistance should be extended under the provisions of this title on credit terms, the Administrator shall allocate funds for the purpose to the Export-Import Bank of Washington, which shall, notwithstanding the provisions of the Export-Import Bank Act of 1945 (59 Stat.   , as amended, make and administer the credit on terms specified by th   _ministrator in consultation with the National Advisory Council on International Monetary and Financial Problems.

*   *   *

(d) The Administrator is authorized to transfer funds directly to any central institution or other organization formed to further the purposes of this Act by two or more participating countries, or to any participating country or countries in connection with the operations of such institution or organization, to be used on terms and conditions specified by the Administrator, in order to facilitate the development of transferability of European currencies, or to promote the liberalization of trade by participating countries with one another and with other countries.

PROTECTION OF DOMESTIC ECONOMY

SEC. 112. (a) The Administrator shall provide for the procurement in the United States of commodities under this title in such a way as to (1) minimize the drain upon the resources of the United States and the impact of such procurement upon the domestic economy, and (2) avoid impairing the fulfillment of vital needs of the people of the United States, and (3) minimize the burden on the American taxpayer by reducing the amount of dollar purchases by the participating countries to the greatest extent possible, consistent with maintaining an adequate supply of the essentials for the functioning of their economies and for their continued recovery.

*   *   *

(d) The term "surplus agricultural commodity" as used in this section is defined as any agricultural commodity, or product thereof, or class, type, or specification thereof, produced in the United States which is determined by the Secretary of Agriculture to be in excess of domestic requirements. In providing for the procurement of any such surplus agricultural commodity for transfer by grant to any participating country in accordance with the requirements of such country, the Administrator shall, insofar as practicable and where in furtherance of the purposes of this title, give effect to the following:

(1) The Administrator shall authorize the procurement of any such surplus agricultural commodity only within the United States: *Provided,* That this restriction shall not be applicable (i) to any agricultural commodity, or product thereof, located in one participating country, and intended for transfer to another participating country, if the Administrator, in consultation with the Secretary of Agriculture, determines that such procurement and transfer is in furtherance of the purposes of this title, and would not create a burdensome surplus in the United States or seriously prejudice the position of domestic producers of such surplus agricultural commodities, or (ii) if, and to the extent that any such surplus agricultural commodity is not available in the United States in sufficient quantities to supply the requirements of the participating countries under this title.

(2) In providing for the procurement of any such surplus agricultural commodity, the Administrator shall, insofar as practicable and applicable, and after giving due consideration to the excess of any such commodity over domestic requirements, and to the historic reliance of United States producers of any such surplus agricultural commodity upon markets in the participating countries, provide for the procurement of each class or type of any such surplus agricultural commodity in the approximate proportion that the Secretary of Agriculture determines such classes or types bear to the total amount of excess of such surplus agricultural commodity over domestic requirements.

(e) Whenever the Secretary of Agriculture determines that any quantity of any surplus agricultural commodity, heretofore or hereafter acquired by Commodity Credit Corporation in the administration of its price-support programs. is available for use in furnishing assistance to foreign countries, he shall so advise all departments, agencies, and establishments of the Government administering laws providing for the furnishing of assistance or relief to foreign countries (including occupied or liberated countries or areas of such countries). Thereafter the department, agency, or establishment administering any such law shall, to the maximum extent practicable, consistent with the provisions and in furtherance of the purposes of such law, and where for transfer by grant and in accordance with the requirements of such foreign country, procure or provide for the procurement of such quantity of such surplus agricultural commodity. The sales price paid as reimbursement to Commodity Credit Corporation for any such surplus agricultural commodity shall be in such amount as Commodity Credit Corporation determines will fully reimburse it for the cost to it of such surplus agricultural commodity at the time and place such surplus agricultural commodity is delivered by it, but in no event shall the sales price be higher than the domestic market price at such time and place of delivery as determined by the Secretary of Agriculture, and the Secretary of Agriculture may pay not to exceed 50 per centum of such sales price as authorized by subsection (f) of this section.

(f) Subject to the provisions of this section, but notwithstanding any other provision of law, in order to encourage utilization of surplus agricultural commodities pursuant to this or any other Act providing for assistance or relief to foreign countries, the Secretary of Agriculture, in carrying out the purposes of clause (1), section 32, Public Law 320, Seventy-fourth Congress, as amended, may make payments, including payments to any government agency procuring or selling such surplus agricultural commodities, in an amount not to exceed 50 per centum of the sales price (basis free along ship or free on board vessel, United States ports), as determined by the Secretary of Agriculture, of such surplus agricultural commodities. The rescission of the remainder of section 32 funds by the Act of July 30, 1947 (Public Law 266, Eightieth Congress), is hereby canceled and such funds are hereby made available for the purposes of section 32 for the fiscal year ending June 30, 1948.

(g) No export shall be authorized pursuant to authority conferred by the Export Control Act of 1949 of any commodity from the United States to any country wholly or partly in Europe which is not a participating country, if the department, agency, or officer in the executive branch of the Government exercising the authority granted to the President by the Export Control Act of 1949 determines that the supply of such commodity is insufficient (or would be insufficient if such export were permitted) to fulfill the requirements of participating countries under this title as determined by the Administrator: Provided, however, That such export may be authorized if such department, agency, or officer determines that such export is otherwise in the national interest of the United States.

(h) In providing for the performance of any of the functions described in subsection (a) of section 111, the Administrator shall, to the maximum extent consistent with the accomplishment of the purposes of this title, utilize private channels of trade.

(i) (1) Insofar as practicable and to the maximum extent consistent with the accomplishment of the purposes of this title, the Administrator shall assist American small business to participate equitably in the furnishing of commodities and services financed with funds authorized under this title by making available or causing to be made available to suppliers in the United States, and particularly to small independent enterprises, information, as far in advance as possible, with respect to purchases proposed to be financed with funds authorized under this title, and by making available or causing to be made available to prospective purchasers in the participating countries information as to commodities and services produced by small independent enterprises in the United States, and by otherwise helping to give small business an opportunity to participate in the furnishing of commodities and services financed with funds authorized under this title.

(2) The Administrator shall appoint a special assistant to advise and assist him in carrying out the foregoing paragraph (1). Each report transmitted to the Congress under section 123 shall include a report of all activities under this subsection.

(j) The Administrator shall, in providing assistance in the procurement of commodities in the United States, make available United States dollars for marine insurance on such commodities where such insurance is placed on a competitive basis in accordance with normal trade practices prevailing prior to the outbreak of World War II.

(k) No funds authorized for the purposes of this title shall be used in the United States for advertising foreign products or for advertising foreign travel.

(l) No funds authorized for the purposes of this title shall be used for the purchase in bulk of any commodities at prices higher than the market price prevailing in the United States at the time of the purchase adjusted for differences in the cost of transportation to destination, quality, and terms of payment. A bulk purchase within the meaning of this subsection does not include the purchase of raw cotton in bales.

*　　*　　*

(n) It is the sense of Congress that no participating country shall maintain or impose any import, currency, tax, license, quota, or other similar business restrictions which discriminate against citizens of the United States or any corporation, partnership, or other association substantially beneficially owned by citizens of the United States, engaged or desiring to engage, in furtherance of the purposes of this title, in the importation into such country of any commodity, which restrictions are not reasonably required to meet balance of payments conditions, or requirements of national security, or are not authorized under international agreements to which such country and the United States are parties. In any case where the Department of State determines that any such discriminatory restriction is maintained or imposed by a participating country or by any dependent area of such country, the Administrator shall take such remedial action as he determines will effectively promote the purposes of this subsection (n).

*　　*　　*

AUTHORIZATION OF APPROPRIATIONS

SEC. 114. (a) Notwithstanding the provisions of any other law, the Reconstruction Finance Corporation is authorized and directed, until such time as an appropriation shall be made pursuant to subsection (c) of this section, to make advances not to exceed in the aggregate $1,000,000,000 to carry out the provisions of this title, in such manner, at such time, and in such amounts as the President shall determine, and no interest shall be charged on advances made by the Treasury to the Reconstruction Finance Corporation for this purpose. The Reconstruction Finance Corporation shall be repaid without interest for advances made by it hereunder, from funds made available for the purposes of this title.

*   *   *

(c) In order to carry out the provisions of this title with respect to those participating countries which adhere to the purposes of this title, and remain eligible to receive assistance hereunder, such funds shall be available as are hereafter authorized and appropriated to the President from time to time through June 30, 1952, to carry out the provisions and accomplish the purposes of this title: *Provided, however,* That for carrying out the provisions and accomplishing the purposes of this title for the period of one year following the date of enactment of this Act, there are hereby authorized to be so appropriated not to exceed $4,300,000,000: *Provided further,* That, in addition to the amount heretofore authorized and appropriated, there are hereby authorized to be appropriated for carrying out the provisions and accomplishing the purposes of this title not to exceed $1,150,000,000 for the period April 3, 1949, through June 30, 1949, and not to exceed $4,280,000,000 for the fiscal year ending June 30, 1950: *Provided further,* That, in addition to the foregoing, any balance, unobligated as of June 30, 1949, or subsequently released from obligation, of funds appropriated for carrying out and accomplishing the purposes of this title for any period ending on or prior to that date is hereby authorized to be made available for obligation through the fiscal year ending June 30, 1950, and to be transferred to and consolidated with any appropriations for carrying out and accomplishing the purposes of this title for said fiscal year: *Provided further,* That, in addition to the amount heretofore authorized and appropriated, there is hereby authorized to be appropriated for carrying out the provisions and accomplishing the purposes of this title not to exceed $2,700,000,000 for the fiscal year ending June 30, 1951: *Provided further,* That $600,000,000 of the funds appropriated hereunder shall be available during the fiscal year 1951 solely for the purpose of encouraging and facilitating the operation of a program of liberalized trade and payments, for supporting any central institution or other organization described in subsection (d) of section 111, and for furnishing of assistance to those participating countries taking part in such program: *Provided further,* That not more than $600,000,000 of such funds shall be available during the fiscal year 1951 for transfer of funds pursuant to subsection (d) of section 111: *Provided further,* That in addition to the foregoing, any balance, unobligated as of June 30, 1950, or subsequently released from obligation, of funds appropriated for carrying out and accomplishing the purposes of this title for any period ending on or prior to that date is hereby authorized to be made available for obligation through the fiscal year ending June 30, 1951, and to be transferred to and consolidated with any appropriations for carrying out and accomplishing the purposes of this title for said fiscal year. Nothing in this title is intended nor shall it be construed as an express or implied commitment to provide any specific assistance, whether of funds, commodities, or services, to any country or countries. The authorizations in this title are limited to the period ending June 30, 1951.

* * *

BILATERAL AND MULTILATERAL UNDERTAKINGS

SEC. 115. (a) The Secretary of State, after consultation with the Administrator, is authorized to conclude, with individual participating countries or any number of such countries or with an organization representing any such countries, agreements in furtherance of the purposes of this title.

* * *

(b) The provision of assistance under this title results from the multilateral pledges of the participating countries to use all their efforts to accomplish a joint recovery program based upon self-help and mutual cooperation as embodied in the report of the Committee of European Economic Cooperation signed at Paris on September 22, 1947, and is contingent upon continuous effort of the participating countries to accomplish a joint recovery program through multilateral undertakings and the establishment of a continuing organization for this purpose. In addition to continued mutual cooperation of the participating countries in such a program, each such country shall conclude an agreement with the United States in order for such country to be eligible to receive assistance under this title. Such agreement shall provide for the adherence of such country to the purposes of this title and shall, where applicable, make appropriate provision, among others, for—

(1) promoting industrial and agricultural production in order to enable the participating country to become independent of extraordinary outside economic assistance; and submitting for the approval of the Administrator, upon his request and whenever he deems it in furtherance of the purposes of this title, specific projects proposed by such country to be undertaken in substantial part with assistance furnished under this title, which projects, whenever practicable, shall include projects for increased production of coal, steel, transportation facilities, and food;

(2) taking financial and monetary measures necessary to stabilize its currency, establish or maintain a valid rate of exchange, to balance its governmental budget as soon as practicable, and generally to restore or maintain confidence in its monetary system;

(3) cooperating with other participating countries in facilitating and stimulating an increasing interchange of goods and services among the participating countries and with other countries and cooperating to reduce barriers to trade among themselves and with other countries;

(4) making efficient and practical use, within the framework of a joint program for European recovery, of the resources of such participating country, including any commodities, facilities, or services furnished under this title, which use shall include, to the extent practicable, taking measures to locate and identify and put into appropriate use, in furtherance of such programs, assets, and earnings therefrom, which belong to

the citizens of such country and which are situated within the United States, its Territories and possessions;

(5) facilitating the transfer to the United States by sale, exchange, barter, or otherwise for stock-piling or other purposes, for such period of time as may be agreed to and upon reasonable terms and in reasonable quantities, of materials which are required by the United States as a result of deficiencies or potential deficiencies in its own resources, and which may be available in such participating country after due regard for reasonable requirements for domestic use and commercial export of such country;

(6) placing in a special account a deposit in the currency of such country, in commensurate amounts and under such terms and conditions as may be agreed to between such country and the Government of the United States, when any commodity or service is made available through any means authorized under this title, and is furnished to the participating country on a grant basis: *Provided,* That the obligation to make such deposits may be waived, in the discretion of the Administrator, with respect to technical information or assistance furnished under section 111 (a) (3) of this title and with respect to ocean transportation furnished on United States flag vessels under section 111 of this title in an amount not exceeding the amount, as determined by the Administrator, by which the charges for such transportation exceed the cost of such transportation at world market rates: *Provided further,* That such special account, together with the unencumbered portions of any deposits which may have been made by such country pursuant to section 6 of the joint resolution providing for relief assistance to the people of countries devastated by war (Public Law 84, 80th Cong.) and section 5 (b) of the Foreign Aid Act of 1947 (Public Law 389, 80th Cong.) shall be used in furtherance of any central institution or other organization formed by two or more participating countries to further the purposes set forth in subsection (d) of section 111 or otherwise shall be held or used for purposes of internal monetary and financial stabilization, for the stimulation of productive activity and the exploration for and development of new sources of wealth, or for such other expenditures as may be consistent with the declaration of policy contained in section 102 and the purposes of this title, including local currency administrative expenditures of the United States within such country incident to operations under this title: *Provided further,* That the use of such special account shall be subject to agreement between such country and the Administrator, who shall act in this connection after consultation with the National Advisory Council on International Monetary and Financial Problems and the Public Advisory Board provided for in section 107 (a): *And provided further,* That any unencumbered balance remaining in such account on June 30, 1952, shall be disposed of within such country for such purposes as may, subject to approval by Act or joint resolution by the Congress, be agreed to between such country and the Government of the United States;

(7) publishing in such country and transmitting to the United States, not less frequently than every calendar quarter after the date of the agreement, full statements of operations under the agreement, including

a report of the use of funds, commodities, and services received under this title;

(8) furnishing promptly, upon request of the United States, any relevant information which would be of assistance to the United States in determining the nature and scope of operations and the use of assistance provided under this title;

(9) recognizing the principle of equity in respect to the drain upon the natural resources of the United States and of the recipient countries, by agreeing to negotiate (a) a future schedule of minimum availabilities to the United States for future purchase and delivery of a fair share of materials which are required by the United States as a result of deficiencies or potential deficiencies in its own resources at world market prices so as to protect the access of United States industry to an equitable share of such materials either in percentages of production or in absolute quantities from the participating countries, and (b) suitable protection for the right of access for any person as defined in paragraph (iii) of subparagraph (3) of section 111 (b) in the development of such materials on terms of treatment equivalent to those afforded to the nationals of the country concerned, and (c) an agreed schedule of increased production of such materials where practicable in such participating countries and for delivery of an agreed percentage of such increased production to be transferred to the United States on a long-term basis in consideration of assistance furnished by the Administrator to such countries under this title; and

(10) submitting for the decision of the International Court of Justice or of any arbitral tribunal mutually agreed upon any case espoused by the United States Government involving compensation of a national of the United States for governmental measures affecting his property rights, including contracts with or concessions from such country.

*   *   *

(d) The Administrator shall encourage each participating country to insure, by an effective follow-up system, that efficient use is made of the commodities, facilities, and services furnished under this title. In order further to insure that each participating country makes efficient use of such commodities, facilities, and services, and of its own resources, the Administrator shall encourage the joint organization of the participating countries referred to in subsection (b) of this section to observe and review the operation of such follow-up systems.

(e) The Administrator shall encourage arrangements among the participating countries in conjunction with the International Refugee Organization looking toward the largest practicable utilization of manpower available in any of the participating countries in furtherance of the accomplishment of the purposes of this title. The Administrator shall also encourage emigration from participating countries having permanent surplus manpower to areas, particularly underdeveloped and dependent areas, where such manpower can be effectively utilized.

(f) The Administrator will request the Secretary of State to obtain the agreement of those countries concerned that such capital equipment as is scheduled for removal as reparations from the three western zones of Germany be retained in Germany if such retention will most effectively serve the purposes of the European recovery program.

(g) It is the understanding of the Congress that, in accordance with agreements now in effect, prisoners of war remaining in participating countries shall, if they so freely elect, be repatriated prior to January 1, 1949.

(h) Not less than 5 per centum of each special local currency account established pursuant to paragraph (6) of subsection (b) of this section shall be allocated to the use of the United States Government for expenditure for materials which are required by the United States as a result of deficiencies or potential deficiencies in its own resources or for other local currency requirements of the United States.

(i) (1) The Administrator shall, to the greatest extent practicable, initiate projects for and assist the appropriate agencies of the United States Government in procuring and stimulating increased production in participating countries of materials which are required by the United States as a result of deficiencies or potential deficiencies in its own resources; and in furtherance of those objectives the Administrator shall, in addition to the local currency allocated pursuant to subsection (h), use such other means available to him under this title as he may deem appropriate.

(2) In furtherance of such objectives and within the limits of the appropriations and contract authorizations of the Bureau of Federal Supply to procure strategic and critical materials, the Administrator, with the approval of the Director of such Bureau, shall enter into contracts in the name of the United States for the account of such Bureau for the purchase of strategic and critical materials in any participating country. Such contracts may provide for deliveries over definite periods, but not to exceed twenty years in any contract, and may provide for payments in advance of deliveries.

(3) Nothing in this subsection shall be deemed to restrict or limit in any manner the authority now held by any agency of the United States Government in procuring or stimulating increased production of the materials referred to in paragraphs (1) and (2) in countries other than participating countries.

(j) The Administrator shall utilize such amounts of the local currency allocated pursuant to subsection (h) as may be necessary, to give full and continuous publicity through the press, radio, and all other available media, so as to inform the peoples of the participating countries regarding the assistance, including its purpose, source, and character, furnished by the American taxpayer.

*   *   *

OTHER DUTIES OF THE ADMINISTRATOR

Sec. 117. (a) The Administrator, in furtherance of the purposes of section 115 (b) (5), and in agreement with a participating country, shall, whenever practicable, promote, by means of funds made available for the purposes of this title, an increase in the production in such participating country of materials which are required by the United States as a result of deficiencies or potential deficiencies in the resources within the United States.

(b) The Administrator, in cooperation with the Secretary of Commerce, shall facilitate and encourage, through private and public travel, transport, and other agencies, the promotion and development of travel by citizens of the United States to and within participating countries.

* * *

(d) The Administrator is directed to refuse delivery insofar as practicable to participating countries of commodities which go into the production of any commodity for delivery to any nonparticipating European country which commodity would be refused export licenses to those countries by the United States in the interest of national security. Whenever the Administrator believes that the issuance of a license for the export of any commodity to any country wholly or partly in Europe which is not a participating country is inconsistent with the purposes and provisions of this title, he shall so advise the department, agency, or officer in the executive branch of the Government exercising the authority with respect to such commodity granted to the President by the Export Control Act of 1949, and, if differences of view are not adjusted by consultation, the matter shall be referred to the President for final decision.

* * *

TERMINATION OF ASSISTANCE

SEC. 118. The Administrator, in determining the form and measure of assistance provided under this title to any participating country, shall take into account the extent to which such country is complying with its undertakings embodied in its pledges to other participating countries and in its agreement concluded with the United States under section 115. The Administrator shall terminate the provision of assistance under this title to any participating country whenever he determines that (1) such country is not adhering to its agreement concluded under section 115, or is diverting from the purposes of this title assistance provided hereunder, and that in the circumstances remedial action other than termination will not more effectively promote the purposes of this title or (2) because of changed conditions, assistance is no longer consistent with the national interest of the United States or (3) the provision of such assistance would be inconsistent with the obligations of the United States under the Charter of the United Nations to refrain from giving assistance to any State against which the United Nations is taking preventative or enforcement action. Termination of assistance to any country under this section shall include the termination of deliveries of all supplies scheduled under the aid program for such country and not yet delivered.

* * *

UNITED NATIONS

SEC. 121. (a) The President is authorized to request the cooperation of or the use of the services and facilities of the United Nations, its organs and specialized agencies, or other international organizations, in carrying out the purposes of this title, and may make payments by advancements or reimbursements, for such purposes, out of funds made available for the purposes of this title, as may be necessary therefor, to the extent that special compensation is usually required for such services and facilities. Nothing in this

Foreign economic aid authorizations and appropriations, 1948-51

| | Fiscal 1947-1948 | | | | Fiscal 1948-1949 | | | |
| | Authorization | | Appropriation | | Authorization | | Appropriation | |
	Amount	Public Law	Amount	Public Law	Amount	Public Law	Amount	Public Law
1. Post-UNRRA relief (Austria, Hungary, Italy, Greece, Poland, Trieste, China)	$350,000,000	[1] 84	$332,000,000	[1] 271				
2. Greece and Turkey [2]	400,000,000	[1] 75	400,000,000	[1] 271	$275,000,000	[1] 472	$225,000,000	[1] 793
3. Interim aid	597,000,000	[1] 389	540,000,000	[1] 393				
4. European recovery program					[3][4] 5,300,000,000 / [3] 1,150,000,000	[1] 472 / 47	[3][4] 5,000,000,000 / [3] 1,074,000,000	[1] 793 / 327
5. China					[5] 463,000,000	[1] 472	[5] 400,000,000	[1] 793
6. Children's Fund	40,000,000	[1] 84	40,000,000	[1] 271	60,000,000	[1] 472	35,000,000	[1] 793
7. Palestine refugees								
8. Institute of Inter-American Affairs								
9. Korea								
10. Point 4								
11. Yugoslav aid								

[1] These public laws are from the 80th Cong. All others are from the 81st Cong.
[2] After 1949, Greece and Turkey aid was incorporated in the ERP and the MDAP.
[3] These combined figures cover a 15-month period.
[4] These figures include a public-debt transaction of $1,000,000,000.
[5] These figures include $125,000,000 for military aid.

Foreign economic aid authorizations and appropriations, 1948-51—Continued

| | Fiscal 1949-1950 | | | | Fiscal 1950-1951 | | | |
| | Authorization | | Appropriation | | Authorization | | Appropriation | |
	Amount	Public Law	Amount	Public Law	Amount	Public Law	Amount	Public Law
1. Post-UNRRA relief (Austria, Hungary, Italy, Greece, Poland, Trieste, China)	. . . . .	. . . . .	. . . . .	. . . . .	. . . . .	. . . . .	. . . . .	. . . . .
2. Greece and Turkey [2]	. . . . .	. . . . .	$45,000,000	327	. . . . .	. . . . .	. . . . .	. . . . .
3. Interim aid	. . . . .	. . . . .	. . . . .	. . . . .	. . . . .	. . . . .	. . . . .	. . . . .
4. European recovery program	[6] $4,430,000,000	47	[6] 3,778,380,000	327	[7] $2,700,000,000	535	[7] $2,250,000,000	759
5. China	([8]) ([8])	47} 447}	. . . . .	. . . . .	([8])	535	. . . . .	. . . . .
6. Children's Fund	([8])	170	. . . . .	. . . . .	15,000,000	535	. . . . .	. . . . .
7. Palestine refugees	16,000,000	25	16,000,000	119	27,450,000	535	27,450,000,000	759
8. Institute of Inter-American Affairs	[9] 35,000,000	283	[10] 4,751,600	179	. . . . .	. . . . .	[10] 5,000,000	759
9. Korea	60,000,000	447	. . . . .	[11] 154	100,000,000	535	90,000,000	759
			. . . . .	[11] 196				
			30,000,000	349				
			30,000,000	430				
			50,000,000	583				
10. Point 4	. . . . .	. . . . .	. . . . .	. . . . .	35,000,000	535	. . . . .	. . . . .
11. Yugoslav aid	. . . . .	. . . . .	. . . . .	. . . . .	[7] (50,000,000)	535	26,900,000	759

[6] These figures include a public-debt transaction of $150,000,000.
[7] $50,000,000 was authorized to be expended for emergency relief to Yugoslavia out of ECA funds previously authorized and appropriated.
[8] Time extension.
[9] This authorization is for a 5-year period.
[10] These appropriations are for a 1-year period.
[11] These laws carried no specific sums for this program, but appropriated funds for short times at the rate of expenditures of the previous fiscal year.

title shall be construed to authorize the Administrator to delegate to or otherwise confer upon any international or foreign organization or agency any of his authority to decide the method of furnishing assistance under this title to any participating country or the amount thereof.

(b) The President shall cause to be transmitted to the Secretary General of the United Nations copies of reports to Congress on the operations conducted under this title.

(c) Any agreements concluded between the United States and participating countries, or groups of such countries, in implementation of the purposes of this title, shall be registered with the United Nations if such registration is required by the Charter of the United Nations.

TERMINATION OF PROGRAM

SEC. 122. (a) After June 30, 1952, or after the date of the passage of a concurrent resolution by the two Houses of Congress before such date, which declares that the powers conferred on the Administrator by or pursuant to subsection (a) of section 111 of this title are no longer necessary for the accomplishment of the purposes of this title, whichever shall first occur, none of the functions authorized under such provisions may be exercised; except that during the twelve months following such date commodities and services with respect to which the Administrator had, prior to such date, authorized procurement for, shipment to, or delivery in a participating country, may be transferred to such country, and funds appropriated under authority of this title may be obligated during such twelve-month period for the necessary expenses of procurement, shipment, delivery, and other activities essential to such transfer, and shall remain available during such period for the necessary expenses of liquidating operations under this title.

(b) At such time as the President shall find appropriate after such date and prior to the expiration of the twelve months following such date, the powers, duties, and authority of the Administrator under this title may be transferred to such other departments, agencies, or establishments of the Government as the President shall specify, and the relevant funds, records, and personnel of the Administration may be transferred to the departments, agencies, or establishments to which the related functions are transferred.

REPORTS TO CONGRESS

SEC. 123. The President from time to time, but not less frequently than once every calendar quarter through June 30, 1952, and once every year thereafter until all operations under this title have been completed, shall transmit to the Congress a report of operations under this title, including the text of bilateral and multilateral agreements entered into in carrying out the provisions of this title. Reports provided for under this section shall be transmitted to the Secretary of the Senate or the Clerk of the House of Representatives, as the case may be, if the Senate or the House of Representatives, as the case may be, is not in session.

JOINT CONGRESSIONAL COMMITTEE

SEC. 124. (a) There is hereby established a joint congressional committee to be known as the Joint Committee on Foreign Economic Cooperation (hereinafter referred to as the committee), to be composed of ten members as follows:

(1) Three members who are members of the Committee on Foreign Relations of the Senate, two from the majority and one from the minority party, to be appointed by the chairman of the committee; two members who are members of the Committee on Appropriations of the Senate, one from the majority and one from the minority party, to be appointed by the chairman of the committee; and

(2) Three members who are members of the Committee on Foreign Affairs of the House, two from the majority and one from the minority party, to be appointed by the chairman of the committee; and two members who are members of the Committee on Appropriations of the House, one from the majority and one from the minority party, to be appointed by the chairman of the committee.

A vacancy in the membership of the committee shall be filled in the same manner as the original selection. The committee shall elect a chairman from among its members.

(b) It shall be the function of the committee to make a continuous study of the programs of United States economic assistance to foreign countries, and to review the progress achieved in the execution and administration of such programs. Upon request, the committee shall aid the several standing committees of the Congress having legislative jurisdiction over any part of the programs of United States economic assistance to foreign countries; and it shall make a report to the Senate and the House of Representatives, from time to time concerning the results of its studies, together with such recommendations as it may deem desirable. The Administrator, at the request of the committee, shall consult with the committee from time to time with respect to his activities under this Act.

*   *   *

◇◇◇◇◇◇

233. YUGOSLAV EMERGENCY RELIEF ASSISTANCE ACT OF 1950

[In addition to helping Western Europe to recover and regain stability, the United States also extended considerable aid to Yugoslavia following Tito's break with the Kremlin in the spring of 1948. In 1949 we granted Yugoslavia some $55,000,000 in Export-Import Bank loans. In 1950, following a severe drought in that country, we made available nearly $70,000,000 in foodstuffs, thus widening still further the break in the Soviet satellite ranks. Fifty million of that amount were authorized in the Yugoslav Emergency Relief Assistance Act of 1950, which set forth the conditions under which aid was to be granted.]

[1] Public Law 897, 81st Cong., 2nd sess., S. 4234, approved December 29, 1950.

AN ACT

To promote the foreign policy and provide for the defense and general welfare of the United States by furnishing emergency relief assistance to Yugoslavia.

Be it enacted by the Senate and House of Representatives of the United States of America in Congress assembled, That this Act may be cited as the "Yugoslav Emergency Relief Assistance Act of 1950".

SEC. 2. The President is hereby authorized to expend not in excess of $50,000,000 of the funds heretofore appropriated for expenses necessary to carry out the provisions of the Economic Cooperation Act of 1948, as amended (Public Law 759, Eighty-first Congress), for the purpose of providing emergency relief assistance to Yugoslavia under the authority of this Act.

SEC. 3. No assistance under authority of this Act shall be made available nor shall any funds appropriated hereunder be expended until an agreement is entered into between Yugoslavia and the United States containing the following undertakings, and any others the President may determine to be desirable, on the part of Yugoslavia:

(a) To make available to the Government of the United States local currency in amounts required by it to meet its local currency administrative and operating expenses in Yugoslavia in connection with assistance supplied under this Act.

(b) To give full and continuous publicity through the press, radio, and all other available media in Yugoslavia to the assistance furnished by the United States; and to allow to the United States, in cooperation with Yugoslavia, the use of such media as may be required to accomplish this purpose.

(c) To permit persons designated by the Government of the United States to observe and supervise without restriction the distribution by Yugoslavia of commodities and other assistance made available under the authority of this Act, and to the extent necessary for this purpose to permit full freedom of movement of such persons within Yugoslavia and full access to communication and information facilities.

(d) To make equitable distribution to the people in Yugoslavia of the commodities made available under this Act, as well as similar commodities produced locally or imported from outside sources, without discrimination as to race or political or religious belief.

(e) Whenever relief supplies furnished under this Act are sold for local currency by the Government of Yugoslavia, to use an equivalent amount of such currency to provide relief to needy persons and to children, and for charitable, medical, and such other purposes as may be mutually agreed upon.

(f) To take all appropriate economic measures to reduce its relief needs, to encourage increased production and distribution of food stuffs within Yugoslavia and to lessen the danger of similar future emergencies.

SEC. 4. All of the funds made available under authority of this Act shall be utilized to the fullest practicable extent in the purchase of the commodities from the surplus commodities in the possession of the Commodity Credit

Corporation at prices authorized by section 112 of the Foreign Assistance Act of 1948, as amended.

SEC. 5. Nothing in this Act shall be interpreted as endorsing measures undertaken by the present Government of Yugoslavia which suppress or destroy religious, political, and economic liberty, and the Yugoslav Government shall be so notified when aid is furnished under this Act.

SEC. 6. At the termination of each three-month period after aid has been extended under this Act the Secretary of State shall make a full and detailed report to the Congress. Said three-month reports shall not be limited to, but shall include (1) information as to whether or not Yugoslavia is abiding by the agreement as provided for under section 3 of this Act; (2) information as to any developments in the attitude of Yugoslavia with respect to basic human rights.

SEC. 7. All or any portion of the funds made available under authority of this Act may be transferred by the President to any department or agency of the executive branch of the Government to be expended for the purpose of this Act. Funds so transferred may be expended under the authority of any provisions of law, not inconsistent with this Act, applicable to the departments or agencies concerned, except that funds so transferred shall not be commingled with other funds of such departments or agencies and shall be accounted for separately.

SEC. 8. Local currency made available to the United States by Yugoslavia under the provisions of the agreement required by section 3 may be used for local currency administrative and operating expenses in Yugoslavia in connection with assistance provided by this Act without charge against appropriated funds.

SEC. 9. At least 50 per centum of the gross tonnage of any equipment, materials, or commodities made available under the provisions of this Act and transported on ocean vessels (computed separately for dry bulk carriers and dry cargo liners) shall be transported on United States flag commercial vessels at market rates for United States flag commercial vessels, if available.

SEC. 10. All or any part of the assistance provided hereunder shall be promptly terminated by the President—

(a) whenever he determines that (1) Yugoslavia is not complying fully with the undertakings in the agreement entered into under section 3 of this Act, or is diverting from the purpose of this Act assistance provided hereunder; or (2) because of changed conditions, continuance of assistance is unnecessary or undesirable, or no longer consistent with the national interest or the foreign policy of the United States;

(b) whenever the Congress, by concurrent resolution, finds termination is desirable.

Termination of assistance to Yugoslavia under this section shall include the termination of deliveries of all supplies scheduled under this Act and not yet delivered.

◇◇◇◇◇◇

234. REPORT TO THE PRESIDENT ON FOREIGN ECONOMIC POLICIES: SUMMARY AND RECOMMENDATIONS [1]

[Congress and the Administration have repeatedly stated that the European Recovery Program should end in 1952. With this in mind, and with the thought that the whole range of foreign economic problems facing the United States should be carefully analyzed, the President on March 31, 1950, asked Mr. Gordon Gray to serve as his special assistant, and to formulate recommendations charting our course in the field of foreign economic policies and programs. While Mr. Gray and his staff were making their study, the Korean aggression and the decision of the free world to rearm considerably altered world economic conditions. The basic nature of the problem remains the same, however, and the summary and recommendations of Mr. Gray's report (released on November 10, 1950) are worth careful study.]

* * *

PROBLEMS FOR THE FUTURE

In the pursuit of the long-run objectives of our foreign policy it has become necessary to emphasize these major goals: (a) To help make possible, politically and economically, a rapid buildup in the defense capabilities of Western Europe; (b) to help develop additional sources of supply for needed materials; (c) to help strengthen the economic and political structures of the free world in general against the intensified pressures of Communist subversion and penetration; and (d) to continue laying the groundwork for world trade and financial relationships which will promote progress on a self-supporting basis.

The following appear to be the major problems in prospect for our foreign economic policy:

(1) In the case of Western Europe, the difficulties now in prospect are no longer ones of finding export markets, but of producing sufficient goods and services to meet the new and enlarged military requirements and minimum civilian needs, including the exports necessary for self-support. In the interest of the common defense, the Western European countries can and undoubtedly will make sacrifices by foregoing consumption and investment, but there are limits beyond which they cannot go without drastically undermining their economic health and their political cohesion. A sufficient rate of rearmament will probably exceed these limits, and to the extent that it forces a reduction in their exports, it reduces the only means they have of becoming self-supporting.

(2) It is important to increase the production of the raw materials necessary for defense. It is not enough simply to buy existing supplies—new capital must flow into the raw material producing countries to increase production. Moreover, it is vital not to lose the sources of these needed raw materials to

[1] Report to the President on Foreign Economic Policies, Washington, November 10, 1950, Government Printing Office, pp. 8-18.

the forces of Communist aggression. Serious dangers are also in prospect with regard to the prices and distribution of primary commodities in the period before measures to increase supplies can become effective. Rapid price increases for many of these commodities cannot significantly increase supplies, but only serve to reinforce the dangerous inflationary pressures which have again emerged throughout the world.

(3) The economic stagnation, political unrest, and extreme poverty of most underdeveloped countries represent a growing threat to the rest of the free world. In general the requirements for adequate economic development are beyond their internal capabilities—in some cases because of inadequate material resources, but more generally because of insufficient technical and administrative ability and the corrosive effects of poverty itself. Despite great obstacles, it is more important than ever to the security and well-being of free countries that social and economic progress be achieved in the underdeveloped areas.

(4) Despite the measures which will be temporarily required to influence the distribution and prices of primary commodities and to assure the needed distribution of manufactured goods, it is still important to continue developing a system of unobstructed international trade and investment that can maximize output and place the major areas of the world on a sound and self-supporting basis.

(5) Major adjustments are needed in some of our own national policies. Especially in the present period of general shortages, a freer flow of imports would be of general benefit in many ways, and at present there exist unreasonable obstructions to such a flow. Administration of any necessary developments with respect to domestic price, allocation, and export controls must take our foreign programs into account if they are not to impair the progress toward our international objectives. Over the longer run, certain policies with regard to agriculture and shipping have an important and unfavorable impact on our foreign economic relations.

(6) There is cause for concern regarding the morale and outlook of peoples in many parts of Western Europe and the underdeveloped areas. Foreign economic policies and programs must be part of a total policy which can generate greater unity, hope, and support for freedom now, while providing the basis for gradual economic improvement in the future....

These various problems are clearly interrelated. From an economic standpoint they all involve the most effective use of the available resources of the free world to support adequate military security, to increase output, to obtain the needed distribution of output, and to develop an international trading and financial pattern which can efficiently serve these goals.

Thus the solution of the problems of Western Europe and Japan—adequate supplies of food and raw materials, adequate markets (both dollar and non-dollar) for exports of manufactured goods, a satisfactory relationship between import and export prices, sufficient total resources to meet the needs of security and stability—is closely related to the development of underdeveloped areas from which many of their raw materials must come, to the achievement of political stability in overseas countries with which Western Europe has responsibilities or close connections, and to United States trade policies.

Similarly, the underdeveloped areas must obtain from the industrialized countries supplies of capital, manufactured goods, and technical aid to achieve needed increases in output and living standards, and assistance in preserving their national independence.

The economic and security interests of the United States itself in the rest of the world are affected not only by economic, political, and social conditions in other countries but also by certain specific requirements—adequate supplies of imported materials essential for security, and of other goods which can contribute to our living standards; self-supporting markets for the output of our farms and factories which the rest of the world needs and which we produce efficiently and in abundance; sufficient ability and will on the part of all free nations to share in the common defense and to participate in an effective system of economic relationships.

RECOMMENDATIONS

Our foreign economic affairs have reached a stage when major policy decisions must be made. The recommendations of this Report are intended to assist in this task. Some of them call for legislative action, others involve only administrative action or reaffirm present policies. They are related to one another, and are designed to equip this country to pursue an economic policy abroad that would best contribute to the attainment of our foreign policy objectives. It should be emphasized again that the latter requires much more than foreign economic measures, which by themselves cannot be effective. It requires adequate military defensive strength, sound political and diplomatic policies, a forceful informational program, and the continual strengthening of our own economy.

A. What should be done about aid to Western Europe and Japan?

The urgent need for rapidly creating defensive strength in Western Europe, as part of a joint effort to provide mutual security, forces a postponement of the time when the United States, consistent with its own interest, can end economic assistance. Adequate rearmament—within the time required by the current situation—will require, not only extensive supplies of military equipment from the United States, but also a substantial diversion of Western European output from other uses and some increases in imports. In view of the mutual interest in achieving security, the Western European countries should be willing to undertake diversion of resources from consumption and investment to the extent possible.

The recent marked improvement in the trade and reserve positions of Western Europe reflects, to some extent at least, the favorable effects on their position of developments in the United States, while they have not yet felt the unfavorable impact of their own accelerated rearmament. It seems clear that a sufficiently large and rapid growth in military strength is beyond the capacity of Western European countries solely through their own efforts or with aid only in the form of military equipment.

Provided that the Western European countries undertake a genuinely adequate defense effort, we should be prepared to extend dollar aid to meet the short-run burden of their own military production, insofar as it exceeds the sacrifices which it is within their ability to make. Western Europe is the most critical area from the standpoint of our own security and the security of the free world.

We should also recognize that, unless Western European exports and earnings are maintained to the maximum extent consistent with accelerated rearmament, Western Europe's inability to support itself and consequently its need for economic aid will be unnecessarily prolonged. At the same time, it is important that the Western European countries utilize their total resources more fully and continue to press toward closer economic and political relationships.

With these considerations in mind, it is recommended that:

1. To facilitate the required expansion of Western European defenses in accordance with joint plans, the United States should be prepared to continue supplying aid, apart from military equipment, for another 3 or 4 years beyond the present time. The needed amount of aid depends upon the rearmament effort actually undertaken by individual countries, and its total impact on their economies, these factors being worked out primarily through the economic and production planning agencies of the North Atlantic Treaty Organization.

2. Aid to Western Europe should be planned on the basis of an over-all assessment of requirements rather than on a specific project basis. It should be administered separately from aid in the form of military equipment shipped from the United States.

3. Such aid should be administered on a basis that will contribute to the fullest possible use of European resources, encourage intra-European trade, and help to integrate the European economic effort. It is recommended that the United States continue to support the development of an effective intra-European payments mechanism. At least for the time being, it should continue to allot to the European Payments Union a portion of the dollar aid it extends to Europe.

4. In the joint planning of security programs, and specifically in helping to increase the defensive strength of Western Europe, adequate consideration should be given to the importance of a high volume of European exports, which are the only means for achieving self-support, although the internal burden of rearming must obviously have an impact on the levels of consumption and investment.

5. In view of the special importance of the pound sterling in world trade and of a strong position of the United Kingdom, the needed rate of increase in British military expenditures should be achieved by means that avoid seriously worsening the external position of the United Kingdom.

Because of its predominant industrial position in the Far East, the potential contribution of a stable and democratic Japan is extremely important for economic growth, the improvement of living standards, and the maintenance of peace in the region. During the last year, with the help of United States Government aid, Japan has been able to add substantially to her dollar reserves, and at the same time has experienced a continued improvement in her balance-of-payments position. This process should continue during fiscal year 1951 with the United States aid already appropriated. Unused resources are still available to permit further increases in output for both exports and domestic use. By fiscal year 1952, with a continuation of present favorable trends, Japan may be self-supporting and may possess substantial dollar and possibly commodity reserves, although living standards will still remain below the prewar level. It is recommended that:

6. Further appropriations for Japanese aid should be carefully considered and measured against the effect of the favorable circumstances brought about by current developments, and also in the light of other recommendations in this report that would increase Japanese export opportunities. However, should Japan for any reason prove unable to increase production for export, it might need external aid.

B. What should be done about underdeveloped areas?

The need for economic development and progress in these areas becomes daily more pressing, not only for their own welfare, but for the security and the well-being of all the free nations. The process of stimulating development is more complicated and slow than that of assisting recovery in developed countries, and there are limits to the capacity of underdeveloped countries to absorb capital. Wide variations in local internal conditions, as well as in resource potential and in vulnerability to aggression, require diversity in method and flexibility in administration. Each type of stimulus—private investment, public loans, technical assistance, and grants—has a significant role to play.

The following recommendations are intended to increase the scope and improve the effectiveness of these forms of assistance. Taken together, they are intended to constitute the outlines of a total program of development assistance that is both possible and necessary to achieve the objectives of United States foreign policy.

7. Private investment should be considered as the most desirable means of providing capital and its scope should be widened as far as possible. It normally carries with it the technological and administrative skills which are an essential ingredient for effectiveness. There should be constant reevaluation of the role which it can play and the burden of public lending should be correspondingly adjusted. Further study should be given to the desirability and possibility of promoting private investment through tax incentives, in areas where economic development will promote mutual interests, but where political uncertainty now handicaps U. S. private investment. The possibilities of measures to improve the United States market for sound foreign dollar securities should also be studied. The following steps should immediately be taken, although the uncertainty of their effectiveness in many areas must be recognized in the light of present world conditions.

(a) The negotiation of investment treaties to encourage private investment should be expedited.

(b) The bill to authorize Government guaranties of private investment against the risks of nonconvertibility and expropriation should be enacted as a worthwhile experiment.

8. Under present conditions a heavy reliance on public lending must be recognized as essential for an aggressive development program. This will require continued vigorous efforts by the International Bank for Reconstruction and Development, supplemented by the Export-Import Bank, and coordinated with effective technical assistance activities. Their combined efforts should aim at a net outflow of capital to underdeveloped areas in the range of 600 to 800 million dollars a year, of which half or more should be supplied by the International Bank from sources other than the United States Treasury. With respect to United States Government lending, the following steps are also needed:

(a) The lending authority of the Export-Import Bank should be increased from the present 3½ to a total of 5 billion dollars, in order to make advance planning effective.

(b) A general policy of permitting United States loans to be spent outside as well as within the United States should be adopted. In this way, loan recipients can buy goods wherever they are cheapest, and other industrial countries will have an opportunity to expand exports and dollar earnings if they are sufficiently competitive. This would also be in the interests of the United States; it would tend to help relieve inflationary shortages at the present time, and in the longer run to support export markets for United States goods which are likely to be most readily available.

(c) In selected cases loans should be permitted to finance some of the local costs of development projects even though these costs do not involve imports and therefore do not directly require foreign exchange. Such local costs frequently cause an indirect foreign exchange drain, which may handicap or prevent successful development.

9. In some cases, grants may appropriately be used for development and technical assistance, where development programs urgently needed from the standpoint of United States objectives cannot be soundly financed by loans, and where grants will be an effective spur to economic development. Furthermore, our present technical assistance programs in underdeveloped areas should be expanded in scope and made more effective. The United States therefore should make further limited funds available for a program of grants for technical assistance and development. It seems probable that a needed, feasible, and effective program would require funds of up to about 500 million dollars a year for several years, apart from emergency requirements arising from military action. This compares with present funds of about 150 million dollars a year for these purposes.

10. The administration of programs to stimulate development in underdeveloped areas—including loans, technical assistance, grants, and measures to encourage private investment—should be much more closely coordinated than is now the case.

C. *What should be done about the procurement and export of goods in short supply?*

The United States is a net importer of many minerals and other commodities which are vital to our national security and our economy, and which are produced predominantly in the underdeveloped areas. Rearmament programs here and abroad greatly increase the requirements for these commodities in the face of supplies which are already in many cases inadequate. The recently enlarged stockpiling program will impose further heavy pressure on world supplies. An unchecked scramble for supplies and the inevitable effects on prices would have serious consequences for the rearmament programs, for our own economy and those of friendly nations. It would adversely affect the balance of payments positions of many Western European countries and Japan, and would introduce an element of instability into the economies of exporting countries. Exports of manufactured goods are also likely to be inadequate to meet all demands, and measures may be required to see that the high priority needs of friendly nations are met. It is recommended that:

11. In addition to necessary and properly administered domestic measures within the United States, methods for international collaboration should be promptly established for guiding supplies of scarce materials among the free nations in the manner best calculated to contribute to the common defense.

12. In administering such export controls as may be necessary, adequate steps should be taken to assure the delivery of goods required by other countries for purposes that support broad United States interests. Cooperative action in assuring a flow of goods needed to support common objectives should be developed with other countries.

13. Efforts should be intensified to effect a rapid expansion in the output of scarce materials, not only through the provision of capital funds and equipment, but also through procurement activities such as long-term contracts.

D. *What should be done to promote our international trade and financial objectives?*

We are working toward the ultimate goal of a peace which rests upon the firm foundations of an expanding world economy. It is, therefore, important that we continue our efforts to encourage world trade and capital investment throughout the world. Only in this way can the nations of the world achieve rising standards of living through sound and self-supporting economies. Despite the restrictions on trade and payments, resulting from persistent dislocations and government policies, or which are likely to become necessary under the strain of rearmament, it is still possible and necessary to make progress in the direction of a system of multilateral and nondiscriminatory trade.

We must, therefore, continue to work for such a system. We must try to establish an adequate system of international payments. We should encourage other countries to adopt the necessary monetary and fiscal measures which can assure sound currencies and obviate the need for direct trade restrictions. We must make sure that our own house is in order—that we have eliminated unnecessary barriers to imports, and that our policies in such fields as agriculture and shipping are so adjusted that they do not impose undue burdens on world trade. In addition, our intensified need for goods in the short-term future makes it desirable to remove barriers to imports as far as possible in order to augment supplies and alleviate upward pressure on prices.

The United States occupies a central position in world agricultural trade, both as an exporter and as an importer. Our policies in this field are of vital concern to other nations. Similarly, as a major maritime nation, our policy with regard to shipping subsidies directly affects the ability of other maritime nations to earn dollars in international trade. In both cases conflicts tend to arise between considerations of domestic and of foreign objectives.

For these reasons, the following recommendations are made:

14. The United States should continue to work for the elimination of discriminatory trade and exchange practices through the General Agreement on Tariffs and Trade, the Reciprocal Trade Act, and the International Monetary Fund. The United States should also become a member of the International Trade Organization.

15. The United States should consider the eventual desirability of assistance, such as stabilization credits, to permit convertibility of currencies for current account, notably the pound sterling. But such credits should not be granted until all requirements for convertibility, with the exception of adequate reserves, have been met. Neither should such credits be extended unless convertibility will be accompanied by a reduction of trade discriminations.

16. With respect to our own import policy we should:

(a) Continue to seek further general tariff reductions under the Reciprocal Trade Agreements Act, renew the Reciprocal Trade Agreements Act for a period of four years, and continue efforts to assure that obligations mutually undertaken are carried out.

(b) Adopt, as an emergency measure, temporary legislation to permit temporary unilateral reductions in specific tariff rates on commodities which are scarce and when conditions of inflationary pressure exist.

(c) Reduce unnecessary and unreasonable regulatory and procedural barriers by administrative action and by passing the proposed Customs Simplification Act.

(d) Initiate as soon as possible, through the Tariff Commission, a study of the feasibility and desirability of a general tariff reclassification, and to make recommendations concerning proper legislative and administrative action.

(e) Repeal existing legislation which requires, in Government procurement, discrimination against imported goods, and in the meantime reduce the impact of such legislation by administrative action.

17. With respect to our own agricultural policies we should, over the long-run, attempt to modify our price support system, and our methods of surplus disposal and accumulation of stocks, in ways which, while consistent with domestic objectives, will be helpful to our foreign relations. In the meantime we should:

(a) Eliminate as soon as possible import embargoes imposed for other than sanitary or similar reasons, and in the interim apply their restrictions in a less rigid manner.

(b) Not encourage increases in the domestic production of crops which have to be protected not only by quotas and tariffs but also by direct subsidies to producers.

18. With respect to our shipping industry, we should limit the use of Government subsidies or other protective measures to the amounts necessary to maintain the operation of shipping facilities required for national security. The United States should negotiate with other governments to remove cargo preferences and other similar types of discrimination.

E. How should our foreign economic programs be administered?

It is continuously necessary to relate the use of resources required by foreign economic programs to other United States needs, and to the capacity of our economy. We must not lose sight of the fact that our economic health is itself vital to attaining the objectives of the free world. In the critical period ahead, when United States resources will be severely strained, United States aid must be channeled to those areas and for those purposes where reasonable performance in the political and economic fields can be achieved. It is important, from this standpoint as well as from others, to develop as far as possible, a cooperative and multilateral approach to foreign programs, notably through the United Nations and associated organizations. In the case of some programs, such an approach may be essential for accomplishing the basic purpose. We should recognize that other countries have contributed and will increasingly contribute to the achievement of objectives mutually shared.

It is also important to improve our own methods and organization for carrying on foreign economic programs. We need a high degree of continuity and consistency in legislative and administrative action, and we need a better organization within the Executive Branch. As the importance of our foreign economic policy has grown, its complexities have increased. Loans, grants, technical assistance, the production and procurement abroad of raw materials for defense, and measures to influence the international flow of goods are all closely related. At the present time, the administration of these various aspects of our foreign economic policy is scattered throughout the Government. While foreign economic policy is a part of our total foreign policy, and the basic decisions must, of course, be made at the highest level, greater efficiency and effectiveness can be achieved by more administrative centralization. (This Report does not attempt to deal with the problem of coordination at broader policy levels, or the relationship of various mechanisms which are now in existence or under discussion for this purpose.)

For these reasons, it is recommended that:

19. Assistance activities should in general be initiated only when requested by other governments and when the latter are prepared to make appropriate contributions and provide cooperative effort.

20. Grants and loans should be made conditional upon agreement as to reasonable standards of performance, and should be used to help achieve these standards. It should be recognized that these conditions will frequently have to relate to broad internal measures and policies.

21. The United States should help to strengthen appropriate international and regional organizations and to increase the scope of their activities. It should be prepared, insofar as practicable, to support their activities as the

best method of achieving the economic and security objectives which it shares with other free nations.

22. An agency or organization should be established within the United States Government to administer foreign economic programs. Its functions should include the administration of all grant and technical assistance programs (except the provision of military equipment) and the administration of other related activities, such as the stimulation of needed materials production abroad. It is also necessary to follow through on present efforts to improve the machinery within the Government for coordinating operations in the foreign economic field with over-all foreign policy.

◇◇◇◇◇

COLLECTIVE SELF-DEFENSE
235. VANDENBERG RESOLUTION [1]
Senate Resolution 239, Eightieth Congress

[During the eightieth Congress, the growing concern of the American people over the expansionist tactics of the Soviet Union was reflected by the introduction of a number of resolutions designed to strengthen the United Nations. The Vandenberg resolution, developed in close coöperation between the State Department and the Senate Foreign Relations Committee, was an outgrowth of these proposals. While it urged the strengthening of the United Nations in various ways, its main purpose was to put the Senate on record as favoring the association by the United States with regional and other collective self-defense arrangements under the United Nations Charter. It thus paved the way for the negotiation of the North Atlantic Treaty. The resolution, which was approved by a vote of 64 to 4, is an excellent example of the Senate's advising the President as to the course he should follow in the conduct of foreign policy.]

Whereas peace with justice and the defense of human rights and fundamental freedoms require international cooperation through more effective use of the United Nations: Therefore be it

Resolved, That the Senate reaffirm the policy of the United States to achieve international peace and security through the United Nations so that armed force shall not be used except in the common interest, and that the President be advised of the sense of the Senate that this Government, by constitutional process, should particularly pursue the following objectives within the United Nations Charter:

(1) Voluntary agreement to remove the veto from all questions involving pacific settlements of international disputes and situations, and from the admission of new members.

(2) Progressive development of regional and other collective arrangements

[1] S. Res. 239, 80th Cong., 2d sess., June 11, 1948.

for individual and collective self-defense in accordance with the purposes, principles, and provisions of the Charter.

(3) Association of the United States, by constitutional process, with such regional and other collective arrangements as are based on continuous and effective self-help and mutual aid, and as affect its national security.

(4) Contributing to the maintenance of peace by making clear its determination to exercise the right of individual or collective self-defense under article 51 should any armed attack occur affecting its national security.

(5) Maximum efforts to obtain agreements to provide the United Nations with armed forces as provided by the Charter, and to obtain agreement among member nations upon universal regulation and reduction of armaments under adequate and dependable guaranty against violation.

(6) If necessary, after adequate effort toward strengthening the United Nations, review of the Charter at an appropriate time by a General Conference called under article 109 or by the General Assembly.

◇◇◇◇◇

236. NORTH ATLANTIC TREATY, APRIL 4, 1949 [1]

[Shortly after the passage of the Vandenberg resolution on June 11, 1948, the State Department began exploratory conversations about the security of the North Atlantic area with representatives of Canada and the Brussels Pact countries—Belgium, France, Luxemburg, the Netherlands, and the United Kingdom. Formal negotiations opened in December, and the North Atlantic Treaty was signed in Washington by the six governments referred to above, as well as by Denmark, Iceland, Italy, Norway, Portugal, and the United States. The main purpose of the Treaty was to strengthen the security system of the North Atlantic area by making clear the determination of the parties to exercise the right of collective self-defense in the event of an attack. Although it is patterned somewhat after the Rio Treaty, it is not, strictly speaking, a regional pact. Rather it is based upon the collective self-defense principle expressed in Article 51 of the United Nations Charter. The Treaty, which is second in importance only to the Charter in our postwar history, was approved by the Senate on July 21, 1949, by a vote of 82 to 13.]

The Parties to this Treaty reaffirm their faith in the purposes and principles of the Charter of the United Nations and their desire to live in peace with all peoples and all governments.

They are determined to safeguard the freedom, common heritage and civilization of their peoples, founded on the principles of democracy, individual liberty and the rule of law.

They seek to promote stability and well-being in the North Atlantic area.

They are resolved to unite their efforts for collective defense and for the preservation of peace and security.

They therefore agree to this North Atlantic Treaty:

[1] The North Atlantic Treaty, Documents relating to the North Atlantic Treaty, published by the Senate Committee on Foreign Relations, 1949, p. 1.

ARTICLE 1

The Parties undertake, as set forth in the Charter of the United Nations, to settle any international disputes in which they may be involved by peaceful means in such a manner that international peace and security, and justice, are not endangered, and to refrain in their international relations from the threat or use of force in any manner inconsistent with the purposes of the United Nations.

ARTICLE 2

The Parties will contribute toward the further development of peaceful and friendly international relations by strengthening their free institutions, by bringing about a better understanding of the principles upon which these institutions are founded, and by promoting conditions of stability and well-being. They will seek to eliminate conflict in their international economic policies and will encourage economic collaboration between any or all of them.

ARTICLE 3

In order more effectively to achieve the objectives of this Treaty, the Parties, separately and jointly, by means of continuous and effective self-help and mutual aid, will maintain and develop their individual and collective capacity to resist armed attack.

ARTICLE 4

The Parties will consult together whenever, in the opinion of any of them, the territorial integrity, political independence or security of any of the Parties is threatened.

ARTICLE 5

The Parties agree that an armed attack against one or more of them in Europe or North America shall be considered an attack against them all; and consequently they agree that, if such an armed attack occurs, each of them, in exercise of the right of individual or collective self-defense recognized by Article 51 of the Charter of the United Nations, will assist the Party or Parties so attacked by taking forthwith, individually and in concert with the other Parties, such action as it deems necessary, including the use of armed force, to restore and maintain the security of the North Atlantic area.

Any such armed attack and all measures taken as a result thereof shall immediately be reported to the Security Council. Such measures shall be terminated when the Security Council has taken the measures necessary to restore and maintain international peace and security.

ARTICLE 6

For the purpose of Article 5 an armed attack on one or more of the Parties is deemed to include an armed attack on the territory of any of the Parties in Europe or North America, on the Algerian departments of France, on the occupation forces of any Party in Europe, on the islands under the jurisdiction of any Party in the North Atlantic area north of the Tropic of Cancer or on the vessels or aircraft in this area of any of the Parties.

Prepared by the Legislative Reference Service,
Library of Congress

——————— **Area defined in Article 6 of the North Atlantic Treaty**

ARTICLE 7

This Treaty does not affect, and shall not be interpreted as affecting, in any way the rights and obligations under the Charter of the Parties which are members of the United Nations, or the primary responsibility of the Security Council for the maintenance of international peace and security.

ARTICLE 8

Each Party declares that none of the international engagements now in force between it and any other of the Parties or any third state is in conflict with the provisions of this Treaty, and undertakes not to enter into any international engagement in conflict with this Treaty.

ARTICLE 9

The Parties hereby established a council, on which each of them shall be represented, to consider matters concerning the implementation of this Treaty. The council shall be so organized as to be able to meet promptly at any time. The council shall set up such subsidiary bodies as may be necessary; in particular it shall establish immediately a defense committee which shall recommend measures for the implementation of Articles 3 and 5.

ARTICLE 10

The Parties may, by unanimous agreement, invite any other European state in a position to further the principles of this Treaty and to contribute to the security of the North Atlantic area to accede to this Treaty. Any state so invited may become a party to the Treaty by depositing its instrument of accession with the Government of the United States of America. The Government of the United States of America will inform each of the Parties of the deposit of each such instrument of accession.

ARTICLE 11

This Treaty shall be ratified and its provisions carried out by the Parties in accordance with their respective constitutional processes. The instruments of ratification shall be deposited as soon as possible with the Government of the United States of America, which will notify all the other signatories of each deposit. The Treaty shall enter into force between the states which have ratified it as soon as the ratifications of the majority of the signatories, including the ratifications of Belgium, Canada, France, Luxembourg, the Netherlands, the United Kingdom and the United States, have been deposited and shall come into effect with respect to other states on the date of the deposit of their ratifications.

ARTICLE 12

After the Treaty has been in force for ten years, or at any time thereafter, the Parties shall, if any of them so requests, consult together for the purpose of reviewing the Treaty, having regard for the factors then affecting peace and security in the North Atlantic area, including the development of universal as well as regional arrangements under the Charter of the United Nations for the maintenance of international peace and security.

ARTICLE 13

After the Treaty has been in force for twenty years, any Party may cease to be a party one year after its notice of denunciation has been given to the Government of the United States of America, which will inform the Governments of the other Parties of the deposit of each notice of denunciation.

ARTICLE 14

This Treaty, of which the English and French texts are equally authentic, shall be deposited in the archives of the Government of the United States of America. Duly certified copies thereof will be transmitted by that Government to the Governments of the other signatories.

In witness whereof, the undersigned plenipotentiaries have signed this Treaty.

Done at Washington, the fourth day of April, 1949.
For the Kingdom of Belgium:
   P. H. SPAAK
   SILVERCRUYS

For Canada:
   LESTER B. PEARSON
   H. H. WRONG

For the Kingdom of Denmark:
   GUSTAV RASMUSSEN
   HENRIK KAUFFMAN

For France:
   SCHUMAN
   H. BONNET

For Iceland:
   BJARNI BENEDIKTSSON
   THORS THORS

For Italy:
   SFORZA
   ALBERTO TARCHIANI

For the Grand Duchy of Luxembourg:
   JOS BECH
   HUGUES LE GALLAIS

For the Kingdom of the Netherlands:
   STIKKER
   E. N. VAN KLEFFENS

For the Kingdom of Norway:
   HALVARD M. LANGE
   WILHELM MUNTHE MORGENSTIERNE

For Portugal:
   JOSÉ CAEIRO DA MATTA
   PEDRO THEÓTONIO PEREIRA

For the United Kingdom of Great Britain and Northern Ireland:
   ERNEST BEVIN
   OLIVER FRANKS

For the United States of America:
   DEAN ACHESON

I CERTIFY THAT the foregoing is a true copy of the North Atlantic Treaty signed at Washington on April 4, 1949 in the English and French languages, the signed original of which is deposited in the archives of the Government of the United States of America.

IN TESTIMONY WHEREOF, I, DEAN ACHESON, Secretary of State of the United States of America, have hereunto caused the seal of the Department of State to be affixed and my name subscribed by the Authentication Officer of the said Department, at the city of Washington, in the District of Columbia, this fourth day of April, 1949.

DEAN ACHESON
Secretary of State

[SEAL]   By M. P. CHAUVIN
Authentication Officer
Department of State

◇◇◇◇◇◇

237. NORTH ATLANTIC TREATY

Report of the Committee on Foreign Relations, June 6, 1949 [1]

[The report of the Senate Foreign Relations Committee on the North Atlantic Treaty is perhaps the best official interpretation of the Treaty from the U.S. point of view. The following excerpts from the report, which was unanimously adopted by the Committee, shed considerable light upon the exact meaning of the specific articles of the Treaty. The Committee's interpretation of our obligations under Article 5, and the President's use of armed forces abroad, is particularly significant.]

*   *   *

PART II. GENERAL NATURE OF THE TREATY

The treaty establishes a collective defense arrangement for the North Atlantic area within the framework of the United Nations Charter and based upon the inherent right of individual or collective self-defense recognized by article 51 of the Charter. In many respects it is similar to and patterned upon the Treaty of Rio de Janeiro.

The 12 signatories of the treaty are Belgium, Canada, Denmark, France, Iceland, Italy, Luxembourg, the Netherlands, Norway, Portugal, the United Kingdom, and the United States.

The treaty is subject to review at any time after 10 years and any party may cease to be a party after 20 years; otherwise it is of indefinite duration.

General objectives of the treaty

The primary objective of the treaty is to contribute to the maintenance of peace by making clear the determination of the parties collectively to resist armed attack upon any of them.

It is designed to strengthen the system of law based upon the purposes and principles of the United Nations. It should go far to remove any uncertainty which might mislead potential aggressors as to the determination of the parties fully to carry out their obligations under the Charter and collectively to resist an armed attack.

[1] Senate Executive Report No. 8, 81st Congress, 1st Session.

The security of the North Atlantic area is vital to the national security of the United States and of key importance to world peace and security. The peoples of the North Atlantic area are linked together not only by the interdependence of their security but by a common heritage and civilization and devotion to their free institutions, based upon the principles of democracy, individual liberty and the rule of law. It is this common heritage and civilization and these free institutions which the signatories are determined to defend.

The treaty is designed to contribute toward the further development of peaceful and friendly international relations, to strengthen the free institutions of the parties and promote better understanding of the principles upon which they are founded, to promote conditions of stability and well-being, and to encourage economic collaboration. It should facilitate long-term economic recovery through replacing the sense of insecurity by one of confidence in the future.

Although it is intended that the general machinery and procedures provided in the Charter would be utilized in cases of disputes between the signatories, the treaty can of course be used as a regional arrangement under the United Nations for dealing with such matters as are appropriate for regional action within the meaning of chapter VIII of the Charter.

The obligations of national defense and advancing the welfare of its people are inherent in any government. The obligations to settle international disputes by peaceful means and to refrain from the threat or use of force, expressly reaffirmed in the treaty, were undertaken by this Government when it ratified the United Nations Charter.

New obligations

The new obligations undertaken by the United States in the treaty are—

1. To maintain and develop, separately and jointly and by means of continuous and effective self-help and mutual aid, the individual and collective capacity of the parties to resist armed attack (art. 3);

2. To consult whenever, in the opinion of any of the parties, the territorial integrity, political independence, or security of any of them is threatened (art. 4);

3. To consider an armed attack upon any of the parties in the North Atlantic area an attack against them all (art. 5); and

4. In the event of such an attack, to take forthwith, individually and in concert with the other parties, such action as the United States deems necessary, including the use of armed force, to restore and maintain the security of the North Atlantic area (art. 5).

The treaty provides for a council and such subsidiary agencies as may be necessary, including a defense committee, to assist the parties in giving effect to the treaty.

Safeguards

The treaty in letter and in spirit is purely defensive. It is directed against no one; it is directed solely against aggression.

The treaty expressly provides that all of its provisions must be carried out in accordance with the respective constitutional processes of the parties.

The provisions of the treaty are expressly subordinated to the purposes, principles, and provisions of the United Nations Charter. The provisions of the Charter, wherever applicable, control every activity undertaken under the treaty.

PART III. ANALYSIS AND INTERPRETATION

PREAMBLE

*   *   *

The purposes and spirit of the treaty

The preamble states clearly and simply the purpose, intent, and spirit of the treaty. The committee endorses this declaration, which is formal recognition of the common interests, developing unity, and increasing interdependence of the North Atlantic community.

It should be emphasized, however, that the preamble is no expression of narrow regionalism for the members' will to live in peace is "with all peoples and all governments"—the primary purpose of the Charter of the United Nations. Moreover, peace, stability, and well-being in the North Atlantic area are of universal advantage in the cause of peace.

While cognizant of the elements of common heritage and civilization, and of mutually acceptable principles, there is no intent to impose these upon other peoples. There is the determination, however, to safeguard the fundamental and dynamic nature of this common heritage which includes, under God, the basic moral principles of democracy, individual liberty, and the rule of law.

ARTICLE 1.—PEACEFUL SETTLEMENT OF DISPUTES

*   *   *

In this article the members of the pact reaffirm the solemn obligations which they have accepted under the United Nations Charter to settle all their international disputes by peaceful means. The committee is convinced that the entire text of the treaty, and particularly this article, makes abundantly clear the will of the signatories for peace and their desire to threaten no one.

*   *   *

By becoming parties to the treaty, countries which are not members of the United Nations, such as Italy and Portugal, accept the obligations set forth in article 2 of the Charter to settle any international disputes in which they may be involved by peaceful means in such a manner that international peace and security and justice are not endangered. Article 33 and other articles of the Charter set forth means of settling such disputes which are available for nonmembers as well as members of the United Nations.

ARTICLE 2.—DEVELOPMENT OF PEACEFUL AND FRIENDLY RELATIONS

*   *   *

Article 2 is a reaffirmation of faith. It demonstrates the conviction of the parties that peace is positive and dynamic, that real peace is far more than the mere absence of war. The parties undertake to strengthen their free institutions, promote conditions of stability and well-being, and encourage economic collaboration.

The unilateral undertaking of the parties to "strengthen their free institutions" recognizes that free institutions have succumbed in many places of the world and that eternal vigilance is still the price of liberty. The effort to secure "better understanding" of the principles upon which these institutions are based is a positive appreciation of the role of public opinion, both among the signatories and throughout the world. Free nations must take affirmative measures to this end, rather than resort to censorship or iron curtains. The gospel of freedom can best be spread by example.

The committee supports these objectives as desirable goals to be sought by the signatory parties. It believes that their progressive attainment will contribute to stability, well-being, and real peace.

No legislative action required

Considerable attention has been given by the committee to the question whether article 2, in stating these objectives, imposes on the United States any obligation to take specific legislative action. Would the references to "strengthening free institutions" and "eliminate conflict in their international economic policies," for example, mean that we would be obligated to enact additional legislation relating to civil rights, the reduction of tariffs, and similar matters?

The committee is completely satisfied that this article involves no obligation on us to take any legislative action whatsoever. In fact, no such obligations were contemplated by the negotiators and no new machinery is envisaged for these purposes under the treaty. The article does, however, provide encouragement for individual or bilateral action or action through such existing agencies as the United Nations, the Brussels pact, and the Organization of European Economic Co-operation.

The committee finds no implication whatever in article 2 that the United States could be called upon under the treaty to contribute toward a long-term recovery program for Europe.

> ARTICLE 3.—SELF-HELP AND MUTUAL AID

*   *   *

Article 3 embodies in the treaty the principle of continuous and effective self-help and mutual aid established by Senate Resolution 239 as a prerequisite to United States association in any collective defense arrangement. * * *

A realistic assessment of the defensive capacity necessary to resist armed attack will be a function of the organization to be established under article 9. On the basis of this assessment each party would determine for itself what it could most effectively contribute in the form of facilities, military equipment, productive capacity, manpower, etc. This decision would be taken in the light of the resources and geographical location of the individual state and with due regard for its economic stability. There is no specific obligation as to the timing, nature, and extent of assistance to be given by any party.

Clearly the capacity of the member states to resist armed attack depends primarily upon their basic economic health. The committee, therefore, fully agrees with the view of the signatories that measures to increase the military strength of the parties must not be permitted to prevent achievement of the objectives of the European recovery program.

It has been suggested in some quarters that article 3 might be interpreted in such a way as to provide the basis for an armaments race. The committee rejects any such interpretation. Capacity to resist armed attack includes all elements, including economic strength, and is relative to the degree of danger and the strength of potential aggressors. If the treaty and the United Nations are successful in providing substantially increased security, it should be possible to have greater capacity to resist armed attack with smaller military forces. The essential objective is increased security, not increased military strength

Questions have also been raised as to whether the United States, under article 3, would be obligated to assist the other parties to develop the capacity of their overseas territories to resist armed attack. The objective of the treaty is to maintain the peace and security of the North Atlantic area. During the negotiations there were no suggestions that this article should be interpreted as applying to any other area. The United States is under no obligation to assist the other parties in building up military establishments for use in their overseas territories, nor to engage in resisting armed attack outside the area defined in article 6.

The committee calls attention to the fact that the United States stands to gain great benefits from the principle of "continuous and effective self-help and mutual aid." Implementation of this principle will not only help deter aggression but will go far, in the event all the efforts of the parties for peace should fail, to assure the successful defense of the United States and the collective strength essential for victory.

ARTICLE 4.—CONSULTATION

* * *

In article 4 the parties undertake to consult whenever any party so requests on the basis that the territorial integrity, political independence, or security of any of them is threatened. A situation arising anywhere might be cause for consultation, provided that it constituted a threat to one or more of the parties and might involve obligations under the treaty. The committee underlines the fact that consultation could be requested only when the element of threat is present and expresses the opinion that this limitation should be strictly interpreted.

Many well-known techniques have been developed whereby internal disorders or coups are deliberately engineered by outside powers to further their own interests. Accordingly, consultation might also be sought under article 4 in the case of an internal disorder where circumstances indicated that such disorder was being aided and abetted by assistance from outside the country affected.

Article 4 carries no obligation other than that of consultation. Whether or not any action was taken following consultation, or what form such action might take, would be matters for each party to decide for itself. It should be emphasized, however, that in no event is collective enforcement action, such as that defined in articles 41 and 42 of the Charter, contemplated.

*   *   *

♪ ARTICLE 5.—ACTION IN THE EVENT OF ARMED ATTACK

*   *   *

Article 5 is the heart of the treaty. In it the parties establish the principle that an armed attack against one or more of them is to be considered an attack against them all. In accepting this principle, the committee believes that the United States is acting on the basis of a realization brought about by its experience in two world wars that an armed attack in the North Atlantic area is in effect an attack on itself. The solemn acceptance of this principle by all the parties should have a powerful deterring effect on any would-be aggressor by making clear to him in advance that his attack would be met by the combined resistance of all the nations in the North Atlantic Pact.

*   *   *

Determination whether attack has occurred

The committee notes that article 5 would come into operation only when a nation had committed an international crime by launching an armed attack against a party to the treaty. The first question which would arise would be whether or not an armed attack had in fact occurred. If the circumstances were not clear, there would presumably be consultation but each party would have the responsibility of determining for itself the answer to this question of fact.

*   *   *

Obviously, purely internal disorders or revolutions would not be considered "armed attack" within the meaning of article 5. However, if a revolution were aided and abetted by an outside power such assistance might possibly be considered an armed attack. Each party would have to decide, in the light of the circumstances surrounding the case and the nature and extent of the assistance, whether, in fact, an armed attack had occurred and article 5 thus brought into play.

"Such action as it deems necessary"

The second problem is the nature and extent of the action contemplated as a result of armed attack. The action specified is that deemed necessary to "restore and maintain the security of the North Atlantic area." The committee emphasizes that this clearly does not commit any of the parties to declare war. Depending upon the gravity of the attack, there are numerous measures short of the use of armed force which might be sufficient to deal with the situation. Such measures could involve anything from a diplomatic protest to the most severe forms of pressure.

In this connection, the committee calls particular attention to the phrase "such action as it deems necessary." These words were included in article 5 to make absolutely clear that each party remains free to exercise its honest judgment in deciding upon the measures it will take to help restore and maintain the security of the North Atlantic area. The freedom of decision as to what action each party shall take in no way reduces the importance of the commitment undertaken. Action short of the use of armed force might suffice, or total war with all our resources might be necessary. Obviously article 5 carries with it an important and far-reaching commitment for the United States; what we may do to carry out that commitment, however, will depend upon our own independent decision in each particular instance reached in accordance with our own constitutional processes.

President and Congress

During the hearings substantially the following questions were repeatedly asked: In view of the provision in article 5 that an attack against one shall be considered an attack against all, would the United States be obligated to react to an attack on Paris or Copenhagen in the same way it would react to an attack on New York City? In such an event does the treaty give the President the power to take any action, without specific congressional authorization, which he could not take in the absence of the treaty?

The answer to both these questions is "No." An armed attack upon any State of the United States by its very nature would require the immediate application of all force necessary to repel the attack. The Constitution itself recognizes the special significance of such a calamity by providing that the United States shall protect each State against invasion. Similarly, the government of any nation party to the treaty would feel itself under obligation and under imminent physical need to give the highest priority to essential countermeasures to meet an armed attack upon its own homeland.

In the event any party to the treaty were attacked the obligation of the United States Government would be to decide upon and take forthwith the measures it deemed necessary to restore and maintain the security of the North Atlantic area. The measures which would be necessary to accomplish that end would depend upon a number of factors, including the location, nature, scale, and significance of the attack. The decision as to what action was necessary, and the action itself, would of course have to be taken in accordance with established constitutional procedures as the treaty in article 11 expressly requires.

Article 5 records what is a fact, namely, that an armed attack within the meaning of the treaty would in the present-day world constitute an attack upon the entire community comprising the parties to the treaty, including the United States. Accordingly, the President and the Congress, each within their sphere of assigned constitutional responsibilities, would be expected to take all action necessary and appropriate to protect the United States against the consequences and dangers of an armed attack committed against any party to the treaty. The committee does not believe it appropriate in this report to undertake to define the authority of the President to use the armed forces. Nothing in the treaty, however, including the provision that an attack against one shall be considered an attack against all, increases or decreases the constitutional powers of either the President or the Congress or changes the relationship between them.

Duration of action

Measures may be taken under article 5 only when an armed attack has occurred and must be terminated whenever the Security Council has taken the measures necessary to restore and maintain international peace and security. Thus action under article 5 will never be necessary unless the Security Council has been unable to meet its responsibilities and must cease whenever the Security Council has regained control of the situation. The treaty, like article 51 of the Charter, provides insurance against a situation which the Security Council is unable to control. The committee is convinced that the treaty, in making clear that an aggressor could not profit from such a situation, provides a valuable supplement to the Charter in reducing the possibility that it might arise.

ARTICLE 6.—DESCRIPTION OF NORTH ATLANTIC AREA

*   *   *

Article 6 specifies the area within which an armed attack would bring the provisions of article 5 into operation. Thus, the obligations under article 5 are strictly limited to the area described.

The word "area" is intended to cover the general region, rather merely the North Atlantic Ocean in a narrow sense, and includes the western part of the Mediterranean as well as the North Sea and most of the Gulf of Mexico. Western Europe faces on the Atlantic even if all the nations of the western European community do not.

In view of the purpose of the treaty to deter armed attack, the area covered by the treaty was deliberately described in general terms rather than defined by lines on a map. The committee agrees that this general description is preferable, for it would seem inconsistent with the spirit of the treaty to provide that article 5 would come into operation in the event of an attack, for example, upon ships or aircraft at a given point but not if the attack occurred a few miles away. If there should be any doubt as to whether or not an armed attack has taken place within the area specified in the treaty, each party would decide for itself, in the light of the facts surrounding the particular situation and the significance of the attack.

Not applicable to overseas territories

*   *   *

The committee wishes to emphasize the fact that article 5 would not apply to any of the overseas territories outside the North Atlantic area as described in article 6. The three Algerian departments of France (which constitute only a small part of the total territory of Algeria) are an integral part of metropolitan France under the French Constitution and are not overseas possessions. The only outlying territories covered are the islands in the North Atlantic area, Alaska, the Aleutian Islands, and the islands of the Canadian Arctic.

ARTICLE 7.—PARAMOUNT AUTHORITY OF THE UNITED NATIONS

* * *

Lest there be any misunderstanding about the relative position of the treaty and the United Nations Charter, article 7 makes clear the overriding character of the Charter with respect to the obligations of the signatories who are also members of the United Nations. This principle is in accordance with the provisions of article 103 of the Charter which stipulates that—

In the event of a conflict between the obligations of the Members of the United Nations under the present Charter and their obligations under any other international agreement, their obligations under the present Charter shall prevail.

The provisions of the Charter thus govern, wherever they may be applicable, any activities undertaken under the treaty.

The Charter also bestows upon the Security Council the primary responsibility for the maintenance of international peace and security. In the opinion of the committee the treaty rightly recognizes the primary responsibility of the Security Council in this field and makes clear the intent of the signatories not to compete with this responsibility or interfere with it in any way.

This desire not to compete with or impair the authority of the United Nations is applicable not only to the Security Council but to other organs of the United Nations, which, the committee understands, the parties intend to use wherever appropriate.

ARTICLE 8.—POSSIBLE CONFLICT WITH OTHER TREATIES

* * *

Before the details of the Atlantic Pact were made public, considerable concern was expressed lest its terms conflict with certain treaties and agreements already in force. Both France and Great Britain, for example, have treaties of alliance negotiated with the Soviet Union during World War II, which obligate the parties to assist one another in the event of an attack by Germany, of any state associated with Germany in the war, and not to conclude any alliance, or take part in any coalition, directed against either party. The Soviet Government asserts that under these treaties France and Britain could not become parties to the pact. The committee thinks it is perfectly obvious that the treaty is not an alliance or coalition directed against any nation, but that it is directed solely against aggression.

* * *

Italian peace treaty

The committee also examined the terms of the Italian peace treaty, which limit the size of the Italian armed forces and the extent to which rearmament will be possible. Given these limitations the question naturally arises as to whether Italy could live up to her obligations under article 3 of the Atlantic Pact to develop her capacity to resist armed attack. The matter is adequately disposed of by the following statement supplied for the record by the State Department:

It is understood by all parties to the treaty that the participation of Italy in the North Atlantic Pact has no effect on the military provisions, or any other provisions, of the Italian peace treaty. Any contribution which Italy makes to the collective capacity for defense of the North Atlantic area must be within the limits fixed by the military provisions of the Italian peace treaty.

ARTICLE 9.—ORGANIZATION UNDER THE TREATY

*   *   *

While some machinery is clearly necessary for the effective implementation of the treaty, it would be inadvisable to attempt to elaborate this machinery in detail in the treaty. On the contrary, it is preferable that the machinery be described only in broad outline in order that the specific organization may be evolved in the light of need and experience. The committee urges that the organization set up be as simple as possible consistent with its function of assisting implementation of the treaty and that maximum use be made of existing organizations.

Unanimous agreement is required to invite other states to join the treaty. Other European states in the North Atlantic area may in the future be considered desirable additions to the pact and in a position to accede to it. Since the other American Republics are already signatories of the Rio Treaty no provision was made for their accession to this pact.

Senate action necessary on new members

Inasmuch as the admission of new members might radically alter our obligations under the pact, the committee examined article 10 very carefully. The question arose whether any United States decision respecting new members would be based solely on Presidential action or would require Senate approval. Consequently, the committee was fully satisfied by the commitment of the President, delivered by the Secretary of State, that he would consider the admission of a new member to the pact as the conclusion of a new treaty with that member and would seek the advice and consent of the Senate to each such admission. The committee considers this an obligation binding upon the Presidential office.

Spain and Germany

The signatory countries did not invite Spain to participate though it is recognized that Spain is strategically important to the defense of the North Atlantic area. Whether Spain will be invited to participate at a later date will depend upon the unanimous decision of the parties.

So many imponderables affect the current position of Germany, which is still under military occupation, that in the negotiations extensive consideration was not given to the inclusion of western Germany. Presumably, Germany will be reunited one day, but time is required so that the German people may prove their attachment to the principles of the treaty. Meanwhile, it should be noted that Germany receives some protection since the treaty covers armed attack upon the occupation forces.

* * *

The committee and the Senate, in Senate Resolution 239, attached great importance to assuring that any such agreement as the pact would not only be ratified in accordance with the "respective constitutional processes" of the signatory nations, but also that all its provisions would be carried out under the same constitutional safeguards. Constitutional processes for giving effect to the will of the people are the very essence of democracy and it is only through wide popular support that the treaty can be given the strength and vitality necessary to assure its success.

The committee wishes to emphasize the fact that the protective clause "in accordance with their respective constitutional processes" was placed in article 11 in order to leave no doubt that it applies not only to article 5, for example, but to every provision in the treaty. The safeguard is thus all-inclusive.

The treaty in no way affects the basic division of authority between the President and the Congress as defined in the Constitution. In no way does it alter the constitutional relationship between them. In particular, it does not increase, decrease, or change the power of the President as Commander in Chief of the armed forces or impair the full authority of Congress to declare war.

Except for the proposed foreign military assistance program, no legislation related to the treaty is presently contemplated or considered necessary. The treaty would constitute legislative authorization for our share of the expenses of the organization contemplated in article 9, but appropriations by Congress would be necessary. As the United States representatives on the council and the defense committee will have no authority to bind the United States Government, the committee believes that officials previously appointed with the confirmation of the Senate will not require further confirmation for these assignments.

Effectiveness of the democratic process

It has been questioned whether a treaty subordinating action to the constitutional processes of 12 democratic nations offers sufficient certainty and immediacy of action effectively to deter aggression. The committee is convinced that it does. The expression of the will of a whole people offers far more certainty than any commitment by a dictator. The action of the democracies in the past great war is concrete evidence of their ability to ict with the necessary speed in the event of an emergency.

* * *

ARTICLE 12.—REVIEW AND AMENDMENT OF TREATY

* * *

The treaty takes into account the processes of peaceful change and the need for flexibility in a rapidly changing world by providing that its terms may be reviewed at any time after it has been in force 10 years. Of course, earlier review is possible by unanimous consent. For purposes of review, the signatories will take into account the factors affecting peace and security in the North Atlantic area. The committee draws particular attention to the explicit reference that developments in the United Nations, including universal as well as regional arrangements, will figure significantly among such factors.

Apart from the general review contemplated in article 12 the treaty makes no provision for particular amendments. If such amendments were advanced, they would require the unanimous approval of the signatory states. In our own case the advice and consent of the Senate would be required. The committee believes that the interests of the United States would be amply protected by these safeguards.

ARTICLE 13.—DURATION OF TREATY

* * *

This article provides that after the treaty has been in effect for 20 years any party may cease to be a party 1 year after notice of denunciation has been given. There is no provision for individual members to withdraw prior to that time.

The committee gave serious thought to the problems involved in the duration of the treaty. In view of the difficulties of forecasting developments in the international situation in the distant future, rigidity for too long a time clearly would be undesirable. On the other hand, the committee agrees that the stability and confidence which are so essential for the security of the North Atlantic area could not adequately be established if the treaty were of short duration. It accepts as a desirable solution, therefore, the indefinite duration of the treaty, with provision for review after 10 years, and for withdrawal after 20 years.

* * *

PART V. CONCLUSIONS AND RECOMMENDATIONS

1. NEED FOR RATIFICATION

The committee believes that our failure to ratify the North Atlantic Treaty would have disastrous consequences abroad. At the present time there is an encouraging momentum of confidence that has been building up in Europe during the past year as a direct result of our interest and assistance. The failure of the political strikes in France, the Communist losses in the Italian and French elections in 1948 and 1949, the recent success of the French internal loan and the increased strength of the western European currencies generally, the recent agreements on Germany, and the success of the recovery program—all these things reflect this growing momentum.

The great retarding factor in the European situation has been the pervading sense of insecurity. This sense of insecurity has been lessened during the past year as a direct result of American interest in common security problems as demonstrated by the passage of Senate Resolution 239 and our willingness to negotiate and sign the North Atlantic Treaty. The decision on the part of some of the European nations, such as Norway and Denmark, to participate in the treaty was not taken without full regard for the risks inherent in making clear their determination to resist aggression.

The committee strongly believes that it would be in the best interests of the United States and indeed, the entire world, to sustain and encourage the momentum of confidence that has been building up in Europe, by ratifying the treaty at an early date.

2. SUMMARY OF REASONS COMMITTEE URGES RATIFICATION

On June 6 the committee unanimously agreed to report the treaty to the Senate for favorable action. Its reasons for recommending ratification include the following:

(1) The treaty should greatly increase the prospect that another war can be averted by making clear in advance the determination of these 12 nations of the North Atlantic area to throw their collective power and influence into the scales on the side of peace.

(2) It expresses in concrete terms the will of the American people, and the other peoples of the North Atlantic area, to work constantly to maintain peace and freedom.

(3) Since the course of action envisaged in the treaty is substantially that which the United States would follow without the treaty, there is great advantage to the United States and the entire world in making clear our intentions in advance.

(4) The treaty is expressly subordinated to the purposes, principles, and provisions of the United Nations Charter and is designed to foster those conditions of peace and stability in the world which are essential if the United Nations is to function successfully.

(5) It is wholly consistent with our Constitution and stipulates that all its provisions shall be carried out in accordance with the constitutional processes of the participating countries.

(6) The treaty is in accordance with the basic interests of the United States, which would be steadfastly served regardless of fluctuations in the international situation or our relations with any country.

(7) In strengthening the security of the North Atlantic area the treaty greatly increases the national security of the United States.

(8) It is strictly in accordance with the Senate's recommendation, expressed last year in Senate Resolution 239, that the United States should associate itself with collective defense arrangements and thus contribute to the maintenance of peace by making clear its determination to defend itself against any armed attack affecting its national security.

(9) The treaty will greatly increase the determination of the North Atlantic states to resist aggression and their confidence that they can successfully do so.

(10) It will free the minds of men in many nations from a haunting sense of insecurity and enable them to work and plan with that confidence in the future which is essential to economic recovery and progress.

(11) By encouraging this feeling of confidence and security it should eventually make possible substantial savings for the United States both in connection with the European recovery program and our domestic Military Establishment.

(12) The treaty is essential to the development of that degree of unity

and security among the North Atlantic states which will make possible the reintegration of Germany into western Europe and the ultimate solution of the German problem.

(13) It will greatly stimulate the efforts of the North Atlantic states to help themselves and to help each other and, through proper coordination of these efforts, to achieve maximum benefits with minimum costs and bring far greater strength than could be achieved by each acting alone.

(14) In the event our efforts for peace are undermined and war is imposed upon us, the treaty assures us that 11 other nations will stand with us to defend our freedom and our civilization.

(15) The treaty is not confined to the prevention of war but reflects the will of the participating nations to strengthen the moral and material foundations of lasting peace and freedom.

*   *   *

In tendering this unanimous report on the North Atlantic Treaty, we do so in furtherance of our Nation's most precious heritage—shared in common with the other signatories—continuing faith in our dependence upon Almighty God and His guidance in the affairs of men and nations.

◇◇◇◇◇◇

238. MUTUAL DEFENSE ASSISTANCE ACT OF 1949, AS AMENDED [1]

[After World War II, the United States extended military aid to various countries. But this aid had been sporadic and was not adequate to restore the defense systems of the States involved to an efficient basis. The Mutual Defense Assistance Act of 1949 provided a coördinated program of assistance not only to the North Atlantic Treaty states but to Greece and Turkey, Iran, Korea, the Philippines, and the general area of China. The most important provisions of the basic law as amended in 1950 are reproduced below. Over $6 billion were appropriated for the purposes of the Act during 1949 and 1950.]

AN ACT

To promote the foreign policy and provide for the defense and general welfare of the United States by furnishing military assistance to foreign nations.

Be it enacted by the Senate and House of Representatives of the United States of America in Congress assembled, That this Act may be cited as the "Mutual Defense Assistance Act of 1949".

FINDINGS AND DECLARATION OF POLICY

The Congress of the United States reaffirms the policy of the United States to achieve international peace and security through the United Nations so that armed force shall not be used except in the common interest. The Congress hereby finds that the efforts of the United States and other countries to promote peace and security in furtherance of the purposes of the Charter

---

[1] Public Law 329, 81st Cong. (approved October 6, 1949), incorporating amendments made by Public Law 621, 81st Cong. (approved July 26, 1950).

of the United Nations require additional measures of support based upon the principle of continuous and effective self-help and mutual aid. These measures include the furnishing of military assistance essential to enable the United States and other nations dedicated to the purposes and principles of the United Nations Charter to participate effectively in arrangements for individual and collective self-defense in support of those purposes and principles. In furnishing such military assistance, it remains the policy of the United States to continue to exert maximum efforts to obtain agreements to provide the United Nations with armed forces as contemplated in the Charter and agreements to achieve universal control of weapons of mass destruction and universal regulation and reduction of armaments, including armed forces, under adequate safeguards to protect complying nations against violation and evasion.

The Congress hereby expresses itself as favoring the creation by the free countries and the free peoples of the Far East of a joint organization, consistent with the Charter of the United Nations, to establish a program of self-help and mutual cooperation designed to develop their economic and social well-being, to safeguard basic rights and liberties and to protect their security and independence.

The Congress recognizes that economic recovery is essential to international peace and security and must be given clear priority. The Congress also recognizes that the increased confidence of free peoples in their ability to resist direct or indirect aggression and to maintain internal security will advance such recovery and support political stability.

Title I: North Atlantic Treaty Countries

Sec. 101. In view of the coming into force of the North Atlantic Treaty and the establishment thereunder of the Council and the Defense Committee which will recommend measures for the common defense of the North Atlantic area, and in view of the fact that the task of the Council and the Defense Committee can be facilitated by immediate steps to increase the integrated defensive armed strength of the parties to the treaty, the President is hereby authorized to furnish military assistance in the form of equipment, materials, and services to such nations as are parties to the treaty and request such assistance. Any such assistance furnished under this title shall be subject to agreements, further referred to in section 402, designed to assure that the assistance will be used to promote an integrated defense of the North Atlantic area and to facilitate the development of defense plans by the Council and the Defense Committee under article 9 of the North Atlantic Treaty and to realize unified direction and effort; and after the agreement by the Government of the United States with defense plans as recommended by the Council and the Defense Committee, military assistance hereunder shall be furnished only in accordance therewith.

Sec. 102. (a) There are hereby authorized to be appropriated to the President for the period through June 30, 1950, out of any moneys in the Treasury not otherwise appropriated, for carrying out the provisions and accomplishing the policies and purposes of this title, not to exceed $500,000,-000, of which not to exceed $100,000,000 shall be immediately available upon appropriation, and not to exceed $400,000,000 shall become available when the President of the United States approves recommendations for an integrated defense of the North Atlantic area which may be made by the Council and the Defense Committee to be established under the North Atlantic Treaty. The recommendations which the President may approve shall be limited, so far as expenditures by the United States are concerned, entirely to the amount herein authorized to be appropriated and the amount authorized hereinafter as contract authority.

(b) In addition to the amounts heretofore authorized to be appropriated, there are hereby authorized to be appropriated to the President for the year ending June 30, 1951, out of any money in the Treasury not otherwise appropriated, for carrying out the provisions and accomplishing the policies and purposes of this title, not to exceed $1,000,000,000.

SEC. 103. In addition to the amount authorized to be appropriated under section 102, the President shall have authority, within the limits of specific contract authority which may be hereafter granted to him in an appropriation Act, to enter into contracts for carrying out the provisions and accomplishing the policies and purposes of this title in amounts not exceeding in the aggregate $500,000,000 during the period ending June 30, 1950, and there are hereby authorized to be appropriated for expenditure after June 30, 1950, such sums as may be necessary to pay obligations incurred under such contract authorization. No contract authority which may be granted pursuant to the provisions of this section shall be exercised by the President until such time as he has approved recommendations for an integrated defense of the North Atlantic area which may be made by the Council and the Defense Committee to be established under the North Atlantic Treaty.

SEC. 104. None of the funds made available for carrying out the provisions of this Act or the Act of May 22, 1947, as amended, shall be utilized (a) to construct or aid in the construction of any factory or of other manufacturing establishment outside of the United States or to provide equipment (other than production equipment, including machine tools) for any such factory or other manufacturing establishment, (b) to defray the cost of maintaining any such factory or other manufacturing establishment, (c) directly or indirectly to compensate any nation or any governmental agency or person therein for any diminution in the export trade of such nation resulting from the carrying out of any program of increased military production or to make any payment, in the form of a bonus, subsidy, indemnity, guaranty, or otherwise, to an owner of any such factory or other manufacturing establishment as an inducement to such owner to undertake or increase production of arms, ammunition, implements of war, or other military supplies, or (d) for the compensation of any person for personal services rendered in or for any such factory or other manufacturing establishment, other than personal services of a technical nature rendered by officers and employees of the United States for the purpose of establishing or maintaining production by such factories or other manufacturing establishments to effectuate the purposes of this Act and in conformity with desired standards and specifications.

TITLE II: GREECE, TURKEY, AND IRAN

SEC. 201 (a) In addition to the amounts heretofore authorized to be appropriated, there are hereby authorized to be appropriated, out of any moneys in the Treasury not otherwise appropriated, not to exceed $211,370,000 to carry out the provisions of the Act of May 22, 1947, as amended, for the period through June 30, 1950.

(b) In addition to the amounts heretofore authorized to be appropriated, there are hereby authorized to be appropriated, out of any moneys in the Treasury not otherwise appropriated, not to exceed $211,370,000 to carry out the provisions of the Act of May 22, 1947, as amended, and for the purpose of furnishing military assistance to Iran as provided in this Act, for the year ending June 30, 1951. Whenever the furnishing of such assistance will further the purposes and policies of this Act, the President is authorized to furnish military assistance as provided in this Act to Iran.

Title III: Other Assistance

Sec. 301. The President, whenever the furnishing of such assistance will further the purposes and policies of this Act, is authorized to furnish military assistance as provided in this Act to the Republic of Korea, and the Republic of the Philippines.

Sec. 302. (a) There are hereby authorized to be appropriated to the President for the period through June 30, 1950, out of any moneys in the Treasury not otherwise appropriated, for carrying out the provisions and accomplishing the purposes of section 301, not to exceed $27,640,000.

(b) In addition to the amounts heretofore authorized to be appropriated, there are hereby authorized to be appropriated to the President for the year ending June 30, 1951, out of any moneys in the Treasury not otherwise appropriated, for carrying out the provisions and accomplishing the purposes of section 301, as amended, not to exceed $16,000,000.

Sec. 303 (a) In consideration of the concern of the United States in the present situation in China, there is hereby authorized to be appropriated to the President, out of any moneys in the Treasury not otherwise appropriated, the sum of $75,000,000 in addition to funds otherwise provided as an emergency fund for the President, which may be expended to accomplish in that general area the policies and purposes declared in this Act. Certification by the President of the amounts expended out of funds authorized hereunder, and that it is inadvisable to specify the nature of such expenditures, shall be deemed a sufficient voucher for the amounts expended.

(b) In addition to the amounts heretofore authorized to be appropriated, there are hereby authorized to be appropriated to the President, out of any moneys in the Treasury not otherwise appropriated, the sum of $75,000,000, to be used as provided in subsection (a) of this section, of which not more than $35,000,000 may be accounted for as therein provided and any amount accounted for in such manner shall, with the exception of $7,500,000, be reported to the Committee on Foreign Relations of the Senate, the Committees on Armed Services of the Senate and of the House of Representatives, and the Committee on Foreign Affairs of the House of Representatives.

Title IV: General Provisions

Sec. 401. Military assistance may be furnished under this Act, without payment to the United States except as provided in the agreements concluded pursuant to section 402, by the provision of any service, or by the procurement from any source and the transfer to eligible nations of equipment, materials, and services: *Provided,* That no equipment or materials may be transferred out of military stocks if the Secretary of Defense, after consultation with the Joint Chiefs of Staff, determines that such transfer would be detrimental to the national security of the United States or is needed by the reserve components of the armed forces to meet their training requirements.

SEC. 402. The President shall, prior to the furnishing of assistance to any eligible nation, conclude agreements with such nation, or group of such nations, which agreements, in addition to such other provisions as the President deems necessary to effectuate the policies and purposes of this Act and to safeguard the interests of the United States, shall make appropriate provision for—

(a) the use of any assistance furnished under this Act in furtherance of the policies and purposes of this Act;

(b) restriction against transfer of title to or possession of any equipment and materials, information or services furnished under this Act without the consent of the President;

(c) the security of any article, service, or information furnished under this Act;

(d) furnishing equipment and materials, services, or other assistance, consistent with the Charter of the United Nations, to the United States or to and among other eligible nations to further the policies and purposes of this Act.

SEC. 403.

*   *   *

(d) Not to exceed $450,000,000 worth of excess equipment and materials may be furnished under this Act or may hereafter be furnished under the Act of May 22, 1947, as amended: *Provided,* That during the fiscal year ending June 30, 1951, an additional $250,000,000 worth of excess equipment and materials may be so furnished. For the purposes of this subsection, the worth of any excess equipment or materials means either the actual gross cost to the United States of that particular equipment or materials or the estimated gross cost to the United States of that particular equipment or materials obtained by multiplying the number of units of such particular equipment or materials by the average gross cost of each unit of that equipment or materials owned by the furnishing agency.

*   *   *

SEC. 405. The President shall terminate all or part of any assistance authorized by this Act under any of the following circumstances:

(a) If requested by any nation to which assistance is being rendered;

(b) If the President determines that the furnishing of assistance to any nation is no longer consistent with the national interest or security of the United States or the policies and purposes of this Act; or

(c) If the President determines that provision of assistance would contravene any decision of the Security Council of the United Nations, or if the President otherwise determines that provision of assistance to any nation would be inconsistent with the obligation of the United States under the

Charter of the United Nations to refrain from giving assistance to any nation against which the United Nations is taking preventive or enforcement action or in respect of which the General Assembly finds the continuance of such assistance is undesirable.

(d) If, in the case of any nation, which is a party to the North Atlantic Treaty, the President determines after consultation with the North Atlantic Treaty Council that such nation is not making its full contribution through self-help and mutual assistance in all practicable forms to the common defense of the North Atlantic area; and in the case of any other nation, if the President determines that such nation is not making its full contribution to its own defense or to the defense of the area of which it is a part.

(e) Assistance to any nation under this Act may, unless sooner terminated by the President, be terminated by concurrent resolution by the two Houses of the Congress: *Provided,* That funds made available under this Act shall remain available for twelve months from the date of such termination for the necessary expenses of liquidating contracts, obligations, and operations under this Act.

* * *

SEC. 408.

* * *

(c) Whenever he determines that such action is essential for the effective carrying out of the purposes of this Act, the President may from time to time utilize not to exceed in the aggregate 10 per centum of the funds and contract authority made available for the purposes of any title of this Act for the purposes of any other title, or in the event of a development seriously affecting the security of the North Atlantic area for the purpose of providing military assistance to any other European nation whose strategic location makes it of direct importance to the defense of the North Atlantic area and whose immediately increased ability to defend itself, the President, after consultation with the governments of the other nations which are members of the North Atlantic Treaty, finds contributes to the preservation of the peace and security of the North Atlantic area and is vital to the security of the United States. Whenever the President makes any such determination he shall forthwith notify the Committee on Foreign Relations of the Senate, the Committees on Armed Services of the Senate and of the House of Representatives, and the Committee on Foreign Affairs of the House of Representatives.

* * *

(e) (1) The President may, from time to time, in the interest of achieving standardization of military equipment and in order to provide procurement assistance without cost to the United States, transfer, or enter into contracts for the procurement for transfer of, equipment, materials or services to: (A) nations eligible for assistance under title I, II, or III of this Act, (B) a nation which has joined with the United States in a collective defense and regional arrangement, or (C) any other nation not eligible to join a collective defense and regional arrangement referred to in clause (B) above, but whose ability to defend itself or to participate in the defense of the area of which it is a part, is important to the security of the United States: *Provided,* That, prior to the transfer of any equipment, materials, or services to a nation under this clause (C), it shall provide the United States with assurance that such equipment, materials, or services are required for and will be used solely to maintain its internal security, its legitimate self-defense, or to permit it to participate in the defense of the area of which it is a part, and that it will not undertake any act of aggression against any other state: *Provided further,* That, in the case of any such transfer, the President shall forthwith notify the Committee on Foreign Relations of the Senate, the Committees on Armed Services of the Senate and of the House of Representatives, and the Committee on Foreign Affairs of the House of Representatives.

(2) Whenever equipment or material is transferred from the stocks of, or services are rendered by, any agency, to any nation as provided in paragraph (1) above, such nation shall first make available the fair value, as determined by the President, of such equipment, materials, or services. The fair value shall not be less for the various categories of equipment or materials than the "value" as defined in subsection (c) of section 403: *Provided* That, with respect to excess equipment or materials the fair value may not be determined to be less than the value specified in paragraph 1 of that subsection plus (a) 10 per centum of the original gross cost of such equipment or materials; (b) the scrap value; or (c) the market value, if ascertainable, whichever is the greater. Before a contract is entered into, such nation shall (A) provide the United States with a dependable undertaking to pay the full amount of such contract which will assure the United States against any loss on the contract, and (B) shall make funds available in such amounts and at such times as may be necessary to meet the payments required by the contract in advance of the time such payments are due, in addition to the estimated amount of any damages and costs that may accrue from the cancellation of such contract: *Provided,* That the total amount of outstanding contracts under this subsection, less the amounts which have been paid the United States by such nations, shall at no time exceed $100,000,000.

(f) Any equipment or materials procured to carry out the purposes of title I of this Act shall be retained by, or transferred to, and for the use of, such department or agency of the United States as the President may determine in lieu of being disposed of to a nation which is a party to the North Atlantic Treaty whenever in the judgment of the President of the United States such disposal to a foreign nation will not promote the self-help, mutual aid, and collective capacity to resist armed attack contemplated by the treaty or whenever such retention is called for by concurrent resolution by the two Houses of the Congress.

SEC. 409. That at least 50 per centum of the gross tonnage of any equipment, materials, or commodities made available under the provisions of this Act, and transported on ocean vessels (computed separately for dry bulk carriers and dry cargo liners) shall be transported on United States flag commercial vessels at market rates for United States flag commercial vessels in such manner as will insure a fair and reasonable participation of United States flag commercial vessels in cargoes, by geographic areas.

SEC. 410. The President, from time to time, but not less frequently than once every six months, while operations continue under this Act, shall transmit to the Congress reports of expenditures and activities authorized under this Act, except information the disclosure of which he deems incompatible with the security of the United States. Reports provided for under this section shall be transmitted to the Secretary of the Senate or the Clerk of the House of Representatives, as the case may be, if the Senate or the House of Representatives, as the case may be, is not in session.

SEC. 411. For the purposes of this Act—

(a) The terms "equipment" and "materials" shall mean any arms, ammunition or implements of war, or any other type of material, article, raw material, facility, tool, machine, supply, or item that would further the purposes of this Act, or any component or part thereof, used or required for use in connection therewith, or required in or for the manufacture, production, processing, storage, transportation, repair, or rehabilitation of any equipment or materials, but shall not include merchant vessels.

(b) The term "mobilization reserve", as used with respect to any equipment or materials, means the quantity of such equipment or materials determined by the Secretary of Defense under regulations prescribed by the President to be required to support mobilization of the armed forces of the United States in the event of war or national emergency until such time as adequate additional quantities of such equipment or materials can be procured.

(c) The term "excess", as used with respect to any equipment or materials, means the quantity of such equipment or materials owned by the United States which is in excess of the mobilization reserve of such equipment or materials.

*   *   *

239. STATEMENT BY GENERAL DWIGHT D. EISENHOWER BEFORE AN INFORMAL MEETING OF THE CONGRESS AT THE LIBRARY OF CONGRESS, FEBRUARY 1, 1951 [1]

[As part of the North Atlantic defense program the Treaty partners agreed at the Brussels Conference in December 1950 to create a united integrated army to defend Western Europe. At the same time they unanimously asked President Truman to designate General Eisenhower as the Supreme Allied Commander in Europe. Following his appointment on December 19 General Eisenhower visited the Atlantic Treaty countries and conferred with various leaders about the problems relating to the joint defense of the area. On his return to the United States he presented his findings in an informal address to the members of Congress. He reported encouraging progress in Europe and urged the full coöperation of the United States in building the collective defense of the North Atlantic community.]

Mr. President, Mr. Speaker, ladies, and gentlemen, I am very deeply aware of the distinction implicit in the invitation to appear before the elected representatives of the people. I am also keenly aware of the responsibility that rests upon me in accepting such an invitation, a responsibility that is not, of course, easy to discharge.

[1] United States Senate, Committee on Foreign Relations. Hearings on S. Con. Res. 8, relating to the assignment of ground forces of the United States to duty in the European area, 1951, pp. 1-8.

The very great problems involved in the defense of the free world are so vast and so complex that no man could hope in a lifetime of study and reflection to solve them all. He can certainly not be sure of the accuracy of his conclusions. In my own case, to a lifetime of professional study I have recently been able to add the observations of a very hurried trip to 13 capitals, but that is most obviously a meager foundation upon which to base the conclusions that I have formed and am about to present to you.

So, aware as I am of this responsibility, I do assure you that I approach you in very deep humility and ask from you only this much on faith, that you do believe in the sincerity of my convictions. I have no end to serve, as I know you have no end to serve, except the good of the United States; and that is the reason I am talking here. And that is the reason I am back in uniform, and it is the reason I have the courage to appear before this body to express my convictions.

I am also aware of the very big responsibilities devolving upon you gentlemen. You will be forced from time to time, and soon to make decisions that are going to be far reaching. In my opinion, they may determine the course of our civilization, whether or not free government is going to continue to exist upon the earth safely, and with all of the rights and privileges that devolve upon the individual citizen under that protection.

As I start this talk I think it would be well to establish a platform of understanding. Let us make certain assumptions. Now, the first, I have already made, that the Members of Congress here assembled and I have one object in common view, the good of the United States.

The next assumption I would like to make is that we are concerned not only with the protection of our territories, of our rights, of our privileges, but we are also concerned with the defense of a way of life. Our own way of life has certain factors that must persist if that way of life itself is to persist for example, the freedom of the individual, his political freedom, his freedom of worship, and that he will have an economy based upon free enterprise. In other words, our system must remain solvent, as we attempt a solution of this great problem of security. Else we have lost the battle from within that we are trying to win from without.

I do not believe, for example, that the United States can pick up the world on its economic, financial, and military shoulders and carry it. We must have cooperation if we are to work with other nations. The results of the effort to be the mutual, the common good, the common security of the free nations of the free world.

Military defense is made up of many things. The things that defend the nation or that act for it on the field of battle are many and varied, and as complex as the nation itself. The fighting forces are but the cutting edge of a very great machine, the inspiration and the power for which are found in the hearts of the citizens. All of the various mechanisms that are necessary are represented in our industrial capacity, our economic processes, and so on, so that when we talk about defending the free world we are not merely talking about defense in the terms of divisions and battleships and planes. We are talking about what is in our hearts, what we understand with our heads, and what we are going to do as a body. And let me here say, gentlemen, that unless this assumption is correct I am out of place.

We are not attempting to build a force that has any aggressive, any belligerent intent; we are concerned only with one thing. In a world in which the power of military might is still too much respected, we are going to build for ourselves a secure wall of peace, of security.

This very moment I think is a good time to bring up this one thought: What we are trying to do cannot honestly be considered by any other nation as a threat to its existence, as a threat to any peaceful purpose it may have. If any such charge is made in the propaganda of the world, it is for a nefarious purpose, and any kind of attempt or announcement to move against us because of the simple modest actions we are trying to take is merely an excuse. I must say to you that that purpose would have been executed anyway if we did not do it, if that is the only reason they have for moving against us.

The NATO organization foresees and plans for the common defense of the free world with specific reference to those nations on the border of the North Atlantic. Since we are approaching this problem from the welfare of the United States, I think it well to pause just for a moment to review certain factors with you. These factors are: What is the importance of Western Europe to us? There are, of course, ties of sentiment; they are the people from whom we drew originally our genius, our bloodstream; they are our relatives, and there are other bonds beyond those of sentiment that appeal to us in this job of protecting ourselves. We must look at all the common factors.

Behind our faith in them, since that is the basic assumption of the NATO organization, first of all in Western Europe there exists the greatest pool of skilled labor in the world. In Western Europe exists a great industrial fabric that is second in its capacity only to that of our Nation. There are more than 200,000,000 people who are related to us. If we take that whole complex with its potential for military exploitation and transfer it from our side to another side, the military balance of power has shifted so drastically that our safety would be gravely imperiled, grossly imperiled. The significance of the Western European group of nations is even greater than that. They have with many areas of the world close blood, political, and economic ties. It is scarcely possible to imagine the fall of Western Europe to communism without the simultaneous fall of certain of these great areas, particularly those, and first those, areas which have a political dependency upon the European powers, the very areas from which we draw the materials which are absolutely essential to our existence, our way of life. No matter how strong we prove in keeping open routes of communication, we must always keep open, clearly we must keep open the areas, keep them open to us when we need their trade in order to exist. Take such items only as manganese, copper, uranium. Could we possibly ever exist without access to them?

I believe that such things as this are tied up in our concern with the Western European complex in our determination—our decision that as I understand it has already been made—that we must defend them. But I refer again to the statement I have made, we cannot do this thing alone. All we would be doing would be to disperse our strength throughout the world unless we were sure first that we were being given full cooperation; and, second, that this strength of ours properly placed in other countries will there inspire the growth of still greater power and multiply every single effort that we make by comparable effort on the part of our friends.

As I said a moment ago, military strength is made up of various things of which the fighting forces are merely the cutting edge. One of the greatest factors in this whole thing is morale, and, ladies and gentlemen, almost the rest of my talk will be made up directly or indirectly in discussions of this question of morale, because morale involves understanding, it involves heart, it involves courage, fortitude, basic purpose.

Where my trip comes in is this: What have I been able to find out about the basic intent, the basic purpose, the basic morale of Europe? It is a complex question; and, again, certainly I do not consider that there is anything sacrosanct about the conclusions I have reached. Again I can only say they are honest.

We have heard for many years, five at least, much about the destruction of the European nations, about their material destruction, but above all about their loss of spirit, their loss of will, their unreadiness to do something for themselves. Of course, I think that Americans in general have not really tried to blame Europeans for this failure as we have seen it. They have tried merely to explain it. After all, Europe was occupied for 4 years; its industries were destroyed and its people lived in fear of the informer next door. They were crushed; their systems of government were overturned, and they lived according to the dictates of an invader.

The effects of the Marshall plan have been marked and have been important to the partial rehabilitation of Europe, but it would be false and idle to say that there does not exist in many strata of society pessimism bordering upon defeatism.

But there is likewise evidence, ladies and gentlemen, of a rejuvenation, a growth of determination, a spirit to resist, a spirit again to try to live the lives of free men to hold their heads up in the world, to do their part and to take the risk. I am going to quote to you a few examples, because I do not ask you to accept such a statement as that at face value; I would rather give you a few examples of the things that influenced my own judgment.

On my arrival in France I talked with the Government there and found this: That to their conscription law they have now added a proviso that permits almost no exemption for any cause whatsoever. They have made it one of the strictest, most inclusive conscription laws that would be possible to devise. As of this moment their tour of service is 18 months, but they pointed out to me the very many factors that have limited it from being greater, and indicated that one of the most important of these was lack of instructors, capable instructors. They cannot get instructors because they are losing many of them each month in Indochina. But as that is relieved and they get more equipment, they will go further and extend the tour to 2 years.

They are determined to stand against communism both internally and externally with courage in their hearts. Most of it has been inspired, at least it has been strengthened by the consummation of the NATO Treaty. There is no question about that.

I moved into Belgium and found similar determination. In Holland I received statements of the increased military preparations that they are going to make.

Denmark, exposed as it is way out between the Baltic and North Seas, likewise is going to do everything that represents their maximum effort.

In Norway there is no question about the determination of their will to resist. Their attitude is that resistance to the point of destruction is preferable.

In Rome it was quite clear that there is a stiffening resolve to meet this issue face on. While they are limited in the amount of their military force by treaty, they have determined to make that force efficient and to put it unreservedly at the command of the NATO powers.

I am not even going to mention my several conversations in Germany and for a very specific reason. I personally think that there has to be a political platform achieved and an understanding reached that will contemplate an eventual and earned equality on the part of that nation before we should start to talk about including units of Germans in any kind of an army. I, certainly, for one commander, want no unwilling contingent, no soldiers serving in the pattern of the Hessians who served in our Revolutionary War, serving in any army I command. Therefore until the political leaders, the diplomats, and the statesmen find the proper answer, it is not for a soldier to delve in too deeply.

In little Luxemburg I had an unusual experience. I think you would like to hear about it as illustrating the readiness of the nations today to try to cooperate. They are very small; there are only 300,000 people there, but they set their jaws and said: "We will have universal military service with no exemptions." They said: "We are very badly handicapped; we have equipment for one battalion only. What we particularly need is more artillery equipment."

When I stopped in Ottawa I told the Canadians about this trouble and the Canadians said: "Why, we have some artillery; we can ship it tomorrow." When I got to West Point a few hours later, I was greeted with the information that the Canadian Government had approved of the transfer and just left the red tape to me and my staff to look after.

What I am trying to say is that out of these conferences I sensed the feeling that there will be a rejuvenation of spirit if we can put ourselves into this thing, not only with the sense that we must do it because there is no acceptable alternative, because standing alone and isolated in a world with the rest completely dominated by communism, our system would have to wither away, our economy could not thrive.

Just stop to consider, ladies and gentlemen, that there are in the free world today—and not counting all of the outlying segments in such places as Australia, New Zealand, South America, and other parts of the free world—in Europe and the North American Continent alone there are 350,000,000 people who represent the highest culture man has been able to achieve upon this earth. They are responsible for every advance of science, the arts, and culture! they possess great reservoirs of leadership that have not been touched; they possess on the average a higher understanding than any other people in the world; they have the greatest productive capacity. Thanks to our great wisdom in keeping the proper strength upon the sea and in the air we have access to the raw materials that we need. Why, then, are we frightened of totalitarian government? For only one reason, because they have a unity of purpose. True, it is a unity achieved by ignorance, by force, by the NKVD.

What we have got to do, the only thing we have to do, is to meet that unity with a higher type of unity, the unity of free men that will not be divided. Someone in achieving that unity has to take the leadership, and I mean some one nation, not some one individual. We cannot either individually or at the national level afford to look over our shoulders with a suspicious thought that our friend is not doing as much as we are. We must by example inspire and insist and get everybody to do his maximum. The fullness of his performance will be limited by his capacity only. All of us must make this problem that of the highest priority.

I do not say, ladies and gentlemen, that that has been achieved. I merely say that, if the presentation I have made of the military situation, the possibilities of development in the whole economic world based upon the loss or the retention of Western Europe within our own wall of security, if those presentations are only reasonably accurate, then it is clear that we must do this. What nation is more capable, more ready for providing this leadership than the United States? We have been spared much of the discouragement, the defeatism, the destruction that has been visited upon Europe. We are younger, we are fresher, and a further important point is that we are farther removed from the immediate threat. We do not dwell in the gray zone. This strength, as I see it, must grow up in the rear and be pushed out. I do not mean pushed out in the sense that as soon as we produce units they must be deployed all over the world. I mean financial, moral, military, and material strength.

Our friends must know it. Inspired by it and living with it they must produce equal amounts of their own, far more than equal in particular areas. Our view in the central position must be directed to many sectors. We cannot concentrate all our forces in any one sector, even one as important as Western Europe. We must largely sit here with great, mobile, powerful reserves ready to support our policies, our rights, our interests wherever they may be in danger in the world.

The point I make is that Western Europe is so important to our future, our future is so definitely tied up with them, that we cannot afford to do less than our best in making sure that it does not go down the drain.

I repeat that, given the premise that we must produce, there is, then, one element left, time. We must accept, we must always accept this disadvantage militarily, internationally, that goes with peaceful intent and defensive purpose only. Any aggressor picks a day on which he intends to strike, and he builds everything to that point. We have to devise a scheme that we can support, if necessary over the next 20 years, 30 years, whatever may be the time necessary, as long as the threat, the announced threat of aggression remains in the world. That means we must be ready at any time. One of the important times is today, and from here on. As long as we are determined to secure the peace we have to use, employ, or resort to force and military power. In so doing let us not forget that there is not a moment to waste.

This brings me to a very important point: One of the great deficiencies in Europe is equipment, military equipment. Not only was all of this taken away from them in the war, but their facilities, destroyed, damaged as they were, have since that time been all occupied in trying to restore some semblance of a decent standard of living to their millions. They have little in the way of munitions productivity, although it is growing, and some of it, indeed, is very good.

I believe that the transfer of certain of our units should be in direct ratio to what Europe is doing so that we know that we are all going forward together, and no one is suspicious of the other.

The great need of the moment, as I say, is equipment. The great, the crying need today, as I see it, is equipment, the impedimenta of armies, of navies, of air forces. It must be furnished quickly and properly adjusted to this purpose of ours, the purpose of peace and security, to our ability to carry it forward without insolvency for year after year. I believe that within those limits we must now go into the production of equipment exactly as if we were preparing for the emergency of war.

We must remember that in World War II we used a system we called lend-lease, and I heard often in my headquarters people criticize this scheme of lend-lease. I never could feel that way about it, and I will tell you why, ladies and gentlemen. It took a rifle and a man to go out and advance the cause of the Allies against the enemies we had. If the United States could provide merely the rifle and get someone else to carry it in order to do the work that was necessary, I was perfectly content.

I believe in this thinking, particularly today. If we can put munitions in the hands of people that we know will serve on the side that is essential to our future security, to the kind of life our grandchildren are going to live, the only thing we need to know is that they are going forward with us. They are not lagging in their hearts or in their efforts.

I would say that in this particular subject of equipment the United States faces again the great proposition of transferring so much of its great productive capacity into the terrible business of producing munitions of war. You gentlemen are going to find it one of your most difficult, but at the same time one of your most important and immediate, tasks.

I believe as of now that with that equipment we will find a great rejuvenation in western morale. What we are trying to do, ladies and gentlemen, is to start a sort of reciprocal action across the Atlantic. We do one thing which inspires our friends to do something, and that gives us greater confidence in their thoroughness, their readiness for sacrifice. We do something more and we establish an upward-going spiral which meets this problem of strength and morale. The only thing that can defeat us is to establish a descending spiral born of suspicion, unreadiness on the part of each of us to do his job, the job that he knows in his own heart he must do.

I should like to bring to your attention a few things that I think are important to remember. Enemy propaganda has among other things, as it is reflected in the European press, tried to make it appear that the whole job is hopeless. He has shouted it from the housetops. If they say it is hopeless, they must have a purpose. Let us not believe too freely enemy propaganda, or the propaganda of somebody who wants to defeat our peaceful, our sane, our utterly just purposes. Let us not forget the strength of America, its great people, its history, its broad acres, its productive capacity, its great capacity for leadership. And then let us keep in our minds the kind of organization we shall have when we bind that up heart and soul and in material ways with our friends across the sea.

I come back again for a moment to the question of morale. Nobody can defend another nation. The true defense of a nation must be found in its own soul, and you cannot import a soul. We must make sure that the heart and soul of Europe is right. That is one of the obligations, gentlemen, that is imposed on me and my staff. I cannot conceive that the United States ever consented to accept the responsibility for acting in Western Europe except with those two reservations, that their representatives would do their utmost to see that they were all advancing together and that the United States was not being made merely an Atlas to carry the world upon its shoulders. I can see that each one of you in your great responsibilities as the lawmakers of this Nation has an element and a part of that responsibility individually. But we must not watch that so closely that we fail to get out in front to provide the leadership that will make this thing a complete success.

So this faith in America is one that lies at the bottom of this whole thing. Faith that the leadership she can provide will inspire the same kind of feeling, the same kind of effort in our friends abroad. And there I am sure we must exercise a bit of patience. It takes some time for our purposes—no matter how plainly we think they may be written upon the wall—it takes some time for others to understand those purposes and to gain faith in them. Remember, we have our own doubts and divisions, and we have our own debates. Think how that is multiplied in Europe where there are 10 of these nations in this organization, and they have all of the nationalistic factors to increase the intensity of the debate. We must have patience. Some of their problems are very, very serious. France, in the war against communism in Indochina, is losing monthly more than half of the men she can produce as instructors, the instructors they need to produce the army in France which they are so desperately trying to do. They have promised in spite of that to have by the end of the year 1953 roughly 25 battle-ready divisions. That is the kind of effort they are making.

Britain has similar things to face. Others, too, have problems. So while we may get a bit impatient when we think they do not see instantly what we are trying to do and what they should do in order to have the effort mutual and equal, we must have patience, ladies and gentlemen. Leadership must have patience or it cannot succeed.

And now there is one other point. I tried desperately to bring to you gentlemen specific types of comparisons that would convince you today of Europe's intent and of Europe's accomplishments, but when I tried to take such items as the proportion of gross national product that is turned into military purposes, when I tried to take the terms of enlistment, or the terms of service under conscription, when I tried to take the number of men that are actually in uniform or the kind of force they were trying to produce, the amount of their national budget that is put into military purposes, I found it impossible to make such comparisons. I started to talk about it in one nation and a man said to me "General, we are amazed at the amount of your national product that you can devote to this great purpose. We understand that you are going to put about 20 percent of your gross national product into military or semimilitary purposes. Come with me, come out to the villages and come to the farms and see what a 5-percent reduction in our standard of living means." I looked at that squarely in the face.

I would like to bring you specific criteria, and I find myself disappointed in being unable to do so. I do come back to this, however, the defense of freedom is exactly like the appreciation for freedom, it is in the heart. It is a job that each of us here can do.

And though I cannot bring you back specific criteria by which you may judge for yourselves in the materialistic way, I do hope earnestly that each of you will take the opportunity to go to Europe and see whether you appreciate and sense this coming rejuvenation, this great determination that I think I sense. I assure you that when I get a headquarters established every one of you will be welcome there. Some of you were in my headquarters some years ago. It will be a nice return visit if you come back.

The cost of peace is going to be a sacrifice, a very great sacrifice individually and nationally. But the total war is tragedy; it is probably the suicide of civilization.

I came back, ladies and gentlemen, with the purpose of rendering just a report. It is not my proper role to be exhorting the Members. I am trying now to make my words those of education; I am trying to make them those of deep conviction that the world, our world, has arrived at a moment of decision. I have come to the conclusion that we can go on following the basic principles of our system safely and surely, subject to the tasks that I have here so briefly tried to outline. We can do it without constituting of ourselves or of our forces a threat to any other nation. Any attempt so to describe it would be for propaganda purposes only.

I close, ladies and gentlemen, on one note only which I have not to this moment mentioned, because it does not lie completely within my province, but it is important. That is our own efforts to let the world understand what we are about, what we are, and sometimes our own efforts to have our own people understand what we are trying to do. In any event, I believe that the United States needs a very, very much stronger information service. In our case I would not call it propaganda, because the truth is all we need. We do not have to fasify the record nor our intentions.

I think most of you know it has been my invariable practice when I appear before a body such as this to ask for a question period. As has been explained to you by your Presiding Officer, it was decided that it was impossible today. But I am, I believe, going to be in joint meetings with four committees of the Congress. I assure you that, so far as it lies within my power to do so, I will answer as honestly and sincerely as I know how every single question which you may choose to ask me.

This has been a very great honor, ladies and gentlemen. I cannot tell you how much it means to me that you have assembled to hear the conclusions that I have drawn and the beliefs that I hold with respect to this very, very great task.

Thank you very much.

❖❖❖❖❖

240. CONNALLY-RUSSELL RESOLUTION [1]

[In addition to implementing the North Atlantic Treaty through aid furnished under the Mutual Defense Program, President Truman announced on September 9, 1950, that he had authorized substantial increases in the strength of our forces to be stationed in Western Europe. When the eighty-first Congress reconvened in January, the so-called Great Debate in the Senate centered around the President's authority to send armed forces abroad. The upshot of that debate was the approval of the Connally-Russell resolution which was adopted by the Senate on April 4 by a vote of 69 to 21. The resolution, which has no binding legal effect, endorsed the appointment of General Eisenhower as Supreme Commander in Europe and approved the plans of the President to send four additional divisions of ground troops to Europe. However, it called for Congressional approval before any additional ground forces could be sent to Europe to implement Article 3 of the Atlantic Pact.]

RESOLUTION

Whereas the foreign policy and military strength of the United States are dedicated to the protection of our national security, the preservation of the liberties of the American people, and the maintenance of world peace; and

Whereas the North Atlantic Treaty, approved by the Senate by a vote of 82-13, is a major and historic act designed to build up the collective strength of the free peoples of the earth to resist aggression, and to preserve world peace; and

Whereas the security of the United Nations and its citizens is involved with the security of its partners under the North Atlantic Treaty, and the commitments of that treaty are therefore an essential part of the foreign policy of the United States; and

Whereas article 3 of the North Atlantic Treaty pledges that the United States and the other parties thereto "separately and jointly, by means of continuous and effective self-help and mutual aid, will maintain and develop their individual and collective capacity to resist armed attack"; and

Whereas recent events have threatened world peace and as a result all parties to the North Atlantic Treaty are individually and collectively mobilizing their productive capacities and manpower for their self-defense; and

Whereas the free nations of Europe are vital centers of civilization, freedom, and production, and their subjugation by totalitarian forces would weaken and endanger the defensive capacity of the United States and the other free nations; and

Whereas the success of our common defense effort under a unified command requires the vigorous action and the full cooperation of all treaty partners in the supplying of materials and men on a fair and equitable basis, and General Eisenhower has testified that the "bulk" of the land forces should be supplied by our European allies and that such numbers supplied should be the "major fraction" of the total number: Now, therefore, be it

[1] S. Res. 99, 82nd Cong., 1st sess., April 4, 1951.

Resolved, That—

1. the Senate approves the action of the President of the United States in cooperating in the common defensive effort of the North Atlantic Treaty nations by designating, at their unanimous request, General of the Army Dwight D. Eisenhower as Supreme Allied Commander, Europe, and in placing Armed Forces of the United States in Europe under his command;

2. it is the belief of the Senate that the threat to the security of the United States and our North Atlantic Treaty partners makes it necessary for the United States to station abroad such units of our Armed Forces as may be necessary and appropriate to contribute our fair share of the forces needed for the joint defense of the North Atlantic area;

3. it is the sense of the Senate that the President of the United States as Commander in Chief of the Armed Forces, before taking action to send units of ground troops to Europe under article 3 of the North Atlantic Treaty, should consult the Secretary of Defense and the Joint Chiefs of Staff, the Committee on Foreign Relations of the Senate, the Committee on Foreign Affairs of the House of Representatives, and the Armed Services Committees of the Senate and the House of Representatives, and that he should likewise consult the Supreme Allied Commander, Europe;

4. it is the sense of the Senate that before sending units of ground troops to Europe under article 3 of the North Atlantic Treaty, the Joint Chiefs of Staff shall certify to the Secretary of Defense that in their opinion the parties to the North Atlantic Treaty are giving, and have agreed to give full, realistic force and effect to the requirement of article 3 of said treaty that "by means of continuous and effective self-help and mutual aid" they will "maintain and develop their individual and collective capacity to resist armed attack," specifically insofar as the creation of combat units is concerned;

5. the Senate herewith approves the understanding that the major contribution to the ground forces under General Eisenhower's command should be made by the European members of the North Atlantic Treaty, and that such units of United States ground forces as may be assigned to the above command shall be so assigned only after the Joint Chiefs of Staff certify to the Secretary of Defense that in their opinion such assignment is a necessary step in strengthening the security of the United States; and the certified opinions referred to in paragraphs 4 and 5 shall be transmitted by the Secretary of Defense to the President of the United States, and to the Senate Committees on Foreign Relations and Armed Services, and to the House Committees on Foreign Affairs and Armed Services as soon as they are received;

6. it is the sense of the Senate that, in the interests of sound constitutional processes, and of national unity and understanding, congressional approval should be obtained of any policy requiring the assignment of American troops abroad when such assignment is in implementation of article 3 of the North Atlantic Treaty; and the Senate hereby approves the present plans of the President and the Joint Chiefs of Staff to send four additional divisions of ground forces to Western Europe, but it is

the sense of the Senate that no ground troops in addition to such four divisions should be sent to Western Europe in implementation of article III of the North Atlantic Treaty without further congressional approval;

7. it is the sense of the Senate that the President should submit to the Congress at intervals of not more than six months reports on the implementation of the North Atlantic Treaty, including such information as may be made available for this purpose by the Supreme Allied Commander, Europe;

8. it is the sense of the Senate that the United States should seek to eliminate all provisions of the existing treaty with Italy which impose limitations upon the military strength of Italy and prevent the performance by Italy of her obligations under the North Atlantic Treaty to contribute to the full extent of her capacity to the defense of Western Europe;

9. it is the sense of the Senate that consideration should be given to the revision of plans for the defense of Europe as soon as possible so as to provide for utilization on a voluntary basis of the military and other resources of Western Germany and Spain, but not exclusive of the military and other resources of other nations.

◇◇◇◇◇◇

TECHNICAL ASSISTANCE FOR ECONOMIC DEVELOPMENT

241. TECHNICAL ASSISTANCE

Resolution of the General Assembly, December 4, 1948 [1]

[Following the creation of the United Nations, representatives of the underdeveloped countries put forth repeated requests for technical assistance so they could develop their resources more effectively and raise their standards of living. Some such aid was extended by the UN specialized agencies, particularly in the fields of health, agriculture, labor, and education. In 1948, the General Assembly took an important step forward when it authorized the Secretary-General (1) to organize teams of experts to advise with governments in connection with their economic development programs, and (2) to develop facilities for training technical experts. The text of the resolution follows.]

The General Assembly,

1. *Taking into account* the action in relation to technical assistance previously taken by the General Assembly (resolutions 52 (I) and 58 (I) of 14 December 1946) and by the Economic and Social Council (resolutions 27 (IV) and 51 (IV) of 28 March 1947, 96 (V) of 12 August 1947, 139 (VII), A, of 26 August 1948 and 149 (VII), C, of 27 August 1948),

2. *Considering* that

(*a*) The promotion of conditions of economic and social progress and

---

[1] United Nations, Official Records of the Third Session of the General Assembly, Part I, September 21-December 12, 1948. Resolutions, pp. 38-40.

development is one of the principal objectives of the Charter of the United Nations,

(*b*) The lack of expert personnel and lack of technical organization are among the factors which impede the economic development of the under-developed areas,

(*c*) The United Nations can extend efficacious and timely help in this connexion for the achievement of the objectives set forth in Chapters IX and X of the Charter,

3. *Decides* to appropriate the funds necessary to enable the Secretary-General to perform the following functions, where appropriate in cooperation with the specialized agencies, when requested to do so by Member Governments:

(*a*) Arrange for the organization of international teams consisting of experts provided by or through the United Nations and the specialized agencies for the purpose of advising those Governments in connexion with their economic development programmes, the organization of such teams, of course, not to preclude the invitation of individual, or groups of, experts from the United Nations or from specialized agencies in connexion with problems in the field of those specialized agencies;

(*b*) Arrange for facilities for the training abroad of experts of under-developed countries through the provision of fellowships for study in those countries or institutions which, in the particular fields of study, have achieved an advanced level of technical competence;

(*c*) Arrange for the training of local technicians within the under-developed countries themselves by promoting visits of experts in various aspects of economic development for the purpose of instructing local personnel and for assisting in the organization of technical institutions;

(*d*) Provide facilities designed to assist Governments to obtain technical personnel, equipment and supplies, and to arrange for the organization of such other services as may be appropriate in the promotion of economic development, including the organization of seminars on special problems of economic development, and the exchange of current information concerning technical problems of economic development;

4. *Instructs* the Secretary-General to undertake the performance of the functions listed in paragraph 3 above, in agreement with the Governments concerned, on the basis of requests received from Governments with due regard to geographical considerations and in accordance with the following policies:

(*a*) The amount of services and the financial conditions under which they shall be furnished to the various Governments shall be decided by the Secretary-General, and shall be reviewed by the Economic and Social Council at each of its sessions;

(*b*) The kind of service mentioned under paragraph 3 to be rendered to each country shall be decided by the Government concerned;

(*c*) The countries desiring assistance should perform in advance as much of the work as possible in order to define the nature and the scope of the problem involved;

(*d*) The technical assistance furnished shall (i) not be a means of foreign economic and political interference in the internal affairs of the country concerned and shall not be accompanied by any considerations of a political nature; (ii) be given only to or through Governments; (iii) be designed to meet the needs of the country concerned; (iv) be provided, as far as possible, in the form which that country desires; (v) be of high quality and technical competence;

(*e*) The sums appropriated for the performance of the functions set forth in paragraph 3 shall not be expended on functions or services which are a special responsibility of a specialized agency except in agreement with the executive head of that agency;

5. *Requests* the Secretary-General to report to each session of the Economic and Social Council on the measures which he has taken in compliance with the terms of the present resolution;

6. *Recommends* to the Economic and Social Council that it review at each session the actions taken under the present resolution and, when necessary, formulate recommendations concerning policy and budgetary action required by the General Assembly to carry on the functions instituted by the present resolution.

242. THE "POINT 4" PROGRAM

Excerpt from the President's Inaugural Address, January 20, 1949 [1]

[In his inaugural address delivered on January 20, 1949, President Truman set forth a four-point program for American foreign policy. In his fourth point he called for a "bold new program" of technical assistance to the underdeveloped areas. While the plans subsequently developed were neither very bold nor very new, his speech put the United States Government in back of the idea of technical assistance and gave considerable impetus to the movement in the United Nations.]

Fourth, we must embark on a bold new program for making the benefits of our scientific advances and industrial progress available for the improvement and growth of underdeveloped areas.

More than half the people of the world are living in conditions approaching misery. Their food is inadequate. They are victims of disease. Their economic life is primitive and stagnant. Their poverty is a handicap and a threat both to them and to more prosperous areas.

For the first time in history, humanity possesses the knowledge and the skill to relieve the suffering of these people.

The United States is preeminent among nations in the development of industrial and scientific techniques. The material resources which we can afford to use for the assistance of other peoples are limited. But our imponderable resources in technical knowledge are constantly growing and are inexhaustible.

I believe that we should make available to peace-loving peoples the benefits of our store of technical knowledge in order to help them realize their as-

---

[1] Department of State Bulletin, January 30, 1949, p. 125.

pirations for a better life. And, in cooperation with other nations, we should foster capital investment in areas needing development.

Our aim should be to help the free peoples of the world, through their own efforts, to produce more food, more clothing, more materials for housing, and more mechanical power to lighten their burdens.

We invite other countries to pool their technological resources in this undertaking. Their contributions will be warmly welcomed. This should be a cooperative enterprise in which all nations work together through the United Nations and its specialized agencies wherever practicable. It must be a worldwide effort for the achievement of peace, plenty, and freedom.

With the cooperation of business, private capital, agriculture, and labor in this country, this program can greatly increase the industrial activity in other nations and can raise substantially their standards of living.

Such new economic developments must be devised and controlled to benefit the peoples of the areas in which they are established. Guaranties to the investor must be balanced by guaranties in the interest of the people whose resources and whose labor go into these developments.

The old imperialism—exploitation for foreign profit—has no place in our plans. What we envisage is a program of development based on the concepts of democratic fair-dealing.

All countries, including our own, will greatly benefit from a constructive program for the better use of the world's human and natural resources. Experience shows that our commerce with other countries expands as they progress industrially and economically.

Greater production is the key to prosperity and peace. And the key to greater production is a wider and more vigorous application of modern scientific and technical knowledge.

Only by helping the least fortunate of its members to help themselves can the human family achieve the decent, satisfying life that is the right of all people.

Democracy alone can supply the vitalizing force to stir the peoples of the world into triumphant action, not only against their human oppressors, but also against their ancient enemies—hunger, misery, and despair.

◇◇◇◇◇

243. TECHNICAL ASSISTANCE PROGRAM FOR UNDER-DEVELOPED AREAS

Message From the President to the Congress, June 24, 1949 [1]

[Following President Truman's inaugural address in which he urged technical assistance for the under-developed areas, there was much speculation both at home and abroad about the nature and extent of the program he had in mind. Six months later the President spelled out his plans in some detail when he sent a message to the Congress requesting legislative authority

[1] H. Doc. 240, 81st Cong., 1st sess., Department of State Bulletin of July 4, 1949, pp. 862-865.

to take the essential first steps in what he called a "constantly growing effort to improve economic conditions in the less developed regions of the world." As the message below makes clear, Mr. Truman emphasized that the program would have to be modest in its initial stages and that the major effort would have to be made by the people of the under-developed countries.]

To the Congress of the United States:

In order to enable the United States, in cooperation with other countries, to assist the peoples of economically underdeveloped areas to raise their standards of living, I recommend the enactment of legislation to authorize an expanded program of technical assistance for such areas, and an experimental program for encouraging the outflow of private investment beneficial to their economic development. These measures are the essential first steps in an undertaking which will call upon private enterprise and voluntary organizations in the United States, as well as the government, to take part in a constantly growing effort to improve economic conditions in the less developed regions of the world.

The grinding poverty and the lack of economic opportunity for many millions of people in the economically underdeveloped parts of Africa, the Near and Far East, and certain regions of Central and South America, constitute one of the greatest challenges of the world today. In spite of their age-old economic and social handicaps, the peoples in these areas have, in recent decades, been stirred and awakened. The spread of industrial civilization, the growing understanding of modern concepts of government, and the impact of two World Wars have changed their lives and their outlook. They are eager to play a greater part in the community of nations.

All these areas have a common problem. They must create a firm economic base for the democratic aspirations of their citizens. Without such an economic base, they will be unable to meet the expectations which the modern world has aroused in their peoples. If they are frustrated and disappointed, they may turn to false doctrines which hold that the way of progress lies through tyranny.

For the United States the great awakening of these peoples holds tremendous promise. It is not only a promise that new and stronger nations will be associated with us in the cause of human freedom, it is also a promise of new economic strength and growth for ourselves.

With many of the economically underdeveloped areas of the world, we have long had ties of trade and commerce. In many instances today we greatly need the products of their labor and their resources. If the productivity and the purchasing power of these countries are expanded, our own industry and agriculture will benefit. Our experience shows that the volume of our foreign trade is far greater with highly developed countries than it is with countries having a low standard of living and inadequate industry. To increase the output and the national income of the less developed regions is to increase our own economic stability.

In addition, the development of these areas is of utmost importance to our efforts to restore the economies of the free European nations. As the economies of the underdeveloped areas expand, they will provide needed products for

Europe and will offer a better market for European goods. Such expansion is an essential part of the growing system of world trade which is necessary for European recovery.

Furthermore, the development of these areas will strengthen the United Nations and the fabric of world peace. The preamble to the Charter of the United Nations states that the economic and social advancement of all people is an essential bulwark of peace. Under article 56 of the Charter, we have promised to take separate action and to act jointly with other nations "to promote higher standards of living, full employment, and conditions of economic and social progress and development."

For these various reasons, assistance in the development of the economically underdeveloped areas has become one of the major elements of our foreign policy. In my inaugural address, I outlined a program to help the peoples of these areas to attain greater production as a way to prosperity and peace.

The major effort in such a program must be local in character; it must be made by the people of the underdeveloped areas themselves. It is essential, however, to the success of their effort that there be help from abroad. In some cases, the peoples of these areas will be unable to begin their part of this great enterprise without initial aid from other countries.

The aid that is needed falls roughly into two categories. The first is the technical, scientific, and managerial knowledge necessary to economic development. This category includes not only medical and educational knowledge, and assistance and advice in such basic fields as sanitation, communications, road building, and governmental services, but also, and perhaps most important, assistance in the survey of resources and in planning for long-range economic development.

The second category is production goods—machinery and equipment—and financial assistance in the creation of productive enterprises. The underdeveloped areas need capital for port and harbor development, roads and communications, irrigation and drainage projects, as well as for public utilities and the whole range of extractive, processing, and manufacturing industries. Much of the capital required can be provided by these areas themselves, in spite of their low standards of living. But much must come from abroad.

The two categories of aid are closely related. Technical assistance is necessary to lay the ground-work for productive investment. Investment, in turn, brings with it technical assistance. In general, however, technical surveys of resources and of the possibilities of economic development must precede substantial capital investment. Furthermore, in many of the areas concerned, technical assistance in improving sanitation, communications, or education is required to create conditions in which capital investment can be fruitful.

This country, in recent years, has conducted relatively modest programs of technical cooperation with other countries. In the field of education, channels of exchange and communication have been opened between our citizens and those of other countries. To some extent, the expert assistance of a number of Federal agencies, such as the Public Health Service and the Department of Agriculture, has been made available to other countries. We have also participated in the activities of the United Nations, its specialized agencies, and other international organizations to disseminate useful techniques among nations.

Through these various activities, we have gained considerable experience in rendering technical assistance to other countries. What is needed now is to expand and integrate these activities and to concentrate them particularly on the economic development of under-developed areas.

Much of the aid that is needed can be provided most effectively through the United Nations. Shortly after my inaugural address, this government asked the Economic and Social Council of the United Nations to consider what the United Nations and the specialized international agencies could do in this program.

The Secretary-General of the United Nations thereupon asked the United Nations Secretariat and the Secretariats of the specialized international agencies to draw up cooperative plans for technical assistance to under-developed areas. As a result, a survey was made of technical projects suitable for these agencies in such fields as industry, labor, agriculture, scientific research with respect to natural resources, and fiscal management. The total cost of the program submitted as a result of this survey was estimated to be about 35 million dollars for the first year. It is expected that the United Nations and the specialized international agencies will shortly adopt programs for carrying out projects of the type included in this survey.

In addition to our participation in this work of the United Nations, much of the technical assistance required can be provided directly by the United States to countries needing it. A careful examination of the existing information concerning the underdeveloped countries shows particular need for technicians and experts with United States training in plant and animal diseases, malaria and typhus control, water supply and sewer systems, metallurgy and mining, and nearly all phases of industry.

It has already been shown that experts in these fields can bring about tremendous improvements. For example, the health of the people of many foreign communities has been greatly improved by the work of United States sanitary engineers in setting up modern water supply systems. The food supply of many areas has been increased as the result of the advice of United States agricultural experts in the control of animal diseases and the improvement of crops. These are only examples of the wide range of benefits resulting from the careful application of modern techniques to local problems. The benefits which a comprehensive program of expert assistance will make possible can only be revealed by studies and surveys undertaken as a part of the program itself.

To inaugurate the program, I recommend a first year appropriation of not to exceed 45 million dollars. This includes 10 million dollars already requested in the 1950 Budget for activities of this character. The sum recommended will cover both our participation in the programs of the international agencies and the assistance to be provided directly by the United States.

In every case, whether the operation is conducted through the United Nations, the other international agencies, or directly by the United States, the country receiving the benefit of the aid will be required to bear a substantial portion of the expense.

The activities necessary to carry out our program of technical aid will be diverse in character and will have to be performed by a number of different government agencies and private instrumentalities. It will be necessary to

utilize not only the resources of international agencies and the United States Government, but also the facilities and the experience of the private business and nonprofit organizations that have long been active in this work.

Since a number of Federal agencies will be involved in the program, I recommend that the administration of the program be vested in the President, with authority to delegate to the Secretary of State and to other government officers, as may be appropriate. With such administrative flexibility, it will be possible to modify the management of the program as it expands and to meet the practical problems that will arise in its administration in the future.

The second category of outside aid needed by the underdeveloped areas is the provision of capital for the creation of productive enterprises. The International Bank for Reconstruction and Development and the Export-Import Bank have provided some capital for underdeveloped areas, and, as the economic growth of these areas progresses, should be expected to provide a great deal more. In addition, private sources of funds must be encouraged to provide a major part of the capital required.

In view of the present troubled condition of the world—the distortion of world trade, the shortage of dollars, and other aftereffects of the war—the problem of substantially increasing the flow of American capital abroad presents serious difficulties. In all probability novel devices will have to be employed if the investment from this country is to reach proportions sufficient to carry out the objectives of our program.

All countries concerned with the program should work together to bring about conditions favorable to the flow of private capital. To this end we are negotiating agreements with other countries to protect the American investor from unwarranted or discriminatory treatment under the laws of the country in which he makes his investment.

In negotiating such treaties we do not, of course, ask privileges for American capital greater than those granted to other investors in underdeveloped countries or greater than we ourselves grant in this country. We believe that American enterprise should not waste local resources, should provide adequate wages and working conditions for local labor, and should bear an equitable share of the burden of local taxes. At the same time, we believe that investors will send their capital abroad on an increasing scale only if they are given assurance against risk of loss through expropriation without compensation, unfair or discriminatory treatment, destruction through war or rebellion, or the inability to convert their earnings into dollars.

Although our investment treaties will be directed at mitigating such risks, they cannot eliminate them entirely. With the best will in the world a foreign country, particularly an underdeveloped country, may not be able to obtain the dollar exchange necessary for the prompt remittance of earnings on dollar capital. Damage or loss resulting from internal and international violence may be beyond the power of our treaty signatories to control.

Many of these conditions of instability in underdeveloped areas which deter foreign investment are themselves a consequence of the lack of economic development which only foreign investment can cure. Therefore, to wait until stable conditions are assured before encouraging the outflow of capital to underdeveloped areas would defer the attainment of our objectives indefinitely. It is necessary to take vigorous action now to break out of this vicious circle.

Since the development of underdeveloped economic areas is of major importance in our foreign policy, it is appropriate to use the resources of the government to accelerate private efforts toward that end. I recommend, therefore, that the Export-Import Bank be authorized to guarantee United States private capital, invested in productive enterprises abroad which contribute to economic development in underdeveloped areas, against the risks peculiar to those investments.

This guarantee activity will at the outset be largely experimental. Some investments may require only a guarantee against the danger of inconvertibility, others may need protection against the danger of expropriation and other dangers as well. It is impossible at this time to write a standard guarantee. The Bank will, of course, be able to require the payment of premiums for such protection, but there is no way now to determine what premium rates will be most appropriate in the long run. Only experience can provide answers to these questions.

The Bank has sufficient resources at the present time to begin the guarantee program and to carry on its lending activities as well without any increase in its authorized funds. If the demand for guarantees should prove large, and lending activities continue on the scale expected, it will be necessary to request the Congress at a later date to increase the authorized funds of the Bank.

The enactment of these two legislative proposals, the first pertaining to technical assistance and the second to the encouragement of foreign investment, will constitute a national endorsement of a program of major importance in our efforts for world peace and economic stability. Nevertheless, these measures are only the first steps. We are here embarking on a venture that extends far into the future. We are at the beginning of a rising curve of activity, private, governmental, and international, that will continue for many years to come. It is all the more important, therefore, that we start promptly.

In the economically underdeveloped areas of the world today there are new creative energies. We look forward to the time when these countries will be stronger and more independent than they are now, and yet more closely bound to us and to other nations by ties of friendship and commerce, and by kindred ideals. On the other hand, unless we aid the newly awakened spirit in these peoples to find the course of fruitful development, they may fall under the control of those whose philosophy is hostile to human freedom, thereby prolonging the unsettled state of the world and postponing the achievement of permanent peace.

Before the peoples of these areas we hold out the promise of a better future through the democratic way of life. It is vital that we move quickly to bring the meaning of that promise home to them in their daily lives.

HARRY S. TRUMAN

THE WHITE HOUSE,
June 24, 1949.

◇◇◇◇◇◇

244. TECHNICAL ASSISTANCE

Resolution of the General Assembly, November 16, 1949 [1]

[Encouraged by the President's inaugural address and the prospects of substantial American aid, the United Nations moved ahead in 1949 with plans for an expanded technical assistance program. The General Assembly resolution of November 16, 1949, approved the guiding principles developed earlier by the Economic and Social Council, and agreed that a technical assistance conference should be convened. This conference was eventually held in the summer of 1950, and the United Nations made a beginning on what may prove to be its most important long-range activity.]

THE GENERAL ASSEMBLY,

HAVING CONSIDERED the Economic and Social Council's resolution 222 (IX) A of 15 August 1949 on an expanded program of technical assistance for economic development,

1. APPROVED the observations and guiding principles set out in Annex I of that resolution and the arrangements made by the Council for the administration of the program;

2. NOTES the decision of the Council to call a Technical Assistance Conference to be convened by the Secretary-General in accordance with the terms of paragraphs 12 and 13 of the Council resolution;

3. AUTHORIZES the Secretary-General to set up a special account for technical assistance for economic development, to be available to those organizations which participate in the expanded program of technical assistance and which accept the observations and guiding principles set out in Annex I of the Council resolution and the arrangements made by the Council for the administration of the program;

4. APPROVES the recommendations of the Council to Governments participating in the Technical Assistance Conference regarding financial arrangements for administering contributions, and authorizes the Secretary-General to fulfill the responsibilities assigned to him in this connection;

5. INVITES all Governments to make as large voluntary contributions as possible to the special account for technical assistance.

◇◇◇◇◇◇

245. ACT FOR INTERNATIONAL DEVELOPMENT [2]

Title IV of the Foreign Economic Assistance Act of 1950, June 5, 1950

[Congress did not respond to the President's "Point 4" appeal until May 1950. The bill which finally emerged—and which passed the Senate by the

[1] General Assembly Roundup, Fourth Regular Session, Press Release GA/600, Part III, pp. 1-2.
[2] Public Law 535, 81st Cong., 2nd sess.

narrow margin of 37 to 36—authorized the expenditure of $45,000,000 for the fiscal year 1950 for technical assistance to the under-developed areas partly through UN channels, and partly through bilateral programs conducted by various United States agencies. As of January 1, 1951, however, the second half of the President's proposal relating to private investment abroad had failed to win committee approval of the Congress.]

TITLE IV

SEC. 401. This title may be cited as the "Act for International Development".

SEC. 402. The Congress hereby finds as follows:

(a) The peoples of the United States and other nations have a common interest in the freedom and in the economic and social progress of all peoples. Such progress can further the secure growth of democratic ways of life, the expansion of mutually beneficial commerce, the development of international understanding and good will, and the maintenance of world peace.

(b) The efforts of the peoples living in economically underdeveloped areas of the world tò realize their full capabilities and to develop the resources of the lands in which they live can be furthered through the cooperative endeavor of all nations to exchange technical knowledge and skills and to encourage the flow of investment capital.

(c) Technical assistance and capital investment can make maximum contribution to economic development only where there is understanding of the mutual advantages of such assistance and investment and where there is confidence of fair and reasonable treatment and due respect for the legitimate interests of the peoples of the countries to which the assistance is given and in which the investment is made and of the countries from which the assistance and investments are derived. In the case of investment this involves confidence on the part of the people of the underdeveloped areas that investors will conserve as well as develop local resources, will bear a fair share of local taxes and observe local laws, and will provide adequate wages and working conditions for local labor. It involves confidence on the part of investors, through intergovernmental agreements or otherwise, that they will not be deprived of their property without prompt, adequate, and effective compensation; that they will be given reasonable opportunity to remit their earnings and withdraw their capital; that they will have reasonable freedom to manage, operate, and control their enterprises; that they will enjoy security in the protection of their persons and property, including industrial and intellectual property, and nondiscriminatory treatment in taxation and in the conduct of their business affairs.

SEC. 403. (a) It is declared to be the policy of the United States to aid the efforts of the peoples of economically underdeveloped areas to develop their resources and improve their working and living conditions by encouraging the exchange of technical knowledge and skills and the flow of investment capital to countries which provide conditions under which such technical assistance and capital can effectively and constructively contribute to raising standards of living, creating new sources of wealth, increasing productivity and expanding purchasing power.

(b) It is further declared to be the policy of the United States that in order to achieve the most effective utilization of the resources of the United States, private and public, which are or may be available for aid in the development of economically underdeveloped areas, agencies of the United States Government, in reviewing requests of foreign governments for aid for such purposes, shall take into consideration (1) whether the assistance applied for is an appropriate part of a program reasonably designed to contribute to the balanced and integrated development of the country or area concerned; (2) whether any works or facilities which may be projected are actually needed in view of similar facilities existing in the area and are otherwise economically sound; and (3) with respect to projects for which capital is requested, whether private capital is available either in the country or elsewhere upon reasonable terms and in sufficient amounts to finance such projects.

SEC. 404. (a) In order to accomplish the purposes of this title, the United States is authorized to participate in multilateral technical cooperation programs carried on by the United Nations, the Organization of American States, and their related organizations, and by other international organizations, wherever practicable.

(b) Within the limits of appropriations made available to carry out the purposes of this title, the President is authorized to make contributions to the United Nations for technical cooperation programs carried on by it and its related organizations which will contribute to accomplishing the purposes of this title as effectively as would participation in comparable programs on a bilateral basis. The President is further authorized to make contributions for technical cooperation programs carried on by the Organization of American States, its related organizations, and by other international organizations.

(c) Agencies of the United States Government on request of international organizations are authorized, upon approval by the President, to furnish services and such facilities as may be necessary in connection therewith, on an advance of funds or reimbursement basis, for such organizations in connection with their technical cooperation programs. Amounts received as reimbursements from such organizations shall be credited, at the option of the appropriate agency, either to the appropriation, fund, or account utilized in incurring the obligation, or to an appropriate appropriation, fund, or account currently available for the purposes for which expenditures were made.

SEC. 405. The President is authorized to plan, undertake, administer, and execute bilateral technical cooperation programs carried on by any United States Government agency and, in so doing—

(a) To coordinate and direct existing and new technical cooperation programs.

(b) To assist other interested governments in the formulation of programs for the balanced and integrated development of the economic resources and productive capacities of economically underdeveloped areas.

(c) To receive, consider, and review reports of joint commissions set up as provided in section 410 of this title.

(d) To make, within appropriations made available for the purpose, advances and grants in aid of technical cooperation programs to any person, corporation, or other body of persons, or to any foreign government or foreign government agency.

(e) To make and perform contracts or agreements in respect of technical cooperation programs on behalf of the United States Government with any person, corporation, or other body of persons however designated, whether within or without the United States, or with any foreign government or foreign government agency: *Provided,* That with respect to contracts or agreements which entail commitments for the expenditure of funds appropriated pursuant to the authority of this title, such contracts or agreements, within the limits of appropriations or contract authorizations hereafter made available may, subject to any future action of the Congress, run for not to exceed three years in any one case.

*   *   *

SEC. 407. In carrying out the programs authorized in section 405 of this title—

(a) The participation of private agencies and persons shall be sought to the greatest extent practicable.

(b) Due regard shall be given, in reviewing requests for assistance, to the possibilities of achieving satisfactory results from such assistance as evidenced by the desire of the country requesting it (1) to take steps necessary to make effective use of the assistance made available, including the encouragement of the flow of productive local and foreign investment capital where needed for development; and (2) to endeavor to facilitate the development of the colonies, possessions, dependencies, and non-self-governing territories administered by such requesting country so that such areas may make adequate contribution to the effectiveness of the assistance requested.

(c) Assistance shall be made available only where the President determines that the country being assisted—

(1) Pays a fair share of the cost of the program.

(2) Provides all necessary information concerning such program and gives the program full publicity.

(3) Seeks to the maximum extent possible full coordination and integration of technical cooperation programs being carried on in that country.

(4) Endeavors to make effective use of the results of the program.

(5) Cooperates with other countries participating in the program in the mutual exchange of technical knowledge and skills.

*   *   *

SEC. 409. The President shall create an advisory board, hereinafter referred to as the "board", which shall advise and consult with the President or such other officer as he may designate to administer the program herein authorized, with respect to general or basic policy matters arising in connection with operation of the program. The board shall consist of not more than thirteen members to be appointed by the President, one of whom, by and with the advice and consent of the Senate, shall be appointed by him as chairman. The members of the board shall be broadly representative of voluntary agencies and other groups interested in the program, including business, labor, agriculture, public health, and education. All members of the board shall be citizens of the United States; none except the chairman shall be an officer or an employee of the United States (including any agency or instrumentality of the United States) who, as such, regularly receives compensation for current services. Members of the board, other than the chairman if he is an officer of the United States Government, shall receive out of funds made available for the purposes of this title a per diem allowance of $50 for each day spent away from their homes or regular places of business for the purpose of attendance at meetings of the board or at conferences held upon the call of the chairman, and in necessary travel, and while so engaged they may be paid actual travel expenses and not to exceed $10 per diem in lieu of subsistence and other expenses. The President may appoint such committees in special fields of activity as he may determine to be necessary or desirable to effectuate the purposes of this title. The members of such committees shall receive the same compensation as that provided for members of the board.

SEC. 410. (a) At the request of a foreign country, there may be established a joint commission for economic development to be composed of persons named by the President and persons to be named by the requesting country, and may include representatives of international organizations mutually agreed upon.

(b) The duties of each such joint commission shall be mutually agreed upon, and may include, among other things, examination of the following:

(1) The requesting country's requirements with respect to technical assistance.

(2) The requesting country's resources and potentialities, including mutually advantageous opportunities for utilization of foreign technical knowledge and skills and investment.

(3) Policies which will remove deterrents to and otherwise encourage the introduction, local development, and application of technical skills and the creation and effective utilization of capital, both domestic and foreign; and the implementation of such policies by appropriate measures on the part of the requesting country and the United States, and of other countries, when appropriate, and after consultation with them.

(c) Such joint commissions shall prepare studies and reports which they shall transmit to the appropriate authorities of the United States and of the requesting countries. In such reports the joint commissions may include recommendations as to any specific projects which they conclude would contribute to the economic development of the requesting countries.

(d) The costs of each joint commission shall be borne by the United States and the requesting country in the proportion that may be agreed upon between the President and that country.

SEC. 411. All or part of United States support for and participation in any technical cooperation program carried on under this title shall be terminated by the President—

(a) If he determines that such support and participation no longer contribute effectively to the purposes of this title, are contrary to a resolution adopted by the General Assembly of the United Nations that the continuance of such technical cooperation programs is unnecessary or undesirable, or are not consistent with the foreign policy of the United States.

(b) If a concurrent resolution of both Houses of the Congress finds such termination is desirable.

*   *   *

SEC. 413. In order to carry out the purposes of this title—

(a) The President shall appoint, by and with the advice and consent of the Senate, a person who, under the direction of the President or such other officer as he may designate pursuant to section 412 hereof to exercise the powers conferred upon him by this title, shall be responsible for planning, implementing, and managing the programs authorized in this title. He shall be compensated at a rate fixed by the President without regard to the Classification Act of 1949 but not in excess of $15,000 per annum.

*   *   *

SEC. 414. No citizen or resident of the United States, whether or not now in the employ of the Government, may be employed or assigned to duties by the Government under this Act until such individual has been investigated by the Federal Bureau of Investigation and a report thereon has been made to the Secretary of State: *Provided, however,* That any present employee of the Government, pending the report as to such employee by the Federal Bureau of Investigation, may be employed or assigned to duties under this Act for the period of three months from the date of its enactment. This section shall not apply in the case of any officer appointed by the President by and with the advice and consent of the Senate.

SEC. 415. The President shall transmit to the Congress an annual report of operation under this title.

SEC. 416. (a) In order to carry out the provisions of this title, there shall be made available such funds as are hereafter authorized and appropriated from time to time for the purposes of this title: *Provided, however,* That for the purpose of carrying out the provisions of this title through June 30, 1951, there is hereby authorized to be appropriated a sum not to exceed $35,000,-000, including any sums appropriated to carry on the activities of the Institute of Inter-American Affairs, and technical cooperation programs as defined in section 418 herein under the United States Information and Educational Exchange Act of 1948 (62 Stat. 6). Activities provided for under this title may be prosecuted under such appropriations or under authority granted in appropriation Acts to enter into contracts pending enactment of such appropriations. Unobligated balances of such appropriations for any fiscal year may, when so specified in the appropriation Act concerned, be carried over to any succeeding fiscal year or years. The President may allocate to any United States Government agency any part of any appropriation available for carrying out the purposes of this title. Such funds shall be available for obligation and expenditure for the purposes of this title in accordance with authority granted hereunder or under authority governing the activities of the Government agencies to which such funds are allocated.

(b) Nothing in this title is intended nor shall it be construed as an expressed or implied commitment to provide any specific assistance, whether of funds, commodities, or services, to any country or countries, or to any international organization.

*   *   *

SEC. 418. As used in this title—

(a) The term "technical cooperation programs" means programs for the international interchange of technical knowledge and skills designed to contribute to the balanced and integrated development of the economic resources and productive capacities of economically underdeveloped areas. Such activities may include, but need not be limited to, economic, engineering, medical, educational, agricultural, fishery, mineral, and fiscal surveys, demonstration, training, and similar projects that serve the purpose of promoting the development of economic resources and productive capacities of underdeveloped areas. The term "technical cooperation programs" does not include such activities authorized by the United States Information and Educational Exchange Act of 1948 (62 Stat. 6) as are not primarily related to economic development nor activities undertaken now or hereafter pursuant to the International Aviation Facilities Act (62 Stat. 450), nor pursuant to the Philippine Rehabilitation Act of 1946 (60 Stat. 128), as amended, nor pursuant to the Foreign Assistance Act of 1948 (62 Stat. 137), as amended, nor activities undertaken now or hereafter in the administration of areas occupied by the United States armed forces or in Korea by the Economic Cooperation Administration.

*   *   *

Index